QuickPass™
More Than a Textbook

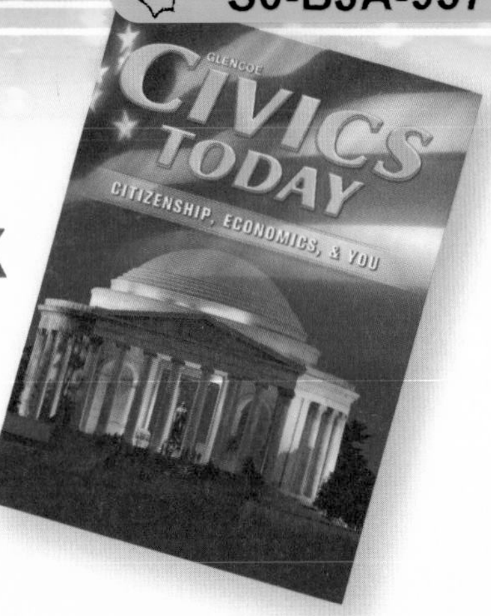

Find it faster.

Visit Civics ONLINE at glencoe.com and enter a QuickPass™ chapter code to go directly to the chapter resources you need.

CIV3093c1

Enter this code with the appropriate chapter number.

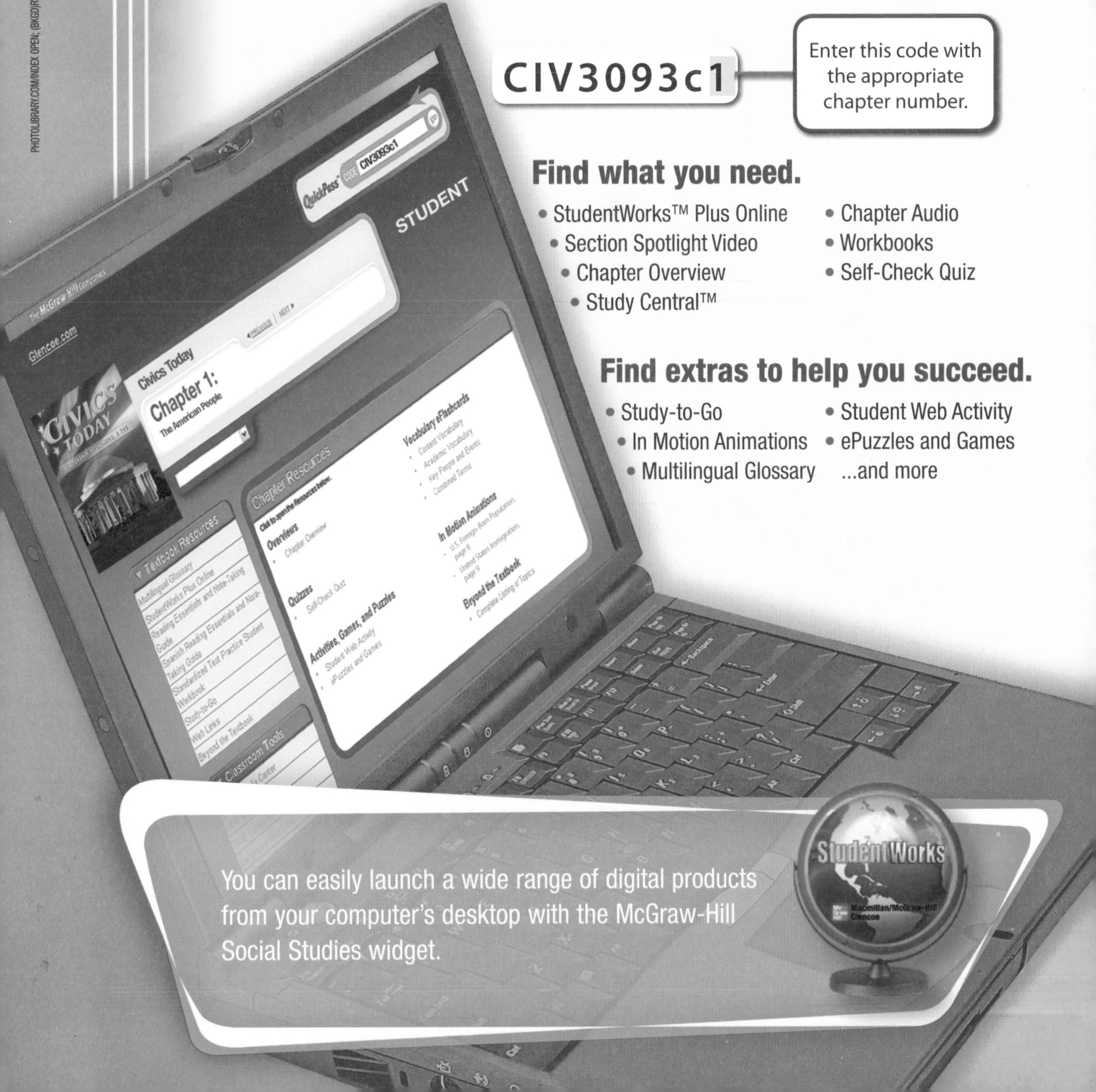

Find what you need.

- StudentWorks™ Plus Online
- Section Spotlight Video
- Chapter Overview
- Study Central™
- Chapter Audio
- Workbooks
- Self-Check Quiz

Find extras to help you succeed.

- Study-to-Go
- In Motion Animations
- Multilingual Glossary
- Student Web Activity
- ePuzzles and Games
- ...and more

You can easily launch a wide range of digital products from your computer's desktop with the McGraw-Hill Social Studies widget.

PHOTOLIBRARY.COM/INDEX OPEN; (BKGD)RYAN MCVAY/GETTY IMAGES

GLENCOE

CIVICS TODAY

CITIZENSHIP, ECONOMICS, & YOU

Richard C. Remy, Ph.D. • John J. Patrick, Ed.D.
David C. Saffel, Ph.D. • Gary E. Clayton, Ph.D.

Authors

Richard C. Remy, Ph.D., is professor emeritus in the College of Education at The Ohio State University, and Senior Consultant on Civic Education with the Mershon Center for International Security and Public Policy at Ohio State. He received his Ph.D. in political science from Northwestern University. His books include: *United States Government: Democracy in Action, Building Civic Education for Democracy in Poland, American Government and National Security*, and *Lessons on the Constitution*. In the 1990s Dr. Remy created and codirected a long-term project with the Polish Ministry of National Education and the Center for Citizenship Education, Warsaw to develop new civic education programs for Polish students, teachers, and teacher educators.

John J. Patrick, Ed.D., is a professor emeritus of Education at Indiana University, Bloomington. He is the author or coauthor of many publications about civics and government, such as *The Oxford Guide to the United States Government, The Supreme Court of the United States: A Student Companion, The Bill of Rights: A History in Documents, Founding the Republic,* and *Constitutional Debates on Freedom of Religion*. He is a member of the Standing Committee on Civics for the National Assessment of Educational Progress (NAEP). Since 1992 he has been involved in several international Civic education projects involving post-Communist countries. In 2002 he received Indiana University's John W. Ryan Award for distinguished achievements in International Programs. In 2003 he received the Sagamore of the Wabash award from the Governor of Indiana in recognition of his long-term contributions to civic education in Indiana. In 2005, he was the original recipient of the Indiana State Bar Association's civic eduation award.

David C. Saffell, Ph.D., received his Ph.D. degree in political science from the University of Minnesota. He has taught at Ohio Northern University since 1972, serving as chair of the Social Science Division for 15 years. Professor Saffell is coauthor of *State of Local Government: Politics and Public Policies,* 7th edition, published by McGraw-Hill. He has authored and edited several other books dealing with American government.

Gary E. Clayton, Ph.D., currently teaches economics at Northern Kentucky University. He received his Ph.D. in Economics from the University of Utah, has taught economics and finance at several universities and internationally, and has authored a number of books. Dr. Clayton appeared on numerous radio and television programs and was a guest commentator for NPR's *Marketplace*. Dr. Clayton has a longstanding interest in economic education. He has participated in numerous economic education workshops, and is a National Council on Economic Education Kazanjian award winner. Dr. Clayton most recently received a year 2000 Leavey Award for Excellence in Private Enterprise Education from the Freedoms Foundation at Valley Forge, and is the recipient of a national teaching award from the National Council on Economic Education. Most recently Dr. Clayton was the recipient of NKU's 2005 Frank Sinton Milburn Outstanding Professor Award.

Contributing Author

Dinah Zike, M.Ed., is an award winning author, educator, and inventor known for designing three-dimensional hands-on manipulatives and graphic organizers known as Foldables™. Foldables are used nationally and internationally by teachers, parents, and educational publishing companies. Dinah has developed over 150 supplemental educational books and materials. She is the author of *The Big Book of Books and Activities,* which was awarded *Learning Magazine's* Teachers' Choice Award. In 2004, Dinah was honored with the CESI Science Advocacy Award. Dinah received her M.Ed. from Texas A&M, College Station, Texas.

The McGraw·Hill Companies

Send all inquiries to:
Glencoe/McGraw-Hill
8787 Orion Place
Columbus, OH 43240-4027

ISBN: 978-0-07-880309-3
MHID: 0-07-880309-8

Printed in the United States of America.
6 7 8 9 10 QDB/LEH 12 11

Table of Contents

U.S. Capitol, Washington, D.C.

Replica of the United States Constitution

Joint session of Congress

Academic Consultants

Brandon Bartels, Ph.D.
Assistant Professor of Political Science
Stony Brook University
Stony Brook, New York

Jody Baumgartner, Ph.D.
Assistant Professor of Political Science
East Carolina University
Greenville, North Carolina

Jeff Biddle, Ph.D.
Professor of Economics
Michigan State University
East Lansing, Michigan

Nancy Lind, Ph.D.
Associate Department Chair, Professor of Political Science
Illinois State University
Normal, Illinois

Scott McClurg, Ph.D.
Assistant Professor of Political Science
Southern Illinois University
Carbondale, Illinois

Carrie Meyer, Ph.D.
Associate Professor of Economics
George Mason University
Fairfax, Virginia

Emmanuel Oritsejafor, Ph.D.
Associate Professor of Political Science
North Carolina Central University
Durham, North Carolina

Bassam Yousif, Ph.D.
Associate Professor of Economics
Indiana State University
Terre Haute, Indiana

Teacher Reviewers

Cliff Avant
Bleckley County High School
Cochran, Georgia

Lori Braunstein
Aurora Central High School
Aurora, Colorado

Heather Bridges
Mills University Studies High School
Little Rock, Arkansas

Nathan Bruck
Greenfield-Central High School
Greenfield, Indiana

Dorothea Bryant
Huron High School
Ann Arbor, Michigan

Michael Clark
Hall High School
Little Rock, Arkansas

Brad Donovan
Willapa Valley High School
Menlo, Washington

Jennifer Goss
Fleetwood Area High School
Fleetwood, Pennsylvania

Jeanne Hamacher
Lake Park High School
Roselle, Indiana

Jodi Howell
West Albany High School
Albany, Oregon

Annette King
Colquitt County High School
Moultrie, Georgia

Vanessa Lal Steinkamp
Adlai Stevenson High School
Lincolnshire, Illinois

Brian Myatt
Oneida High School
Oneida, New York

Bill Schreier
Wheaton Warrenville South High School
Wheaton, Illinois

Russell Sousa
Fort Myers High School
Fort Myers, Florida

Brian Stevens
Coldwater High School
Coldwater, Michigan

Diane Stewart
Chester County High School
Henderson, Tennessee

John Sullivan
Belmont High School
Belmont, Massachusetts

Stephen Venezia
Marblehead High School
Marblehead, Massachusetts

TABLE OF CONTENTS

▼ Convenient ATM banking

▼ The New York Stock Exchange

▼ United Nations Headquarters in New York City

Appendix

TIME™ Features

TIME™ Political Cartoons

TIME™ Teens in *Action*

TIME REPORTS

TIME REPORTS

The White House

An intricate model takes visitors behind the scenes at 1600 Pennsylvania Avenue

Described by former President Gerald Ford as "the best public housing in the world" and by former President Harry Truman as a "glamorous prison," the White House was first occupied by President John Adams in 1800. Two centuries later, the White House is a village of 6,000 busy souls: On a typical day, the President and First Lady, journalists, cooks, cops, gardeners, and tourists operate in harmony on 18 acres.

In 1962, John and Jan Zweifel of Orlando, Florida, set out to bring the White House to the American people by constructing the detailed model shown at right. Except for the location of the library, which was pushed forward for show purposes, the Zweifels' White House is a faithful recreation of the original, down to TVs, furniture, and paintings. The Zweifels contact the White House every few weeks to find out if anything has changed. The 60-foot by 20-foot, 10-ton model, which includes the East and West wings (not shown), took more than 500,000 hours to construct and cost more than

1 SITTING ROOM Generally claimed by the First Lady, this room was allocated one of the building's first indoor toilets in 1801.

2 MASTER BEDROOM Nancy Reagan, who served as First Lady from 1981 to 1989, decorated this bedroom in hand-painted paper that was imported from China.

3 PRESIDENT'S STUDY Franklin Delano Roosevelt used this study as a bedroom; the Reagans liked to have quiet dinners here in front of the television.

4 YELLOW OVAL ROOM One of the most historic rooms in the house, it took on the color yellow during the tenure of First Lady Dolley Madison.

5 TREATY ROOM Originally a large bedroom, this room served as Bill Clinton's office in the residence.

6 LINCOLN BEDROOM Abraham Lincoln signed the Emancipation Proclamation here.

7 LINCOLN SITTING ROOM William McKinley's war room during the Spanish-American War.

8 STATE DINING ROOM Gilbert Stuart's portrait of George Washington (which was later used on the one-dollar bill) hung here when the British torched the mansion in 1814. (The portrait survived the fire.)

9 RED ROOM John Adams's breakfast room was where Rutherford B. Hayes took the oath of office in 1877.

10 BLUE ROOM Where Grover Cleveland married Frances Folsom, in 1886.

11 GREEN ROOM Thomas Jefferson's dining room is now used for receptions.

12 EAST ROOM The largest room in the mansion, it was used by First Lady Abigail Adams to dry the family wash.

13 LIBRARY Placed here by the replica designers, the presidential library is actually located behind the Vermeil Room.

14 MAP ROOM Decorated with Chippendale furniture imported from England, this room was inspired by Winston Churchill's World War II map room.

15 DIPLOMATIC RECEPTION ROOM Site from which F.D.R. broadcast his fireside chats (though the fireplace at that time was fake).

16 CHINA ROOM Edith Wilson, First Lady from 1915 to 1921, used this area to display china.

17 VERMEIL (ver-MAY) ROOM This room takes its name from a display of vermeil (gilded silver).

A Long Road

The Zweifels' quest to create a replica of the White House took decades. After going on hundreds of public tours of the mansion, they finally persuaded President Gerald Ford to let them look behind the

American Biography

Landmark Supreme Court Case Studies

Issues to Debate

Financial Literacy

Reading Social Studies

Analyzing Primary Sources

Historical Documents

Skills Handbook

Charts and Graphs

UNIT 1

UNIT 2

UNIT 3

UNIT 4

UNIT 5

UNIT 6

UNIT 7

UNIT 8

Maps

Primary Sources

Ed. = Editor **Tr. = Translator** **V = Volume**

CHAPTER 6

CHAPTER 7

CHAPTER 8

CHAPTER 9

Scavenger Hunt

Civics Today contains a wealth of information. The trick is to know where to look in the text to access all this information. If you complete this Scavenger Hunt exercise with your teacher or parents, you will see how the textbook is organized, and how to get the most out of your reading and study time. Let's get started!

1. How many units and how many chapters are in the book?
2. What topic does Unit 4 cover?
3. Where can you quickly find a definition of the word *communism*?
4. What is the topic of the *Real World Civics* item on page 292?
5. What is the topic of "Analyzing Primary Sources" at the end of Unit 2?
6. What does the Web site call-out found on page 439 tell you to do?
7. How are the content vocabulary words *microeconomics*, *scarcity*, and *trade-off* in Chapter 18 called out?
8. Who is the topic of Teens in *Action* on page 152?
9. What does the Foldables™ exercise on page 655 ask you to do?
10. Where do you find graphic data about all of the United States, including the presidents?

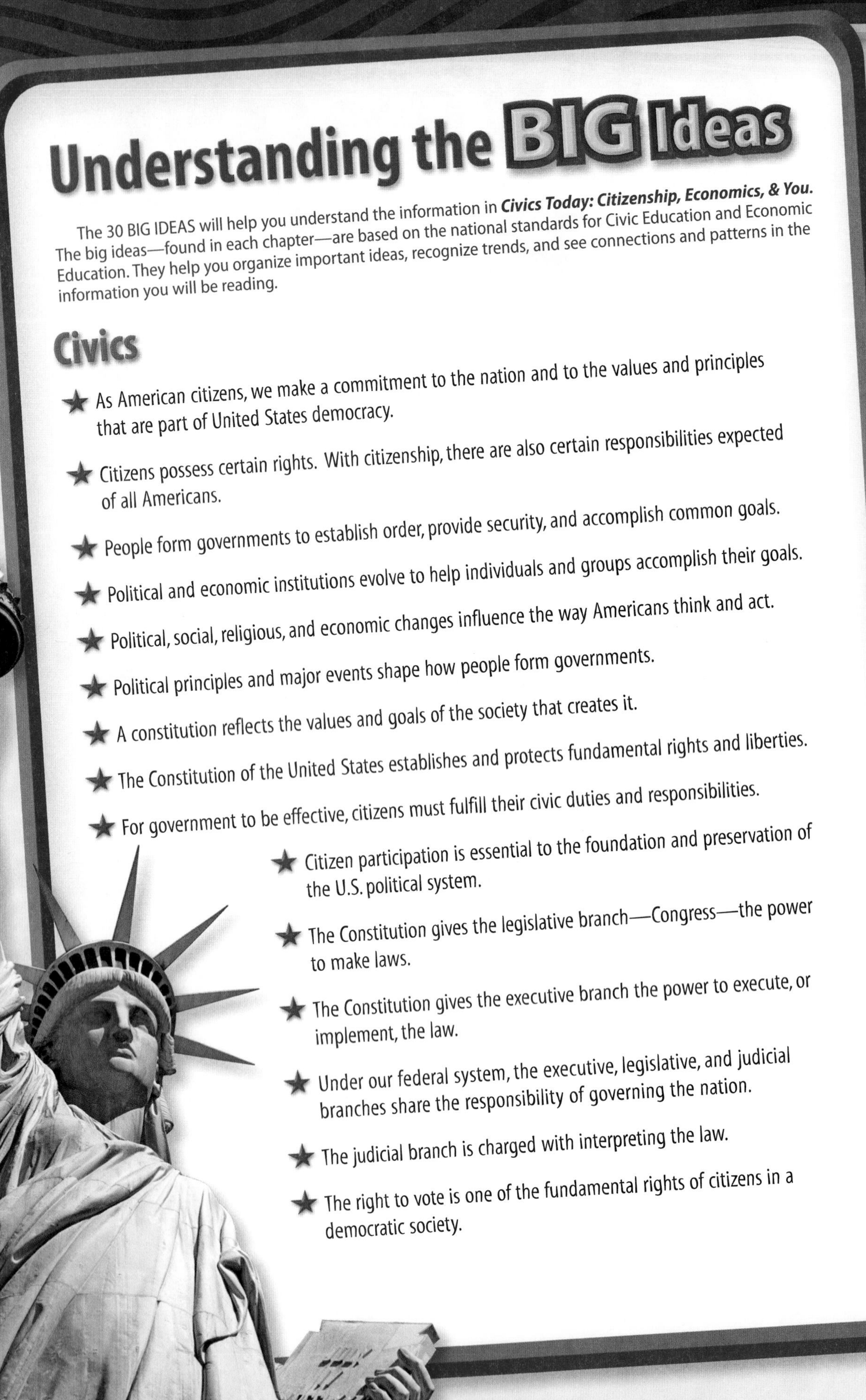

Understanding the BIG Ideas

The 30 BIG IDEAS will help you understand the information in ***Civics Today: Citizenship, Economics, & You.*** The big ideas—found in each chapter—are based on the national standards for Civic Education and Economic Education. They help you organize important ideas, recognize trends, and see connections and patterns in the information you will be reading.

Civics

- ★ As American citizens, we make a commitment to the nation and to the values and principles that are part of United States democracy.
- ★ Citizens possess certain rights. With citizenship, there are also certain responsibilities expected of all Americans.
- ★ People form governments to establish order, provide security, and accomplish common goals.
- ★ Political and economic institutions evolve to help individuals and groups accomplish their goals.
- ★ Political, social, religious, and economic changes influence the way Americans think and act.
- ★ Political principles and major events shape how people form governments.
- ★ A constitution reflects the values and goals of the society that creates it.
- ★ The Constitution of the United States establishes and protects fundamental rights and liberties.
- ★ For government to be effective, citizens must fulfill their civic duties and responsibilities.
- ★ Citizen participation is essential to the foundation and preservation of the U.S. political system.
- ★ The Constitution gives the legislative branch—Congress—the power to make laws.
- ★ The Constitution gives the executive branch the power to execute, or implement, the law.
- ★ Under our federal system, the executive, legislative, and judicial branches share the responsibility of governing the nation.
- ★ The judicial branch is charged with interpreting the law.
- ★ The right to vote is one of the fundamental rights of citizens in a democratic society.

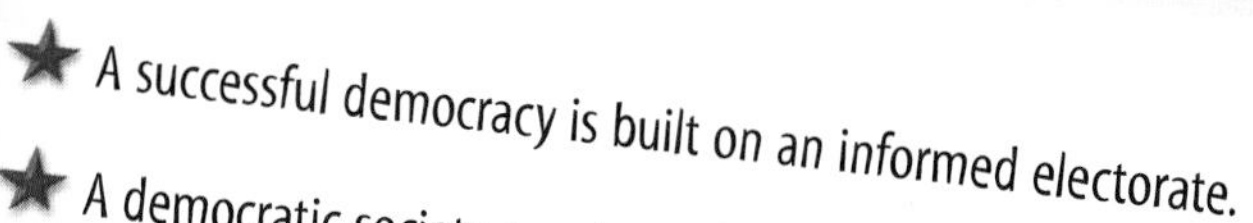

★ A successful democracy is built on an informed electorate.

★ A democratic society requires the active participation of its citizens.

★ In a democratic society, various forces shape people's ideas.

★ Under our federal system, power is shared between the national government and the state governments.

Economics

★ Scarcity requires individuals and groups to make choices about using goods and services to satisfy their wants.

★ Throughout history, civilizations have developed systems of laws to meet their needs.

★ An economic system is the way a society organizes the production and consumption of goods and services.

★ The basis of the market economy is voluntary exchange. In the American economy, the exchange usually involves money in return for a good or service.

★ Free enterprise is the freedom of individuals and businesses to operate and compete with a minimum of government interference or regulation.

★ You and everyone around you are consumers and, as such, play an important role in the economic system.

★ We all make economic choices. Opportunity cost, scarcity, and supply and demand influence the decisions we make.

★ Supply and demand in a market interact to determine price and the quantities bought and sold.

★ Market economies rest upon the fundamental principle of individual freedom for consumers, producers, and workers.

★ The exchange of goods and services helps create economic interdependence among peoples in different places and different countries.

★ Economic, social, and political changes create new traditions, values, and beliefs.

UNIT 1

Foundations of American Citizenship

Fourth of July parade, New York City

★ **Chapter 1** **The American People**

★ **Chapter 2** **Roots of American Democracy**

★ **Chapter 3** **The Constitution**

★ **Chapter 4** **The Bill of Rights**

★ **Chapter 5** **Citizenship and Government in a Democracy**

CITIZENSHIP Be an Active Citizen

Find out the purposes of government firsthand. Contact a government leader, such as a state representative, a city council member, or a school board member, and ask how the government he or she represents serves American citizens.

UNIT 1

Reading Social Studies

Making Connections

1 Learn It!

As a reader, you are constantly making connections between what you are reading and what you already know. The more connections you make, the better you are able to comprehend. You may make connections between the text and an experience you have had in your life (text-to-self), the text and another text (text-to-text), or the text and something that happened in school, your community, or the world (text-to-world).

- Read the paragraph below.
- Which statements in the paragraph create a connection in your mind?
- Think about any connections related to the text, such as the examples given below.

> Conflicts are unavoidable when people live together in a community. Governments make laws to prevent conflicts and to settle those conflicts that do arise.
>
> *—from page 22*

Graphic Organizer

Statement from text	Connection
Conflicts are unavoidable when people live together in a community.	Our neighbors got into a big argument once about loud music.
Governments make laws to prevent conflicts.	My uncle once went to court to settle a conflict he had with a company.

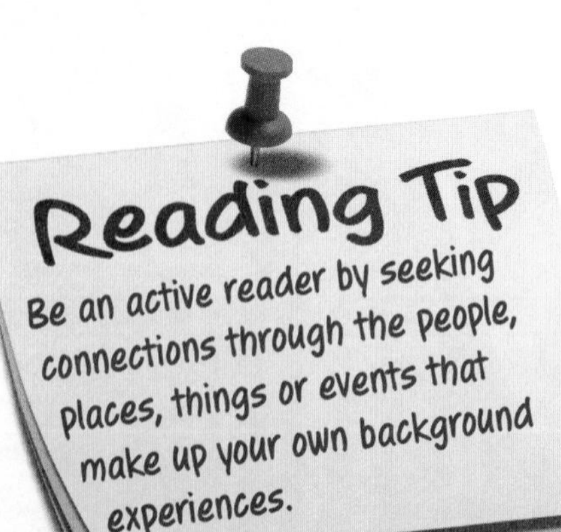

2 Practice It!

Read the following paragraph from this unit.

- Draw a graphic organizer like the one shown below.
- In the left-hand column, write at least three statements from the paragraph with which you can make a connection. You do not need to copy the entire sentence.
- In the right-hand column, write your connections beside each statement.

> Throughout our nation's history, people still in their teens have bravely fought for our country. By law, however, they were not old enough to vote for the leaders who sent them into battle. Although the Constitution did not specify, or mention, a minimum age for voters, most states set the minimum at 21.
>
> That standard finally changed in 1971, a year when many young Americans were fighting in the Vietnam War.
>
> *—from page 137*

Statement from text	Connection

Read to Write Activity

Read the section titled *New Taxes and a Tea Party* in Chapter 2, Section 4, page 53. As you read, jot down any statement with which you make a connection. Write a paragraph about one connection you made and how it relates to the text.

3 Apply It!

Your mind will be busy making connections as you read the chapters in this unit. At the end of each chapter, create a graphic organizer such as the one above to help you tie your connections to an important concept from the chapter. Use your organizer to help you remember important facts as you study for tests.

Chapter 1 The American People

Why It Matters

Our Declaration of Independence proclaims that "all men are created equal." This does not mean that everyone is born with the same wealth, intelligence, strength, or ambition. Each one of us has a unique combination of qualities and characteristics. The words of the Declaration mean that all people should have equal *rights,* which is the cornerstone of the democratic ideal.

Civics ONLINE
Visit glencoe.com and enter QuickPass™ code CIV3093c1 for Chapter 1 resources.

BIG Ideas

Section 1: The Diversity of Americans

As American citizens, we make a commitment to the nation and to the values and principles that are part of United States democracy. In addition to the common values and civic unity, the United States benefits from its rich diversity.

Section 2: Who Are America's Citizens?

Citizens possess certain rights. With citizenship, Americans also have certain responsibilities. In the United States, there are two ways to become a citizen: by birth and by a process called naturalization.

Section 3: Government and the People

People form governments to establish order, provide security, and accomplish common goals. Democratic governments perform necessary functions so citizens can live together peacefully.

Jorge and Carlos Urbina, and others, take the oath of allegiance to become American citizens

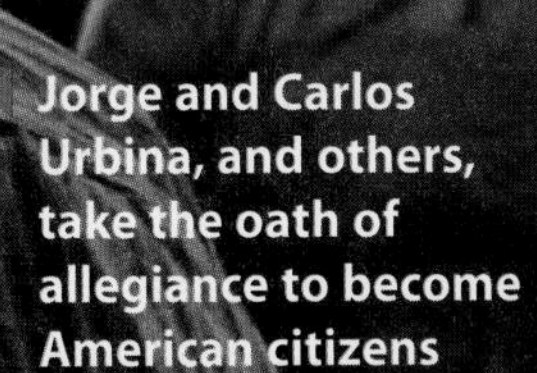

Comparing Information Study Foldable Make the following Foldable to help you compare information about citizenship and government in a democracy.

Step 1 Use one sheet of paper folded in half the long way.

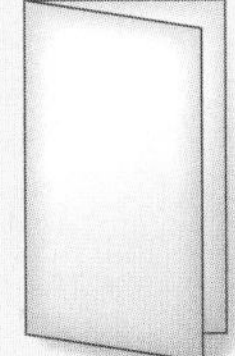

Step 2 Fold in half again to create cutting lines.

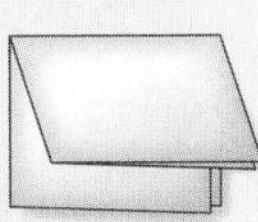

Step 3 Cut the folded top sheet in half to create two tabs.

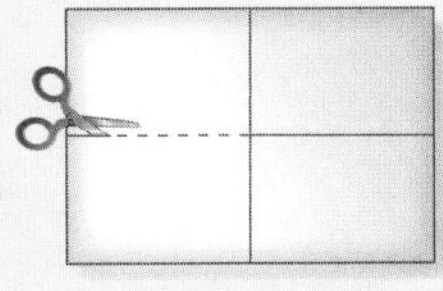

Step 4 Label the tabs as shown.

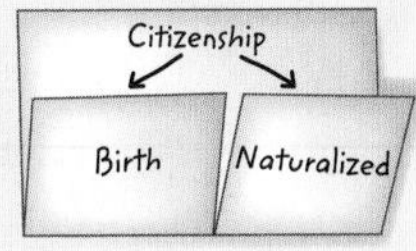

Reading and Writing

As you read the chapter, note details about the processes of becoming a citizen from birth or by naturalization.

Section Audio

Spotlight Video

The Diversity of Americans

Guide to Reading

Big Idea
As American citizens, we make a commitment to the nation and to the values and principles that are part of United States democracy.

Content Vocabulary
- civics *(p. 7)*
- citizenship *(p. 7)*
- citizen *(p. 7)*
- service economy *(p. 10)*
- value *(p. 11)*
- popular sovereignty *(p. 12)*
- institution *(p. 13)*

Academic Vocabulary
- diverse *(p. 8)*
- ethnic *(p. 9)*
- principle *(p. 11)*

Reading Strategy
Identifying As you read, note on the diagram below the major changes in the population of the United States that have taken place since its beginning.

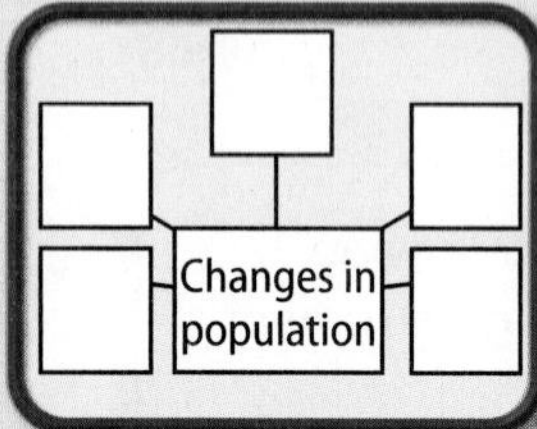

Real World Civics Does your vote count? Enthusiastic young people like those pictured volunteered for the America Votes National Day of Action. Both political parties worked to register as many citizens as possible to vote, especially minorities and immigrants who might not feel that their voice matters. Why? When you do not vote, you let others speak for you.

▼ **Stacey Brayboy and Alvin Anderson prepare to canvass a neighborhood in Miami, Florida.**

What Is Civics?

Main Idea **Civics is the study of the rights and duties of citizens.**

Civics & You As an American citizen, did you know you have certain rights as well as responsibilities? Read to find out what it means to be a citizen of a country.

When Americans vote or serve on a jury, their actions are based on ideas that people had in the fourth century B.C. In examining how people act, Greek philosopher Aristotle wrote:

> *"If liberty and equality, as is thought by some, are chiefly to be found in democracy, they will be best attained when all persons alike share in the government to the utmost."*
>
> —Aristotle, *Politics*

Ancient Roots

Civics is the study of the rights and duties of citizens. The concept of **citizenship** dates back more than 2,500 years to ancient Greece and Rome. In those days, only a few people could be **citizens.** Only men with property possessed the right to vote and to take part in government.

Today gender and wealth are no longer requirements for citizenship. Indeed, most people are citizens of the country in which they live. Citizens have certain rights and duties. They are community members who owe loyalty to the government and are entitled to protection from it.

However, being a citizen means much more than just living in a country. American citizens who live abroad are still citizens of the United States. Citizens are a part of a country. They may share a common history, common customs, or common beliefs. They agree to follow a set of rules and to accept the government's authority.

Reading Check **Explaining** As a citizen, what do you agree to do?

Diversity Native Americans from Taos, New Mexico, perform a dance that represents one of their cultural traditions. ***Discussing*** **How do you think diversity has influenced our nation and its culture?**

A Changing Society

Main Idea **American society has undergone many changes in the past, and these changes continue today.**

Civics & You What would make you want to move to a new place? Read on to find out why people immigrated to the Americas.

On the back of every American coin, you will find the Latin words *E pluribus unum,* meaning "Out of many, one." This phrase reminds us that the many **diverse,** or different, citizens of the United States have joined together to make a single, strong nation. For all our differences, we are linked by shared values and experiences. More than 300 million people live in the United States today. All of us are descendants from families that immigrated at one time or another. Most scholars believe that even the first Native Americans arrived here thousands of years ago by crossing over a "land bridge" that once connected Asia and North America.

A Nation of Immigrants

Until the mid-1900s, most immigrants came from Europe. The first Europeans to settle permanently in North America arrived from Spain during the 1500s. They lived in what is now Florida, California, and the Southwest. By the time the United States won its independence from England, the Spanish had founded Tucson, Albuquerque, San Antonio, and San Diego.

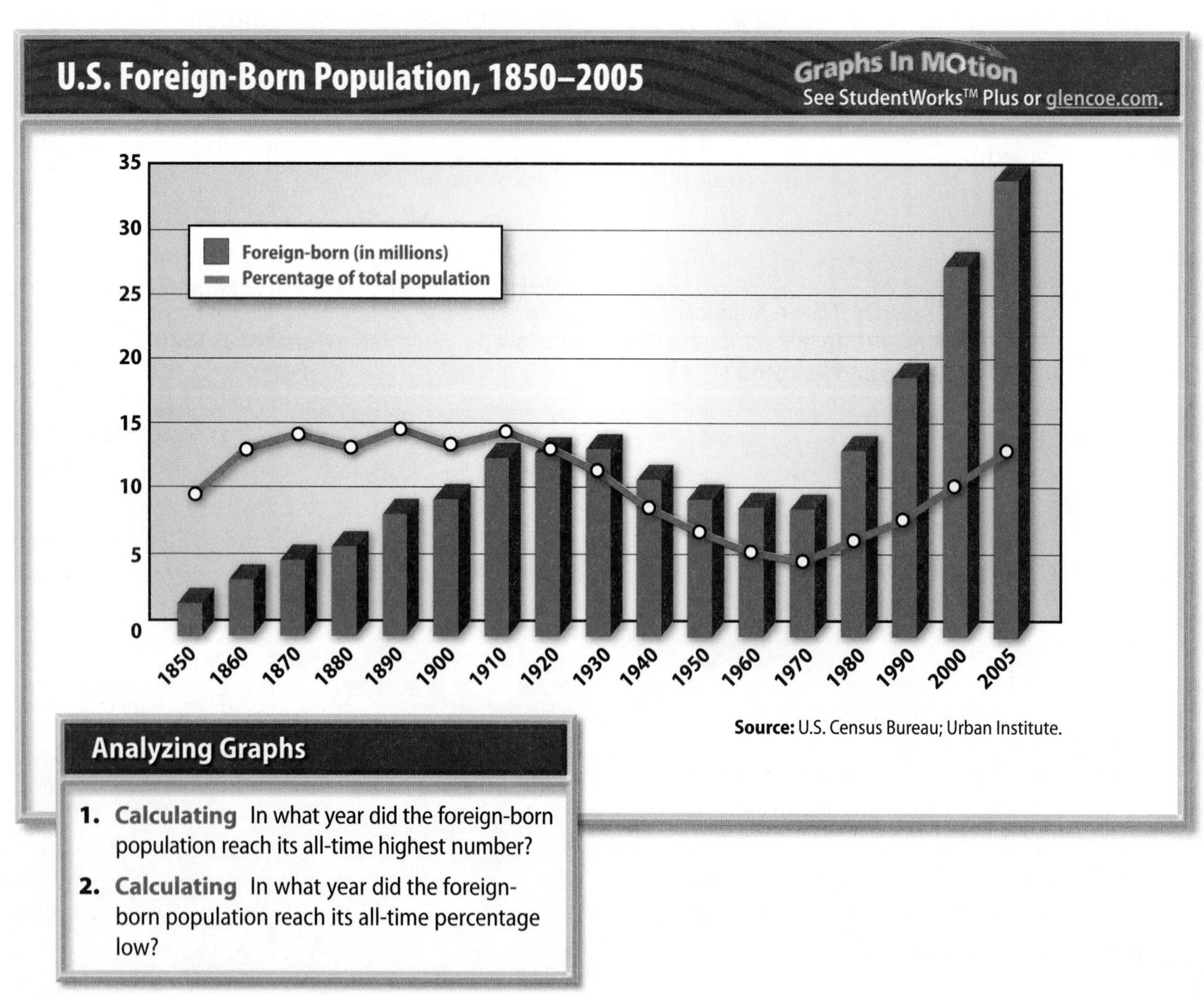

Source: U.S. Census Bureau; Urban Institute.

Analyzing Graphs

1. **Calculating** In what year did the foreign-born population reach its all-time highest number?
2. **Calculating** In what year did the foreign-born population reach its all-time percentage low?

Early Immigration Beginning in the 1600s, people from France and England came to North America. The French settled primarily in Canada, but they also clustered around the Mississippi River. English immigrants settled mainly along the east coast of North America, creating the thirteen colonies that became the United States. During the late 1600s and the 1700s, immigrants from Germany, the Netherlands, Ireland, Scotland, and Sweden joined these English settlers.

After Independence After the United States gained its independence, it became known throughout Europe as a land of promise. The number of immigrants grew from 600,000 in the 1830s to more than 2 million by the 1850s. Between 1860 and 1890, more than 10 million Europeans—many of them from Denmark, Norway, and Sweden—streamed into this country.

A Shift in Immigration Another flood of immigrants—about 22 million—reached our shores between 1890 and 1924. Most of them came from southern and eastern Europe, from countries such as Italy, Greece, Poland, and Russia.

During the past 50 years, immigration from Europe to the United States has lagged far behind immigration from the rest of the world. Asia now accounts for the largest share of foreign newcomers, followed by Latin America.

Enslaved Africans Among the early immigrants to America were some who did not come willingly. Western and central Africans were taken by force from their homes, shipped across the Atlantic Ocean, and sold as slaves in the Caribbean Islands and North and South America. Between 1619 and 1808, before it became illegal to bring enslaved persons into the United States, some 500,000 people were brought to the country in this way. Most African Americans today are descendants of enslaved persons. Others are immigrants from various countries in Africa and the Caribbean region.

Immigration Patterns Until the mid-1900s most American immigrants came from Europe. Today the largest numbers of immigrants, like these girls taking part in the Latino celebration of Cinco de Mayo in New York City, have come from Spanish-speaking countries. ***Speculating*** **Why do people from other countries want to live in the United States?**

A Diverse Population

The American population is extraordinarily diverse in terms of **ethnic,** or racial, backgrounds. Many Americans today do not identify themselves as members of a single ethnic group. However, whites of European descent number more than 234 million. There are about 37 million African Americans, over 12 million Asians and Pacific Islanders, and almost 2.8 million Native Americans. More than 39 million people are Latinos—people of any race who trace their ancestry to the Spanish-speaking countries of the Western Hemisphere.

Religious Diversity Our ethnic diversity is matched by religious diversity. More than 200 million people practice some form of Christianity. Jews, Muslims, Buddhists, and many other religious groups are also free to worship according to their conscience. Those who do not practice any religion are equally at home here.

Many Traditions As people with different beliefs and backgrounds have made lives for themselves in the United States, many of their "old country" traditions have become part of the American culture. The American culture is a rich blend of varied influences.

Transforming America

Between 1830 and 1930, the nation's population grew from about 12 million people to about 120 million people. About 40 million of those new Americans were immigrants.

Over the years, the American population has changed in many ways. In the mid-1800s, for example, people began moving from rural areas to cities. The higher wages paid in the cities attracted workers. Many of those moving to the cities found work in newly opened factories. These workers became known as blue-collar workers. Others found jobs in offices, schools, stores, and other nonfactory settings and were called white-collar workers. By 1920 more than half of all Americans lived in towns or cities.

Another significant change was the shift to service industry jobs. In the past few decades, manufacturing has lost ground to what we call the **"service economy."** Many Americans now earn a living by providing services—practicing law or medicine, programming computers, teaching, and so forth. There are also more women and at-home workers in the labor force than ever before.

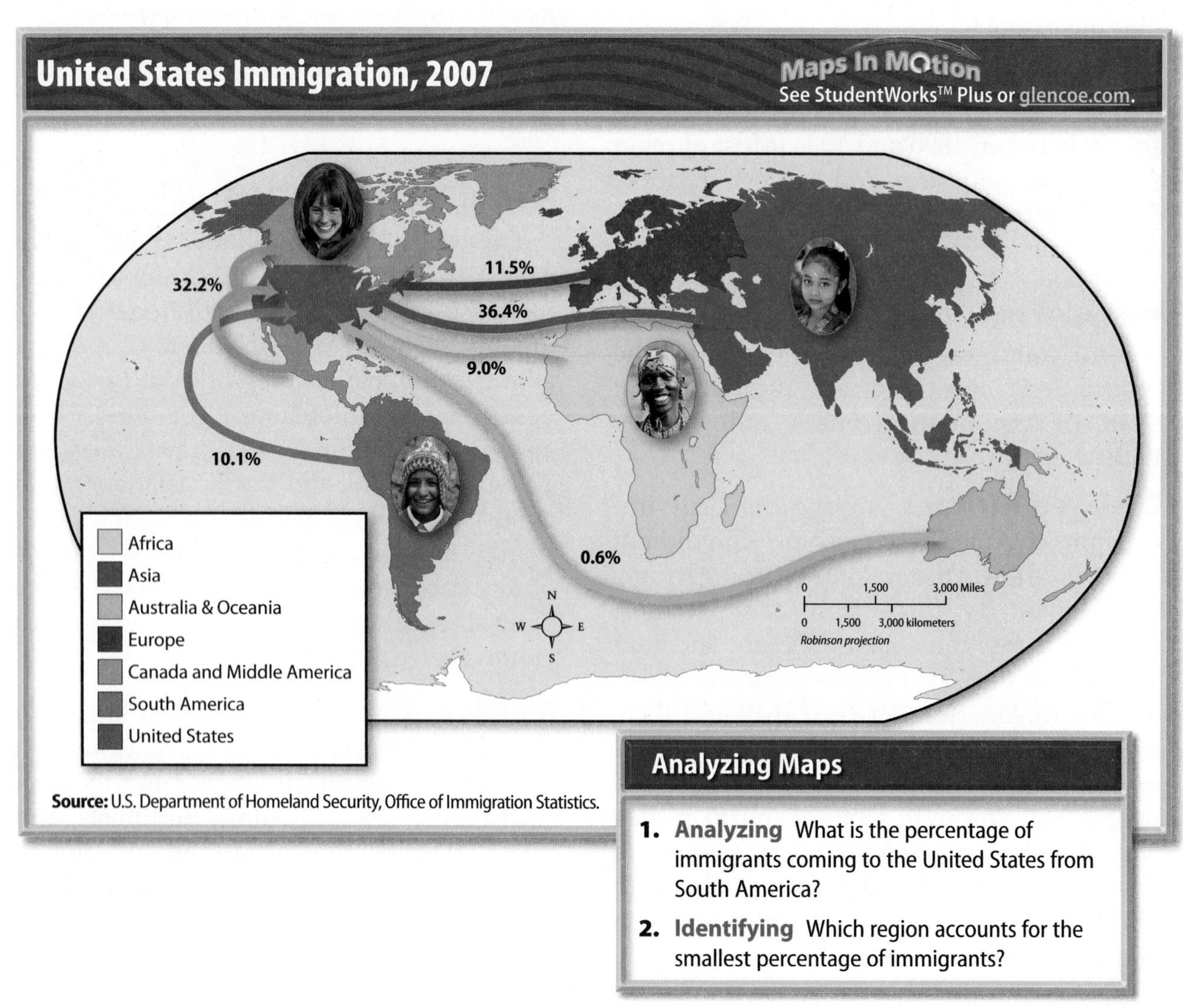

Source: U.S. Department of Homeland Security, Office of Immigration Statistics.

Analyzing Maps

1. **Analyzing** What is the percentage of immigrants coming to the United States from South America?
2. **Identifying** Which region accounts for the smallest percentage of immigrants?

Cultural Diversity Americans enjoy foods, music, sports, and holiday traditions brought to the United States by immigrants from around the world. This Chicago parade marks the Chinese New Year. ***Analyzing*** **Why is it important for American citizens to share cultural traditions?**

The places where we live are changing too. For example, shortly after the Civil War, African Americans, freed from slavery, headed for northern cities, seeking jobs and a new way of life. The result was a migration, or mass movement, of African Americans from the South to the North. For much of our history, the Northeast was the most populous part of the country. Today, the South claims that distinction, and the population there and in the West is growing faster than in any other regions.

The population is changing in other ways, including the following:

- The average age of citizens is climbing upward as people live longer and have fewer children.
- Record numbers of Americans are now earning college and graduate degrees.
- Latinos, commonly referred to as Hispanic Americans, are the fastest-growing ethnic group.

Indeed, if current patterns continue, Latinos and other minority groups, taken as a whole, will soon be in the majority.

Reading Check **Summarizing** In what ways is the American population changing?

American Values and Institutions

Main Idea **Americans share key values, and these values are reflected in the important institutions of American life.**

Civics & You What do you think makes a person an American? Read to find out about the values we share and how they have shaped the character of the American people.

Even though American society is more diverse than ever, certain shared ideas help unite Americans of different backgrounds. Two of these important ideas are our values and our institutions.

What Are Values?

Do you agree with most of your classmates on what is good and what is bad? The general **principles,** or beliefs, you use to make these judgments are your **values.** Values are broad ideas about what is good or desirable, and are shared by people in a society. Values are important because they influence the way we act.

TIME Political Cartoons

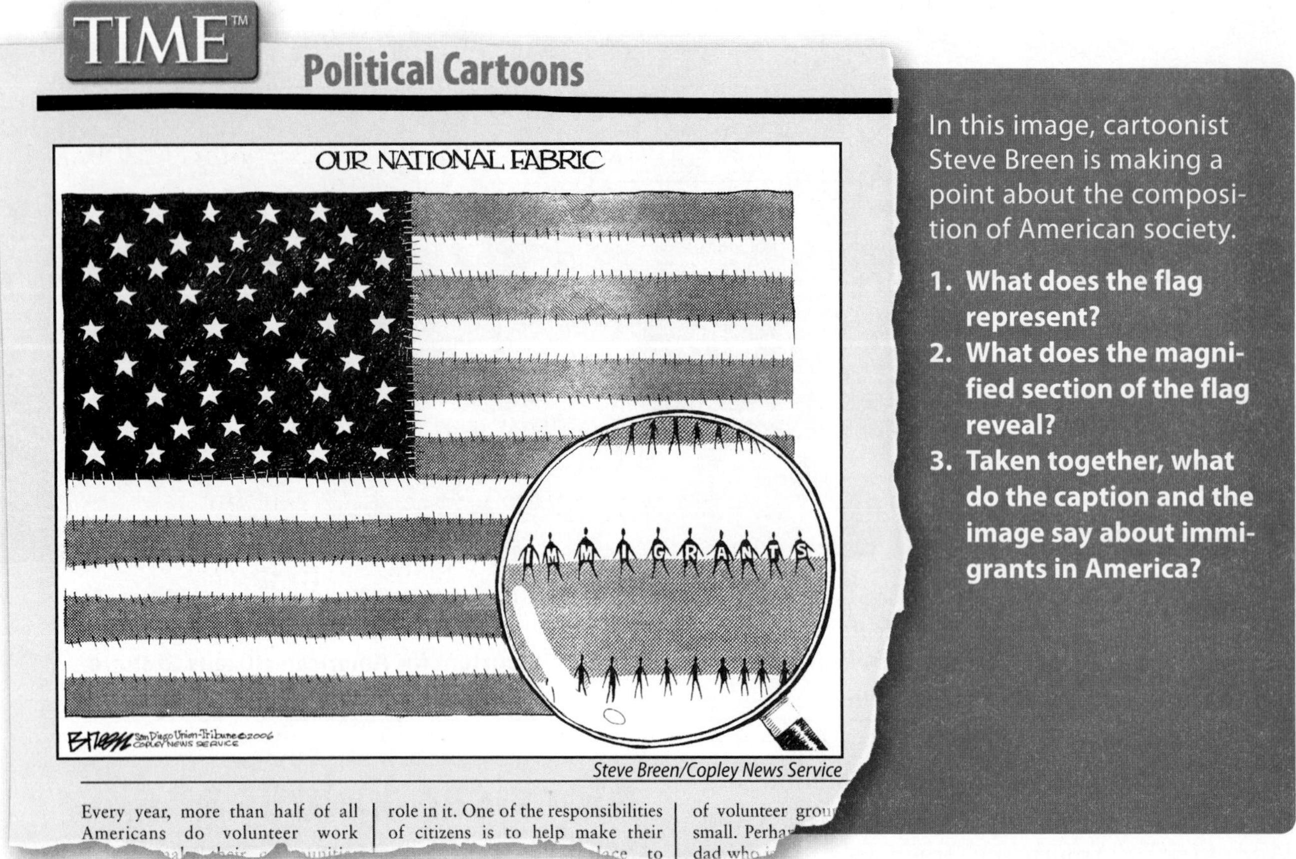

Steve Breen/Copley News Service

In this image, cartoonist Steve Breen is making a point about the composition of American society.

1. **What does the flag represent?**
2. **What does the magnified section of the flag reveal?**
3. **Taken together, what do the caption and the image say about immigrants in America?**

Basic American Values

Everyone's list of basic American values will include different ideas. However, some values would appear on almost every list. These include freedom, equality, opportunity, justice, democracy, unity, respect, and tolerance. Some of these values, such as equality and opportunity, and respect and tolerance, are linked. Can you think of other values to include on this list?

Shared Values Unite Americans

Another important effect of having a set of shared values is the unity it builds among Americans. For example, one very important source of American unity is a common civic and political heritage based on the country's founding documents. These key documents include the Declaration of Independence, the U.S. Constitution of 1787, and the Bill of Rights of 1791. American ideals of individual rights to "life, liberty, and the pursuit of happiness" are in these founding documents. So are such values as **popular sovereignty** (government by consent of the governed) through

- fair, free, and regular elections;
- equal justice under the law;
- majority rule through the people's representatives in government.

A second significant source of unity is a single language, English, which generally is accepted as the primary means of communication in education, government, and business. Americans are free to speak any language. However, some people think that the United States is strengthened by the common and public use of one language, which can be used by diverse groups of Americans to communicate freely with one another. Can you think of other values that have helped unite Americans throughout history?

American Institutions

Each society has its own social **institutions.** These are not buildings or places but sets of ideas that people have about relationships, obligations, roles, and functions. As in every society, the most important institution in American life is the *family.* The family is the core of social life: it produces new generations, socializes the young, offers care and affection, and provides economic support. Parents and caregivers are also transmitters of values, both personal and national, to their children.

Other important institutions in American life, which also reflect our nation's shared values, are religious, educational, and social. *Religious institutions,* such as churches, temples, and mosques, can promote social unity and provide a sense of meaning and belonging. *Educational institutions* at all levels reflect our society's culture, history, and learning, create a common identity, and promote personal growth and development. *Social institutions,* such as clubs and volunteer service organizations, can be another way we share our common values.

The different parts of our government are also institutions. *Governmental institutions* were created, and have developed over time, based on important shared American values. As Abraham Lincoln explained in his first Inaugural Address in 1861:

> ***"This country, with its institutions, belongs to the people who inhabit it. Whenever they shall grow weary of the existing government, they can exercise their constitutional right of amending it, or their revolutionary right to dismember, or overthrow it."***
>
> —Abraham Lincoln, *First Inaugural Address*

With these words, Lincoln underscored the most important concept of American government: the people, not the government, are in control.

Reading Check **Identifying** What are some types of important American institutions?

Vocabulary

1. **Define** the following terms and use them correctly in sentences: *civics, citizenship, citizen, service economy, value, popular sovereignty, institution.*

Main Ideas

2. **Describing** What do people of a nation share as citizens?
3. **Explaining** What impact do American values have on society?

Critical Thinking

4. **BIG Ideas** What do you think is the most important source of American unity? Explain your answer.
5. **Sequencing** On a diagram similar to the one below, identify the period when various ethnic groups immigrated to the United States.

To 1500	
1600–1700	
1800–1900	
2000–today	

CITIZENSHIP Activity

6. **Expository Writing** Review the discussion of values in this section. Is there a value not listed that you think should be included? What is it? Why would you include it?

Study Central™ To review this section, go to glencoe.com.

Section Audio Spotlight Video

Who Are America's Citizens?

Guide to Reading

Big Idea

Citizens possess certain rights. With citizenship, Americans also have certain responsibilities.

Content Vocabulary

- naturalization *(p. 15)*
- alien *(p. 16)*
- immigrant *(p. 16)*
- deport *(p. 19)*

Academic Vocabulary

- deny *(p. 17)*
- obtain *(p. 17)*
- priority *(p. 18)*

Reading Strategy

Defining As you read, complete a diagram like the one below that shows the different paths to U.S. citizenship and who qualifies for each.

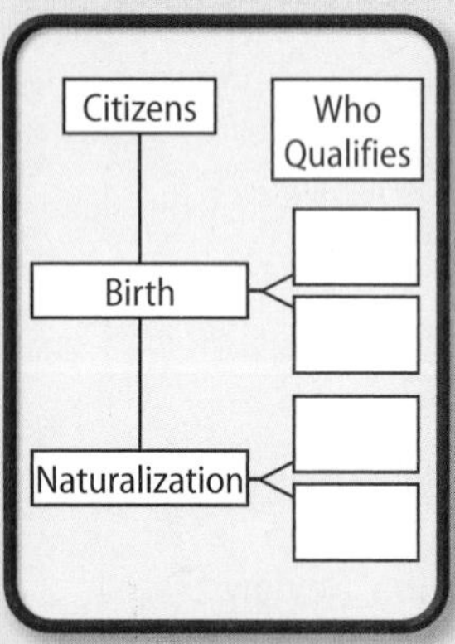

Real World Civics What does your U.S. citizenship mean to you? The aircraft carrier USS *Midway* set the scene for Navy sailor Hugston Brooks from Liberia and 80 other Marine and Navy service members from 25 countries to become U.S. citizens on Veterans Day in 2004. The San Diego ceremony was held during a military celebration of Veterans Day. For many people around the world, becoming a U.S. citizen is a lifelong dream. With nearly 12,500 noncitizen active-duty sailors, the Navy now provides a streamlined route to naturalized citizenship for many recruits.

▼ **U.S. Navy sailor Hugston Brooks**

Path to Citizenship

Main Idea **In the United States, there are two ways to become a citizen: by birth and by a process called naturalization.**

Civics & You What should people who want to become U.S. citizens know about our country? Read to find out about the process of becoming a citizen.

You learned that citizens are community members who owe loyalty to the government and are entitled to protection from it. Every country has rules about how people gain citizenship. The U.S. Constitution establishes two ways to become a citizen: by birth and, for foreign-born people who choose to become citizens, by a legal process called **naturalization.**

Citizenship by Birth

If you were born in any of the 50 states or the District of Columbia, you automatically became an American citizen at birth. The same is true if you were born outside the country but in American territory, such as Puerto Rico or Guam, or on a U.S. military base overseas. Even if you were born elsewhere, you could still claim American citizenship if your parents are both citizens or if one is a citizen who has lived in the United States. Children born on American soil to non-U.S. citizens also acquire U.S. citizenship at birth.

Americans may hold dual citizenship. This means that they enjoy rights in the United States and in another country. For example, a child born abroad to American parents may be both a U.S. citizen and a citizen of the country of his or her birth.

Shared Opportunities Both native-born and naturalized citizens can vote in America. In his room at Camp Eagle in Baghdad, Iraq, U.S. Army Sergeant George Scheufele fills out an absentee ballot for a presidential election. ***Defining*** **U.S. citizens are encouraged to vote. Is this more a right or responsibility of citizenship? Explain.**

The Naturalization Process

Several million noncitizens, or **aliens,** live in the United States. Some come to study, to work, or to visit relatives. They remain citizens of their own countries and eventually return home. Other aliens plan to settle here and become naturalized citizens. More than half a million **immigrants**—people who move permanently to a new country—gain American citizenship each year.

Beginning the Process Aliens who want to become United States citizens must first sign a statement saying just that. This Declaration of Intention is then filed with the U.S. Citizenship and Immigration Services (USCIS), an agency of the national government. For most aliens, the next step comes after living in the United States at least five years. (Aliens who are married to citizens wait only three years.) During this time, many immigrants take special classes to prepare for citizenship. Then, if they are at least 18 years old and have lived for at least three months in the state where they seek naturalization, they may file an application for citizenship.

Naturalized Citizens President George W. Bush poses with new American citizens at their swearing in on Ellis Island, New York. ***Reviewing*** **What are the steps that aliens must take to become citizens of the United States?**

Interview and Examination After the paperwork is checked, the alien has an interview with a USCIS official. Agency officials want to be sure the alien meets the necessary requirements and is of good moral character. The applicant must also take a citizenship exam that consists of questions about reading, writing, and speaking English and basic facts about the history and government of the United States. Afterward, the USCIS makes its decision.

Oath of Allegiance If the application is granted, the final step in naturalization is attending a ceremony and pledging an oath of allegiance. The alien swears to be loyal to this country above all others, to obey the Constitution and other laws, and to perform military or other duties if needed. Then the person signs a document and is declared a citizen of the United States. If he or she has children under 18, they automatically become naturalized citizens, too.

Native Americans For a long time, most Native Americans were excluded from citizenship. A few groups became citizens through treaties with the federal government. Later, Congress offered citizenship to individual Native Americans who gave up their traditional culture. Not until 1924 did Congress make all Native Americans citizens of the United States.

A Lifelong Privilege

Whether they are naturalized or native-born, most Americans keep their citizenship forever. Only the federal government can both grant citizenship and take it away. State governments can **deny,** or refuse, a convicted criminal some of the privileges of citizenship, such as voting, but they do not have the power to deny citizenship itself.

The government may strip naturalized citizens of citizenship if it was improperly **obtained,** or gained. Citizens can lose citizenship in three ways: through denaturalization, through expatriation, or by being convicted of certain crimes. Native-born U.S. citizens can lose citizenship only through their own actions and cannot be denaturalized.

Denaturalization The loss of citizenship through fraud or deception during the naturalization process is called denaturalization. For example, former Nazis who engaged in war crimes during World War II and later lied about their wartime activities were denaturalized after they entered the United States or when they applied for citizenship.

Expatriation The simplest way to lose citizenship is through expatriation, or giving up one's citizenship by leaving one's native country to live in a foreign country. Expatriation may be voluntary or involuntary. For example, a person who becomes a naturalized citizen of another country automatically loses his or her American citizenship. Involuntary expatriation would occur in the case of a child whose parents become citizens of another country.

Punishment For a Crime A person may lose citizenship when convicted of certain federal crimes that involve extreme disloyalty. These crimes include treason, participation in a rebellion, and attempts to overthrow the government through violent means.

Reading Check **Summarizing** Describe the two methods of obtaining U.S. citizenship.

TIME™ Teens in *Action*

Chris Garrett

Meet Chris Garrett, a 16-year-old who lives near Key West, Florida. Thanks to his work to protect our natural resources, Chris has received an Environmental Hero Award from the National Oceanic & Atmospheric Administration—and a Congressional Certificate of Recognition.

QUESTION: How do you make a difference?

ANSWER: I helped start Team Panda—a youth conservation organization sponsored by the World Wildlife Fund. There are now 16 students in the group helping to preserve the environment.

Q: Do you work with elected officials?

A: Definitely. Much of our work is geared to changing government policies to help further conservation efforts. Elected officials want to hear what students have to say. It's really great to see officials making huge decisions that will protect our environment because we got involved.

Q: What inspires you?

A: I believe the more we give to help others, the more we gain for ourselves. And growing up in the Florida Keys, you learn the environment is very special and it's important to preserve it.

Q: What would you tell other teens who want to help conserve the environment?

A: Find an organization that's dedicated to conservation and that sounds appealing to you. Or start your own.

Team Panda members

Making a Difference CITIZENSHIP

What do you think motivated Chris to start Team Panda?

Aliens in America

Main Idea **Even though the United States controls the admission of aliens to this country, each year millions of people enter America illegally.**

Civics & You Why do you think so many people want to come to the United States? Read to find out why our country is such a magnet to people around the world.

The United States restricts the number of immigrants who can enter the country. Millions apply, but only about one million are admitted each year. Traditionally, the relatives of U.S. citizens and people with needed job skills receive the highest **priority,** or first consideration. Family members still get special consideration, but because of the Immigration Act of 1990, emphasis has shifted toward welcoming "those who want to work and produce and contribute," as one member of Congress put it. The new policy benefits people with particular skills, talents, or the money to invest in our economy.

Illegal Aliens

Despite immigration limits, more than 12 million aliens are living in the United States illegally. Some were refused permission to immigrate; others never applied for permission because they feared a long, slow process or being turned down.

Illegal aliens come to the United States in a variety of ways. A few enter the country as temporary visitors but never leave. Others risk arrest by illegally crossing our borders with Mexico and Canada. Other illegal aliens are foreigners who have stayed in the United States after their legal permits expired.

Whatever the method, the reason is usually the same. "I came for work and for a better life," explained one Mexican immigrant. Yet illegal aliens often have a difficult time in the United States. Many have no

Border Security A U.S. Immigration and Naturalization Service agent searches a Mexican fishing boat for people who may be entering the country illegally. ***Discussing*** **Why do people enter the United States illegally?**

friends or family here, no place to live, and no sure way to earn money. It is against the law to hire illegal aliens, and those who do find work usually receive little pay and no benefits. Every day they live with the fear that government officials will discover and **deport** them—send them back to their own countries.

The United States Border Patrol is the law-enforcement unit of the USCIS. Its primary responsibility is to detect and prevent the illegal entry of aliens into the United States. The Border Patrol guards the 6,000 miles of Mexican and Canadian international land borders and 2,000 miles of coastal waters surrounding the Florida Peninsula and the island of Puerto Rico.

Legal Aliens

United States law classifies aliens into different categories. A resident alien is a person from a foreign country who has established permanent residence in the United States. Resident aliens may stay in the United States as long as they wish without becoming American citizens. A nonresident alien is a person from a foreign country who expects to stay in the United States for a short, specified period. A Turkish journalist who has come to report on a presidential election is an example of a nonresident alien. Refugees are another category. Refugees are people fleeing their country to escape persecution.

Aliens who have entered the United States legally lead lives much like those of American citizens. Aliens may hold jobs, own property, attend public schools, and receive other government services. They pay taxes and are entitled to legal protection.

Aliens do not have full political rights, however. They may not vote in elections or run for office. They may not serve on juries or work in most government jobs. In addition, unlike U.S. citizens, aliens must carry identification cards at all times.

Reading Check **Contrasting** How do the rights of legal aliens differ from those of U.S. citizens?

Vocabulary

1. **Explain** how each of the following terms relates to citizenship in the United States: *naturalization, alien, immigrant, deport.*

Main Ideas

2. **Explaining** What is dual citizenship? How can an American obtain dual citizenship?
3. **Analyzing** Why do you think the United States puts a limit on the number of immigrants who may enter the country?

Critical Thinking

4. **Synthesizing** If you were a government official, how would you prevent illegal aliens from entering the United States?
5. **BIG Ideas** On a chart like the one below, list the sequence of steps in the naturalization process.

Naturalization
Step 1 ______
Step 2 ______
Step 3 ______

CITIZENSHIP Activity

6. **Descriptive Writing** Interview an American who became a citizen through the naturalization process. Write a one-page paper in which you answer these questions: What reasons brought him or her to the United States? Why did he or she want to become an American citizen?

Study Central™ To review this section, go to glencoe.com.

Government and the People

Guide to Reading

Big Idea

People form governments to establish order, provide security, and accomplish common goals.

Content Vocabulary

- government *(p. 21)*
- public policy *(p. 22)*
- budget *(p. 22)*
- democracy *(p. 23)*
- direct democracy *(p. 23)*
- representative democracy *(p. 24)*
- republic *(p. 24)*
- monarchy *(p. 24)*
- majority rule *(p. 25)*
- authoritarian *(p. 25)*
- totalitarian *(p. 26)*

Academic Vocabulary

- community *(p. 21)*
- enforce *(p. 21)*
- constrain *(p. 25)*

Reading Strategy

Organizing Create a chart like the one below. Then list the different types of government and a brief description of each.

Types of Government	Description
1. Democracy	
2.	
3.	
4.	

Real World Civics Curious teens scramble over rocks as they near the spectacular Fiery Furnace in Arches National Park and are careful to leave the park the way they found it. This park is one of nearly 400 national parks in 49 states to which lawmakers are considering cutting services. About 118 million people visit these precious gems for fun, recreation, inspiration, and renewal. However, rising costs for maintenance and staffing, which is provided by the national government, may cause some national parks to reduce tours and public access, cut back on hours, and in some cases close parkland.

▼ **Ranger Clay Parcels leads a group through the Fiery Furnace of Arches National Park in Moab, Utah.**

The Need for Government

Main Idea **The different levels of government provide many different services.**

Civics & You When was the last time a government provided you with a service? Read to find out how local, state, and national governments serve the public.

A **government** is the ruling authority for a **community,** or society. Any organization that has the power to make and **enforce,** or carry out, laws and decisions for its members acts as a government.

For hundreds of years, people have formed governments. The earliest Native Americans had tribal councils. Thomas Hobbes, an English political thinker during the 1600s, believed that without government, life would be "solitary, poor, nasty, brutish, and short." If each of us could do just as he or she pleased, fighting probably would be common, and survival would depend on strength and skill.

Think about trying to play basketball with no rules or referees. The game would probably be a chaotic free-for-all. Similarly, if there were no government to make and enforce laws, we would live in a state of confusion, violence, and fear. Government can make it possible for people to live together peacefully and productively.

What Governments Do

The most important purpose of a government is to provide laws, or rules of conduct. These laws help prevent conflicts between individuals, groups, or nations and help settle any conflicts that do occur.

Government Services This fire station protects the community and also serves as a place where these citizens can cast their votes in their neighborhoods. ***Identifying*** **What other types of public services does government provide?**

Functions of Government

KEEP ORDER
• Pass and enforce traffic laws
• Establish courts
PROVIDE SECURITY
• Prevent crime
• Protect citizens from foreign attacks
PROVIDE SERVICES
• Provide libraries, schools, hospitals, parks, water, utilities
GUIDE THE COMMUNITY
• Manage the economy
• Conduct foreign relations

Analyzing Charts

1. **Classifying** Under what function of government would you find setting up fire departments?
2. **Explaining** How do courts keep order?

Keep Order Conflicts are unavoidable when people live together in a community. Governments make laws to help prevent conflicts and to settle those conflicts that do arise.

Governments have the power to enforce the laws. For example, to make sure that drivers obey traffic regulations, police officers are empowered to ticket or arrest violators. Courts decide whether those accused of crimes are guilty and how they should be punished if found guilty.

Provide Security Along with the need for law and order come concerns about community security—defending citizens and their land from enemies. For this reason, governments set up armed forces and agencies that watch for likely sources of trouble.

Provide Public Services Governments provide many services that would not be available otherwise. Governments create and manage libraries, schools, hospitals, parks, and recreation centers. Government workers build and repair streets, erect bridges, collect garbage, and deliver the mail.

Many government services are aimed at keeping the public healthy and safe. Local communities set up fire departments and ambulance services. States license drivers and doctors. Other government agencies protect us from dangerous medicines and spoiled food. Government inspectors check for safety problems in everything from factories to amusement park rides.

Governments also give help to needy people. For example, in each of the 50 states, poor families and people who are out of work can receive food, aid, or cash. Government agencies also supply affordable housing, health care, job training, and special programs for people with disabilities.

Guide the Community Another function of government is to formulate **public policy,** or a course of government action to achieve community goals. When government leaders decide they want to protect consumers, for example, or strengthen national security, they are setting public policy goals. When they pass laws or develop guidelines to reach these goals, they are making public policy.

Most public policy decisions involve financial planning. Governments have limited amounts of money, and they must use it wisely. Creating a **budget,** or a plan for collecting and spending money, is key to the success of the community.

Another part of guiding the community is developing relations with the community's neighbors and other outsiders. Governments often take responsibility for communicating and cooperating with other governments on matters of trade, travel, and military agreements for the benefit of their citizens.

Levels of Government

Many levels of government exist, each representing a particular collection of people. Each of the 50 states has its own government; so do most counties, cities, and towns. The students in your school may have their own student government.

National Government Although each of the above is a government, when most people talk about "the government," they are talking about the national government—the government of an entire country. In the United States, the national government is made up of three branches of government. These branches are the legislative, the executive, and the judicial branches. A national government is different from other levels of government in two important ways.

First, a national government has the highest level of authority over its citizens. A city or state government cannot make any laws that would go against the laws of the national government. The national government, however, has the power to make whatever laws it feels would benefit the country. Second, a national government provides the basic framework for citizenship.

State and Local Government The national government makes and enforces laws for the entire country. Each state decides matters for the people in that state.

The level of government closest to Americans is local government. Local governments include counties, cities, and towns. Your school may have a student government, and if you choose to belong to a club like Girl Scouts or 4-H, you respect that organization's governing body, too.

However, state and local governments, as well as governments of organizations, cannot take actions that go against the laws and authority of the national government.

Reading Check **Describing** How do governments keep order and provide security?

Types of Government

Main Idea **The people are the ultimate rulers of democratic countries, while in totalitarian states, a single person or small group holds all the power.**

Civics & You Did you know there is more than one type of democracy? Read to find out about other kinds of democracies.

Democratic Government

The foundations of **democracy** are more than 2,500 years old. Democracy began in the ancient Greek city of Athens. Athens had a **direct democracy**—all the citizens met to debate government matters and vote firsthand. Direct democracy is not practical for most countries today because of their large areas and populations.

Public Safety Government inspectors regularly check amusement park rides to ensure that they meet safety requirements. ***Identifying*** **In what other ways does the government protect your health and safety?**

What Is a Republic? Many countries have a **representative democracy** instead. The citizens choose a smaller group to represent them, make laws, and govern on their behalf. For most Americans today, the terms representative democracy, **republic,** and constitutional republic mean the same thing: a system of limited government in which the people are the ultimate source of governmental power. The United States is the oldest representative democracy in the world.

Constitutional Monarchy Another kind of democracy is the constitutional monarchy. The word **monarchy** describes a government with a hereditary ruler—a king, queen, or other royal figure who inherits this position of power. In most countries with monarchs, the power of the hereditary ruler is limited by the country's constitution and laws.

Modern constitutional monarchies generally follow democratic practices. The monarchs are heads of state only, presiding at ceremonies and serving as symbols of unity. The queen of Great Britain and the emperor of Japan are two examples of constitutional monarchs.

Principles of American Democracy

RULE OF LAW
• All people, including those who govern, are bound by the law.
LIMITED GOVERNMENT
• Government is not all-powerful—it may do only those things that the people have given it the power to do.
CONSENT OF THE GOVERNED
• American citizens are the source of all government power.
INDIVIDUAL RIGHTS
• In the American democracy, individual rights are protected by government.
REPRESENTATIVE GOVERNMENT
• People elect government leaders to make the laws and govern on their behalf.

Analyzing Charts

1. **Identifying** Who is the source of power in direct and representative democracies?
2. **Explaining** What binds the governed together in a democracy?

Democratic Principles

Abraham Lincoln described our democracy as a "government of the people, by the people, for the people." His words make three important points. First, the power of the government comes from the citizens. Second, Americans themselves, acting through their representatives, run their government. Third, the purpose of the government is to make the United States a better place for those who live here.

Voting and Democracy All genuine democracies have free, fair, and competitive elections. Everyone's vote must carry the same weight. This principle is often expressed in the phrase "one person, one vote." All candidates have the right to express their views freely to the public, and citizens are free to support any candidate or issue.

The legal requirements for voting must be kept to a minimum. For example, our voting laws center on age, residence, and citizenship, while other factors, such as wealth, race, and ethnic and religious background, cannot be used to restrict voting. Finally, citizens may vote freely by secret ballot, without fearing punishment for their voting decisions.

Civics ONLINE

Student Web Activity Visit glencoe.com and complete the Chapter 1 Web Activity.

Comparing Democratic and Authoritarian Systems

	Selection of Leaders	Extent of Government Power	Means of Ensuring Compliance	Political Parties
Democracy	Leaders are chosen in fair elections with universal suffrage	The government is limited in power by the constitution and laws; citizens' rights and freedoms are protected	The government relies on the rule of law	Multiple parties exist
Authoritarianism (including absolute monarchy, dictatorship, and totalitarianism)	Rulers inherit their positions or take power by force	Rulers have unlimited power; the government may impose an official ideology and control all aspects of political, economic, and civic life	The government relies on state control of the media, propaganda, military or police power, and terror	Power lies with a single party

Analyzing Charts

1. **Explaining** Why do you think dictators control their military and police forces?
2. **Comparing** How do the leaders gain their positions of power in each form of government?

Voters Have Choices Competitive elections and competing political parties are an important element in democracies. A political party is a group of individuals with broad, common interests who organize to support candidates for office and determine public policy. Competing political parties give voters a choice among candidates. Also, parties out of power serve as watchdogs of parties in power.

Majority Rule Another principle of our democracy is **majority rule.** French philosopher Jean-Jacques Rousseau promoted this idea in the late 1700s. According to this principle, citizens agree that when differences of opinion arise, they will abide by what most people want. At the same time, they respect the rights of those in the minority.

Respect for minority rights is sometimes difficult, though, especially if society is under a great deal of stress. For example, after the terrorist attacks of 2001, President George W. Bush realized that many Americans might turn their anger against Muslims in the United States. He explained that Islam is a peaceful religion and urged Americans to treat Muslim Americans fairly.

Authoritarian Government

In democratic regimes, the people rule. In **authoritarian** regimes, power is held by an individual or a group not accountable to the people.

Absolute Monarchy Until about the 1600s, monarchs were mostly absolute monarchs. That is, they had unlimited authority to rule as they wished. Many countries still have monarchs, but absolute monarchy is almost nonexistent today. In the Middle East, however, the king of Saudi Arabia and the emir of Qatar might still be considered "absolute." Their power is technically unrestricted, although they do consult with advisers and are **constrained,** or bound, by Islamic law.

Dictatorships Another form of authoritarian government is a dictatorship. Dictators, like absolute monarchs, exercise complete control over the state. Unlike absolute monarchs, who usually acquire their power through inheritance, dictators usually take power by force. At times, when a crisis situation demands a strong leader, authorities may place them in charge. To stay in power, most dictators rely on the police and military. They often tamper with elections or refuse to hold them. They also limit freedoms of speech, assembly, and the press.

Scores of dictators have ruled throughout history. Those who seek only personal gain are often overthrown quickly. With the help of the United States, Panamanian dictator Manuel Noriega was overthrown in 1989. Other dictators endure for decades. Fidel Castro led Cuba from 1959 until he retired in 2008. Saddam Hussein ruled Iraq from 1979 until he was overthrown in 2003. Hussein was convicted of crimes against humanity and executed in 2007.

Totalitarianism Many dictators impose totalitarian rule on their people. In a **totalitarian** state, the government's control extends to almost all aspects of people's lives. Totalitarian leaders ban political opposition. They regulate what industries and farms produce. They suppress individual freedom, dictating what people should believe and with whom they may interact. The people lack the power to limit their rulers.

To enforce their ideology, or ideas about life and society, totalitarian leaders control the media and use propaganda, scare tactics, and violence. Three of the most notorious totalitarian regimes arose in the 1920s and 1930s. They were Nazi Germany under Adolf Hitler, Fascist Italy under Benito Mussolini, and the Soviet Union under Joseph Stalin. Today, the nations of China, Cuba, and North Korea are usually considered totalitarian states.

Reading Check **Describing** What is a totalitarian government?

Review

Vocabulary

1. **Write** complete sentences that demonstrate the meaning of each of the following terms: *government, public policy, budget, democracy, direct democracy, representative democracy, republic, monarchy, majority rule, authoritarian, totalitarian.*

Main Ideas

2. **Identifying** Name three public services that governments provide.
3. **Comparing** What is the difference between rulers in a democracy and rulers in a totalitarian state?

Critical Thinking

4. **BIG Ideas** What do you think would happen if there were no governments anywhere in the world? Describe such a situation, then explain why governments are necessary.
5. **Organizing** On a diagram like the one below, write the functions of government.

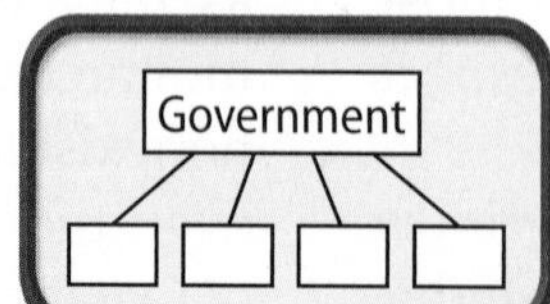

6. **Analyzing Visuals** Review the principles of American democracy on page 24. How does the American government carry out the principle of consent of the governed?

CITIZENSHIP Activity

7. **Descriptive Writing** In a one-page essay, explain how you think your life would be different if you were living in a country ruled by a monarch.

Study Central™ To review this section, go to glencoe.com.

Chapter 1 Visual Summary

The American People

- Because of its heritage, the United States is often called "a nation of immigrants."
- Until the mid-1900s, most immigrants came from Europe.
- Asia now accounts for the largest share of immigrants to the United States.
- The United States is a diverse nation, reflecting the values of many groups.

American Values and Institutions

- Values are ideas about what is good or desirable that are shared by people in a society.
- Our basic values include freedom, equality, opportunity, justice, and tolerance.
- Every society has institutions that help it transmit its values.
- Important American institutions are the family, religious, educational, social, and governmental institutions.

Yosemite National Park

Citizenship

- According to the U.S. Constitution, people can become American citizens by birth and through naturalization.
- Millions of illegal aliens live in the United States. Legal aliens have entered the country lawfully.

Government

- People need governments to make and enforce laws and to help us meet our needs.

The purposes of government include the following:

- Providing order and security
- Providing public services
- Guiding the community
- Although all governments carry out the same basic functions, there are differences in the ways governments can be organized.
- The main types of government are democratic government and authoritarian government.
- In a democracy, the supreme political authority rests with the people.

School crossing guard

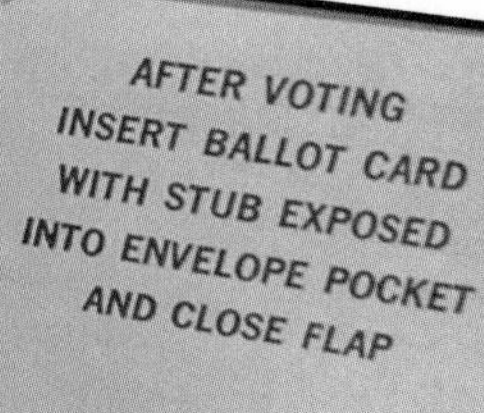

Official ballot

Study anywhere, anytime! Download quizzes and flash cards to your PDA from glencoe.com.

Chapter 1

Assessment

Standardized Test Practice

TEST-TAKING TIP

Keep daily notes to review for tests and examinations. It often helps you retain information if you review your notes with a study partner.

Reviewing Vocabulary

Directions: Choose the word(s) that best completes the sentence.

1. ______ are broad ideas about what is good and desirable.

A public policies
B institutions
C values
D budgets

2. Government by consent of the governed is ______.

A community
B majority rule
C naturalization
D popular sovereignty

3. People from foreign countries who plan to stay in the United States for a short time are called ______.

A citizens
B immigrants
C aliens
D institutions

4. The people are the ultimate source of government power in a ______.

A monarchy
B dictatorship
C republic
D totalitarian state

Reviewing Main Ideas

Directions: Choose the best answer for each question.

Section 1 *(pp. 6–13)*

5. Which is the fastest growing ethnic group in the United States today?

A Native Americans
B African Americans
C European Americans
D Latino Americans

6. Which value is part of Americans' common civic and political heritage?

A fair elections
B volunteerism
C caring parents
D cultural education

Section 2 *(pp. 14–19)*

7. Which person is NOT a United States citizen?

A a child born in Guam to Japanese parents
B a girl born in Yemen to an American mother
C a boy born in Illinois to Mexican parents
D a child born in Great Britain to Irish parents

8. What is the primary responsibility of the National Border Patrol?

A to deport aliens with expired visas
B to prevent illegal entry of aliens
C to naturalize resident aliens
D to issue visas to legal aliens

Section 3 *(pp. 20–26)*

9. Which function of government do public libraries fulfill?

A keeping order
B providing public security
C providing services
D guiding the community

10. Which factor is a legal restriction on voting in the United States?

A age
B race
C wealth
D religion

GO ON

Critical Thinking

Directions: Base your answers to questions 11 and 12 on the chart below and your knowledge of Chapter 1.

Rule of Law
All people, including those who govern, are bound by the law.
Limited Government
Government is not all powerful—it may do only those things that the people have given it the power to do.
Consent of the Governed
American citizens are the source of all governmental power.
Individual Rights
In the American democracy, individual rights are protected by government.
Representative Government
People elect leaders to make the laws and govern on their behalf.

11. Which principle of American democracy prevents a president from serving more terms than allowed in Amendment XXII of the Constitution?

A rule of law

B limited government

C individual rights

D representative government

12. Which practice best reflects the principle of representative government?

A serving on a jury

B voting for mayor

C writing to the editor

D polling public opinion

Document Based Questions

Directions: Analyze the following document and answer the short-answer questions that follow.

The passage is from *The Social Contract* by Jean Jacques Rousseau, the eighteenth-century political theorist, who believed that real democracy was impossible.

Nothing is more dangerous than the influence of private interests on public affairs; and the abuse of the laws by the government is a lesser evil than the corruption of the legislator [lawmaker], which is the infallible result of the pursuit of private interests. For when the State is changed in its substance all reform becomes impossible. A people which would never abuse the government would likewise never abuse its independence; a people which always governed well would not need to be governed.

—Jean Jacques Rousseau

13. How might the corruption of a legislator who pursues his or her private interests endanger the democratic principle of majority rule? Give an example.

14. What do you think Rousseau means by a government's independence?

Extended Response

15. Many American citizens confuse legal and illegal aliens. Write a brief essay comparing and contrasting the situations of illegal aliens with that of resident aliens.

STOP

For additional test practice, use Self-Check Quizzes—Chapter 1 on glencoe.com.

Need Extra Help?

If you missed question...	1	2	3	4	5	6	7	8	9	10	11	12	13	14	15
Go to page...	11	12	16	24	9	12	15	19	22	24	24	24	25	24	18

Chapter 2

Roots of American Democracy

Why It Matters

The American colonies were settled by individuals from many nations. Nonetheless, the majority of American settlers came from England. Many of the rights that American citizens enjoy can be traced to the political and legal traditions of England. When English people began settling in the Americas, they brought with them a tradition of limited and representative government.

Civics ONLINE Visit glencoe.com and enter QuickPass™ code CIV3093c2 for Chapter 2 resources.

BIG Ideas

Section 1: Our English Heritage

Political and economic institutions evolve to help individuals and groups accomplish their goals. The English colonists brought with them ideas about government that had been developing in England for centuries.

Section 2: The English Colonies

Political, social, religious, and economic changes influence the way Americans think and act. The English established thirteen colonies along the East Coast of North America.

Section 3: Colonial Society

Political, social, religious, and economic changes influence the way Americans think and act. The English colonists created a prosperous economy and learned to govern themselves.

Section 4: Birth of a Democratic Nation

Political principles and major events shape how people form governments. The Declaration of Independence explained why the colonies were founding a new nation.

The Lincoln Memorial is an important symbol of American democracy.

Sequencing Information Study Foldable Make the following Foldable to help you sequence information about the roots of American democracy.

Step 1 Fold the paper in half from side to side.

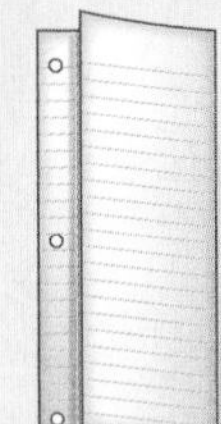

Step 2 Turn the paper and fold it in half and in half again.

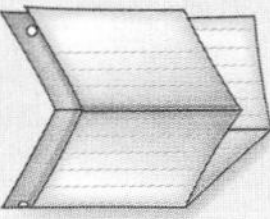

Step 3 Cut the top layer of the paper only along the fold lines.

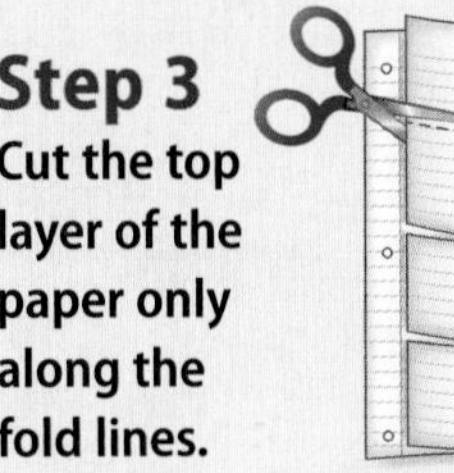

Step 4 Label each tab as shown.

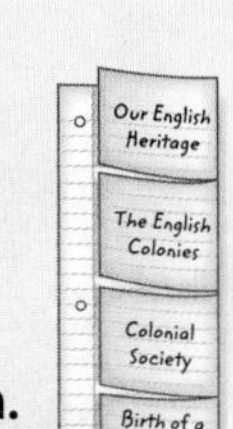

Reading and Writing
As you read the chapter write details of the sequence of events that unfolded as democracy developed in America under the tabs.

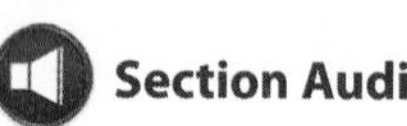

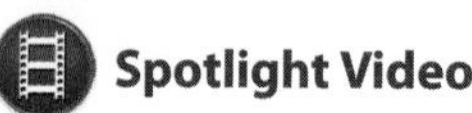

Section 1

Section Audio   Spotlight Video

Our English Heritage

Guide to Reading

Big Idea

Political and economic institutions evolve to help individuals and groups accomplish their goals.

Content Vocabulary

- Enlightenment *(p. 33)*
- monarch *(p. 33)*
- legislature *(p. 33)*
- precedent *(p. 34)*
- common law *(p. 34)*
- natural rights *(p. 34)*
- social contract *(p. 35)*
- colony *(p. 36)*
- joint-stock company *(p. 36)*
- charter *(p. 36)*
- compact *(p. 36)*

Academic Vocabulary

- document *(p. 33)*
- authority *(p. 33)*
- grant *(p. 33)*

Reading Strategy

Organizing As you read, complete a web diagram like the one below by listing six sources of American law.

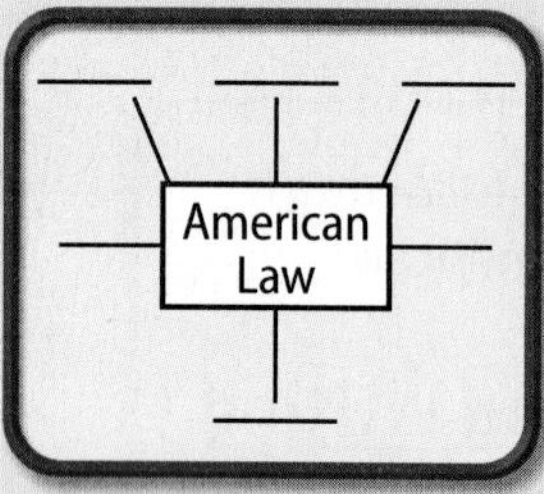

Real World Civics For many of us, town meetings seem like something from another century—and for the most part they are. The first settlers in this country, most of whom were English, brought with them their traditional forms of government, which relied on local involvement. Town meetings are a form of direct democracy, giving citizens a clear voice in decision making. The purpose of the town meeting has not changed in over 200 years.

▼ **Town meeting in Bridgeport, Vermont**

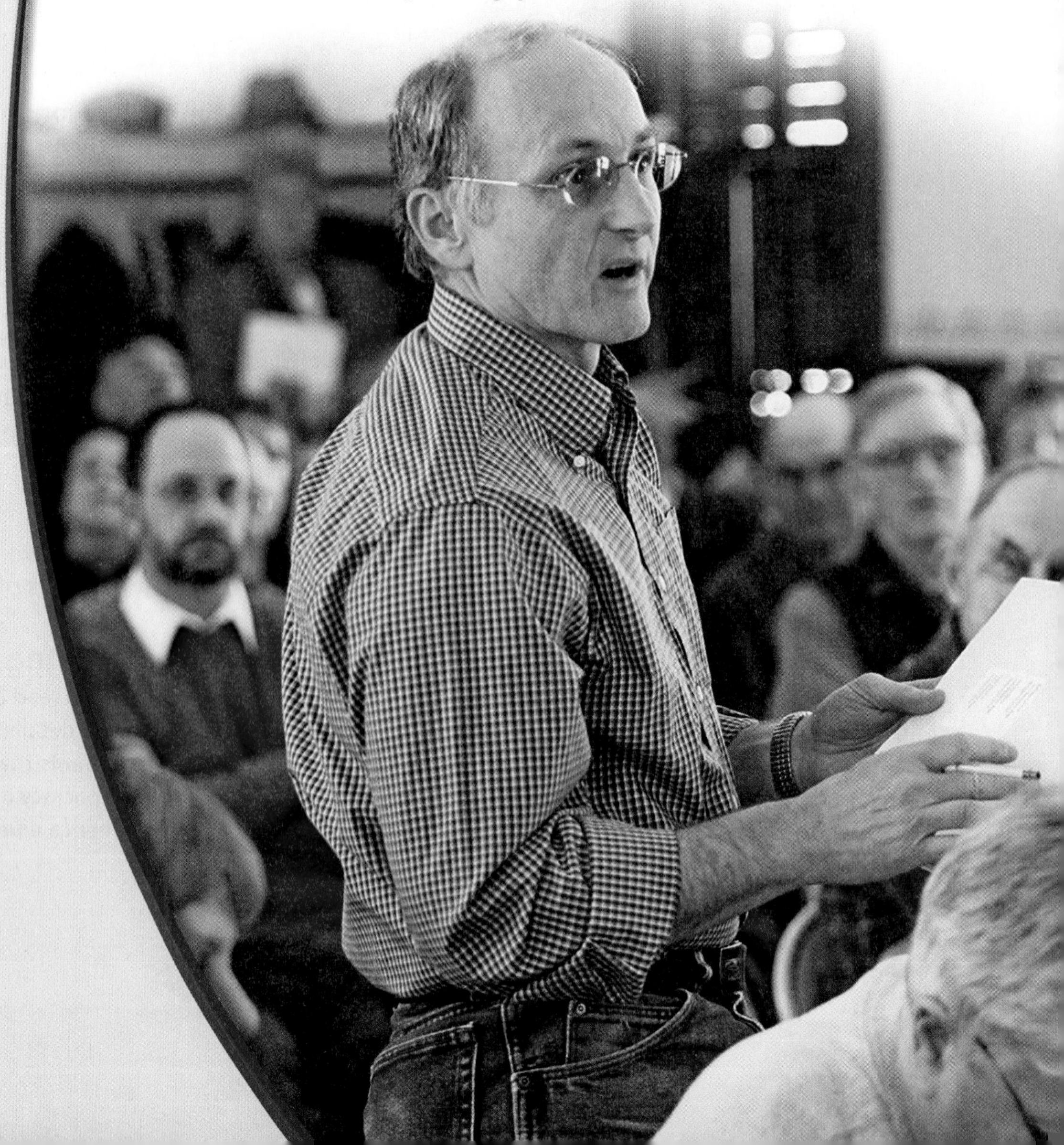

What Influenced Colonial Government?

Main Idea **Science and the influence of reason led to new innovations in political thought.**

Civics & You What helps people get along with each other? Do they need rules, a strong leader, or to share the same goals? Read to learn how thinkers in Europe answered these questions.

Many of the rights that American citizens enjoy today can be traced to the political and legal traditions of England and to the ideas of a cultural movement called the **Enlightenment.** When English people began settling here in the 1600s, they brought with them a history of limited and representative government. They also brought with them new ideas about law, society, and the rights people possessed.

For centuries, England had been ruled by a **monarch**—a king or queen. However, noble families also had considerable power. The monarch gave them ownership and control of vast lands in exchange for their loyalty, tax payments, and promises of military support.

The Magna Carta

In 1215, nobles rebelled against King John, who had treated them harshly. They forced the king to sign an agreement called the Magna Carta (Latin for "Great Charter"). This **document,** or deed, protected the nobles' privileges and **authority,** or control. It also **granted,** or allowed, certain rights to all landholders—rights that eventually came to apply to all English people. These rights included equal treatment under the law and trial by one's peers. The Magna Carta limited the power of the monarch by guaranteeing that no one would be above the law, not even the king or queen. (See the Appendix to read this document.)

Parliament

Kings who followed John met regularly with nobles and church officials to get their advice. Gradually, this group grew in size and power, expanding to include representatives of the common people. By the late 1300s, it had developed into a **legislature**—a lawmaking body—known as Parliament.

For the next few centuries, English monarchs cooperated with Parliament. In the mid-1600s, however, serious power struggles began. In 1688, Parliament removed King James II from the throne and invited his daughter Mary and her husband William to rule instead. In doing so, Parliament demonstrated that it was now stronger than the monarch.

This peaceful transfer of power, known as the Glorious Revolution, changed government in England. From that time on, no ruler would have more power than Parliament.

Authority From the end of the seventeenth century on, English monarchs, such as George III, shared the powers of government with Parliament. ***Describing*** **How did the authority of English monarchs change?**

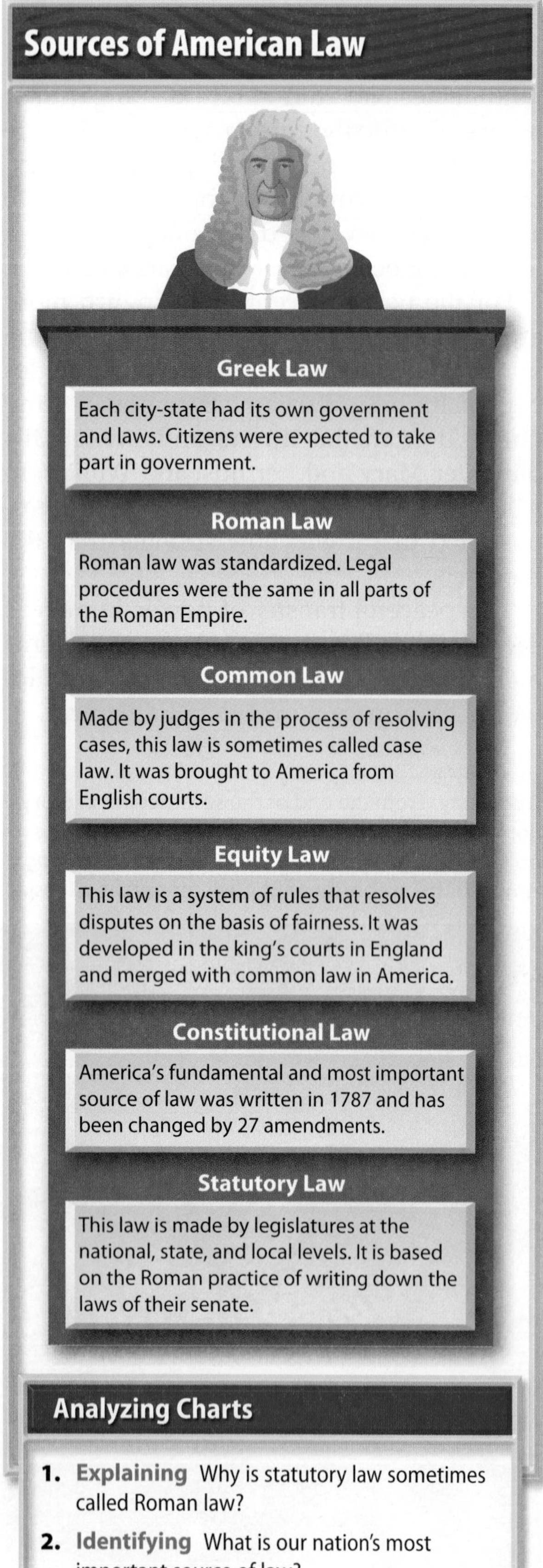

Analyzing Charts

1. **Explaining** Why is statutory law sometimes called Roman law?
2. **Identifying** What is our nation's most important source of law?

English Bill of Rights To clarify this relationship, Parliament drew up the English Bill of Rights in 1689. This document further restricted the monarch's power. It also guaranteed free elections to Parliament, the right to a fair trial, and the elimination of cruel and unusual punishments.

Common Law

In its earliest days, England had no written laws. People developed rules to live by, however, and these customs came to have the force of law. In addition, as a court system developed, the courts' decisions became the basis of a body of law. When judges were asked to decide a case, they would look for a **precedent,** or a ruling in an earlier case that was similar. The judge would then make a consistent ruling.

This system of law is known as **common law.** It rests on court decisions rather than regulations written by lawmakers. Although England's system of common law came about without being planned, it worked well and has remained in place to this day. Our own laws about property, contracts, and personal injury are based on English common law.

Philosophical Influences

John Locke (1632–1704) was an English writer who supported the Glorious Revolution. Locke argued that people were born free, equal, and independent. They also possessed rights, called **natural rights,** to life, liberty, and property that no government could take away. In *The Second Treatise of Government,* Locke wrote:

> ***"All mankind . . . being all equal and independent, no one ought to harm another in his life, health, liberty, or possessions."***
>
> —John Locke, *The Second Treatise of Government*

What Is a Social Contract? Locke also believed that if a government tried to take away people's natural rights, it was breaking the social contract. A **social contract** is an agreement among the people in a society. They agree to give up part of their freedom to a government in exchange for protection of natural rights. The people agree to obey the government as long as it protects their rights.

French philosopher Jean-Jacques Rousseau (1712–1778) wrote in *The Social Contract*, published in 1762, that "man is born free, yet everywhere he is found in chains." Rousseau was referring to the large number of people in Europe living under oppressive governments. He argued that the people alone had the right to determine how they should be governed.

Separation of Powers A French writer, Baron de Montesquieu (1689–1755), developed the idea about dividing the branches of government into different parts to balance each other so that no one part can become too strong or threaten individual rights. His ideas on the separation of powers, along with Locke's ideas on the social contract and natural rights, became cornerstones of the Declaration of Independence and the U.S. Constitution.

Ideas of Enlightenment Locke and Montesquieu are considered Enlightenment thinkers. Building on the scientific discoveries of the 1600s, these thinkers believed that God had created an orderly universe. The laws of this universe could be discovered through the use of human reason. Enlightenment thinkers argued that the laws that governed nature also applied to human life and society. As you will read, the ideas of the Enlightenment had a profound effect on Americans.

Reading Check **Evaluating** Why was the English Bill of Rights important to English citizens?

Social Contract The Mayflower Compact, signed by the Pilgrims in 1620, stands as the first example of many colonial plans for self-government. ***Explaining*** **Why is the Mayflower Compact considered a social contract?**

Colonial Traditions of Self-Government

Main Idea **The American colonists accepted the idea of representative government.**

Civics & You What do you do when you face a difficult problem? Do you try to solve it yourself? Do you ask other people for help? Read to learn about the development of representative government in the colonies.

In the 1600s and 1700s, England established colonies in America. A **colony** is a group of people in one place who are ruled by a parent country elsewhere.

The Capitol at Williamsburg Williamsburg was the capital of Virginia from 1699 to 1780. Those who met here included Patrick Henry, George Washington, Thomas Jefferson, and George Mason. ***Explaining*** **How were the members of the House of Burgesses chosen?**

The early colonists remained loyal subjects of England, with a strong sense of English political traditions. They accepted common law and believed that the ruler was not above the law. They also expected to have a voice in government and other basic rights.

Representative Government

The first permanent English settlement in North America was Jamestown, in what is now Virginia. It was founded in 1607 by the Virginia Company, a group of London merchants. Jamestown was organized as a **joint-stock company,** which provided investors partial ownership and a share in future profits. The merchants also received a charter from King James I. A **charter** is a written document granting land and the authority to set up colonial governments.

At first Jamestown was managed by a governor and council appointed by the Virginia Company. In 1619, however, the colonists formed the House of Burgesses, the first representative assembly, or legislature, in the English colonies. The House of Burgesses had little power, but it marked the beginning of self-government in colonial America.

The Mayflower Compact In 1620, shortly after the House of Burgesses was formed, another group of colonists from England, known as the Pilgrims, arrived in America. They built a settlement called Plymouth hundreds of miles north of Virginia. Today Plymouth is in Massachusetts, a part of New England.

Even before their ship, the *Mayflower,* reached America, the Plymouth colonists realized they needed rules to govern themselves if they were to survive in a new land. They drew up a written plan for government. Forty-one of the men aboard signed the Mayflower Compact. (See the Appendix to read this document.) A **compact** is an agreement, or contract, among a group of people.

Town Meetings The Mayflower Compact established a tradition of direct democracy. Throughout the colonial period—and in New England today—citizens held town meetings to address local problems and issues. These town meetings developed into the local town government. Although anyone in the town could attend and express an opinion, voting was limited to men who had been granted land by the town.

Fundamental Orders of Connecticut By 1639 a number of Pilgrims were being persecuted for their religious beliefs. They left Massachusetts and colonized the area that is now Connecticut. There, they developed America's first written constitution—the Fundamental Orders of Connecticut. This document called for an assembly of elected representatives from each town to make laws. It also called for the popular election of a governor and judges.

Early Legislatures The success of the Jamestown and Plymouth colonies led to other settlements in America. By 1733, thirteen English colonies stretched from Massachusetts (which included what is now Maine) in the north to Georgia in the south. Each new colony set up its own government.

Each colony had a governor, who was elected by the colonists or appointed by the English king. Each colony also had a legislature, with representatives elected by the free adult males.

As years passed, the colonial governments took on more responsibility while the king and Parliament dealt with matters in Great Britain (the country was renamed the United Kingdom of Great Britain in 1707 when England unified with Scotland). The colonists in America soon grew used to making their own decisions.

Reading Check **Concluding** How did Great Britain's tending to matters in that country affect the colonists?

Review

Vocabulary

1. **Write** complete sentences using each of these key terms: *Enlightenment, monarch, legislature, precedent, common law, natural rights, social contract, colony, joint-stock company, charter, compact.*

Main Ideas

2. **Explaining** Describe two influences that changed colonial thought.

3. **Hypothesizing** Why were colonists so eager to put self-government into practice?

Critical Thinking

4. **BIG Ideas** Explain the reasons for and the effects of the English Bill of Rights by completing a graphic organizer like the one that follows.

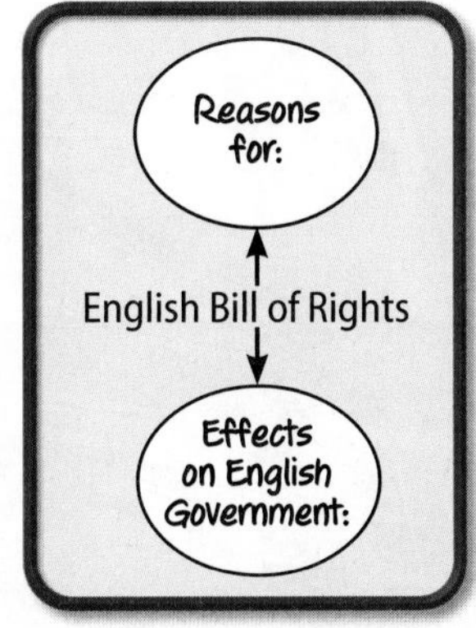

5. **Drawing Conclusions** Explain the significance of the Glorious Revolution.

6. **Comparing** Read the Mayflower Compact in the Appendix. What ideas do you see in the compact that also exist in the government of the United States?

CITIZENSHIP Activity

7. **Persuasive Writing** Imagine you are an English noble in favor of the Magna Carta. Write a letter to the king explaining why he should sign the document.

Study Central™ To review this section, go to glencoe.com.

Section Audio

The English Colonies

Guide to Reading

Big Idea

Political, social, religious, and economic changes influence the way Americans think and act.

Content Vocabulary

- proprietary colony *(p. 39)*
- royal colony *(p. 39)*
- religious dissenters *(p. 41)*
- Puritans *(p. 41)*
- Pilgrims *(p. 41)*
- toleration *(p. 41)*
- indentured servant *(p. 42)*
- plantation *(p. 43)*
- triangular trade *(p. 43)*

Academic Vocabulary

- acquire (p. 39)
- decade (p. 39)

Reading Strategy

Identifying On a web diagram like the one below, identify reasons that people immigrated to the English colonies.

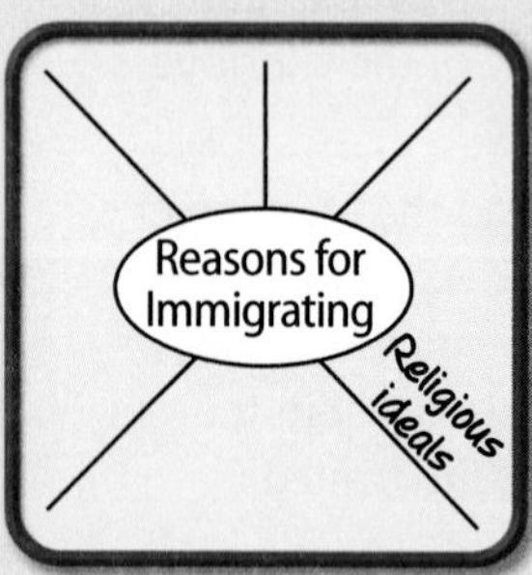

Real World Civics During the American Revolution, the drum and fife called the soldiers to action! Julie Phelps keeps the tradition alive. She practices the fife, whose shrill notes strengthened soldiers' orders to march, turn, change formation, or halt. The fife, and its companion the drum, have marched to war with soldiers since the twelfth century. During the Revolutionary War, the fife and drum were well known to colonist-soldiers. The rat-a-tat tat-a-pan of the drums provided a beat for marching and for signaling battle. So, even though colonists worked to escape from English rule, they brought an English military custom into battle.

▼ **Julie Phelps, playing the fife, keeps tradition alive**

Settling the Colonies

Main Idea **The English established thirteen colonies along the East Coast of North America.**

Civics & You How far would you travel to live in a new place? What would it be like if you did not know what to expect? Read to learn about the early settlements in North America.

Although several European nations had claims in North America, it was the English who eventually dominated the continent. By 1733, there were thirteen colonies along the eastern seaboard under English control. These colonies had been founded in a variety of ways and for a variety of reasons. Despite these differences, the colonies had one thing in common—their English heritage.

New England Colonies

Nine years after the Pilgrims arrived at Plymouth, another group of investors received a royal charter to start a colony north of Plymouth. In 1630, about 900 men, women, and children landed at Massachusetts Bay and built a town they called Boston. During the 1630s, more than 15,000 people journeyed to the new colony of Massachusetts. By the mid-1600s, the New England colonies of Rhode Island, Connecticut, and New Hampshire had been founded.

The Middle Colonies

A second group of colonies grew up south of New England. Known as the Middle Colonies, they included New York, New Jersey, Pennsylvania, and Delaware.

The first of these, New York, was originally the Dutch colony of New Netherland. An English fleet seized the important harbor town of New Amsterdam on Manhattan Island in 1664. The English King Charles II gave the colony to his brother, the Duke of York.

The newly **acquired,** or obtained, colony of New York became a **proprietary colony,** in which the owner, or proprietor, owned the land and controlled the government. The Duke of York gave the southern part of his colony to two men, who named it New Jersey. For several **decades,** or ten-year spans, New Jersey was a proprietary colony. In 1702, it became a **royal colony,** one owned and ruled directly by the king.

Another proprietary colony was started in 1680. William Penn received a large parcel of land west of the Delaware River from King Charles. Penn saw his colony, Pennsylvania, as a place to put his Quaker ideals of peace, equality, and justice to work. By offering freedom of religion, Penn drew many settlers to his new city of Philadelphia. In 1704, the southernmost three counties of the colony separated and became known as Delaware.

Southern Colonies

A third set of colonies formed in the South after Jamestown, Virginia, was founded as a joint-stock colony in 1607 (it became a royal colony in 1624). North of Virginia, Maryland was founded in 1734. To Virginia's south, another group of proprietors started Carolina. The two parts of Carolina developed differently, and they officially became two royal colonies, North and South Carolina, in 1729.

Boston By the 1660s, Boston was one of the largest cities in the English colonies. ***Specifying*** **In what year did the first English settlers come to Boston?**

The English Colonies

Maps In MOtion
See StudentWorks™ Plus or glencoe.com.

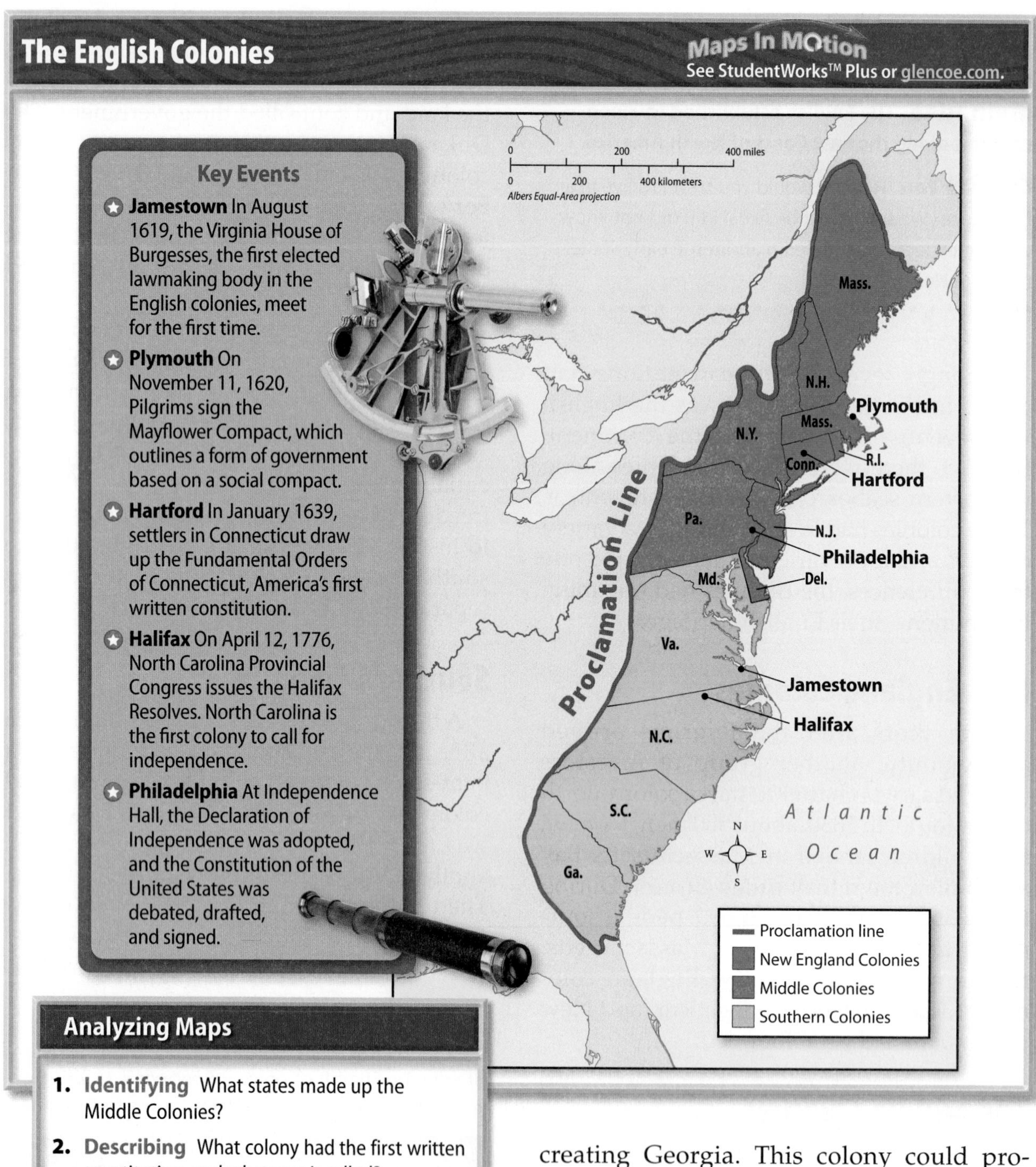

Key Events

- **Jamestown** In August 1619, the Virginia House of Burgesses, the first elected lawmaking body in the English colonies, meet for the first time.
- **Plymouth** On November 11, 1620, Pilgrims sign the Mayflower Compact, which outlines a form of government based on a social compact.
- **Hartford** In January 1639, settlers in Connecticut draw up the Fundamental Orders of Connecticut, America's first written constitution.
- **Halifax** On April 12, 1776, North Carolina Provincial Congress issues the Halifax Resolves. North Carolina is the first colony to call for independence.
- **Philadelphia** At Independence Hall, the Declaration of Independence was adopted, and the Constitution of the United States was debated, drafted, and signed.

Analyzing Maps

1. **Identifying** What states made up the Middle Colonies?
2. **Describing** What colony had the first written constitution, and what was it called?

Georgia The last English colony founded in America was Georgia. A group led by James Oglethorpe received a charter to create a colony where English debtors and poor people could make a fresh start. In Great Britain, debtors were often thrown into prison. The British government had another reason for creating Georgia. This colony could protect the other British colonies from Spanish attack. Great Britain had been at war in the early 1700s, and new conflicts over territory in North America were always breaking out. Located between Spanish Florida and South Carolina, Georgia could serve as a military barrier.

Reading Check **Comparing** How did proprietary and royal colonies differ?

People of the Colonies

Main Idea **Throughout the colonies, people adapted their traditions to the new conditions of life in America.**

Civics & You Would you be willing to move across the ocean to unexplored, possibly dangerous territory to gain certain freedoms or perhaps just to get a new start on life? Read to find out why English settlers came to North America.

English colonists settled in America for different reasons. Some immigrated to escape religious persecution in England. Others came in search of economic gain. Still others, such as criminals, prisoners, and enslaved Africans, did not come willingly. Colonists' reasons for immigration helped shape the types of colonies they created.

Why Did Colonists Immigrate?

Many colonists in New England and the Middle Colonies were **religious dissenters,** those who followed a faith other than the official religion of England, the Anglican religion. For example, the founders of Massachusetts were called **Puritans,** because they wanted to reform, or purify, the Anglican Church.

Religious Havens These Puritans also considered themselves **Pilgrims,** or people on a religious journey. The rulers of Massachusetts did not believe in **toleration,** or acceptance, of other religions.

New York City Colonists settled where economic opportunities were available. New York became a leading center for commerce and trade. ***Explaining*** **What natural feature made New York an economic center?**

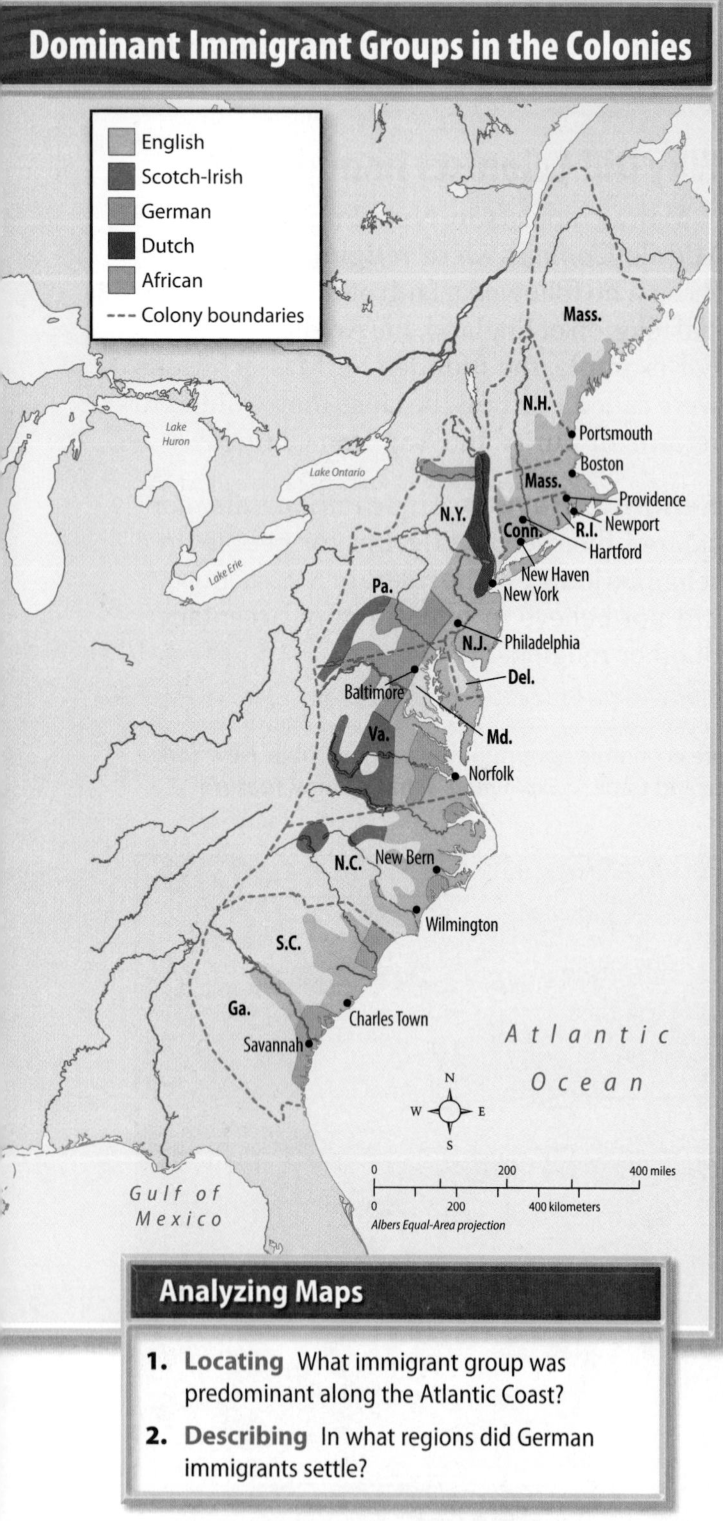

Analyzing Maps

1. **Locating** What immigrant group was predominant along the Atlantic Coast?
2. **Describing** In what regions did German immigrants settle?

In the late 1600s, devout Puritans in Salem and other Massachusetts towns held trials of people accused of witchcraft. In the town of Salem alone, 19 residents were convicted and hanged, and five died in prison before the trials were discontinued in 1693.

Other groups sought religious freedom. The Quakers founded Pennsylvania as a safe place to practice their religion. A proprietor named George Calvert founded Maryland in 1634 as a safe home for Catholics. In 1636, a minister named Thomas Hooker led his church congregation to Connecticut, south of Massachusetts, in search of religious freedom. Another minister, Roger Williams, was forced to leave Massachusetts for his religious views and his belief that it was wrong to take land from Native Americans. In 1644, Williams received a charter to found the colony of Rhode Island. Rhode Island became the first place in America to welcome people of all faiths.

Economic Opportunity Especially in the South, many settlers came to the colonies for economic reasons. Early Virginians struggled until they began successfully to raise and sell their tobacco crop. Carolina was strongly influenced by immigrants from the English colony of Barbados in the West Indies. There, many settlers became involved in growing rice and indigo, a valuable blue dye.

The system of **indentured servants** made it possible for poor people to come to the colonies. Colonists in America agreed to pay the cost of transporting the servants to the colonies and promised to provide food, clothing, and shelter to them until their indentures, or labor contracts, expired.

Conflict Over Land Throughout the colonies, the spread of settlements led to conflicts with Native Americans over land. In some colonies, such as Pennsylvania, relations were fairly peaceful. In Virginia, they were not. In the 1640s, Virginia Governor William Berkeley agreed to keep settlers from taking Native American land. A planter named Nathaniel Bacon disagreed strongly with this policy and led attacks on the colonial government. Bacon's Rebellion showed that many settlers were not willing to be restricted by government policy.

The Beginnings of Slavery

In the Southern Colonies, a form of large-scale agriculture developed, based on the **plantation,** or large estate. This system for growing tobacco, rice, and indigo demanded more workers than immigration and the system of indentured servants could provide. Southern farmers began using enslaved Africans. Enslaved workers, unlike indentured servants, did not have to be freed and therefore would never need their own land.

At first it was not clear that enslaved Africans were to be treated differently from white indentured servants. Gradually, legal distinctions were adopted. Indentured servants retained the rights of English people and the protection of the law. Africans were protected by no law or tradition.

The trade in enslaved Africans was at the heart of what came to be called the **triangular trade**—the pattern of trade that developed among the Americas, Africa, and Europe. The colonists shipped rum to Africa, where traders exchanged it for enslaved people and gold. The enslaved were shipped to the West Indies and traded for sugar and molasses, which was used to make rum in America. The Africans' horrendous journey across the Atlantic was known as the Middle Passage. A young African, Olaudah Equiano, described the voyage:

> ***"I was soon put down under the decks . . . . The closeness of the place, and the heat of the climate, added to the number in the ship, which was so crowded that each had scarcely room to turn himself, almost suffocated us . . . . The shrieks of the women, and the groans of the dying, rendered [made] the whole a scene of horror."***
>
> —Olaudah Equiano, *The Interesting Narrative of the Life of Olaudah Equiano*

Reading Check **Evaluating** How did the system of indentured servants help both business owners and workers?

Vocabulary

1. **Write** a paragraph in which you use the following terms: *proprietary colony, royal colony, religious dissenters, Puritans, Pilgrims,* and *toleration.* Then write a second paragraph using these terms: *indentured servant, plantation,* and *triangular trade.*

Main Ideas

2. **Identify** the Southern Colonies and their location.
3. **Describe** three main reasons why colonists came to America. Which do you think was most important? Why?

Critical Thinking

4. **BIG Ideas** Use a graphic organizer similar to the one below to discuss the reasons the colony was founded.

Colony	Why was it founded?
New York	
Pennsylvania	
Georgia	

5. **Analyzing** Why did slavery become more prevalent in the Southern Colonies than in New England?
6. **Explaining** What was the main reason immigrants settled in the Southern Colonies?

CITIZENSHIP Activity

7. **Descriptive Writing** Pretend you have decided to move from England to America in the 1700s. Write a letter to your family and friends explaining why you have chosen to settle in a particular colony.

Study Central™ To review this section, go to glencoe.com.

Section Audio Spotlight Video

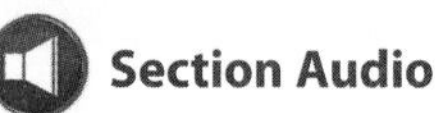

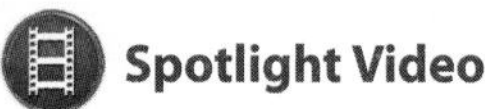

Section 3

Colonial Society

Guide to Reading

Big Idea
Political, social, religious, and economic changes influence the way Americans think and act.

Content Vocabulary
- Tidewater *(p. 46)*
- egalitarianism *(p. 48)*

Academic Vocabulary
- adapt *(p. 45)*
- assist *(p. 48)*

Reading Strategy
Organizing Use a graphic organizer like the one below to describe the differences in the economies of the New England, Middle, and Southern Colonies.

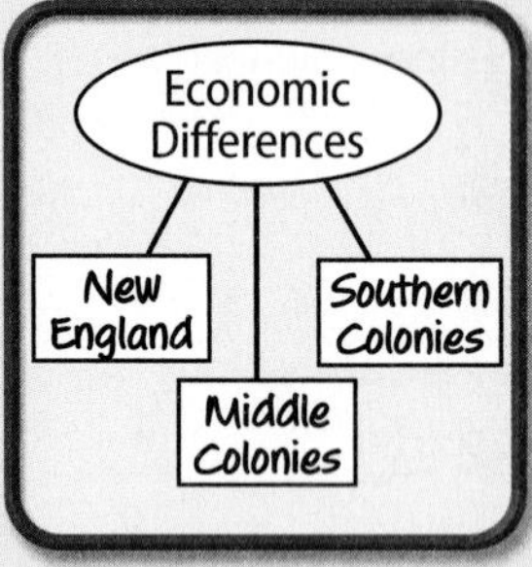

Real World Civics Six U.S. presidents graduated from Harvard University, a remarkable record for a school founded before the Revolutionary War and designed to train ministers. Most early schools in America were established on the ideals of freedom of religion and freedom of education. In 1940, John F. Kennedy, one of those Harvard graduates, prepared to leave college to visit Britain, where his father was the U.S. Ambassador. Kennedy later returned to the United States during the early rumblings of World War II and went on to be, in just over two decades, the 35th president of the United States.

▼ **A youthful John F. Kennedy**

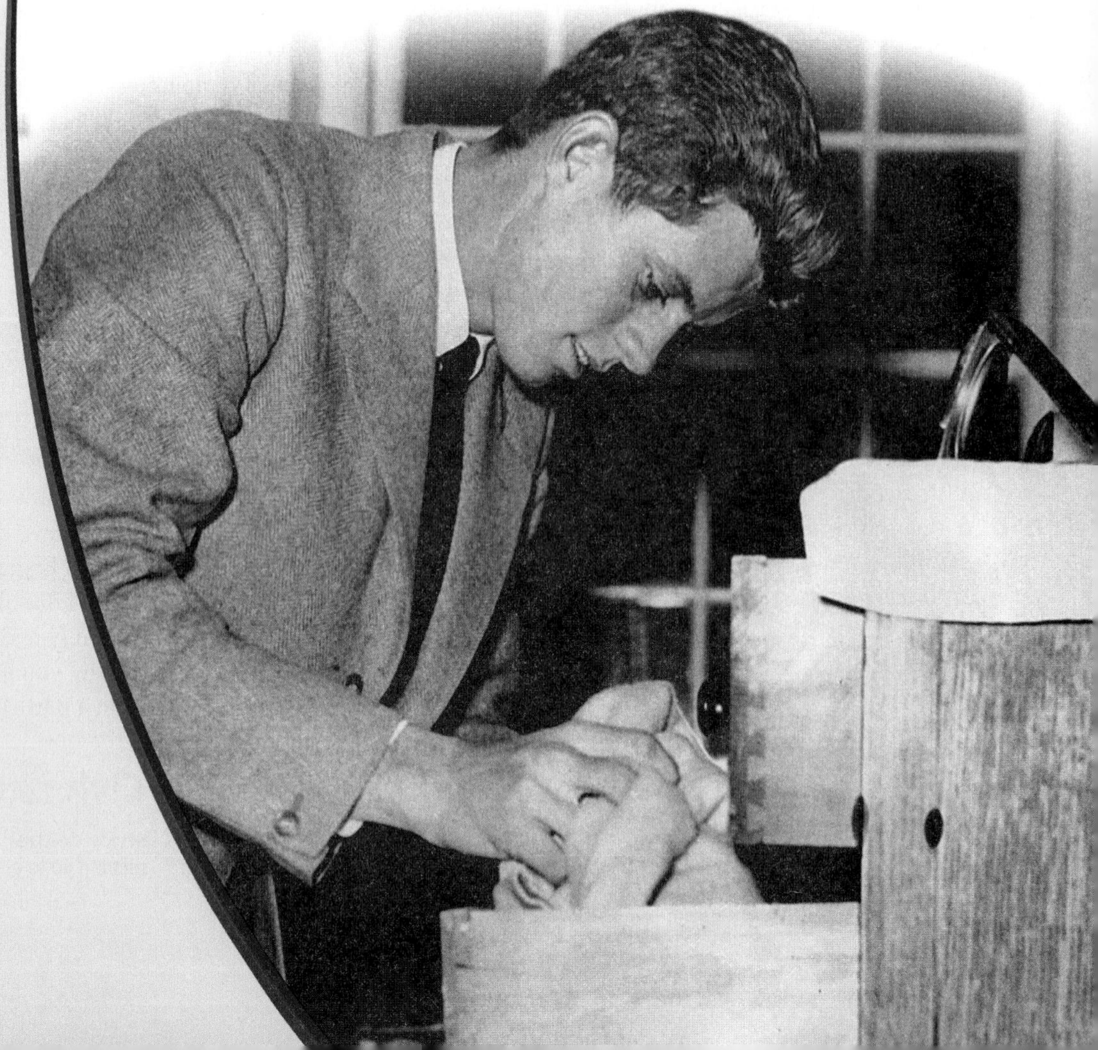

The Economy

Main Idea **The people in the colonies developed different ways of living.**

Civics & You Is your community or region known for any special product, either agricultural or manufactured? Read to find out how the economies of the New England, Middle, and Southern Colonies differed.

From the beginning, geography played a key role in how colonies developed. Colonists in the different regions had to **adapt,** or adjust, to the climate, soil, terrain, availability of rivers and harbors, natural resources, and other factors.

New England

Most people in New England, including farmers, lived in towns. Farms were small and located on the towns' outskirts. Long winters and rocky, infertile soil made large-scale farming difficult. Other New Englanders worked in small businesses, milling grain, sewing clothes, or making furniture. Some worked as blacksmiths, shoemakers, or shopkeepers.

Shipbuilding was an important industry. The region's forests provided wood for boats, and fishing and whaling also employed many New Englanders. The Puritan religion of early New England emphasized hard work, modest living, and personal virtues such as honesty, thriftiness, and obedience. These personal characteristics became known as the Puritan ethic.

The Middle Colonies

In contrast to New England, the soil and climate in New York, Pennsylvania, New Jersey, and Delaware were more suited to agriculture. Farmers in the Middle Colonies grew large amounts of wheat and other cash crops, which they sold in markets and overseas. This foreign trade spurred the growth of busy ports, such as New York and Philadelphia. Industries such as sawmills, mines, and ironworks were developed to take advantage of the region's abundant natural resources. Industry and agriculture also improved through the ideas and energy of immigrants from Germany, Holland, Sweden, and other European countries.

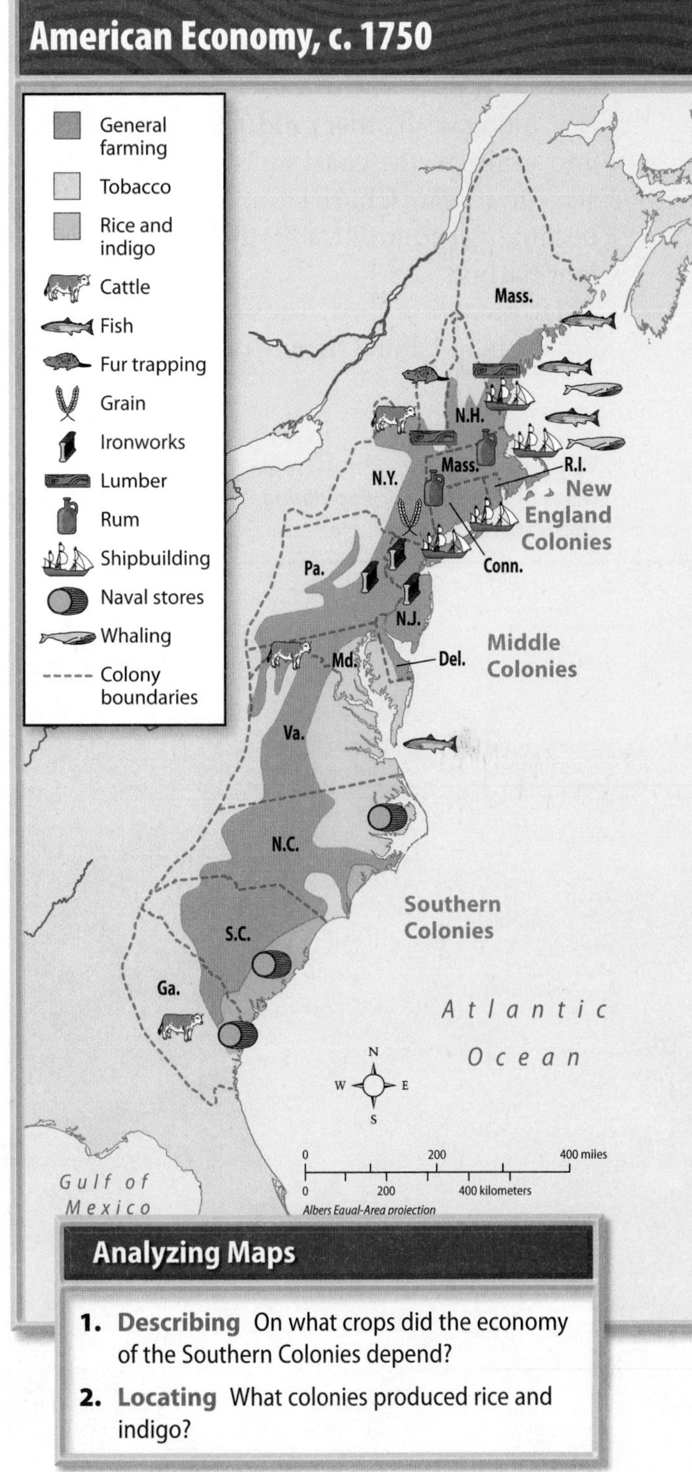

Analyzing Maps

1. **Describing** On what crops did the economy of the Southern Colonies depend?
2. **Locating** What colonies produced rice and indigo?

The Southern Colonies

A warm climate, long growing season, and rich soil spurred the growth of large-scale agriculture in the Southern Colonies. In Maryland, Virginia, and North Carolina, tobacco was the leading crop. Rice dominated in South Carolina and Georgia. Both crops were grown in the **Tidewater,** areas of flat, low plains, near the seacoast of Virginia and North Carolina. The region's rivers made it easy to transport the harvested tobacco and rice, along with other products such as indigo and grain, to the coast for shipment to overseas markets. Charleston, South Carolina, became a leader in trade, thanks to its excellent harbor.

Tidewater crops required very large amounts of labor. Owners of plantations, the large estates of the Southern Colonies, came to depend on enslaved African workers. Smaller-scale agriculture also existed, mainly in inland areas. Independent small farmers grew tobacco, corn, and other crops and were less dependent on enslaved workers.

Small farmers outnumbered the large plantation owners. The plantation owners, however, had greater wealth and more influence. They controlled the economic and political life of the region. Because large-scale agriculture was dominant in the South, the region did not develop much industry or commerce. It traded its many agricultural products for the manufactured goods it needed.

Reading Check **Explaining** Why did the plantation system develop in the South but not in the New England or the Middle Colonies?

The Southern Economy Large-scale farming grew in South Carolina and in many parts of the South. ***Explaining*** **Why did slavery become the labor system for large plantations?**

An American Identity

Main Idea **The colonies continued to grow and developed their own culture and beliefs.**

Civics & You What are some things you consider truly American? Read to find out how the colonists began to form a culture that was different from other cultures.

In 1760, an English traveler in America, Andrew Burnaby, wrote that the colonies were as different from one another as "fire and water." He felt their differences in character, manners, religion, and interests would prevent them from ever uniting. Burnaby noted:

> "*In short, such is the difference of character, manners, religion, and interest of the different colonies that if they were left to themselves, there would soon be a civil war from one end of the continent to another.*"
>
> —Andrew Burnaby, *Burnaby's Travels Through North America*

But in spite of the opinion of Burnaby and others, by the mid-1700s, colonists were already developing an American identity.

Religion

The desire for religious freedom was the reason many settlers first came to America, and religion remained a key element of the emerging American identity. In several colonies, such as Massachusetts, religious leaders were often also the leaders of the government. Puritans passed laws that supported their beliefs about religion and society, and they had the power to expel those who did not share these beliefs.

In other colonies, however, religion became separate from government, and toleration became the official policy. In colonies such as Pennsylvania and Rhode Island, toleration of other religions drew settlers of many different faiths. Religious tolerance gradually spread to other colonies during the 1700s.

Religion Revival Massachusetts minister Jonathan Edwards preached throughout the colonies urging renewed faith. ***Explaining*** **What was the Great Awakening?**

The Great Awakening While some Americans turned away from religion in the 1700s, others renewed their faith. In the 1720s, a powerful religious revival known as the Great Awakening swept through the colonies. Fiery preachers stressed the importance of a personal religious experience and questioned the commitment and authority of some established religious leaders. Congregations were torn apart, and new religious groups, such as Baptists and Methodists, grew strong. In the South, enslaved workers found hope in Christianity, which strongly influenced the development of a new African American culture.

Education

Religious feeling also led to the founding of America's first colleges and schools. Colleges such as Harvard in Massachusetts, Princeton in New Jersey, and William and Mary in Virginia were created for the

TIME™ Teens in *Action*

Bita Emrani

Bita Emrani, 17, who lives in Greensboro, North Carolina, knows the power of words. To help immigrants and disadvantaged kids in her area, she started a program called English Learning with Love (ELL).

QUESTION: Why did you create a language-tutoring program?

ANSWER: I started ELL in 2005 after a visit to Iran. I was haunted by the poverty there and decided to help the disadvantaged in my own city. I think education is an important way to battle poverty. Plus, I have a real passion for languages (I'm bilingual in Persian and English and able to get by in Spanish).

Q: What does ELL do?

A: ELL is an English for Speakers of Other Languages (ESOL) program and it's held after school in three local elementary schools. We help newcomers to the area become members of the community by working to improve their English. ELL works with about 30 to 35 students.

Q: Who are the tutors?

A: I recruit high school kids who volunteer their time to help. These teens discover that they can have a huge impact on their community.

Q: What difference do you see in the participants after they take the program?

A: ELL has not only improved kids' English, but it's also improved their attitude toward learning.

Q: What does the future hold for you?

A: I want to pursue a degree in public policy. I'd also like to volunteer for a nonprofit international medical organization, such as Doctors Without Borders.

ACTION FACT: Emrani loves learning dances from other countries.

Making a Difference — CITIZENSHIP

Why did Bita start the ELL program?

purpose of training ministers. Religious groups also set up schools for children to make sure that people could read the Bible for themselves. In some colonies, taxes were levied to pay for public education. Not all colonial Americans enjoyed the benefits of education, however. Slave codes—strict laws governing the treatment of enslaved people—made it illegal to teach enslaved workers to read or write.

Family Life

The family formed the foundation of colonial society. Men were the formal heads of their families, which were often large. Wives looked after children and worked on household chores. On farms, men and women often worked together, **assisted,** or helped, by older children.

In towns, women sometimes held jobs outside the home. They worked as maids, cooks, nurses, teachers, shopkeepers, or seamstresses. Families often arranged for their sons to work as apprentices, or learning assistants, to craft workers who taught them a trade. Married women had few rights, while widows and unmarried women could run businesses and own property. Women, however, could not vote, and men managed all community and church affairs.

Ideas About Government

In spite of the inequalities that existed in colonial America between whites and African Americans and between men and women, a new spirit was growing. The Enlightenment reinforced the idea of natural rights and individualism. The Great Awakening encouraged Christians to question traditional authority and to rely on their own insights about God. Together these two powerful influences helped create a spirit of **egalitarianism,** or equality. One element of this spirit of egalitarianism was the belief of many colonists that they possessed all the traditional rights of native English people.

Americans viewed the growth of the power of Parliament in the 1700s with approval. They considered the British legislature the protector of the people's rights against royal power. At the same time, America's colonies were governed by officials appointed by the British crown, a decision in which Americans had no say. British trade and tax policies protected British interests at the expense of American businesses.

Government in the Colonies The English government had permitted new patterns of land ownership, new types of worship, and new kinds of government in its colonies. Once established, these practices became fixed principles. The colonists became used to self-government and gradually came to think of it as their right.

By 1733, all thirteen English colonies had been established, each with its own constitution. The Massachusetts Body of Liberties, adopted in 1641, protected individual rights and became part of colonial law. In 1683 the Pennsylvania Frame of Government was passed. This document, along with the 1701 Pennsylvania Charter of Privileges, established part of the basis for the U.S. Constitution and the Bill of Rights. By the time the colonies gained independence in 1776, each colony had its own representative government, one that had been operating for more than 100 years.

Growing Discontent Yet, by the mid-1700s, many Americans felt they did not possess the rights of English citizens. They read Enlightenment writings in which the rights of the individual were proclaimed. Yet many British policies toward the colonies did not follow these ideals. In particular, colonists accepted John Locke's idea that government derives its power from the consent of the people. As the century wore on, Americans looked for answers to the problem of a distant and unresponsive British government. To a growing number, one answer seemed to make the most sense: independence.

Reading Check **Concluding** How did religious beliefs influence American ideas about government?

Vocabulary

1. **Write** a paragraph about life in the Southern Colonies using these terms: *Tidewater, egalitarianism.*

Main Ideas

2. **Identifying** What were the main crops grown in the Southern Colonies?
3. **Describing** What was the purpose of the first colleges?

Critical Thinking

4. **Determining Cause and Effect** How did the geography of the New England and the Middle Colonies contribute to their economic development?
5. **BIG Ideas** Use a graphic organizer similar to the one below to show the effects of the Great Awakening on the American colonies.

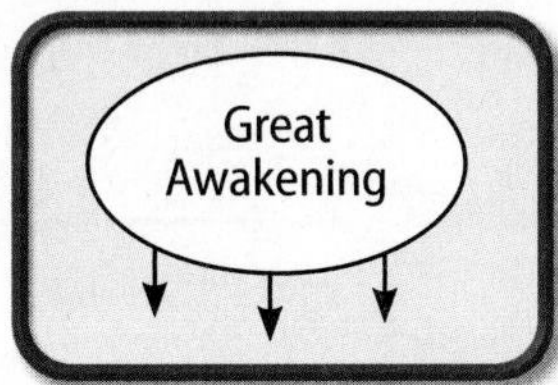

6. **Analyzing Visuals** Study the map on page 45 that shows the economic activity of the colonies. On what crops did the economy of the Middle Colonies depend?

CITIZENSHIP Activity

7. **Expository Writing** Describe the founding of at least two colonies in a short essay.

Study Central™ To review this section, go to glencoe.com.

Section 4: Birth of a Democratic Nation

Guide to Reading

Political principles and major events shape how people form governments.

Content Vocabulary

- mercantilism *(p. 51)*
- boycott *(p. 52)*
- repeal *(p. 52)*
- delegate *(p. 54)*
- independence *(p. 54)*

Academic Vocabulary

- challenge *(p. 54)*
- restore *(p. 54)*

Reading Strategy

Determining Cause and Effect As you read, complete a chart like the one below by explaining how the colonists responded to British actions.

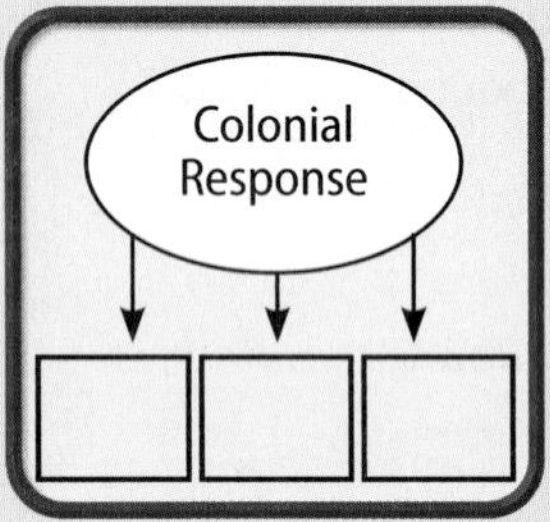

Real World Civics The air was hot and muggy, the sun beating down at midday, and the windows were tightly shut. As July 1776 began, dozens of men sat around these tables in Independence Hall in Philadelphia debating Thomas Jefferson's Declaration of Independence. They were British subjects living in a British colony, so each man agreeing to this document was committing treason against his country. Treason was punishable by death. Yet 56 men signed the Declaration, which outlines the reason why America should declare itself a new and independent nation. On the Fourth of July, these men announced to the world : "We mutually pledge to each other our lives, our fortunes and our sacred honor," in the hope that they one day would be free.

▼ **Room where Declaration of Independence was signed**

New York Harbor New York served as an economic center of activity for the Northern Colonies, receiving ships from all over the world. ***Analyzing*** **How did the British policy of salutary neglect affect the colonies?**

Colonial Resistance

Main Idea The American colonists began to fight against British control.

Civics & You Have you ever stopped buying a product, perhaps because the manufacturer changed the product or raised its price? Read to find out why American colonists refused to buy British products.

Separated from Great Britain by more than 3,000 miles (4,828 km) of vast ocean and left largely to their own devices, the American colonists gained valuable experience in self-government. They learned how to manage their own affairs. This policy of loose control by the British was known as salutary, or healthy, neglect. Under this policy, the British did not insist on strict enforcement of laws.

Mercantilism Around 1760, when George III took the throne, Britain's policy toward the American colonies began to change. The British adopted a program called mercantilism. **Mercantilism** is the theory that a country's power depends on its wealth. A nation should sell more goods to other countries than it buys. A favorable balance of trade—more exports and fewer imports—brings money into the country. For mercantilism to be successful, Great Britain needed the colonies to be a source of cheap, raw materials. The Navigation Acts were a series of laws, passed in the early 1660s, that put the theory of mercantilism into practice.

Growing Tensions

Since the late 1600s, the British and the French had battled for supremacy in Europe and other parts of the world. After several wars in Europe, the fighting spilled over into North America. At a conference in Albany, New York, in 1754, the colonies debated a plan for a federal union. The plan, proposed by a committee led by Benjamin Franklin, was rejected. However, the Albany Plan showed that many colonists were already thinking about joining together for their common defense.

TIME™

Political Cartoons

THE HORSE AMERICA, throwing his Master.

—Library of Congress

This cartoon was created in Great Britain in 1779.

1. **What does the horse represent?**
2. **Whom does the rider stand for?**
3. **What action is taking place in this image, and what does it symbolize?**
4. **What historical event do you think inspired this image?**

From 1754 to 1763, Great Britain fought a long, costly war against France—the French and Indian War—winning French territory in North America. In order to prevent conflict with Native Americans over land, colonial settlers were forbidden to settle west of the Appalachian Mountains without permission from the British government. This Proclamation of 1763 enraged many farmers and others who wanted the land. To pay off its heavy war debts, Britain placed steep taxes and new restrictions on the American colonies. The Stamp Act of 1765 required colonists to attach expensive tax stamps to all newspapers and legal documents. The Quartering Act required the colonies to provide barracks and supplies to British troops.

Worsening Relations

In protest, many colonists decided to **boycott,** or refuse to buy, British goods. Organizations known as the Sons of Liberty were formed throughout the colonies in opposition to the Stamp Act.

Stamp Act Congress In October of 1765, nine of the thirteen colonies sent representatives to the Stamp Act Congress held in New York City. The representatives prepared a declaration against the new British actions, which was sent to King George III. This action marked the first time that a majority of the colonies joined together to oppose British rule. As a result, the British Parliament **repealed,** or cancelled, the Stamp Act.

The same day it repealed the Stamp Act, Parliament passed the Declaratory Act of 1766, which stated that Parliament had the right to tax and make decisions for the American colonies "in all cases." Then, in 1767, Parliament passed a set of laws that came to be known as the Townshend Acts. One of the Townshend Acts legalized the use of writs of assistance to assist customs officers in arresting smugglers.

The writs were general search warrants that enabled customs officers to enter any location to look for evidence of smuggling. Angered by these laws, colonists caused trouble for British officials. The worst incident of violence took place in Boston. On March 5, 1770, British soldiers fired into a crowd, killing five. The shootings became known as the Boston Massacre.

New Taxes and a Tea Party

The colonists resented the new taxes. Because they had no representatives in Parliament, as people living in Great Britain did, the colonists believed that Parliament had no right to tax them. They summed up their feelings with the slogan "No taxation without representation!"

In 1773 Parliament passed another measure. The Tea Act gave the British East India Company the right to ship tea to the colonies without paying most of the taxes usually placed on tea. This made the East India Company tea cheaper than any other tea in the colonies, giving the British company an advantage over colonial merchants. In December 1773, a group of angry colonists dressed as Native Americans dumped 342 chests of British tea into Boston Harbor. In reaction to this protest, known as the Boston Tea Party, Parliament passed the Coercive Acts, which Americans called the Intolerable Acts. These laws restricted the colonists' civil rights, including the right to trial by jury.

Reading Check **Explaining** Why were the colonists angry about the new taxes?

American Biography

Thomas Jefferson (1743–1826)

Thomas Jefferson disliked public life. "I had rather be shut up in a very modest cottage, with my books, my family and a few old friends," he once wrote.

Jefferson acquired his lifelong love of books on science, philosophy, and literature from his childhood teachers and as a student at William and Mary College. His enormous library later became the basis of the Library of Congress.

Jefferson had the wealth and social status to live as he wished. However, abuses of power by the British pulled Jefferson from his beloved home at Monticello, Virginia, and launched him into a lifelong political career.

Jefferson held a variety of offices. They included governor of Virginia, secretary of state, vice president, and president of the United States. Yet, when writing the words for his gravestone, Jefferson mentioned none of these offices. Instead he wrote: *Here was Buried Thomas Jefferson, Author of the Declaration of Independence, of the Statute of Virginia for Religious Freedom and Father of the University of Virginia.*

Making a Difference CITIZENSHIP

Speculating Jefferson is considered one of the greatest writers of early America. Why do you think Jefferson wrote what he did for his gravestone?

Moving Toward Independence

Main Idea **The colonists began to take steps toward independence from Great Britain.**

Civics & You How might you protest a new community or school rule that you believed was unfair? Read to find out how Americans protested British measures.

The colonial governments banded together to fight the Intolerable Acts. In September 1774, twelve of the colonies sent **delegates,** or representatives, to Philadelphia to discuss their concerns. These representatives—from every colony except Georgia—wanted to establish a political body to represent American interests and **challenge,** or question, British control.

The First Continental Congress

The meeting in Philadelphia, known as the First Continental Congress, lasted seven weeks. During that time, the delegates sent a document to King George III demanding that the rights of the colonists be **restored,** or given back. They also made plans to extend the boycott of British goods. When the Congress ended, the delegates vowed to hold another meeting if their demands were not met by the following year.

King George responded with force. In April 1775, two battles between British and colonial soldiers took place in Massachusetts at Lexington and Concord. These became the first battles of the Revolutionary War. Until this time, most colonists still thought of themselves as loyal subjects of Great Britain. Now, with British soldiers shooting at Americans, many colonists began to question their attachment to Britain. More people began talking about **independence,** or self-reliance and freedom from outside control.

Years after the first battle, Ralph Waldo Emerson wrote this poem to immortalize the colonists who fought at Concord:

> *"By the rude bridge that arched the flood, Their flag to April's breeze unfurled, Here once the embattled farmers stood; And fired the shot heard round the world."*
>
> —Ralph Waldo Emerson, "The Concord Hymn"

The Second Continental Congress

In May 1775, colonial leaders met at the Second Continental Congress in Philadelphia. Not every member of the Congress favored independence. Some believed the colonists could never win a war against Great Britain. Others were still loyal to their home country. The Congress spent many months debating the best course of action.

Meanwhile, support for independence grew. In January of 1776, an American colonist named Thomas Paine inspired many other colonists by publishing a pamphlet titled *Common Sense.* In it Paine called for complete independence from Britain. He argued that it was simply "common sense" to stop following the "royal brute," King George III. Paine called the colonists' actions a struggle for freedom. By 1776 more than half of the delegates of the Second Continental Congress agreed with Paine that the colonies must break away from Britain.

The Congress, acting now as a government for the colonies, appointed a committee to write a document that would officially announce the independence of the United States. Thomas Jefferson, a delegate from Virginia, did most of the work. His draft of the Declaration explained why the United States of America should be a free nation.

Reading Check **Explaining** Why did colonists gather at the Second Continental Congress?

Citizen Warriors Many women, including Molly Pitcher, fought side by side with other colonial soldiers during the American Revolution. ***Comparing*** **How does the colonial fighting force compare with the makeup of modern army groups?**

The Declaration of Independence

Main Idea **The Declaration of Independence used traditional English political rights to call for independence for the colonies.**

Civics & You Why do you think governments are formed? Read to find out how the writer of the Declaration of Independence addressed this question.

The Declaration argued that the British government did not look after the interests of the colonists. The authors included a long list of abuses by King George III and called him a "Tyrant . . . unfit to be the Ruler of a free People." However, the document was much more than a list of complaints.

Democratic Ideals

The second paragraph of the Declaration of Independence set forth the colonists' beliefs about the rights of individuals. It said:

> *"We hold these truths to be self-evident, that all men are created equal, that they are endowed by their Creator with certain unalienable Rights, that among these are Life, Liberty and the pursuit of Happiness."*
>
> —The Declaration of Independence

Civics ONLINE

Student Web Activity Visit glencoe.com and complete the Chapter 2 Web Activity.

The paragraph quoted from the Declaration went on to say:

> "*. . . to secure these rights, Governments are instituted among Men, deriving their just powers from the consent of the governed, That whenever any Form of Government becomes destructive of these ends, it is the Right of the People to alter or abolish it, and to institute new Government. . . .*"
>
> —The Declaration of Independence

In other words, the purpose of a government is to protect the rights of the people. Moreover, government is based on the consent, or agreement, of the people. It only has the powers that the governed give it. The people are also entitled to change a government if it disregards their rights or their combined wishes.

These ideas were not new. Remember as you read earlier, the ideas about democracy and freedom originated with the ancient Greeks. Jefferson was influenced by John Locke and other writers. As you learned earlier, Locke wrote that good government is based on a social contract between the people and the rulers. Locke also wrote that all people should equally enjoy the rights to life, liberty, and property.

An Uncertain Future

The Second Continental Congress approved the Declaration of Independence, with a few changes, on July 4, 1776. The American colonies were now independent states—at least in theory. True freedom, though, would not come until the war ended and Great Britain officially recognized the United States as an independent nation.

Reading Check **Summarizing** According to the Declaration, what is the purpose of government?

Vocabulary

1. **Write** complete sentences that include these groups of terms: *merchant, boycott, repeal; delegates,* and *independence.*

Main Ideas

2. **Explaining** Why did Great Britain show control by raising taxes on the American colonists after 1763? What effect did this have on the colonists?
3. **Identifying** What British legislation prompted colonists to hold the First Continental Congress in a show of independence?

Critical Thinking

4. **Persuasive Writing** Assume the role of a British government official in 1774, and write a press release explaining why the Coercive Acts (Intolerable Acts) were necessary.
5. **BIG Ideas** In a web diagram like the one below, list the ideas of government found in the Declaration of Independence.

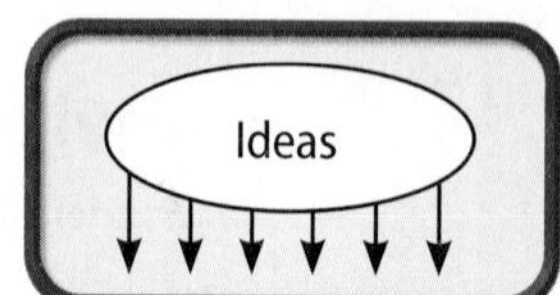

Citizenship Activity

6. **Expository Writing** Read the Declaration of Natural Rights in the Declaration of Independence (second, third, and fourth paragraphs). Select what you think is the single most important idea and explain in a paragraph how that idea affects your life today.

Study Central™ To review this section, go to glencoe.com.

Chapter 2

Visual Summary

1600–1649

1607 Jamestown is founded

1619 House of Burgesses meets for first time

1620 Pilgrims found Plymouth

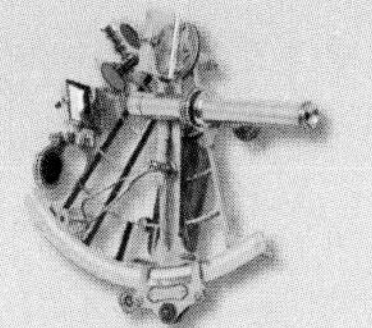

1630 Puritans settle Massachusetts Bay Colony

1649 Maryland passes Toleration Act

1650–1699

1676 Bacon's Rebellion

1681 William Penn founds Pennsylvania

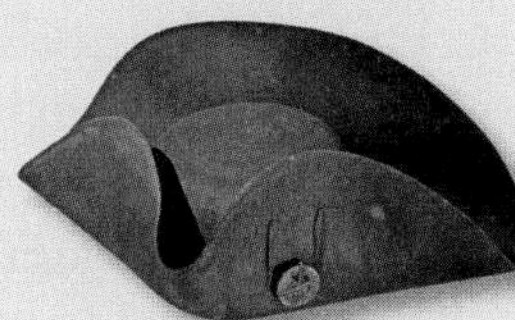

1689 English Bill of Rights signed

1700–1749

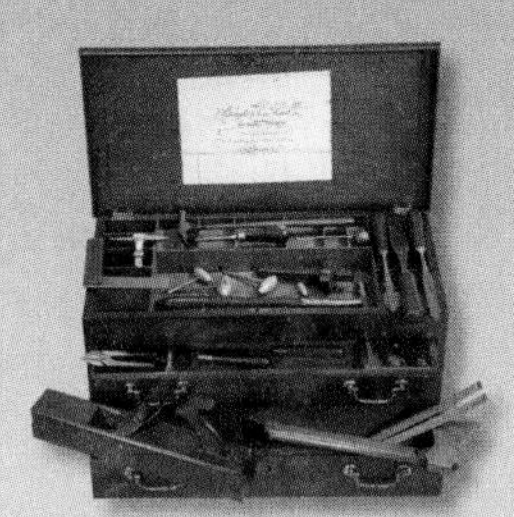

1729 Carolina is divided into separate colonies

1733 Georgia settled last of thirteen English colonies

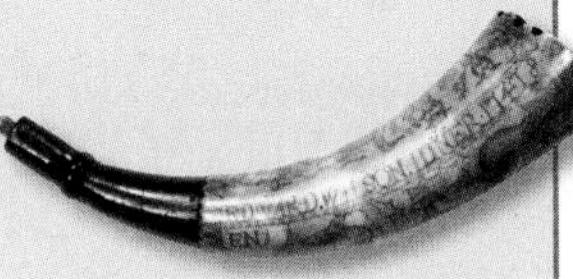

1740 Great Awakening peaks

1750–1783

1754 French and Indian War begins; Ben Franklin proposes Albany Plan of Union

1763 Proclamation of 1763 established

1765 Stamp Act protests

1770 Boston Massacre

1773 Boston Tea Party

1775 Battles fought at Lexington and Concord

1776 Declaration of Independence signed

1781 British surrender at Yorktown

1783 With Treaty of Paris, the United States officially wins independence

Study anywhere, anytime! Download quizzes and flash cards to your PDA from glencoe.com.

Chapter 2

ASSESSMENT

TEST-TAKING TIP

Get eight or more hours of sleep the night before a test.

Reviewing Vocabulary

Directions: Choose the word(s) that best completes the sentence.

1. If a government tried to take away a people's ______, it was breaking the social contract.

A legislature
B natural rights
C charter
D compact

2. The Duke of York owned and governed the ______ of New York.

A Tidewater
B royal colony
C proprietary colony
D joint-stock company

3. The founders of Massachusetts were ______.

A enslaved people
B plantation owners
C indentured servants
D religious dissenters

4. The Navigation Acts put ______ into practice.

A toleration
B mercantilism
C egalitarianism
D triangular trade

Reviewing Main Ideas

Directions: Choose the best answer for each question.

Section 1 *(pp. 32–37)*

5. Which innovation allowed rights to land holders in England?

A Magna Carta
B common law
C English Bill of Rights
D Locke's social contract

6. Which institution or document established a tradition of direct democracy in New England?

A Virginia Company
B House of Burgesses
C Mayflower Compact
D Fundamental Orders of Connecticut

Section 2 *(pp. 38–43)*

7. Which English colony became the first to welcome people of all faiths?

A Massachusetts
B Rhode Island
C Pennsylvania
D Maryland

8. Why did Southern farmers begin using enslaved Africans?

A Africans were more willing workers than Europeans.
B Long indentures placed huge financial burdens on planters.
C Plantations demanded more workers than immigration provided.
D The triangular trade was more humane than indentured servitude.

Section 3 *(pp. 44–49)*

9. What about the Middle Colonies spurred the growth of ports such as New York and Philadelphia?

A soil and climate suited to cash crops
B rivers for easy transport to the coast
C abundant wood for use in shipbuilding
D an ideal location for fishing and whaling

10. How would you characterize the Great Awakening of the 1700s?

A a religious revival
B a political upheaval
C an economic revolution
D an educational movement

Section 4 *(pp. 50–56)*

11. Which legislation passed by Parliament restricted colonists' right to trial by jury?

A Stamp Act
B Townsend Acts
C Declaratory Act of 1766
D Coercive Acts

GO ON

12. Who published *Common Sense,* a pamphlet calling for complete independence from Britain?

A Benjamin Franklin

B Thomas Paine

C Thomas Jefferson

D John Locke

Critical Thinking

Directions: Base your answers to questions 13 and 14 on the cartoon below and your knowledge of Chapter 2.

13. What does the cartoonist imply by using darker print for the word *men*?

A Women are excluded.

B All people are included.

C All slaves are excluded.

D Male slaves are included.

14. Why does the cartoonist include a washerwoman?

A to contrast rulers and workers in the colonies

B to suggest gender inequality in colonial times

C to show the industriousness of colonial women

D to imply the protection of even poor people's rights

Document-Based Questions

Directions: Analyze the document and answer the short-answer questions that follow.

This passage from the Declaration of Independence includes some of the colonists' complaints about King George III.

> *He has combined with others to subject us to a jurisdiction foreign to our constitution, and unacknowledged by our laws; giving his Assent to their Acts of pretended Legislation:*
>
> *For quartering large bodies of troops among us:*
>
> *For protecting them, by a mock Trial, from punishment for any Murders which they should commit on the Inhabitants of these States:*
>
> *For cutting off our Trade with all parts of the world:*
>
> *For imposing Taxes on us without our Consent:*
>
> *For depriving us in many cases, of the benefits of Trial by Jury:*
>
> *For transporting us beyond Seas to be tried for pretended offences:*
>
> —the Declaration of Independence

15. The Declaration refers to King George combining with "others" and "giving his assent to their Acts of pretended Legislation." Who are these others?

16. Choose two of the complaints. What legislation or event from the chapter is related to each complaint?

Extended Response

17. The colonists tried other means of resolving their differences with the British before declaring their independence. Write a brief essay describing their efforts.

For additional test practice, use Self-Check Quizzes—Chapter 2 on glencoe.com.

Need Extra Help?

If you missed questions...	1	2	3	4	5	6	7	8	9	10	11	12	13	14	15	16	17
Go to page...	35	39	41	51	33	37	39	43	45	47	53	54	48	48	55	51	51

The Declaration of Independence

In Congress, July 4, 1776. The unanimous Declaration of the thirteen united States of America,

Words spelled as originally written.

What It Means

The Preamble The Declaration of Independence has four parts. The Preamble explains why the Continental Congress drew up the Declaration.

[Preamble]

When in the Course of human events, it becomes necessary for one people to dissolve the political bands which have connected them with another, and to assume among the Powers of the earth, the separate and equal station to which the Laws of Nature and of Nature's God entitle them, a decent respect to the opinions of mankind requires that they should declare the causes which **impel** them to the separation.

impel: force

What It Means

Natural Rights The second part, the Declaration of Natural Rights, lists the rights of the citizens. It goes on to explain that, in a republic, people form a government to protect their rights.

[Declaration of Natural Rights]

We hold these truths to be self-evident, that all men are created equal, that they are **endowed** by their Creator with certain unalienable Rights, that among these are Life, Liberty, and the pursuit of Happiness.

endowed: provided

That to secure these rights, Governments are instituted among Men, deriving their just powers from the consent of the governed,

That whenever any Form of Government becomes destructive of these ends, it is the Right of the People to alter or to abolish it, and to institute new Government, laying its foundation on such principles and organizing its powers in such form, as to them shall seem most likely to effect their Safety and Happiness. Prudence, indeed, will dictate that Governments long established should not be changed for light and transient causes; and accordingly all experience hath shown, that mankind are more disposed to suffer, while evils are sufferable, than to right themselves by abolishing the forms to which they are accustomed. But when a long train of abuses and **usurpations,** pursuing invariably the same Object evinces a design to reduce them under absolute **Despotism**, it is their right, it is their duty, to throw off such Government, and to provide new Guards for their future security.

usurpations: unjust uses of power

despotism: unlimited power

What It Means

List of Grievances The third part of the Declaration lists the colonists' complaints against the British government. Notice that King George III is singled out for blame.

[List of Grievances]

Such has been the patient sufferance of these Colonies; and such is now the necessity which constrains them to alter their former Systems of Government. The history of the present King of Great Britain is a history of repeated injuries and usurpations, all having in direct object the establishment of an absolute Tyranny over these States. To prove this, let Facts be submitted to a candid world.

He has refused his Assent to Laws, the most wholesome and necessary for the public good.

He has forbidden his Governors to pass Laws of immediate and pressing importance, unless suspended in their operation till his Assent should be obtained; and when so suspended, he has utterly neglected to attend to them.

He has refused to pass other Laws for the accommodation of large districts of people, unless those people would **relinquish** the right of Representation in the Legislature, a right **inestimable** to them and formidable to tyrants only.

relinquish: give up
inestimable: priceless

He has called together legislative bodies at places unusual, uncomfortable, and distant from the depository of their Public Records, for the sole purpose of fatiguing them into compliance with his measures.

He has dissolved Representative Houses repeatedly, for opposing with manly firmness his invasions on the rights of the people.

He has refused for a long time, after such dissolutions, to cause others to be elected; whereby the Legislative Powers, incapable of **Annihilation**, have returned to the People at large for their exercise; the State remaining in the mean time exposed to all the dangers of invasion from without, and **convulsions** within.

annihilation: destruction

convulsions: violent disturbances

He has endeavoured to prevent the population of these States; for that purpose obstructing the **Laws for Naturalization of Foreigners;** refusing to pass others to encourage their migrations hither, and raising the conditions of new Appropriations of Lands.

Laws for Naturalization of Foreigners: process by which foreign-born persons become citizens

He has obstructed the Administration of Justice, by refusing his Assent to Laws for establishing Judiciary Powers.

He has made Judges dependent on his Will alone, for the **tenure** of their offices, and the amount and payment of their salaries.

tenure: term

He has erected a multitude of New Offices, and sent hither swarms of Officers to harass our people, and eat out their substance.

He has kept among us, in times of peace, Standing Armies without the Consent of our legislature.

He has affected to render the Military independent of and superior to the Civil Power.

He has combined with others to subject us to a jurisdiction foreign to our constitution, and unacknowledged by our laws; giving his Assent to their acts of pretended legislation:

quartering: lodging

For **quartering** large bodies of troops among us:

For protecting them, by a mock Trial, from Punishment for any Murders which they should commit on the Inhabitants of these States:

For cutting off our Trade with all parts of the world:

For imposing taxes on us without our Consent:

For depriving us in many cases, of the benefits of Trial by Jury:

For transporting us beyond Seas to be tried for pretended offences:

render: make

For abolishing the free System of English Laws in a neighbouring Province, establishing therein an Arbitrary government, and enlarging its Boundaries so as to **render** it at once an example and fit instrument for introducing the same absolute rule into these Colonies:

For taking away our Charters, abolishing our most valuable Laws, and altering fundamentally the Forms of our Governments:

For suspending our own Legislature, and declaring themselves invested with Power to legislate for us in all cases whatsoever.

abdicated: given up

He has **abdicated** Government here, by declaring us out of his Protection and waging War against us.

He has plundered our seas, ravaged our Coasts, burnt our towns, and destroyed the lives of our people.

perfidy: violation of trust

He is at this time transporting large armies of foreign mercenaries to compleat the works of death, desolation and tyranny, already begun with circumstances of Cruelty & **perfidy** scarcely paralleled in the most barbarous ages, and totally unworthy the Head of a civilized nation.

He has constrained our fellow Citizens taken Captive on the high Seas to bear Arms against their Country, to become the executioners of their friends and Brethren, or to fall themselves by their Hands.

insurrections: rebellions

He has excited domestic **insurrections** amongst us, and has endeavoured to bring on the inhabitants of our frontiers, the merciless Indian Savages, whose known rule of warfare, is an undistinguished destruction of all ages, sexes and conditions.

petitioned for redress: asked formally for a correction of wrongs

In every stage of these Oppressions We have **Petitioned for Redress** in the most humble terms: Our repeated Petitions have been answered only by repeated injury. A Prince, whose character is thus marked by every act which may define a Tyrant, is unfit to be the ruler of a free People.

unwarrantable jurisdiction: unjustified authority

Nor have We been wanting in attention to our British brethren. We have warned them from time to time of attempts by their legislature to extend an **unwarrantable jurisdiction** over us. We have reminded them of the circumstances of our emigration and settlement here. We have appealed to their native justice and magnanimity, and we have conjured them by the ties of our common kindred to disavow these usurpations, which, would inevitably interrupt our connections and correspondence. They too have been deaf to the voice of justice and of **consanguinity**. We must, therefore, acquiesce in the necessity, which denounces our Separation, and hold them, as we hold the rest of mankind, Enemies in War, in Peace Friends.

consanguinity: originating from the same ancestor

[Resolution of Independence by the United States]

What It Means

Resolution of Independence The final section declares that the colonies are "Free and Independent States" with the full power to make war, to form alliances, and to trade with other countries.

We, therefore, the Representatives of the united States of America, in General Congress, Assembled, appealing to the Supreme Judge of the world for the **rectitude** of our intentions, do, in the Name, and by Authority of the good People of these Colonies, solemnly publish and declare, That these United Colonies are, and of Right ought to be Free and Independent States; that they are Absolved from all Allegiance to the British Crown, and that all political connection between them and the State of Great Britain, is and ought to be totally dissolved; and that as Free and Independent States, they have full Power to levy War, conclude Peace, contract Alliances, establish Commerce, and to do all other Acts and Things which Independent States may of right do.

rectitude: rightness

And for the support of this Declaration, with a firm reliance on the Protection of Divine Providence, we mutually pledge to each other our Lives, our Fortunes and our sacred Honor.

John Hancock
President from Massachusetts

Georgia
Button Gwinnett
Lyman Hall
George Walton

North Carolina
William Hooper
Joseph Hewes
John Penn

South Carolina
Edward Rutledge
Thomas Heyward, Jr.
Thomas Lynch, Jr.
Arthur Middleton

Maryland
Samuel Chase
William Paca
Thomas Stone
Charles Carroll of Carrollton

Virginia
George Wythe
Richard Henry Lee
Thomas Jefferson
Benjamin Harrison
Thomas Nelson, Jr.
Francis Lightfoot Lee
Carter Braxton

Pennsylvania
Robert Morris
Benjamin Rush
Benjamin Franklin
John Morton
George Clymer
James Smith
George Taylor
James Wilson
George Ross

Delaware
Caesar Rodney
George Read
Thomas McKean

New York
William Floyd
Philip Livingston
Francis Lewis
Lewis Morris

New Jersey
Richard Stockton
John Witherspoon
Francis Hopkinson
John Hart
Abraham Clark

New Hampshire
Josiah Bartlett
William Whipple
Matthew Thornton

Massachusetts
Samuel Adams
John Adams
Robert Treat Paine
Elbridge Gerry

Rhode Island
Stephen Hopkins
William Ellery

Connecticut
Samuel Huntington
William Williams
Oliver Wolcott
Roger Sherman

What It Means

Signers of the Declaration The signers, as representatives of the American people, declared the colonies independent from Great Britain. Most members signed the document on August 2, 1776.

Chapter 3

The Constitution

Why It Matters

The Constitution outlines the ideals of American government and describes how they should be achieved. It tells you what your rights and privileges are. The Constitution affects you, your family, and your friends as much today as it affected those who wrote it more than 200 years ago.

Civics ONLINE
Visit glencoe.com and enter QuickPass™ code CIV3093c3 for Chapter 3 resources.

Chapter Audio

BIG Ideas

Section 1: The Nation's First Governments

Political principles and major events shape how people form governments. Americans faced the task of forming independent governments at both the state and national levels.

Section 2: The Road to the Constitution

Political principles and major events shape how people form governments. American leaders decided that a new constitution was needed.

Section 3: The Structure of Our Constitution

A constitution reflects the values and goals of the society that creates it. The Constitution is this nation's fundamental law.

Section 4: Principles Underlying the Constitution

A constitution reflects the values and goals of the society that creates it. The Constitution sets forth the basic principles of government.

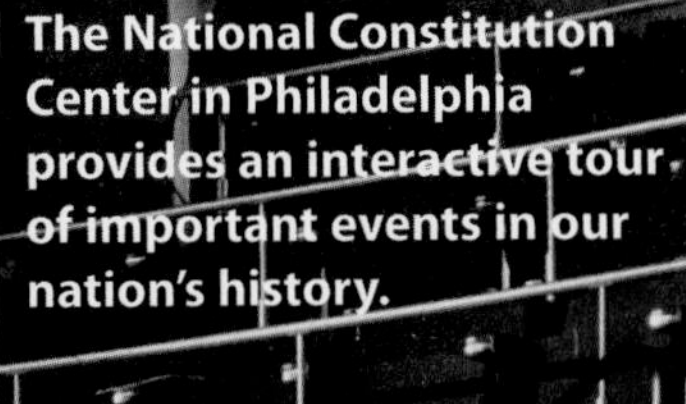

The National Constitution Center in Philadelphia provides an interactive tour of important events in our nation's history.

FOLDABLES™ Study Organizer

Sequencing Information Study Foldable Make the following Foldable to help you analyze information about the Constitution.

Step 1 Mark the midpoint of a sheet of paper. Then fold in the outside edges to touch the midpoint.

Step 2 Fold paper in half from top to bottom.

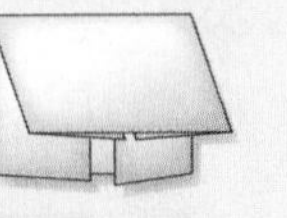

Step 3 Open and cut along the inside fold lines to form four tabs. Label your Foldable as shown.

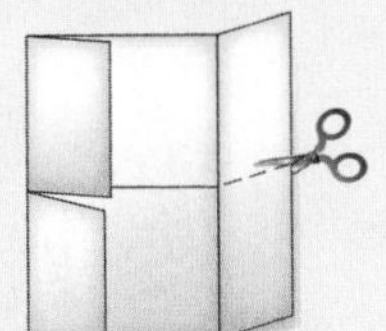

Reading and Writing As you read the chapter, note details about the Constitution, showing each major idea of the document under the tabs.

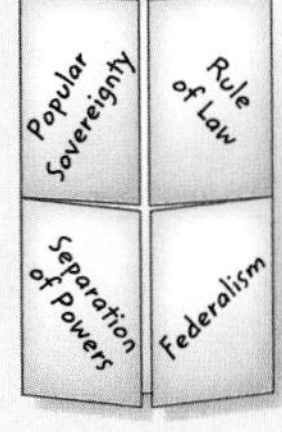

The Nation's First Governments

Guide to Reading

Big Idea
Political principles and major events shape how people form governments.

Content Vocabulary
- constitution *(p. 67)*
- bicameral *(p. 67)*
- confederation *(p. 68)*
- ratify *(p. 68)*

Academic Vocabulary
- convert *(p. 67)*
- area *(p. 69)*
- impact *(p. 69)*

Reading Strategy
Comparing As you read, create a diagram like the one below identifying four important documents of government that preceded the Constitution.

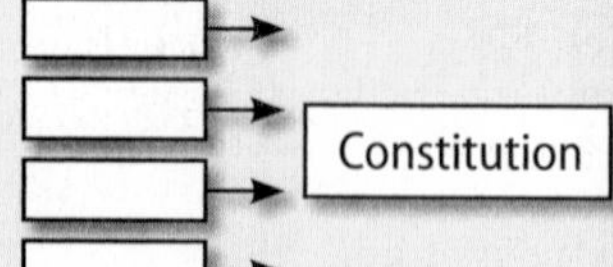

Real World Civics It has a crack—and it no longer rings. The Liberty Bell, on display in Philadelphia today, brings to the minds of every American student what independence and freedom mean. Tradition tells us that the Liberty Bell last rang in July 1776, to announce the first public reading of the Declaration of Independence. This was a time when there was no television, radio, or Internet; it announced to the people that John Hancock and Benjamin Franklin, William Ellery, Josiah Bartlett, and the other 52 people had signed the Declaration.

▼ **Several students marvel at the Liberty Bell in Philadelphia, Pennsylvania**

The First State Constitutions

Main Idea **Americans faced the task of forming independent governments at both the state and national levels.**

Civics & You Would you be surprised to learn that the Constitution of the United States was not our first plan of government? Read to find out about the nation's first constitution.

Even before the Declaration of Independence was signed, American colonists discussed the possibility of independence, and American leaders began preparing new state constitutions to replace the old colonial charters. In May of 1776, the Second Continental Congress urged colonists to form state governments,

> *"as shall . . . best conduce [contribute] to the happiness and safety of their constituents [voters]."*
>
> —Continental Congress

In January 1776, New Hampshire became the first colony to organize as a state and craft a detailed, written plan for government, or **constitution.** Within a few years, every former colony had a new constitution or had **converted,** or changed, its colonial charters into a state constitution.

From Colonies to States

The states set up similar systems of government. Each state had a legislature to create laws. Most of these legislatures were **bicameral,** like the English Parliament; that is, they were divided into two parts, or houses. The members of each house or state legislature were chosen by different methods.

Each state also had a governor, who was elected either by the legislature or by the citizens. The governor's job was to carry out the laws. Finally, each state had judges and courts to decide what the laws meant and how they applied to each new situation.

Preserving Rights

Many of the new state governments were based upon ideals expressed in the Declaration of Independence. American ideals of individual rights to "life, liberty, and the pursuit of happiness" are in the Declaration. Most state constitutions included a bill of rights, guaranteeing certain basic freedoms and legal protections to the state's citizens. Some of these rights, such as trial by jury and protection of personal property, can be traced back to the Magna Carta and the English Bill of Rights.

Reading Check **Describing** What documents did the new state constitutions replace?

Early Statehood New Hampshire's state capitol building is one of the oldest in the country.
Discussing **Why were state governments based on the ideals of the Declaration of Independence?**

The Articles of Confederation

Main Idea **The weaknesses of the Articles of Confederation created problems for the new country.**

Civics & You You make a plan but the plan is not working—what do you do? Find out what action American leaders took when their plan of government was not working.

Although each state was well prepared to govern itself when independence was declared, a state could not do some things on its own. It could not raise and maintain a large army, for example, and Americans realized that 13 small, separate forces would be no match for the mighty British army. Americans concluded that if they wanted to win the war with Great Britain, they needed a single, strong army under central control.

For this and other reasons, the Second Continental Congress made plans for a union of the states. In 1777 the Congress detailed these plans in a document called the Articles of Confederation, the first constitution of the United States of America.

Land Ordinance Some Midwestern boundaries still reflect those drawn by the Ordinance of 1785. ***Explaining*** **What are the dimensions of townships? Of sections?**

Forming a Confederation A **confederation** is a group of individual state governments that band together for a common purpose. The Articles of Confederation established a system for cooperation, or "league of friendship," among independent states. By 1781 all 13 states had **ratified,** or approved, the Articles of Confederation.

The Articles set up a one-house legislature in which each state had one vote. This Confederation Congress, as it came to be called, was the only government body with control over the army and authority to deal with foreign countries on behalf of the states. These central powers were quite limited, though.

As a result of the colonial experience under the British government, the 13 states refused to give the Confederation Congress two important powers. It had no power to enforce its laws and no power to tax. The Articles allowed the Congress to ask the states for money but not to demand it. The Congress could not, in fact, require the states to do anything.

Accomplishments

The Confederation Congress laid the foundations for the administration of the national government. It also provided for the systematic growth and development of the United States.

Ordinance of 1785 When the American Revolution began, only a few thousand white settlers lived west of the Appalachian Mountains. By the 1790s, their numbers had increased to about 120,000.

Through the Ordinance of 1785, Congress created a system for surveying—taking a detailed measurement of an area of land—and selling the western lands. It arranged the land into townships six miles square. Each township was divided into 36 sections of each one square mile. The Ordinance of 1785 at first applied only to what was then called the Northwest Territory—present-day Ohio, Indiana, Illinois, Michigan, and Wisconsin. It established a system of land surveying and settlement that we still use today.

Northwest Ordinance Once the policy for settlement of western lands was established, Congress turned to the problem of governing this **area,** or region. In 1787, the Northwest Ordinance, perhaps the most significant achievement of Congress under the Articles, was passed. It laid the basis for the organization of new territorial governments and set a precedent for the method of admitting new states to the Union. The Northwest Ordinance also included a specific provision outlawing slavery:

> *"There shall be neither slavery nor involuntary servitude in said territory."*
>
> —the Northwest Ordinance

This provision would have an important **impact,** or effect, on the history of America in the 1800s. The Confederation's western ordinances had an enormous effect on American expansion and development. The Ordinance of 1785 and the Northwest Ordinance opened the way for settlement of the Northwest Territory in a stable and orderly manner.

Weaknesses of the Articles

It soon became clear that the Articles had some serious problems. To begin with, the Congress could not pass a law unless nine states voted in favor of it. Any attempt to amend, or change, the Articles required a unanimous vote of all 13 states. These strict voting requirements made it difficult for the Congress to accomplish anything.

Even when the Congress managed to pass laws, it could not enforce them. Unlike the state constitutions, the Articles did not provide for a governor or for courts. If a state decided to ignore a law, the Congress could do nothing about it.

Weaknesses of the Articles of Confederation

LACK OF POWER AND MONEY
• Congress had no power to collect taxes.
• Congress had no power to regulate trade.
• Congress had no power to enforce its laws.
LACK OF CENTRAL POWER
• No single leader or group directed government policy.
• No national court system existed.
RULES TOO RIGID
• Congress could not pass laws without the approval of 9 states.
• The Articles could not be changed without the agreement of all 13 states.

Analyzing Charts

1. **Discussing** Did Congress have the power to enforce its laws? Explain.
2. **Analyzing** Why was it so difficult to pass laws under the Articles of Confederation?

A Time of Crisis

The United States was able to overcome the weaknesses of the Articles. The states secured their independence by winning the Revolutionary War against Great Britain. A peace agreement called the Treaty of Paris was signed in 1783.

Debt Independence, however, did not put an end to the struggles of the United States. For one thing, the country faced serious financial troubles. Unable to collect taxes, the Congress had borrowed money to pay for the Revolutionary War. It had run up a debt that would take years to repay.

The state governments had also fallen into deep debt. They taxed their citizens heavily as a result, driving many farmers out of business and sparking widespread resentment. The states also taxed goods imported from other states and foreign countries, hurting trade. The Confederation Congress had no power to remedy these problems.

Shays's Rebellion Even worse, the Congress could do nothing about the public's insecurity. Americans feared that the government could not protect their safety. During 1786 and 1787, riots broke out in several states. Daniel Shays, a farmer who had fallen into debt because of heavy state taxes, led one of the most alarming disturbances. When Massachusetts courts threatened to take his farm as payment for his debts, Shays felt the state had no right to punish him for a problem it had created. Many others agreed. Shays armed about 1,200 farmers in an attack on a federal arsenal. Although the rebellion, known as Shays's Rebellion, was quickly stopped, it sent a wake-up call throughout the country.

Many political leaders, merchants, and others began arguing for a stronger national government. As George Washington wrote,

> *"I do not conceive we can exist long as a nation, without having lodged somewhere a power which will pervade the whole Union."*
>
> —George Washington's papers

In 1787, only 12 of the states sent delegates to a meeting in Philadelphia to revise the Articles of Confederation.

Reading Check **Explaining** What financial troubles did the young nation face?

Section 1 Review

Vocabulary

1. **Write** a paragraph in which you use each of the following vocabulary terms: *constitution, bicameral, confederation, ratify.*

Main Ideas

2. **Explaining** Why did the colonies decide they needed a national government in addition to state governments?
3. **Describing** What problems did the colonists come up against because of the weaknesses of the Articles of Confederation?

Critical Thinking

4. **BIG Ideas** Why was the Ordinance of 1785 important?
5. **Categorizing** On a graphic organizer like the one below, list the characteristics of bicameral legislatures—the one adopted by most colonies.

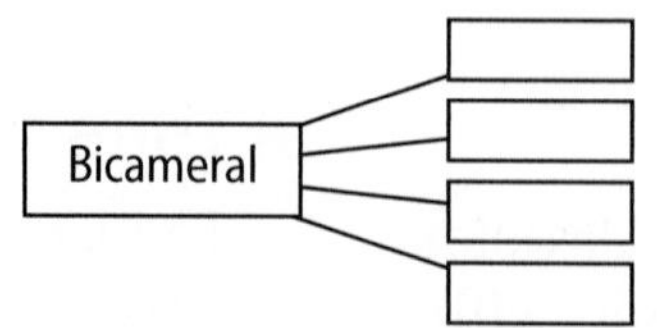

6. **Analyzing** Why did the states approve the Articles of Confederation despite its many weaknesses?

CITIZENSHIP Activity

7. **Expository Writing** Imagine you are on a committee to write a new state constitution. List three freedoms you want attached to your state's constitution. Explain why it is important to guarantee these rights.

Study Central™ To review this section, go to glencoe.com.

Section Audio Spotlight Video

The Road to the Constitution

Guide to Reading

Big Idea

Political principles and major events shape how people form governments.

Content Vocabulary

- Constitutional Convention *(p. 73)*
- Great Compromise *(p. 75)*
- Three-Fifths Compromise *(p. 75)*
- Electoral College *(p. 76)*
- Federalists *(p. 77)*
- federalism *(p. 77)*
- Anti-Federalists *(p. 78)*

Academic Vocabulary

- process *(p. 72)*
- despite *(p. 73)*

Reading Strategy

Identifying As you read, compare the Virginia Plan to the New Jersey Plan by completing a Venn diagram like the one below.

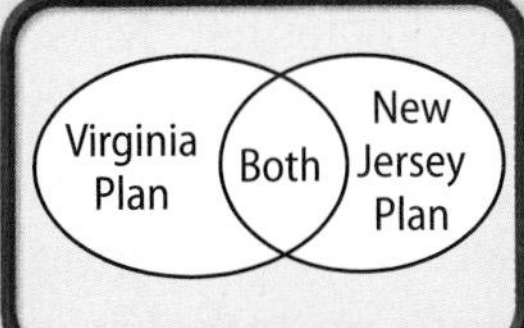

Real World Civics When the U.S. Constitution was ratified in 1787, there were no parades, no wild celebration, and certainly no bulletproof glass to shield the president. But in 1987, then president Ronald Reagan had to be protected from harm when he led the celebration for the 200th birthday of the Constitution. He asked Americans to think back to the time when the document was drafted. The colonies were surrounded by unfriendly powers, some colonies had unbearably high taxes, others had crushing debts, and still others were involved in trade disagreements.

▼ **Americans celebrate the 200th birthday of the Constitution outside the Capitol**

The Philadelphia Convention

Main Idea **American leaders decided to create a new plan of government.**

Civics & You Why is it important for a nation to establish a set of laws? Read to find out the issues American leaders faced in organizing a new plan of government.

Ten years of living under the Articles of Confederation had shown Americans that the loose association of 13 independent states was not working. By early 1787, it was clear that the national government had to be strengthened. Each state was asked to send delegates to a convention in Philadelphia to fix the flaws. This meeting was to become the Constitutional Convention. Only Rhode Island chose not to take part, because its leaders opposed a stronger central government.

New Government Colonial reenactors perform a scene at Independence Hall. ***Explaining*** **Would you have waited outside the hall for word of your new government? Why or why not?**

The Work Begins

The convention began in Philadelphia's Independence Hall on May 25, 1787. Rain fell heavily during the opening week, leaving the roads to the city choked with mud. Many delegates had to travel long distances and arrived late. Once all were assembled, however, they were an extraordinary group.

The Delegates Most of the 55 men present were well-educated lawyers, merchants, college presidents, physicians, generals, governors, and planters with considerable political experience. Eight of the delegates had signed the Declaration of Independence. Seven had been governors of their states, and 41 were or had been members of the Continental Congress. Native Americans, African Americans, and women were not considered part of the political **process,** or movement, so none attended.

Benjamin Franklin of Pennsylvania, 81, was the oldest delegate. He was famous as a diplomat, writer, inventor, and scientist. Most delegates, however, were still young men in their thirties or forties with great careers ahead of them. Two delegates, George Washington and James Madison, would go on to become presidents of the United States. Nineteen would become U.S. senators, and 13 served in the House of Representatives. Four men would become federal judges, and four others would become Supreme Court justices.

A few notable leaders were not at the convention. Thomas Jefferson and John Adams were both in Europe as representatives of the American government—Jefferson in Paris and Adams in London. Patrick Henry, a prominent Virginian leader during the American Revolution, was also missing. Although elected as a delegate, Henry was against the convention and did not attend.

Key Decisions

The delegates unanimously chose George Washington to preside over the convention. Widely respected for his leadership during the American Revolution, Washington would now call on speakers and make sure that the meetings ran in an orderly, efficient manner. At the start, he reminded the delegates of the importance of their task. He warned that if they could not come up with an acceptable plan of government, "perhaps another dreadful conflict is to be sustained."

Operating Procedures At the very start of the convention, the delegates made several important decisions. They agreed that each state would have one vote, no matter how many delegates represented that state. They also agreed that a simple majority—in this case, seven votes—would decide any issue.

The delegates decided to keep the work of the convention secret. This was a key decision because it made it possible for the delegates to talk freely. The public was not allowed to attend meetings, the doors were guarded, and the windows were kept tightly shut **despite,** or in spite of, the summer heat. Each delegate promised not to tell outsiders what was going on inside.

Because of this secrecy, we have virtually no written records of the convention. The only details we have came from a notebook kept by James Madison, a delegate from Virginia.

Need for a New Constitution The Congress gave delegates the job of revising the Articles of Confederation. The call to revise the Articles of Confederation came while the young nation faced difficult problems. Many Americans believed that the Confederation government was too weak to deal with these challenges. Many national leaders had become dissatisfied with the weaknesses of the Confederation. They quickly agreed, that changing the Articles was not enough. They decided instead to dispose of the Articles and write a new constitution. All the delegates set out to strengthen the national government by creating a new plan of government. Thus the meeting in Philadelphia came to be known as the **Constitutional Convention.**

Who Were the Delegates?

- Practically all of the 55 delegates had experience in colonial and state government.
- Eight delegates had signed the Declaration of Independence.

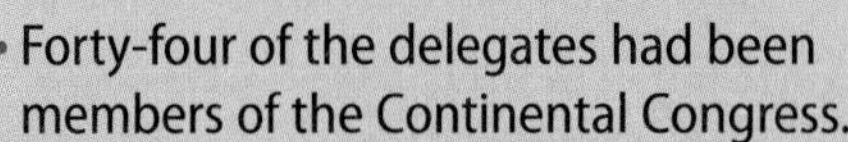

- Forty-four of the delegates had been members of the Continental Congress.
- Virtually every individual had taken part in the American Revolution, and at least 29 served in the military.
- George Washington and James Madison became president of the United States.

- The delegates ranged in age from Jonathan Dayton (left) of New Jersey, aged 26, to Benjamin Franklin (above), aged 81.

Analyzing Charts

Inferring Why do you think delegates came from so many different backgrounds and professions?

Reading Check **Explaining** Why did the delegates decide to keep the work of the Constitutional Convention a secret?

Creating the Constitution

Main Idea **Many of the provisions of the Constitution were arrived at through a series of compromises.**

Civics & You Have you and a rival ever set aside your differences to work for a common cause? This happened when the delegates resolved their differences to create the Constitution.

The delegates to the Constitutional Convention were determined to create a framework of government that all states could accept. Everyone knew that failure could mean disaster. According to James Madison's notes of the Convention, George Mason of Virginia said the following:

> *"[I] would bury [my] bones in this city rather than [leave] . . . the Convention without any thing being done."*
>
> —George Mason, remarks at the Constitutional Convention

On May 29, 1787, shortly after the convention began, the Virginia delegates proposed a plan for the new government. James Madison had designed what became known as the Virginia Plan.

The Virginia Plan

The Virginia Plan described a federal government very similar to the one we have today. It included a president, courts, and a congress with two houses. Representation in each house of congress would be based on each state's population. Large states would have more votes than smaller states.

Birthplace of the Nation Independence Hall was originally built to serve as the Pennsylvania state capitol. ***Speculating*** **What other important event occurred here? Why do you think it was chosen as the site of the Constitutional Convention?**

The Virginia Plan appealed to delegates from the more heavily populated states such as Massachusetts, Pennsylvania, and New York, as well as Virginia. The small states, however, feared that a government dominated by the large states would ignore their interests.

The New Jersey Plan

After two weeks of heated discussion, delegates from the smaller states submitted their own plan. On June 15, William Paterson presented an alternative plan. The New Jersey Plan called for a government similar to the one under the Articles of Confederation. It included a one-house congress in which states would have equal representation and therefore equal votes. Under this plan, Congress could set taxes and regulate trade—powers it did not have under the Articles.

Delegates from Delaware, New Jersey, and Maryland approved of this plan. It made their states equal in power to the big states. Of course, the large states would not accept this plan. They thought larger states should have more power than smaller states.

The Great Compromise

For six weeks the delegates debated the merits of the two plans. A committee headed by Roger Sherman of Connecticut finally came up with an answer. The committee proposed that Congress have two houses—a Senate and a House of Representatives—that would be structured differently from each other. Each state would have equal representation in the Senate, which would please the smaller states. In the House, representation would be based on population, which would please the larger states.

No group was completely happy, but this was a solution with which all could live. Historians call Sherman's plan the Connecticut Compromise, or the **Great Compromise.** (A compromise is a way of resolving disagreements in which each side gives up something but gains something else.)

Counting Population The delegates decided representation in a new government would be based on population but could not decide how to count the many slaves in America. ***Explaining*** **What compromise answered this question?**

The Three-Fifths Compromise

Although the Great Compromise settled the structure of Congress, other questions remained. At the time of the Constitutional Convention, more than 550,000 African Americans, mostly in the South, were enslaved. The Southern states wanted to count these people as part of their populations to increase their voting power in the House of Representatives. The Northern states, which had few enslaved persons, opposed the idea. They argued that because enslaved persons were not allowed to vote or otherwise participate in government, they should not be used to give Southern states a stronger voice in Congress.

In the **Three-Fifths Compromise,** delegates agreed that every five enslaved persons would count as three free persons. Thus three-fifths of the slave population in each state would be used in determining representation in Congress.

American Biography

James Madison (1751–1836)

Even in his day, **James Madison** was known as the "Father of the Constitution." Madison protested: "You give me credit to which I have no claim. . . . It ought to be regarded as the work of many heads and many hands."

When it came to creating a constitution, however, Madison had few equals. Madison, though, at first opposed the addition of a bill of rights. He feared that future governments might honor only those rights listed in the bill. When some leaders continued to insist on a bill of rights, Madison finally agreed.

To make sure the amendments did not weaken the new government, he helped write them himself. Then, as the U.S. representative from Virginia, Madison pushed the amendments through Congress, fulfilling the Constitution's promise to create a "more perfect union."

At the Constitutional Convention, Madison served his nation well. In the years to come, the nation would call on him again. In 1801 he became President Thomas Jefferson's secretary of state. In 1808 Madison was elected the fourth president of the United States.

Making a Difference

James Madison wrote that "Liberty may be endangered by the abuse of liberty, but also by the abuse of power." ***Explaining*** **Put this statement in your own words.**

Other Compromises Northern and Southern delegates to the convention compromised on trade matters, too. The Northern states felt that Congress should be able to regulate both foreign trade and trade between the states. The Southern states, however, feared that Congress would use this power to tax exports—goods sold to other countries. If this happened, the Southern economy would suffer because it depended heavily on exports of tobacco, rice, and other products.

Southerners also feared that Congress might stop slave traders from bringing enslaved people into the United States. Thus, Southern delegates objected because Southern plantations depended on the labor of slaves. Again a compromise among the delegates would settle the issue.

After some discussion, the Southern states agreed that Congress could regulate trade between the states, as well as with other countries. In exchange, the North agreed that Congress could not tax exports, nor could it interfere with the slave trade before 1808.

The delegates also compromised on issues concerning their new government. Some delegates thought members of Congress should choose the president; others believed that the people should vote to decide the presidency. The solution was the **Electoral College,** a group of people who would be named by each state legislature to select the president and vice president. The Electoral College system is still used today, but the voters in each state, not the legislatures, now choose electors.

Balancing Viewpoints

Main Idea **Writing the new Constitution and getting the American people to approve it was not an easy task.**

Civics & You Did you ever work on a committee in which many people had to decide on one solution to a problem? That is a similar situation to what faced the writers of the new U.S. Constitution.

Throughout the summer, the delegates to the Constitutional Convention hammered out the details of the new government. As their work drew to an end, some delegates headed home, but 42 remained out of the original 55. On September 17, 1787, they gathered for the last time. A committee headed by Gouverneur Morris had put its ideas in writing, and the Constitution was ready to be signed. All but three delegates signed their names at the bottom.

The delegates at Philadelphia had produced the Constitution, but its acceptance depended upon the will of the American people. The next step was to win ratification, or approval, of the Constitution. The delegates had decided that each state would set up a ratifying convention to vote "yes" or "no." When at least nine of the 13 states had ratified it, the Constitution would become the supreme law of the land.

Who Were the Federalists? Americans reacted to the proposed Constitution in different ways. Supporters of the document called themselves **Federalists.** They chose this name to emphasize that the Constitution would create a system of **federalism,** a form of government in which power is divided between the federal, or national, government and the states.

Civics ONLINE

Student Web Activity Visit glencoe.com and complete the Chapter 3 Web Activity.

Ratification of the Constitution

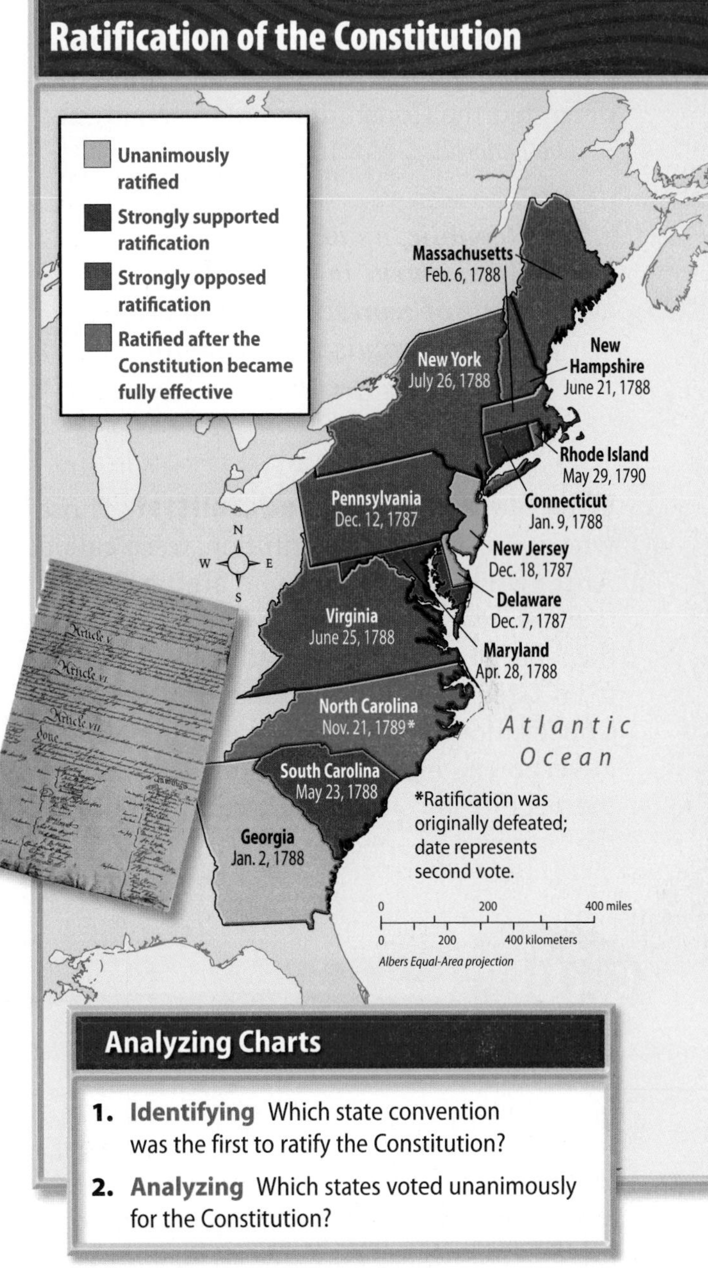

Analyzing Charts

1. **Identifying** Which state convention was the first to ratify the Constitution?
2. **Analyzing** Which states voted unanimously for the Constitution?

To win support, the Federalists reminded Americans of the flaws in the Articles of Confederation. They argued that the United States would not survive without a strong national government. Supporters of the Federalists included large landowners who wanted the property protection a strong national government could provide. The Federalists claimed that only a strong national government could protect the new nation from enemies abroad and solve the country's internal problems.

The Federalist Papers In a series of essays known as *The Federalist*, Alexander Hamilton, James Madison, and John Jay defended the Constitution. Madison argued in *The Federalist*, No. 10:

> "*A Republic, by which I mean a Government in which the scheme of representation takes place . . . promises the cure for which we are seeking. . . .*"
>
> —*James Madison, The Federalist,* No. 10

Who Were the Anti-Federalists? Those who opposed the Constitution were called **Anti-Federalists.** Their main argument was that the new Constitution would take away the liberties Americans had fought to win from Great Britain. They believed the new Constitution would create a strong national government, ignore the will of the states and the people, and favor the wealthy few over the common people.

Perhaps the strongest criticism of the Constitution was that it lacked a bill of rights to protect individual freedoms. Many feared they would lose the liberties gained during the Revolution. Several state conventions took a stand and announced they would not ratify the Constitution without the addition of a bill of rights.

Launching a New Nation The Federalists eventually agreed with the Anti-Federalists that a bill of rights was necessary. They promised that if the Constitution was adopted, the new government would add a bill of rights to it.

That promise helped turn the tide. Several states had already voted for ratification. On June 21, 1788, New Hampshire became the ninth state to do so, and the Constitution took effect. In time, the four remaining states ratified the Constitution, the last being Rhode Island in 1790. The 13 independent states were now one nation, the United States of America.

Reading Check **Explaining** Why did Anti-Federalists oppose the Constitution?

Vocabulary

1. **Write** short paragraphs about the Constitutional Convention using these terms: *Great Compromise, Three-Fifths Compromise, Electoral College, Federalists, federalism, Anti-Federalists.*

Main Ideas

2. **Explaining** Why did delegates think the Articles of Confederation needed to be replaced?
3. **Describing** What issue did the Three-Fifths Compromise solve?
4. **Analyzing** What was the biggest obstacle the delegates faced when getting the Constitution approved?

Critical Thinking

5. **BIG Ideas** Why was the Electoral College established? What power did it have?
6. **Comparing** On a graphic organizer like the one below, list the details of the Great Compromise that many delegates supported.

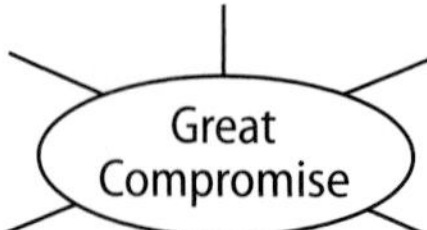

CITIZENSHIP Activity

7. **Expository Writing** Conduct a survey of at least 10 adults in which you ask them whether they favor continuing the Electoral College or amending the Constitution to have the presidency determined by the popular vote. Ask respondents to explain their answers. Then, summarize your findings in a short paper.

Study Central™ To review this section, go to glencoe.com.

Spotlight Video

The Structure of Our Constitution

Guide to Reading

Big Idea

A constitution reflects the values and goals of the society that creates it.

Content Vocabulary

- Preamble *(p. 80)*
- legislative branch *(p. 80)*
- executive branch *(p. 80)*
- judicial branch *(p. 81)*
- amendment *(p. 82)*

Academic Vocabulary

- consist *(p. 80)*
- assume *(p. 84)*

Reading Strategy

Categorizing As you read, complete the diagram below listing the major powers the Constitution allows each branch.

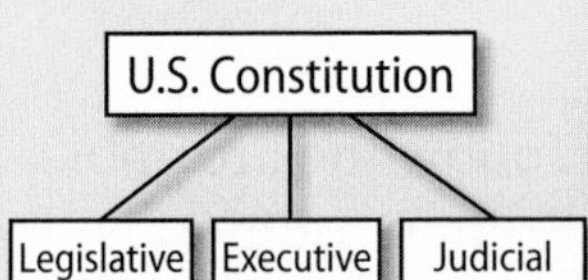

Real World Civics What does the word government mean to you? The military? Many, many documents? Laws and rules? Lynne Cheney, wife of former Vice President Dick Cheney, supports the idea that school children need to know the government is made up of living, breathing people who represent their right to freedom. Mrs. Cheney, hosting a Constitution Day party for dozens of Washington, D.C., second graders, stressed the importance of knowing history and that, "One of the important [history] lessons we can learn is that freedom isn't inevitable."

▼ **Lynne Cheney hosts Constitution Day in Washington, D.C.**

The Sections of the Constitution

Main Idea **The Constitution is a remarkable document that serves as an adaptable blueprint for governing the United States.**

Civics & You Have you ever read some instructions that did not make sense? Did you wish they were better organized so you could follow them? Read how the Constitution was organized.

Although the main purpose of the Constitution is to provide a framework for government, it does much more than that. It is the highest authority in the nation. It is the basic law of the United States. The powers of the branches of government come from it. Like the American flag, the Constitution is a symbol of our nation. It represents our system of government and our basic ideals, such as liberty and freedom.

The Constitution has three main parts. First is the **Preamble,** an introduction that states the goals and purposes of the government. Next are seven articles that describe the structure of the government. Third are 27 amendments, or additions and changes, to the Constitution.

The Preamble

The Preamble **consists,** or is expressed by, a single concise sentence that begins and ends as follows:

> *"We the People of the United States . . . do ordain and establish this Constitution for the United States of America."*
>
> —Preamble of the U.S. Constitution

These carefully chosen words make clear that the power of government comes from the people. The government depends on the people for its power and exists to serve them. The middle part of the Preamble states six purposes of the government:

1. "To form a more perfect Union"—to unite the states so they can operate as a single nation, for the good of all
2. "To establish Justice"—to make certain that all citizens are treated equally
3. "To insure domestic Tranquility"—to maintain peace and order, keeping citizens and their property safe from harm
4. "To provide for the common defense"—to be ready militarily to protect the country and its citizens from attack
5. "To promote the general Welfare"— to help people live healthy, happy, and prosperous lives
6. "To secure the Blessings of Liberty to ourselves and our Posterity"—to guarantee the basic rights of all Americans, including future generations (posterity)

The Articles

The seven articles that follow the Preamble are identified by the Roman numerals I through VII. The first three articles describe the powers and responsibilities of each branch of government.

Article I Article I outlines the lawmaking powers of the **legislative branch,** or Congress. The Article states that Congress, made up of two houses—the Senate and the House of Representatives—will have all lawmaking authority. The article then describes how members of each house will be chosen and what rules they must follow in making laws. You will learn more about Congress in Chapter 6.

Article II Article II provides for an **executive branch,** or law-enforcing branch of government headed by a president and vice president. Article II explains how these leaders are to be elected and how they can be removed from office.

Article II goes on to list the president's powers, including the power to command the armed forces and to make treaties with other nations. You will learn more about the executive branch in Chapter 7.

Article III The **judicial branch** is the part of government that interprets the laws and sees that they are fairly applied. Article III calls for "one Supreme Court" and such lower courts as Congress deems appropriate. Article III then lists the powers of the federal courts and describes the kinds of cases they may hear. You will read about our federal judiciary in Chapter 8.

Articles IV–VII Article IV of the Constitution explains the relationship between the states and the national government. Article V specifies under what conditions the Constitution can be changed. Article VI contains a key statement declaring the Constitution the "supreme Law of the Land."

In Article VII, the Framers dealt with practical matters. The Constitution would take effect, they wrote, when nine states ratified it.

Reading Check **Describing** What is the main purpose of Article I of the U.S. Constitution?

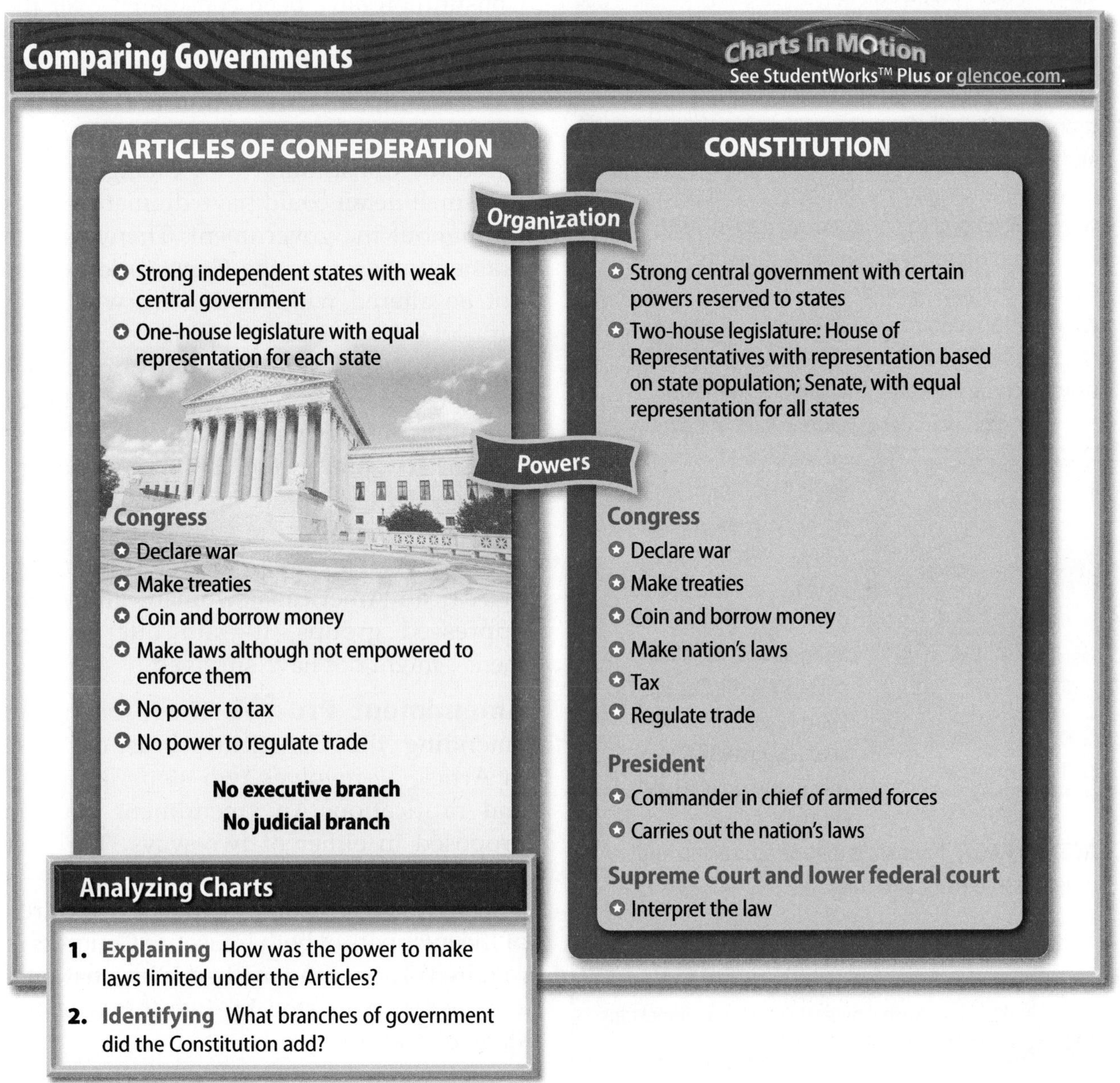

Analyzing Charts

1. **Explaining** How was the power to make laws limited under the Articles?
2. **Identifying** What branches of government did the Constitution add?

TIME™ Teens in Action

We the People

We caught up with Kushal Kadakia, 17, in his hometown of Fremont, California. He had just taken part in a competition called "We the People."

QUESTION: What is We the People?

ANSWER: It's the first three words of the United States Constitution—but it's also a civics competition.

Q: How does that work?

A: Teams of students compete in a simulated congressional testimony. There are question-and-answer sessions on constitutional principles. It promotes an understanding of the Constitution and how it applies to historical and current events. According to We the People's Web site, www.civiced.org, the program started in 1987 and served more than 28 million students.

Q: How did your team do?

A: We finished fourth in California. But beyond the awards, We the People has motivated many of us to become involved with politics by making us more aware of how our government functions.

Kushal encourages voting

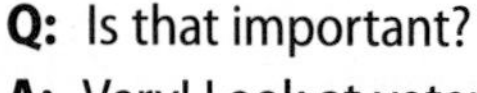

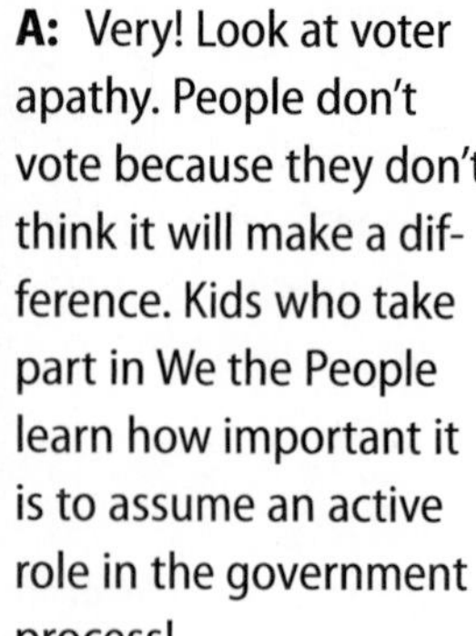

Q: Is that important?

A: Very! Look at voter apathy. People don't vote because they don't think it will make a difference. Kids who take part in We the People learn how important it is to assume an active role in the government process!

ACTION FACT: Kadakia is a huge sports fan and runs cross-country and track.

Making a Difference — CITIZENSHIP

Why does Kushal believe voting is an important responsibility?

Amending the Constitution

Main Idea **The Framers wrote the Constitution so that it could be adapted to meet changing needs.**

Civics & You How do you think the Constitution and our government have changed over time? Read to find out how the Framers planned for change.

Any change in the Constitution is called an **amendment.** Would it surprise you to know that thousands of amendments to the Constitution have been considered over the years? Only 27 have become law because the Framers deliberately made the amendment process difficult. After months of debate and compromise, they knew how delicately balanced the Constitution was. Changing even one small detail could have dramatic effects throughout the government. Therefore, the Framers made sure the Constitution could not be altered without the overwhelming support of the people.

At the same time, the ability to amend the Constitution is necessary. Constitutional amendments safeguard many of our freedoms. For example, the abolition of slavery and the right of women to vote were added as amendments. If the Constitution could not have been amended to protect the rights of African Americans, women, and other oppressed groups, it—and our government—might not have survived.

Amendment Process The process for amending the Constitution, as outlined in Article V, involves two steps: proposal and ratification. An amendment may be proposed in either of two ways. The first method—used for all amendments so far—is by congressional action. A vote of two-thirds of the members of both houses of Congress is required. The second method is by a national convention requested by two-thirds of the state legislatures.

Ratifying an Amendment Once a national amendment has been proposed, three-fourths of the states must ratify it. The states have two ways to do this: by a vote of either the state legislature or by a special state convention. Only one amendment, the Twenty-first Amendment, has been ratified by means of state conventions.

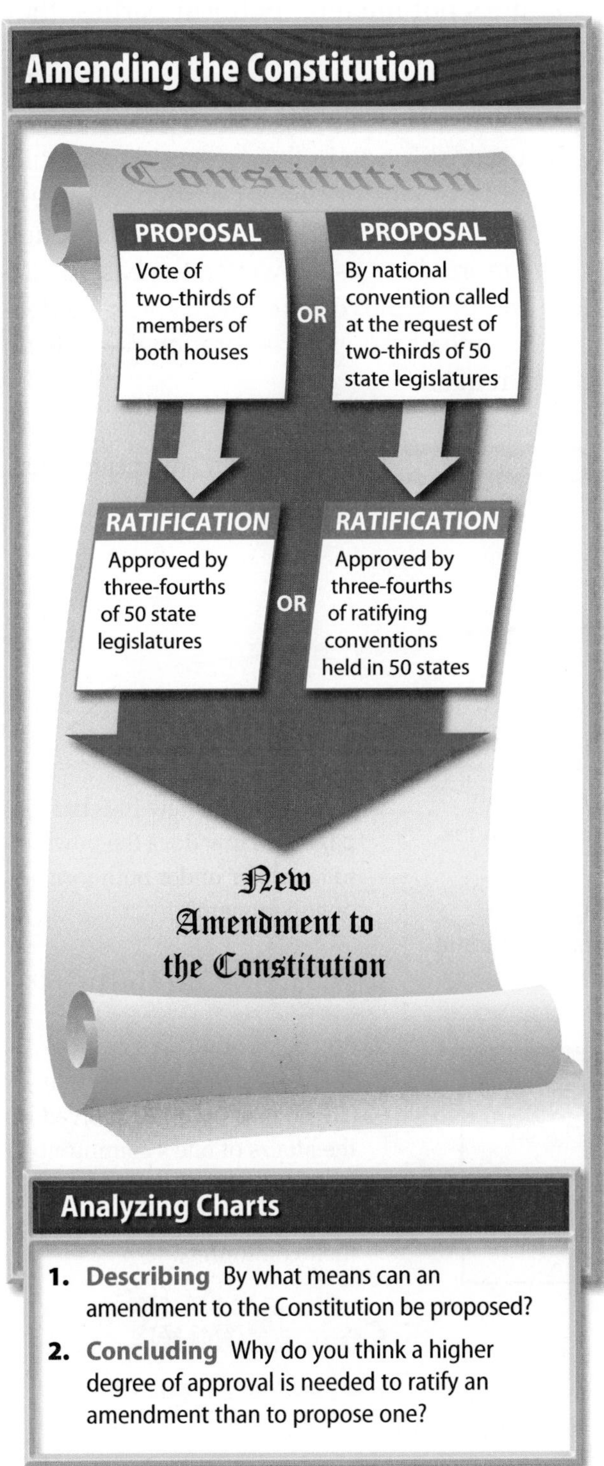

Analyzing Charts

1. **Describing** By what means can an amendment to the Constitution be proposed?
2. **Concluding** Why do you think a higher degree of approval is needed to ratify an amendment than to propose one?

Interpreting the Constitution

The writers of the Constitution knew that the world would change in ways they could not predict. For this reason, they attempted to keep the document as general as possible. Although they went into great detail about some matters, they left other matters open to interpretation.

The Necessary and Proper Clause Article I lists the powers of Congress. In this article, the Constitution gives Congress the power "to make all Laws which shall be necessary and proper" to carry out its duties. The necessary and proper clause allows Congress to exercise powers not specifically listed in the Constitution. These powers are known as "implied powers." Much of what the federal government does today—from licensing television stations to regulating air pollution—is based on the implied powers of Congress.

Of course, not everyone agrees which laws are "necessary and proper" and which laws are not. Some people feel Congress should be allowed to make any laws the Constitution does not specifically forbid. These people believe in a loose interpretation of the Constitution. Others believe in a strict interpretation. They feel Congress should make only the kinds of laws mentioned by the Constitution.

Court Decisions The final authority for interpreting the Constitution rests with the Supreme Court. Over the years, the Supreme Court has interpreted the Constitution in different ways—sometimes strictly, sometimes loosely. With each new interpretation, our government changes.

Legislative and Presidential Actions The actions of Congress and the executive branch have also caused new interpretations of the Constitution. The Constitution allows the House of Representatives to impeach, or accuse, federal officials, while the Senate determines the person's guilt or innocence.

How have actions by the president informally amended the Constitution? In 1841 William Henry Harrison became the first president to die in office. Vice President John Tyler **assumed,** or accepted, the powers of the president according to the provisions in the Constitution. The Constitution, however, was unclear on whether Tyler automatically became president or whether he was merely acting as president until the next election. Tyler went ahead and took the presidential oath. Not until 1967, when the Twenty-fifth Amendment was ratified, was Tyler's action officially part of the Constitution.

There are other examples as well. Nowhere in the Constitution does it state that the president should propose bills or budgets to Congress. Yet since the presidency of Woodrow Wilson (1913–1921), each year the president proposes hundreds of bills to Congress. Presidents interpret the Constitution in other ways, too. Not only does the president make agreements with other countries without congressional approval, the president also requests legislation from Congress. The Constitution does not direct the president to take these actions.

Interpretation Through Custom The interpretation of the Constitution has also changed through customs that have developed. For example, although the Constitution does not mention political parties, they are an important part of today's political system. These days, parties help organize the government and conduct elections.

The Constitution in the present day is quite different from the document written in 1787. In the next 200 years, it will probably go through many more changes. However, the basic structure and principles of our government—a delicate balance among three branches—will no doubt remain.

Reading Check **Inferring** Why are amendments to the Constitution necessary?

Vocabulary

1. **Write** a paragraph about the Constitution in which you use these terms: *Preamble, legislative branch, executive branch, judicial branch, amendment.*

Main Ideas

2. **Explaining** Why has the Constitution been called a blueprint for governing the United States?
3. **Describing** How are the states involved in the process of ratifying an amendment?

Critical Thinking

4. **BIG Ideas** Why have only 27 amendments been added to the Constitution?
5. **Summarizing** Complete the chart below by listing important details of each part of the Constitution.

Part	Details
Preamble	
Articles	
Amendments	

Analyzing Visuals

6. **Comparing** Review the chart on page 81. How does the power to tax differ under both forms of government?

CITIZENSHIP Activity

7. **Creative Writing** One responsibility of being an American citizen is to become involved in the affairs of one's community. Make a poster showing how students can get involved in their community.

Study Central™ To review this section, go to glencoe.com.

Section 4

Principles Underlying the Constitution

Guide to Reading

Big Idea

A constitution reflects the values and goals of the society that creates it.

Content Vocabulary

- popular sovereignty *(p. 86)*
- rule of law *(p. 87)*
- separation of powers *(p. 88)*
- checks and balances *(p. 88)*
- expressed powers *(p. 89)*
- reserved powers *(p. 89)*
- concurrent powers *(p. 89)*

Academic Vocabulary

- ensure *(p. 87)*
- assign *(p. 88)*

Reading Strategy

Organizing List information about the way the Constitution divides powers by completing a graphic organizer like the one below.

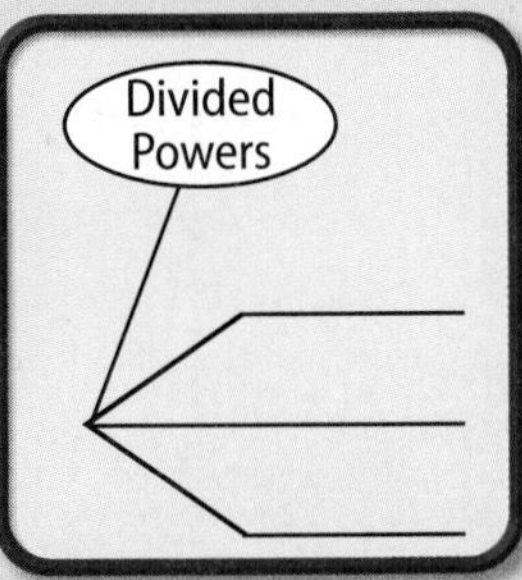

Real World Civics When young people leave home to go to college, where do they vote? At home or in the city where they go to school for nine months of the year? Young Han, a student at Hamilton College in Utica, New York, believed that state and federal law should grant him the right to vote in the town where he lived while going to school. The county election board in Utica did not agree, claiming that students living in dorms were not permanent residents. Han organized the national Student Voting Rights campaign to fight for college students who wanted to vote at the location of their colleges.

▼ **Young Han, founder of Student Voting Rights, a grass roots voting campaign**

Major Principles of Government

Main Idea The Constitution sets forth the basic principles of government.

Civics & You What principles do you live by? Read to discover how the basic principles of the Constitution have remained the same for more than 200 years.

While the Constitution may seem filled with many details about how our nation should be governed, these details fall under five fundamental principles of government: popular sovereignty; the rule of law; separation of powers; checks and balances; and federalism. These principles are the foundation on which our government is built.

Article IV of the Constitution guarantees the American people "a Republican Form of Government." Today the word *republic* can mean any representative government headed by an elected president or similar leader rather than a leader who inherits the position. To the Framers of the Constitution, though, a republic was a representative democracy. In a representative democracy, the power belongs to the people, who express their will through elected representatives. This idea was important to the early English colonists who came to America.

Popular Sovereignty

The idea that the power of government lies with the people is called **popular sovereignty.** (*Sovereignty* means "the right to rule"; *popular*, in this case, means "the population or public.") The Declaration of Independence is really a statement about popular sovereignty. It says that governments should draw their powers "from the consent of the governed." The same idea is echoed in the "We the People" phrase with which the Constitution begins.

—Scott Stantis/Copley News Service

In this image, cartoonist Scott Stantis is making a comment on security and liberty in the United States.

1. **What figure is depicted, and what document is he holding?**
2. **What does the pencil stand for?**
3. **What do you think the figure means when he asks, "So . . . where do I draw the line?"**

Further, the Constitution includes several provisions that protect and **ensure,** or guarantee, the sovereignty of the people. Under the Constitution, the will of the people is expressed most strongly through elections. By a majority vote, citizens decide who will represent them in Congress. Through the Electoral College, they also choose the president and vice president.

Elected officials are always accountable to the people. Elections are regularly scheduled, and voters can reject and replace representatives who serve them poorly.

Rule of Law

The Framers firmly believed that the government should be strong, but not too strong. They therefore included in the Constitution the principle of limited government, which means that government can do only what the people allow it to do.

As James Madison put it,

> ***"In framing a government which is to be administered by men over men, the great difficulty lies in this: you must first enable the government to control the governed; and in the next place oblige it to control itself."***
>
> —James Madison, *The Federalist,* No. 51

To limit the power of both the federal government and the states, the Constitution specifies what they may and may not do. English monarchs, prior to the Magna Carta, had unlimited government. There were few restrictions on what they did.

Under the Constitution, the government is also limited by the **rule of law.** This means that the law applies to everyone, even those who govern. No one may break the law or escape its reach.

Foundations of Rights

Charts In MOtion
See StudentWorks™ Plus or glencoe.com.

RIGHTS AND FREEDOMS	Magna Carta (1215)	English Bill of Rights (1689)	Virginia Declaration of Rights (1776)	Bill of Rights (1791)
Trial by jury	★	★	★	★
Due process	★	★	★	★
Private property	★		★	★
No unreasonable searches or seizures	★		★	★
No cruel punishment	★	★	★	★
No excessive bail or fines		★	★	★
Right to bear arms		★		★
Right to petition		★		★
Freedom of speech				★
Freedom of the press			★	★
Freedom of religion			★	★

Analyzing Charts

1. **Identifying** Which documents granted freedom of religion?
2. **Analyzing** Which rights or freedoms were included in all four documents?

A System of Checks and Balances

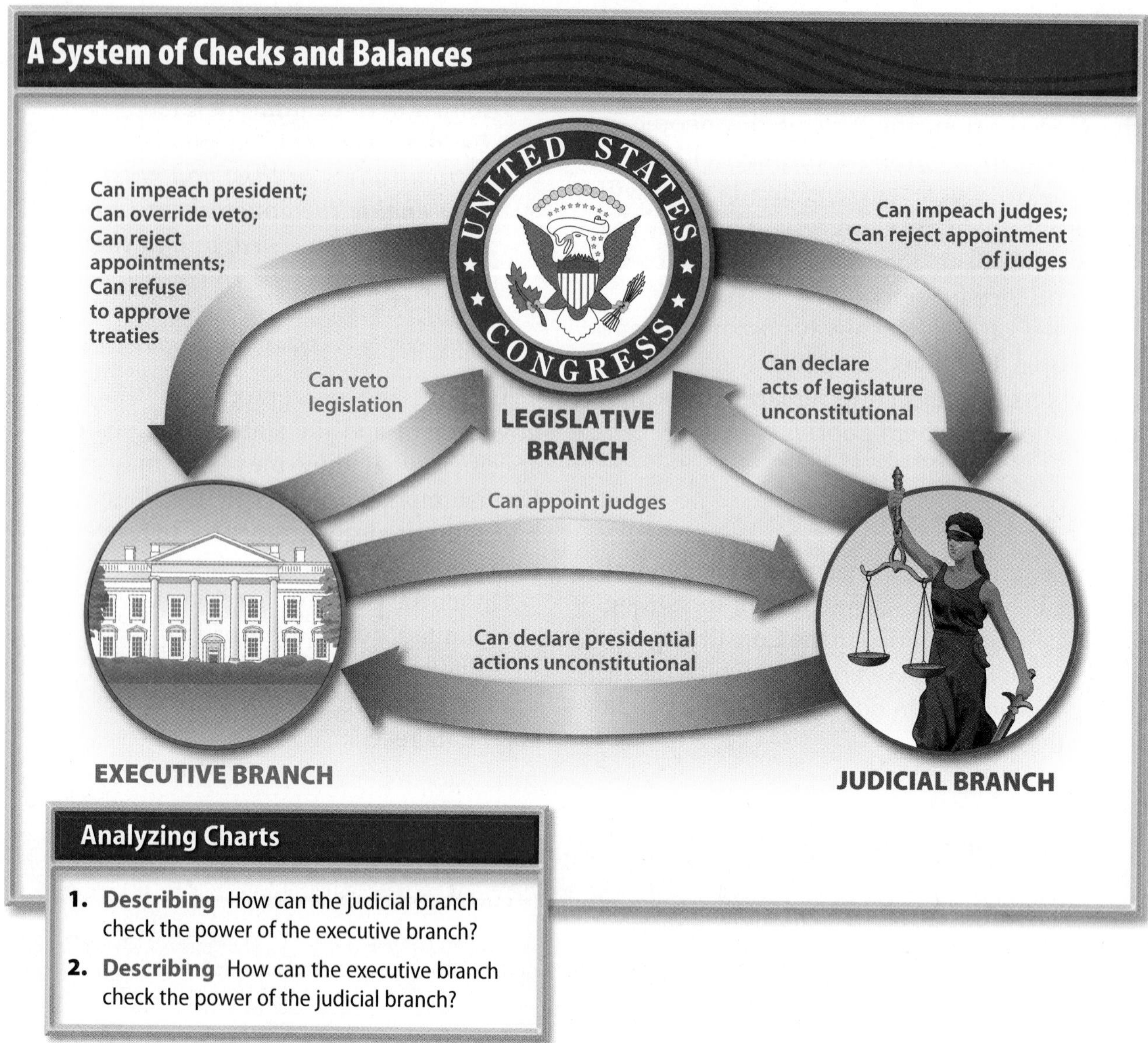

Analyzing Charts

1. **Describing** How can the judicial branch check the power of the executive branch?
2. **Describing** How can the executive branch check the power of the judicial branch?

Separation of Powers

To protect against abuse of power and the possibility of one person or group gaining too much power, the Framers divided the federal government into three branches, each with different functions. The Framers were influenced by the ideas of French philosopher Baron de Montesquieu.

Montesquieu believed that the best way to safeguard the liberty of the people was to clearly separate the legislative, executive, and judicial functions of government and **assign,** or appoint, each to a separate branch of government. This division of authority is called **separation of powers.**

Checks and Balances

Even with the separation of powers, the Framers feared that one branch of government could dominate the other two. In order to prevent any one of the three branches from becoming too powerful, the Framers of the Constitution also included a system of **checks and balances.** Under this system, each branch of government is able to check, or limit, the power of the others. Look at the chart of checks and balances on this page and you can see how this is done.

Reading Check **Explaining** Why did the Framers divide the government into three branches?

The Principle of Federalism

Main Idea **The Constitution created a federal system of government. Under federalism, power is divided between national and state governments.**

Civics & You As you read, think about how the writers of the Constitution divided powers between the federal and state governments.

Further limits on government arise from our Federal system. Under federalism, as you read in Section 3, power is shared by the national government and the states. Each level of government—national and state—has independent authority over people at the same time. Americans must obey both federal and state laws.

Three Types of Power

In setting up a federal system, the writers of the Constitution divided the powers of government into three types. The powers specifically granted to the national government are called the enumerated powers, or **expressed powers.** You will read more about them in Chapter 6. Powers that the Constitution does not give to the national government are kept by the states. These **reserved powers,** as they are called, include regulating trade within state borders, establishing schools, and making rules for marriage and divorce.

In some areas, the authority of the states and the national government overlaps. Powers that both levels of government can exercise are **concurrent powers.** Examples include the power to collect taxes, borrow money, and set up courts and prisons.

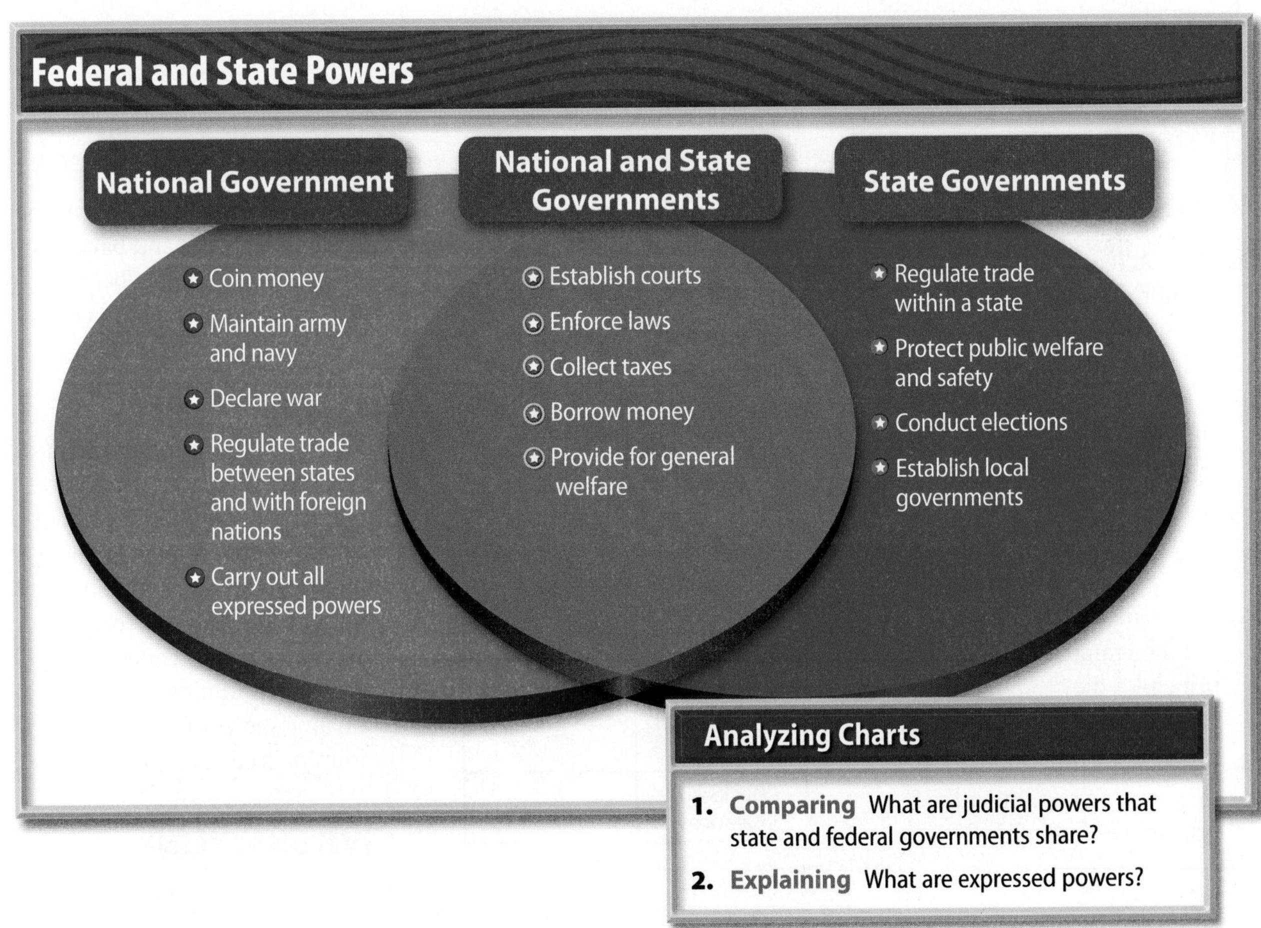

Analyzing Charts

1. **Comparing** What are judicial powers that state and federal governments share?
2. **Explaining** What are expressed powers?

The Supremacy Clause

In a federal system, the laws of a state and the laws of the nation may conflict. To deal with this possibility, the Framers included the supremacy clause. Found in Article VI, the supremacy clause states that the Constitution and other laws and treaties made by the national government "shall be the supreme Law of the Land."

Because the Constitution is the highest law, the national government is not supposed to act in violation of it. Likewise, states may do nothing that goes against either the Constitution or federal law.

Thomas Jefferson admired the Constitution. He wrote,

> ***"I am persuaded no constitution was ever before so well calculated as ours for . . . self-government."***
>
> —Thomas Jefferson's letter to James Madison

The Constitution Today

The entire system of federal government in the United States rests on a single document: the Constitution. It has served as the "supreme law of the land" for more than 200 years. The Constitution is both durable and adaptable. The principles that underpin it—popular sovereignty, the rule of law, separation of powers, checks and balances, and federalism—ensure government restraint as well as power. The Constitution gives our chosen representatives enough power to defend our country's freedom and to keep order. At the same time, it sets limits so that Americans need never fear tyranny. The United States Constitution stands as a powerful symbol of American values and a source of pride and unity.

Explaining What are reserved powers?

Vocabulary

1. **Write** at least three paragraphs about the U.S. Constitution using the group of words that follow: *popular sovereignty, rule of law, separation of powers, checks and balances, expressed powers, reserved powers, concurrent powers.*

Main Ideas

2. **Identifying Central Issues** Why did the Framers include the principles they did in writing the Constitution?
3. **Explaining** How is the power to govern shared under the principle of federalism?

Critical Thinking

4. **BIG Ideas** What are the five principles of government embodied in the United States Constitution?
5. **Summarizing** Give an explanation of each of the listed Constitutional principles in a graphic organizer like the one below.

Popular Sovereignty	
Rule of Law	
Separation of Powers	
Checks and Balances	

6. **Analyzing** In what ways has the system of checks and balances helped avoid conflict between the branches of government?

CITIZENSHIP Activity

7. **Expository Writing** Part of your responsibility as an American citizen is to be informed about what the government is doing and to voice your opinion about its actions. Draft a speech you would give at a schoolwide meeting, outlining your views on an issue your school or community is currently facing.

Study Central™ To review this section, go to glencoe.com.

Chapter 3

Visual Summary

Constitutional Convention, 1787

The Constitution

The Constitution is this nation's fundamental law. It established that our nation is a republic that includes:

- an elected president;
- a bicameral legislature;
- a system of courts.

The Constitution is made up of three parts:

- the Preamble
- the Articles
- the Amendments

Independence Hall

The Constitution sets forth the five basic principles upon which the American system of government rests.

1. popular sovereignty
2. the rule of law
3. separation of powers
4. checks and balances
5. federalism

In setting up a federal system, the writers of the Constitution divided the powers of government into three types:

- Enumerated powers are those powers the Constitution specifically gives to the national government.
- Reserved powers are those that the Constitution gives to the states.
- Concurrent powers are those that the national and state governments share.

The Supremacy Clause

Found in Article VI, the supremacy clause states that the Constitution and the laws of the national government are the "supreme law of the land." In any conflict between national law and state law, the national law has the higher authority.

Amending the Constitution

Any change in the Constitution is called an amendment. The Constitution has 27 amendments.

Viewing the Declaration of Independence

Study anywhere, anytime! Download quizzes and flash cards to your PDA from glencoe.com.

Chapter 3

Standardized Test Practice

ASSESSMENT

TEST-TAKING TIP

Note the kinds of topics and ideas covered in a test to determine what to study for the next examination.

Reviewing Vocabulary

Directions: Choose the word(s) that best completes the sentence.

1. The Second Continental Congress made plans for a _______.

A confederation
B constitutional convention
C bill of rights
D territorial government

2. The agreement about how to represent enslaved persons was known as the _______.

A rule of law
B Electoral College Compromise
C Great Compromise
D Three-Fifths Compromise

3. According to the Constitution, establishing schools is a(n) _______.

A expressed power
B reserved power
C concurrent power
D enumerated power

4. The president and vice president head the _______.

A judicial branch
B executive branch
C legislative branch
D all three branches

Reviewing Main Ideas

Directions: Choose the best answer for each question.

Section 1 *(pp.66–70)*

5. How were most early state governments different from the British government?

A They guaranteed trial by jury.
B They had written constitutions.
C They had bicameral legislatures.
D They protected private property.

6. What was a significant achievement under the Articles of Confederation?

A payment of all Revolutionary War debts
B economic security for American farmers
C establishment of a plan for organizing territories
D uniform enforcement of laws throughout the states

Section 2 *(pp. 71–78)*

7. Which proposal at the Constitutional Convention described a system with a president, courts, and bicameral legislature?

A Albany Plan
B Virginia Plan
C New Jersey Plan
D Connecticut Compromise

8. Which person defended the Constitution in *The Federalist*?

A John Jay
B John Tyler
C Roger Sherman
D Baron de Montesquieu

Section 3 *(pp. 79–84)*

9. What does Article I of the Constitution outline?

A the purposes of the federal government
B the lawmaking powers of the legislative branch
C the law-enforcing powers of the executive branch
D the relationship of the state and national governments

GO ON

Section 4 *(pp. 85–90)*

10. Which principle divides the functions of government among three branches?

A federalism

B rule of law

C popular sovereignty

D separation of powers

11. What does the supremacy clause state?

A The Constitution is the highest law of the land.

B Only the national government can raise an army.

C States keep powers not given to the federal government.

D The federal and state governments share the power to tax.

Critical Thinking

Directions: Base your answers to questions 12 and 13 on the diagram below and your knowledge of Chapter 3.

Amending the Constitution	
Proposal By	Proposal By
2/3 vote of Congress	Conventions called by 3/4 of states
Ratification	Ratification
By 2/3 of state legislatures	By 3/4 of state conventions

12. Either process for amending the Constitution involves representatives from ______.

A half of the states

B states who entered the union before 1900

C all of the states

D states with populations over 12 million

13. Of those asked, how many state legislatures must approve an amendment for it to be ratified?

A three-fifths

B two-thirds

C all

D half

Document-Based Questions

Directions: Analyze the following document and answer the short-answer questions that follow.

The preamble to the United States Constitution describes the writers' vision for a new kind of government.

> *We the People of the United States, in Order to form a more perfect Union, establish Justice, insure domestic Tranquility, provide for the common defence, promote the general Welfare, and secure the Blessings of Liberty to ourselves and our Posterity, do ordain and establish this Constitution for the United States of America.*
>
> —Preamble of the U.S. Constitution

14. What is meant by the phrase to "promote the general Welfare"?

15. Which phrase indicates the source of the government's power? Explain.

Extended-Response Question

16. Write a brief essay explaining why leaders of the United States decided to replace the Articles of Confederation.

For additional test practice, use Self-Check Quizzes—Chapter 3 on glencoe.com.

Need Extra Help?

If you missed question...	1	2	3	4	5	6	7	8	9	10	11	12	13	14	15	16
Go to page...	68	75	89	80	67	68	74	78	80	88	90	82	83	80	80	69

The Constitution of the United States

The Constitution of the United States is truly a remarkable document. It was one of the first written constitutions in modern history. The Framers wanted to devise a plan for a strong central government that would unify the country, as well as preserve the ideals of the Declaration of Independence. The document they wrote created a representative legislature, the office of president, a system of courts, and a process for adding amendments. For over 200 years, the flexibility and strength of the Constitution has guided the nation's political leaders. The document has become a symbol of pride and a force for national unity.

The entire text of the Constitution and its amendments follows. For easier study, those passages that have been set aside or changed by the adoption of amendments are printed in blue. Also included are explanatory notes that will help clarify the meaning of each article and section.

U.S. Capitol

Preamble

We the People of the United States, in Order to form a more perfect Union, establish Justice, insure domestic Tranquility, provide for the common defence, promote the general Welfare, and secure the Blessings of Liberty to ourselves and our Posterity, do ordain and establish this Constitution for the United States of America.

Article I

Section 1

All legislative Powers herein granted shall be vested in a Congress of the United States, which shall consist of a Senate and House of Representatives.

Section 2

[1.] The House of Representatives shall be composed of Members chosen every second Year by the People of the several States, and the Electors in each State shall have the Qualifications requisite for Electors of the most numerous Branch of the State Legislature.

[2.] No person shall be a Representative who shall not have attained the Age of twenty five Years, and been seven Years a Citizen of the United States, and who shall not, when elected, be an Inhabitant of that State in which he shall be chosen.

[3.] Representatives and direct Taxes shall be apportioned among the several States which may be included within this Union, according to their respective Numbers, which shall be determined by adding to the whole Number of free Persons, including those bound to Service for a Term of Years, and excluding Indians not taxed, three fifths of all other Persons. The actual Enumeration shall be made within three Years after the first Meeting of the Congress of the United States, and within every subsequent Term of ten Years, in such Manner as they shall by Law direct. The Number of Representatives shall not exceed one for every thirty Thousand, but each State shall have at Least one Representative; and until such enumeration shall be made, the State of New Hampshire shall be entitled to chuse three; Massachusetts eight, Rhode-Island and Providence Plantations one, Connecticut five, New-York six, New Jersey four, Pennsylvania eight, Delaware one, Maryland six, Virginia ten, North Carolina five, South Carolina five, and Georgia three.

The Preamble introduces the Constitution and sets forth the general purposes for which the government was established. The Preamble also declares that the power of the government comes from the people.

The printed text of the document shows the spelling and punctuation of the parchment original.

What It Means

Article I. The Legislative Branch The Constitution contains seven divisions called articles. Each article covers a general topic. For example, Articles I, II, and III create the three branches of the national government—the legislative, executive, and judicial branches. Most of the articles are divided into sections.

What It Means

Representation The number of representatives from each state is based on the size of the state's population. Each state is entitled to at least one representative. ***What are the qualifications for members of the House of Representatives?***

Vocabulary

preamble: introduction

constitution: principles and laws of a nation

enumeration: census or population count

[4.] When vacancies happen in the Representation from any State, the Executive Authority thereof shall issue Writs of Election to fill such Vacancies.

[5.] The House of Representatives shall chuse their Speaker and other Officers; and shall have the sole Power of Impeachment.

What It Means

Electing Senators Originally, senators were chosen by the state legislators of their own states. The Seventeenth Amendment changed this, so that senators are now elected by the people. There are 100 senators, 2 from each state. The vice president serves as president of the Senate.

Section 3

[1.] The Senate of the United States shall be composed of two Senators from each State, chosen by the Legislature thereof, for six Years; and each Senator shall have one Vote.

[2.] Immediately after they shall be assembled in Consequence of the first Election, they shall be divided as equally as may be into three Classes. The Seats of the Senators of the first Class shall be vacated at the Expiration of the second Year, of the second Class at the Expiration of the fourth Year, and of the third Class at the Expiration of the sixth Year, so that one third may be chosen every second Year; and if Vacancies happen by Resignation, or otherwise, during the Recess of the Legislature of any State, the Executive thereof may make temporary Appointments until the next Meeting of the Legislature, which shall then fill such Vacancies.

▲ **John Adams, the first vice president**

[3.] No Person shall be a Senator who shall not have attained to the Age of thirty Years, and been nine Years a Citizen of the United States, and who shall not, when elected, be an Inhabitant of that State for which he shall be chosen.

[4.] The Vice President of the United States shall be President of the Senate, but shall have no Vote, unless they be equally divided.

[5.] The Senate shall chuse their other Officers, and also a President pro tempore, in the Absence of the Vice President, or when he shall exercise the Office of the President of the United States.

What It Means

Impeachment One of Congress's powers is the power to impeach—to accuse government officials of wrongdoing, put them on trial, and if necessary remove them from office. ***Which body has the power to decide the official's guilt or innocence?***

[6.] The Senate shall have the sole Power to try all Impeachments. When sitting for that Purpose, they shall be on Oath or Affirmation. When the President of the United States is tried, the Chief Justice shall preside: And no Person shall be convicted without the Concurrence of two thirds of the Members present.

[7.] Judgment in Cases of Impeachment shall not extend further than to removal from Office, and disqualification to hold and enjoy any Office of honor, Trust or Profit under the United States: but the Party convicted shall nevertheless be liable and subject to Indictment, Trial, Judgment and Punishment, according to Law.

Vocabulary

impeachment: bringing charges against an official

president pro tempore: presiding officer of Senate who serves when the vice president is absent

indictment: charging a person with an offense

Section 4

[1.] The Times, Places and Manner of holding Elections for Senators and Representatives, shall be prescribed in each State by the Legislature thereof; but the Congress may at any time by Law make or alter such Regulations, except as to the Places of chusing Senators.

[2.] The Congress shall assemble at least once in every Year, and such Meeting shall be on the first Monday in December, unless they shall by Law appoint a different Day.

Section 5

[1.] Each House shall be the Judge of the Elections, Returns and Qualifications of its own Members, and a Majority of each shall constitute a Quorum to do Business; but a smaller Number may adjourn from day to day, and may be authorized to compel the Attendance of absent Members, in such Manner, and under such Penalties as each House may provide.

[2.] Each House may determine the Rules of its Proceedings, punish its Members for disorderly Behaviour, and, with the Concurrence of two thirds, expel a Member.

[3.] Each House shall keep a Journal of its Proceedings, and from time to time publish the same, excepting such Parts as may in their Judgment require Secrecy; and the Yeas and Nays of the Members of either House on any question shall, at the Desire of one fifth of those Present, be entered on the Journal.

[4.] Neither House, during the Session of Congress, shall, without the Consent of the other, adjourn for more than three days, nor to any other Place than that in which the two Houses shall be sitting.

Section 6

[1.] The Senators and Representatives shall receive a Compensation for their Services, to be ascertained by Law, and paid out of the Treasury of the United States. They shall in all Cases, except Treason, Felony and Breach of the Peace, be privileged from Arrest during their Attendance at the Session of their respective Houses, and in going to and returning from the same; and for any Speech or Debate in either House, they shall not be questioned in any other Place.

[2.] No Senator or Representative shall, during the Time for which he was elected, be appointed to any civil Office under the Authority of the United States, which shall have been created, or the Emoluments whereof shall have been encreased during such time; and no Person holding any Office under the United States, shall be a Member of either House during his Continuance in Office.

What It Means

Congressional Salaries To strengthen the federal government, the Founders set congressional salaries to be paid by the United States Treasury rather than by members' respective states. Originally, members were paid $6 per day. In 2006, all members of Congress received a base salary of $165,200.

Vocabulary

quorum: minimum number of members that must be present to conduct sessions

adjourn: to suspend a session

immunity privilege: members cannot be sued or prosecuted for anything they say in Congress

emoluments: salaries

What It Means

Where Tax Laws Begin All tax laws must originate in the House of Representatives. This ensures that the branch of Congress that is elected by the people every two years has the major role in determining taxes.

What It Means

How Bills Become Laws A bill may become a law only by passing both houses of Congress and by being signed by the president. The president can check Congress by rejecting—vetoing—its legislation. ***How can Congress override the president's veto?***

What It Means

Powers of Congress Expressed powers are those powers directly stated in the Constitution. Most of the expressed powers of Congress are listed in Article I, Section 8. These powers are also called enumerated powers because they are numbered 1–18. ***Which clause gives Congress the power to declare war?***

Vocabulary

bill: draft of a proposed law

revenue: income raised by government

resolution: legislature's formal expression of opinion

naturalization: procedure by which a citizen of a foreign nation becomes a citizen of the United States.

Section 7

[1.] All Bills for raising Revenue shall originate in the House of Representatives; but the Senate may propose or concur with Amendments as on other Bills.

[2.] Every Bill which shall have passed the House of Representatives and the Senate, shall, before it become a Law, be presented to the President of the United States; If he approve he shall sign it, but if not he shall return it, with his Objections to that House in which it shall have originated, who shall enter the Objections at large on their Journal, and proceed to reconsider it. If after such Reconsideration two thirds of that House shall agree to pass the Bill, it shall be sent, together with the Objections, to the other House, by which it shall likewise be reconsidered, and if approved by two thirds of that House, it shall become a Law. But in all such Cases the Votes of both Houses shall be determined by yeas and Nays, and the Names of the Persons voting for and against the Bill shall be entered on the Journal of each House respectively. If any Bill shall not be returned by the President within ten Days (Sundays excepted) after it shall have been presented to him, the Same shall be a Law, in like Manner as if he had signed it, unless the Congress by their Adjournment prevent its Return, in which Case it shall not be a Law.

[3.] Every Order, Resolution, or Vote to which the Concurrence of the Senate and House of Representatives may be necessary (except on a question of Adjournment) shall be presented to the President of the United States; and before the Same shall take Effect, shall be approved by him, or being disapproved by him, shall be repassed by two thirds of the Senate and House of Representatives, according to the Rules and Limitations prescribed in the Case of a Bill.

Section 8

[1.] The Congress shall have the Power To lay and collect Taxes, Duties, Imposts and Excises, to pay the Debts and provide for the common Defence and general Welfare of the United States; but all Duties, Imposts and Excises shall be uniform throughout the United States;

[2.] To borrow Money on the credit of the United States;

[3.] To regulate Commerce with foreign Nations, and among the several States, and with the Indian Tribes;

[4.] To establish an uniform Rule of Naturalization, and uniform Laws on the subject of Bankruptcies throughout the United States;

[5.] To coin Money, regulate the Value thereof, and of foreign Coin, and fix the Standard of Weights and Measures;

[6.] To provide for the Punishment of counterfeiting the Securities and current Coin of the United States;

[7.] To establish Post Offices and post Roads;

[8.] To promote the Progress of Science and useful Arts, by securing for limited Times to Authors and Inventors the exclusive Right to their respective Writings and Discoveries;

[9.] To constitute Tribunals inferior to the supreme Court;

[10.] To define and punish Piracies and Felonies committed on the high Seas, and Offences against the Law of Nations;

[11.] To declare War, grant Letters of Marque and Reprisal, and make Rules concerning Captures on Land and Water;

[12.] To raise and support Armies, but no Appropriation of Money to that Use shall be for a longer Term than two Years;

[13.] To provide and maintain a Navy;

[14.] To make Rules for the Government and Regulation of the land and naval Forces;

[15.] To provide for calling forth the Militia to execute the Laws of the Union, suppress Insurrections and repel Invasions;

[16.] To provide for organizing, arming, and disciplining, the Militia, and for governing such Part of them as may be employed in the Service of the United States, reserving to the States respectively, the Appointment of the Officers, and the Authority of training the Militia according to the discipline prescribed by Congress;

[17.] To exercise exclusive Legislation in all Cases whatsoever, over such District (not exceeding ten Miles square) as may, by Cession of particular States, and the Acceptance of Congress, become the Seat of Government of the United States, and to exercise like Authority over all Places purchased by the Consent of the Legislature of the State in which the Same shall be, for the Erection of Forts, Magazines, Arsenals, dock-Yards, and other needful Buildings, —And

[18.] To make all Laws which shall be necessary and proper for carrying into Execution the foregoing Powers, and all other Powers vested by this Constitution in the Government of the United States, or in any Department or Officer thereof.

Section 9

[1.] The Migration or Importation of such Persons as any of the States now existing shall think proper to admit, shall not be prohibited by the Congress prior to the Year one thousand eight hundred and eight, but a Tax or duty may be imposed on such Importation, not exceeding ten dollars for each Person.

[2.] The Privilege of the Writ of Habeas Corpus shall not be suspended, unless when in Cases of Rebellion or Invasion the public Safety may require it.

[3.] No Bill of Attainder or ex post facto Law shall be passed.

[4.] No Capitation, or other direct, Tax shall be laid, unless in Proportion to the Census or Enumeration herein before directed to be taken.

[5.] No Tax or Duty shall be laid on Articles exported from any State.

What It Means

Elastic Clause The final enumerated power is often called the "elastic clause." This clause gives Congress the right to make all laws "necessary and proper" to carry out the powers expressed in the other clauses of Article I. It is called the elastic clause because it lets Congress "stretch" its powers to meet situations the Founders could never have anticipated.

What does the phrase "necessary and proper" in the elastic clause mean? Almost from the beginning, this phrase was a subject of dispute. The issue was whether a strict or a broad interpretation of the Constitution should be applied. The dispute was first addressed in 1819, in the case of *McCulloch* v. *Maryland*, when the Supreme Court ruled in favor of a broad interpretation.

What It Means

Habeas Corpus A writ of habeas corpus issued by a judge requires a law official to bring a prisoner to court and show cause for holding the prisoner. A bill of attainder is a bill that punished a person without a jury trial. An "ex post facto" law is one that makes an act a crime after the act has been committed. ***What does the Constitution say about bills of attainder?***

Vocabulary

tribunal: a court

insurrection: rebellion

[6.] No Preference shall be given by any Regulation of Commerce or Revenue to the Ports of one State over those of another: nor shall Vessels bound to, or from, one State, be obliged to enter, clear, or pay Duties in another.

[7.] No Money shall be drawn from the Treasury, but in Consequence of Appropriations made by Law; and a regular Statement and Account of the Receipts and Expenditures of all public Money shall be published from time to time.

[8.] No Title of Nobility shall be granted by the United States: And no Person holding any Office of Profit or Trust under them, shall, without the Consent of the Congress, accept of any present, Emolument, Office, or Title, of any kind whatever, from any King, Prince, or foreign State.

What It Means

Limitations on the States Section 10 lists limits on the states. These restrictions were designed, in part, to prevent an overlapping in functions and authority with the federal government.

Section 10

[1.] No State shall enter into any Treaty, Alliance, or Confederation; grant Letters of Marque and Reprisal; coin Money; emit Bills of Credit; make any Thing but gold and silver Coin a Tender in Payment of Debts; pass any Bill of Attainder, ex post facto Law, or Law impairing the Obligation of Contracts, or grant any Title of Nobility.

[2.] No State shall, without the Consent of the Congress, lay any Imposts or Duties on Imports or Exports, except what may be absolutely necessary for executing its inspection Laws: and the net Produce of all Duties and Imposts, laid by any State on Imports and Exports, shall be for the Use of the Treasury of the United States; and all such Laws shall be subject to the Revision and Controul of the Congress.

[3.] No State shall, without the Consent of Congress, lay any Duty of Tonnage, keep Troops, or Ships of War in time of Peace, enter into any Agreement or Compact with another State, or with a foreign Power, or engage in War, unless actually invaded, or in such imminent Danger as will not admit of delay.

What It Means

Article II. The Executive Branch Article II creates an executive branch to carry out laws passed by Congress. Article II lists the powers and duties of the presidency, describes qualifications for office and procedures for electing the president, and provides for a vice president.

Article II

Section 1

[1.] The executive Power shall be vested in a President of the United States of America. He shall hold his Office during the Term of four Years, and, together with the Vice President, chosen for the same Term, be elected, as follows.

[2.] Each State shall appoint, in such Manner as the Legislature thereof may direct, a Number of Electors, equal to the whole Number of Senators and Representatives to which the State may be entitled in the Congress: but no Senator or Representative, or Person holding an Office of Trust or Profit under the United States, shall be appointed an Elector.

Vocabulary

appropriations: funds set aside for a specific use

emolument: payment

impost: tax

duty: tax

[3.] The Electors shall meet in their respective States, and vote by Ballot for two Persons, of whom one at least shall not be an Inhabitant of the same State with themselves. And they shall make a List of all the Persons voted for, and of the Number of Votes for each; which List they shall sign and certify, and transmit sealed to the Seat of the Government of the United States, directed to the President of the Senate. The President of the Senate shall, in the Presence of the Senate and House of Representatives, open all the Certificates, and the Votes shall then be counted. The Person having the greatest Number of Votes shall be the President, if such Number be a Majority of the whole Number of Electors appointed; and if there be more than one who have such Majority, and have an equal Number of Votes, then the House of Representatives shall immediately chuse by Ballot one of them for President; and if no person have a Majority, then from the five highest on the List the said House shall in like Manner chuse the President. But in chusing the President, the Votes shall be taken by States, the Representation from each State having one Vote; A quorum for this Purpose shall consist of a Member or Members from two thirds of the States, and a Majority of all the States shall be necessary to a Choice. In every Case, after the Choice of the President, the Person having the greatest Number of Votes of the Electors shall be the Vice President. But if there should remain two or more who have equal Votes, the Senate shall chuse from them by Ballot the Vice President.

[4.] The Congress may determine the Time of chusing the Electors, and the Day on which they shall give their Votes; which Day shall be the same throughout the United States.

[5.] No Person except a natural born Citizen, or a Citizen of the United States, at the time of the Adoption of this Constitution, shall be eligible to the Office of President; neither shall any Person be eligible to that Office who shall not have attained to the Age of thirty five Years, and been fourteen Years a Resident within the United States.

[6.] In Case of the Removal of the President from Office, or of his Death, Resignation, or Inability to discharge the Powers and Duties of the said Office, the Same shall devolve on the Vice President, and the Congress may by Law provide for the Case of Removal, Death, Resignation or Inability, both of the President and Vice President, declaring what Officer shall then act as President, and such Officer shall act accordingly, until the Disability be removed, or a President shall be elected.

[7.] The President shall, at stated Times, receive for his Services, a Compensation, which shall neither be encreased nor diminished during the Period for which he shall have been elected, and he shall not receive within that Period any other Emolument from the United States, or any of them.

What It Means

Previous Elections The Twelfth Amendment, added in 1804, changed the method of electing the president stated in Article II, Section 3. The Twelfth Amendment requires that the electors cast separate ballots for president and vice president.

What It Means

Qualifications The president must be a citizen of the United States by birth, at least 35 years of age, and a resident of the United States for 14 years.

What It Means

Vacancies If the president dies, resigns, is removed from office by impeachment, or is unable to carry out the duties of the office, the vice president becomes president. The Twenty-fifth Amendment sets procedures for presidential succession.

What It Means

Salary Originally, the president's salary was $25,000 per year. The president's current salary is $400,000 plus a $50,000 nontaxable expense account per year. The president also receives living accommodations in two residences—the White House and Camp David.

What It Means

The Cabinet Mention of "the principal officer in each of the executive departments" is the only suggestion of the president's cabinet to be found in the Constitution. The cabinet is an advisory body, and its power depends on the president. Section 2, Clause 1 also makes the president—a civilian—the head of the armed services. This established the principle of civilian control of the military.

What It Means

Presidential Powers An executive order is a command issued by a president to exercise a power which he or she has been given by the U.S. Constitution or by a federal statute. In times of emergency, presidents sometimes have used the executive order to override the Constitution and Congress. During the Civil War, President Lincoln suspended many fundamental rights, such as closing down newspapers that opposed his policies and imprisoning people who disagreed with him. Lincoln said that these actions were justified to preserve the Union.

▲ President Bill Clinton during impeachment proceedings

[8.] Before he enter on the Execution of his Office, he shall take the following Oath or Affirmation:—"I do solemnly swear (or affirm) that I will faithfully execute the Office of President of the United States, and will to the best of my Ability, preserve, protect and defend the Constitution of the United States."

Section 2

[1.] The President shall be Commander in Chief of the Army and Navy of the United States, and of the Militia of the several States, when called into the actual Service of the United States; he may require the Opinion, in writing, of the principal Officer in each of the executive Departments, upon any Subject relating to the Duties of their respective Offices, and he shall have Power to grant Reprieves and Pardons for Offences against the United States, except in Cases of Impeachment.

[2.] He shall have Power, by and with the Advice and Consent of the Senate, to make Treaties, provided two thirds of the Senators present concur; and he shall nominate, and by and with the Advice and Consent of the Senate, shall appoint Ambassadors, other public Ministers and Consuls, Judges of the supreme Court, and all other Officers of the United States, whose Appointments are not herein otherwise provided for, and which shall be established by Law: but the Congress may by Law vest the Appointment of such inferior Officers, as they think proper, in the President alone, in the Courts of Law, or in the Heads of Departments.

[3.] The President shall have Power to fill up all Vacancies that may happen during the Recess of the Senate, by granting Commissions which shall expire at the End of their next Session.

Section 3

He shall from time to time give to the Congress Information of the State of the Union, and recommend to their Consideration such Measures as he shall judge necessary and expedient; he may, on extraordinary Occasions, convene both Houses, or either of them, and in Case of Disagreement between them, with Respect to the Time of Adjournment, he may adjourn them to such Time as he shall think proper; he shall receive Ambassadors and other public Ministers; he shall take Care that the Laws be faithfully executed, and shall Commission all the Officers of the United States.

Section 4

The President, Vice President and all civil Officers of the United States, shall be removed from Office on Impeachment for, and Conviction of, Treason, Bribery, or other high Crimes and Misdemeanors.

Article III

Section 1

The judicial Power of the United States, shall be vested in one supreme Court, and in such inferior Courts as the Congress may from time to time ordain and establish. The Judges, both of the supreme and inferior Courts, shall hold their Offices during good Behaviour, and shall, at stated Times, receive for their Services, a Compensation, which shall not be diminished during their Continuance in Office.

Section 2

[1.] The judicial Power shall extend to all Cases, in Law and Equity, arising under this Constitution, the Laws of the United States, and Treaties made, or which shall be made, under their Authority;—to all Cases affecting Ambassadors, other public Ministers and Consuls;—to all Cases of admiralty and maritime Jurisdiction;—to Controversies to which the United States shall be a Party;—to Controversies between two or more States;—between a State and Citizens of another State;—between Citizens of different States,—between Citizens of the same State claiming Lands under Grants of different States, and between a State, or the Citizens thereof, and foreign States, Citizens or Subjects.

[2.] In all Cases affecting Ambassadors, other public Ministers and Consuls, and those in which a State shall be Party, the supreme Court shall have original Jurisdiction. In all the other Cases before mentioned, the supreme Court shall have appellate Jurisdiction, both as to Law and Fact, with such Exceptions, and under such Regulations as the Congress shall make.

[3.] The Trial of all Crimes, except in Cases of Impeachment, shall be by Jury; and such Trial shall be held in the State where the said Crimes shall have been committed; but when not committed within any State, the Trial shall be at such Place or Places as the Congress may by Law have directed.

What It Means

Article III. The Judicial Branch The term *judicial* refers to courts. The Constitution set up only the Supreme Court, but provided for the establishment of other federal courts. The judiciary of the United States has two different systems of courts. One system consists of the federal courts, whose powers derive from the Constitution and federal laws. The other includes the courts of each of the 50 states, whose powers derive from state constitutions and laws.

What It Means

Statute Law Federal courts deal mostly with "statute law," or laws passed by Congress, treaties, and cases involving the Constitution itself.

What It Means

The Supreme Court A Court with "original jurisdiction" has the authority to be the first court to hear a case. The Supreme Court has "appellate jurisdiction" and mostly hears cases appealed from lower courts.

Vocabulary

original jurisdiction: authority to be the first court to hear a case

appellate jurisdiction: authority to hear cases that have been appealed from lower courts

Section 3

[1.] Treason against the United States, shall consist only in levying War against them, or in adhering to their Enemies, giving them Aid and Comfort. No Person shall be convicted of Treason unless on the Testimony of two Witnesses to the same overt Act, or on Confession in open Court.

[2.] The Congress shall have Power to declare the Punishment of Treason, but no Attainder of Treason shall work Corruption of Blood, or Forfeiture except during the Life of the Person attainted.

What It Means

Article IV. Relations Among the States Article IV explains the relationship of the states to one another and to the national government. This article requires each state to give citizens of other states the same rights as its own citizens, addresses admitting new states, and guarantees that the national government will protect the states.

Article IV

Section 1

Full Faith and Credit shall be given in each State to the public Acts, Records, and judicial Proceedings of every other State. And the Congress may by general Laws prescribe the Manner in which such Acts, Records and Proceedings shall be proved, and the Effect thereof.

Section 2

[1.] The Citizens of each State shall be entitled to all Privileges and Immunities of Citizens in the several States.

[2.] A Person charged in any State with Treason, Felony, or other Crime, who shall flee from Justice, and be found in another State, shall on Demand of the executive Authority of the State from which he fled, be delivered up, to be removed to the State having Jurisdiction of the Crime.

[3.] No Person held to Service of Labour in one State, under the Laws thereof, escaping into another, shall, in Consequence of any Law or Regulation therein, be discharged from such Service or Labour, but shall be delivered up on Claim of the Party to whom such Service or Labour may be due.

What It Means

New States Congress has the power to admit new states. It also determines the basic guidelines for applying for statehood. Two states, Maine and West Virginia, were created within the boundaries of another state. In the case of West Virginia, President Lincoln recognized the West Virginia government as the legal government of Virginia during the Civil War. This allowed West Virginia to secede from Virginia without obtaining approval from the Virginia legislature.

Section 3

[1.] New States may be admitted by the Congress into this Union; but no new State shall be formed or erected within the Jurisdiction of any other State; nor any State be formed by the Junction of two or more States, or Parts of States, without the Consent of the Legislatures of the States concerned as well as of the Congress.

[2.] The Congress shall have Power to dispose of and make all needful Rules and Regulations respecting the Territory or other Property belonging to the United States; and nothing in this Constitution shall be so construed as to Prejudice any Claims of the United States, or of any particular State.

Vocabulary

treason: violation of the allegiance owed by a person to his or her own country, for example, by aiding an enemy

Section 4

The United States shall guarantee to every State in this Union a Republican Form of Government, and shall protect each of them against Invasion; and on Application of the Legislature, or of the Executive (when the Legislature cannot be convened) against domestic Violence.

Article V

The Congress, whenever two thirds of both Houses shall deem it necessary, shall propose Amendments to this Constitution, or, on the Application of the Legislatures of two thirds of the several States, shall call a Convention for proposing Amendments, which, in either Case, shall be valid to all Intents and Purposes, as Part of this Constitution, when ratified by the Legislatures of three fourths of the several States, or by Conventions in three fourths thereof, as the one or the other Mode of Ratification may be proposed by the Congress; Provided that no Amendment which may be made prior to the Year One thousand eight hundred and eight shall in any Manner affect the first and fourth Clauses in the Ninth Section of the first Article; and that no State, without its Consent, shall be deprived of its equal Suffrage in the Senate.

Article VI

[1.] All Debts contracted and Engagements entered into, before the Adoption of this Constitution, shall be as valid against the United States under this Constitution, as under the Confederation.

[2.] This Constitution, and the Laws of the United States which shall be made in Pursuance thereof; and all Treaties made, or which shall be made, under the Authority of the United States, shall be the supreme Law of the Land; and the Judges in every State shall be bound thereby, any Thing in the Constitution or Laws of any State to the Contrary notwithstanding.

[3.] The Senators and Representatives before mentioned, and the Members of the several State Legislatures, and all executive and judicial Officers, both of the United States and of the several States, shall be bound by Oath or Affirmation, to support this Constitution; but no religious Test shall ever be required as a Qualification to any Office or public Trust under the United States.

What It Means

Republic Government can be classified in many different ways. The ancient Greek Philosopher Aristotle classified government based on the question: Who governs? According to Aristotle, all governments belong to one of three major groups: (1) autocracy—rule by one person; (2) oligarchy—rule by a few persons; or (3) democracy—rule by many persons. A republic is a form of democracy in which the people elect representatives to make the laws and conduct government.

What It Means

Article V. The Amendment Process Article V spells out the ways that the Constitution can be amended, or changed. All of the 27 amendments were proposed by a two-thirds vote of both houses of Congress. Only the Twenty-first Amendment was ratified by constitutional conventions of the states. All other amendments have been ratified by state legislatures. ***What is an amendment?***

What It Means

Article VI. National Supremacy Article VI contains the "supremacy clause." This clause establishes that the Constitution, laws passed by Congress, and treaties of the United States "shall be the supreme Law of the Land." The "supremacy clause" recognized the Constitution and federal laws as supreme when in conflict with those of the states.

Vocabulary

amendment: a change to the Constitution

ratification: process by which an amendment is approved

What It Means

Article VII. Ratification Article VII addresses ratification and declares that the Constitution would take effect after it was ratified by nine states.

Article VII

The Ratification of the Conventions of nine States, shall be sufficient for the Establishment of this Constitution between the States so ratifying the Same.

Done in Convention by the Unanimous Consent of the States present the Seventeenth Day of September in the Year of our Lord one thousand seven hundred and Eighty seven and of the Independence of the United States of America the Twelfth. In witness whereof We have hereunto subscribed our Names,

Signers

George Washington, President and Deputy from Virginia

New Hampshire
John Langdon
Nicholas Gilman

Massachusetts
Nathaniel Gorham
Rufus King

Connecticut
William Samuel Johnson
Roger Sherman

New York
Alexander Hamilton

New Jersey
William Livingston
David Brearley
William Paterson
Jonathan Dayton

Pennsylvania
Benjamin Franklin
Thomas Mifflin
Robert Morris
George Clymer
Thomas FitzSimons
Jared Ingersoll
James Wilson
Gouverneur Morris

Delaware
George Read
Gunning Bedford, Jr.
John Dickinson
Richard Bassett
Jacob Broom

Maryland
James McHenry
Daniel of St. Thomas Jenifer
Daniel Carroll

Virginia
John Blair
James Madison, Jr.

North Carolina
William Blount
Richard Dobbs Spaight
Hugh Williamson

South Carolina
John Rutledge
Charles Cotesworth Pinckney
Charles Pinckney
Pierce Butler

Georgia
William Few
Abraham Baldwin

Attest: *William Jackson,* ***Secretary***

Re-creating colonial response to the signing at Indepencence Hall

Amendment I

Congress shall make no law respecting an establishment of religion, or prohibiting the free exercise thereof; or abridging the freedom of speech, or of the press; or the right of the people peaceably to assemble, and to petition the Government for a redress of grievances.

Amendment II

A well regulated Militia, being necessary to the security of a free State, the right of the people to keep and bear Arms, shall not be infringed.

Amendment III

No Soldier shall, in time of peace be quartered in any house, without the consent of the Owner, nor in time of war, but in a manner to be prescribed by law.

Amendment IV

The right of the people to be secure in their persons, houses, papers, and effects, against unreasonable searches and seizures, shall not be violated, and no Warrants shall issue, but upon probable cause, supported by Oath or affirmation, and particularly describing the place, to be searched, and the persons or things to be seized.

Amendment V

No person shall be held to answer for a capital, or otherwise infamous crime, unless on a presentment or indictment of a Grand Jury, except in cases arising in the land or naval forces, or in the Militia, when in actual service in time of War or public danger; nor shall any person be subject for the same offence to be twice put in jeopardy of life or limb; nor shall be compelled in any criminal case to be a witness against himself, nor be deprived of life, liberty, or property, without due process of law; nor shall private property be taken for public use without just compensation.

What It Means

The Amendments This part of the Constitution consists of amendments, or changes. The Constitution has been amended 27 times throughout the nation's history.

What It Means

Bill of Rights The first 10 amendments are known as the Bill of Rights (1791). These amendments limit the powers of government. The First Amendment protects the civil liberties of individuals in the United States. The amendment freedoms are not absolute, however. They are limited by the rights of other individuals. ***What freedoms does the First Amendment protect?***

What It Means

Rights of the Accused This amendment contains important protections for people accused of crimes. One of the protections is that government may not deprive any person of life, liberty, or property without due process of law. This means that the government must follow proper constitutional procedures in trials and in other actions it takes against individuals. ***According to Amendment V, what is the function of a grand jury?***

Vocabulary

quarter: to provide living accommodations

warrant: document that gives police particular rights or powers

probable cause: police must have a reasonable basis to believe a person is linked to a crime

What It Means

Rights to a Speedy, Fair Trial A basic protection is the right to a speedy, public trial. The jury must hear witnesses and evidence on both sides before deciding the guilt or innocence of a person charged with a crime. This amendment also provides that legal counsel must be provided to a defendant. In 1963, the Supreme Court ruled, in *Gideon* v. *Wainwright*, that if a defendant cannot afford a lawyer, the government must provide one to defend him or her. ***Why is the right to a "speedy" trial important?***

Amendment VI

In all criminal prosecutions, the accused shall enjoy the right to a speedy and public trial, by an impartial jury of the State and district wherein the crime shall have been committed, which district shall have been previously ascertained by law, and to be informed of the nature and cause of the accusation; to be confronted with the witnesses against him; to have compulsory process for obtaining Witnesses in his favor, and to have the assistance of counsel for his defence.

Amendment VII

In Suits at common law, where the value in controversy shall exceed twenty dollars, the right of trial by jury shall be preserved, and no fact tried by a jury, shall be otherwise reexamined in any Court of the United States, than according to the rules of common law.

Amendment VIII

Excessive bail shall not be required, nor excessive fines imposed, nor cruel and unusual punishments inflicted.

What It Means

Powers of the People This amendment prevents government from claiming that the only rights people have are those listed in the Bill of Rights.

Amendment IX

The enumeration in the Constitution, of certain rights, shall not be construed to deny or disparage others retained by the people.

What It Means

Powers of the States The final amendment of the Bill of Rights protects the states and the people from an all-powerful federal government. It establishes that powers not given to the national government—or denied to the states—by the Constitution belong to the states or to the people.

Amendment X

The powers not delegated to the United States by the Constitution, nor prohibited by it to the States, are reserved to the States respectively, or to the people.

What It Means

Suits Against States The Eleventh Amendment (1795) limits the jurisdiction of the federal courts. The Supreme Court had ruled that a federal court could try a lawsuit brought by citizens of South Carolina against a citizen of Georgia. This case, *Chisholm* v. *Georgia*, decided in 1793, raised a storm of protest, leading to passage of the Eleventh Amendment.

Amendment XI

The Judicial power of the United States shall not be construed to extend to any suit in law or equity, commenced or prosecuted against one of the United States by Citizens of another State, or by Citizens or Subjects of any Foreign State.

Amendment XII

The electors shall meet in their respective states and vote by ballot for President and Vice-President, one of whom, at least, shall not be an inhabitant of the same state with themselves; they shall name in their ballots the person voted for as President, and in distinct ballots the person voted for as Vice-President, and they shall make distinct lists of all persons voted for as President, and of all persons voted for as Vice-President, and of the number of votes for each, which lists they shall sign and certify, and transmit sealed to the seat of the government of the United States, directed to the President of the Senate;—The President of the Senate shall, in the presence of the Senate and House of Representatives, open all the certificates and the votes shall then be counted;—The person having the greatest number of votes for President, shall be the President, if such number be a majority of the whole number of Electors appointed; and if no person have such majority, then from the persons having the highest numbers not exceeding three on the list of those voted for as President, the House of Representatives shall choose immediately, by ballot, the President. But in choosing the President, the votes shall be taken by states, the representation from each state having one vote; a quorum for this purpose shall consist of a member or members from two-thirds of the states, and a majority of all the states shall be necessary to a choice. And if the House of Representatives shall not choose a President whenever the right of choice shall devolve upon them, before the fourth day of March next following, then the Vice-President shall act as President, as in the case of the death or other constitutional disability of the President. The person having the greatest number of votes as Vice-President, shall be the Vice-President, if such number be a majority of the whole number of Electors appointed, and if no person have a majority, then from the two highest numbers on the list, the Senate shall choose the Vice-President; a quorum for the purpose shall consist of two-thirds of the whole number of Senators, and a majority of the whole number shall be necessary to a choice. But no person constitutionally ineligible to the office of President shall be eligible to that of Vice-President of the United States.

What It Means

Elections The Twelfth Amendment (1804) corrects a problem that had arisen in the method of electing the president and vice president. This amendment provides for the Electoral College to use separate ballots in voting for president and vice president. ***If no candidate receives a majority of the electoral votes, who elects the president?***

Vocabulary

common law: law established by previous court decisions

bail: money that an accused person provides to the court as a guarantee that he or she will be present for a trial

majority: more than half

devolve: to pass on

What It Means

Abolition of Slavery Amendments Thirteen (1865), Fourteen (1868), and Fifteen (1870) often are called the Civil War amendments because they grew out of that great conflict. The Thirteenth Amendment outlaws slavery.

What It Means

Rights of Citizens The Fourteenth Amendment (1868) originally was intended to protect the legal rights of the freed slaves. Today it protects the rights of citizenship in general by prohibiting a state from depriving any person of life, liberty, or property without "due process of law." In addition, it states that all citizens have the right to equal protection of the law in all states.

What It Means

Representation in Congress This section reduced the number of members a state had in the House of Representatives if it denied its citizens the right to vote. Later civil rights laws and the Twenty-fourth Amendment guaranteed the vote to African Americans.

Vocabulary

apportionment: distribution of seats in House based on population

abridge: to reduce

Amendment XIII

Section 1

Neither slavery nor involuntary servitude, except as a punishment for crime whereof the party shall have been duly convicted, shall exist within the United States, or any place subject to their jurisdiction.

Section 2

Congress shall have power to enforce this article by appropriate legislation.

Amendment XIV

Section 1

All persons born or naturalized in the United States, and subject to the jurisdiction thereof, are citizens of the United States and of the State wherein they reside. No State shall make or enforce any law which shall abridge the privileges or immunities of citizens of the United States; nor shall any State deprive any person of life, liberty, or property, without due process of law; nor deny to any person within its jurisdiction the equal protection of the laws.

Section 2

Representatives shall be apportioned among the several States according to their respective numbers, counting the whole number of persons in each State, excluding Indians not taxed. But when the right to vote at any election for the choice of electors for President and Vice President of the United States, Representatives in Congress, the Executive and Judicial officers of a State, or the members of the Legislature thereof, is denied to any of the male inhabitants of such State, being twenty-one years of age, and citizens of the United States, or in any way abridged, except for participation in rebellion, or other crime, the basis of representation therein shall be reduced in the proportion which the number of such male citizens shall bear to the whole number of male citizens twenty-one years of age in such State.

Section 3

No person shall be a Senator or Representative in Congress, or elector of President and Vice President, or hold any office, civil or military, under the United States, or under any State, who, having previously taken an oath, as a member of Congress, or as an officer of the United States, or as a member of any State legislature, or as an executive or judicial officer of any State, to support the Constitution of the United States, shall have engaged in insurrection or rebellion against the same, or given aid or comfort to the enemies thereof. But Congress may by a vote of two-thirds of each House, remove such disability.

Section 4

The validity of the public debt of the United States, authorized by law, including debts incurred for payment of pensions and bounties for service in suppressing insurrection or rebellion, shall not be questioned. But neither the United States nor any State shall assume or pay any debt or obligation incurred in aid of insurrection or rebellion against the United States, or any claim for the loss or emancipation of any slave; but all such debts, obligations and claims shall be held illegal and void.

Section 5

The Congress shall have power to enforce, by appropriate legislation, the provisions of this article.

Amendment XV

Section 1

The right of citizens of the United States to vote shall not be denied or abridged by the United States or by any State on account of race, color, or previous condition of servitude.

Section 2

The Congress shall have power to enforce this article by appropriate legislation.

Amendment XVI

The Congress shall have power to lay and collect taxes on incomes, from whatever source derived, without apportionment among the several States and without regard to any census or enumeration.

Amendment XVII

Section 1

The Senate of the United States shall be composed of two Senators from each State, elected by the people thereof, for six years; and each Senator shall have one vote. The electors in each State shall have the qualifications requisite for electors of the most numerous branch of the State legislatures.

What It Means

Public Debt The public debt acquired by the federal government during the Civil War was valid and could not be questioned by the South. However, the debts of the Confederacy were declared to be illegal. ***Could former slaveholders collect payment for the loss of their slaves?***

What It Means

Right to Vote The Fifteenth Amendment (1870) prohibits the government from denying a person's right to vote on the basis of race. Despite the law, many states denied African Americans the right to vote by such means as poll taxes, literacy tests, and white primaries. During the 1950s and 1960s, Congress passed successively stronger laws to end racial discrimination in voting rights.

What It Means

Election of Senators The Seventeenth Amendment (1913) states that the people, instead of state legislatures, elect United States senators. ***How many years are in a Senate term?***

Vocabulary

insurrection: rebellion against the government

emancipation: freedom from slavery

▲ Dumping illegal liquor

What It Means

Prohibition The Eighteenth Amendment (1919) prohibited the production, sale, or transportation of alcoholic beverages in the United States. Prohibition proved to be difficult to enforce. This amendment was later repealed by the Twenty-first Amendment.

What It Means

Woman Suffrage The Nineteenth Amendment (1920) guaranteed women the right to vote. By then women had already won the right to vote in many state elections, but the amendment put their right to vote in all state and national elections on a constitutional basis.

Section 2

When vacancies happen in the representation of any State in the Senate, the executive authority of such State shall issue writs of election to fill such vacancies: *Provided,* That the legislature of any State may empower the executive thereof to make temporary appointments until the people fill the vacancies by election as the legislature may direct.

Section 3

This amendment shall not be so construed as to affect the election or term of any Senator chosen before it becomes valid as part of the Constitution.

Amendment XVIII

Section 1

After one year from ratification of this article, the manufacture, sale, or transportation of intoxicating liquors within, the importation thereof into, or the exportation thereof from the United States and all territory subject to the jurisdiction thereof for beverage purposes is hereby prohibited.

Section 2

The Congress and the several States shall have concurrent power to enforce this article by appropriate legislation.

Section 3

This article shall be inoperative unless it shall have been ratified as an amendment to the Constitution by the legislatures of the several States, as provided in the Constitution, within seven years from the date of the submission hereof to the States by the Congress.

Amendment XIX

Section 1

The right of citizens of the United States to vote shall not be denied or abridged by the United States or by any State on account of sex.

Section 2

Congress shall have power by appropriate legislation to enforce the provisions of this article.

Amendment XX

Section 1

The terms of the President and Vice President shall end at noon on the 20th day of January, and the terms of the Senators and Representatives at noon on the 3d day of January, of the years in which such terms would have ended if this article had not been ratified; and the terms of their successors shall then begin.

Section 2

The Congress shall assemble at least once in every year, and such meeting shall begin at noon on the 3d day of January, unless they shall by law appoint a different day.

Section 3

If, at the time fixed for the beginning of the term of the President, the President elect shall have died, the Vice President elect shall become President. If a President shall not have been chosen before the time fixed for the beginning of his term, or if the President elect shall have failed to qualify, then the Vice President elect shall act as President until a President shall have qualified; and the Congress may by law provide for the case wherein neither a President elect nor a Vice President elect shall have qualified, declaring who shall then act as President, or the manner in which one who is to act shall be selected, and such person shall act accordingly until a President or Vice President shall have qualified.

Section 4

The Congress may by law provide for the case of the death of any of the persons from whom the House of Representatives may choose a President whenever the right of choice shall have devolved upon them, and for the case of the death of any of the persons from whom the Senate may choose a Vice President whenever the right of choice shall have devolved upon them.

Section 5

Section 1 and 2 shall take effect on the 15th day of October following the ratification of this article.

What It Means

"Lame-Duck" Amendments The Twentieth Amendment (1933) sets new dates for Congress to begin its term and for the inauguration of the president and vice president. Under the original Constitution, elected officials who retired or who had been defeated remained in office for several months. For the outgoing president, this period ran from November until March. Such outgoing officials had little influence and accomplished little, and they were called lame ducks because they were so inactive. ***What date was fixed as Inauguration Day?***

What It Means

Succession This section provides that if the president-elect dies before taking office, the vice president-elect becomes president.

Vocabulary

president elect: individual who is elected president but has not yet begun serving his or her term

Section 6

This article shall be inoperative unless it shall have been ratified as an amendment to the Constitution by the legislatures of three-fourths of the several States within seven years from the date of its submission.

What It Means

Repeal of Prohibition The Twenty-first Amendment (1933) repeals the Eighteenth Amendment. It is the only amendment ever passed to overturn an earlier amendment. It is also the only amendment ratified by special state conventions instead of state legislatures.

Amendment XXI

Section 1

The eighteenth article of amendment to the Constitution of the United States is hereby repealed.

Section 2

The transportation or importation into any State, Territory, or possession of the United States for delivery or use therein of intoxicating liquors, in violation of the laws thereof, is hereby prohibited.

Section 3

This article shall be inoperative unless it shall have been ratified as an amendment to the Constitution by conventions in the several States, as provided in the Constitution, within seven years from the date of the submission hereof to the States by the Congress.

What It Means

Term Limit The Twenty-second Amendment (1951) limits presidents to a maximum of two elected terms. It was passed largely as a reaction to Franklin D. Roosevelt's election to four terms between 1933 and 1945.

Amendment XXII

Section 1

No person shall be elected to the office of the President more than twice, and no person who had held the office of President, or acted as President, for more than two years of a term to which some other person was elected President shall be elected to the office of the President more than once. But this Article shall not apply to any person holding the office of President when this Article was proposed by the Congress, and shall not prevent any person who may be holding the office of President, or acting as President, during the term within which this Article becomes operative from holding the office of President or acting as President during the remainder of such term.

Section 2

This article shall be inoperative unless it shall have been ratified as an amendment to the Constitution by the legislatures of three-fourths of the several States within seven years from the date of its submission to the States by the Congress.

Amendment XXIII

Section 1

The District constituting the seat of Government of the United States shall appoint in such manner as the Congress may direct:

A number of electors of President and Vice President equal to the whole number of Senators and Representatives in Congress to which the District would be entitled if it were a State, but in no event more than the least populous State; they shall be in addition to those appointed by the States, but they shall be considered, for the purposes of the election of President and Vice President, to be electors appointed by a State; and they shall meet in the District and perform such duties as provided by the twelfth article of amendment.

Section 2

The Congress shall have power to enforce this article by appropriate legislation.

What It Means

Electors for the District of Columbia The Twenty-third Amendment (1961) allows citizens living in Washington, D.C., to vote for president and vice president, a right previously denied residents of the nation's capital. The District of Columbia now has three presidential electors, the number to which it would be entitled if it were a state.

Amendment XXIV

Section 1

The right of citizens of the United States to vote in any primary or other election for President or Vice President, for electors for President or Vice President, or for Senator or Representative in Congress, shall not be denied or abridged by the United States or any State by reason of failure to pay any poll tax or other tax.

Section 2

The Congress shall have power to enforce this article by appropriate legislation.

What It Means

Abolition of Poll Tax The Twenty-fourth Amendment (1964) prohibits poll taxes in federal elections. Prior to the passage of this amendment, some states had used such taxes to keep low-income African Americans from voting. In 1966 the Supreme Court banned poll taxes in state elections as well.

Amendment XXV

Section 1

In case of the removal of the President from office or his death or resignation, the Vice President shall become President.

Section 2

Whenever there is a vacancy in the office of the Vice President, the President shall nominate a Vice President who shall take the office upon confirmation by a majority vote of both Houses of Congress.

What It Means

The Vice President The Twenty-fifth Amendment (1967) established a process for the vice president to take over leadership of the nation when a president is disabled. It also set procedures for filling a vacancy in the office of vice president.

This amendment was used in 1973, when Vice President Spiro Agnew resigned from office after being charged with accepting bribes. President Richard Nixon then appointed Gerald R. Ford as vice president in accordance with the provisions of the Twenty-fifth Amendment. A year later, President Nixon resigned during the Watergate scandal and Ford became president. President Ford then had to fill the vice presidency, which he had left vacant upon assuming the presidency. He named Nelson A. Rockefeller as vice president. Thus individuals who had not been elected held both the presidency and the vice presidency. ***Whom does the president inform if he or she cannot carry out the duties of the office?***

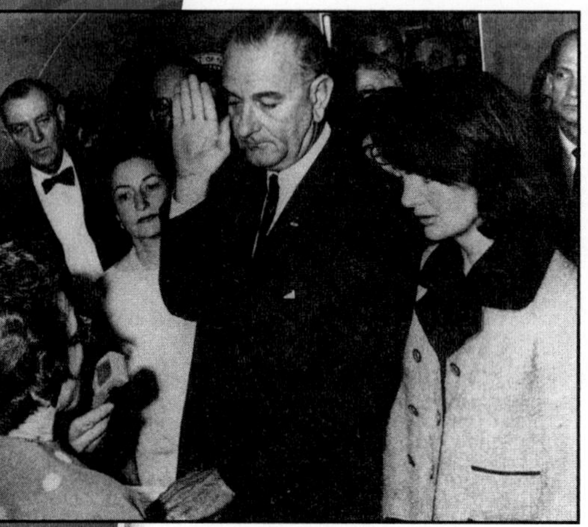

▲ Lyndon B. Johnson is sworn into office after the assassination of President John F. Kennedy.

Section 3

Whenever the President transmits to the President pro tempore of the Senate and the Speaker of the House of Representatives his written declaration that he is unable to discharge the powers and duties of his office, and until he transmits to them a written declaration to the contrary, such powers and duties shall be discharged by the Vice President as Acting President.

Section 4

Whenever the Vice President and a majority of either the principal officers of the executive departments or of such other body as Congress may by law provide, transmit to the President pro tempore of the Senate and the Speaker of the House of Representatives their written declaration that the President is unable to discharge the powers and duties of his office, the Vice President shall immediately assume the power and duties of the office of Acting President.

Thereafter, when the President transmits to the President pro tempore of the Senate and the Speaker of the House of Representatives his written declaration that no inability exists, he shall resume the powers and duties of his office unless the Vice President and a majority of either the principal officers of the executive department or of such other body as Congress may by law provide, transmit within four days to the President pro tempore of the Senate and the Speaker of the House of Representatives their written declaration that the President is unable to discharge the powers and duties of his office. Thereupon Congress shall decide the issue, assembling within forty-eight hours for that purpose if not in session. If the Congress, within twenty-one days after receipt of the latter written declaration, or, if Congress is not in session, within twenty-one days after Congress is required to assemble, determines by two-thirds vote of both Houses that the President is unable to discharge the powers and duties of his office, the Vice President shall continue to discharge the same as Acting President; otherwise, the President shall resume the power and duties of his office.

What It Means

Voting Age The Twenty-sixth Amendment (1971) lowered the voting age in both federal and state elections to 18.

Amendment XXVI

Section 1

The right of citizens of the United States, who are eighteen years of age or older, to vote shall not be denied or abridged by the United States or by any State on account of age.

Section 2

The Congress shall have power to enforce this article by appropriate legislation.

Amendment XXVII

No law, varying the compensation for the services of Senators and Representatives, shall take effect, until an election of representatives shall have intervened.

What It Means

Congressional Pay Raises The Twenty-seventh Amendment (1992) makes congressional pay raises effective during the term following their passage. James Madison offered the amendment in 1789, but it was never adopted. In 1982 Gregory Watson, then a student at the University of Texas, discovered the forgotten amendment while doing research for a school paper. Watson made the amendment's passage his crusade.

▼ **Joint meeting of Congress**

Chapter 4 The Bill of Rights

Why It Matters

Americans have the right to speak out on issues and make their feelings known. The Bill of Rights—the first 10 amendments to the U.S. Constitution—guarantees certain basic rights to all Americans. Among the most important is freedom of speech. It guarantees that people will not be punished for stating their beliefs even if most people disagree with those beliefs.

Civics ONLINE
Visit glencoe.com and enter QuickPass™ code CIV3093c4 for Chapter 4 resources.

Chapter Audio

BIG Ideas

Section 1: The First Amendment

The Constitution of the United States establishes and protects fundamental rights and liberties. The First Amendment protects five basic freedoms that are essential to the American way of life.

Section 2: The Bill of Rights

The Constitution of the United States establishes and protects fundamental rights and liberties. The first 10 amendments to the Constitution describe the rights of American citizens.

Section 3: Extending the Bill of Rights

A constitution reflects the values and goals of the society that creates it. Some Americans have not always enjoyed the full rights of United States citizens.

Section 4: The Civil Rights Struggle

Political, social, religious, and economic changes influence the way Americans think and act. In the 1950s and 1960s, many African Americans began an organized fight for their rights as citizens.

◀ Rally for immigrant rights, Oakland, California

FOLDABLES™ Study Organizer

Organizing Information Study Foldable

Make the following Foldable to help you organize information about the Bill of Rights.

Step 1 Fold a sheet of paper in half from side to side.

Step 2 Turn the paper and fold it in fifths.

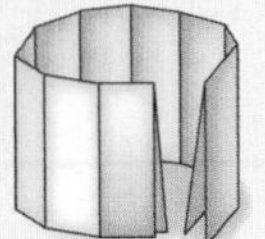

Step 3 Unfold and cut the top layer only along both folds. Then cut each of the five tabs in half. This will make 10 tabs.

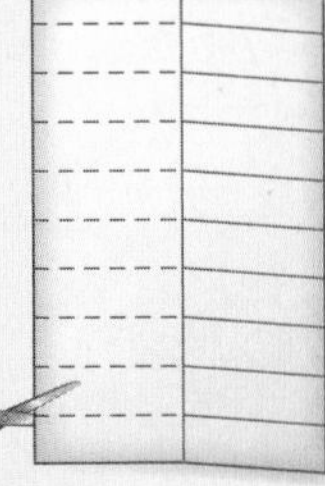

Step 4 Label your Foldable as shown.

1st Amendment
2nd Amendment
3rd Amendment
4th Amendment
5th Amendment
6th Amendment
7th Amendment
8th Amendment
9th Amendment
10th Amendment

Reading and Writing As you read, select key facts about each amendment to the Constitution and write them under the tabs of your Foldable.

Section Audio

Spotlight Video

Section 1

The First Amendment

Guide to Reading

Big Idea
The Constitution of the United States establishes and protects fundamental rights and liberties.

Content Vocabulary
- civil liberties *(p. 121)*
- censorship *(p. 122)*
- petition *(p. 123)*
- slander *(p. 124)*
- libel *(p. 124)*

Academic Vocabulary
- media *(p. 122)*
- imply *(p. 123)*

Reading Strategy
Identifying As you read, identify the main rights outlined in the First Amendment.

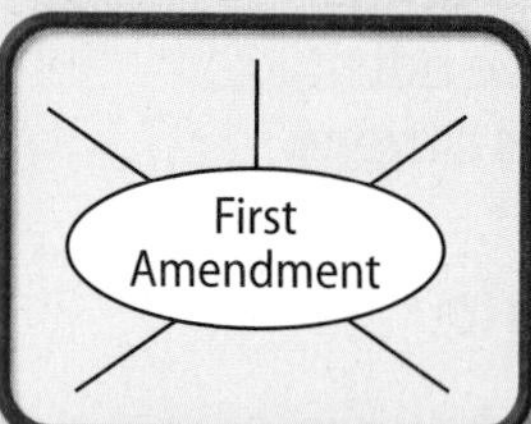

Real World Civics Today it is not unusual to see a minority or a woman delivering the news on national television. This was not always the case. Former CNN correspondent Maria Hinojosa led a panel discussion among important artists of color about this issue. Even though the Bill of Rights gives Americans the right to free speech, free press, and free expression, it did not ensure these opportunities would be given to all Americans. Hinojosa's career success, and that of other minorities, represented an acceptance of multicultural voices in mainstream media, music, and the arts that is relatively recent in American history.

▼ **Latina CNN correspondent, Maria Hinojosa, speaks on a panel about multicultural music in Washington, D.C.**

First Amendment Freedoms

Main Idea **Soon after ratification of the Constitution, the First Amendment was added to guarantee basic freedoms essential to American democracy.**

Civics & You As you learn about the First Amendment, think about how life in the United States might be different if we did not have these rights.

The Founders of the United States believed that protecting individual rights and providing for the safety and well-being of citizens were important purposes of government. The Constitution might not have been ratified had the Bill of Rights not been promised. Added in 1791, the 10 amendments in the Bill of Rights place strict limits on how the national government can use its power over the people.

Civil Liberties The Bill of Rights protects our **civil liberties**—the freedoms we have to think and to act without government interference or fear of unfair treatment. These civil liberties are the cornerstone of our democracy. They ensure that each of us can develop our own beliefs, express ourselves freely, meet openly with others, and have our views on public matters heard by those who govern.

The First Amendment to the Constitution protects five basic freedoms: freedom of religion, freedom of speech, freedom of the press, freedom of assembly, and freedom to petition the government.

Freedom of Religion

Intolerance of different beliefs in their homelands forced many colonists to come to America in the first place. The First Amendment safeguards religious freedom in two ways. First, the amendment prohibits Congress from establishing an official religion in the United States. This is known as the establishment clause. In 1802 President Thomas Jefferson referred to the First Amendment's establishment clause as a "wall of separation between church and state."

This makes the United States different from countries in which a state religion is established. It also makes us different from nations that have in the past strongly discouraged the practice of religion at all, such as the former Soviet Union and People's Republic of China.

The First Amendment

Analyzing Charts

1. **Identifying** What rights are listed in the First Amendment?
2. **Explaining** What is meant by the "press" in this amendment?

Second, this amendment guarantees Americans the right to practice their faith as they wish. The government may not favor one religion over another or treat people differently because of their personal beliefs.

Freedom of Speech

In some countries, people can be jailed for criticizing the government or for expressing their ideas, even if they do so in private conversations. The First Amendment guarantees that we can say what is on our minds, in public or in private, without fear of punishment by the government.

Face-to-face discussions, telephone conversations, lectures, and radio and TV broadcasts are covered by the guarantee of free speech; so are other forms of expression besides the spoken word. As interpreted by the Supreme Court, "speech" can mean Internet communication, art, music, and even clothing.

Freedom of the Press

The First Amendment allows Americans to express themselves in print as well as in speech. When the Bill of Rights was written, "the press" referred to printed publications such as books, newspapers, and magazines. Today the press includes many other sources of **media,** such as radio, television, and computer networks.

Freedom of the press ensures that the American people are exposed to a wide variety of viewpoints. The government cannot practice **censorship;** that is, it cannot ban printed materials or films merely because they contain alarming or offensive ideas. It also cannot censor information before it is published or broadcast.

Buddhist New Year Buddhist monks in San Francisco's Chinatown celebrate the 2006 Chinese New Year by bringing families together, sharing food, and praying for good health and prosperity. A Sikh woman (inset) prays during a weekly religious ceremony. ***Inferring*** **Why do you think the Framers included freedom of religion in the First Amendment?**

The Zenger Case In 1733, publisher John Peter Zenger, in his paper the *New-York Weekly Journal,* was arrested and imprisoned for criticizing the governor of New York. Andrew Hamilton, Zenger's lawyer, argued that only a press free to criticize the government could prevent that government from abusing its power. Zenger was acquitted. At the time, the case attracted little attention, but today it is regarded as a landmark in the development of free press in America.

After the American Revolution, several states provided for the freedom of the press in their state constitutions. Later, the First Amendment of the U.S. Constitution provided for a free press in American society as a whole. The mass media—newspapers, magazines, television, radio, and the Internet—however, are not totally free of government regulation.

Many reasonable restrictions can be placed on rights of the media. For example, no person has the right to use printed words to injure another person's character or reputation. Supreme Court rulings allowed the press to be limited when the printed materials might threaten national security. Laws also prohibit the printing and distribution of obscene materials.

A POPULAR TRIUMPH CELEBRATED.

Freedom of the Press Supporters celebrate John Peter Zenger's acquittal. ***Explaining*** **Why is the Zenger case significant?**

Freedom of Assembly

The First Amendment protects our right to gather in groups for any reason, so long as the assemblies are peaceful. We have the right to attend meetings, parades, political rallies, and public celebrations. Governments may make rules about when and where such activities can be held, but they cannot ban them.

The Supreme Court has decided that freedom of assembly **implies,** or suggests, freedom of association. Thus the First Amendment also protects our right to form and join social clubs, political parties, labor unions, and other organizations. Even if we never assemble with fellow members, we have the right to belong to such groups.

Freedom to Petition

Finally, the First Amendment guarantees all Americans the right to petition the government. A **petition** is simply a formal request. Often we use the word to refer to a specific kind of document—a brief, or written statement signed by hundreds or thousands of people. Even a simple letter or e-mail written by an individual, however, could be considered a petition.

The right to petition means the right to express one's ideas to the government. If you want to complain about overcrowded schools, for example, or suggest that a skating park be built in your community, you can write to your elected representatives. If enough people express similar views, government leaders may take action.

Reading Check **Summarizing** What is meant by a "petition" in freedom to petition?

First Amendment Limits

Main Idea **All constitutional rights are limited. These limitations are necessary to ensure our other rights are protected.**

Civics & You The First Amendment protects free speech, but does it protect speech that damages a person's character or reputation? Read to find out what limits are placed on our First Amendment freedoms.

The First Amendment guarantees Americans the right to express their thoughts and opinions. However, this is not an absolute freedom. Freedom of speech, for example, does not include the right to endanger our government or other Americans. You do not have freedom to provoke a riot. You are not free to speak or write in a way that immediately leads to criminal activities or efforts to overthrow the government by force.

Citizens should use their civil liberties responsibly, which means they should not interfere with the rights of others. For example, you are free to talk with your friends in the street, but you must not block traffic. You may campaign for causes, but you may not disturb your neighbors with blaring loudspeaker broadcasts. You may criticize government officials, but you may not spread lies that harm a person's reputation. Spreading spoken lies is a crime called **slander.** It is called **libel** if lies are printed.

The First Amendment was never intended to allow Americans to do whatever they please. The rights of one individual must be balanced against the rights of others and against the rights of the community. When there is a conflict, the rights of the community often come first. Otherwise, the society would break apart.

Reading Check **Explaining** Why are your First Amendment rights limited?

Vocabulary

1. **Define** the following terms and use them in sentences related to the First Amendment: *civil liberties, censorship, petition, slander, libel.*

Main Ideas

2. **Analyzing** Why was the First Amendment added to the Constitution immediately?
3. **Explaining** What is the difference between libel and slander?

Critical Thinking

4. **BIG Ideas** Which First Amendment right do you think is the most important? Explain your view.
5. **Classifying** In a chart like the one below, list two limitations to our First Amendment freedoms.

Limitations to First Amendment Freedoms
1.
2.

6. **Analyzing** Why do you think the right to petition is considered an important basic freedom?

CITIZENSHIP Activity

7. **Persuasive Writing** How do you think the First Amendment's freedom of the press protections should be applied during wartime? Do you think that the government should be allowed to censor press coverage or that the press should be allowed to report on what it sees? Write an essay expressing your view. Give reasons to support your answers.

Study Central™ To review this section, go to glencoe.com.

Schools place restrictions on computers to protect students from visiting undesirable Internet sites. Some consider this a form of surveillance.

Is the Patriot Act an infringement of privacy?

A terrorist attack shocked the United States on September 11, 2001. Congress quickly responded to the Attorney General's call for changes in the law to combat terrorism. President George W. Bush signed the Patriot Act as a new tool to fight "a threat like no other our Nation has ever seen." Later, some members of Congress and concerned citizens said some parts of the act violated the Fourth Amendment's protection against unreasonable searches and seizures. Before most searches, officers must obtain a warrant from a judge, showing "probable cause" and describing the place to be searched and the persons or things to be seized. The Patriot Act made exceptions to these requirements. Section 215 permitted the FBI to go before the Foreign Intelligence Surveillance Court for an order to search for "any tangible things" connected to a terrorism suspect.

YES

In November 2003, the American Civil Liberties Union contended that the Patriot Act contains "flaws that threaten your fundamental freedoms by giving the government the power to access to your medical records, tax records, information about the books you buy or borrow without probable cause, and the power to break into your home and conduct secret searches without telling you for weeks, months, or indefinitely." In 2004 the ACLU filed a lawsuit to overturn a Patriot Act provision that gave the government authority to obtain customer records from Internet service providers and other businesses without a warrant.

—American Civil Liberties Union

NO

Senator Orrin Hatch of Utah voted for the Patriot Act and defended it when Congress voted to renew most of its provisions. In 2003 he said, "The Patriot Act has not eroded any of the rights we hold dear as Americans. I would be the first to call for corrective action, were that the case. Yet not one of the civil liberties groups has cited one instance of abuse of our constitutional rights. . . . We should not undermine or limit our law enforcement and intelligence agencies' efforts by imposing requirements that go above and beyond those required by the Constitution. That would only have the effect of protecting terrorists and criminals while endangering the lives of innocent Americans."

—Senator Orrin Hatch

Debating the Issue

1. **Describing** How does the Fourth Amendment attempt to protect Americans' privacy?
2. **Describing** What must an officer of the law do to obtain a warrant for a search?
3. **Explaining** Why were some people concerned about the provisions in Section 215?
4. **Concluding** Were the concerns of people who opposed some provisions of the Patriot Act justified? Explain.

Section 2

The Bill of Rights

Guide to Reading

Big Idea

The Constitution of the United States establishes and protects fundamental rights and liberties.

Content Vocabulary

- search warrant *(p. 127)*
- indictment *(p. 128)*
- grand jury *(p. 128)*
- double jeopardy *(p. 128)*
- due process *(p. 128)*
- eminent domain *(p. 128)*
- bail *(p. 129)*

Academic Vocabulary

- proportion *(p. 129)*
- involve *(p. 131)*

Reading Strategy

Summarizing On a graphic organizer like the one below, discuss four ways that the Bill of Rights protects the rights of the accused.

Real World Civics Some dogs are pets and some dogs perform a civic duty during a legal search. Below, police officer Tom Kolbert and his K-9 partner, Reggie, check student lockers in a Cheektowaga, New York, high school for contraband. Most dogs have a sense of smell that is 1,000 times more sensitive than a human's. With proper training, sniffer dogs can detect explosives, weapons, and illegal drugs. The Supreme Court holds that an individual's right to privacy does not extend to illegal activities and has ruled that K-9 searches are legal.

▼ **A drug-sniffing dog and police officer search lockers**

Protecting the Rights of the Accused

Main Idea **In addition to the important civil liberties protected by the First Amendment, the other nine amendments in the Bill of Rights guarantee the right to fair legal treatment, as well as other freedoms.**

Civics & You How well do you know what constitutional protections you enjoy as a United States citizen? Read about your rights under the Bill of Rights.

The First Amendment freedoms are among our most important civil liberties. Equally precious, however, is the right to fair legal treatment. This is the subject of several amendments in the Bill of Rights.

Suppose someone accuses you of committing a crime. In some countries, government agents might ransack your home, drag you off to jail, beat you, and hold a trial without even letting you respond to the charges. In the United States, the Fourth, Fifth, Sixth, and Eighth Amendments help prevent such a scenario from occurring.

The Fourth Amendment

The Fourth Amendment protects Americans "against unreasonable searches and seizures." No soldier, government agent, or police officer can search your home or take your property without probable, or a valid, cause.

If law enforcement officers believe you have committed a crime, they can ask a judge to issue a **search warrant.** This is a court order allowing law enforcement officers to search a suspect's home or business and take specific items as evidence. Judges do not give out search warrants easily. They must be convinced that a search will probably turn up evidence of criminal activity.

Rights of the Accused

FIFTH AMENDMENT
• No trial may be held unless a person is formally charged, or indicted, by the grand jury.
• A person found not guilty may not be put on trial again for the same crime.
• Accused persons may not be forced to testify against themselves.
• Every person is entitled to due process of law.
• No one may be deprived of their property by the government without compensation.
SIXTH AMENDMENT
• The accused must be informed of the nature of the charges.
• The accused must be allowed a speedy and public trial by an impartial jury.
• If possible, the trial must be held in the area where the crime took place.
• The accused must be permitted to hear and question all witnesses.
• The accused is entitled to a lawyer and to call witnesses for his or her defense.

Analyzing Charts

1. **Identifying** Which amendment guarantees that if you are arrested, you will be informed of the charges against you?
2. **Explaining** What is due process of law?

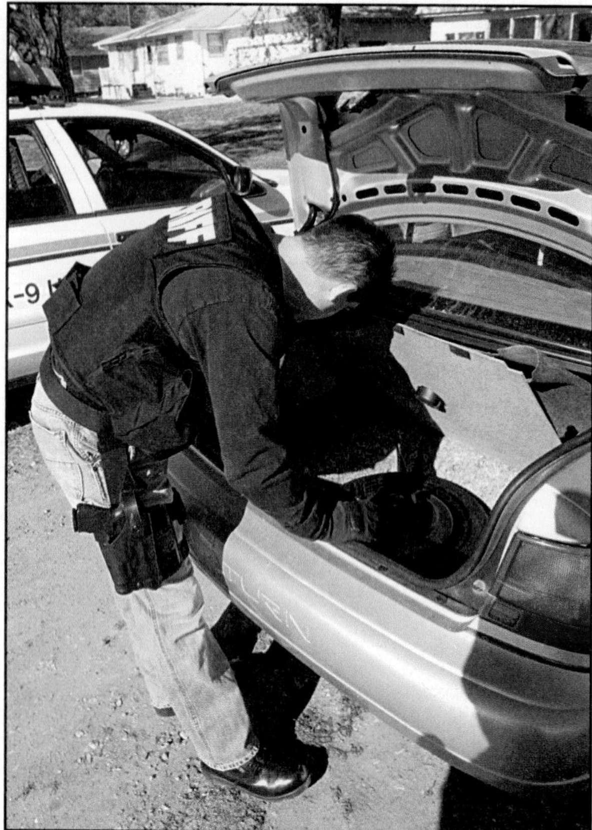

Legal Searches Reasonable searches can take place when the county police have cause to suspect a crime has been committed. ***Analyzing*** **How does a search warrant help protect the rights of a person accused of a crime?**

If warrants were issued frivolously, the Fourth Amendment would give us little sense of security. Anytime of the day or night, the police could invade our privacy and confiscate our possessions.

The Fifth Amendment

The Fifth Amendment protects the rights of people accused of crimes. It states that no one can be put on trial for a serious federal crime without an **indictment**—a formal charge by a group of citizens called a **grand jury,** who review the evidence against the accused.

A person who is indicted is not necessarily guilty of a crime. An indictment simply indicates the grand jury's belief that an individual *may* have committed a crime.

The Fifth Amendment also protects people from **double jeopardy.** This means that people who are accused of a crime and judged not guilty may not be put on trial again for the same crime.

In addition, the Fifth Amendment protects an accused person's right to remain silent. Throughout history, innocent people have been threatened, tortured, or bullied into confessing to crimes they did not commit. To prevent this, the Fifth Amendment states that people cannot be forced to testify against themselves. This is called protection against self-incrimination.

The Fifth Amendment goes on to say that no one may be denied life, liberty, or property "without due process of law." **Due process** means following established legal procedures. It also includes the idea that the laws themselves must be reasonable.

The Fifth Amendment also protects a citizen's property rights. It limits the government's power of eminent domain. **Eminent domain** is the right of the government to take private property—usually land—for public use.

For example, if your home lies in the path of a proposed highway, the government may legally take the land and destroy your house. The Fifth Amendment limits this power and requires the government to pay a fair price for the property.

The Sixth Amendment

The Sixth Amendment guarantees additional rights to people accused of crimes. It requires that they be told the exact nature of the charges against them. It also requires that the accused be allowed a trial by jury, although they may ask to be tried by only a judge instead.

If an accused person asks for a jury trial, the trial must be speedy and public, and jurors must be impartial. If possible, the trial should be held in the same area in which the crime took place.

Accused individuals have the right to hear and question all witnesses against them. They must also be permitted to call witnesses in their own defense. Finally, they are entitled to have a lawyer. Since the Sixth Amendment was written, the Supreme Court has ruled that if an accused person cannot afford a lawyer, the government must provide one and pay his or her fees.

The Eighth Amendment

Although the Sixth Amendment guarantees a speedy trial, sometimes months go by before a case can be heard. During that time, the accused may have two choices: stay in jail or remain free by paying bail. **Bail** is a sum of money used as a security deposit. If the accused person comes to court for the trial, the bail is returned. If the person fails to appear, though, the bail is forfeited.

The judge decides how much bail a person must pay. The Eighth Amendment, however, forbids "excessive" bail—that is, an amount that is much too high. Excessive does not just refer to what a person can afford to pay. In determining bail, a judge considers various factors, including the type of crime committed, the record of the accused person, and the likelihood that the accused will appear in court. In some cases, bail may be denied, as when a defendant is likely to flee.

When a person is convicted of a crime, the Eighth Amendment protects him or her against having to pay excessive fines. Fines may vary, however, depending on the seriousness of the crime.

The Eighth Amendment forbids "cruel and unusual punishments." For many years, Americans have debated what kinds of punishment are cruel and unusual. It is generally agreed that punishment should be in **proportion,** or balanced, to the crime committed. For example, a sentence of life imprisonment for stealing a loaf of bread would be too harsh. People disagree strongly, however, about whether the death penalty for very serious crimes is cruel and unusual punishment.

Reading Check **Identifying** Which amendment protects a person accused of a crime from double jeopardy?

Gun Ownership Individuals may own firearms if laws are obeyed. At this firing range in Massachusetts, gun owners are trained on weapon safety. ***Speculating*** **Why did the Framers think the right to bear arms was an important right to protect?**

TIME™ Teens in *Action*

Jackie Fernandez

You can probably find Jackie Fernandez, 17, of Alexandria, Virginia, in a local bookstore. She is one of the writers of a new book published by Bill Rhatican, her AP government teacher at West Potomac High School.

QUESTION: Can you tell us about the book?

ANSWER: It's called *The Constitution: Written in Sand or Etched in Stone?* The book is a collection of essays written by students about the U.S. Constitution and the Bill of Rights.

Q: What's your essay in the book about?

A: Fanfiction, or fictional stories about characters from books and movies that are already copyrighted. For example, if I wanted to write a story about what the character Yoda did between *Star Wars: Episode III* and the original Star Wars movies—that would be fanfiction.

Q: How does this relate to the Bill of Rights?

A: I think the First Amendment protects the fanfiction author's freedom of speech, while the Fifth Amendment protects the original creator's right to property. In other words, one part of the Bill of Rights allows me to write about Yoda, but another part of the Bill of Rights protects the person who thought Yoda up. So fanfiction is both condemned and protected by the Bill of Rights.

Q: Is the Bill of Rights a "living" document?

A: Yes! If the Bill of Rights wasn't "alive," it wouldn't be applicable to modern-day inventions.

Q: How will it feel to see the book in stores?

A: Amazing. I've always wanted to be published. It's like a dream come true!

Making a Difference 

Write a paragraph on how freedom of expression has taken place in your life.

Other Protections

Main Idea **In addition to the First Amendment freedoms and due process guarantees, the Bill of Rights includes other protections for American citizens.**

Civics & You Several of the first 10 amendments deal with the rights of people accused of committing a crime. Why do you think the constitution protects the rights of the accused?

There is debate over what rights, exactly, are guaranteed by the Second Amendment. Some argue that it provides only for each state to maintain "a well-regulated militia" by allowing the members of those militias to carry arms. When the Second Amendment was written, a militia was a small, local army made of volunteer soldiers.

Other people hold that the Second Amendment guarantees the right of all individual citizens to "keep and bear arms" without the interference of the government. The courts have generally ruled that the government can pass laws to control, but not prevent, the possession of weapons. For example, federal and state laws determine who can be licensed to own firearms.

The Third Amendment

One cause of the American Revolution was the colonists' resentment of the law requiring them to house and feed British soldiers. The Third Amendment makes it unlikely that Americans will ever be forced to shelter the military again. The amendment says that, in peacetime, soldiers may not move into private homes without the consent of the homeowner.

Student Web Activity Visit glencoe.com and complete the Chapter 4 Web Activity.

The Seventh Amendment

The Fifth, Sixth, and Eighth Amendments deal with people's rights in criminal cases. The Seventh Amendment concerns civil cases—lawsuits that **involve**, or contain, disagreements between people rather than crimes. The Seventh Amendment provides for the right to a jury trial in federal courts to settle all disputes about property worth more than $20. When both parties in a conflict agree, however, a judge rather than a jury may hear evidence and settle the case.

The Ninth Amendment

The Ninth Amendment states that all other rights not spelled out in the Constitution are "retained by the people." This amendment prevents the government from claiming that the only rights people have are those listed in the Bill of Rights. The Ninth Amendment makes it clear that citizens have other rights beyond those listed in the Constitution, and those rights may not be taken away.

The Tenth Amendment

The first eight amendments grant the people rights. The Ninth Amendment states that the rights guaranteed in the Constitution are not the only rights the people have.

Unlike the other amendments, the Tenth Amendment did not add anything to the ratified Constitution. The Tenth Amendment states that any powers the Constitution does not specifically give to the national government are reserved for the states and for the people. (This amendment is the source of many of the reserved powers you learned about in Chapter 3.) The amendment expresses the idea that the federal government is limited only to the powers it is granted in the Constitution.

In this way, the Tenth Amendment prevents Congress and the president from becoming too strong. The government of the United States can have only the powers the people give it.

Reading Check **Describing** What is the purpose of the Tenth Amendment?

Vocabulary

1. **Write** sentences related to the Bill of Rights using the following terms: *search warrant, indictment, grand jury, double jeopardy, due process, eminent domain, bail.*

Main Ideas

2. **Hypothesizing** Why do you think the Framers of the Constitution addressed the legal treatment of the accused in so many amendments?
3. **Explaining** How do the Ninth and Tenth Amendments limit the power of government?

Critical Thinking

4. **BIG Ideas** Which of the first 10 amendments do you think is the most important? Why?
5. **Organizing** In a web diagram similar to the one below, identify important rights in the Fifth Amendment.

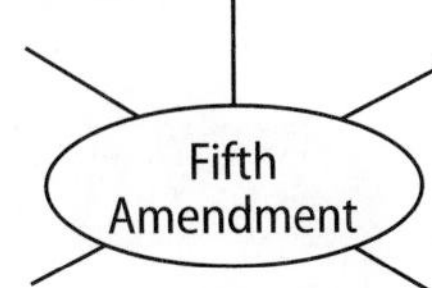

CITIZENSHIP Activity

6. **Persuasive Writing** Select an issue related to the amendments in this section, such as the death penalty or gun control. Write a letter to the editor of your local newspaper expressing your views on the issue.

Study Central™ To review this section, go to glencoe.com.

Landmark Supreme Court Case Studies

Tinker v. Des Moines School District

Public school officials set standards of behavior that students are expected to follow. Does this arrangement leave students with any rights? Sometimes the Supreme Court must decide.

Background of the Case

One night in December 1965, a group of public school students, led by high school sophomores Christopher Eckhardt and John Tinker, and eighth-grader Mary Beth Tinker, wore black armbands to protest the Vietnam War. As other students joined the armband protest, principals and members of the school board met the growing protest with a ban on armbands—to prevent "disturbing influences."

On December 16, 1965, Christopher, John, and Mary Beth were suspended for wearing their armbands to school. Their parents protested the suspensions in federal courts. They contended the students' First Amendment free-speech rights had been violated.

Lorena, Paul, and Mary Beth Tinker hear their case has been settled in their favor.

The Decision

On February 24, 1969, the United States Supreme Court in a 7–2 decision declared the school suspensions unconstitutional. Justice Abe Fortas, who wrote the majority opinion, first established that the students' action was "akin to pure speech." Even though their protest involved no speaking, it deserved "protection under the First Amendment." Then he wrote:

> ***"It can hardly be argued that either students or teachers shed their constitutional rights to freedom of speech or expression at the schoolhouse gate."***
>
> —Justice Abe Fortas

Why It Matters

Supporters saluted the decision that "students are entitled to freedom of expression of their views." Critics predicted harmful consequences. Dissenter Justice Hugo Black suggested that the Court's decision was "the beginning of a new revolutionary era of permissiveness in this country fostered by the judiciary." He argued that no one has a complete right to freedom of speech and expression. Later decisions, such as *Bethel School District* v. *Fraser* (1986) and *Hazelwood School District* v. *Kuhlmeier* (1988), narrowed students' First Amendment rights while expanding the authority of school officials.

Analyzing the Court Decision

1. **Explaining** Why did the students' lawyers argue that the armbands were protected by the First Amendment?
2. **Inferring** How did Judge Fortas's concept of "pure speech" extend First Amendment free-speech rights?

Guide to Reading

Big Idea
A constitution reflects the values and goals of the society that creates it.

Content Vocabulary
- suffrage *(p. 135)*
- poll tax *(p. 137)*

Academic Vocabulary
- violate *(p 134)*
- specify *(p. 137)*

Reading Strategy
Explaining As you read, complete a graphic organizer like the one below to identify and explain the Civil War amendments.

Section 3

Section Audio Spotlight Video

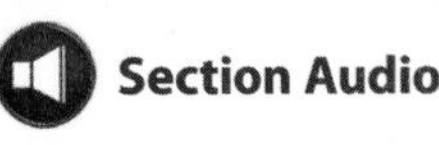

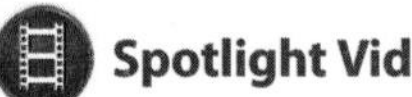

Extending the Bill of Rights

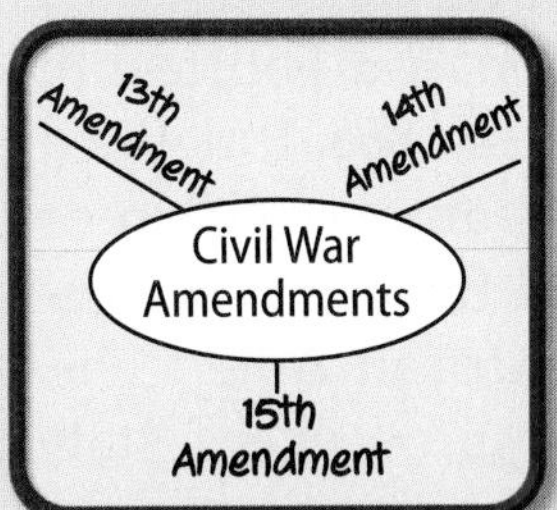

Real World Civics In the 1948 primary elections, thousands of African Americans across the country stood in line to exercise their right to vote for the first time since 1876. They faced possible violence, name calling—even losing their jobs. Although the Fifteenth Amendment guarantees the right to vote, some states created obstacles such as poll taxes, passing a literacy test, or proving property ownership to avoid letting minorities vote. In 1944, the Supreme Court ruled that these requirements, specifically designed to exclude African Americans, were illegal.

▼ **African American voters line up to receive ballots in Columbia, South Carolina, in 1948**

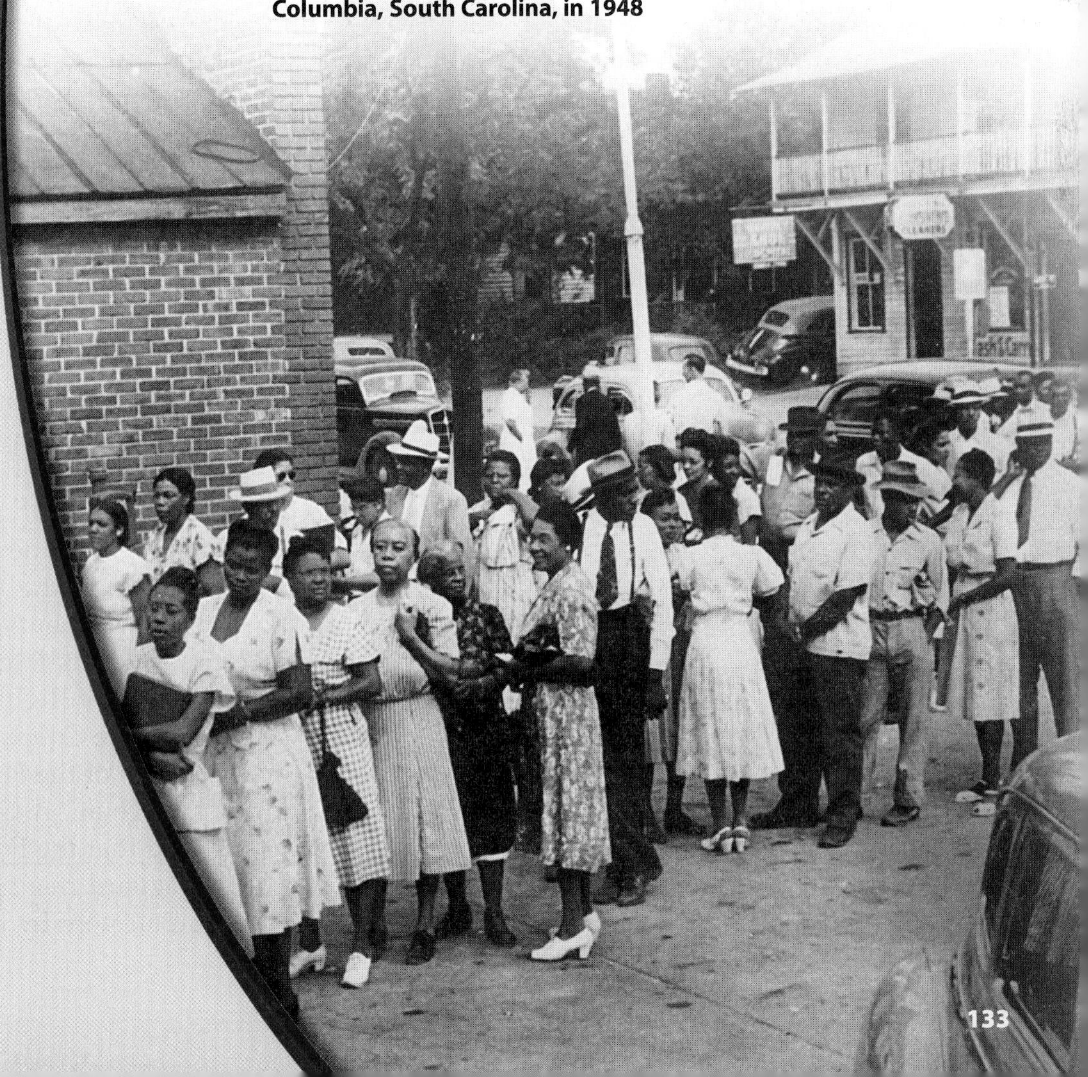

Civil War Amendments

Main Idea **The Thirteenth, Fourteenth, and Fifteenth Amendments are called the Civil War amendments because they grew out of that war.**

Civics & You In our country, freedom and the right to express our opinions are precious rights. Read to learn about efforts to extend these rights.

The Bill of Rights was intended originally to constrain only the national government. For many years, local and state governments were not bound by its terms. As a result, states sometimes used their reserved powers to pass laws that **violate,** or disobey, civil liberties. In most parts of the country, for example, women and African Americans could not vote. Before 1865, many states had laws that sanctioned the enslavement of African Americans, who were treated as property and had almost no rights at all.

Three amendments were passed after the Civil War to extend civil liberties to African Americans. However, the promise of these Civil War amendments was not fulfilled for almost 100 years. Many states were slow to change their customs; some actively resisted. The federal government and the Supreme Court often seemed indifferent.

The Right to Vote Following the Civil War, African Americans across the South voted for the first time. Many states tried to make it difficult for them to exercise this right. ***Identifying*** **Who else besides African Americans were prevented from voting after the Civil War?**

The Thirteenth Amendment

The Thirteenth Amendment officially outlawed slavery in the United States and thus freed thousands of African Americans. It also outlawed any sort of forced labor, except as punishment for a crime.

The Fourteenth Amendment

Although the Thirteenth Amendment ensured the freedom of African Americans, it did not guarantee them full rights. After the Civil War, many Southern states passed "black codes" that excluded African Americans from certain jobs, limited their property rights, and restricted them in other ways.

To remedy this situation, the Fourteenth Amendment was enacted in 1868. It defined a United States citizen as anyone "born or naturalized in the United States," a definition that included most African Americans. The amendment also required every state to grant its citizens "equal protection of the laws." In recent years, this clause has been used to benefit women, people with disabilities, and other groups whose rights have not always been protected fairly.

The Fourteenth Amendment also forbids state governments from interfering with the "privileges or immunities of citizens of the United States." Further, state governments may not take an individual's "life, liberty, or property, without due process of law." These provisions made the Bill of Rights binding for state governments as well as the federal government. This is called the nationalization of the Bill of Rights.

The Supreme Court, however, ignored this interpretation of the Fourteenth Amendment until 1925. Then, in *Gitlow* v. *New York,* the Court ruled that the Fourteenth Amendment could safeguard free speech and a free press "from impairment by the states."

Constitutional Amendments

ELEVENTH AMENDMENT (1795)
• Places limits on suits against states
TWELFTH AMENDMENT (1804)
• Revises procedure for electing the president and vice president
THIRTEENTH AMENDMENT (1865)
• Abolishes slavery
FOURTEENTH AMENDMENT (1868)
• Defines United States citizenship; guarantees all citizens "equal protection of the laws"
FIFTEENTH AMENDMENT (1870)
• Prohibits restrictions on the right to vote based on race and color
SIXTEENTH AMENDMENT (1913)
• Gives Congress the power to levy an income tax
SEVENTEENTH AMENDMENT (1913)
• Enables voters to elect senators directly
EIGHTEENTH AMENDMENT (1917)
• Prohibits making, drinking, or selling alcoholic beverages (Prohibition)

NINETEENTH AMENDMENT (1920)
• Gives women the right to vote
TWENTIETH AMENDMENT (1933)
• Changes the dates of congressional and presidential terms
TWENTY-FIRST AMENDMENT (1933)
• Repeals Prohibition (Eighteenth Amendment)
TWENTY-SECOND AMENDMENT (1951)
• Limits presidents to two terms in office
TWENTY-THIRD AMENDMENT (1961)
• Gives residents of the District of Columbia the right to vote
TWENTY-FOURTH AMENDMENT (1964)
• Abolishes poll taxes
TWENTY-FIFTH AMENDMENT (1967)
• Establishes procedures for succession to the presidency
TWENTY-SIXTH AMENDMENT (1971)
• Sets voting age at 18 years
TWENTY-SEVENTH AMENDMENT (1992)
• Delays congressional pay raises until the term following their passage

Analyzing Charts

1. **Identifying** Which is the amendment that specifically deals with women's rights?
2. **Explaining** Why do you think the Framers made the amendment process so difficult?

Since the *Gitlow* case, the Supreme Court has used the Fourteenth Amendment to apply other rights in the Bill of Rights to the states. This "incorporation" of the Bill of Rights by the Fourteenth Amendment's due process clause means that U.S. citizens in every part of the country have the same basic rights.

The Fifteenth Amendment

The last of the Civil War amendments, the Fifteenth, says that no state may take away a person's voting rights on the basis of race, color, or previous enslavement. The amendment clearly aimed to guarantee **suffrage**—the right to vote—to African Americans. Still, many states found ways to keep African Americans away from the polls.

The Fifteenth Amendment, in reality, protected only men. The various states had the power to decide whether women could vote. Women, regardless of their race, could not vote in most federal or state elections.

Reading Check **Explaining** What did the Thirteenth Amendment outlaw in addition to slavery?

Later Amendments

Main Idea **Amendments added to the Constitution in the twentieth century deal with a wide range of topics.**

Civics & You Our Constitution has endured for more than 200 years with only 27 amendments. Read to find out about the amendments added to the Constitution in the twentieth century.

Gradually, the Bill of Rights came to cover all Americans equally and to limit government power at all levels. Additional amendments to the Constitution and court rulings extended the rights of Americans to participate fully in the democratic process. A number of amendments deal with voting rights.

18-Year-Olds Get the Vote In 1971 President Richard Nixon, before a group of young people, signed the Twenty-sixth Amendment. ***Explaining*** **What role did the Vietnam War play in the passing of this amendment?**

The Seventeenth Amendment

According to Article I of the Constitution, the people were to elect members of the House of Representatives, but the state legislatures were to choose members of the Senate. Ratified in 1913, the Seventeenth Amendment allows voters to elect their senators directly. This change in the election process gave Americans a greater voice in their government.

The Nineteenth Amendment

Although the Constitution did not guarantee women the right to vote, it did not explicitly deny them suffrage. As a result, states made their own laws on the matter, using the powers reserved to them under the Tenth Amendment. The territory of Wyoming permitted women to vote in 1869, and several other territories and states did so as well in the years that followed.

Anthony and Stanton However, national support for woman suffrage was slow in coming. Woman suffrage leaders Susan B. Anthony and Elizabeth Cady Stanton had insisted as early as 1848 that women belonged at the polls. Many who believed that women should not have the same rights as men opposed them, however. It was only in 1920 that the Nineteenth Amendment protected the right of women to vote in all national and state elections.

The Twenty-third Amendment

African Americans and women were not the only citizens who were denied voting rights for many years. Residents of our nation's capital, Washington, D.C., also fell into this group.

As you may know, "D.C.," stands for the District of Columbia, an area between Maryland and Virginia. Because the District is not a state, the people who lived there were not initially allowed to vote in national elections. The Twenty-third Amendment changed that in 1961. The amendment says that residents of the District of Columbia may vote for the president and vice president, just as other Americans do.

The Twenty-fourth Amendment

Although the Fifteenth Amendment gave African Americans the right to vote, many had trouble exercising this right. One reason was that several Southern states had **poll taxes.** In other words, they required voters to pay a sum of money before casting a ballot. Because the tax had to be paid not only for the current year, but also for previous unpaid years as well, it was a financial burden for many. Because many African Americans could not afford the tax, they could not vote. Poor whites were in the same situation.

In 1964, the Twenty-fourth Amendment made poll taxes illegal in national elections. Two years later, the Supreme Court ruled that poll taxes were illegal in state elections as well. The elimination of the poll tax allowed many African American citizens to enjoy their full rights as voters for the first time.

The Twenty-sixth Amendment

Throughout our nation's history, people still in their teens have bravely fought for our country. By law, however, they were not old enough to vote for the leaders who sent them into battle. Although the Constitution did not **specify,** or mention, a minimum age for voters, most states set the minimum at 21.

That standard finally changed in 1971, a year when many young Americans were fighting in the Vietnam War. The Twenty-sixth Amendment guaranteed the right to vote to citizens 18 and older for all national and state elections. As a result, millions more Americans can exercise their right to vote and enjoy the rights of full citizenship.

Reading Check **Explaining** Who benefitted most from the passing of the Twenty-third Amendment?

Review

Vocabulary

1. **Write** sentences related to voting rights using the following terms: *suffrage, poll tax.*

Main Ideas

2. **Explaining** How was the promise of the Civil War amendments fulfilled in the mid-twentieth century?
3. **Identifying** One topic covered in the later amendments is the right to vote. Whose voting rights did the twentieth century amendments specifically address?

Critical Thinking

4. **BIG Ideas** How do you account for the fact that even though the Fifteenth Amendment guaranteed suffrage to African Americans, many were not allowed to vote?
5. **Explaining** On a chart like the one below, explain how each of these amendments extended voting rights.

Amendment	Effect
17th	Voters elect senators directly
19th	
23rd	
24th	
26th	

6. **Analyzing Visuals** Review the chart on page 135. Which amendment guaranteed the right to vote to citizens 18 and older?

CITIZENSHIP Activity

7. **Persuasive Writing** Because many 18- to 21-year-olds do not vote, some believe the Twenty-sixth Amendment should be repealed. Write a one-page essay expressing your views on this topic.

Study Central™ To review this section, go to glencoe.com.

Financial Literacy

Cash or Credit?

Debbie is shopping and sees a jacket she really likes on sale for $300. However, she has a problem—no cash. Since she is 18, she has her own credit card. The card carries an 18 percent annual percentage rate on unpaid balances. Debbie calculates she can afford to pay $15 a month on the account. Should she buy the jacket or not?

How Credit Cards Work

Credit is using tomorrow's money to pay for something you get today. A credit card is a useful financial tool. It can be more convenient to use and carry than cash, and it offers valuable consumer protections under federal law.

Credit card advantages:
- Buy needed items now
- Do not have to carry cash
- Creates a record of purchases
- Consolidates bills into one payment

Credit card pitfalls:
- Higher cost of items (interest and finance charges)
- Financial problems may occur if you lose track of how much you are spending each month
- Leads to impulse buying

Credit has both advantages and disadvantages. By using it wisely, you emphasize the advantages.

Checklist for Buying on Credit
There are no hard-and-fast rules to tell you whether or not to buy on credit. Answer these questions to help you determine if you are making a wise decision:
1. Do I really require this item? Can I postpone purchasing the item until later?
2. If I pay cash, what will I be giving up that I could buy with this money?
3. Have I done comparison shopping for credit?
4. Can I afford to borrow or use credit now?

Analyzing Economics

1. **Describing** What are three ways to avoid credit card debt?
2. **Defending** To qualify for a personal credit card, a person must be 18 years old or older. Should the age restriction remain the same or be changed? Defend your response.

Section Audio

Spotlight Video

Section 4

The Civil Rights Struggle

Guide to Reading

Big Idea

Political, social, religious, and economic changes influence the way Americans think and act.

Content Vocabulary

- discrimination *(p. 140)*
- segregation *(p. 140)*
- civil rights *(p. 140)*
- affirmative action *(p. 143)*
- racial profiling *(p. 143)*

Academic Vocabulary

- section *(p. 140)*
- gender *(p. 141)*

Reading Strategy

Identifying As you read, complete the chart below by filling in key laws achieved by the civil rights movement.

Important Laws
Civil Rights Acts of 1964

Real World Civics In September 1957, after weeks of violence, Little Rock Central High School accepted nine African American students—the only black students in the public high school. The teenagers, and their families, could not have imagined how their determination would affect the lives of millions of students who came after them. Now, more than 50 years later, their bravery is marked by *Testament*, a monument on the Arkansas State Capitol grounds. The former students, Elizabeth Eckford (right), Melba Pattillo Beals (left), and the other students were reunited for the dedication.

▼ **Elizabeth Eckford, right, unveils her *Testament* statue in 2005**

Struggle for Rights

Main Idea **Although amendments to the Constitution guaranteed rights to Americans, African Americans and other groups still did not enjoy civil rights.**

Civics & You What would you do if you were denied equal rights when using public transportation or while sitting in a movie theater? Read to find out how the civil rights movement reacted.

Despite the advances made after the Civil War, African Americans routinely faced **discrimination,** or unfair treatment based on prejudice against a certain group. Southern states, for example, passed so-called "Jim Crow" laws requiring African Americans and whites to be separated in most public places, such as schools. Later, African Americans had to ride in the back of buses and sit in separate **sections,** or parts, of restaurants and theaters. They even had to use separate public restrooms. The social separation of the races was known as **segregation.** African Americans in the North fared better. They could vote freely, and segregation was less noticeable. Even so, prejudice restricted opportunities for many. It would take more than 100 years for African Americans to secure their **civil rights**—the rights of full citizenship and equality under the law.

The *Brown* Decision An important gain came in 1948, when President Harry S. Truman ordered an end to segregation in the nation's armed forces. A bigger victory was the Supreme Court's decision in *Brown* v. *Board of Education of Topeka, Kansas* (1954). In this landmark case, the Supreme Court ruled that racial segregation in the public schools was unconstitutional. Segregation violated the Fourteenth Amendment's principle of equal protection under the law.

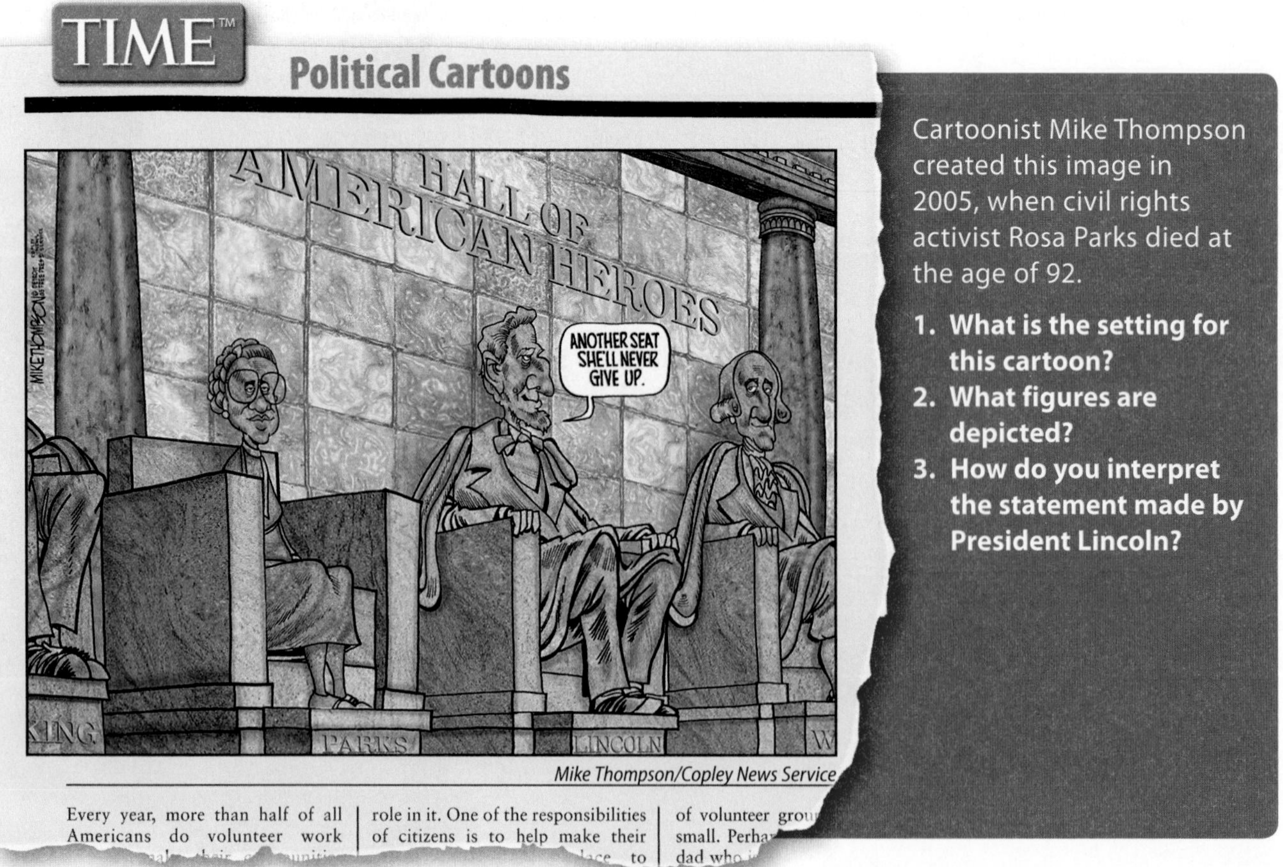

Cartoonist Mike Thompson created this image in 2005, when civil rights activist Rosa Parks died at the age of 92.

1. **What is the setting for this cartoon?**
2. **What figures are depicted?**
3. **How do you interpret the statement made by President Lincoln?**

American Biography

Martin Luther King, Jr. (1929–1968)

Born in Atlanta, Georgia, in 1929, **Martin Luther King, Jr.,** riveted the country's conscience as a leader of the civil rights movement. He was selected as Man of the Year by *TIME* magazine in 1963. King received the Nobel Peace Prize in 1964, making him the youngest man and third African American ever to receive this international award. His words and efforts moved many to join in the struggle for equal rights. What drove him into this demanding role in history?

The son of a Baptist minister, King attended Morehouse College and, when he was 18 years old, decided on a career in the ministry. By the time he first arrived in Montgomery in September 1954 as pastor of the Dexter Avenue Baptist Church, he had also met and married Coretta Scott.

From the beginning of the Montgomery bus boycott, King encouraged his followers to use nonviolent resistance. This meant that those who carried out the demonstrations should not fight with authorities. In spite of his stand on nonviolence, King often became the target of violence.

In April 1968, King was in Memphis, Tennessee, to support a strike of sanitation workers. There, the minister was shot and killed.

Making a Difference CITIZENSHIP

In what way does Dr. King's religious training show itself in his leadership of the civil rights movement?

Montgomery Bus Boycott In 1955, one year after the *Brown* decision, an African American woman named Rosa Parks was arrested for refusing to give up her seat to a white man on a Montgomery, Alabama, bus. Parks was arrested for violating Alabama's segregation laws. Her refusal and arrest spurred the local African American community to organize a boycott of the Montgomery bus system. A year later, the Supreme Court ruled that public bus segregation was unconstitutional. Both Parks and Dr. Martin Luther King, Jr., a leader of the boycott, gained national prominence.

Peaceful Protests A Baptist minister and stirring speaker, King believed in nonviolent resistance—the peaceful protest of unfair laws. He helped organize marches, boycotts, and demonstrations that opened many people's eyes to the need for change.

African American students began staging "sit-ins" at lunch counters that served only whites. White and African American "Freedom Riders" traveled together on buses to protest segregation. In his 1963 "I Have a Dream" speech, King inspired thousands with his hopes for racial equality.

Civil Rights Act of 1964 In response to the growing demand for government action, Congress passed the Civil Rights Act of 1964. This far-reaching law prohibited discrimination in public facilities, employment, education, and voter registration. It also banned discrimination not only by race and color but also by sex, or **gender,** religion, and national origin.

Reading Check **Describing** Through what means did Martin Luther King, Jr., hope to change unfair laws?

The Struggle Continues

Main idea **The struggle for equality in America has persisted and has extended to include many groups.**

Civics & You Regardless of your race, religion, or political beliefs, you have the right to be treated equally under the law. Read more about the efforts to fight discrimination.

Although the Fifteenth Amendment to the Constitution gave African American males the right to vote, that right was not always respected. By the 1960s, several states had found ways, such as the poll tax, to discourage African Americans from registering and voting.

Ratified in 1964, the Twenty-fourth Amendment outlawed poll taxes. The Voting Rights Act of 1965 took further steps to ensure that all citizens would have the opportunity to vote, regardless of race. As President Lyndon Johnson said when he signed the act,

> "*Millions of Americans are denied the right to vote because of their color. This law will ensure them the right to vote. The wrong is one which no American, in his heart, can justify.*"
>
> —President Lyndon B. Johnson

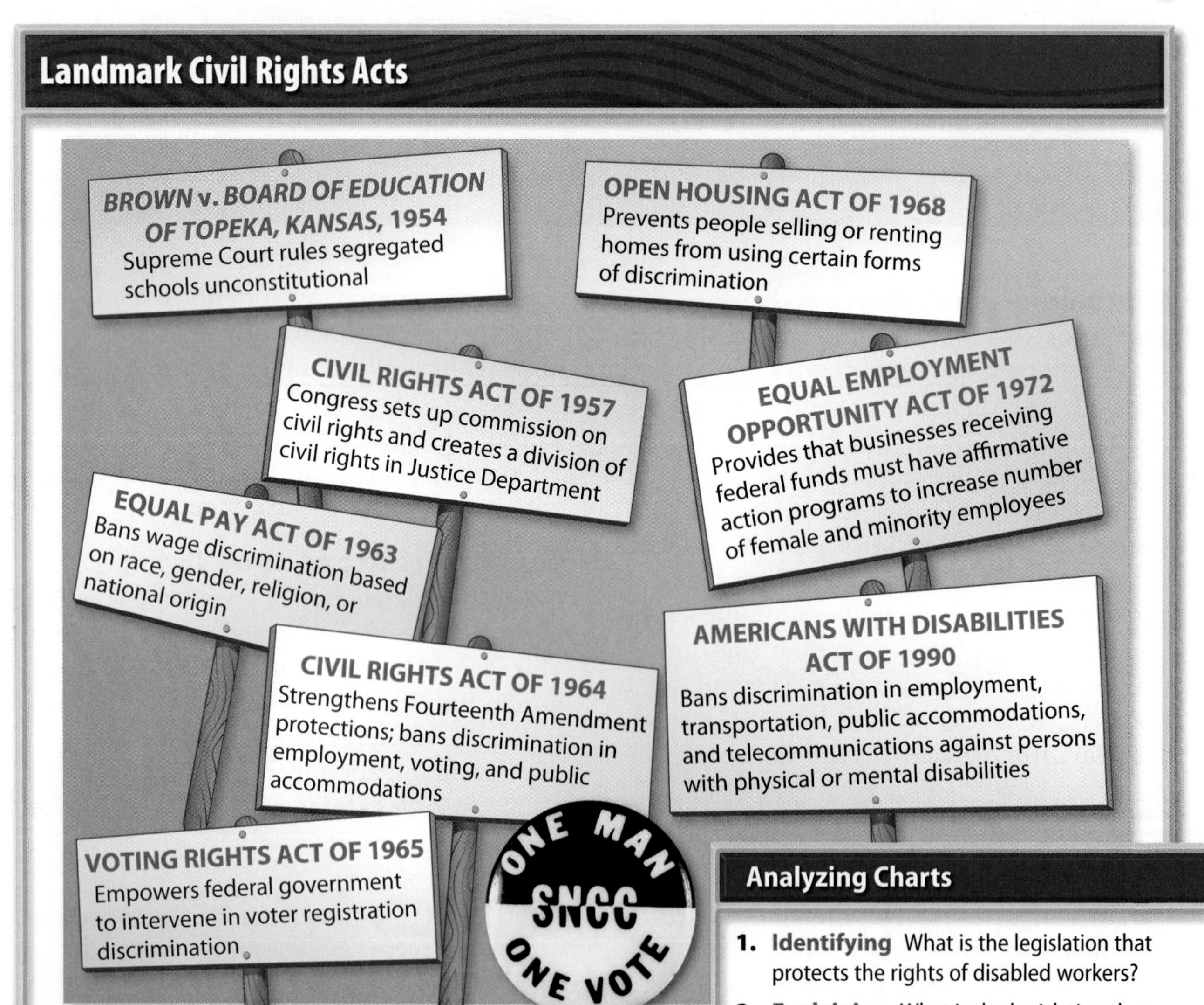

Analyzing Charts

1. **Identifying** What is the legislation that protects the rights of disabled workers?
2. **Explaining** What is the legislation that banned wage discrimination?

Civil Rights Gains

In 2006, the United States Senate renewed the Voting Rights Act of 1965, hailing it as one of the most effective pieces of civil rights legislation in history. The civil rights laws of the 1960s were instrumental in opening more doors for minorities. African Americans, Latinos, and other minorities have made striking gains in educational achievement. They increasingly hold professional and managerial jobs and serve in government, yet whites still tend to have more opportunities.

Affirmative Action

In the 1970s, the federal government began **affirmative action** programs to try to make up for past discrimination. These programs encouraged the hiring and promoting of minorities and women in fields that were traditionally closed to them. Colleges, too, practiced affirmative action to help minority students gain admission.

From the start, affirmative action was controversial. Critics complained that giving preferential treatment to women and minorities amounted to discrimination against men and whites. The Supreme Court case of *Gratz* v. *Bollinger* (2003) centered on affirmative action. The Court struck down a University of Michigan point-based admission policy, stating that it gave excessive points to minority applicants.

The struggle for equal rights continues. Each year, the federal government receives more than 75,000 complaints of workplace discrimination. Many Americans and others are sometimes subject to **racial profiling** by law enforcement officers—being singled out as suspects because of the way they look. Some Americans even become the victims of hate crimes—acts of violence based on a person's race, color, national origin, gender, or disability.

Reading Check **Explaining** What is the purpose of affirmative action programs?

Review

Vocabulary

1. **Write** a paragraph using the following terms to summarize the civil rights movement: *discrimination, segregation, civil rights, affirmative action, racial profiling.*

Main Ideas

2. **Identifying** List examples of the discrimination that African Americans faced after the Civil War.
3. **Describing** What other groups besides African Americans are struggling for equality under the law today?

Critical Thinking

4. **BIG Ideas** Why was the civil rights movement started?
5. **Identifying** Use the graphic organizer below to identify the areas of American life where affirmative action has been used.

6. **Analyzing Visuals** Reexamine the chart on page 142 that lists some landmark acts achieved by civil rights activists. What was the purpose of the Americans with Disabilities Act?

CITIZENSHIP Activity

7. **Persuasive Writing** Do you think that affirmative action laws are a fair way to change past discrimination? Write your opinion in a letter to the editor.

Study Central™ To review this section, go to glencoe.com.

Dred Scott v. Sandford

Before the Civil War, Americans were asking: Are African Americans citizens of the United States? May Congress prohibit enslavement of African Americans in U.S. territories?

Background of the Case

Dred Scott, an enslaved African American, worked for a physician. A member of the military, the physician moved often, taking Scott with him. As a result, Scott lived for a time in the state of Illinois and in the territory of Wisconsin, both slave-free zones. Both zones were also north of the boundary set by Congress in the Missouri Compromise of 1820. The Missouri Compromise permitted slavery south of the line and prohibited slavery north of it.

By 1846, the physician died, and Scott was again living in Missouri. There he continued to work for the physician's widow and her brother John Sanford, who was from New York. Scott sued for his freedom. He claimed that his earlier residence in a free state and a free territory made him free. Missouri's courts denied Scott, however. In order to claim federal court jurisdiction, Scott's lawyers then stated that Scott was a citizen of Missouri bringing suit against Sanford, a citizen of New York.

Dred Scott

The Decision

The Supreme Court decided the case on March 6–7, 1857. Chief Justice Roger B. Taney spoke for the seven-justice majority. Taney first asserted his own view of the Framers' so-called original intent: "The only rights and privileges African Americans were meant to have were those granted by their so-called 'owners' or by the government. Therefore, Dred Scott could not be a citizen." He wrote further:

> ***"[I]t is the opinion of the Court that the act of Congress which prohibited . . . [slaveholding] north of the line therein mentioned is . . . void; and that neither Dred Scott himself, nor any member of his family were made free by being carried into this territory."***
>
> —Chief Justice Roger B. Taney

The Court was saying that the suit of noncitizen Scott and the Missouri Compromise were unconstitutional. Therefore, Scott was not free.

Why It Matters

The ruling added to the tensions that led to the Civil War. In 1868, three years after the end of the war, the Fourteenth Amendment to the United States Constitution overruled the *Dred Scott* decision.

Analyzing the Court Decision

1. **Explaining** Why was Dred Scott not freed as a result of the Supreme Court's decision?
2. **Inferring** What is your opinion of Justice Taney's view of the Framers' "original intent"?

Chapter 4

Visual Summary

Rights of Citizens

The Bill of Rights—the first 10 amendments to the U.S. Constitution—guarantees certain basic rights to all Americans. The Bill of Rights ensures constitutional guarantees of

- freedom of expression and belief;
- individual security; and
- equal and fair treatment before the law.

First North Carolina sit-in, 1960s

Limits on Rights

- An individual's rights must be balanced with the rights of others and the community's health and safety.

Equality Under the Law

- Limits on rights must be reasonable and apply equally to all.
- This is especially critical in the courtroom, which is where the right to due process comes into play.
- Due process means that government may not act unfairly or arbitrarily but must follow a set of reasonable, fair, and standard procedures.

Civil Rights

- Civil rights are the protections granted in the Constitution that recognize all citizens must be treated equally under the law.
- In the United States at one time, there were widespread segregation laws.

Suffragist parade, 1913

Civil Rights march on Washington, D.C., 1963

- In *Plessy* v. *Ferguson* (1896), the Supreme Court ruled that separate-but-equal facilities were constitutional.
- In *Brown* v. *Board of Education of Topeka* (1954), the Court ruled for complete desegregation.
- The civil rights movement made possible the passage of legislation guaranteeing basic civil rights for all Americans.

STUDY TO GO

Study anywhere, anytime! Download quizzes and flash cards to your PDA from glencoe.com.

Chapter 4

Standardized Test Practice

Assessment

TEST-TAKING TIP

For effective recall at exam time, study in one-half-hour intervals for a week before the test.

Reviewing Vocabulary

Directions: Choose the word(s) that best completes the sentence.

1. The First Amendment guarantees the right to ________.

A libel
B slander
C petition
D due process

2. The right of the government to take private property for public use is called ________.

A suffrage
B civil right
C eminent domain
D double jeopardy

3. ________ in Southern states prevented many African Americans from voting.

A poll taxes
B age requirements
C civil rights
D search warrants

4. Sometimes law enforcement officials single out suspects unfairly through ________.

A indictments
B racial profiling
C censorship
D affirmative action

Reviewing Main Ideas

Directions: Choose the best answer for each question.

Section 1 *(pp.120–124)*

5. Which of the following does the Bill of Rights protect?

A the right to provoke a riot for a good cause
B the power of government to operate efficiently
C the freedom to act without government interference
D the choice to overthrow an unjust government by force

6. What does the First Amendment prohibit?

A assembly of groups such as communists
B establishment of an official state religion
C criticism of the government or its officials
D dissemination of alarming or offensive ideas

Section 2 *(pp. 126–131)*

7. How does the Fifth Amendment help accused persons?

A by requiring a speedy trial
B by requiring a search warrant
C by guaranteeing a trial by jury
D by protecting against self incrimination

8. Which amendment states that all rights not spelled out in the Constitution are "retained by the people"?

A Second Amendment
B Third Amendment
C Seventh Amendment
D Ninth Amendment

Section 3 *(pp. 133–137)*

9. Which amendment guaranteed African American men the right to vote?

A Thirteenth Amendment
B Fourteenth Amendment
C Fifteenth Amendment
D Nineteenth Amendment

10. Whose right to vote did the Twenty-sixth Amendment guarantee?

A poor people in the South
B women across the country
C residents of Washington, D.C.
D citizens 18 years old and older

GO ON

Section 4 *(pp. 139–143)*

11. Which sphere of American life was desegregated in the 1940s?

A schools

B work places

C armed forces

D lunch counters

12. Which measure outlawed poll taxes?

A Civil Rights Act of 1957

B Civil Rights Act of 1954

C Voting Rights Act of 1965

D Twenty-fourth Amendment

Critical Thinking

Directions: Base your answers to questions 13 and 14 on the table below and your knowledge of Chapter 4.

Rights and Freedoms in the Bill of Rights
Trial by jury
Due process
Private property
No unreasonable searches or seizures
No cruel punishment
No excessive bail or fines
Right to bear arms
Right to petition
Freedom of speech
Freedom of the press
Freedom of religion

13. Which amendment protects freedom of speech?

A First Amendment

B Fifth Amendment

C Thirteenth Amendment

D Twenty-fourth Amendment

14. Which right or freedom best reflects the humane intent of Anglo-American law?

A the right to bear arms

B the freedom of the press

C the right to private property

D the freedom from cruel punishment

Document-Based Questions

Directions: Analyze the following document and answer the short-answer questions that follow.

> Amendment XXII
>
> Section 1
>
> *No person shall be elected to the office of the President more than twice, and no person who had held the office of President, or acted as President, for more than two years of a term to which some other person was elected president shall be elected to the office of President more than once.*
>
> —the Constitution

15. A presidential term lasts four years. According to the Twenty-second Amendment, what is the longest time one person may serve as president?

16. Why do you think Congress and the state legislatures considered the Twenty-second Amendment necessary?

Extended-Response Question

17. Write a brief essay explaining how the Ninth and Tenth Amendments prevent the national government from becoming too strong.

STOP

For additional test practice, use Self-Check Quizzes—Chapter 4 on glencoe.com.

Need Extra Help?

If you missed question...	1	2	3	4	5	6	7	8	9	10	11	12	13	14	15	16	17
Go to page...	121	128	134	143	121	124	128	131	135	137	140	142	122	129	135	135	131

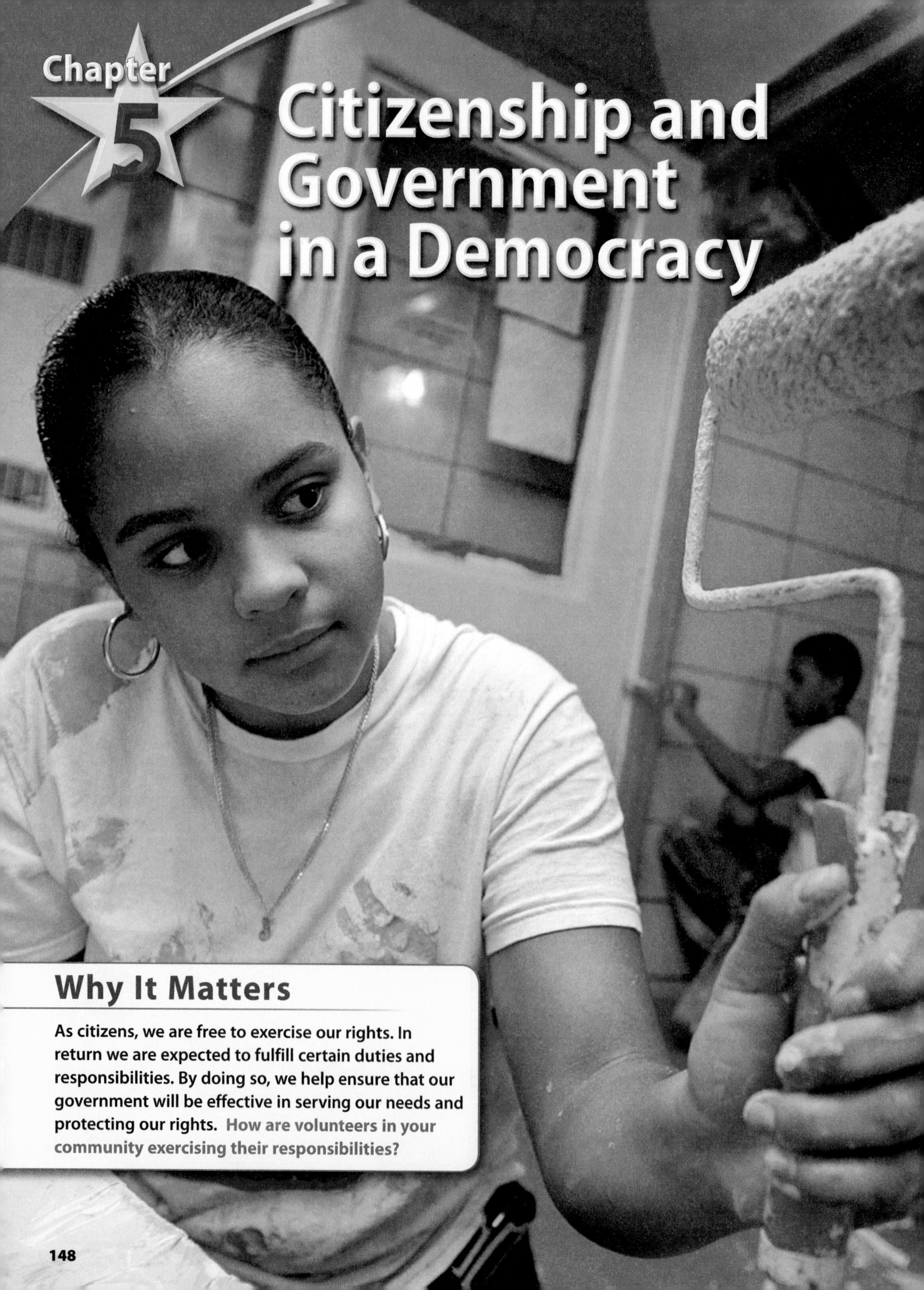

Chapter 5

Citizenship and Government in a Democracy

Why It Matters

As citizens, we are free to exercise our rights. In return we are expected to fulfill certain duties and responsibilities. By doing so, we help ensure that our government will be effective in serving our needs and protecting our rights. How are volunteers in your community exercising their responsibilities?

Civics ONLINE
Visit glencoe.com and enter QuickPass™ code CIV3093c5 for Chapter 5 resources.

Chapter Audio

BIG Ideas

Section 1: Duties and Responsibilities

For government to be effective, citizens must fulfill their civic duties and responsibilities. As American citizens, we enjoy many rights under our system of government. Along with those rights, we also share many responsibilities. These responsibilities help protect our rights.

Section 2: Citizens and the Community

Citizen participation is essential to the foundation and preservation of the U.S. political system. Good citizenship does not depend on each of us doing only what we are required to do by law. The American ideal of citizenship has always stressed each citizen's responsibility to participate in his or her community.

◀ Young volunteer in the Publicolors Paint Club spruces up her New York City school

Comparing Information Study Foldable Make this Foldable to help you compare responsibilities of the citizen and the community.

Step 1 Fold one sheet of paper in half from side to side.

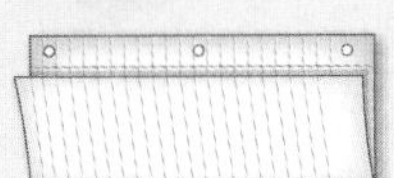

Step 2 Turn the paper and fold it into thirds.

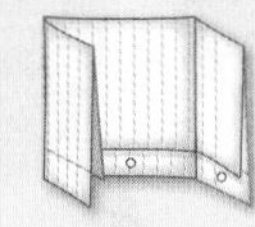

Step 3 Unfold and draw two overlapping ovals, and label them as shown.

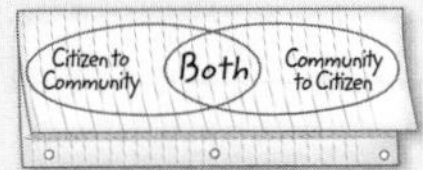

Step 4 Cut only the top layer along both fold lines.

Reading and Writing
As you read this chapter, list the responsibilities the citizen has to the community and those that the community has to the citizen under the appropriate tabs of your Foldable. Be sure to fill out the "Both" area, too.

Section Audio · Spotlight Video

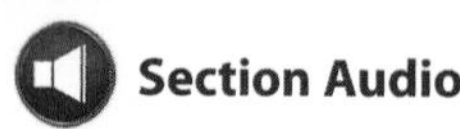

Section 1

Duties and Responsibilities

Guide to Reading

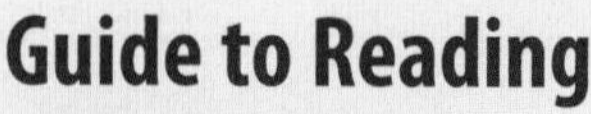

Big Idea
For government to be effective, citizens must fulfill their civic duties and responsibilities.

Content Vocabulary
- responsibility *(p. 151)*
- duty *(p. 151)*
- draft *(p. 152)*
- tolerance *(p. 154)*

Academic Vocabulary
- global *(p. 151)*
- income *(p. 152)*

Reading Strategy
Summarizing Information
As you read, on a web diagram like the one below, list the legal duties of U.S. citizens.

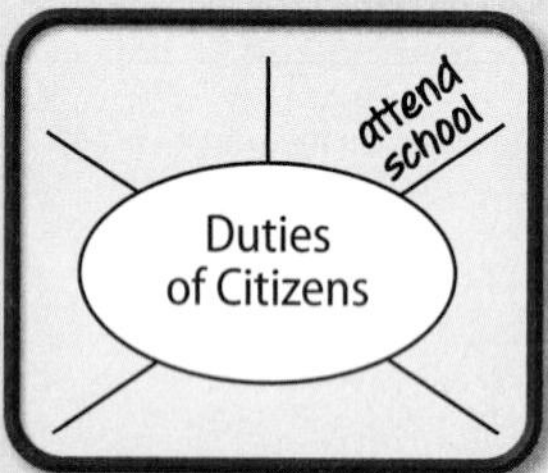

Real World Civics Kirk Bauer is no stranger to a challenge. As a young soldier in Vietnam in 1969, Bauer lost his leg to a grenade blast. Today, after years of surgeries and rehabilitation, Bauer is the executive director of Disabled Sports USA, an organization dedicated to providing sports rehabilitation to persons with permanent disabilities. Because Bauer was introduced to skiing by other Vietnam veterans, he has focused his energy on providing rehabilitation opportunities for veterans injured in conflicts in Iraq and Afghanistan.

▼ **Kirk Bauer competes at the Hartford Ski Spectacular in Breckenridge, Colorado.**

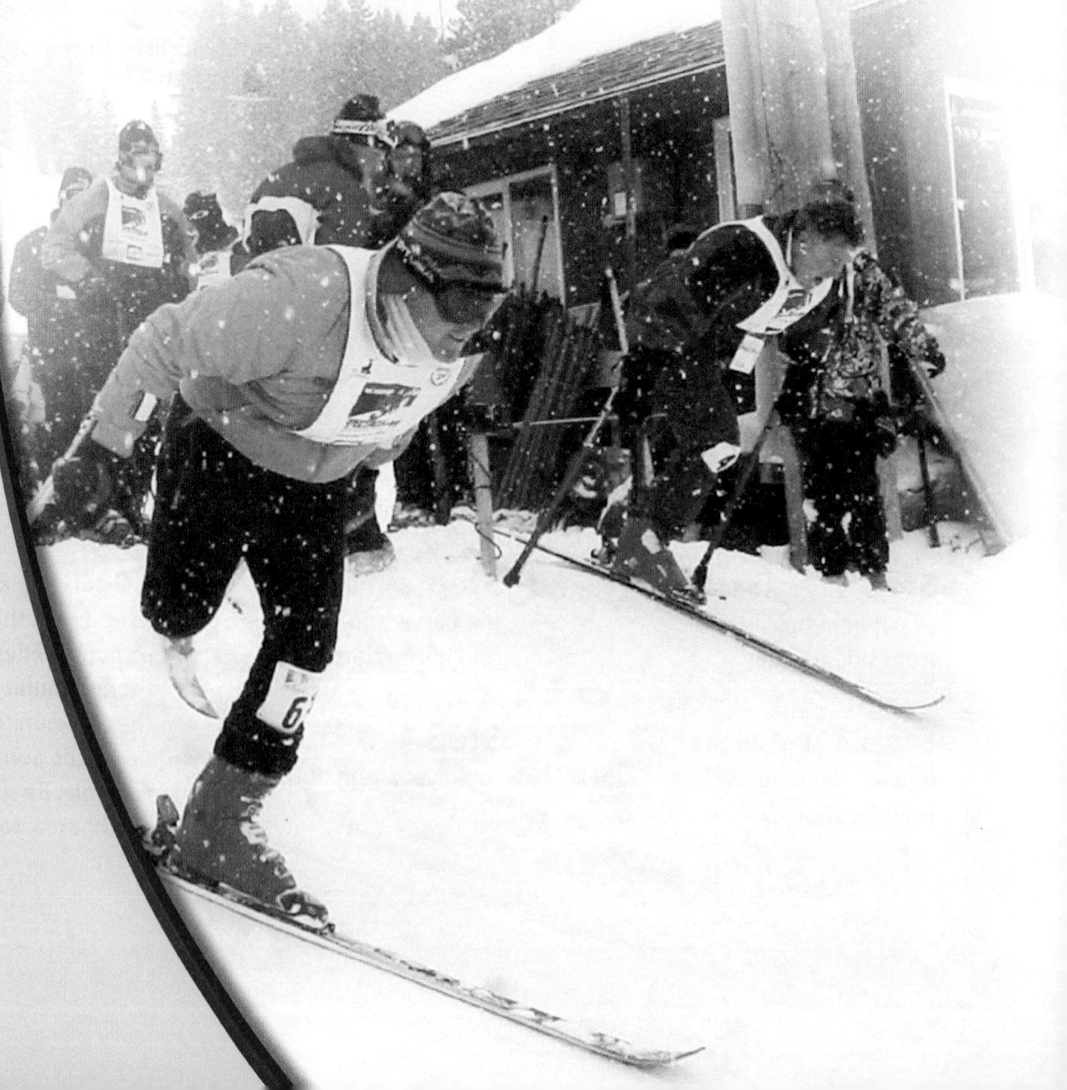

Duties of Citizens

Main Idea **The privilege of U.S. citizenship brings with it certain duties and responsibilities.**

Civics & You Are you a good citizen? What are the duties and the responsibilities of citizenship? Read on to find out why American citizens have a responsibility to their communities, the environment, and the law.

What comes to mind when you hear the word "community"? Do you think of your neighborhood or perhaps your town? Actually, each of us belongs to many communities—our school or workplace; our church, synagogue, or mosque; our state; and our country. On the broadest level, we are also members of the **global,** or worldwide, community becoming more connected than ever before with people around the world.

We all play a part in making our communities safe and successful. All of us have certain responsibilities to fulfill. **Responsibilities** are things we should do; they are obligations that we fulfill voluntarily. As American citizens, we also have legal duties that we are required to perform. **Duties** are things that we are required to do.

National, state, and local governments require Americans to perform certain duties established by laws. If we fail to perform them, we are subject to legal penalties, such as fines or imprisonment.

Some countries require much from their citizens. In some countries, for example, citizens must serve in the armed forces for a period of time each year. The United States government asks much less of its citizens than many other countries. Nonetheless, the government does require its citizens to perform the following duties.

Civics ONLINE

Student Web Activity Visit glencoe.com and complete the Chapter 5 Web Activity.

Duties As citizens of the United States, we all have certain duties, such as defending the nation. ***Explaining*** **Why is it important to fulfill our duties as citizens?**

Obey Laws

This is a citizen's most important duty. Our laws are designed for specific purposes—to help people get along, to prevent accidents, to see that resources are used fairly, and so on. If we do not obey the law, then communities cannot maintain order or protect our health, safety, and property.

Pay Taxes

Another duty of citizens is to pay taxes. Taxes provide most of the money government needs to keep functioning. Without taxes, the federal government could not pay its employees, maintain armed forces to defend the country, and help those in need. Your local community probably could not hire police or firefighters, and your state could not pave roads or maintain prisons.

The federal government and some states and cities collect **income,** or earnings, in the form of taxes—a percentage of what people earn. Most states and some cities collect taxes on the sale of goods and services. Your school district collects taxes on the residential and commercial property within the district.

Defend the Nation

Under the law, men aged 18 to 25 are required to register with the government in case the country needs to **draft,** or call up, men for military service. Since the end of the Vietnam War, there has been no draft, and America's military has been made up of volunteers. The draft is typically used only in the event of war or extreme national emergency.

Serve in Court

The Constitution guarantees the right to a trial by jury. Every adult citizen must be prepared to serve on a jury. People can be excused from jury duty if they have a valid reason, but service is usually rewarding. People involved in court cases depend on their fellow citizens to reach a fair verdict. Another duty of citizens is to serve as witnesses at a trial if called to do so.

Attend School

All young people have access to free public schools and, in most states, are required to attend school until the age of 16. This benefits both you and the government because you need knowledge and skills to be a good citizen. In school you not only gain an understanding of history, government, and other important subjects, but you also learn to think through problems, to form opinions, and to express your views clearly.

Reading Check **Explaining** Why must all citizens pay taxes?

TIME™ Teens in *Action*

Bring It On!

Geneva Johnson, 17, runs a group in New York City that gives hope and guidance to inner-city kids.

Geneva Johnson was 14 when she and her two siblings watched in horror as a stranger shot a man waiting for a parking space outside their Bronx apartment. "We were so scared," she says. "We just hit the floor." Living in a neighborhood so dangerous her parents forbade her to use the local playground, Johnson was determined to give other kids options—and hope.

To do that, Johnson founded Bring It On! (www.bringitonnyc.org). It is a youth group that tries to fire up the dreams and ambitions of underprivileged kids. Although she gets some money as donations from corporations and local businesses, Johnson also contributes money from her own pocket. With siblings Jeremiah, 18, and Christina, 14, she runs a neighborhood art gallery. For the 50 or so members of Bring It On!—most are from her Eastchester Heights neighborhood—Johnson runs seminars on starting up businesses and ways to make money. Johnson also hosts monthly panels called You Go Girl Go!! where women who have overcome obstacles tell their stories to girls.

Geneva Johnson helps inner-city kids create art in New York City.

Making a Difference — CITIZENSHIP

Write a paragraph explaining how Geneva Johnson's project has helped others and Geneva herself.

Civic Responsibilities

Main Idea **The voluntary responsibilities of U.S. citizens include participating in the political process and being informed.**

Civics & You As a citizen, what do you think is your most important responsibility? Read to find out what voluntary actions are part of good citizenship.

Be Informed

Keep in mind that government decisions affect your life. The state legislature, for example, might pass a law changing the rate of sales tax you pay. Your school board might vote to start the school day earlier. Your town council might set aside funds for a new recreation center. You have a responsibility to know what the government is doing so that you can voice your opinions on matters about which you feel strongly.

Speak Up and Vote

Our government is based on the principle of "consent of the governed." This means that people are the source of all governmental power; that is, government exists to serve you. If you expect public officials to act in your interests, you can make your concerns known by contacting your elected representatives, working for a particular cause, or, above all, by voting.

Voting is one of American citizens' most important responsibilities. By electing leaders and voting on proposed measures, Americans give their consent to the government. As former President Franklin D. Roosevelt said,

> *"The ultimate rulers of our democracy are not a President and Senators and Congressmen and Government officials but the voters of this country."*
>
> —Franklin D. Roosevelt, *Address at Marietta*

Citizens' Duties and Responsibilities

RIGHTS
• **Security**—protection by government
• **Equality**—equal treatment under the law
• **Liberty**—rights guaranteed under the Constitution
DUTIES
• Obey the law
• Pay taxes
• Defend the nation
• Serve in court
• Attend school
RESPONSIBILITIES
• Be informed and vote
• Participate in your community and government
• Respect the rights and property of others
• Respect different opinions and ways of life

Analyzing Charts

1. **Recognizing** Is voting a right or a responsibility of American citizens?
2. **Comparing** How do duties differ from responsibilities?

In the United States today, all citizens of at least 18 years of age have the right to vote. Each Election Day, citizens have the chance to shape the future of our communities, states, and nation by voting. Thoughtful voters study the candidates and issues carefully before marking their ballots. They also regularly check on what their elected leaders are doing. If an official's performance falls short, it is up to the voters to choose someone else in the next election. Voting responsibly ensures that leadership is changed in a peaceful and orderly manner.

Respect Others' Rights

In order for you to enjoy your rights, you have a responsibility to respect the rights of others. For example, if you own a dog, you have an obligation to keep it from becoming a nuisance to your neighbors. In a democratic society like ours, with such a diverse population, it is especially important to respect the civil liberties of others. Although you may disagree with people or disapprove of their lifestyles, they have an equal right to their beliefs and practices. Respecting and accepting others, regardless of their beliefs, practices, or differences, is called **tolerance.** Treating others politely and respectfully is thus part of being a good citizen. Many of our laws encourage people to respect each other's rights.

You also have a responsibility to respect public and private property. Some people might claim that "no one gets hurt" when they litter in a park or paint graffiti on a school wall, yet such public property belongs to us all, and we all pay if it is damaged.

Contribute to the Common Good

Responsible citizens show concern for others as well as for themselves. They are willing to give time, effort, and money to improve community life for all.

The members of a community must be actively concerned with promoting the health and welfare of every one of its members so that each member can contribute to the common good, or the things that benefit all members of the community. For example, everyone benefits from having safe streets, good schools, and a clean environment.

Think about what your community would be like if no one donated to charities, volunteered in after-school programs, or lent a hand at the local health clinic. What if no one ever spoke out about community problems? Communities and governments need people to participate.

Reading Check **Explaining** Why is being informed about your government an important responsibility?

Vocabulary

1. **Define** *responsiblity, duty, draft,* and *tolerance.* Use them in sentences related to U.S. citizenship.

Main Ideas

2. **Identify** three duties of U.S. citizens.
3. **Describing** What are the responsibilities of American citizens?

Critical Thinking

4. **BIG Ideas** Why are citizens' responsibilities to their communities an important part of our democratic system?
5. **Explaining** Why is it important to respect the rights of others?
6. **Describing** On a graphic organizer like the one below, describe three ways you can express your views and influence government.

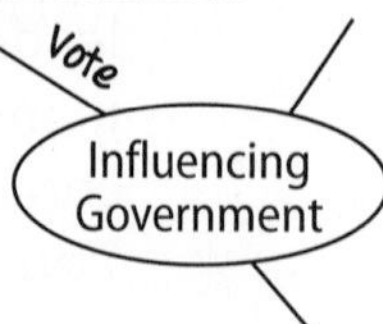

CITIZENSHIP Activity

7. **Expository Writing** What do you think would happen if the legal duties of citizens became voluntary? Write a paragraph explaining your answers.

Study Central™ To review this section, go to glencoe.com.

Financial Literacy

Federal Revenues and Expenditures

"The only constants in life are death and taxes." Perhaps you have heard someone utter that line. At the federal level, there are three major taxes: the individual income tax, the corporate income tax, and the Social Security tax. Many people do not know how their tax dollars are being used. Where does the money go?

Where Your Tax Dollars Go

Social Security 21.1%

National Defense 17.2%

Income Security 14.0%

Medicare 12.0%

Health Benefits 10.4%

Net Interest 7.2%

Education and Other Health Services 3.9%

Other 14.2%

Where Your Tax Dollars Come From

Individual Income Taxes 45.4%

Corporate Income Taxes 11.5%

Other Taxes 3.8%

Social Security Taxes, other Retirement, Insurance 39.3%

Source: Department of the Treasury; Congressional Budget Office, 2006.

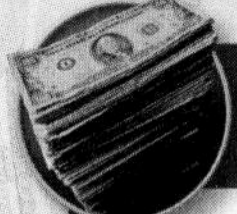

Analyzing Economics

1. **Concluding** Should we be required to pay taxes? Why or why not?
2. **Prioritizing** How would you change the top diagram if you were able to assign how your tax money would be spent? Why?

 Section Audio  Spotlight Video

Section 2

Citizens and the Community

Guide to Reading

Big Idea
Citizen participation is essential to the foundation and preservation of the U.S. political system.

Content Vocabulary
- bureaucracy *(p. 157)*
- welfare *(p. 158)*
- volunteerism *(p. 158)*

Academic Vocabulary
- percent *(p. 158)*
- register *(p. 160)*
- domestic *(p. 160)*
- annual *(p. 162)*

Reading Strategy
Organizing Information
As you read, complete a graphic organizer like the one below in which you list ways that people can take action and contribute to their community.

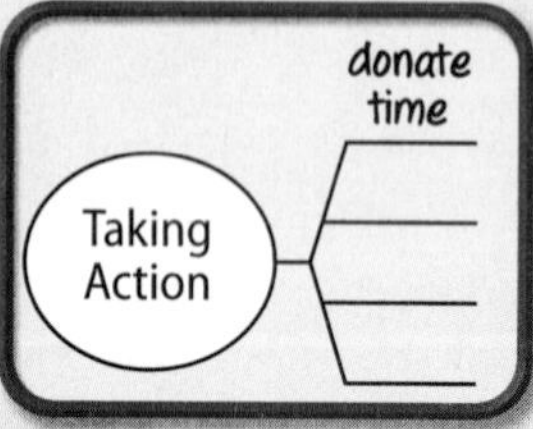

Real World Civics The "Dragon Slayers" are teen members of the Aniak Volunteer Fire Department in Alaska. All members must undergo extensive training. In addition to fire fighting, the teens are trained as medics. Contributing to their tiny community located near Anchorage is uppermost in the minds of these young people. All volunteers must vow to abstain from drugs and alcohol and maintain passing grades in school.

▼ **The group's volunteers—the youngest is 13—serve on the only emergency medical team within 10,000 square miles of Aniak, Alaska.**

Civic Responsibility Volunteer crews rescue a Mississippi family trapped by flooding caused by 2005's Hurricane Katrina. ***Explaining*** **Why is it important that citizens support their communities?**

Citizen Involvement

Main Idea **By volunteering, we make our communities better places to live, gain new opportunities to solve problems, and learn new things.**

Civics & You Have you volunteered to help out at school or in your community? Read on to find out why it is important for citizens to volunteer.

Why do volunteers such as the Dragon Slayers do so much work without pay? John Gatus, a retired steamfitter who volunteers in an anti-gang neighborhood patrol, explains his reason:

> *"Volunteer work brings real change, change you can be a part of, change you can see with your own eyes."*
>
> —John Gatus, as quoted in "America's Voluntary Spirit"

Every year, more than half of all Americans do volunteer work to help make their communities better places to live. A community is a group of people who share the same interests and concerns. These volunteers include more than 14 million students in grades 6 through 12. Without the efforts of so many private citizens, many pressing social needs simply would not be met.

In the United States, federal, state, and local government provides many different services. We rely on government for everything from local police protection to national defense, from collecting household trash to ensuring clean water and air nationwide.

Citizens, though, also share responsibility for meeting community needs. The government, after all, has limited resources. In addition, governments are **bureaucracies**—complex systems with many departments, many rules, and many people in the chain of command.

TIME™

Political Cartoons

Marshall Ramsey/Copley News Service

In 2005, Hurricane Katrina dealt devastating blows to communities in Louisiana and Mississippi. Cartoonist Marshall Ramsey shows help arriving.

1. **Based only on the first panel of the cartoon, what would you imagine Ramsey sees as "the most powerful force in nature"?**
2. **Looking at the second panel, what event do you think inspired this cartoon, which was drawn in the summer of 2005?**
3. **How does Ramsey feel about volunteerism?**

Because of this, government cannot always respond quickly or efficiently to problems. In many cases, the best solutions come from private citizens. Good citizens are concerned about the **welfare**—the health, prosperity, and happiness—of all members of the community.

In 1961 President John F. Kennedy issued a challenge: "Ask not what your country can do for you; ask what you can do for your country." President George W. Bush in 2005 noted that we can show "the world the true values of America through the gathering momentum of a million acts of responsibility and decency and service."

Donating Time and Money

People help their communities in many ways, working independently or as part of volunteer groups both large and small. Neighbors might gather to spend a Saturday cleaning up a highway or preparing holiday baskets for needy families. Retirees mentor schoolchildren, record books for the blind, and lead museum tours. You and your fellow students might visit nursing home patients, volunteer in an animal shelter, or collect canned goods for a local food pantry.

Giving your time to work on community projects is the core of **volunteerism**—the practice of offering your time and services to others without payment. However, Americans may also support worthy causes by contributing money. Annually, individual Americans give more than $250 billion to charity. Much of this money comes from small donations by average citizens. The typical American donates about 2 **percent,** or portion of an amount in hundredths, of his or her income to charity.

Reading Check **Defining** What is volunteerism?

American Biography

Marian Wright Edelman (1939–)

Marian Wright Edelman once told an interviewer that she "never for a moment lacked a purpose worth fighting, living, or dying for." At first, Edelman found her purpose in the civil rights movement of the 1950s and 1960s. Then, in 1973, she organized the Children's Defense Fund (CDF). The CDF's mission is to institute programs to keep children healthy, in school, and out of trouble.

Edelman, the youngest of five children, credits her parents with teaching her to help other people. "Working for the community was as much a part of our existence as eating and sleeping," Edelman recalled. With her parents' support, she obtained a law degree and went on to become the first African American woman to practice law in Mississippi. She also served as a leader in the NAACP Legal Defense and Education Fund.

Edelman's work with the CDF earned her the reputation as "the children's crusader." Today the CDF is the leading lobby on behalf of children, especially the more than 12 million children who live in poverty. In 2000, Edelman received the Presidential Medal of Freedom, the nation's highest civilian award. In 2005, Edelman and the CDF responded to the destruction along the Gulf Coast caused by Hurricane Katrina by aiding hurricane survivors and helping displaced families locate their loved ones.

Making a Difference CITIZENSHIP

Edelman wrote that "service is the rent we pay to be living." ***Explaining*** **How does this apply to Edelman's life and work?**

Volunteers in Action

Main Idea **Young people can make a difference by volunteering.**

Civics & You Is it okay to want some benefits for yourself from volunteering? Think about this question as you read.

Responsible citizens are concerned about the welfare of the community as a whole. They may be concerned about the environment, or surroundings of the community, or about the quality of life.

Safeguarding these things may require government action. It could mean cleaning up a toxic waste dump that is polluting the water, adding more police officers to combat drug trafficking, or building more parks.

Having concern for our communities is not enough, however. Our concern must be supported by our action. No community or government has the money or resources to provide for the welfare of all its people or to solve all its problems. It counts on volunteers to help.

Community Involvement

Community involvement tends to be rooted in individual action and informal groups. People are more likely to participate when they feel a connection to a cause or know others involved. Thus they join their Neighborhood Watch or become active at their child's school. They reach out to the community through their religious congregations or their work through service clubs such as the Lions and Kiwanis. Some people, however, volunteer through more formal channels.

Charitable Organizations

More than 1 million charities are officially **registered,** or recorded, with the federal government. Many are small and locally based. These organizations often work on one or two projects, such as helping the victims of **domestic,** or home, abuse or preserving a historic building. Other organizations are large national charities serving millions of people.

School-Based Programs

More than half of all United States middle and high schools now arrange community service for students in grades 6 through 12. Several hundred school districts in various states even require it. In Atlanta, Chicago, and the entire state of Maryland, for example, high school students must volunteer a set number of hours to earn a graduation diploma.

National Service Programs

During his Inaugural Address in 1961, President John F. Kennedy challenged Americans to work together to fight poverty, disease, and war in the poorest corners of the world. Less than two months later, Kennedy signed an executive order establishing the Peace Corps.

Since that time, the Peace Corps has sent more than 180,000 Americans to 138 countries, where they advise farmers, teach children and young adults, help start small businesses, and fight the spread of AIDS.

AmeriCorps Here in the United States, AmeriCorps members help meet the nation's needs in education, public safety, health, and the environment. More than 50,000 Americans participate each year in AmeriCorps. In return for a year of full-time service, organization members receive an allowance to live on and money to help pay for college.

Global Responsibility Peace Corps volunteers learn about installing toilet bowls in preparation for work in Western Samoa. ***Explaining*** **Why is it important that people support communities around the world?**

American Volunteers in Action

Graphs In MOtion
See StudentWorks™ Plus or glencoe.com.

Source: *Statistical Abstract of the United States,* 2006.

National Service Programs	
USA Freedom Corps	Brings together Peace Corps, AmeriCorps, and Senior Corps
Peace Corps	Advises farmers, teaches children, starts small businesses, and fights serious diseases worldwide
Ameri-Corps	Meets community needs, helps victims of natural disasters, cleans polluted rivers, and assists disabled people
Senior Corps	Volunteer opportunities for Americans 55 and older: • Foster Grandparents—help special-needs kids • Senior Companions—help other seniors at home • Retired and Senior Volunteer Program (RSVP)—connects seniors to volunteer opportunities in their own communities

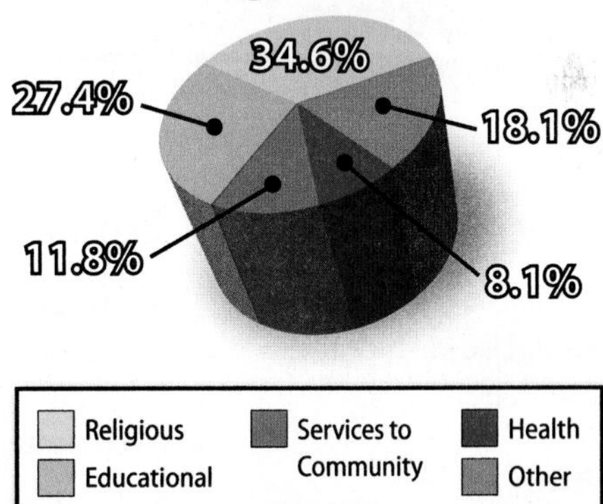

Source: *Statistical Abstract of the United States,* 2005.

Analyzing Graphs

1. **Identifying** What national service organization provides help for people in other countries?
2. **Comparing** Which age group of Americans has the highest percentage of people volunteering? Why do you think this is so?

Senior Corps The Senior Corps provides volunteer opportunities to Americans aged 55 or older. These senior citizens take part in three main programs. Foster Grandparents work one-on-one with children with special needs. Senior Companions help other seniors meet their daily needs while living independently in their own homes. The Retired and Senior Volunteer Program provides seniors with volunteer opportunities in their communities.

USA Freedom Corps On January 29, 2002, in his **annual,** or yearly, State of the Union address, President Bush asked Americans to join together and help, saying, "If you aren't sure how to help, I've got a good place to start."

Bush described a new program, called USA Freedom Corps. The program brings together the Peace Corps, AmeriCorps, and Senior Corps. Freedom Corps was designed to focus on three areas of need: responding to national emergencies, rebuilding our communities, and extending American compassion throughout the world.

Voluntary Spirit

Americans have a long history of volunteering. When Alexis de Tocqueville, a French political writer, visited America in the 1830s, he was amazed to see citizens pitching in to solve community problems rather than relying on the government. He explained it as "self-interest rightly understood." In other words, by banding together to serve the community, we really serve ourselves. For example, more than 50,000 Americans participate each year in AmeriCorps. Most work through local and national organizations such as Habitat for Humanity.

Reading Check **Identifying** What organization provides opportunities for volunteers 55 years of age or older?

Vocabulary

1. **Define** *bureaucracy, welfare,* and *volunteerism.* Use each of these terms in sentences.

Main Ideas

2. **Explaining** Why is it important for citizens to volunteer?
3. **Describing** Provide at least two examples of useful services provided by volunteer groups and organizations in a community.

Critical Thinking

4. **BIG Ideas** Explain why citizens have a responsibility to turn their concerns for their community into action.
5. **Identifying** On a graphic organizer like the one below, list channels through which an individual can volunteer.

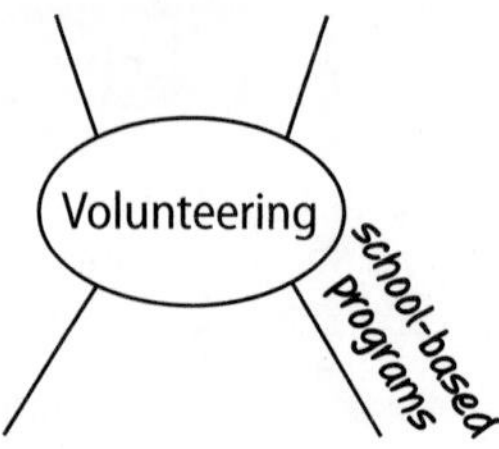

CITIZENSHIP Activity

6. **Expository Writing** Do research or contact a local volunteer organization that was mentioned in Section 2 of this chapter. Find out what projects or problems they are working on in your community and how they use volunteers. Write a one-page essay in which you provide answers to these questions.

Study Central™ To review this section, go to glencoe.com.

Visual Summary

Citizenship

- The combination of rights, responsibilities, and duties characterizes what it means to be a citizen of a free democratic society.
- As citizens, we are free to exercise our rights.
- In return, we are expected to fulfill certain duties and responsibilities.

Why Should I Participate?

- A key part of being a good citizen is taking an active and engaged role in your community.
- A well-planned project gives you opportunities to practice your rights and responsibilities as a citizen.
- You make a difference by participating. Your efforts are needed, valued, and respected.
- When you share your knowledge and skills to help others, you develop new skills and cultivate new knowledge.

Neighborhood crime prevention

NEIGHBORHOOD CRIME WATCH
TAKE A BITE OUT OF CRIME
WE IMMEDIATELY REPORT ALL SUSPICIOUS ACTIVITIES TO OUR POLICE DEPARTMENT
IN COOPERATION WITH OUR LOCAL POLICE DEPARTMENT

Registering to vote

Our Duties

Duties are things we are required to do by law.

- One of the duties of all Americans is to obey the law.
- Americans have a duty to pay taxes.
- Another duty of citizenship is to defend the nation.

Our Responsibilities

Responsibilities are things we should do. Civic responsibilities include:

- being informed;
- speaking up and voting;
- respecting others' rights;
- respecting diversity; and
- contributing to the common good.

Active Citizens

- Participate in community service
- Do their part to make their schools, communities, and the world a better place

City street cleanup

Study anywhere, anytime! Download quizzes and flash cards to your PDA from glencoe.com.

Chapter 5

Assessment

TEST-TAKING TIP

When reviewing for a test, pay special attention to bold type, questions, and summary paragraphs in your text.

Reviewing Vocabulary

Directions: Choose the word(s) that best completes the sentence.

1. Men 18 to 25 years of age are required to register in case the country needs to draft them for ______.

A military duty **C** jury duty
B volunteer service **D** school attendance

2. Listening to a neighbor in a different political party shows ______.

A tolerance **C** compassion
B obedience **D** responsibility

3. Recording books for the blind is an example of ______.

A civic duty **C** civic responsibility
B volunteerism **D** government activity

4. Your neighborhood is a kind of ______.

A charity **C** bureaucracy
B community **D** congregation

Reviewing Main Ideas

Directions: Choose the best answer for each question.

Section 1 *(pp.150–154)*

5. What is the most important civic duty of Americans?

A to pay taxes
B to obey laws
C to serve in court
D to attend school

6. Which civic responsibility does reading the metropolitan section of a newspaper fulfill?

A being informed
B respecting others
C speaking up and voting
D contributing to the common good

7. When was the last time the United States instituted a military draft?

A World War II
B World War I
C Korean War
D Vietnam War

Section 2 *(pp. 156-162)*

8. Which service do volunteers perform?

A ensuring clean water
B mentoring schoolchildren
C collecting household trash
D providing for national defense

9. Which group is a national charity?

A United Way
B Freedom Corps
C church food pantry
D Neighborhood Watch

10. Which national service program sends volunteers overseas?

A AmeriCorps
B Peace Corps
C Senior Corps
D Foster Grandparents

GO ON

Critical Thinking

Directions: Base your answers to questions 11 and 12 on the table below and your knowledge of Chapter 5.

Reason for Not Voting in Last Presidential Election	Percent Who Sited Reason
Not registered	31
Didn't like candidates	10
Not interested in politics	8
No particular reason	8
Illness	7
Inconvenient	7
Working	7
Other reasons	7
Not a citizen	6
Out of town	5
Couldn't get to the polls	3
Didn't get absentee ballot	1

11. Which generalization can you make based on this chart?

A Political parties are nominating uninspiring candidates.

B Most people in this survey are shirking their civic duty.

C Most people in this survey are neglecting an important civic responsibility.

D The sample is too small to draw any valid conclusions about why people do not vote.

12. Which prediction is supported by the chart?

A Fast-track naturalization laws could double voter turnout.

B Providing shuttle buses to the polls would not increase voter participation.

C Improving the absentee voting system might raise voter turnout by 10 percent.

D Declaring voting day a national holiday could boost voter participation up to 7 percent.

Document-Based Questions

Directions: Analyze the following document and answer the short-answer questions that follow.

The following paragraph is the current oath for commissioned officers in the United States Army.

> *I, (name), having been appointed an officer in the Army of the United States, as indicated above in the grade of (rank) do solemnly swear (or affirm) that I will support and defend the Constitution of the United States against all enemies, foreign or domestic, that I will bear true faith and allegiance to the same; that I take this obligation freely, without any mental reservations or purpose of evasion; and that I will well and faithfully discharge the duties of the office upon which I am about to enter; So help me God.*
>
> —United States Army

13. Which of the five civic duties does an army officer perform?

14. Give an example of domestic enemies of the Constitution of the United States.

Extended-Response Question

15. Anthropologist Margaret Mead wrote: "Never doubt that a small group of thoughtful, committed citizens can change the world. Indeed, it is the only thing that ever has." Write a brief essay explaining why you agree or disagree with Mead's statement. Use examples from the chapter to support your opinion.

For additional test practice, use Self-Check Quizzes—Chapter 5 on glencoe.com.

Need Extra Help?

If you missed question...	1	2	3	4	5	6	7	8	9	10	11	12	13	14	15
Go to page...	152	154	158	159	151	153	152	158	160	160	153	153	151	151	157

Analyzing Primary Sources

Active Citizenship

Reading Focus

Have you ever thought about the things that bind people together? What values and beliefs do they share? The American ideal of citizenship has always stressed each citizen's responsibility to participate in political life.

Read to Discover

As you read, think about the following:

- What are the things that unite people in a common cause?
- What values and beliefs do people in a society share?

Reader's Dictionary

self-interest: a concern for one's own advantage or well-being

complacency: self-satisfaction

disinterested: free of bias; impartial

ruthless: without mercy

unbridled: uncontrolled

abridged: cut short

servitude: lack of personal freedom

Democracy in America

In *Democracy in America,* Alexis de Tocqueville vividly described nineteenth-century American life, politics, and morals.

The Americans, on the other hand, are fond of explaining almost all the actions of their lives by the principle of **self-interest** rightly understood; they show with **complacency** how an enlightened regard for themselves constantly prompts them to assist one another and inclines them willingly to sacrifice a portion of their time and property to the welfare of the state. In this respect I think they frequently fail to do themselves justice, for in the United States as well as elsewhere people are sometimes seen to give way to those **disinterested** and spontaneous impulses that are natural to man; but the Americans seldom admit that they yield to emotions of this kind; they are more anxious to do honor to their philosophy than to themselves.

—Alexis de Tocqueville, *Democracy in America*

The Spirit of Liberty

In his essay "The Spirit of Liberty," United States Circuit Court Judge Learned Hand promoted the ideal of ethical and committed citizens.

What do we mean when we say that first of all we seek liberty? I often wonder whether we do not rest our hopes too much upon constitutions, upon laws, and upon courts. These are false hopes; believe me, these are false hopes. Liberty lies in the hearts of men and women; when it dies there, no constitution, no law, no court can save it; no constitution, no law, no court can even do much to help it. And what is this liberty which must lie in the hearts of men and women? It is not the **ruthless,** the **unbridled** will; it is not freedom to do as one likes. That is the denial of liberty, and leads straight to its overthrow. A society in which men recognize no check upon their freedom soon becomes a society where freedom is the possession of only a savage few; as we have learned to our sorrow.

—Judge Learned Hand, "The Spirit of Liberty"

The Right to Vote

Many groups struggled to win the right to vote. Several amendments to the U.S. Constitution deal with suffrage.

The right of citizens of the United States to vote shall not be denied or **abridged** by the United States or by any State on account of race, color, or previous condition of **servitude.**

—Fifteenth Amendment (1870)

The right of citizens of the United States to vote shall not be denied or abridged by the United States or by any State on account of sex.

—Nineteenth Amendment (1920)

The right of citizens of the United States to vote in any primary or other election . . . shall not be denied or abridged . . . by reason of failure to pay any poll tax or other tax.

—Twenty-fourth Amendment (1964)

The right of citizens of the United States, who are eighteen years of age or older, to vote shall not be denied or abridged by the United States or by any State on account of age.

—Twenty-sixth Amendment (1971)

Photographs as Primary Sources What does this photograph tell you about women's rights in the early 1900s? For what right is this woman campaigning?

DBQ Document-Based Questions

1. **Connecting** What connections did de Tocqueville make between the interests of individuals and the interests of groups?
2. **Responding** What do you think Judge Hand meant when he said, "Liberty lies in the hearts of men and women"?
3. **Predicting** How do you think people would respond to a compulsory voting law in the United States? Explain.
4. **Evaluating and Connecting** The privilege of U.S. citizenship brings with it certain responsibilities. Some responsibilities, such as obeying laws, are required. Other responsibilities, such as participating in political life, are voluntary. Make a list of the voluntary responsibilities you found in these readings. Then write a paragraph in response to the question: What do you think would happen if the voluntary responsibilities you listed became required by law?

TIME REPORTS

A Nation of Givers

Through charities, churches, and foundations, Americans put their money where their cause is

Comstock

Every year, nearly two-thirds of all Americans donate money to charity. Some citizens contribute only a few dollars, while others give away millions. On average, each American contributes $1,894.

All those donations add up. Americans donated a total of $248.5 billion to U.S. charities in 2004. Of this amount, about a third went to religious groups; less than 10% was donated to organizations that directly help the poor (see "Donation Nation" at right).

So why is the U.S. the most generous nation on earth? Its tax code encourages private giving in place of spending more public money on social programs. But tax breaks can't account for all the generosity. The deduction for charitable giving cost the government $40 billion in 2004. Americans gave away more than six times that amount.

The Top Three

The largest total philanthropic gifts by individuals in 2004

Bill and Melinda Gates
The Microsoft chairman and his wife's pledge to the Gates Foundation—which committed more than $1 billion to global health alone in 2004—increased its endowment to nearly $32 billion, by far the largest in the world.

Susan T. Buffett
The wife of Berkshire Hathaway founder Warren Buffett left 31,707 shares of company stock largely to her foundation dedicated to college scholarships and medical research.

John M. Templeton
The former investor pledged the money to his foundation to investigate the relationship among science, religion, and health.

Generosity's Deep Roots

Wealthy Americans have been creating ways to give away their time and money for generations

Culver Pictures

1873
Johns Hopkins (1795-1873), a railroad investor and merchant, leaves $7 million to found a university and hospital.

1907
Margaret Olivia Slocum Sage (1828-1918), a banking heiress, creates the Russell Sage Foundation, which offers grants to improve living conditions. Her total gift is estimated at $80 million.

Time Life Pictures/Getty Images

1911
Andrew Carnegie (1835-1919), a Scottish-born steel baron, defines charity as a moral imperative and gives away more than $350 million in his lifetime through the Carnegie Corporation.

Donation Nation

About two-thirds of Americans give to charity each year. The average gifts:

Most generous region: $2,252

Most likely to give to religious causes: $2,146

Highest percentage of donors: 82%: $1,648

$1,903

$2,204

$1,615

$1,404

$1,986

$1,927

Lowest percentage of donors: 61%

U.S. average: $1,894

Regional figures are from 2002 data, the most recent available

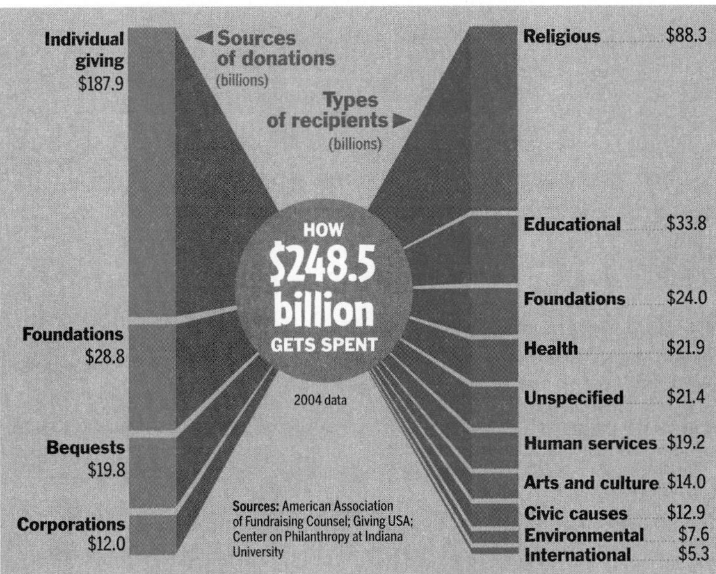

Star Power

Big names are changing the face of philanthropy

Brooks Kraft/Corbis

U.S. contributions to disaster relief through Dec. 2005

Former Presidents and rivals **George H.W. Bush** and **Bill Clinton** formed an unlikely partnership that turned into a friendship, raising millions after the Asian tsunami and the devastating hurricanes in the U.S.

The Bono Effect? Since 2001, development aid for poor nations has increased from $67 billion to $80 billion and is projected to rise 60% by 2010. Many European countries are committed to giving 0.7% of their gross domestic product for aid; the U.S. currently gives only 0.1%.

Ethan Miller/Getty Images

Time Life Pictures/Getty Images

1913

John D. Rockefeller (1839-1937) is the founder of Standard Oil and the richest man of his time. His $450 million in contributions to public health through the Rockefeller Foundation sets a precedent for the Gates Foundation.

1919

Madam C.J. Walker (1867-1919), an African American self-made millionaire, supports social and educational institutions with the profits from her hair-care and cosmetics business.

1936

Bettmann/Corbis

Henry Ford (1863-1947), the automotive pioneer, establishes the Ford Foundation in Dearborn, Michigan, with $25,000. Now a nationwide force, it has more than $11 billion in assets.

1977

John D. (1897-1978) and **Catherine T. MacArthur** (1909-1981) start their namesake foundation with the vast wealth from his insurance company, Bankers Life. Today the foundation's assets are estimated at $5 billion.

UNIT 2

The National Government

Aerial view of Washington, D.C., the Capitol, and the National Mall

★ **Chapter 6** **The Legislative Branch**

★ **Chapter 7** **The Executive Branch**

★ **Chapter 8** **The Judicial Branch**

Be an Active Citizen

CITIZENSHIP The Constitution states that the power in government lies with the people. In our federal system of government, the executive, legislative, and judicial branches share the responsibility of governing the nation. Read about your responsibilities as a citizen in preparing to vote for officials who express your point of view.

UNIT 2

Reading Social Studies

Finding the Main Idea

1 Learn It!

Main ideas are the most important ideas in a paragraph, section, or chapter. Supporting details are facts or examples that explain the main idea.

- Read the paragraph below. Notice how the main idea is identified.
- The sentences that follow are the supporting details.

Main Idea

Supporting Details

Our Constitution explains not only what Congress may do but also what it may *not* do. Some limitations are imposed by the Bill of Rights. The purpose of the Bill of Rights was to limit or deny certain powers to the federal government. For example, Congress may not pass laws that restrict freedom of speech, or ban freedom of religion.

—from page 188

Web Diagram

A web diagram can organize the main idea and supporting details.

Our Constitution explains not only what Congress may do but also what it may *not* do.

Some limitations are imposed by the Bill of Rights.

The purpose of the Bill of Rights was to limit or deny certain powers to the federal government.

For example, Congress may not pass laws, restrict freedom of speech, or ban freedom of religion.

Reading Tip

Often, the first sentence in a paragraph will contain a main idea. However, main ideas can also appear in the middle or at the end of a paragraph.

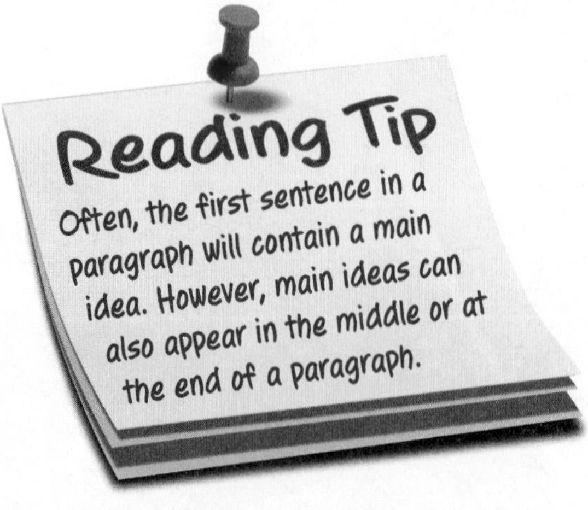

2 Practice It!

Read the paragraph. Draw a graphic organizer like the one below to show the main idea and supporting details.

> People contribute to their communities in countless ways, working independently or as part of volunteer groups both large and small. Perhaps you know a mom or dad who is active in the PTA (Parent Teacher Association) or leads a Scout troop. Your friends and you might spend a Saturday cleaning up a highway or preparing holiday baskets for needy families. Retirees mentor school children, record books for the blind, and lead museum tours.

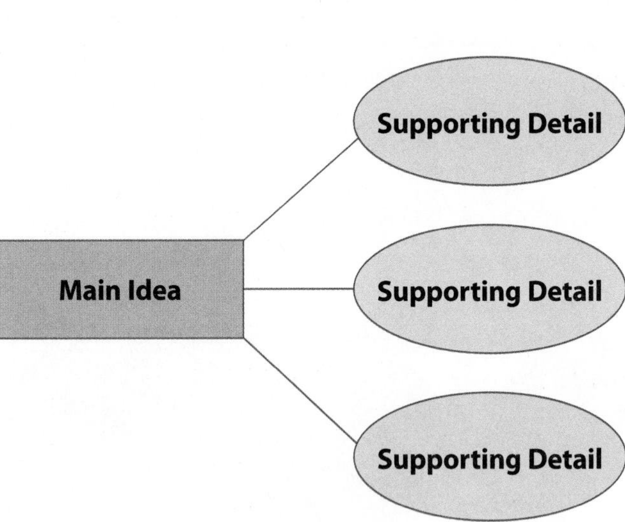

Read to Write Activity

Read the Main Idea on page 185. Use it as a topic sentence and add supporting details to create a complete paragraph.

▲ A volunteer highway cleanup crew

3 Apply It!

Identify one main idea and its supporting details for:

- **Chapter 7; Section 2**
- **Chapter 8; Section 3**

The Legislative Branch

Why It Matters

Our nation's Constitution gives the power to make laws to the legislative branch. Citizens participate in the lawmaking process by expressing their views to Congress. Find out what legislation is pending in Congress and your representatives' positions on the issues. **Do you agree with your representatives?**

Chapter Audio

Civics ONLINE
Visit glencoe.com and enter QuickPass™ code CIV3093c6 for Chapter 6 resources.

BIG Ideas

Section 1: How Congress Is Organized

The Constitution gives the legislative branch—Congress—the power to make laws. In Congress, members of each party select their own leaders and work mainly in committees to carry out their duties.

Section 2: Powers of Congress

The Constitution gives the legislative branch—Congress—the power to make laws. While the Constitution limits the powers of Congress, it also gives Congress the powers it needs to conduct its business and to accomplish its goals.

Section 3: Representing the People

The Constitution gives the legislative branch—Congress—the power to make laws. Congress employs many staffers who help with the workload.

Section 4: How a Bill Becomes a Law

The Constitution gives the legislative branch—Congress—the power to make laws. Several complex steps are involved in taking an idea and turning it into a law.

The U.S. Capitol, Washington, D.C.

FOLDABLES™ Study Organizer

Summarizing Information Study Foldable Make the following Foldable to help you summarize information about the national government of the United States.

Step 1 Collect three sheets of paper and place them on top of each other about an inch apart.

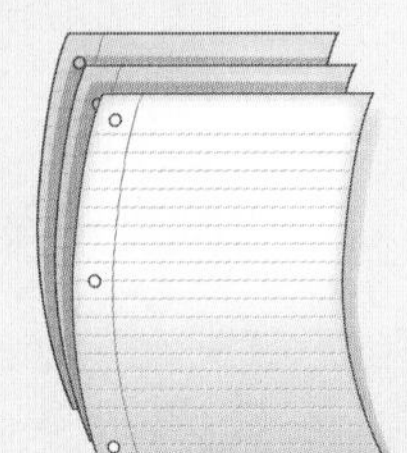

Step 2 Fold up the bottom edges of the paper to form six tabs.

Step 3 When all the tabs are the same size, crease the paper to hold the tabs in place and staple the sheets together. Label each tab as shown.

Presidential Action
Voting on a Bill
Floor Debate and Action
Committee Action
Bill Introduced
How a Bill Becomes a Law

Reading and Writing
As you read the chapter, write the details of the different stages that a bill goes through to become a law as it passes through Congress.

Guide to Reading

Big Idea

The Constitution gives the legislative branch—Congress—the power to make laws.

Content Vocabulary

- bicameral *(p. 177)*
- census *(p. 179)*
- constituent *(p. 179)*
- gerrymander *(p. 179)*
- majority party *(p. 180)*
- minority party *(p. 180)*
- standing committee *(p. 181)*
- seniority *(p. 182)*

Academic Vocabulary

- occur *(p. 178)*
- adjust *(p. 179)*

Reading Strategy

Comparing and Contrasting Create graphic organizers similar to the ones below. As you read, fill in the information about the House of Representatives and the Senate.

Section 1

Section Audio

Spotlight Video

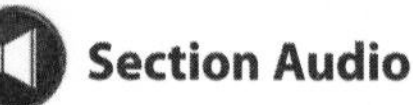

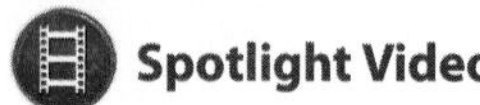

How Congress Is Organized

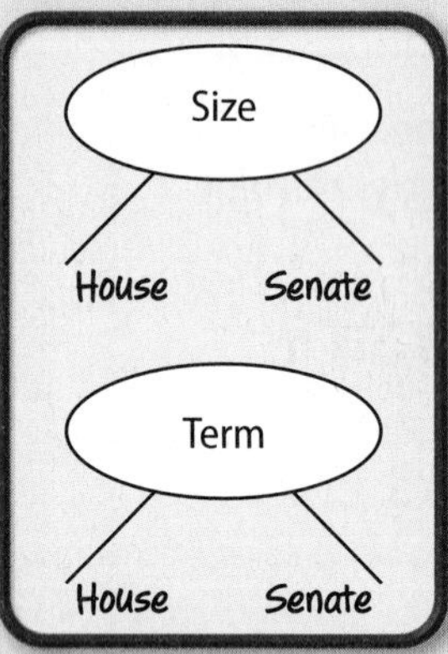

Real World Civics Politics in Illinois—the heartland of America—are the same as everywhere else in the country. Members of Congress speak to and listen to the people they represent so they can do their jobs in Washington. Here, as a senator, Barack Obama speaks to constituents at a town hall meeting in Carrollton, Illinois. Members of Congress meet with their constituents to find out how they feel about important issues.

▼ **Former Illinois U.S. senator Barack Obama**

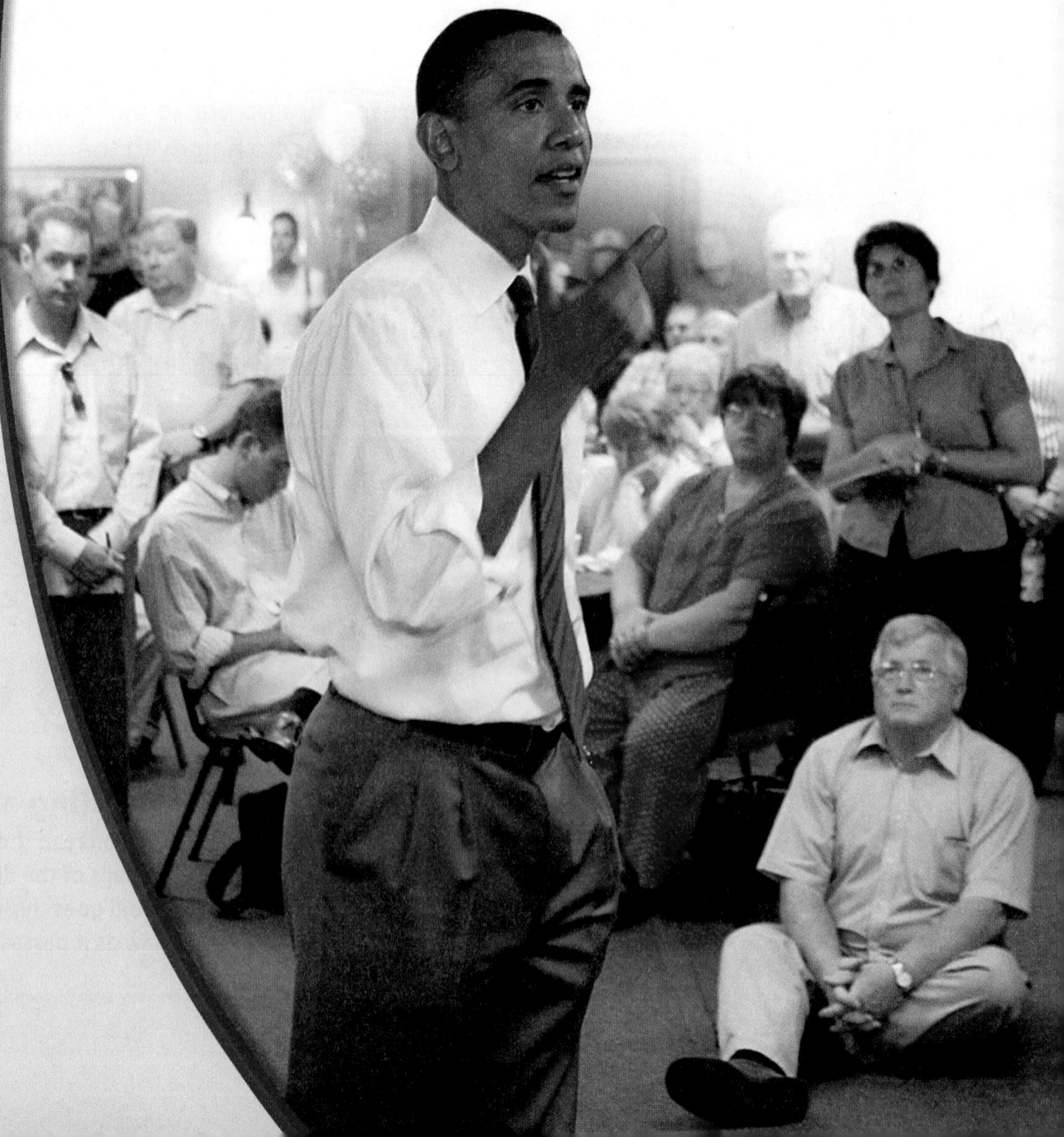

A Bicameral Legislature

Main Idea **Congress is the legislative, or lawmaking, branch of government.**

Civics & You What type of person would you choose to represent you in government? Read to find out how congressional leadership is determined.

The Framers wanted to establish a Congressional voting body, but one of the conflicts at the Constitutional Convention in 1787 concerned state representation. While delegates from the smaller states wanted equal representation, delegates from the larger states wanted representation to be based on population, which would give them a greater voice in government. As you will recall from Chapter 3, the Great Compromise established Congress as a two-part, or **bicameral,** body. In the Upper House, the Senate, each state would have an equal number of representatives—two. In the lower house, the House of Representatives, each state's population would determine its representation.

The Framers of the U.S. Constitution intended to make the legislative branch of government more powerful than any other branch. In fact, Congress is described in the first part of the Constitution, Article I. As James Madison said, Congress is "the First Branch of this Government."

Every year, inside the U.S. Capitol in Washington, D.C., 535 of our fellow citizens gather to make new laws and address countless issues facing our country. These are our elected representatives, the members of Congress.

Joint Session A special session of Congress in New York City marks only the second time in 200 years that Congress has met outside the nation's capital. ***Explaining*** **Why did the Framers establish a bicameral legislature?**

Congressional Apportionment, Selected Years

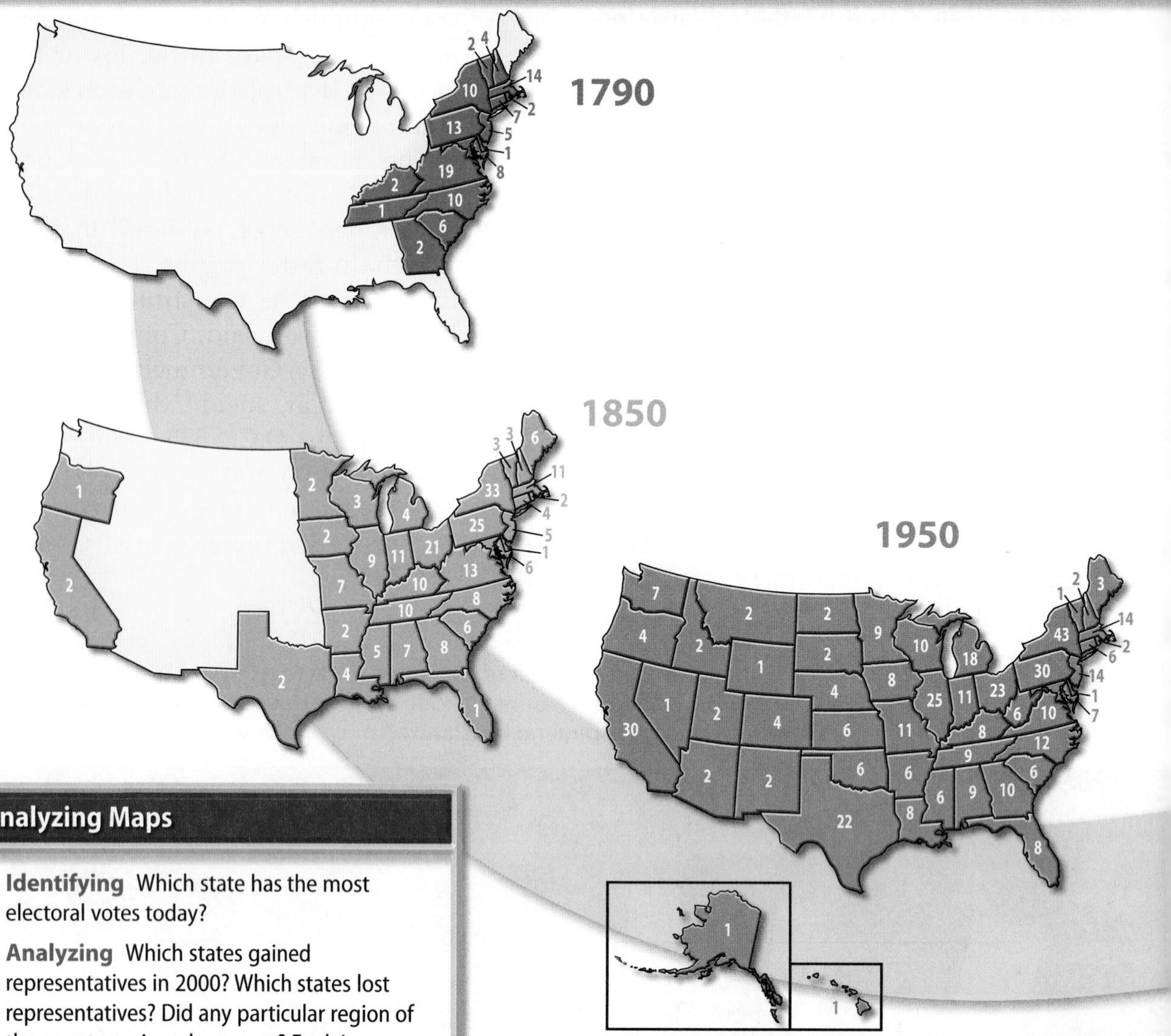

Analyzing Maps

1. **Identifying** Which state has the most electoral votes today?
2. **Analyzing** Which states gained representatives in 2000? Which states lost representatives? Did any particular region of the country gain or lose seats? Explain.

Terms of Congress

The government calendar is set by law. Each Congress lasts for a meeting period, or a term, of two years. Each term of Congress starts on January 3rd of odd-numbered years (unless a different day is appointed) and lasts for two years.

Each "new" Congress is given a number to identify its two-year term. For example, the first Congress met in 1789, and the 111th Congress is in session from January 2009 to January 2011.

Congressional Sessions Each term of Congress is divided into two sessions, or meetings. A typical session of Congress today lasts from January until November or December. Congress may also meet during special sessions or in times of crisis. A joint session **occurs,** or takes place, when the House and Senate meet together.

Civics ONLINE

Student Web Activity Visit glencoe.com and complete the Chapter 6 Web Activity.

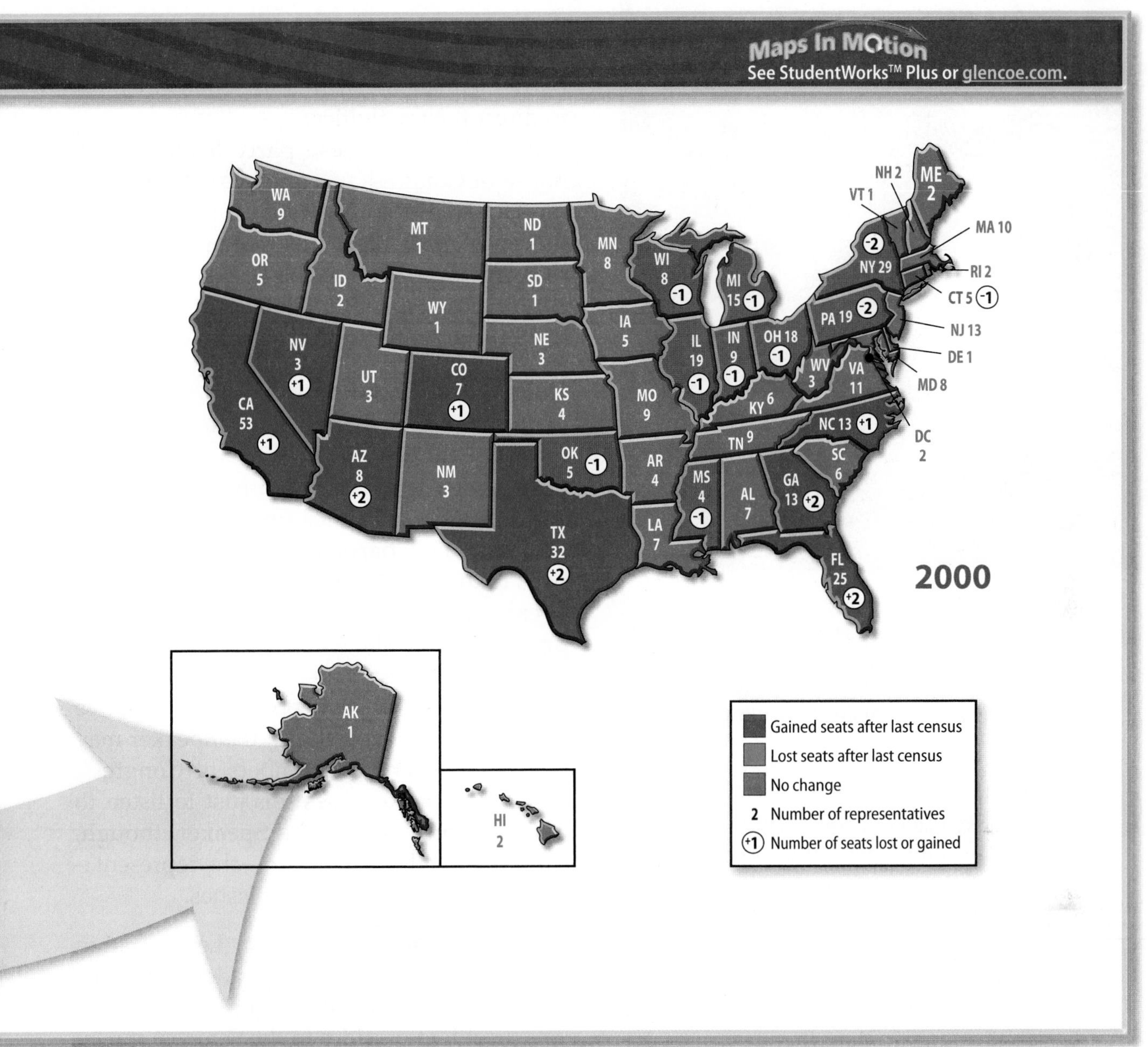

The House of Representatives

The House of Representatives, the larger body of Congress, has 435 voting members allotted to the states according to population. The Constitution guarantees each state at least one representative, no matter how small its population. After each 10-year **census,** or population count taken by the Census Bureau, Congress **adjusts,** or changes, the number of representatives given to each state. Representatives serve two-year terms and usually focus on concerns in their districts.

Congressional Districts Each state is divided into one or more congressional districts, with one representative elected from each district. State legislatures must draw the boundaries so that the districts include roughly the same number of **constituents,** or people represented. Sometimes states abuse this process by gerrymandering. A **gerrymander** is an oddly shaped district designed to increase the voting strength of a particular group. Laws have reduced but not eliminated gerrymandering.

House and Senate Cooperation Senator Barbara Boxer (left) and former Representative Stephanie Tubbs Jones (right), both Democrats, collaborated often. ***Speculating*** **Why do you think female members of Congress remain in the minority?**

For example, if most of a state's representatives are Republican, they might draw the lines so that as many districts as possible have more Republican than Democratic voters.

The Senate

The Senate has 100 members—2 from each of the 50 states. Each senator represents his or her entire state rather than a particular district. Senators serve six-year terms, but the elections are staggered so that no more than one-third of the senators are up for reelection at any one time. This ensures a certain amount of stability and continuity.

If a senator dies or resigns before the end of the term, the state legislature may authorize the governor to appoint someone to fill the vacancy until the next election.

Leaders in Congress

In both the House and the Senate, the political party to which more than half the members belong is known as the **majority party.** The other party is called the **minority party.** At the beginning of each term, the party members in each house choose leaders to direct their activities.

In addition to these party leaders, each house of Congress has one overall leader. In the House of Representatives, this leader is the Speaker of the House. Members of the majority party choose the Speaker at a caucus, or closed meeting. The rest of the House then approves the choice of Speaker.

Role of the Speaker As presiding officer of the House and the leader of the majority party, the Speaker has great power. The Speaker steers legislation through the House and leads floor debates (in which all representatives may participate). If anything happens to the president and vice president, the Speaker is next in line to become president, provided he or she is legally qualified.

Speakers rely on their powers of persuasion and the power of their positions to exercise influence. On a typical day, the Speaker may talk with dozens of members of Congress. Often the Speaker does this just to listen to requests for a favor. The Speaker, though, expects something in return—the representatives' support on important issues.

Congressional Leadership Leadership in the Senate closely parallels leadership in the House, but the Senate has no speaker. The vice president presides in the Senate but may only vote to break a tie. The president pro tempore—meaning "for the time being"—usually acts as chairperson of the Senate. He or she is from the majority party and is usually its most senior member.

Other powerful leaders are the floor leaders. The majority and minority floor leaders in each house speak for their parties on issues, push bills along, and try to sway votes. Party "whips" help the floor leaders. They make sure legislators are present for key votes.

Reading Check **Identifying** Which article of the Constitution describes Congress?

Committee Work

Main Idea **Much of the actual work of legislating is performed by committees and subcommittees within Congress.**

Civics & You Have you served on a committee? What are their advantages and disadvantages? Read to find out about congressional committees.

Each house of Congress must consider thousands of bills, or proposed laws, in the course of a session. To make it possible to handle so many bills at one time, each house has developed a system of committees.

Congressional Committees

Congress has three types of committees: standing committees, select committees, and joint committees. **Standing committees** are permanent committees. For example, both the Senate and the House have standing committees to deal with agriculture, commerce, and veterans' affairs.

The House and Senate sometimes form temporary committees to deal with special issues. These select committees meet for a limited time until they complete their assigned task. Occasionally, the Senate and the House form joint committees, which include members of both houses. Joint committees meet to consider specific issues.

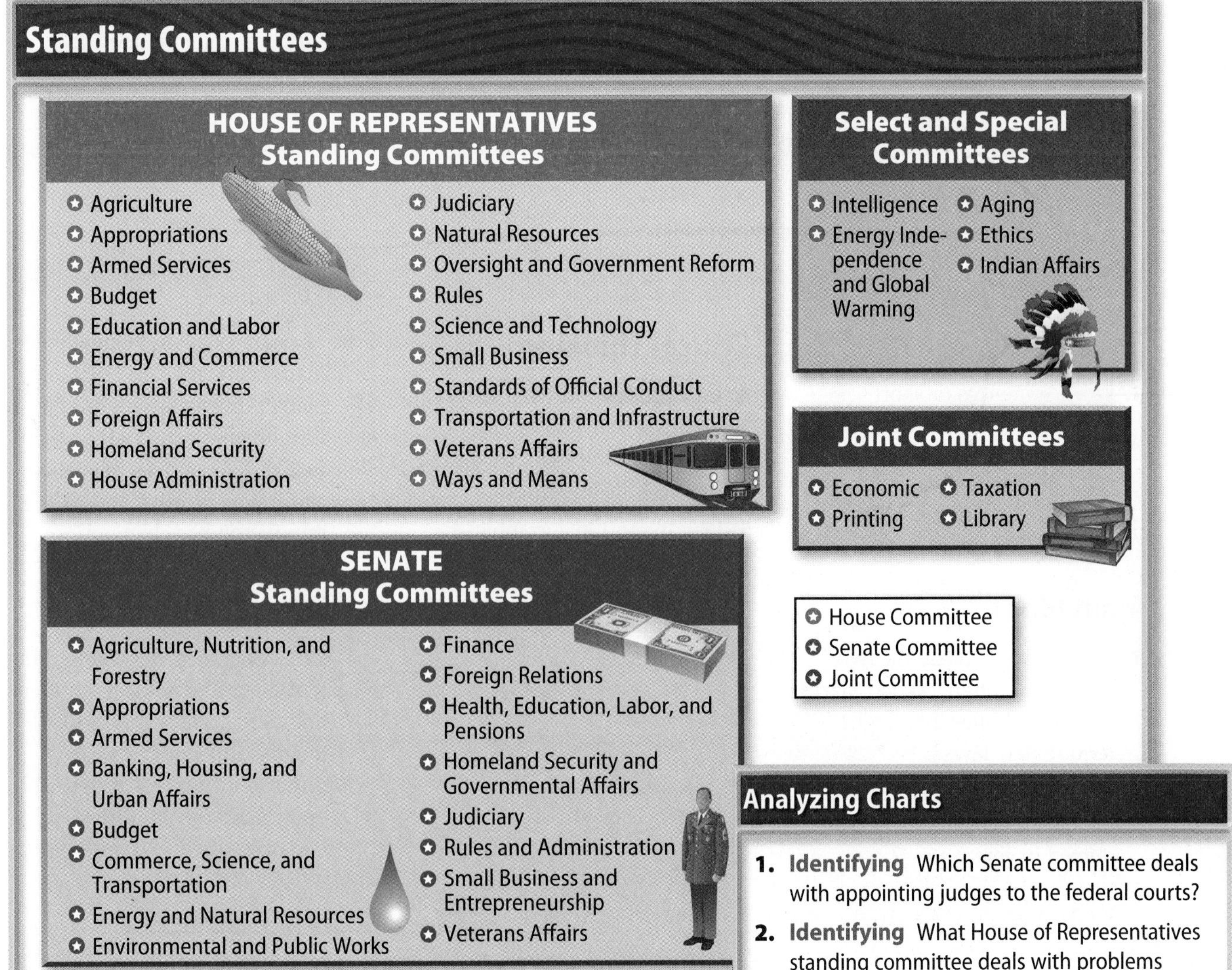

Analyzing Charts

1. **Identifying** Which Senate committee deals with appointing judges to the federal courts?
2. **Identifying** What House of Representatives standing committee deals with problems facing the airline industry?

Committee Assignments

When senators and representatives first come to Congress, they try to get assigned to important committees that affect the people who elected them. For example, members of Congress from farm areas might want to serve on agriculture committees. Those with many factories in their districts might be interested in serving on labor committees.

What Is The Seniority System? Party leaders make committee assignments. In doing so, they consider members' preferences, expertise, and loyalty to the party. Another key factor is **seniority,** or years of service. The senators and representatives who have been in Congress longest usually get the preferred committee spots. The longest-serving committee member from the majority party traditionally becomes chairperson. Chairpersons decide when and if a committee will meet, what bills will be studied, and who will serve on which subcommittees.

Some people think the seniority system is a good idea. They say it prevents fights over committee jobs and ensures that chairpersons will have experience. Other people complain that talented people may be overlooked in favor of those who have simply been around for a while. There has been so much criticism of the seniority system over the years that both political parties have moved slightly away from it. The senior majority party member on a committee still usually wins the role of chairperson, but it is no longer guaranteed.

Reading Check **Explaining** What is the difference between a standing committee and a select committee?

Vocabulary

1. **Write** sentences or short paragraphs in which you use the following terms: *bicameral, census, constituent, gerrymander, majority party, minority party, standing committee,* and *seniority.*

Main Ideas

2. **Describing** Why are the two houses of Congress good places to discuss issues that might require new laws?
3. **Explaining** Why is so much of the business of Congress conducted in committees?

Critical Thinking

4. **BIG Ideas** In what ways do the Senate and House of Representatives work together to pass bills into laws?
5. **Identifying** On a graphic organizer like the one below, identify the different types of committees established in Congress.

6. **Analyzing Visuals** Review the maps on pages 178–179. How many representatives did North Carolina have in 1790? In 1950? In 2000? What does this tell you about how North Carolina's population has changed?

CITIZENSHIP Activity

7. **Persuasive Writing** Do you think that government by committee makes the role of individual members of Congress less important? Express your opinion on this question in a one-page essay.

Study Central™ To review this section, go to glencoe.com.

Financial Literacy

What Is a Lemon Law?

You save money for your first car, and you find a great deal. From the beginning, however, problems start. It stalls at traffic lights. You take it in for repair. In most cases, the manufacturer's warranty will provide the coverage you need to have your car repaired at no cost to you. However, what if your car spends more time in the repair shop than on the road? In some cases, the dealer may be unable to fix your car's problem. Did you get a "lemon"?

What Is a Lemon? A "lemon" is a vehicle that has a defect that the dealer has not fixed within a reasonable number of chances.

State Lemon Laws State lemon laws provide some protection. In most states, to qualify as a lemon, the problem has to be serious enough that it "substantially impairs the use, value, or safety" of the vehicle, and the vehicle has not been properly repaired within a "reasonable number of attempts."

In North Carolina, for example, this reasonable number is four attempts or if the car has been out of service awaiting repair for a total of 20 or more business days during any 12-month period of the warranty. Most state lemon laws stipulate that a manufacturer must provide a refund or replacement for a defective new vehicle when a substantial defect cannot be fixed.

Checklist for Buying a Vehicle

Your best protection against a lemon happens before you buy. These tips will help you:

- Have a reliable technician thoroughly inspect the vehicle—whether it is new or used.
- Check what is covered by the service warranty. A used car may still be covered under the original manufacturer's warranty. Also, some dealers offer their own limited warranties for used cars.
- Check various dealers for the reputation of their service departments. Your warranty usually allows you to take your car to any dealer selling that make of car.

Analyzing Economics

1. **Describing** What is the purpose of a lemon law?
2. **Specifying** Write three questions you should ask yourself before you buy a vehicle.

Guide to Reading

Big Idea
The Constitution gives the legislative branch—Congress—the power to make laws.

Content Vocabulary
- expressed powers *(p. 185)*
- implied powers *(p. 185)*
- elastic clause *(p. 185)*
- impeach *(p. 187)*
- writ of habeas corpus *(p. 188)*
- bill of attainder *(p. 188)*
- ex post facto law *(p. 188)*

Academic Vocabulary
- regulate *(p. 185)*

Reading Strategy
Explaining As you read, complete a graphic organizer like the one below to explain the main areas of Congressional legislative powers.

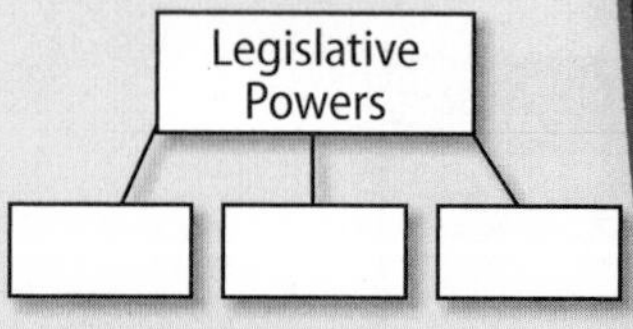

 Section Audio  Spotlight Video

Section 2

Powers of Congress

Real World Civics Who represents the people of America and protects their safety around the world? Congress. Powers granted to Congress by Article I, Section 8, of the Constitution include the ability to raise an army and a navy and to declare war. All men between the ages of 18 and 25 are required to register for military service, even though there is currently no active draft. Many young men and women choose to enlist voluntarily in the military, which makes the draft unnecessary.

▼ **These young marines are training at Camp Pendleton in California, the busiest military base in the country**

Legislative Powers

Main Idea **The Constitution provides that all powers to make laws for the United States government shall be given to Congress.**

Civics & You Did you know that no government agency can spend money without the approval of Congress? Read to find out about the legislative powers of Congress.

Most of the powers delegated to the Congress are enumerated, or clearly listed, in Article I, Section 8. These are called **expressed powers.** There are 18 separate clauses enumerating different powers specifically given to Congress. Clause 5, for example, says, "The Congress shall have the Power . . . To coin Money."

Certain powers are given to the national government even though they are not expressly presented in the Constitution. Their constitutional basis is found in Article I, Section 8, Clause 18, which states that Congress shall have the power to do whatever is "necessary and proper" to carry out the expressed powers. The powers that Congress has because of Clause 18 are called **implied powers** because they are not stated explicitly in the Constitution. Clause 18 is often called the **elastic clause** because it has allowed Congress to stretch its powers to meet new needs. For instance, you will not find the power to create an air force written in the Constitution. However, the elastic clause has allowed Congress to do so as part of its expressed powers to support armies.

Most of Congress's powers are related to making laws. Some of the most important legislative powers involve raising and spending money, **regulating** (or managing) commerce, and dealing with foreign countries.

Reading Check **Explaining** Why is the "necessary and proper" clause also called the elastic clause?

Congress Funds Defense Military weaponry stored on the deck of the USS *Harry S. Truman* is supplied by funds from Congress. ***Specifying*** **How is maintaining an air force an example of an implied power of Congress?**

Powers of Congress

Charts In MOtion
See StudentWorks™ Plus or glencoe.com.

SELECTED EXPRESSED POWERS	SELECTED IMPLIED POWERS
Money Powers	
• Lay and collect taxes to provide for the defense and general welfare of the United States (Clause 1) • Borrow money (Clause 2) • Establish bankruptcy laws (Clause 4) • Coin, print, and regulate money (Clause 5) • Punish counterfeiters of American currency (Clause 6)	• Lay and collect taxes implies the power to support public schools, welfare programs, public housing, etc. • Borrow money implies the power to maintain the Federal Reserve Board
Commerce Powers	
• Regulate foreign and interstate commerce (Clause 3)	• Regulate commerce implies the power to prohibit discrimination in restaurants, hotels, and other public accommodations
Military and Foreign Policy Powers	
• Declare war (Clause 11) • Raise, support, and regulate an army and navy (Clauses 12, 13, & 14) • Provide, regulate, and call into service a militia, known as the National Guard (Clauses 15 &16) • Punish acts committed on international waters and against the laws of nations (Clause 10)	• Raise and support an army implies the right to draft people into the armed services
Other Legislative Powers	
• Establish laws of naturalization (Clause 4) • Establish post offices and post roads (Clause 7) • Grant copyrights and patents (Clause 8) • Create lower federal courts (Clause 9) • Govern Washington, D.C. (Clause 17) • Provide for laws necessary and proper for carrying out of all other listed powers (Clause 18)	• Establish laws of naturalization implies the power to limit the number of immigrants to the United States

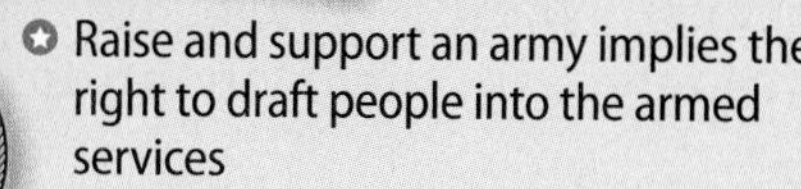

Source: *Congress A to Z*, 4th ed. (Washington, D.C.: CQ Press 2003.).

Analyzing Charts

1. **Identifying** Which clause gives Congress the power to declare war?
2. **Contrasting** What is the difference between the expressed and implied powers of Congress?

Nonlegislative Powers

Main Idea **The Constitution gives Congress a number of nonlegislative duties.**

Civics & You Has a friend ever asked you to check over something after it was completed? Congress often checks over other departments of government as part of its nonlegislative powers.

As the legislative branch, the most important duty of Congress is to make laws. Congress also holds a number of duties besides lawmaking. Among Congress's most important nonlegislative powers are those it uses to check the other branches of government. Some of these are set forth in the Constitution; others have developed over time. One such power is to propose amendments to the Constitution.

The Senate has the power to approve or reject the president's nominees for various offices, including Supreme Court justices, federal judges, and ambassadors.

The Constitution also allows Congress to remove from office any federal official who has committed serious wrongdoing. The House has the sole authority to **impeach,** or accuse officials of misconduct in office. If a majority of the House votes to impeach a public official, the Senate then has the power to hold a trial and to act as a jury and decide the official's guilt or innocence. A two-thirds vote is necessary to convict and to remove a person from office.

The House uses its impeachment power sparingly, most often with federal judges. Only two presidents have been impeached: Andrew Johnson in 1868 and Bill Clinton in 1998. Both presidents were tried by the Senate and acquitted (they were not removed from office).

Senate Approval The Constitution gives the Senate the power to approve Supreme Court justices such as John G. Roberts, Jr., in an open hearing. ***Hypothesizing*** **Why do you think the Framers did not leave judicial appointments to the president alone?**

Power Limitations

Our Constitution explains not only what Congress may do but also what it may *not* do. Some limitations are imposed by the Bill of Rights. The purpose of the Bill of Rights was to limit or deny certain powers to the federal government. For example, Congress may not pass laws that restrict freedom of speech or ban freedom of religion.

According to Article I of the Constitution, Congress may not favor one state over another, tax interstate commerce, or tax exports. Article I also forbids Congress from enacting laws that would interfere with the legal rights of individuals. Congress cannot suspend the **writ of habeas corpus.** This is a court order that requires police to bring a prisoner to court to explain why they are holding the person. Congress is also banned from passing **bills of attainder,** or laws that punish a person without a jury trial.

Further, Congress may not pass **ex post facto laws.** These are laws that make an act a crime after the act has been committed.

The Constitution also reserves many powers for the states. Congress cannot interfere with these powers, such as the right to regulate public school systems. The Bill of Rights and other amendments also deny Congress certain powers.

Checks and Balances Other restrictions come from the Constitution's system of checks and balances. The Supreme Court can declare laws established by Congress as unconstitutional. The president can veto bills passed by Congress before they become laws. If both houses of Congress can muster a two-thirds vote, they can override the president's action.

Reading Check **Concluding** How does the Bill of Rights limit Congress's powers?

Review

Vocabulary

1. **Explain** how each of the following terms relates to Congress: *expressed powers, implied powers, elastic clause, impeach, writ of habeas corpus, bill of attainder, ex post facto law.*

Main Ideas

2. **Hypothesizing** Why do you think Congress, rather than the states, is given most lawmaking powers?

3. **Describe** three nonlegislative powers given to Congress.

Critical Thinking

4. **Comparing** What do writs of habeas corpus, bills of attainder, and ex post facto laws have in common?

5. **BIG Ideas** In a graphic organizer like the one below, list the different offices for which Congress has the right to approve appointees.

6. **Analyzing Visuals** Reexamine the powers of Congress on page 186. Which clause gives Congress the power to borrow money?

CITIZENSHIP Activity

7. **Persuasive Writing** Should representatives always vote the way their constituents want, or should they vote according to their own best judgment? Write an essay in which you express your view. Give reasons for your answer.

Study Central™ To review this section, go to glencoe.com.

Does a public library have the right to censor Internet information?

In its early stages of development, the Internet raised a number of issues. Hackers can access private information. Many people are concerned about spyware, adware, and offensive sites. Congress first addressed the issue of offensive Internet sites in the Communications Decency Act of 1996. The Supreme Court ruled that law an unconstitutional violation of free speech. In December 2000, Congress passed the Children's Internet Protection Act (CIPA) to address concerns about access to offensive Internet content on school and library computers. Almost immediately, civil liberties groups challenged the law.

On the Internet Students in Brownsville, Texas, work together on a project with information they are obtaining from Internet research.

YES

In 2003 the Supreme Court ruled that the Children's Internet Protection Act was constitutional. The act allows the federal government to withhold funds from schools and public libraries that do not have a safety policy to "block or filter Internet access to pictures that: (a) are obscene, or (b) are harmful to minors, for computers are accessed by minors." Chief Justice Rehnquist wrote, "A library's need to exercise judgment in making collection decisions depends on its traditional role in identifying suitable and worthwhile material; it is no less entitled to play that role when it collects material from the Internet than when it collects material from any other source."

—William Rehnquist, October 2002

NO

One interest group that opposed the new law was the Online Policy Group, Inc. It filed a "friend of the court" brief with the Supreme Court during the CIPA case. The group said that blocking of information was similar to "prior restraint," because it allowed prepublication censorship and gave local officials the authority to make such judgments: "Indeed, commercial blocking software is even more troubling because it effectively delegates censorship decisions to private individuals, who . . . have no obligation to uphold the Constitution or narrowly tailor (fit) their censorship to comply with the First Amendment."

—*Brief of Amici Curiae* Online Policy Group, Inc., 2002

Debating the Issue

1. **Identifying** What are three important issues related to the use of the Internet?
2. **Naming** What was the first attempt by Congress to address the issue of offensive Internet sites?
3. **Explaining** How did Congress attempt to control the use of the Internet by schools and public libraries?
4. **Concluding** Is the censorship of some Internet sites similar to a library's decision to purchase certain books and exclude others?

Representing the People

Guide to Reading

Big Idea

The Constitution gives the legislative branch—Congress—the power to make laws.

Content Vocabulary

- franking privilege *(p. 192)*
- lobbyist *(p. 192)*
- casework *(p. 195)*
- pork-barrel project *(p. 196)*

Academic Vocabulary

- draft *(p. 193)*
- complex *(p. 193)*
- estimate *(p. 193)*

Reading Strategy

Analyzing On a chart like the one below, write the basic requirements for running for Congress.

Requirements

Real World Civics Shake up in the halls of Congress! The results of the 2006 national election made it possible for the first woman Speaker of the House—Nancy Pelosi of California—to lead the 110th Congress in 2007. Also, after 12 years of Republican control, in 2007 the Democrats held majorities in both the House of Representatives and the Senate. This Democratic hold on Congress, however, was only by a narrow margin. The Democrats did not have enough votes to override President George W. Bush's vetoes of their legislation, and the President did not have enough Republican votes to carry out his legislative plans. It was apparent that little would be accomplished until after the 2008 elections.

▼ **Rep. Nancy Pelosi celebrates 2007 Democratic control of Congress**

Qualifications and Privileges

Main Idea **The Constitution sets forth the qualifications for election to the House and to the Senate.**

Civics & You Have you applied for a job? What set of qualifications did you need for the job? Read to find out about the qualifications for Congress.

Each American is represented by a congressperson and two senators. Many others help these elected representatives. Thousands of people work full-time for Congress, keeping the wheels of government turning.

Qualifications The legal qualifications for our congressional representatives are spelled out in the Constitution. To run for senator, you must be at least 30 years old, live in the state you plan to represent, and have been a U.S. citizen for at least nine years before being elected. Members of the House of Representatives must be at least 25 years old, live in the state they represent, and have been a U.S. citizen for at least seven years before being elected.

Makeup of Congress The members of Congress have more in common than legal qualifications. Nearly half are lawyers. Almost all have college degrees. They also tend to be "joiners." Members of Congress are more likely than the average citizen to be active in community organizations.

Campaign Trail Many members of the House, such as Representative Harold Ford, Jr., of Tennessee, run for the Senate later in their careers. ***Identifying*** **What qualities do you think representatives and senators have in common?**

Representing Voters Senator Ted Kennedy from Massachusetts responds to students lobbying for funds for higher education. ***Explaining*** **How do members of Congress keep voters informed about issues that the members are supporting?**

Salary Members of Congress receive an annual salary, currently $169,300 for both senators and representatives. Further, they receive free office space, parking, and trips to their home states. Senators and representatives can send job-related mail without paying postage. This is called the **franking privilege.** Members of Congress also have low-cost life insurance and the use of a gymnasium, special restaurants, and a medical clinic.

Other Privileges The Constitution also grants senators and representatives immunity, or legal protection, in certain situations. This allows them to say and do what they believe is right without fear of interference from outsiders. The guarantee of immunity does not mean that members of Congress are free to break the law.

Behind-the-Scene Helpers

Serving in Congress is a full-time job. To get help with their workload, members of Congress hire a staff of clerks, secretaries, and special assistants.

Personal Staff The personal staffs of members of Congress run offices in Washington, D.C., as well as one or more offices in the congressional member's home district. Why are personal staffs needed? These workers gather information on new bills and issues. They handle requests for help from voters. They deal with news reporters and **lobbyists**—people hired by private groups to influence government decision makers. They also work for the re-election of the congressional member, even though the law requires them to do this on their own time.

In addition to professional staffers, many members of Congress hire students from their home states or districts to serve as interns and pages. Interns typically help with research and office duties; pages deliver messages and run other errands. This experience gives young people a firsthand look at the political process. One former congressional intern commented, "I felt like I had a backstage pass to the greatest show in the world."

Committee Staff Congressional committees also need staffs. Committee staff members do many of the various day-to-day lawmaking chores of Congress. They **draft,** or outline, bills, gather information, organize committee hearings, and negotiate with lobbyists. In short, they keep the long and **complex,** or difficult, lawmaking process moving.

Support Services Congress has created several agencies to support its work. The Library of Congress is one of the largest libraries in the world. Did you know that one copy of every book published in the United States is kept there? The Library of Congress is an important source of information for members of Congress and their staffs.

Finance and Budget The General Accounting Office (GAO) is the investigative arm of Congress in financial issues. It reviews the spending activities of federal agencies, studies federal programs, and recommends ways to improve the financial performance of the government.

The Congressional Budget Office (CBO) provides Congress with information and analysis for making budgetary decisions. It makes no policy recommendations but rather **estimates,** or guesses, the costs and possible economic effects of programs. It also helps Congress come up with—and stick to—a budget plan.

Reading Check **Explaining** Why are members of Congress granted some immunity?

TIME™ Teens in *Action*

Sarah Seufer

Take a page from this teen's book! Sarah Beth Seufer, 18, of Newland, North Carolina, took part in the United States House of Representatives Page Program. Here is what she had to say about her experiences living and working in Washington, D.C.

QUESTION: How did you become involved?

ANSWER: Last summer, after submitting an application, I was nominated by my congressional representative to the office of the Speaker of the House. I was chosen to be a Cloakroom Page. It was my responsibility to answer phone calls related to the activities on the House floor, and to relay messages to representatives.

Pages and representatives leaving a House session

Q: Did you have a good time?

A: I've always loved learning about American government—seeing it in action was incredible! The goal is that pages will return home from Washington, D.C., with a newfound sense of American history and politics.

ACTION FACT: Seufer wants to become a lawyer and eventually run for public office.

Making a Difference CITIZENSHIP

What steps did Sarah take to become a page?

American Biography

Ileana Ros-Lehtinen (1952–)

In 1822, Joseph Marion Hernandez of Florida became the first Latino to serve in Congress. In 1989, **Ileana Ros-Lehtinen** was the first Cuban American to be elected to the United States Congress. Born in 1952, Ileana and her family fled Cuba in 1959 after Fidel Castro's Communist revolution. After completing her studies, she began her career as an educator. She founded a private school, Eastern Academy, where she served as a teacher and administrator.

Ros-Lehtinen entered politics in 1982, serving as a Republican member of the Florida House of Representatives and later in the state senate. Since 1989 she has served in the United States House of Representatives, representing Florida's Eighteenth Congressional District.

Ros-Lehtinen has been one of the leaders in defending the U.S. embargo on Cuba. She also plays a leading role promoting the spread of human rights to countries like Lebanon, Syria, Iran, Saudi Arabia, and China. Ros-Lehtinen was part of a congressional delegation that visited Iraq to understand how the war has affected Iraqi women and their families and to encourage them to get "involved in all levels of their government."

Making a Difference — CITIZENSHIP

Ileana Ros-Lehtinen was an educator before she turned to politics. ***Explaining*** **Why do you think Ros-Lehtinen is such a strong supporter of the U.S. embargo on Cuba?**

Congress at Work

Main Idea **The 535 members of Congress have several different but closely related roles.**

Civics & You What do you think is the most important work for members of Congress? Read on to find out about the three major jobs of Congress.

The basic job of senators and representatives is to represent the people of their states and districts. They are responsible for reflecting and translating into action their constituents' interests and concerns. Congress does its work in regular time periods, or sessions, that begin each January 3 and continue through most of the year.

Lawmaking

In carrying out the responsibility of representing the people of their states and districts, members of Congress perform three major jobs. Making laws is perhaps the best known task of Congress.

Congress considers several different kinds of legislation each year. Most pieces of legislation are in the form of bills. Bills are drafts of laws presented to the House and Senate for enactment. Members of the Senate and the House of Representatives write and introduce bills, take part in committee work, listen to the input of people for and against a bill, and then vote on the floor of the House or Senate. You will learn more about this process in Section 4 of this chapter.

Casework

Members of Congress often act as troubleshooters for people from their home districts and states who request help in dealing with the federal government. This help is called **casework.** Over the course of a year, some congressional offices receive as many as 10,000 requests for information or services.

What drives representatives to help their constituents? Senator Olympia Snowe of Maine explains:

> *"Out of my experiences in life has grown a conviction that no pursuit is as valuable as, or worthier than, the simple idea of helping others—of enabling individuals to improve their lives, to soften the hardest days and brighten the darkest."*
>
> —Olympia Snowe quoted in *Nine and Counting: The Women of the Senate*

Most requests for help are handled by the senator's or representative's office staff. If a staffer cannot get results, the senator or representative usually steps in. Senator Dianne Feinstein of California said,

> *"It's one of the most important things we do . . . . We respond to constituents. . . . I insist on responding promptly, because it's a matter of accountability to our constituency."*
>
> —Dianne Feinstein quoted in *Nine and Counting: The Women of the Senate*

Why do lawmakers spend so much of their time on casework? First, casework helps lawmakers to get reelected. Helping voters increases popular support. Second, casework helps lawmakers get a closer look at how well the executive branch is handling programs such as Social Security or veterans' benefits. Third, casework provides a way to help average citizens deal with federal agencies.

TIME™

Political Cartoons

Michael Ramirez/Copley News Service

Every year, more than half of all Americans do volunteer work ... role in it. One of the responsibilities of citizens is to help make their ... of volunteer grou... small. Perha... dad who...

With this 2006 cartoon, Michael Ramirez is making a point about earmarking—the Congressional practice of setting aside specific funds for a special project in a spending bill, often without public review.

1. **How is Congress depicted in this cartoon?**
2. **Why do you think Ramirez chose this symbol?**
3. **How is earmarking represented?**
4. **Do you think Ramirez supports or opposes earmarking? Explain.**

Helping the District or State

Besides providing services for their constituents, members of Congress also try to bring federal government projects and money to their districts and states. Lawmakers do this in several ways.

Public Works Every year through public works bills, Congress appropriates billions of dollars for a variety of local projects. These projects might include things such as post offices, dams, military bases, veterans' hospitals, and mass transit system projects. Such government projects can bring jobs and money into a state or district.

Grants and Contracts Lawmakers also try to make sure their districts or states get their fair share of the available federal grants and contracts which are funded through the federal budget. Federal grants and contracts are very important to lawmakers and their districts or states. These contracts are a crucial source of money and jobs and can greatly affect the economy of a state.

All members of Congress work to give their constituents a share in the money the national government spends every year. A contract to make army uniforms, for example, might mean lots of money for a local business. Government projects and grants that primarily benefit the home district or state are known as **pork-barrel projects.** To understand this term, think of a member of Congress dipping into the "pork barrel" (the federal treasury) and pulling out a piece of "fat" (a federal project for his or her district).

Using Influence Lawmakers do not have direct control over grants and contracts. Instead, agencies of the executive branch, such as the Department of Labor, award federal grants and contracts.

Lawmakers, however, may try to influence agency decisions. They may pressure agency officials to give a favorable hearing to their state's requests. Lawmakers may also encourage their constituents to contact agency officials in order to make their needs known.

Reading Check **Describing** What are the three major jobs of a congressperson?

Vocabulary

1. **Write** a true and a false statement for each term below. Beside each false statement, explain why it is false: *franking privilege, lobbyist, casework, pork-barrel project.*

Main Ideas

2. **Explaining** What are the qualifications for members of the House of Representatives and the Senate?
3. **Summarizing** What action does Congress take after a bill is introduced in Congress?

Critical Thinking

4. **Analyzing** Why do you think the Constitution did not include other qualifications for members of Congress?
5. **BIG Ideas** On a graphic organizer like the one below, write the major responsibilities Congress has in the lawmaking process.

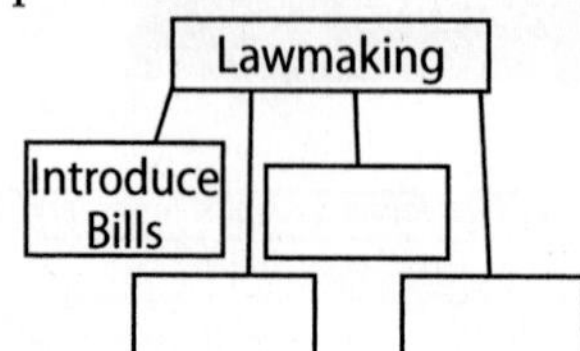

CITIZENSHIP Activity

6. **Creative Writing** Describe the job of a member of the House or Senate by creating a want ad for a congressperson. In the ad, include qualifications, benefits and salary, and skills needed. Also include facts that demonstrate the typical responsibilities of members.

Study Central™ To review this section, go to glencoe.com.

Section Audio

Spotlight Video

How a Bill Becomes a Law

Guide to Reading

Big Idea
The Constitution gives the legislative branch—Congress—the power to make laws.

Content Vocabulary
- joint resolution *(p. 198)*
- special-interest group *(p. 199)*
- filibuster *(p. 200)*
- cloture *(p. 200)*
- voice vote *(p. 202)*
- standing vote *(p. 202)*
- roll-call vote *(p. 202)*
- veto *(p. 202)*
- pocket veto *(p. 202)*

Academic Vocabulary
- element *(p. 198)*
- category *(p. 198)*

Reading Strategy
Sequencing Information
As you read, create a graphic organizer similar to the one below to track the major steps an idea takes to become a law.

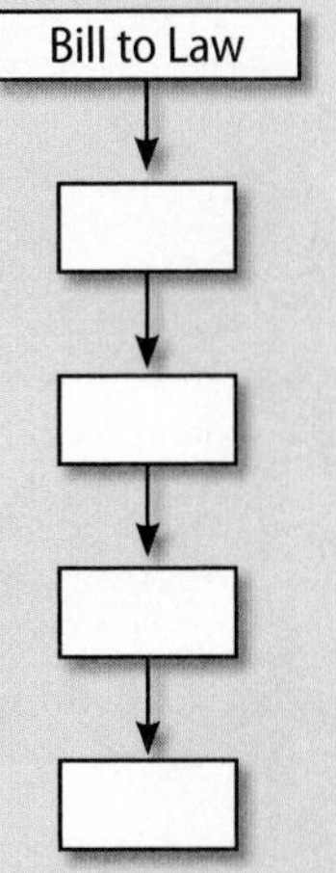

Real World Civics For most of our nation's history, African Americans throughout the South were prevented from voting by local officials. President Lyndon B. Johnson had assured Dr. Martin Luther King, Jr., that he would push for a Voting Rights Act in time. In March of 1965, Dr. King decided to change things himself by marching from Selma to Montgomery, Alabama, demanding the right to vote. When Dr. King's original 600 marchers reached Montgomery, they had become 25,000 strong. Less than five months later, President Johnson signed a law assuring every citizen the right to vote. Passing laws such as the Voting Rights Act is one of Congress's most important roles.

▼ **Dr. Martin Luther King, Jr., (center), wife Coretta, and others in the 1965 peace march**

Bills Congress Considers

Main Idea **Congress considers several different kinds of legislation each year. Most pieces of legislation are in the form of bills.**

Civics & You How do you think Congress should make decisions about bills? What factors should have the greatest influence on its decision making?

Have you heard people say there are two things you should never watch being made—sausages and laws? Strange **elements,** or factors, may go into the final product, and the process requires patience. More than 10,000 bills are often introduced during each term of Congress, yet only several hundred pass all the hurdles and become law.

Bills generally fall into two **categories,** or types. Private bills concern individual people or places. They usually deal with people's claims against the government. Public bills apply to the entire nation and involve general matters such as taxation.

Along with bills, Congress considers different kinds of resolutions, or formal statements expressing lawmakers' opinions or decisions. Many resolutions do not have the force of law. **Joint resolutions,** however, which are passed by both houses of Congress, do become laws if signed by the president. Congress uses joint resolutions to propose constitutional amendments and to designate money for a special purpose.

Reading Check **Analyzing** Why might public bills take months to debate?

Protecting Parkland Part of the money Congress designates for the upkeep of federal parks goes to Yellowstone National Park, which is visited by thousands each year. ***Analyzing*** **Why do you think the power for funding of federal parkland is not given to the states?**

Presidential Signing The majority of bills passed by Congress are signed into law by the president. In 1962, President John F. Kennedy signed a bill designating the home of abolitionist Frederick Douglass as a national monument as his descendants looked on. ***Speculating*** **Why might a president refuse to sign a bill?**

From Bill to Law

Main Idea **To become a law, a bill must be passed in identical form by both chambers of Congress.**

Civics & You As a bill is considered, both houses of Congress keep a check on it. Read to find out why the houses must agree on each law.

Every bill starts with an idea. The ideas for new bills come from private citizens, the White House, or from **special-interest groups**—organizations made up of people with common interests.

Whatever its source, a senator or representative must introduce a bill before Congress will consider it. Every bill is given a title and a number when it is submitted. For example, during the first session of Congress, the first bill introduced is called S.1 in the Senate and H.R.1 in the House.

Committee Action

After a bill is introduced, it is sent to the standing committee that is related to the subject of the bill. Standing committees have life-and-death power over bills. The committee can (1) pass the bill, (2) mark up a bill with changes and suggest that it be passed, (3) replace the original bill with a new bill, (4) ignore the bill and let it die (which is called "pigeonholing" the bill), or (5) kill the bill outright by majority vote.

Debating a Bill

Bills approved in committee are ready for consideration by the full House or Senate. When bills do reach the floor of the House or Senate, the members argue their pros and cons and discuss amendments. The House accepts only amendments relevant to the bill. The Senate, however, allows riders—completely unrelated amendments—to be tacked onto the bill.

Rules of Debate In the House, the Rules Committee sets the terms for debate. It usually puts time limits on the discussion, for example, to speed up action. The Senate, because it is smaller, has fewer rules. Senators can speak as long as they wish. At times they take advantage of this custom to **filibuster,** or talk a bill to death. One member can speak—holding the floor for hour after hour, delaying a vote until the bill's sponsor withdraws the measure. The Senate can end a filibuster if three-fifths of the members vote for **cloture.** Under this procedure, no one may speak for more than one hour. Senators rarely resort to cloture, though. In 1964, during debate on the Civil Rights Act, the Senate waited out a 74-day filibuster by senators opposed to the legislation.

Reading Check **Speculating** What is a rider to a bill? Why do you think Senators attach riders to bills?

Profile of the 111th Congress*

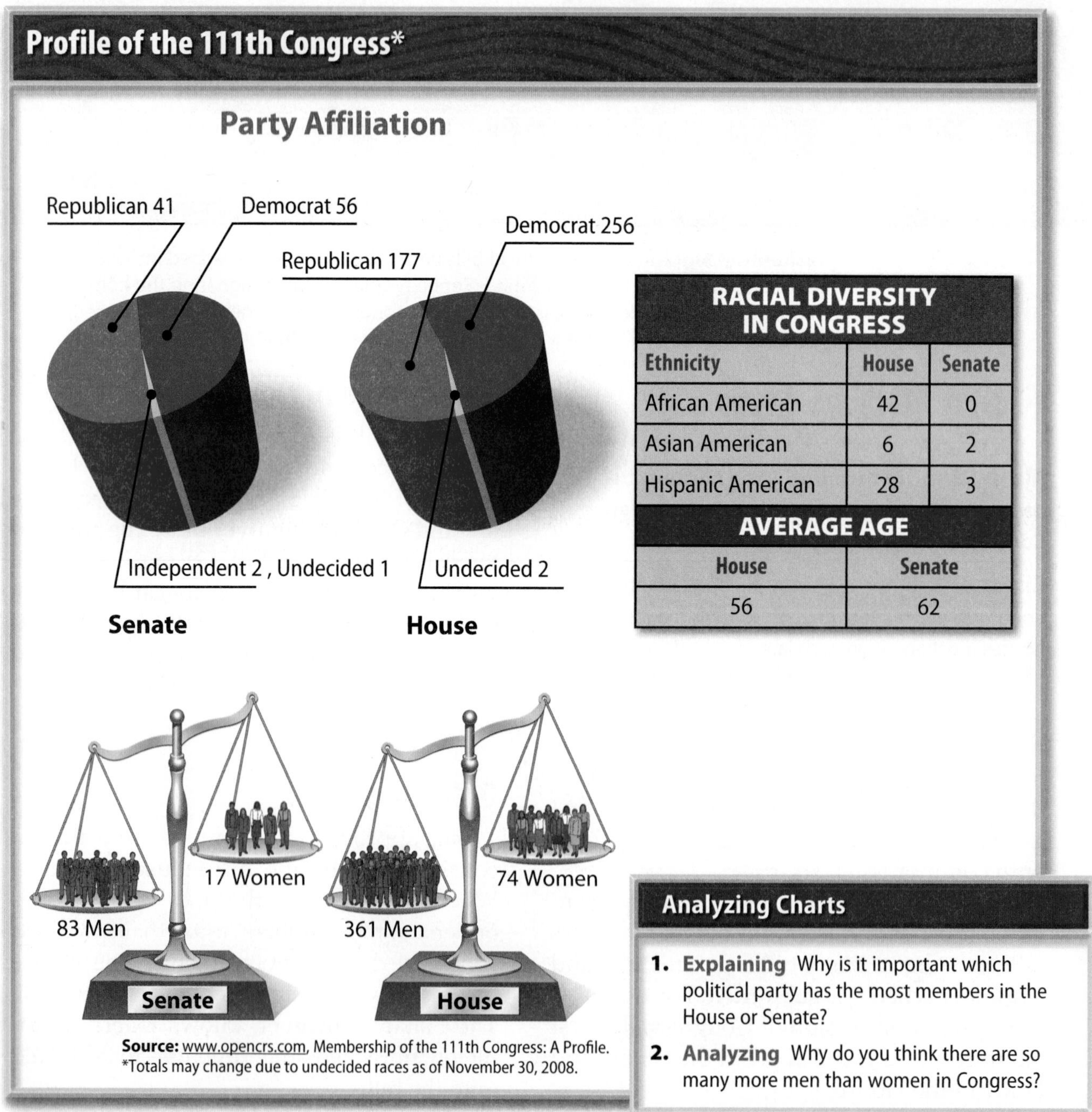

RACIAL DIVERSITY IN CONGRESS		
Ethnicity	House	Senate
African American	42	0
Asian American	6	2
Hispanic American	28	3

AVERAGE AGE	
House	Senate
56	62

Source: www.opencrs.com, Membership of the 111th Congress: A Profile.
*Totals may change due to undecided races as of November 30, 2008.

Analyzing Charts

1. **Explaining** Why is it important which political party has the most members in the House or Senate?
2. **Analyzing** Why do you think there are so many more men than women in Congress?

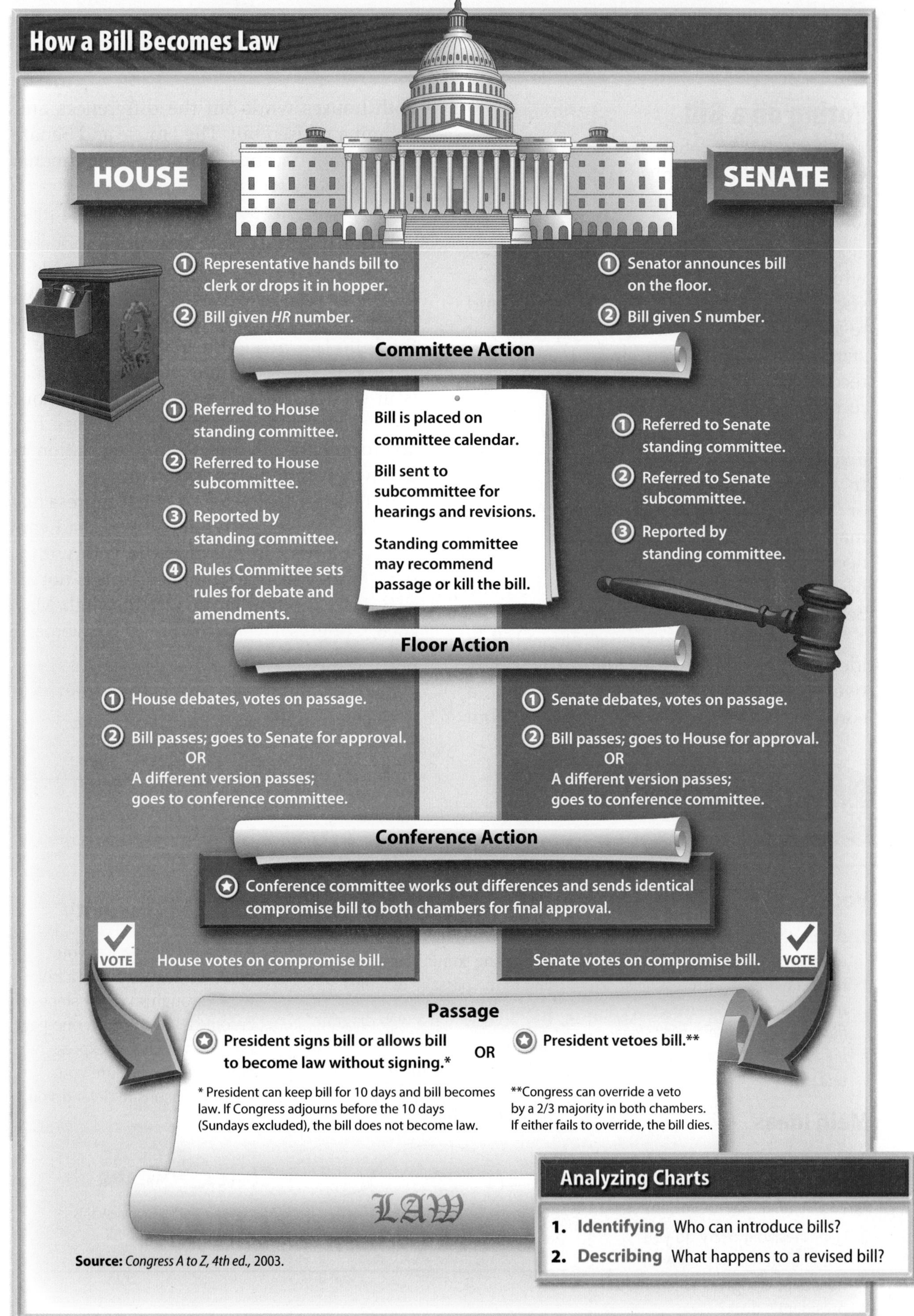

Source: *Congress A to Z, 4th ed.*, 2003.

Analyzing Charts

1. **Identifying** Who can introduce bills?
2. **Describing** What happens to a revised bill?

Voting on a Bill

After a bill is debated, it is brought to a vote. Voting in the House is done in one of three ways. The simplest is a **voice vote,** in which those in favor say "Yea" and those against say "No." The Speaker determines which side has the most voice votes. In a **standing vote,** those in favor of a bill stand to be counted, and then those against it stand to be counted. The third method is a recorded vote, in which members' votes are recorded electronically.

The Senate has three methods of voting: a voice vote, a standing vote, and a roll call. In a **roll-call vote,** senators respond "Aye" or "No" as their names are called. A simple majority of all members that are present is needed to pass a bill. If a bill passes in one house, it is sent to the other. If either the Senate or the House rejects a bill, it dies.

The Senate and House must pass a bill in identical form before it becomes law. When two versions of the same bill are passed, a conference committee with members from both houses work out the differences and submit a revised bill. The House and Senate must either accept it without amendments or completely reject it.

Action by the President After a bill is approved, it goes to the president. One of four things may then happen. The president may sign the bill and declare it a new law. The president may **veto,** or refuse to sign, the bill. The president may also do nothing for 10 days. At that point, if Congress is in session, the bill becomes law without the president's signature. If Congress has adjourned, the bill dies. Killing legislation in this way is called a **pocket veto.**

If the president vetoes a bill, Congress has one last chance to save it. As you read earlier, Congress can override the veto with a two-thirds vote of each house. This is not an easy task, though. From 1789 through May 2008, Congress overturned only 108 vetoes.

Reading Check **Explaining** When is a conference committee formed and what is its purpose?

Review

Vocabulary

1. **Define** the following terms and use them in sentences that relate to the lawmaking process: *joint resolution, special-interest group, filibuster, cloture, voice vote, standing vote, roll-call vote, veto, pocket veto.*

Main Ideas

2. **Contrasting** What is the difference between public and private bills? What are resolutions?
3. **Hypothesizing** Why do you think a bill has to pass both houses of Congress to reach the president's desk?

Critical Thinking

4. **Explaining** Why is the action of a standing committee so important to the passage of a bill?
5. **BIG Ideas** On a web diagram like the one below, write the different actions the president can take when deciding on the passage of a bill.

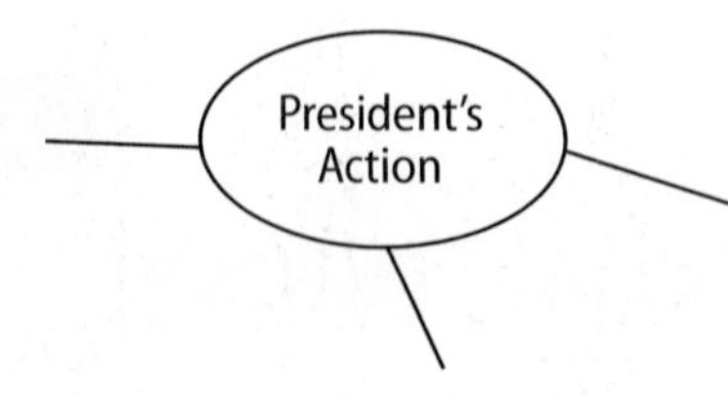

CITIZENSHIP Activity

6. **Persuasive Writing** Do you think it is necessary for a bill to go through so many steps to become a law? Write a one-page essay in which you express your view. Make sure you include reasons to defend your view.

Study Central™ To review this section, go to glencoe.com.

Chapter 6

Visual Summary

Comparing the House and the Senate

The Congress of the United States was created by Article I, Section 1, of the Constitution, providing that "All legislative Powers herein granted shall be vested in a Congress of the United States, which shall consist of a Senate and a House of Representatives."

HOUSE*	SENATE
Members chosen from local districts	Members chosen from an entire state
Two-year term	Six-year term
A representative must be at least 25 years of age and must have been a citizen of the United States for at least 7 years	A senator must be at least 30 years of age and must have been a citizen of the United States for at least 9 years
House members must be residents of the state from which they are chosen	Senate members must be residents of the state from which they are chosen
435 voting members; the number representing each state is determined by population	Composed of 100 members; 2 from each state
Originally elected by voters	Originally (until 1913) elected by state legislatures
May impeach federal officials	May convict federal officials of impeachable offenses
More formal rules	Fewer rules and restrictions
Debate limited	Debate extended
Floor action controlled	Unanimous consent rules
Less prestige and less individual notice	More prestige and media attention
Originates bills for raising revenues	Power of "advice and consent" on presidential appointments and treaties
Local or narrow leadership	National leadership
The Speaker of the House is the presiding officer	The vice president of the United States is the presiding officer

*Some of these differences, such as terms of office, are provided for in the Constitution, while others, such as debate rules, are not.

Study anywhere, anytime! Download quizzes and flash cards to your PDA from glencoe.com.

Chapter 6

ASSESSMENT

TEST-TAKING TIP

Answer the questions you know first and go back to those for which you need more time.

Directions: Choose the word(s) that best completes the sentence.

1. _______ choose the Speaker of the House.

A Lobbyists
B Constituents
C Standing committees
D Majority party members

2. _______ requires police to bring a prisoner to court to explain why they are holding him or her.

A A bill of attainder
B The franking privilege
C An ex post facto law
D A writ of habeas corpus

3. Members of Congress bring government funds to their state through _______.

A casework
B special-interest groups
C gerrymandering
D pork-barrel projects

4. The simplest way to vote in the House and the Senate is a _______.

A voice vote
B standing vote
C roll-call vote
D computerized vote

Reviewing Main Ideas

Directions: Choose the best answer for each question.

Section 1 *(pp. 176–182)*

5. The House and Senate meet as one body in _______.

A a standing committee
B odd-numbered years
C caucuses
D a joint session

6. The _______ is the most powerful leader in the House of Representatives.

A Speaker of the House
B president pro tempore
C vice president
D minority leader

Section 2 *(pp. 184–188)*

7. Which of the following legislative powers is implied by the elastic clause?

A coining money
B creating an air force
C regulating foreign trade
D establishing post offices

8. What nonlegislative power resides in the House of Representatives?

A trying public officials
B impeaching federal judges
C establishing bankruptcy laws
D approving presidential nominees

Section 3 *(pp. 190–196)*

9. Which of the following is a requirement for representatives in the House?

A be at least 30 years old
B live in the state they represent
C live in the district they represent
D be U.S. citizens for at least 9 years

10. What is NOT a major responsibility of representatives?

A writing and introducing bills
B voting on the floor of the House
C troubleshooting for people in their district
D providing analysis for the IRS

GO ON

Section 4 *(pp. 197–202)*

11. What is the term for ignoring a bill and letting it die?

A earmarking

B cloture

C gerrymandering

D pigeonholing

12. What may happen to a bill in the House after the bill leaves committee?

A Representatives add riders to the bill.

B The House clerk assigns a number to the bill.

C Representatives add amendments related to the bill.

D Representatives vote for cloture to limit debate on the bill.

Critical Thinking

Directions: Base your answers to questions 13 and 14 on the cartoon below and your knowledge of Chapter 6.

13. Determine the cartoonist's point of view. How would he describe politicians?

A extremely ruthless

B easily manipulated

C scrupulously honest

D fiercely independent

14. Analyze the symbols in the cartoon. What does the wagon most likely represent?

A casework

B legislation

C franking privileges

D campaign contributions

Document-Based Questions

Directions: Analyze the following document and answer the short-answer questions that follow.

Article 1, Section 7, U.S. Constitution

In this section of the Constitution the passing of a bill is discussed.

> *Every bill which shall have passed the House of Representatives and the Senate, . . . [and] Every order, resolution, or vote to which the concurrence of the Senate and House of Representatives may be necessary (except on a question of adjournment) shall be presented to the President. . .*
>
> —U.S. Constitution

15. Why do you think the Framers decided that all three arms of the government—the House of Representatives, the Senate, and the president—must be made aware of all bills and issues discussed in Congress?

16. What issue is the exception to this plan of review?

Extended Response

17. Write a brief essay describing two ways a president might stop a bill from becoming law.

STOP

Civics ONLINE

For additional test practice, use Self-Check Quizzes—Chapter 6 on glencoe.com.

Need Extra Help?

If you missed question. . .	1	2	3	4	5	6	7	8	9	10	11	12	13	14	15	16	17
Go to page. . .	180	188	196	202	178	180	185	187	191	194	199	201	192	195	201	202	202

Chapter 7

The Executive Branch

Delegates to the 2008 National Republican Convention prepare to nominate their

Why It Matters

The Framers did not state specifically in the Constitution what the role of the president should be. The nation's first president, George Washington, established many traditions that shaped the presidency. Every president since Washington has followed and built upon these traditions, refining the president's role within the government.

Civics ONLINE
Visit glencoe.com and enter QuickPass™ code CIV3093c7 for Chapter 7 resources.

Chapter Audio

BIG Ideas

Section 1: The President and Vice President

The Constitution gives the executive branch the power to execute, or implement, the law. The president holds one of the most powerful and important elective offices in the world.

Section 2: The President's Job

The Constitution gives the executive branch the power to execute, or implement, the law. The president fills many different roles.

Section 3: Making Foreign Policy

Under our federal system, the executive, legislative, and judicial branches share the responsibility of governing the nation. The president and Congress have important roles in making foreign policy.

Section 4: Presidential Advisers and Executive Agencies

The Constitution gives the executive branch the power to execute, or implement, the law. Thousands of employees and advisers help the president.

FOLDABLES™ Study Organizer

Organizing Information Study Foldable Make the following Foldable to help you organize information about the U.S. president and the executive branch of government.

Step 1 Fold a sheet of paper in half from top to bottom with edges evenly together.

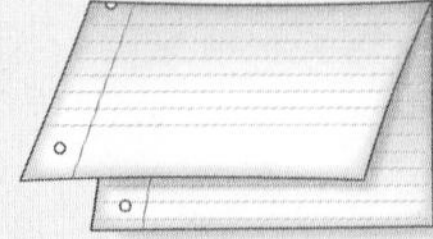

Step 2 Then fold the paper in half from side to side.

Step 3 Label the Foldable as shown.

Reading and Writing
As you read the chapter, record the different roles the president plays in government as he or she fulfills the requirements of this office.

Section Audio

Spotlight Video

Section 1

The President and Vice President

Guide to Reading

Big Idea
The Constitution gives the executive branch the power to execute, or implement, the law.

Content Vocabulary
- Electoral College *(p. 210)*
- elector *(p. 210)*

Academic Vocabulary
- display *(p. 210)*
- outcome *(p. 210)*

Reading Strategy
Describing As you read this section, describe the qualifications and terms of office for the president by completing the graphic organizer below.

Real World Civics Any child born in the United States can grow up to be president. It is considered to be the most powerful job in the world. Would you want it? Barack Obama did. After serving in the U.S. Senate representing Illinois, he decided to run for the presidency in 2008. After becoming the nominee of his party, he chose Senator Joseph Biden as his running mate. Together they campaigned in a history-making election. Barack Obama succeeded at becoming the first African American elected to the U.S. presidency.

Barack Obama (right) and Joe Biden claim the nominations for president and vice president at the 2008 Democratic convention.

The Office of the President

Main idea **As the head of the executive branch of our federal government, the president holds one of the most powerful and important elective offices in the world.**

Civics & You What qualifications do you think a president should have? Read this section to find out what Americans have come to expect from their presidents.

The president heads the executive branch of the United States government. The presidency is the top political job in the country. Because of the power and global influence of the United States, the president is generally considered to hold the most important job in the world. Our country's first president was George Washington. Just as the nation has grown tremendously since that time, so has the office of the presidency.

The U.S. Constitution lists only three rules about who, by law, can become president of the United States. A person must be (1) at least 35 years old, (2) a native-born American citizen, and (3) a resident of the United States for at least 14 years.

Characteristics of Presidents Almost all our presidents have shared similar characteristics. So far, every American president has been male. All but one have been Protestant Christians. Most have had a college education. Many have been lawyers. Most came from states with large populations.

Only in the past few decades has the presidency become a possibility for a wider group of Americans. John F. Kennedy became the first Catholic president in 1960. In 1984 the Democratic Party nominated Geraldine Ferraro as its first female vice-presidential candidate. In 2000 the Democrats nominated Connecticut senator Joseph Lieberman as the first Jewish candidate for vice president. The first African American president, Barack Obama, was elected in 2008.

President for Life Former presidents are often called upon to attend official ceremonies as former presidents Carter, Bush, Clinton, and Ford do here. ***Identifying*** **What would happen if a person who came to this country as an immigrant wanted to run for president?**

Presidential Elections

Presidential elections take place every four years in years evenly divisible by the number four—for example, 2000, 2004, and 2008. The Constitution provides for an indirect method of election called the **Electoral College.** The Constitution says that each state "shall appoint" **electors,** who then vote for one of the major candidates. Although the ballot will **display,** or show, the names of the presidential candidates, you are actually voting for a list of presidential electors pledged to that candidate.

Each state has as many electoral votes as the total of its U.S. senators and representatives. (Washington, D.C., has three electoral votes.) The Electoral College includes 538 electors. In almost every state, the Electoral College is a "winner-take-all" system. Even if a candidate wins the popular vote by just a tiny majority, that candidate usually gets all of the state's electoral votes. Thus, the electoral votes of a few small states can decide the **outcome,** or result, of a close election.

To be elected, a candidate must receive half of the 538 electoral votes available, or 270 votes to win. If no candidate gets an electoral college majority, the House of Representatives votes on the candidates, with each state delegation casting only a single vote. This has happened twice—in 1800 and in 1824.

Although the winning presidential candidate is usually announced on the same evening as the popular election, the formal election by the Electoral College does not take place until December. The electors meet in each state capital to cast their ballots. Then Congress officially counts the electoral votes.

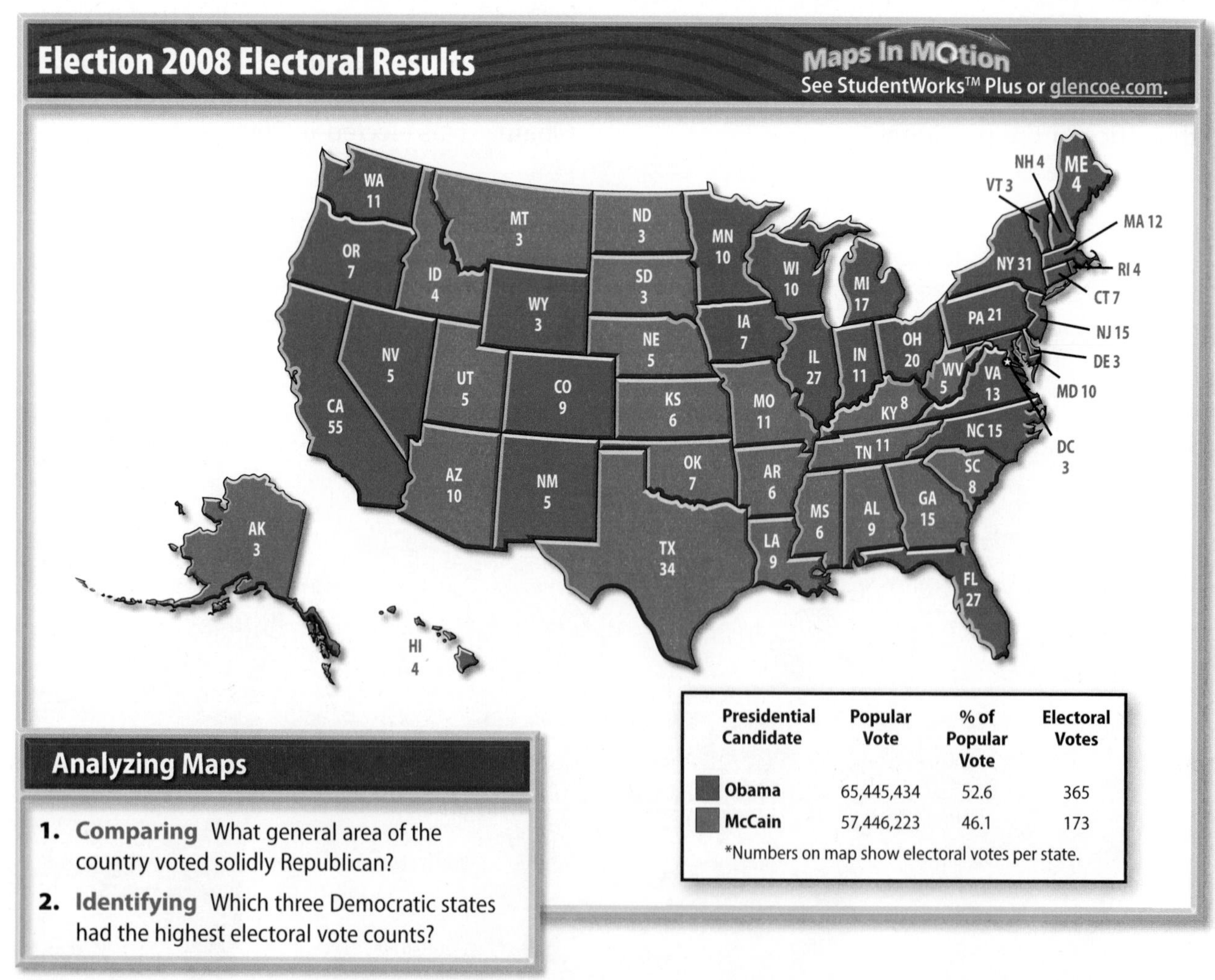

Presidential Candidate	Popular Vote	% of Popular Vote	Electoral Votes
Obama	65,445,434	52.6	365
McCain	57,446,223	46.1	173

*Numbers on map show electoral votes per state.

Analyzing Maps

1. **Comparing** What general area of the country voted solidly Republican?
2. **Identifying** Which three Democratic states had the highest electoral vote counts?

Presidential Succession

Graphs In MOtion
See StudentWorks™ Plus or glencoe.com.

ORDER OF SUCCESSION

1. Vice President
2. Speaker of the House
3. President *pro tempore* of the Senate
4. Secretary of State
5. Secretary of the Treasury
6. Secretary of Defense
7. Attorney General
8. Secretary of the Interior
9. Secretary of Agriculture
10. Secretary of Commerce
11. Secretary of Labor
12. Secretary of Health and Human Services
13. Secretary of Housing and Urban Development
14. Secretary of Transportation
15. Secretary of Energy
16. Secretary of Education
17. Secretary of Veterans Affairs
18. Secretary of Homeland Security*

*The order of this position may change, pending congressional legislation.

Source: Nelson, Ed. *The Presidency A to Z*, 3rd ed. (Washington, D.C.: CQ Press, 2003).

Fourteen vice presidents have become president. Five former vice presidents were elected president. Four vice presidents succeeded to the presidency upon the assassination of the incumbent: Andrew Johnson for Abraham Lincoln in 1865, Chester Arthur for James Garfield in 1881, Theodore Roosevelt for William McKinley in 1901, and Lyndon Johnson for John F. Kennedy in 1963.

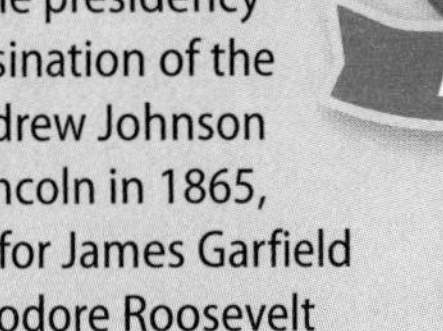

A. Lincoln

A. Johnson

Four vice presidents inherited the presidency after the natural death of the incumbent: John Tyler for William Henry Harrison in 1841, Millard Fillmore for Zachary Taylor in 1850, Calvin Coolidge for Warren Harding in 1923, and Harry S. Truman for Franklin Roosevelt in 1945.

F.D. Roosevelt

H.S. Truman

Ratified in 1967, the Twenty-fifth Amendment established the order of succession to the presidency and spelled out what happens when the vice presidency becomes vacant. In 1974, Gerald Ford became the first president to take office under its provisions. Ford succeeded to the presidency after Richard Nixon resigned during the Watergate scandal.

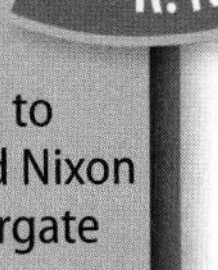

R. Nixon

G. Ford

Analyzing Charts

1. **Evaluating** Why is a line of succession for the presidency important?
2. **Explaining** Why did Andrew Johnson succeed President Lincoln?

Term of Office

Presidents serve four-year terms. Originally the Constitution placed no limits on how many terms a president could serve. The nation's first president, George Washington, served for eight years and then refused to run for a third term. Following Washington's example, no president served more than two terms until 1940, when Franklin D. Roosevelt ran for and won a third term. In 1944 Roosevelt won a fourth term. The Twenty-second Amendment, ratified in 1951, limits each president to two elected terms in office, or a maximum of 10 years if the presidency began during another president's term.

Salary and Benefits

The president receives a salary of $400,000 per year, plus money for expenses and travel. The president lives and works in the White House. A domestic staff of more than 80 people takes care of the president's family.

The president has use of Camp David, an estate in the Catoctin Mountains of Maryland, about 60 miles north of Washington, D.C. When presidents travel, they command a fleet of special cars, helicopters, and airplanes. For long trips, the president uses *Air Force One*, a specially equipped jet.

The Vice President

The vice president is elected with the president through the Electoral College system. The qualifications for the office are the same as those for the presidency. The Constitution gives little authority to the vice president. Article I states that the vice president shall preside over the Senate and vote in that body in case of a tie. If the president dies, is removed from office, falls seriously ill, or resigns, the vice president becomes president.

Reading Check **Identifying** What is the maximum number of years that a U.S. president can serve?

Presidential Succession

Main Idea **The office of the president has an established order of succession.**

Civics & You Do you know what happens when a president dies or is forced to leave office? Read to find out how the Constitution answers this question.

In 1841 William Henry Harrison became the first president to die in office. His death raised many questions. While the Constitution says that the vice president should assume the "powers and duties" of the presidency, no one was sure what that meant. Should the vice president remain as vice president while doing the president's job? Should the vice president become president? Should a special election be called to elect a new president?

Vice President John Tyler settled these questions. He declared himself president, took the oath of office, and served out the remainder of Harrison's term. Since Tyler's time, eight other vice presidents have taken over the presidency following the death or resignation of a president.

Executive Travel President Bush walks from the White House to *Marine One* to fly to a fund-raiser within an hour. ***Speculating*** **How might this be different than an early president's travel?**

Presidential Succession Act

In 1947 Congress passed the Presidential Succession Act, which indicates the line of succession after the vice president. According to this law, if both the president and vice president die or leave office, the Speaker of the House becomes president. Next in line is the president pro tempore of the Senate, then the secretary of state and other members of the cabinet.

Twenty-fifth Amendment

Remaining questions about presidential succession were answered by the passage of a constitutional amendment. The Twenty-fifth Amendment, ratified in 1967, says that if the president dies or leaves office, the vice president becomes president. The new president then chooses another vice president. Both the Senate and House of Representatives must approve the choice. This amendment also gives the vice president a role in determining whether a president is disabled and unable to do the job. Should that occur, the vice president would serve as acting president until the president is able to go back to work.

The Twenty-fifth Amendment has been used only three times. In 1973 Vice President Spiro Agnew resigned. President Richard Nixon replaced him with Gerald Ford, a representative from Michigan, and Congress approved the nomination. When Nixon resigned from the presidency in 1974, Ford became the new president. Ford then nominated Nelson A. Rockefeller, former governor of New York, to be his vice president. In 1985 President Ronald Reagan informed Congress that he would need to undergo surgery and would be unable to carry out his presidential duties. As a result, Vice President George H.W. Bush served as acting president for about eight hours.

Reading Check **Describing** What was the purpose of the Twenty-fifth Amendment?

Review

Vocabulary

1. **Write** complete sentences about the United States presidency using each of the following terms: *Electoral College, elector.*

Main Ideas

2. **Analyzing** Why do you think the president is elected rather than appointed by Congress?
3. **Identifying** Who are the first four officers in the line of succession to the presidency? Who is last in line?

Critical Thinking

4. **Analyzing** Candidates for president are not usually drawn to the office because of the salary. Why do you think these people run for office?
5. **BIG Ideas** In a graphic organizer like the one below, identify the main qualifications for running for the office of president of the United States.

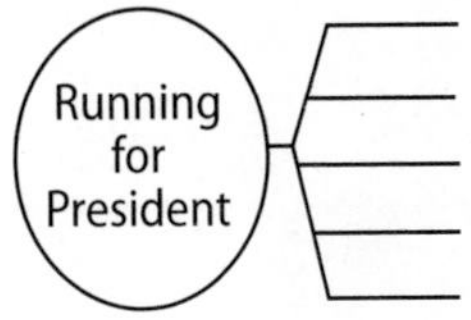

CITIZENSHIP Activity

6. **Expository Writing** What qualifications or characteristics do you think a president should have? Which of the recent presidents, if any, have had these qualifications or characteristics? Write a one-page essay in which you answer these questions.

Study Central™ To review this section, go to glencoe.com.

Guide to Reading

Big Idea

The Constitution gives the executive branch the power to execute, or implement, the law.

Content Vocabulary

- executive order *(p. 216)*
- pardon *(p. 217)*
- reprieve *(p. 217)*
- amnesty *(p. 217)*

Academic Vocabulary

- require *(p. 215)*
- impact *(p. 216)*
- policy *(p. 217)*

Reading Strategy

Summarizing As you read, in a chart like the one below, list the different duties that are part of the president's role as chief executive.

Section 2

Section Audio

Spotlight Video

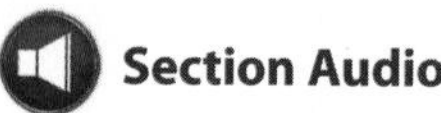

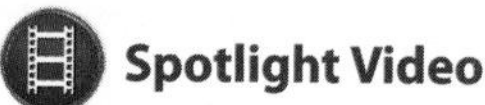

The President's Job

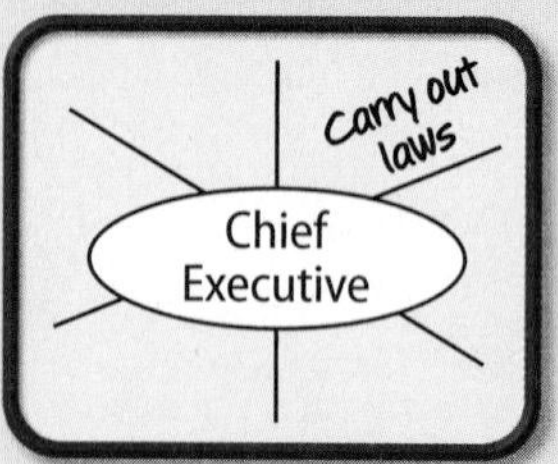

Real World Civics The president is the commander in chief of the U.S. armed forces. He or she is also one of the most important hosts of one of the most impressive houses in the world—the White House. The president must maintain good relationships with other world leaders and often entertains dignitaries. Here President Bill Clinton hosts Spain's King Juan Carlos in 2000, engaging in a ceremonial troop review of U.S. Marines. The south lawn of the White House is a popular location for such honorary troop reviews and other greetings of foreign leaders.

▼ **Former president Clinton honors the king of Spain**

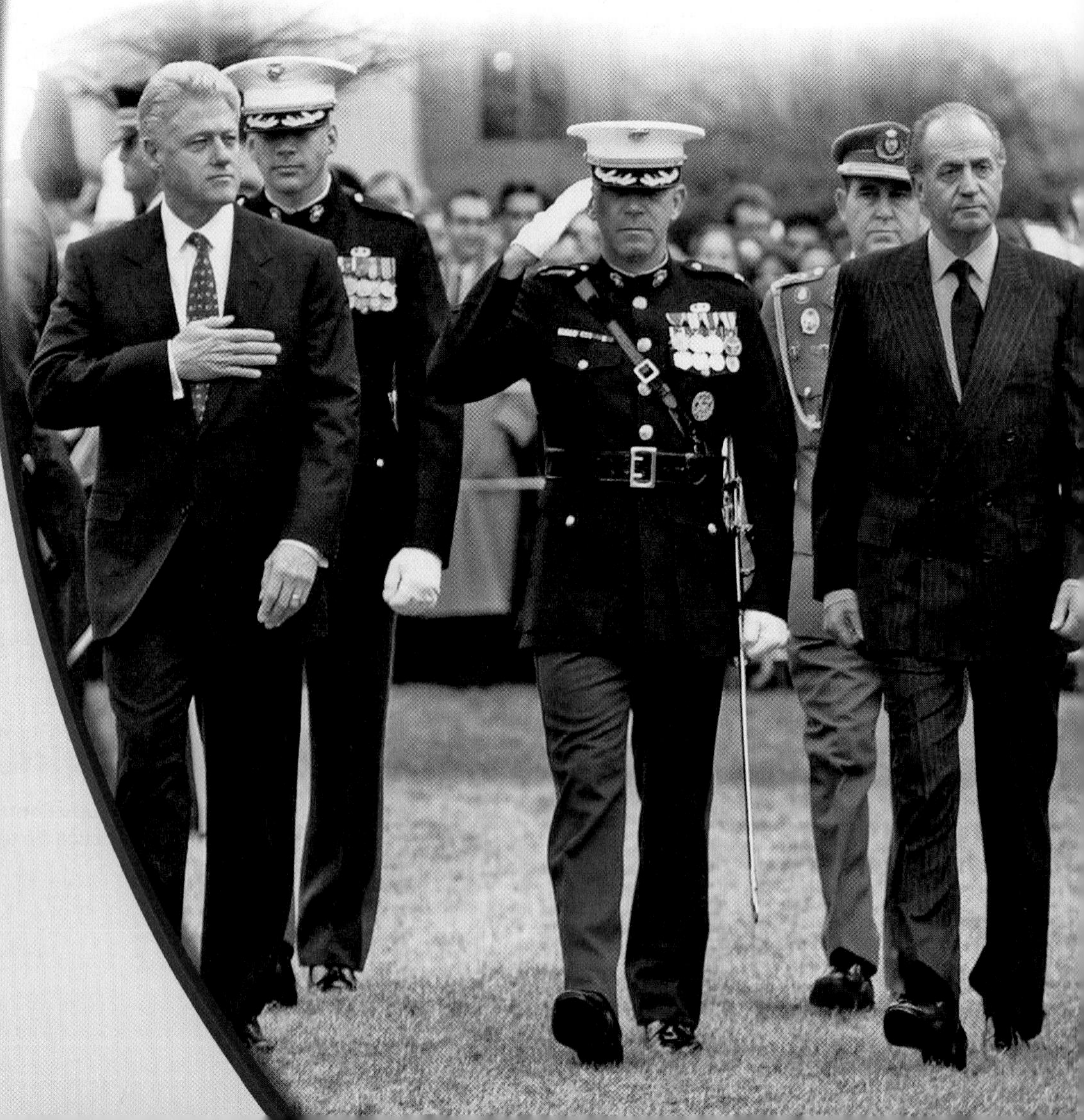

Constitutional Powers

Main Idea **The source for the president's authority is Article II of the Constitution.**

Civics & You What qualifications or characteristics do you think a president should have? Which of the recent presidents, if any, have had these qualifications or characteristics?

Fewer than 50 men have been able to say what it feels like to be president of the United States. Some former presidents' thoughts are revealing.

> "*The presidency has made every man who occupied it, no matter how small, bigger than he was; and no matter how big, not big enough for its demands.*"
>
> —Lyndon B. Johnson

Duties of the President

Although the president is the head of just one of the three branches of government, he or she, with the exception of the vice president, is the only official of the federal government elected by the entire nation. As a result, the president stands as a symbol not only of the federal government, but of the entire nation as well. Even so, the thirty-eighth president, Gerald Ford, pointed out that not even the president can do the impossible.

> "*You know, the President of the United States is not a magician who can wave a wand or sign a paper that will instantly end a war, cure a recession, or make bureaucracy disappear.*"
>
> —Gerald Ford

The president is the most powerful public official in the United States. The U.S. Constitution is the basis of the president's power. Article II says,

> "*Executive Power shall be invested in a President. . . .*"

Thus, the president's main job is to execute, or carry out, the laws passed by Congress.

The Constitution also gives the president the power to

- veto, or reject, bills passed in Congress.
- call Congress into special session.
- serve as commander in chief of the armed forces.
- receive leaders and other officials of foreign countries.
- make treaties with other countries (with Senate approval).
- appoint heads of executive agencies, federal court judges, ambassadors, and other top government officials (also subject to Senate approval).
- pardon or reduce the penalties against people convicted of federal crimes.

Because the Constitution **requires,** or calls for, the president to give Congress information about the "state of the union," the president gives several speeches to Congress each year. The most important is the State of the Union address, in which the president discusses the most important issues facing the nation.

The constitutional duties of the nation's first president, George Washington, and those of a modern president are much the same. For example, the Constitution makes the president the commander in chief of the nation's armed forces. In Washington's administration this meant calling out a militia of 15,000 volunteers. Today the president oversees a military divided into five major units and makes the decision on how to deploy troops stationed around the world.

Reading Check **Analyzing** What are the powers of the president as expressed in the Constitution?

Roles of the President

Main Idea **The president fills many roles that are important to the functioning of the United States government.**

Civics and You The Constitution grants broad powers to the president. Do you think the president has too much power? Read about the president's many roles.

The Constitution holds one person—the president—responsible for carrying out the duties of the executive branch. As the nation has grown, the duties and responsibilities of the executive branch have grown.

Chief Executive

The most important job of the president is to carry out the nation's laws. To do this, the president is in charge of 15 cabinet departments and the approximately 3 million civilians who work for the federal government. The president appoints the heads of the cabinet departments and of other large government agencies, with the Senate's approval.

Use of Executive Orders Presidents have several tools to influence how laws are carried out. One is the executive order. An **executive order** is a rule or command that has the force of law. Only Congress has the authority to make laws. Issuing executive orders, however, is generally considered to fall under the president's constitutional duty to "take care that the laws are faithfully executed."

Many executive orders deal with simple administrative problems. Some, however, have had a great **impact,** or influence. President Harry S. Truman, for instance, used an executive order in 1948 to racially integrate the armed forces. This gave Americans of all races the opportunity to serve in the armed forces.

TIME™ Teens in Action

Shauna Fleming

What is it like to meet the president of the United States? Just ask Shauna Fleming, 17, of Orange, California. She received the President's Volunteer Service Award for her work as founder of "A Million Thanks."

QUESTION: What does A Million Thanks do?

ANSWER: Our goal is to collect thank-you letters for the U.S. military. I started the campaign in 2004 and have collected 2 million letters so far.

Q: Why did you start it?

A: I saw a need for a morale boost for our troops. We've sent millions of letters and e-mails to U.S military men and women stationed all over the world. If you put all the paper together, it would weigh 8,000 pounds and fill two large semi trucks. Our Web site has had over 4 million hits and thousands of great responses from soldiers who received letters.

Q: Because of your work, you were invited to the White House. What was that like?

A: I've met some of the most powerful people in the world. But the highlight has to be meeting President George W. Bush in a private meeting with my family in the Oval Office. I presented the president with the one millionth thank-you letter received by my campaign. I discussed many things with him and he even gave us a tour of the office, pointing out objects that were important to him.

Making a Difference — **CITIZENSHIP**

What qualities does Shauna display that makes her volunteer work successful?

Power of Appointment The Constitution gives the president the power to appoint judges to the Supreme Court and other federal courts. This is an important power because the Supreme Court has the final authority to determine whether a law is constitutional. Because the power to interpret laws is important, most presidents try to appoint Supreme Court justices who share views similar to their own.

The Constitution also gives the president the power to grant pardons. A **pardon** is a declaration of forgiveness and freedom from punishment. The president may also issue a **reprieve,** an order to delay a person's punishment until a higher court can hear the case, or grant **amnesty,** a pardon toward a group of people.

Chief Diplomat

The president directs the foreign **policy,** or strategy, of the United States, making key decisions about how the United States acts toward other countries in the world.

Commander in Chief

The Constitution makes the president commander in chief of the armed forces of the United States. This role gives presidents the ability to back up their foreign policy decisions with force, if necessary. The president is in charge of the army, navy, air force, marines, and coast guard. The top commanders of all these branches of service are subordinate to the president.

The president shares with Congress the power to make war. The Constitution gives Congress the power to declare war, but only the president can order American soldiers into battle. Congress has declared war five times: the War of 1812, the Mexican War, the Spanish-American War, World War I, and World War II. Presidents, however, have sent troops into action overseas more than 150 times since 1789. For example, although Congress never declared war in Korea or in Vietnam, American troops were involved in conflicts in those countries because they were sent there by U.S. presidents.

In 1973, after the Vietnam War, Congress passed the War Powers Resolution. According to this law, the president must notify Congress within 48 hours when troops are sent into battle. These troops must be brought home after 60 days unless Congress gives its approval for them to remain longer or declares war.

European Union President Bush and advisers meet with leaders in Europe to discuss trade. ***Identifying*** **What official role of the president is this an example of?**

Legislative Leader

Only members of Congress have the power to introduce bills for consideration, but in practice Congress expects the executive branch to propose the legislation it would like to see enacted.

Every president has a legislative program. These are new laws that the president wants Congress to pass. The president makes speeches to build support for this program and meets with key senators and representatives to try to persuade them to support the proposed laws.

Civics ONLINE

Student Web Activity Visit glencoe.com and complete the Chapter 7 Web Activity.

The president and Congress have often disagreed over what new laws Congress should adopt. One reason for this is that presidents represent the entire United States, while members of Congress represent only the people of their states or districts.

The difference in the lengths of time that presidents and members of Congress can hold office also contributes to this conflict. While presidents can serve no more than two elected terms, members of Congress can be elected over and over again for decades. Therefore, many members of Congress may not want to move as quickly on programs as the president does.

Head of State

The president is the living symbol of the nation. In this role, the president aids diplomacy by greeting visiting kings and queens, prime ministers, and other foreign leaders. The president also carries out ceremonial functions for Americans, such as lighting the national Christmas tree and giving medals to the country's heroes.

Economic Leader

Every president tries to help the country's economy prosper. Voters expect the president to deal with such problems as unemployment, rising prices, and high taxes. One key task the president must accomplish each year as economic leader is to plan the federal government's budget. The president meets with budget officials to decide what programs to support and what programs to cut back. Budget decisions have a great effect on the national economy.

Party Leader

The president is generally regarded as the leader of his or her political party. Members of the president's party work hard to elect the president. In turn, the president gives speeches to help fellow party members who are running for office as members of Congress, governors, and mayors. The president also helps the party raise money.

Reading Check **Defining** What is a president's legislative program?

Review

Vocabulary

1. **Define** the following terms and use them in complete sentences related to the presidency: *executive order, pardon, reprieve, amnesty.*

Main Ideas

2. **Identifying** According to the Constitution, what is the president's duty to Congress?
3. **Describing** As commander in chief, what responsibilities does the president have? Which is most important?

Critical Thinking

4. **Drawing Conclusions** Which of the roles of the president do you think is the most important? Least important? Why?
5. **BIG Ideas** In a web diagram like the one below, classify the roles filled by the president as leader of his or her party.

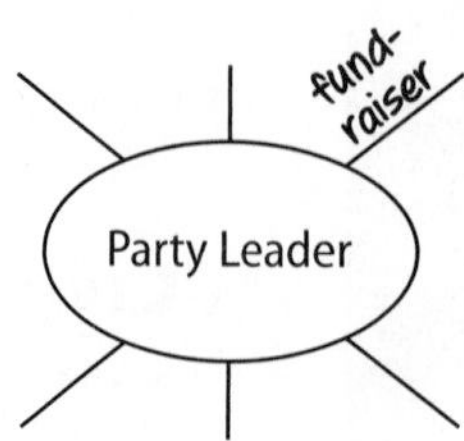

CITIZENSHIP Activity

6. **Creative Writing** Imagine a typical day in the life of a United States president. Prepare an agenda for the president's day. Be sure to keep the duties of the president in mind when creating the agenda.

Study Central™ To review this section, go to glencoe.com.

Section 3

Making Foreign Policy

Guide to Reading

Big Idea

Under our federal system, the executive, legislative, and judicial branches share the responsibility of governing the nation.

Content Vocabulary

- foreign policy *(p. 220)*
- national security *(p. 220)*
- treaty *(p. 222)*
- executive agreement *(p. 222)*
- ambassador *(p. 222)*
- trade sanction *(p. 223)*
- embargo *(p. 223)*

Academic Vocabulary

- method *(p. 222)*
- target *(p. 223)*

Reading Strategy

Comparing and Contrasting As you read, complete a graphic organizer like the one below showing the president's four goals in foreign policy.

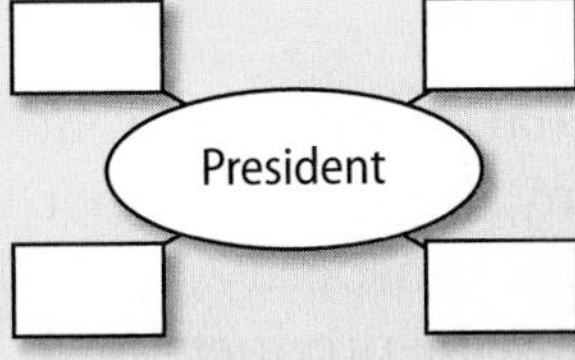

Real World Civics The president's long arm of foreign policy stretches around the world in the form of U.S. ambassadors. The president cannot be everywhere spreading good will. So he or she appoints ambassadors to major countries to maintain diplomatic relationships with other governments. Great Britain has been one of the United States's closest allies. Here, Prince Charles, accompanied by U.S. Ambassador William S. Farish, signs a book of condolences following the terrorist attacks on New York City and the Pentagon in 2001. Ambassadorships are often awarded to people for their hard work and support of the president.

▼ **Prince Charles of Wales signs Remembrance Book with U.S. Ambassador Farish in London**

TIME™

Political Cartoons

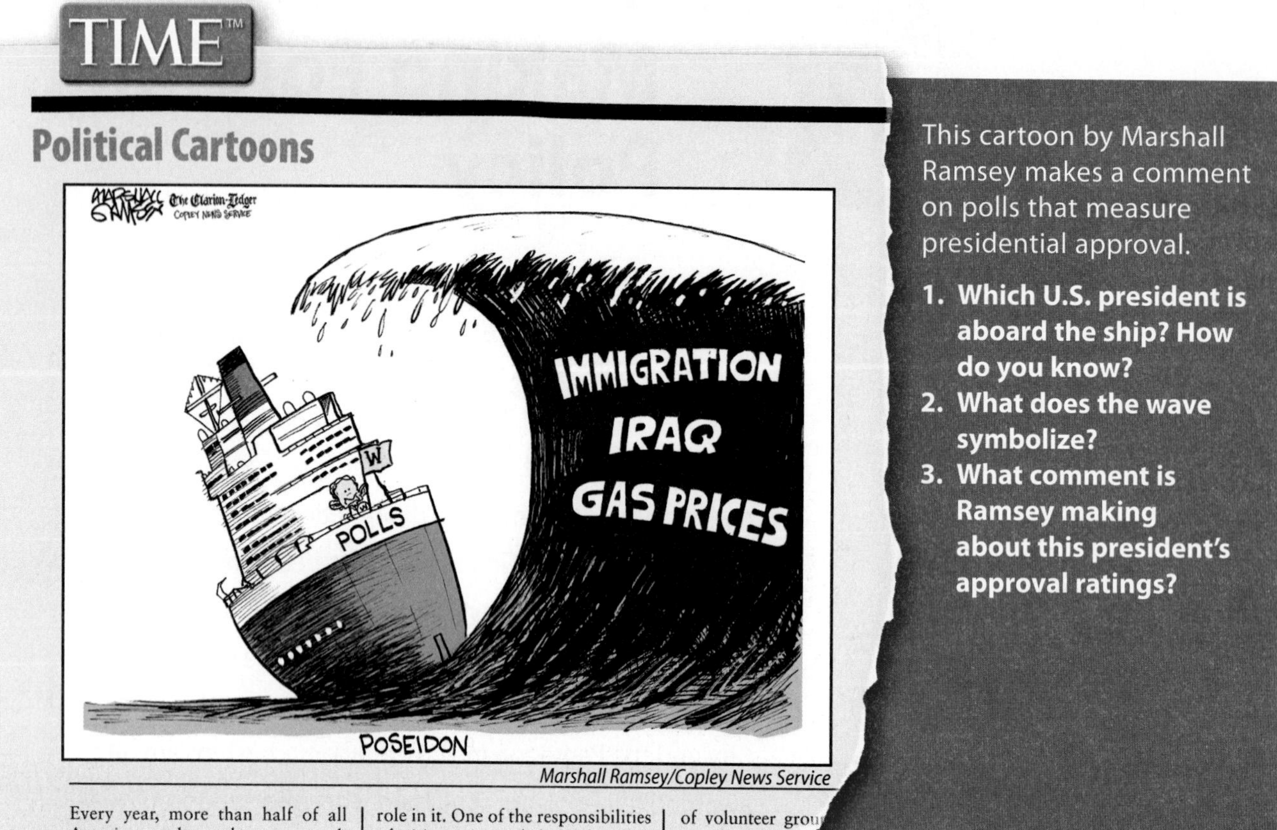

Marshall Ramsey/Copley News Service

This cartoon by Marshall Ramsey makes a comment on polls that measure presidential approval.

1. **Which U.S. president is aboard the ship? How do you know?**
2. **What does the wave symbolize?**
3. **What comment is Ramsey making about this president's approval ratings?**

The President and Foreign Policy

Main Idea **As commander in chief and chief diplomat, the president leads the nation's armed forces and directs U.S. foreign policy.**

Civics & You Just as the president very often has to deal with people outside our country, you have to deal with people outside your family. Think about times when that has been a challenge for you. What did you do?

A nation's plan for dealing with other nations is called its **foreign policy.** The president directs the foreign policy of the United States, making the key decisions about the relations the United States has with other countries in the world. The primary goal of American foreign policy is **national security,** the ability to keep the country safe from attack or harm. This goal is vital. No government can effectively meet other important goals, such as better health care or cleaning up the environment, if the nation is under attack.

Another important goal is international trade. In today's economy, trade with other nations is vital to economic prosperity. Trade creates markets for American products and jobs for American workers.

A third goal is promoting world peace. Even a war far from the United States can disrupt trade and put national security at risk. When other nations are at peace, the United States runs no risk of being drawn into a foreign war.

A fourth goal of foreign policy is to promote democracy around the world. Promoting democracy and basic human rights in other countries encourages peace and thus helps protect our own national security.

American Biography

Condoleezza Rice (1954–)

Condoleezza Rice juggles numbers of missiles and tanks as confidently as any general. An expert on Russia and arms control, Rice launched her foreign policy career while only a teenager.

Born in Birmingham, Alabama, Rice lived through the early years of the civil rights movement. While Rice was in junior high school, her father took a job in Denver, Colorado. There she skipped two grades and entered college at age 15. Rice had many interests and was not sure about a future career. As Rice shopped for a major, she sat in on a lecture about the former Soviet Union.

All the governmental maneuvers by the Communists fascinated her. Rice was hooked. A talented piano player, Rice once joked, "I was saved from [becoming] a music major by Russia."

Rice went on to earn a Ph.D. and by her late 20s was teaching political science at Stanford University in California. In 2001 President Bush appointed Rice as the first woman to head the National Security Council. In 2005 he appointed her to serve as Secretary of State. Rice became the first African American woman to hold that position. At her confirmation hearing, Rice stated "we must use American diplomacy to help create a balance of power in the world that favors freedom. And the time for diplomacy is now."

Making a Difference — CITIZENSHIP

What positions has Rice held in the federal government?

"I make American foreign policy," President Harry S. Truman declared in 1948. The president is indeed a very important foreign-policy decision maker. Americans and others throughout the world look to the president to represent our country in foreign affairs.

Foreign-Policy Bureaucracy The president, along with White House assistants, works with a large foreign-policy bureaucracy in the executive branch. This bureaucracy includes the State Department, the Defense Department, the Central Intelligence Agency, and the National Security Council. These agencies assist the president in foreign affairs. They can carry out presidential decisions around the world and give the president valuable information. At the same time, presidents must make the final decision. President Harry S. Truman noted,

> ***"No one who has not had the responsibility can really understand what it is like to be President, not even his closest aides. . . . [H]e is never allowed to forget that he is President."***
>
> —Harry S. Truman

Congress v. the President

The president is chief diplomat and commander in chief, but Congress has the power to declare war, to prohibit certain military actions, and to spend—or withhold—money for defense. The Constitution does not clearly spell out how the legislative and the executive branches can use their powers. As a result, there has always been competition between Congress and the president over who controls foreign policy.

In this struggle, one branch or the other has controlled foreign policy at various times. After World War II, Congress lost much of its control over foreign policy to the president. Then, in the late 1960s and early 1970s, during the Vietnam conflict, Congress regained some of its war powers. In starting the American war on global terrorism in 2001, President George W. Bush tipped the balance back toward the presidency.

Tools of Foreign Policy

The president and Congress have several approaches they can use to carry out American foreign policy. These **methods,** or procedures, include creating treaties; appointing ambassadors; and directing foreign aid, international trade, and military forces.

Treaties and Executive Agreements Formal agreements between the governments of two or more countries are called **treaties.** Some treaties are based on defense. One of the most important is the North Atlantic Treaty Organization (NATO), a mutual defense treaty between the United States, Canada, and the nations of Europe.

The Senate must approve a treaty by a two-thirds vote. However, the president can bypass the Senate by making an **executive agreement.** This is an agreement between the president and the leader of another country. Most agreements deal with fairly routine matters.

Appointing Ambassadors An official representative of a country's government is an **ambassador.** The president appoints about 150 ambassadors, who must be confirmed by the Senate. Ambassadors are sent only to those countries where the United States recognizes, or accepts, the legal existence of the government. If the government of a certain country is thought to hold power illegally,

Teamwork President George W. Bush's advisers—namely his cabinet, who often met at his retreat, Camp David—helped him announce decisions about foreign policy. ***Hypothesizing*** **Why is the president's power to make treaties through executive power an important part of his foreign policy powers?**

the president can refuse to recognize that government.

Foreign Aid Foreign aid is money, food, military assistance, or other supplies given to help other countries. One of this nation's greatest examples of foreign aid was the Marshall Plan, a program created to help restore Western Europe after World War II.

International Trade As the leader of a great economic power, the president can make agreements with other nations about what products may be traded and the rules for such trading. Sometimes trade measures include **trade sanctions,** or efforts to punish another nation by imposing trade barriers. Another punishing tool is the **embargo,** which is an agreement among a group of nations that prohibits them from trading with a **target** nation. Congress takes the lead in other areas, such as tariffs—taxes on imported goods—and membership in international trade groups, such as the North American Free Trade Agreement (NAFTA) and the World Trade Organization (WTO).

Military Force As commander in chief of the armed forces, presidents may use the military to carry out some foreign-policy decisions. Numerous times in the history of the United States, presidents have sent troops to troublesome spots on the globe, even though Congress had not declared war. This is a powerful tool of foreign policy, but one that must be used with great care. President George Washington summoned troops to put down the Whiskey Rebellion in 1794. President Bill Clinton ordered cruise missiles to be launched at terrorist facilities in Afghanistan and Sudan in 1998. In 2003 President George W. Bush ordered the American armed forces to invade Iraq and remove the nation's dictator Saddam Hussein.

Reading Check **Concluding** What foreign policy tools does the president have to deal with international terrorism?

Vocabulary

1. **Define** the following terms and use them in sentences related to U.S. foreign policy: *foreign policy, national security, treaty, executive agreement, ambassador, trade sanction, embargo.*

Main Ideas

2. **Describing** In what way is the president the country's chief diplomat? What duties does this include?
3. **Defining** Why are trade sanctions and embargoes considered tools of foreign policy?

Critical Thinking

4. **Analyzing** Should Congress or the president have more power in conducting foreign affairs? Explain your answer.
5. **BIG Ideas** Compare and contrast the responsibilities and roles of the president and Congress on a chart like the one below.

Foreign Policy	
President	Congress

CITIZENSHIP Activity

6. **Expository Writing** Interview several adults, all of whom have different jobs, about the North American Free Trade Agreement (NAFTA). Find out why they think it is good or bad foreign policy. Share your results in an essay.

Study Central™ To review this section, go to glencoe.com.

Guide to Reading

Big Idea

The Constitution gives the executive branch the power to execute, or implement, the law.

Content Vocabulary

- cabinet *(p. 226)*
- federal bureaucracy *(p. 228)*
- independent agency *(p. 229)*
- government corporation *(p. 229)*
- political appointee *(p. 229)*
- civil service worker *(p. 229)*
- civil service system *(p. 229)*
- spoils system *(p. 230)*
- merit system *(p. 230)*

Academic Vocabulary

- monitor *(p. 225)*
- role *(p. 225)*

Reading Strategy

Categorizing As you read, complete a chart similar to the one below to categorize information about the president's cabinet.

President's Cabinet	
No. of Depts.	
Dept. Head's Role	
Newest Dept.	
Cabinet Meets When	

Presidential Advisers and Executive Agencies

Real World Civics What is the proper role of the First Lady? At one time, the spouse of the president served as a ceremonial hostess at White House events. Eleanor Roosevelt changed all that when she became active in political causes during her husband's presidencies in the 1940s. Jacqueline Kennedy, Lady Bird Johnson, Rosalynn Carter and Barbara Bush continued to revolutionize the role of the First Lady. Here President George H.W. Bush celebrates Thanksgiving with the U.S. Marines in Saudi Arabia during the Persian Gulf War in 1990. Now, First Ladies are seen as advisers to their husbands, as well as having their own agendas as public figures.

▼ **Former president George H.W. Bush and Barbara Bush visit U.S. troops in Saudi Arabia**

Organization of the Federal Branch

Main Idea **The executive branch is made up of the top advisers and assistants who help the president carry out major duties.**

Civics & You The executive branch has grown tremendously over the years. What advantages and disadvantages can you see in having a large executive staff?

The executive branch is organized like a pyramid. The president, as chief executive, is at the very top of the pyramid. Directly below the president are a number of powerful officials, usually handpicked by the president. Below these are many levels of lesser officials and managers. In general, the people at the top of the pyramid are the ones who set goals and make important decisions.

In 1801 President Thomas Jefferson did his job with the help of a few advisers, a messenger, and a part-time secretary. Today thousands of highly trained specialists, secretaries, and clerks assist the president. Most of these people work in the Executive Office of the President (EOP). These people are often referred to as a president's administration.

Franklin D. Roosevelt's administration created the EOP in 1939 to help the president do his job. The office has been growing ever since. Currently it has about 2,000 employees and a budget of more than $100 million.

The Executive Office

The core of the Executive Office of the President is the White House Office, which is comprised of about 500 people who work directly for the president. Among them are 10 to 12 people who serve as the president's closest political advisers. The most powerful among this group is the chief of staff. Other top advisers are the deputy chief of staff and the press secretary. (The press secretary provides the public with news about and statements from the president.) As a group, such advisers make up the White House staff.

Management and Budget

The Office of Management and Budget (OMB) prepares the federal budget and **monitors,** or oversees, spending in hundreds of government agencies. The director of the OMB works closely with the president. The federal budget is the clearest statement of the administration's plans and goals for the coming year.

National Security Council (NSC)

The National Security Council (NSC) helps the president direct United States military and foreign policy. It handles matters affecting the security of the country. It includes the vice president, the secretaries of state and defense, and the chairman of the Joint Chiefs of Staff, which includes the top commander from each of the armed services. The National Security Advisor heads the NSC. The NSC also supervises the Central Intelligence Agency (CIA), which gathers information about the governments of other countries.

Other Offices

The Office of Administration provides administrative services to the executive offices of the president. The Office also responds to individuals who are seeking records under the Freedom of Information Act.

The Council of Economic Advisers (CEA) helps the president carry out the **role,** or position, of economic leader. The president names the CEA's members, and the Senate approves them. The CEA's primary duty involves giving the president advice about complex economic matters such as employment, inflation, and foreign trade.

Reading Check **Identifying** What are the duties of a president's press secretary?

The Cabinet

Main Idea **The cabinet is an advisory group chosen by the president to help accomplish the work of the executive branch.**

Civics & You Some presidents have followed their cabinets' opinion on many matters. Other presidents have not. Do you think strong presidents rely more or less on their cabinets' advice?

The EOP is only a small part of the president's administration. Many more people work in the cabinet. The **cabinet** is a group of presidential advisers that includes the heads of the 15 top-level executive departments. The head of the Department of Justice is called the attorney general; all the other department heads are called secretaries. The president may also ask the vice president and other top officials to join the cabinet.

Department of Homeland Security

On November 25, 2002, President Bush signed the Homeland Security Act of 2002. The act created the Department of Homeland Security to improve the nation's defenses against terrorism and coordinate counterterrorism intelligence. It is the first new department established since the Department of Veterans Affairs was created in 1989.

Cabinet Responsibilities

As cabinet members, the secretaries advise the president on issues related to their departments. The secretary of agriculture, for instance, might keep the president and White

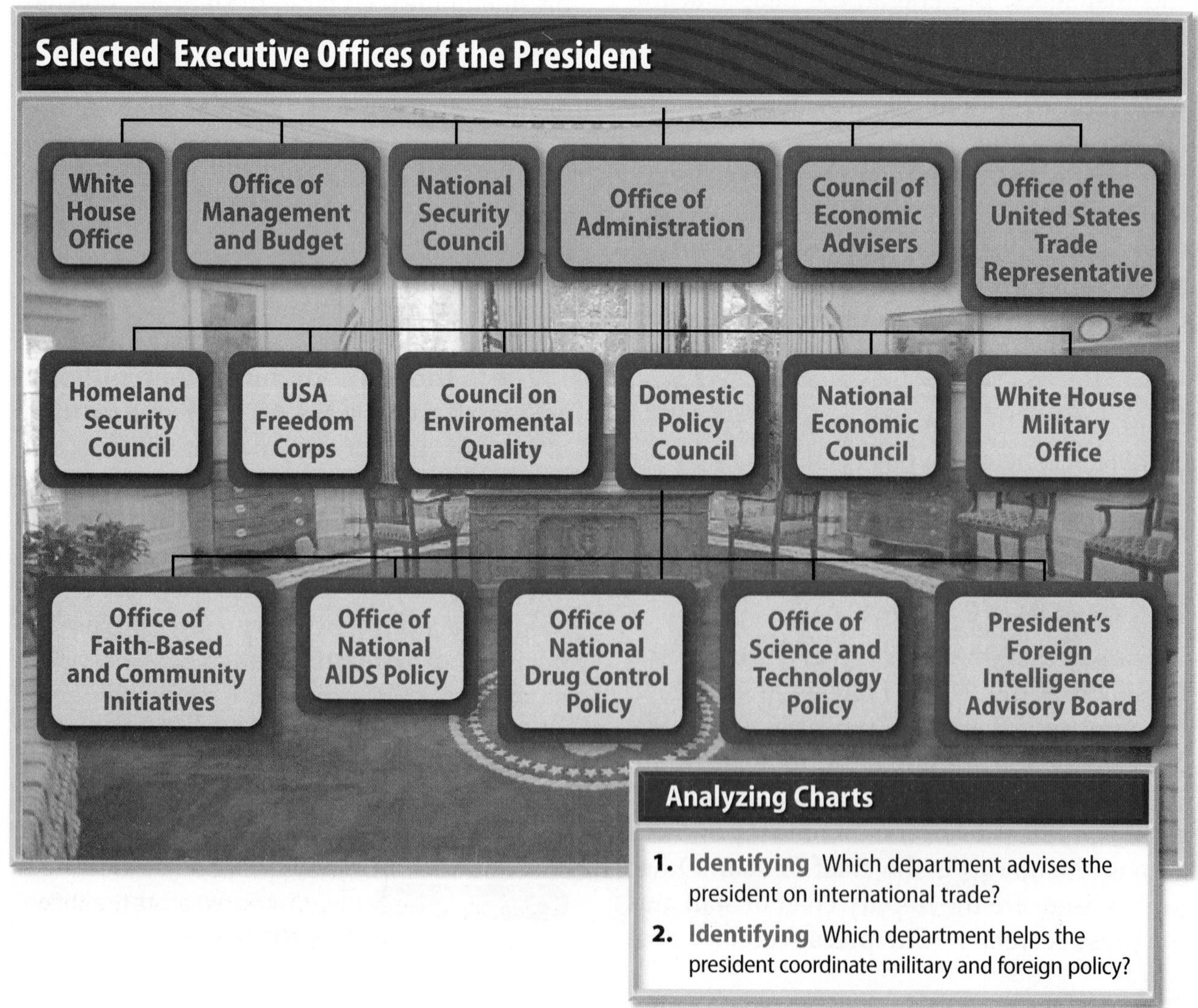

Analyzing Charts

1. **Identifying** Which department advises the president on international trade?
2. **Identifying** Which department helps the president coordinate military and foreign policy?

The President's Cabinet

Department	Role
Department of State (1789)	Plans and carries out the nation's foreign policy
Department of the Treasury (1789)	Collects, borrows, spends, and prints money
Department of Defense (1789 as War Department; renamed in 1949)	Manages the armed forces
Department of Justice (1870)	Responsible for all aspects of law enforcement
Department of the Interior (1849)	Manages and protects nation's public lands and natural resources
Department of Agriculture (1889)	Assists farmers and consumers of farm products
Department of Commerce (1903)	Supervises trade, promotes U.S. business, tourism
Department of Labor (1913)	Deals with working conditions, wages of U.S. workers
Department of Health and Human Services (1953)	Works for the well-being and health of all Americans
Department of Housing and Urban Development (1965)	Deals with the special needs and problems of cities
Department of Transportation (1966)	Manages nation's highways, railroads, airlines, and sea traffic
Department of Energy (1977)	Directs overall energy plan for the nation
Department of Education (1979)	Provides advice and funding for schools
Department of Veterans Affairs (1989)	Directs services for armed forces veterans
Department of Homeland Security (2002)	Oversees America's defenses against terrorist attacks

Analyzing Charts

1. **Identifying** Which department manages public lands? In what year was this department created?
2. **Analyzing** Why might the president call on the secretary of transportation to deal with drug smuggling along the Pacific coast?

House staff informed about matters of concern to American farmers. Cabinet secretaries often make important policy decisions.

No mention of the cabinet appears in the Constitution. Instead, this body developed when George Washington began to meet regularly with the heads of the first four executive departments. These were the attorney general and the secretaries of state, war, and the treasury.

The cabinet meets whenever the president determines that it is necessary. This may be as often as once a week or hardly at all. Many presidents have not relied heavily on their cabinets and have felt free to ignore cabinet advice. As heads of executive agencies, these department secretaries must spend most of their time coordinating those departments' activities. Department heads of the cabinet must be approved by the Senate.

Vice President and First Lady

Most presidents have delegated little authority to their vice presidents. Recently, however, some have tried to give their vice presidents more responsibility. Vice President Al Gore, for example, served as a close adviser to President Bill Clinton on environmental issues, and Vice President Dick Cheney advised President George W. Bush closely on foreign policy issues.

The Constitution does not mention the spouse of a president. First Ladies, though, have served the country in many ways. Eleanor Roosevelt worked tirelessly for the young and the disadvantaged. Nancy Reagan spoke out for drug abuse prevention, Hillary Clinton worked to improve health care for all Americans, and Laura Bush promoted education and reading. Today First Ladies have an office in the White House.

Reading Check **Stating** When does the cabinet meet?

The Federal Bureaucracy

Main Idea **The federal bureaucracy has grown over the years and assumes an important role in making public policy.**

Civics & You With every new administration, new people are named to hold positions within the federal bureaucracy. Why might it be a problem for new people to always be taking these jobs?

Below the cabinet departments are hundreds of agencies that deal with everything from setting standards for the hot dogs you eat to running the space shuttle program. About 3 million civilians work in these many departments and agencies. Taken together, the agencies and employees of the executive branch are often called the **federal bureaucracy.** The people who work for these organizations are called bureaucrats, or civil servants.

Federal Staffing President Bush watches as Trade Representative Susan Schwab is sworn into office as a new member of the federal civil servant corps. ***Explaining*** **Why do you think such position holders are sworn in rather than simply hired like other government workers?**

The Bureaucracy in Action

The executive branch of government must carry out the many programs that Congress has created to serve the American people. Executive departments and agencies do this by performing three basic jobs. First, they turn new laws into action by deciding how to apply the laws to daily life. When Congress writes new laws, it often uses very general language. Federal agencies then must develop specific rules and procedures to put the laws into practice.

Second, departments and agencies administer the day-to-day operations of the federal government. Agencies deliver the mail, collect taxes, send out Social Security checks, and perform thousands of other services.

Regulatory Functions Third, with authority from Congress, federal agencies regulate various activities. They regulate, or police, the activities of broadcasting companies, labor unions, banks, airlines, nuclear power plants, and many other enterprises and organizations.

In doing these jobs, federal agencies help shape government policy. By deciding how to run a government program or what to do in a certain situation, federal agencies often determine what government policy will be.

Independent Agencies

The executive branch includes hundreds of **independent agencies.** They are called independent because they are not part of the cabinet. In general, however, these agencies can be divided into three types: executive agencies, government corporations, and regulatory commissions.

Executive Agencies These are independent agencies responsible for dealing with certain specialized areas within the government. The National Aeronautics and Space Administration (NASA) is an example. It operates the United States space program.

Government Corporations More than 50 independent agencies are **government corporations.** These are like private businesses, except that the government rather than individuals owns and operates them. With Senate approval, the president chooses a board of directors and a general manager to run each corporation. Like private businesses, these corporations charge fees for their services and products, but they are not supposed to make a profit. The United States Postal Service, for example, is a government corporation.

Regulatory Boards and Commissions These units differ from other independent agencies. They do not have to report to the president, who appoints the members but cannot fire them. Only Congress can remove them through impeachment.

Regulatory commissions are supposed to protect the public. They make and enforce rules for certain industries or groups. For instance, the Federal Communications Commission (FCC) makes broadcasting rules for the nation's television and radio stations.

Government Workers

Every executive department has thousands of employees. The top leadership jobs generally go to **political appointees**—people whom the president has chosen because they have proven executive ability or were important supporters of the president's election campaign. Their employment usually ends when the president leaves office.

About 90 percent of all national government employees are **civil service workers.** Unlike political appointees, civil service workers usually have permanent employment. These are people, ranging from clerks to doctors and lawyers, employed by the federal government through the **civil service system**—the practice of hiring government workers on the basis of open, competitive examinations and merit.

Development of the Civil Service System

Originally, the executive branch was small enough for presidents to be able to choose most of their employees personally. Early presidents tried to appoint the most qualified people to federal jobs. They also, however, tended to appoint members of their own party, who shared similar views.

The Spoils System Before 1883 a great many federal jobs fell under the **spoils system.** In this system, government jobs went to people as a reward for their political support. Each newly elected president would sweep out most of the old federal workers and replace them with his own political supporters and friends. The idea was "To the victor belong the spoils [jobs]." Public dissatisfaction with abuses of the spoils system, and public outrage over the assassination of President James Garfield in 1881 by a man who was refused a job under the system, led Congress to pass the Pendleton Act.

The Merit System The Pendleton Act, also known as the Civil Service Reform Act of 1883, created the civil service system and placed limits on the number of jobs a new president could hand out to friends and backers. The Office of Personnel Management (OPM) directs the civil service system today. It sets standards for federal jobs, and it gives demanding written tests to people who want those jobs. The civil service system is a **merit system.** Government officials hire new workers from lists of people who have passed the tests or otherwise met civil service standards.

Reading Check **Describing** What is the purpose of regulatory commissions?

Review

Vocabulary

1. **Write** complete sentences related to the federal government using the following vocabulary terms: *cabinet, federal bureaucracy, independent agency, government corporation, political appointee, civil service worker, civil service system, spoils system, merit system.*

Main Ideas

2. **Discuss** the role of the Office of Management and Budget.
3. **Describing** Name three cabinet departments and describe their main duties.
4. **Comparing** Why has the federal bureaucracy grown over the years?

Critical Thinking

5. **Making Inferences** What part of the EOP do you think is the most important? Why?
6. **BIG Ideas** In the Venn diagram below, compare and contrast the types of workers employed by the federal government under the civil service system and those who are political employees.

Civil Service	Both	Political Employees

7. **Analyzing Visuals** Review the cabinet departments of the executive branch on page 227. Why are there so many cabinet departments under the president of the United States?

CITIZENSHIP Activity

8. **Creative Writing** Imagine that you are on a presidential commission looking into establishing a new executive department. Decide on an important issue facing the country today. Think of a new executive department to deal with this issue. Present your suggestion in a one-page report.

Study Central™ To review this section, go to glencoe.com.

Chapter 7

Visual Summary

The Presidency

- The president is head of the executive branch of the federal government and is our nation's top political leader.
- The source for the president's authority is Article II of the Constitution, which says that "the executive power shall be vested in the president of the United States of America."

John F. Kennedy, 1940 Harvard yearbook

Electing the President

- Presidents are elected through an indirect method called the Electoral College.

Responsibilities

- According to the Constitution, the president's main job is to carry out the laws passed by Congress.
- As head of the executive branch of government, the president must make decisions that affect the lives of all Americans.

Roles of the President

In carrying out the responsibilities of the office, the president must play a number of different roles. These roles are:

- Chief executive
- Chief diplomat
- Commander in chief
- Legislative leader
- Head of state
- Economic leader
- Party leader

President Lyndon B. Johnson

Tools of Foreign Policy

The president and Congress use many tools to carry out American foreign policy. These tools include:

- Treaties and executive agreements
- Appointing ambassadors
- Foreign aid
- International trade
- Military force

President's official helicopter

Organization of the Federal Government

- President
- Vice president
- Executive Office of the President
- Executive departments
- Federal bureaucracy

Study anywhere, anytime! Download quizzes and flash cards to your PDA from glencoe.com.

ASSESSMENT

TEST-TAKING TIP

When taking a test, watch for *usually, never, most,* and other qualifying words that indicate under what circumstances an answer is correct.

Reviewing Vocabulary

Directions: Choose the word(s) that best completes the sentence.

1. The Constitution provides an indirect method of electing a president called the _______.

A merit system
B Electoral College
C spoils system
D executive agreement

2. The president can delay the punishment of a person by issuing a (n) _______.

A pardon
B amnesty
C reprieve
D executive order

3. The nation's plan for dealing with other nations is called its _______.

A foreign policy
B national security
C trade sanctions
D federal bureaucracy

4. Most national government employees are _______.

A ambassadors
B civil service workers
C cabinet members
D political appointees

Reviewing Main Ideas

Directions: Choose the best answer for each question.

Section 1 *(pp. 208–213)*

5. Which president was elected to four terms?

A George Washington
B Abraham Lincoln
C Franklin Roosevelt
D George W. Bush

6. Why was the Twenty-fifth Amendment passed?

A to create the Electoral College
B to limit presidents to two terms
C to establish the order of presidential succession
D to clarify when a vice president becomes president

Section 2 *(pp. 214–218)*

7. Which of the following powers does the Constitution give the president?

A to declare war on other nations
B to appoint judges to federal courts
C to ignore laws passed by Congress
D to strike down unconstitutional laws

8. How does a president fulfill the role of economic leader?

A by planning the federal budget
B by meeting with foreign leaders
C by raising funds for his or her party
D by proposing legislation to Congress

Section 3 *(pp. 219–223)*

9. Which of the following is NOT a primary goal of American foreign policy?

A world peace
B national security
C better health care
D international trade

Section 4 *(pp. 224–230)*

10. What part of the Executive Office of the President supervises the Central Intelligence Agency?

A Office of Administration
B National Security Council
C Council of Economic Advisers
D Office of Management and Budget

11. What is the responsibility of the Department of the Interior?

A school funding
B natural resources
C problems of cities
D trade, business, and tourism

GO ON

Critical Thinking

Directions: Choose the best answer for each question.

Base your answers to questions 12 and 13 on the chart below and your knowledge of Chapter 7.

Order of Succession

1	Vice President
2	Speaker of the House
3	President *pro tempore* of the Senate
4	Secretary of State
5	Secretary of the Treasury
6	Secretary of Defense
7	Attorney General
8	Secretary of the Interior
9	Secretary of Agriculture
10	Secretary of Commerce
11	Secretary of Labor
12	Secretary of Health and Human Services
13	Secretary of Housing and Urban Development
14	Secretary of Transportation
15	Secretary of Energy
16	Secretary of Education
17	Secretary of Veterans Affairs
18	Secretary of Homeland Security

12. How many office holders listed on the chart are elected officials?

A none **B** one

C three **D** eighteen

13. The offices in the line of succession are ordered according to the dates they were created. What would it take to change that order?

A an executive order

B a law passed by Congress

C a Supreme Court decision

D a Constitutional Amendment

Document-Based Questions

Directions: Analyze the following document and answer the short-answer questions that follow.

The passage below is from George Washington's Farewell Address given at his retirement.

> *Observe good faith and justice toward all nations. Cultivate peace and harmony with all. . . .*
>
> *In the execution of such a plan, nothing is more essential than that permanent, inveterate antipathies [deep-rooted hatred] against particular nations and passionate attachments for others should be excluded, and that in place of them just and amicable feelings toward all should be cultivated. . . .*
>
> —George Washington, "Washington Bids Farewell"

14. Which role of the president does Washington discuss in the passage?

15. Which member of the cabinet would most likely assist Washington's successor in achieving the goals described in the passage?

Extended Response

16. Which do you think is the most effective foreign diplomacy tool: foreign aid, trade sanctions, or military force? Write a brief essay giving reasons for your choice.

STOP

For additional test practice, use Self-Check Quizzes—Chapter 7 on glencoe.com.

Need Extra Help?

If you missed question...	1	2	3	4	5	6	7	8	9	10	11	12	13	14	15	16
Go to page...	210	217	220	229	212	213	215	218	220	225	227	227	213	216	216	222

The White House

An intricate model takes visitors behind the scenes at 1600 Pennsylvania Avenue

Described by former President Gerald Ford as "the best public housing in the world" and by former President Harry S. Truman as a "glamorous prison," the White House was first occupied by President John Adams in 1800. Two centuries later, the White House is a village of 6,000 busy souls: On a typical day, the President and First Lady, journalists, cooks, cops, gardeners, and tourists operate in harmony on 18 acres.

In 1962, John and Jan Zweifel of Orlando, Florida, set out to bring the White House to the American people by constructing the detailed model shown at right. Except for the location of the library, which was pushed forward for show purposes, the Zweifels' White House is a faithful recreation of the original, down to TVs, furniture, and paintings. The Zweifels contact the White House every few weeks to find out if anything has changed. The 60-foot by 20-foot, 10-ton model, which includes the East and West wings (not shown), took more than 500,000 hours to construct and cost more than $1 million. It is built on a scale of 1 inch to 1 foot.

1 SITTING ROOM
Generally claimed by the First Lady, this room has an unusual distinction: It was allocated one of the building's first indoor toilets in 1801.

2 MASTER BEDROOM
Nancy Reagan, who served as First Lady from 1981 to 1989, decorated this bedroom in hand-painted paper that was imported from China.

3 PRESIDENT'S STUDY
Franklin Delano Roosevelt used this study as a bedroom; the Reagans liked to have quiet dinners here in front of the television.

4 YELLOW OVAL ROOM
One of the most historic rooms in the house, it took on the color yellow during the tenure of First Lady Dolley Madison.

5 TREATY ROOM
Originally a large bedroom, this room served as Bill Clinton's office in the residence.

6 LINCOLN BEDROOM
Abraham Lincoln signed the Emancipation Proclamation here.

7 LINCOLN SITTING ROOM
William McKinley's war room during the Spanish-American War.

8 STATE DINING ROOM
Gilbert Stuart's portrait of George Washington (which was later used on the one-dollar bill) hung here when the British torched the mansion in 1814. (The portrait survived the fire.)

9 RED ROOM
John Adams's breakfast room was where Rutherford B. Hayes took the oath of office in 1877.

Steven P. Widoff for TIME

10 BLUE ROOM
Where Grover Cleveland married Frances Folsom, in 1886.

11 GREEN ROOM
Thomas Jefferson's dining room is now used for receptions.

12 EAST ROOM
The largest room in the mansion, it was used by First Lady Abigail Adams to dry the family wash.

13 LIBRARY
Placed here by the replica designers, the presidential library is actually located behind the Vermeil Room.

14 MAP ROOM
Decorated with Chippendale furniture imported from England, this room was inspired by Winston Churchill's World War II map room.

15 DIPLOMATIC RECEPTION ROOM
Site from which F.D.R. broadcast his fireside chats (though the fireplace at that time was fake).

16 CHINA ROOM
Edith Wilson, First Lady from 1915 to 1921, used this area to display china.

17 VERMEIL *(ver-MAY)* ROOM
This room takes its name from a display of vermeil (gilded silver).

A Long Road

The Zweifels' quest to create a replica of the White House took decades. After going on hundreds of public tours of the mansion, they finally persuaded President Gerald Ford to let them look behind the scenes.

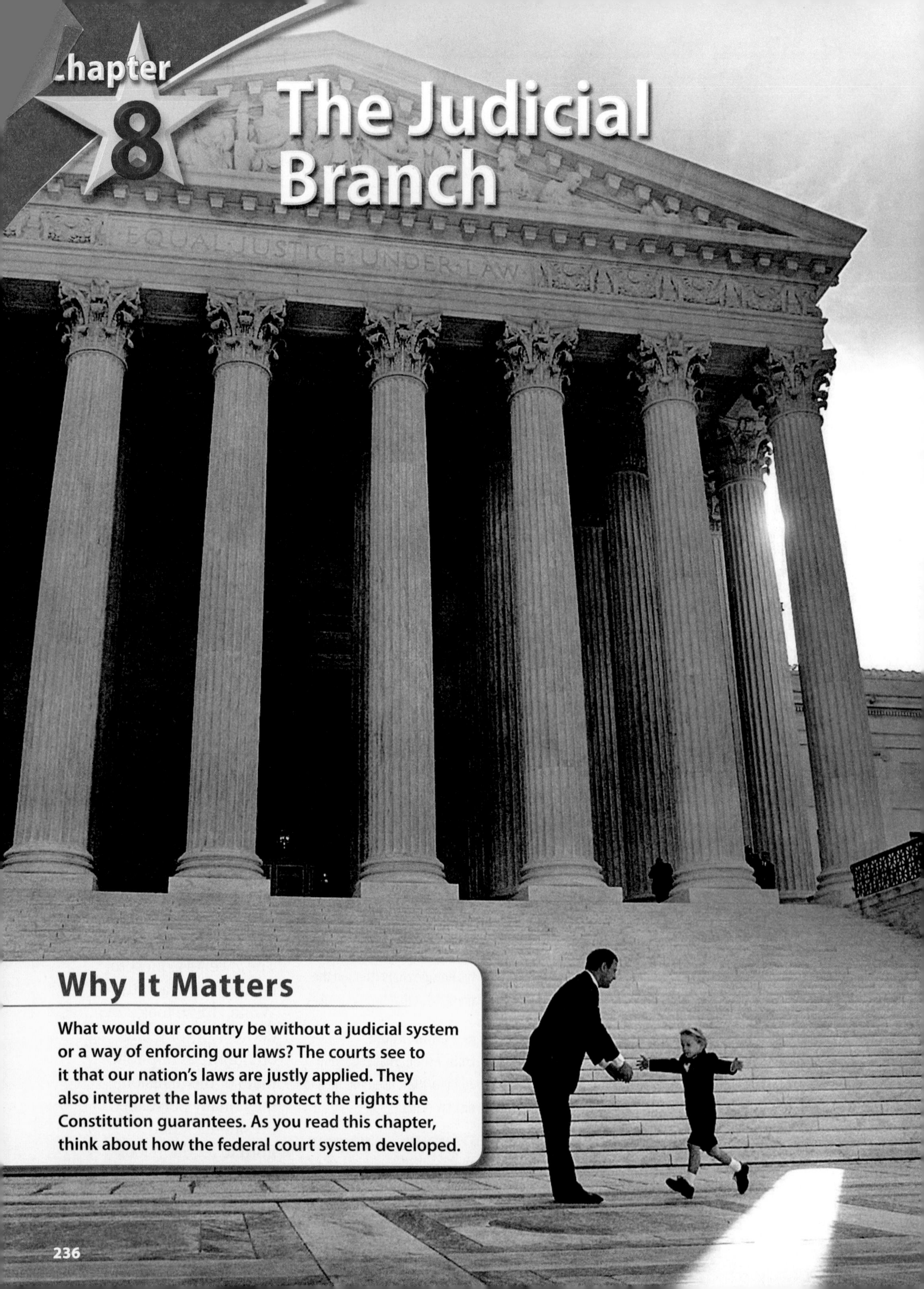

Chapter 8 The Judicial Branch

Why It Matters

What would our country be without a judicial system or a way of enforcing our laws? The courts see to it that our nation's laws are justly applied. They also interpret the laws that protect the rights the Constitution guarantees. As you read this chapter, think about how the federal court system developed.

Chapter Audio

Civics ONLINE
Visit glencoe.com and enter QuickPass™ code CIV3093c8 for Chapter 8 resources.

BIG Ideas

Section 1: The Federal Courts

Under our federal system, the executive, legislative, and judicial branches share the responsibility of governing the nation. Three levels of federal courts try to ensure that everyone in the United States receives equal justice under the law.

Section 2: How Federal Courts Are Organized

Under our federal system, the executive, legislative, and judicial branches share the responsibility of governing the nation. The different levels of federal courts each deal with a different caseload, ensuring all citizens receive a speedy trial or day in court.

Chief Justice John Roberts, Jr., and his son on the steps of the U.S. Supreme Court

Section 3: The Supreme Court

The judicial branch is charged with interpreting the law. The Supreme Court's decisions have wide-ranging effects because court justices interpret the meaning of the U.S. Constitution.

Section 4: The Supreme Court at Work

The judicial branch is charged with interpreting the law. Supreme Court justices weigh many factors and go through several complex steps before making a decision.

Sequencing Information Study Foldable Make the following Foldable to help you analyze and sequence key influences and responsibilities of the judicial branch of government.

Step 1 Fold a sheet of paper in half from the long way with edges evenly together.

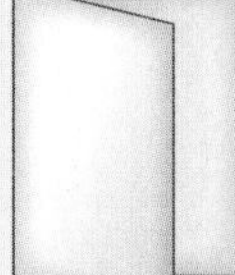

Step 2 Turn the paper and fold it into thirds.

Step 3 Unfold and cut along the two folds on the front flap to make three tabs.

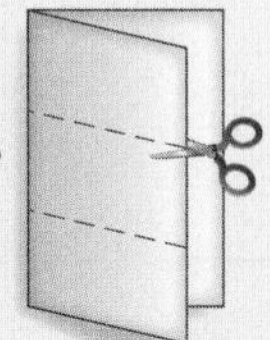

Step 4 Label as shown, including arrows.

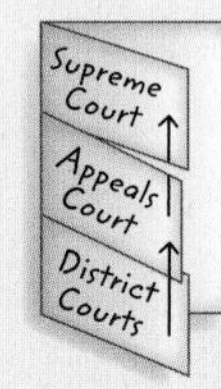

Reading and Writing
As you read the chapter, compare and note the details of the responsibilities of each level of the court system from least influence to greatest influence.

Section Audio

Spotlight Video

Section 1

The Federal Courts

Guide to Reading

Big Idea
Under our federal system, the executive, legislative, and judicial branches share the responsibility of governing the nation.

Content Vocabulary
- circuit *(p. 240)*
- jurisdiction *(p. 240)*
- exclusive jurisdiction *(p. 242)*
- concurrent jurisdiction *(p. 242)*

Academic Vocabulary
- acknowledge *(p. 239)*
- circumstance *(p. 242)*

Reading Strategy
Organizing As you read, complete a graphic organizer like the one below to identify the three levels of courts in the U.S. justice system.

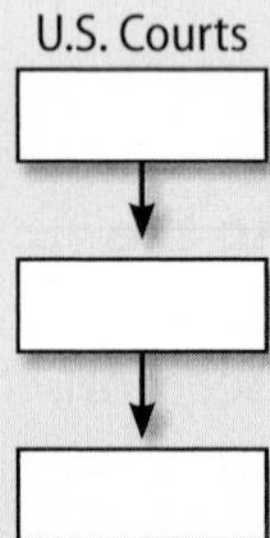

Real World Civics Can you imagine being forced to live in a strange place simply because of your nationality? That is exactly what happened to these young boys during World War II. During the United States war with Japan, President Roosevelt ordered Japanese Americans to be sent to internment camps so that they could not spy on America. More than half of those interned in the "camps" were naturalized American citizens. By the 1980s the U.S. admitted it had acted too harshly, apologized to those who had been wrongly interned, and paid them damages.

▼ **Young Japanese children interned at Manzanar War Relocation Center in California during World War II**

Right to Trial The judicial system provides fair trials to all accused, even if the crimes involve attacks against the United States, as in the case of accused al-Qaeda conspirator Zacarias Moussaoui. ***Predicting*** **What difficulties might arise in finding a fair jury to judge a crime such as terrorism?**

Equal Justice for All

Main Idea The courts that make up the judicial branch try to ensure that our nation's laws are justly enforced.

Civics & You Do you think a society could exist without a court system that determines in a fair manner if laws have been broken? Read about the powers of the courts as established in the Constitution.

A native-born citizen, Mitsuye Endo was fired from a California state job in 1942 and sent to a relocation center like the boys discussed on the previous page. Her lawyer challenged the War Relocation Board's right to intern a loyal American citizen.

Endo took the matter to the Supreme Court and won her case. In 1944, the Court ruled that Endo "should be given her liberty." Justice William O. Douglas proclaimed that

> ***"A citizen who is concededly loyal presents no problem of espionage or sabotage. Loyalty is a matter of the heart and mind not of race, creed, or color."***
>
> —*Ex parte Endo,* 1944

Later the United States government would **acknowledge,** or admit to, the injustice of the internment camps and apologize. Shortly after the Court made its decision in the *Ex-parte Endo* case, many detained Japanese Americans were released and returned home.

Role of the Courts

Federal courts, such as the Supreme Court, make up the third branch of the U.S. government. Courts use the law to settle civil disputes and to decide the guilt or innocence of people accused of crimes.

Whether a civil dispute is between two private parties (people, companies, or organizations), between a private party and the government, or between the United States and a state or local government, both sides come before a court. Each side presents its position. The court then applies the law to the facts that have been presented and makes a decision in favor of one or the other. The courts also hold criminal trials in which witnesses present evidence and a jury or a judge delivers a verdict.

Equal Treatment

The United States Supreme Court is at the top of the federal court system. If you visit the Court, you will see the words "Equal Justice Under Law" on the face of its marble building. Our legal system is based on this important ideal. The goal of the legal system is to treat every person the same. Under the Constitution, every person accused of breaking the law has the right to have a public trial and a lawyer. If an accused person cannot afford a lawyer, the court will appoint and pay for one. Each person is presumed innocent until proven guilty and has the right to ask for a review of his or her case if, in that person's view, the courts have made a mistake.

The ideal of equal justice is difficult to achieve. Judges and juries are not free from personal prejudices or the prejudices of their communities. Poor people do not have the money to spend on the best available legal help, unlike wealthy citizens and large companies. Nonetheless, American courts try to uphold the ideal of equal justice.

Reading Check **Describing** Under the Constitution, what rights does every accused person have?

Federal Courts

Main Idea **The Constitution gives the federal courts the authority to hear and decide certain types of cases.**

Civics & You Do you know anyone who has had to go to court or has served on a jury? Read to learn about what kinds of cases are heard in federal courts.

From 1781 to 1789, when the United States was governed by the Articles of Confederation, there was no national court system. Each state had its own laws and its own courts. There was no way to guarantee that people would receive equal justice in all the states.

To deal with this problem, the writers of the Constitution provided for a federal judiciary. Article III of the Constitution established a national Supreme Court. It also gave Congress the power to establish lower federal courts.

Over the years, Congress has created two kinds of lower courts. In 1789 it passed the Judiciary Act, which established federal district courts and circuit courts of appeals. Much later, in 1891, Congress created a system of federal appeals courts and the **circuits** or districts they serve. Thus, the federal court system has three levels—the district courts at the lower level, the appeals courts in the middle, and the Supreme Court at the top.

Our federal court system exists alongside 50 separate state court systems. Each state has its own laws and courts. The state courts get their powers from state constitutions and laws. You will read more about state courts in Chapter 12.

Federal Court Jurisdiction

Article III of the Constitution gives federal courts **jurisdiction**—the authority to hear and decide a case—only in cases that involve one of the following:

Federal Judicial Circuits

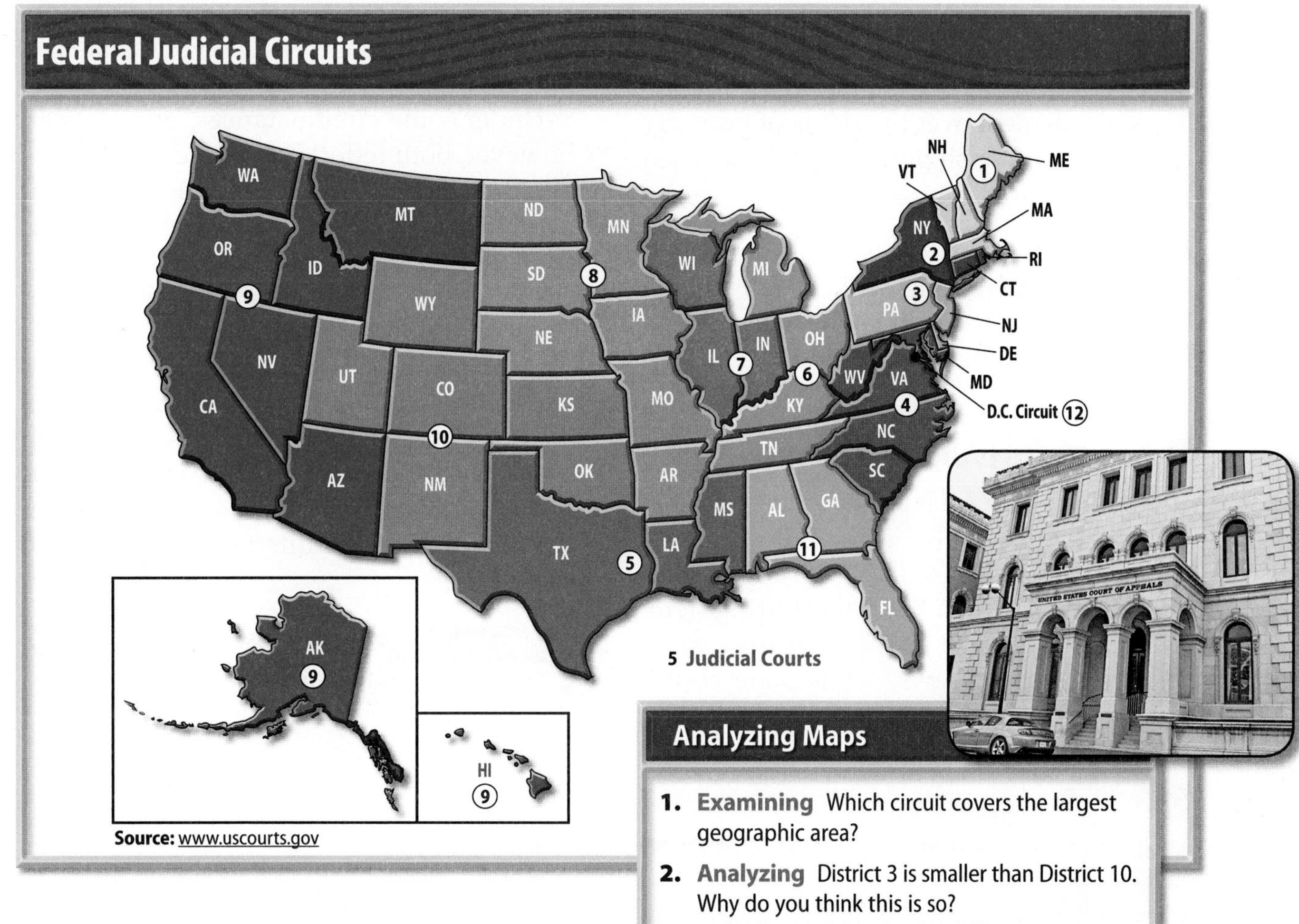

Source: www.uscourts.gov

Analyzing Maps

1. **Examining** Which circuit covers the largest geographic area?
2. **Analyzing** District 3 is smaller than District 10. Why do you think this is so?

The Constitution For example, if a person believes a constitutional right, such as freedom of speech, has been violated, that person has a right to be heard in a federal court.

Federal Laws Federal courts try people accused of federal crimes such as kidnapping, tax evasion, and counterfeiting. Federal courts also hear civil cases that involve federal laws.

Disputes Between States Disagreements between state governments are resolved in federal courts. If Colorado and California, for example, disagree over rights to water in the Colorado River, it is a federal case.

Citizens from Different States Lawsuits between citizens of different states also come under the federal courts. For example, Ms. Jones of Maine may bring suit in a federal court against Mr. Smith of Iowa for not fulfilling his part of a business agreement.

The Federal Government The U.S. government, for example, could take a company to court for failing to live up to a contract to deliver supplies to a government department. Individuals or companies can also take the government to court. For instance, if a United States Army van struck your car or the Department of the Interior failed to pay your company for equipment, you could sue the government.

Foreign Governments and Treaties In any dispute between a foreign government and the United States government, an American company, or an American citizen, the case will be heard in a federal court.

Admiralty and Maritime Laws These laws concern crimes and accidents outside territorial waters. For example, a case involving disagreement over the rights of property recovered from a shipwreck would be tried in federal court.

U.S. Diplomats If, for example, an American diplomat working in the U.S. embassy in France is accused of breaking an American law, the case would go to a federal court.

Types of Jurisdiction

For most of the areas just described, federal courts have **exclusive jurisdiction,** which means that only the federal courts may hear and decide cases. In the dual court system, federal courts have jurisdiction over cases involving federal laws, while state courts have jurisdiction over cases involving state laws. Most U.S. court cases involve state law and are tried in state courts.

Under some **circumstances,** or instances, however, both federal and state courts have jurisdiction, a situation known as **concurrent jurisdiction.** Either court may try crimes that violate both state and federal law. Concurrent jurisdiction also applies when citizens of different states are involved in a dispute concerning at least $50,000. In such a case, a person may sue in either a federal court or a state court. If the person being sued insists, however, the case must be tried in a federal court. Such appeals might eventually reach the United States Supreme Court.

Reading Check **Identifying** Which article of the Constitution lists the jurisdiction of federal courts?

Review

Vocabulary

1. **Define** *jurisdiction*. Then explain the difference between *exclusive* and *concurrent jurisdiction*.

Main Ideas

2. **Explaining** What is meant by the words that are inscribed on the United States Supreme Court building: "Equal Justice Under Law."

3. **Describing** Why do you think federal courts rule on disputes between states? What would be an example of such a case?

Critical Thinking

4. **Describing** How did the federal court system develop?

5. **BIG Ideas** On a chart like the one below, write four kinds of cases for which federal courts have jurisdiction and give an example of each kind of case.

Kinds of Cases	Examples
Cases involving the Constitution	Person believes First Amendment right is violated

6. **Analyzing Visuals** Study the map of federal judicial circuits and districts on page 241. In which judicial circuit is your state?

CITIZENSHIP Activity

7. **Expository Writing** Do research on the United States Supreme Court in the library or online. Select a famous case decided by the Supreme Court. Of the eight kinds of cases for which federal courts have jurisdiction, under which kind does your case fall? Write a paragraph explaining your choice.

Study Central™ To review this section, go to glencoe.com.

Section 2

How Federal Courts Are Organized

Guide to Reading

Big Idea
Under our federal system, the executive, legislative, and judicial branches share the responsibility of governing the nation.

Content Vocabulary
- district court *(p. 244)*
- original jurisdiction *(p. 244)*
- appeals court *(p. 244)*
- appellate jurisdiction *(p. 244)*
- remand *(p. 245)*
- opinion *(p. 245)*
- precedent *(p. 245)*

Academic Vocabulary
- affect *(p. 244)*
- submit *(p. 246)*

Reading Strategy
Analyzing As you read, take notes on a Venn diagram like the one below to compare the similarities and differences between two branches of the courts.

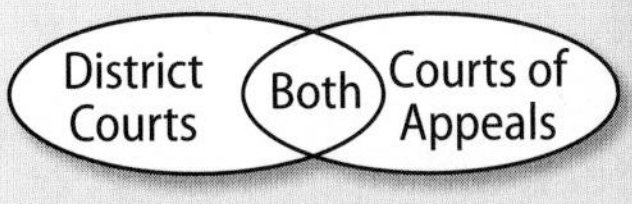

District Courts | Both | Courts of Appeals

Real World Civics For more than one hundred years, the Supreme Court justices have carried on the tradition of the "conference handshake." When they gather before taking the bench, each justice shakes hands with each of the other eight. Chief Justice Melvin Fuller instituted this practice in the late 1800s. It serves as a reminder that their differences of opinion do not prevent the justices from working harmoniously toward a common purpose.

▼ **Newly appointed Supreme Court Justice Samuel Alito, Jr., receives congratulations from Attorney General Alberto Gonzales.**

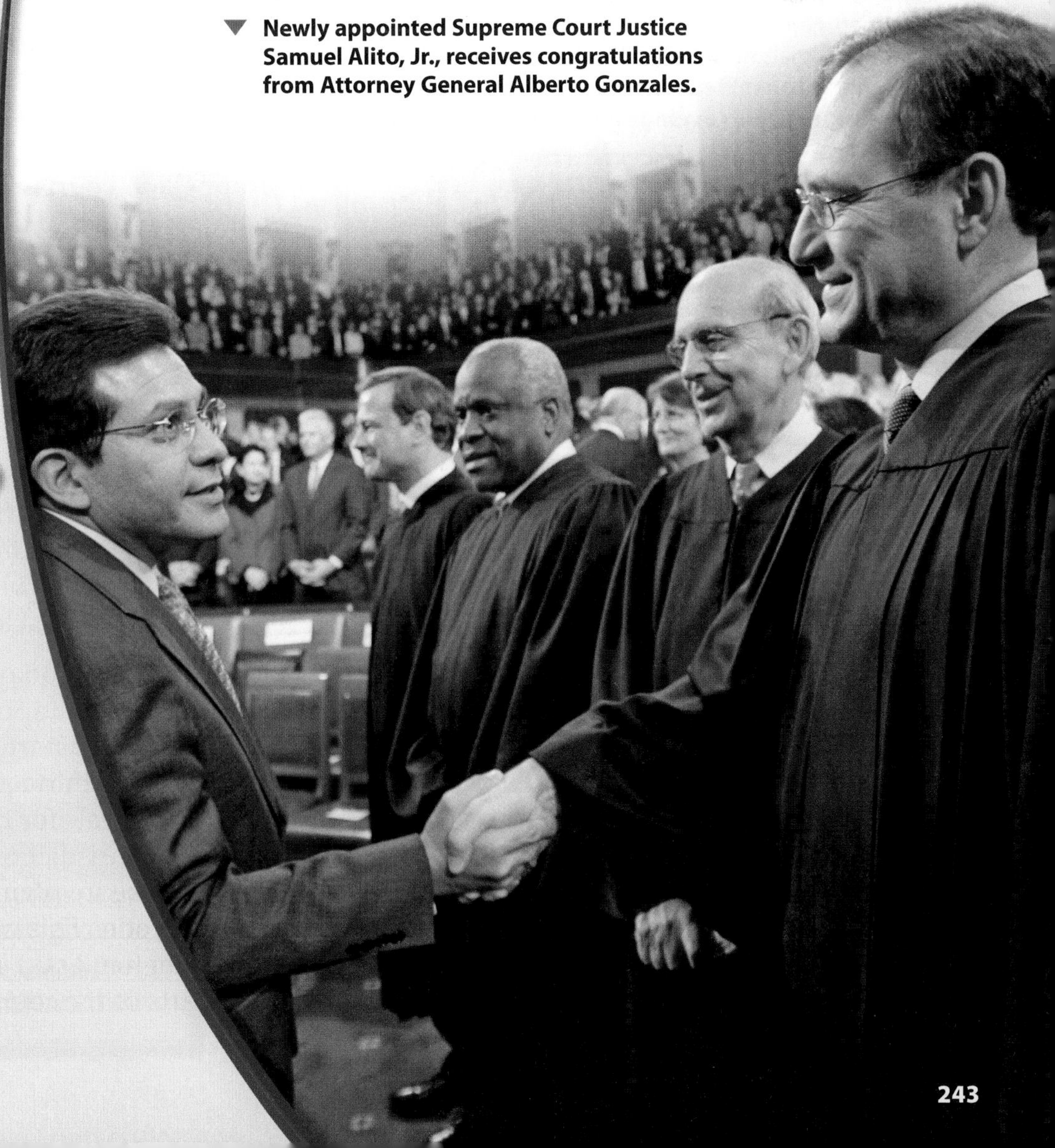

The Lower Federal Courts

Main Idea **There are three types of federal courts: district courts, courts of appeals, and the Supreme Court.**

Civics & You What makes the U.S. court system effective? Read to learn how the federal court system is organized.

At the top of the federal court system is the Supreme Court. Below the Supreme Court are two lower courts—the district courts and the appeals courts.

Media Coverage The media often film trials as they happen. Federal court buildings are located in each state and trials must be held in the state where the crime was committed. ***Analyzing*** **In what way can extensive media coverage help ensure a fair trial?**

U.S. District Courts

District courts are the federal courts in which trials are held and lawsuits are begun. There are 94 district courts in all. Every state has at least one district court, and some states have more. All federal cases must begin in a district court, because district courts have **original jurisdiction,** the authority to hear cases for the first time. District courts are responsible for determining the facts of a case; they are the trial courts for both criminal and civil federal cases. Thus, in a criminal case, a district court will decide if a person is guilty or innocent based on the evidence presented. District courts are the only federal courts in which witnesses testify and juries hear cases and reach verdicts.

U.S. Courts of Appeals

Above the district courts in the federal court system are the United States courts of appeals. These courts are also referred to as federal appeals courts, circuit courts of appeals, or appellate courts. The job of the **appeals courts** is to review decisions made in lower district courts. This is referred to as **appellate jurisdiction,** or the authority of a court to hear a case appealed from a lower court.

Lawyers usually appeal when they feel that the district court judge in their case followed the wrong procedure or did not apply the law. Some appeals may be based on new evidence that could **affect,** or impact, the verdict. Appeals courts may also review federal regulatory agency rulings if those involved believe the agency acted unfairly.

Organization Today, each of the 12 United States courts of appeals has jurisdiction over a circuit, or particular geographic area. In addition, a thirteenth appeals court, the Court of Appeals for the Federal Circuit, has nationwide jurisdiction to hear special cases, such as those involving patent law or international trade. This court's headquarters is in Washington, D.C., but it can hear cases in other parts of the country.

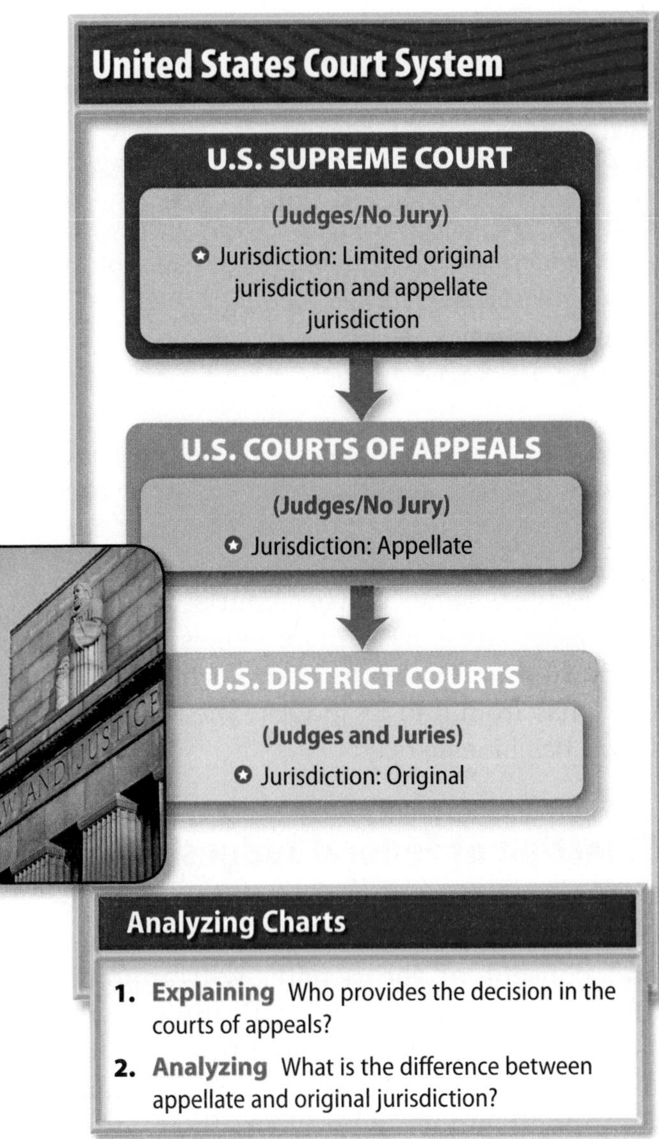

Analyzing Charts

1. **Explaining** Who provides the decision in the courts of appeals?
2. **Analyzing** What is the difference between appellate and original jurisdiction?

Making a Decision

Appeals courts do not hold trials. Instead, these courts may decide an appeal in one of three ways: by upholding the original decision, by reversing that decision, or by **remanding** the case, that is, by sending the case back to the lower court to be tried again. A panel of three or more judges reviews the record of the case being appealed and listens to arguments. The judges then meet and make a decision by majority vote.

The judges do not decide the guilt or innocence of a defendant in a criminal case or which side should win in a civil lawsuit. They rule on only whether the defendant's rights have been protected and on whether he or she received a fair trial. Unless appealed to the Supreme Court, decisions of the courts of appeals are final.

Announcing the Decision

When an appeals court makes a decision, one judge writes an opinion for the court. The **opinion** offers a detailed explanation of the legal thinking behind the court's decision. The opinion sets a precedent for all courts and agencies within the district.

A **precedent** gives guidance to other judges by offering a model upon which to base their own decisions on similar cases. A precedent does not have the force of law, but it is a very powerful argument to use in court. Judges and courts follow precedents in nearly all cases.

Early Precedents

Certain judicial principles were established early in the nation's history. Neither any federal court nor the Supreme Court may initiate action. A judge or justice may not seek out an issue and ask both sides to bring it to court. The courts must wait for litigants, or people engaged in a lawsuit, to come before them.

Judicial precedents derive their force from a common law principle. This principle states that the decisions of the highest court in the jurisdiction are binding on all lower courts in the jurisdiction. Thus, all courts in the United States are bound by precedent to follow the decisions of the United States Supreme Court. Furthermore, each panel of judges on the courts of appeals for a circuit is bound to follow the prior appellate decisions of the same circuit. You will read more about this precedent in Section 4.

Reading Check **Explaining** Why are precedents important to the enforcement of laws?

Student Web Activity Visit glencoe.com and complete the Chapter 8 Web Activity.

TIME™ Teens in *Action*

Clayton G. Lillard

Clayton G. Lillard, 17, from San Antonio, Texas, decided to do something good for kids who had a parent in prison. So he started Clayton's Backyard Crew.

QUESTION: What does your group do?

ANSWER: Clayton's Backyard Crew is made up of volunteers, usually teenagers. Each year we solicit donations for gently used bicycles and cash donations for new bikes and parts. We refurbish the used bikes and distribute them to children whose parents are in prison.

Q: When do you hand out the bikes?

A: Each year I deliver the bikes on my birthday, December 23. I get to play Santa—it's amazing!

Q: How did the group start?

A: In 1999, my mom and I saw two bikes in the trash. I thought I'd fix them up and give them to needy children. Then we set a goal of giving out 25 bikes. I contacted the radio stations and they put out the word. The response from the community was overwhelming. We ended up getting 100 bikes the first year.

Q: How many bikes have you given away?

A: About 800 bikes. Parents in prison really miss their children at Christmas, and the children are really sad with their parents gone during the holidays. On one occasion, we delivered bikes to two brothers. We told them the bikes were from their father in prison. One boy jumped up and down with joy. He kept shouting, "I knew he wouldn't forget me, I just knew he wouldn't forget me!" It brought tears to everyone's eyes.

For more info, check out www.claytonsbackyardcrew.com.

ACTION FACT: Music is Lillard's passion—water polo and swimming play big parts in his life as well.

Making a Difference

Why does a community need organizations like Clayton's Backyard Crew?

Federal Judges

Main Idea **Federal judges interpret the laws and protect the rights the Constitution guarantees.**

Civics & You What qualifications do you think are important in selecting a person for a position of responsibility? Read on to find out about how federal judges are selected.

The chief decision makers in the judicial branch are the federal judges. There are more than 650 judges who preside over the district courts. Each district court has at least two judges. Some district courts in high-population areas have more judges because there are more cases to hear. Each appeals court has from 6 to 28 judges. The Supreme Court has nine justices.

Selection of Federal Judges

Article II, Section 2, of the Constitution provides that the president, with the advice and consent of the Senate, will appoint all federal judges. The Constitution, however, sets no particular qualifications for federal judges. In general, presidents want to appoint judges who share their ideas about politics and justice. Thus, presidents usually choose people who belong to their political parties.

When naming judges, presidents usually follow a practice called senatorial courtesy. Under this system, a president **submits,** or presents, the name of a candidate to the senators from the candidate's state before submitting it to the entire Senate for approval. If either or both senators object to the candidate, the president usually withdraws the name and nominates another candidate. The practice of senatorial courtesy usually applies only to the selection of judges to the district courts and other trial courts, not to the selection of judges to courts of appeals or the Supreme Court.

Tenure Once appointed, federal judges may have their jobs for life. A judge can be removed from office only through the process of impeachment. The writers of the Constitution gave federal judges this sort of job security because they wanted judges to be able to decide cases free from public or political pressures.

Other Court Officials

Judges do not work alone. They have help from clerks, secretaries, court reporters, probation officers, and other workers.

Magistrates Each district court has magistrate judges. These officials take care of much of a judge's routine work. They issue court orders, such as search and arrest warrants, in federal cases. They hear preliminary evidence in a case to determine whether the case should be brought to trial. They also decide whether people under arrest should be held in jail or released on bail. Magistrates may also hear minor cases.

U.S. Attorneys Each judicial district has a United States attorney and one or more deputies. U.S. attorneys are government lawyers who prosecute people accused of breaking federal laws. They look into complaints of crime, prepare formal charges, and then present evidence in court. It is the U.S. attorney's job to represent the nation in civil cases in which the government is involved. U.S. attorneys are appointed to four-year terms by the president, with consent of the Senate.

U.S. Marshals Each federal judicial district also has a United States marshal. Marshals and their staffs make arrests, collect fines, and take convicted persons to prison. They protect jurors, keep order in federal courts, and serve legal papers, including subpoenas. A subpoena is a court order requiring someone to appear in court.

Reading Check **Defining** What is senatorial courtesy?

Review

Vocabulary

1. **Write** sentences using each of the following key terms: *district court, original jurisdiction, appeals court, appellate jurisdiction, remand, opinion, precedent.*

Main Ideas

2. **Describing** What are the responsibilities of judges in district courts?
3. **Explaining** Why do federal judges serve for life? Who appoints them to these terms?

Critical Thinking

4. **Analyzing** A judge who shares a president's views when first appointed may rule differently on cases later. Why?
5. **BIG Ideas** On a graphic organizer like the one below, identify the people who help federal court judges with their duties.

6. **Analyzing Visuals** Review the organization of the U.S. courts system on page 245. What type of jurisdiction do U.S. Courts of Appeals have? Explain what this means.

CITIZENSHIP Activity

7. **Creative Writing** Write a job description for a federal district judge. Include the qualifications you believe federal judges should have.

Study Central™ To review this section, go to glencoe.com.

Section Audio

Spotlight Video

The Supreme Court

Guide to Reading

Big Idea
The judicial branch is charged with interpreting the law.

Content Vocabulary
- judicial review *(p. 252)*
- constitutional *(p. 252)*

Academic Vocabulary
- philosophy *(p. 250)*
- conflict *(p. 252)*

Reading Strategy
Summarizing On a graphic organizer similar to the one below, describe the powers of the Supreme Court and give an example of each.

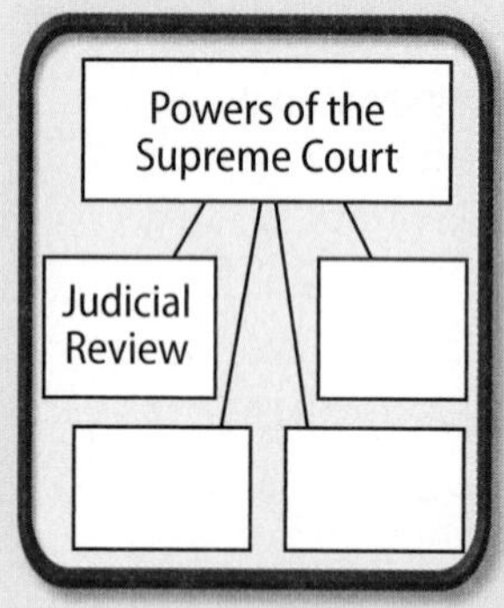

Real World Civics How many people are appointed to a job for life? U.S. Supreme Court justices are. William O. Douglas served on the Court for 36 years, longer than any other justice. John Marshall served longest as chief justice, 34 years. Since justices can serve a lifetime, many different groups want a say in their confirmation. When Justice Sandra Day O'Connor announced she was stepping down in 2005, the White House saw its chance to select a judge who supports President Bush's views. Samuel Alito, Jr., was confirmed and sworn in following a tough confirmation battle in the Senate.

▼ **Justices Souter, Thomas, and Ginsburg attending the swearing in of Justice Alito**

Jurisdiction and Powers

Main Idea **The Supreme Court is composed of nine justices: the chief justice of the United States and eight associate justices.**

Civics & You What qualities do you think a judge should have? Read on to find out how the justices of the Supreme Court are selected.

Chief Justice of the Supreme Court John G. Roberts, Jr., summarized his view of the Court's role in the following way:

> "*What Daniel Webster termed, 'the miracle of our Constitution' is not something that happens in every generation. But every generation in its turn must accept the responsibility of supporting and defending the Constitution, and bearing true faith and allegiance to it.*"
>
> —Chief Justice John G. Roberts, Jr.

As Justice Roberts noted, all Americans are called upon to support the Constitution. It stands above all other courts. The Supreme Court's main job is to decide whether laws are allowable under the U.S. Constitution.

Jurisdiction

Like the federal government, the power of the Supreme Court is limited. Article III of the U.S. Constitution established the boundaries of federal judicial power.

The Supreme Court has original jurisdiction in only two instances. It can preside over cases that involve diplomats from foreign countries and in disputes between states. In all other instances, the Supreme Court hears cases that have been appealed from lower district courts or federal regulatory agencies.

The Supreme Court does not hear all the cases it receives. It chooses the cases it hears. It has final authority in any case involving the Constitution, acts of Congress, and treaties with other nations. The decisions of the Court are binding on all lower courts. When the Court refuses to hear a case, the decision of the lower court stands.

The Supreme Court Seated left to right: Anthony Kennedy, John Paul Stevens, Chief Justice John G. Roberts, Jr., Antonin Scalia, David Souter. Standing left to right: Stephen Breyer, Clarence Thomas, Ruth Bader Ginsburg, Samuel Alito, Jr. ***Describing*** **Why do you think Congress keeps the number of justices an uneven number?**

American Biography

Sandra Day O'Connor (1930–)

When a Supreme Court vacancy opened up in 1981, President Ronald Reagan decided to fulfill his campaign promise to name the first woman justice. He chose **Sandra Day O'Connor,** an Arizona appeals court judge.

Unlike most Supreme Court justices, O'Connor also had broad political experience. After earning a law degree in 1952, she found that most law firms would not hire a woman—except as a legal secretary. She went into public service, had three sons, and practiced law privately. Appointed to a state senatorial vacancy in 1969, she successfully ran for the position and became its first woman majority leader in 1972. O'Connor won the election for superior court judge in 1974 and was later appointed to the appeals court.

Her nomination to the Supreme Court had strong support, but was opposed by some because she had supported the Equal Rights Amendment (ERA) and refused to back an antiabortion amendment. Others, however, praised her legal judgment.

O'Connor's years on the Court marked her as a conservative jurist; however, she often occupied the Court's "middle ground," by casting the deciding vote on many controversial issues.

Making a Difference — CITIZENSHIP

Justice O'Connor once said, "The power I exert on the Court depends on the power of my arguments, not on my gender." ***Explain*** **What is the meaning of this statement?**

Organization and Duties

The Supreme Court is made of eight associate justices led by a chief justice. Congress sets this number and has the power to change it. The justices are important political decision makers. Their rulings often affect citizens as much as do presidential or congressional decisions.

The main duty of justices is to hear and rule on cases. They choose which cases to hear from among the thousands appealed to the Court each year, then decide the case itself and issue a written explanation for the decision, called the Court's opinion.

Selecting the Justices

The president appoints Supreme Court justices, with the approval of the Senate. Vacancies in the Court open up due to the resignation or death of a justice. In 2005, for example, President Bush appointed John G. Roberts, Jr., as chief justice, following the death of Chief Justice William Rehnquist. He also selected Samuel Alito, Jr., to replace Sandra Day O'Connor, who resigned.

Presidents are careful to choose nominees who are likely to be approved by the Senate. The president's decision is often influenced by the attorney general and other Justice Department officials, other Supreme Court justices, the American Bar Association, and interest groups, such as labor and civil rights groups.

Senators typically give the president advice in appointing new justices, which he is free to accept or ignore. The Senate also has rejected nominees based on doubts about the qualifications or the legal **philosophy** (system of beliefs) of the persons nominated.

Background of the Justices

Supreme Court justices are always lawyers, although there is no legal requirement that they must be lawyers. They have had careers practicing or teaching law, serving as judges in lower courts, or holding other public positions prior to appointment.

Political support and agreement with the president's ideas are important factors in who gets appointed. Of course, once appointed, a justice may make rulings with which the president does not agree.

The first African American justice, Thurgood Marshall, joined the Court in 1967. The first female justice, Sandra Day O'Connor, was appointed in 1981.

Reading Check **Identifying** Who makes up the Supreme Court?

Powers of the Court

Main Idea **The Supreme Court is the final court to which anyone can appeal a legal decision.**

Civics & You How do you feel when someone makes a decision that you feel is against the law? Read to find out about the Supreme Court and the constitutionality of the law.

The Supreme Court enjoys a great deal of power and prestige. The legislative and executive branches of government must follow the Supreme Court's rulings. The fact that the Supreme Court is removed from politics and from the influences of special-interest groups makes it more likely that the parties involved in a case will get a fair hearing.

Special Rulings The Supreme Court ruled on whether these residents of Washington, D.C., burning their federal tax statements could vote in federal elections. ***Identifying*** **Which branches of the federal government must follow Supreme Court rulings?**

Judicial Review

One of the most important powers of the Supreme Court is the power of judicial review. **Judicial review** means that the Court can review any federal, state, or local law or action to see if it is **constitutional,** or allowed by the Constitution. If the Court decides a law is unconstitutional, it has the power to nullify, or cancel, that law or action. Chief Justice John Marshall described the great power of judicial review when he said,

> "*It is emphatically the province and duty of the judicial department to say what the law is. Those who apply the rule to particular cases, must of necessity expound and interpret that rule. If two laws conflict with each other, the courts must decide on the operation of each.*"
>
> —Chief Justice John Marshall

Marbury* v. *Madison The Constitution does not give the Supreme Court the power of judicial review. A provision of the Judiciary Act of 1789 gave the Court the power of judicial review for acts of state governments. In 1803 the case of *Marbury* v. *Madison* established that the Supreme Court had the power to decide whether laws passed by Congress were constitutional.

(See Landmark Supreme Court Case Studies on page 260 for information about this case.)

John Marshall's opinion set forth three principles of judicial review:

- The Constitution is the supreme law of the land.
- If there is a **conflict,** or a disagreement, between the Constitution and any other law, the Constitution rules.
- The judicial branch has a duty to uphold the Constitution. Thus, it must be able to determine when a law conflicts with the Constitution and to nullify unconstitutional laws.

In this drawing, cartoonist Joseph Mirachi is making a statement about the U.S. Supreme Court.

1. **What is the setting for this cartoon, and what figures are depicted?**
2. **What is the Supreme Court's role in determining the constitutionality of a law?**
3. **What happens if the Supreme Court rules that a law is unconstitutional?**

The power of judicial review is an important check on the legislative and executive branches of government. It prevents them from straying too far from the Constitution when they make and carry out laws.

Limits on the Supreme Court

Under the system of checks and balances, there are limits on the power of the federal courts, including the Supreme Court. The Court depends on the executive branch as well as state and local officials, such as governors or police officers, to enforce its decisions.

The executive branch usually follows Court rulings, but there have been exceptions. President Andrew Jackson refused to obey a Court ruling in the case of *Worcester* v. *Georgia,* in which Chief Justice John Marshall ordered the state of Georgia to stop violating federal land treaties with the Cherokee Nation in 1832. Because most citizens agreed with President Jackson, there was no public pressure to force him to uphold the Court's decision.

Congress can get around a Court ruling by passing a new law or changing a law ruled unconstitutional by the Court. Congress and state legislatures can also try to undo Court rulings by adopting a new amendment to the Constitution.

Another limit is the fact that the Court can only hear and make rulings on the cases that come to it. All cases submitted to the Court must be actual legal disputes. A person cannot simply ask the Court to decide whether a law is constitutional. The Court will not rule on a law or action that has not been challenged on appeal. The Court also accepts only cases that involve a federal question.

Traditionally, the Court has refused to deal with political questions because it believes that these are issues the executive or legislative branch of the government should resolve. However, in the 2000 presidential election, the Supreme Court for the first time heard two cases involving the recounting of votes in the state of Florida.

Reading Check **Explaining** How does the Supreme Court receive the cases it considers?

Review

Vocabulary

1. **Write** a true statement *and* a false statement for the terms: *judicial review, constitutional.* Beside each false statement explain why it is false.

Main Ideas

2. **Describe** the selection process for Supreme Court justices.
3. **Analyzing** What is the significance of the case of *Marbury* v. *Madison* and how it relates to Congress?

Critical Thinking

4. **Interpreting** Former Chief Justice Charles Evans Hughes once said, "The Constitution is what the judges say it is." Explain the meaning of this statement.
5. **BIG Ideas** On a graphic organizer like the one below, list the kinds of laws that can be reviewed in judicial review and what they are reviewed for.

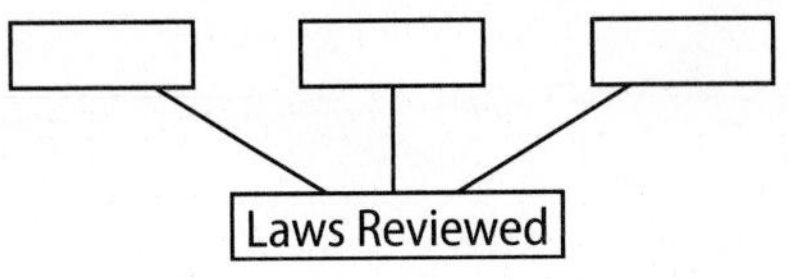

CITIZENSHIP Activity

6. **Expository Writing** Select one Supreme Court Justice, either past or current. Research more about and write a report on the justice.

Study Central™ To review this section, go to glencoe.com.

Section Audio   Spotlight Video

The Supreme Court at Work

Guide to Reading

Big Idea
The judicial branch is charged with interpreting the law.

Content Vocabulary
- docket *(p. 255)*
- brief *(p. 256)*
- majority opinion *(p. 256)*
- unanimous opinion *(p. 256)*
- concurring opinion *(p. 256)*
- dissenting opinion *(p. 256)*
- stare decisis *(p. 257)*

Academic Vocabulary
- communicate *(p. 256)*
- attitude *(p. 257)*

Reading Strategy
Contrasting As you read, use a graphic organizer similar to the one below to take notes on the differences between dissenting opinions and concurring opinions.

Supreme Court Decisions
- Dissenting Opinions
- Concurring Opinions

Real World Civics At times, the Supreme Court has changed its mind due to changing social conditions. In the 1890s, the Supreme Court ruled that segregation in America was legal. But in the 1950s, nine African American students won a lower court case to desegregate Central High School in Little Rock, Arkansas. In 1958, Thurgood Marshall, a lawyer for the National Association for the Advancement of Colored People (NAACP), helped convince the Supreme Court that Little Rock had to proceed with integration.

▼ **Thurgood Marshall with Little Rock students on the steps of the Supreme Court building in Washington, D.C., in 1958**

Court Procedures

Main Idea **The Supreme Court is not required to hear all cases presented before it and carefully chooses the cases it will consider.**

Civics & You In a dispute, why might it be helpful to have an impartial third party decide who is right and who is wrong? Read to find out the process the Supreme Court uses to make an unbiased decision.

The Supreme Court meets for about nine months each year. Each term begins the first Monday in October and runs as long as the business before the Court requires. A term is named after the year in which it begins. The 2009 term, for example, began in October 2009 and ended in July 2010. Special sessions may be called to deal with urgent matters that cannot wait until the next term. Between terms the justices study new cases and catch up on other Court work.

How Cases Reach the Court

An important task of Supreme Court justices is to decide whether to hear a case. The justices review a list of possible cases and consider their merits. The Court will accept a case if four of the nine justices agree to do so. Accepted cases go on the Court **docket,** or calendar.

Caseload The number of cases handled in a given period is called the caseload. Thousands of cases are filed with the Supreme Court each year. Nearly 8,900 cases were appealed to the Supreme Court in 2006. The Court may decide several hundred cases, but, for example, it gave full hearings and written opinions in only 67 cases in 2006.

In the opinions that accompany this small number of cases, the Court sets out general principles that apply to the nation as well as to the specific parties in the case. It is mainly through these cases that the Court interprets the law and shapes public policy.

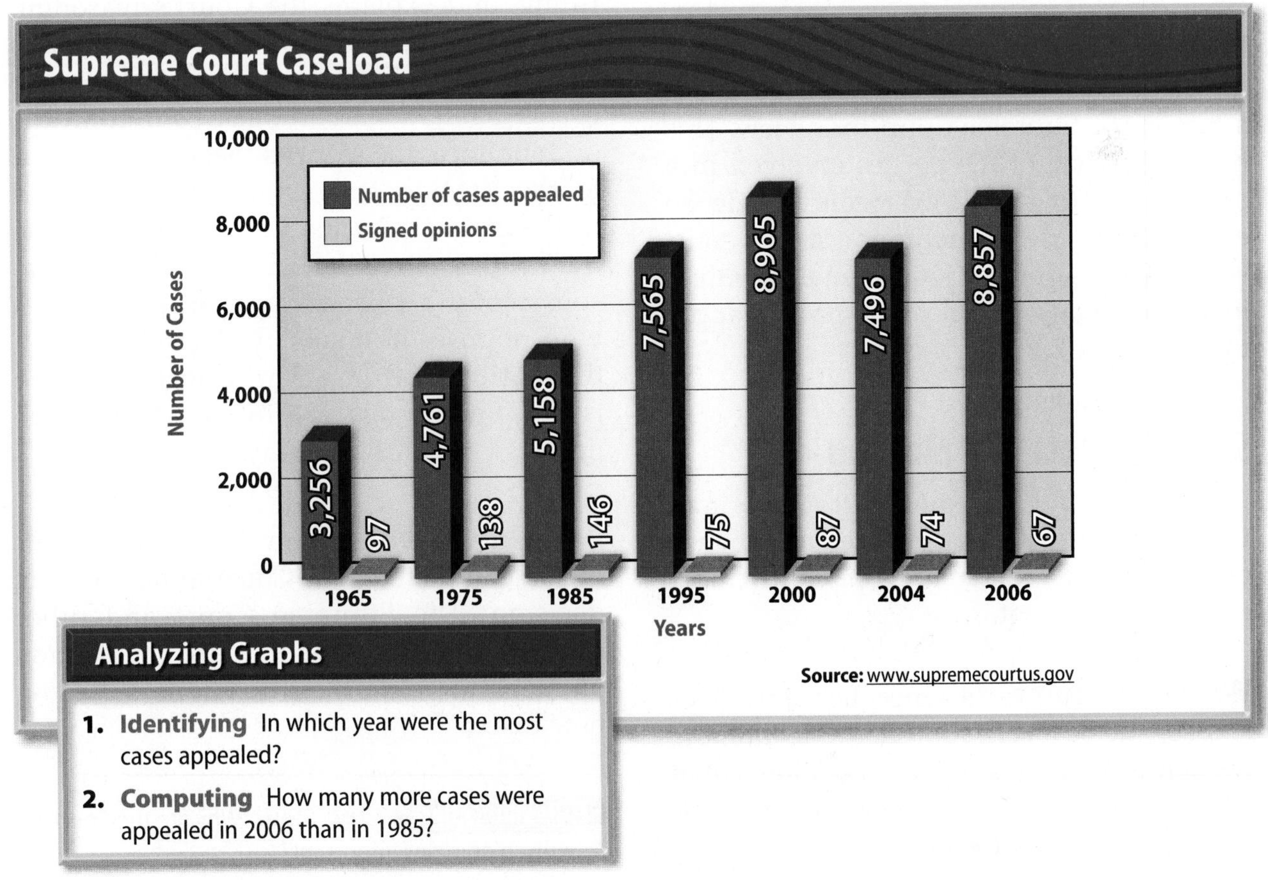

Analyzing Graphs

1. **Identifying** In which year were the most cases appealed?
2. **Computing** How many more cases were appealed in 2006 than in 1985?

Selecting Cases

Supreme Court justices decide to hear only certain kinds of cases. They usually decide to hear a case if it involves a significant constitutional question. In most instances, such questions center around the Bill of Rights and other amendments and deal with issues such as freedom of speech, equal protection of the laws, and fair trial.

The justices always choose cases that involve a real dispute between two adversaries, or opposing sides. In other words, the cases must deal with real people and events.

Supreme Court justices also tend to select cases that involve legal, rather than political issues, as well as those that affect the entire country rather than isolated individuals or groups.

You have already learned that nearly all cases come to the Supreme Court on appeal from a lower court. Most of the appeals reach the Court by a request for a writ of certiorari (Latin for "to make more certain").

Writ of Certiorari A writ of certiorari directs a lower court to send its records on a case to the Supreme Court for review. This happens if one of the parties involved in a case claims that the lower court made an error in the case. Sometimes a lower court will ask the Supreme Court to make a ruling in a case because it is not sure how to apply the law to the case.

Steps in Decision Making

Every case the Supreme Court accepts goes through a series of steps: written arguments, oral arguments, conference, opinion writing, and announcement.

Written Arguments Once the Court takes a case, the lawyers for each side prepare a brief. A **brief** is a written document that explains one side's position on the case. The justices then study the briefs.

Oral Arguments Next, lawyers for each side present oral arguments. Each side gets only 30 minutes to summarize its case. The justices often ask the lawyers very tough questions about the case.

Conference On Fridays the justices get together to make their first decisions about the cases they have been studying. These meetings take place in secret; no audience is present and no meeting minutes are kept. The chief justice presides over the discussion of the case. A majority—at least five votes when all nine justices are participating—decides a case. At least six justices must be present for a decision.

Opinion Writing Once the Court has reached a decision on a case, one justice gets the job of writing the majority opinion. A **majority opinion** presents the views of the majority of the justices on a case. The opinion states the facts of the case, announces the ruling, and explains the Court's reasoning in reaching the decision. Written opinions are important. They set a precedent for lower courts to follow, and they also **communicate,** or announce, the Court's view to Congress, to the president, to interest groups, and to the public. The justice who agrees with the majority decision but has different reasons writes a **concurring opinion.** Justices who oppose the majority decision issue a **dissenting opinion.** The Court may also issue a **unanimous opinion** in which all the justices vote the same way.

Announcement When the opinion writing is completed, the Court announces its decision. The Supreme Court and other courts around the country use the written opinions to guide their decisions regarding new cases.

Reading Check **Explaining** Why are the Court's written opinions important?

Reasons for Decisions

Main Idea **The law, social conditions, and legal and personal views are among the factors that influence the decisions of the Supreme Court.**

Civics & You The Supreme Court hears cases appealed to it by everyone from prisoners in jail to presidents. What influences the justices' decisions?

Many factors, such as precedents, the social atmosphere in the country, and the justices' own legal and personal views, influence justices when they decide a case that comes before the Court.

The Law Law is the foundation for deciding cases that come before the Supreme Court. A guiding principle for all judges is called **stare decisis,** a Latin term that means "let the decision stand." By following precedent, courts make the law predictable.

At the same time, the law needs to be flexible to adapt to changing times. Social conditions, public ideas and **attitudes,** or feelings, and technology change over the years. As the highest court in the land, the Supreme Court is in a position to overrule outdated precedents.

The Supreme Court sometimes reviews a case to clarify the meaning of the Constitution for an important issue. This happened with disputes over manually recounting the Florida ballots in the presidential election of 2000. The dispute led the Court to address a question involving the Fourteenth Amendment: did all recounted votes have to be treated equally? In *Bush* v. *Gore* (2000), the Court ordered the recount to stop. This decision ensured that George W. Bush would receive Florida's electoral votes and win the election.

Changing Social Conditions Although the Supreme Court is somewhat protected from public and political pressures, the social situation can also influence Court decisions. When social conditions change, the Court may make new interpretations of the law.

Constitutional Question Demonstrators gathered outside the Supreme Court building in Washington, D.C., while justices considered the recount question of the 2000 presidential election.
Analyzing **Why did the Supreme Court rule on the issue rather than a state court?**

Landmark Decisions of the Supreme Court

FEDERAL POWER

- ***Marbury* v. *Madison* (1803)** established the Supreme Court's power of judicial review
- ***McCulloch* v. *Maryland* (1819)** ruled that in a conflict between national and state power, the national government is supreme
- ***Gibbons* v. *Ogden* (1824)** established that Congress has sole authority to regulate interstate commerce

CIVIL LIBERTIES

- ***Brown* v. *Board of Education* (1954)** overturned ***Plessy* v. *Ferguson* (1896),** which said African Americans could be provided with "separate but equal" public facilities; began school integration
- ***Reed* v. *Reed* (1971)** held that a state law that discriminated against women was unconstitutional
- ***Roe* v. *Wade* (1973)** legalized a woman's right to an abortion under certain circumstances
- ***Bush* v. *Gore* (2000)** ruled that Florida recount of presidential votes violated Fourteenth Amendment; recount stopped and Bush became president

FIRST AMENDMENT RIGHTS

- ***Brandenburg* v. *Ohio* (1969)** expanded the protection of political speech unless it is linked to immediate lawless behavior
- ***Near* v. *Minnesota* (1931)** ruled against censorship of information, defining "prior restraint" of written material as unconstitutional
- ***DeJonge* v. *Oregon* (1937)** reinforced peaceable assembly and association protection of the First Amendment
- ***Engel* v. *Vitale* (1962)** held that a public school district's practice of starting the day with prayer violates the establishment clause
- ***United States* v. *Eichman* (1990)** struck down Federal Flag Protection Act; held that flag burning is expressive speech

RIGHTS OF THE ACCUSED

- ***Gideon* v. *Wainwright* (1963)** declared that a person accused of a major crime had the right to legal counsel during a trial
- ***Miranda* v. *Arizona* (1966)** ruled that at the time of arrest suspects cannot be questioned until informed of their rights
- ***Hamdan* v. *Rumsfeld* (2006)** ruled that special military courts for foreign prisoners violated U.S. military law and international laws

Analyzing Charts

1. **Analyzing** What earlier decision did *Brown* v. *Board of Education* overturn?
2. **Concluding** Why do you think these decisions are called "landmark" decisions?

In the 1890s, many restaurants, schools, and trains were separate for whites or for African Americans. In Louisiana, Homer Plessy, an African American, decided to sit in a section of a train marked "For Whites Only." When he refused to move, Plessy was arrested.

Plessy was convicted of violating Louisiana's segregation law. The Supreme Court upheld the Louisiana law as constitutional in *Plessy* v. *Ferguson*. "Legislation is powerless to eradicate racial instincts or to abolish distinctions," the Court concluded. The Court ruled that the equal protection clause of the Fourteenth Amendment permitted "separate but equal" facilities for whites and for African Americans. The "separate but equal" doctrine was used to justify segregation in many areas of American life for the next 50 years.

Reversing *Plessy* However, by the 1950s, society's views on racial segregation were beginning to change. World War II made it harder to support segregation openly because many African Americans had fought and died for American ideals. In addition, civil rights groups were demanding an end to racial discrimination. In 1954, in the case of *Brown* v. *Board of Education of Topeka, Kansas,* the Court overturned the precedent of "separate but equal."

On May 17, 1954, Chief Justice Earl Warren read the decision of the unanimous Court:

> ***"We conclude that in the field of public education the doctrine of 'separate but equal' has no place. Separate educational facilities are inherently unequal."***

The justices ruled that racially separate schools are unequal simply because they are separate. The Court found that segregation was a violation of the equal protection clause of the Fourteenth Amendment.

Differing Legal Views Justices have varying views of the law and the proper role of the courts in our society. Some justices, for example, believe that the Court should be very active and hear many different kinds of cases. Others believe that the Court should hesitate to use the power of judicial review to promote new ideas or policies. Political checks limit the extent to which courts can exercise judicial review.

Personal Beliefs Finally, justices are human beings. Each sees the world based on his or her own life experiences. Justice Benjamin Cardozo once said,

> ***"We may try to see things as objectively as we please. Nonetheless, we can never see them with any eyes except our own."***
>
> —Benjamin Cardozo, *The Nature of the Judicial Process* (1921)

Reading Check **Summarizing** Why do you think the Court relies on the concept of stare decisis?

Vocabulary

1. **Define** the following terms and use them in sentences that relate to the Supreme Court: *docket, brief, majority opinion, concurring opinion, dissenting opinion, unanimous opinion, stare decisis.*

Main Ideas

2. **Describing** What are the steps of a writ of certiorari?
3. **Explaining** Why does the Supreme Court sometimes reverse its earlier decisions?

Critical Thinking

4. **Concluding** Do you think it is a good idea that Supreme Court justices are appointed for life? Explain your answer.
5. **BIG Ideas** On a web diagram like the one below, identify the factors that must be part of a majority decision made by the Supreme Court.

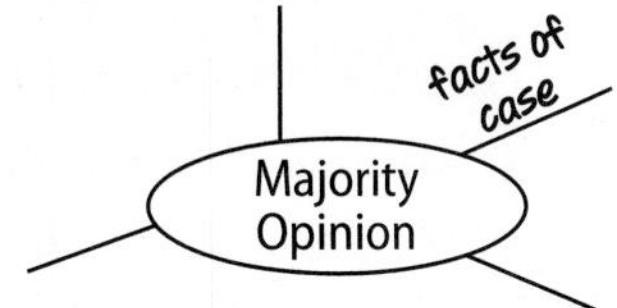

6. **Analyzing Visuals** Review the chart on page 258. Which ruling guarantees you the right to be informed of your rights if you are arrested?

CITIZENSHIP Activity

7. **Expository Writing** Read more about *Brown* v. *Board of Education of Topeka, Kansas.* Summarize the facts in the case.

Study Central™ To review this section, go to glencoe.com.

Landmark Supreme Court Case Studies

Marbury v. Madison

By the early 1800s, the role of the judicial branch was unclear and its influence small. How did the Supreme Court establish its power of judicial review of Congress?

Background of the Case

As President John Adams' term expired in 1801, Congress passed a bill—the Judiciary Act of 1789—giving the president a chance to appoint 42 new justices of the peace in the District of Columbia. The Senate approved the new appointees, and the Secretary of State, James Madison, delivered the paperwork to all but four of the new judges before the next president—Thomas Jefferson—was sworn in. Because Jefferson wanted to stop any action by the previous officeholder, his first act as president was to stop delivery of those last four appointments. William Marbury was one of those who did not receive his appointment in time. He filed a suit in the Supreme Court under the Judiciary Act against the person who was to deliver the paperwork—James Madison. Marbury claimed he should have received his appointment as declared by Congress.

President Adams spent his last night in office signing commissions.

The Decision

The Supreme Court heard the case in 1803. Chief Justice John Marshall announced the ruling. He stated that Marbury's rights had been violated under the Judiciary Act. The Court further ruled, however, that the act gave the Supreme Court rights it should not have, according to the Constitution. Thus, they ruled that the law itself—the one that gave Marbury his appointment—was unconstitutional. Even though Marbury was ruled the winner, the Court could not force the president to give him the appointment because the law allowing the whole appointment was constitutionally false.

Marshall wrote:

> ***"It is emphatically the province and duty of the judicial department to say what the law is. Those who apply the rule to particular cases, must of necessity expound and interpret the rule."***
>
> —Chief Justice John Marshall

Why It Matters

The Supreme Court claimed its right to declare acts of the legislative and executive branches unconstitutional for the first time in *Marbury* v. *Madison.* It defined its role as the final authority on what the Constitution means. By doing so, it established a model of judicial independence.

Analyzing the Court Decision

1. **Explaining** Why is *Marbury* v. *Madison* a landmark case?
2. **Describing** Why did the Supreme Court refuse to allow the appointment of the last judges?

Chapter 8

Visual Summary

The Judicial Branch

- The Constitution provided for a Supreme Court of the United States as part of a court system that would balance the powers of the other two branches of government.
- The United States judiciary consists of parallel systems of federal and state courts.

Chief Justice John Marshall

Federal Court System

- District Courts are the federal courts where trials are held and lawsuits are begun.
- Courts of Appeals review decisions made in lower district courts.
- Once appointed, federal judges may have their jobs for life.

The Supreme Court

- The Supreme Court is the final authority in the federal court system.
- Most of the Supreme Court cases come from appeals of lower court decisions.
- Judicial review gives the Supreme Court the authority to determine the constitutionality of government laws and actions.

Justice Samuel Alito, Jr., being sworn in

- The Supreme Court is made up of eight associate justices and a chief justice.
- The Supreme Court does not have unlimited powers. The Constitution provides that the legislative and executive branches of the national government have several ways to check the Supreme Court's power.

Decisions of the Court

- The Court's decisions are written in an opinion.
- When all justices unanimously agree on an opinion, it is written for the entire Court in a unanimous opinion.
- When there is not a unanimous opinion, a majority opinion is written.
- One or more dissenting opinions are usually written by those justices who do not agree with the majority.

Study anywhere, anytime! Download quizzes and flash cards to your PDA from glencoe.com.

Chapter 8

Standardized Test Practice

ASSESSMENT

TEST-TAKING TIP

When answering multiple-choice questions, your first answer is usually correct. Do not change an answer unless you are absolutely certain your first answer is wrong.

Reviewing Vocabulary

Directions: Choose the word(s) that best completes the sentence.

1. A situation in which both federal and state courts have authority to hear a case is known as ________.

A appellate jurisdiction

B concurrent jurisdiction

C original jurisdiction

D exclusive jurisdiction

2. A past decision on which judges base their decisions in similar cases is a(n) ________.

A circuit
C docket
B opinion
D precedent

3. Judicial review gives the Supreme Court the power to ________.

A declare a law unconstitutional

B remand a case to a lower court

C reject a brief

D hear an appeal

4. When all the justices vote the same way, the Supreme Court issues a(n) ________.

A majority opinion
C dissenting opinion
B concurring opinion
D unanimous opinion

Reviewing Main Ideas

Directions: Choose the best answer for each question.

Section 1 *(pp. 238–242)*

5. According to the Constitution, what does every accused person have a right to?

A a lawyer

B a civil trial

C the best legal help

D a Supreme Court hearing

6. Which of the following cases would be tried in a federal court?

A A state sues another state over water rights.

B A Houstonian kills a person in Los Angeles.

C An Illinois state worker is accused of forgery.

D The U.S. ambassador to Russia breaks a Russian law.

Section 2 *(pp. 243–247)*

7. In which federal courts do juries try cases?

A district courts

B appellate courts

C the Supreme Court

D all levels of federal courts

Section 3 *(pp. 248–253)*

8. How might a president limit the powers of the Supreme Court?

A submit an appeal to the Court

B veto Court decisions

C appoint federal judges

D refuse to enforce a Supreme Court decision

Section 4 *(pp. 254–259)*

9. What kind of case does the Supreme Court usually decide to hear?

A a case that concerns political issues

B a case that involves the Bill of Rights

C a case that poses hypothetical questions

D a case that affects only a few individuals

10. What major factor influenced the Court to overturn the "separate but equal" precedent?

A stare decisis

B conservatism

C racial prejudice

D societal changes

GO ON

Critical Thinking

Directions: Base your answers to questions 11 and 12 on the chart below and your knowledge of Chapter 8.

11. Which decision might lead you to infer that the Constitution protects your right to protest war by wearing a black armband?

- **A** *Engle* v. *Vitale*
- **B** *DeJonge* v. *Oregon*
- **C** *Brandenberg* v. *Ohio*
- **D** *United States* v. *Eichman*

First Amendment Rights

***Brandenburg* v. *Ohio* (1969)** expanded scope of political speech by protecting all political speech unless it is linked to immediate lawless behavior

***Near* v. *Minnesota* (1931)** ruled against censorship of information, defining "prior restraint" of written material as unconstitutional

***DeJonge* v. *Oregon* (1937)** reinforced peaceable assembly and association protection of the First Amendment

***Engle* v. *Vitale* (1962)** held that a public school district's practice of starting the day with prayer violates the establishment clause

***United States* v. *Eichman* (1990)** struck down Federal Flag Protection Act; held that flag burning is expressive speech

12. What First Amendment freedom did *Near* v. *Minnesota* uphold?

- **A** freedom to petition
- **B** freedom of religion
- **C** freedom of the press
- **D** freedom to assemble

Document Based Questions

Directions: Analyze the document and answer the short-answer questions that follow.

The following document is a summation of the Supreme Court's decision in *Reed* v. *Reed* (1971).

Facts of the Case

The Idaho Probate Code specified that "males must be preferred to females" in naming administrators of estates. After the death of their adopted son, both Sally and Cecil Reed sought to be named the administrator of their son's estate. According to the Probate Code, Cecil was appointed administrator and Sally challenged the law in court.

Question Presented

Did the Idaho Probate Code violate the Equal Protection Clause of the Fourteenth Amendment?

Conclusion

In a unanimous decision, the Court held that the law's dissimilar treatment of men and women was unconstitutional. The Court argued that "[t]o give a mandatory preference to members of either sex over members of the other . . . is to make the very kind of arbitrary legislative choice forbidden by the Equal Protection Clause of the Fourteenth Amendment. . .[T]he choice in this context may not lawfully be mandated solely on the basis of sex."

—Reed *v.* Reed

13. How many Supreme Court justices agreed with the decision in *Reed* v. *Reed*?

14. What is the main idea of the Court's conclusion?

Extended Response

15. Write a brief essay describing the procedure that Supreme Court justices follow in hearing important cases.

STOP

For additional test practice, use Self-Check Quizzes—Chapter 8 on glencoe.com.

Need Extra Help?

If you missed question. . .	1	2	3	4	5	6	7	8	9	10	11	12	13	14	15
Go to page. . .	242	245	252	256	240	241	244	253	256	259	258	258	256	256	256

Analyzing Primary Sources

The Federal Branch of Government

Reading Focus

Each of the excerpts are from persons who have served in the legislative, executive, or judicial branches. Each excerpt provides a view on the workings of that particular branch.

Read to Discover

As you read, think about

- how political and judicial leaders view their roles.
- what values and beliefs these leaders share.

Reader's Dictionary

character assassination: the slandering of a person with the goal of destroying his or her public image

exemplary: showing or illustrating by example

comity: a friendly social atmosphere

usurpation: taking hold of by force and without right

pervasive: spread throughout

The Role of Congress

Senator Margaret Chase Smith of Maine was a senator who believed in the idea of true Americanism—those who believe in the freedom of America. Robert Byrd, who has served longer than any other U.S. senator, argues that the American people need statespeople in Congress, not politicians.

Those of us who shout the loudest about Americanism in making **character assassinations** are all too frequently those who, by our own words and acts, ignore some of the basic principles of Americanism—

- The right to criticize
- The right to hold unpopular beliefs
- The right to protest
- The right of independent thought

The exercise of these rights should not cost one single American citizen his reputation or his right to a livelihood nor should he be in danger of losing his reputation or livelihood merely because he happens to know someone who holds unpopular beliefs. Who of us doesn't? Otherwise none of us could call our souls our own. Otherwise thought control would have set in.

—from "Declaration of Conscience" by Margaret Chase Smith, June 1, 1950

In the real world, **exemplary** personal conduct can sometimes achieve much more than any political agenda. **Comity,** courtesy, charitable treatment of even our political opposites, combined with a concerted effort to not just occupy our offices, but to bring honor to them, will do more to inspire our people and restore their faith in us, their leaders, than millions of dollars of 30-second spots or glitzy puff-pieces concocted by spinmeisters.

—Address by Robert C. Byrd, September 15, 1998

The Role of the Executive Branch

Two presidents write about the power of the executive branch.

I have used every ounce of power there was in the office and I have not cared a rap for the criticisms of those who spoke of my '**usurpation** of power'; for I knew that the talk was all nonsense and that there was no usurpation . . . I have felt not merely that my action was right in itself, but that in showing the strength of, or in giving strength to, the executive, I was establishing a precedent of value.

—Theodore Roosevelt, letter to George Otto Trevelyan

[T]he government of the United States has become too big, too complex, and too **pervasive** in its influence on all our lives for one individual to pretend to direct the details of its important and critical programming. Competent assistants are mandatory; without them the Executive Branch would bog down.

—Dwight Eisenhower, letter to Henry Robinson Luce

The Role of the Supreme Court

Two justices write about the role of the Court.

A dissent in a court of last resort is an appeal to the brooding spirit of the law, to the intelligence of a future day, when a later decision may possibly correct the error into which the dissenting judge believes to court to have been betrayed.

—Chief Justice Charles Evans Hughes

[The Supreme Court is] somewhat of an umpire. It considers what the Congress proposes, or what the executive proposes, or what some individual claims, and rules upon these laws . . . by comparing them with the law as laid down by the Constitution . . . and then calls the strikes and the balls.

—Associate Justice Tom Clark

Photographs as Primary Sources
President Lyndon Johnson (right) discusses strategy with adviser Abe Fortas. What does this photograph tell you about Johnson's leadership style? Do you think his style was effective or not?

DBQ Document-Based Questions

1. **Explaining** Do you think Smith's stand was courageous? Explain.
2. **Comparing and Contrasting** How are the views expressed by Roosevelt and Eisenhower alike and how are they different?
3. **Explaining** What purpose does the dissenting opinion in a Supreme Court decision play?
4. **Evaluate and Connect** Select one of the passages that expresses a view that you agree with and select one with which you disagree. Write two paragraphs explaining your position.

UNIT 3

Political Parties and Interest Groups

DEAF Rights!

Hearing-impaired students rally at Gallaudet University, Washington, D.C.

★ Chapter 9 Political Parties and Politics

★ Chapter 10 Voting and Elections

★ Chapter 11 Influencing Government

Be an Active Citizen

CITIZENSHIP The United States is the first modern nation in which citizens deliberately took governmental power into their own hands. They created a governmental system in which the people—rather than a monarch, a dictator, or ruling party—have ultimate power. To ensure the continuation of democracy in this country, Americans must constantly involve themselves in their government.

UNIT 3

Reading Social Studies

Summarizing Information

1 Learn It!

Summarizing is an important skill that helps you clarify text and understand key points, especially if the text is difficult.

- Read the paragraph below. What are the key points in the paragraph?
- In your mind, summarize the key points in complete thoughts.

> The Progressive Party promoted the direct primary to allow the people a more direct role in government. Two other Progressive ideas—the initiative and referendum—were intended to give voters more power to make laws. Although the Populists and the Progressives never won the presidency, the Democratic and Republican Parties adopted many of their ideas.
>
> —*from page 275*

Graphic Organizer

A graphic organizer can help to organize key points to summarize.

Key Points

- There are two major parties: Republican and Democratic
- Both parties have millions of supporters.
- Since 1860, one or the other has always held the presidency.
- Together they have held most seats in Congress.

↓

Summary

The Republican and Democratic Parties are the two major political parties. Both parties have millions of supporters. Since 1860, one or the other has always held the presidency. Together, they have also held most seats in Congress.

Reading Tip

Reading a summary before reading the actual text will help with your comprehension of new concepts.

2 Practice It!

Read the following paragraph from this unit. Draw a graphic organizer like the one below to show key points and a summary.

> There are important reasons to exercise your right to vote. Voting gives citizens a chance to choose their government leaders. It gives them an opportunity to voice their opinions on past performances of public officials. If voters are dissatisfied, they can elect new leaders. Voting also allows citizens to express their opinions on public issues.
>
> —*from page 299*

Key Points

↓

Summary

Read to Write Activity

Read the section titled "Forming Public Opinion" pages 318–324. Then, write a paragraph that uses key points to summarize the argument *for* public opinion polling or *against* public opinion polling.

3 Apply It!

Identify one summary with supporting key points for:

- **Chapter 11, Section 2**

Chapter 9

Political Parties and Politics

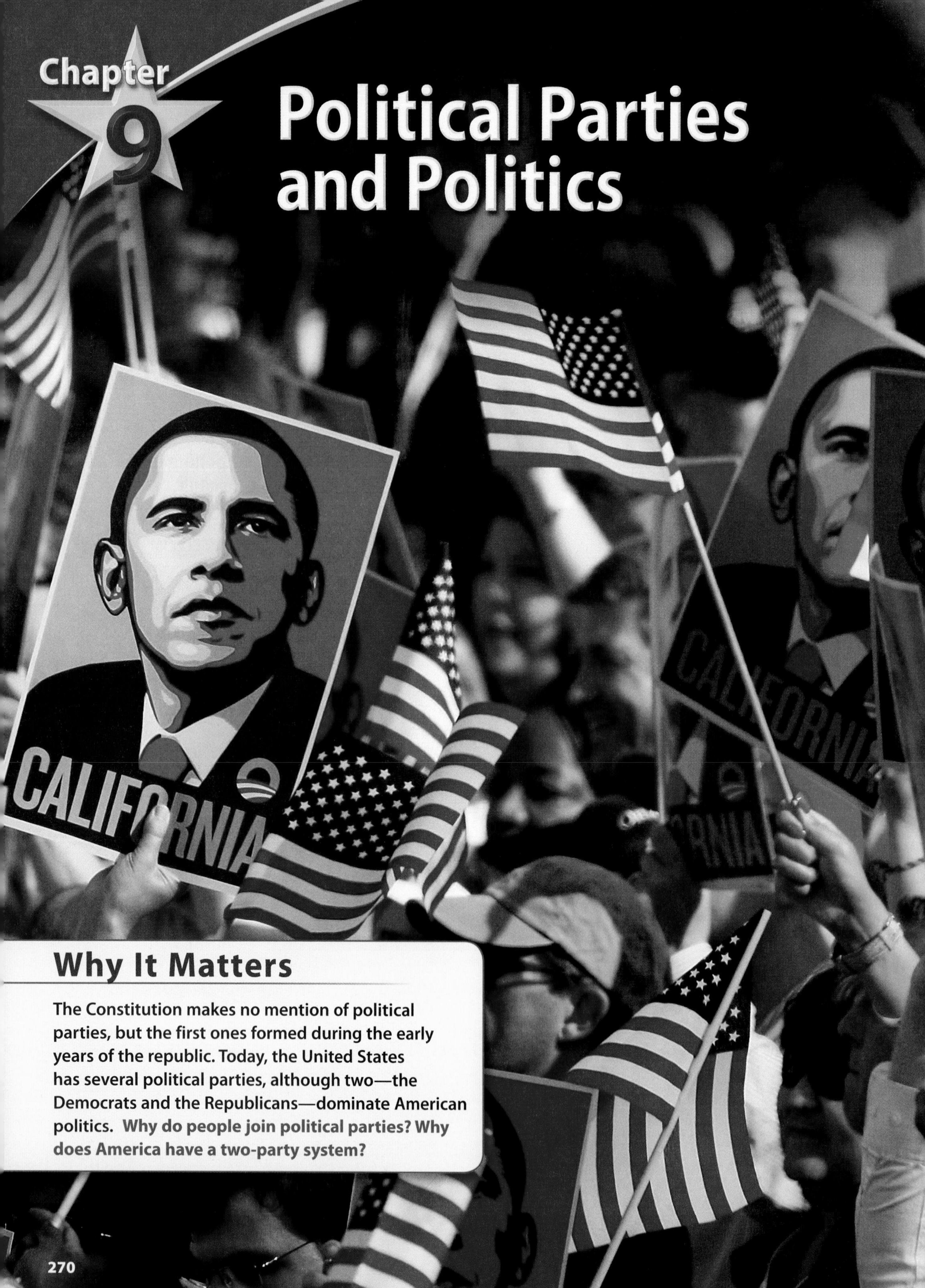

Why It Matters

The Constitution makes no mention of political parties, but the first ones formed during the early years of the republic. Today, the United States has several political parties, although two—the Democrats and the Republicans—dominate American politics. **Why do people join political parties? Why does America have a two-party system?**

Civics ONLINE
Visit glencoe.com and enter QuickPass™ code CIV3093c9 for Chapter 9 resources.

Chapter Audio

BIG Ideas

Section 1: Development of Political Parties

Political and economic institutions evolve to help individuals and groups accomplish their goals. The United States has had a two-party system since its early days as a nation.

Section 2: Role of Political Parties Today

Political and economic institutions evolve to help individuals and groups accomplish their goals. Political parties play a large role in the decisions made by government.

◀ **Delegates cheer for the first African American presidential candidate at the 2008 Democratic Convention**

FOLDABLES™ Study Organizer

Comparing Information Study Foldable Make the following Foldable to help you compare how political parties work.

Step 1 Fold a sheet of paper in half from the long way with edges evenly together.

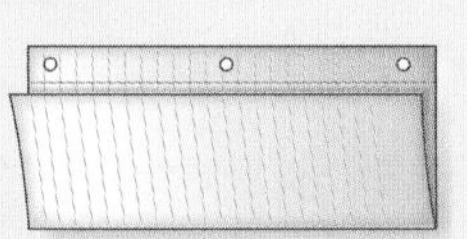

Step 2 Turn the paper and fold it into thirds.

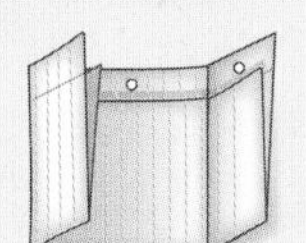

Reading and Writing As you read the chapter, compare and contrast the duties and roles of political parties at different levels.

Step 3 Unfold and draw two overlapping ovals. Cut the top layer along both fold lines.

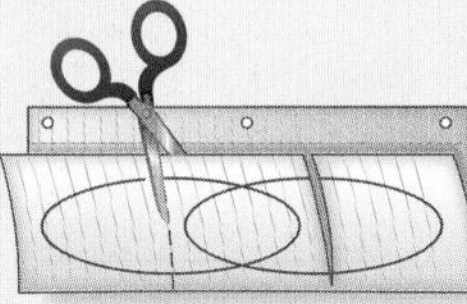

Step 4 Label as shown.

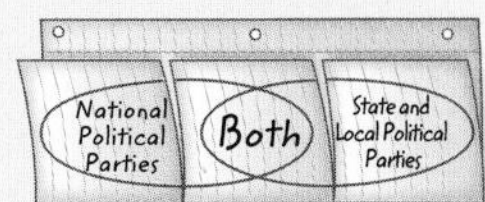

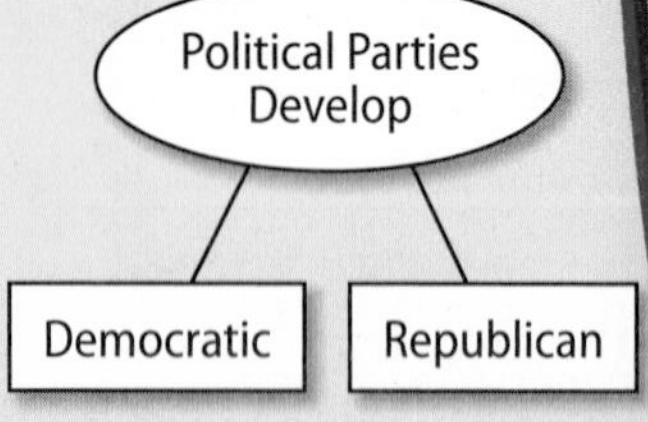

Section Audio   Spotlight Video

Development of Political Parties

Guide to Reading

Big Idea

Political and economic institutions evolve to help individuals and groups accomplish their goals.

Content Vocabulary

- political party *(p. 273)*
- two-party system *(p. 273)*
- third party *(p. 274)*
- platform *(p. 277)*
- plank *(p. 277)*

Academic Vocabulary

- stress *(p. 273)*
- promote *(p. 274)*

Reading Strategy

Comparing As you read, complete a web diagram similar to the one below by detailing the development of today's major political parties in the United States: the Democratic and Republican.

Political Parties Develop

Democratic | Republican

Real World Civics Despite the dominance of the two major political parties, third parties have often influenced American politics. Many important issues have been brought to the public's attention by third parties. Theodore Roosevelt's Progressive Party split the Republican Party, taking many of its votes and causing it to lose the election in 1912. Democratic candidate Woodrow Wilson was elected.

▼ **In 1912, Theodore Roosevelt became the presidential candidate for the newly formed Progressive Party**

Political Participation As American citizens, each of us has the right to participate in the political process and express our opinions on government policy. Political parties are one of the major vehicles of participation in our political system. ***Describing*** **What is the function of political parties?**

Political Parties

Main Idea **Political parties play a vital role in our democratic system.**

Civics & You Many of us demand to have a say in the governmental decisions that affect us. Read on to find out how political parties help meet this demand.

A **political party** is an organization of individuals with broad, common interests who organize to win elections, to operate the government, and to thereby influence government policy. During most of American history there have been two major political parties. Other parties have sometimes run in elections, but they have seldom won. For these reasons, the United States is said to have a **two-party system.**

Growth of American Parties

The U.S. Constitution says nothing about political parties. In fact, many delegates to the Constitutional Convention were against them. In his Farewell Address of 1796, President George Washington warned against the "baneful [very harmful] effects of the spirit of the party." Even so, by the late 1790s, two rival political groups had organized in opposition to one another.

Secretary of State Thomas Jefferson led one group, and Secretary of the Treasury Alexander Hamilton led the other. They disagreed strongly about how the U.S. government should operate.

Hamilton believed that individual rights were at risk if the government was too weak, so he favored a strong national government. Jefferson wanted to limit the power of the national government. Contrary to Hamilton, he argued for more power for state governments, which were closer to the citizens.

The Democratic Party At first Jefferson's group was called the Democratic-Republican Party. From 1800 to 1816 Jefferson's party grew stronger, while Hamilton's, the Federalist Party, weakened. In 1824 all four presidential candidates had run as Democratic-Republicans. By 1828, however, the party had split. Those who supported candidate Andrew Jackson took the name Democratic Party to **stress,** or play up, their ties to the common people. In 1830 a new party, the Whigs (or National Republicans), rose to compete with the Democrats. The Whigs and the Democrats remained the two major parties until the 1850s.

Evolution of American Political Parties

Party	Years	Description
Federalist	1789–1820	Promoted a strong central government
Democratic-Republican	1796–1832	Formed to oppose Federalist policies
National Republican	1828–1836	Split from the Democratic-Republican Party to promote strong national government and oppose Andrew Jackson's campaign for presidency
Democratic	1832–Present	Party formed in support of Andrew Jackson
Whig	1834–1864	Included critics of Andrew Jackson, states' rights advocates, and supporters of internal improvements
Republican	1856–Present	Formed to oppose the Democratic Party's support of the institution of slavery

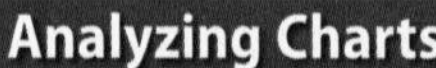

Analyzing Charts

1. **Identifying** According to the chart, which political party had the shortest life span?
2. **Sequencing** When did the modern Republican Party get its start?

The Republican Party In 1854 a group of Democrats and Whigs, many of whom opposed slavery, left their parties to form new ones. These parties took many different names, including the Fusion Party, the Peoples Party, and the Independent Party. The most popular name for the new coalition was the Republican Party.

Republicans did not agree on whether slavery should be abolished in the Southern states, but they did agree that it had to be kept out of the Northern territories. A large majority of Northern voters seemed to agree, enabling the Republican Party to make great strides in the congressional elections of 1854. In 1860 Abraham Lincoln won election as the first Republican president. Since then, Republicans and Democrats have been the major parties in our system.

Reading Check **Explaining** Why did Washington not want political parties to form?

Third Parties

Main Idea **Throughout American history, additional parties have arisen to influence politics.**

Civics & You As you read, think about how third parties influence American politics.

Throughout American history, smaller minor parties, sometimes called **third parties,** have competed for power in the nation's two-party system. While most Americans do not support third parties or vote for their candidates, third parties have influenced American politics in several important ways.

Third parties have often **promoted,** or advanced, ideas that were at first unpopular or hotly debated. The Populist Party of the 1890s, a combination of farmers and laborers, called for the direct election of senators and an eight-hour working day.

The Progressive Party promoted the direct primary to allow the people a more direct role in government. Two other Progressive ideas—the initiative and referendum—were intended to give voters more power to make laws. Although the Populists and the Progressives never won the presidency, the Democratic and the Republican Parties adopted many of their ideas. (You will read about the initiative and referendum in Chapter 10.)

Single-Issue Parties Some third parties form to promote a social, economic, or moral issue. For example, the Prohibitionist Party, formed in 1872, wanted to ban the sale of alcohol. A single-issue party usually does not last long. It may fade away when the issue is no longer important or if a major party adopts the issue.

Ideological Parties An ideology is a set of beliefs about human nature and government institutions. Ideological parties are those that support a particular philosophy or political doctrine. For example, the Socialist Labor Party and the Communist Party USA believe that our free enterprise system should be replaced by one in which government or workers own the factories, transportation, and resources. In contrast, an ideological party such as the Libertarian Party opposes government interference in private enterprise in order to increase individual freedoms.

Independent Candidates Sometimes third parties form around leaders with strong personalities who cannot get support from one of the two major parties. Such parties usually do not survive beyond the defeat of their candidates.

In 1992 wealthy business leader H. Ross Perot challenged both major-party candidates as an independent. Perot ran again in 1996, under the banner of the Reform Party.

Obstacles to Third Parties Third parties rarely win major elections because of the nation's two-party tradition. While the names of the Republican and Democratic candidates are automatically placed on the ballot in many states, third-party candidates must obtain a large number of voter signatures in order to get on the ballot. Third parties also often have trouble raising sufficient amounts of money to compete in campaigns against the major-party candidates.

Other Party Systems

Political parties exist in most countries. Two-party systems, however, are rare. The role that political parties play differs with each nation's political system.

Third Parties Former professional wrestler and Reform Party candidate Jesse Ventura was elected governor of Minnesota in 1998. ***Explaining*** **Why are some political parties called third parties?**

Leading Third-Party Presidential Candidates, 1952–2008

ELECTION YEAR	CANDIDATE	POLITICAL PARTY	VOTES (in thousands)
1952	Vincent Hallinan	Progressive	104
1956	T. Coleman Andrews	States' Rights	111
1960	Eric Hass	Socialist Labor	48
1964	Eric Hass	Socialist Labor	45
1968	George Wallace	American Independent	9,906
1972	John Schmitz	American	1,099
1976	Eugene McCarthy	Independent	757
1980	John Anderson	Independent	5,720
1984	David Bergland	Libertarian	228
1988	Ron Paul	Libertarian	432
1992	H. Ross Perot	Independent	19,742
1996	H. Ross Perot	Reform	8,085
2000	Ralph Nader	Green	2,883
2004	Ralph Nader	Independent	464
2008	Ralph Nader	Independent	698

Analyzing Charts

1. **Identifying** Which of the candidates listed was most successful in gaining popular votes?
2. **Comparing** Which third-party candidates received more than 5 million votes?

Multiparty Systems Many democracies have multiparty systems. In these systems, three or more parties compete for control of the government. For example, Canada has three major parties, Germany has five, and Israel has more than 20.

In multiparty systems, one party rarely wins enough support to control the government, so several parties often must work together. This is a situation that may easily break down and become politically unstable because of so many competing interests of the parties.

One-Party System Another type of party system is the one-party system. In such a system, the party and the government are nearly the same thing. In the People's Republic of China, for instance, only one party—the Communist Party—is allowed to exist, and only Communist candidates may run for office. As a result, only Communist Party members fill government positions. In a one-party system, the main job of party members is to recruit new members, maintain party discipline, and carry out the party's orders. Elections are an empty exercise because there are no rival candidates. One-party systems, obviously, are not democratic systems.

Reading Check **Describing** Name three different types of third parties and explain why they were formed.

How the Parties Differ

Main Idea **Political parties play a large role in the decisions made by government.**

Civics & You People who share common goals often join political parties. Read on to find out about the basic differences between the major parties.

Competing political parties are a necessary part of democratic government. They are a key link between citizens and their elected officials. They give voters a choice among candidates and ideas.

A basic difference between the major parties is their belief in how much the government should be involved in the lives of Americans. For example, the Democrats tend to believe that the federal government should be more directly involved in regulating the economy and in providing housing, income, education, and jobs for the poor. The Republicans tend to believe that if they help the nation's economy grow, poor people will have a better chance of finding jobs on their own. They favor less government regulation of the economy as the best way to promote the growth of production.

Sometimes the differences between the two major parties seem small. Both try to appeal to as many voters as possible. By adopting moderate and mainstream positions and avoiding extreme or radical positions, the major parties hope to attract votes and win elections. The parties are also similar because the majority of American people generally agree about many political and social issues.

One way to identify the differences between the parties is to read the political document, or platform, that each party writes at its presidential nominating convention, held every four years. The **platform** is a series of statements expressing the party's principles, beliefs, and positions on election issues. Each individual part of the platform is called a **plank.** The platform communicates to voters what the party claims it will do if it wins.

Reading Check **Explaining** Why do the two major parties seem so similar?

Section 1 Review

Vocabulary

1. **Write** sentences or short paragraphs about political parties in which you use the following terms: *political party, two-party system, third party, platform, plank.*

Main Ideas

2. **Identifying** What were the first two major political parties in the United States?

3. **Explaining** What are the characteristics of one-party systems?

Critical Thinking

4. **Comparing** Describe the basic differences between the views of Thomas Jefferson and Alexander Hamilton regarding how government should operate.

5. **BIG Ideas** In a diagram like the one below, identify at least three obstacles third parties face.

CITIZENSHIP Activity

6. **Expository Writing** Prepare for a debate on the following statement: The two-party system has outlived its usefulness. Choose either the pro or con side of the issue and prepare arguments for the side you choose. Pair up with a classmate who has prepared arguments opposing yours and debate the issue.

Study Central™ To review this section, go to glencoe.com.

Section Audio Spotlight Video

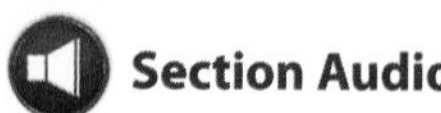

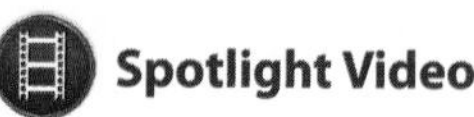

Section 2

Role of Political Parties Today

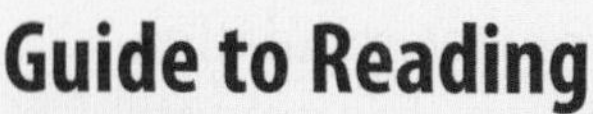

Guide to Reading

Big Idea

Political and economic institutions evolve to help individuals and groups accomplish their goals.

Content Vocabulary

- national committee *(p. 279)*
- caucus *(p. 279)*
- precinct *(p. 281)*
- ward *(p. 281)*
- political machine *(p. 282)*
- direct primary *(p. 283)*
- closed primary *(p. 283)*
- open primary *(p. 283)*
- plurality *(p. 284)*
- majority *(p. 284)*
- petition *(p. 284)*

Academic Vocabulary

- range *(p. 279)*
- adjacent *(p. 281)*

Reading Strategy

Identifying As you read, identify four functions of political parties.

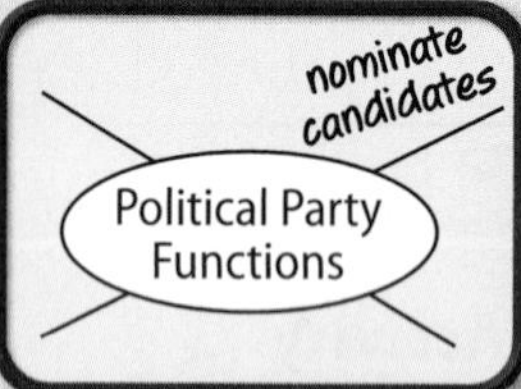

Real World Civics On the campaign trail, who manages travel for the candidates? Who makes sure there are facilities available? And who makes up the cheering crowds? The answer is the loyal members of each candidate's political party. The party supporters are whom the candidates want to reach out to, but also whom they depend upon. The heart of any campaign for national office is the support and organization of the major political parties.

▼ **John McCain and Sarah Palin reach out to supporters during the 2008 presidential campaign.**

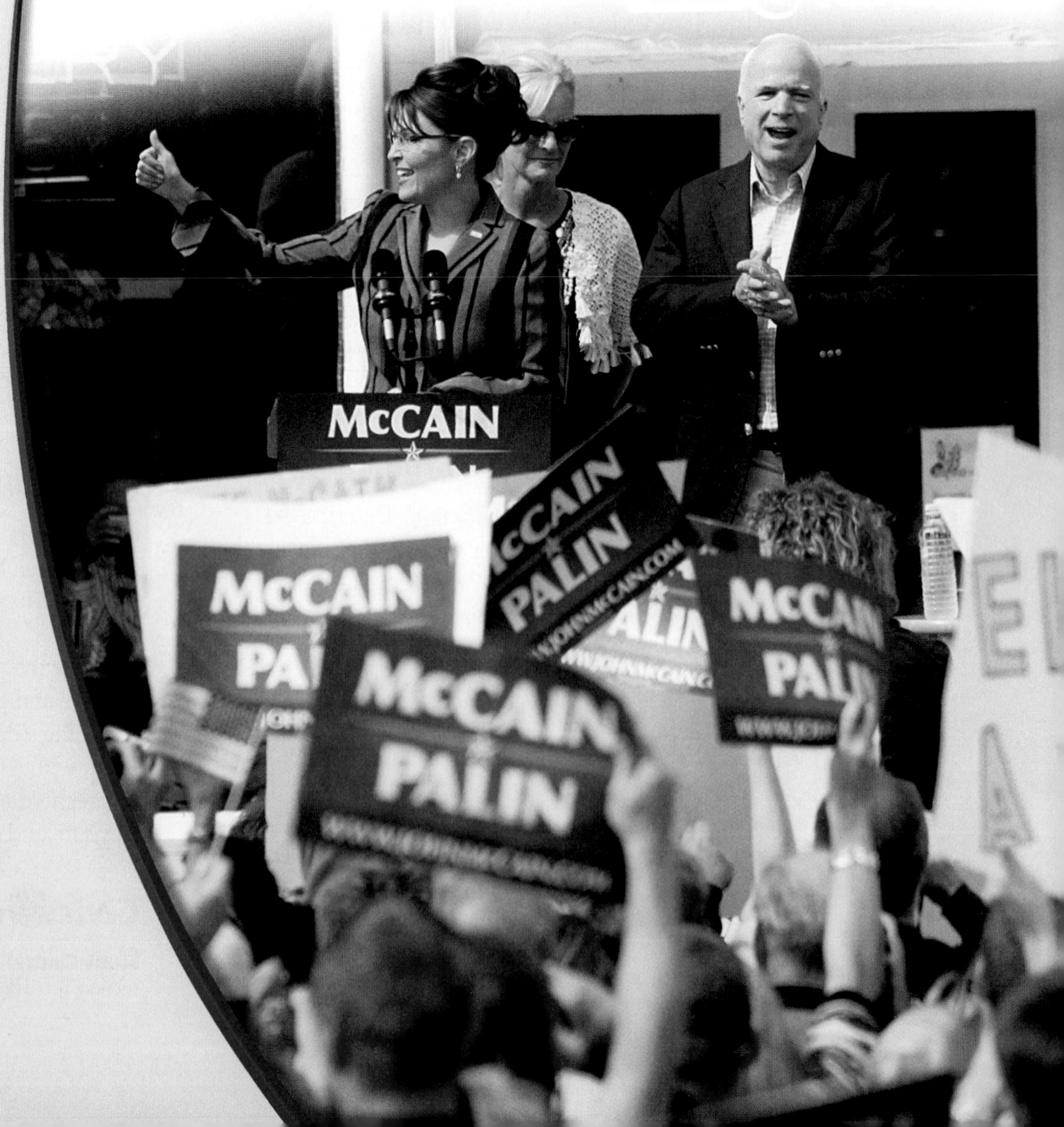

National Conventions Every four years, political party delegates gather to select a ticket—candidates for president and vice president as they did in 1948 in Philadelphia. ***Explaining*** **What is the first task for the delegates?**

Organization of Political Parties

Main Idea **Democrats and Republicans are organized into 50 state parties and thousands of local parties that operate independently of the national organization.**

Civics & You Do you support one of the political parties? Political parties do everything they can to attract supporters.

The two major parties are organized at the local, state, and national levels. These levels are only loosely tied together. There is no chain of command that lets the national organization control state or local party leaders. All the levels, however, have roughly the same political beliefs, and they are united in their ultimate goal—to help the party win election to as many offices as possible.

National Organization

Each party has a **national committee** made of representatives from every state. This committee helps raise funds for presidential elections and organizes the party's national convention. A national party chairperson runs the committee. The chairperson's main jobs are to manage the office, to direct the committee staff, and to lead fund-raising efforts.

National Convention The national convention is one of the most important responsibilities of the national committee. Held once every four years, the national convention is where party members nominate their candidates for president and vice president of the United States. Each party chooses its delegates through a combination of presidential primary elections and **caucuses,** or meetings, of state and local party organizations.

The delegates' first job is to write the platform. This task can be difficult because each party includes members with a wide **range,** or variety, of positions on key issues.

Nominating the Candidate After the platform has been prepared and approved, delegates nominate the party's presidential candidate. The nominating speech for each candidate sets off a demonstration, as supporters parade around the convention hall. Historically, conventions were suspenseful events where delegates from around the country decided upon their presidential candidate. The conventions were a grand spectacle on television. Today the increasing use of early primary elections, where voters narrow down the list of candidates, has caused the nomination for president to be almost entirely decided by the time of the convention.

Campaign Committees The major parties also have campaign committees made up of members of Congress. These committees work to elect party members and raise money.

State and Local Organization

Each major party has 50 state committees or organizations. In some states the parties are well organized, have large staffs, and spend a lot of money each year. In others the organization is weak. State committees focus on electing party candidates to state offices—governor, attorney general, state legislators, and others. They also work to elect their parties' candidates to national offices.

Analyzing Charts

1. **Identifying** At what level of organization is a precinct? Who controls the precinct workers?
2. **Explaining** Why do you think political parties have three levels: national, state, and local?

Local party organizations consist of thousands of city, town, and county committees across the country. These committees include people elected by their fellow party members.

What Is a Precinct? Each city or county is divided into election districts or precincts. A **precinct** is a geographic area that contains a specific number of voters. A precinct may consist of an entire small town or, in a large city, a group of **adjacent,** or neighboring, neighborhoods. All voters in a precinct cast their ballots at the same voting place.

For each precinct, the local party committee appoints a precinct captain, whose job is to organize other party members during campaigns and encourage voters on Election Day. The volunteers distribute leaflets, register voters, and try to convince voters to support the party's candidates.

Several geographically connected precincts make up a larger election unit called a **ward.** Party members in each ward typically elect a volunteer to represent the ward at the local party's next level of organization—the county committee.

County Committees

Counties are the largest political units within a state. Both major parties have county committees. A county chairperson, who runs the committee, often has a great deal of political power in the county. If the county is large, state party leaders such as the governor or a U.S. senator may consult with the county chairperson about important appointments, such as judgeships.

Higher-level party leaders depend on precinct and ward leaders to build the party at the "grassroots," or neighborhood, level. These local leaders have to know what issues their neighbors are worried about and keep track of how local political sentiment is running. At election time they must "deliver the vote" for party candidates at every level of government.

TIME™ Teens in Action

Emily Nguyen

Emily Nguyen, 16, from Morristown, New Jersey, knows debate is a big part of politics. That is one reason she takes part in the Junior Statesmen of America (JSA).

QUESTION: What's JSA?

ANSWER: It's a group for high school students that promotes interest in government, politics, debate, law, and global affairs.

Q: How does it do all that?

A: JSA hosts discussions about contemporary issues, conventions for students, and summer school programs. The group encourages all teenagers to stand up and be heard with its motto "Democracy is not a spectator sport!"

Q: Sounds intense. But is it fun?

A: Yes! The chapter at my school is extremely active. We attend the triannual regional conventions, hold debates at our weekly meetings, organize community service projects—and take part in many other activities.

Q: How will it help your future?

A: Members of JSA learn leadership, managerial, and public speaking skills. JSA works solely to educate America's youth, with the knowledge that one day they will become lawmakers, lawyers, activists, and politicians.

Q: How can other teens get involved with JSA?

A: If there isn't a chapter at their school, students can visit www.jsa.org for more information.

ACTION FACT: Nguyen can often be found playing soccer with a team or refereeing youth soccer.

Making a Difference — CITIZENSHIP

What is the motto of JSA?

Political Cartoons

Michael Ramirez/Copley News Service

Every year, more than half of all Americans do volunteer work

role in it. One of the responsibilities of citizens is to help make their

of volunteer grou small. Perha

In this cartoon, Michael Ramirez makes a comment on the campaign-finance reform movement, whose aim is to regulate donations to political candidates.

1. **How are "special interests" represented?**
2. **Why do you think Ramirez chose this symbol?**
3. **Why is money falling off the back of the truck?**
4. **Do you think Ramirez is optimistic or pessimistic that new campaign-finance reform measures will become law? Explain.**

Political Machines

Sometimes a local party organization becomes so powerful that, year after year, its candidates sweep almost every election. Such a strong party organization is called a **political machine.** One of the most famous—and notorious—political machines was New York City's Tammany Hall.

This organization ruled New York City in the late 1800s and early 1900s. Its leader, William Marcy "Boss" Tweed, and his friends grew rich from bribes and kickbacks—extra payments—given by building contractors seeking to do business with the city. Eventually, many members of the Tweed group ended up in prison.

At a time in American history when few social service agencies existed to help poor people and immigrants, political machines often served a useful purpose. The machines provided needy citizens with jobs, food, fuel, and help with medical care in return for their votes. Today most people think of political machines as harmful. They believe when one party is in power for too long, it may become unresponsive to the needs of the community. Political leaders are less accountable to citizens when the leaders do not have to worry about getting reelected.

Joining a Political Party

You do not need to join a political party in the United States to vote. However, political parties offer every citizen a great way to get involved in politics. Political parties do everything they can to attract members, and they welcome whomever wishes to belong. Party membership involves no duties or obligations other than voting. If a member of a party chooses to do more, then he or she may contribute money, do volunteer work, or participate in other activities, especially during election campaigns. The parties depend on citizen involvement to accomplish their goals.

Reading Check **Concluding** Why is it important to build grassroots support for a party?

Nominating Candidates

Main Idea **Political parties nominate candidates to run for public office.**

Civics & You Have you ever run for an office at school? Did you choose to run or did someone nominate you? Read to find out the role political parties play in selecting nominees for public office.

The individuals who take part in the work of political parties play an important role in the American system of government. They select candidates for office. They keep people informed and interested in the issues and the candidates. They try to see that party members elected to office do a good job. They keep an eye on the opposition party, publicly criticizing many of its actions. They also act as a link between different branches and levels of government.

The parties carry out these activities throughout the year. They are busiest, however, at election time. Political parties are the only organizations that select and present candidates for public office. They do this through the nomination process.

Primary Elections

Today major parties in all states nominate candidates at all levels of government. The method most commonly used today to nominate candidates is the direct primary. The **direct primary** is an election in which voters choose candidates to represent each party in a general election. In recent years, these elections have been very competitive, and the winner of the most primaries is often nominated by his or her party. There are two main forms of the direct primary: closed and open.

Most states hold a **closed primary,** in which only the declared members of a party are allowed to vote for that party's nominees. For example, only Republicans can vote in the Republican Party's primary.

Rules for how voters declare their party affiliation vary by state. In some states you must declare your party when you register. In others, you do not have to declare your party preference until you actually vote.

A few states hold an **open primary,** in which voters do not need to declare their party preference in order to vote for the party's nominees. In most open-primary states, you choose a party in the privacy of the voting booth.

Campaigning Candidates for president begin organizing their campaigns long before the election. Representative Dennis Kucinich of Ohio, campaigning for the 2004 Democratic nomination, talks to New Hampshire students before the state's primary election.
Explaining **Why do candidates bother to talk to students who cannot vote?**

Closed Primaries People who support the closed primary believe that it helps keep the members of one party from crossing over into the other party's primary to try to promote weak candidates (who would then be easy to defeat). An argument against the closed primary is that it does not permit a truly secret ballot, since voters must first declare a party preference. It also prevents unaffiliated voters from taking part in primary elections in most states.

What Is a Plurality? Sometimes a political office can have more than one vacancy, and thus each party can nominate more than one candidate. Most offices, however, are open to only one winner. In these cases, the candidate who gets the *most* votes obtains a **plurality** (the largest number), and wins the election, even if this means less than 50 percent of the votes cast.

What Is a Majority? In a few states, however, the winner must have a **majority.** (A majority is more than 50 percent of the total votes.) If no candidate receives a majority, the party holds a runoff primary between the two leading candidates with the most votes. The winner then becomes the party's candidate in the general election.

Unaffiliated Candidates Candidates who are not affiliated with either of the two major parties can get on the ballot for the general election in most states by **petition.** If enough qualified voters sign papers declaring support for a candidate, he or she goes on the ballot for the general election.

Reading Check **Contrasting** What is the difference between an open and a closed primary?

Student Web Activity Visit glencoe.com and complete the Chapter 9 Web Activity.

Other Party Roles

Main Idea **In addition to nominating candidates for office, political parties have many other responsibilities.**

Civics & You Taking part in political parties is an important way for citizens to affect government decision making. Read to find out the impact of political parties on government.

Although the main purpose of political parties in the United States is to elect candidates to office, they also play an important role in helping the people of the United States practice self-government. The parties enable people to communicate with their government leaders and help ensure that government remains responsive to the people. The parties fulfill this role in a number of ways. Nominating candidates for office is just one of many tasks that political parties perform.

Political parties have several functions that help them fulfill their role in government. Political parties do the following:

- select and support candidates
- inform citizens
- carry the message of the people to the government
- operate the government
- act as a watchdog over government
- serve as a link between different levels and branches of government

Campaigning for Candidates After a political party nominates its candidates for office, it begins to campaign for them in the general election. The parties raise money for the campaign. They also help candidates inform voters about their ideas and views on public issues. A key role for party volunteers is to make sure party supporters are registered to vote and to ensure that on Election Day these voters go to the polls.

Informing Citizens Running a campaign serves another important purpose in a democracy: it informs citizens about public issues and the way government works. To get their views across, party candidates make speeches, publish and distribute pamphlets, and place ads in newspapers and magazines and on television and radio.

Carrying the People's Message In addition to presenting their views to the people, the parties listen to what the people have to say. Voters have ideas and concerns of their own and issues they want leaders to address.

Sometimes people in different areas feel very strongly about an issue. They may oppose a government policy or want stronger laws to protect the environment. A political movement that begins with the people is known as a grassroots movement. When a grassroots movement becomes strong enough, its ideas will probably be taken over by a political party.

Operating the Government Political parties play a key role in running and staffing the government. Congress and the state legislatures are organized and carry on their work on the basis of party affiliation. Party leaders in the legislature make every effort to see that their members support the party's position when considering legislation.

Many government jobs are civil service jobs gained on the basis of open, competitive examinations and merit. However, the president, governors, and some mayors have the power to appoint their trusted supporters to many high-level jobs.

Spreading the Message Concerned citizens use various tactics to make the public aware of their concerns. These California citizens hand out information before a special election. ***Explaining*** **What is a grassroots movement?**

These supporters will usually be party members who believe in their party's ideas and want the opportunity to serve in government. If a chief executive has jobs to fill but does not have enough high-level supporters to fill them, he or she often seeks recommendations from party leaders.

Linking the Different Levels of Government Just as political parties carry the people's message to the government, they also help different levels and branches of government cooperate with one another. For example, suppose the mayor of Columbia, South Carolina, and the governor of South Carolina are both Democrats. They are likely to have similar goals and ideas. They may be personal friends. Perhaps they have worked together on election campaigns or party business in the past. These connections may make it easier for them to join forces to tackle mutual problems. Likewise, when a majority of legislators belongs to the same party as a chief executive, cooperation between the two branches is likely to be better than if they belong to opposing parties.

Acting as a Watchdog Between elections, political parties act as "watchdogs" over government activities. The party that is out of power—the party that lost the election for president, governor, or Congress—watches the actions of the party in power for any mistakes or misuse of power. This opposition party may criticize the party in power and offer its own solutions to political problems. In this way, the opposition party hopes to attract voters. Competition between parties forces the party in power to pay attention to the will of the people.

Reading Check **Explaining** What is a political party's connection to legislation?

Review

Vocabulary

1. **Explain** the following terms by using each in a complete sentence: *national committee, caucus, precinct, ward, political machine, direct primary, closed primary, open primary, plurality, majority,* and *petition.*

Main Ideas

2. **Explaining** What is the purpose of a party's national convention?
3. **Explaining** In what way do political parties help manage the government?
4. **Identify** three ways in which parties and their candidates inform the public.

Critical Thinking

5. **Evaluating** In your opinion, which is a better system, the open primary or the closed primary? Explain.
6. **BIG Ideas** On a web diagram like the one below, write the campaigning roles that political party members play in supporting their party.

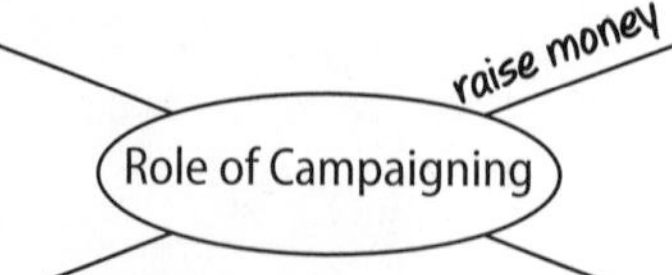

7. **Understanding Cause and Effect** The two major parties are criticized as being out of touch with the needs of many Americans. How might a successful third party affect the two major parties?

CITIZENSHIP Activity

8. **Creative Writing** Create a poster that presents a democratic and cost-efficient system for selecting nominees for president.

Study Central™ To review this section, go to glencoe.com.

Chapter 9

Visual Summary

What Is a Political Party?

A political party is a group of individuals outside of government that organizes to win elections, to operate the government, and to determine policy.

Candidates are ready to answer questions

Political Parties Form

- Shortly after our nation began, two political parties formed.
- The basic difference between the two parties today is their beliefs in how much the government should be involved in Americans' lives.
- In the United States, we have a two-party system, which means that two major parties—the Democrats and the Republicans—dominate national politics.

Students speak out on issues

Organization

- Each party has a national committee and congressional campaign committees. Each party also has 50 state committees and many local party organizations.
- In the past, some local party organizations became so powerful that their candidates won almost every election. These were known as political machines.

What Political Parties Do

- Select candidates
- Inform the public
- Coordinate policy making
- Balance competing interests
- Run campaigns

Comparing Parties

- One way to compare political parties is to study their party platforms, which are declarations of each party's beliefs and positions on major issues.
- The platform is made of planks, which are the party's official positions on specific issues such as education, crime, and foreign policy.

The president leads his political party

Study anywhere, anytime! Download quizzes and flash cards to your PDA from glencoe.com.

Chapter 9

Assessment

Standardized Test Practice

TEST-TAKING TIP

Preconceived ideas about what will be on the test may lead you to assume the meaning of a question before you finish reading it. Read every word in each question to avoid wrong answers based on false assumptions.

Reviewing Vocabulary

Directions: Choose the word(s) that best completes the sentence.

1. A political party's belief, position, or principle on an election issue is called a(n) ______.

A idea
B platform
C plank
D ideology

2. Each party chooses its delegates to the national convention through a combination of elections and ______.

A petitions
B caucuses
C political machines
D national committees

3. All voters in a ______ cast their ballots at the same voting place.

A ward
B precinct
C political party
D direct primary

4. An election in which only the declared members of a party are allowed to vote for that party's nominees is a(n) ______.

A direct primary
B general election
C open primary
D closed primary

Reviewing Main Ideas

Directions: Choose the best answers to the following questions.

Section 1 *(pp. 272–277)*

5. In what year did Democrats and Republicans become the major political parties in the United States?

A 1824

B 1828

C 1854

D 1860

6. Which third party would like to replace capitalism with worker-owned factories?

A Reform Party

B Libertarian Party

C Communist Party

D Prohibitionist Party

Section 2 *(pp. 278–286)*

7. What is the delegates' first job at a party's national convention?

A nominating candidates

B writing the party platform

C raising large amounts of money

D listening to nominating speeches

8. How do candidates unaffiliated with either of the two major parties get on the ballot in a general election?

A by winning an open primary

B by running in a direct primary

C by collecting voters' signatures

D by receiving a majority of votes

9. What political organization of the past used to win elections consistently?

A idealogical party

B whig party

C precinct organization

D political machine

GO ON

Critical Thinking

Directions: Base your answers to questions 10 and 11 on the diagram below and your knowledge of Chapter 9.

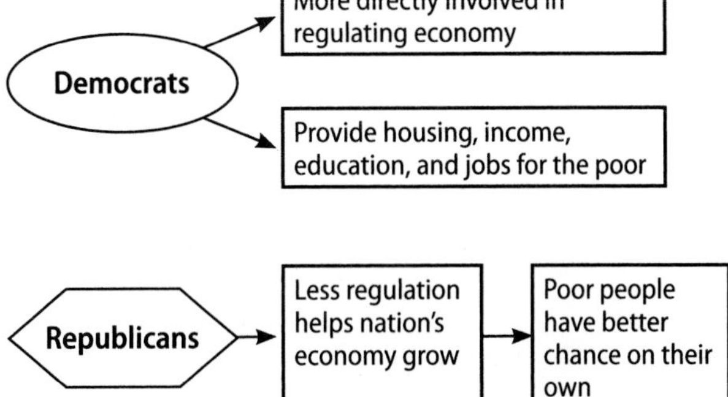

10. Consider how different persons might view the two major parties. Which voter would most likely support the Republican Party?

A a homeless senior

B a low-income student

C a corporate executive

D a government regulator

11. Compare the discussion of third parties in the chapter with the facts in the diagram. Which third party has goals similar to those of Republicans?

A Libertarian Party

B Communist Party

C Prohibitionist Party

D Socialist Labor Party

Document Based Questions

Directions: Analyze the following document and answer the short-answer questions that follow.

The following passage is from the keynote speech by senatorial candidate Barack Obama given at the Democratic National Convention in 2004.

> *For alongside our famous individualism, there's another ingredient in the American saga. A belief that we are connected as one people.*
>
> *If there's a child on the south side of Chicago who can't read, that matters to me, even if it's not my child. If there's a senior citizen somewhere who can't pay for their prescription and having to choose between medicine and the rent, that makes my life poorer, even if it's not my grandparent. If there's an Arab American family being rounded up without benefit of an attorney or due process, that threatens my civil liberties. It's that fundamental belief—I am my brother's keeper, I am my sister's keeper— that makes this country work. It's what allows us to pursue our individual dreams, yet still come together as a single American family. "E pluribus unum." Out of many, one.*
>
> —Barack Obama

12. What two priorities of the Democratic Party are alluded to in Obama's speech?

13. How does Obama suggest that the Democratic Party is the party of diversity? Back up your answer with proof from the passage.

Extended Response

14. Write a short description of the state and local organization of the political parties. Discuss the differences from state to state, the divisions of the organization, and the common focus in all the states.

STOP

For additional test practice, use Self-Check Quizzes—Chapter 9 on glencoe.com.

Need Extra Help?

If you missed question...	1	2	3	4	5	6	7	8	9	10	11	12	13	14
Go to page...	277	279	281	283	274	275	279	284	282	277	275	279	279	280

Chapter 10

Voting and Elections

Why It Matters

The right to vote is a major responsibility of citizenship. By voting, citizens can influence all levels of government as well as the laws under which we live. Yet many Americans do not exercise this fundamental right and responsibility of our democratic way of life.

Civics ONLINE
Visit glencoe.com and enter QuickPass™ code CIV3093c10 for Chapter 10 resources.

BIG Ideas

Section 1: Who Can Vote?

The right to vote is one of the fundamental rights of citizens in a democratic society. Voting is a basic political right of all U.S. citizens who meet certain qualifications set by law.

Section 2: Election Campaigns

A successful democracy is built on an informed electorate. The success of an election campaign depends on the people who organize it.

Section 3: Paying for Election Campaigns

A successful democracy is built on an informed electorate. The sophisticated vote-getting techniques that candidates use have made campaigning very expensive.

Governor Arnold Schwarzenegger campaigns in California

FOLDABLES™ Study Organizer

Evaluating Information Study Foldable Make the following Foldable to help you evaluate the voting process and who can vote, how election campaigns are run, and how campaigns are financed.

Step 1 Fold a sheet of paper in thirds as shown.

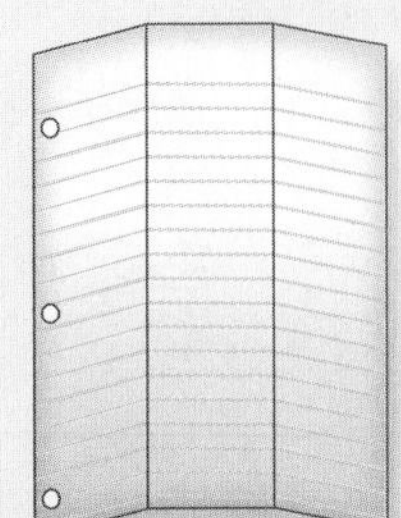

Step 2 Open up the paper and label each of the columns created by folds with these headings:
Who Can Vote?
Election Campaigns
Paying for Election Campaigns

Who Can Vote? | Election Campaigns | Paying for Election Campaigns

Reading and Writing
As you read the chapter, evaluate the information you read about the voting process, taking notes on the rules of voting and how election campaigns are run. Use your notes to understand the entire process of an election.

 Section Audio

 Spotlight Video

Section 1

Who Can Vote?

Guide to Reading

Big Idea
The right to vote is one of the fundamental rights of citizens in a democratic society.

Content Vocabulary
- polling place *(p. 295)*
- precinct *(p. 295)*
- ballot *(p. 296)*
- absentee ballot *(p. 297)*
- returns *(p. 297)*
- exit poll *(p. 297)*
- electorate *(p. 299)*
- apathy *(p. 299)*

Academic Vocabulary
- ultimate *(p. 293)*
- devote *(p. 297)*

Reading Strategy
Sequencing As you read, complete a chart like the one below by listing the steps in the voting process.

Voting Process
1. register to vote when qualified
2. go to polling place
3.
4.
5.
6.

Real World Civics Wheelchairs can help many people with disabilities live more independent daily lives. However, if you are disabled, can you get out and vote? Polling places have been accused of not being "disabled-friendly." The Constitution promises everyone the right to vote regardless of race, color, gender, or age (as long as they are 18). It is up to each state to find ways to make polling places accessible for all voters. Despite the Help America Vote Act of 2002, some people still face obstacles to voting. Organizations at the state level work to help these voters overcome such obstacles.

▼ **Voters at Parker Jewish Geriatric Institute in New York**

Qualifying to Vote

Main Idea **The right to vote is the foundation of American democracy.**

Civics & You Many of you will have the opportunity to vote for the first time in the not-too-distant future. As you read, think about why so many people have sacrificed so much to gain the right to vote.

Voting is an important right of American citizenship. Without it, citizens would not be able to choose the people who will run their government. Voting is also a major responsibility. Those who do not vote are failing to carry out a civic responsibility. They are also handing over their share of political power to voters whose views they may oppose. President Franklin D. Roosevelt reminded Americans of the importance of voting when he said, "Let us never forget that government is ourselves. The **ultimate** [fundamental] rulers of our democracy . . . are the voters of this country."

Early Restrictions

During the early years of our nation, most voters were white, adult males, and property owners. People often barred from voting included white adult males who could not afford to buy property, women, African American males, Native American males, and people under 21 years of age. Today, however, property ownership is no longer a consideration, and the U.S. Constitution states that no state may deny the right to vote because of race, color, gender, or age—if the person is at least 18 years old. Most states deny individuals convicted of serious crimes the right to vote until they have served their prison sentences.

In most states, you must be registered to vote. To be eligible to vote, you must be at least 18, a resident of the state for a specified period, and a citizen of the United States.

Registering Citizens must register in order to vote. ***Explaining*** **What responsibilities do citizens have when they register for the first time?**

Voter Registration

Most states require registration at least 25 days before an election. In a few states, however, the deadline is later—10 or even fewer days before the election.

Registration requirements vary. Registration applications may be obtained from county offices. Some states make the process easier, permitting registration by mail or offering more convenient times and places for in-person registration such as allowing registration at public libraries or high schools.

Extending the Right to Vote

ACTION AND IMPACT

1870 Fifteenth Amendment
Prohibits denying a person's right to vote on the basis of race

1920 Nineteenth Amendment
Guarantees women the right to vote

1924 Congressional Act
All Native Americans given citizenship

1944 *Smith* v. *Allwright*
Supreme Court rules prohibiting African Americans from voting in primary elections is unconstitutional

1957 Civil Rights Act of 1957
Justice Department can sue to protect voting rights in various states

1960 Civil Rights Act of 1960
Introduces penalties against anybody who obstructs an individual's voting rights

1961 Twenty-third Amendment
Residents of District of Columbia given right to vote

1964 Twenty-fourth Amendment
Outlaws poll tax in national elections

1965 Voting Rights Act of 1965
Literacy tests prohibited; Federal voter registrars authorized in seven southern states

1970 Voting Rights Act Amendments of 1970
Lowers the minimum voting age to 18 in federal elections

1971 Twenty-sixth Amendment
Minimum voting age reduced to 18 for all elections

1975 Voting Rights Act Amendments of 1975
Bans literacy tests and mandates bilingual ballots in certain areas

1982 Voting Rights Act Amendment of 1982
Extends provisions of two previous voting rights act amendments

1992 Voting Rights Language Assistance Act
Extends use of bilingual ballots and voting assistance

1993 National Voter Registration Act
Makes it easier to register to vote and to maintain registration

2006 Voting Rights Act Reauthorization and Amendments Act of 2006
Prohibits use of tests or devices to deny the right to vote; requires certain jurisdictions to provide voting materials in multiple languages

Analyzing Charts

1. **Explaining** Why were the Civil Rights Acts necessary?
2. **Identifying** What amendment gave the right to vote to 18-year-olds?

American Biography

Carrie Chapman Catt (1859–1947)

Carrie Chapman Catt declared, "Everybody counts in a democracy." She worked to help women gain the right to vote. Catt felt that self-government would never be safe until "every responsible and law-abiding adult" possessed the vote.

Catt, born Carrie Clinton Lane, grew up along the Iowa frontier. She put herself through college by washing dishes, teaching, and working in the library. She went on to become one of the nation's first female school superintendents. In 1885 Lane married Leo Chapman and helped coedit his newspaper. Widowed a year later, she joined the suffrage movement. When her second husband, George Catt, died in 1902, Carrie Chapman Catt went overseas to help spread the movement worldwide.

With the support of Susan B. Anthony, one of the founders of the suffrage movement, she led the campaign to add the Nineteenth Amendment to the Constitution when she returned to America. Victory came in 1920. To prepare some 20 million women for "political independence," Catt founded the League of Women Voters. Today the League honors its founder by educating all citizens on the importance of voting in a democracy.

Making a Difference CITIZENSHIP

Carrie Catt was one of the earliest female education reformers. ***Identifying*** **What organization did Catt found to prepare women for "political independence"?**

How to Register The National Voter Registration Act requires states to let people register when they renew their drivers' licenses. Citizens may also mail in registrations or register at various state and welfare offices, and agencies that serve people with disablilities.

Registration forms ask for your name, address, age, and often your party preference. You may register as a member of a political party or as an unaffiliated voter. If you register as a Democrat or a Republican, you may vote in primary elections in which you choose candidates for the general election.

To register, first-time voters must show proof of citizenship, address, and age using a driver's license or birth certificate. Voters are then assigned to an election district.

Reading Check **Identifying** What requirements must you meet to qualify to vote?

Steps in Voting

Main Idea **Voting is a basic political right of all U.S. citizens who meet certain qualifications set by law.**

Civics & You Once you take the initiative to vote, there is a process you must follow in order to cast your ballot.

Once the campaign is over, it is up to the voters to decide who will win or lose. On Election Day, voters go to the polling place in their precincts to cast their votes. A **polling place** is the location where voting is carried out, and a **precinct** is a voting district. Polling places are usually set up in town halls, schools, fire stations, community centers, and other public buildings.

The Right to Vote African Americans rallied to be allowed to vote in 1965 in Montgomery, Alabama. Led by Dr. Martin Luther King, Jr., they faced a line of police officers barring their way. ***Explaining*** **Why did it require protests to allow African Americans to vote?**

At the Polls

Polling places are generally open from early morning until 7 or 8 P.M. When you first arrive, you can study a sample ballot posted near the entrance. A **ballot** is the list of candidates on which you cast your vote. Once inside, you write your name and address and sign an application form at the clerk's table. The clerk reads your name aloud and passes the form to a challenger's table.

A challenger—there are challengers representing each party—looks up your registration form and compares the signature on it with the signature on your application. If the two do not appear to match, the challenger may ask you for additional identification. When the challenger is convinced that you are eligible to vote, he or she initials the application form and returns it to you.

Casting Your Vote

You then go to the voting booth where you hand the application form to an election judge. Judges oversee the operation of the voting booths, ensuring that everyone votes in secret and helping voters who are physically challenged, elderly, or unable to read.

Types of Voting Machines

You will cast your ballot by using a voting machine. The two most common types are the punch-card machine and the lever machine. Because election methods are left to the states, the kinds of voting machines used vary widely. Whatever machine you use, you will usually have a ballot with the candidates' names listed according to their political party and the office they are seeking.

"Butterfly Ballot" It is always important to read the ballot carefully. In the 2000 presidential election, many voters in Florida were confused by the "butterfly ballot," a paper ballot in which opposing candidates were listed across from each other instead of vertically. The 2000 election in Florida also proved that some machines were more reliable than others.

Punch-Card Ballots Punch-card ballots, in which voters punched a hole next to the name of a candidate, were run through machines and misread much more often than computerized, scanned ballots. Since the 2000 election, many states are converting to upgraded voting machines.

The Secret Ballot

All types of voting machines allow voters to cast a secret ballot. We recognize the secret ballot as a protection of our right to make our electoral choices unhindered and without fear. Some machines also allow voters to vote for a straight ticket, which means voting for all the candidates in one political party. If you choose some candidates from one party and some from another, you are voting a split ticket. You may even decide to cast a write-in vote by writing in the name of someone who is not on the ballot.

Absentee Voting

Citizens who cannot get to the polls on Election Day can vote by **absentee ballot.** People who know they will be out of town that day, those who are too sick to get to the polls, and military personnel serving away from home often use absentee ballots. Voters must request an absentee ballot from their local election board sometime before Election Day. They mark this ballot and return it to the election board. On Election Day, or shortly thereafter, election officials open and count the absentee ballots.

Counting the Vote

When the polls close, election workers count the votes at the polling place and take the ballots and the results—called **returns**—to the election board. The board then collects and counts the returns for the entire city or county. If the voting machines are not computerized, gathering all the returns and tallying the results can take several hours or longer. Then the board sends the returns to the state canvassing authority. A few days after the election, the state canvassing authority certifies the election of the winner.

In a major election, the news media and party workers try to predict winners as soon as possible. One way they do this is to ask a sample of voters leaving selected polling places how they voted. This is known as an **exit poll.** Through exit polling, specialists can often predict the winners long before all the votes have been officially counted.

The Media and Elections

Major television networks always **devote,** or dedicate, the entire evening to covering the vote during presidential elections. They use computerized predictions based on the past voting history of key precincts. Through this process, the media "call" winners of Senate, House, and governors' seats, as well as the electoral vote in the race for president.

In some cases the networks make these calls with as little as 10 percent of the vote counted. Their projections are usually correct, but some of the major networks were embarrassed by an early and incorrect call on the presidential vote in the 2000 election in the decisive state of Florida.

Some political commentators have criticized these early projections. The predictions usually come when millions of Americans in the Western time zones have yet to vote and the polls there are still open. These observers charge that such early projections may persuade great numbers of West Coast voters not to bother going out to vote. This not only reduces overall voter turnout but also may affect the outcome of local, state, and congressional elections.

Student Web Activity Visit glencoe.com and complete the Chapter 10 Web Activity.

Reading Check **Explaining** What does it mean to vote a split ticket?

Why Your Vote Matters

Main Idea **Through our vote, we directly participate in governing.**

Civics & You Each person's vote counts. If you doubt it, think about how many elections have been decided by just a few votes.

Registering is only one part of getting ready to vote. It is equally important to prepare to vote. It is important to stay informed about candidates and public issues. Newspapers, TV, radio, newsmagazines, and the Internet carry useful information. Other good sources include the Voters' Information Bulletin, published by the League of Women Voters; literature distributed by each political party; and information published by interest groups, such as the American Conservative Union or the AFL-CIO Committee on Political Education.

Preparing to Vote As you read about candidates and the issues they support, read carefully to separate facts from opinions. Everyone has different reasons for supporting particular candidates. As you read about various candidates, answer the following questions to help you decide whom to support with your vote:

- Does the candidate stand for the things I think are important?
- Is the candidate reliable and honest?
- Does the candidate have relevant past experience?
- Will the candidate be effective in office?
- Does the candidate have a real chance of winning? Sometimes Americans vote for candidates, even though they do not have a real chance of winning the election, because they wish to show their support for a certain point of view.

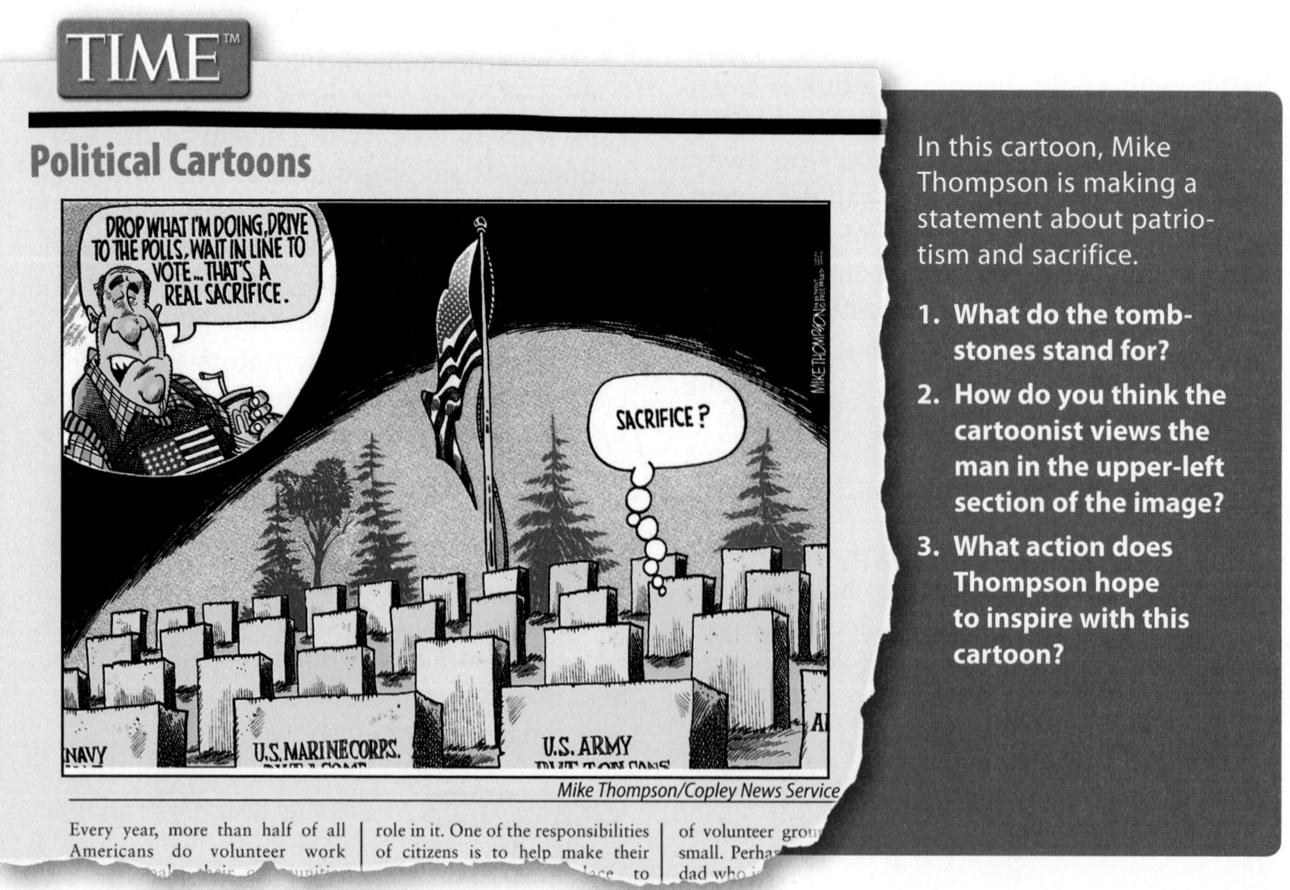

Mike Thompson/Copley News Service

In this cartoon, Mike Thompson is making a statement about patriotism and sacrifice.

1. **What do the tombstones stand for?**
2. **How do you think the cartoonist views the man in the upper-left section of the image?**
3. **What action does Thompson hope to inspire with this cartoon?**

All the people who are eligible to vote are called the **electorate.** Each person's vote counts. If you doubt it, consider this. The 2000 presidential election was decided by about 500 votes in the state of Florida. In the 2006 mid-term elections, which party took control of Congress was decided by a few thousand votes.

Why Some People Do Not Vote

Despite the fact that voting gives Americans a chance to participate in their government, not everyone votes. Some citizens do not vote because they do not meet state voting requirements, or they have not reregistered after changing residences. Others do not think that any of the candidates represent their feelings on issues, or they think that their vote will not make a difference. Another reason is **apathy,** or lack of interest. Even among those who are registered to vote, many fail to do so.

Why Some People Do Vote

The citizens who do vote share some characteristics. These citizens generally have positive attitudes toward government and citizenship. Usually the more education a citizen has, the more likely it is that he or she will be a regular voter. Middle-aged citizens have the highest voting turnout rate of all age groups. The higher a person's income, the more likely he or she is to vote.

Reasons for Voting There are important reasons to exercise your right to vote. Voting gives citizens a chance to choose their government leaders. It gives them an opportunity to voice their opinions on past performances of public officials. If voters are dissatisfied, they can elect new leaders. Voting also allows citizens to express their opinions on public issues.

Reading Check **Summarizing** What are two important reasons to exercise your right to vote?

Review

Vocabulary

1. Write a true statement *and* a false statement for each term below. For each false statement explain why it is false. *polling place, precinct, ballot, absentee ballot, returns, exit poll, electorate,* and *apathy.*

Main Ideas

2. Identifying In the early days of our nation, what was the only group of people eligible to vote?

3. Explaining Why is the secret ballot important?

4. Identify three reasons that some citizens do not exercise their right to vote.

Critical Thinking

5. Drawing Conclusions Do you think the federal government should prohibit exit polls during presidential elections? Why or why not?

6. BIG Ideas On a graphic organizer like the one below, identify four different places a citizen may register to vote.

7. Making Inferences American statesman John Jay (1745–1829) said, "The people who own the country ought to govern it." Would Jay have supported or opposed the extension of voting rights? Explain.

CITIZENSHIP Activity

8. Creating Voter apathy is an issue in the United States today. Draw a political cartoon that depicts a reason people give for not voting.

Study Central™ To review this section, go to glencoe.com.

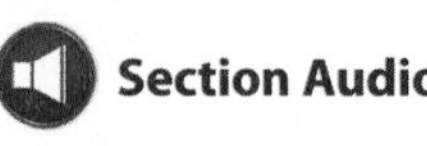

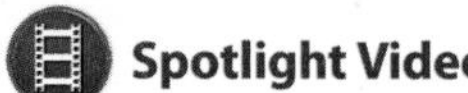

Section 2

Section Audio   Spotlight Video

Election Campaigns

Guide to Reading

Big Idea
A successful democracy is built on an informed electorate.

Content Vocabulary
- Electoral College *(p. 301)*
- initiative *(p. 301)*
- proposition *(p. 301)*
- referendum *(p. 301)*
- recall *(p. 301)*
- elector *(p. 303)*
- winner-take-all system *(p. 303)*

Academic Vocabulary
- issue *(p. 301)*
- odd *(p. 301)*

Reading Strategy
Organizing As you read this section, complete a graphic organizer like the one below by listing the features of three types of elections.

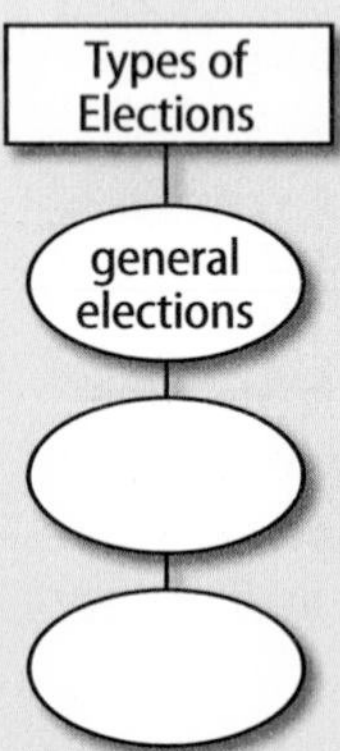

Real World Civics Candidates on the campaign trail face long days, trip delays, meals at odd times, uncomfortable sleeping conditions, and lots of handshaking. Senator Hillary Clinton ran for president in 2008 in a tough primary race for the democratic nomination. The road to the nominations is long. Campaigning often starts a year ahead of the first primary in New Hampshire, which is two years before the actual election.

▼ **Hillary Clinton campaigns in 2008**

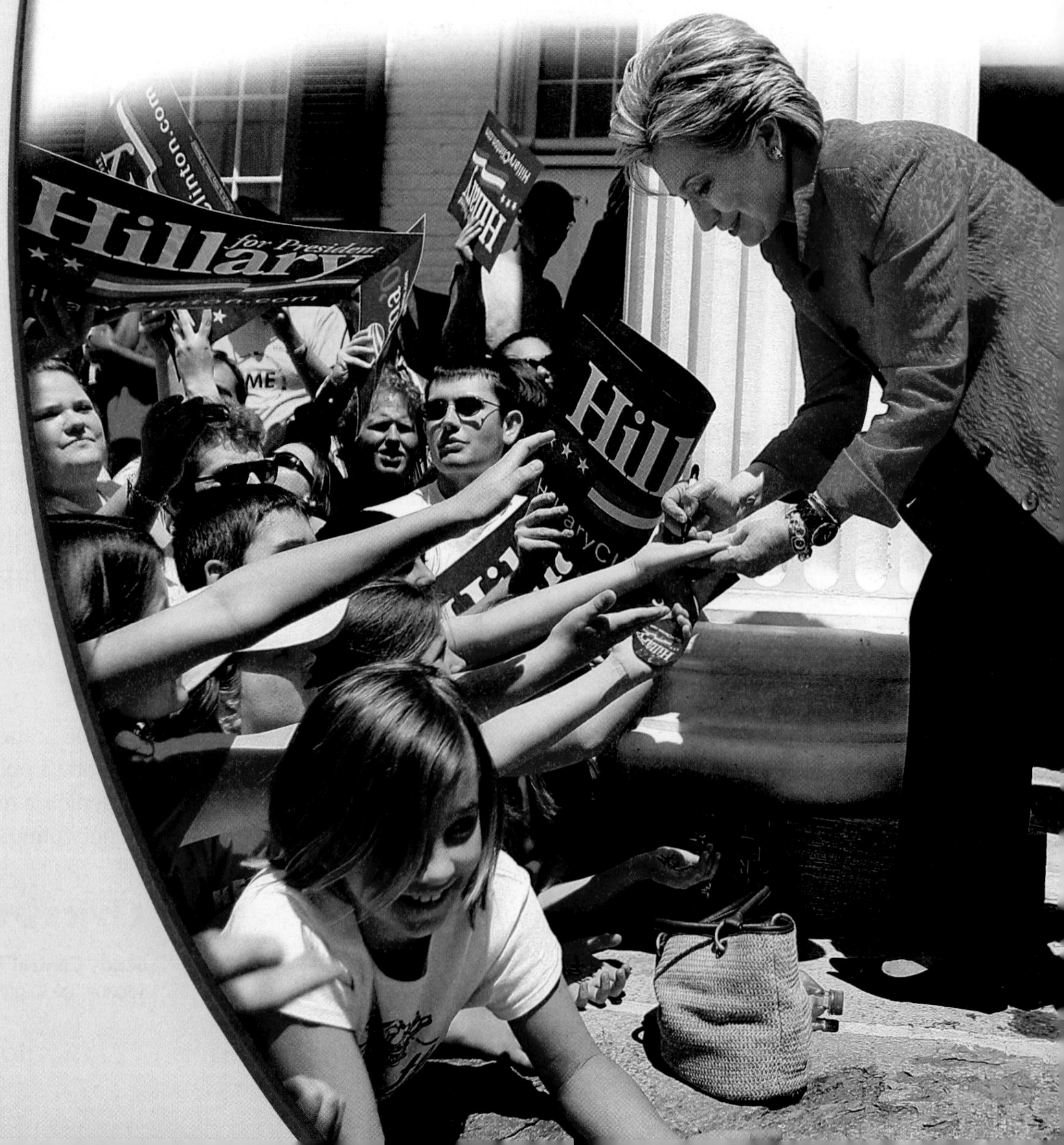

Types of Elections

Main Idea **There are different types of elections in the United States political system.**

Civics & You Americans have been voting since the earliest colonial governments. As you read, identify the differences among the different types of elections.

The **Electoral College** is part of the process that Americans use to select their president. Americans also vote in many other elections. There are about half a million elected officials in the United States. In addition, Americans have many opportunities to vote on **issues,** or topics of concern, as well as candidates. Besides primary elections, there are three other types of elections in the United States: general elections, elections on issues, and special elections.

General Elections

Under the United States political system, every election is a two-part process. The first part is the nomination of candidates in a primary election. Primary races help to narrow the field of candidates. Then, in a general election, the voters choose candidates for various offices. General elections always take place on the first Tuesday after the first Monday in November. All seats in the U.S. House of Representatives and about one-third of the seats in the Senate are at stake in general elections every even-numbered year.

Presidential elections occur every four years. In these elections the ballot often includes candidates for governor, the state legislature, county government, and local offices. In some states, however, elections for mayor and other city offices take place in **odd**-numbered, or uneven, years.

For all races except the presidential race, the candidate who wins most of the popular vote is elected to office. If an election is very close, the loser has the right to demand a recount of the votes. Occasionally, a disputed election cannot be resolved through a recount and another election must be held. In the case of a national election, a dispute may be referred to Congress for settlement. If it is a presidential election and neither candidate wins a majority of electoral votes, the House of Representatives elects the president. This happened in the elections of 1800 and 1824.

Voting on Issues

In some elections at the state or local level, voters may decide on issues as well as candidates. The **initiative,** for example, is a way that citizens can propose new laws or state constitutional amendments. Citizens who want a new law gather signatures of qualified voters on a petition. If enough people sign the petition, the proposed law, or **proposition,** is put on the ballot at the next general election.

The **referendum** is a way for citizens to approve or reject a state or local law. Citizens in more than half the states have the right to petition to have a law referred, or sent back, to the voters for their approval at the next general election.

Special Elections

From time to time, state or local governments also hold certain kinds of special elections. Runoff elections may be held when none of the candidates for a particular office wins a majority of the vote in the general election. The runoff is held to determine the winner.

The **recall** is another type of special election. In a recall, citizens in some states can vote to remove a public official from office. Like the initiative, the recall starts with a petition. Voters may recall an official because they do not like his or her position on issues or because the official has been charged with wrongdoing.

Reading Check **Comparing** What is the difference between an initiative and a referendum?

TIME™ Teens in *Action*

Kids Voting USA

One vote can make a difference—and Sam Hay, 18, of Charlotte, North Carolina, is spreading the word!

QUESTION: What is Kids Voting USA?

ANSWER: It's a group that teaches kids about citizenship and voting through classroom activities—and by asking them to go to the polls with their parents on Election Day. I'm on the Student Advisory Board of the group.

Q: Why is it so important to vote?

A: Many people think their vote doesn't matter, but it does. There have been elections where the winner has been decided by only a few votes. By taking part in our democracy you show our leaders what you think.

Q: How does getting kids involved in voting and politics affect parents?

A: Conversations at the dinner table may become more political if a child takes part in Kids Voting. To keep up, parents may follow politics closer.

Q: How many kids do you reach?

A: Thousands in 27 states and the District of Columbia. The program reaches out to every student because voter apathy stretches across all ethnic and socioeconomic boundaries.

Making a Difference 

Why do you think Sam decided to become involved in Kids Voting USA?

Presidential Elections

Main Idea **Presidential elections have three major steps: (1) nomination of candidates, (2) the campaign, and (3) the vote.**

Civics & You As you read, ask yourself: What issues are important for a candidate to address?

Candidates for president begin organizing their campaigns long before the election. In the past, both major parties held national conventions in the summer of the election year to choose their candidates. Delegates came to these conventions from each state, the District of Columbia, and U.S. territories.

These conventions were dramatic events full of behind-the-scenes negotiations. Backers of various candidates would move around the convention floor, promising future political favors to state delegations in hopes of stealing their votes away from a rival. The political dealings would be interrupted for suspenseful and colorful state-by-state roll-call votes to see if any contender had rounded up enough support to win the nomination.

In recent years, however, the conventions have lost their main purpose—choosing the nominee. So much campaigning now goes on in the primary elections that by convention time one contender has already wrapped up the nomination. The parties use the conventions mainly to kick off the campaign and to rally party members across the country for the work ahead.

Campaigns

Presidential campaigns are usually in full swing by early September. Candidates travel across the country giving speeches, appearing on TV, and holding news conferences—even though there is seldom any real news to announce.

Candidates may face their opponents in televised debates. They meet with state and local political leaders, and they give pep talks to lower-level members of the party who are working for them.

Electoral Votes and the States

For all races except the presidential race, the candidate who wins a majority of the popular vote—votes cast directly by the people—is elected to office. In a presidential race, the voters are actually electing people called **electors,** who hold electoral votes and are part of the Electoral College system.

In every state, a slate, or list, of electors is pledged to each candidate. The purpose of the popular vote in each state is to choose one of these slates of electors. The candidate who wins the popular vote in a state usually receives all of the state's electoral votes. This is called the **winner-take-all system.**

The winning electors meet in their state capitals in December to cast the state's electoral votes for president and vice president. The electors send their votes to Congress, which counts them. Because every state has one elector for each of its U.S. senators and representatives, the total number of votes in the Electoral College is 538. (Washington, D.C., has three electoral votes.) The candidate who receives a majority of these votes—270 or more—wins the election.

Article II, Section 1, established the Electoral College. It was a compromise measure. Some of the Framers wanted the American people to have direct control over the new national government.

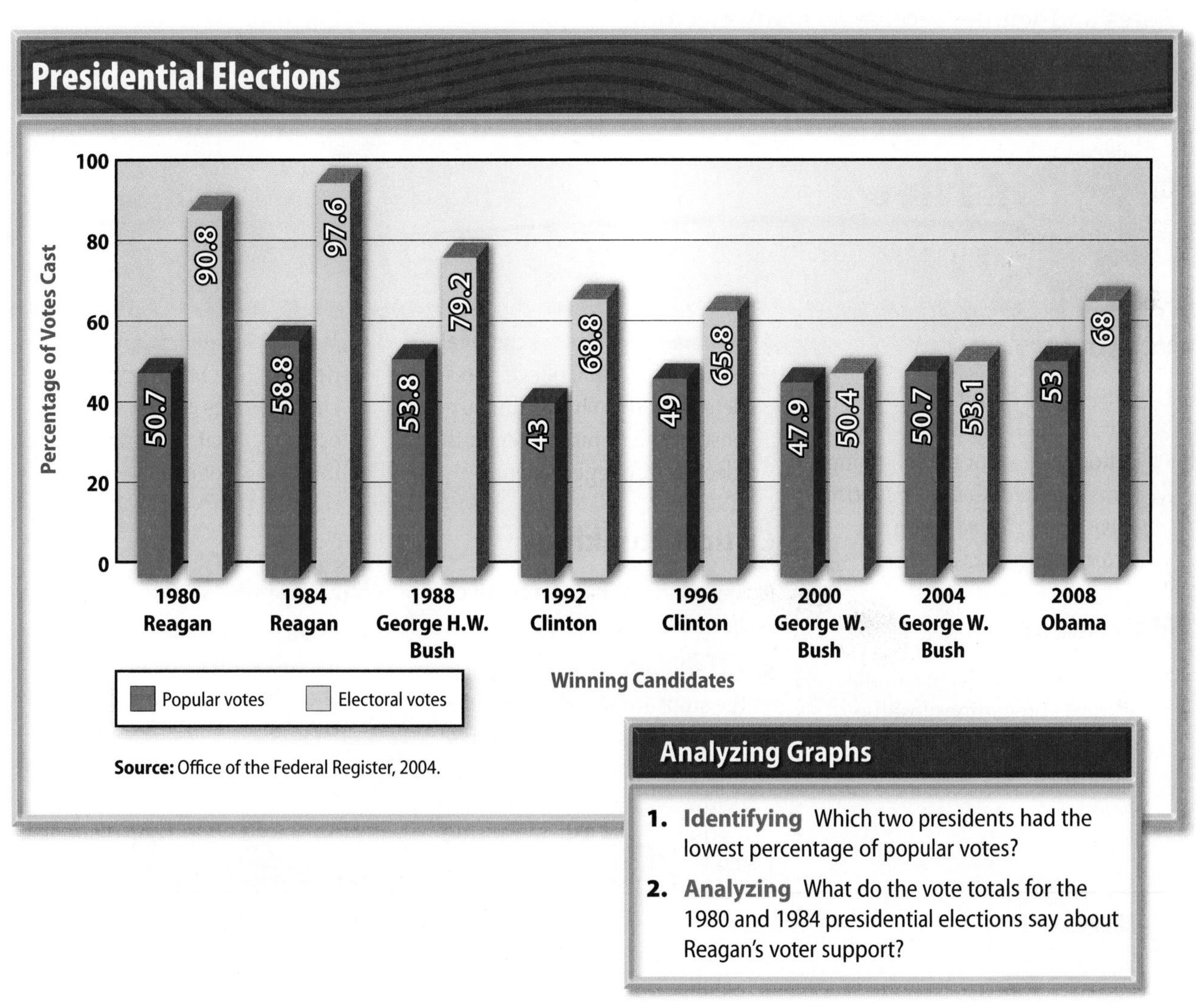

Source: Office of the Federal Register, 2004.

Analyzing Graphs

1. **Identifying** Which two presidents had the lowest percentage of popular votes?
2. **Analyzing** What do the vote totals for the 1980 and 1984 presidential elections say about Reagan's voter support?

Others strongly believed that the government must be able to function without having to give in to popular whims. The first group demanded a direct popular election of the president. Their opponents pushed to have Congress name the president. The compromise was to have the legislatures in each state choose presidential electors. Today, the voters in each state directly choose the electors.

Electoral College Issues

Some people think that the Electoral College should be changed or eliminated. They charge that large states—such as California and Texas, which have many more electoral votes than smaller states—have too much influence in deciding the election. One candidate might win five or six small states and yet not receive as many electoral votes as the candidate who wins just one large state.

If a candidate wins the largest number of popular votes in a state, that person receives all the state's electoral votes. Under the winner-take-all system, a candidate who loses the popular vote can still win the electoral vote and the presidency. This has happened four times in our nation's history, most recently in 2000. The winner-take-all system also makes it extremely difficult for third-party candidates to be represented in the electoral vote.

Ideas for Reform There have been several suggestions for reform. Under one plan, electoral votes would be based on the percentage of the popular vote. If a candidate won 54 percent of a state's popular vote, for example, he or she would also get 54 percent of the electoral votes. Any change in the Electoral College system requires a constitutional amendment.

Reading Check **Inferring** When you vote for the U.S. president, for whom are you actually voting?

Vocabulary

1. **Write** a paragraph that summarizes the key points of this section. Use all of the following terms: *Electoral College, initiative, proposition, referendum, recall, elector, winner-take-all system.*

Main Ideas

2. **Explaining** Why have national political conventions lost the main purpose of choosing nominees?

3. **Summarizing** How is the total of 538 Electoral College votes determined? What is the purpose of the popular vote in the Electoral College system?

Critical Thinking

4. **Explaining** What is a recall election? Describe the process.

5. **BIG Ideas** List and explain the steps involved in presidential elections by completing a graphic organizer like the one below.

6. **Making Generalizations** The right to vote belongs to every United States citizen. In your opinion, what do citizens forfeit if they do not exercise their right to vote?

CITIZENSHIP Activity

7. **Persuasive Writing** Should the Electoral College be kept, abolished, or reformed in some way? State your views in a letter to the editor of your local newspaper.

Study Central™ To review this section, go to glencoe.com.

 Section Audio  Spotlight Video

Section 3

Paying for Election Campaigns

Guide to Reading

Big Idea
A successful democracy is built on an informed electorate.

Content Vocabulary
- propaganda *(p. 307)*
- political action committee (PAC) *(p. 308)*
- soft money *(p. 308)*
- incumbent *(p. 309)*

Academic Vocabulary
- image *(p. 307)*
- fee *(p. 307)*

Reading Strategy
Explaining Use a graphic organizer like the one below to explain the main part of the Federal Election Campaign Act (FECA).

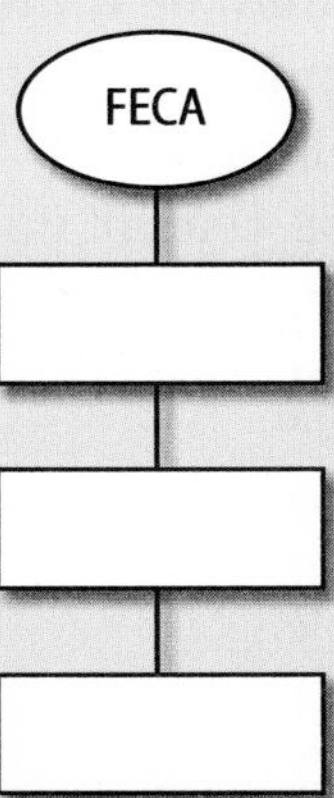

Real World Civics Citizens take action when they believe in an issue. Doris "Granny D" Haddock, 91, walked across the country to register voters and to protest the use of corporate money in political campaigns. Ms. Haddock, like many Americans, was concerned that within the current system only the rich can run for office. Inspired by Haddock and others, Senators Russell Feingold and John McCain teamed up in 2001 to present to Congress the McCain-Feingold bill to limit the money spent on campaigns. Although it passed, the 2004 presidential election cost nearly a billion dollars.

▼ **John McCain, Doris Haddock, and Russell Feingold at the Capitol**

Running for Office

Main Idea **Running for public office is the first step in the election process.**

Civics & You Would you run for public office if given the chance? As you read, ask yourself: What are the reasons an individual runs for public office?

Americans spend more than $3 billion on national, state, and local elections every four-year period. Former House Speaker Tip O'Neill once said, "There are four parts to any campaign. The candidate, the issues . . . , the campaign organization, and the money. Without money you can forget the other three."

It takes a great deal of money to run a successful campaign for a major office today. Once candidates are nominated, they spend weeks and even months campaigning.

The purpose of campaigns is to convince the public to vote for a particular candidate. Each campaign has a campaign organization. An organization for a local candidate may have only a few workers. Presidential campaigns, though, have thousands of workers. Campaign workers must acquaint voters with the candidate's name, face, and positions on issues, and convince voters to like and trust the candidate. Campaign workers use several techniques to accomplish their goals.

Canvassing

When candidates or campaign workers travel through neighborhoods asking for votes or taking public opinion polls, they are canvassing. At the local level, candidates often go door-to-door to solicit votes and hand out campaign literature. At the national level, campaign organizations conduct frequent polls to find out how their candidates are doing.

Endorsements

When a famous and popular person supports or campaigns for a candidate, it is an endorsement. The endorser may be a movie star, a famous athlete, a popular politician, or some other well-known individual. The idea behind endorsements is that if voters like the person making the endorsement, they may decide to vote for the candidate.

Running for Office Shepherd University student Frank Salzano campaigned and won election in 2006 to a seat on the Shepherdstown, West Virginia, town council. ***Comparing*** **In what ways are running for local office and running for national office similar and in what ways are they different?**

Grass Roots Mayor Antonio Villaraigosa, the first Latino mayor of Los Angeles since 1872, gained national attention for progress in his city. ***Describing*** **Where do popular candidates like Villaraigosa get funds for their campaigns?**

Endorsements are a kind of propaganda technique. **Propaganda** is an attempt to promote a particular person or idea. Candidates use propaganda techniques to try to persuade or influence voters to choose them over another candidate.

Advertising and Image Molding

Campaign workers spend much time and money to create the right **image,** or impression, for a candidate. Much of that money goes to advertising. Political advertisements allow a party to present only its candidate's position or point of view. They also enable a candidate to attack an opponent without offering an opportunity to respond.

Candidates for a local election may use newspaper advertisements or posters, while state and national candidates spend a great deal of money advertising on television. Why? Television ads can present quick and dramatic images of a candidate and his or her ideas. Such television images tend to stay in the viewer's mind.

Campaign Expenses

The sophisticated vote-getting techniques that candidates use have made campaigning very expensive. Television commercials are a very effective way to win votes, but they cost tens of thousands of dollars per minute. Other campaign costs include airfare and other transportation, salaries of campaign staff members, and **fees,** or payments, to professional campaign consultants, such as public opinion pollsters. There are also computer, telephone, postage, and printing costs.

A small-town mayoral race may cost only a few hundred or a few thousand dollars. A state legislative or congressional race may cost several hundred thousand dollars or more. In recent elections, spending for each seat in Congress has averaged about $1.5 million. Some congressional candidates spent $15 million or more. A presidential race can cost hundreds of millions of dollars.

Reading Check **Describing** What is the purpose of election propaganda?

Financing a Campaign

Main Idea **Candidates spend considerable time and effort raising campaign funds.**

Civics & You Have you read about campaign finance issues? As you read, think about questions you may have about campaign spending.

The methods used to finance election campaigns have been established by congressional legislation and Supreme Court decisions. In recent years, a push to reform how candidates raise money has led to many changes in the law.

Federal Election Campaign Act

In 1971 Congress passed the Federal Election Campaign Act (FECA) in an effort to place some controls on campaign financing. FECA and its amendments in 1974, 1976, and 1979 established many key rules for campaign finance. The law required public disclosure of each candidate's spending. It limited the amount—called hard money—that individuals or groups could donate directly to a candidate or a political party. It also tried to limit how much other individuals and groups could spend.

Federal Election Commission The 1974 amendment to FECA created the Federal Election Commission (FEC)—an independent agency of the executive branch—to administer all federal election laws and to monitor campaign spending. All candidates and political parties must keep records of campaign contributions. Candidates are now required to report all individual contributions that exceed $200 to the FEC.

Limiting Contributions In 1976 the Supreme Court ruled in *Buckley* v. *Valeo* that the government, through laws like FECA, could set limits on campaign contributions because of its need to keep corruption out of elections. The Court did find, however, that it was a violation of free speech to limit how much of their own money candidates could spend on their election campaigns.

Public Funding

FECA also set up public funding for presidential elections by creating the Presidential Election Campaign Fund. This fund allows taxpayers, by checking a box on their federal income tax return, to designate $3 of their annual taxes to go to the fund. In general, major-party presidential candidates can qualify for some of this money to campaign in the primary elections if they have raised $100,000 on their own. After the national conventions, the two major-party candidates can receive equal shares of money from the fund, so long as they agree not to accept any other direct contributions. Third-party candidates can also qualify for this funding if their party received more than 5 percent of the popular vote in the previous presidential election.

Soft Money and PACS

Most campaign money comes from private sources rather than public funding. These sources include individual citizens, corporations, labor unions, interest groups, and **political action committees (PACs).** PACs are organizations set up by interest groups especially to collect money to support favored candidates. FECA limited direct donations from PACs and other private sources.

In the late 1970s, complaints grew that campaign finance legislation was making fund-raising difficult. Congress responded with new laws enabling political parties to raise **soft money**—unlimited amounts of money for general purposes, not designated to particular candidates. By law this money was supposed to be used for general party-building purposes, such as voter registration drives or direct mailings on behalf of the party.

Soft money could come from individuals or PACs. FECA placed no limits on these contributions, and in the 2002 national elections, they totaled about $500 million.

Spending on Media There is also the issue of money spent by interest groups for radio and television ads that support the groups' positions on issues. These ads do not ask people to vote for or against a specific candidate, but they might show a candidate's name or image. They are powerful tools for interest groups to help candidates they like. FECA placed no limits on how much money could be spent on such ads.

A Reluctance for Reform In response to these developments, Congress repeatedly discussed reforming campaign finance laws. Changes, though, were difficult to achieve. PACs gave most of their money to **incumbents**—politicians who have already been elected to office. As a result, many of these incumbent lawmakers were reluctant to change the rules in ways that might help their opponents in the next election.

Campaign Reform

Change came in 2002, however, when Congress passed legislation aimed at better controlling the money flowing into national campaigns. The Bipartisan Campaign Reform Act—also known as the McCain-Feingold Act—prohibits national political parties, federal officeholders, and federal candidates from raising soft money.

The law also places time restrictions on broadcasting political ads. Corporations, unions, and interest groups are banned from running ads aimed at a candidate for federal office within 60 days of a general election or 30 days of a primary election. Finally, the law raises the limits on hard money contributions, stating that candidates may collect up to $2,000 per donor in each election. Political parties can collect $25,000 per donor in each year.

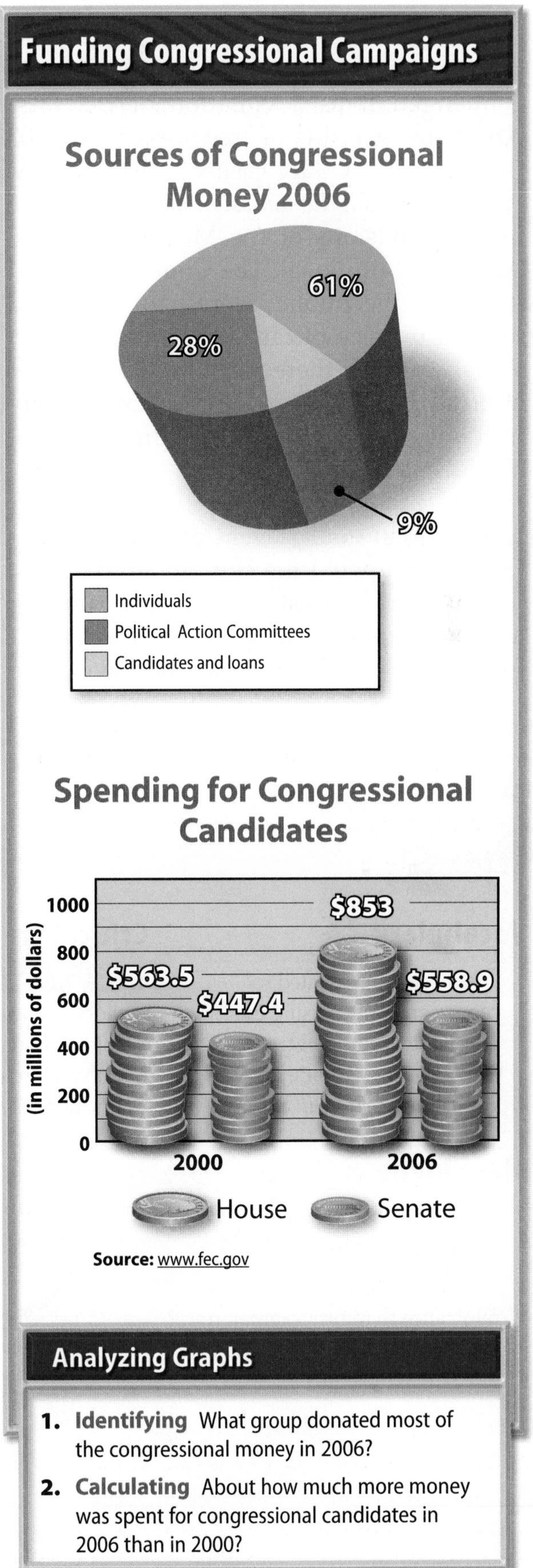

Analyzing Graphs

1. **Identifying** What group donated most of the congressional money in 2006?
2. **Calculating** About how much more money was spent for congressional candidates in 2006 than in 2000?

New Law Upheld

Critics of the new law immediately challenged it as a violation of the First Amendment rights of free speech. In 2003 the Supreme Court case of *McConnell* v. *Federal Election Commission* upheld all the major provisions of the McCain-Feingold Act as constitutional. The Court stated that it was in the public interest for Congress to limit the size of campaign contributions. Without limits, there would always be the appearance that big donors were able to buy influence with policymakers in ways not available to ordinary citizens.

The majority opinion, written by Justices John Paul Stevens and Sandra Day O'Connor, upheld the ban on corporations, unions, and interest groups from running advertisements for or against a candidate for federal office within a certain period of time before general and primary elections, The Court also supported the McCain-Feingold Act's setting restrictions on campaign advertisements disguised as "issue ads."

Looking to the Future

The Court's decision set the rules for the 2004 elections and beyond. It will affect how candidates go about raising funds. For example, there will be a new emphasis on getting many small donations rather than a few large ones. As a result, the Internet will play a larger role in political fund-raising. The Internet gives politicians and their supporters an inexpensive way to quickly reach millions of people who might be willing to make the smaller contributions.

Reading Check **Identifying** How did the McCain-Feingold Act change campaign finance?

Vocabulary

1. **Write** sentences related to campaign finance using the following terms: *propaganda, political action committee (PAC), soft money, incumbent.*

Main Ideas

2. **Describing** What is the purpose of a political campaign?
3. **Describing** Why was there some reluctance to reform campaign financing? What groups were most in favor of this reform?

Critical Thinking

4. **BIG Ideas** Explain the two sides in the campaign spending reform issue. With which side do you agree? Explain your position.
5. **Summarizing** On a graphic organizer like the one below, list the different private sources of campaign contributions.

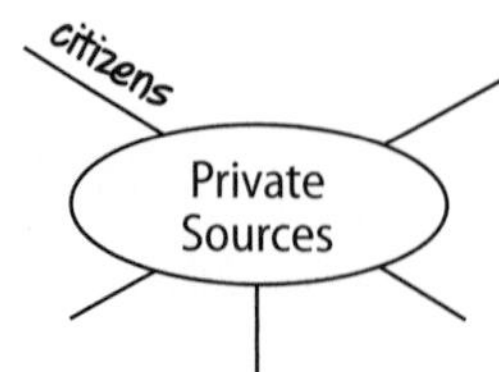

6. **Evaluating** What qualities of competence and leadership do you think are important in a presidential candidate?

CITIZENSHIP Activity

7. **Persuasive Writing** Should the media be required to provide equal coverage for all candidates and for all political parties? Is it fair that the two major political parties can obtain greater coverage in the news than the minor parties? Write a one-page paper explaining your view on these issues.

Study Central™ To review this section, go to glencoe.com.

Chapter 10

Visual Summary

Voting

Voting is a basic political right of all citizens in a democracy who meet certain qualifications set by law.

Voting allows citizens to take positive actions to influence or control government.

You are qualified to vote if you are not a convicted felon or legally insane, and you are:

- a citizen of the United States
- at least 18 years old
- Most states also require that you be a resident of the state for a specified period and that you register to vote.

Registering to Vote

Registration requirements are set by state law and differ from state to state.

When you register to vote for the first time, you must show proof of citizenship, address, and age.

President John F. Kennedy votes

Students register to vote

Voting Procedures

- You vote at a polling place in your home precinct. A precinct is a voting district.
- You will cast your ballot by using a voting machine.
- Citizens who cannot get to the polling place on Election Day can vote by absentee ballot.

The Electoral College

Presidents are not chosen by direct popular vote but by a body known as the Electoral College.

While the presidential candidates' names are printed on the ballot, the voters are not actually voting directly for president and vice president. Rather, they are voting for all of their party's electors in their state.

Political Campaigns

- Running for office costs money.
- Campaigns are funded privately and publicly.
- Campaign finance reform remains an important issue.

Campaign worker monitors voters

STUDY TO GO

Study anywhere, anytime! Download quizzes and flash cards to your PDA from glencoe.com.

Chapter

10 ASSESSMENT

Standardized Test Practice

TEST-TAKING TIP

Neatness counts even in objective questions. Fill in ovals carefully and print legibly.

Reviewing Vocabulary

Directions: Choose the word(s) that best completes the sentence.

1. The results of an election are called ______.

A returns **C** exit polls
B ballots **D** electorates

2. Citizens can propose a new law through a(n) ______.

A recall **C** referendum
B initiative **D** proposition

3. Citizens can approve or reject a local or state law with a(n) ______.

A recall **C** referendum
B initiative **D** proposition

4. Much of the money from election campaigns comes from ______.

A returns **C** incumbents
B electors **D** political action committees

Reviewing Main Ideas

Directions: Choose the best answer for each question.

Section 1 *(pp. 292–299)*

5. What does the National Voter Registration Act require states to do?

A deny felons the right to vote
B give the vote to citizens 18 and older
C record voters' party affiliation when they register
D allow people to register when renewing their licenses

6. Which group has the highest rate of voter turnout?

A middle-aged people
B disgruntled citizens
C low-income earners
D high school dropouts

Section 2 *(pp. 300–304)*

7. How many electoral votes does a presidential candidate need to win?

A 100
B 270
C 435
D 538

8. Why is a runoff election held?

A citizens want to remove an elected official
B parties want to narrow a field of candidates
C no candidate in a state election wins a majority
D no presidential candidate wins enough electoral votes

Section 3 *(pp. 305–310)*

9. How do campaign organizations canvass on a national level?

A by going door to door
B by advertising on television
C by conducting frequent polls
D by seeking celebrity endorsements

10. Why does the federal government set limits on direct campaign contributions?

A to limit candidates' free speech
B to keep corruption out of elections
C to create public funding for third parties
D to increase the soft money contributions

GO ON

Critical Thinking

Directions: Base your answers to questions 11 and 12 on the diagram below and your knowledge of Chapter 10.

Table 1: Voter Turnout Among Citizens November 2000 and 2004		
	2000	2004
18–24	36%	47%
25–34	51%	56%
35–44	60%	64%
45–54	66%	69%
55–64	70%	73%
65–74	72%	73%
75+	67%	69%
All ages	***60%***	***64%***

Source: Authors' Tabulations from the CPS Nov. Voting and Registration Supplements, 1972-2004.

11. Compare the percentage point differences between the 2000 and 2004 elections. Which age group showed the greatest increase in its rate of voter turnout?

A 18–24

B 25–34

C 35–44

D 45–54

12. What can you conclude based on data in the chart?

A More people 65–74 years old voted in 2000 than in 2004.

B Voters 75 and older outnumbered voters between 25 and 34.

C Voters between 18 and 24 had the lowest rates of voter turnout.

D Voters between 45 and 74 made up 72% of the total voters in 2004.

Document-Based Questions

Directions: Analyze the following document and answer the short-answer questions that follow.

The following passage is from a campaign debate between presidential candidates Al Gore and George Bush in 2000.

> ***GORE:*** *One of the serious problems, hear me well, is that our system of government is being undermined by too much influence coming from special-interest money. We have to get a handle on it. And like John McCain, I have learned from experience, and it's not a new position for me. Twenty-four years ago I supported full public financing of all federal elections. And anybody who thinks I'm just saying it, it will be the first bill I send to the Congress. . . .*
>
> ***BUSH:*** *All right, let me just say one thing!*
>
> ***GORE:*** *I care passionately about this, and I will fight until it becomes law.*
>
> ***BUSH:*** *I want people to hear what he just said! He is for full public financing of Congressional elections! I'm absolutely, adamantly opposed to that! I don't want the government financing Congressional elections!*
>
> *—Presidential Debate, October 3, 2000*

13. What are Gore's and Bush's positions on full public financing of federal elections?

14. Why might wealthy special-interest groups object to candidates using only federal funding for their campaigns?

Extended Response

15. Write a brief essay about the kinds of activities that political campaigns include. Also explain why candidates need large amounts of money to run their campaigns.

STOP

For additional test practice, use Self-Check Quizzes—Chapter 10 on glencoe.com.

Need Extra Help?

If you missed question...	1	2	3	4	5	6	7	8	9	10	11	12	13	14	15
Go to Page...	297	301	301	308	295	299	303	301	306	308	299	299	303	303	306

TIME REPORTS

The Machinery of Democracy

With no national balloting system, the U.S. is a patchwork of voting methods

Unlike India and Canada, America does not have a national system for running elections or counting votes. That's because the Constitution left election procedures to the states. They in turn have passed the responsibility down to counties and cities—some 13,000 of them—which choose and pay for their preferred methods of counting ballots.

The imperfect patchwork of voting methods in use around the U.S. causes hundreds of thousands of ballots to be discarded each year. About 2% of all votes in presidential elections are marked for more than one candidate or for none, mostly as a consequence of voter confusion. Sometimes that confusion has serious consequences. In 2000, George W. Bush was declared President based on a 537-vote lead in Florida. Later analysis revealed that Al Gore lost more than 6,000 votes—and the White House—because some Florida voters marked more than one name on Palm Beach County's "butterfly ballot." On that ballot, the names of 10 presidential candidates alternated on two pages. "Voters' confusion with ballot instruction and design and voting machines appears to have changed the course of U.S. history," concluded a post-election analysis by a group of newspapers.

How Americans Vote: An imperfect system

A look at the various methods used throughout the United States*

1 Optical Scan

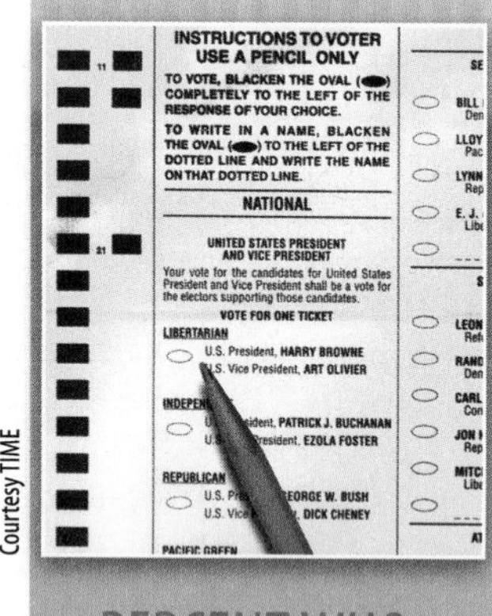

Courtesy TIME

PERCENT WHO VOTE THIS WAY: **35%**

HOW IT WORKS: Voters fill in rectangles, circles, ovals, or incomplete arrows next to their candidate. A computer selects the darkest mark as the choice.

PROS/CONS: Easy for voters to use, and double-marked ballots are immediately rejected, allowing voters to revise their ballots. But the equipment is expensive and can have problems reading sloppily marked forms.

2 Electronic

Tim Boyles/Stringer/Getty Images

PERCENT WHO VOTE THIS WAY: **29%**

HOW IT WORKS: Voters directly enter choices into the machine using a touchscreen or push buttons. Votes are stored via a memory cartridge.

PROS/CONS: Though as easy as using an ATM, this technology is still fairly expensive. There is no "paper trail" in the event of a recount. And the machines are subject to programming error, malfunction, and tampering.

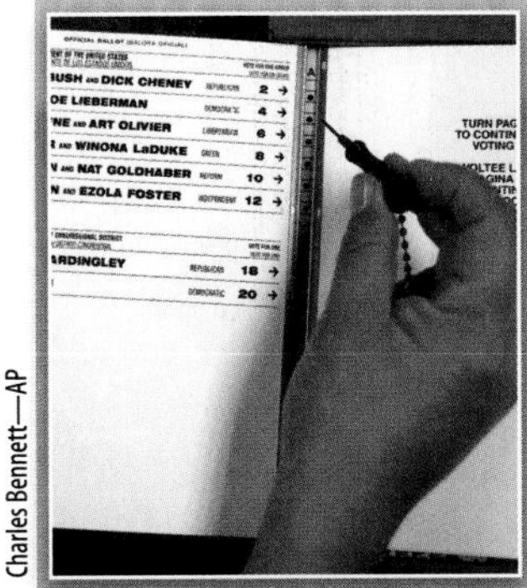

Charles Bennett—AP

Punch Card 3

HOW IT WORKS: Voters insert blank cards into clipboard-size devices, then punch the hole opposite their choice. Ballots are read by a computer tabulator.

PROS/CONS: An economical method, but holes are often incompletely punched. The dangling bits of cardboard, known as "chads," can lead to inaccurate tabulation of votes. And the notorious "butterfly ballot" caused massive confusion among Florida voters in 2000.

PERCENT WHO VOTE THIS WAY:
14%

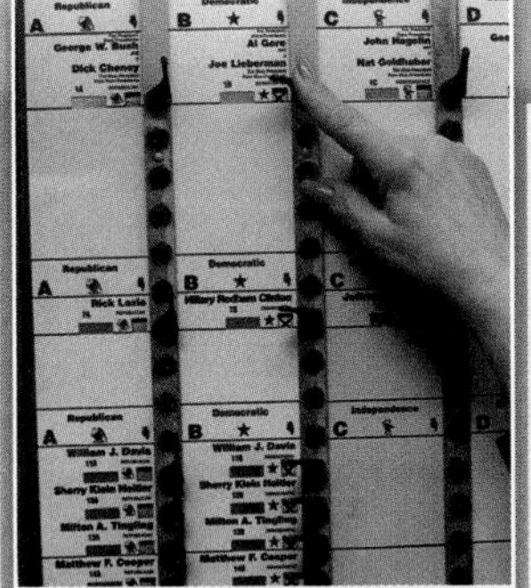

Stuart Ramson

Lever Machine 4

HOW IT WORKS: Each candidate is assigned a lever, which voters push down to indicate their choices.

PROS/CONS: Once the most popular form of voting, lever machines are simple to use but heavy, old, and no longer manufactured. There is no paper trail if recounts are necessary.

PERCENT WHO VOTE THIS WAY:
14%

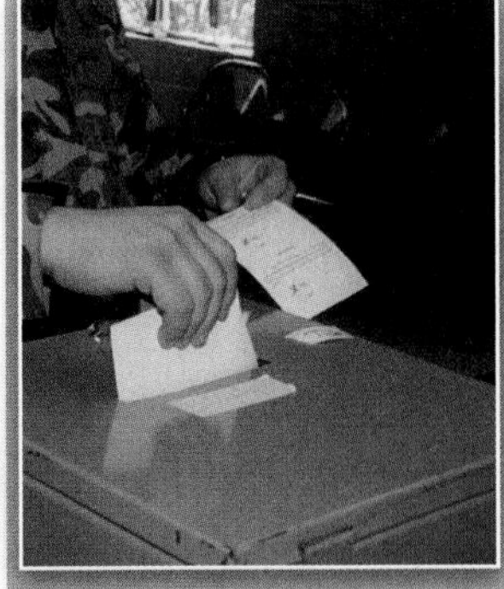

Vincent Lerz—AP

Paper Ballot 5

HOW IT WORKS: Voters record their choices in private by marking the boxes next to the candidate and then drop ballots in a sealed box.

PROS/CONS: An inexpensive and straightforward method that dates back to 1889. Counting and recounting can be slow.

PERCENT WHO VOTE THIS WAY:
1%

* Note: Figures are for the presidential election held in November 2004. Additional 7% is made up of voters in counties where more than one voting method is used. **Sources:** Election Data Services, Federal Election Commission.

Is There a Better Way of Balloting Ahead?

A UNIFORM BALLOT

Some think there should be a single ballot design for all federal elections—same type, style, and size, with ballot marks in the same place.

MOVE ELECTION DAY

Should it be a holiday or moved to the weekend so more people don't have to squeeze in their civic responsibility around work? It's a nice idea, but voters might just take a vacation.

VOTING BY MAIL

Oregon has tried this concept, with mixed success. If the kinks can be worked out, though, it could relieve the crowding on Election Day and boost turnout by giving people more time to vote.

COMPUTERIZED VOTING

Some experts see elections being eventually held entirely over the Internet. Security problems have to be solved first, though. And what about voters who are not computer-literate?

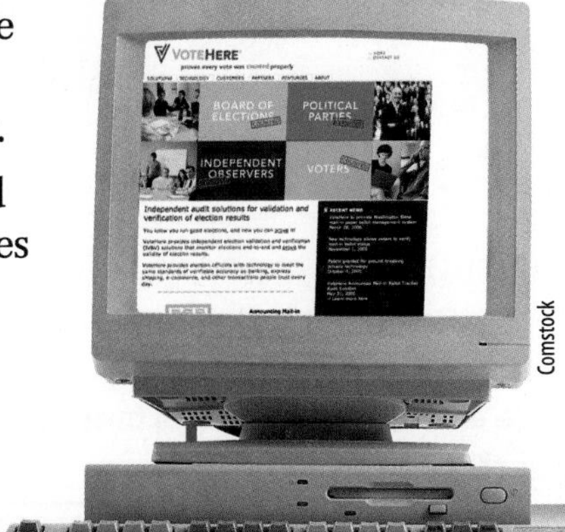

Comstock

Chapter 11

Influencing Government

Why It Matters

In America, different groups of people hold many different viewpoints. Some groups form to try to persuade government officials to support their views. These groups are exercising the important rights of freedom of speech and assembly.

Civics ONLINE
Visit glencoe.com and enter QuickPass™ code CIV3093c11 for Chapter 11 resources.

Chapter Audio

BIG Ideas

Section 1: Forming Public Opinion

A democratic society requires the active participation of its citizens. Individuals, interest groups, the mass media, and government officials all play a role in shaping public opinion.

Section 2: The Mass Media

In a democratic society, various forces shape people's ideas. The media have a profound influence on the ideas and behavior of the American people and their government.

Section 3: Interest Groups

Political and economic institutions evolve to help individuals and groups accomplish their goals. Interest groups, a powerful force in our democracy, use various techniques to influence public opinion and policy.

Antiwar protesters march past the White House in 2005

Comparing Information Study Foldable Make the following Foldable to help you compare the ideas and attitudes that influence government representatives in their decision making.

Step 1 Fold two sheets of paper in half from top to bottom.

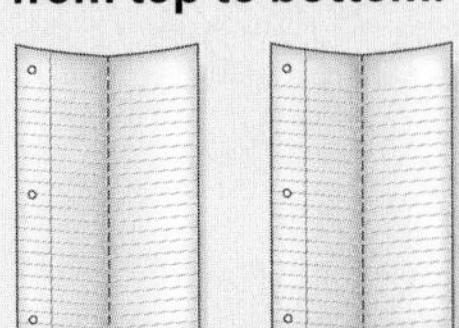

Step 2 Cut each sheet of paper in half the long way. Fold in half again.

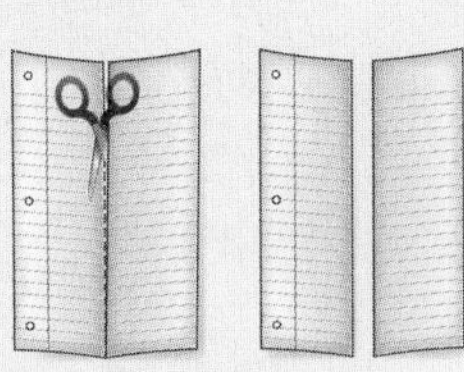

Step 3 Place three of the folded papers one on top of each other and label the top side of each: Public Opinion, The Mass Media, and Interest Groups.

Step 4 Cut the labeled sides of the folded sheets as shown. Staple here.

Reading and Writing
As you read the chapter, take notes and compare how each of the three groups discussed in the chapter influence decision makers in government.

Section Audio   Spotlight Video

Forming Public Opinion

Guide to Reading

Big Idea
A democratic society requires the active participation of its citizens.

Content Vocabulary
- public opinion *(p. 319)*
- mass media *(p. 320)*
- interest group *(p. 321)*
- public opinion poll *(p. 323)*
- pollster *(p. 323)*

Academic Vocabulary
- uniform *(p. 319)*
- gender *(p. 319)*
- survey *(p. 323)*

Reading Strategy
Identifying As you read, complete a graphic organizer like the one below by identifying the three features of public opinion.

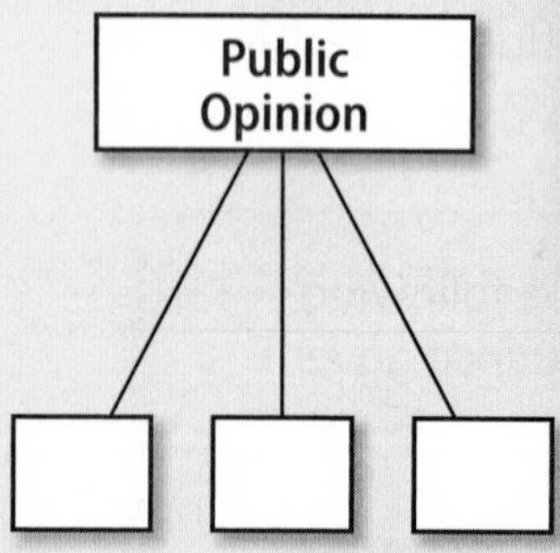

Real World Civics Have you heard about all the opinion polls that roll out during election time? Internet blogs are everywhere. In politics, voter opinion is constantly monitored. Students are often part of these polls, as during the Kerry-Bush debates in their 2004 race for president. Pollsters gathered information in pre-debate polls and then in post-debate polls to evaluate shifts in opinion as a result of the debate. Overnight approval ratings of the candidates can rise or drop dramatically because of these polls.

▼ **Students in Pennsylvania post online opinions following 2004 presidential debates**

Public Opinion

Main Idea **Public opinion, the ideas and attitudes most people hold, plays a vital role in our democracy.**

Civics & You How often have you heard that a president's popularity is up or down? Whose opinion does this represent? Read to find out how public opinion is created and how it, in turn, shapes the way our country is governed.

Public opinion is a term that refers to the ideas and attitudes that most people hold about a particular issue or person. Public opinion plays a key role in a democracy.

Role of Public Opinion For example, public opinion helps shape the decisions of every president. Presidents know they need the support of the public to carry out presidential programs. They also need the support of Congress. Presidents are more likely to have this support if their popularity with the public is high.

Understanding public opinion can also help presidents make effective, timely decisions. Successful presidents have a good sense of when the public is ready for a new idea and when it is not. Franklin D. Roosevelt expressed this idea when he said, "I cannot go any faster than the people will let me."

Diversity Public opinion is not **uniform,** or alike, however. In fact, most Americans agree on very few issues. On any given issue, different groups of the "public" often hold different viewpoints. For example, some Americans support increasing the nation's military forces, while others strongly disagree and wish to minimize military spending. Between these two positions are many shades of opinions. Enough people must hold a particular opinion, however, to make government officials listen to them.

Protecting Animals Activist Tony Madsen protests the treatment of animals by the Ringling Bros. and Barnum & Bailey Circus. ***Analyzing*** **How might a person's age or residence have an effect on his or her opinions?**

Sources of Public Opinion

Where does public opinion come from? Why do people often hold widely differing opinions about a particular issue or government action? Among the factors that influence public opinion are a person's background, the mass media, public officials, and interest groups.

Personal Background People's lives and experiences have a major influence on their opinions. Age, **gender,** income, race, religion, occupation, and place of residence play important roles. For example, a wealthy young person who lives in a big city may have very different opinions about the government's role in providing social services than might a poor elderly person who lives in a small town or rural area.

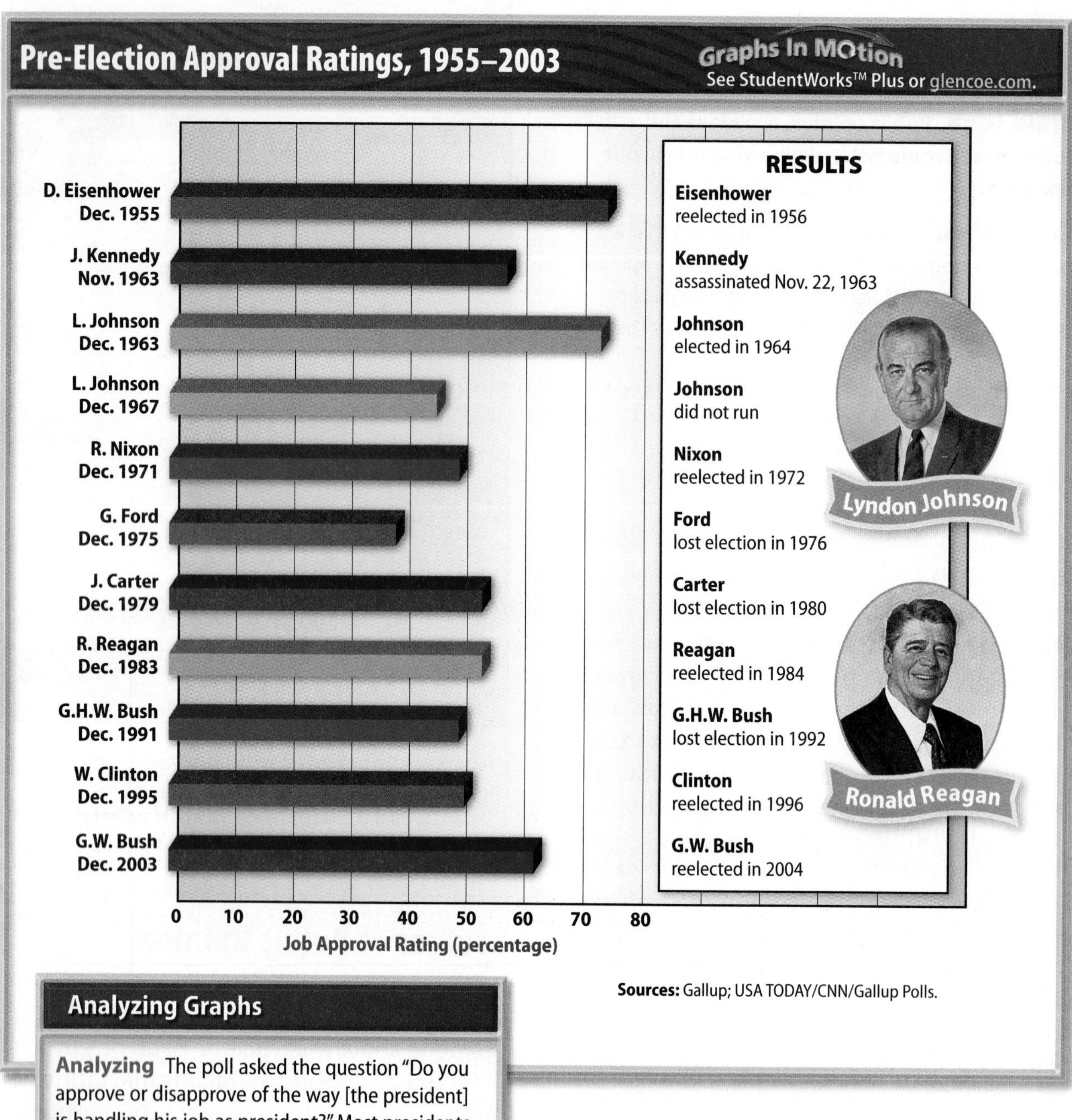

Analyzing Graphs

Analyzing The poll asked the question "Do you approve or disapprove of the way [the president] is handling his job as president?" Most presidents who ended their third year in office with a job approval rating above 50 percent and ran for another term were reelected. Who was not? What presidents had approval ratings of more than 70 percent? Were they reelected?

The Mass Media A medium is a means of communication. (The plural form of the word is *media*.) A letter you send to a friend, for example, is a private medium of communication between the two of you. Television, radio, newspapers, magazines, recordings, movies, Internet Web sites, and books are called the **mass media** because they communicate broadly to masses of people.

Public Officials Political leaders and government officials can influence public opinion. When voters elect people to office, they are indicating that they trust those officials and rely on their opinions. When public officials state their views, they hope to persuade as many people as possible to support their positions.

Interest Groups Individuals who share a point of view about an issue sometimes unite to promote their beliefs. They form what is called an **interest group.** Interest groups work at influencing public opinion by trying to persuade people—including public officials—toward their point of view. Interest groups are sometimes called pressure groups. This refers to their attempts at putting pressure on government to act in their interests.

Features of Public Opinion

Public opinion is often described in terms of three features: *direction, intensity,* and *stability.* These terms are discussed in the following paragraphs.

Direction One important question is whether public opinion on any given topic is positive or negative. For example, are people for or against spending more money on national defense? Do people support or oppose a cut in taxes? On most topics, public opinion is mixed, with some people expressing positive opinions and other people holding negative opinions.

Intensity Intensity refers to the strength of an opinion on a given issue. When Americans do have strong feelings, many are often willing to act upon them by voting for or against a candidate, working in an election campaign, or even participating in demonstrations.

Powerful Photos Images shown in the media are often meant to catch attention or change people's opinions about an issue. The baseball player needs funding for a better ballpark. This duck is covered in oil. ***Explaining*** **What interest group would want to publicize this image of the duck?**

American Biography

Ethel Percy Andrus (1884–1967)

Ethel Percy Andrus spent her life as an educator, becoming the first female principal of a California high school at age 32. When she retired at age 60 in 1944, Andrus volunteered to direct California's Retired Teachers Association. What she discovered troubled her. Many retired teachers struggled to survive on small pensions, often with no health insurance.

Andrus decided to form retired teachers into an alliance that would force lawmakers to listen to them. In 1947 she founded the National Retired Teachers Association.

In 1956 the organization won the first health insurance program for educators over age 65. Two years later, Andrus founded the American Association for Retired Persons, now known as the AARP.

Under the direction of Andrus, the AARP became a powerful lobby, focused on meeting the needs of all Americans over age 50. Today the AARP has more than 34 million members. The AARP advises the government on age-related issues and protects programs like Social Security. Staffed mostly by volunteers, the AARP tries to fulfill the motto given to it by Andrus: "To Serve; Not to be Served!"

Making a Difference — CITIZENSHIP

Ethel Andrus was active in education her whole life. ***Identifying*** **What contributions did Andrus make that benefited older Americans?**

Stability The stability of public opinion—meaning how firmly people hold to their views—may differ greatly from issue to issue. People's opinions are less likely to change when they have a firm belief. For example, most people's opinions about civil rights are more stable than their opinions about political candidates. Evidence suggests that most Americans hold the strongest convictions about issues that directly affect their lives. It is one thing to support more aid to the poor if you are poor. It is quite another if you are extremely well off. In some campaigns, voters change their minds many times before Election Day. Thus, public opinion on candidates is relatively unstable.

Reading Check **Describing** Why is public opinion of interest to government officials?

Measuring Public Opinion

Main Idea **The most common way of measuring public opinion is with public opinion polls.**

Civics & You Have you ever taken part in an opinion poll? Did you think about why the poll was being taken? Read to find out the role of opinion polls in measuring public attitudes.

If public opinion is to affect public policy, then political leaders must be made aware of it. One way to measure public opinion is by looking at election results. If voters elect a candidate, presumably many of them agree with most of the candidate's ideas.

Public Opinion Polls

Measuring public opinion by looking at election results is not always reliable, though. People vote for particular candidates for a variety of reasons. Perhaps they liked how a candidate looked; they supported some, but not all, of the candidate's views; or they voted a straight ticket, that is, for only Republicans or only Democrats. Election results show only a broad measure of public opinion.

A more accurate measure is to request individuals answer questions in a **survey,** or a **public opinion poll.** Today hundreds of organizations conduct public opinion polls. Every major elected official uses polls to closely monitor public opinion.

What Do Pollsters Do?

Most presidents, for example, have a specialist—a pollster—whose job is to conduct polls regularly. The **pollster** measures the president's popularity or public attitudes toward possible White House proposals, such as a tax increase or change in immigration policy.

Random Samples Pollsters usually question a group of people selected at random from all over the United States. Such a sample, often of about 1,500 people, will usually include both men and women of nearly all races, incomes, ages, and viewpoints. A well-constructed sample will reflect the characteristics of the entire population so that it can present a reasonably accurate picture of public opinion as a whole.

To find out people's true opinions, pollsters must be careful how they word their questions. By changing the wording of the questions, pollsters can manipulate the process to get nearly any answers they want. For example, the question "Do you favor cutting taxes?" might produce one kind of answer from a person. "Do you favor cutting taxes if it means letting poor people go hungry?" might make the same person respond differently.

TIME™ Teens in *Action*

Alix Olian

Alix Olian, 17, of Highland Park, Illinois, knows that public awareness of an issue is often the key to change. She was one of three students in charge of the annual Highland Park High School (HPHS) Charity Drive. The month-long drive raised $162,000 for the Children's Neuroblastoma Cancer Foundation (CNCF).

QUESTION: What is neuroblastoma?

ANSWER: It is one of the most common childhood cancers. As of now, there is no cure. Yet it gets almost no government funding.

Q: Why is awareness of this form of cancer so important?

A: When leukemia research first began, it was at the point where neuroblastoma is today in terms of its mortality rate and lack of research. Then government funding for leukemia research increased, and doctors made strides toward finding a cure. We hope that by raising awareness, we will inspire the government to take similar action with neuroblastoma research.

Alix Olian with other fundraisers

Q: What happened at the school assembly at the end of the charity drive?

A: We announced the amount of money we had raised. The mothers of children who had died from neuroblastoma were in tears, and so were a number of students and teachers. It was a moment I will never forget.

Making a Difference — CITIZENSHIP

Analyzing What do you think led Alix to provide her time and efforts to support the CNCF cause?

Push Polls Polls in which the questions are worded so as to influence a person's responses one way or another are called push polls. Push polls are condemned by responsible scientific pollsters. When they are considering poll results, thoughtful citizens should ask themselves whether the questions were, in fact, fair and unbiased.

Support for Polls Some people believe that public-opinion polling serves a useful purpose. Polling, they argue, allows officeholders to keep in touch with citizens' changing ideas about issues. With polls, officials do not have to wait until the next election to see if the people approve or disapprove of government policies.

Problems With Polls Some claim polling makes our elected officials more concerned with pleasing the public rather than exercising political leadership and making wise decisions. Many people also worry that polls affect elections. The media conduct polls constantly during campaigns so they can report who is ahead. Critics argue that these polls treat an election like a horse race, ignoring the candidates' views on issues to concentrate on who is winning or losing at the moment. Furthermore, polls may discourage voting. If they show one candidate far ahead of another, some people may decide not to bother voting because they think the election has already been won or lost.

Our government is responsive to public opinion—to the wishes of the people. However, public opinion is not the only influence on public policy. Interest groups, political parties, the mass media, other institutions of government, and individuals also shape public policy.

Reading Check **Explaining** Why do some people criticize public opinion polls?

Vocabulary

1. **Define** the following terms and use them correctly in a paragraph about a recent election: *public opinion, mass media, interest group, public opinion poll,* and *pollster.*

Main Ideas

2. **Explaining** What are three components of public opinion and what do they describe?
3. **Describing** In polling, what are random samples?

Critical Thinking

4. **BIG Ideas** Do you think political polling provides accurate results? Useful results? Explain your opinion.
5. **Identifying** In a graphic organizer like the one below, list different forms of mass media.

6. **Analyzing Visuals** Examine the graph—Pre-Election Approval Ratings—on page 320. Write a paragraph summarizing the general trends you feel the results indicate.

CITIZENSHIP Activity

7. **Persuasive Writing** Supporters of polling argue that it is a tool for democracy. Critics of polling think that it makes politicians into reactors rather than leaders. In a short essay, explain which opinion you agree with and why.

Study Central™ To review this section, go to glencoe.com.

Hazelwood School District v. Kuhlmeier

The Supreme Court's 1969 ruling in Tinker v. Des Moines *affirmed students' First Amendment rights to freedom of expression in public schools (see the* Tinker *decision in Chapter 4, page 132). How far did those rights extend?*

Background of the Case

Hazelwood East High School near St. Louis, Missouri, sponsored a student newspaper as part of its journalism classes. Before each issue, principal Robert Reynolds reviewed the pages.

Reynolds objected to two articles he read in the pages for an issue. One article discussed three pregnant students. The other described a certain student's experience with divorcing parents. Although actual names were not used, Reynolds felt readers could easily identify the featured individuals. Reynolds cancelled the two pages on which the articles appeared.

Kathy Kuhlmeier and two other students who worked on the newspaper sued the school claiming their First Amendment rights had been denied. Many others wore armbands in support.

High school students all over the country learn about freedom of the press rights as they publish their school newspapers.

The Decision

Relying on the Supreme Court's earlier *Tinker* decision, a lower court upheld Kuhlmeier's claim. On January 8, 1988, however, the Supreme Court reversed this ruling. The Court did not overturn the *Tinker* decision. Instead it drew a sharp line between individual expression—as in the wearing of armbands in *Tinker*—and the content of a school-sponsored newspaper. Justice Byron R. White wrote:

> ***"A school must be able to set high standards for the student speech that is disseminated [distributed] under its [sponsorship] . . . and may refuse to disseminate student speech that does not meet those standards."***
>
> —Justice Byron R. White

Why It Matters

Although students still have some First Amendment protections, the Hazelwood decision brought on cries of censorship among advocates of free speech and student interest groups. The Student Press Law Center reports that a number of schools, fearing lawsuits, have done away with student newspapers. Schools have also applied the Hazelwood decision to prevent the publication of student yearbooks, to stop stage performances, and to censor the content of student-based Internet Web pages.

Analyzing the Court Decision

1. **Analyzing** Why did the students on the school newspaper sue their school?
2. **Concluding** How do you think Hazelwood could affect a school's responsibility to educate?

Section Audio

Spotlight Video

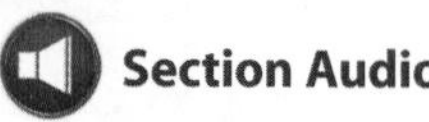

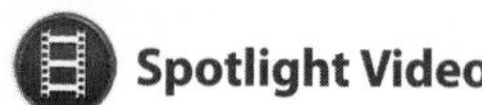

Section 2

The Mass Media

Guide to Reading

Big Idea
In a democratic society, various forces shape people's ideas.

Content Vocabulary
- print media *(p. 327)*
- electronic media *(p. 327)*
- public agenda *(p. 327)*
- leak *(p. 328)*
- prior restraint *(p. 329)*
- libel *(p. 330)*
- malice *(p. 330)*

Academic Vocabulary
- acknowledge *(p. 328)*
- benefit *(p. 328)*
- regulatory *(p. 330)*

Reading Strategy
Organizing As you read, note the impact of each of the types of media and list them on a chart like the one below.

Most Powerful Media
1.
2.
3.
4.
5.

Real World Civics If you see it on the news, or read it in the newspaper, it must be true—right? News media cameras track politicians' every move. But competition for the best photos and newest news is tremendous. While it is the job of the media to report the facts, there are many ways to see the facts. The media can act as a "watchdog," but they also can "spin" the news to present a specific point of view. Remembering that those in the media have their own viewpoints of government and politics can help citizens better understand the messages the media are sending.

▼ **Photographers and reporters swarm presidential candidates**

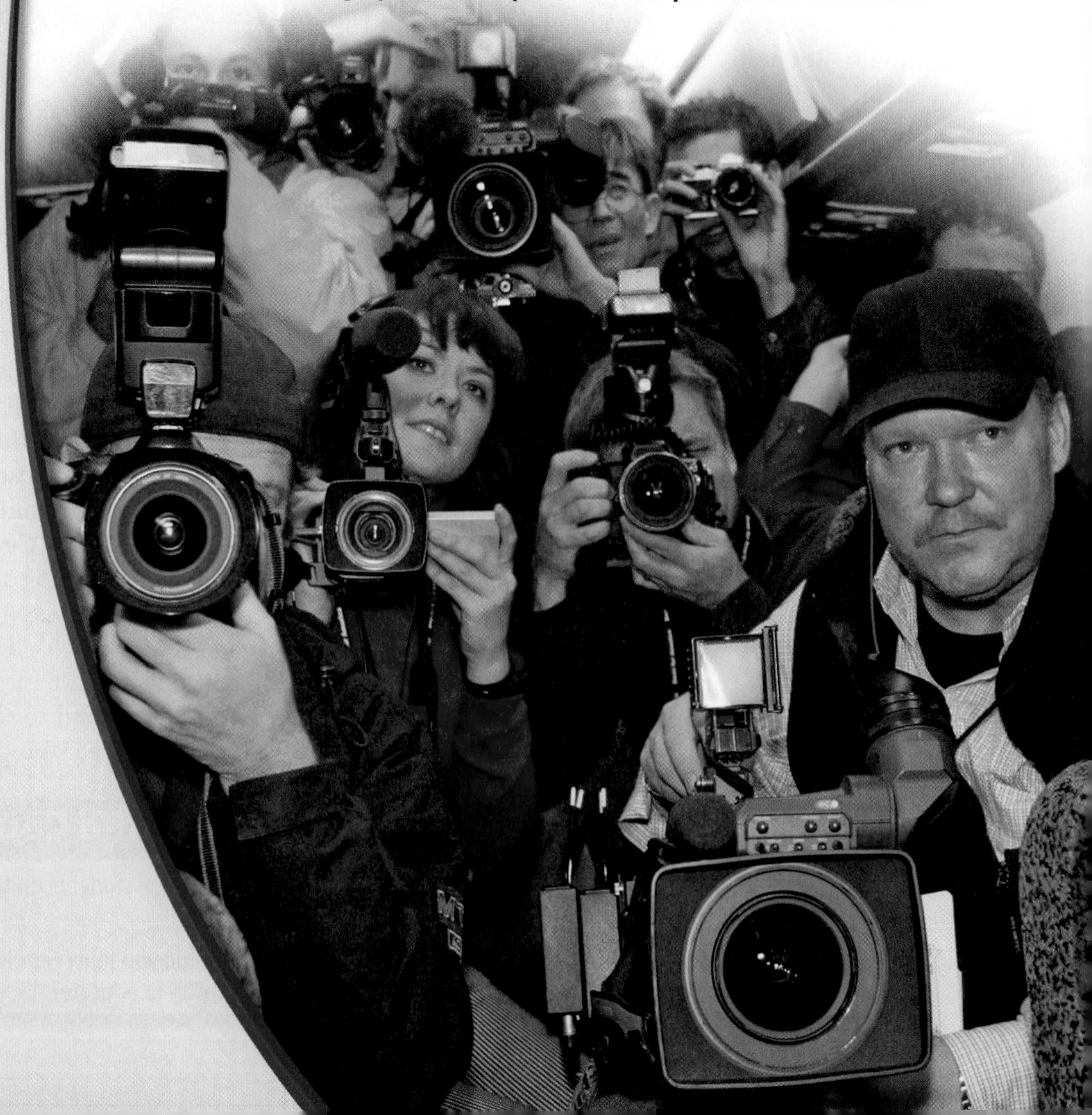

You Are There Television reporting of news events, such as the damage done by Hurricane Katrina in 2005, takes people right to the event. ***Predicting*** **How might television affect people's thoughts about how serious an event is?**

The Media's Impact

Main Idea **The nation's media are an important influence on politics and government and also help set the public agenda.**

Civics & You Where do you get your news? How reliable is this source? Read to find out how Americans depend on the media for information.

In the United States the mass media play an important role in influencing politics and government. They also form a link between the people and elected officials.

Types of Media

Newspapers, magazines, newsletters, and books are examples of **print media.** The **electronic media** are radio, television, and the Internet. In the United States, most media outlets are private businesses, run to make a profit. For that reason, media managers often decide what news to run based on what will attract the most viewers, listeners, or readers. The larger the audience, the more money the media can charge for advertising.

Public Agenda

The government must deal with many problems and issues. The ones that receive the most time, money, and effort from government leaders make up what is often called the **public agenda.**

The media have great influence on which problems governments consider important. When the media publicize a problem, such as immigration, white-collar crime, or pollution, people begin to worry about it and to expect that government officials will deal with the problem.

Watchdogs The media track and report bad behavior and corruption by politicians. ***Explaining*** **What positive things about politicians do the media report?**

Coverage of Candidates

Today's modern media, especially television, make it possible for some people to run for office who might never have done so in an earlier time. Previously, candidates were usually experienced politicians who had spent many years working their way up through their political parties. Today sports, media, and Hollywood celebrities with little or no political experience can quickly move into major political positions, based on the fame they earned in other fields.

Media and Elected Officials

The relationship between journalists and politicians is complicated. They need one another, yet they often clash. One presidential assistant explained it this way: "Politicians live—and sometimes die—by the press. The press lives by politicians."

Politicians may also secretly pass on, or **leak,** information to friendly reporters about proposed actions. Leaks allow them to test public reaction to a proposal without having to **acknowledge,** or admit, that the government is considering it. If the public reacts favorably, the government might officially move ahead with the idea. If the public reaction is negative, they can quietly drop it. Politicians also use leaks to change public opinion on an issue, or to gain favor with a reporter.

Leaking information is part of politics. Many journalists go along with the practice because they **benefit,** or profit, from being able to report "inside" information. When they can get hot news from politicians and "scoop" their rivals—break a story first—they become more successful as journalists.

Watchdog Role

The mass media also play an important "watchdog" role over government activities. Journalists are eager to expose government waste or corruption. They know that stories about government misconduct will attract a large audience. Throughout American history the media have served both their own interests and the public interest by exposing misconduct in government.

Media and National Security

A tension exists between the American citizens' need for information and the need for the government to keep secrets to protect national security. The government can control information the media reports by classifying information as secret and limiting press coverage of military actions. In the war in Iraq, "embedded," or implanted, journalists went with American troops into battle. They reported live on clashes with the enemy as well as on the daily life of the troops. Most journalists welcomed this opportunity. Some critics, however, felt the arrangement made it too easy for the government to control news reporting on the war.

Reading Check **Explaining** Why would a government official leak information to the media?

Civics ONLINE

Student Web Activity Visit glencoe.com and complete the Chapter 11 Web Activity.

Media Safeguards

Main Idea **Freedom of the press is protected by the U.S. Constitution, although some regulation is permitted.**

Civics & You Have you ever seen something on TV or heard something on the radio that you thought "went too far"? What do you think should be done about it? Read to find out what the Constitution says and how courts have interpreted it.

Democracy requires a free flow of information and ideas in order to thrive. In the United States the government plays an important role in protecting the ability of the mass media to operate freely. The Constitution extends freedom of speech to the media.

The First Amendment to the U.S. Constitution states, in part,

> *"Congress shall make no law . . . abridging the freedom . . . of the press."*

Today, "press" in this usage refers not only to print media but to radio, television, and the Internet as well. In the United States, the First Amendment means that the media are free from **prior restraint,** or government censorship of material *before* it is published. Generally the government cannot tell the media what or what not to publish. This means that reporters and editors are free to decide what they will say, even if it is unpopular or embarrassing to the government or to individual politicians.

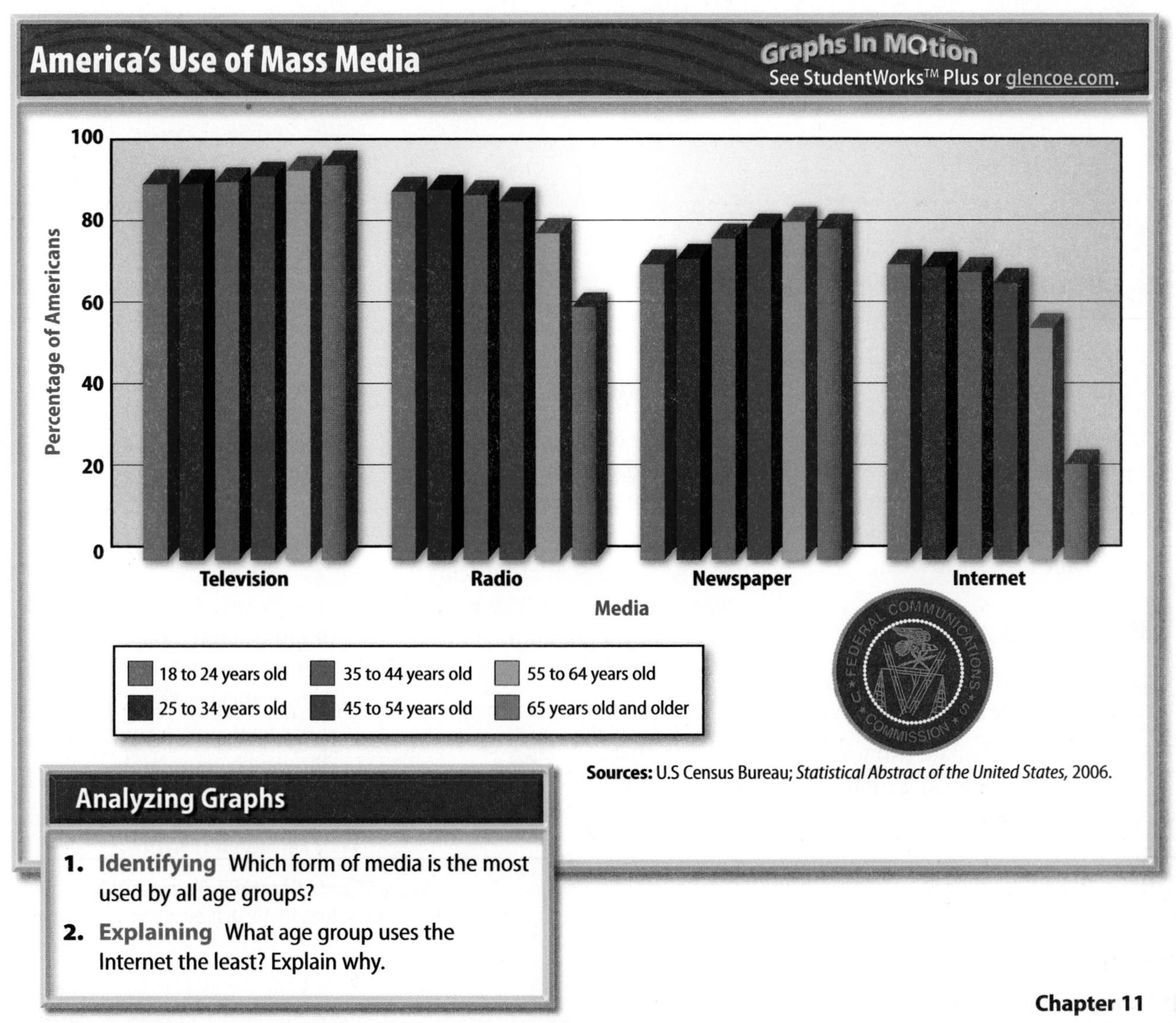

Sources: U.S Census Bureau; *Statistical Abstract of the United States,* 2006.

Analyzing Graphs

1. **Identifying** Which form of media is the most used by all age groups?
2. **Explaining** What age group uses the Internet the least? Explain why.

Freedom Within Limits Freedom of the press is not, however, unlimited. For example, no one is free to publish false information that will harm someone's reputation. This action is called **libel.** Anyone who believes a written story has damaged him or her may sue for libel. Unlike ordinary people, however, government officials rarely win libel lawsuits. In *New York Times Co.* v. *Sullivan* (1964), the Supreme Court ruled that public officials must prove actual **malice,** or evil intent—meaning that the publisher either knew that the material was false or showed a reckless disregard for the truth.

Protecting Sources Success in gathering news may depend on getting information from those who do not want their names made public. The press and the United States government have fought many battles over the media's right to keep sources secret. Thirty-one states and the District of Columbia have media shield laws to protect reporters from having to reveal their sources. For the most part, however, reporters have no more right to avoid presenting evidence than do other citizens.

Regulating the Media

The federal government possesses some power to regulate the broadcast media. This is because the government decides who gets access to the limited number of airwaves available for radio and television broadcasting. One way the government regulates broadcasting is through the Federal Communications Commission (FCC). The FCC is a **regulatory,** or managing, commission of the federal bureaucracy. The FCC cannot censor broadcasts, but it can penalize stations that violate its rules. A well-known example is the fine for the broadcast of the 2004 Super Bowl halftime show featuring singer Janet Jackson.

Reading Check **Describing** How does prior restraint protect the media?

Vocabulary

1. **Write** a short paragraph about mass media using each of these terms: *print media, electronic media, public agenda, leak, prior restraint, libel, malice.*

Main Ideas

2. **Explaining** How do the media set the public agenda?
3. **Describing** What are two ways freedom of the press is limited?

Critical Thinking

4. **Analyzing** Explain how the media and public officials are dependent on one another.
5. **BIG Ideas** Describe the roles the media plays in influencing government and politics by completing a graphic organizer like the one below.

6. **Analyzing Visuals** Examine the chart on page 329. What general statements can you make about those 18 to 24 years old?

CITIZENSHIP Activity

7. **Interviewing** Contact a local TV or radio station. Ask them to identify a recent broadcast that drew criticism. Have the station describe its procedure for handling such complaints.

Study Central™ To review this section, go to glencoe.com.

Issues to Debate

Do the media have a political bias?

In the past, most Americans watched the major television networks—CBS, NBC, and ABC—for their news. Today fewer Americans rely on the three major networks and their local newspapers. Many receive their news from a wide variety of sources, including cable television and the Internet. The issue of bias—or prejudice—in the news has become a topic for debate. Interest groups have organized to report on media bias. Some groups report that the media are generally liberal; others say they are more often conservative. Obviously, the bias of the interest group helps determine how it sees the media. Is news reporting in America generally biased?

A cartoon shows that it seems the media produced slanted or biased reports.

YES

The nonpartisan Center for Media and Public Affairs published a study in 1981 showing that the majority of network journalists identified themselves as liberal. Rupert Murdoch founded the Fox News cable channel to counterbalance what he saw as liberal bias at the big three networks. More recently, a CBS broadcast journalist, Bernard Goldberg, wrote a book called *Bias* in which he claimed that a one-sided opinion dominates the mainstream news media. He identified three network anchors: "I said out loud what millions of TV news viewers all over America know and have been complaining about for years: that too often, Dan (Rather) and Peter (Jennings) and Tom (Brokaw) and a lot of their foot soldiers don't deliver the news straight, that they have a liberal bias."

—Bernard Goldberg, Center for American Progress

NO

Network anchors, like former CBS anchorman Dan Rather, claim to be unbiased and above politics. In 1995, Rather said that most reporters did not know whether they were Republican or Democrat. He thought that most were probably moderates. In his recent book *What Liberal Media?* Eric Alterman accused conservatives of using the myth of liberal bias to gain a political advantage. "The myth of the 'liberal media' empowers conservatives to control debate in the United States to the point where liberals cannot even hope for a fair shake anymore. However immodest my goal, I aim to change that." He added that the 47 percent of people polled who believed that the media are "too liberal" were influenced by the myth of liberal bias.

—Eric Alterman, *What Liberal Media?*

Debating the Issue

1. **Identifying** What three networks captured most of the news viewers in the past?
2. **Recalling** How has the way Americans receive their news changed in recent years?
3. **Contrasting** Explain the difference between Goldberg's and Rather's views of network anchors.
4. **Evaluating** Why do many people believe news reporting is biased?

Spotlight Video

Section 3

Interest Groups

Guide to Reading

Big Idea

Political and economic institutions evolve to help individuals and groups accomplish their goals.

Content Vocabulary

- public interest group *(p. 334)*
- nonpartisan *(p. 334)*
- political action committee (PAC) *(p. 334)*
- lobbyist *(p. 335)*

Academic Vocabulary

- primary *(p. 334)*
- guarantee *(p. 337)*

Reading Strategy

Summarizing As you read, complete a web diagram like the one below to show how interest groups influence governmental decision making.

Real World Civics Since our country began, the right to assemble has been a basic freedom. When labor union members such as those in the AFL-CIO get together to support issues, they hope people listen. Labor unions formed early in America to give workers a more powerful voice. Although not all Americans agree with unions, all people have a right to be heard. The AFL-CIO was formed in the 1950s to give labor unions its most powerful voice.

▼ **Steelworkers and postal workers at an AFL-CIO Solidarity rally**

Types of Interest Groups

Main Idea **Interest groups are an important part of our democratic process because they influence public policy.**

Civics & You If you wanted to change a policy at your school, do you think you would have more influence as an individual or as a part of a large group? Read to see how many Americans have answered this question on the national level.

As you learned earlier, interest groups are organizations of people who unite to promote their ideas. People form, join, or support interest groups, also called special-interest groups, because they believe that by pooling their resources, they can increase their influence on decision makers. The First Amendment protects your right to belong to interest groups by guaranteeing "the right of the people peaceably to assemble and to petition the government."

Economic Interest Groups

Some of the most powerful interest groups are based on economic interests. The U.S. Chamber of Commerce, which promotes free enterprise, is one of the largest. Others represent specific types of businesses, such as the Tobacco Institute, which represents cigarette manufacturers. Such groups try to influence government decisions on issues that affect their industries.

Interest groups representing workers have been some of the most influential. They are concerned with wages, working conditions, and benefits. The American Federation of Labor and Congress of Industrial Organizations (AFL-CIO), an alliance of labor unions, is the largest of these groups. Professionals such as lawyers, doctors, and accountants have their own interest groups. The American Medical Association, for instance, represents doctors.

Energy Protest Demonstrators protest President Bush's energy policy in 2003. ***Comparing*** **How are public interest groups different than economic interest groups who protest?**

Other Interest Groups

People have also organized to promote an ethnic group, age group, religious group, or gender. The National Association for the Advancement of Colored People (NAACP) works to improve the lives of African Americans. The National Organization for Women (NOW) represents women's interests. AARP promotes the interests of older Americans.

Another category of interest groups works for special causes. For example, the Sierra Club is concerned with protecting nature. The National Rifle Association (NRA) looks after the interests of gun owners.

Public Interest Groups All the interest groups described earlier are private groups because they promote only the special interests of their own members. Some groups, however, work to benefit all, or at least most, of society. These are **public interest groups.** These groups support causes that affect the lives of Americans in general. For example, the League of Women Voters is a **nonpartisan,** or impartial, group that educates voters about candidates and issues. Other public interest groups have worked for consumer rights and the rights of the disabled.

Interest Groups and Government

Interest groups are an important part of our democratic process because their **primary,** or first, goal is to influence public policy. To do this, interest groups focus their efforts on elections, the courts, and lawmakers.

Elections Some interest groups use political resources to support certain candidates at election time. For example, the Sierra Club might back candidates who support laws to protect nature and oppose those who disagree with its beliefs. Many interest groups, including most labor unions and many corporations and trade associations, have formed **political action committees (PACs).** PACs collect money from the members of their groups and use it to support some candidates and oppose others.

Going to Court Trying to influence public policy by bringing cases to court is another option. For example, when a law—in the opinion of an interest group—is not being properly enforced, the group may sue the party who is breaking the law. A group may also use the courts to argue that a law or government policy is unconstitutional.

Peaceful Demonstrations Many special-interest groups protest peacefully, just asking citizens to read materials or sign petitions. ***Describing*** **What kinds of actions by the government are special-interest groups hoping for?**

TIME™

Political Cartoons

—Steve Breen/Copley News Service

Every year, more than half of all Americans do volunteer work ... role in it. One of the responsibilities of citizens is to help make their ... of volunteer grou... small. Perha...

In this cartoon, Steve Breen comments on the relationship between special interests and Congress by making reference to the movie *King Kong.*

1. **Define special interests.**
2. **Why do you think the cartoonist represents special interests as a giant?**
3. **How does Breen portray Congress?**
4. **Do you think Breen views this relationship as positive or negative? Explain.**

Lobbying Government

Interest groups use lobbyists to help them influence government officials, especially at the national and state levels. **Lobbyists** are representatives of interest groups who contact lawmakers or other government officials directly. Lobbyists operate at all levels of government—local, state, and national.

The term *lobbyist* was first used in the 1830s to describe people who waited in the lobbies of statehouses to ask politicians for favors. Today lobbyists use a variety of strategies to influence lawmakers. Lobbyists have a good understanding of how the government functions. Good lobbyists know which government department to contact about a particular concern. They are also talented public relations agents who know how to make friends and talk persuasively.

One of the lobbyist's most important resources is information. The most effective lobbyists are able to supply to lawmakers useful information that helps their own cases. They suggest solutions to problems and issues. Lobbyists sometimes prepare their own drafts of bills for lawmakers to consider and even testify in legislative hearings on bills. All of these activities provide lawmakers with a tremendous amount of information. This is important because lawmakers deal with thousands of bills each year.

The work of lobbyists does not end once a law is passed. Their interest groups also try to make sure the laws are enforced and upheld in court. For example, if an oil exploration bill is approved, environmental groups are likely to watch the whole operation carefully. If oil companies do not observe provisions aimed at protecting the environment, lobbyists for the environmental groups will lobby various government departments or agencies to see that the law is enforced.

Reading Check **Explaining** Why do some people form interest groups?

Propaganda Techniques

THE BANDWAGON

"Polls show our candidate is pulling ahead, and we expect to win in a landslide."

NAME-CALLING

"Candidate A is a dangerous extremist."

ENDORSEMENT

Popular beauty queen says, "I'm voting for Candidate B and so should you."

STACKED CARDS

"Candidate C has the best record on the environment."

GLITTERING GENERALITY

"Candidate B is the one who will bring us peace and prosperity."

JUST PLAIN FOLKS

"My parents were ordinary, hardworking people, and they taught me those values."

TRANSFER

Associating a patriotic symbol with a candidate.

Analyzing Charts

1. **Explaining** How does name-calling differ from the other techniques?
2. **Evaluating** In your opinion, which propaganda techniques, if any, are more acceptable than others in political campaigns?

Techniques Interest Groups Use

Main Idea **Interest groups use various techniques to influence public opinion and policy.**

Civics & You Are you more likely to support a cause because a famous singer supports it? Read to find out how groups and office seekers try to gain your support.

All interest groups want to influence public opinion, both to gain members and to convince people of the importance of their causes. Many use direct-mail campaigns to recruit. Interest groups also advertise. Maybe you have seen ads urging you to drink milk, use ethanol in your car, or buy American-made products. Trade associations sponsor these types of ads. Interest groups also stage protests and organize public events to get coverage in the media.

Beware Propaganda!

Interest groups use propaganda techniques to promote a particular viewpoint or idea. Citizens need to recognize the different types of propaganda described in the chart on this page. Many political and special-interest groups apply the same techniques used to market products to consumers.

Regulating Interest Groups

Although the Constitution **guarantees,** or promises, Americans the right to participate in interest groups, state and federal governments regulate their activities. Laws have limited the amount of money PACs may contribute to candidates and have required lobbyists to register with congressional officials who have authority to monitor them. Lobbyists must also disclose who hired them, how much they are paid, and how they spend money related to their work.

Federal and state laws also require a waiting period before former government officials can become lobbyists. For example, a person who just ended a term as a representative cannot immediately become a lobbyist for some special-interest group or organization that wants to hire that person. These laws are meant to prevent ex-public officials from taking unfair advantage of inside knowledge and friendships with former associates on behalf of interest groups. Laws regulating lobbyists have had only limited success.

Pros and Cons Interest groups have both their critics and their defenders. Some people argue that interest groups and lobbyists have too much say in government. Critics claim that campaign contributions give interest groups improper influence over officeholders. Many critics point to the example of Jack Abramoff, one of Washington's most powerful lobbyists. In January 2006, Abramoff admitted corrupting government officials and stealing millions of dollars from his lobbying clients.

Those who defend interest groups say that they make government more responsive. They provide necessary and important services by communicating the people's wishes to their representatives. They also enable Americans to organize and participate in the political system, and pressure the government to follow policies they want.

Reading Check **Explaining** What are the main tasks of lobbyists?

Vocabulary

1. **Define** the following terms and use them in sentences related to interest groups: *public interest group, nonpartisan, political action committee (PAC), lobbyist.*

Main Ideas

2. **Describing** What are three ways interest groups can be organized?
3. **Explaining** How have laws regulated the activities of interest groups, PACs, and lobbyists?

Critical Thinking

4. **Making Judgments** Which of the marketing techniques discussed in this section do you think is the most effective among consumers and citizens? Why?
5. **BIG Ideas** On a graphic organizer like the one below, compare and contrast the benefits and dangers of interest groups and lobbyists in our political system.

Benefits	Dangers

6. **Analyzing Visuals** Examine the chart of propaganda techniques on page 336. Work with a partner to list an example you have seen, heard, or read in the media of each.

CITIZENSHIP Activity

7. **Expository Writing** You have studied about political parties and about interest groups. Write a one-page paper in which you compare interest groups and political parties. How are they similar? How are they different?

Study Central™ To review this section, go to glencoe.com.

Financial Literacy

Shopping on the Internet

Shopping on the Internet has become increasingly popular because of the ease with which it can be done. Anybody with access to the Internet and a valid credit card can order on the Web.

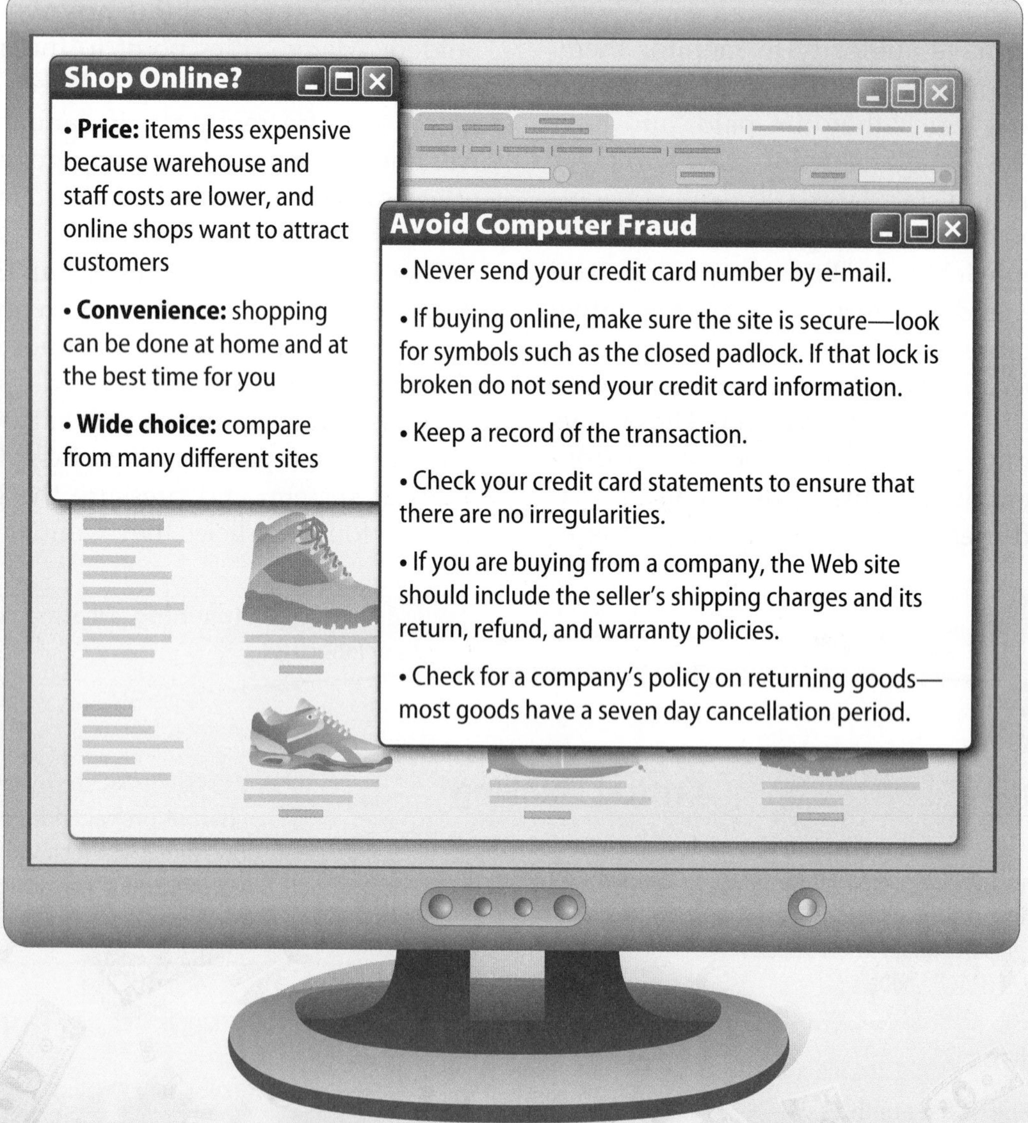

Analyzing Economics

1. **Comparing and Contrasting** Make a chart comparing the advantages and disadvantages of shopping on the Internet. In your opinion, do the advantages outweigh the disadvantages or vice versa? Why?
2. **Applying** What are three ways that you and your family can make shopping on the Internet safer for yourselves?

Chapter 11

Visual Summary

The AARP is a strong special-interest group.

American daily newspapers

INFLUENCING GOVERNMENT

Interest groups influence government decision making.

Public opinion helps shape the decisions of government officials.

The mass media help set the public agenda, publicize candidates, and present information to the public. The mass media also monitor government activities.

A person's background, the mass media, public officials, and interest groups all play a role in shaping public opinion.

Citizens often join together in a common cause.

Study anywhere, anytime! Download quizzes and flash cards to your PDA from glencoe.com.

Chapter 11

ASSESSMENT

Standardized Test Practice

TEST-TAKING TIP

When answering an essay question, give specific details to support your main ideas.

Reviewing Vocabulary

Directions: Choose the word(s) that best completes the sentence.

1. A(n) ______ measures public attitudes toward possible White House proposals.

A pollster
B interest group
C regulatory commission
D political action committee

2. Issues that receive the most time and money from government leaders make up the ______.

A mass media
B public opinion
C public agenda
D public interest group

3. Government censorship of material before it is published is called ______.

A libel
B malice
C partisanship
D prior restraint

4. Representatives of interest groups who contact public officials directly are called ______.

A celebrities
B journalists
C lobbyists
D white-collar criminals

Reviewing Main Ideas

Directions: Choose the best answer for each question.

Section 1 *(pp. 318–324)*

5. How do public officials try to persuade as many people as possible to support their positions?

A by conducting public opinion polls
B by promoting their views in the mass media
C by changing their positions based on public opinion
D by forming groups with others who share their beliefs

6. Why do responsible pollsters condemn push polls?

A Push polls discourage voting.
B Push poll questions are biased.
C Push polls use too few respondents.
D Push poll samples are seldom random.

Section 2 *(pp. 326–330)*

7. How do mass media act as a "watchdog" over government?

A by covering leaks from public officials
B by airing news that attracts more viewers
C by exposing public officials' misconduct
D by publicizing entertainers running for office

8. How does the Federal Communications Commission regulate radio and television?

A by penalizing stations for breaking rules
B by suing scriptwriters for committing libel
C by monitoring programmers suspected of malice
D by censoring objectionable material in broadcasts

Section 3 *(pp. 332–337)*

9. What interest group would most likely back a candidate who supports laws to protect nature?

A Sierra Club
B Tobacco Institute
C Chamber of Commerce
D League of Women Voters

10. What do critics of interest groups claim?

A Interest groups have too much influence.
B Interest groups provide necessary services.
C Interest groups enable Americans to organize.
D Interest groups communicate the people's wishes.

GO ON

Critical Thinking

Directions: Base your answers to questions 11 and 12 on the diagram below and your knowledge of Chapter 11.

Techniques	How to Recognize It
Name-calling	Referring to an opponent with an unpleasant label or description, such as "un-American"
Glittering generality	Vague or broad statement containing little substance
Card stacking	Giving only one side of the facts to support a position
Transfer of symbol	Associating a patriotic symbol with a point of view or person
Just plain folks	Identifying a person as "just one of the common people"
Testimonial or endorsement	A celebrity endorses a person or point of view
The bandwagon	Urging people to support a position or person because everyone else is

11. Analyze the following passages from special-interest Web sites. Which uses glittering generalities?

A The Sierra Club's members are more than 750,000 of your friends and neighbors.

B Hispanic-American Soldiers have embodied the army's core values for generations.

C The arrogance of anti-gun politicians and their hate of freedom will churn your stomach.

D Robert Redford urges Americans to call on their representative to vote against any bill that would plunder the Arctic Refuge.

12. Which passage uses name-calling?

A The Sierra Club's members are more than 750,000 of your friends and neighbors.

B Hispanic-American Soldiers have embodied the Army's core values for generations.

C The arrogance of anti-gun politicians and their hate of freedom will churn your stomach.

D Robert Redford urges Americans to call on their representative to vote against any bill that would plunder the Arctic Refuge.

Document-Based Questions

Directions: Analyze the following document and answer the short-answer questions that follow.

The following passage discusses reporting on the occupation of Iraq.

> *There were photos of the platoon, guns over shoulders, praying for the fallen buddy. The* Times *is careful not to ruin the heroic mood, so there is no photograph of pieces of corporal Smith's shattered head. Instead, there's an old, smiling photo of the wounded soldier.*
>
> *The reporter, undoubtedly wearing the Kevlar armor of the troop in which he's "embedded," quotes at length the thoughts of the military medic: "I would like to say that I am a good man. But seeing this now, what happened to Smith, I want to hurt people. You know what I mean?"*
>
> *The reporter does not bother — or dare — to record a single word from any Iraqi in the town of Karma where Smith's platoon was, "performing a hard hit on a house."*
>
> *And if we asked, I'm sure the sniper would tell us, "I am a good man, but seeing what happened, I want to hurt people."*
>
> —Greg Palast, "I Want to Hurt Somebody"

13. Why do you think the author mentions that the reporter is "embedded"?

14. In the third paragraph, the author implies that the reporter used a propaganda technique. Which one?

Extended Response

15. Write a brief essay about requirements for a well-constructed public opinion poll.

For additional test practice, use Self-Check Quizzes—Chapter 11 on glencoe.com.

Need Extra Help?

If you missed question...	1	2	3	4	5	6	7	8	9	10	11	12	13	14	15
Go to page...	323	327	329	335	320	324	328	330	333	336	336	336	328	336	323

Analyzing Primary Sources

Extending the Right to Vote

Reading Focus

On Election Day, every citizen over the age of 18 is able to cast a vote. It is a right that defines our nation as a democracy. But universal suffrage—letting everyone vote—did not appear overnight with the ratification of our Constitution. Many Americans struggled to gain the right to vote.

Read to Discover

As you read, think about the following:

- Why did it take so long for many people to win voting rights?
- How were voting rights extended?

Reader's Dictionary

peer: a person who has equal standing with another or others

comply: meet the terms

The Fight for Woman Suffrage

Susan B. Anthony was a leader in the fight for legal rights for women.

It may be delayed longer than we think; it may be here sooner than we expect; but the day will come when man will recognize woman as his **peer,** not only at the fireside but in the councils of the nation. Then, and not until then, will there be . . . the ideal union between the sexes that shall result in the highest development of the race. What this shall be we may not attempt to define, but this we know, that only good can come to the individual or to the nation through the rendering of exact justice.

—Susan B. Anthony, article on woman suffrage

Promoting Voting Rights

Martin Luther King, Jr., explains why the right to vote is vital.

"We know that Americans of good will have learned that no nation can long continue to flourish or to find its way to a better society while it allows any one of its citizens . . . to be denied the right to participate in the most fundamental of all privileges of democracy—the right to vote."

—Dr. Martin Luther King, Jr., "Civil Rights No. 1: The Right to Vote"

Native American Suffrage

Native Americans also were denied equal rights.

The Indian Citizenship Act of 1924 granted Native Americans citizenship. However, it still took more than 40 years for all 50 states to allow Native Americans to vote.

In order to exercise the right of suffrage, Indians must of course **comply** with the conditions equally required of other voters, and may be denied the privilege of voting if they fail to comply with the requirements of the law as to registration, payment of poll tax, or do not meet the educational or other qualifications for electors, etc., as provided by the State laws.

—Indian Citizenship Act of 1924

The Voting Rights Act

The purpose of this Act is to ensure that the right of all citizens to vote, including the right to register to vote and cast meaningful votes, is preserved and protected as guaranteed by the Constitution. . . .

The record compiled by Congress demonstrates that, without the continuation of the Voting Rights Act of 1965 protections, racial and language minority citizens will be deprived of the opportunity to exercise their right to vote, or will have their votes diluted, undermining the significant gains made by minorities in the last 40 years.

—H. R. 9, the bill to extend the 1965 Voting Rights Act

Photographs as Primary Sources What can you learn from the photo about the people who demonstrated in Selma, Alabama, in the 1950s? What kind of demonstration did they hold?

Civil rights leader John Lewis, who helped organize voter registration drives in the 1960s, spoke out in favor of extending the Voting Rights Act.

"The Voting Rights Act is the heart and soul of our Democracy. The Voting Rights Act literally ushered in the possibility of transforming electoral politics. In the American South, you had millions who could not vote because of the color of their skin."

—John Lewis on the renewal of the Voting Rights Act

Why I Vote

A college student explains why voting is important.

As a child growing up with parents who were immigrants and had no voice in their country, I was able to see the importance of voting. When my parents became American citizens they took me and my siblings into the voting booth with them every time.

—Sonia Zobdeh, student at Brooklyn College

DBQ Document-Based Questions

1. **Interpreting** What did Anthony mean when she argued that women should be recognized as peers to men "not only at the fireside but in the councils of the nation"?
2. **Explaining** What did King mean when he called the right to vote "the most fundamental of all privileges of a democracy"?
3. **Explaining** Why was the right to vote not extended to all Native Americans, despite passage of the Indian Citizenship Act?
4. **Evaluating and Connecting** If Susan B. Anthony and Martin Luther King, Jr., were alive today, what issues do you think they might be addressing? Why?

UNIT 4

State and Local Government

Charlottesville, Virginia, students take part in school activity

★ Chapter 12 State Government

★ Chapter 13 Local Government

★ Chapter 14 Dealing With Community Issues

Be an Active Citizen

CITIZENSHIP State and local government issues are closest to citizens. Identify a local issue in your community that concerns you. Find out facts about it, and form an opinion about it. Make a poster expressing this opinion to put in your classroom.

UNIT 4 Reading Social Studies

Distinguishing Fact from Opinion

1 Learn It!

A fact is something that can be proven or documented and does not change unless new evidence disproves it. On the other hand, an opinion is what you believe based upon your own viewpoints or feelings. Opinions can change from person to person, but everyone agrees that facts are true. When you read, it is important to distinguish fact from opinion.

- Read the paragraph below.
- Identify the facts in the paragraph.
- Read how one student used the facts to form an opinion about state lotteries.

> In a recent year Americans spent $50 billion on state lotteries—more money than on reading materials or attending movies. Half of that money was returned to the winners. After paying their other costs, the states kept about $15 billion. Many states use the money to help finance education.
>
> —*from page 361*

Chart

Facts	Opinion
1. Americans spent $50 billon on state lotteries. 2. Half of the money was returned to the winners. 3. States kept about $15 billion. 4. Many states use the money to help finance education.	Lotteries are a good way to raise money for education. People like to play the lottery, and at the same time they are helping their state with education costs.

② Practice It!

Read the following paragraph from this unit.

- Draw a chart like the one shown below.
- Write facts from the paragraph in the column on the left.
- Write your opinion about cities in the paragraph in the column on the right.

> . . . City leaders [in Galveston] decided that a commission government was the best way to handle the emergency.
>
> Since that time, however, other cities have found that a commission government is not always efficient in running a city. Without clear leadership, a commission is often unable to set and meet goals. Each commissioner is likely to concentrate primarily on his or her own department, without considering the problems of the city as a whole.
>
> —*From page 381*

Facts	Opinion

Read to Write Activity

Read *Teens in Action* on page 354. Jot down facts about Prateek Peres-da-Silva. Then, write a paragraph in which you express your opinion about his activities in the Governor's Page Program.

③ Apply It!

There are many facts presented in Chapters 12, 13, and 14 about state government. You may have no opinion about some of the facts, but others may cause you to think about your own beliefs or feelings. At least three times in each chapter, stop reading and write your opinion about a fact in the text. Share your opinions with others in the class.

Chapter 12

State Government

Why It Matters

State governments mirror the federal government in their organization. State governments, being closer to the citizens, have a great influence on people's daily lives and activities.

Chapter Audio

Civics ONLINE
Visit glencoe.com and enter QuickPass™ code CIV3093c12 for Chapter 12 resources.

BIG Ideas

Section 1: The Federal System

Under our federal system, power is shared between the national government and the state governments. Our federal system also establishes a special relationship between the national government and those of the individual states.

Section 2: The State Legislative Branch

The Constitution gives the legislative branch—Congress—the power to make laws. State governments, which generally mirror the federal government in organization, address problems closer to citizens.

Texas State troopers receive their commission

Section 3: The State Executive Branch

The Constitution gives the executive branch the power to execute, or implement, the law. Like the president on the national level, governors are the chief executives of the states.

Section 4: The State Judicial Branch

The judicial branch is charged with interpreting the law. Different levels of state courts administer justice.

FOLDABLES™ Study Organizer

Organizing Information Study Foldable Make the following Foldable to organize information about the branches of state government.

Step 1 Mark the midpoint of the side edge of one sheet of paper. Then fold in the outside edges to touch the midpoint.

Step 2 Fold the paper in half from side to side.

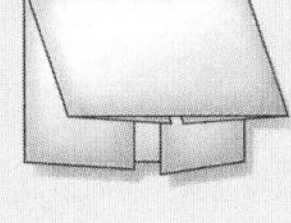

Cut along the fold lines on both sides.

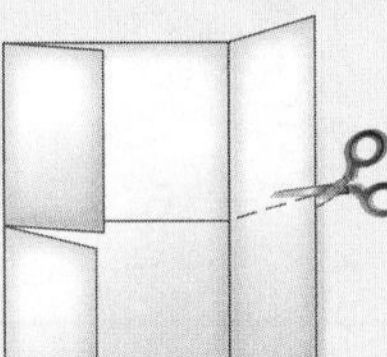

Step 3 Open and cut along the inside fold lines to form four tabs. Label the Foldable as shown.

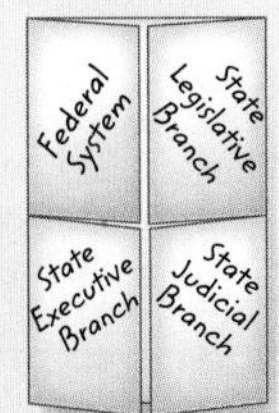

Reading and Writing Fill out your Foldable as you read the chapter. You will organize information about the federal system and the three branches of state government.

Section Audio

Spotlight Video

The Federal System

Guide to Reading

Big Idea

Under our federal system, power is shared between the national government and the state governments.

Content Vocabulary

- federal system *(p. 351)*
- reserved powers *(p. 352)*
- concurrent powers *(p. 353)*
- grants-in-aid *(p. 353)*

Academic Vocabulary

- consent *(p. 351)*
- expanded *(p. 353)*

Reading Strategy

Summarizing On a web diagram like the one below, summarize the important features of the federal system of government.

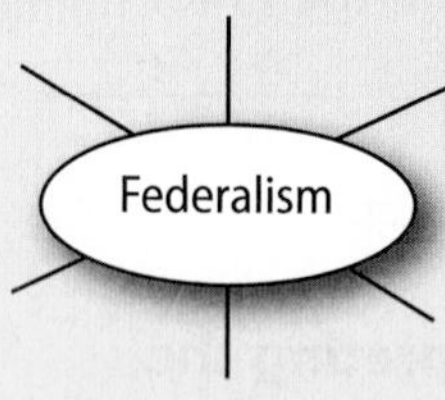

Real World Civics Did you know that your state has its own military force? The National Guard of each state, like these troops from Louisiana, is commanded by the governor of that state. The Framers established the National Guard as a way to balance state and federal power. A governor may call up the Guard during a natural disaster, such as Hurricane Katrina, or activate it to keep the peace during a civil disturbance. But the president can also federalize the Guard when needed for national interests.

▼ **National Guard patrols New Orleans, 2006**

Public Safety The states have the power to build and regulate roads as part of guarding the welfare of citizens. ***Hypothesizing*** **Why do you think control of roadways was not left with the federal government?**

Constitutional Basis for Federalism

Main Idea **The U.S. Constitution created a federal system of government in which the central government and the state governments share power.**

Civics & You Can you think of a way the state government affects your daily activities? Read more to find out what these state activities are and why the state pursues them.

The Constitution created a **federal system** of government, or federalism. The Constitution established an arrangement that gives the national government certain powers and reserves others for the states. There are also powers that the Constitution denies to each level of government. In addition, there are some powers that are shared by the national government and by the state governments. The sharing, however, is not equal. If a state law conflicts with a national law, the national law must be followed. Federalism is a middle position between having an all-powerful central government and a system in which the states dominate. The writers of the Constitution wanted to place some limits on national power and yet not allow the states to be so strong that the central government would be ineffective.

Protecting States

The Constitution protects states in several ways. For example, no state can be divided or merged with another state without the states' **consent,** or approval. States can maintain a militia—a military force called the National Guard—under the control of each state's governor. In a national emergency, however, the president may federalize the National Guard, putting it under control of the U.S. armed forces.

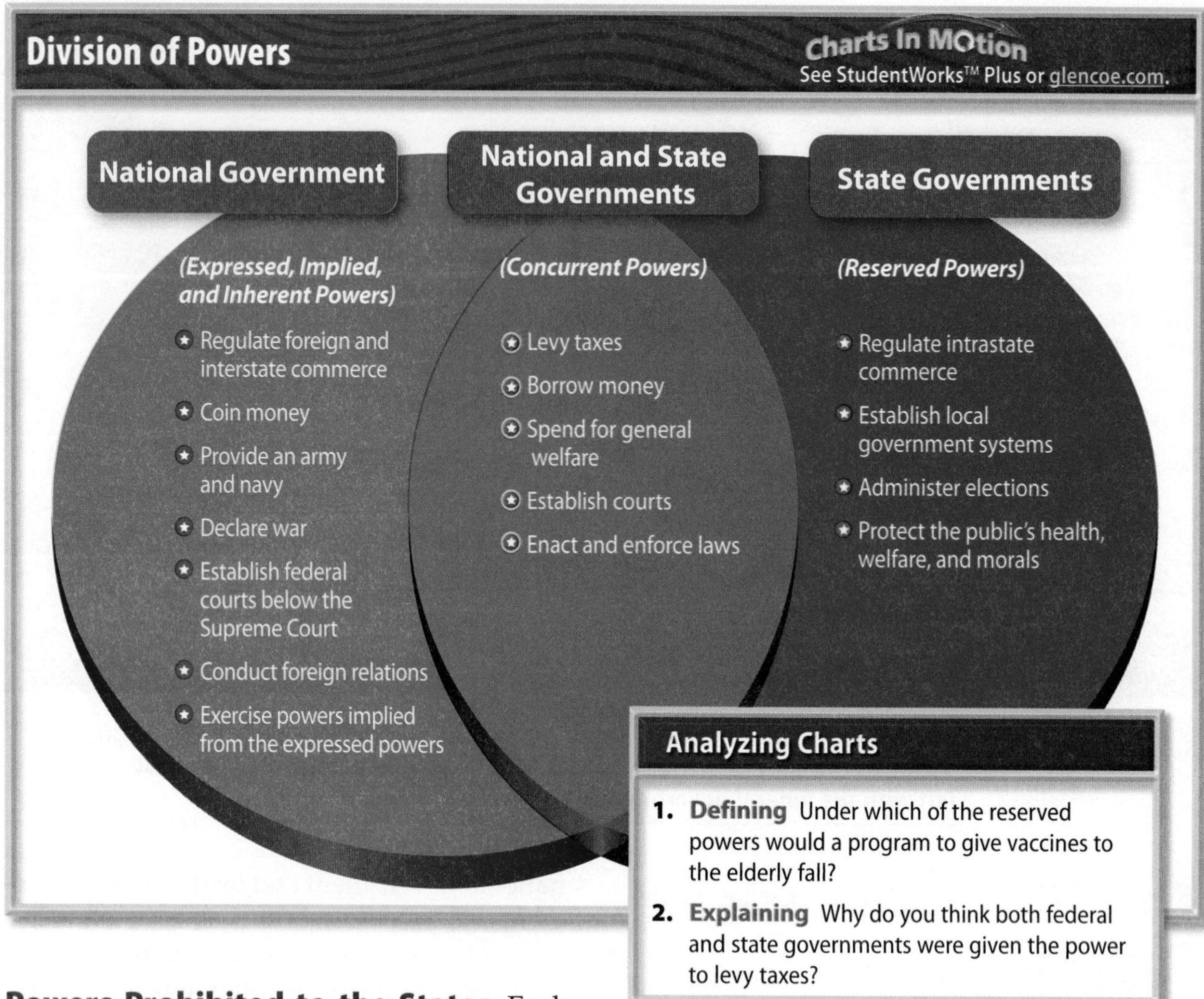

Analyzing Charts

1. **Defining** Under which of the reserved powers would a program to give vaccines to the elderly fall?
2. **Explaining** Why do you think both federal and state governments were given the power to levy taxes?

Powers Prohibited to the States Each state is largely free to govern itself the way its citizens consider best. Just as the U. S. Constitution denies certain powers to the national government, it also specifies what the state governments may not do. The explicit prohibitions are found in Article I, Section 10, as well as in many of the amendments to the Constitution. For example, the Constitution forbids states to declare war, to issue their own money, or to impose taxes on imports from other countries or states. The Constitution forbids any state from entering into a treaty on its own with another country. In addition, several constitutional amendments prevent state governments from taking away rights granted by the federal government. The most important of these is the Fourteenth Amendment, which guarantees all Americans equal protection of the laws.

Reserved Powers

The Tenth Amendment to the U.S. Constitution establishes that state governments may exercise *all* powers *not* given to the federal government or denied to the states. These powers are called **reserved powers** because they are reserved to the states. Among them are the powers to make marriage laws, to regulate education, and to hold elections.

In general, each state is responsible for the public health, safety, and welfare of its citizens. States and their governments set up police forces and other law enforcement operations. They build roads and bridges. They set educational requirements and provide money to run the schools. They organize local governments.

Federal Supremacy

The Constitution grants some **concurrent powers**—those shared by state governments and the federal government. Both, for example, may impose taxes and borrow money. If, however, conflicts arise between the states and the federal government, the Supreme Court decides the case. Article VI of the Constitution states that the laws that Congress makes shall be the "supreme law of the land." This clause is called the supremacy clause.

States' Rights v. Nationalists Throughout history, Americans have argued over how federalism should operate. One view—the states' rights position—argues that because the states created the national government, all of the national government's powers should be limited. Those who favor states' rights believe that state governments are closer to the people and better reflect the people's wishes than the national government can. On the other hand, Americans who support the nationalist position argue that the people, not the states, created the national government and the states. Therefore, the powers granted to the national government should be **expanded,** or developed, as needed to carry out the people's will.

Supporters of this nationalist position argue that the "necessary and proper" clause in Article I of the Constitution means that Congress has the right to adopt any means it needs to carry out its delegated powers. Supporters of the nationalist position look to the national government to take the lead in solving major social and economic problems.

A Balancing Act The balance of powers between the national and state governments has shifted through the years. The national government's ability to wage war, to regulate commerce, and to levy taxes has strengthened the national government's authority. However, some people believe that state and local governments will always be important because Americans identify more closely with their local communities and look to these communities to understand their needs.

Governmental Cooperation

Since the 1930s, state governments and the federal government have increasingly cooperated to fund and administer a wide variety of programs. Although the money is allotted by Congress, the funds are meant to aid state and community citizens. These include funds for highways, education, and welfare. Usually the federal government provides **grants-in-aid**—awards of money—to the states to help them pay for some of their programs. States must contribute some of their own money, and they must obey rules set by Congress in order to receive these grants. The federal government gives some *grants-in-aid* directly to cities and counties. In other cases federal grants "pass through" state governments to cities.

States Provide State agencies provide things such as special telephones for physically challenged citizens. ***Explaining*** **How do states pay for programs to help the disabled?**

TIME™ Teens in Action

Prateek Peres-da-Silva

Paging all future politicians! Check out this story about Prateek Peres-da-Silva, 16, of Carrboro, North Carolina. He spent one week in the North Carolina Governor's Page Program.

QUESTION: What's the Governor's Page Program all about?
ANSWER: High school students get the chance to spend a week in the state capital and learn about how government functions. Pages, students in the program, are assigned to help state workers with various tasks.
Q: How many pages are there?
A: About 1,000 kids from different counties around the state participate each year—20 each week. In addition to the daily responsibilities, pages attend press conferences, tour historic landmarks like the capitol and the legislative building—and they can meet the governor.
Q: Speaking of the governor, did you work with elected officials?
A: Yes! I attended meetings at the senate and spoke to several state senators. I also delivered mail and filed documents in the State Office of Management and Budget.
Q: How were you chosen for the program?
A: I filled out an application form and requested a reference letter from my district senator.

North Carolina state legislature

ACTION FACT: A music and sports lover, Peres-da-Silva was born in Goa, India.

Making a Difference — CITIZENSHIP

1. **Describing** What might be some of the goals of students who take part in the page program?

Cooperation Among States The Constitution ensures that states cooperate with one another. Article IV encourages interstate cooperation by requiring states to give "full faith and credit" to the public laws and court decisions of other states. For example, a car registration or corporation charter issued by one state must be accepted in all other states.

Form of Government Article IV also requires every state to have a "republican form of government." The federal government will protect each state against invasion and domestic violence. When a state or local police force cannot control violent incidents within a state, the governor may call for the assistance of federal troops. In return, states provide certain services to the federal government, such as conducting elections for state officials.

Extradition Article IV also ensures another type of cooperation. Often, someone who breaks the law in one state will flee to another state to avoid punishment. A state cannot legally punish a person for breaking the laws of another state. If requested to do so, however, a governor usually orders that a person charged with a crime be returned to the state where the crime was committed. Returning a suspected criminal is called extradition.

Sharing Responsibilities States cooperate in other ways as well, especially when they share a border. The neighboring states of New York and New Jersey, for example, are partners in an agency called the Port Authority. The Port Authority manages bridges, airports, and other transportation facilities that serve both states.

Reading Check **Defining** What are reserved powers?

Civics ONLINE

Student Web Activity Visit glencoe.com and complete the Chapter 12 Web Activity.

State Constitutions

Main Idea **While differing in details, all state constitutions share many characteristics.**

Civics & You Did you know that your state has a constitution that is similar to the U.S. Constitution? Read to find out how this document can affect your life.

Each state has its own constitution. Like the United States Constitution, a state constitution is a plan of government.

Typical Form and Content

State constitutions are similar in many ways to the U.S. Constitution. Every state constitution provides for separation of powers among three branches of government—legislative, executive, and judicial. The state constitutions outline the organization of each branch, the powers and terms of various offices, and the method of election for state officials. States have also included their own bills of rights in their constitutions, which include all or most of the protections of the Bill of Rights in the U.S. Constitution.

Often, they also include rights not provided in the national Constitution, such as workers' right to join unions and protections for the physically challenged.

State constitutions also establish different types of local governments, including counties, townships, municipalities, special districts, parishes, and boroughs. State constitutions also regulate the ways state and local governments can raise and spend money. Finally, state constitutions establish independent state agencies and boards.

Just as the U.S. Constitution is the highest law in the nation, a state's constitution is the highest law in that state. State constitutions, however, cannot include provisions that clash with the U.S. Constitution.

Reading Check **Comparing** What do all state constitutions have in common?

Vocabulary

1. **Define** the following terms and use them in complete sentences related to the way state and federal governments work together: *federal system, reserved powers, concurrent powers, grants-in-aid.*

Main Ideas

2. **Describing** What happens in a federal system, like that of the United States, if a state law conflicts with a national law?

3. **Identifying** What are three areas usually covered in state constitutions?

Critical Thinking

4. **BIG Ideas** How are reserved powers different from concurrent powers?

5. **Identifying** On a chart like the one below, identify the reserved powers given to states.

Reserved Powers
1.
2.
3.
4.

CITIZENSHIP Activity

6. **Persuasive Writing** Do you think there should be term limitations for every elected government official at all levels—local, state, and federal? Why or why not? Express your views in an essay.

Study Central™ To review this section, go to glencoe.com.

What Information Is on Your Paycheck?

If you work 40 hours a week and receive $15 an hour, you earn $600. When you get your paycheck, one thing is obvious: Your net pay—the amount of money you take home—is not the same amount as your earnings. Your take-home pay is total earnings minus the deductions.

Period Ending: June 15, 2006

Name: Olivia Detwiler

	This Period
Gross pay	**$1,041.60**
Deductions:	
Federal Income Tax	-$82.19
Social Security Tax	-$64.59
Medicare Tax	-$15.11
State Income Tax	-$34.27
City Income Tax	-$3.14
Net Pay	**$842.30**

Confirming your net pay is important, but what other information is provided on a typical pay stub?

- Pay period is how often you are paid.
- Gross pay is your pay before deductions.
- Net pay is your pay after deductions.
- Federal income tax withheld is shown.
- You might also choose to withhold a percentage of your gross income to put into a retirement account.

Analyzing Economics

1. **Explaining** How does net pay differ from gross pay?
2. **Analyzing** Why is it important to keep track of all the amounts on your pay stub?

Section 2

Section Audio

Spotlight Video

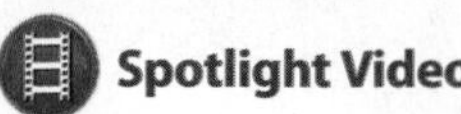

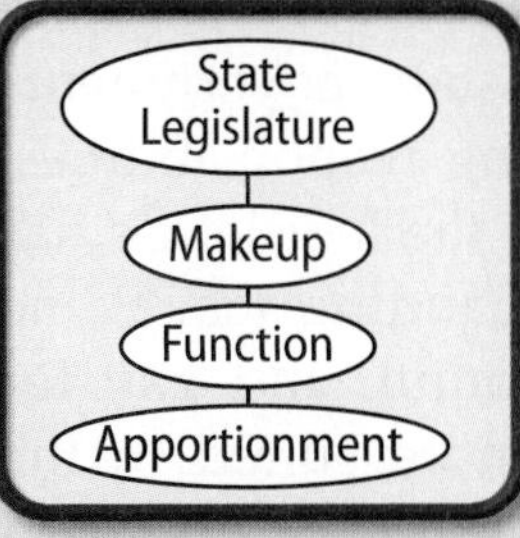

The State Legislative Branch

Guide to Reading

Big Idea

The Constitution gives the legislative branch—Congress—the power to make laws.

Content Vocabulary

- unicameral *(p. 358)*
- bicameral *(p. 358)*
- census *(p. 359)*
- apportion *(p. 359)*
- malapportionment *(p. 359)*

Academic Vocabulary

- revise *(p. 359)*
- whereas *(p. 360)*

Reading Strategy

Summarizing As you read, take notes by completing a web diagram like the one below by adding details under each of the three secondary heads.

Real World Civics As a country of immigrants, people who represent you in government come from many different backgrounds. Pedro Colón is the first Latino representative in the Wisconsin State Legislature. His district is 39 percent Latino, making it the majority ethnic group in that district. Colón's job is to represent all Wisconsin citizens in his district, however. Who represents your interests in your state?

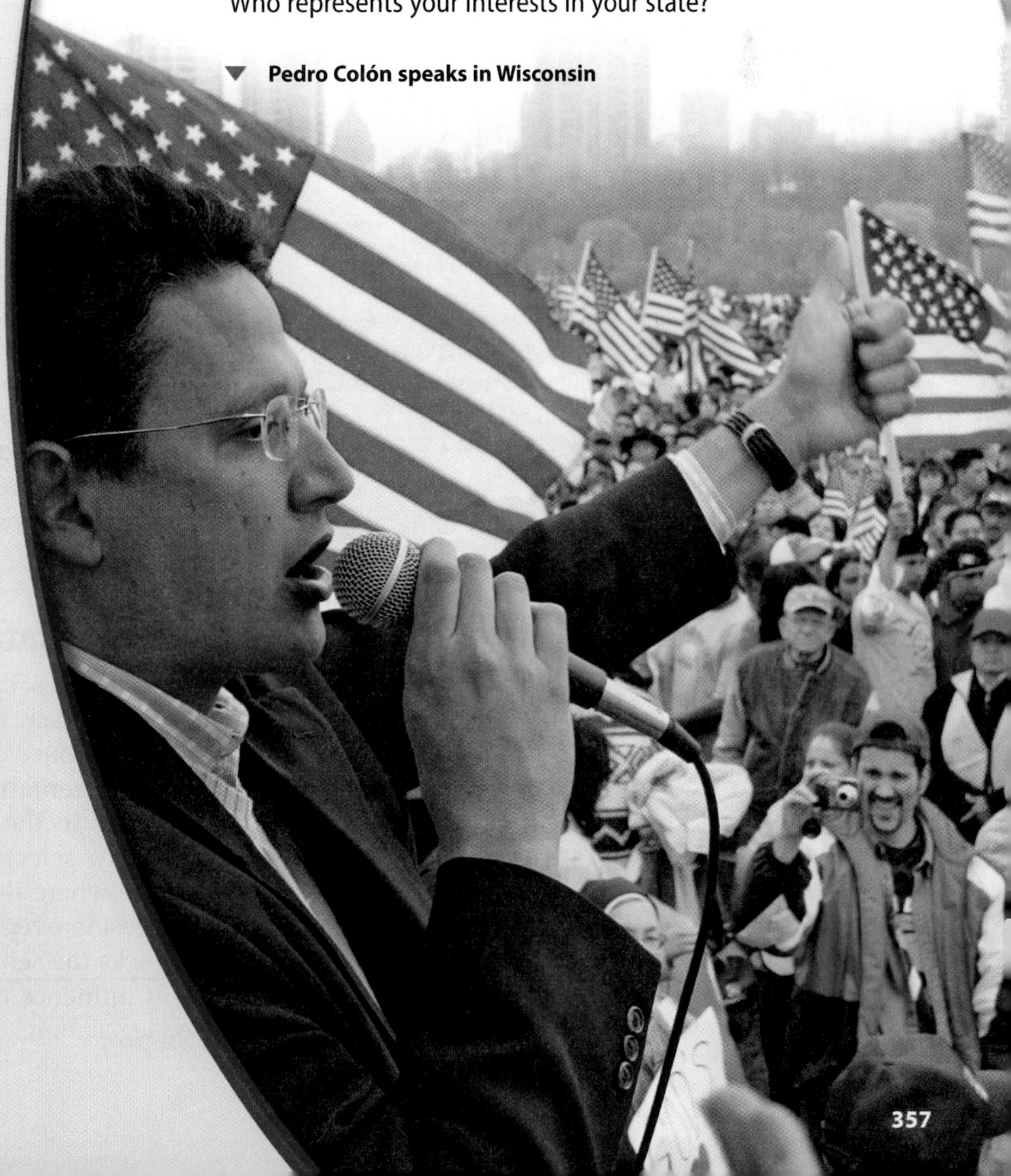

▼ **Pedro Colón speaks in Wisconsin**

Legislative Sessions The New Jersey legislature gives Governor Corzine a standing ovation following his speech about budget issues in 2006. ***Describing*** **What is a bicameral legislature?**

How Legislatures Function

Main Idea **State legislatures pass the laws that govern the states.**

Civics & You Can you name your state representative or senator? Read to find out what these important people do for your state's government.

State lawmaking bodies vary in name and size. In some states the legislature is called the general assembly. Most states, however, call it the legislature. New Hampshire, one of the nation's smallest states in area and population, has the largest legislature—more than 400 members. Nebraska has the smallest, with only 49 members.

Organization

Except for Nebraska's **unicameral,** or one-house, legislature, every state has a **bicameral** legislature, with an upper house, called the senate, and a lower house, usually called the house of representatives. Senators typically serve four-year terms, and representatives two-year terms. Generally, members must be American citizens and live in the district they represent. In most states, representatives must be at least 18 years old, while the minimum age for senators ranges from 18 to 30.

Originally, service in the state legislature required little time. As state governments have gained ever-growing responsibilities, however, membership in the legislature has become a far more demanding job. Some legislatures meet year-round, and pay for members is becoming more suited to the level of work.

What Do Legislatures Do?

State legislatures operate much like the U.S. Congress. Each house has a leader. A speaker of the house directs business in the house of representatives, and a president does the same in the senate. The majority political party selects the house speaker, and in states where the lieutenant governor does not preside over the senate, the majority party picks the senate president. Leaders have great influence over what happens to proposed legislation.

How Bills Become State Law Ideas for bills come from many sources, including the governor, individuals, and the legislators themselves. After a member in either house introduces a bill, it goes to the appropriate committee of that house.

The committees study bills, hold hearings, and **revise,** or change, the bills if necessary. In many cases, bills die in committee, never making it to a vote. Otherwise, a committee may send a bill to the full house, with a recommendation that it be passed or rejected. If the two houses pass differing versions of the same bill, it goes to a conference committee, which works out agreeable language. Both houses must approve the final version of a bill, and the governor must sign it before it becomes a law.

Legislative Districts Representatives to the U.S. Congress and the state legislatures are elected from districts. In most states, legislatures draw the boundary lines for each election district.

The U.S. Census Bureau takes a national **census,** or population count, every 10 years. So every 10 years, state legislatures set up or reexamine congressional districts.

Unequal Representation For many years, state senate districts were based roughly on land area, and state house districts were **apportioned,** or divided into districts, based on population. Area-based districts often produced **malapportionment,** or unequal representation, in many state legislatures. For example, a city district and a rural district might each have had one senator, even though the city district had 10 times as many people. U.S. Supreme Court rulings in the 1960s established that state legislatures must be apportioned on the basis of equal population. As a result, many states had to reapportion their legislatures.

Reading Check **Defining** What is a census?

TIME™

Political Cartoons

—Chris Britt/Copley News Service

Every year, more than half of all Americans do volunteer work ... role in it. One of the responsibilities of citizens is to help make their ... of volunteer grou... small. Perha... dad who...

Chris Britt, the creator of this cartoon, is commenting on a Supreme Court decision on *eminent domain,* which is the right of the government to take private property for public use.

1. **What does the crane represent?**
2. **On what foundation is the house sitting?**
3. **What details in the cartoon convey the cartoonist's opinion of this Supreme Court ruling?**

Problems Facing States

Main Idea **Today's state governments face many difficult challenges.**

Civics & You When you do not have enough money to do or buy everything you want, how do you decide what to spend your money on? Read to find out how state legislators address this thorny problem.

Americans expect a great deal from their state governments. They demand better public transportation, better schools, and better services for disabled and disadvantaged people. They also expect state governments to protect the environment, regulate business, and reduce crime and drug abuse.

Paying for Service State governments, however, are finding it difficult to pay for these services. Many legislators refuse to vote to raise taxes. Also, **whereas** federal grants paid for many of these services in the past, the federal government has eliminated many grants because of its own budget concerns.

A Tough Choice

As a result, state governments face a difficult choice: Should they cut programs or raise taxes to pay for them? Legislators fear they may be defeated in the next election if they raise taxes. They also want to avoid cutting essential services. Cutting services at a time when challenges are mounting may be considered irresponsible.

The U.S. Supreme Court's rulings of the 1960s also increased the representation of city dwellers in state legislatures. Since the larger cities are where crime, drug abuse, and unemployment are often highest, today's state legislators face great pressure in dealing with these issues.

Reading Check **Describing** What issues face state legislators today?

Vocabulary

1. **Write** complete sentences for each of the following terms related to state legislatures: *unicameral, bicameral, census, apportion, malapportionment.*

Main Ideas

2. **Concluding** Who are the leaders in state legislatures and what do they do?

3. **Evaluating** Which problem facing your state do you feel is the most serious? Why? What do you think the state government should do about the problem?

Critical Thinking

4. **BIG Ideas** Originally most state legislatures required only part-time lawmakers. Today many state legislators work full time. Do you think this is a good development? Why or why not?

5. **Sequencing** On a graphic organizer like the one below, write the steps a bill takes on its way to becoming a law.

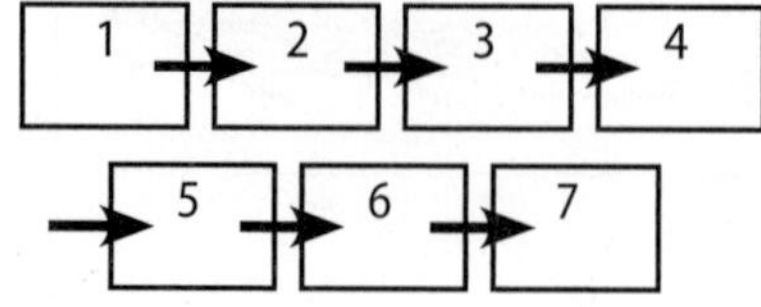

6. **Inferring** What is one problem the legislature of New Hampshire might face because of its large size? Nebraska's because of its small size?

CITIZENSHIP Activity

7. **Expository Writing** Choose one of your state representatives or senators to research. Write a brief biography of the person, focusing on his or her legislative priorities.

Study Central™ To review this section, go to glencoe.com.

An attendant rings up lottery ticket sales in Indiana for the multistate lottery drawing.

Is a lottery a good way to raise state revenue?

In a recent year Americans spent $50 billion on state lotteries—more money than on reading materials or attending movies. Half of that money was returned to the winners. After paying their other costs, the states kept about $15 billion. Many states use the money to help finance education. Although gambling is a controversial way to raise money, about four of every five states today uses the lottery. Some states feel pressure to use a lottery because of the fear that their citizens will gamble in a neighboring state. Studies have shown that the poor spend a higher portion of their income on lotteries than do middle- and upper-income people. Because the lottery is a substitute for other forms of taxation, the question has been raised, "Is a lottery a good way to raise state revenue?"

YES

State lotteries are not new. Between 1790 and 1860 more than half the states used them to finance things such as hospitals, libraries, jails, and schools. Usually, states adopt the lottery as a way to avoid raising taxes. State legislators consider the lottery a voluntary tax because people do not have to play. Executive Director Alan R. Yandow's report on the Vermont lottery is typical of many states: "As much fun as our games are, and as much fun as we have bringing them to you, we're just as serious about the good we do for Vermont. Every year since 1998, all Vermont Lottery profits go exclusively to support the Vermont Education Fund. Last year alone, that meant more than $19 million for the state's Education Fund."

—Alan R. Yandow, Executive Director of Vermont Lottery Commission

NO

Opponents of state lotteries cite the rising number of people addicted to gambling and studies that show the lottery hurts people with low incomes. Andy Rooney of CBS *60 Minutes* said, "There ought to be a law making it compulsory for anyone who reports the name of the winner of a lottery, to also give the name of all the losers. . . . Lower income people in Massachusetts . . . spent 15 times as much on gambling as people who make a decent living. . . . We approve of using some of our tax money for welfare to help the helpless. What I don't approve of is any government agency buying radio commercials to encourage the poor to waste what we give them on lottery tickets."

—Andy Rooney, CBS *60 Minutes*

Debating the Issue

1. **Identifying** About how many states use the lottery to raise money?
2. **Recalling** What income group spends the greatest percentage of its money on lottery tickets?
3. **Explaining** Why do legislators and governors often support the lottery as a means of raising state money?
4. **Concluding** What arguments for and against the lottery are most convincing?

Section Audio

Spotlight Video

The State Executive Branch

Guide to Reading

Big Idea

The Constitution gives the executive branch the power to execute, or implement, the law.

Content Vocabulary

- line-item veto *(p. 364)*
- commute *(p. 364)*
- parole *(p. 364)*

Academic Vocabulary

- issue *(p. 363)*
- guideline *(p. 364)*

Reading Strategy

Organizing As you read, identify three qualifications for governor required by most states.

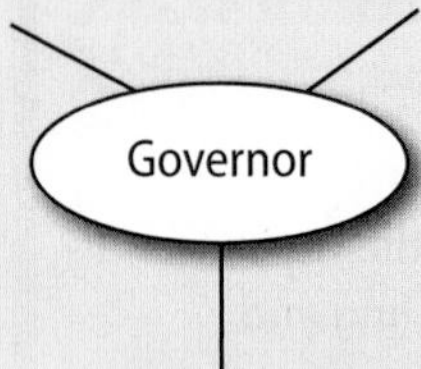

Real World Civics The most powerful job in your state is the office of governor. Who runs for this office? In the past it was men, with wives sometimes taking over the office if their husbands died while serving. In 2002, Jennifer Granholm became the first female governor elected in Michigan. Like the president of the United States, Governor Granholm runs a large government with budgets and a bicameral legislature. A major focus of her successful campaign was a "Jobs Today, Jobs Tomorrow" plan, which she promotes across the state.

▼ **Governor Granholm promotes her agenda across Michigan**

Governors Meet Governors from Iowa, Delaware, Virginia, and Arkansas grill meat at the national governors' meeting in Iowa. ***Comparing*** **What do the offices of president and governor have in common?**

Powers and Duties of the Governor

Main Idea **Governors are the chief executives in all state governments.**

Civics & You What do you know about your state's governor? Read to find out how he or she got the job.

Like the federal government, every state has an executive branch consisting of a chief executive—the governor—and a number of departments and agencies.

Becoming a Governor

Each state constitution lists the qualifications for the office of governor. In most states a governor must be an American citizen, at least 30 years old, and a resident of the state for at least 5 years. Most governors have previously been elected to other public offices or been active in state politics.

Almost all potential governors begin by gaining the nomination of a major political party, usually by winning a primary. Then that party nominee runs in the general election, usually with a lieutenant governor. Most governors serve four-year terms. In nearly every state, a governor can be impeached and removed from office for committing a crime. In some of the states, the voters themselves can take steps to unseat their governor by demanding a special "recall" election. In 2003, California voters recalled their governor and replaced him with actor Arnold Schwarzenegger.

Head of the Executive Branch

Like the president of the United States, a governor heads the executive branch of state government and fills many of the same kinds of roles. A governor is the state's chief executive, responsible for carrying out the laws of the state. To help with this job, the governor **issues,** or distributes, executive orders to a large state bureaucracy.

Powers/Duties of Governor

Charts In MOtion
See StudentWorks™ Plus or glencoe.com.

Judicial Leader
Offers pardons and reprieves; Grants parole

Ceremonial Leader
Greets important visitors; Represents the state

Chief Executive
Carries out state laws; Appoints officials; Prepares a budget

Chief Legislator
Proposes legislation; Approves or vetoes legislation

Commander in Chief
In charge of the National Guard (state militia)

Party Leader
Leads the political party in the state

Analyzing Charts

1. **Explaining** What connection does the governor have to the National Guard?
2. **Comparing** Which role of the governor would probably take the most time? Why?

The governor appoints some of the state's top officials. In most states the governor is also responsible for preparing a budget and winning its approval from the legislature. Governors also exercise various legislative and judicial duties and responsibilities.

Legislative and Judicial Duties The governor can suggest new bills and try to persuade the legislature to pass them. All governors have the power to veto bills the legislature has passed. Governors in 43 states have the power to veto specific parts of a bill—an action called a **line-item veto.** State legislatures may override governors' vetoes. Usually, however, overrides require a two-thirds ratio and are rare.

Governors also have judicial powers. A governor may grant pardons to criminals or **commute**—reduce—a sentence. Governors also have the power to grant prisoners **parole,** an early release from prison, within certain **guidelines,** or rules.

One Office, Many Roles Governors play other roles as well. Every governor heads the state National Guard. The governor is the state leader of his or her political party. The governor also serves as ceremonial leader of the state.

Until recently nearly all governors were white males. Since the 1960s, more than half the states have elected female governors. Several Southwestern states have elected Latino governors. Washington State and Hawaii have had Asian American governors. The first Asian American governor was George R. Ariyoshi of Hawaii, elected in 1974. The nation's first elected African American governor was Lawrence Douglas Wilder. He served as governor of Virginia from 1990 to 1994.

Reading Check **Recalling** What judicial powers does a governor have?

Executive Departments

Main Idea **Top officials in charge of executive departments assist the governor.**

Civics & You Have you ever needed help doing a tough job? Read to find out about the people who help the governor run the state.

Not every governor has a cabinet, but every state has a number of top officials who are in charge of executive departments and who advise the governor on important issues. Governors appoint many of these officials. In most states, however, some of these officials are elected.

While the top officials vary from state to state, most states have a few in common. In most states, a secretary of state manages elections and maintains the state's official records. An attorney general represents the state in lawsuits and gives legal advice to the governor, state agencies, and the legislature. A superintendent of public instruction (sometimes called a commissioner of education) sets educational standards and oversees the state's public schools. A treasurer collects taxes and invests state funds. An auditor reviews the record-keeping of state agencies to make certain that money is used according to state law.

In addition, every state has a number of executive departments, agencies, boards, and commissions. Some, such as departments of justice, agriculture, and labor, are like their federal counterparts. Others exist only at the state level. Most states have a department or board of health, which runs programs in disease prevention and health education. Most of the states also have departments of public works and highways, which are responsible for building and maintaining roads, bridges, and public buildings. Many states have a state welfare board to help the unemployed and people living in poverty.

Reading Check **Describing** What does a secretary of state do?

Vocabulary

1. **Define** the following terms and use each in a sentence or short paragraph related to state governors: *line-item veto, commute, parole.*

Main Ideas

2. **Identifying** What legislative powers do governors have?
3. **Describing** What role does an attorney general perform in state governments?

Critical Thinking

4. **BIG Ideas** Do you think a governor should have the power to pardon or commute the sentence of a person convicted of a crime? Why or why not?
5. In a graphic organizer like the one below, list the major roles a governor must fill.

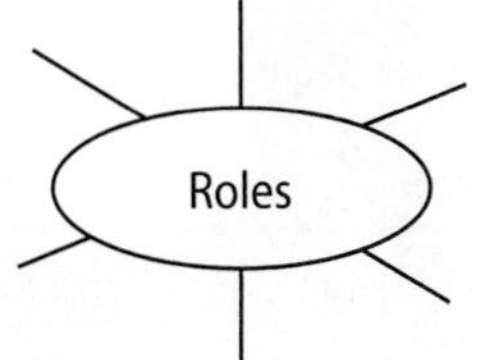

CITIZENSHIP Activity

6. **Expository Writing** Some people consider that the governorship is excellent preparation for the presidency. In what ways do you think it would prepare someone for the presidency? In what ways do you think it would not? Answer these questions in a one-page essay.

Study Central™ To review this section, go to glencoe.com.

 Section Audio

 Spotlight Video

The State Judicial Branch

Guide to Reading

Big Idea

The judicial branch is charged with interpreting the law.

Content Vocabulary

- justice of the peace *(p. 367)*
- misdemeanor *(p. 367)*
- magistrate court *(p. 367)*
- civil case *(p. 367)*
- plaintiff *(p. 368)*
- defendant *(p. 368)*
- felony *(p. 368)*

Academic Vocabulary

- portion *(p. 367)*
- intermediate *(p. 368)*
- confirm *(p. 369)*

Reading Strategy

Classifying As you read, identify each level of state courts and an example of a type of case heard in each. Write your information on a diagram like the one below.

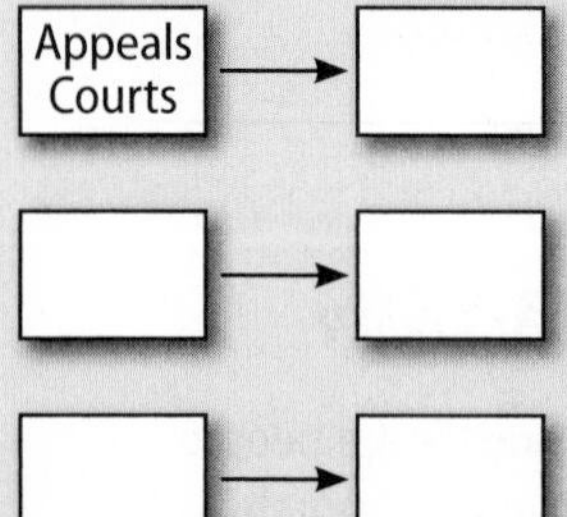

Real World Civics Most state courts are organized in the same way as the federal courts. The highest position is the chief justice of the state supreme court. When Henry Frye was appointed to that position by the governor of North Carolina in 1999, he became the first African American to serve as chief justice in the state's history. Like the U.S. Supreme Court, the North Carolina Supreme Court does not make law or rule on the facts of a case, but it does rule on errors in legal procedures and on judicial decisions regarding existing law. Chief Justice Frye presided for two years alongside six other justices in reviewing cases.

▼ **Chief Justice Henry Frye congratulated by granddaughters**

Courtroom Judges Judges are in charge of their courtrooms whether they are dealing with municipal, state, civil, or criminal cases. ***Speculating*** **Is this courtroom most likely a city or state court? Why?**

The State Court System

Main Idea **Most legal matters within a state are handled by the state's court system.**

Civics & You Would you like to serve on a trial jury? Why or why not? Read to find out how your state's court system operates.

The federal court system handles only a small **portion,** or part, of the nation's judicial business. The overwhelming majority of legal matters are settled in state courts.

How State Courts Are Organized

Most state courts are organized like the federal court system. They have a three-level system that includes courts for minor law violations and lawsuits, courts for serious crimes and large-scale civil cases, and appeals courts.

Rural Areas and Small Towns In many rural areas and small towns, the local court is called a justice court, and the judge is called a **justice of the peace.** These courts almost always handle less serious crimes, known as **misdemeanors.** An example of such a crime would be a minor theft or breaking and entering. Justice courts operate without juries. Instead, a judge or justice of the peace hears and decides each case. In most communities the voters elect these judges.

Larger Towns and Cities Larger towns may have police courts or **magistrate courts.** These courts handle minor cases such as traffic violations or disturbing the peace. They may also hear civil cases involving small sums of money, usually less than $1,000. **Civil cases** occur when a person or group takes legal action against another person or group. People convicted in these courts usually receive a small fine or a short jail term.

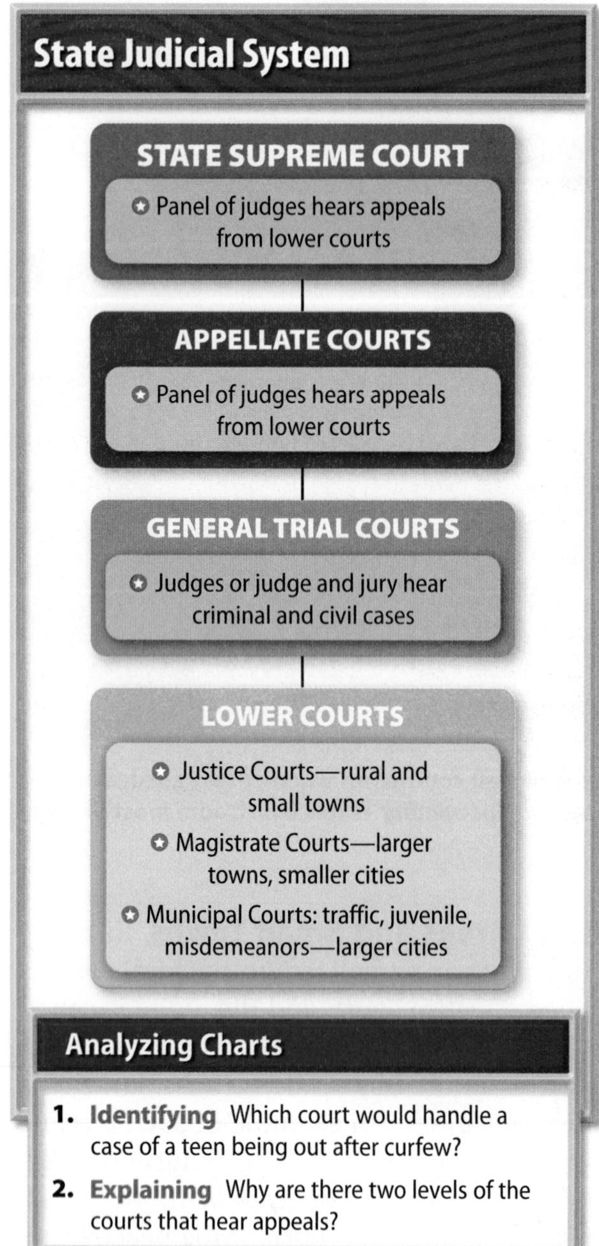

Analyzing Charts

1. **Identifying** Which court would handle a case of a teen being out after curfew?
2. **Explaining** Why are there two levels of the courts that hear appeals?

Municipal Courts Large cities may have municipal courts that serve the same purpose. These are often divided into specialized areas, such as traffic, juvenile, and small claims courts. Small claims courts decide civil cases usually involving less than $1,000. **Plaintiffs** (people filing lawsuits) and **defendants** (people being sued) speak for themselves with no lawyers present for either side.

Higher State Courts

The second level of state courts deals with more serious crimes, called felonies, and with civil cases involving large amounts of money. The third level of state courts consists of courts that consider appeals of lower-court decisions.

General Trial Court Defendants charged with **felonies**—murder, armed robbery, drug trafficking, and other major crimes—go on trial in general trial courts. Depending on the state, such a court may be called a district court, county court, common pleas court, circuit court, or superior court.

Trials in these courts may be held before a jury. In such cases, the judge's job is to make sure the trial is conducted fairly and lawfully. The judge does this by ruling on whether certain evidence or testimony is permissible, ruling on objections by attorneys in the case, and guiding the jury on points of law. In many states, the judge also decides on the penalty in case of a guilty verdict.

Appellate Courts Most states have a level of **intermediate** appeals courts. These courts review decisions made by trial courts. Appeals courts do not have juries. Instead, a panel of judges decides cases by a majority vote. If the judges find evidence that the defendant did not have a fair trial, they can overturn the lower court's decision.

Supreme Court The court of last resort in most states is the state supreme court. It reviews decisions of appeals courts and is responsible for supervising all courts in the state. State supreme courts also interpret the state's constitution and laws. A successful appeal at this level requires a majority vote of the judges hearing the case. Except for cases involving federal law or the United States Constitution, the decisions of the state supreme courts are final.

Reading Check **Explaining** Why do you think state supreme courts are called courts of last resort?

Selection of Judges

Main Idea **State judges can be elected, appointed, or chosen in a way that combines both methods.**

Civics & You Have you ever heard someone described as having good judgment? What does that phrase mean to you?

State judges are selected in different ways. Some are elected by popular vote in either partisan elections (affiliated with a political party) or nonpartisan elections (unaffiliated with a political party). Others are elected by the state legislature or appointed by the governor. Some states appoint judges for life; others for a set number of years. Still other states select judges through a combination of appointment and popular election. Under this plan, the governor appoints a judge from a list prepared by a commission, and voters either reject or **confirm** (approve) the appointed judge.

Many people think judges should not be elected. These critics fear that judges may be more concerned with pleasing voters than administering the law impartially. Other people argue that popular election of judges ensures a government "of the people, by the people, and for the people." Popular election is still commonly used to select judges. According to the American Bar Association, 38 states use some form of election at the highest level of state judiciary.

State judges usually have longer terms of office—6 to 12 years—than legislators or governors. In theory, the longer their terms, the more independent they can be.

Judges can be removed from office by impeachment. Impeachment, though, can be time-consuming. Most states have created boards to investigate any complaints about judges. If the board finds that a judge has acted improperly, it makes a recommendation to the state supreme court. The court may then suspend or remove the judge.

Reading Check **Explaining** How can state judges be removed from office?

Review

Vocabulary

1. **Use** all of the following terms to write a paragraph that summarizes the main points of this section: *justice of the peace, misdemeanor, magistrate court, civil cases, plaintiff, defendant, felony.*

Main Ideas

2. **Identifying** Of the three tiers of state courts, which one uses juries to decide guilt or innocence or to settle civil suits?
3. **Describing** What are three ways state judges are chosen in this country?

Critical Thinking

4. **BIG Ideas** In your opinion, should judges be elected, as they usually are at the state level, or appointed, as they are at the federal level? Explain.
5. **Organizing Information** On a diagram like the one below, note the three types of lower courts and where each is found.

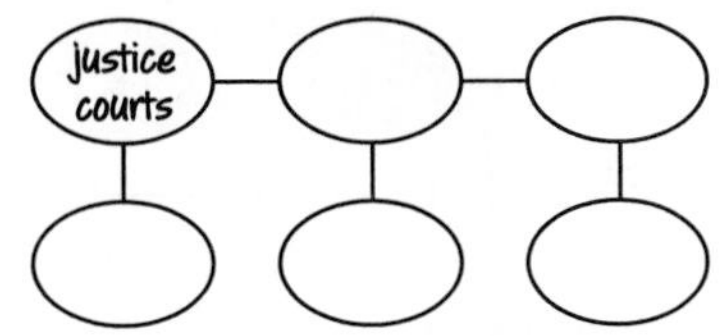

CITIZENSHIP Activity

6. **Reporting** On the Internet, do a search to find opinions on the election-versus-the-selection-of-judges argument. Summarize the main points of both sides and share your findings with the class.

Study Central™ To review this section, go to glencoe.com.

Landmark Supreme Court Case Studies

Mapp v. Ohio

The Fourth Amendment aims to protect citizens from unreasonable searches by requiring government officials to first obtain search warrants. In 1914 the U.S. Supreme Court declared that any evidence obtained without this protection cannot be used in federal court trials. How did this "exclusionary" rule find its way into state courts as well?

Background of the Case

In 1957 police officers arrived at the Cleveland, Ohio, apartment of Dollree Mapp. They were looking for evidence linking her with a gambling operation. Mapp asked to see a search warrant. The police flashed a piece of paper, but it never became clear whether the paper was actually a warrant. Although the police found no evidence of gambling, they did discover some pieces of alleged pornography. Ohio courts sentenced Mapp to prison for possession of illegal goods. They held that the pornography could be used against her in court even though the police were not searching for it under their supposed warrant.

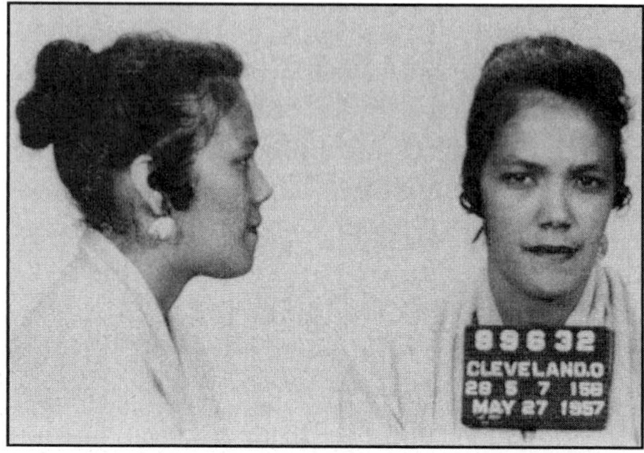

Police arrested Dollree Mapp in 1957 for possession of illegal goods found during a questioned search.

The Decision

With Justice Tom C. Clark writing the 5–4 decision, the Supreme Court issued its ruling on June 19, 1961. Clark first called on the Fourteenth Amendment's protection against certain state actions. From there he argued:

> ***"Having once recognized that the right to privacy embodied in the Fourth Amendment is enforceable against the States, and that the right to be secure against rude invasions of privacy by state officers is, therefore, constitutional . . . we can no longer permit it to be revocable [able to be canceled] at the whim of any police officer who . . . chooses to suspend [it]. . . ."***
>
> —Justice Clark, 1961

The Court declared that the presentation of evidence obtained through improper police searches is unconstitutional in state criminal courts.

Why It Matters

The *Mapp* case marked a shift in Supreme Court thinking. The Court had argued that the Bill of Rights governed only the actions of the federal government. During the 1960s, though, the Court included the states in more protections under the Bill of Rights as implied under the Fourteenth Amendment. After this case, evidence seized in violation of the Fourth Amendment could not be used by the prosecution as evidence of a defendant's guilt in any court—federal, state, or local.

Analyzing the Court Decision

1. **Explaining** On what basis did Justice Clark establish citizens' right to privacy?
2. **Concluding** How might you answer the criticism that the *Mapp* decision could hamper law enforcement?

Chapter 12

Visual Summary

The Federal System

- We live in a federal system in which there are 50 separate state governments and one federal government.
- The U.S. Constitution gives a broad range of powers to state governments.

Connecticut state capitol

State Constitutions

State constitutions are similar in structure to the U.S. Constitution. They include the following:

- A preamble
- A bill of rights
- An outline of the framework of government
- A listing of state powers and responsibilities
- A provision for local government
- The methods of amending the constitution

Florida state seal

State Legislative Branch

- State legislators are chosen by popular vote.
- The lawmaking machinery in the state legislatures is similar to that used in the U.S. Congress.
- All state legislatures, except Nebraska's, are bicameral.

State Executive Branch

- The governor is the chief executive officer in each of the 50 states.
- Important executive powers of the governor include appointing and removing officials, administering laws, planning and carrying out the budget, and commanding the National Guard.

State Judicial Branch

- State courts interpret and apply state and local laws.
- State judges are selected by the governor, by the legislature, or by the people.
- Crimes are defined by state statutes, which are laws enacted by state legislatures.

Maryland state trooper guards children

Study anywhere, anytime! Download quizzes and flash cards to your PDA from glencoe.com.

Chapter 12 ASSESSMENT

TEST-TAKING TIP

To prepare for a major exam, save weekly tests and review the questions.

Reviewing Vocabulary

Directions: Choose the word(s) that best completes the sentence.

1. ______ powers belong to the state and are NOT shared with the federal government.

A reserved
B concurrent
C bicameral
D unicameral

2. Area-based legislative districts often produce ______.

A civil cases
B misdemeanors
C felonies
D malapportionment

3. Governors have the power to ______ prisoners.

A parole
B commute
C apportion
D line-item veto

4. A ______ is a person who files a lawsuit.

A defendant
B magistrate
C plaintiff
D justice of the peace

Reviewing Main Ideas

Directions: Choose the best answer for each question.

Section 1 *(pp. 350–355)*

5. What power do the state and national governments share?

A the power to declare war
B the power to collect taxes
C the power to issue money
D the power to administer elections

Section 2 *(pp. 357–360)*

6. On what basis do states today apportion their legislatures?

A area
B parties
C population
D legislation

Section 3 *(pp. 362–365)*

7. Which of the following is a legislative duty of the governor?

A preparing a budget
B suggesting new bills
C commanding the National Guard
D all of the above

8. What state official manages elections?

A auditor
B treasurer
C attorney general
D secretary of state

Section 4 *(pp. 366–369)*

9. What courts handle traffic violations?

A trial courts
B appeals courts
C magistrate courts
D state supreme courts

10. Who selects state judges in many states?

A voters
B governors
C legislatures
D all of the above

GO ON

Critical Thinking

Directions: Base your answers to questions 11 and 12 on the cartoon below and your knowledge of Chapter 12.

11. Which of the following statements best expresses the cartoon's main idea?

A Joblessness is the root cause of most problems in society.

B States lack the resources to handle essential social services.

C Too many federal dollars are dumped into job programs.

D States farm out their job programs to small-time entrepreneurs.

12. What caused the dilemma illustrated in the cartoon?

A an increase in state taxes

B an elimination of grants-in-aid

C the outsourcing of manufacturing jobs

D the Supreme Court rulings of the 1960s

Document-Based Questions

Directions: Analyze the following document and answer the short-answer questions that follow.

The following principles are guidelines for child welfare workers in North Carolina.

- Enhancing a parent's safety enhances the child's safety.
- Domestic violence perpetrators may cause serious harm to children.
- Domestic violence perpetrators, and not their victims, should be held accountable for their action and the impact on the well-being of the adult and child victims.
- Appropriate services, tailored to the degree of violence and risk, should be available for adult victims leaving, returning to, or staying in abusive relationships and for child victims and perpetrators of domestic violence.
- Children should remain in the care of their non-offending parent whenever possible.
- When the risk of harm to the children outweighs the detriment of being separated from non-offending parents, alternative placement should be considered.

—North Carolina Well-Being and Domestic Violence Task Force

13. Which problems facing states do you think contribute to domestic violence?

14. How do you think cutting social services in North Carolina might affect children in homes with domestic violence?

Extended Response

15. Write a brief essay about the pros and cons of long terms for state judges. Include a discussion of how most states handle complaints about judges' improper conduct.

For additional test practice, use Self-Check Quizzes—Chapter 12 on glencoe.com.

Need Extra Help?

If you missed question...	1	2	3	4	5	6	7	8	9	10	11	12	13	14	15
Go to page...	352	359	364	368	353	359	364	365	367	369	353	353	360	360	369

Chapter 13 Local Government

Why It Matters

City, county, town, township, and village governments are local governments. These forms of government are closest to the everyday lives of people and have a great effect on their daily activities.

Civics ONLINE
Visit glencoe.com and enter QuickPass™ code CIV3093c13 for Chapter 13 resources.

Chapter Audio

BIG Ideas

Section 1: City Governments

People form governments to establish order, provide security, and accomplish common goals. A variety of forms of city government has been developed to meet different needs.

Section 2: County Governments

People form governments to establish order, provide security, and accomplish common goals. County governments somewhat mirror city governments but also meet different needs and provide different services.

Section 3: Towns, Townships, and Villages

Political and economic institutions evolve to help individuals and groups accomplish their goals. Town meetings and township governments developed early in U.S. history and have remained active to the present.

Main Street, Northampton, Massachusetts

FOLDABLES™ Study Organizer

Identifying Main Ideas Foldable Make the following Foldable to help you identify the main ideas about city, county, and township governments and their responsibilities and roles.

Step 1 Fold down the paper from the top right corner so edges line up. Cut off the leftover piece.

Step 2 Fold the triangle in half. Then unfold the top layer one inch from the left edge.

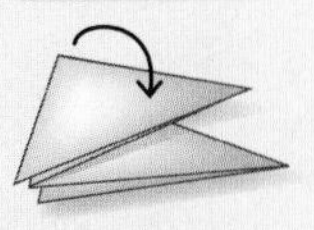
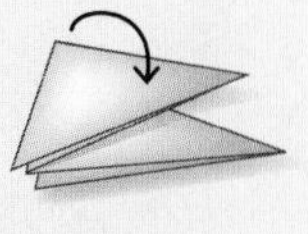

The fold will form an X making four equal sections.

Step 3 Cut on the fold, stopping in the middle. Draw an X on one tab and label the other three as shown.

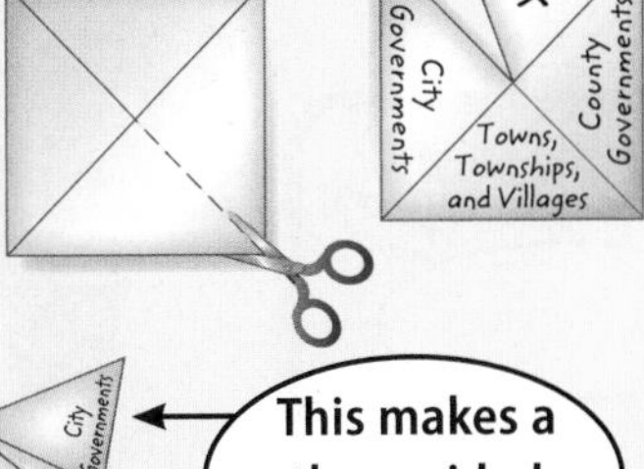

Step 4 Fold the X flap under the flap and glue or tape together.

This makes a three-sided pyramid.

Reading and Writing As you read the chapter, make note of the details of the different levels of government for cities, counties, and townships. Write a summary paragraph of your details.

Section Audio   Spotlight Video

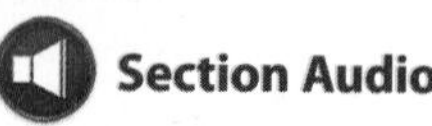

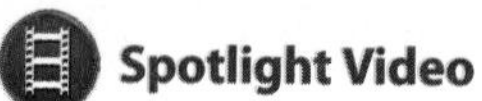

Section 1

City Governments

Guide to Reading

Big Idea

People form governments to establish order, provide security, and accomplish common goals.

Content Vocabulary

- incorporate *(p. 377)*
- city charter *(p. 377)*
- home rule *(p. 377)*
- ordinance *(p. 378)*
- strong-mayor system *(p. 379)*
- weak-mayor system *(p. 379)*
- at-large election *(p. 380)*
- special district *(p. 382)*
- metropolitan area *(p. 382)*
- suburb *(p. 382)*

Academic Vocabulary

- dominate *(p. 379)*
- furthermore *(p. 379)*
- reluctant *(p. 379)*

Reading Strategy

Organizing As you read, complete a web diagram like the one below by listing services that city governments provide.

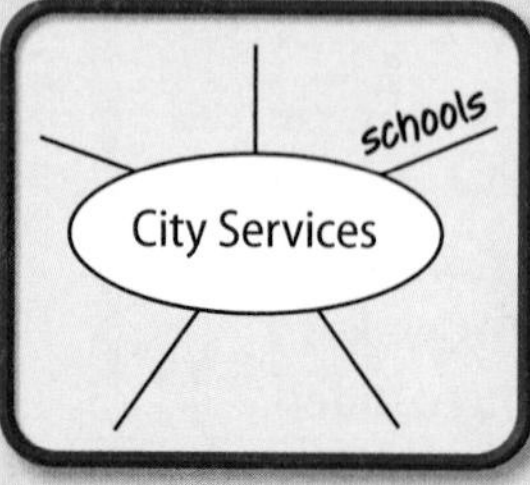

Real World Civics On September 8, 1900, Galveston, Texas, was overrun with water from the Gulf of Mexico. Hurricane winds traveling over 100 miles (161 km) per hour swept through Galveston Island in what residents have often called the "worst disaster" in America. Thousands died. The city rallied immediately. Emergency meetings were called to provide necessary services to residents. The city government then built a seawall and raised the entire city. Engineers and construction workers have made every effort to ensure that this tragedy never happens again.

▼ **Topsy-turvy destruction in Galveston, Texas**

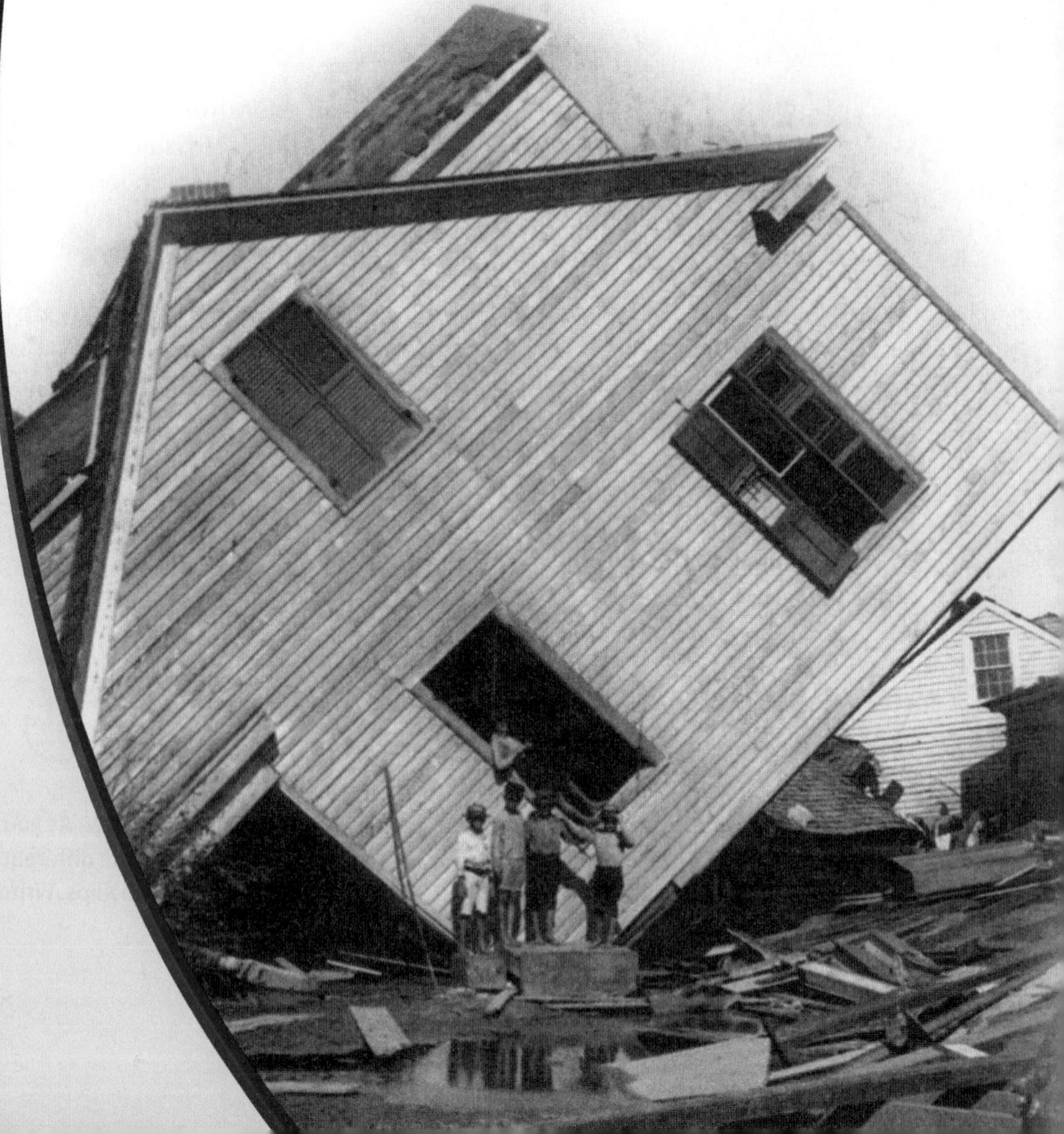

Chokoloskee, Florida This city hall houses the various departments of city government. ***Identifying*** **What document grants the power of a local government to become a city?**

How Are Local Governments Formed?

Main Idea **Local governments are created by the states.**

Civics & You What has your city or town government done for you lately? Read more to find out how local governments are created.

The United States has become a mostly urban nation over the past century. In 1900 only about one-third of the nation's 76 million people lived in urban areas. Today about three-fourths of the 300 million Americans do. Although they are the closest units of government to the people, local governments have no legal independence. The U.S. Constitution does not even mention the existence of local governments. They are created by, and are entirely dependent on, the state. State constitutions usually establish the powers and duties of local governments.

The City Charter Most states define a municipality as an **incorporated** place—a locality with an officially organized government that provides services to residents. A city is a municipal government. New cities are created every year as people who live in urban communities incorporate. They do this by applying to the state legislature for a **city charter,** a document that grants power to a local government. A community must meet certain general requirements to obtain a charter. For example, the community may be required to have a population of a certain minimum size. A city charter is much like a constitution, describing the type of city government, its structure, and its powers.

Home Rule For many decades there has been a movement to grant home rule to cities. **Home rule** allows cities to write their own charters, to choose their own type of government, and to manage their own affairs, although they still have to follow state laws.

Reading Check **Summarizing** How are city governments created?

The Mayor-Council Form

Main Idea **A common form of city government features an executive and a legislature.**

Civics & You Can you name your mayor or a council member? Read to find out what these officials do.

Every municipal charter provides for the type of government the community will have. Today urban areas in the United States use one of three basic forms of municipal government. These are the mayor-council form, the commission form, and the council-manager form.

A Division of Power

Until the early twentieth century, almost all American cities had a mayor-council form of government, which remains a common form of government today. It is the form of government preferred by the largest cities.

The mayor-council form follows the traditional concept of separation of powers. Executive power belongs to a mayor, and legislative power to a council. Voters elect a mayor and the members of a city council. The mayor is the chief executive of the city government and is responsible for overseeing the operation of administrative offices. Often the mayor appoints the heads of departments, such as public works, planning, police and fire protection, and other offices.

The City's Legislature The council acts as the legislature, approving the city budget and passing city laws, which are usually known as **ordinances.** Most city councils have fewer than 10 members, who usually serve four-year terms. Some cities are divided into voting districts called wards. Each ward elects a representative to the city council. In other cities, some or all of the council members are known as members-at-large, elected by the entire city.

Strong Mayors Two main types of mayor-council government exist, depending on the power given to the mayor. These two types are the strong-mayor system and the weak-mayor system.

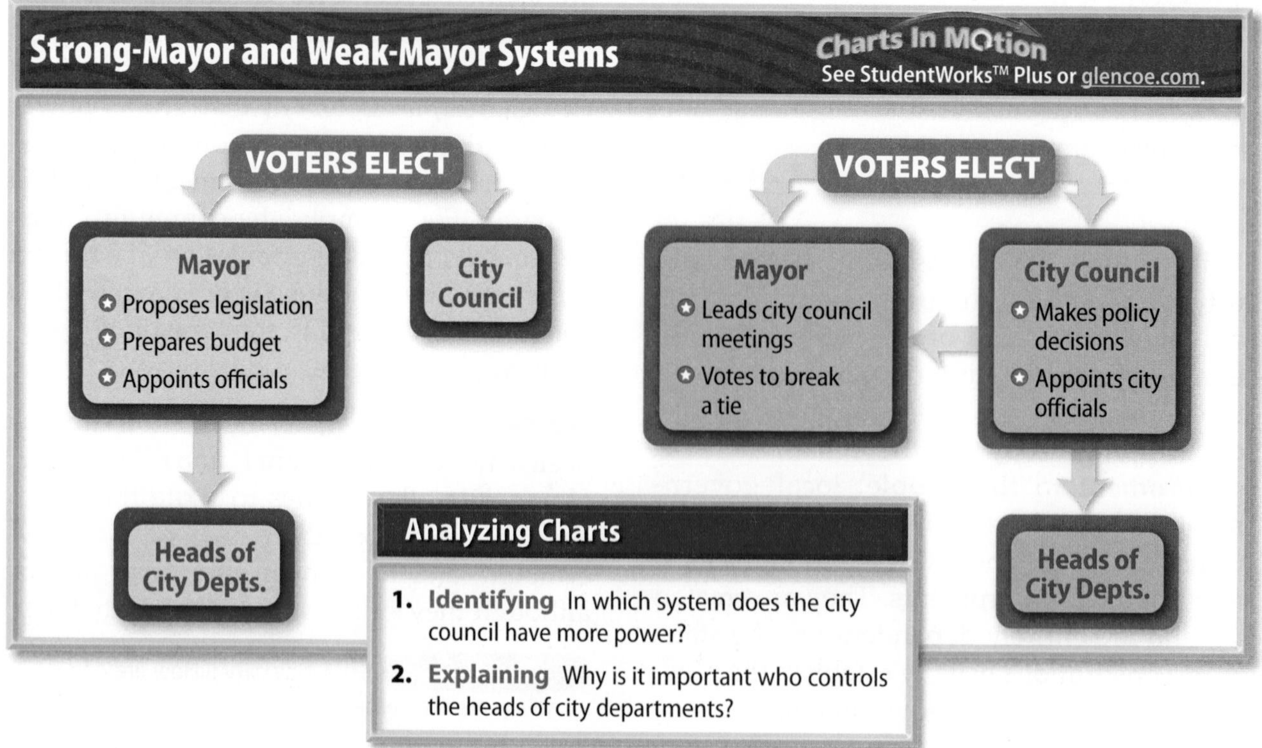

Analyzing Charts

1. **Identifying** In which system does the city council have more power?
2. **Explaining** Why is it important who controls the heads of city departments?

Most large cities operate under a **strong-mayor system.** The mayor has strong executive powers, such as the power to veto ordinances the city council passes, appoint various city officials, and write the city budget. Strong mayors tend to **dominate,** or control, city government because membership on the city council, even in large cities, is usually a part-time job. **Furthermore,** because council members are elected by wards, they focus on issues that are important to their parts of town. By contrast, a strong mayor usually works full-time, has assistants, and represents the entire city.

Weak Mayors Under a **weak-mayor system,** the mayor's authority is limited. The council, not the mayor, appoints department heads and makes most policy decisions. The mayor usually presides over council meetings but votes only in case of a tie. The weak-mayor system dates from the nation's earliest days. Former colonists, tired of the injustices they suffered at the hands of the British government, were **reluctant,** or unwilling, to grant any official too much power.

Successful Mayor-Council Governments The success of the mayor-council form of government depends to a large extent on the individual who serves as mayor. In the strong-mayor system, a politically skillful mayor can provide effective leadership. Under the weak-mayor plan, because official responsibility is in many hands, success depends upon the cooperation of the mayor and the council.

Reading Check **Analyzing** What are the mayor and council's roles in decision-making under a weak-mayor form of government?

Student Web Activity Visit glencoe.com and complete the Chapter 13 Web Activity.

TIME™ Teens in *Action*

A Mayor with Class

Michael Sessions, 18, has a new after-school activity: he is running a small town! Sessions was sworn in as the mayor of Hillsdale, Michigan, in 2005. He joined the race as a write-in candidate and beat the former mayor by just two votes.

The young mayor has been involved in politics ever since a fourth-grade trip to the state capitol in Lansing. But it was not until 2003, when his dad lost his job when the auto plant he worked for moved to Mexico, that Michael was moved to take action. "The people of Hillsdale are hard-working, and I knew I had to try to bring jobs here and retain them," he says. "I ran because I wanted to get involved."

When Sessions walks the halls of Hillsdale High School, kids greet him with "Hello, Mayor" and high fives. He is managing to keep a 3.25 GPA in courses that include Spanish, computer science, and accounting, while working as a part-time teacher's aide. All that, plus he is running a town with a $20 million annual budget. "I'll be a student from 7:50 to 2:30," Sessions says. "And then I'll work on mayor stuff from 3 to 6."

Among his duties are signing off on the budget, running Hillsdale's city council meetings, and exercising emergency powers in the event of a crisis.

Sessions serving as mayor

Making a Difference — **CITIZENSHIP**

Explaining Why did Michael decide to run for mayor?

American Biography

John Liu (1967–)

In the Flushing, Queens, section of New York City, voters made history in 2001. They elected John C. Liu to represent their district on the City Council. Liu became the first Asian American to win elected office in New York City—or anyplace else in New York State. "We are in a new era," Liu declared in his victory speech.

Liu, who describes himself as a "Flushing boy," immigrated to Queens from Taiwan at age 5. He attended New York City public schools and, later, State University of New York, before taking a job at an accounting firm. Public service paved his way to the city council. Liu did volunteer work in junior high and high school. In college, he took part in student government. As an adult, Liu worked to improve Flushing by forming community action groups.

As a member of the city council, Liu faced the task of not only representing Flushing but of uniting one of the city's most diverse districts. In a post-election pep talk, Liu told supporters, "The issues facing this district affect us all, and we will solve these issues together." As a member of the Council's Committee on Education, Liu worked to raise standards in public schools and invest city resources in the students. He also instituted programs to fund high-tech upgrades to local schools.

Making a Difference — CITIZENSHIP

John Liu has lived most of his life and participated in public service in the New York City area.

Explaining **How did Liu make history in 2001?**

The Council-Manager and Commission Forms

Main Idea **Two other local government types are the council-manager and the commission.**

Civics & You Do you think a town can be run like a business? Read to find out what form of government adopts this idea.

Two forms of government that started in the early 1900s are the council-manager and commission forms. The council-manager form of government is a popular form of city government today. When it first appeared in 1912, it was seen as a way to reform corrupt or inefficient mayor-council governments.

Under the council-manager form, the city council, as the legislative body, appoints the manager in much the same way that a school board might appoint a superintendent. The manager recommends a budget, oversees city departments, and deals with personnel matters. The manager reports to the council as a whole. The council can hire and remove the manager by a majority vote. Most managers have specialized training in areas such as budgeting, financial management, and planning.

In many smaller cities with managers, council members are elected in **at-large elections.** This means they run in citywide elections rather than representing only one district. Some people believe this system forces members to consider the interests of the entire city instead of only looking out for the concerns of their own neighborhoods.

The Commission Form

The commission form of government was invented a few years before the council-manager form. Only a handful of cities continue to use it.

Executives and Legislators A commission government has no separation of legislative and executive powers. Instead, separate departments, each of which handles a different set of responsibilities, govern the city. Some of the most common departments are police, fire, finance, and health.

The elected heads of these departments, called commissioners, perform executive duties for their particular departments. They also meet together as a commission, with legislative power to pass city ordinances and make policy decisions.

Serious Flaws The commission form of municipal government developed after a devastating hurricane struck Galveston, Texas, in 1900. Thousands died and the city was nearly destroyed. City leaders decided that a commission government was the best way to handle the emergency.

Since that time, however, other cities have found that a commission government is not always efficient in running a city. Without clear leadership, a commission is often unable to set and meet goals. Each commissioner is likely to concentrate primarily on his or her own department, without considering the problems of the city as a whole.

Recognizing its drawbacks, most cities that once used a commission system have switched to a council-manager or mayor-council form of government.

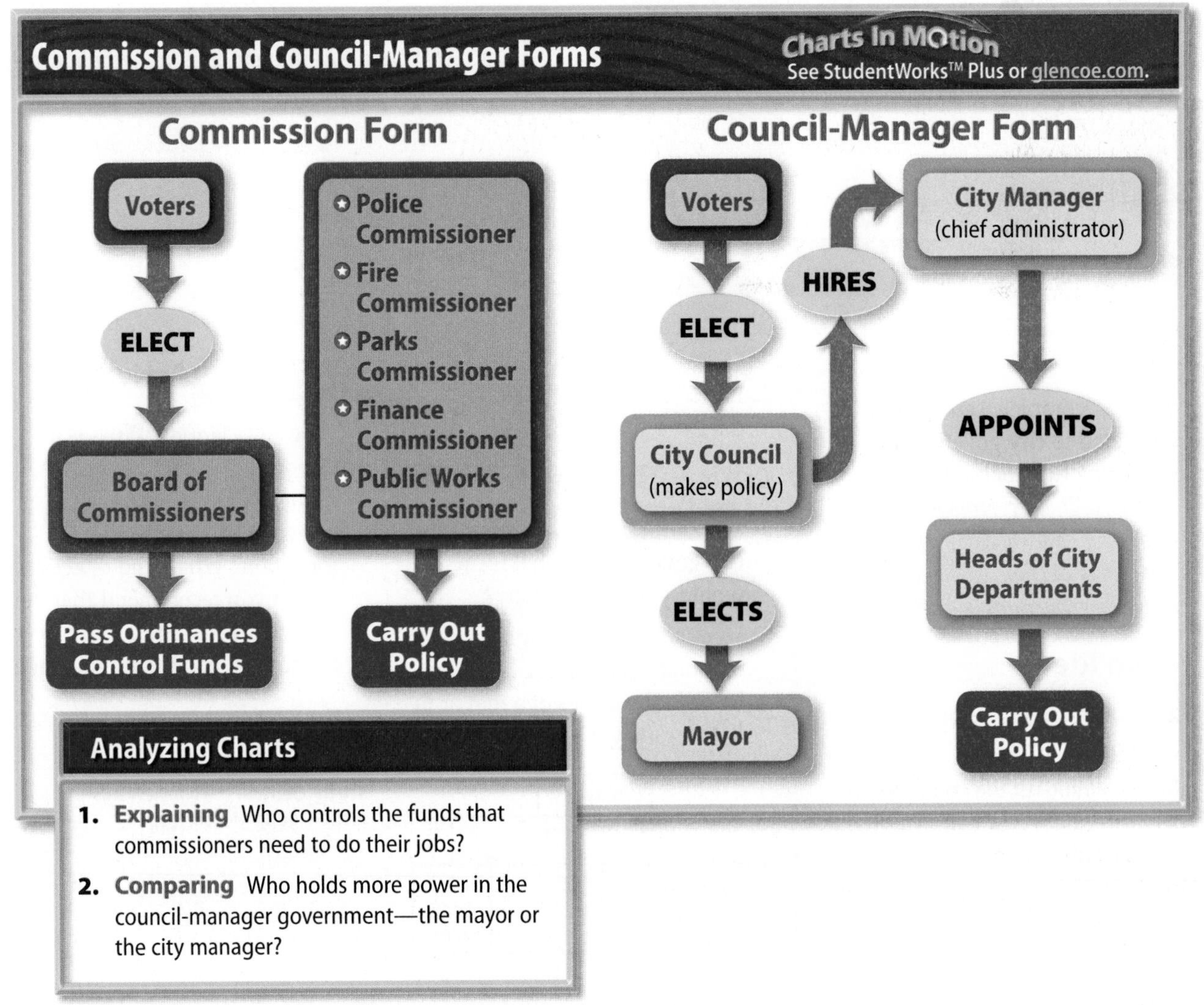

Analyzing Charts

1. **Explaining** Who controls the funds that commissioners need to do their jobs?
2. **Comparing** Who holds more power in the council-manager government—the mayor or the city manager?

Other Units of Government

Two other important concepts in municipal government are the special district and the metropolitan area. The **special district** is a unit of government that deals with a specific function, such as education, water supply, or transportation. A board or commission, which may be elected or appointed, runs a special district. Special districts are the most numerous types of local government, because in some states several kinds of special districts overlap most cities. The local school district is the most common example of a special district.

A **metropolitan area** is a central city and its surrounding suburbs. **Suburbs** are communities near or around cities. A metropolitan area may also include small towns that lie beyond the suburbs. The U.S. Census Bureau has an official name for urban concentrations made up of a central city and suburbs with a combined population of 50,000 or more—Metropolitan Statistical Areas.

Growing Suburbs In the United States since the 1950s, suburbs have expanded around central cities. As a result, often the suburban population has become much greater than that of the central city. For example, Detroit's population dropped from nearly 2 million in 1950 to about 870,000 in 2006, while its suburbs now have more than 3 million people.

The growth in population and the expansion of business in metropolitan areas have created problems in transportation, pollution, law enforcement, and land management. Some metropolitan areas have created a council whereby the central city joins with its suburbs to make area-wide decisions about growth and services, such as mass transit. Today, with fuel supplies and costs at issue, mass transit systems are under consideration in many cities.

Reading Check **Contrasting** How does the council-manager government differ from the mayor-council government?

Vocabulary

1. **Write** complete sentences related to city government: *incorporate, city charter, home rule, ordinance, strong-mayor system, weak-mayor system, at-large election, special district, metropolitan area, suburb.*

Main Ideas

2. **Describing** What is the purpose of city charters?
3. **Explaining** In the commission form of government, who holds legislative power?
4. **Explaining** Why was the council-manager form of city government developed?

Critical Thinking

5. **BIG Ideas** If you created a city government, what form would you use and why?
6. **Identifying** Use a graphic organizer like the one below to identify the duties of a mayor in a strong-mayor government.

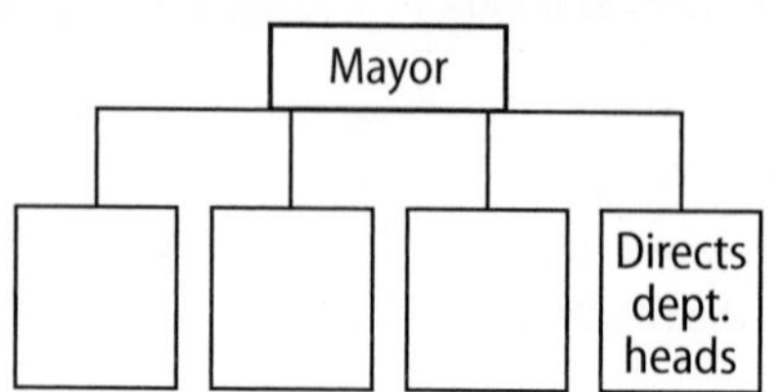

CITIZENSHIP Activity

7. **Expository Writing** What is an important issue in your community that you would like to bring before the city council for action? What kind of action would you recommend that the council take? Write a letter to the council addressing the issue.

Study Central™ To review this section, go to glencoe.com.

Guide to Reading

Big Idea
People form governments to establish order, provide security, and accomplish common goals.

Content Vocabulary
- county *(p. 384)*
- county seat *(p. 384)*

Academic Vocabulary
- levy *(p. 385)*
- estimate *(p. 386)*

Reading Strategy
Identifying As you read, identify the county officials elected by voters in most counties on a graphic organizer like the one below.

Section Audio　Spotlight Video

County Governments

Real World Civics Counties provide many enjoyable moments and services to their residents—especially the elderly. County departments that serve seniors often have Web sites that allow residents to browse through a list of helpful resources such as long-term care facilities, transportation options, hotlines, and other services. County departments also provide access to information about laws that affect the lives of seniors. In addition, counties provide a wealth of recreational outlets for older citizens, from field trips to classes that offer lifelong learning opportunities.

▼ **Seniors share activities at a county-run senior center**

Protection and Safety County sheriffs provide protection and enforce laws meant to keep residents safe. Highway patrol is one protection. ***Speculating*** **Why do you think it is necessary to have county sheriffs in addition to city police?**

Organization

Main Idea **The nation's more than 3,000 counties show great variety in size, population, and government.**

Civics & You Have you ever had to call 911 or buy a license for your dog? Read to find out what level of government handles these activities in most states.

The **county** is normally a state's largest territorial and political subdivision. The U.S. Census Bureau recognizes more than 3,000 counties or countylike units in the nation. All states, except Connecticut and Rhode Island, are divided into counties. There is great variety among American counties. Los Angeles County, California, for example, has about 10 million residents, while 67 people live in Loving County, Texas, according to the 2000 census. San Bernardino County, California, has more land area than the states of Vermont and New Hampshire combined. Texas has 254 counties, and Delaware and Hawaii have 3 each. Alaska and Louisiana do not even use the word *county.* In Alaska, counties are called boroughs; in Louisiana, they are known as parishes.

What Is a County Seat?

When many Midwestern and Southern states were mapping out counties during the nineteenth century, officials were concerned that all citizens would have access to county services. The idea was that residents who lived in the farthest corners of a county should be able to get to the county courthouse and back by horse and buggy in the same day. That is why states in these regions have so many relatively small counties. The county courthouse was the center of government, serving as a headquarters for law enforcement, record keeping, and road construction as well as courts. The towns where the county courthouse is located are called **county seats.**

Reading Check **Explaining** How were county seats originally chosen?

Functions

Main Idea **County governments perform many different duties and provide an array of services to residents.**

Civics & You What does the word *sheriff* mean to you? Read to find out what a modern-day sheriff does.

With modern transportation and the growth of cities, county government has changed. In some areas, cities now provide many of the services that counties once handled. However, county governments have grown in importance and assumed functions that city governments once handled, from sewer and water service to mass transit systems.

Who Runs a County?

A board of three to five elected commissioners, or supervisors, governs most counties. Most board members serve four-year terms. The board acts as a legislature, adopting ordinances and the annual budget, **levying** taxes, and enforcing laws. County governments have a variety of organizations. These include the commission-manager, commission-elected executive, and strong commission forms.

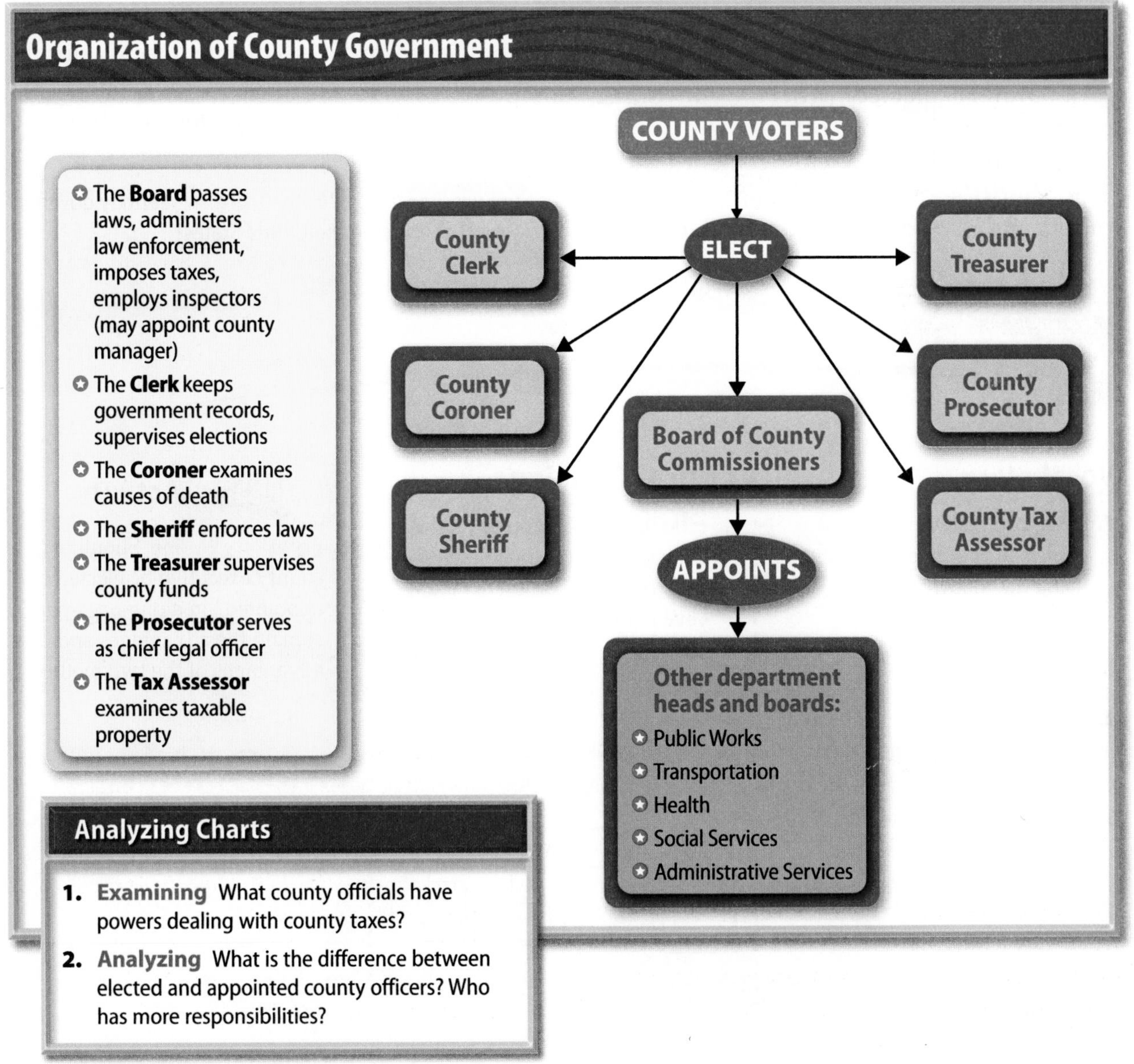

Analyzing Charts

1. **Examining** What county officials have powers dealing with county taxes?
2. **Analyzing** What is the difference between elected and appointed county officers? Who has more responsibilities?

Like a City—but Different As their responsibilities have grown, many counties have adopted a form of government in which the county board operates only as a legislature. In some cases, the board of commissioners appoints a county manager, who acts much like a city manager in running the county government.

In other cases, counties have created a new elective office, that of a chief administrative official. This person, often called the county executive, handles all executive responsibilities. Whether appointed or elected, the county manager or executive appoints top officials and manages the organization. The board of commissioners functions alongside this leader, but only as a legislative body.

Sheriffs, DAs, and More

Separately elected officials run some county administrative offices. The sheriff is a county's chief law enforcement officer. The sheriff's department enforces court orders and manages the county jail. In some counties, the sheriff's department shares law enforcement duties with a separate police department. The district attorney (DA) is the county's prosecutor. The DA investigates crimes, brings charges against suspected lawbreakers, and prosecutes the cases in court.

Other county functions are led by officials who may be appointed or elected. The assessor examines all taxable property within the county and **estimates,** or approximately values, how much it is worth. The county's property tax is based on the assessor's estimate. The county finance director or treasurer supervises the county's funds. An auditor makes sure that the county's money is spent within the requirements of state and local law. A county clerk keeps official government records. A coroner works closely with the police department to establish the causes of unusual or suspicious deaths.

Reading Check **Identifying** What body governs most counties in the United States?

Vocabulary

1. **Write** complete sentences related to county government using the following terms: *county, county seat.*

Main Ideas

2. **Explaining** Why are counties relatively small in the South and Midwest?
3. **Identifying** Many counties today provide services that cities used to handle. What are some services counties often provide today?

Critical Thinking

4. **BIG Ideas** Do you think the United States needs both city and county governments today? Give reasons to support your answer.
5. **Identifying** In a graphic organizer like the one below, list the other boards the county commissioners appoint.

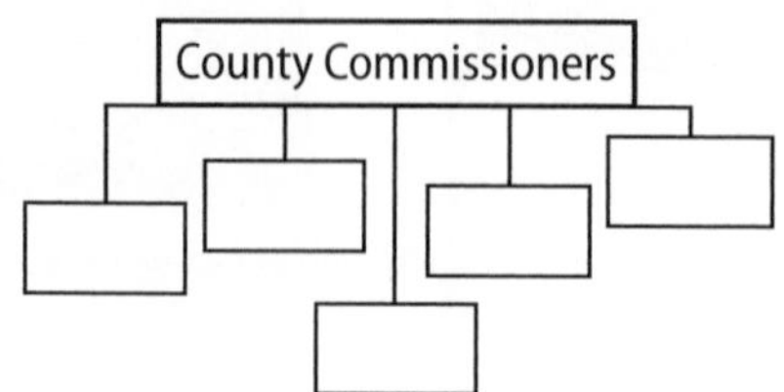

CITIZENSHIP Activity

6. **Expository Writing** Should a county executive be elected or appointed? In a one-page paper explain the advantages and disadvantages of the two methods.

Study Central™ To review this section, go to glencoe.com.

Section 3

Towns, Townships, and Villages

Guide to Reading

Big Idea

Political and economic institutions evolve to help individuals and groups accomplish their goals.

Content Vocabulary

- town *(p. 388)*
- town meeting *(p. 388)*
- township *(p. 389)*
- village *(p. 390)*

Academic Vocabulary

- complex *(p. 389)*
- similar *(p. 389)*
- decline *(p. 390)*

Reading Strategy

Identifying As you read, name the different forms of government below the county level by completing a graphic organizer like the one below.

Forms of Government

Real World Civics Neither snow nor hail nor sleet can stop the people of Woodbury, Vermont, from casting their votes in a town meeting. The citizens here have a history of participation in local government that started in 1806. The town meeting provides a forum for community members to voice their feelings on matters ranging from local issues—such as school budgets—to world events. Vermonters are known for their strong sense of civic duty as well as military service during wartime, dating back to the Revolutionary War.

▼ Citizens of Woodbury, Vermont

Town Government

Main Idea **New England town government is one of the oldest forms of government in the United States.**

Civics & You Think about a meeting you attended recently. Was it well organized and productive? Read to learn about a meeting that served as a government.

In 1654 a group of men in Sudbury, Massachusetts, gathered to discuss how to divide the land. The town has seen many changes since that day, but some things have not changed. Today people in Sudbury still meet to discuss issues.

Towns in New England

Just as most states are divided into counties, counties are often divided into smaller political units. In the New England states, these units are called **towns.** In many other states, especially in the Midwest, they are called townships. Like county and city governments, town governments receive their authority from the state.

The relationship between town or township governments and their surrounding counties varies. In New England, town governments handle the needs of most small communities, while counties are mainly judicial districts. In all other states that have townships, county and township governments share authority. County governments tend to be more important in the South and the West where there may be no townships.

New England town government is one of the oldest forms of government in the United States. In early **town meetings,** citizens—rather than elected representatives—made the important decisions. Town meetings are an exercise in direct democracy—as opposed to the representative democracy common throughout most of the United States. Residents in New England still come together once a year to discuss and vote on local ordinances, taxes, and budgets.

Citizens Speak A town meeting in Grafton, New Hampshire, is held in a fire station because of the huge crowd. ***Hypothesizing*** **Why do you think so many people want to attend town meetings?**

TIME™

Political Cartoons

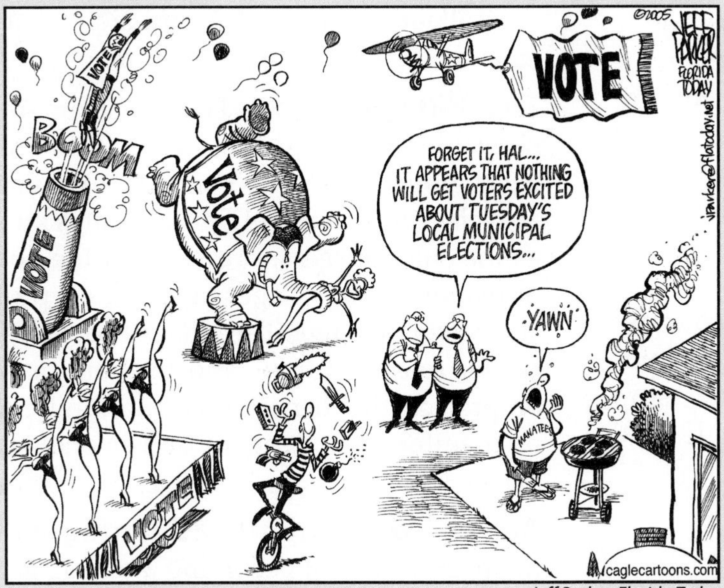

—Jeff Parker, Florida Today

Every year, more than half of all Americans do volunteer work

role in it. One of the responsibilities of citizens is to help make their

of volunteer grou… small. Perha… dad who…

In this image, cartoonist Jeff Parker focuses on turnout for local elections.

1. **Whom do the two men wearing neckties represent?**
2. **What do all the performers symbolize?**
3. **How is the voter depicted?**
4. **What do you think explains the voter's attitude?**

Limitations Because town meetings occur so rarely, they are useful only for broad policy making, not the everyday details of government. So each New England town elects a group of officials called "selectmen" to run local government. Selectman, a very old title, now applies to women as well as to men. Towns may also elect executives such as a clerk and a treasurer.

Over the years, as New England towns grew and their governments became more **complex,** or involved, direct democracy became impractical. Some New England towns have replaced the traditional town meetings with representative town meetings. In these meetings, elected representatives make the decisions instead of the people as a whole. Other towns have eliminated the meetings altogether and instead have a town council that runs the local government.

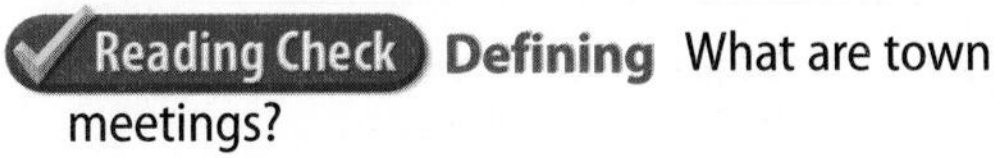

Reading Check **Defining** What are town meetings?

Townships and Villages

Main Idea **Townships and villages are the smallest units of local government.**

Civics & You Did you know that there are villages all over America? Read to find out more about this type of government.

New York, New Jersey, and Pennsylvania were organized somewhat differently from New England. Their counties are divided into **townships,** which are smaller than New England towns but have **similar,** or almost the same, governments.

As the United States expanded westward, it acquired new land. Congress divided the land into uniform square blocks, usually six miles wide and six miles long—originally designed to be an hour's buggy ride to the township hall for any resident.

Responsibilities As settlers moved west, they set up local governments called civil townships. Midwestern townships kept the borders established by Congress, so today many appear perfectly square on a map.

Most townships elect a small body of officials known as a township committee, board of supervisors, or board of trustees. They have legislative responsibilities and usually hold regular meetings citizens may attend.

Townships have **declined,** or become less, in importance as cities and counties have taken on more of township functions. In some instances, county and township governments work together to provide local services.

Village Government

A **village** is the smallest unit of local government. Villages almost always lie within the boundaries of other local governments, such as townships or counties. Communities with small populations often have no need for their own government; county or township governments provide for most of their needs. Occasionally, however, community members may be dissatisfied with the services the county provides, or they may want to set up their own school system. In that case, they may organize the community as a village and request permission from the state to set up a village government.

The Village Board The government of most villages consists of a small board of trustees elected by the voters. Some villages also elect an executive. This official is known as the chief burgess, president of the board, or mayor. Large villages might hire a professional city manager. The village board has the power to collect taxes and to spend money on projects that benefit the community, such as maintaining streets or sewer and water systems.

Advantages and Disadvantages The main drawback of becoming a village is that residents often have to pay higher taxes to support the extra layer of government. In return, however, they usually receive better services. Becoming a village also tends to upgrade the community's status, making it more attractive to visitors and potential new residents and businesses.

Reading Check **Explaining** What is an advantage in setting up a village government?

Vocabulary

1. **Explain** how the following terms differ: *town, town meeting, township, village.*

Main Ideas

2. **Describing** How did town government begin in the United States?
3. **Explaining** What are the basic responsibilities of village government?

Critical Thinking

4. **BIG Ideas** If you lived in a small community, would you support the establishment of a village government? Why or why not?
5. **Comparing** On a Venn diagram like the one below, compare township and village governments.

CITIZENSHIP Activity

6. **Expository Writing** Do you think that too many smaller local governments, such as townships and villages, in an area reduces or improves the quality of services residents receive? Explain your answer in a short paper.

Study Central™ To review this section, go to glencoe.com.

Chapter 13

Visual Summary

Local Government

- Local governments provide many important services.
- When residents of a community find some particular reason to organize legally, they seek to incorporate a municipality, which may be called a village, city, or town.

City Governments

- Cities develop local governments when they are granted special legal status by the state legislature through incorporation.
- The major forms of city government are the mayor-council form, the council-manager form, and the commission form.

Buying a house in a town

- A special district is a unit of government created to deal with a specific function, such as education or transportation.
- A metropolitan area is a central city and its surrounding suburbs.

Cityscape of Chicago, Illinois

County Governments

- County governments were first set up to provide a few basic services that residents could not provide for themselves.
- The responsibilities of a county are usually determined by the state constitution and state laws.

Towns and Villages

- Counties are often divided into smaller political units. These units are called towns or townships.
- A village is the smallest unit of local government.

Fire departments serve townships

STUDY TO GO

Study anywhere, anytime! Download quizzes and flash cards to your PDA from glencoe.com.

Chapter

13 ASSESSMENT

Standardized Test Practice

TEST-TAKING TIP

When taking an exam, follow instructions exactly.

Reviewing Vocabulary

Directions: Choose the word(s) that best completes the sentence.

1. A city law is known as a(n) ______.

A council
B home rule
C charter
D ordinance

2. A unit of government that deals with a specific function is called a(n) ______.

A suburb
B county
C special district
D metropolitan area

3. A state's largest territorial and political subdivision is normally a(n) ______.

A suburb
B county
C special district
D metropolitan area

4. ______ governments handle the needs of most small communities in New England.

A town
B village
C city
D township

Reviewing Main Ideas

Directions: Choose the best answer for each question.

Section 1 *(pp. 376–382)*

5. In which form of city government does the city council appoint department heads?

A commission form
B weak-mayor system
C strong-mayor system
D council-manager form

6. What has established the power and duties of most local governments?

A home rule
B city charters
C state constitutions
D the United States Constitution

Section 2 *(pp. 383–386)*

7. Which state has boroughs rather than counties?

A Texas
B Alaska
C California
D Louisiana

8. Which county official enforces court orders?

A sheriff
B coroner
C assessor
D district attorney

Section 3 *(pp. 387–390)*

9. What are New England town meetings used for?

A trying civil cases
B governing day-to-day
C making general policy
D electing representatives

10. Which of the following is the smallest unit of local government?

A city
B village
C township
D board of trustees

GO ON

Critical Thinking

Directions: Base your answers to questions 11 and 12 on the cartoon below and your knowledge of Chapter 13.

11. Based on the cartoon and facts in Chapter 13, who most likely enacted the ban in the headline?

A a city council

B a county sheriff

C a county assessor

D a board of trustees

12. Which of the following statements best reflects the cartoonist's viewpoint?

A He objects to the ban on cell phone use.

B He thinks the ban will prevent accidents.

C He is undecided about the need for the ban.

D He believes citizens should know local laws.

Document-Based Questions

Directions: Analyze the document and answer the short-answer questions that follow.

The following passage is from the 2006 State of the City address by Salt Lake City's Mayor Ross C. "Rocky" Anderson.

> *In its 6th edition,* Places Rated Almanac *rated Salt Lake City as the best place to live in North America. That is as true today as in 1999, when the rating was published. As part of a dazzlingly vibrant and diverse community, we benefit from a strong economy and myriad cultural and artistic opportunities. With its captivating scenery, brilliant vistas, and incomparable recreational opportunities, Salt Lake City has long been an international destination for outdoor enthusiasts. We are unique in having such convenient access to so many remarkable, different aspects of life.*
>
> *People around the country are taking note of our extraordinary quality of life. Just a few months ago,* Outside *magazine listed Salt Lake City as one of 18 "new American Dream Towns." The Sierra Club commended our efforts to preserve the character of our neighborhoods and prevent sprawl development. Moreover,* Men's Health *magazine named Salt Lake City the most smoke-free city in the country, and ranked Salt Lake City as the 5th best city in the nation for men, with an A+ ranking.*
>
> —Mayor Ross C. "Rocky" Anderson

13. What qualities do the mayor, magazines, and the Sierra Club attribute to Salt Lake City?

14. How might these qualities benefit the city's economy?

Extended-Response Question

15. Compare and contrast the strong-mayor and weak-mayor systems of city government. Mention a benefit of each system.

STOP

For additional test practice, use Self-Check Quizzes—Chapter 13 on glencoe.com.

Need Extra Help?

If you missed question...	1	2	3	4	5	6	7	8	9	10	11	12	13	14	15
Go to page...	378	382	384	388	378	377	384	386	388	390	378	378	378	378	378

Chapter 14

Dealing With Community Issues

Why It Matters

Communities across America face a variety of public policy issues every day. Among the most critical are those involving education; crime prevention; social programs to help poor, elderly, sick, and disabled citizens; and environmental issues.

Civics ONLINE Visit glencoe.com and enter QuickPass™ code CIV3093c14 for Chapter 14 resources.

Chapter Audio

BIG Ideas

Section 1: How a Community Handles Issues

A democratic society requires the active participation of its citizens. When dealing with public policy, a community and its leaders must consider many factors in making their plans.

Section 2: Education and Social Issues

A democratic society requires the active participation of its citizens. Solving educational and social problems, including crime, requires the input of all members of a community.

Section 3: Environmental Issues

Scarcity requires individuals and groups to make choices about using goods and services to satisfy their wants. Many environmental problems that communities face stem from overuse and misuse of natural resources.

Parade celebrating New York City American Legion post

FOLDABLES™ Study Organizer

Comparing Foldable Make the following Foldable to help you compare the different educational, social, and environmental issues faced by communities.

Step 1 Fold a sheet of paper in half from top to bottom. Cut the paper in half across the middle fold line.

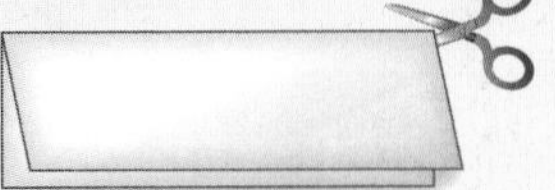

Step 2 Fold the two papers in half from top to bottom.

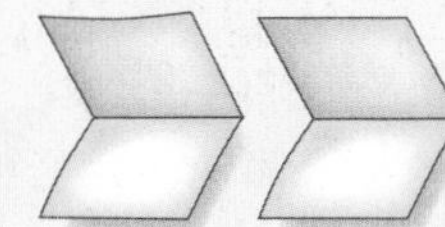

Step 3 Tape the edges of pieces together as shown (overlapping the edges slightly) to make an accordion-like paper line. Label each chapter section as shown.

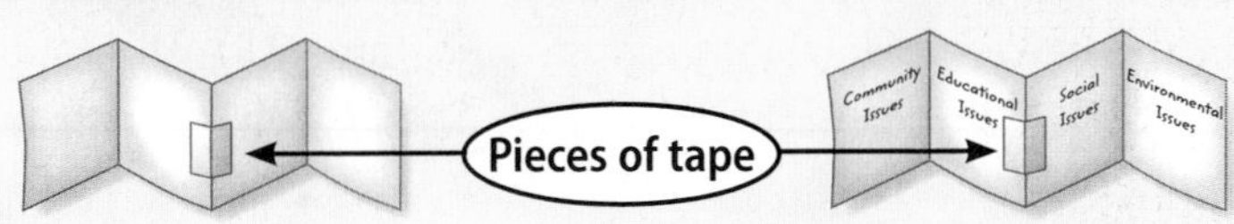

Reading and Writing
As you read the chapter, make notes on the back of each corresponding section about the issues faced by communities. Compare the details for each issue to identify common problems.

Guide to Reading

Big Idea
A democratic society requires the active participation of its citizens.

Content Vocabulary
- policy *(p. 397)*
- public policy *(p. 397)*
- planning commission *(p. 398)*
- short-term plan *(p. 398)*
- long-term plan *(p. 398)*
- infrastructure *(p. 399)*
- priority *(p. 399)*
- resource *(p. 399)*
- master plan *(p. 399)*

Academic Vocabulary
- convince *(p. 397)*
- professional *(p. 398)*
- specific *(p. 399)*

Reading Strategy
Analyzing As you read, list on a web diagram like the one below the people who might serve on a community planning commission.

Section Audio   Spotlight Video

Section 1

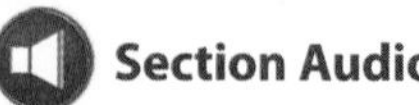

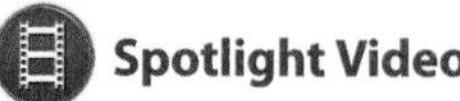

How a Community Handles Issues

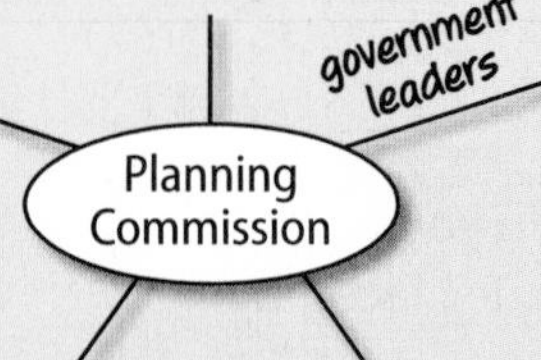

Real World Civics If you disagree with laws, you can change them. Wendy Hamilton lost her sister and nephew in a car accident with a drunk driver more than 20 years ago. Even before that, she lost an 18-year-old cousin who was riding with a friend who had been drinking. Since then, Hamilton has worked to lower the blood alcohol level that indicates drunkenness and to raise the legal drinking age. She has served as president of MADD (Mothers Against Drunk Driving).

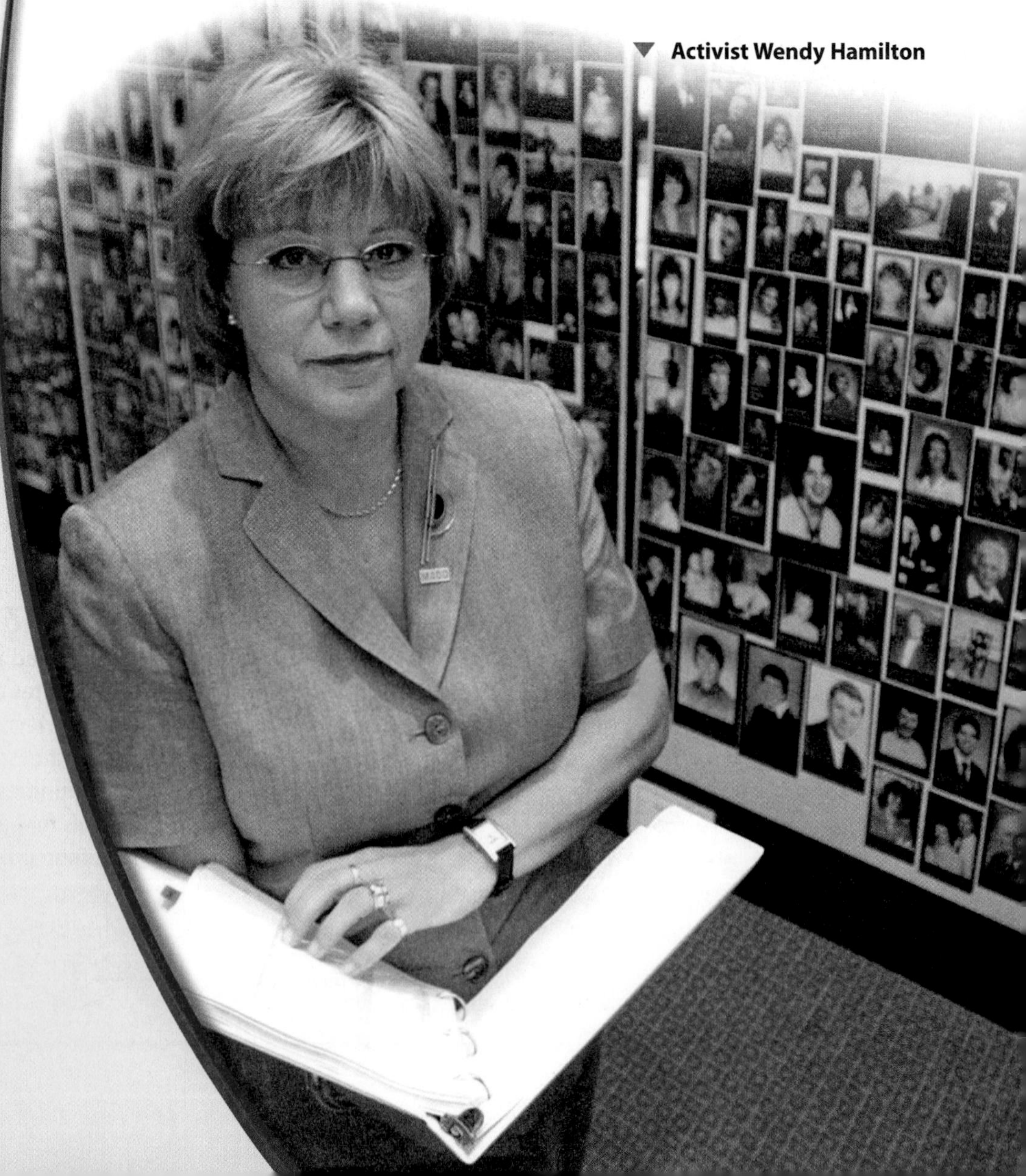
▼ Activist Wendy Hamilton

Public Policy

Main Idea **Public policy, or how a community deals with issues, has many sources.**

Civics & You Do you disagree with something your community has decided that affects your life? Read to find out how some people worked to change their communities' approaches to problems.

Do you think going to school should make you sick? A group of families in Sugar Hill, Georgia, did not think so. When they found out a new school would be built between two garbage landfills, the families began to study possible health risks. They formed a group called Community Awareness Regarding Education and Safety (CARES).

The organization sets up committees to continue research and contact the media. Although the school did open, the organization **convinced,** or persuaded, the school board to monitor toxic substances in the building. Mindy Clark, a cofounder of CARES, explained, "We're going to fight. We know too much to walk away."

Mindy Clark and CARES worked to change a policy. All organizations, such as schools, businesses, and governments, have **policies,** or sets of rules or guidelines they follow when making decisions and carrying out actions. Most businesses, for example, have policies about hiring, promoting, and firing employees.

What Is Public Policy? **Public policy** is concerned with the decisions and actions of government as it deals with issues and problems that affect the entire community. Public policy may deal with a specific issue; the decision to build or not build a road is an example. Public policy also deals with issues that are wider in scope, such as health care and the environment. A public policy is not necessarily a law. It may not even be written down.

Volunteering Citizens, such as these volunteers in Miami, support many public cleanup programs.
Identifying **What issues need volunteer support in your community?**

Sources of Public Policy

Where do ideas for public policy originate? They may come from the government. Political parties, interest groups, or the media may suggest them. Another important source of policy ideas, especially at the local level, is private citizens.

Often a single person can have a great impact on government policies. In 1980, after a drunk driver killed her 13-year-old daughter, Cari, a California woman named Candy Lightner launched a campaign to change government policy toward drunk driving. Lightner explained, "I promised myself on the day of Cari's death that I would fight to make this needless homicide count for something positive in the years ahead." She founded Mothers Against Drunk Driving (MADD), which soon became a nationwide organization. Lightner helped MADD bring about the passage of more than 1,000 tough new laws against drunk driving.

Reading Check **Contrasting** What is the difference between a law and public policy?

TIME™ Teens in *Action*

Amelia Pennewell

When it comes to helping her community, Amelia Pennewell, 16, of Livermore, California, believes in jumping in feet first.

QUESTION: You started an organization called Amelia's Socks. How did you get started?

ANSWER: When I was nine, I was on my way to my aunt's for Thanksgiving dinner. We drove past people who were lined up outside a building. Some people didn't have socks. My mom explained that they were homeless or hungry, and when the doors opened they would get a hot meal. I wanted to help. I thought I could use my money to buy them some socks to help keep them warm. I asked my teacher, Mr. Menendez, to help. I started Amelia's Socks, which is now a nonprofit organization. People help by donating clothing to the group.

Q: How has it worked out?

A: The first year I collected more than 3,000 pairs of new socks, about 1,000 hats, and 450 pairs of mittens. I have given more than 80,000 pairs of new socks over the past seven years. And I've sent socks to Iraq, Mexico, Afghanistan, and to victims of Hurricane Katrina.

Amelia and her volunteers

ACTION FACT:
Pennewell was a finalist in the Do Something 2005 Brick Awards. When she's not collecting socks and mittens, Pennewell runs track and plays soccer.

Making a Difference — CITIZENSHIP

What was the result of Amelia's efforts in the first year?

Future Plans

Main Idea **When ideas for public policy come before a community, leaders must consider many factors.**

Civics & You Have you ever had to decide between two things you wanted to do or buy? How did you make your decision? Read to find out how many communities approach this dilemma.

Many who formulate public policy look at what is likely to happen in the future and plan for it now. A growing number of local governments have planning commissions to oversee community growth. A **planning commission** is an advisory group that may include government leaders, businesspeople, local residents, and **professionals,** or skilled people, such as architects and traffic engineers.

Short-Term and Long-Term Plans

Local governments and their planning commissions make both short-term and long-term plans. A **short-term plan** is a policy meant to be carried out over the next few years. For example, granting a builder a permit to construct apartments is a short-term plan.

A **long-term plan** is a broader policy meant to serve as a guide over the next 10, 20, or even 50 years. To make long-term plans, a planning commission makes educated guesses about a community's future needs.

For example, the population of a community is growing, and forecasts show great growth in the future. A situation like this one raises questions for local government. Will heavier traffic overload roads? Should the town build new highways or promote public transportation?

Civics ONLINE

Student Web Activity Visit glencoe.com and complete the Chapter 14 Web Activity.

What other demands will the growing population put on the town's **infrastructure**—its systems of roads, bridges, water, and sewers? How will the town pay for needed improvements?

Evaluating Priorities and Resources

The answers to these questions about planning usually depend on two things—priorities and resources.

Priorities are the goals a community considers most important or most urgent. In setting priorities, a community must decide what it values most. For example, is it more important to have a thriving commerce center or a peaceful place to live? A community must also determine its **specific,** or exact, goals and rank them in order of importance. It may decide, for example, that its top goal is to attract new businesses. Lesser goals may include improving services, preserving open spaces, and upgrading schools.

After a community sets its priorities, it must determine what resources it has and how to use them. **Resources** are the money, people, and materials available to accomplish the community's goals. Suppose, for example, that a community has decided to improve its public transportation system. Is there enough money to build and maintain a new fleet of buses for busy routes?

Creating a Master Plan

After setting priorities and calculating resources, a planning commission makes concrete decisions about the community's future. It usually spells these out in a **master plan.** This plan states a set of goals and explains how the government will carry them out to meet changing needs over time. If the local government accepts the plan, it becomes public policy, and the government is responsible for carrying it out.

Reading Check **Explaining** What should be considered when deciding on the priorities of a community?

Vocabulary

1. **Define** the following terms and use them in sentences related to public policy: *planning commission, short-term plan, long-term plan, infrastructure, priority, resource, master plan.*

Main Ideas

2. **Identifying** Provide two examples of public policies that deal with specific issues.
3. **Explaining** What is the purpose of a master plan?

Critical Thinking

4. **Discussing** What role does setting priorities play in planning for the future?
5. **BIG Ideas** In a graphic organizer like the one below, identify four ways that ideas for public policy are initiated.

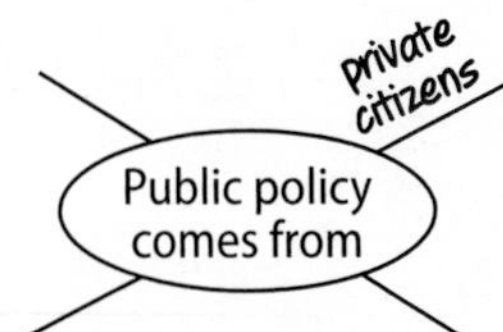

CITIZENSHIP Activity

6. **Descriptive Writing** Imagine you are a community leader creating a master plan for a city park. You want to plan for new attractions. You also want to ensure that the park retains its natural beauty. How do you balance the two goals? Describe your plan in a one- to two-page paper.

Study Central™ To review this section, go to glencoe.com.

 Section Audio  Spotlight Video

Guide to Reading

Big Idea

A democratic society requires the active participation of its citizens.

Content Vocabulary

- charter school *(p. 402)*
- tuition voucher *(p. 403)*
- community policing *(p. 405)*
- welfare *(p. 406)*

Academic Vocabulary

- role *(p. 401)*
- impose *(p. 401)*
- ratio *(p. 404)*

Reading Strategy

Summarizing As you read, on a web diagram like the one below, list four challenges that schools face.

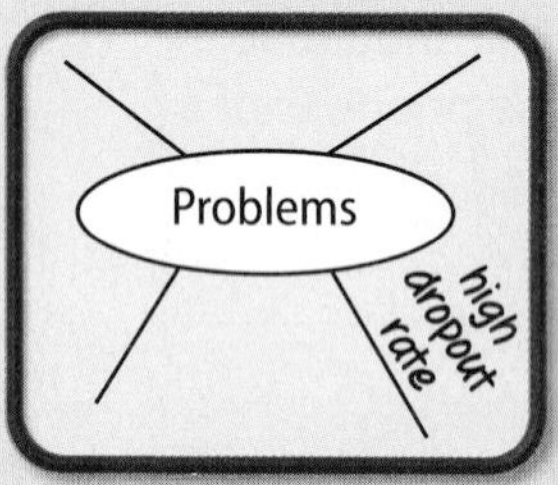

Education and Social Issues

Real World Civics Community issues usually affect all citizens and sometimes include education. The Navajo Nation chose President Joe Shirley and his wife, Vikki Shirley, to guide the largest Native American tribe in the United States. Many issues are on President Shirley's agenda, including alcohol education in the Navajo Nation. Vikki Shirley lost her 29-year-old daughter to a drunk driver. Using her status as a Navajo leader, Vikki Shirley has devoted much of her time to touring other tribes' reservations with her anti-drunk-driving message and encouraging a ban on drinking on the reservations.

▼ **Vikki Shirley speaks to Navajo groups**

TIME™

Political Cartoons

—Marshall Ramsey/Copley News Service

Marshall Ramsey, the creator of this cartoon, is making a comment on higher education.

1. **What does the yellow crane stand for, and what impact is it having?**
2. **How is this situation affecting students?**
3. **Does Ramsey support or oppose increases in college tuition? How do you know?**

Public Education

Main Idea **Schools today are trying to solve a variety of difficult challenges with innovative solutions.**

Civics & You Is your school doing a good job of educating students? How do you know? Read to find out how the federal government is trying to grade schools like yours.

Since the U.S. Constitution does not mention education, public education has always been under the general control of the individual states. In colonial times, some local governments took the lead and began offering free public education to children. The practice spread until it became almost universal after the Civil War. Today about 55 million students attend the nation's public elementary and secondary schools. Some 7 million other students go to private schools.

As public education grew, local school districts raised most of the money for schools and determined how students would be taught. In 1816, Indiana set up the first modern public school system. Today in most states, elementary and secondary education remains a local responsibility under state guidelines. The basic administrative unit for public schools is the local school district.

The federal government, though, plays an important **role,** or function, in education, providing aid to local schools in several forms. Its share of the total funding is less than 10 percent, but it **imposes,** or demands, certain rules on local schools. These rules include prohibiting gender discrimination in school activities and saying how schools must meet the needs of students with disabilities.

The steadily increasing role of the federal government in public education has been a source of controversy. Some critics claim that the federal government is overstepping its constitutional bounds.

A Landmark Law

In 2001 President George W. Bush signed a landmark education bill known as the "No Child Left Behind Act." This law authorized $26.5 billion in federal spending on education, but it also added to the rules that local schools must follow. For example, all students in grades three through eight must take a series of state tests in reading, science, and math. Bush hoped this law would establish a system of new accountability measures for schools that do not perform well. Bush claimed that "[t]he fundamental principle of this bill is that every child can learn. We expect every child to learn, and you must show us whether or not every child is learning."

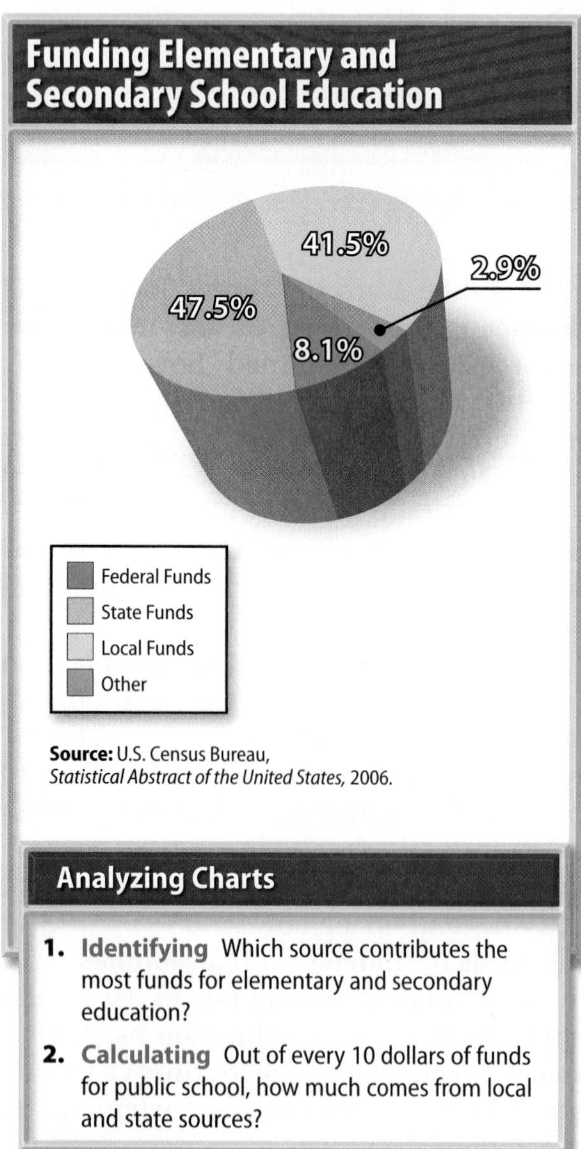

Source: U.S. Census Bureau, *Statistical Abstract of the United States*, 2006.

Analyzing Charts

1. **Identifying** Which source contributes the most funds for elementary and secondary education?
2. **Calculating** Out of every 10 dollars of funds for public school, how much comes from local and state sources?

Closing the Gap The biggest education issue facing state governments is how to equally provide high-quality schooling to all students. Currently there is a large spending gap between wealthy and poor school districts. The gap occurs because many districts depend heavily on property taxes to fund the schools, and property values vary greatly from one district to another. A community with a healthy, expanding tax base, for example, has far more to spend per student than a community that has not benefited from the same growth in property tax values.

To raise more money, some schools have turned to businesses. The placement of soft drink vending machines in schools is a controversial example of alternative ways to raise money for education.

Challenges to Schools and Teachers

Among the nonfinancial problems facing schools today are low test scores, high dropout rates, and crime and violence on school property. Dealing with dropout rates and violence requires a wide range of remedies, many of which necessarily occur outside the schools. Remedies must take place outside schools because the problems are rooted in broader social problems of poverty, broken families, drug abuse and alcoholism, and crime and violence in the streets.

Charter Schools To combat poor academic performance, more than 30 states now permit the creation of **charter schools.** These schools receive state funding, but they are excused from meeting many public school regulations. Some educators believe that this freedom will encourage charter schools to be more innovative than conventional public schools. Former public school teachers and community groups may establish and run charter schools.

American Biography

Charlotte Hawkins Brown (1883–1961)

The life of **Charlotte Hawkins Brown** from her birth in Henderson, North Carolina, until her death, was centered on education and helping others. The granddaughter of slaves, Brown and her family moved to Massachusetts, where she attended Massachusetts public schools in Cambridge and the State Normal School in Salem.

In 1900, Charlotte Brown met Alice Freeman Palmer, the president of Wellesley College, who became her lifelong trusted friend and adviser. Palmer provided funds for Brown's education to become a teacher. In 1901 Charlotte Brown, just 18 years old, began her teaching career in a missionary school, the Bethany Institute, in Sedalia, North Carolina. When the mission school closed because of a lack of money, the town's residents asked her to stay and start a new school.

Brown agreed and opened the Palmer Memorial Institute. Through her efforts, the Palmer Institute became one of the leading academies for African American children in the nation.

Beyond being a pioneer of African American education, Brown was an eloquent spokesperson for equal rights and woman suffrage.

Making a Difference

Charlotte Hawkins Brown made important contributions in many fields. ***Comparing*** **What do you think was Brown's most important accomplishment? Explain.**

Pros and Cons Opponents of charter schools argue that they take away funds from public schools and that they are likely to enroll many of the better students, leaving "problem" students behind in the public schools. Supporters of charter schools, however, claim that charter schools simply offer alternatives to public schools, and there seems to be no sign that they are luring away the best students from public schools.

The Voucher Controversy Another educational alternative is for cities and states to give parents **tuition vouchers**—a kind of government money order. Parents can use these vouchers to pay for their children to attend private schools. Only a few places, such as Cleveland (Ohio), Milwaukee (Wisconsin), and the state of Vermont, have experimented with vouchers.

Teachers' unions oppose vouchers because they feel vouchers funnel education funds out of the public school system and into private schools. Other opponents contend that vouchers violate the First Amendment because they can be used to pay tuition at religious schools. The Supreme Court has ruled that it is constitutional to use public money (vouchers) at religious schools as long as the funds are granted directly to the parents or guardians, and are not used to promote the religious mission of the school.

Privatization A more extreme alternative to the traditional management of schools by school boards is for private companies to contract with local districts to run the schools. These corporations promise to improve the quality of education and to do it more cheaply than public school administrations, while making a profit for themselves.

Community Center "Drums not Drugs" is the theme of this teen performance in Seymour, Connecticut. ***Explaining*** **What teen programs do community centers offer?**

The Rise of Mass Testing As mentioned earlier, the 2001 federal education bill requires states to test all students in reading, math, and science, in grades three through eight. Some states also require students to pass competency tests in order to be promoted to the next grade or to receive a high school diploma at the end of the 12th grade.

Competency tests and other forms of mass testing are given to provide certain measures. These tests are used to:

- provide comparative scores for individual students
- indicate a student's strengths or weaknesses
- assess the effectiveness of teachers, schools, and even entire districts.

Supporters of competency testing claim that it holds schools and teachers to high levels of accountability, but many teachers' organizations oppose such testing. They claim that it forces teachers to spend valuable classroom time teaching students how to pass tests instead of how to understand the subjects they are supposed to be learning.

Describing What is a school voucher?

Crime and Social Programs

Main Idea **Battling crime and ending social problems associated with poverty are two of the biggest challenges governments face.**

Civics & You Think about how crime affects the community where you live. What do you believe should be done about it?

Federal and state prisons hold more than 2 million inmates. The **ratio,** or percentage, of prisoners per 100,000 population in the United States is among the highest in the world.

Crime and Poverty

Crime rates are usually highest in large cities, where poverty and crime often go hand in hand. For poor people who have struggled with dead-end, minimum-wage jobs, robbery or drug dealing may seem like an easier way to make a living. For others, having a normal job may not seem possible.

Many of the poorest inner-city residents drop out of school early and spend much of their time on the streets. Crime is often the only way of life they know.

Police Forces

America's large cities have many more police officers than in all the nation's state, county, and small-town law enforcement units combined. As a result, urban police are the main crime-fighting force in the nation.

Police Functions More than 3,000 county sheriffs and their deputies are the main law enforcement presence in rural areas. In addition, every state has a law enforcement agency known as the highway patrol or state police. These agencies' main responsibility is highway safety, but they often play an important role in investigating crimes and capturing suspects.

A major function of police departments is to enforce the law, but most of the daily work of uniformed police officers involves keeping the peace. Peacekeeping activities might include handling neighborhood disputes and providing services, such as directing traffic. Much of the credit for the recent drop in crime is given to the use of **community policing.** Under this program, police become a visible presence in neighborhoods, walking or riding bicycles, and getting to know local residents. The program also works to get residents involved in neighborhood watch efforts.

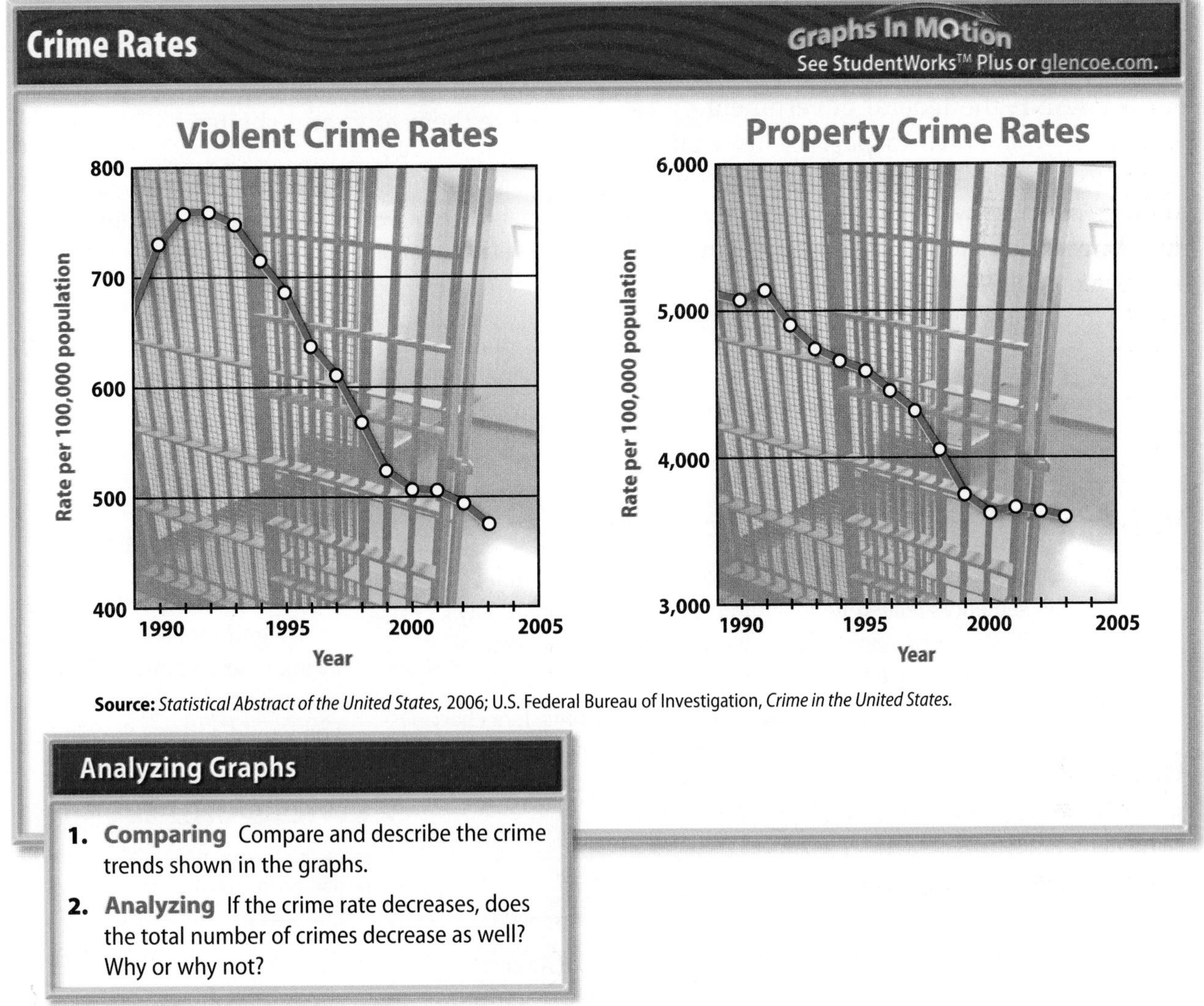

Source: *Statistical Abstract of the United States,* 2006; U.S. Federal Bureau of Investigation, *Crime in the United States.*

Analyzing Graphs

1. **Comparing** Compare and describe the crime trends shown in the graphs.
2. **Analyzing** If the crime rate decreases, does the total number of crimes decrease as well? Why or why not?

Social Programs

Our government tries to help Americans who suffer from ill health, old age, poverty, and physical disabilities with **welfare** programs. Policymakers have long struggled over the problems of reducing poverty and administering government financial aid to the best effect. Critics of welfare claim that it undermines self-respect among the poor and encourages dependency. Defenders of welfare assert that it is the only way many poor families can avoid homelessness and hunger.

Welfare Reform After years of debate, in 1996 Congress created a program called Temporary Assistance for Needy Families (TANF). It ended Aid to Families with Dependent Children, a 60-year-old federal program, and gave more power to the states to set the rules for future welfare eligibility. Under TANF, the federal government gives money to the states to pass on as welfare payments. Each state has considerable authority to decide who is eligible for welfare and how much money each person gets, but there are some federal rules attached. There is a five-year lifetime limit on receiving welfare, and states are required to develop job-training programs for the poor to help them leave the welfare rolls.

The number of people on welfare dropped tremendously following passage of TANF. In 1995 about 14.2 million people received welfare benefits. By 2007 there were slightly fewer than 4 million recipients. In 45 states, welfare caseloads dropped by more than 50 percent.

Some critics of the law claim, however, that its successes result mostly from the booming economy of the late 1990s. The labor shortage of the period made it relatively easy for unemployed welfare recipients to find work. Some observers fear that if the economy were to slump, as it did in 2001, people being forced off the welfare rolls will be helpless—without jobs *and* without the so-called safety net of welfare to at least ensure them food and shelter.

Reading Check **Explaining** According to defenders of welfare, who benefits most from welfare programs?

Vocabulary

1. **Define** the following terms and use them in sentences related to public education: *charter school, tuition voucher, community policing, welfare.*

Main Ideas

2. **Defining** What is the privatization of schools?
3. **Explaining** Why do some critics believe the voucher program violates the First Amendment?

Critical Thinking

4. **BIG Ideas** Do you think the federal government plays too great a role in education? Explain.
5. **Making Comparisons** In a chart like the one below, compare the argument for and against charter schools.

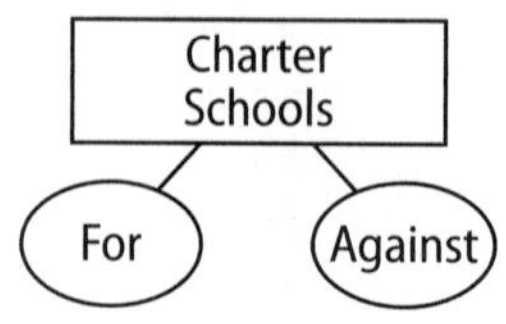

CITIZENSHIP Activity

6. **Expository Writing** What is the most significant social issue facing your community? In a one-page paper, discuss how you would address the issue.

Study Central™ To review this section, go to glencoe.com.

Financial Literacy

College Costs: Planning Ahead

If you want to go to college, it pays to plan ahead. The cost of tuition, fees, and room and board for a year of undergraduate education ranges from $12,127 at the average four-year public university to $29,026 at private universities.

How can I meet the cost of college? A scholarship and other financial aid can help, but most of us still need to save more and spend less. Here are some possibilities to consider:

- **Create a budget and keep to it** Budget the items that are under your control.
- **Work** You can attend school full-time and still work part-time, or work full-time and attend school part-time.
- **Get your degree in less than four years** Completing a bachelor's degree in less than four years is difficult, but it is possible.
- **Save regularly** Set a goal to put a specific amount in a savings account monthly.
- **Federal student aid** If you do not have the resources to pay for college, you may apply for financial aid. Different forms include federal grants, student loans, and college work-study. Check with your school to find out which programs are available.

Average Annual College Costs

Public Institutions	
Tuition and mandatory fees	$5,491
Room and board	$6,636
Total College Base Costs	**$12,127**
Books and supplies	$894
Transportation	$852
Other expenses	$1,693
Total College Expenses	**$15,566**

Source: The College Board, Trends in College Pricing 2005.

Analyzing Economics

Researching Select a college you would like to attend and contact the financial aid office. Through the office, gather information on all types of financial aid available to incoming freshmen students. Report your findings.

Environmental Issues

Guide to Reading

Big Idea
Scarcity requires individuals and groups to make choices about using goods and services to satisfy their wants.

Content Vocabulary
- environmentalism *(p. 409)*
- solid waste *(p. 409)*
- landfill *(p. 409)*
- NIMBY *(p. 409)*
- toxic *(p. 409)*
- recycle *(p. 410)*
- conservation *(p. 410)*

Academic Vocabulary
- authority *(p. 409)*
- attitude *(p. 409)*
- federal *(p. 411)*

Reading Strategy
Identifying As you read, use a diagram like the one below to identify three sources of air and water pollution.

Real World Civics Can you breathe easily every morning when you leave your home? Does the air around you look clear? The people living in the San Francisco Bay area face many days that look smoggy and polluted. Much has been done by the county and city to try to limit air pollution for citizens and protect the environment. During the summer, the city and county of San Francisco sponsor "Spare the Air" days. On days when dangerous smog levels exist, bay area residents and companies are urged to refrain from activities that cause pollution, such as burning wood, and are asked to take public transportation.

▼ **San Francisco skyline at dawn**

Dealing With Concerns

Main Idea **Protecting the environment is an important issue with which community leaders must deal.**

Civics & You Can a single individual like you make a difference in protecting the environment? Read more to find out some ways you can.

Matt Bell lives near the Cincinnati-Northern Kentucky Airport. The stream behind his home, he explained, "used to be crystal clear." Now the stream is filled with a thick white haze and no aquatic life can live in it.

This was caused by the runoff of de-icing fluid from the nearby airport. Around 600 planes a day take off from the busy transportation hub, and in the winter, they must be deiced with a special chemical. This chemical has found its way into the creek behind Matt Bell's home. No one disagrees that airplanes need to be deiced—but could it be done without destroying a nearby stream?

What Is Environmentalism?

We pay a high price for living in an industrialized society. Every time we turn on a light or throw away trash, we may harm our environment. **Environmentalism,** or protecting our environment, is a national and worldwide concern, but most often it is up to local communities to address environmental problems.

Until the 1970s, state and local **authorities,** or experts, paid little attention to environmental problems. The focus changed in 1970 when Congress passed the Clean Air Act and established the Environmental Protection Agency (EPA). While the EPA has taken the lead in setting goals and standards, the states have implemented the programs by monitoring air and water quality and inspecting industrial facilities.

Dumping Garbage Landfills of solid waste are filling up across the country. ***Analyzing*** **Why is it difficult to find new sites for waste landfills?**

Solid Waste

Managing the disposing of **solid waste**—the technical name for garbage—is a huge problem for cities. Americans produce about 250 million tons of solid waste each year, and most places where it can be dumped, called **landfills,** are filling up fast. Some landfills have been closed because rainwater seeping through them has damaged underground water reservoirs and streams.

Complicating the search for new landfill sites is the fact that no one wants a garbage dump in his or her general area. Indeed, there is a name for this **attitude**—**NIMBY,** meaning "not in my backyard." Opposition from citizens' groups makes it difficult to find new landfill sites.

Incineration As an alternative to landfills, much solid waste is burned in huge incinerators. These, however, cause problems of their own: **toxic,** or poisonous, substances in the smoke from incineration can cause serious air pollution. New ways to "scrub" pollutants from incinerator stacks are being developed. Current pollution-control devices for incinerator smokestacks are expensive.

Recycling

A second alternative to landfills is **recycling,** which means reusing old materials to make new ones. Most communities across the United States have recycling programs. Many Americans recycle materials such as paper, metal cans, plastic and glass bottles, and plastic bags in their homes, schools, and workplaces.

Paper is the number one material that we throw away. For every 100 pounds (45 kg) of trash we throw away, about 35 pounds (16 kg) is paper. When paper is recycled, it saves our forests and reduces our air and water pollution. Recycling paper also means lower disposal costs. Unfortunately, not all waste is recyclable. Furthermore, many people do not bother to participate in recycling efforts.

Conservation **Conservation** is the preservation and protection of our natural resources. For example, some stores offer customers a rebate when they return bags or use their own shopping bags. Businesses are encouraged, and sometimes required by law, to eliminate unnecessary packaging of products.

Many communities depend on private citizens and local businesses to promote conservation. People can conserve electricity by buying energy-efficient appliances and turning off unnecessary lights. They can conserve oil and natural gas by adjusting thermostats, installing more efficient furnaces, and insulating their homes. Many gas companies also offer competitive fees. Similarly, water use in many communities is being reduced significantly through the efforts of private citizens. As conservation becomes a way of life for more Americans, the nation may come closer to solving its environmental problems.

Reading Check **Explaining** What elements of daily life are people encouraged to conserve?

Motor City Makeover This Detroit, Michigan, family spends time cleaning city park grounds and planting flowers. ***Speculating*** **What recycled products might they be using in their tasks?**

Protecting the Air, Water, and Land

Main Idea **Sources of pollution include the activities of both industries and individuals.**

Civics & You Has a parent or teacher ever reminded you to clean up after yourself? Read to find out how the same good advice applies to communities as well.

Much air, water, and land pollution comes from industrial sources. However, individuals are responsible for pollution as well.

Industrial Pollution

Water pollution comes mainly from factories, which produce all sorts of chemical waste. For generations, some factories pumped this waste directly into rivers and streams. Others buried it, which allowed it to seep into underground water supplies. Factory smokestacks emit many different toxic gases into the air. The EPA has done much to stop industrial pollution of air and water. **Federal,** or national, regulations limit the amounts and kinds of waste that factories may discharge. However, budget limitations keep many of these regulations from being strictly enforced.

Pollution from Individuals

Pollution from factories, nevertheless, is far easier to regulate than pollution from the activities of individuals. In most cities, cars and trucks are the worst air polluters. To reduce the pollution they cause, the federal government mandated the removal of lead from gasoline. It also required the automobile industry to develop more efficient engines and to equip cars with devices to remove pollutants from exhaust gases.

Another important way to reduce urban air pollution is to persuade people to drive less. Many local governments are trying to build or improve public transportation systems to get more people to use subways and buses. They encourage drivers to carpool by creating carpool lanes.

Controlling Pollution Constant monitoring of seawater helps scientists trying to ease pollution. ***Comparing*** **Whom do you think pollutes more—individuals or industries? Why?**

A serious threat to *indoor* air quality is smoking. Many cities and counties have passed no-smoking ordinances. Almost all states regulate smoking in public buildings.

Threat of Hazardous Waste

Hazardous waste is a major environmental danger. Perhaps the most serious form is radioactive waste from nuclear power plants. Hazardous waste also includes runoff from pesticides that farmers and gardeners spray on plants and residues from improperly discarded motor oil, auto engine coolant, and batteries. Until 1970, much toxic waste was put in metal containers, which were then encased in concrete and dumped into the ocean.

Today, land disposal is the only way to dispose of hazardous waste. Disposal facilities are filling up fast. There is currently no completely safe method of disposing of hazardous waste. Sometimes entire communities are affected by a site. The town of Love Canal, New York, had to be abandoned because residents had so many serious health problems as a result of exposure to toxic waste that began in 1978.

A Grassroots Effort

Beginning in the 1960s, citizens formed groups to do something about protecting the environment. The Sierra Club, the Audubon Society, and the Wilderness Society gained prominence. These organizations worked to protect the environment and promote the conservation of natural resources.

Many communities and businesses responded to the efforts of these organizations and started including sustainable development in their planning. City planners tried to reduce urban sprawl and expand green spaces, builders included energy efficiency in their designs, and the forestry industry started reforestation programs.

Government Actions With the environmental movement gaining support, the federal government took action. The National Environmental Policy Act, which created the Environmental Protection Agency (EPA), was signed into law in 1970. The EPA took on the job of setting and enforcing pollution standards and coordinating antipollution activities with state and local governments.

The Clean Air Act of 1970 established emissions standards for factories and automobiles. In following years, Congress passed two more pieces of important environmental legislation. The Clean Water Act (1972) restricted the discharge of pollutants into the nation's lakes and rivers. The Endangered Species Act (1973) established measures for saving threatened animal species.

Reading Check **Identifying** What have individual citizens done to protect the environment?

Section 3 Review

Vocabulary

1. **Define** the following terms and use them in sentences related to environmental problems in American communities: *environmentalism, solid waste, landfill, NIMBY, toxic, recycle, conservation.*

Main Ideas

2. **Defining** What is environmentalism?
3. **Explaining** Why is the threat of hazardous waste a serious problem?

Critical Thinking

4. **Evaluating** Which of the environmental issues discussed do you think is most critical today? Explain.
5. **BIG Ideas** In a graphic organizer like the one below, describe three ways to limit pollution caused by individuals.

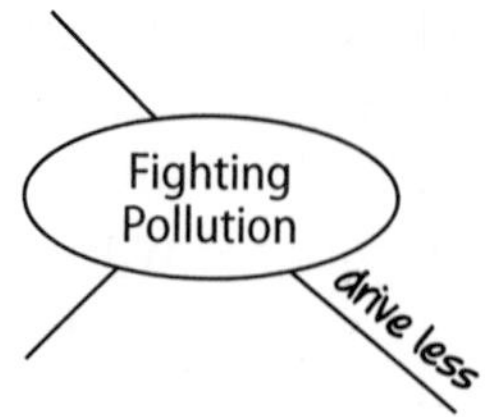

CITIZENSHIP Activity

6. **Expository Writing** Make a list of five ways that you could change your everyday activities to reduce the amount of waste you create.

Study Central™ To review this section, go to glencoe.com.

Chapter 14 Visual Summary

Public Policy

- Government leaders make public policy, which is a general agreement among leaders about how to deal with particular issues.
- One goal of public policy is to anticipate and prevent problems.
- Governments and planning commissions make both short-term and long-term plans.
- Priorities are the goals a community considers most important or most urgent.
- A master plan spells out decisions about a community's future.

Education

- Elementary and secondary education is a local responsibility under state guidelines. Even so, the federal government plays an important role in education, providing aid to local schools in several forms.
- Local school leaders face funding issues, low test scores, high dropout rates, and crime and violence on school property.

Crime and Social Issues

- Crime rates are usually highest in large cities, where poverty and crime often go hand in hand.
- Federal, state, and local law enforcement agencies fight crime, although most of the daily work is done by uniformed police officers.

Community volunteers clean up their neighborhood

- Policymakers have long struggled over the problems of how to reduce poverty and to best administer government financial aid.

The Environment

- Environmentalism is the concern that our environment must be protected.
- Through the EPA, the government tries to reduce air and water pollution.

North Carolina students work to earn college math credits

Factory wastes cause pollution

STUDY TO GO

Study anywhere, anytime! Download quizzes and flash cards to your PDA from glencoe.com.

Chapter

14 Assessment

TEST-TAKING TIP

When answering an essay question on a test, set off lists of facts with numbers or bullets.

Reviewing Vocabulary

Directions: Choose the word(s) that best completes the sentence.

1. Granting a builder a permit to construct apartments is an example of a ______.

A master plan **C** public policy
B long-term plan **D** short-term plan

2. The money, people, and materials available to accomplish a community's plan are its ______.

A policies **C** priorities
B resources **D** infrastructure

3. Critics of ______ claim they undermine self-respect among the poor.

A charter schools **C** welfare programs
B tuition vouchers **D** community policing programs

4. ______ is environmentally friendly because it requires reusing solid waste.

A recycling **C** landfills
B incineration **D** conservation

Reviewing Main Ideas

Directions: Choose the best answer for each question.

Section 1 *(pp. 396–399)*

5. Who suggests public policy ideas?

A media
B interest groups
C political parties
D all of the above

6. What do members of a planning committee consider when formulating a master plan?

A priorities
B resources
C future needs
D all of the above

Section 2 *(pp. 400–406)*

7. What do opponents of charter schools claim?

A Charter schools have high dropout rates.
B Charter schools only enroll problem students.
C Charter schools take funds from public schools.
D Charter schools produce poor academic performance.

8. Which program set a five-year lifetime limit on receiving welfare?

A Drums not Drugs
B No Child Left Behind
C Temporary Assistance to Needy Families
D Aid to Families with Dependent Children

Section 3 *(pp. 408–412)*

9. How can businesses help conserve forests?

A by adjusting thermostats in stores
B by selling energy-efficient furnaces
C by eliminating unnecessary packaging
D by accepting cans and bottles for recycling

10. How can cities reduce air pollution?

A by improving public transportation
B by dumping toxic waste in the ocean
C by eliminating runoff from pesticides
D by mandating the use of lead in gasoline

GO ON

Critical Thinking

Directions: Base your answers to questions 11 and 12 on the graph below and your knowledge of Chapter 14.

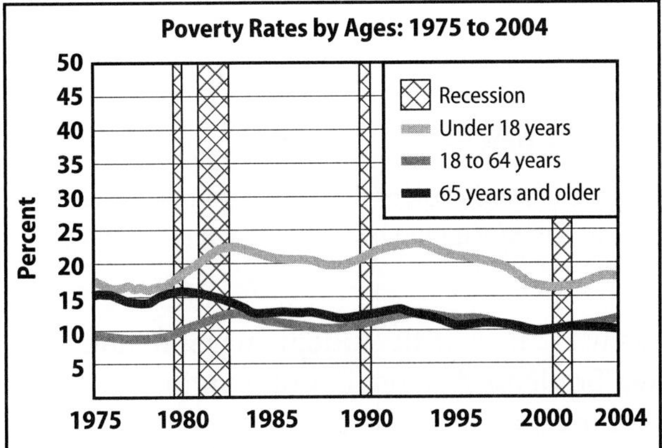

Note: The data points are placed at the midpoints of the respective years.
Source: U.S. Census Bureau, Current Population Survey, 1960 to 2005; Annual Social and Economic Supplements.

11. Which of the following conclusions might you draw based on the graph?

A The percentage of elderly poor has increased since 1965.

B Poverty among working age people has increased since 1975.

C Poverty among children has been greatly reduced since 1975.

D Recessions have no effect on poverty among children.

12. During which period did poverty increase among children and people between 18 and 65?

A 1985–1990

B 1975–1979

C 1996–2000

D 2000–2004

Document-Based Questions

Directions: Analyze the document and answer the short-answer questions that follow.

The following passage is from the Clean Air Act.

> *(b) The purposes of this title are -*
>
> *(1) to protect and enhance the quality of the Nation's air resources so as to promote the public health and welfare and the productive capacity of its population;*
>
> *(2) to initiate and accelerate a national research and development program to achieve the prevention and control of air pollution;*
>
> *(3) to provide technical and financial assistance to State and local governments in connection with the development and execution of their air pollution prevention and control programs; and*
>
> *(4) to encourage and assist the development and operation of regional air pollution prevention and control programs.*
>
> *(c) Pollution Prevention—A primary goal of this Act is to encourage or otherwise promote reasonable Federal, State, and local governmental actions, consistent with the provisions of this Act, for pollution prevention.*
>
> —[42 U.S.C. 7401]

13. According to the passage, how does the federal government help state and local governments clean their air?

14. Refer to the first part of the passage. What goal in the preamble to the U.S. Constitution does the Clean Air Act help to achieve?

Extended-Response Question

15. Briefly explain why providing equal education to all students presents a challenge in many states.

STOP

For additional test practice, use Self-Check Quizzes—Chapter 14 on glencoe.com.

Need Extra Help?

If you missed question...	1	2	3	4	5	6	7	8	9	10	11	12	13	14	15
Go to page...	398	399	406	410	397	399	403	406	410	411	406	406	411	412	401

Analyzing Primary Sources

Making A Difference

Reading Focus

Recall an individual who made a difference in your life or a group that inspired you. The efforts of Rosa Parks, Rachel Carson, and Bob Anastas spurred action on a large scale.

Read to Discover

As you read, think about the following:

- What encourages individuals to take action?
- What values are important to those individuals who want to improve society?

Reader's Dictionary

moribund: approaching death

The Founding of SADD

Students Against Destructive Decisions (SADD) is a school-based organization dedicated to preventing behaviors that are harmful to young people.

Bob Anastas was direct with students when telling them why he created Students Against Drunk Driving.

"I lost two of my students to drunk driving four days apart," Anastas said. "After two kids died, I said 'Never again.' It is not a game. There is no instant replay."

That was in 1981 when two Wayland [Mass.] High School students died in separate drunk driving auto accidents. Anastas taught and coached both students. He said he has dedicated himself to spreading the word on the evils of drunk driving ever since. . . .

Anastas founded SADD in 1981. The name changed to Students Against Destructive Decisions in 1997 to broaden the organization's mission.

The problem at Wayland, Anastas said, was the lack of a plan for young students. He said 28 percent of the school sent students to college while most schools in the area were sending 98 percent.

"The only difference was that my students believed they couldn't get there," Anastas said. "Seventy-five percent of the student population would drink, do drugs, be depressed and not motivated and I said we're going to fight this."

Anastas sent another message to the students. He told them to be in the top 25 percent of students instead of the bottom 75 percent that take the easy way out and find excuses. He said students who are partying and drinking instead of studying are in a bad position.

—Steve Lettau, "SADD Founder Visits Campus"

Challenging Segregation

Rosa Parks was arrested and fined for refusing to give up her seat on a Montgomery, Alabama, bus. Her simple act of protest sparked a new chapter of the civil rights movement.

One evening in early December 1955 I was sitting in the front seat of the colored section of a bus in Montgomery, Alabama. The white people were sitting in the white section. More white people got on, and they filled up all the seats in the white section. When that happened, we black people were supposed to give up our seats to the whites. But I didn't move. The white driver said, "Let me have those front seats." I didn't get up. I was tired of giving in to white people.

"I'm going to have you arrested," the driver said.

"You may do that," I answered.

Two white policemen came. I asked one of them, "Why do you push us around?"

He answered, "I don't know, but the law is the law and you're under arrest."

—Rosa Parks, *Rosa Parks: My Story*

Photographs as Primary Sources After the Supreme Court decision outlawing segregation on city buses, Rosa Parks rides at the front of the bus. Who are the people in the photograph? What are they doing? What is the photographer trying to communicate to the viewer?

The Beginnings of Environmentalism

In the early 1960s, Rachel Carson warned about the dangers of environmental pollution.

There was a strange stillness. The birds, for example—where had they gone? . . . The feeding stations in the backyards were deserted. The few birds seen anywhere were **moribund;** they trembled violently and could not fly. It was a spring without voices. . . only silence lay over the fields and woods and marsh.

—Rachel Carson, *Silent Spring*

Environmentalist Rachel Carson

DBQ Document-Based Questions

1. **Explaining** How did Anastas's personal experience lead to action?
2. **Connecting** What is a boycott and what effect did the bus boycott have on Alabama's business community?
3. **Examining** How do you think that Rosa Parks, an individual who was relatively uninvolved in the civil rights movement, could have become such an important figure in that movement?
4. **Analyzing** What environmental problem do you think is the most pressing problem we face today? Explain your response.
5. **Evaluating and Connecting** Think about the actions these individuals took to effect change. What is your opinion of their approaches to instituting political and social change? Give reasons for your opinion.

TIME REPORTS

The House of the Future

By harnessing the power of the sun, new designs can save money—and the planet

It sounds like a far-off dream: The home that heats and cools itself for free and actually generates more energy than it consumes, so that the local utility company might even send families a check for supplying power to the community grid. But with commonsense design principles and a little help from the sun, the house of the future can be yours.

Solar energy is the key to the system shown here, which could power a three-bedroom house. The sun's heat is captured in special panels on the home's roof. Pipes carry liquid heated by the solar panels into the house. This heated liquid, a water-alcohol mixture to prevent freezing, is then used to warm the home's air and water.

The hefty up-front cost of this system—about $20,000—is eased by state and federal rebates, and typically pays for itself in 10 years. In the long run, energy-efficient houses like this one would free cash for home improvements and consumer spending, providing a big—and sunny—boost to the economy.

Fast Facts on Solar Power

- All the energy stored in the Earth's reserves of oil, coal, and natural gas is equivalent to the energy from 20 days of sunshine.
- All new homes and apartments in Israel are required to use solar power to heat their water.
- In the U.S., residential and commercial buildings account for one-third of all energy use. Solar power, improved insulation, and more efficient appliances could reduce this demand by up to 80%.

Source: Union of Concerned Scientists

Sources: Union of Concerned Scientists; Solar Energy Industries Association; Department of Energy; U.S. Green Building Council; Build It Green; David Arkin/ArkinTilt Architects TIME Graphic by Lon Tweeten. Text by Amanda Bower.

UNIT 5

The Individual, the Law, and the Internet

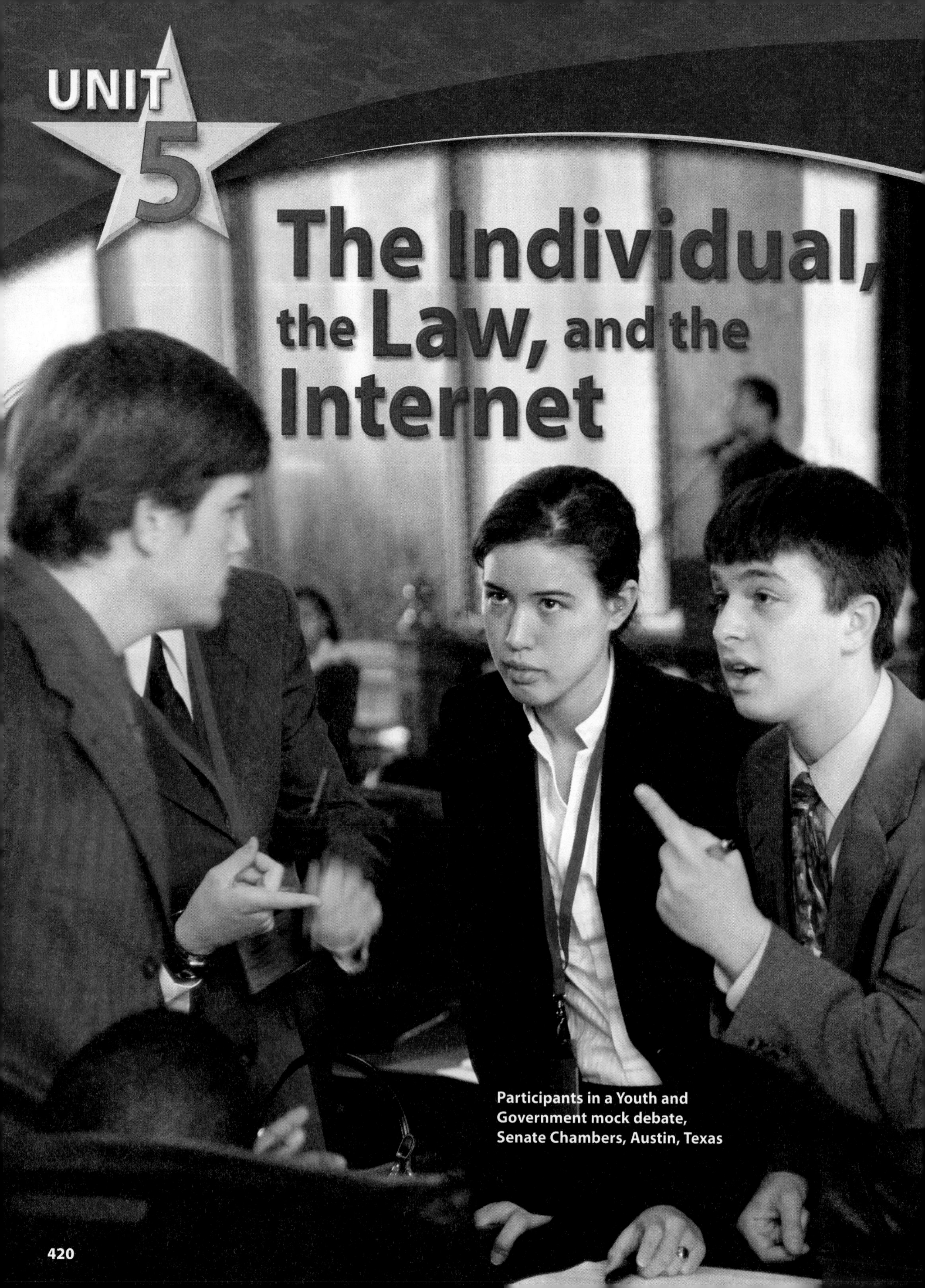

Participants in a Youth and Government mock debate, Senate Chambers, Austin, Texas

Be An Active Citizen

CITIZENSHIP What laws protect property owners in your community? With a group of students, imagine you are all part owners of a grocery store. Someone slips and is injured in your store. Research the Internet and community laws to find out what problems you might or might not face in this situation. Report your findings to the class.

UNIT 5

Reading Social Studies

Identifying Cause and Effect

1 Learn It!

Almost everything that happens in life is based upon cause and effect. For example, if you strike a match (cause) a flame appears (effect). Clue words to look for are: *as a result* or *due to.*

- Read the sentences below.
- Identify the cause of the expansion of Roman Law.
- Identify one effect Napoleon had on Louisiana.

> Napoleon updated the Justinian Code and called it the Napoleonic Code. Like the ancient Romans, Napoleon carried his laws to all the lands he controlled. One of those lands was Louisiana, an American territory which France eventually sold to the United States in 1803. The laws of the state of Louisiana are still based on the Napoleonic Code.
>
> —*from page 429*

A chart like the one below will help you identify cause and effect.

Cause: Napoleon conquered lands and brought the Napoleonic Code with him. → **Effect:** Louisiana adopted the Napoleonic Code

Reading Tip

If you can restate the ideas in a sentence using the word because, the writer is probably using cause and effect to explain what happened.

2 Practice It!

Read the following paragraph from this unit.

- Draw a chart like the one shown below.
- Identify one cause and effect from the paragraph to write in the chart.

> In November 2000, residents of Palm Beach County in Florida filed, or registered, a civil lawsuit against the Palm Beach County Canvassing Board, their election authority. The residents argued that a flaw in the ballot format caused them to vote for candidates other than the candidate for whom they intended to vote. This civil suit led to a recounting of votes and reached the Supreme Court. The Court's ruling led to George W. Bush's winning the presidency in 2000.
>
> —*from page 449*

Cause	→	Effect

Read to Write Activity

Read the section titled "What Happens in a Civil Case" in Chapter 15, Section 2. Write a paragraph where you provide examples of actions people may take (*causes*) that might result in a civil law case (*effect*).

3 Apply It!

Identify a cause and the resulting effects you can find in:

- **Chapter 16, Section 2**
- **Chapter 17, Section 1**

Chapter 15

Legal Rights and Responsibilities

Why It Matters

The Constitution and the Bill of Rights contain important provisions, or laws, safeguarding the rights of Americans. In return, our system of laws gives American citizens a number of responsibilities.

Civics ONLINE
Visit glencoe.com and enter QuickPass™ code CIV3093c15 for Chapter 15 resources.

BIG Ideas

Section 1: Sources of Our Laws

Throughout history, civilizations have developed systems of laws to meet their needs. Our laws today can be traced back to early legal systems such as the Code of Hammurabi and English common law.

Section 2: Types of Laws

The Constitution of the United States establishes and protects the individual's fundamental rights and liberties. A variety of laws protects people and their property, and helps settle disputes between parties.

Section 3: The American Legal System

The Constitution of the United States establishes and protects the individual's fundamental rights and liberties. All Americans have basic constitutional legal rights and responsibilities as well as important protections if they are accused of a crime.

Durango, Colorado, police officer writes a traffic ticket

FOLDABLES™ Study Organizer

Evaluating Information Study Foldable

Make the following Foldable to help you evaluate the sources and types of American laws, and the rights and responsibilities they protect.

Step 1 Mark a point in the middle of the paper top to bottom. Fold in each side of the paper to meet that point.

Step 2 Unfold the paper and in the center section draw a T diagram.

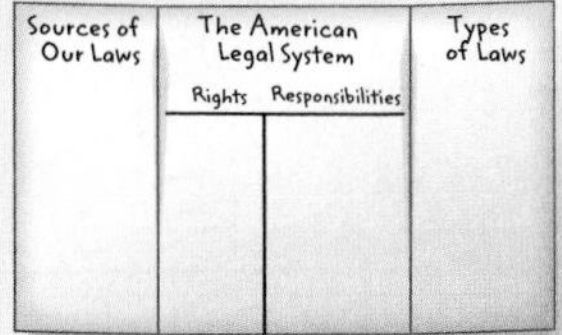

Step 3 Label all three sections as shown.

Reading and Writing

As you read the chapter, make notes under each heading about main ideas, key terms, and supporting facts for each topic. Write a paragraph summarizing the types of laws in America.

Section Audio

Spotlight Video

Sources of Our Laws

Guide to Reading

Big Idea

Throughout history, civilizations have developed systems of laws to meet their needs.

Content Vocabulary

- common law *(p. 429)*
- precedent *(p. 429)*
- statute *(p. 429)*

Academic Vocabulary

- potential *(p. 427)*
- resolve *(p. 427)*
- tradition *(p. 427)*

Reading Strategy

Identifying As you read, identify the characteristics of good laws.

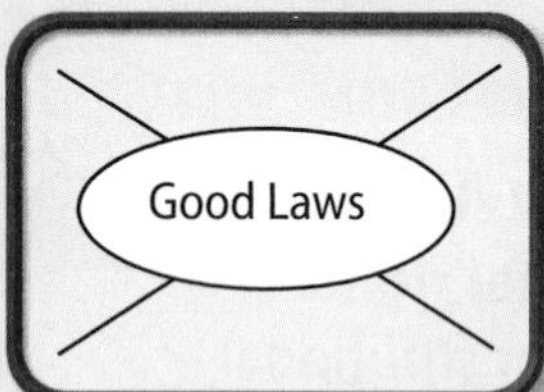

Real World Civics In 2003 Kamala Harris made history, becoming the first woman and the first person of African and East Indian American descent to become a district attorney in the state of California. Now working as the district attorney in San Francisco, Harris represents activism in government. In addition to fighting crime, she works to protect children and improve their lives by pairing them with mentors. She also strives to protect the rights of immigrants, people living in poverty, women, and people of all races.

▼ **Kamala Harris uses her public office to improve the lives of citizens**

Functions of Laws

Main Idea **Laws are sets of rules that allow people in a society to live together.**

Civics & You Have you ever wondered why certain laws exist? Read to learn their purpose.

> *"If fire break[s] out in a house, and some one . . . take[s] the property of the master of the house, he shall be thrown into that self-same fire."*
>
> —Code of Hammurabi, c. 1780 B.C.E.

Does this law strike you as harsh? It comes from the Code of Hammurabi, the first known system of written law.

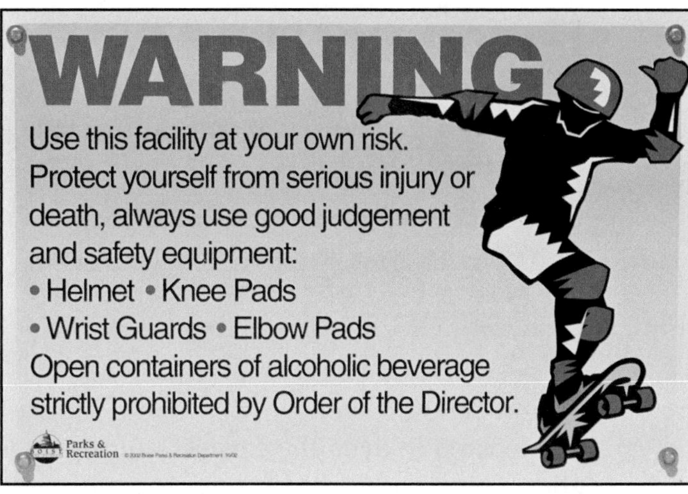

Laws Protect This skateboarding sign in a park in Idaho suggests rules for the use of skateboards. ***Comparing*** **What is the difference between a warning and a law?**

What Should Laws Do?

Laws are sets of rules that allow people to live together. Laws affect nearly everything we do—the food we eat, how we drive our cars, how we buy and sell things, and even what happens when we are born and when we die. People, organizations, and governments can deal with one another because everyone knows which actions are permissible and which are not.

A major purpose of laws is to keep the peace and prevent violent acts. Laws set punishments that are meant to discourage **potential,** or future, criminals. Laws include the administration of justice in the form of law enforcement agencies (police) and courts. Laws also set the rules for **resolving,** or answering, disagreements over money, property, contracts, and other noncriminal matters.

What Makes a Law a Good Law?

Although not all laws are beneficial, good laws share certain characteristics. Good laws are fair. People in similar circumstances will be treated equally under the law.

Good laws are also reasonable. In England in the 1700s, a person who stole a loaf of bread might have had his or her hand cut off. Today such harsh punishment for a similar crime would be considered unreasonable.

Good laws must be understandable. If laws are too complicated, people may break them without meaning to or realizing it. Ignorance of a law is no excuse for not obeying it. If most people understand the laws and believe they are reasonable and fair, then they will tend to obey the laws.

Finally, good laws are enforceable by communities, state authorities, or federal authorities. The government's ability to enforce a law often depends on the people's willingness to obey it.

A Nation of Laws

When the writers of the Constitution created our government, they based the nation's system of laws on ideas, **traditions** (customs), and laws passed down from generation to generation. Some of these ideas date back thousands of years.

Explaining What are fair laws?

History of Law

Main Idea **Law systems of early societies influence us today.**

Civics & You Have you ever seen a courtroom trial? Read more to find out how the judges' rulings also help make law.

Legal scholars believe that some kind of law existed in even the earliest human societies. They trace its beginnings to prehistoric people, who used unwritten rules of behavior to help people avoid or cope with social conflict. These earliest laws were probably passed orally from one generation to the next. Later, people began to write down their laws.

Code of Hammurabi

The first known system of written law was the Code of Hammurabi. King Hammurabi of Babylonia, an ancient Middle Eastern empire, compiled his code in about 1760 B.C. By today's standards, the Code of Hammurabi prescribed very harsh penalties.

Another set of early laws is the Ten Commandments found in the Hebrew Bible. Hebrews living in ancient Palestine followed these laws. Moral rules of the Commandments, such as "thou shalt not steal" and "thou shalt not kill," are reflected in our laws today.

Roman Law

The first code of Roman law was published in 450 B.C. As in the Code of Hammurabi, Roman penalties for offenses were drastic by later standards. Over centuries the Roman senate adopted a great many laws, and Roman judges wrote commentaries on them, which often became part of the law.

Roman Law Spreads As the Roman Empire grew, its laws spread to Europe, Africa, and Asia. In A.D. 533 Emperor Justinian I, ruler of the Byzantine Empire, also known as the Eastern Roman Empire, boiled down the confusing mass of Roman laws into an orderly body of rules called the Justinian Code. This code became the basis of law for the Byzantine Empire. Roman law also became part of the laws of the Roman Catholic Church, known as canon law.

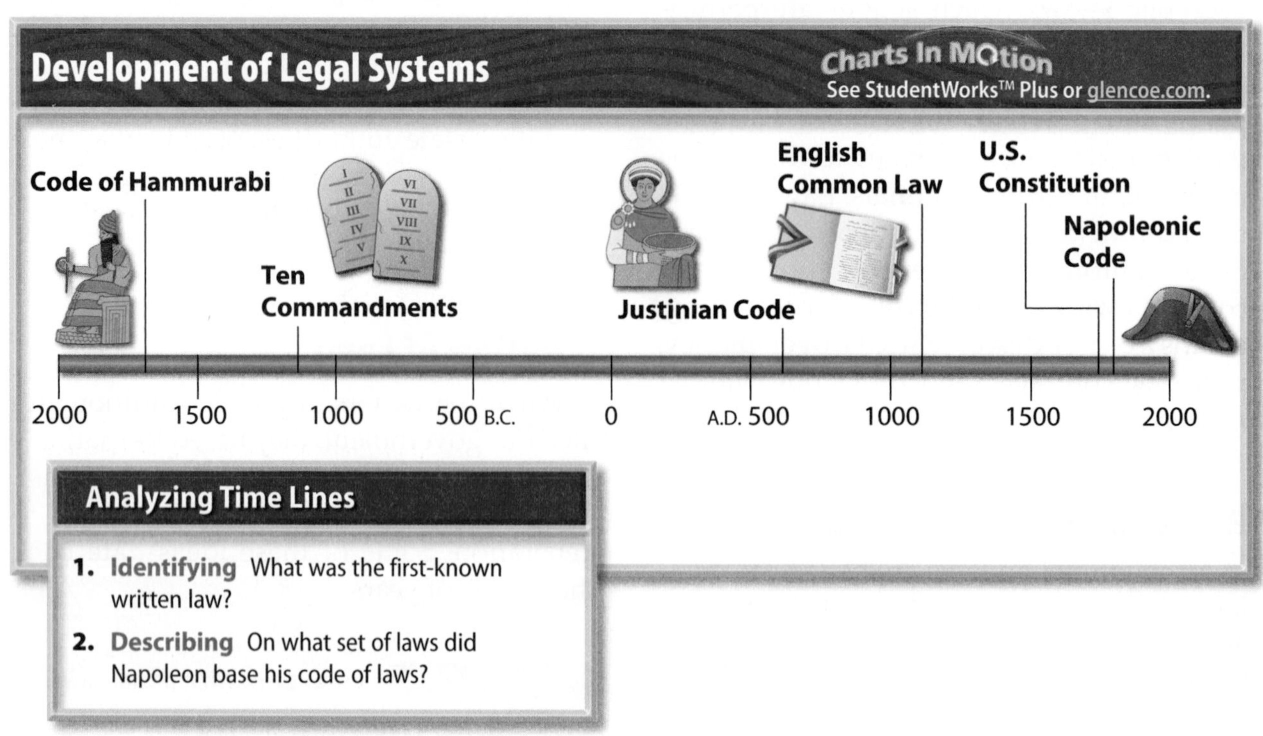

Analyzing Time Lines

1. **Identifying** What was the first-known written law?
2. **Describing** On what set of laws did Napoleon base his code of laws?

More than twelve hundred years after the Justinian Code was written, its ideas were taken over by the French emperor Napoleon Bonaparte. Napoleon updated the Justinian Code and called it the Napoleonic Code. Like the ancient Romans, Napoleon carried his laws to all the lands he controlled. One of those lands was Louisiana, an American territory which France eventually sold to the United States in 1803. The laws of the state of Louisiana are still based on the Napoleonic Code.

English Law

The most important source of American laws is English law. Perhaps the greatest contribution is the English system of **common law,** or law based on court decisions rather than on a legal code. In other words, it is a system of analyzing how a previous judge applied a law, and using it later in the same manner. After the Norman conquest of England in 1066, English kings sent judges into the countryside to hold trials and administer the law. When judges decided a new case, they looked in the books for a similar case and followed the earlier ruling, or **precedent.** Precedents are legal opinions that became part of the common law. English judges were familiar with Roman law and canon law, and they blended these into the body of common law. The law came to include basic principles of individual's rights, such as trial by jury and the concept that people are considered innocent until proven guilty.

Although acts of Parliament—written **statutes**—came to dominate the English legal system, common law continued to have a strong influence. When English settlers came to North America in the 1600s and 1700s, they brought with them their traditions of common law and individual's rights. The common-law tradition of following precedents still survives in our U.S. courts.

Reading Check **Concluding** Why was the Justinian Code important?

Vocabulary

1. **Define** the following terms and use them in sentences related to law and legal systems: *common law, precedent, statute.*

Main Ideas

2. **Explaining** What is the purpose of laws?
3. **Identifying** What are two early legal systems that have influenced the development of our laws?

Critical Thinking

4. **BIG Ideas** How did English law influence the development of American law?
5. **Making Comparisons** Using a graphic organizer like the one below, compare early systems of law.

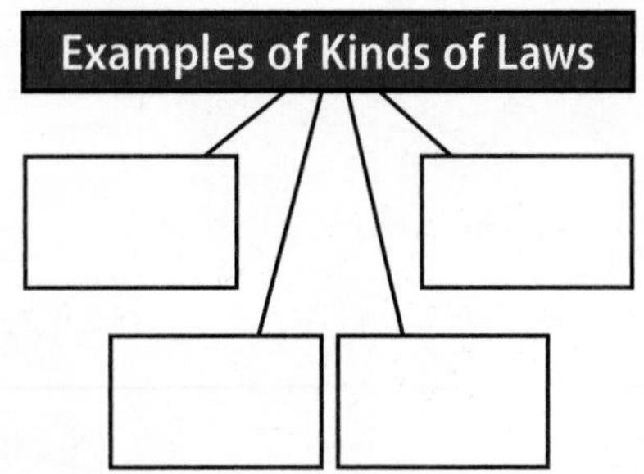

6. **Analyzing Visuals** Look at the time line on page 428. The U.S. Constitution was written about how many years after the Justinian Code was written?

CITIZENSHIP Activity

7. **Expository Writing** John Adams wrote in 1779 that Massachusetts should have "a government of laws, and not of men." What do you think he meant by this?

Study Central™ To review this section, go to glencoe.com.

Section 2

Types of Laws

Guide to Reading

Big Idea
The Constitution of the United States establishes and protects the individual's fundamental rights and liberties.

Content Vocabulary
- plaintiff *(p. 431)*
- defendant *(p. 431)*
- felony *(p. 432)*
- misdemeanor *(p. 432)*
- larceny *(p. 432)*
- robbery *(p. 432)*
- burglary *(p. 432)*
- lawsuit *(p. 432)*
- tort *(p. 433)*
- libel *(p. 433)*
- constitutional law *(p. 434)*

Academic Vocabulary
- prohibition *(p. 431)*
- recover *(p. 433)*

Reading Strategy
Comparing As you read, explain on a graphic organizer like the one below the difference between constitutional, administrative, and statutory law.

Types of Law

Real World Civics Moviegoers are thrilled to watch a car chase on the screen . . . but real-life speeding is a crime. The state and federal governments set laws to help protect people from such crimes. In 1995 the national interstate speed limit of 55 miles per hour—which had been federally imposed in 1974 to save fuel—was lifted, and each state set its own speed limits. Most states raised their interstate limits to 65 or 70 miles per hour. Safety is an issue, but motorists have supported the higher speed limits.

▼ A South Carolina highway crew "ups" the speed limit

Criminal and Civil Law

Main Idea **Criminal laws help maintain a peaceful and orderly society, while civil laws involve disputes between people or groups.**

Civics & You What would you do if your bicycle were stolen? Read more to find out how our legal system handles such a case.

Most people are familiar with criminal laws, such as **prohibitions,** or bans, against drunk driving, robbing a store, or selling drugs. Other kinds of laws exist as well. Civil law is concerned with disputes between people (or groups of people) or between the government and its citizens. Public law concerns alleged violations of constitutional rights and disputes involving the actions of government agencies.

Two types of law affect Americans directly—criminal law and civil law. These laws help maintain a peaceful and orderly society. People who break these laws are likely to find themselves in a courtroom.

Criminal Law

Criminal laws seek to prevent people from deliberately or recklessly harming one another or one another's property. American courts operate on an adversary system. Under this system, the courtroom serves as an arena in which lawyers for opposing sides try to present their strongest cases. The judge has an impartial role and should be fair to both sides. Critics of the adversary system argue that it encourages lawyers to ignore evidence that is not favorable to their sides. Supporters, though, claim that it is the best system to bring out the facts of a case.

In criminal cases, the government is always the **plaintiff**—the party that brings the charges against the accused. The basis for this tradition is that the American system of justice assumes that society—everyone—is the victim when a crime is committed.

We Are All Victims The individual or group accused of a crime is the **defendant.** About 95 percent of criminal trials in the United States are for violations of state laws. Most criminal cases are titled in terms of the

Felonies Serious crimes, such as arson, burglary, and murder, are considered felonies. Arson is also categorized as a crime against property. ***Identifying*** **What are other examples of crimes against property?**

TIME™ Teens in *Action*

Jeremy Verbit

Jeremy Verbit, 18, of Warren, Michigan, was saddened and angry over deaths caused by drunk drivers in his community and decided to take action. Jeremy, who believes, "We're not born with responsibility; it is learned," decided to join Students Against Destructive Decisions (SADD). Now he is spreading an important message.

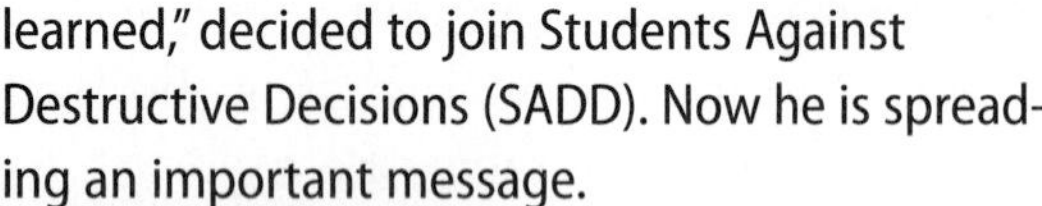

SADD meeting

QUESTION: How did you turn your anger into something positive?

ANSWER: I became a freshman representative with SADD. My school's chapter works to prevent drunk driving. We wanted to help tomorrow's high school students by starting Peer Resistance Training.

Q: Peer Resistance Training? What's that?

A: It's a program designed to train high school students to go to local fifth-grade classrooms. The older kids serve as role models to promote an alcohol-free lifestyle and let kids know there are lots of ways to have fun that don't involve drinking.

Q: How many younger kids do you speak to?

A: Each year, the program reaches about 300 fifth graders and trains around 20 high school students as role models. And it's working. When we leave the school after our presentations, we can hear fifth graders talking to their friends about how underage drinking is "irresponsible."

ACTION FACT: Verbit's other interests include computers and the Detroit Pistons basketball team.

Making a Difference — CITIZENSHIP

What is the purpose of Peer Resistance Training?

state against the defendant—for example, *State of California* v. *John Jones*. This way of naming cases shows that the government, rather than an individual crime victim, is bringing action against the defendant.

Felonies and Misdemeanors Crimes are graded as either **felonies** or **misdemeanors.** Murder, rape, arson, robbery, and other serious crimes are felonies because they have serious consequences for the victim and the criminal. Misdemeanors are offenses such as vandalism or stealing inexpensive items. Typically, misdemeanors are punishable with a fine or a jail sentence of less than one year.

Crimes Against Property Crimes against property are the most common type of crime. The category of crimes against property includes crimes in which property is destroyed and crimes in which property is stolen or taken against the owner's will. Arson and vandalism are examples of crimes involving the destruction of property.

There are other categories of crimes that involve taking property against the will of the owner. **Larceny** is the unlawful taking away of another person's property with the intent never to return it. **Robbery** is the taking of property from a person's possession by using force or threats, while **burglary** is the unlawful entry into any dwelling or structure with the intention to commit a crime.

Civil Law

Civil law is concerned with disputes between people or groups in which no criminal laws have been broken. These disputes are not viewed as a threat to the social order, so the state will not take legal action. When a civil case goes to court, it is called a **lawsuit.** A lawsuit is a legal action whereby a person or group sues to collect damages for some harm that is done. Individuals who think they have been wronged must take action themselves by filing a lawsuit. The person suing is the plaintiff, while the person or organization being sued is the defendant.

What Happens in a Civil Case? Individuals believe they have lost something of value or suffered some damage because of someone else's blameworthy actions. A case may be a dispute over a contract in which one party believes that the other has not fulfilled the terms of an agreement.

Suppose, for example, that you order something from a mail-order catalog and charge it to your credit card. The mail-order company has, in effect, made a contract with you. If you do not receive the merchandise, the mail-order company has broken the contract. If the company fails to return your money, you can take it to court.

Tort Law Civil law also covers **torts,** or civil wrongs. In tort law a person may suffer an injury and claim that another party is responsible because of negligence. Suppose, for example, that you slip on ice on your neighbor's sidewalk and break a leg. According to your local law, property owners are responsible for keeping their sidewalks clear of ice. If your neighbor does not do this and you are injured as a result, you have a right to sue and **recover,** or get back, the costs of your medical treatment and other damages.

Family Law The basic social unit is the family. Not surprisingly, much civil law involves rules applied to the relationship between members of the family unit. The legality of marriage is regulated by state law. Typically, a state requires a person to be at least 18 years of age to be married unless there is parental consent. Typical family law cases involve divorce, child custody, adoption, alimony, child support, and spousal and child abuse.

Battles for Legal Rights

One of the earliest individuals to fight for people's rights was John Peter Zenger (1697–1746). Zenger was a New York newspaper editor who, in 1732, published stories about the colony's corrupt royal governor. At the time no newspapers had the freedom to criticize government officials. The governor charged Zenger with **libel,** the printing of false and damaging information, and threw him into jail. When the case came to trial in 1735, however, it took the jurors just 10 minutes to reach a "not guilty" verdict.

Another journalistic trailblazer was Ida Wells-Barnett (1862–1931). The daughter of slaves, she crusaded against lynching and for equal rights for all Americans. Her career was launched when she was forcibly removed from a railroad car reserved for whites in Memphis in 1884. For the rest of her life, she fought against segregation and for women's rights. In 1909 she helped found the National Association for the Advancement of Colored People (NAACP).

Statutory Law Statutes are the source of many of our rights. The Americans with Disabilities Act states that employees are to be provided "reasonable accommodations" necessary to assist them in doing their jobs. ***Analyzing*** **What would be "reasonable accommodations" for a person in a wheelchair?**

Reading Check **Comparing** What is the difference between a felony and a misdemeanor?

Other Types of Law

Main Idea **Laws protect your rights and enforce rules and statutes.**

Civics & You When you buy a snack, do you ever worry it might contain ingredients that could make you sick? Read to find out what kind of law ensures that your snack is safe to eat.

Laws that govern our lives and protect our rights come from many sources. These are state and federal constitutions, administrative agencies, and lawmaking bodies.

Constitutional Law The Constitution is the most fundamental and important source of law in the United States. The term **constitutional law** applies to that branch of the law dealing with the formation, construction, and interpretation of constitutions. For the most part, cases involving constitutional law decide the limits of the government's power and the rights of the individual.

Administrative Law If the Federal Aviation Administration issued an order requiring commercial airlines to install a new type of safety device, that would be an example of administrative law. Administrative law refers to the rules and regulations that the executive branch must make to carry out its job. It might include an individual charging a government agency with wrongdoing.

Statutory Law Recall from Section 1 that a statute is a law written by a legislative branch of government. The U.S. Congress, state legislatures, and local legislatures write thousands of these laws. Statutes regulate our behavior by setting speed limits and specifying rules for inspecting food products. Statutes are also the source of many of the rights and benefits we take for granted, such as the right to get a Social Security check, to enter a veterans' hospital, to get a driver's license, and to return merchandise you bought at a store.

Reading Check **Identifying** What is an example of a statutory law?

Vocabulary

1. **Define** the following terms and use them in sentences related to different kinds of laws: *plaintiff, defendant, felony, misdemeanor, larceny, robbery, burglary, lawsuit, tort, libel, constitutional law.*

Main Ideas

2. **Describing** Give at least two reasons a person might file a civil lawsuit.
3. **Classifying** What does administrative law deal with? Why is administrative law considered part of public law?

Critical Thinking

4. **BIG Ideas** Which type of law that you have read about in this section do you feel has the greatest influence on your daily life? Why?
5. **Organizing Information** In a graphic organizer like the one below, give two examples of each kind of law.

Criminal Laws	Civil Laws
Drunk driving	

6. **Evaluating** Describe the contribution of either John Peter Zenger or Ida Wells-Barnett to the rights you enjoy today as an American.

CITIZENSHIP Activity

7. **Creative Writing** Write a newspaper article about an imaginary case involving one of the types of laws you read about in this section.

Study Central™ To review this section, go to glencoe.com.

Section Audio

Spotlight Video

The American Legal System

Guide to Reading

Big Idea

The Constitution of the United States establishes and protects the individual's fundamental rights and liberties.

Content Vocabulary

- stare decisis *(p. 436)*
- writ of habeas corpus *(p. 436)*
- bill of attainder *(p. 436)*
- ex post facto law *(p. 436)*
- due process of law *(p. 437)*
- search warrant *(p. 438)*
- double jeopardy *(p. 439)*
- grand jury *(p. 439)*
- plea bargain *(p. 440)*
- bail *(p. 440)*

Academic Vocabulary

- interpret *(p. 436)*
- factor *(p. 437)*
- presume *(p. 438)*

Reading Strategy

Identifying On a diagram like the one below, list three rights that help ensure a fair trial.

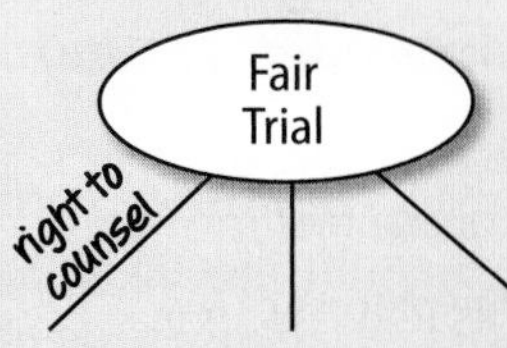

Real World Civics From watching television and movies, nearly everyone knows they have the right to remain silent when arrested. Do you know why it is called the Miranda warning? In 1963, Ernesto Miranda was arrested for kidnap and rape. During a two-hour interrogation, he confessed to the crime. He was never told that he could remain silent or that he had the right to an attorney, as provided by the Fifth and Sixth Amendments in the Bill of Rights. Miranda appealed his conviction, and in 1966 the Supreme Court ruled that his rights had been violated. Do you know your other rights that are guaranteed by the Constitution?

▼ **Defendant Ernesto Miranda (left) speaks with his attorney, 1967**

Protections in the U.S. Constitution

Main Idea **All Americans have basic legal rights and responsibilities.**

Civics & You Have you ever thought a law was wrong or unfair? Read to find out what you can do about it.

Early settlers in the American colonies enjoyed a degree of liberty found in few countries in the eighteenth century. They owed their rights to legal principles that developed in England and were transferred to America with the colonists. Colonial lawyers studied from English law books, and judges used English common law as the basis for their decisions.

As in England, however, American law increasingly became a law of written statutes, which are the work of Congress and state legislatures. Although legislation has replaced common law, courts still refer to common-law principles when no statutes exist to deal with a given legal issue.

Individual Rights

The U.S. Constitution is the basic law of our nation. It gives each branch of government a role in making, enforcing, and **interpreting,** or defining, the law. The legislative branch of government makes the laws of the nation. The executive branch carries out these laws and, in doing so, makes laws as well. The judicial branch applies the law to specific cases. Courts base their rulings on written laws and on the precedents of earlier cases. The rulings are then used to build decisions about similar cases in the future. This process is called **stare decisis,** which is Latin for "let the decision stand."

Several basic legal rights that belong to Americans are included in Article I of the Constitution. One of the most important is the **writ of habeas corpus.** A writ is a written legal order; *habeas corpus* is a Latin phrase that roughly means "you should have the body." The writ of habeas corpus requires an official who has arrested someone to bring that person to court and explain why he or she is being held. This writ is a safeguard against being kept in jail unlawfully.

Article I also forbids enactment of **bills of attainder** and **ex post facto laws.** A bill of attainder is a law that punishes a person

Constitutional Rights of the Accused

ARTICLE I, SECTION 9
• to be granted habeas corpus (released until trial)
FIFTH AMENDMENT
• to have a grand jury hearing
• to be protected from double jeopardy
• to refuse to answer questions that may be incriminating
SIXTH AMENDMENT
• to be informed of the accusation
• to hear and question witnesses
• to be able to subpoena witnesses
• to be represented by an attorney
• to have a speedy and public trial by an impartial jury
• to be represented by a lawyer
FOURTEENTH AMENDMENT
• to have due process of law
• to have equal protection of the laws

Analyzing Charts

1. **Describing** What protections does the Fourteenth Amendment guarantee?
2. **Analyzing** How does due process of law limit what government can do?

accused of a crime without a trial or a fair hearing in court. An ex post facto law is a law that would allow a person to be punished for an action that was not against the law when it was committed.

A Guarantee of Rights The Constitution's Bill of Rights further guarantees the freedoms of individuals. Several of these amendments spell out the rights of Americans in relation to the administration of justice. After the Civil War, Congress proposed and the states ratified the Fourteenth Amendment, extending these rights to formerly enslaved persons. The amendment also requires the states to provide equal protection under the law to all persons.

The Fifth and Fourteenth Amendments guarantee **due process of law.** Due process means, in part, that government may not take our lives, liberty, or property except according to the proper exercise of law. The law requires, for example, that accused people have the opportunity for a trial by jury.

The equal-protection clause in the Fourteenth Amendment requires governments to treat all people equally. It forbids unfair or unequal treatment based on **factors,** or influences such as gender, race, and religion. Since the 1950s, this clause has been the major civil rights tool of minorities and women when challenging laws or government policies that discriminate against them.

Legal Responsibilities

The Declaration of Independence states, "All men are created equal." This democratic ideal of equality means that all people are entitled to equal rights and treatment before the law. Americans have a number of legal responsibilities. By fulfilling them, we ensure that our legal system works as it should and that our legal rights are protected.

Reading Check **Explaining** What two amendments guarantee the due process of law?

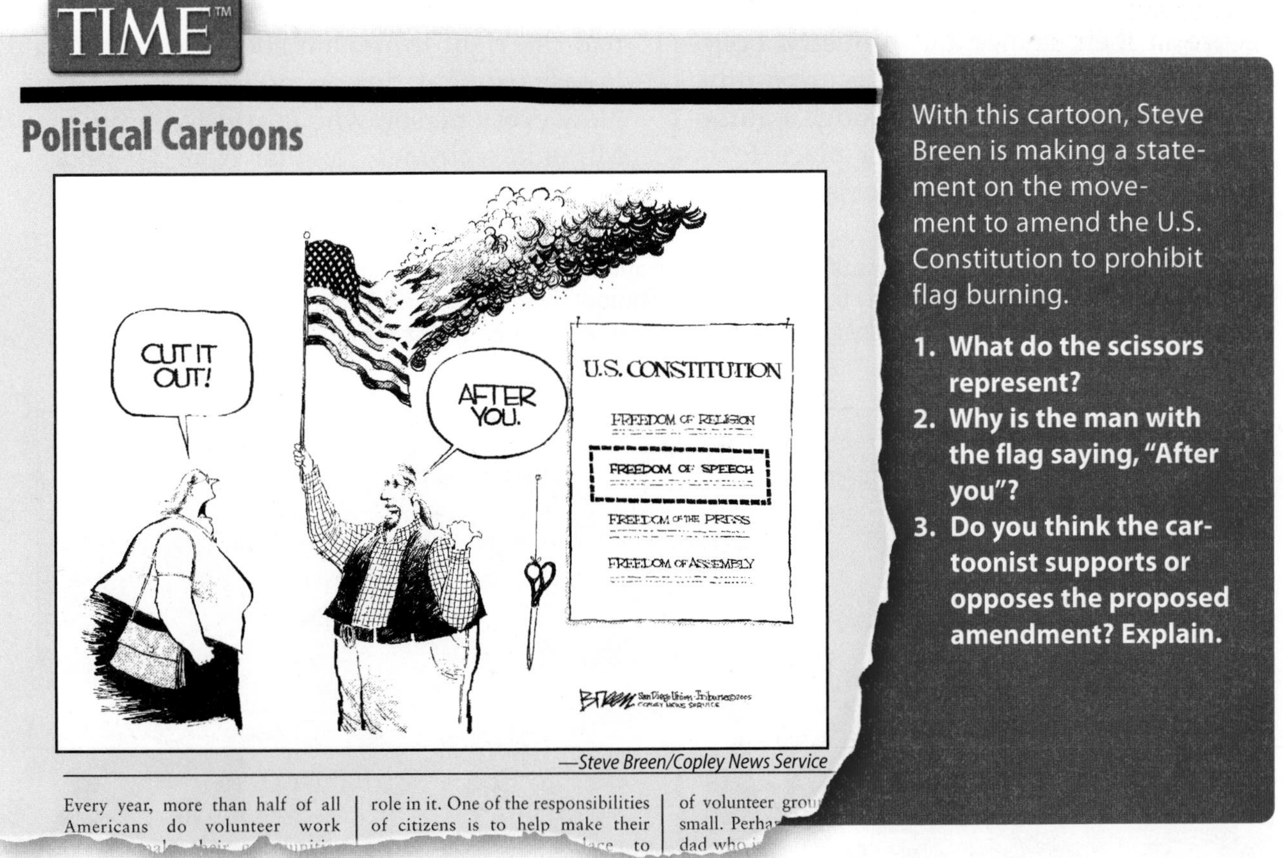

—*Steve Breen/Copley News Service*

Every year, more than half of all Americans do volunteer work ... role in it. One of the responsibilities of citizens is to help make their ... of volunteer grou... small. Perha... dad who...

With this cartoon, Steve Breen is making a statement on the movement to amend the U.S. Constitution to prohibit flag burning.

1. **What do the scissors represent?**
2. **Why is the man with the flag saying, "After you"?**
3. **Do you think the cartoonist supports or opposes the proposed amendment? Explain.**

Guaranteed Rights of Those Accused

Main Idea **The U.S. Constitution includes several protections for Americans accused of a crime.**

Civics & You Have you ever received a punishment that seemed too drastic for what you did wrong? Read to find out what the Constitution says about this.

The Constitution includes several specific rights that protect citizens accused of crimes. These rights make sure that accused people are treated fairly and receive every chance to defend themselves. Each right is based on the idea that a person is **presumed,** or believed to be, innocent until proven guilty in a court of law.

The Fourth Amendment

The Fourth Amendment protects citizens against "unreasonable searches and seizures." It gives Americans a fundamental right to be secure in their homes and property. Police seeking to intrude on this security must first get a **search warrant**—a judge's authorization—specifying the exact place to be searched and describing what objects may be seized. Police must show the judge that they have probable cause—a good reason—that their search will prove useful. In the 1961 case *Mapp* v. *Ohio,* the Supreme Court adopted what is called the exclusionary rule. This rule says that if the police gain evidence in a way that violates the Fourth Amendment, that evidence may not be used in a trial.

The Fifth Amendment

The Fifth Amendment states that "no person . . . shall be compelled in any criminal case to be a witness against himself." This means that a person does not have to answer questions that may incriminate that person, or show his or her involvement in a crime. Before the 1960s, police often questioned suspects, sometimes under great pressure, to push them to confess to a crime before they saw a lawyer or appeared in court.

In 1966, in *Miranda* v. *Arizona,* the Supreme Court held that police must inform suspects that they have the right to "remain silent"—to refuse to answer police questions. Ernesto Miranda claimed he had not realized he had the right to remain silent or to have a lawyer present during police questioning. Now every person who is arrested hears the Miranda warnings, familiar from TV police programs.

Enforcing Laws An arrested person is taken to a police station where the charges are recorded. At this time, the suspect may be fingerprinted, photographed, or put in a lineup to be identified by witnesses. ***Explaining*** **What are the Fifth Amendment rights of a person accused of a crime?**

The Fifth Amendment also protects an accused person from **double jeopardy.** This means that a person who is tried for a crime and found not guilty may not be placed in jeopardy—put at risk of criminal penalty—a second time by being retried for the same crime.

What Is a Grand Jury? The Fifth Amendment says, furthermore, that people accused of serious federal crimes must be brought before a **grand jury** to decide whether the government has enough evidence to bring them to trial. (In some states, a preliminary hearing is used instead of a grand jury indictment.) A grand jury is a group of 12 to 23 citizens that hears evidence presented by a prosecutor. It decides whether there is enough evidence to indicate that the accused has committed a crime. If the grand jury finds sufficient evidence to proceed to trial, it indicts the accused person, or issues a formal charge that names the suspect and states the charges against him or her.

The Sixth Amendment

The Sixth Amendment grants an accused person the right to be defended by a lawyer. In 1963 the Supreme Court, in *Gideon* v. *Wainwright,* interpreted the amendment to mean that if a defendant cannot afford a lawyer, the state must provide one. Previously the federal government provided lawyers for poor defendants, but some states did not if the case did not involve capital punishment.

The Sixth Amendment also guarantees that accused people must be informed of the nature and cause of the accusations against them and have "the right to a speedy and public trial, by an impartial jury" and the right to confront, or question, witnesses against them. This right protects defendants against being held in jail for an unreasonably long time. It also means that trials usually may not be closed to the public or the news media.

Right to a Trial A person accused of a crime also has the right to a trial by an impartial jury. *Impartial* means that jury members will be people who do not know anyone involved in the case and have not already made up their minds about the case. Jury members usually must be drawn from the area where the crime was committed.

Although everyone charged with a crime has a right to a jury trial, defendants may choose to appear before only a judge, without a jury. This kind of trial is called a bench trial.

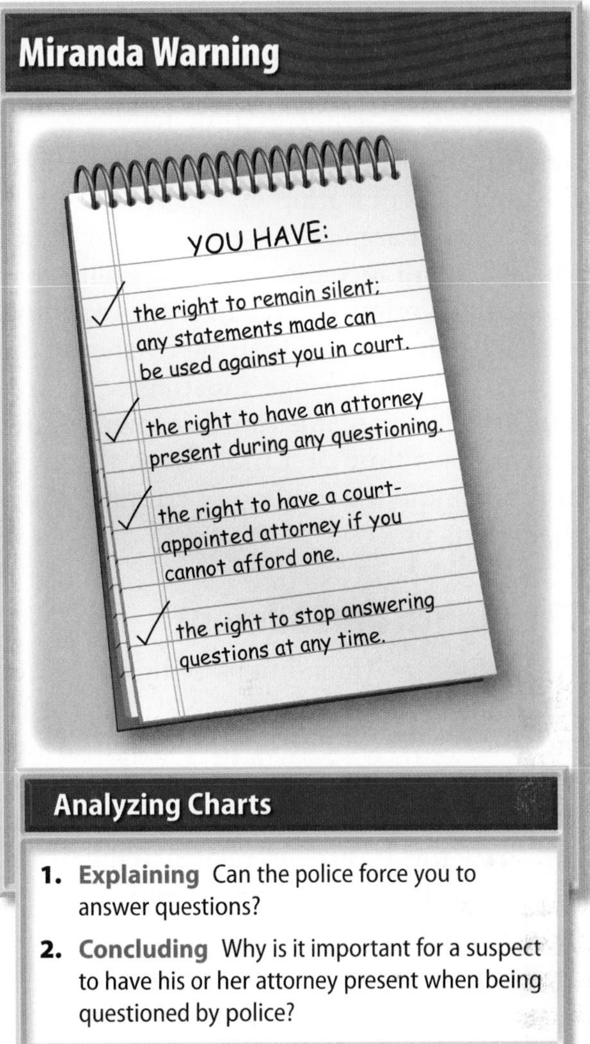

Analyzing Charts

1. **Explaining** Can the police force you to answer questions?
2. **Concluding** Why is it important for a suspect to have his or her attorney present when being questioned by police?

Student Web Activity Visit glencoe.com and complete the Chapter 15 Web Activity.

Even so, many criminal prosecutions do not come to trial at all—with or without a jury—because of plea bargains. **Plea bargaining** is a negotiation between the defense attorney and the prosecutor, who is the government's attorney.

In a plea bargain, the government offers the defendant a chance to plead guilty to a less serious crime in exchange for receiving a less severe penalty than he or she might receive at trial. A judge must agree to any bargain. Plea bargains can cut down on the expense and time of a trial. They also help judges handle the volume of criminal cases that courts process.

The Eighth Amendment

The Eighth Amendment outlaws "cruel and unusual punishments." Also, a punishment may not be out of proportion to the crime, such as imposing a life sentence for shoplifting. There is controversy, however, over how this protection relates to the death penalty. In 1972 the Supreme Court ruled in *Furman* v. *Georgia* that the death penalty as then administered was not constitutional. The Court found that the death penalty was being imposed in unfair ways, for a wide variety of crimes, and mainly on African Americans and poor people.

After the *Furman* decision, most states revised their death penalty laws to comply with the Supreme Court's guidelines. Some states have established a two-stage process to deal with death penalty cases. First, a jury trial determines the guilt or innocence of the defendant. A separate hearing then determines the degree of punishment.

What Is Bail? The Eighth Amendment also prohibits "excessive bail." **Bail** is a sum of money an arrested person pays to a court to win release from jail while awaiting trial.

In determining the amount of bail, the judge considers the seriousness of the case, the criminal record of the accused, and the ability of the accused to post bail.

Reading Check **Explaining** What effect did the *Furman* decision have?

Vocabulary

1. **Define** the following terms and use them in sentences related to constitutional legal protections and rights of the accused: *writ of habeas corpus, bill of attainder, ex post facto law, double jeopardy, bail.*

Main Ideas

2. **Describing** How is the Bill of Rights related to protecting citizens?
3. **Explaining** Why is a writ of habeas corpus an important right?

Critical Thinking

4. **BIG Ideas** Why do you think it is important for arrested persons to be informed of their Miranda rights?
5. **Summarizing** On a web diagram like the one below, list four legal protections that are included in the Bill of Rights and in the Fourteenth Amendment of the Constitution.

6. **Analyzing Visuals** Review the chart on page 436. Which part of the U.S. Constitution includes the guarantee that if you are arrested you must be informed of the charges against you?

CITIZENSHIP Activity

7. **Persuasive Writing** Which of the rights guaranteed to people accused of a crime do you think is the most important? Explain.

Study Central™ To review this section, go to glencoe.com.

Chapter 15

Visual Summary

Sources of Our Laws

- The set of rules and standards by which a society governs itself is known as law.
- Laws keep the peace and prevent violent acts.
- Laws set punishments and rules for resolving disputes.
- To be fully effective, laws must be fair and must treat all people equally.

Early Systems of Law

- The earliest laws were probably passed from one generation to the next by word of mouth.
- Early laws, such as the Code of Hammurabi, the Ten Commandments, Roman law, and English law, have influenced our laws today.

Lady Justice symbolizes impartiality

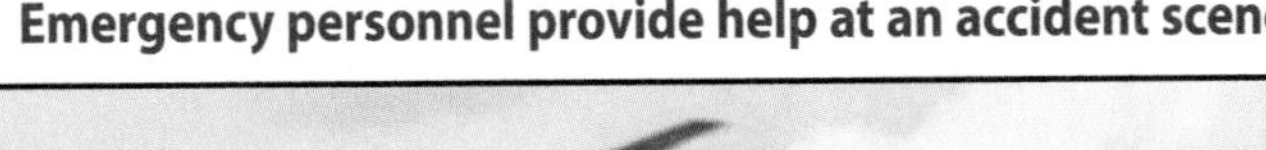

Emergency personnel provide help at an accident scene

The American Legal System

- The Constitution is our most fundamental and important source of law.
- Many types of law exist, including criminal and civil law.
- Whereas criminal law deals with criminal acts, civil law deals with disputes between people or groups.
- Article I of the U.S. Constitution and the Bill of Rights include several protections for those accused of a crime.

STUDY TO GO

Study anywhere, anytime! Download quizzes and flash cards to your PDA from glencoe.com.

Chapter 15 Assessment

TEST-TAKING TIP

Make sure the number of answer spaces on the answer sheet matches the number of questions on the test you are taking.

Reviewing Vocabulary

Directions: Choose the word(s) that best completes the sentence.

1. The system of _______ law is based on court decisions rather than on a legal code.

A criminal
B constitutional
C administrative
D common

2. The system of civil law dealing with civil wrongs, or _______, has a long history.

A torts
B felonies
C libels
D plaintiffs

3. A person charged with a crime and tried in court is the _______.

A plaintiff
B defendant
C tort
D judge

4. A _______ is a negotiation between the prosecutor and defense attorney to avoid a trial.

A verdict
B due process of law
C plea bargain
D search warrant

Reviewing Main Ideas

Directions: Choose the best answer for each question.

Section 1 *(pp. 426–429)*

5. On which of the following did the writers of the U.S. Constitution base the system of laws?

A Russian law
B new laws they created
C ancient laws passed down through generations
D warnings from King George

6. The oldest system of laws known to the modern world is the _______.

A Justinian Code
B Napoleonic Code
C Roman Code
D Code of Hammurabi

Section 2 *(pp. 430–434)*

7. A crime that is considered less serious and requires a short jail sentence is a _______.

A misdemeanor
B felony
C plaintiff
D lawsuit

8. Which of the following might result in a lawsuit?

A A person is attacked and a wallet is stolen.
B A person has his or her garage painted with graffiti.
C A company breaks a contract to build someone's house.
D A person is hit by a hit-and-run driver.

Section 3 *(pp. 435–440)*

9. With a writ of habeas corpus, the person arrested has a right to know _______.

A why he or she is being held
B who the prosecutor is
C who brought the lawsuit against him or her
D how many people will be on his or her jury

GO ON

Critical Thinking

Directions: Choose the best answer for each question.

Base your answers to questions 10 and 11 on the chart below and your knowledge of Chapter 15.

Misdemeanors and Felonies
Minor crimes and misdemeanors are tried in the lower state courts.
• Running a red light • Littering • Shoplifting small items • Vandalism
Felonies are tried in the higher state courts.
• Murder • Arson • Robbery • Drug trafficking

10. What type of law deals with the examples in this chart?

A civil law

B criminal law

C constitutional law

D administrative law

11. Which of the following offenses would most likely be punished with a fine?

A arson

B murder

C robbery

D littering

Document-Based Questions

Directions: Analyze the following document and answer the short-answer questions that follow.

Justice Oliver Wendell Holmes, Jr., who served 30 years on the U.S. Supreme Court stated the following about evidence against the accused in his dissenting opinion to the court ruling in *Olmstead* v. *United States*, 1928.

> *The government ought not to use evidence obtained and only obtainable by a criminal act. . . For my part I think it is a less evil that some criminals should escape than that the Government should play some ignoble [corrupt] part.*
>
> —Justice Oliver Wendell Holmes, Jr.

12. To which Constitutional amendment is Justice Holmes referring in this statement?

A First Amendment

B Fourth Amendment

C Fifth Amendment

D Sixth Amendment

13. Do you agree with Justice Holmes in his statement? Why or why not?

Extended-Response Question

14. Briefly explain what makes a law a good law. Give at least three characteristics.

STOP

For additional test practice, use Self-Check Quizzes—Chapter 15 on glencoe.com.

Need Extra Help?

If you missed question. . .	1	2	3	4	5	6	7	8	9	10	11	12	13	14
Go to page. . .	429	433	431	440	428	428	432	432	436	431	432	438	438	427

TIME REPORTS

New Laws on Immigration

In the absence of national legislation, lawmakers are formulating local statutes

Fed up with all the Congressional talk and the lack of national legislation on immigration, lawmakers in cities across the U.S. have been taking matters into their own hands. To deter illegal immigrants from coming to town, they've been passing local laws. In Vista, California, a new ordinance requires employers to register with the city before using day laborers, many of whom are illegal immigrants. They must also report whom they hire. The coal town of Hazleton, Pennsylvania (population 31,000), passed the nation's toughest illegal-immigration law in 2006. Hazleton's regulations impose fines on employers who knowingly hire illegal immigrants and on landlords who rent to them. "Our quality of life is at stake, and I'm not going to sit back and wait for the Federal Government to do something about it," said Mayor Louis Barletta. "I know that other cities across the country feel the same way."

The Puerto Rican Legal Defense and Education Fund filed a lawsuit to overturn Hazleton's ordinance, which Cesar Perales, president of the New York City-based advocacy group, calls "unconstitutional and discriminatory." Perales cites a legal analysis by the bipartisan Congressional Research Service that suggests Hazleton's ordinance, by creating penalties for those who aid immigrants, may be trampling on an area of law that is under federal jurisdiction. "You can't have every little town deciding the conditions under which illegal immigrants are going to live there," he says. For now, at least, some communities seem determined to try.

ON THE JOB Landscaping attracts immigrants, both legal and illegal, in East Hampton, New York, a wealthy community on Long Island.

Samantha Appleton—Aurora for TIME

How the Influx Is Changing the U.S.

Illegal immigrants in the U.S. are largely from Mexico ...

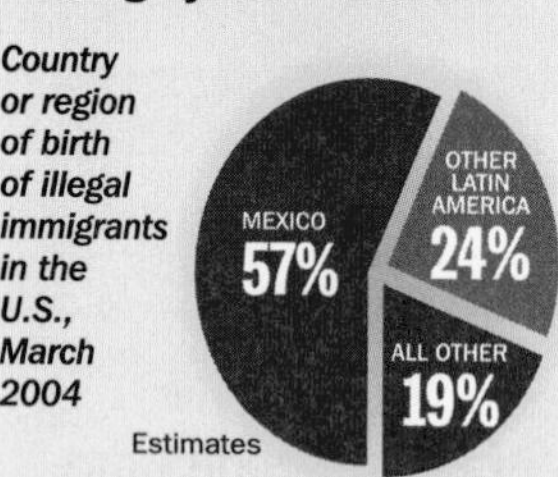

... Their numbers are growing ...

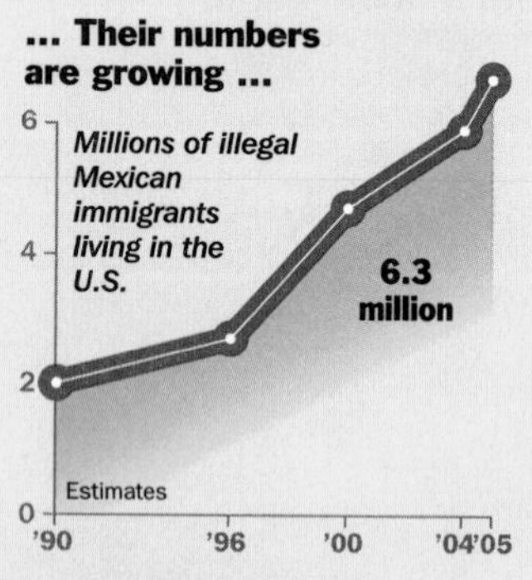

... and they are sending more and more money back home

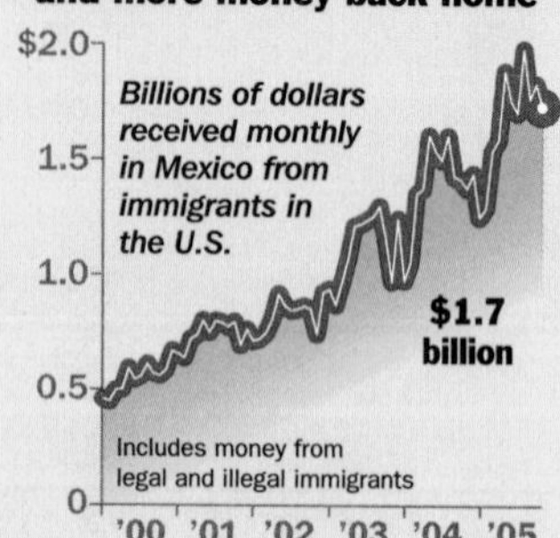

PROFILE OF IMMIGRATION

1 in 10
Proportion of Mexicans born in Mexico who now reside in the U.S.

80% to 85%
Percentage of new immigrants from Mexico who lack legal documentation

$9
Median hourly wage of Mexican-born workers in the U.S. in 2004

$1.86 (21 pesos)
Median hourly wage in Mexico in 2004

$450 billion
Estimated combined annual gross income of all U.S. workers born in Latin America, of both legal and illegal immigration status, according to a 2004 report*

93%
Percentage of that $450 billion that was spent in the U.S.*

*From the Inter-American Development Bank

Sources: Pew Hispanic Center; National Immigration Law Center; National Conference of State Legislatures; INEGI (Instituto Nacional de Estadística, Geografía e Informática)

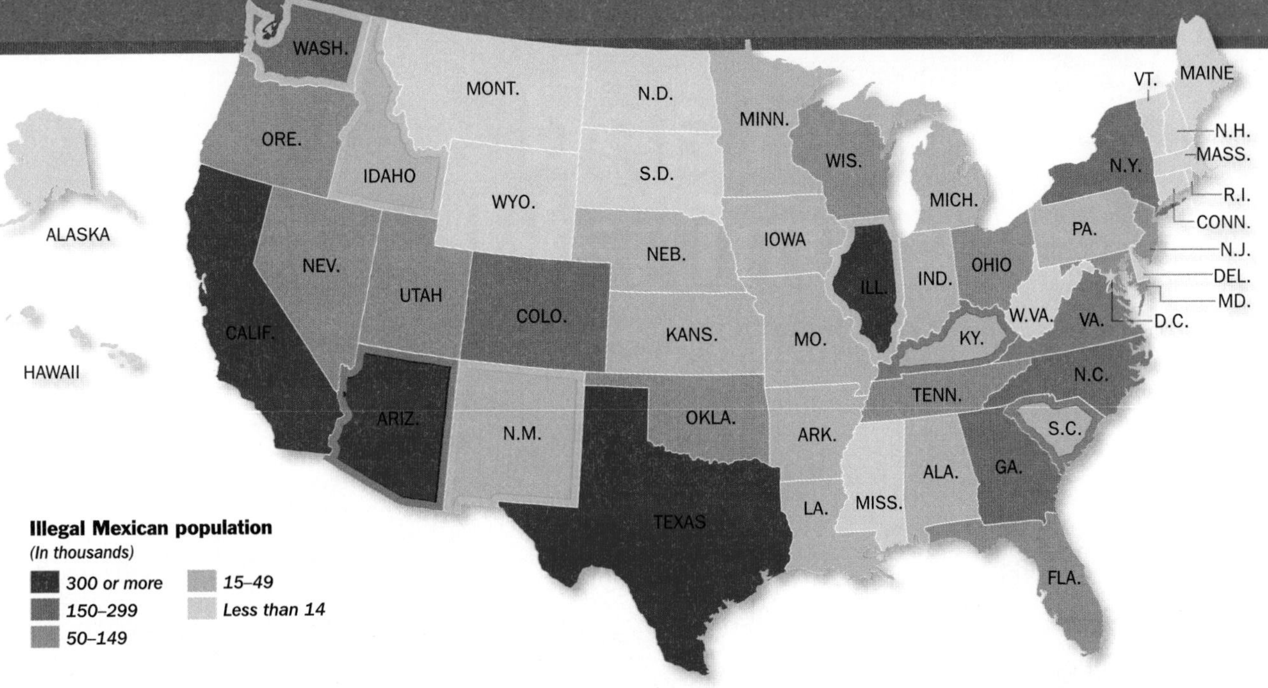

Where unauthorized Mexican immigrants go

About 6.3 million illegal immigrants from Mexico live in the U.S., according to the Pew Hispanic Center, and an average of 485,000 more arrive every year. In response, state legislatures considered nearly 300 bills on immigration policy in the first half of 2005 alone, but passed just 47. While some states address the challenges facing migrant workers with families, others are trying to crack down on illegal immigration.

SUPPORTIVE LEGISLATION

Washington State Reversed a 2002 measure and restored health-care coverage to children regardless of their immigration status.

Idaho Rejected a bill that would have required counties to pay for transportation of undocumented workers back to their home countries.

Illinois Governor Rod Blagojevich set up an office to study immigrants' contributions and needs; a new law allows illegal immigrant children to obtain health insurance.

New Mexico Became the ninth state to extend in-state tuition benefits to undocumented immigrant students.

CRACKING DOWN

Virginia A recent bill would make it the first state to prohibit illegal immigrants from attending state colleges; a new law restricts other benefits.

Kentucky Enacted a law requiring anyone seeking licenses for various professions to show proof of immigration status.

South Carolina A bill passed the state house and senate requiring Medicaid applicants to present proof of legal residency if asked.

Arizona Passed a law prohibiting cities from maintaining public day-laborer centers, where migrant workers congregate to seek employment.

TIME POLL

A majority say illegals are a real problem ...

How serious a problem is illegal immigration into the U.S.?

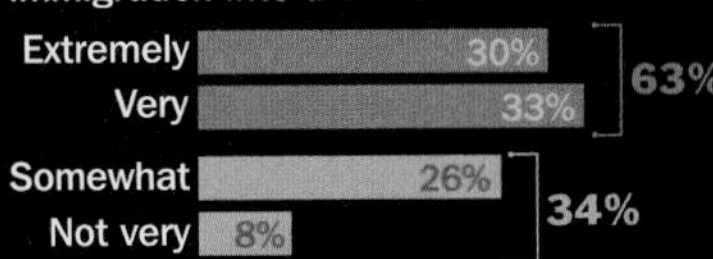

83% are concerned that providing social services for illegal immigrants costs taxpayers too much

71% are concerned that illegal immigrants increase crime

56% think illegal immigrants are taking jobs that citizens don't want

... although few say they are personally affected ...

Do you pay less for some items or services because of low-wage illegal-immigrant labor?

61% said they have had some kind of contact with people they believed to be illegal immigrants

5% said they had hired someone they thought might be illegal to work around the house

14% said they had hired a contractor or company that may have used illegal immigrants

... they still want more done about it

Is the government doing enough to keep illegal immigrants from entering the U.S.?

50% said all illegal immigrants should be deported, but:

76% think illegal immigrants should be able to earn citizenship

73% favor guest-worker registration for those already here

64% favor issuing temporary work visas for seasonal work

*Includes 7% who think the government is doing "too much"

This TIME poll was conducted by telephone Jan. 24-26, 2006 among 1,002 adult Americans by SRBI Public Affairs. The margin of error is 3 percentage points. "Don't know" answers omitted

Chapter 16

Civil and Criminal Law

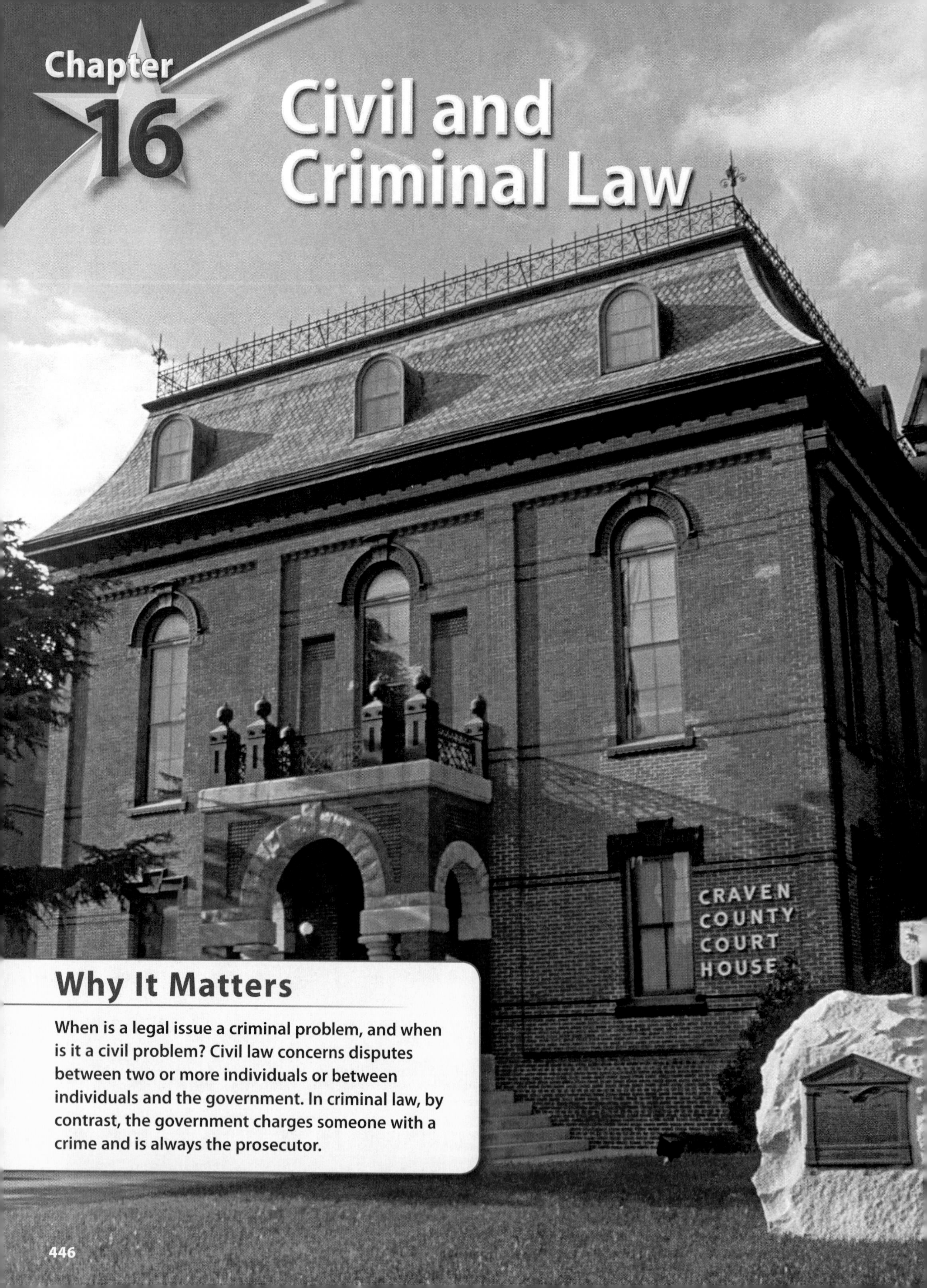

CRAVEN COUNTY COURT HOUSE

Why It Matters

When is a legal issue a criminal problem, and when is it a civil problem? Civil law concerns disputes between two or more individuals or between individuals and the government. In criminal law, by contrast, the government charges someone with a crime and is always the prosecutor.

Civics ONLINE
Visit glencoe.com and enter QuickPass™ code CIV3093c16 for Chapter 16 resources.

BIG Ideas

Section 1: Civil Cases

The judicial branch of government is charged with interpreting the law. America's courts decide thousands of civil cases each year.

Section 2: Criminal Cases

The Constitution of the United States establishes and protects the individual's fundamental rights and liberties. Thousands of criminal cases each year help define Americans' rights and enforce law and order.

Section 3: Young People and the Courts

The Constitution of the United States establishes and protects the individual's fundamental rights and liberties. A separate legal system, the juvenile justice system, handles the cases of young people in trouble with the law.

◀ Craven County Courthouse, New Bern, North Carolina

FOLDABLES™ Study Organizer

Comparing Foldable Make the following Foldable to help you compare the details and procedures of the juvenile and adult justice systems.

Step 1 Fold a sheet of paper in half from side to side.

Step 2 Fold into thirds. Unfold the paper.

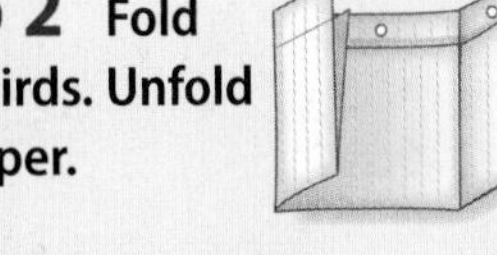

Step 3 Draw intersecting circles on the front as shown. Cut along the fold lines to make three flaps.

Step 4 Label the circles as shown.

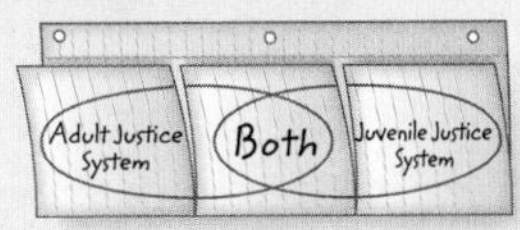

Reading and Writing As you read the chapter, make notes under each flap about the processes of the different justice systems. Under the flap labeled "both," put anything the two justice systems have in common.

Guide to Reading

Section 1

Big Idea
The judicial branch of government is charged with interpreting the law.

Content Vocabulary
- complaint *(p. 450)*
- summons *(p. 450)*
- discovery *(p. 450)*
- settlement *(p. 450)*

Academic Vocabulary
- file *(p. 449)*
- retain *(p. 450)*
- respond *(p. 450)*

Reading Strategy
Sequencing Use a graphic organizer like the one below to show the steps in a civil lawsuit.

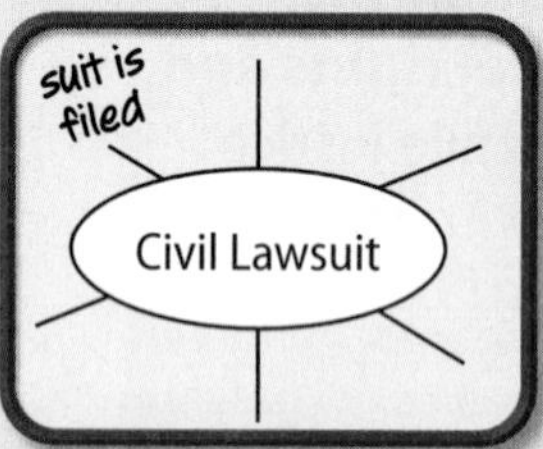

Civil Cases

Real World Civics Would you like to be judged for some wrongdoing by a group of your peers . . . people your own age? Students all over the world see what it is like to be in a court of law by engaging in a mock trial competition in the YMCA Youth and Government program. The mock trials give young people a chance to practice resolving problems in a democratic manner and to learn about the court system. Over 44 teams across the nation compete, along with high school students from Guam, the Marianna Islands, and South Korea.

▼ **Teens argue a mock trial case**

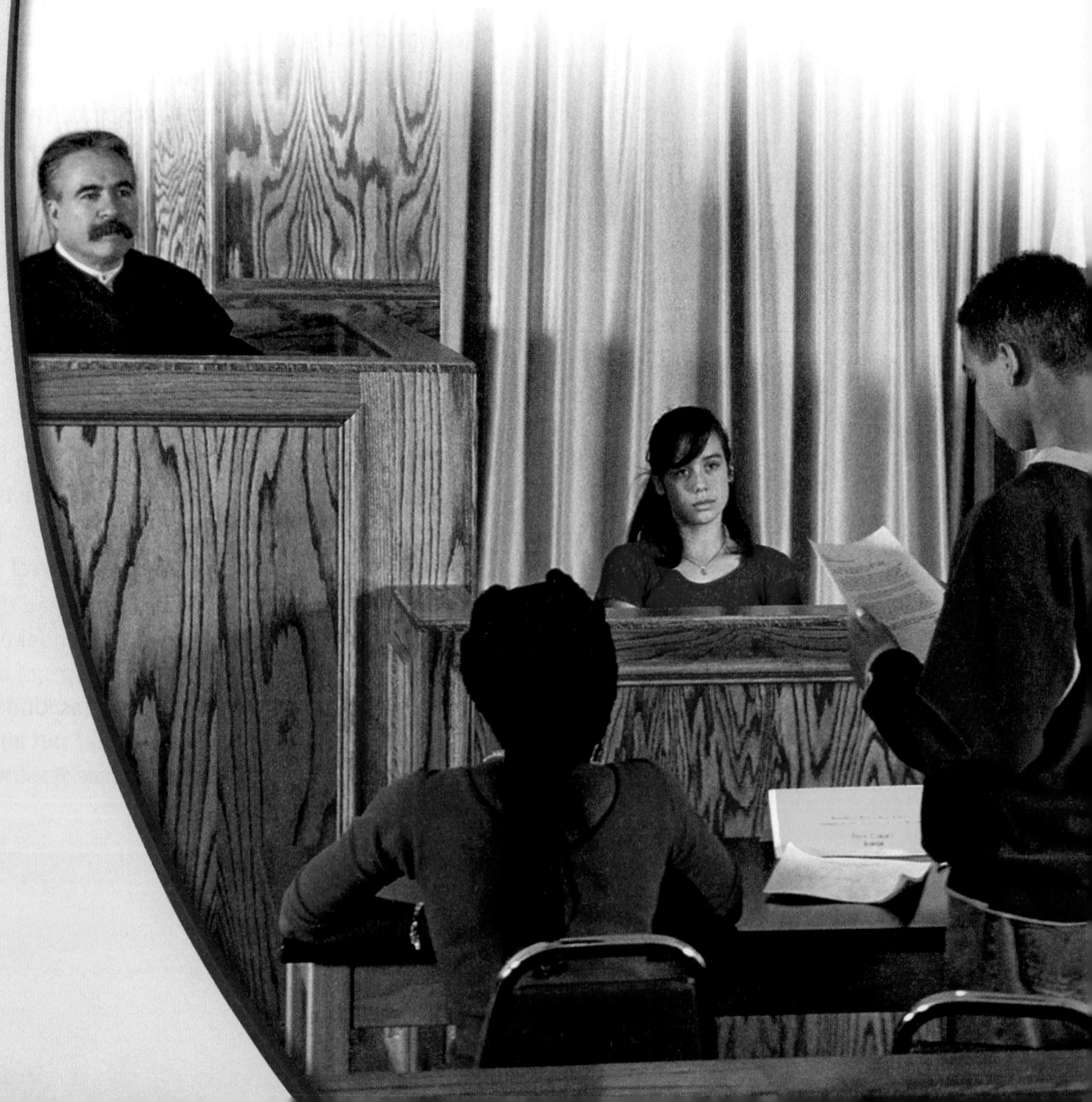

TIME™

Political Cartoons

—Chris Britt/Copley News Service

Every year, more than half of all Americans do volunteer work | role in it. One of the responsibilities of citizens is to help make their | of volunteer grou small. Perha

Chris Britt, the creator of this cartoon, is making a comment on laws that require drivers to wear seatbelts.

1. **Why might the driver consider the seatbelt law "a stupid idea"?**
2. **What proves him wrong?**
3. **Does the cartoonist favor or oppose seat-belt laws?**
4. **What is your position on seatbelt laws? Explain.**

Civil Lawsuits

Main Idea **Civil lawsuits may involve property disputes, a breach of contract, family matters, or personal injury.**

Civics & You The presidential election of 2000 was a disputed election. Read to find out why it ended up in the Supreme Court.

In November 2000, residents of Palm Beach County in Florida **filed,** or registered, a civil lawsuit against the Palm Beach County Canvassing Board, their election authority. The residents argued that a flaw in the ballot format caused them to vote for candidates other than the candidate for whom they intended to vote. This civil suit led to a recounting of votes and reached the Supreme Court. The Court's ruling led to George W. Bush's winning the presidency in 2000.

Why Do People File Civil Suits?

In civil cases the plaintiff—the party bringing a lawsuit—claims to have suffered a loss or injury to themselves and usually seeks damages, an award of money from the defendant. The defendant—the party being sued—argues either that the loss or injury did not occur or that the defendant is not responsible for it. The court's job is to provide a place to resolve the differences between the plaintiff and the defendant.

Courts hear many different kinds of civil lawsuits. Lawsuits may involve property disputes, breaches of contract, or family matters involving two or more parties. Many lawsuits deal with negligence, or personal injury. A negligence suit is filed when someone has been injured or killed or when property has been destroyed because someone else has been careless, or negligent.

Reading Check **Identifying** Who is the plaintiff in a civil lawsuit?

The Process in a Civil Case

Main Idea **Civil lawsuits follow a specified legal procedure.**

Civics & You Despite what you see on TV, lawsuits do not always end up dramatically in court. Read to find out what happens to most of them.

Let us look at how a lawsuit proceeds through the court system. Suppose you are riding in a city bus one day and suffer head injuries and a broken arm when the bus is in an accident. You decide to file a lawsuit against the city to recover the costs of hospital and doctor bills, lost income from days missed at work, and other expenses. You become the plaintiff, or person filing the lawsuit. The party you are suing, in this case the city, is the defendant.

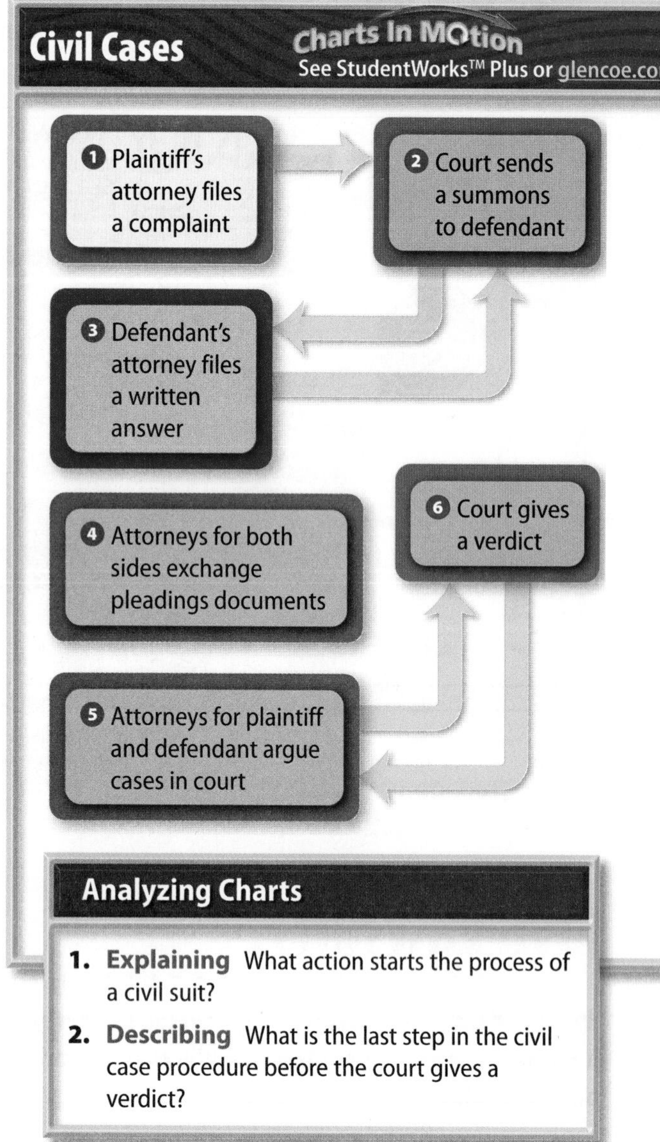

Analyzing Charts

1. **Explaining** What action starts the process of a civil suit?
2. **Describing** What is the last step in the civil case procedure before the court gives a verdict?

Bringing Suit

You start the process by **retaining,** or hiring, a lawyer, who files a **complaint** with the court. The complaint is a statement naming the plaintiff and the defendant and describing the lawsuit. The court sends the defendant (the city) a **summons,** a document that announces that the defendant is being sued, and sets a date and time for an appearance in court.

The Defendant's Response The defendant's attorneys may **respond,** or react, to the charges by filing an "answer" to the complaint. The answer will either admit to the charges or offer reasons the defendant is not responsible for the injuries the plaintiff is claiming. The complaint and the answer together are referred to as pleadings. Before going to trial, the lawyers on each side have an opportunity to check facts and to gather evidence by questioning the other party and possible witnesses. This process is called **discovery.**

Pretrial Hearing Before the trial, the judge might call a conference to help clarify differences between the two sides. At this stage you and your lawyer might decide that your case looks weak, and you may want to drop the suit. Or the city may conclude that your case is very strong and that you are likely to win your suit. The city may, therefore, offer you a **settlement,** in which the parties agree on an amount of money that the defendant will pay to the plaintiff.

Another way to resolve disputes is by a process called mediation. During mediation, each side is given the opportunity to explain its side of the dispute and must listen to the other side. A trained mediator helps the two sides find a solution.

The two sides may also agree to submit their dispute to arbitration. This is a process conducted by a professional arbitrator who acts somewhat like a judge by reviewing the case and resolving the dispute.

Most civil cases are settled before trial. Because trials are time-consuming and expensive, all the major participants—the defendant, the insurer, the plaintiff, the judge, and the attorneys—are likely to prefer a settlement.

Trial

If the parties do not reach a settlement, the case goes to trial. There may be a jury, or more likely, a judge who will hear the case alone. Both sides present their cases.

In criminal trials the prosecution must prove the defendant guilty "beyond a reasonable doubt." In a civil case the plaintiff has to present only a "preponderance of evidence"—enough to convince the judge or jury that the defendant *more likely than not* was responsible for the incident that caused the damages or injury.

After all evidence has been presented, the judge or jury considers the case and decides on a verdict, or decision, in favor of one party. If the plaintiff wins, a remedy is set. In the case of the bus accident, the remedy might be for the defendant—the city—to pay your medical costs, replace your lost earnings, and compensate you for your pain and suffering with a cash payment. If the defendant wins, the plaintiff—you—gets nothing and must pay court costs for both sides of the lawsuit.

Appeal If the losing side believes the judge made errors during the trial or that some other type of injustice took place, it may appeal the verdict to a higher court. Remember that in the hierarchy of the court system, each district has Courts of Appeals to hear local disputes of this nature. In cases in which the plaintiff wins a large cash award, the defendant or the defendant's insurance company often appeals to have the award reduced. As a result, a winning plaintiff may have to wait years before seeing any of the money the court awarded or, depending on the outcome of the appeals, may end up with nothing.

Reading Check **Explaining** When can the defendant appeal a verdict of a civil lawsuit?

Section 1 Review

Vocabulary

1. **Write** complete sentences using each of the following terms: *complaint, summons, discovery, settlement.*

Main Ideas

2. **Describing** In civil cases, what is the plaintiff usually seeking?
3. **Identifying** What is the purpose of the discovery phase of a civil trial?

Critical Thinking

4. **BIG Ideas** In your opinion, should civil cases be tried before a jury? Why or why not?
5. **Sequencing** Use a graphic organizer similar to the one below to summarize the reasons that most civil cases are settled before trial.

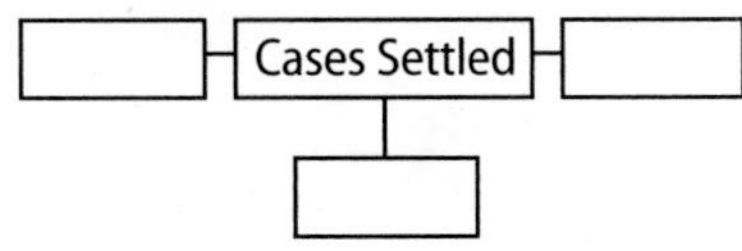

CITIZENSHIP Activity

6. **Expository Writing** Find a newspaper story about a civil lawsuit. Write a summary about the nature of the dispute and the way the lawsuit was resolved. Use the information in this section to make sure the details of your summary are accurate.

Study Central™ To review this section, go to glencoe.com.

Section Audio

Spotlight Video

Guide to Reading

Big Idea

The Constitution of the United States establishes and protects the individual's fundamental rights and liberties.

Content Vocabulary

- prosecution *(p. 453)*
- crime *(p. 453)*
- penal code *(p. 453)*
- parole *(p. 454)*
- mandatory sentencing *(p. 454)*
- arraignment *(p. 456)*
- testimony *(p. 457)*
- cross-examine *(p. 457)*
- acquittal *(p. 458)*
- hung jury *(p. 458)*

Academic Vocabulary

- function *(p. 453)*
- confine *(p. 453)*
- sufficient *(p. 456)*

Reading Strategy

Sequencing Outline the procedures that take place in a criminal case after an arrest is made.

1. hearing
2.
3.
4.
5.

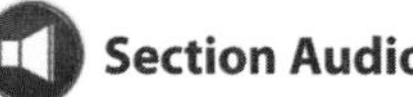

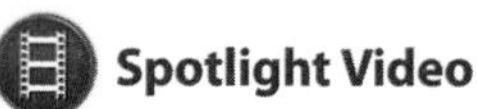

Section 2

Criminal Cases

Real World Civics Those serving time in prison do not have a lot of choices, but most can get their high school diplomas if they take courses offered. Almost half the inmates in state prisons do not have a high school degree. These Arkansas prisoners received their GED diplomas through a tutoring program provided by the state prison system. Why is this an important service for the state governments to provide?

▼ **Inmates achieve high school graduation**

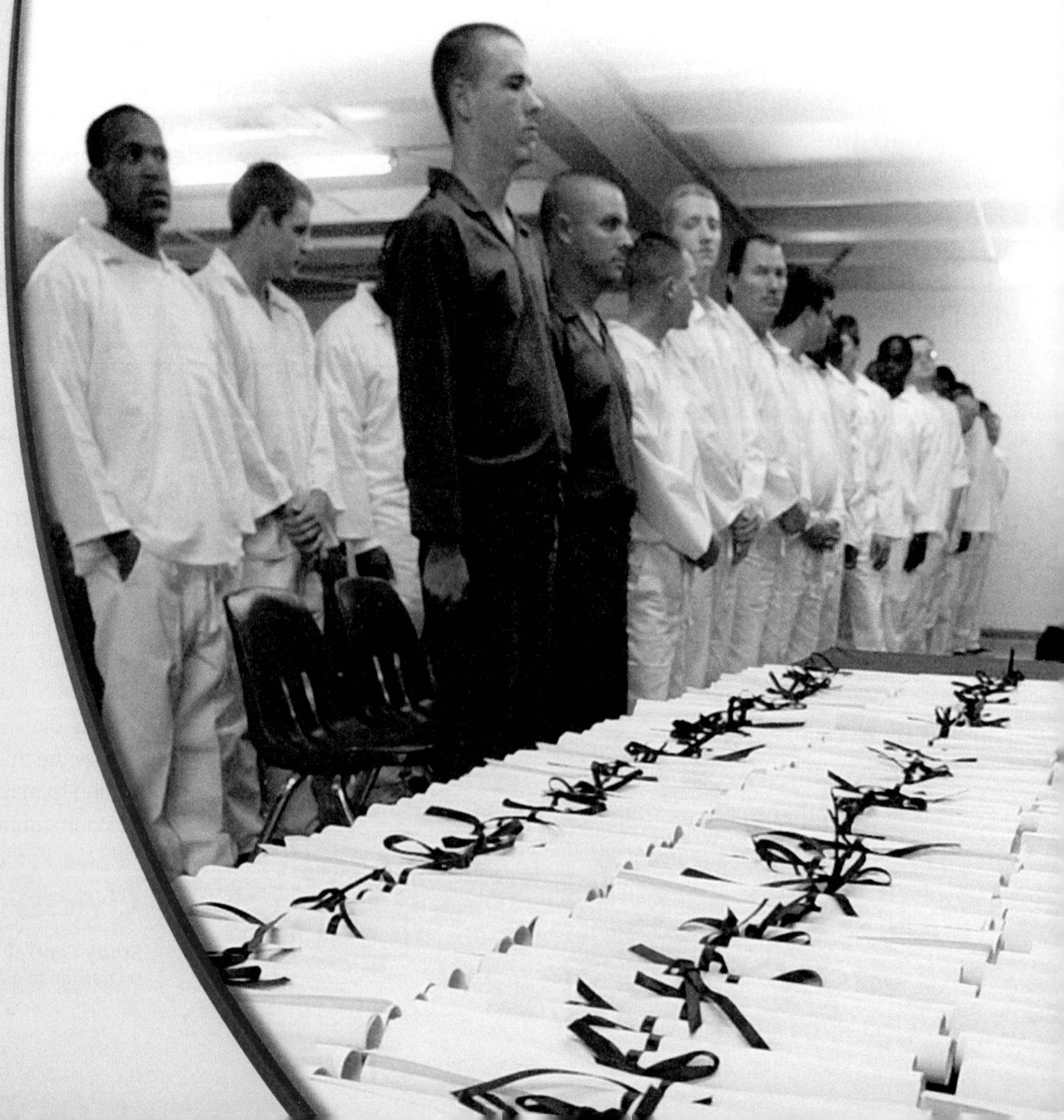

What Is a Criminal Case?

Main Idea **In criminal cases, defendants are charged with crimes, and if convicted, they are sentenced as punishment.**

Civics & You Have you ever received a punishment for something you did? Read to find out how society deals with punishment.

Criminal law cases are those in which the state or federal government charges someone with a crime. The government is always the **prosecution**—the party who starts the legal proceedings against another party for a violation of the law. The person accused of the crime is the defendant. A **crime** is an act that breaks a federal or state criminal law and causes harm to people or society.

The Criminal Justice System The state and federal courts, judges, lawyers, police, and prisons that have the responsibility for enforcing criminal law make up the criminal justice system. There is a separate juvenile justice system with special rules and procedures for handling cases dealing with juveniles, who in most states are people under the age of 18. You will read about the juvenile justice system in Section 3.

The Penal Code Crimes are defined in each state's written criminal laws, called the **penal code.** A state's penal code also spells out the punishments that go with each crime. In general, the more serious the crime, the harsher the punishment will be. The federal government also has a penal code that defines federal crimes such as income tax evasion, kidnapping, and drug smuggling.

Types of Crime

Persons convicted of misdemeanors may be fined or sentenced to one year or less in jail. Some misdemeanors, such as illegal gambling, are considered victimless crimes—no one individual has been harmed, and often no direct punishment is enacted. Serious crimes, such as burglary, kidnapping, arson, manslaughter, and murder, are considered felonies. These crimes are punishable by imprisonment for a year or more. In the case of murder, the punishment could be death.

People convicted of felonies may also lose certain civil rights such as the right to vote, possess a firearm, and serve on a jury. Further, they may lose employment opportunities in some careers such as the military, law, teaching, and law enforcement.

Misdemeanors may sometimes be treated as felonies. Drunk driving, for example, is often a misdemeanor. However, if a person has been arrested for drunk driving before and has been convicted of the same offense, that person may be charged with a felony.

Penalties for Crimes

Criminal penalties serve several **functions,** or purposes. They provide punishment so that a criminal pays for an offense. They help protect society by keeping dangerous lawbreakers **confined,** or enclosed, in prison. Criminal penalties can also keep other people from committing the same crimes by serving as warnings to deter others.

GPS Global Positioning Systems, electronic devices such as the one being attached below, monitor those under house arrest and are often attached to the ankle. ***Speculating*** **What kinds of crimes are punished by this method?**

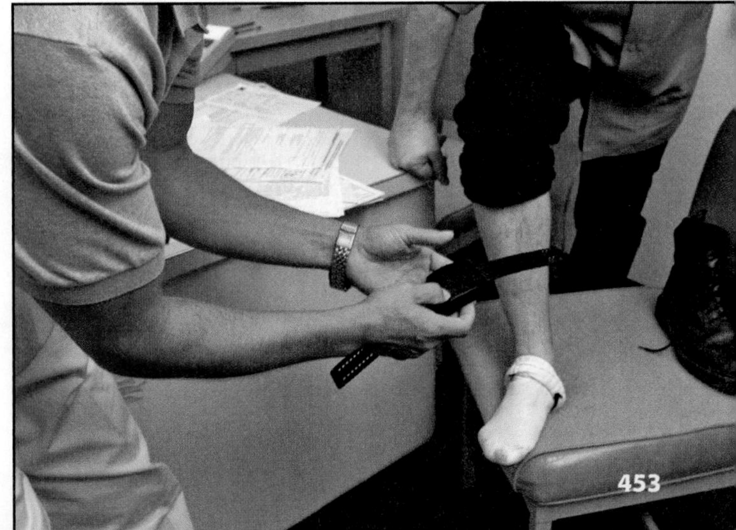

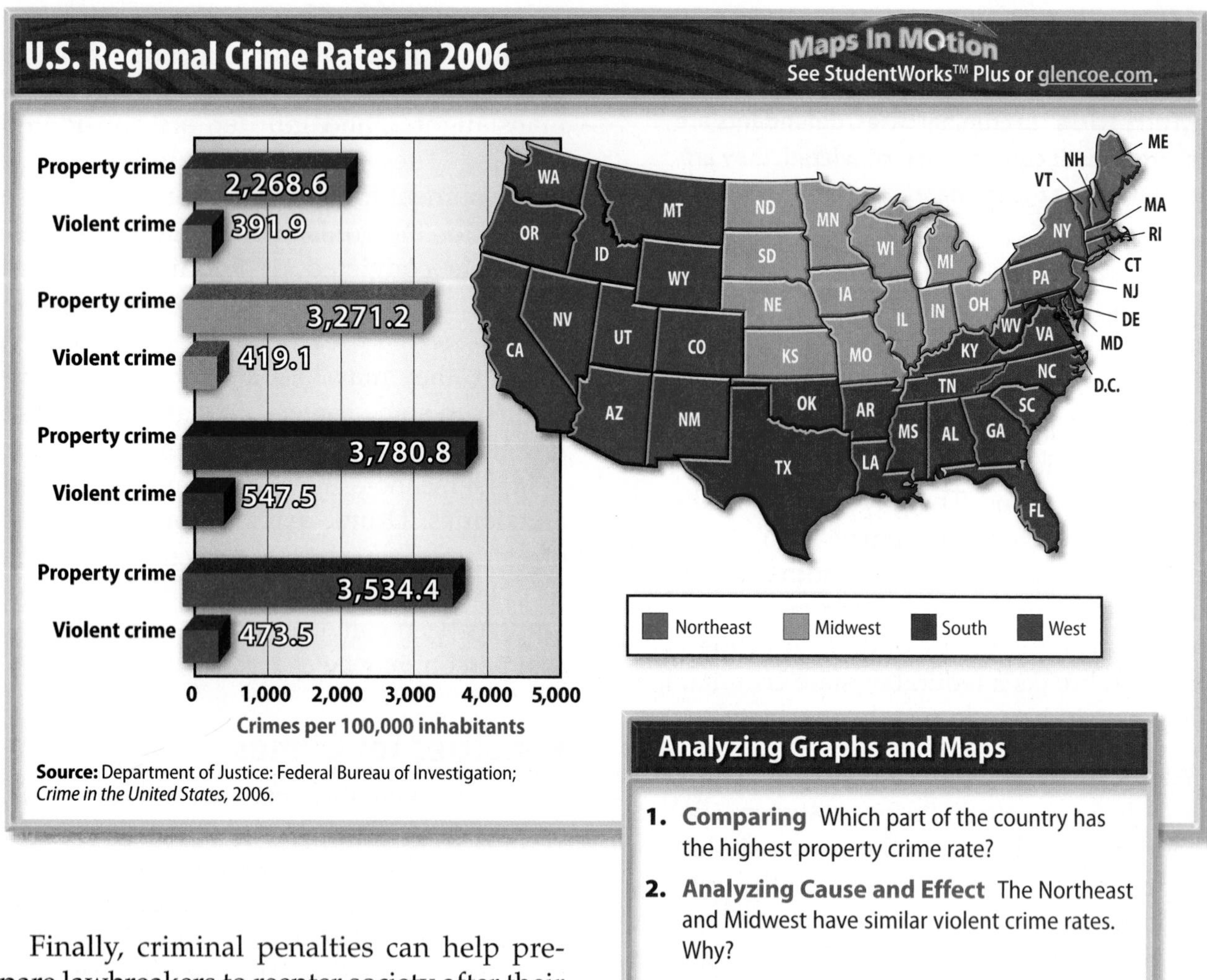

Source: Department of Justice: Federal Bureau of Investigation; *Crime in the United States,* 2006.

Analyzing Graphs and Maps

1. **Comparing** Which part of the country has the highest property crime rate?
2. **Analyzing Cause and Effect** The Northeast and Midwest have similar violent crime rates. Why?

Finally, criminal penalties can help prepare lawbreakers to reenter society after their prison terms have ended. Through counseling, education, and job training, some prisons help inmates learn skills that will help them lead productive, noncriminal lives after prison. Some prisons even support money-making businesses from inmate-made items prisoners have been trained to produce.

Sentencing Determining the sentence, or punishment, of a person convicted of a crime is one of the more complicated and difficult aspects of the criminal justice system. Because the circumstances in each case are different, judges may hand down very different sentences for similar crimes.

In the past, many states used a system of indeterminate sentences in penalizing criminals. An indeterminate sentence is one in which a judge gives a minimum and maximum sentence.

Some prisoners become eligible for **parole** after serving part of their sentences. A parole board decides whether or not to grant a prisoner early release from prison. If parole is granted, the person must report to a parole officer until the sentence expires.

Mandatory Sentencing Critics of the parole system claim that many sentences end up much shorter than intended. In answer to this criticism, some states have established **mandatory sentencing,** which means that judges must impose whatever sentence the law directs. Opponents of mandatory sentencing, though, claim that in some cases, the judge should be able to impose harsher sentences than the law directs.

Sentencing Options Judges follow basic sentencing options (from least serious to most serious): suspended sentence—a sentence is given but not served at that time; probation—the defendant has supervised release; home confinement—defendant is required to serve his or her sentence at home, closely monitored; a monetary fine—damages are paid; restitution—the defendant is required to pay back or make up for damages; work release—the defendant is allowed to work but must return to prison at night and on weekends; imprisonment—the defendant is confined to an institution to serve the sentence; death—the defendant is sentenced to die for his or her crime in the state where this is mandated.

Many states are giving judges more sentencing options. Among these are shock incarceration, intensive-supervision probation or parole, and house arrest. Shock incarceration involves shorter sentences in a highly structured environment where offenders participate in work, community service, education, and counseling.

Intensive-supervision probation or parole keeps high-risk offenders in the community but remaining under close supervision that involves frequent home visits or even nightly curfew checks. The offender often wears an electronic device that continually signals his or her location. A related alternative sentence is house arrest, which requires an offender to stay at home except for certain functions the court permits.

Reading Check **Explaining** Why have some states established mandatory sentencing?

Criminal Evidence Brooklyn, New York, authorities collected evidence of criminal gambling activities that will be presented in court. ***Explaining*** **Why is illegal gambling considered a victimless crime?**

Criminal Case Procedure

Main Idea **Criminal cases follow several steps, including arrest, hearing, indictment, arraignment, verdict, sentencing, and appeal.**

Civics & You Do you ever have trouble making up your mind? Read to find out what happens when a jury in a criminal trial has this problem.

You learned earlier that the criminal justice system has the responsibility for enforcing criminal law. Criminal cases follow several steps. At each step defendants are entitled to the protections of due process guaranteed in the Bill of Rights.

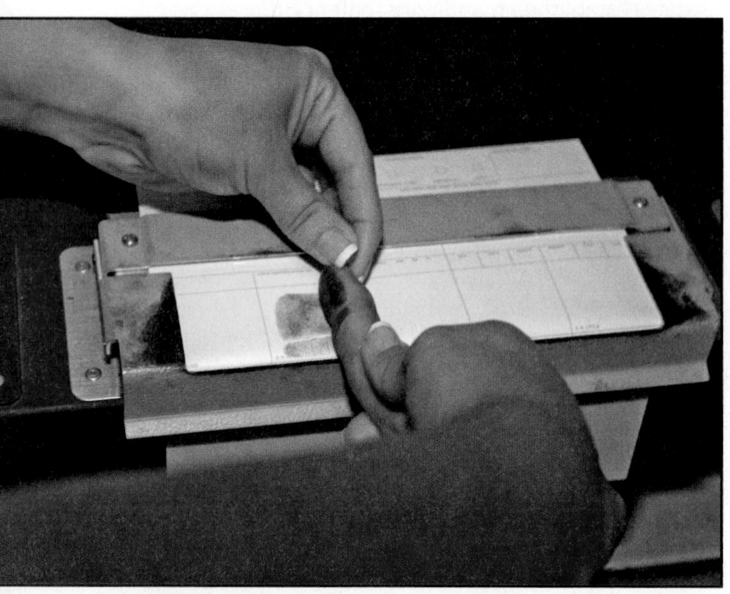

Fingerprinting Once a criminal suspect is arrested, fingerprints and photographs of them are taken. ***Analyzing*** **Why do the police take fingerprints and what do you think they use the fingerprints for?**

Arrest

Criminal cases begin when police or other law enforcement officers arrest a person on suspicion of having committed a crime. Officers make arrests if they have witnessed a suspected crime, if a citizen has made a complaint or a report of a crime, or if a judge has issued an arrest warrant. When they make the arrest, the officers are required to read the suspect his or her Miranda rights, which you learned about in Chapter 15.

The suspect is taken to a local police station and booked, or charged with a crime. As part of the booking process, the police fingerprint and photograph the suspect. During that time he or she is allowed to call a lawyer. If the suspect cannot afford a lawyer, the state must provide one.

Hearing, Indictment, and Arraignment

A few hours after being booked, the suspect appears in court and is informed of the charges against him or her. At this time the prosecution must show the judge that there is probable cause—a good reason—for believing the accused committed the crime. The judge then either sends the accused back to jail, sets bail, or releases the accused on his or her own recognizance, or control.

As noted in Chapter 15, in federal courts and many state courts, grand juries decide whether a person should be indicted—formally charged with a crime. Some states use a preliminary hearing instead of a grand jury indictment. In some cases, the prosecutor files an "information," which claims that there is **sufficient,** or enough, evidence to bring the accused person to trial.

The defendant then appears in court for a procedure called an **arraignment.** He or she is formally presented with the charges and asked to enter a plea. If the defendant pleads not guilty, the case continues. If the defendant pleads guilty, he or she stands convicted of the crime, and the judge determines a punishment. Another option is for the defendant to plead no contest. A no contest plea means that he or she does not admit guilt but will not fight the prosecution's case. The effect is much the same as for a guilty plea.

Trial

If the case goes to trial, the defense lawyer interviews witnesses, studies the laws affecting the case, and gathers information. Although criminal defendants have a constitutional right to a jury trial, many give up that right and have their cases tried before a judge alone in what is called a bench trial.

If the defense asks for a jury trial, the first step when the trial starts is to choose the jurors. Both sides select potential jurors from a large pool of residents within the court's jurisdiction. In most states, residents are called randomly for jury duty. A specific excuse or acceptable reason must be presented for a person to be excused from jury duty. Both sides try to avoid jurors who might be unfavorable to their side. Either side can reject a certain number of jury candidates without giving reasons and can ask the judge to dismiss others for various causes.

Presenting the Case After the jury has been selected, the lawyers for each side make opening statements in which they outline the cases they will present. The prosecution and defense then present their cases in turn. Each side calls witnesses who swear that their **testimony**—the answers they give while under oath—will be "the truth, the whole truth, and nothing but the truth."

After a witness testifies for one side, the other side is allowed to **cross-examine.** The questions asked in cross-examination are meant to clarify testimony but are usually designed to make the witness's original testimony appear unreliable or untrue. Finally, each side makes a closing statement highlighting the testimony and evidence that support it and questioning the other side's testimony and evidence. The judge then "instructs" the jury, or explains the law that relates to the case.

Civics ONLINE

Student Web Activity Visit glencoe.com and complete the Chapter 16 Web Activity.

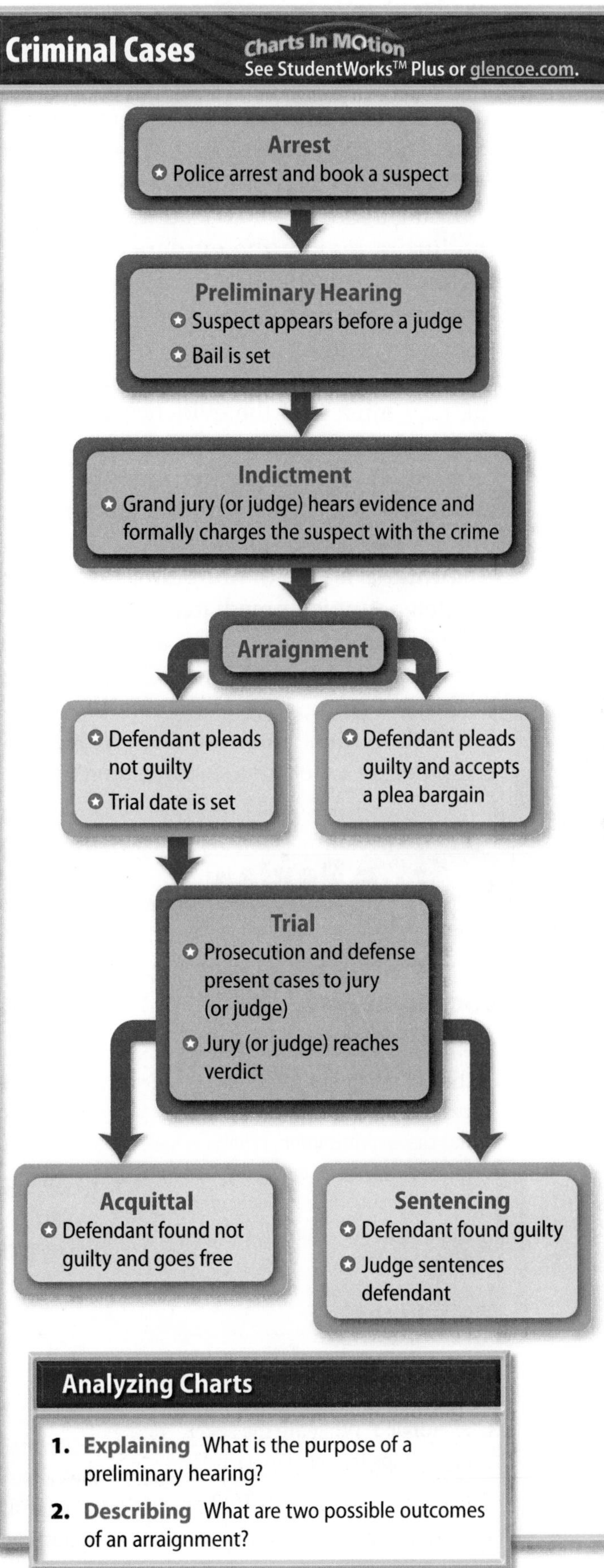

Analyzing Charts

1. **Explaining** What is the purpose of a preliminary hearing?
2. **Describing** What are two possible outcomes of an arraignment?

The Verdict, Sentencing, and Appeal

After the judge gives the jury a set of instructions, the jury goes to the jury room to discuss the case and reach a verdict. After choosing a foreperson to lead the discussion, the jurors review the evidence and legal arguments. Jury deliberations are secret and have no set time limit. Finally, the jurors vote on whether the defendant is guilty or not guilty. To decide that a person is guilty, the jury must find the evidence convincing "beyond a reasonable doubt." In nearly all criminal cases, the verdict must be unanimous. If a jury feels the prosecution has not proven its case, it can decide on acquittal. **Acquittal** is a vote of not guilty, after which the defendant is immediately released.

Sometimes a jury cannot agree on a verdict, even after many votes. Then the judge declares a **hung jury** and rules the trial a mistrial. With a mistrial, the prosecution must decide whether to ask for a retrial.

Sentencing If a defendant is found guilty, the judge sets a court date for sentencing. In some cases, a jury recommends a sentence. More often, however, the judge decides on the sentence after considering the defendant's family situation, previous criminal record, employment status, and other information. Sentences often specify a period of time to be spent in prison. Victims of the crime are often allowed to make statements about the sentence, and judges may take those statements into account. Sentences may include a variety of options as discussed earlier in this chapter.

Appeal If the defendant is found guilty, the defense may, and often does, appeal the verdict to a higher court. (If the case is a capital case, or one involving the death penalty, the appeal could go directly to the state supreme court.) Usually an appeal contends that the judge made errors or that the defendant's constitutional rights were violated.

Reading Check **Explaining** If a defendant is found guilty, who or what decides his or her sentence?

Vocabulary

1. **Write** a paragraph using six of the following key terms in a paragraph that relates to criminal cases: *prosecution, crime, penal code, parole, mandatory sentencing, arraignment, testimony, cross-examine, acquittal, hung jury.*

Main Ideas

2. **Describing** What is included in a state's penal code?
3. **Identifying** What are the seven basic steps in a criminal case?

Critical Thinking

4. **Concluding** Why do you think judges allow some suspects to be released on their own recognizance?
5. **BIG Ideas** Using a graphic organizer like the one below, list the major participants in a trial.

6. **Analyzing Visuals** Review the crime rate map/graph on page 454. How does your region compare with others?

CITIZENSHIP Activity

7. **Persuasive Writing** Should judges be allowed to hand down sentences based on the characteristics of individual cases and defendants, or should they follow mandatory sentencing guidelines? Write a newspaper editorial on the subject.

Study Central™ To review this section, go to glencoe.com.

Landmark Supreme Court Case Studies

Gideon v. Wainwright

In the 1930s, the Supreme Court ruled that the Sixth Amendment requires the government to supply lawyers for defendants who cannot otherwise afford one in all federal cases. How did poor defendants acquire Sixth Amendment rights in state courts?

Background of the Case

In 1942 the Supreme Court, in *Betts* v. *Brady,* ruled that the Sixth Amendment did not require states to appoint attorneys for people who could not afford them. By way of the Fourteenth Amendment, however, it held that states were required to supply lawyers in cases that held the death penalty.

Clarence Earl Gideon

In June 1961, Clarence Earl Gideon of Florida was accused of theft, a nondeath-penalty crime. Gideon mistakenly believed the Supreme Court had entitled him to court-appointed counsel and so asked for a lawyer. His request was denied, so Gideon defended himself in an intelligent but inadequate manner. The jury found him guilty and the judge sentenced him to five years in prison.

Gideon appealed his conviction claiming, "I knew the Constitution guaranteed me a fair trial, but I didn't see how a man could get one without a lawyer to defend him." The state supreme court refused to review Gideon's case. Gideon appealed his case to the U. S. Supreme Court.

The Supreme Court heard the case after Gideon sent his own petition claiming his Sixth and Fourteenth Amendment rights were violated. Because only lawyers may speak before the Supreme Court, a Washington, D.C., attorney was appointed for Gideon. A Florida lawyer represented Louie Wainwright, head of the state's prisons.

The Decision

The Supreme Court's ruling came on March 18, 1963. Justice Hugo L. Black wrote the unanimous decision:

> "*We accept* Betts *v.* Brady's *assumption . . . that a provision of the Bill of Rights which is 'fundamental and essential to a fair trial' is made obligatory upon the States by the Fourteenth Amendment. We think the Court in* Betts *was wrong, however, in concluding that the Sixth Amendment's guarantee of counsel is not one of these fundamental rights. . . . [A]ny person hauled into court, who is too poor to hire a lawyer, cannot be assured a fair trial unless counsel is provided for him.*"
>
> —Justice Hugo L. Black

The Court thus overturned *Betts.* Under the "due process" clause of the Fourteenth Amendment, it found the Sixth Amendment guarantee of counsel binding on state as well as federal courts.

Why It Matters

Although some states by 1963 already had court-appointed lawyers in nondeath-penalty cases, the *Gideon* decision assured this protection for all. Gideon was retried and found not guilty.

Analyzing the Court Decision

1. **Explaining** What protection did the *Gideon* decision guarantee?
2. **Describing** How would you summarize the importance of the decision?

Section Audio

Spotlight Video

Young People and the Courts

Guide to Reading

Big Idea

The Constitution of the United States establishes and protects the individual's fundamental rights and liberties.

Content Vocabulary

- juvenile *(p. 461)*
- juvenile delinquent *(p. 461)*
- rehabilitate *(p. 462)*

Academic Vocabulary

- emphasis *(p. 463)*
- preliminary *(p. 463)*
- equivalent *(p. 463)*

Reading Strategy

Summarizing Judges have options when sentencing juvenile offenders. List these options in a graphic organizer like the one below.

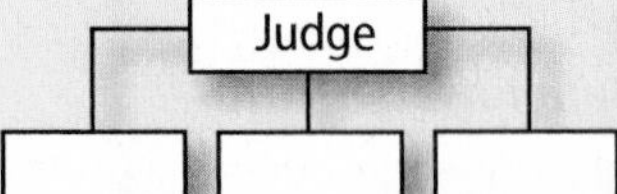

Citizens in Action California Youth Authority

Juvenile boot camps are one approach to the problem of dealing with teens in trouble. Sent to a boot camp as the result of a court decision, teens here are taught techniques for managing anger and receive treatment for emotional problems. This alternative sentence is meant to help teens who need counseling and education as well as discipline. They are called boot camps due to their similarity to military organizations.

▼ **Juvenile offenders line up at California boot camp**

Causes of Juvenile Delinquency

Main Idea **All states and the federal government have a separate justice system for young people.**

Civics & You Have you heard the term *juvenile delinquent?* Read to find out what this term means.

Every state establishes a certain age at which people are considered adults in the eyes of the criminal justice system. Anyone under that age—18 in most states—is considered a **juvenile.** Our system treats young people who commit crimes—called **juvenile delinquents**—somewhat differently from adults. All states and the federal government, however, allow older juveniles who are charged with very serious crimes or already have criminal records to be tried as adults.

This treatment of juveniles was not always the case historically. Even in the late 1800s children were thrown into jail with adults. Long prison terms and physical punishment—such as striking the individual—were common for children and adults, often for crimes we consider minor today.

Children and teenagers currently commit many crimes each year. Some of these crimes are misdemeanors, such as shoplifting. Others, however, are serious crimes, such as armed robbery, rape, and murder. Studies show that children who are abused or neglected, or who suffer emotional or mental problems, are more likely than others to get into trouble with the law. The studies also show that children who grow up in poverty, in overcrowded and rundown neighborhoods where drug and alcohol abuse are common, are more likely to become delinquents.

Although these factors may contribute to juvenile delinquency, they do not explain why some young people commit crimes. Many children who suffer abuse and live amid poverty never have trouble with the law, whereas children from all backgrounds can become juvenile delinquents.

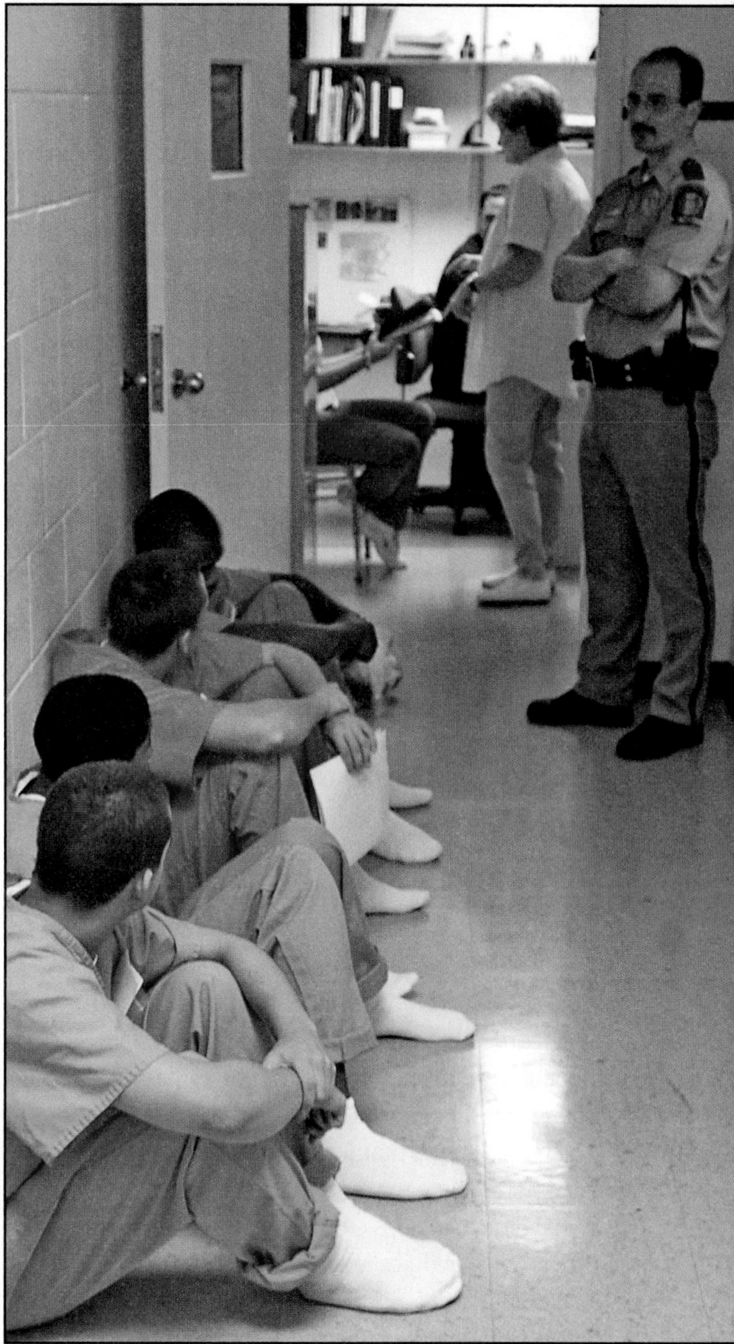

Counseling Services Texas youth offenders await psychological testing before being assigned to specific institutions. ***Analyzing*** **Why are young offenders kept separate from adult offenders?**

Reading Check **Explaining** What effect can abuse and neglect have on young people?

TIME™ Teens in *Action*

The Real Thing

Sarah Carr

Teens around the United States are acting as official judges, jurors, and lawyers.

Hear ye! Hear ye! Youth Court in Colonie, New York, is in session. Prosecutor Sarah Carr, 16, is questioning Andrew G., 17, the defendant. Carr asks, "Didn't you know it was wrong?" Andrew G. nods shyly. He knows that shoplifting a $4.97 popular action figure is not only a petty crime but also a geeky one in the eyes of his high school peers, some of whom are serving on the jury.

In this youth court, the jurors, judge, and lawyers are all teens. The real defendants are limited to first-time offenders who are under the age of 19 and who admit guilt to minor crimes. Sentences are generally creative forms of community service—such as washing police cars—but never jail terms. The record shows that 99 percent of those sentenced complete the required tasks. Doing so keeps their criminal records clean, which is advantageous when completing college and job applications.

Volunteer defenders and prosecutors, like Carr, undergo eight weeks of training to learn about the judicial process. They serve for at least a year and rotate among the other court roles: judge, bailiff, and jury foreperson. Jurors are untrained volunteers in grades 7 through 12.

Many experts say youth court, which is becoming an institution across the U.S., is helping to relieve the clogged criminal-court systems. Some are run by schools, others by police departments or nonprofit groups.

Making a Difference

Explain why it takes a strong commitment to take part in this program.

The Juvenile Justice System

Main Idea **The juvenile justice system is similar to the adult system, with some important differences.**

Civics & You The juvenile court system is modeled after the adult court system. Read on to find out how justice is administered in the juvenile court system.

When juveniles are charged with violating the law, their cases are handled in separate courts called juvenile courts. The primary goal of juvenile courts is to try to **rehabilitate,** or correct a person's behavior, rather than punish a person. Juvenile courts aim to do whatever is in the best interests of the young people.

Most juvenile court cases begin when police make an arrest. Other cases result from petitions to the courts that school administrators, store managers, or others in contact with children have filed. Parents who cannot control their children's behavior also may petition a court for help.

Neglect and Delinquency

Juvenile courts handle two types of cases. Cases of *neglect* involve juveniles whose caregivers neglect or abuse them. A juvenile court has the power to place these youths with other families in foster homes. *Delinquency* cases involve juveniles who commit crimes. Juvenile courts also handle cases in which juveniles perform acts that are illegal for juveniles but not for adults, such as running away from home or violating curfew laws.

Diversion or Detention?

Most police departments have officers who handle juvenile cases. These officers often have the authority to divert juveniles away from court and into special programs.

Because the **emphasis,** or importance, is on rehabilitation rather than punishment, the juvenile system offers counseling, job training, and drug-treatment programs to which young people can be diverted.

The Trial

For juveniles who continue to be held for a crime, the next stage is a **preliminary** hearing, as in the adult system. The court procedure for juveniles is similar to adult trials, but with important differences. First, juveniles are not entitled to a jury trial. The judge alone makes the determination as to whether the juvenile is delinquent. Secondly, juvenile cases are normally closed to the public.

The juvenile court system keeps offenders' identities and criminal records secret. In addition, juveniles are not fingerprinted or photographed when they are arrested.

Sentencing If a juvenile is found delinquent, or guilty, the court holds another hearing—the **equivalent,** or equal, to sentencing. Juvenile court judges can sentence offenders in different ways. They may send them home with a stern lecture, or they may place offenders with a previous history of delinquency in a special training school, reformatory, treatment center, or teen shelter.

If the young person successfully completes probation, the charges will be dropped and removed from the record. Juveniles who are neglected may become wards of the court. The court becomes their guardian and can supervise them until adulthood.

Supreme Court Rules

The Supreme Court has established several rules for juvenile criminal cases. In general, juveniles have the same or similar rights as adults accused of crimes: the right to counsel, the right to confront witnesses, and the right not to be forced to incriminate themselves. In 1967, the Court stated, ". . . neither the Fourteenth Amendment nor the Bill of Rights is for adults alone."

Reading Check **Describing** What does it mean to "divert" a juvenile from the court system?

Vocabulary

1. **Define** the following terms and use them in a paragraph about the justice system for young people: *juvenile, juvenile delinquent, rehabilitate.*

Main Ideas

2. **Explaining** Can juveniles be tried as adults?
3. **Describing** What is the primary goal of juvenile courts?

Critical Thinking

4. **BIG Ideas** Do you agree that some young people should be tried as adults? Why or why not?
5. **Describing** Rehabilitation is the goal of the juvenile justice system. On a graphic organizer like the one below, list the programs youths can be diverted into to reach this goal.

CITIZENSHIP Activity

6. **Creative Writing** Write a series of journal entries from the point of view of someone involved in the juvenile justice system: a young person, a police officer, a parent or caregiver, a crime victim, a judge, or a parole officer. Use details from this chapter to make sure your entries are accurate with regard to the juvenile justice system.

Study Central™ To review this section, go to glencoe.com.

Computer blog speech has become more sophisticated and harder to monitor.

Can schools punish students for undesirable blog speech?

The word *blog* is a blend of *web* and *log*. Individuals with access to the Internet can post comments on blog pages for anyone to read and respond to. In the last few years "blogging" has exploded in popularity for all age groups, especially young people. Today millions of blogs are posted around the world. Blogging was in its early stages when a Missouri school district suspended a student for posting a personal Web page criticizing his school. Since then, the courts have decided a number of cases involving student use of the Internet from locations outside their schools. Should a school be allowed to punish blog speech?

YES

A federal district court ruled a Missouri high school student blogger's criticism of school officials was protected speech. However, not all such speech is protected by the First Amendment. Advising the Association of School Administrators, attorneys Robert Ashmore and Brian Herman noted that, "Student blogs are protected by the First Amendment as long as their content does not constitute a material disruption to classwork or involve substantial disorder or invasion of the rights of others. . . . [T]he U.S. District Court for the Western District of Pennsylvania recently refused to stop a school district from suspending a student, placing him in an alternative school. . . . " The student's Web site had mocked his principal. The court said that, at trial, the Web site probably would be considered a material disruption.

—Robert Ashmore and Brian Herman, "Abuse in Cyberspace"

NO

The American Civil Liberties Union (ACLU) and the Student Press Law Center (SPLC) often come to the defense of student bloggers who believe their free speech is being violated. With their support, students often win court cases against their schools. In a 1999 case U.S. District Judge Barbara Jacobs Rothstein ruled that a school had violated the First Amendment rights of a student when it expelled him for the content of a poem he wrote about school violence. "'Last Words' was not a sincere expression of intent to harm or assault, and the poem therefore falls squarely within the purview of the First Amendment's core protections," Rothstein said in her decision. "The Supreme Court has repeatedly held that both teachers and students retain their Constitutional rights to freedom of speech and expression. . . . Poetry . . . falls within the core speech protected by the Constitution."

—U.S. District Judge Barbara Jacobs Rothstein, *LaVine* v. *Blaine School District*, 2000

Debating the Issue

1. **Defining** What is a blog?
2. **Identifying** What are three organizations that have an interest in student blog speech?
3. **Explaining** What does a school have to prove in order to punish a student for blog speech?
4. **Analyzing** Why would courts rule that content on a personal blog is protected by the First Amendment but that classroom speech is less likely to be?

Chapter 16

Visual Summary

Civil Law

- Civil law includes disputes over rights, property, and agreements.
- In a civil lawsuit, the plaintiff files a complaint against the defendant, and the defendant responds.
- The legal system has established a procedure that everyone must follow to settle civil disputes.

Divorce and family law is part of civil law

Criminal Law

- In criminal law cases, the government charges someone with a crime.
- A crime is an act that breaks a federal or state criminal law and causes harm to people or society in general.
- Criminal cases are divided into two main groups—felonies and misdemeanors.

Students try a case in peer court

Juveniles and the Court System

- When a juvenile is arrested, the police must notify his or her parents or caregivers.
- A preliminary hearing is held, followed by a court appearance.

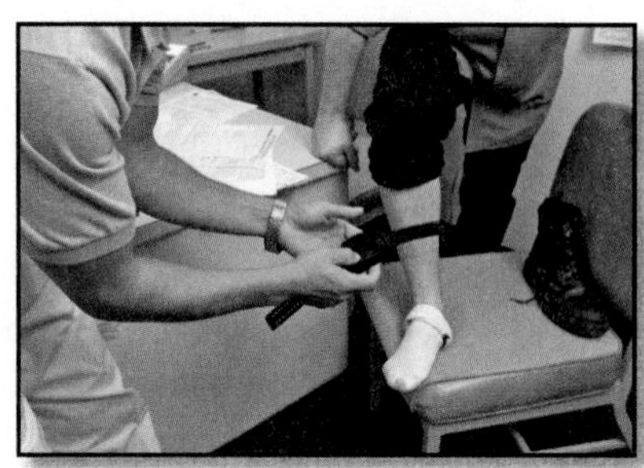

Offender gets tracking device

- At sentencing, juveniles may be sent home, put on probation, made a ward of the court, or sent to a reformatory.
- There is no jury in juvenile court cases.
- The primary goal of juvenile courts is to try to rehabilitate, or correct the behavior of, offenders.

STUDY TO GO

Study anywhere, anytime! Download quizzes and flash cards to your PDA from glencoe.com.

Chapter 16 Assessment

Standardized Test Practice

Chapter 16 Assessment

TEST-TAKING TIP

When reviewing for a civics exam, divide material into easy-to-remember categories such as civic duties, civil rights, and types of law.

Reviewing Vocabulary

Directions: Choose the word(s) that best completes the sentence.

1. A statement naming the defendant and plaintiff and announcing the lawsuit is called a ______.

A summons **C** settlement
B complaint **D** penal code

2. A ______ spells out the punishments that go with each crime.

A summons **C** settlement
B complaint **D** penal code

3. After serving parts of their sentences, some prisoners become eligible for early release, or ______.

A parole **C** discovery
B acquittal **D** arraignment

4. The primary role of juvenile courts is to ______.

A punish **C** acquit
B arraign **D** rehabilitate

Reviewing Main Ideas

Directions: Choose the best answer for each question.

Section 1 *(pp. 448–451)*

5. Which of the following situations may lead to a negligence suit?

A parents argue over custody of their children
B neighboring farmers disagree over boundaries
C a football player quits before his contract expires
D a worker is killed on the job when equipment fails

Section 2 *(pp. 452–458)*

6. What is meant by indeterminate sentencing?

A a set amount of time that the law directs for a specific crime
B probation with intensive supervision
C different sentences for similar crimes under different circumstances
D a sentence that ranges from a minimum to a maximum term

7. When does an accused person enter his or her plea of guilt or innocence?

A on being arrested
B during booking
C at the arraignment
D during cross examination

Section 3 *(pp. 460–463)*

8. According to studies, which young people are most likely to get in trouble with the law?

A older juveniles
B abused children
C mediocre students
D middle-class teenagers

9. What right do accused juveniles NOT share with adults?

A the right to counsel
B the right to a jury trial
C the right to confront witnesses
D the right to refuse to incriminate themselves

GO ON

Critical Thinking

Directions: Base your answers to questions 10 and 11 on the chart below and your knowledge of Chapter 16.

Average Prison Sentences and Time Served for Criminal Cases		
Type of offense	Average sentence given	Percent of sentence served
Murder	12.4 years	48%
Kidnapping	8.7 years	50%
Robbery	8 years	46%
Assault	5.1 years	48%
Other	5 years	47%

10. What conclusion can you draw from the chart?

A More than half of all convicted felons serve their full sentences.

B On average, convicted robbers are sentenced to four years.

C Criminals serve only about half their sentences in prison.

D Convicted murderers spend the rest of their life in prison.

11. What judgment might you make based on the chart?

A Murderers should be in prison for life.

B Robbery is a more serious crime than assault.

C All felonies are equally detrimental to society.

D Society considers kidnapping the most heinous crime.

Document-Based Questions

Directions: Analyze the following document and answer the short-answer questions that follow.

The federal government and 38 states allow the death penalty for certain crimes such as murder and kidnapping. The following passage is by Sister Helen Prejean, the author of Dead Man Walking *and an advocate for abolition of the death penalty.*

To shackle conscious, imaginative human beings and bring them to the death house with the clock ticking away the days and hours of their lives is mental torture. To prepare human beings for execution by diapering them, shackling them, and forcibly injecting them with valium to lower resistance, then strapping them onto a gurney and injecting them with chemicals that first paralyze them so they can't cry out and then throw them into cardiac arrest is mental torture and in all probability physical torture too. We've been trying over the last 30 years to sanitize death, make it look like we're not really killing them, we're "putting them to sleep."

The death penalty always involves torture. There's no way to kill a human being without causing them extreme pain. Legalizing death doesn't change anything.

—Sister Helen Prejean

12. According to Helen Prejean's characterization, which constitutional freedom does the death penalty negate?

13. What is the main idea of the passage?

Extended-Response Question

14. Describe mediation and arbitration in civil cases, and point out the differences between the two.

STOP

For additional test practice, use Self-Check Quizzes—Chapter 16 on glencoe.com.

Need Extra Help?														
If you missed question...	1	2	3	4	5	6	7	8	9	10	11	12	13	14
Go to page...	450	450	454	462	449	454	456	461	463	454	454	453	453	450

Chapter 17

Citizenship and the Internet

Why It Matters

In a democracy, citizens must be willing to take part in civic life. The Internet increases the opportunities to do just that. Accessing the Internet promises to strengthen democracy, but it may also present serious challenges to democracy.

Visit glencoe.com and enter QuickPass™ code CIV3093c17 for Chapter 17 resources.

Chapter Audio

BIG Ideas

Section 1: Civic Participation

A democratic society requires the active participation of its citizens. The Internet has changed the way people communicate, get information, and participate in democracy.

Section 2: Challenges for Democracy

A democratic society requires the active participation of its citizens. The Internet can both strengthen and threaten our democracy.

Section 3: Regulating the Internet

Citizens possess certain rights. Citizenship also carries certain responsibilities that all Americans are expected to fulfill. The Internet has become a battleground over the issue of free speech, both in society and in America's schools.

◀ **Students take part in computer technology camp in Fairfield, Connnecticut**

FOLDABLES™ Study Organizer

Organizing Foldable Make the following organizing Foldable to help you identify and organize information about each application of the Internet and who would use each.

Step 1 Fold a sheet of paper in thirds from top to bottom. This forms three rows.

Step 2 Open the paper and refold it into fourths from side to side.

This forms four rows.

Step 3 Unfold the paper and draw lines along the folds.

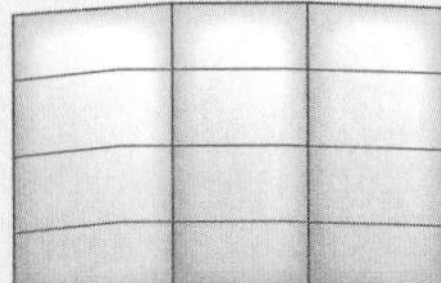

Step 4 Label your table as shown.

Internet	Who	What
Civic Participation		
Challenges for Democracy		
Regulating the Internet		

Reading and Writing
As you read the chapter, make notes about how the Internet can be used for each of these civic issues.

Section Audio

Spotlight Video

Section 1

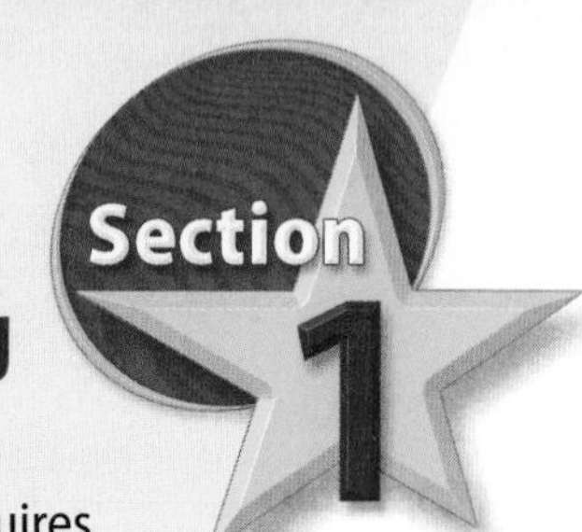

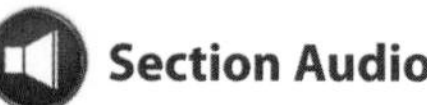

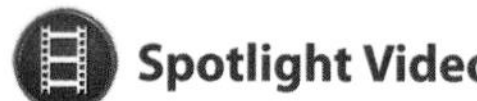

Civic Participation

Guide to Reading

Big Idea

A democratic society requires the active participation of its citizens.

Content Vocabulary

- Internet *(p. 471)*
- World Wide Web *(p. 471)*
- Web site *(p. 471)*
- archives *(p. 471)*
- nonpartisan *(p. 471)*
- newsgroup *(p. 472)*

Academic Vocabulary

- network *(p. 471)*
- interact *(p. 471)*
- version *(p. 473)*

Reading Strategy

Describing As you read, complete a graphic organizer like the one below, listing ways the Internet helps citizens become well informed.

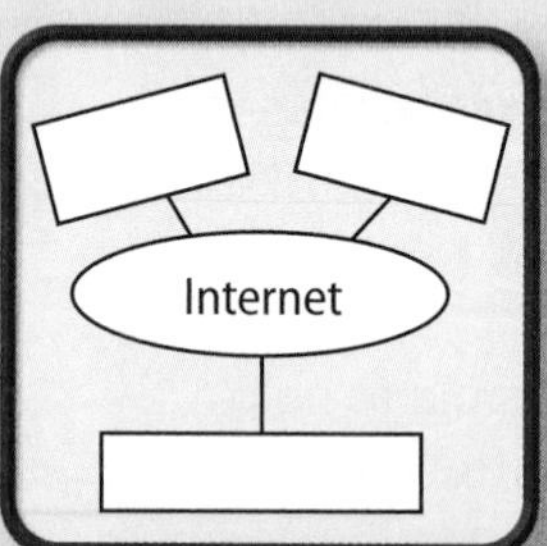

Real World Civics First-time national convention bloggers—online journal writers—worked on their Web log stories at the 2004 Democratic National Convention, revolutionizing campaigning forever. Bloggers posted their reports to the Web audience, providing instant images and thoughts to their readers. Many consider this use of the Internet a type of online "town meeting." It also provides a way for thousands of disabled and homebound voters to participate in politics. One thing is certain: As bloggers continue to express themselves, citizens will have more unfiltered access to information.

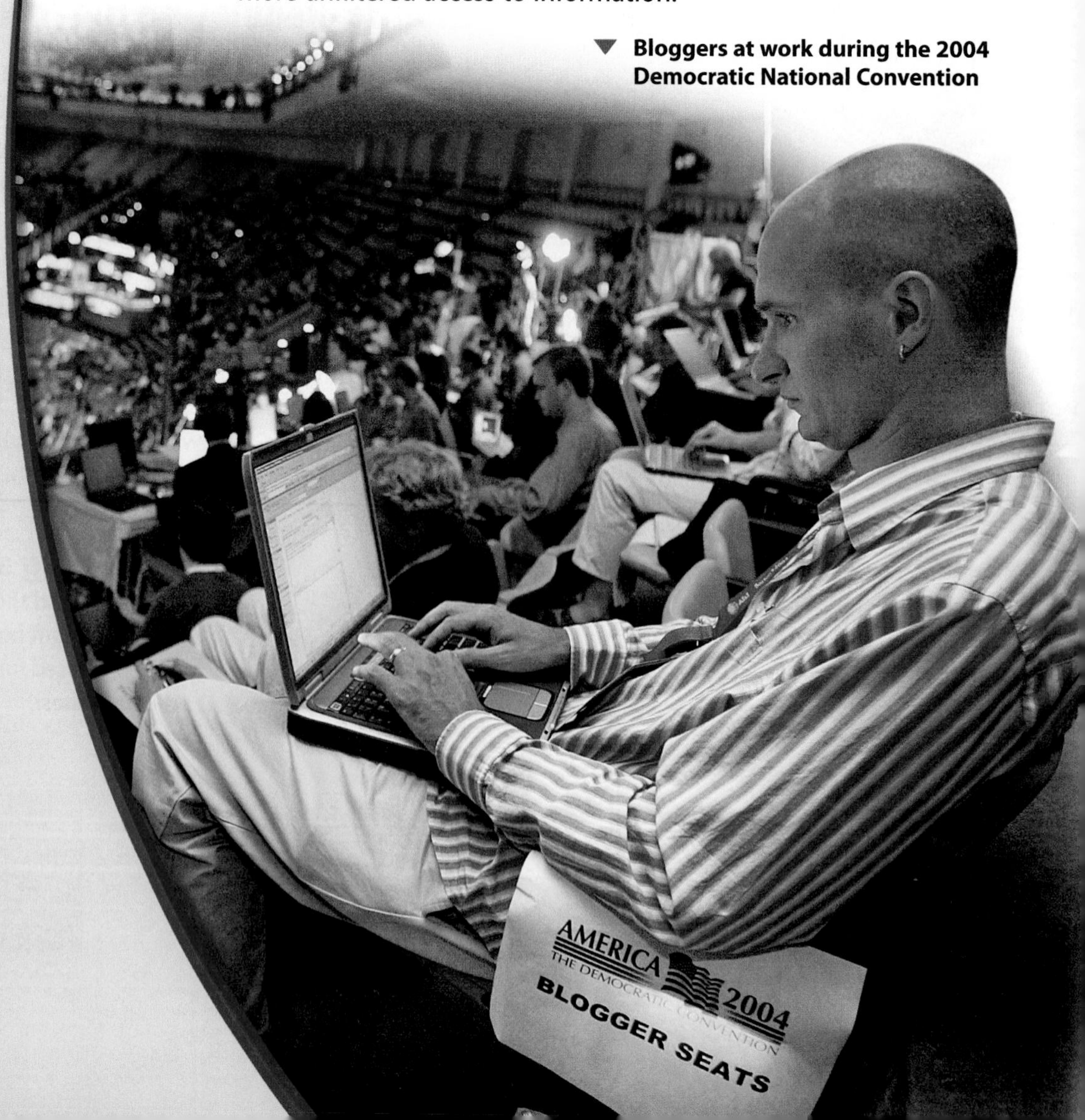

Bloggers at work during the 2004 Democratic National Convention

A Tool for Action

Main Idea **The Internet has changed the way people communicate, get information, and participate in democracy.**

Civics & You What was the last Web site you visited? Read to find out how Web sites have changed the way we communicate.

The **Internet** and the **World Wide Web** allow people to communicate and collaborate across borders. The Internet is a mass communication system of millions of **networked,** or connected, computers and databases all over the world. The World Wide Web is a system for browsing Internet sites, allowing users to **interact,** or work, with the billions of documents stored on computers across the Internet. These include the vast array of **Web sites**—"pages" on the World Wide Web that contain text, images, audio, and video.

A Billion Users

Currently the Internet has more than a billion users, and more are added daily. The first Web sites started in 1993. Today there are many millions, with the number doubling every few months. Almost three-fourths of the U.S. population has access to the Web. Soon half the population of the world will access the Web, many through wireless devices.

The Internet has created opportunities for citizens to stay informed and to participate thoughtfully in their democracy. Much of what is posted on the Internet is not accurate, however. Before believing what you read, be sure to evaluate the credibility of the source.

Gathering Information

Many citizens use the Internet for information about current events. Most national newspapers and newsmagazines publish online every day and keep **archives,** or files of older stories. Your hometown newspaper may have a Web site as well, as do television and radio networks. Research and educational institutes also have informative Web sites. Be aware, though, that not all "think tanks" are **nonpartisan;** that is, they are not free from political party ties or bias. Many, like the Brookings Institution (liberal) and the Heritage Foundation (conservative), have an ideological bias.

The Internet Monks surf the World Wide Web at an Internet café in Lhasa, Tibet. Millions of people obtain information from the Internet. ***Explaining*** **Why is it important to assess the reliability of the sources of Internet information?**

E-Government

Many agencies of government at all levels—federal, state, county, and local—have their own Web sites. E-government makes it easy for citizens to learn about public policy, to check on elected officials, to request services, and to directly participate in government.

Government Web sites help people do everything from obtain marriage licenses to comment on public services. North Carolina's citizens, for example, can use their state government's Web site to register to vote, request an absentee ballot, and learn how their representatives voted on an issue.

Group Action Online

One way to influence government is by supporting a special-interest group. The Internet can help you find groups with goals and values similar to your own. Most significant interest groups today have Web sites. Examples of these groups are the Sierra Club, the American Society for the Prevention of Cruelty to Animals (ASPCA), and the National Education Association (NEA). **Newsgroups,** or Internet discussion forums, provide another way to exchange information and ideas with people who share your concerns. Whether you want to protect the environment, curb TV violence, or help homeless children, you can find a related newsgroup.

Reading Check **Explaining** What is the relationship between the Internet and the World Wide Web?

Political Monitoring A member of a political action group uses a computer to tally contributions. Many political action groups as well as many political parties and candidates have Web sites. ***Analyzing*** **What is the goal of these Web sites? Why do viewers need to exercise caution when viewing them?**

Election Campaigns

Main Idea **The Internet has become a key tool in politics.**

Civics & You Have you ever read a blog? Read to find out how they are changing elections.

The Internet is also changing elections. A campaign manager recently said, "We see the Web as the best campaign tool since the phone and the television."

Political Parties and the Web

The Republican and Democratic Parties, along with many minor parties, have Web sites, as does nearly every candidate for higher political office. Many sites feature an electronic newsletter about the candidate's activities. Some candidates even list their campaign contributors online and answer e-mail questions.

When you visit these Web sites, though, you must use caution, because political party and candidate Web sites do not present a wide range of opinions. The goal of these Web sites is to build support for their own ideas and candidates, not to explain both sides of an issue.

Political Blogs

Blogging has become a widely used way for citizens to take part in politics both during and between elections. Blog is short for Web log. "Bloggers" are people who have their own publicly accessible Web sites. Blogs are their personal online journals, a kind of electronic diary that allows others to comment. Bloggers publish their own ideas —more or less continuously—on any topic of interest to them. Political blogs have quickly become popular with people who are trying to express opinions about candidates, issues, and politics in general.

Bloggers have begun to be recognized as a political influence. Keep in mind anyone can create a blog. Bloggers can, and do, post any messages they want—true or false.

Grassroots Web Sites

Another use of the Internet in politics is grassroots Web sites: citizens set up independent Web sites to support candidates. These sites are the cyberspace **version,** or form, of people putting political signs in their yards. Grassroots Web sites provide an easy way for citizens to get directly involved in an election.

Grassroots Web sites raise some concerns for the major parties and their candidates. The sites may contain misinformation or have links to extremist groups that a candidate would not want to be associated with. Further, it can be hard to tell the difference between official and unofficial sites.

Students at many schools across the country have begun using the Internet to vote in school elections. Using a computer at home or school, students vote online for class officers, student government issues, and prom and homecoming courts. Students are given identification and passwords that prevent them from voting twice in an election.

In most systems, students go online to view an election information page. This page allows student voters to review information about each candidate's background and campaign platform. Students then make their choices, review them, and vote. After organizing her school's first e-election, one California teacher said, "It was very easy to use. . . . The students liked being able to vote anywhere. And it was our most accurate election."

Reading Check **Concluding** What role do grassroots Web sites play in elections?

Vocabulary

1. **Write** a paragraph related to electronic communication using the following terms: *Internet, World Wide Web, Web site, archives, nonpartisan, newsgroup.*

Main Ideas

2. **Explaining** How does e-government allow citizens easier access to government services?
3. **Analyzing** What is a political blog? Why do some people criticize political blogs?

Critical Thinking

4. **BIG Ideas** The Internet offers many advantages for gathering information. What do you think is the biggest disadvantage or danger?
5. **Analyzing** In a graphic organizer like the one below, describe how the Internet and electronic communication have become part of political campaigning.

6. **Researching** Look up the Web site of your representative to Congress or one of your senators. What kind of information can you gather from the site? Share your findings with the class.

CITIZENSHIP Activity

7. **Descriptive Writing** Write a paragraph about your recent use of the Internet to find some information. Describe what you wanted to find out, how you searched for it, and where you found it.

Study Central™ To review this section, go to glencoe.com.

 Section Audio

Spotlight Video

Challenges for Democracy

Guide to Reading

Big Idea
A democratic society requires the active participation of its citizens.

Content Vocabulary
- authoritarian *(p. 475)*
- dissident *(p. 475)*
- extremist group *(p. 476)*
- propaganda *(p. 476)*

Academic Vocabulary
- contrary *(p. 476)*
- isolate *(p. 476)*
- enable *(p. 476)*

Reading Strategy
Summarizing As you read, list on a diagram like the one below three ways to protect your privacy when you use the Internet.

Real World Civics It has been said that the law is a living, breathing animal, but can it keep up with the Internet? Can privacy be protected? What about national security? In today's climate of fighting terrorism, the debate of privacy versus security is at its peak. Bryan Martin runs an Internet phone service that is seeking the same protections of Internet communication as of private phone services. During times of national crisis, national security has often won out over individual privacy. Online communication has opened up new ways to communicate, and many believe the law has not kept pace.

▼ **Bryan Martin calls for Internet privacy protections**

Divisions in Society

Main Idea **The Internet can both strengthen and threaten our democracy.**

Civics & You Have you ever used a computer whose access to the Internet was restricted in some way? How do you feel about such restrictions?

When the Internet and the World Wide Web started, many people assumed innovations like these would promote the expansion of democracy. Information and opinions would flow freely across national borders. By spreading democratic ideas worldwide, the Internet would help undermine **authoritarian** regimes. An authoritarian regime is a government in which one leader or group of people holds absolute power.

Restricting Internet Access

Authoritarian governments, however, are finding ways to limit online political communications. They have begun building electronic borders similar to the "firewalls" that protect business networks from intruders.

China, for example, encourages its citizens to get on the Internet. However, the government strictly controls access to the Web sites of human rights groups, foreign newspapers, and similar organizations. Messages that Chinese users post online are closely watched. Furthermore, the government has shut down the Web sites of some dissident groups. A **dissident** group includes people who disagree with the established political or religious system.

Two Dangers

For Americans, the Internet aids the free exchange of knowledge and ideas. Yet the Internet may still pose challenges to democracy. Some people fear that the Internet is widening the gap between the "haves" and "have-nots" and empowering intolerant extremist groups that seek to splinter society. Another concern is that the Internet leaves citizens vulnerable to invasions of privacy.

Democracy does not guarantee everyone equal wealth. It does aim to give all citizens an equal opportunity to develop their talents, though. It also emphasizes equality before the law for all Americans, regardless of gender, race, or religion. How does the Internet affect these two key ingredients of a democratic community?

A Digital Divide

The Internet is becoming a necessity in today's world. People who do not have effective access to the Internet risk being shut out of a key method of gathering information, participating in civic life, and earning money. A report released in 2006 found striking—but shrinking—differences in access by race, education, and family income level.

Impact of the Internet The Internet is becoming a necessity in economics, helping small business owners establish an online presence. ***Explaining*** **What is the risk of not being "wired"?**

World Wide Web Chinese police inspect an Internet café crowded with students in Guangzhou, the capital of China's southern Guangdong province. ***Identifying*** **What institutions help provide equal access to computers?**

The wealthiest families were more likely to have computers and Internet access at home than were households at the lowest income level. Still, a 2006 survey by the Pew Memorial Trust found that almost three-fourths of all Americans report they are Internet users.

Access at School Schools and public libraries help equalize access to computers. Almost all schoolchildren, in every ethnic and income group, now use computers at school. Some have access to the Internet with fast broadband connections. Business, community, and political leaders have also begun to address the technology gap. Some suggest creating nonprofit organizations to provide training and Internet access to millions of low-income Americans. Congress is considering legislation that would support a number of programs.

Extremist Groups

Just as the Internet can communicate and advance democratic values, it can also aid the spread of ideas that are **contrary,** or opposed, to democracy. The Internet has become an important tool for many hate groups and extremist political organizations. **Extremist groups** are those whose ideas are the farthest from the political center. In the past, these people might have been **isolated,** or set apart, from one another. The Internet **enables,** or allows, extremists to find one another, band together electronically, spread propaganda, and recruit new members. **Propaganda** is the spreading and promoting of certain ideas and may involve misleading messages designed to manipulate people. (See the descriptions of propaganda techniques in Chapter 11.)

To the extent that the Internet helps strengthen intolerant extremist movements, it may weaken our sense of national unity. Most Americans, however, still take pride in our country's diversity and believe in freedom of speech and expression and equal rights for all Americans.

Terrorists also use the Internet. U.S. Army officials explain that al-Qaeda is making very effective use of the Internet to conduct the war on terror, especially its activities in Iraq. Al-Qaeda raises money, gets recruits, and coordinates attacks through Web sites and blogs. Army officials say such online activities are nearly impossible to shut down.

Reading Check **Explaining** Why do authoritarian regimes limit Internet communication?

Threats to Privacy

Main Idea **The Internet poses some significant threats to Americans' privacy.**

Civics & You Did you know that businesses and government agencies can keep records of Web sites you visit? Read to find out more about these activities.

The Internet is creating a growing number of threats to privacy. In our digital world, governments, businesses, and even your neighbor can watch what you are doing online.

Personal Information You need to be cautious with information about yourself whenever you go online to make purchases or visit sites with advertisements. You also need to be very careful when e-mailing, blogging, and visiting chat rooms—social network Web sites.

Businesses and the government are able to mix information about you from different sources to create huge "data warehouses." These detailed profiles of people may include your address, income, age, health, what you buy and read, and much more. All of this information can be for sale to nearly anybody willing to pay for it.

Some Legal Protection Current privacy laws provide only limited safeguards and are hard to enforce. Congress tried to protect younger Web users by passing the Children's Online Privacy Protection Act (1998). This law requires Web site companies to establish a privacy policy describing the information they are collecting from children and how they will use it. The companies must also get permission from parents to collect information from children under 13 years of age.

Government Surveillance

The Internet has become a tool for all kinds of crime and for terrorism. As a result, the federal government conducts a great deal of online surveillance. Online data is being used to solve crimes. In St. Louis, for example, records of a suspect's online searches led to his arrest for a series of murders. The government also monitors electronic communications in an effort to stop terrorist attacks before they occur.

Federal government agencies like the Department of Justice or the National Security Agency collect electronic information in two ways. First, they work with companies that provide Internet services and run Web sites. Second, they develop and operate their own surveillance technology.

Internet Companies Many Web sites keep a log of all user activity and record the Internet Protocol (IP) address of each. Internet companies regularly hand over information about users in response to requests from police and from attorneys involved in lawsuits. The online provider America Online®, for example, receives nearly 1,000 requests a month for information in civil and criminal cases.

In January 2006, the U.S. Justice Department asked search engine companies to turn over records on searches made by millions of their users. The government was collecting data on how often Web searches turn up material harmful to children. In this instance, the government did not ask companies to provide the names of the people making the searches. Three companies—Yahoo!®, MSN®, and AOL® Internet Services—provided some information. Google™ resisted.

Privacy experts warned that search engines could become mechanisms that allow the government to spy on citizens. Some Internet users worried that in the age of terrorism innocent searches related to Islam or

Student Web Activity Visit glencoe.com and complete the Chapter 17 Web Activity.

Middle Eastern countries could be misinterpreted by government officials. On the other hand, supporters said the request for user information was for a good cause. One user argued, "For the government to catch people that prey on children, or fight the war on terror, they are going to need the help of search engines."

Government Tools The federal government has also been developing its own techniques for monitoring electronic communications. The National Security Agency (NSA), for example, has technology that can silently monitor millions of e-mail messages an hour. Not long after the terrorist attacks of September 11, 2001, President Bush secretly ordered the NSA to eavesdrop on Americans and others in the United States without getting court-approved search warrants.

Such activities illustrate the tension in a democracy between the need for the government to protect our national security and the need to guard citizens' constitutional rights. Former House Majority Leader Dick Armey of Texas worried that surveillance infringes on basic "constitutional protections against unwarranted search." Others argue that powerful tools are needed to fight terrorists and criminals using cyberspace. "You can't outlaw this technology," one expert stated. "All you can do is set strict legal standards."

Legal Limits Standards for government online surveillance are not clear. The Fourth Amendment protects citizens against "unreasonable searches." However, to what extent does that amendment apply to Internet activities? The 1996 Electronic Communications Privacy Act sets forth some legal standards for protecting online information. For example, the law generally requires a court order for investigators to read e-mail. At the same time, the USA Patriot Act allows some protections to be waived if lives are at risk.

Reading Check **Explaining** What does the Children's Online Privacy Protection Act require Web site companies to do?

Vocabulary

1. **Define** the following terms and use them in sentences related to the Internet and democracy: *authoritarian, dissident, extremist group, propaganda.*

Main Ideas

2. **Explaining** What is meant by the "digital divide"? Why is it a problem?
3. **Explaining** Why does the government monitor electronic communications? Why do some Americans criticize this action?

Critical Thinking

4. **BIG Ideas** How do you think our society should balance the need for fighting terrorism through activities such as Internet wiretapping against the need to protect the privacy of innocent individuals?
5. **Analyzing Information** In a chart like the one below, describe three effects of threats to privacy posed by the Internet.

Citizenship Activity

6. **Creative Writing** Research and write a letter to the editor of your local newspaper about one of the issues raised in this section. Explain your opinion on the issue and discuss what you believe should be done.

Study Central™ To review this section, go to glencoe.com.

Protecting Yourself Against Identity Theft

What is the nation's fastest-growing crime? According to the U.S. Federal Trade Commission, it is identity theft. Identity theft is a crime in which an imposter obtains key pieces of information, such as Social Security and driver's license numbers, and uses it for personal gain. Nearly 10 million U.S. adults were victims in 2005.

What does the identity thief want?

- Your Social Security card
- Your driver's license
- Your account numbers (bank, credit card, and others), PIN(s), and passwords

Even if you never use a computer, you can fall victim to identity theft. Others may be able to get personal information (such as credit card numbers, phone numbers, account numbers, and addresses) by stealing your wallet, overhearing a phone conversation, poking through your trash (a practice known as Dumpster diving), or "phishing"—an e-mail scam that aims to steal personal information.

Tips for Preventing Identity Theft

- Protect your Social Security number (SSN).
- Always take credit card receipts with you. Never toss them into a public trash container.
- Do not give out personal information on the phone, through the mail, or over the Internet unless you know with whom you are dealing.
- Carry only the identification information and the credit and debit cards you will actually need when you go out. If your wallet is stolen or if you lose it, report it immediately to the card issuers and the local police.

Identity Theft Is Affecting Online Shopping

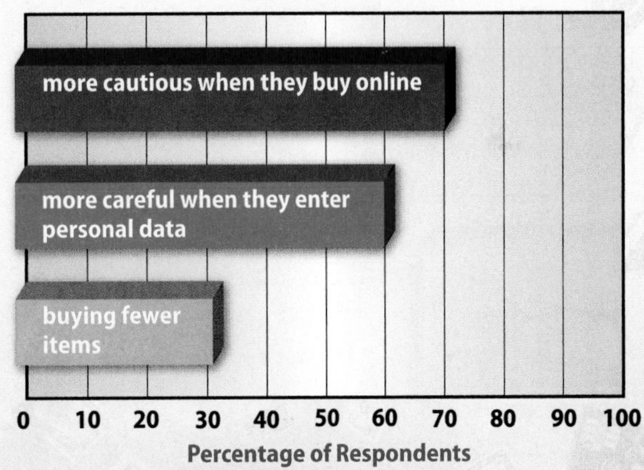

Source: *Business Week,* March 20, 2006; Gartner, Inc.

Analyzing Economics

1. **Explaining** A friend says, "No one can steal my identity because I don't use a computer." Is your friend correct?
2. **Summarizing** How has the increase in identity theft affected online shoppers?

Section Audio

Regulating the Internet

Guide to Reading

Big Idea

Citizens possess certain rights. Citizenship also carries certain responsibilities that all Americans are expected to fulfill.

Content Vocabulary

- intellectual property *(p. 482)*
- copyright *(p. 483)*
- revenue *(p. 485)*

Academic Vocabulary

- nonetheless *(p. 482)*
- erode *(p. 483)*

Reading Strategy

Summarizing The Internet raises many issues that the Framers of the Constitution could not have imagined. As you read, discuss three free-speech issues that are associated with the Internet. Place your answers on a web diagram like the one below.

Real World Civics Are modern-day pirates threatening what may be available on the Internet? Today many people listen to music and play movies on their computers. Sometimes, users download entertainment for free, without paying any fee to the people who created it. Is this fair use? The Senate Government Affairs Committee is acting as watchdog, holding hearings to determine what is fair use of movies, music, and videos on the Internet. The unfair use of such media has been labeled computer "piracy" because it goes against traditional copyright laws.

▼ **Recording and film representatives testify against unauthorized downloading**

TIME

Political Cartoons

Gary Markstein/Copley News Service

This cartoon, drawn by Gary Markstein, makes a comment on efforts to control spam on the Internet.

1. **What is Internet spam?**
2. **Does the cartoonist consider the antispam law effective?**
3. **What details in the image reveal the cartoonist's point of view?**

Internet Speech

Main Idea **The Internet has become a battleground over the issue of free speech.**

Civics & You Do you know someone who has downloaded music from an Internet site? Read to find out how this activity has been at the eye of a huge storm.

Free speech is a key democratic right, spelled out in the First Amendment to the Constitution. The Internet promotes free speech by giving anyone with a computer the chance to spread his or her views across the world. Unfortunately, this freedom has also enabled hate groups and others to fill the Internet with offensive material.

For more than a decade, governments from your local school board to the U.S. Congress have been scrambling for some control over speech on the Internet. In regulating the Internet, though, does the government infringe on the right of free speech?

Safeguards Computer users can block objectionable Web sites by installing filtering software. Lawmakers have also enacted laws to censor some online speech. In 1996 Congress passed the Communications Decency Act. This law made it a federal crime to send or display indecent or obscene material over the Internet "in a manner available" to those under the age of 18.

Challenge to Internet Censorship

Several groups challenged the law in court. They argued that it violated the rights of adults, who can lawfully view graphic material considered inappropriate for children. In *Reno* v. *American Civil Liberties Union* (1997), the Supreme Court declared the indecency portions of the law unconstitutional. The Court held that speech on the Internet should have the highest level of First Amendment protection, similar to the protection given to books and newspapers. This decision was a strong endorsement of free speech on the Internet.

TIME™ Teens in *Action*

Keegan Flynn

The Internet can be a powerful tool to get people involved in good causes. Just ask Keegan Flynn, 14, of Port Chester, New York.

QUESTION: You've said that Hurricane Katrina changed your life. How?

ANSWER: The hurricane, which destroyed much of New Orleans and the Gulf Coast, was very personal for my family. My mom's college roommate and some of our cousins lost their homes and their businesses. They had resources to start over, but I wondered what was going to happen to all those other people who didn't have the same resources. My mom saw on the news that backpacks were needed in Houston, Texas. I decided that this could be a way for me to make a difference.

Q: What happened next?

A: I collected and assembled "school-ready" backpacks for kids in Houston who were victims of Hurricane Katrina who didn't have the ability or funds to gather their own supplies.

Q: How did other people know where to make donations?

A: My mother writes and edits Rye [New York] High School's E-news. I got the word out by posting an announcement there. My mom has a list with over 600 e-mail addresses—all belonging to Rye High School faculty and parents. It was amazing the way people responded to my electronic request.

Flynn's efforts make a difference

Making a Difference — CITIZENSHIP

What steps did Keegan take to request help from volunteers?

In response to the Court's decision, Congress passed the Child Online Protection Act (COPA) in 1998. This law made it a crime for a commercial Web site to knowingly make indecent material available to anyone under the age of 17. The law required Web sites to require all users to verify their ages as a way to keep children from harmful material on their sites.

The Supreme Court stopped enforcement of this law in 2004. In *Ashcroft* v. *American Civil Liberties Union,* the Court ruled that age verification was too harsh of a restriction on the free-speech rights of adults. The justices said filtering software on home computers might be a way to keep children from viewing offensive material while preserving the right of adults to view whatever they want.

Limiting Free Speech in Schools

Although the Supreme Court has ruled that Internet speech is protected by the First Amendment, this protection is not applicable everywhere. **Nonetheless,** restrictions may apply to school-sponsored newspapers on the World Wide Web.

In 1988 the Supreme Court ruled that school administrators can regulate the content of student print publications if doing so serves an educational purpose (see the *Hazelwood School District* v. *Kuhlmeier* case on page 325). Several lower courts have found that students who produce online papers in school with school equipment may be subject to regulation.

Intellectual Property

Americans have always believed in the right of individuals to own property and to use it as they see fit. You can freely sell your old bike, loan your jacket to a friend, or trade away part of your baseball card collection if you so choose. However, special rules apply to **intellectual property**—things that people create, such as songs, movies, books, poetry, art, and software.

American Biography

The Birth of Yahoo!®

In 1994, two Stanford University graduate students wanted a better way to keep track of their favorite Internet sites. The students, **Jerry Yang** and **David Filo,** started keeping lists on a computer. Other students began logging on to check out their lists and using them to find their way around the World Wide Web.

The two students named their site "Jerry and David's Guide to the World Wide Web." They understood that others wanted a single "point of entry" to the quickly growing Web. In the fall of 1994, the site had its first one millionth hit, and Yang and Filo decided to start a business. Yahoo!® was born in March 1995, and the pair raised money to expand their idea. The name they chose for their new business appealed to them because it meant "a rude, unsophisticated person." They hired employees and sold stock to raise more money. Today, Yahoo!® receives about 350 million visits every day, making it the most popular site on the Web.

Jerry Yang recently explained how his company's focus has changed:

"Ten years ago, we were focused on a simple yet vast problem: finding better ways to aggregate and organize information so people can find it. [Today,] . . . it's no longer enough to simply provide a structure for users to find what they want on the Web. Today, people expect to find precisely what they're looking for exactly as it relates to them."

—Jerry Yang, "Jerry's Take on What's Next in Search"

Jerry Yang

Making a Difference — CITIZENSHIP

Describing In a sentence, express what you think is the key to the success of Yahoo!®

The Power of Copyright When you purchase a CD by Christina Aguilera or a *Harry Potter* book, you do not gain ownership rights to the artistic product. Only the artist or author who created the work has a right to sell it or let others use it.

Over the years, many traditions, court decisions, and legal devices such as copyrights have developed to protect the creators of intellectual property. A **copyright** is the owner's exclusive right to control, publish, and sell an original work. Copyrights are designed to prevent people from taking or copying someone else's creation without permission. Computers and the Internet, however, make it easy to copy and widely distribute all kinds of intellectual property, thus threatening to **erode,** or wear away, copyright protection. As a result, the Internet has become a major battleground for intellectual property rights.

In 1998 Congress passed a law aimed at protecting the holders of intellectual property in the Internet age. The Digital Millennium Copyright Act (DMCA) makes it a crime for someone to develop or spread software that will bypass computer codes that protect copyrighted material.

File-Sharing Battles The fight over using file sharing to download music and movies illustrates how the Internet is challenging old rules protecting intellectual property. Grokster and StreamCast Internetworks developed software that allowed Internet users to share computer files on "peer to peer" networks. Such networks connect computers across the globe, making it easy for people to download copyrighted songs and movies without paying for them. Billions of files were being shared over Grokster and similar networks every month.

Metro-Goldwyn-Mayer and other entertainment companies sued Grokster. MGM claimed Grokster encouraged people to use its free software to download copyrighted music without paying for it. Grokster argued its software could be used to swap any kind of computer file and thus had many legitimate uses. It was not responsible for those who used its technology to violate copyrights.

The Supreme Court ruled unanimously against Grokster and StreamCast (*Metro-Goldwyn-Mayer* v. *Grokster*, 2005). The justices found the companies "clearly voiced the objective that recipients use the software to download copyrighted works." The ruling set forth a basic legal principle that will govern intellectual property law for some time. It is not illegal to create an Internet technology that makes copyright theft possible. However, encouraging people to use such technology for copyright violation is prohibited. Companies that promote copyright violations can be held liable for the result.

The music industry said the ruling was a major victory. Still, the Court's decision did not mean the end of online swapping, a global practice. Rather, it is only the latest example of a continuing battle between copyright holders and Internet users. Even as Grokster announced it was stopping distribution of its software, other companies across the world were developing new types of file sharing networks. So-called darknets, for example, allow groups of users to share information without revealing their identity to outsiders who are not part of the group.

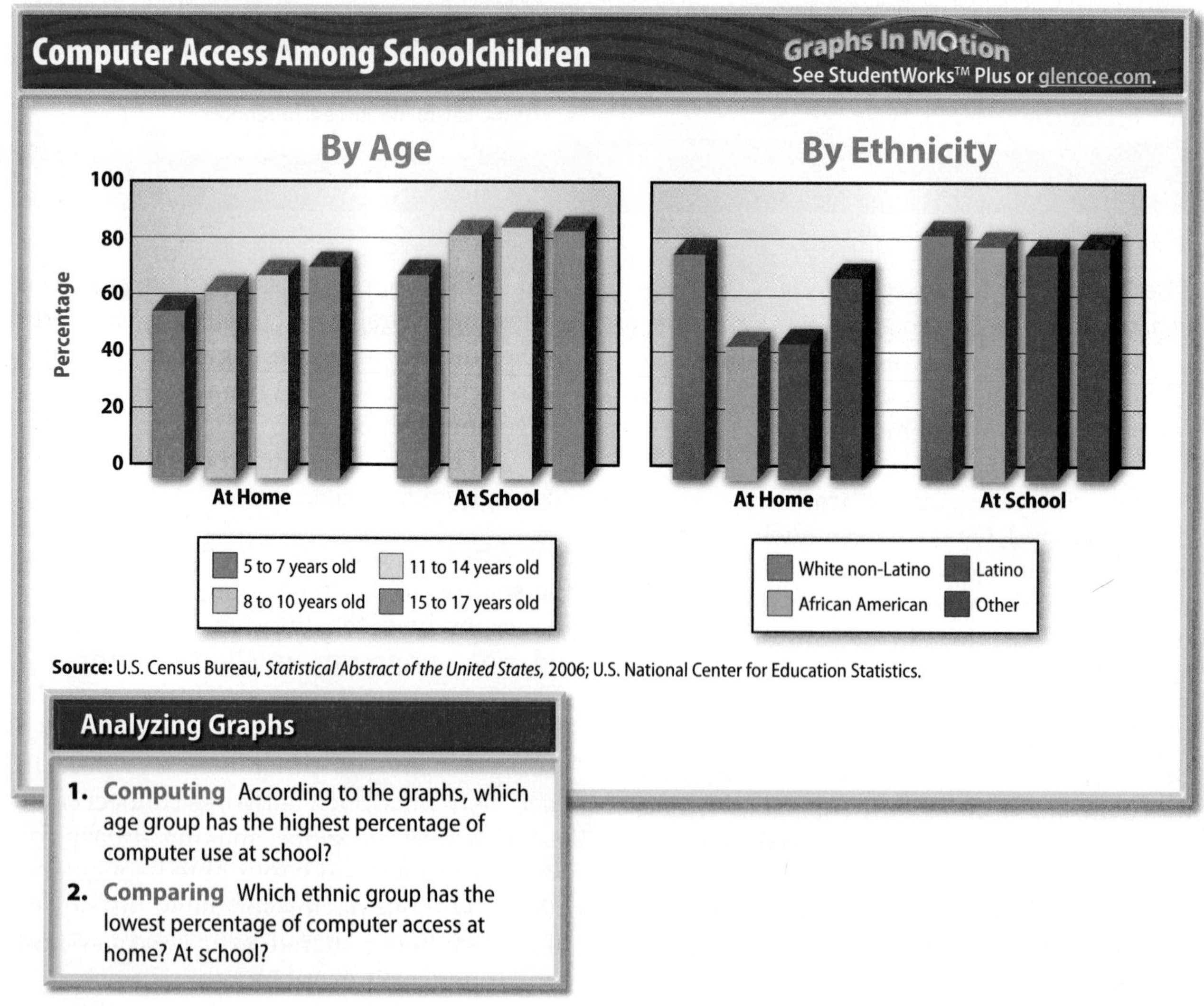

Source: U.S. Census Bureau, *Statistical Abstract of the United States*, 2006; U.S. National Center for Education Statistics.

Analyzing Graphs

1. **Computing** According to the graphs, which age group has the highest percentage of computer use at school?
2. **Comparing** Which ethnic group has the lowest percentage of computer access at home? At school?

Taxing E-Commerce

E-commerce involves using the Internet for purchase and sales transactions. Because e-commerce involves numerous computers communicating, purchase and sales transactions occur very quickly and are often unidentified. How to tax goods and services purchased over the Internet is another important issue. Each year, consumers spend billions of dollars buying goods and services over the Internet. Online shopping is not only convenient, but it also allows customers to avoid paying local sales taxes. Although many states require online consumers to report purchase amounts on income tax forms, state and local governments often lose out on a prime source of **revenue.** Revenue is the income that a government or business collects.

An Unfair Burden? Many state governors and other politicians favor taxation of e-commerce; so do traditional retail stores. After all, the stores lose business if you shop online instead of at your local mall. Many Internet merchants and policy analysts, however, believe that collecting sales taxes would unfairly burden online companies. Because sales taxes vary from state to state, online businesses would have to charge different rates depending on where customers live and then send the funds back to different state governments. Collecting taxes would thus be unusually costly for Internet companies. Furthermore, unlike local merchants, they would share in none of the benefits those taxes pay for, such as police and fire protection, roads, and other government services.

An advisory group created by Congress recently proposed that all state and local tax systems be simplified and made more uniform. Efforts could then be made to develop a fair Internet sales tax.

Reading Check **Explaining** Why may people who hold copyrights be concerned about Internet use?

School and the Internet Teachers and students use laptop computers at the Mary McDowell Center for Learning in Brooklyn, New York. The Center is a Quaker independent school for children with learning disabilities. ***Explaining*** **Why do many schools use filtering software?**

The Internet at School

Main Idea **Growing use of the Internet in schools is creating new controversies.**

Civics & You Have you used the Internet at school? Read to find out why this issue has become a focus of intense debate.

Tens of millions of American students spend classroom time online. Use of the Internet at school is creating new issues for lawmakers and educators.

School Filters

In 2000 Congress passed the Children's Internet Protection Act. This law requires nearly all schools in the United States to install technology that blocks student access to offensive or dangerous Web materials.

Many schools use filtering software that allows school officials to decide what material is harmful. The software also monitors the school's Internet traffic. It can identify anyone who tries to use the Internet for prohibited activities, such as drug dealing. One school official reported that since his town installed the filtering software, "access of unauthorized Internet sites probably dropped by 98 percent."

The Issue of Parental Review

Many schools also keep records of the Web sites that students and staff visit. Should parents be able to look at these records? James Knight, the father of four students in New Hampshire, sued his local school district to win that right. Knight said, "If we can find out what books are on the shelves of the school library or what textbooks are being used in the classroom, it seems consistent that we should be able to know where kids are going on the Internet."

Knight's attorneys argued that the school was not doing enough to keep students away from questionable Web sites. School officials argued that releasing students' Internet records would violate their right to privacy. A New Hampshire judge ruled, however, that a parent could inspect the school district's Internet records as long as administrators removed any information that would identify individual students.

As the Internet becomes more fully integrated into American schools, policies and regulations for its use will continue to evolve. School leaders must determine what level of disclosure of student information is safe and appropriate while maintaining their instructional goals. Parents must then approve or disapprove of the disclosure standards. School officials and lawmakers will keep trying to balance concerns about privacy, censorship, and the safety of young Internet users.

Reading Check **Explaining** What is parental review? What issues are at stake?

Review

Vocabulary

1. **Define** the following terms and use them in sentences related to the Internet: *intellectual property, copyright, revenue.*

Main Ideas

2. **Describing** What is e-commerce?
3. **Explaining** What is the purpose of the Children's Internet Protection Act of 2000?

Critical Thinking

4. **Analyzing** Why have issues such as taxing e-commerce and regulating the Internet in schools arisen?
5. **BIG Ideas** In a diagram like the one below, identify examples of intellectual property.

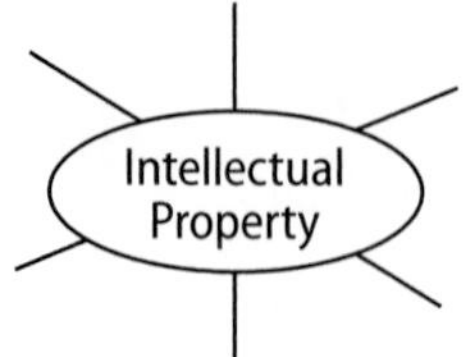

CITIZENSHIP Activity

6. **Expository Writing** Contact your school's computer teacher. Interview him or her about what your school does to monitor Internet use of school computers. Share your findings with the class. Summarize the highlights of your interview in a one-page paper. Then lead a discussion about how your school's policies might be improved.

Study Central™ To review this section, go to glencoe.com.

Chapter 17

Visual Summary

David and Catherine Cook, creators of MyYearbook.com

Regulating the Internet

Many issues surround Internet usage, including the following:

- limits on free speech
- protection of intellectual property
- taxation of e-commerce
- regulation of the Internet in schools

Effects of the Internet

- Millions of people have access to computers, the Internet, and the World Wide Web.
- Electronic communications enable us to instantly access information, to purchase goods and services, and to share ideas around the globe.
- The Internet can help us increase our knowledge about political and social issues.

Issues

- People who do not have access to the Internet cannot enjoy the opportunities it offers.
- Internet users' privacy can be threatened by government and business surveillance.
- Just as the Internet can help advance democratic values, it can also aid the spread of ideas that may run counter to democracy.

California business owner using the Internet

Internet café, China

STUDY TO GO

Study anywhere, anytime! Download quizzes and flash cards to your PDA from glencoe.com.

Chapter

17 ASSESSMENT

TEST-TAKING TIP

Learn the meanings of certain words—such as evaluate, enumerate, and illustrate—that appear in many exam questions.

Reviewing Vocabulary

Directions: Choose the word(s) that best completes the sentence.

1. An Internet discussion forum is called a ______.

A Web site **C** newsgroup
B data warehouse **D** think tank

2. A government in which a leader or group holds absolute power is ______.

A dissident **C** nonpartisan
B extremist **D** authoritarian

3. Misleading messages designed to misinform people are known as ______.

A cookies **C** surveillance
B propaganda **D** broadband connections

4. A(n) ______ bars people from using someone else's creation without permission.

A copyright **C** revenue
B software filter **D** intellectual property

Reviewing Main Ideas

Directions: Choose the best answer for each question.

Section 1 *(pp. 470–473)*

5. What is a disadvantage of using the Internet for information?

A It offers few sources on most topics.
B The Internet lacks a diversity of viewpoints.
C Internet access is limited to computer experts.
D Facts from the Internet are sometimes inaccurate.

6. Why do political candidates have Web sites?

A to hold elections online
B to build support for their ideas
C to present diverse opinions on issues
D to exchange information with opponents

Section 2 *(pp. 474–478)*

7. According to the U.S. Army, how does al-Qaeda use the Internet?

A to recruit new members
B to conduct training programs
C to spread democratic ideas worldwide
D to widen the gap between haves and have-nots

8. Who monitors millions of e-mail messages and other online communications?

A Chinese dissidents
B al-Qaeda terrorists
C National Security Agency
D eighth graders in New York

Section 3 *(pp. 480–486)*

9. What did the Supreme Court declare in *Reno* v. *American Civil Liberties Union* (1997)?

A Users can install filters to block Web sites.
B Indecent material on the Internet is unlawful.
C The First Amendment protects speech on the Internet.
D Users must verify their age to view certain Web sites.

GO ON

10. In which case did the Supreme Court decision prohibit companies from encouraging people to use their technology for copyright violations?

A *Metro-Goldwyn-Mayer* v. *Grokster*

B *Reno* v. *American Civil Liberties Union*

C *Hazelwood School District* v. *Kuhlmeier*

D *Ashcroft* v. *American Civil Liberties Union*

Critical Thinking

Directions: Base your answers to questions 11 and 12 on the cartoon below and your knowledge of Chapter 17.

Tribune Media Services, Inc.

11. What does the highway in the cartoon represent?

A Internet traffic

B corporate America

C government censorship

D interstate expressways

12. Which of the following statements best expresses the cartoonist's point of view?

A Some citizen protections need to be waived if lives are at risk.

B Surveillance of online communications endangers people's privacy.

C Powerful tools are needed to fight terrorists and criminals using cyberspace.

D The government needs to catch people who use the Internet to prey on children.

Document-Based Questions

Directions: Analyze the following document and answer the short-answer questions that follow.

On February 15, 2006, the Senate discussed amending parts of the USA Patriot Act that violate citizens' constitutional rights in the name of the war on terrorism. During the discussion, Senator Robert Byrd from West Virginia made the following statement:

Attorney General Gonzales refused to divulge whether purely domestic communications have also been caught up in this warrantless surveillance, and he refused to assure the Senate Judiciary Committee and the American public that the administration has not deliberately tapped Americans' telephone calls and computers or searched their homes without warrants. Nor would he reveal whether even a single arrest has resulted from the program.

What about the first amendment? What about the chilling effect that warrantless eavesdropping is already having on those law-abiding American citizens who may not support the war in Iraq, or who may simply communicate with friends or relatives overseas? Eventually, the feeling that no conversation is private will cause perfectly innocent people to think carefully before they candidly express opinions or even say something in jest.

—Senator Byrd

13. How would you sum up Senator Byrd's objections to the government's warrantless surveillance program in the first paragraph?

14. Senator Byrd suggests that warrantless eavesdropping permitted by the USA Patriot Act violates First Amendment freedoms. According to the chapter, what other amendment and freedom may be violated by warrantless searches?

Extended-Response Question

15. Explain why standards for government online surveillance are not clear.

For additional test practice, use Self-Check Quizzes—Chapter 17 on glencoe.com.

Need Extra Help?

If you missed question...	1	2	3	4	5	6	7	8	9	10	11	12	13	14	15
Go to page...	472	475	476	483	471	472	476	477	481	484	471	477	477	478	477

Analyzing Primary Sources

Sources of American Law

Reading Focus

The set of rules and standards by which a society governs itself is known as law. Laws serve several functions in every society. The law is used to resolve conflict, to protect rights, to limit government, to promote general welfare, to set social goals, and to control crime.

Read to Discover

As you read, think about the following:

- How has early law influenced American law?
- What is the importance of common law?

Reader's Dictionary

proprietor: an owner

dowry: the money and goods that a woman brings to her husband in marriage

maxim: a general truth

heretofore: up to this time

repugnant: hostile or opposed to

Code of Hammurabi

The most well-known of the earliest written laws was the Code of Hammurabi, assembled in the 1700s B.C. This code was made up of 282 legal cases that spelled out relationships among individuals as well as punishments in areas that we would now call property law, family law, civil law, and criminal law.

22. If any one is committing a robbery and is caught, then he shall be put to death. . . .

117. If any one fail to meet a claim for debt, and sell himself, his wife, his son, and daughter for money or give them away to forced labor: they shall work for three years in the house of the man who bought them, or the **proprietor,** and in the fourth year they shall be set free. . . .

142. If a woman quarrels with her husband . . . the reasons for her prejudice must be presented. If she is guiltless, and there is no fault on her part, but he leaves and neglects her, then no guilt attaches to this woman, she shall take her **dowry** and go back to her father's house. . . .

196. If a man put out the eye of another man, his eye shall be put out. . . .

—"Code of Hammurabi," L.W. King, trans.

The Ten Commandments

An early set of written laws that has influenced our legal system is the Ten Commandments found in the Hebrew Bible and Christian Bible.

1. Do not worship any god except me.
2. Do not . . . bow down and worship idols.
3. Do not misuse my name.
4. Remember that the Sabbath Day belongs to me.
5. Respect your father and your mother.
6. Do not murder.
7. Be faithful in marriage.
8. Do not steal.
9. Do not tell lies about others.
10. Do not want anything that belongs to someone else.

—Exodus 20:3–17

The Justinian Code

In the A.D. 530s, the Roman emperor Justinian had scholars reorganize and simplify all the laws into a Roman legal code called the Justinian Code.

Book I. Of Persons

I. Justice and Law.

3. The **maxims** of law are these: to live honesty, to hurt no one, to give every one his due.
4. The study of law is divided into two branches; that of public and that of private law. Public law regards the government of the Roman empire; private law, the interest of the individuals.

II. Natural, Common, and Civil Law.

1. Civil law is thus distinguished from the law of nations. Every community governed by laws and customs uses partly its own law, partly laws common to all mankind. The law which a people makes for its own government belongs exclusively to that state and is called the civil law. . . .

—"The Institutes," 535 C.E.

Monuments as Primary Sources This stone monument shows Hammurabi (standing) holding his code. What does the monument tell you about the place and time it was created? What do you think was the artist's purpose in creating this monument?

Common Law

The law of the United States was largely derived from the common law of the system of English law. Common law is law based on the concept of precedence—on how the courts have interpreted the law previously—rather than on a legal code. By A.D. 1776 common law was being used throughout the American colonies along with laws created there.

Constitution

ART. 25. The common law of England, as-well as so much of the statute law as has been **heretofore** adopted in practice in this State, shall remain in force, unless they shall be altered by a future law of the legislature; such parts only excepted as are **repugnant** to the rights and privileges contained in this constitution, and the declaration of rights, . . . agreed to by this convention.

—Constitution of Delaware, 1776

DBQ Document-Based Questions

1. **Connecting** Consider this statement: Whether Hammurabi's laws were fair or cruel, the culture benefited from having a written code that applied to everyone. Do you agree or disagree? What would it be like to live in a society with no written rules?
2. **Connecting** How does common law differ from statutory law?
3. **Analyzing** How many of the commandments tell people how to interact with other people? How many tell them how to worship and show respect for God?
4. **Evaluating and Connecting** Consider this statement: Liberty depends upon the power of laws. Write a paragraph explaining what the statement means to you.

UNIT 6

The Economy and the Individual

Young women making individual economic choices at a California shopping mall

Be An Active Citizen

CITIZENSHIP **What do you think economics is? Describe how, in your opinion, economics affects you. After you complete your study of Unit 6, compare your initial ideas with the new information you learn.**

UNIT 6

Reading Social Studies

Comparing and Contrasting

1 Learn It!

When you compare people, things, or ideas you show the similarities among them. When you contrast these things you point out their differences.

- Read the following paragraph. Note how the writer compares fixed costs to variable costs.
- How does the writer contrast fixed costs to variable costs?

> The first kind of cost is fixed costs—costs, or expenses, that are the same no matter how many units of a good are produced. Mortgage payments and property taxes are two examples of fixed costs. It makes no difference whether your company produces one bicycle helmet or a very large number. Your fixed costs, such as your mortgage and property taxes, remain the same. . . . Another kind of cost is variable costs. Variable costs are expenses that change with the number of items produced. Wages and raw materials are examples of variable costs.
>
> —*from page 506*

People, Things, or Ideas	Compare	Contrast
Fixed costs and variable costs	*Both are expenses	*Fixed costs remain the same *Variable costs change with the number of items produced

2 Practice It!

Read the following sentences from this unit that compare and contrast microeconomics to macroeconomics. Draw a chart like the one shown below.

> . . . economics is divided into two branches. In microeconomics, economists look at the small picture. They study the behavior and decision making of small (the meaning of the prefix *micro-*) units such as individuals and businesses. . . . On the other hand, macroeconomics looks at the big (the meaning of the prefix *macro-*) picture. It deals with the economy as a whole and decision making by large units such as governments or whole industries or societies.
>
> —*from page 500*

People, Things, or Ideas	Compare	Contrast
Microeconomics Macroeconomics		

Read to Write Activity

Read the section titled "Circular Flow of Economic Activity" in Chapter 19, Section 2. Choose any two of the sectors (consumer, business, government, or foreign) to compare and contrast. Once you decide which two sectors you will write about, jot down facts about each and write a few sentences to show how they compare or contrast.

3 Apply It!

As you read look for people, things, or ideas that you can compare and contrast in:

- **Chapter 20, Section 1**
- **Chapter 21, Section 2**

Chapter 18

What Is Economics?

Why It Matters

As American citizens, we live in a land of economic opportunity. Our economy provides us with a great variety of jobs, goods, and services. The United States has a free enterprise system under which consumers and producers make the major economic decisions. We can contribute to the nation's economic success by taking advantage of economic opportunities.

Civics ONLINE
Visit glencoe.com and enter QuickPass™ code CIV3093c18 for Chapter 18 resources.

Chapter Audio

BIG Ideas

Section 1: How Economic Systems Work

An economic system is the way a society organizes the production and consumption of goods and services. Economics is the study of how we make decisions in a world in which resources are limited as well as the study of how things are made, bought, sold, and used.

Section 2: Making Economic Decisions

An economic system is the way a society organizes the production and consumption of goods and services. Economic decision making requires us to understand all the different costs and all the benefits of a choice.

An abundance of Florida citrus products for sale in open-air markets

FOLDABLES™ Study Organizer

Defining Study Foldable Make the following Foldable to help you define the content vocabulary that you will encounter in this chapter.

Step 1 Stack four sheets of paper, one on top of the other. On the top sheet of paper, trace a large circle.

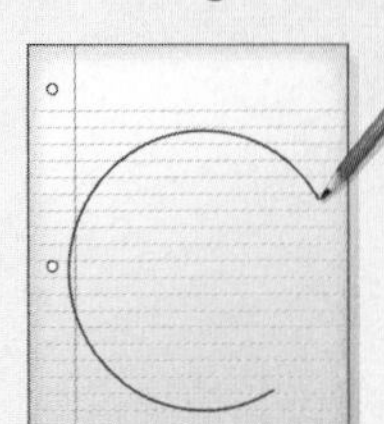

Step 2 With the papers still stacked, cut along the circle line you traced.

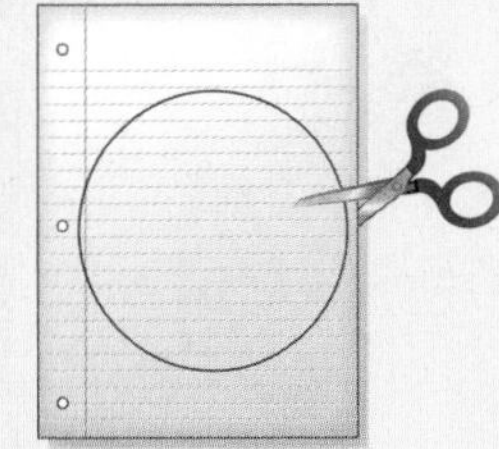

Step 3 Staple the paper circles together at one point around the edge.

Step 4 Label the front circle Content Vocabulary.

Reading and Writing As you read the chapter, record the content vocabulary terms with definitions for each section of Chapter 18 on the fronts and backs of the sheets of your booklet for easy reference.

Section Audio

Spotlight Video

Guide to Reading

Big Idea

An economic system is the way a society organizes the production and consumption of goods and services.

Content Vocabulary

- need *(p. 499)*
- want *(p. 499)*
- economics *(p. 499)*
- microeconomics *(p. 500)*
- macroeconomics *(p. 500)*
- economic model *(p. 500)*
- economic system *(p. 500)*
- resource *(p. 501)*
- scarcity *(p. 501)*

Academic Vocabulary

- rational *(p. 499)*
- capable *(p. 501)*
- generate *(p. 502)*

Reading Strategy

Comparing As you read the section, compare the two ways of defining economics: microeconomics and macroeconomics.

Section 1

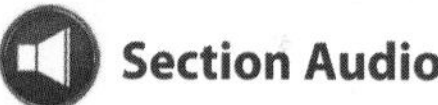

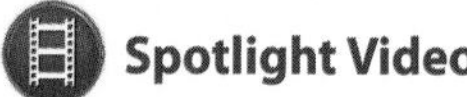

How Economic Systems Work

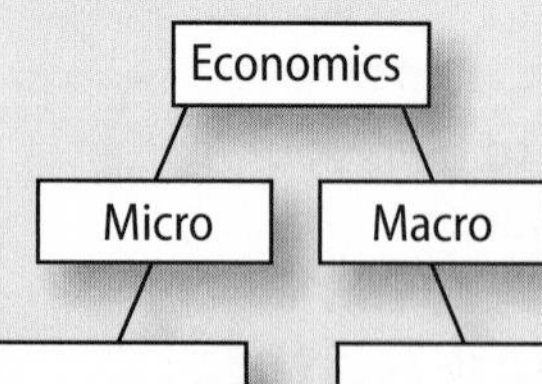

Real World Economics Have you ever gone to the grocery store and found the shelves empty? Sometimes natural disasters can cause huge economic problems from food shortages to the disruption of gas supplies. Hurricane Rita, on the heels of 2005's Hurricane Katrina, shook the economic roots of not only the South but the entire United States. Because Louisiana and Texas are producers of oil and gas, energy needs all across the nation were affected. Both national and state governments provided help in the form of emergency services, health care, information, and supplies.

▼ **Scarcity of products determines purchase prices following a disaster**

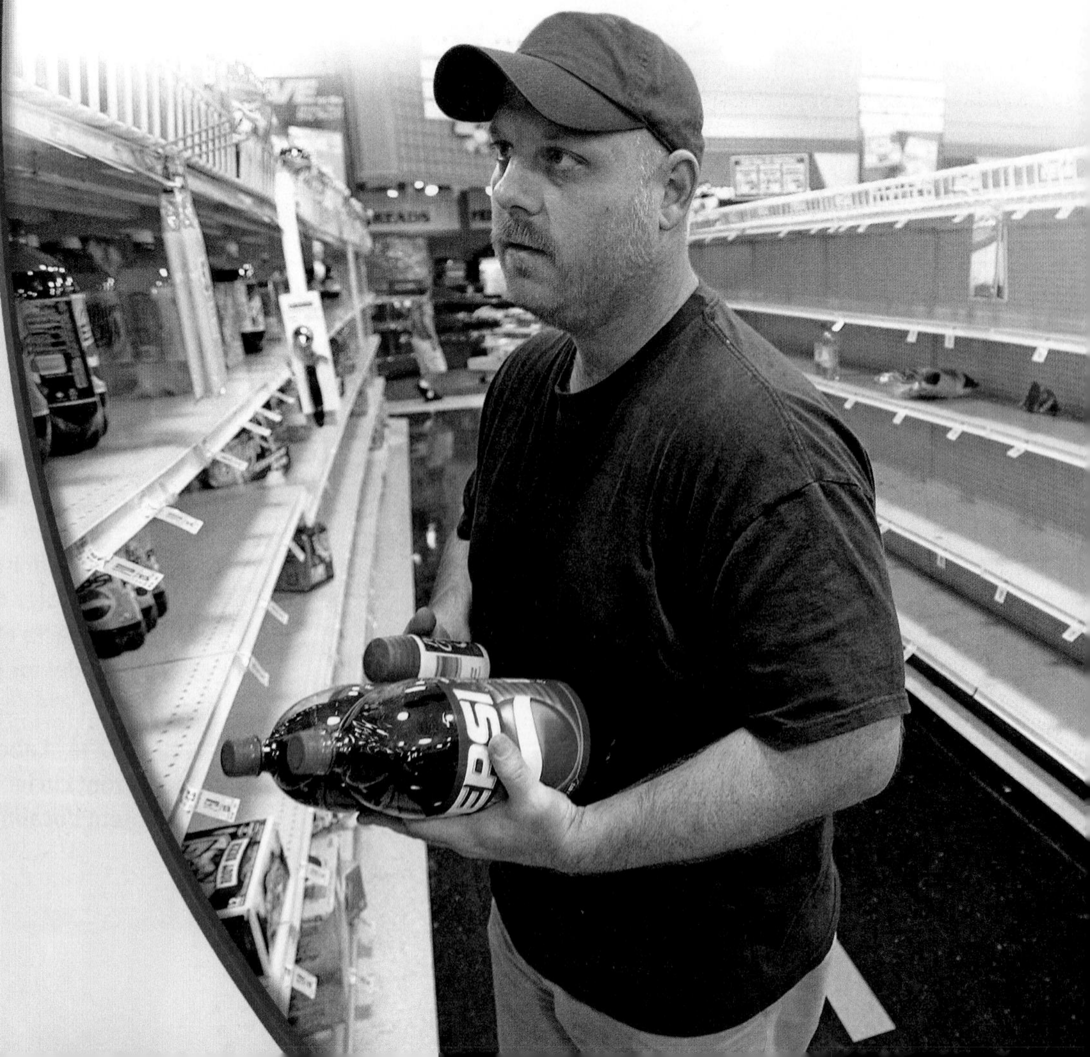

Foreign-Made Products Needs and wants are often satisfied by products made in other countries. These auto imports have just been unloaded at the port in Portland, Oregon. ***Contrasting*** **What is the difference between an economic need and a want?**

Economic Choices

Main Idea **Economics is the study of how we make decisions in a world in which resources are limited as well as the study of how things are made, bought, sold, and used.**

Economics & You Have you ever found it difficult to tell the difference between something you wanted and something you needed? Read to find out how these two ideas influence the science of economics.

To be a well-informed citizen, it is important to have a good understanding of economics and the American economic system. Well-informed citizens do more than make choices in the voting booth. They also make **rational,** or reasonable, economic choices, and they make these choices every day. For example, imagine you have $10 to spend on Saturday night. Do you rent a movie, go to a movie, order a pizza, go to a restaurant, buy snacks for a party, put gas in the car, or make any of a dozen other possible choices? You will quickly discover that your $10 will not cover everything you might want to do. Therefore, you must choose.

Needs and Wants

As individuals, we have many **needs** that are required for survival, such as food, clothing, and shelter. In addition, we also have an enormous number of **wants,** or things we would like to have, such as entertainment, vacations, and other items that make life more comfortable and enjoyable.

The choices we face, as individuals and as a society, are based on the fact that we do not have enough productive resources to satisfy all our wants and needs. Even a seemingly plentiful resource such as water is considered scarce because it is not free; we pay to use it.

Economics: A Definition

Economics is the study of how we make decisions in a world in which resources are limited. The study of economics will help you think about the process of making decisions.

Economics is also the study of how things are made, bought, sold, and used. It helps answer questions such as these: Where do these products come from? Who makes them? How do they get to the stores? Who buys them? Why do people buy them?

American Biography

John H. Johnson (1918–2005)

John H. Johnson began his career in 1942 at the age of 24. He used a $500 loan on his mother's furniture to start *Negro Digest,* a magazine devoted to the accomplishments of African Americans. Today, Johnson Publishing Company, Inc., is the world's largest African American-owned publishing company. This media empire includes many magazines, such as *Ebony* and *Jet,* and Johnson Publishing Company Book Division.

Like many minority-owned companies, Johnson faced many hurdles:

"[The difficulties include] trying to get circulation and to break through in advertising to get large companies to recognize that black consumers had money and would respond to advertising directed to them. . . . The first 20 years or so in business, we couldn't get a bank loan."

Many start-up companies face the same hurdles, but in his autobiography, Johnson expressed a message of hope.

In 1995 Johnson received the Presidential Medal of Freedom, America's highest civilian honor, from former president Bill Clinton. Clinton said Johnson gave "African-Americans a voice and a face, in his words, 'a new sense of somebody-ness,' of who they were and what they could do, at a time when they were virtually invisible in mainstream American culture."

Making a Difference — CITIZENSHIP

Johnson's businesses support all minorities.
Analyzing **What qualities did Johnson possess that made him a leader and a success in business?**

Micro and Macro As you read, keep in mind that economics is divided into two branches. In **microeconomics,** economists look at the small picture. They study the behavior and decision making of small (the meaning of the prefix *micro-*) units such as individuals and businesses. Microeconomics helps explain how individual economic decisions are made. On the other hand, **macroeconomics** looks at the big (the meaning of the prefix *macro-*) picture. It deals with the economy as a whole and decision making by large units such as governments or whole industries or societies. Think of other terms you know that start with the prefixes *micro-* and *macro-*.

Micro- and macroeconomics are examples of economic models. An **economic model** is a theory that tries to explain human economic behavior.

Economic Systems

Every country has its own **economic system,** or way of producing the things its people want and need. A country's economic system helps determine how basic economic decisions will be made. In the United States and many other countries, the economic system is called free enterprise capitalism. All free enterprise systems use more or less the same general methods of making economic decisions and producing things their people want and need. Under this system, businesses are allowed to compete for profit with a minimum of government interference. You will learn more about our economic system, along with other economic systems, later in this unit.

Reading Check **Explaining** On what does microeconomics focus?

The Problem of Scarcity

Main Idea **The limits on, or scarcity of, resources forces people to make careful economic choices.**

Economics & You Have you ever wondered why we do not have more schools, parks, and highways? Read to find out why we have to make choices.

The goods and services a country can produce depend on its resources. **Resources** are the things used in making goods and providing services. They include tools; natural resources such as wood, soil, and water; and human resources—the people who provide the necessary labor, skills, and knowledge to produce the country's goods and services.

A country with many resources is **capable,** or able, of satisfying its people's wants and needs better than a country with few resources. A scarcity of resources affects the economic decisions a country and its people make. Scarcity affects decisions concerning what and how much to produce, how goods and services will be produced, and who will get what is produced.

Scarcity and the Need to Choose

Scarcity occurs whenever we do not have enough resources to produce all the things we would like to have. The United States possesses abundant resources such as fertile soil, trained workers, forests, and water. No country, however, has all the resources it needs. Even a country as rich as the United States does not have enough productive resources to produce all the goods and services it needs.

Scarcity is the result. Because of scarcity, we have to make choices among alternatives. For example, a rational consumer compares prices and makes choices based on his or her limited resources. A rational consumer asks whether or not he or she can afford to buy a small car or a big car, own a home or rent, purchase brand-name items or generic ones, and so on.

What to Produce

One of the choices a society has to face is that of *what* to produce. As you have learned, we live in a world of scarcity. If more of one particular item is produced, then less of something else will be produced.

A Variety of Options For example, if resources are limited, we may have to choose between making weapons for defense or producing services for people who are retired or are too ill to work. Or we may have to choose between improving our roads or schools or even a nearby stadium for athletic events. Any civic leader in any community in the United States could extend this list almost indefinitely, given the wants and needs people have in their own communities.

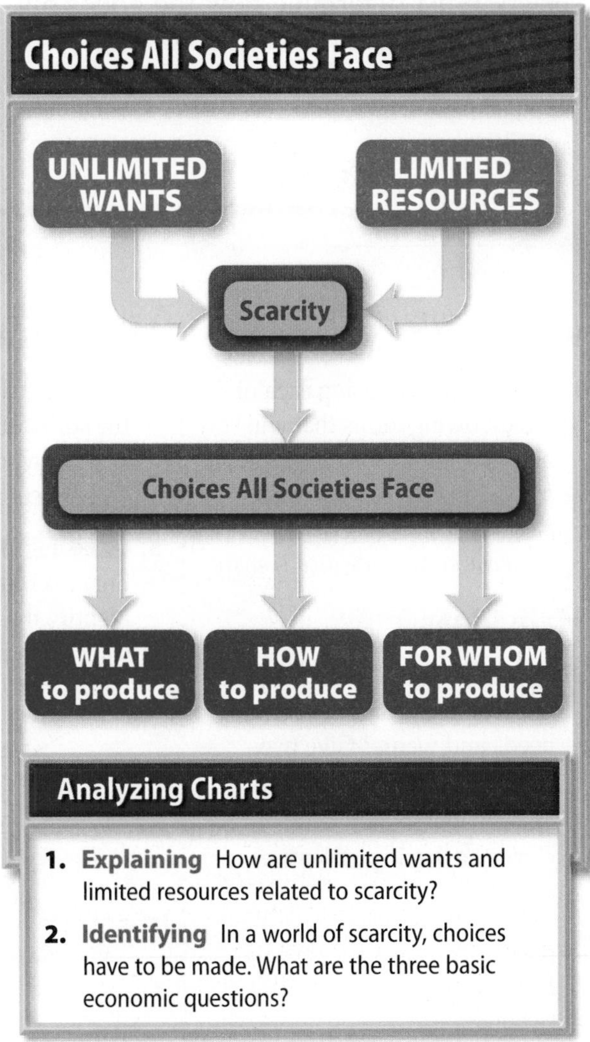

Analyzing Charts

1. **Explaining** How are unlimited wants and limited resources related to scarcity?
2. **Identifying** In a world of scarcity, choices have to be made. What are the three basic economic questions?

How to Produce

After deciding what to produce, a society must then decide *how* these goods and services will be produced. If we need more crude oil to satisfy our energy needs, should we allow drilling in an Alaskan wildlife sanctuary? Or should we restrict oil recovery to less fragile areas? How much pollution should we allow manufacturing firms to **generate,** or create? After all, businesses like to produce as cheaply as possible, and that sometimes means leaving waste behind that may pollute the environment. As you can see, every producer of a good or service faces the question of *how* to produce.

For Whom to Produce

After goods and services are produced, a society must determine how the goods and services will be distributed among its members. *Who* receives the new cars? *Who* benefits from a new school? Will anyone who is able and willing to pay the prices for the goods be able to obtain them, or will government decide who will have the goods?

As you will read, most goods and services in the United States are distributed to individuals and businesses through a price system. Other economies may distribute products through majority rule, a lottery, on a first-come-first-served basis, by sharing equally, by military force, and in a variety of other ways.

These questions concerning what, how, and for whom to produce are not easy for any society to answer. Nevertheless, as long as there are not enough resources to satisfy people's unlimited wants, they must be answered.

Reading Check **Explaining** Why does scarcity lead to the need for making choices?

Vocabulary

1. **Write** sentences using each of the following terms that will help explain its meaning: *need, want, economics, microeconomics, macroeconomics, economic model, economic system, resource, scarcity.*

Main Ideas

2. **Defining** What is the difference, in economic terms, between needs and wants? Give two examples of each.
3. **Explain** why scarcity and choice are basic problems of economics.

Critical Thinking

4. **Evaluating** In what ways can the study of economics help you and your family in your daily lives?
5. **BIG Ideas** On a graphic organizer like the one below, identify the three economic choices every society must make.

CITIZENSHIP Activity

6. **Analyzing** Interview a parent or adult about how the ideas in this section (needs, wants, and scarcity) influence his or her economic decision making. Share your findings in a short essay.
7. **Creative Writing** Write a short story, poem, or song about one of the economic ideas discussed in this section. For example, you might write a humorous song about someone choosing between a need and a want. Share your writing with the class.

Study Central™ To review this section, go to glencoe.com.

Section Audio   Spotlight Video

Making Economic Decisions

Guide to Reading

Big Idea

An economic system is the way a society organizes the production and consumption of goods and services.

Content Vocabulary

- trade-off *(p. 504)*
- opportunity cost *(p. 505)*
- marginal cost *(p. 507)*
- marginal benefit *(p. 508)*
- cost-benefit analysis *(p. 508)*

Academic Vocabulary

- previous *(p. 504)*
- compute *(p. 506)*
- diminish *(p. 509)*

Reading Strategy

Identifying As you read, identify the four types of costs and an example of each on a graphic organizer like the one below.

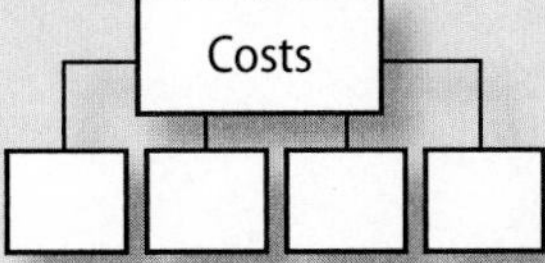

Real World Economics Have you heard the saying "Necessity is the mother of invention"? As the supply of fuel for automobiles becomes more scarce and citizens become more concerned about global warming, the push for developing new energy sources becomes ever stronger. These Wisconsin high school students explored new ideas for fuel efficiency in a contest called the "High Mileage Vehicle Challenge" sponsored by the University of Wisconsin. The team of Eau Claire North High School electronics students competed with a car of their own design and achieved 1,610 miles (2,591 km) per gallon—which propelled them into first place.

▼ **The North High School Hybrid Vehicle Team**

Trade-Offs

Main Idea **Economic decision making requires us to understand all the costs and all the benefits of a choice.**

Economics & You Have you ever had to choose one thing instead of another? Read to find out what economists call this common dilemma.

Economic decision making is surprisingly simple. It involves only a few terms and rules. In fact, you probably already think about many problems in the same way that economists do. As you learned **previously,** or earlier, scarcity forces people to make choices about how they will use their resources. Economic decision making requires that we take into account all the costs and all the benefits of an action.

Making Trade-Offs

The economic choices people make involve exchanging one good or service for another. If you choose to buy a DVD player, you are exchanging your money for the right to own the DVD player rather than something else that might cost the same amount. A **trade-off** is the alternative you face if you decide to do one thing rather than another.

It is important to remember that a trade-off does not apply only to decisions involving money. Here is an example: Suppose you have an economics test tomorrow. Your friends invite you to a party at their house. Total time at the party and traveling to and from your house is four hours. You calculate you need at least three hours to study for the test. You also need to sleep eight hours that night. How do you make trade-offs with your time—what do you give up—studying time, time with friends, or sleep?

Part-Time Jobs Many young people need to have jobs after school so they have some money with which to make economic choices. ***Explaining*** **Why is a type of economic choice called a trade-off?**

Political Cartoons

Steve Breen/Copley News Service

Every year, more than half of all Americans do volunteer work | role in it. One of the responsibilities of citizens is to help make their | of volunteer grou small. Perha dad who

The creator of this cartoon, Steve Breen, is making a statement on consumers' decisions regarding methods of transportation.

1. **What is the setting for this cartoon?**
2. **What "new interest" is the man on the right pursuing?**
3. **What is the primary factor that prompted this interest?**
4. **Do you think there might be benefits to society if people drive less and cycle more? Explain.**

Think about a trade-off on a larger scale. A country wants to put more money into education. This strategy may be a good one, but putting more money into education means having less money available for space exploration or national defense. Individuals, families, businesses, and societies make trade-offs every time they choose to use their resources in one way and not in another.

Opportunity Cost

Suppose you decide to go to college after you graduate from high school. If you do, you will quickly discover that the cost of college is more than the cost of books, transportation, tuition, and other fees. One of the biggest costs is the full-time income that you will not be able to earn because of the time you will spend studying and going to classes.

Economists have a term for this broad measure of cost. **Opportunity cost** is the cost of the next best use of your time or money when you choose to do one thing rather than another.

People tend to think of *cost* only in terms of dollars and cents. Note that opportunity cost includes more than just money. It also involves all the possible discomforts and inconveniences linked to the choice. The opportunity cost of cleaning the house, for example, is not just the price of cleaning products. It also includes the time you could spend doing other things, such as listening to music or visiting with your friends.

A good way to think about opportunity cost is to realize that when you make a trade-off, you lose. What do you lose? You lose the ability to engage in your next highest valued alternative. In economics, therefore, opportunity cost is always an opportunity that is given up.

Reading Check **Explaining** What does making a trade-off require you to do?

Costs Businesses, such as this farm, incur both fixed costs and variable costs. ***Describing*** **Is the farmland used for crops a fixed or a variable cost? How about equipment such as tractors, combines, and plows? Is the fuel to operate the machinery a fixed or a variable cost?**

Costs and Revenues

Main Idea **Economists have developed ways of measuring different types of costs and revenues.**

Economics & You Have you wondered why goods from places like China usually cost less than goods made in the United States? Read to discover why this is so.

Suppose you are in the business of producing bicycle helmets. Do you know how many helmets you would produce? Would it be 100, 500, or 10,000? You may have a feeling that you should not produce too few or too many, but how would you know what were too few and what were too many? To begin to answer these questions, we need to look more closely at costs and revenues.

Types of Costs

All businesses have costs, but not all costs are the same type. Anyone in business must understand several different ways of **computing,** or figuring, cost.

Fixed Costs The first kind of cost is fixed costs—costs, or expenses, that are the same no matter how many units of a good are produced. Mortgage payments and property taxes are two examples of fixed costs. It makes no difference whether your company produces one bicycle helmet or a very large number. Your fixed costs, such as your mortgage and property taxes, remain the same.

Variable Costs Another kind of cost is variable costs. Variable costs are expenses that change with the number of items produced. Wages and raw materials are examples of variable costs.

Variable costs increase as production grows. Conversely, these expenses will decrease when production decreases. For example, the more helmets you make, the more plastic you must buy.

Total Costs When we add fixed costs to variable costs, we arrive at total costs. Suppose you want to compute total costs for a month. If fixed costs are $1,000 for the month and variable costs are $500, then total costs are $1,500 for the month. Many businesses focus on average total cost. To arrive at average total cost, simply divide the total cost by the quantity produced. For example, if the total cost of making bicycle helmets is $1,500 and the company produces 50, then average total cost is $30 ($1,500/50 = $30).

Marginal Costs One final cost concept remains—**marginal cost.** Marginal cost is the additional cost of producing one additional unit of output. Suppose total cost is $1,500 to produce 30 bicycle helmets and $1,550 to produce 31 helmets. What is the marginal cost of the additional (31st) unit? The change in total cost is $50 and the change in the number of units is 1, so the marginal cost is $50.

Types of Revenue

Businesses use two key measures of revenue to decide what amount of output will produce the greatest profits. The first is total revenue, and the second is marginal revenue.

Total revenue is the number of units sold multiplied by the average price per unit. If 42 units of a product are sold at $2 each, the total revenue is $84.

When a business is thinking about a change in output, it considers how its revenue will change as a result of that change in output. What will be the additional revenue from selling another unit of output? Marginal revenue is the change in total revenue—the extra revenue—that results from selling one more unit of output.

TIME™ Teens in *Action*

Jessica Painter

Jessica Painter, 18, of Yucaipa, California, shares her coupon-clipping know-how with people in need.

QUESTION: How did you become a "coupon queen"?

ANSWER: When my mom was out of work and pregnant with me, stretching cash with coupons was a necessity. Stores nearby doubled the value of coupons, and Mom matched coupons with their weekly sales, and items became free or almost free.

Q: How did this lead to your group Food For Love?

A: Growing up, we had more than we could use. We'd donate the extra items to other needy individuals and families. This was the start of the food program. When I was seven, my mom became ill and couldn't do a lot of things that she needed to do to continue with the program. I didn't want to let the people who depended on us down. I helped with shopping, sorting, and deliveries. I became a community leader and a "coupon queen" to help carry on Food For Love.

Q: What would you tell other teens interested in helping out?

A: Action volunteering is about changing the way people live. I'm hoping to help young people see they can make a difference at any age. Passing volunteerism on to future generations is the goal of my Web Site www.actionvolunteering.com.

ACTION FACT: Painter and her family go to animal shelters and cheer up the animals. At one time the family had nine cats!

Delivering goods to a food bank

Making a Difference — **CITIZENSHIP**

Why is volunteer work an important part of Jessica's life?

Measuring Revenue

On page 507, you learned that total revenue is defined as the price of a good multiplied by the quantity sold. For example, if the price of a book at your local bookstore is $5 and 100 are sold, then total revenue is $500. Consider another example:

- MRT is a retail store that sells DVDs for a price of $10 each.
- MRT currently sells 100 DVDs a month.
- This means that MRT's total revenue is $1,000.

If MRT sells one more DVD for $10, what is the change in total revenue that results from the change in output sold?

To answer this question, we first calculate what the total revenue is when MRT sells 101 DVDs instead of 100: it is $1,010. We conclude that the total revenue changes from $1,000 to $1,010 when an additional DVD is sold. In other words, there is a change in total revenue of $10.

The change in total revenue that results from selling an additional DVD is marginal revenue. In the example, $10 is the marginal revenue. If the company sells 2 additional DVDs, the marginal revenue is $20.

This situation provides an example in which marginal revenue is constant (marginal revenue = $10 per DVD sold). This will not always be the case. Businesses often find that marginal revenues start high and then decrease as more and more units are produced and sold.

Marginal Benefit Finally, we usually do something because we expect to achieve some benefit. In other words, we are concerned with the **marginal benefit,** the *additional* satisfaction or benefit received when one more unit is produced.

Cost-Benefit Analysis

Oftentimes, the best decision is made by comparing the *marginal* benefits against the *marginal* costs. To do so, economists use a type of decision making called **cost-benefit analysis.** Rational economic decision making tells us to choose an action when the benefits are greater than the costs. If the costs outweigh the benefits, we should reject the chosen option.

Using Cost-Benefit Analysis The graph on this page shows a sample cost-benefit analysis. Suppose you are a farmer trying to decide how much of your 25 acres to plant with wheat. Assume that the marginal (or extra) cost of planting and harvesting the wheat is the same for all 25 acres. As a result, the line showing marginal cost would be a horizontal line.

Cost-Benefit Analysis

Marginal Benefits

Marginal Costs

0 5 10 15 20 25

Acres

Analyzing Graphs

Calculating As long as the marginal benefit of farming more acres exceeds the marginal cost, the farmer is better off farming more acres. At what point should the farmer stop farming more acres?

Student Web Activity Visit glencoe.com and complete the Chapter 18 Web Activity.

Diminishing Marginal Benefit Assume, though, that some of your land is better than the rest. As a result, the size of the harvest you can expect from each acre goes down as the number of acres increases. After all, you would plant the most fertile land first.

As more land is planted, you must use land that is less productive. As the graph on page 508 shows, the line representing marginal benefit would be downward-sloping, indicating **diminishing,** or declining, marginal benefits.

How Much Should You Plant? The information in the graph makes it easy to decide how much land you should plant. Clearly, you should plant the first 5 acres, because the marginal cost is low when compared to the marginal benefits to be gained. It would also be beneficial to plant 10 acres, even though the benefits are a bit lower. In fact, it would make sense to plant up to 15 acres, because to that point the marginal benefit is greater than the marginal cost. You would not, however, want to plant more than 15 acres. After 15 acres, the extra cost is greater than the extra benefit.

Answering the Basic Questions The previous example represents how to use cost-benefit analysis to answer the question of how much to produce. This is an issue all businesses must deal with—not just farmers. The same method can be used to answer other basic economic questions.

For instance, you can also use this method to decide *for whom* to produce. Think of the costs and benefits of selling your wheat in a town that is close to your farm, compared to selling it in a town 100 miles away. Shipping the wheat farther will probably cost more than trucking it locally, so that makes the marginal benefit of selling it nearby greater.

Reading Check **Explaining** What economic model helps answer the question of *what* to produce?

Vocabulary

1. **Write** sentences that demonstrate the meanings of *trade-off, opportunity cost, marginal cost, marginal benefit, cost-benefit analysis.*

Main Ideas

2. **Explaining** Give two examples of an economic trade-off decision.
3. **Explaining** What is the purpose of cost-benefit analysis?

Critical Thinking

4. **Describe** the relationship between trade-offs and opportunity costs.
5. **BIG Ideas** Identify a large purchase you would like to make. What opportunity costs can you identify if you go ahead with the choice? What is your final decision, based on analyzing the opportunity costs? Illustrate your decision on a grid like the one below.

Choice	Opportunity Cost	Final Decision

Writing

6. **Expository Writing** Because your time is limited, you are constantly facing trade-offs. Write a paragraph or two about the trade-offs you have made in choosing how to use your time during a one-week period. What activities did you choose to do? What were the opportunity costs involved in your choices?

Study Central™ To review this section, go to glencoe.com.

Financial Literacy

Simple and Compound Interest

When you deposit money in a savings account, the bank pays you interest for the use of your money. The amount of interest is expressed as a percentage, such as 6 percent, for a time period, such as a year. One type of interest is simple interest. **Simple interest** is figured on only the principal, or original deposit, not on any interest earned. **Compound interest** is paid on the principal plus any interest that has been earned. In other words, you are earning interest on interest. Over time, there is a significant difference in earnings between simple and compound interest.

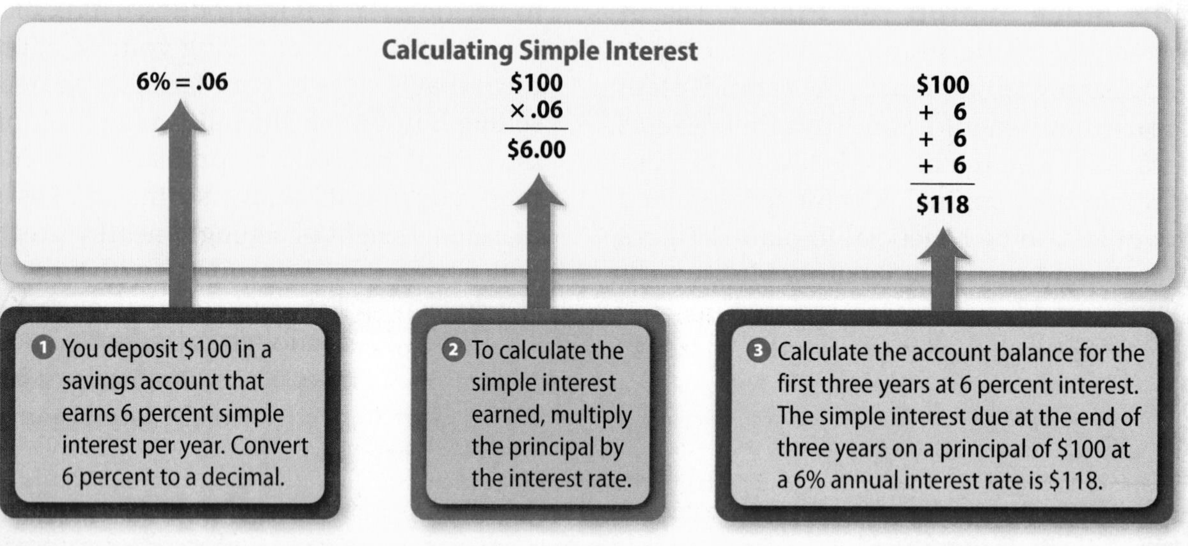

	Simple Interest	Compound Interest
Principal	$1,000	$1,000
Account Balance After One Year	1,100	1,100
Account Balance After Two Years	1,200	1,210 ($1,100 plus 10% of $1,100)
Account Balance After Three Years	1,300	1,331 ($1,210 plus 10% of $1,210)

Analyzing Economics

1. **Calculating** How much interest would you earn if you deposited $300 at 6 percent simple interest for three years?
2. **Concluding** Banks often pay higher rates of interest on money you agree to keep in the bank for longer periods of time. Explain why this might be.

Chapter 18 Visual Summary

Crowded college campus

Economics

Economics is the study of how we make decisions in a world in which resources are limited.

Microeconomics deals with decision making by small units such as individuals and firms.

Macroeconomics deals with the economy as a whole and decision making by large units such as government.

Making Economic Decisions

Individuals satisfy their unlimited wants in a world of limited resources by making choices.

The need to make choices arises because of scarcity, the basic problem in economics.

Every society must answer the three basic economic questions:

- What to produce
- How to produce
- For whom to produce

Individuals are forced to make trade-offs every time they use their resources in one way and not in another.

The cost of making a trade-off is known as opportunity cost—the value of the next best alternative that has to be given up to do the action that is chosen.

Shoppers look for bargains

Costs and Revenue

Four important measures of cost are total cost, fixed cost, variable cost, and marginal cost.

A key measure of revenue is marginal revenue, which is the change in total revenue when one more unit of output is sold.

Economic Systems

Every type of economic system must answer the three basic economic questions.

The United States has a free enterprise, or capitalist, economic system.

Assembly-line worker in Taiwan

STUDY TO GO Study anywhere, anytime! Download quizzes and flash cards to your PDA from glencoe.com.

Chapter 18 Assessment

TEST-TAKING TIP

When you come across an unfamiliar word in an exam, look at the word's parts—root, prefix, and/or suffix—to figure out its meaning.

Reviewing Vocabulary

Directions: Choose the word(s) that best completes the sentence.

1. Economics is the study of how we make decisions in a world of limited _______.

A needs
B wants
C choices
D resources

2. Capitalism is an example of a(n) _______.

A economic model
B economic decision
C economic system
D branch of economics

3. The income from a full time job that you give up when you go to college is called a(n) _______.

A trade-off
B opportunity cost
C marginal cost
D marginal benefit

4. The additional profit obtained from producing one more unit in a factory is called a(n) _______.

A trade-off
B opportunity cost
C marginal cost
D marginal benefit

Reviewing Main Ideas

Directions: Choose the best answer for each question.

Section 1 *(pp. 498–502)*

5. What does microeconomics deal with?

A the production of whole industries
B the distribution of goods worldwide
C the economic decisions of individuals
D the allocation of resources by governments

6. Which of the following items is a want?

A food
B videos
C shelter
D clothing

7. Which of the following is a natural resource?

A water
B skills
C machinery
D knowledge

Section 2 *(pp. 503–509)*

8. What is an example of a fixed cost of doing business?

A wages
B cost of fuel
C price of materials
D mortgage payment

9. What is the formula for total costs?

A fixed costs + variable costs
B fixed costs + marginal costs
C variable costs + marginal costs
D fixed costs + variable costs + marginal costs

10. Why do businesses use cost-benefit analysis?

A to compute total costs
B to measure total revenues
C to decide how much to produce
D to compare marginal cost and marginal revenue

GO ON

Critical Thinking

Directions: Base your answers to questions 11 and 12 on the pie graph below and your knowledge of Chapter 18.

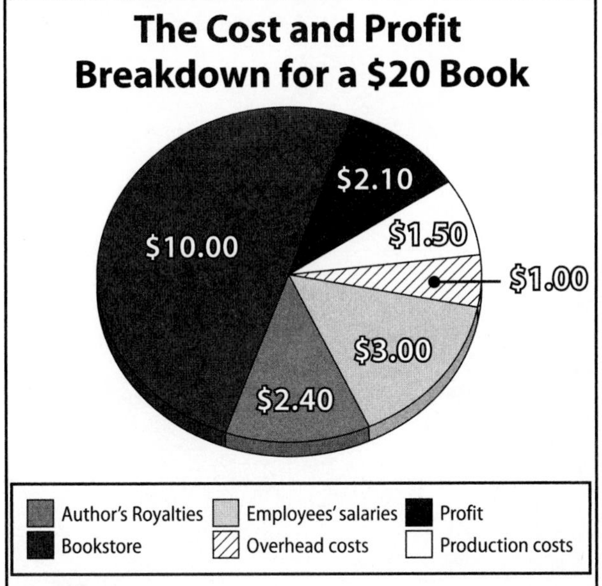

11. The publisher is thinking about printing one thousand more books but would have to hire another employee to do so. What would help her decide?

A tabulating the fixed and variable costs of new books

B comparing her marginal benefit to her marginal cost

C determining the marginal revenue for one more book

D calculating the total revenue from the sale of new books

12. What fixed cost paid by the bookstore owner comes in part from his share of the book's price?

A property tax payment

B the author's royalties

C wages for store clerks

D profit for the storeowner

Document-Based Questions

Directions: Analyze the document and answer the short-answer questions that follow.

In the following excerpt from his book *Capitalism and Freedom,* well-known economist Milton Friedman speaks about capitalism and the free enterprise system in the United States.

> *History suggests only that capitalism is a necessary condition for political freedom. Clearly it is not a sufficient condition. . . .*
>
> *Freedom in economic arrangements is itself a component of freedom broadly understood, so economic freedom is an end in itself. . . . Economic freedom is also an indispensable means toward the achievement of political freedom.*
>
> —Milton Friedman

13. What does Friedman say is the connection between capitalism and political freedom?

14. What is the main idea of the second paragraph?

15. What do you think Friedman would expect to happen to the United States if it were not a capitalist country?

Extended-Response Question

16. Compare and contrast microeconomics and macroeconomics.

For additional test practice, use Self-Check Quizzes—Chapter 18 on glencoe.com.

Need Extra Help?

If you missed question...	1	2	3	4	5	6	7	8	9	10	11	12	13	14	15	16
Go to page...	499	500	505	508	500	499	501	506	507	508	507	506	500	500	500	500

Chapter 19 The American Economy

Why It Matters

An economic system is a set of rules that governs what goods and services to produce, how to produce them, and for whom they are produced. In this chapter, you will learn how the economic system of the United States answers these questions.

Civics ONLINE
Visit glencoe.com and enter QuickPass™ code CIV3093c19 for Chapter 19 resources.

BIG Ideas

Section 1: Economic Resources

An economic system is the way a society organizes the production and consumption of goods and services. Four different key factors of production are necessary to produce goods and services.

Section 2: Economic Activity

The basis of the market economy is voluntary exchange. In the American economy, the exchange usually involves money in return for a good or service. Economic growth occurs when a nation's total output of goods and services, flowing in a circular motion among several sectors, increases.

Section 3: Capitalism and Free Enterprise

Free enterprise is the freedom of individuals and businesses to operate and compete with a minimum of government interference or regulation. The American economic system is the most successful in the history of the world.

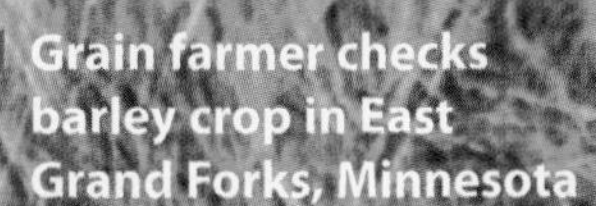

Grain farmer checks barley crop in East Grand Forks, Minnesota

FOLDABLES™ Study Organizer

Categorizing Information Study Foldable Make the following Foldable to help you categorize information about the different sectors of economic activity.

Step 1 Fold a sheet of paper from side to side, leaving a 2-inch tab uncovered along the side.

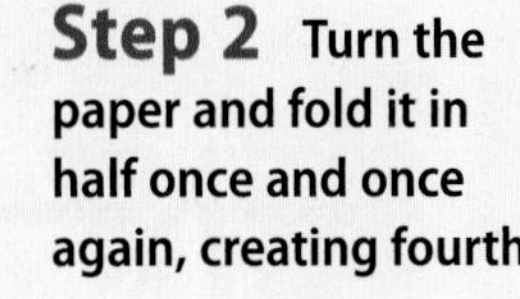

Step 2 Turn the paper and fold it in half once and once again, creating fourths.

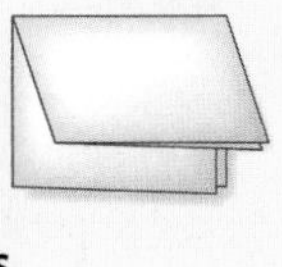

Step 3 Unfold and cut along the three fold lines through the top side of the paper.

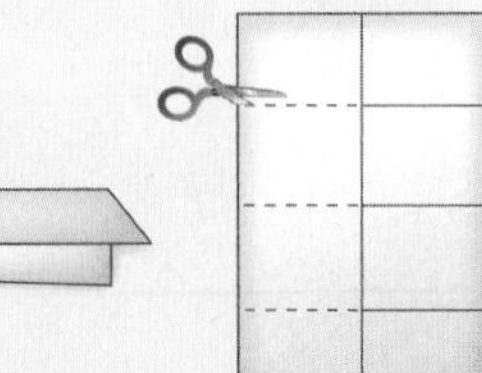

Step 4 Label the flaps as shown.

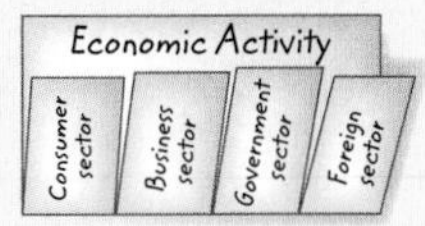

Reading and Writing
As you read the chapter about economic activity, categorize information about each part of the economy under each flap.

Section Audio   Spotlight Video

Economic Resources

Guide to Reading

Big Idea

An economic system is the way a society organizes the production and consumption of goods and services.

Content Vocabulary

- goods *(p. 517)*
- services *(p. 517)*
- factors of production *(p. 517)*
- natural resources *(p. 517)*
- labor *(p. 517)*
- capital *(p. 517)*
- entrepreneur *(p. 517)*
- Gross Domestic Product (GDP) *(p. 518)*
- standard of living *(p. 518)*

Academic Vocabulary

- output *(p. 517)*
- innovate *(p. 517)*

Reading Strategy

Categorizing As you read the section, complete a diagram like the one below by identifying the four factors of production.

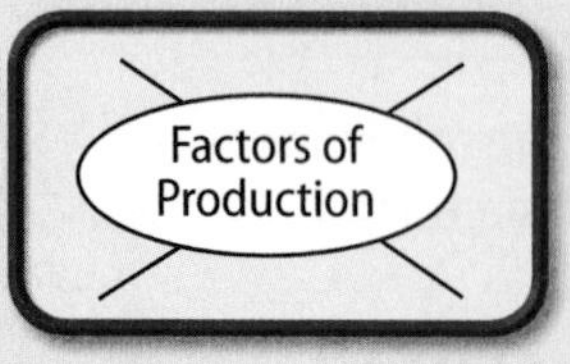

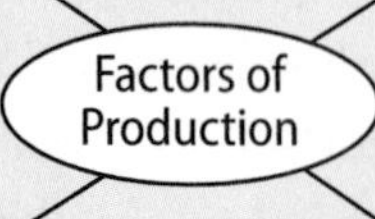

Real World Economics Do you know what an entrepreneur is? Mylan Murphy knows, because he became one when he started his own line of sports-themed clothing while still in the eighth grade. Mylan turned his love of basketball and his talent as an artist into a real business. Although he is too young to sign a contract, Mylan has enlisted his older brother, Mark, to be his business partner. The American economy depends on entrepreneurs, like the Murphys, as one of the four essential factors of production that keep the economy running.

▼ Athlete Mylan Murphy is also a sports apparel entrepreneur

Goods and Services

Main Idea **Four factors of production are necessary to produce goods and services.**

Economics & You What goes into making your CD player or your backpack? Read to find out what four production elements are necessary.

In 2007, the United States's annual **output,** or amount produced, totaled nearly 25 percent of the world's total output. Some of this production is in the form of **goods,** such as books and automobiles. More of this production is in the form of **services,** or work performed for someone else. Services include haircuts, home repairs, and entertainment.

Factors of Production

There are four **factors of production,** or resources necessary to produce goods and services. These are natural resources, labor, capital, and entrepreneurs.

Natural Resources The first factor, **natural resources,** refers to all the "gifts of nature" that make production possible. Natural resources include actual surface land and water as well as fish, animals, forests, and mineral deposits.

Labor The nation's workforce, **labor,** is its human resources. Labor includes anyone who works to produce goods and services.

Capital Another factor of production is **capital,** which are the manufactured goods used to make other goods and services. The machines, buildings, and tools used to assemble automobiles, for example, are *capital goods.*

Capital goods are unique in that they are the *result* of production. For example, we cannot find a hammer in the forest the way we can find a tree—someone actually has to make a hammer. Capital goods differ from consumer goods. Consumer goods directly satisfy wants—things such as clothes, clocks, foods, and radios. Capital goods satisfy wants indirectly by aiding production of consumer goods.

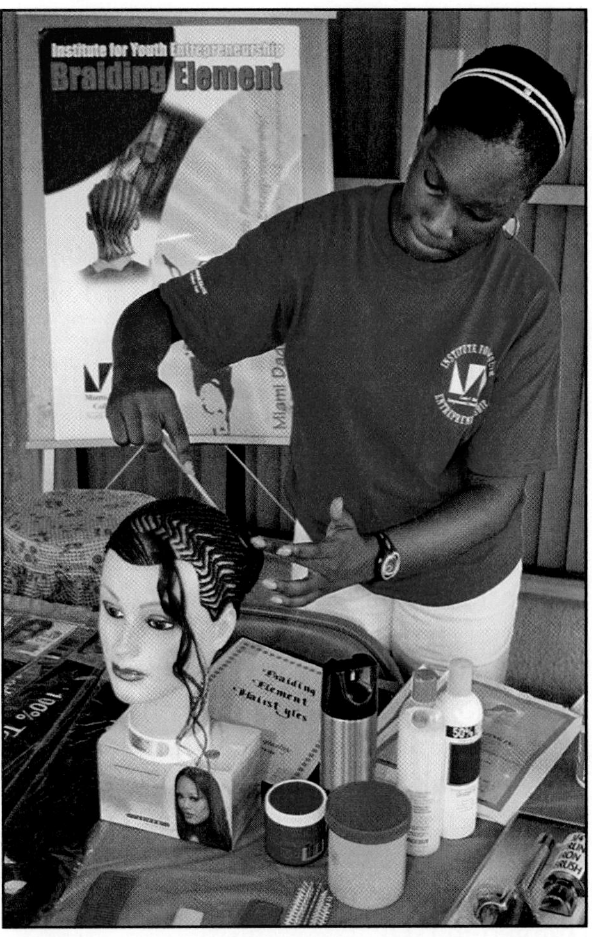

Entrepreneurs A Miami, Florida, teenage entrepreneur owns and operates a hair care business. ***Explaining*** **Why do entrepreneurs start new businesses?**

Entrepreneurs The **entrepreneur** is the fourth factor of production. This is an individual who starts a new business, introduces new products, and improves processes. Being an entrepreneur involves being **innovative,** or original, and being willing to take risks in order to make profits.

Reading Check **Classifying** Under what factor of production would you classify oil deposits? A diamond-cutting machine?

Gross Domestic Product

Main Idea **GDP is the total value of all the *final* goods and services produced in a country in one year.**

Economics & You Have you ever heard the United States described as a rich country? Read to find out how a nation's wealth is measured.

People often measure their economic well-being by the amount of their incomes and their ability to provide for themselves and their families. The success of the overall economy is measured in a similar way. One measure of the economy's size is **Gross Domestic Product (GDP).** This is the total value, in dollars, of all the *final* goods and services produced in a country during a single year. A final good is a good, such as a loaf of bread, that is sold to its user. The intermediate goods that go into making a loaf of bread—flour or wheat, sugar—are not counted in GDP.

In addition, the sale of used goods is not counted as part of GDP. When ownership of products already produced is transferred from one person or group to another, no new production is generated. Although the sale of a used car, chair, or CD player may give someone cash, only the original sale is included in GDP.

Measuring GDP

Remember that GDP is a measure based on money. If we are to compare the number of goods and services produced, it is helpful to get a meaningful idea of their relative worth. Look at the diagram at the top of the page for an example. Suppose there is a tiny economy in which only three goods are produced, in these quantities: 10 bicycles, 10 computers, and 10 watches. Furthermore, suppose the price of a bicycle is $200, the price of a computer is $1,500, and the price of a watch is $100. To find GDP of this economy, we multiply the price of each good by the quantity of that good produced and then add the amounts.

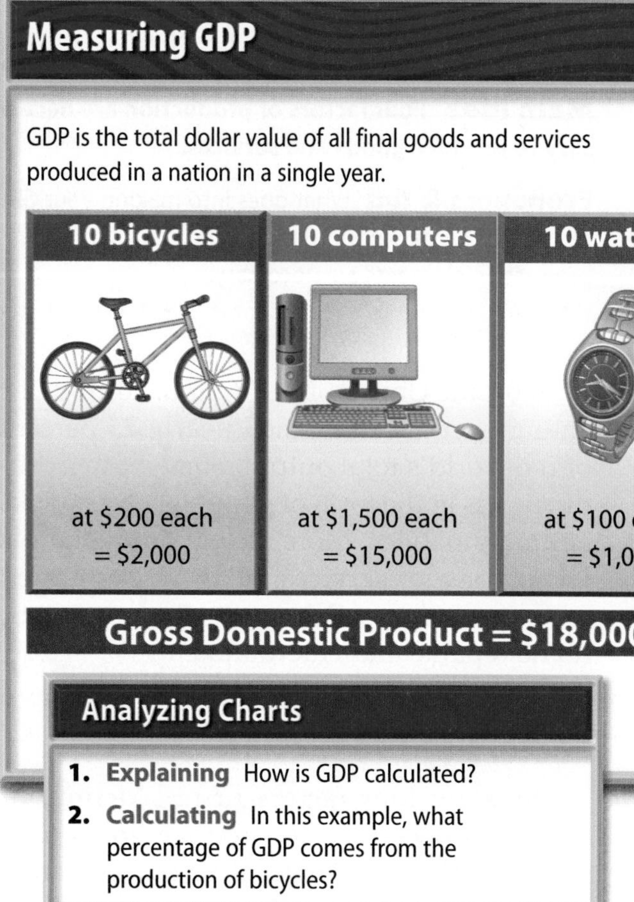

Analyzing Charts

1. **Explaining** How is GDP calculated?
2. **Calculating** In this example, what percentage of GDP comes from the production of bicycles?

How Is GDP Used? Economists study GDP figures regularly to analyze how the economy is doing. GDP is an important indicator of **standard of living,** the quality of life based on the possession of necessities and luxuries that make life easier.

Weaknesses of GDP GDP is a reasonably accurate and useful measure of economic performance. It is not a measure of society's overall well-being, though. Many things might make a country better off without raising GDP, such as reductions in crime or in drug and alcohol abuse.

Keep in mind that the statistics used in computing GDP are accurate only to a point. Statistics about easily measurable things, such as government purchases, are reliable. Some workers, however, are given food, fuel, or housing as part of their wages. To minimize error in calculating GDP, economists must take into account that GDP can include only an estimate of the value of such goods and services.

Quantity vs. Quality Remember that GDP measures *quantity*. It does not reflect improvements in the *quality* of products. There is a great difference between a $1,000 computer purchased today and a computer costing the same amount just a few years ago. Because of this, economists must take great care to account for quality improvement. Greater production of goods and services is only one of the many factors that contribute to raising the standard of living of any country.

Net Domestic Product

The loss of value because of wear and tear to durable goods, such as automobiles and refrigerators, is called depreciation. The same concept applies to capital goods—machinery and equipment. GDP does not take into account that some production merely keeps machines and equipment in working order and replaces them when they wear out.

Net domestic product (NDP)—another way of measuring the economy—accounts for the fact that some production is only due to depreciation. NDP takes GDP and subtracts the total loss in value of capital goods caused by depreciation.

Reading Check **Contrasting** What is the difference between final goods and intermediate goods?

Vocabulary

1. **Write** a paragraph in which you use these key terms: *goods, services, factors of production, natural resources, labor, capital, entrepreneur, Gross Domestic Product (GDP), standard of living.*

Main Ideas

2. **Identify** each of the following as one of the four factors of production:
   - carpenter
   - hammer
   - forest
3. **Describing** What is gross domestic product and how is it measured?

Critical Thinking

4. **Comparing** How does the factor of production of entrepreneurship differ from the factor of labor?
5. **BIG Ideas** Create a diagram like the one below and label the center oval as shown. Fill in an example of each factor of production that went into developing this service.

6. **Applying** Think like an entrepreneur. Identify a new product or service that you believe many people will want to buy. Outline the details of the new product or service. Then explain why you think people will want to buy it.

CITIZENSHIP Activity

7. **Persuasive Writing** Which of the four factors of production do you think has had the greatest impact on the development and enduring strength of the U.S. economy? Why? Write a position paper stating and supporting your reasons.

Study Central™ To review this section, go to glencoe.com.

Section Audio   Spotlight Video

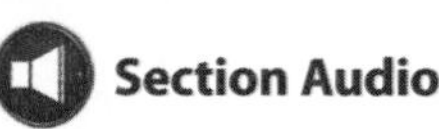

Section 2

Economic Activity

Guide to Reading

Big Idea

The basis of the market economy is voluntary exchange. In the American economy, the exchange usually involves money in return for a good or service.

Content Vocabulary

- market *(p. 521)*
- factor market *(p. 521)*
- product market *(p. 522)*
- productivity *(p. 524)*
- specialization *(p. 524)*
- division of labor *(p. 524)*
- economic interdependence *(p. 525)*

Academic Vocabulary

- sector *(p. 521)*
- consume *(p. 522)*
- input *(p. 523)*

Reading Strategy

Categorizing As you read the section, complete a diagram like the one below by identifying the four sectors of the economy.

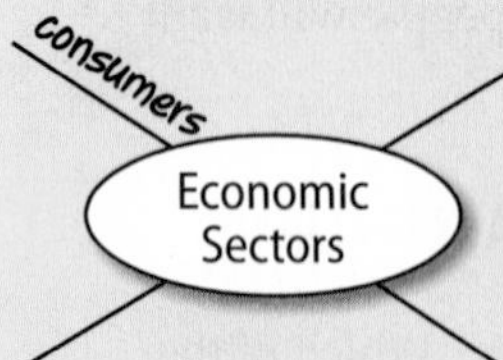

Real World Economics Would you know to shop on the Internet for shoes if you had really large feet? When Neil Moncrief started www.2bigfeet.com, specializing in large-sized shoes, the search engine Google listed his site first on searches for "big feet." Soon Moncrief was getting 95 percent of his business from the Internet. Later Google changed the way its search engines worked and sales decreased dramatically. Moncrief's experience is an example of how business success is based on many factors, including economic interdependence.

▼ **Neil Moncrief stands outside his Albany, Georgia, store**

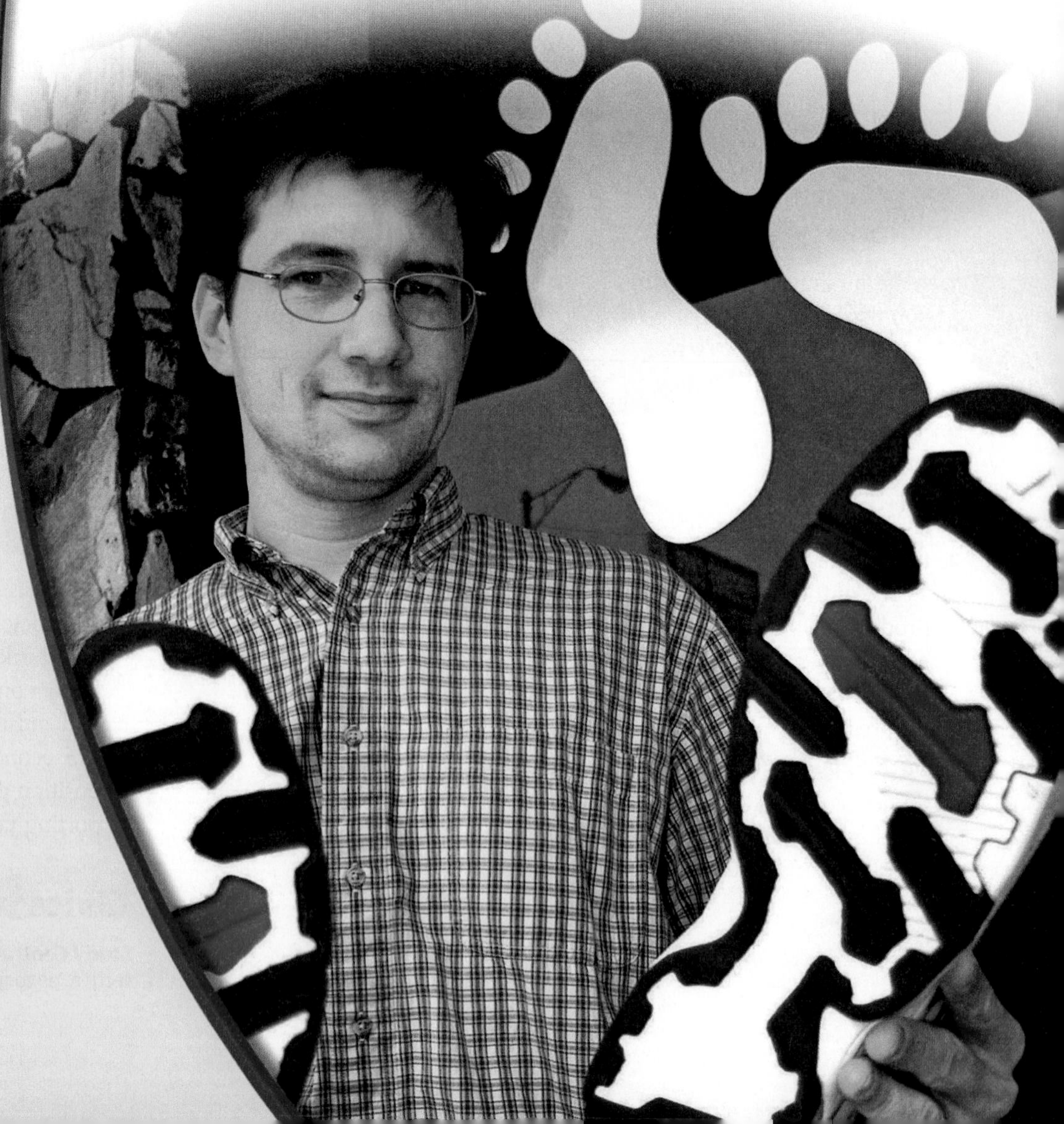

Economic Sectors and Circular Flow

Main Idea **Resources, goods and services, and money flow in a circular motion among several sectors.**

Economics & You The term *market* may mean to you a place to buy fresh fruits and vegetables, but it has a special meaning to economists. Read to find out more.

In the study of economics, a **market** is not necessarily a place. Rather, it is the free and willing exchange of goods and services between buyers and sellers. In other words, markets are places where people come together. Markets may be local, regional, national, or global. In this section, you will learn about the major groups of decision makers and the major markets in the market system. For example, a market exchange may take place in a worldwide market for a good such as crude oil. It may also take place in a neighborhood market for services such as paper delivery, snow shoveling, and babysitting.

Circular Flow of Economic Activity

In a market system, the flow of resources, goods and services, and money is actually circular, as shown in the diagram on page 522. Economists use this model to show how economic decision making in the market system works. The consumer **sector,** or part, makes up one group of economic decision makers, but there are others—the business, government, and foreign sectors.

The Consumer Sector

What role do consumers play in the circular flow? Consumers earn their income in **factor markets**—the markets where productive resources are bought and sold. Here, workers earn wages, salaries, and tips in exchange for their labor. People who own land may loan it in return for a type of income called rent. Finally, people who own capital exchange it for interest.

Economic Activity Within the circular flow of economic activity, consumers buy goods from businesses, and sell resources to businesses. ***Explaining*** **Is the house builder a member of the consumer sector, the business sector, or both?**

The Business Sector

After individuals receive their incomes, they spend them in **product markets**—markets where producers offer goods and services for sale. The business sector receives payments in the product markets where they sell goods and services to consumers. Businesses use these payments to pay for the natural resources, labor, and capital they use. These resources are then used to manufacture additional products that are sold in the product markets.

As the diagram shows, the business sector purchases some of the output it produces—primarily capital goods—so that it can continue to produce more goods and services. These purchases include things such as tools, factories, and other goods needed for current production. In actual practice, the business sector is much smaller than the consumer sector. While the consumer sector purchases about two-thirds of all output, the business sector usually **consumes,** or uses, only about 15 to 20 percent of our GDP.

The Government Sector

The government sector is another sector that plays a part in economic decision making. This sector is made up of all three levels of government—federal, state, and

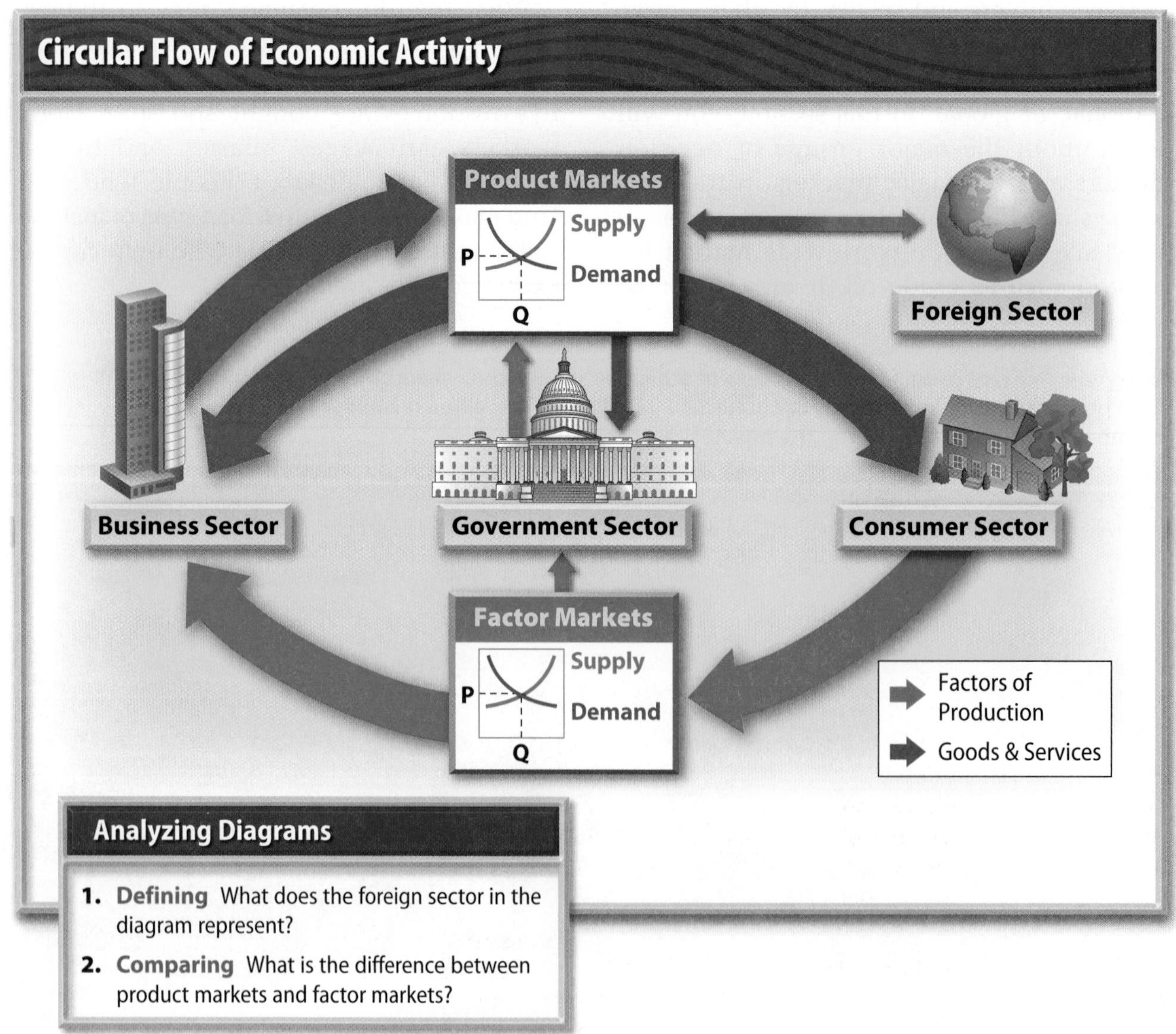

Analyzing Diagrams

1. **Defining** What does the foreign sector in the diagram represent?
2. **Comparing** What is the difference between product markets and factor markets?

local. Because the government sector also produces goods and services, it purchases productive **inputs,** or resources, in the factor markets. Since the time of World War II, the government has become a bigger part of the economy.

Revenues and Expenditures The government receives revenue from the services it sells. For example, public universities charge tuition, public hospitals charge fees, and city buses charge fares. The total cost of government services is seldom covered by fees alone, however. The government sector receives most of its revenues from taxes on businesses and individuals.

Government also uses its revenue to purchase final goods and services in the product markets. School systems, for example, purchase books, buses, and computers while the military purchases trucks, fighter planes, and ships. Historically, the government is the second-largest sector in our economy, purchasing approximately 20 percent of our GDP.

The Foreign Sector

The foreign sector in the diagram represents all the countries in the world. Notice on the diagram on page 522 that this sector is the only one with a line that has an arrow at both ends. The reason is that we both sell products to and buy products from other countries.

The value of the goods and services the United States purchases from other countries and the value of the goods and services it sells to other countries tend to offset one another. As a result, the foreign sector generally accounts for less than 4 percent of our nation's GDP.

Reading Check **Describing** In the circular flow of activity, in what economic activities is the consumer involved?

Civics ONLINE

Student Web Activity Visit glencoe.com and complete the Chapter 19 Web Activity.

TIME™ Teens in Action

Erika Fields

Erika Fields, 17, of Cleveland, Ohio, wondered why public schools in some urban areas get less state money than some schools in suburban areas. To help bring about change, and to make school funding more fair, Fields combined her voice with others in "Our Voice."

QUESTION: What is Our Voice?

ANSWER: Our Voice is a group of students who study school funding issues. We try to make a difference by testifying before education committees, holding rallies, and speaking out for fairness in how tax money is distributed to schools.

Q: Tell us about your newspaper.

A: *Our Voices: Students Speak Out* is a student-produced, statewide paper that talks about funding for public schools in Ohio.

Q: Do only teens from your school work on the paper?

A: No. Students from different schools contribute articles and illustrations. We open it up to everyone who has something to say about public schools—negative or positive.

Q: What is the paper's goal?

A: We are working to get our state lawmakers to produce an equal school funding system—to make sure that each and every student has an equal education.

"Our Voice" teens speak out

ACTION FACT: Fields enjoys singing—and is planning to become a doctor.

Making a Difference **CITIZENSHIP**

What is the purpose and goal of Our Voice, the group?

Promoting Economic Growth

Main Idea **Economic growth occurs when a nation's total output of goods and services from all economic areas increases.**

Economics & You You have probably told yourself at some time or another that you need to be more productive. Find out what productivity means in our nation's economy.

Economic growth occurs when a nation's total output of goods and services increases over time. This increase means that the circular flow becomes larger. Economic growth is important because it raises people's standard of living. This growth is a major goal of our economy and is a way officials can tell if our economy is healthy.

Division of Labor A quality control engineer at a South Carolina plant inspects the fan assembly of a gas-fired turbine. ***Explaining*** **In what way is the engineer's job an example of the division of labor?**

Productivity

When scarce resources are used efficiently, everyone benefits. Efficient use of resources is described by the term **productivity.** This is a measure of the amount of output (goods and services) produced by a given level of inputs (land, labor, capital, and entrepreneurship) in a specific period of time. Productivity goes up whenever more output can be produced with the same amount of input in the same amount of time, or when the same output can be produced with less input.

Productivity is often discussed in terms of labor, but it applies to all factors of production. For this reason, business owners try to buy the most efficient capital goods, and farmers try to use the most fertile land for their crops.

Specialization

Specialization takes place when people, businesses, regions, or even countries concentrate on goods or services that they can produce better than anyone else. As a result, nearly everyone depends upon others to produce many of the things that he or she consumes. Specialization is important because it improves productivity.

Few individuals or households seriously consider producing their own food, shelter, and clothing. When people specialize, they are usually far more productive than if they attempt to do many things. For example, Maria is a carpenter who wants to build a house. Even if Maria is capable of building the entire house without any help, she would likely be better off to hire other workers who specialize in foundations, plumbing, and electrical wiring.

Division of Labor

Division of labor is breaking down a job into small tasks performed by different workers. Division of labor makes use of differences in skills and abilities.

For example, you and your coworker would each do the tasks for which you are best suited. Even if your abilities are identical, specialization can be advantageous. By applying all your time to a single task, you are more likely to discover better techniques. Division of labor improves productivity.

Human Capital

Productivity also tends to increase when businesses invest in human capital—the sum of people's skills, abilities, and motivation. Employers are usually rewarded with higher-quality products and higher profits. Workers often benefit from higher pay, better jobs, greater motivation, and more satisfaction with their work.

Economic Interdependence

Because of specialization, our economy displays a strong degree of **economic interdependence.** This means that we rely on others, and others rely on us, to provide goods and services.

Events in one region of the country or the world often have a dramatic impact elsewhere. For example, bad weather in a country where sugarcane is grown can affect sugar prices in the United States, which in turn can affect the demand for sugar substitutes elsewhere.

Interdependence and Trade-Offs Today, economic technology usually describes the use of science to develop new products and new methods of producing and distributing goods and services. Without satellite technology, for example, it would be impossible to buy and sell goods and services with nations around the world.

This example does not mean that economic interdependence is necessarily bad. The gain in productivity and income that results from increased specialization usually offsets the cost associated with the loss of self-sufficiency.

Reading Check **Explaining** What are the benefits of specialization?

Review

Vocabulary

1. **Write** a paragraph in which you use the following terms: *productivity, specialization, division of labor, economic interdependence.* Then, write a second paragraph using these terms: *market, factor market, product market.*

Main Ideas

2. **Describing** What is a factor market?
3. **Explain** Why is productivity important to economic growth?

Critical Thinking

4. **BIG Ideas** Describe how either you or a relative of yours who has a job fits into the circular-flow model. Be sure to discuss both the factor market and the product market.
5. **Explaining** On a chart like the one below, define *division of labor* and explain how it improves the efficiency of production.

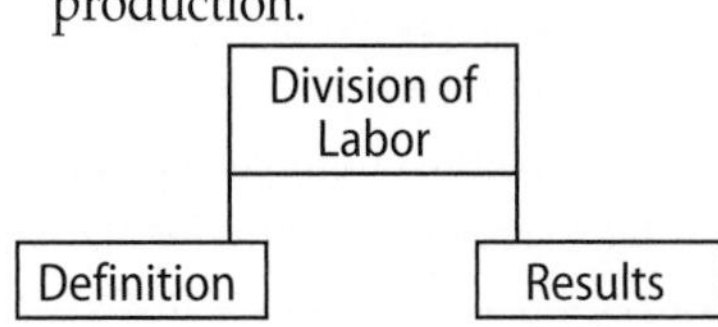

CITIZENSHIP Activity

6. **Expository Writing** Use the information in this section to write a short speech you could give to fourth graders on the topic "Why Economic Growth Is Important." Remember to make your explanation simple enough for younger students to understand.

Study Central™ To review this section, go to glencoe.com.

Financial Literacy

Education and Earning Power

As you probably already know, levels of education and income are related. High-income workers generally have more education than low-income workers. For example,

- high school dropouts earn less than high school graduates;
- high school graduates earn less than college graduates;
- college graduates with bachelor's degrees earn less than those with advanced degrees.

Not only is it likely that income will rise with further education, but also the chances of becoming unemployed are reduced. Unemployment rates for high school graduates are twice that for college graduates. For example, in April 2006, the unemployment rate for workers with a bachelor's degree or higher was 2.2 percent, 3.8 percent for workers with some college or an associate degree, 4.4 percent for those with a high school diploma, and 7 percent for workers with less than a high school diploma.

Level of Education	Median Income*	
	Female	Male
Not a high school graduate	$18,938	$26,468
High school graduate	26,074	35,412
Some college	30,142	41,348
Bachelor's degree	41,327	56,502
Master's degree	50,163	70,640
All full-time workers	**$31,565**	**$41,939**

*The median income is the middle income in a series of incomes ranked from smallest to largest.

Source: National Center for Education Statistics.

Did You Know?

"More than two-thirds of the new jobs being created in our economy are in occupations that require some kind of post-secondary education."

—Secretary of Labor Elaine Chao, May 31, 2006

Source: US Dept of Labor: www.dol.gov/sec/media/speeches/20060531_miami.htm

Analyzing Economics

1. **Comparing** What are the median incomes for men and for women who are employed full-time?
2. **Calculating** What is the difference in median income between female high school graduates and females who attain bachelor's degrees?

 Section Audio  Spotlight Video

Capitalism and Free Enterprise

Guide to Reading

Big Idea

Free enterprise is the freedom of individuals and businesses to operate and compete with a minimum of government interference or regulation.

Content Vocabulary

- capitalism *(p. 528)*
- free enterprise *(p. 528)*
- consumer sovereignty *(p. 529)*
- private property rights *(p. 529)*
- competition *(p. 530)*
- profit *(p. 530)*
- profit motive *(p. 530)*
- voluntary exchange *(p. 530)*
- laissez-faire economics *(p. 531)*

Academic Vocabulary

- accumulate *(p. 528)*
- dispose *(p. 529)*
- incentive *(p. 529)*

Reading Strategy

Organizing As you read the section, complete a diagram like the one below by identifying the features of capitalism. Then provide an example of each feature.

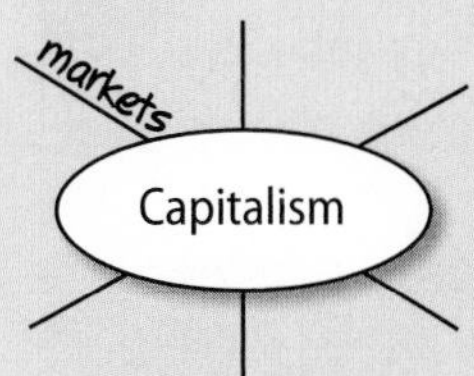

Real World Economics Where would you guess the world's busiest McDonald's restaurant is located? Los Angeles? New York? Tokyo? The answer is Moscow, in the former Soviet Union. How does this American restaurant do so well in a former Communist country? In Russian cities, McDonald's caters to the local citizens, not to American tourists. Teens in Moscow hang out at fast-food places in the same way teens in other countries do. Economic reforms in Russia have moved the country more toward a capitalistic, market-oriented system.

▼ **A McDonald's on St. Petersburg's main avenue, Nevsky Prospekt**

Capitalism

Main Idea **The economic system of the United States is known as capitalism, in which private citizens own and use the factors of production to seek a profit.**

Economics & You Do you feel that the products you want to buy are available? Read to find out what power you have as a consumer.

The economy of the United States is built largely on free markets and private ownership. It is known as **capitalism,** an economic system in which private citizens own and use the factors of production in order to seek a profit.

Free enterprise is another term to describe the American economy. In a free enterprise economy, competition is allowed to flourish with a minimum of government interference. One of the most remarkable characteristics of our nation's economy is its ability to grow and **accumulate,** or collect, wealth. No other economic system in the history of the world has been as successful.

What Makes Capitalism Work?

Several unique features of capitalism combine to contribute to its success in the United States and in other countries. These features are the use of markets, economic freedom, private property rights, competition, profit motive, and voluntary exchange.

Markets Markets are one important part of our economic system. Markets are the places where the prices of goods and services are determined as exchange takes place. Markets may be local, regional, national, or global. Markets also connect the different sectors of the economy. To illustrate, review the chart on page 522. It shows that consumers and businesses interact primarily in the product and factor markets.

TIME™

Political Cartoons

Gary Markstein/Copley News Service

Every year, more than half of all Americans do volunteer work | role in it. One of the responsibilities of citizens is to help make their | of volunteer grou small. Perha

With this cartoon, Gary Markstein is making a point about consumer credit. Examine the first panel of the cartoon.

1. **What "immediate action" would it be logical for the consumer to take in light of his financial situation?**
2. **Now look at the second panel. How are credit card companies depicted?**
3. **Why might credit card companies offer high-interest cards to consumers who are already in debt?**

American Biography

David Hernandez (1969 –)

David Hernandez was only 5 years old when his family left their home in Cuba and moved to the United States. When Hernandez's father died, David delivered newspapers, mowed lawns, and took on odd jobs to help his family. It would have been easy for him to give up on his dream to attend college. Instead, he worked his way through college and graduated magna cum laude from Palm Beach Atlantic University with a degree in accounting. He later earned an MBA from New York University.

When his employer, the energy giant Enron, collapsed, David Hernandez lost his job and his 401(K), but not his entrepreneurial spirit. Along with his brother, Eliezer, and two former colleagues, Hernandez saw an opportunity to build his own company. His plan was to provide small- and mid-sized businesses, with low-cost electric power and great customer support. In less than 4 years, Liberty Power grew from grossing less than $1 million in its first year to more than $100 million in 2005, making it the largest Latino-owned electricity provider in the country.

The company's corporate responsibility does not end with its customers. In January 2004 Hernandez created the Liberty Power Foundation to support education in the communities the company serves.

Making a Difference — CITIZENSHIP

"It's not only important to do well; philosophically, I believe that it's important to do good." ***Discuss the meaning of this quote by David Hernandez.***

When you go to work, your labor is being sold in the factor markets. When you go shopping, the goods and services you buy are being purchased in product markets. In our economic system, the consumer is especially important because businesses usually try to produce the products that people want most. Because of the effort to match products to wants, we use the term **consumer sovereignty** to describe the consumer as the "king," or ruler, of the market, the one who determines what products will be produced.

Economic Freedom In the United States, we place a high value on the freedom to make our own economic decisions. Each of us can choose the type of job or occupation we would like to have, and we can choose when and where we would like to work.

As consumers, we have the right to choose the products we will buy. Businesses have the right to choose the products they will produce and offer for sale. However, along with this freedom come certain costs. In particular, individuals must normally accept the consequences of their decisions in our free enterprise system. If an entrepreneur starts a business that fails, the government usually does not help out.

Private Property Rights Another major feature of capitalism is **private property rights.** These rights mean that we have the freedom to own and use, or **dispose** of, or throw away, our own property as we choose as long as we do not interfere with the rights of others. Private property rights give us the **incentive,** or drive, to work, save, and invest because we know we can keep any gains that we might earn. In addition, people tend to take better care of things if they actually own them.

Competition Cloth making was primarily a home-based craft during colonial times. By the early 1800s, power-loom technology mechanized cloth making, and prices for cloth came down. ***Explaining*** **What are the benefits of competition?**

Competition Capitalism thrives on **competition**—the struggle between buyers and sellers to get the best products at the lowest prices. The competition between sellers keeps the cost of production low and the quality of the goods higher than they would otherwise be. Buyers likewise compete among themselves to find the best products at the lowest prices.

Competition thus rewards the most efficient producers. Competition also forces the least efficient producers out of business or into other industries. The result is that competition makes for efficient production, higher-quality products, and more satisfied customers.

The Profit Motive Under free enterprise and capitalism, people are free to risk their savings or any part of their wealth in a business venture. If the venture goes well, the people will earn rewards for their efforts. If things go poorly, they could lose part or even all of the investment. The possibility of financial gain, however, leads many to take risks in hopes of earning a profit.

Profit is the amount of money left over after all the costs of production have been paid. The **profit motive**—the driving force that encourages individuals and organizations to improve their material well-being—is largely responsible for the growth of a free enterprise system based on capitalism.

Voluntary Exchange **Voluntary exchange** is the act of buyers and sellers freely and willingly engaging in market transactions. Who benefits when you buy something—you or the seller? Both are giving something up to gain something else. As long as the transaction involves a voluntary exchange, both you and the seller benefit—or the exchange would not have happened in the first place.

The exchange takes place because both parties feel they will make a profit. Voluntary exchange, then, is both a characteristic of capitalism and a way for us to improve our economic well-being.

Reading Check **Explaining** What force pushes people to improve their financial well-being?

History of Capitalism

Main Idea **Capitalism developed gradually in Europe and had a powerful influence on America's constitutional Framers.**

Economics & You If you have a job, why do you work? Read to find out how a famous economist answers this question.

In 1776 Adam Smith, a Scottish philosopher and economist, provided a philosophy for the capitalist system in his book *The Wealth of Nations*. Smith's book offered a detailed description of life and trade in British society. It also scientifically described the basic principles of economics for the first time.

Smith wrote that individuals left on their own would work for their own self-interest. In doing so, they would be guided as if by an "invisible hand" to use resources efficiently. From the writings of Smith and others came the idea of **laissez-faire economics.** Laissez-faire, a French term, means "to let alone." According to this philosophy, government should not interfere in the marketplace. The government's role is confined to those actions necessary to ensure free competition.

Many of America's Framers were influenced by *The Wealth of Nations*. James Madison read it, and Alexander Hamilton borrowed heavily from it in his writings. In a 1790 letter he sent, Thomas Jefferson wrote, ". . . in political economy I think Smith's *Wealth of Nations* is the best book extant [in existence] . . ."

Reading Check **Explaining** What is the role of government, according to the laissez-faire philosophy?

Review

Vocabulary

1. **Explain** what *free enterprise* means, then explain how each of the following terms relates to free enterprise: *capitalism, consumer sovereignty, private property rights, competition, profit, profit motive, voluntary exchange, laissez-faire economics.*

Main Ideas

2. **Describing** What does the idea of consumer sovereignty express?
3. **Explaining** What are the limits of private property rights?

Critical Thinking

4. **Explaining** According to Adam Smith, what are the results of individuals working for their own self-interest?
5. **Determining** Under capitalism, how would you answer the question: For whom are goods produced?
6. **BIG Ideas** There are six features of capitalism mentioned in this section. On a diagram like the one below, identify the two features that you think are most important. Explain your answer.

CITIZENSHIP Activity

7. **Analyzing** Survey five fellow students, friends, and neighbors to discover what the term *free enterprise* means to them. Review your findings and analyze why people might have different views of free enterprise.
8. **Descriptive Writing** Adam Smith said that people work for self-interest. Do you agree? Write a paragraph describing someone who works for this reason or for another reason.

Study Central™ To review this section, go to glencoe.com.

Landmark Supreme Court Case Studies

Gibbons v. Ogden

In the early years of the nation, each state jealously guarded its own commerce. Trade barriers among the states restricted commerce and stood in the way of a strong national economy. What changed this situation?

Background of the Case

In the early 1800s, the state of New York licensed Robert Fulton and his partner to operate a steamboat monopoly along its waterway. The partners then used their license to grant Aaron Ogden a monopoly on ferryboat travel between New York City and Elizabethtown, New Jersey. Thomas Gibbons, however, had a federal license to run boats between New York and New Jersey.

Ogden wanted to shut down his competition. He sued to close down Gibbons' operation. It was up to the Supreme Court to decide which would prevail—Ogden's state license or Gibbons' federal license.

New York Harbor, painted by Thomas Birch, 1827

The Decision

John Marshall delivered the Court's unanimous opinion on March 4, 1824. His decision rested on the power of Congress to "regulate commerce," as granted in Article I, Section 8, of the U.S. Constitution. Marshall interpreted *commerce* to mean "every species of commercial [interaction]," including navigation.

> ***"This power [to regulate commerce], like all others vested in Congress, is complete in itself, may be exercised to its utmost extent, and acknowledges no limitations other than are prescribed in the Constitution. . . . [However, this rule does not apply to] . . . commerce, which is completely internal, which is carried on between man and man in a State, or between different parts of the same State. . . ."***
>
> —Justice John Marshall

The decision gave the federal government sole power to regulate all possible forms of commerce between states. It also affirmed Congress's right to regulate trade with foreign nations. States retained the right to regulate trade entirely inside their borders, and Ogden lost his license.

Why It Matters

The *Gibbons* decision took on more significance in later years than it did at the time. Marshall's broad interpretation of the commerce clause, in fact, helped pave the way for today's strong national government. It allowed Congress to prevent companies from fixing prices. In 1964, Congress was able to prohibit racial discrimination in businesses serving the public because such discrimination was seen as affecting interstate commerce.

Analyzing the Court Decision

1. **Describing** How did Marshall define the commerce clause?
2. **Analyzing** How did this Supreme Court ruling affect states' control of economic activities?

Chapter 19 Visual Summary

Economic Resources

- The four factors of production (natural resources, labor, capital, and entrepreneurs) provide the means for a society to produce its goods and services.
- Gross Domestic Product (GDP) is the total value of all the *final* goods and services produced in a country in one year.

Economic Activity

- Productivity relates to the efficient use of resources, and tends to go up when workers specialize in the things they do best.
- Resources, goods and services, and money flow in a circular motion among several sectors, and economic growth occurs when a nation's total output of goods and services increases.

Capitalism and Free Enterprise

- The economic system of the United States is based on capitalism and free enterprise.
- Important characteristics are markets, economic freedom, competition, private property rights, the profit motive, and voluntary exchange.

Mother and daughter shop for clothes

Worker stitches American flags onto baseball caps at a Buffalo, New York, factory

Twin sisters check items on sale

STUDY TO GO Study anywhere, anytime! Download quizzes and flash cards to your PDA from glencoe.com.

Chapter

19 ASSESSMENT

Standardized Test Practice

TEST-TAKING TIP

Skim through a test before you start to answer questions. That way you can decide how to pace yourself.

Reviewing Vocabulary

Directions: Choose the word(s) that best completes the sentence.

1. Machines, buildings, and tools used to make other goods and services are _______ goods.

A consumer **C** factor
B capital **D** manufactured

2. The total value of all the final goods and services produced in a country in one year is its _______.

A income **C** GDP
B VAT **D** resources

3. Consumers earn their income in _______ markets where productive resources are bought and sold.

A factor **C** resource
B product **D** consumer

4. The _______ between sellers keeps the cost of production low and quality of goods high.

A profit motive **C** exchange
B interdependence **D** competition

Reviewing Main Ideas

Directions: Choose the best answer for each question.

Section 1 *(pp. 516–519)*

5. The four factors of production are natural resources, labor, capital and

A entrepreneurs.
B services.
C goods.
D specialization.

6. A nation's standard of living is a measure of not only the quantity of its products, but also

A the value of its resources.
B of its people.
C the quality of its goods and services.
D of how the products are produced.

Section 2 *(pp. 520–525)*

7. The four sectors, business, consumer, government, and foreign are all part of

A the GDP.
B the factors of production.
C the circular flow of economic activity.
D a nation's standard of living.

8. When workers receive additional training for their jobs, this increases

A the cost of production.
B human capital.
C economic interdependence.
D the division of labor.

Section 3 *(pp. 527–531)*

9. In a free enterprise economy, competition is allowed to flourish with a minimum of

A government interference.
B voluntary exchange.
C specialization.
D division of labor.

10. In our economy businesses try to produce goods and services that people want most; this is an example of

A private property rights.
B specialization.
C the factors of production.
D consumer sovereignty.

GO ON

Critical Thinking

Directions: Choose the best answer for each question.

Base your answers to questions 11 and 12 on the chart below and your knowledge of Chapter 19.

Level of Education	Median Income*	
	Female	Male
Not a high school graduate	$18,938	$26,468
High school graduate	26,074	35,412
Some college	30,142	41,348
Bachelor's degree	41,327	56,502
Master's degree	50,163	70,640
All full-time workers	**$31,565**	**$41,939**

Source: National Center for Education Statistics.

*The median income is the middle income in a series of incomes ranked from smallest to largest.

11. If most of the new jobs being created in our economy require a post-secondary education, it is likely that

A higher education will reduce your chances of unemployment.

B the cost of education will continue to fall.

C unemployment will continue to decrease in the larger cities.

D capital goods production will not keep up with consumer goods production.

12. The chart shows that education improves the earning power of almost everyone, but

A it benefits all full time workers equally.

B advanced degrees are very expensive.

C males benefit more than females.

D fewer females work fulltime.

Document-Based Questions

Directions: Analyze the following document and answer the short-answer questions that follow.

In 1776 Adam Smith wrote *The Wealth of Nations*, explaining the foundations of capitalism. Here he describes the advantages of a division of labor.

> *The greatest improvements in the productive powers of labour, and the greater part of the skill, dexterity, and judgment, with which it is anywhere directed, or applied, seem to have been the effects of the division of labour.*
>
> *. . . This great increase in the quantity of work, which, in consequence of the division of labour, the same number of people are capable of performing, is owing to three different circumstances; first, to the increase of dexterity in every particular workman; secondly, to the saving of the time which is commonly lost in passing from one species of work to another; and lastly, to the invention of a great number of machines which facilitate and abridge labour, and enable one man to do the work of many.*
>
> —Adam Smith

13. According to Adam Smith, what are two advantages that are gained when a task is divided among different workers?

14. Why does the invention of machines depend on the division of labor?

Extended-Response Question

15. A division of labor also assumes that the workers will produce an excess of goods—more than they can use. Write an essay explaining how this excess production relates to free markets.

For additional test practice, use Self-Check Quizzes—Chapter 19 on glencoe.com.

Need Extra Help?

If you missed question...	1	2	3	4	5	6	7	8	9	10	11	12	13	14	15
Go to page...	517	518	521	530	517	518	521	525	528	529	525	525	524	524	524

Chapter 20

Personal Finance and Economics

Why It Matters

Whatever goals or dreams you may have, the way you live your life will be determined, at least in part, by your relationship to money: how you get it and how you use it. The opportunities you create for yourself are greatly affected by the money habits you form when you are young. **Why is it important for you to make rational buying decisions?**

Chapter Audio

Civics ONLINE
Visit glencoe.com and enter QuickPass™ code CIV3093c20 for Chapter 20 resources.

BIG Ideas

Section 1: Managing Your Money

You and everyone around you are consumers and, as such, play an important role in the economic system. As a consumer and a citizen, you will make many economic decisions every day.

Family spending their vacation dollars camping

Section 2: Planning and Budgeting

We all make economic choices. Opportunity cost, scarcity, and supply and demand influence the decisions we make. Following a budget can be valuable to you.

Section 3: Saving and Investing

We all make economic choices. Opportunity cost, scarcity, and supply and demand influence the decisions we make. It is important for financial security to start the habit of saving.

Section 4: Achieving Your Financial Goals

We all make economic choices. Opportunity cost, scarcity, and supply and demand influence the decisions we make. Our personal interests, wants, and abilities affect our career choices.

FOLDABLES™ Study Organizer

Comparing Information Study Foldable Make the following Foldable to help you compare the rights and responsibilities of consumers with regards to their personal finances.

Step 1 Lay three sheets of paper on top of one another, about one inch apart at the top.

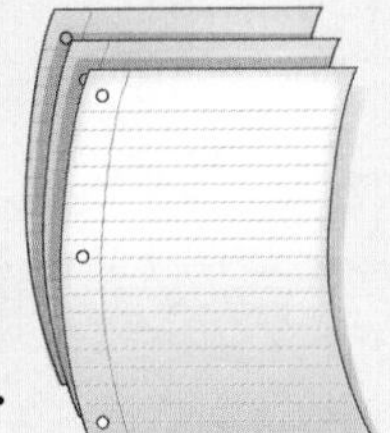

Step 2 Fold up the bottom edges of the paper to form 6 tabs.

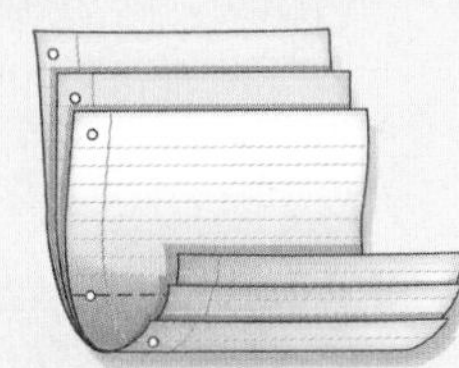

consumer number
consumer income
consumer task
consumer expectations
substitutes
complements

Staple together along the fold.

Step 3 When the tabs are all the same size, crease the paper to hold the tabs in place and staple the sheets together. Label the Tabs as shown.

Reading and Writing As you read the chapter, organize information about the different forces that affect the impact of demand on the economy. Write facts under each appropriate tab.

Section Audio

Spotlight Video

Managing Your Money

Guide to Reading

Big Idea

You and everyone around you are consumers and, as such, play an important role in the economic system.

Content Vocabulary

- consumer *(p. 539)*
- disposable income *(p. 539)*
- discretionary income *(p. 539)*
- consumerism *(p. 540)*
- comparison shopping *(p. 541)*
- warranty *(p. 542)*

Academic Vocabulary

- reject *(p. 539)*
- alternative *(p. 541)*

Reading Strategy

Identifying As you read, create a diagram like the one below to list your rights as a consumer.

Real World Economics Do you make smart decisions when you shop? Making the best use of your money is a skill you can learn and practice throughout your life. Food shopping is a prime example of a way to shop economically. This young woman is looking at two different brands of cereal. This strategy, called comparison shopping, can help a consumer find the best product for the price. As it becomes more difficult for families to meet their basic budgetary needs, smart shopping techniques become more necessary to stretch the family dollar.

▼ **Comparing prices can help you find the best buy**

Right to a Safe Product A new worker gets on-the-job training at a California restaurant. Restaurants must meet standards of cleanliness and quality assurance for the protection of their clientele. ***Analyzing*** **What is the purpose of the Consumer Bill of Rights?**

Consumer Rights

Main Idea **To make good economic decisions as consumers, we need to be aware of our rights and responsibilities.**

Economics & You Have you ever bought a product or service that did not work the way it was advertised? What did you do? Read to find out more about your rights as a consumer.

The American free enterprise system gives numerous economic rights and protections to individuals such as you, your teachers, your relatives, and your friends. You have the right to enter into just about any profession or business in which you are interested. You have the right to buy the products and brands that you like and to **reject,** or pass on, others. As a **consumer,** or someone who buys a product or service, you also have responsibilities.

Two Types of Income

One of your fundamental rights as a consumer is to spend the money you earn as you wish. Your role as a consumer depends on your available income and how much of it you choose to spend or save. There are two basic types of income: disposable income and discretionary income.

Disposable income is the money that remains after all taxes on it have been paid. People spend their disposable income on many kinds of goods and services. First, they usually buy necessities, such as food, clothing, and housing.

Discretionary income is the money remaining after paying for necessities. Discretionary income can be used to satisfy wants, including luxury items and savings accounts. Regardless of the size of a person's income, spending one's income requires, or needs, constant decision making. As a consumer, each person has choices to make.

Protecting Consumer Rights

Throughout much of history, consumer rights could be summed up in one Latin phrase: *caveat emptor,* or "let the buyer beware." In this section, you will learn how **consumerism**—a movement to educate buyers about the purchases they make and to demand better and safer products from manufacturers—affects you personally.

Over the years, Congress has passed a number of laws to protect consumer rights. Many of the laws involve labeling. For example, the Fair Packaging and Labeling Act requires every package to have a label identifying its contents and its weight. The Food, Drug, and Cosmetic Act requires packages to list their ingredients according to the amount of each. Other laws protect consumers' health and safety. An early example is the Pure Food and Drug Act, passed in 1906. It requires manufacturers of foods, cosmetics, and drugs to prove that their products are safe.

Many private groups and organizations have taken on the task of protecting individual consumers. One of the oldest groups is the Better Business Bureau (BBB). In 2005, there were more than 120 Better Business Bureaus located in principal cities in the United States. Surprisingly, business groups rather than consumers run these organizations. These businesspeople recognize that the key to success lies in earning the trust of their customers. They provide information about local businesses and warn consumers about dishonest business practices. They also investigate consumer complaints.

Food Labels The U.S. Food and Drug Administration requires packaged foods to display labels giving key information about their contents. ***Explaining*** **How does this information help consumers?**

Consumer Bill of Rights

In the 1960s, a special effort was made to help consumers. President John F. Kennedy and, later, President Richard Nixon emphasized five consumer rights:

1. Consumers have the *right to a safe product,* one that will not harm their health or lives.
2. Consumers have the *right to be informed* for protection against fraudulent, deceitful, or grossly misleading information, advertising, labeling, or other practices, and to be given the facts necessary for making informed choices.
3. Consumers have the *right to choose* to have available a variety of products and services at competitive prices.
4. Consumers have the *right to be heard*—the guarantee that consumer interests will be listened to when laws are being written.
5. Consumers have the *right to redress*—the ability to obtain from the manufacturer adequate payment if a product causes financial or physical damage.

Reading Check **Summarizing** What is the purpose of the Better Business Bureau?

Consumer Responsibilities

Main Idea **In addition to rights, consumers also have responsibilities.**

Economics & You Have you ever regretted spending money on something? Read more to find out how you can make sure you do not make mistakes when it comes to making purchases.

In earlier chapters, you discovered that with every right comes certain responsibilities. With the right to vote, for example, comes the responsibility of staying informed. In the same way, our rights as consumers require some responsibilities on our part.

Protecting Consumers The president of Consumers for Auto Reliability, Rosemary Shahan (right), and Assemblywoman Cindy Montanez of San Fernando, California, promote a bill designed to protect used car buyers. ***Describing*** **What is your first step if you purchase a faulty product?**

Smart Buying Strategies

Many consumer responsibilities might also be described as smart buying strategies. These are among the most important:

- Gathering information and finding out as much as we can about the products we buy so that we recognize good quality. Consumer magazines and Web sites often provide trustworthy information about product quality and other consumers' experiences.
- Using advertising carefully to help us learn about products and services and the best places to buy them. At the same time, we must be sure we are not swayed by advertising that appeals to our emotions, tries to get us to buy things we do not need or want, or uses questionable techniques to convince us to buy certain products.
- After you have gathered the information about the product you want, you must decide *where* to buy it. It is generally worthwhile to get information on the types and prices of products available from different stores or companies. This process is known as **comparison shopping.** To comparison shop effectively, read newspaper advertisements, make telephone calls, and visit different stores.
- Looking at both brand-name and usually cheaper but nearly identical generic products
- Balancing the costs and benefits of buying used items, ordering by mail, and **alternative,** or different, methods of making purchases

We cannot always rely on stores and businesses to protect us. We must take steps to protect ourselves.

Other Responsibilities

What are some other consumer responsibilities? Here is an important one: If a product or service is faulty, it is the consumer's responsibility to initiate the problem-solving process.

Reporting a Faulty Product If you purchase a faulty product or service, you should do the following:

- Report the problem immediately.
- Do not try to fix a product yourself; home repair may cancel the **warranty,** the promise of a manufacturer or a seller to repair or replace a faulty product within a certain time period.
- Contact the seller or manufacturer, state the problem, and suggest a fair solution.
- Keep an accurate record of your efforts to get the problem solved. Include the names of the people you speak or write to.
- Allow each person reasonable time, such as three weeks, to solve the problem before contacting another source.
- If you need to contact the manufacturer in writing, type your letter or send an e-mail directly.
- Keep a copy of all communications.
- Keep your composure. The person who will help you solve your problem is probably not responsible for the problem.

Making Fair Complaints Another responsibility of consumers is to exhibit ethical behavior by respecting the rights of producers and sellers. For example, a responsible consumer does not try to return a used item because it has been advertised elsewhere for a lower price or claim it is faulty if he or she has broken it.

Buyers feel they have a right to expect honesty from sellers. In turn, sellers feel they have a right to expect honesty from buyers. For example, suppose you purchase a DVD player from a store but drop it on the way to your house. Because you dropped it, it does not play as well as it would have. You could, of course, go back to the store and tell the seller that the DVD player you bought does not work properly—without mentioning the fact that you dropped it—but that would be dishonest. You have a responsibility when making a complaint to provide the seller with the whole truth as you know it.

Seeking Help If you have a complaint that you cannot settle with the seller, you have a responsibility to report this fact to the appropriate government agency. Remember, as a consumer, you have the right to voice your complaints, and you also have a responsibility to exercise your rights.

Making Purchases Shopping online or by telephone saves time. ***Evaluating*** **What do you think is the main disadvantage of shopping from home?**

Reading Check **Explaining** What is a warranty and why is it important to consumers?

Civics ONLINE

Student Web Activity Visit glencoe.com and complete the Chapter 20 Web Activity.

Making Buying Decisions

Main Idea **Buying a product or service costs more than money; it also costs the time it takes to make the purchase and the opportunity cost of *not* buying something else.**

Economics & You How do you make the decision about whether to buy a product or service? Read to find out what factors consumers should take into account when making a purchase.

The first decision a consumer must make is whether or not to buy an item. How many times do you actually think about the reasons for the purchase you are about to make? Do you think about whether you really need the item? Should you wait until there is a sale on the item you want? Do you consider the trade-offs involved?

After you have decided to make a purchase, at least two scarce resources are involved—income and time. Before you spend your discretionary income, you need to invest time in obtaining information about the product you wish to buy. Suppose you decide to buy a mountain bike. The time you spend visiting stores and checking models and prices is a cost to you.

Second, virtually all the steps in consumer decision making involve an opportunity cost. Remember that opportunity cost is the value of the highest alternative choice you did *not* make. Suppose your friend recently purchased athletic shoes. You want to buy a pair yourself. Before you do, however, ask yourself, "What can't I buy or do if I buy these shoes?" In other words, you must decide if the shoes are worth what you must give up to buy them.

Reading Check **Explaining** How does opportunity cost affect the decision to buy something?

Vocabulary

1. **Define** the following terms and use them to write a short essay about making buying decisions: *consumer, disposable income, discretionary income, consumerism, comparison shopping, warranty.*

Main Ideas

2. **Explaining** What is the right to redress?
3. **Describing** How does comparison shopping help the consumer?
4. **Explaining** What scarce resources are involved in making a buying decision?

Critical Thinking

5. **BIG Ideas** Describe two examples of how you educate yourself about a product before buying it.
6. **Identifying** As you read, create a diagram like the one below to list your responsibilities as a consumer.

CITIZENSHIP Activity

7. **Expository Writing** Which of the consumer responsibilities do you think is the most important? Why? Explain your choice in a one-page essay.

Study Central™ To review this section, go to glencoe.com.

Section Audio | Spotlight Video

Planning and Budgeting

Guide to Reading

Big Idea
We all make economic choices. Opportunity cost, scarcity, and supply and demand influence the decisions we make.

Content Vocabulary
- budget *(p. 545)*
- income *(p. 545)*
- expense *(p. 546)*
- credit *(p. 547)*
- annual percentage rate (APR) *(p. 547)*
- collateral *(p. 547)*
- bankruptcy *(p. 549)*

Academic Vocabulary
- exceed *(p. 545)*
- status *(p. 547)*

Reading Strategy
Describing As you read, use a graphic organizer like the one below to describe the steps in making a budget.

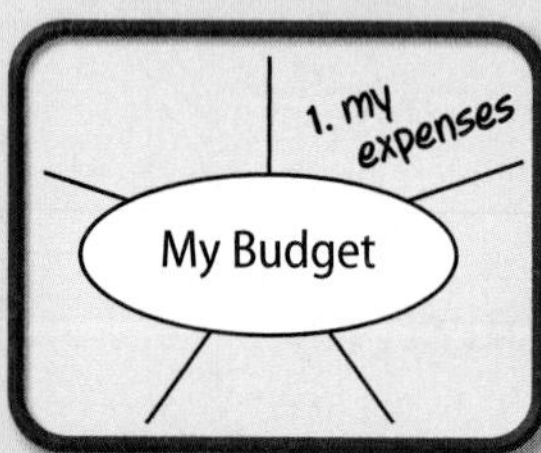

Real World Economics Do you know how to create a budget? College students often have to learn to budget for the first time in their lives. This Clemson University student is shocked by the cost of his textbooks. Over the last twenty years, the price of textbooks has risen at twice the rate of inflation. With textbooks becoming so much more expensive, many students resort to using credit cards to purchase their books. That can add to their accumulating debt.

▼ **Freshman student Noel Cole of Asheville, North Carolina**

Making a Budget—and Sticking to It!

Main Idea **Making and following a budget can help you organize your financial life.**

Economics & You Have you ever had to say no to a concert, dance, game, or other event because you did not have enough money? If so, learning more about budgets can help you make sure there is enough money in your wallet for the things you would really like to do.

The best way to get a handle on your spending is to make a **budget.** What is a budget? It is a careful record of all the money you earn and spend. A budget tells you exactly where your money goes. Using a budget can help you make your expenses match your income.

Mr. Micawber, a famous character from Charles Dickens' novel *David Copperfield,* made it very clear to young David why a budget is important: "Annual income twenty pounds, annual expenditure nineteen six, result happiness. Annual income twenty pounds, annual expenditure twenty pounds ought and six, result misery." Mr. Micawber meant that if your expenses **exceed,** or go beyond, your income by even sixpence [six pennies], you are in big trouble.

A budget is more than a record. It can also be a tool. It can help you plan and cut down on unwise spending and provide a road map toward saving for things you really want.

Basic Budgeting Terms The basic terms used in making and using a budget are the same, whether you are a high school student or the president of a giant company. Your **income** is the money you earn.

Budgeting A family works out their monthly budget. As a student, you might think you do not earn enough money to need a budget. You might be surprised to learn how much further your money goes when you budget. ***Defining*** **What is income?**

TIME™

Political Cartoons

Chris Britt/Copley News Service

The high cost of gasoline was the inspiration for this cartoon by Chris Britt.

1. **What is the setting for this cartoon?**
2. **How does the cartoonist use exaggeration to help make his point?**
3. **Why do you think Britt decided to have the driver own an SUV?**
4. **Do you think the cartoonist is making a statement about high gas prices, SUVs, or both?**

Your **expenses** are the money you spend on everything, including what you choose to save. Balance is the amount of money you have left over after you subtract all your expenses. A surplus means you have more income than expenses; a deficit means you have more expenses than income. This unhappy situation—deficit—is also known as a negative balance.

How to Make a Budget

Creating and organizing a personal budget is not difficult. Anyone who knows addition, subtraction, multiplication, and division, can accomplish it. Follow these steps to organize a budget:

1. Make a list of everything you spend for a couple of weeks. Include entertainment, clothing, food, personal items, gifts, transportation, contributions and donations, and savings. You might also want to have a category, or group listing, for other or miscellaneous expenses. It is important to record *everything* you spend.
2. For the same time period, record everything you earn and its source. Sources might be your allowance, job earnings, payment for household chores, or gifts; again, include a category for other or miscellaneous income.
3. Now that you have recorded your data, analyze it. Do you need to reduce expenses? Where could you cut costs? Would you rather increase your income? Can you work extra hours at your job or advertise your services to neighbors?
4. It is a good idea to have a little surplus for emergency expenses or extra contributions to your savings account.
5. Monitor your spending; use your budget data as a tool for taming any unruly finances. Make changes as needed.

Reading Check **Defining** What is a budget?

Credit

Main Idea **Credit can be a valuable item in your financial toolbox; however, as with all tools, you have to know how to use it correctly.**

Economics & You Have you ever received a credit card offer in the mail? Did you know how to evaluate it? Read more to find out what to look for the next time an offer for a credit card shows up.

A character in a play by William Shakespeare gave some famous advice when he warned, "Neither a borrower nor a lender be." However, it is not very practical today; in fact, almost everyone, along with almost all businesses, sometimes borrows money. Many of us also lend it. The key is using **credit**—borrowing money to pay for something now while promising to repay it later.

Offers Through the Mail Do you receive "pre-approved" credit card offers in the mail, some with low introductory rates? ***Speculating*** **Is it important to compare terms and fees before you agree to open a credit card account? Explain.**

Recognizing Credit Terms

Understanding how credit works in our society requires knowing some important terms.

- A lender is the person who loans someone the money to buy an item.
- A borrower receives the loaned money.
- Interest is the cost for the use of the money.
- The **annual percentage rate (APR)** is the annual cost of credit expressed as a percentage of the amount borrowed.
- A credit rating is an evaluation of the likelihood of a borrower to default on, or be unable to repay, a loan. It is based on the borrower's previous credit experiences, financial situation, job history, **status,** or rank, and other information.
- **Collateral** is property, such as a house, car, or other valuable item, that a borrower pledges as security for a loan. If a borrower fails to repay a loan, the lender can seize the collateral as payment.

Sources of Credit

Banks, credit unions, and finance companies all offer credit to consumers. So do stores that sell relatively expensive merchandise, such as clothing, electronics, appliances, or furniture. Home mortgages and car loans are other popular types of credit. Large credit purchases usually require a down payment, or a part of the purchase price, when you make the purchase. The remaining unpaid balance is then divided into equal monthly payments.

Credit Cards Perhaps the most common type of credit today is the credit card. Issued by banks, credit card companies, and stores, a credit card allows you to charge, or pay using borrowed money, for goods and services up to the value of a preset monthly limit.

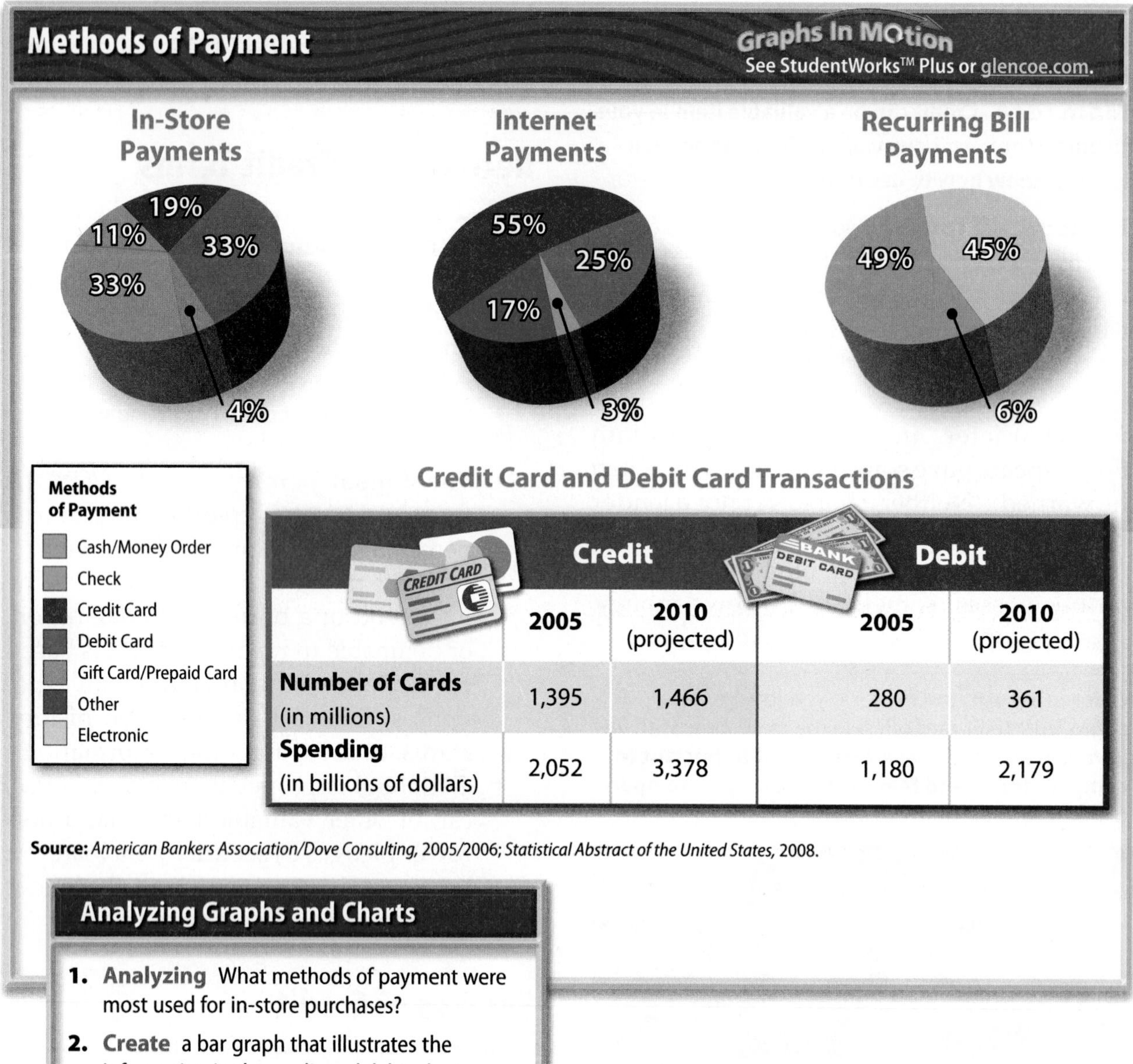

Credit Card and Debit Card Transactions

	Credit		Debit	
	2005	2010 (projected)	2005	2010 (projected)
Number of Cards (in millions)	1,395	1,466	280	361
Spending (in billions of dollars)	2,052	3,378	1,180	2,179

Source: *American Bankers Association/Dove Consulting, 2005/2006; Statistical Abstract of the United States,* 2008.

Analyzing Graphs and Charts

1. **Analyzing** What methods of payment were most used for in-store purchases?
2. **Create** a bar graph that illustrates the information in the credit and debit chart.

When you apply for a credit card, the issuer checks your credit rating and assigns a dollar limit based on what it thinks you can afford to pay back. To avoid interest charges, you must pay off your full credit balance each month. You are charged a fee if your monthly payment is late. High interest charges on unpaid balances add up quickly and have even brought financial ruin to some unlucky or careless consumers.

Here is an eye-opening example: Say you buy an item that costs $2,000 with a credit card that charges 18 percent interest. If you pay off the entire bill immediately, you pay $0 in interest. If you make only the minimum 4 percent payment, over time, it will take you more than 10 years to pay for the item, and you will have paid $1,142 in interest. Thus, the $2,000 item will have cost you $3,142.

Credit: Benefits and Drawbacks

Americans use credit to make many purchases. The total amount of funds borrowed and lent each year is enormous. Used wisely, credit can be a valuable tool for consumers. It allows you to obtain something you want without waiting until you can save the entire purchase price.

Making monthly payments on time can teach you financial discipline. Analyzing your financial situation to see if you can afford to use credit for something you want is an important life skill.

However, credit also carries serious dangers. Many people have gotten in over their heads because they bought more than they could afford. The easy availability of credit, followed by lack of income to pay back the borrowed money, has left millions of people in **bankruptcy,** or the inability to pay debts. A bankruptcy judgment remains on your credit rating from seven to ten years, making it almost impossible for you to get a loan or to receive credit during that time.

Your Responsibilities as a Borrower

Being a responsible borrower means having a plan to make all the payments on your loan or credit purchase in a timely manner. Your budgeting skills will help make sure you can afford a monthly loan or credit payment, along with other necessities. The time to make sure you can afford a credit purchase is *before* you close the deal. You also need to understand all aspects of the agreement: What is the APR? How long will you make payments? What are the penalties for late payments? Are there extra fees?

Tips for Students As long as they are over 18 years old, students can get a credit card without asking their parents to cosign. Debt advisers say students should hold a credit card on which they can carry only a small balance and must pay off monthly. They should pay more than the minimum on credit cards. Furthermore, they should not charge purchases they can pay for in cash, such as food and gas.

Reading Check **Explaining** Why do you need to know the APR of your loan or credit purchase?

Section 2 Review

Vocabulary

1. **Write** a paragraph about planning and budgeting in which you use at least five of these terms: *budget, income, expense, credit, annual percentage rate (APR), collateral, bankruptcy.*

Main Ideas

2. **Explain** the difference between a surplus and a deficit.
3. **Identify** three sources of credit.

Critical Thinking

4. **Describing** What can a budget help you do?
5. **BIG Ideas** Create a table like the one below to list three questions you should consider when deciding whether to use credit.

Decision to Use Credit
1.
2.
3.

6. **Explaining** Why is it important to maintain a good credit rating?

Citizenship Activity

7. **Expository Writing** Think of an item for which you have been saving. How long will it take you to save the funds needed to purchase this item? What are you not buying in the meantime? Explain what you are giving up to buy that particular item. Answer these questions in a one-page paper.

Study Central™ To review this section, go to glencoe.com.

Financial Literacy

Making a Budget

A good budget is a useful tool. It can help you
- understand your actual financial situation.
- fill your basic and material needs.
- gradually achieve your objectives.
- avoid debt.
- save.

In this activity, you will design a strategy for earning, spending, and investing your resources.

Step A: Tools Needed

√ Copies of Table "My Monthly Budget"
√ Newspapers with advertisements for apartment rentals and auto sales
√ Ads from local grocery stores
√ Magazines with photos of apartments, automobiles, and furniture
√ Pencil
√ Calculator

Step B: Procedures to Follow

1. Annually you make $16,640, of which $1,800 goes to pay taxes. Monthly you earn $1,236.66. Your total expenditures will include the items listed in the table.
2. Analyze the newspaper ads to select an apartment to rent. List the rental fee in the table. Also consider the cost of rental insurance.
3. Plan your weekly menus. Then multiply supplies by 4 to budget your food expenses for one month. Use the ads from grocery stores to select and price the food products needed for your menus.
4. Decide on a type of car to buy. Analyze the newspaper ads to obtain the approximate monthly payment for an automobile.
5. From the magazines, select items of furniture to furnish your apartment.
6. Call the following places or ask family members to obtain prices or monthly fees for other necessities: phone company, electric company, gas company, auto insurance, furniture store, medical insurance, and other costs.
7. Fill in your costs in the table. When you complete the table, subtract the total expenses from your earnings for the month to find out how much money you have remaining.

My Monthly Budget

CATEGORIES OF EXPENSES	MONTHLY COST
Rent	
Rental insurance	
Telephone	
Electricity	
Gas heat	
Car payment	
Car insurance	
Car expenses (gas and repairs)	
Furniture expenses	
Clothing expenses	
Groceries	

CATEGORIES OF EXPENSES	MONTHLY COST
Medical insurance	
Medical expenses	
Credit card bill	
Entertainment and dining out	
Laundry and toiletries	
Other	
Monthly earnings	$ 1,236.66
Subtract total monthly expenses	
Total remaining	

Analyzing Economics

1. **Identifying** What is your largest monthly expense?
2. **Calculating** How much money did you have left at the end of the month?
3. **Explaining** What expense(s) surprised you the most? Why?
4. **Calculating** What expenditures did you have to reduce to be able to pay your other monthly expenses?

Section Audio

Spotlight Video

Saving and Investing

Guide to Reading

Big Idea

We all make economic choices. Opportunity cost, scarcity, and supply and demand influence the decisions we make.

Content Vocabulary

- save *(p. 553)*
- interest *(p. 554)*
- principal *(p. 555)*
- return *(p. 557)*
- stock *(p. 557)*
- dividend *(p. 557)*
- bond *(p. 557)*
- mutual fund *(p. 558)*

Academic Vocabulary

- establish *(p. 553)*
- fund *(p. 553)*
- interval *(p. 557)*

Reading Strategy

Comparing and Contrasting As you read, use a chart like the one below to explain how savings accounts, checking accounts, and money market accounts are similar and how they differ.

Type of Account	Similarities/ Differences
Savings accounts	
Checking accounts	
Money Market accounts	

Real World Economics For most teenagers, getting a driver's license and a first car marks a major move into adulthood. But how will they pay for that car? Heather Kimble's mother, Lorene, helped Heather get a debit card, a checking account, and a savings account to learn how to manage the money she earns from an after-school job in Corning, New York. Buying a car was her goal. Learning to save money can be hard, but this is one lesson from which most people will benefit.

▼ **Heather Kimble gets backup from mother, Lorene**

Saving for the Future

Main Idea **Saving part of your income is the key to meeting many of your short-term and long-term financial goals.**

Economics & You Do you know the old fable of the grasshopper and the ants? Unlike the industrious ants, the grasshopper did not bother to put aside food for the winter, and he was left hungry. Read more to find out how you can avoid being a financial grasshopper.

Everyone has long-term goals: what you want to do, where you want to live, how you want to spend your time. One way to help you reach your long-term *purchasing* goals is to save. To **save** means to set aside income for a time so you have it to use later. It is that part of your income that you do not spend. You may already be saving some of your income for a future use, such as buying a car or continuing your education.

Think of saving as a regular "expenditure" item; think of what you "buy" with it. Many people simply save what is left over at the end of the month. This attitude downgrades saving to a less important position than purchasing goods and services.

Why Save?

Saving money can be a difficult habit to **establish,** or create. There are many good reasons for saving. Most people cannot make major purchases, such as a car or a house, without putting aside money to help pay for them. Saving also comes in handy in emergencies. In addition, people can save for luxuries, such as a nicer car or a vacation.

When individuals save, the economy as a whole benefits. Your saving makes money available for others to invest or spend. Saving also allows businesses to borrow from a savings bank to expand, which provides greater income for consumers and raises the standard of living.

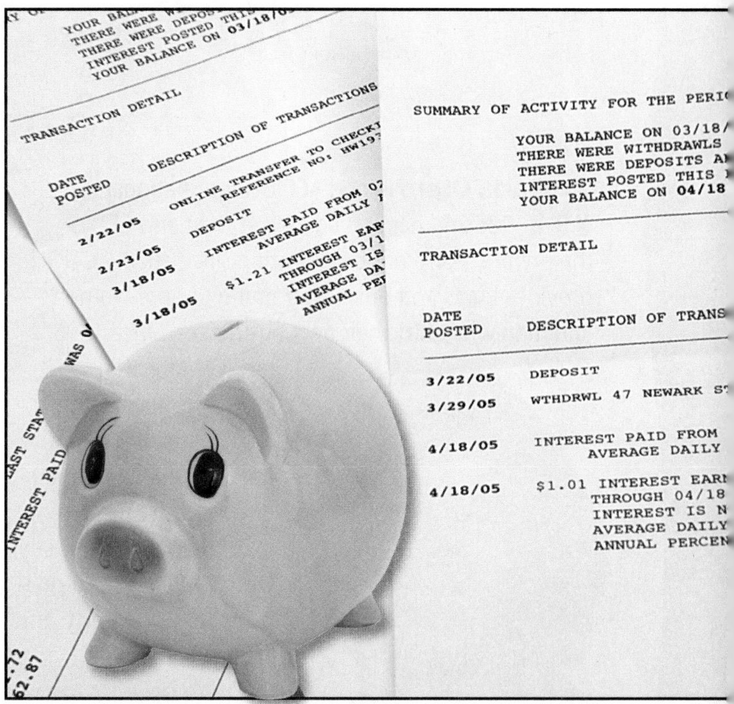

Deciding to Save No matter how you do it, it is important to save some of your money. ***Explaining*** **What is an advantage of making regular deposits to a savings account?**

Saving Regularly

To make it easier for people to save, some employers will withhold a fixed amount from employees' paychecks. This money is automatically deposited into the participating employees' savings accounts. Many people, however, handle the responsibility themselves. Each week or month, they budget a specific amount of money to put aside for savings. There is a budget line for savings right next to the lines for food, movies, gas, and other necessities.

Easy Availability Generally, when people think of saving, they think of putting their **funds,** or money, in a savings bank or a similar financial institution. A major appeal of savings accounts is that they offer easy availability of funds. The depositor can usually withdraw funds at any time without paying a penalty—forfeiting any money.

American Biography

María Otero (1950–)

María Otero joined ACCIÓN International in 1986 and has served as president and CEO of the private, nonprofit organization since 2000. ACCIÓN provides loans and business training to poor women and men who start their own businesses. Since 1996, ACCIÓN-affiliated programs have issued $9.4 billion in loans to nearly 4 million people.

"We don't need to give people charity," says Otero. "We need to give people opportunity and access."

Otero believes the programs not only help businesses get started now, but will "manifest . . . in the education and choices that will open up for their children. . . . The power of putting capital in the hands of poor people enables them to create their own wealth and invest in their children."

Born in La Paz, Bolivia, Otero and her family moved to Washington, D.C., when she was 12. After attending Johns Hopkins University, Otero returned to Bolivia to work. She says, "I really had to determine who I was. Living in Bolivia as an adult and preparing myself to then come back and do more graduate work in economics was very significant. That's what helped me accept that I could be both Bolivian and American."

Making a Difference CITIZENSHIP

At first, Otero studied literature but decided to give up literature for political economics. ***Speculating*** **Why do you think she made this decision?**

Earning Interest Another advantage of depositing your money in a savings account is that it will earn interest. **Interest** is the payment people receive when they lend money, or allow someone else to use their money. In this case, the financial institution pays interest to the person with the savings account. The institution can lend these funds to someone else, who will in turn pay interest to the financial institution for the use of the money. A person receives interest on his or her savings for as long as funds are in the account.

Deciding About Your Saving

It is important to remember that the more money you put in a savings account, and the longer you keep the money deposited, the more interest you will earn, and the larger your account will grow.

Saving and Trade-Off Saving involves a trade-off, as does every other activity. The more you save today, the more you can buy a year from now, 10 years from now, or 30 years from now. You will, however, have less to spend today.

Deciding how much to save depends on your answer to several questions: How much do you spend on your everyday expenses? What are your reasons for saving? How much interest can you earn on your savings and, therefore, how fast will your savings grow? How much income do you think you will be earning in the future? If you expect to make a much higher income tomorrow, you have less reason to save a large percentage of your income today. It is a good idea, however, to have some type of savings plan.

Reading Check **Explaining** How do the savings of individuals benefit the entire economy?

Types of Savings

Main Idea **A variety of options is available to allow you to save money.**

Economics & You Benjamin Franklin said, "A penny saved is a penny earned." Read to find out how this advice applies to you and your financial future.

While savings accounts are probably the best-known way to save, there are other ways, too.

Saving and Checking Accounts

You can open a savings account at a bank, savings and loan, or credit union. These institutions accept people's money, pay them a fairly low rate of interest, and loan the money on deposit to other customers of the institution. You can withdraw your money at any time, and the interest you earn is added automatically to your **principal,** or the amount you initially deposited. You cannot write a check on a savings account. To do that, you will need a checking account.

Just as with a savings account, you make deposits into a checking account. When you write a check, the banking institution pays out of the funds in your checking account. You must be careful not to write checks that exceed the amount of money in your checking account. The way to protect yourself from "bouncing" a check is to keep a record of each check you write.

Some institutions pay a small amount of interest on checking accounts, but most do not. Some charge you a per-check or monthly fee, while others do not. Some institutions require you to keep a minimum amount in your checking account.

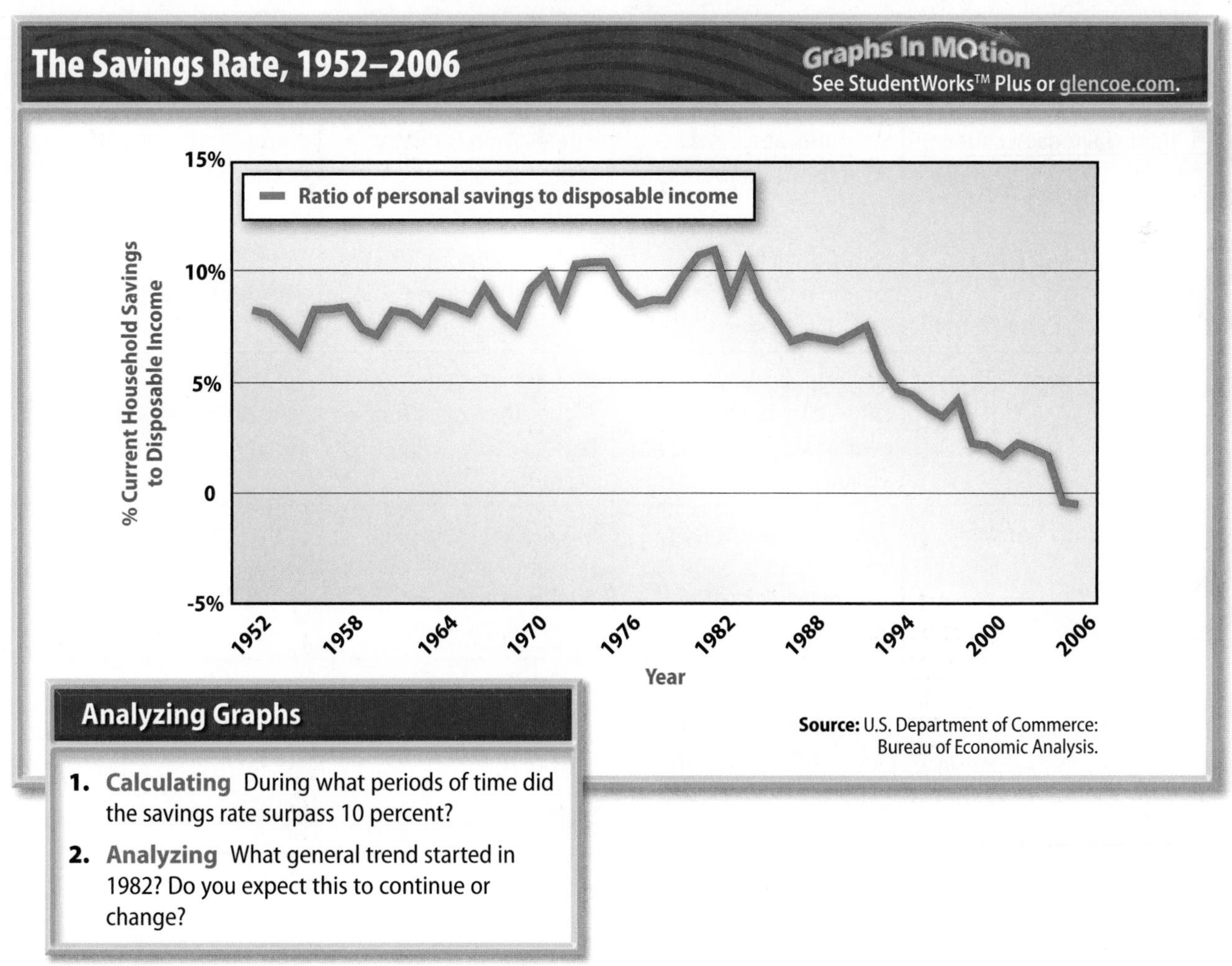

Source: U.S. Department of Commerce: Bureau of Economic Analysis.

Analyzing Graphs

1. **Calculating** During what periods of time did the savings rate surpass 10 percent?
2. **Analyzing** What general trend started in 1982? Do you expect this to continue or change?

If your funds fall below the minimum, they charge you a monthly fee. Many institutions now offer a debit card. This allows you to pay for a purchase directly from your checking account instead of writing a paper check.

Money Market Funds and Certificates of Deposit

A money market account is similar to a checking account in that it allows you to write checks, usually for larger amounts, against the money you have deposited. It is like a savings account because it pays interest, often a little higher than that on savings accounts. Yet another way to save is with certificates of deposit (CDs).

CDs are a kind of time deposit, in which you agree to deposit a sum of money with a financial institution for a certain amount of time, usually at least a year. In return, the institution guarantees you a set rate of interest that will be added to your principal when the CD matures, or comes due. The rate of interest on a CD is almost always higher than that on a savings account. Why? You have less flexibility to withdraw your money; if you want to withdraw it before the stated date, you must pay a substantial penalty. In general, longer-term CDs pay you a higher rate of interest as a reward for locking up your money for a longer period of time.

Reading Check **Contrasting** What are some differences between checking and savings accounts?

Types of Savings Accounts

	DEFINITION	RETURN	TIME FRAME
Bank Savings Accounts	Accounts at a bank, savings association, or credit union	Interest rate is relatively low	Depositor can withdraw money at any time
Certificates of Deposit	Bank notes for a set period of time at a fixed rate of interest	Interest rates are usually higher than rates for bank savings accounts	Vary, generally from 6 months to 5 years
Money Market Accounts	Savings accounts offered by banks that require a high minimum balance	Interest rates are usually higher than rates for regular bank savings accounts	Depositor may withdraw funds at any time
U.S. Savings Bonds	The U.S. government issues savings bonds as one of its ways of borrowing money.	Interest rate is usually higher than rates on bank savings accounts	Good for medium- and long-term savings goals

Analyzing Charts

1. **Comparing** How do bank savings accounts and certificates of deposit differ?
2. **Explaining** What is an advantage of a money market account? What is a disadvantage?

Investments

Main Idea **Making wise investments in a variety of stocks and bonds is an important part of achieving long-term financial goals.**

Economics & You Have you ever gone together with friends and pooled your money to buy something you could all use? Read to find out how this idea is the foundation for many key investment practices.

Savings accounts, money market accounts, and CDs are considered investments, but their **return,** or profit earned by the investor, is usually low. Almost all investors also invest in stocks and bonds, which have averaged a higher return over the years than savings accounts, money market accounts, and CDs. If people are willing to take a chance on earning a higher rate of return, however, they can invest their savings in other ways, such as in stocks and bonds.

Stocks

When you buy shares of **stock,** you are buying partial ownership in a company. If the company does well, the value of your share will probably go up. If the company does not do well, your share will likely be worth less than you paid for it. You can sell it at any time, hopefully for more than you paid, and the difference is your profit.

Dividends Some companies also pay shareholders a portion of company earnings at regular **intervals,** or periods, based on the number of shares people hold. This payment, called a **dividend,** can substantially increase your profit from owning stock.

Greater Risk Stocks generally earn a higher return than other investments because they carry greater risk. There is no guarantee, as with government-protected savings accounts (protected by the Federal Deposit Insurance Corporation [FDIC]) and CDs, that you will make money on your stock investment. In fact, if the company goes out of business, you will lose your entire investment.

Bonds

Whereas stocks represent ownership of a company, buying a **bond** is lending money to a company or government. Unlike buying stock, buying a bond does not make a bondholder part owner of the company or government that issued the bond.

Company Bonds Companies issue bonds to raise money for new equipment, research, or other business expenses. Companies pay bondholders a certain rate of interest over a set number of years. Bonds also carry risk; the company could become unable to pay you your interest or make final repayment of the principal.

Stock as an Investment Millions of people all over the world buy and sell shares of stock every day. Stock certificates like these are issued to people who have invested in a corporation. ***Describing*** **What are two ways stockholders can make money from their investments?**

Government Bonds The U.S. government, along with cities and states, also borrows money to pay for its expenses. The United States issues savings bonds, along with other bonds called Treasury bills, notes, and bonds. U.S. government bonds are considered among the safest of all investments because they are backed by the financial strength of the U.S. government. The government pays interest on these bonds, but it builds the interest into the redemption price rather than sending checks on a regular basis.

A person buying a savings bond pays half the bond's face value. You could purchase a $50 bond for only $25. The bond increases in value every six months until its full face value is reached. (The *Rule of 72* tells you how long it takes for the bond to mature: Divide the number 72 by the interest rate.) If you redeem a U.S. savings bond before it matures you are guaranteed the interest rate, which changes depending on the rates of interest in the economy.

Mutual Funds

Many investors find it easier to invest in stocks and bonds using **mutual funds.** Mutual funds are pools of money from many people. Their money is invested in a selection of individual stocks and/or bonds chosen by financial experts. Your return is based on the experts' choices of investments. Mutual funds are less risky than investments in individual stocks and bonds. Mutual funds usually own several hundreds—or thousands—of different stocks and bonds. Spreading your investment among many stocks or bonds limits the loss if one individual stock or bond performs poorly.

Many popular mutual funds are tracked by a government regulated index. An index is a measuring system that tracks stock prices over the long term. The Dow Jones Industrial Average (DJIA) and the Standard & Poor's (S&P) are the two most common indexes.

Reading Check **Explaining** What is the relationship of an investment's risk to its potential return?

Vocabulary

1. **Write** a paragraph about saving and investing in which you use at least five of these terms: *save, interest, principal, return, stock, dividend, bond, mutual fund.*

Main Ideas

2. **Explain** how the decision to save involves trade-offs.
3. **Comparing** How is a money market account similar to a checking account?
4. **Contrasting** What is the basic difference between a stock and a bond?

Critical Thinking

5. **BIG Ideas** Saving affects you as well as others. On a graphic organizer like the one below, list three results of saving.

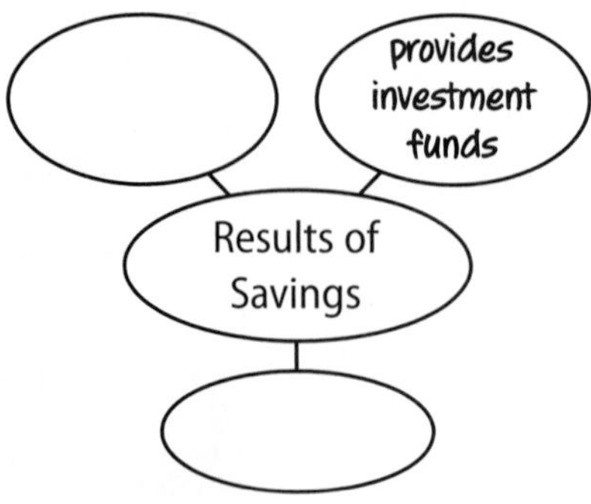

6. **Explaining** Why are certificates of deposit described as time deposits?
7. **Explaining** How does buying a U.S. savings bond increase the United States government's debt?

CITIZENSHIP Activity

8. **Expository Writing** List your short-term savings goals, such as saving to buy a new iPOD. Then list your long-term savings goals, such as saving for a house. In a short essay, explain the major differences between the two kinds of saving.

Study Central™ To review this section, go to glencoe.com.

Section Audio

Spotlight Video

Achieving Your Financial Goals

Guide to Reading

Big Idea
We all make economic choices. Opportunity cost, scarcity, and supply and demand influence the decisions we make.

Content Vocabulary
- impulse buying *(p. 561)*

Academic Vocabulary
- evaluate *(p. 560)*
- commit *(p. 562)*
- eliminate *(p. 562)*

Reading Strategy
Describing As you read, use a diagram like the one below to describe three ways to keep impulse buying in check.

Real World Economics James Meredith struggled to be admitted to the University of Mississippi in 1962, at that time an all-white school in the South. It took a federal court order to get him into the segregated college of his choice. Forty years later, his son, Joseph, completed a PhD in business administration at the same school. But race was not the big problem anymore. It was rather how to pay for this college education. With tuition costs increasing as much as 50 percent over three years in some states, saving to pay for college requires financial planning.

▼ **James and Joseph Meredith**

What Kind of Spender Are You?

Main Idea **Careful spenders avoid pitfalls, such as impulse buying, on their way to meeting their financial goals.**

Economics & You Have you ever bought something expensive on the spur of the moment and regretted it later? Read to find out more about how to avoid budget breakers like this.

As you learned, managing your money, budgeting, and saving and investing money are aimed at the same target: helping you reach your financial goals. These goals today may be modest—things such as being able to afford a movie every weekend, taking a skiing or rafting trip, or saving ten dollars a week. However, as you get older, you can be sure that your goals will get bigger. You may want to buy a car or a house or to continue your education. All of these things take a lot of money. That is why, when setting and monitoring, or examining, your current financial goals, it is useful to **evaluate,** or review, your spending habits.

Impulse Buying

Do you know what it means to be impulsive? One definition is "acting on feelings or emotions without thinking about consequences." When it is paired with buying, it is easy to see how the combination can ruin a carefully organized budget.

Analyzing Advertising

Advertising claim	Why they are misleading
• "Our battery lasts twice as long." • "Detwiler Cheese—33% more flavor."	These ads make **unfinished claims:** the product has "more" or is "better" but does not finish the comparison.
• "With regular use, Beachfront Shampoo helps control dandruff." • "Plews Cleaner makes your sink virtually spotless."	Often words in ads such as *help* and *virtually* draw the reader's attention away from the facts: the shampoo does not eliminate dandruff; it *helps* control it with *regular use.* These terms are called **weasel words.**
• "You're worth it—so our new automobile is the only car for you." • "Our cola is the official thirst quencher of the American League."	These ads are based on **snob appeal.** By purchasing the product, you are one of a select group.
• Quarterback Sammy Sutcliffe says, "I eat Harbor Mist Cereal every morning."	The **testimonial** says that a well-known public figure uses the product or service, so you should, too.

Analyzing Charts

1. **Analyzing** What advertising technique uses a famous person to sell a product?
2. **Explaining** How is a testimonial meant to convince a consumer to use a product?

Marketers know that many consumers buy on impulse. That is why there is such a dazzling display of inexpensive items near the checkout line at the grocery or department store. One of your greatest challenges as a careful consumer is to avoid **impulse buying.**

Danger Signals Here are signals you may be an impulse buyer:

- You buy lots of things you do not really want and do not need.
- Buying things makes you feel better.
- You are always borrowing money from friends because you have spent yours.
- You quickly lose interest in something you have bought.

Even rational consumers can fall prey to the danger of impulse buying.

Tips Here are some tips to keep your impulse buying under control and keep it from ruining your budget.

- Have a line in your spending budget for impulse items of any kind. You will then know how much you have to spend—if anything—on impulse purchases.
- Make a list of things you really need—and take the list when you shop.
- If you see something very tempting, take a break. Leave the store, walk around, and decide whether you really need the item. Better yet, go away and come back tomorrow, after thinking hard about the purchase.
- If you have decided you really do need something, comparison-shop. You may find a better price somewhere else.
- Be careful with online buying. It is easy to charge things online.
- Record all impulse purchases in the spending part of your budget. You need to know how much you are spending on impulse items so you can try to control it.

Reading Check **Explaining** How can impulse buying ruin your budget?

TIME™ Teens in *Action*

Fuel for Thought

Looking for a little "fuel" for thought? Jon Russell, 17, of Scarborough, Maine, might have just what you are looking for!

QUESTION: Your club is called ECOS. What does it stand for?

ANSWER: Environmental Club of Scarborough. I started the group three years ago with four friends to promote environmental awareness.

Q: How are you doing that?

A: We traveled through our school with a rolling Dumpster on Friday afternoons, collecting paper waste and bottles for recycling. With the steadily increasing price of oil, we will soon need a cheaper form of fuel. So ECOS is converting a small school bus to run on waste vegetable oil.

Q: Did you say vegetable oil?

A: Yes. At a fraction of the cost per gallon of gasoline, it's a very thrifty solution. Our nation is too dependent on oil and other nonrenewable sources of energy. I hope our biofuel bus will help others understand that change toward renewable sources of energy is both possible and economical. We'll use data collected from the biofuel bus to introduce our project to local and state governments. We hope our work will have an impact on their lawmaking decisions.

ECOS members work on school bus

Making a Difference **CITIZENSHIP**

Why does Jon believe we should use renewable energy sources?

Your Goals and Your Buying Decisions

Main Idea **The buying decisions you make can have a major impact on your life and career choices.**

Economics & You Do you have a long-term plan for meeting your financial goals? Read to find out how the decisions you make can play a key role in achieving these goals.

It is important to consider your economic goals when you make buying decisions. The kinds of buying decisions you make help reveal what kind of a decision-maker you are and how **committed,** or dedicated, you are to your goals.

Now or Later?

Suppose you work after school and on weekends to save money for a new computer. That is your long-term goal. You also see many things that you would like to buy now. If you buy these things, you will find it harder to accomplish your long-term goal. Which option do you choose? You could buy what you want now and reduce, postpone, or even **eliminate,** or throw out, the chances of buying the computer. Or you could buy less of what you want now and increase the chances of buying the computer later. Long-term goals often conflict with short-term spending decisions.

Long-term planning becomes even more crucial the farther out you go. For example, many students need to save as well as borrow money to further their education. Statistics show that people with more post-high school education earn significantly more money over their working lives than those who complete only high school. Therefore, making the financial sacrifices necessary to continue your education is likely to pay off in a big way later.

Reading Check **Explaining** In what way can long-term goals conflict with short-term spending decisions?

Vocabulary

1. **Define** *impulse buying.* Provide an example of impulse buying.

Main Ideas

2. **Identify** three ways you can cut down on impulse buying.
3. **Explaining** Why is it important to consider your goals when making a buying decision?

Critical Thinking

4. **Concluding** Explain whether you think impulse buying is more common when purchasing expensive or inexpensive items.
5. **BIG Ideas** "You should always shop until you find exactly what you are looking for at the lowest possible price." Do you agree or disagree? Explain your answer.
6. **Classifying** On a chart like the one below, provide two examples of short-term buying goals and two examples of long-term buying goals.

Short Term	Long Term
1.	1.
2.	2.

CITIZENSHIP Activity

7. **Creative Writing** Write a conversation between you and a telemarketer who is trying to sell you something you do not want or need. What does the telemarketer say? What do you say?

Study Central™ To review this section, go to glencoe.com.

Chapter 20 Visual Summary

Buying Strategy

- Making consumer decisions involves deciding the following:
  - whether to spend your money
  - what you will purchase
  - how to use your purchase.
- Comparison shopping involves making comparisons among brands, sizes, and stores.

Consumerism

Consumer rights include

- the right to safety
- the right to be informed
- the right to choose
- the right to be heard
- the right to redress

Negotiation to purchase a car

Budget

- A budget is an organized plan for spending and saving money.
- What you do with the information in a budget is up to you. No one can force you to spend less and save more unless you want to.

Credit

- When buying on credit, the amount you will owe is equal to the principal plus interest.
- Financial institutions that provide credit include commercial banks, savings and loan associations, and credit unions.

Department store shopping in Paris

Saving and Investing

- It is important to get into the habit of saving.
- Individuals have many places to invest their savings, including savings accounts and certificates of deposit.
- Shares of stock entitle the buyer to a certain part of the future profits and assets of the corporation that is selling the stock.

Entertainment spending

Study anywhere, anytime! Download quizzes and flash cards to your PDA from glencoe.com.

Chapter 20 Assessment

Standardized Test Practice

TEST-TAKING TIP

Pay attention to other test questions as you read. Sometimes the information in one question contains help for another.

Reviewing Vocabulary

Directions: Choose the word(s) that best completes the sentence.

1. The cost of credit expressed as a percentage of the amount borrowed is the ______.

A surplus
B APR
C credit rating
D interest

2. A ______ remains on a person's credit rating for at least seven years, making it almost impossible to get a loan.

A warranty
B deficit
C charge
D bankruptcy

3. A bank adds the interest you earn to your ______, the amount you initially deposited.

A mortgage
B debit card
C principal
D loan

4. Some companies pay shareholders a ______ at regular intervals, based on the number of shares they hold.

A dividend
B return
C time deposit
D bond

Reviewing Main Ideas

Directions: Choose the best answer for each question.

Section 1 *(pp. 538–543)*

5. The Pure Food and Drug Act and the Fair Packaging and Labeling Act are examples of ______.

A smart buying strategies
B extended warranties
C protecting consumer rights
D comparison shopping

6. The value of the highest alternative choice that a consumer did not make is the ______.

A time deposit
B down payment
C balance of payments
D opportunity cost

Section 2 *(pp. 544–549)*

7. To avoid interest charges on a credit card, a consumer must ______.

A pay off the full balance each month
B make no charges at the end of the month
C pay the minimum monthly amount
D pay half the monthly balance

8. Millions of people have been left in bankruptcy by the ______.

A lack of collateral
B easy availability of credit
C annual percentage rate
D high down payment requirement

Section 3 *(pp. 552–558)*

9. Because certificates of deposit (CDs) require investors to lock up their money for a longer period of time than a regular savings account ______.

A banks rarely sell CDs
B there is no penalty for cashing them in
C CDs pay a higher rate of interest
D CDs pay lower rates of interest

10. Compared to stocks and bonds, mutual funds are generally ______.

A less risky investments
B longer term investments
C higher risk investments
D shorter term investments

GO ON

Section 4 *(pp. 559–562)*

11. If you are an impulse buyer, you may find that

A you quickly lose interest in things you buy.

B you buy things that you do not need.

C you buy things that make you feel better.

D all of the above.

Critical Thinking

Directions: Base your answers to questions 12 and 13 on the chart below and your knowledge of Chapter 20.

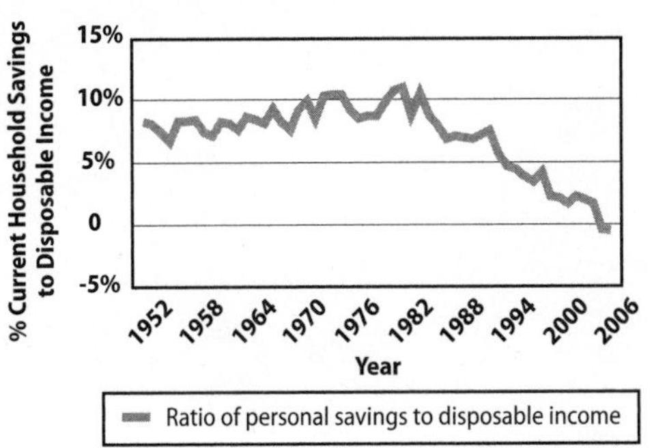

Source: U.S. Department of Commerce: Bureau of Economic Analysis.

12. Because savings not only benefit investors but also provide capital for businesses to grow, the chart indicates that in the future ______.

A business will hire more people soon

B consumers have little money to spend

C business growth could slow down

D interest rates will begin to fall

13. Which of the following economic conditions characterized the United States between 1980 and 2006?

A Consumer credit and savings increased.

B Savings increased; consumer credit decreased.

C Consumer credit increased, savings decreased.

D Savings and consumer credit decreased.

Document-Based Questions

Directions: Analyze the following document and answer the short-answer questions that follow.

Bankrate.com asked economist Joel Naroff whether America's negative savings rate was a problem. The following is his reply.

> *To some extent we're spending way beyond our means. We're drawing down on wealth that has come from equities or, more importantly, our homes. Economists worry because we've gone through an environment where housing prices have soared, and we've spent a lot of the wealth that was generated.*
>
> *The probability that over the next three years we'll see that same increase in property values is pretty low, and there's the possibility that prices will fall. What that says to economists is that the probability that we'll draw that kind of money from equity again is small. If we spend a lot of the wealth and we don't have that money going forward, consumer spending slows and the economy slows.*
>
> —Joel Naroff

14. According to Naroff, where are Americans getting the money to spend that they are not earning? Why are some economists worried?

15. How could spending our wealth today affect tomorrow's economy?

Extended-Response Question

16. Is consumer debt still rising? At what rate? Do research to determine how fast such debt is growing and make some predictions about how it will affect the future.

STOP

For additional test practice, use Self-Check Quizzes—Chapter 20 on glencoe.com.

Need Extra Help?

If you missed question...	1	2	3	4	5	6	7	8	9	10	11	12	13	14	15	16
Go to page...	547	549	555	557	540	543	548	549	556	558	560	553	553	553	553	548

Chapter 21

Demand and Supply

Why It Matters

Two forces work together in markets to establish prices for all the goods and services we buy. They are demand—the desire, willingness, and ability to buy a good or service—and supply—the quantities of a good or service that producers are willing to sell at all possible market prices.

Chapter Audio

Civics ONLINE
Visit glencoe.com and enter QuickPass™ code CIV3093c21 for Chapter 21 resources.

BIG Ideas

Section 1: Demand

Supply and demand in a market interact to determine price and the quantities bought and sold. Demand is the desire, willingness, and ability to buy a good or service.

San Diego drivers find lower gas prices at the co-op gas station

Section 2: Factors Affecting Demand

Supply and demand in a market interact to determine price and the quantities bought and sold. Several factors can cause market demand for a product or service to change.

Section 3: Supply and the Supply Curve

Supply and demand in a market interact to determine price and the quantities bought and sold. Supply is the willingness and ability to produce and sell a good or service.

Section 4: Demand and Supply at Work

Supply and demand in a market interact to determine price and the quantities bought and sold. In our economy, the forces of supply and demand work together to establish prices.

FOLDABLES™ Study Organizer

Organizing Information Study Foldable Make the following Foldable to help you compare the aspects of supply and demand and where they overlap.

Step 1 Fold a sheet of paper in half from the long way with one inch edge left.

Step 2 Turn the paper and fold it into halves.

Cut along the fold on the front flap to make 2 tabs.

Step 3 Unfold and cut the top layer only along the middle fold.

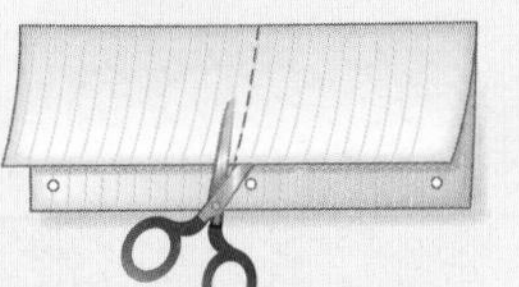

Step 4 Label as shown, including drawing ovals for a Venn diagram.

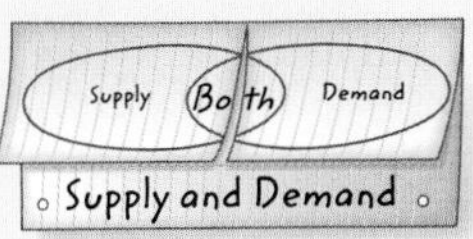

Reading and Writing As you read the chapter, compare and contrast supply and demand.

Section Audio

Spotlight Video

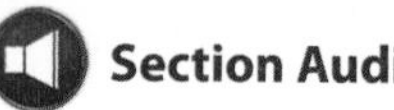

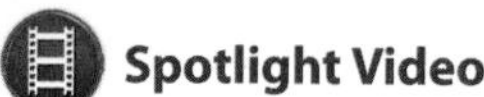

Section 1

Demand

Guide to Reading

Big Idea

Supply and demand in a market interact to determine price and quantities bought and sold.

Content Vocabulary

- demand *(p. 569)*
- demand schedule *(p. 569)*
- demand curve *(p. 569)*
- law of demand *(p. 569)*
- market demand *(p. 570)*
- utility *(p. 570)*
- marginal utility *(p. 572)*

Academic Vocabulary

- identify *(p. 570)*
- illustrate *(p. 572)*
- likewise *(p. 572)*

Reading Strategy

Analyzing As you read the section, complete the diagram below to illustrate how change in prices affects the quantity demanded.

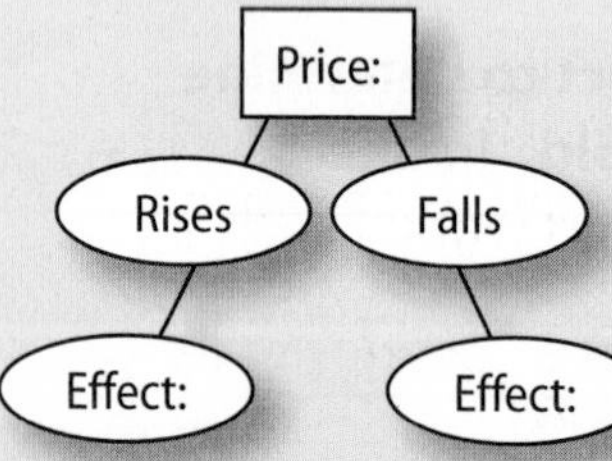

Real World Economics With recent heating and oil prices at all-time highs, people began to look for alternative sources of heat. All across New England—especially—people are turning to wood as fuel, and the price for it has risen. Reed's Firewood in Durham, Maine, supplies its customers who want to supplement their heating sources and to use wood as backup if their power goes out. As wood use increases over time, its price will rise more, and consequently, its demand will diminish.

▼ **Paul Reed, Sr., loads firewood for customers in Maine**

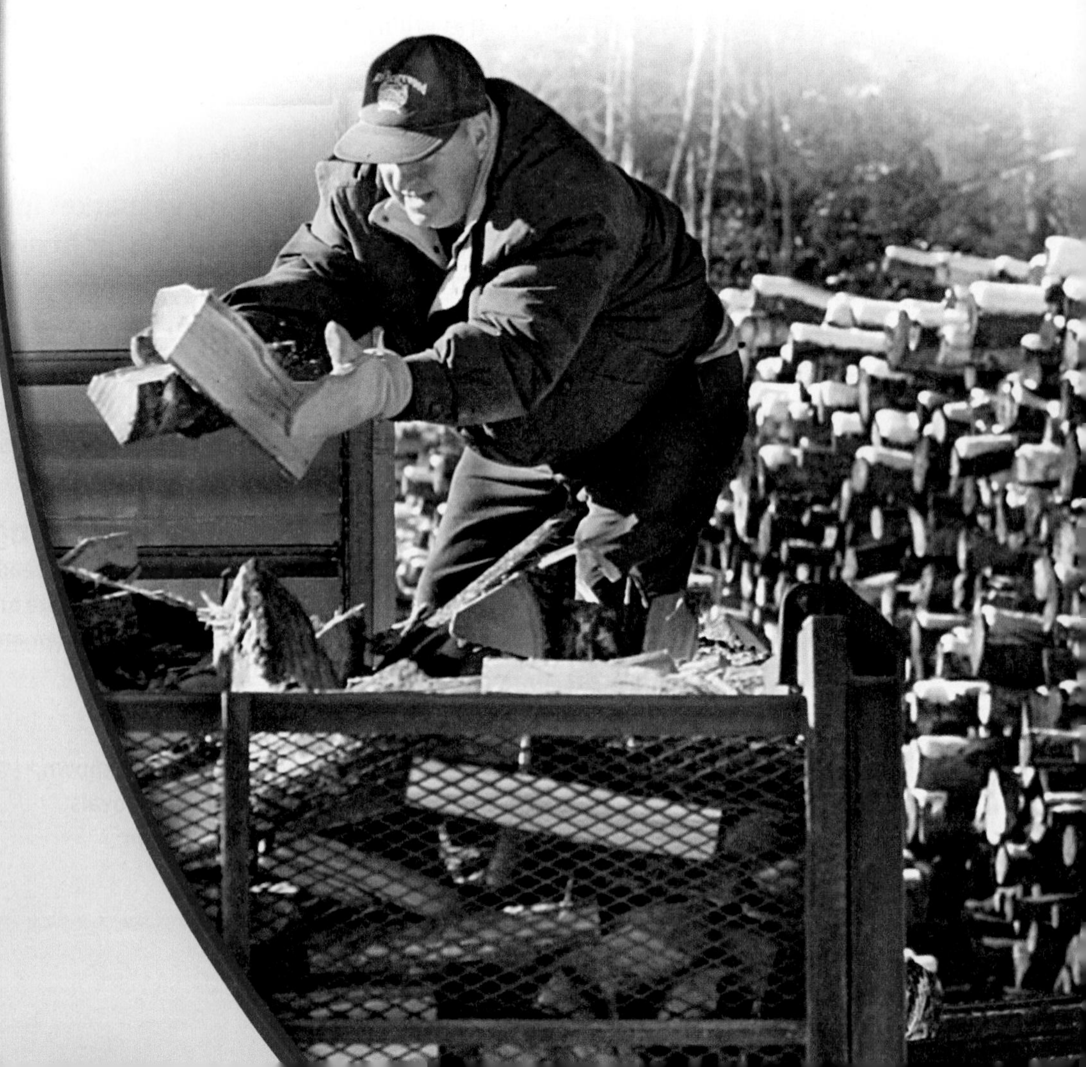

An Introduction to Demand

Main Idea **Demand is the desire, willingness, and ability to buy a good or service.**

Economics & You Do your ears perk up when something you want goes on sale? Read to find out which economic principle is at work.

What is **demand?** In economics, it refers to the desire, willingness, and ability to buy a good or service. For demand to exist, a consumer must *want* a good or service. The consumer has to be *willing* to buy the good or service. Finally, the consumer needs the *resources* to buy it.

The Individual Demand Schedule

When you buy something, do you wonder why it sells at a particular price? A **demand schedule** is a table that lists the various quantities of a product or service that someone is willing to buy over a range of prices. Look at the demand schedule on page 571. It shows how many video games a person—we will call him Ryan—would be willing to buy at different prices. For example, Ryan would not purchase any video games if they cost $50 each. If the price were $20 per game, though, he would be willing to buy two.

The Individual Demand Curve

Demand can also be shown graphically. A **demand curve** is a graph that shows the amount of a product that would be bought at all possible prices in the market. The curve is drawn with prices on the vertical axis and quantities on the horizontal axis. Each point on the curve shows how many units of the product or service an individual will buy at a particular price.

Look at the demand curve on page 571. Notice that each point on the graph matches the quantity listed in the demand schedule.

Desire to Buy New technology for video games available at computer stores is always in high demand. ***Explaining*** **How does the price of an item affect the demand?**

Ryan would buy five video games if the price were $5 each, three games at $10 each, and so on.

The Law of Demand

Look at the graph again. As you see, demand curves usually slope downward because people are normally willing to buy less of a product if the price is high and more of it if the price is low. According to the **law of demand,** quantity demanded and price move in opposite directions. This is the way people behave in everyday life. People ordinarily do buy more of a product at a low price than at a high price. All we have to do is to observe the increased traffic and purchases at the mall whenever there is a sale. This is just common sense. Are you not more interested in buying more of something when the price is lower than when the price is higher?

Reading Check **Comparing** Describe the relationship between the demand schedule and the demand curve.

TIME™ Teens in *Action*

Daniel Lawrence

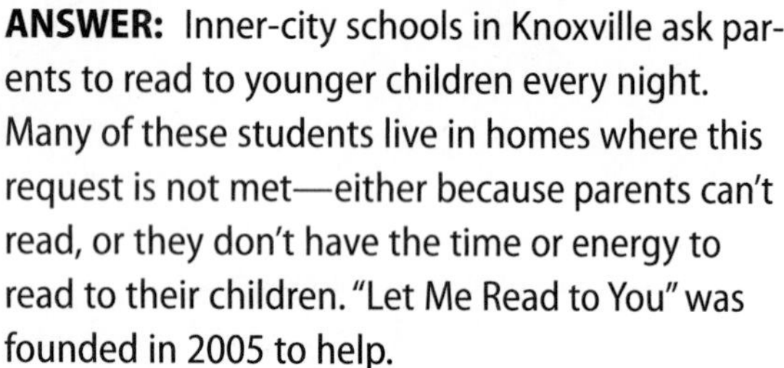

Daniel Lawrence, 15, of Knoxville, Tennessee, did not have to read between the lines to see that his city had a literacy problem. He decided to help out!

QUESTION: Why did you start "Let Me Read to You"?

ANSWER: Inner-city schools in Knoxville ask parents to read to younger children every night. Many of these students live in homes where this request is not met—either because parents can't read, or they don't have the time or energy to read to their children. "Let Me Read to You" was founded in 2005 to help.

Q: How does it work?

A: Commercial audiobooks already exist—but these families can't afford them. So our organization records early reader books onto CDs and donates the books and CDs to inner-city schools. The students are typically in first through third grades. They can read and hear the books at school or take them home for the night.

Q: How will the CDs help these kids?

A: They help them develop good reading skills—a very important thing in today's world. These students will have a better chance to succeed in life.

Q: What's next?

A: Once in high school I am going to start a program to fight Knoxville's litter problem.

Making a Difference — CITIZENSHIP

Daniel's group helped children look at the books and listen to them. Why do you think both looking and listening are important?

Market Demand

Main Idea **Market demand is the total demand of all consumers for a product or service.**

Economics & You Does your ninth slice of pizza taste just as good as the first? Read to find out what economic principle this example illustrates.

So far we have been looking at only one person's demand for a product or service. Companies hope to sell to many people, though. They are interested in the **market demand**—the total demand of all consumers for their product or service. Market demand can also be shown as a demand schedule or as a demand curve (see page 571).

An Example of Demand

Imagine you are opening a bicycle repair shop. Before you begin, you need to know where the demand is. You want to set up your shop in a neighborhood with many bicycle riders and few repair shops. After you **identify,** or establish, an area in which to locate the shop, how do you measure the demand for your services? You may visit other shops and gauge the reactions of consumers to different prices. You may poll consumers about prices. You could study data compiled over past years, which would show consumer reactions to prices. All of these methods would give you a general idea as to the desire, willingness, and ability of people to pay.

Marginal Utility

Almost everything that we buy provides **utility,** meaning the pleasure, usefulness, or satisfaction we get from using the product. The utility of a good or service may vary from one person to the next. For example, you may get a great deal of enjoyment from a home computer, but your friend may get very little. A good or service does not have to have utility for everyone, only for some.

The Law of Demand

Individual Demand Schedule	
Price per video game	**Quantity**
$50	0
$40	1
$30	1
$20	2
$10	3
$ 5	5

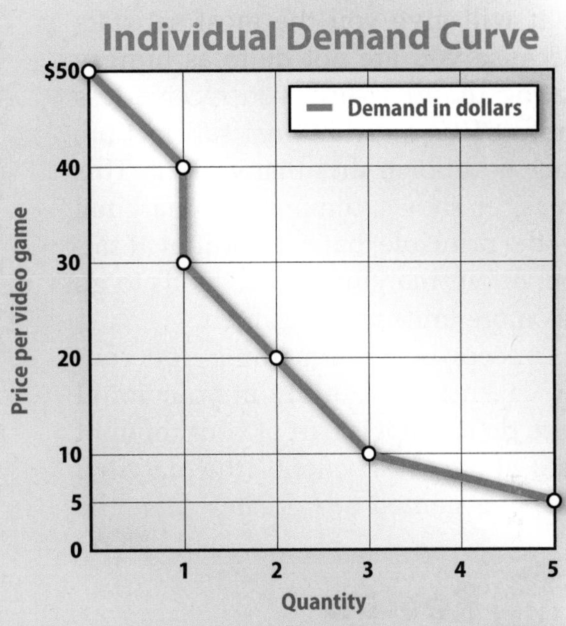

Market Demand Schedule	
Price per video game	**Total Quantity Demanded**
$50	100
$40	150
$30	180
$20	230
$10	300
$ 5	400

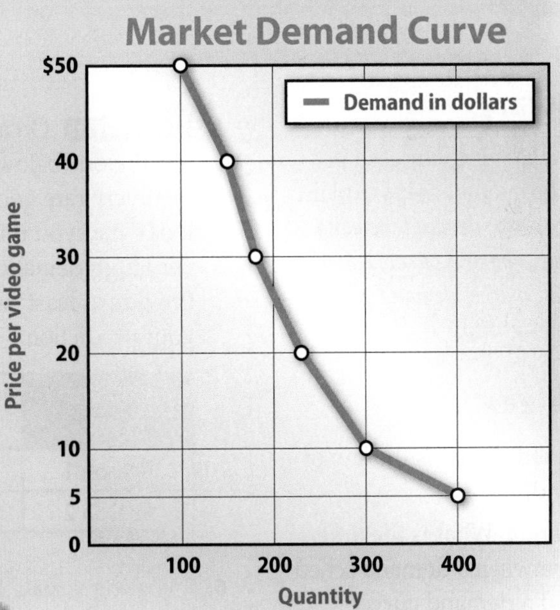

Analyzing Charts and Graphs

1. **Calculating** How many video games is the market willing to purchase at a price of $30? What happens to market demand if the price falls to $20 per video game?
2. **Explaining** The demand curve is the graphic representation of the law of demand. Why does the demand curve slope downward?

Diminishing Marginal Utility

Our satisfaction usually changes as we consume more of a particular product. For example, when eating pizza, you may be very hungry before you eat the first slice, and so it will give you the most satisfaction. Because you are not quite as hungry after eating the first slice, you receive less **marginal utility,** or additional satisfaction, from each additional slice that you eat. This **illustrates,** or shows, diminishing marginal utility—the principle that our additional satisfaction, or our marginal utility, tends to go down as more units are consumed.

This concept is not something you consciously call marginal utility in your mind when you do it, but it is part of your thought processes. If the extra benefits (the marginal utility) to be gained are greater than the marginal cost (the money given up or paid) then we make the purchase. Otherwise we keep our money.

Because our marginal utility diminishes when we consume more of a product, it stands to reason that we would not be as willing to pay as much for the second item as we did for the first. **Likewise,** we would not be willing to pay as much for the third item as we did for the second. When the demand curve slopes downward, it simply tells us that we would be willing to pay the highest price for the first unit we consume, a slightly lower price for the next, an even lower price for the third, and so on.

Reading Check **Comparing** What is the difference between individual demand and market demand?

Vocabulary

1. **Write** a sentence for each of these terms that helps explain its meaning: *demand, demand schedule, demand curve, law of demand, market demand, utility, marginal utility.*

Main Ideas

2. **Explaining** What is the law of demand?
3. **Comparing** What is the difference between a demand schedule and a demand curve?

Critical Thinking

4. **Analyzing** Explain how the principle of diminishing marginal utility is related to the law of demand.
5. **BIG Ideas** On a diagram like the one below, identify a relatively rare good or service today that you think will be in very high demand in 20 years. Provide at least two reasons for your prediction.

Good or Service	
Reason 1	
Reason 2	

6. **Analyzing Visuals** Study the schedule and graph illustrating the law of demand on page 571. What is the quantity demanded at $40? What happens to the total quantity demanded as the price increases?

CITIZENSHIP Activity

7. **Interview** a local merchant to determine the demand for a particular product or service at a specific period of time. Present your findings in graph form. Write a paragraph explaining what factors most affected demand for the product or service.
8. **Expository Writing** Suppose the boss of a company you work for has asked you how to estimate the demand for a new product the company is introducing. Write a memo outlining how you would approach this assignment.

Study Central™ To review this section, go to glencoe.com.

Section Audio Spotlight Video

Guide to Reading

Section 2

Main Idea

Supply and demand in a market interact to determine price and the quantities bought and sold.

Content Vocabulary

- substitute *(p. 575)*
- complement *(p. 576)*
- demand elasticity *(p. 577)*

Academic Vocabulary

- immigration *(p. 574)*
- phenomenon *(p. 577)*

Reading Strategy

Organizing As you read the section, complete a diagram like the one below by identifying six factors that affect demand.

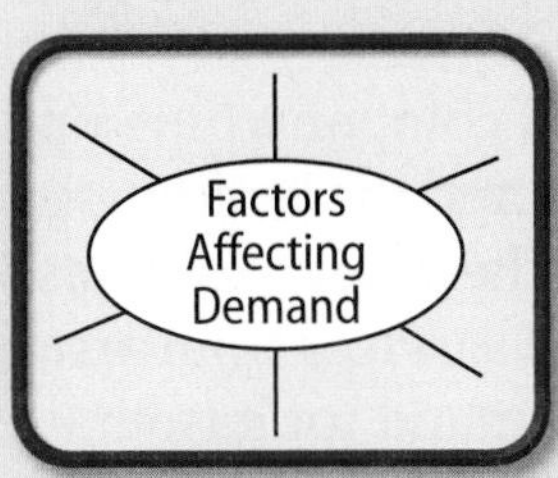

Factors Affecting Demand

Real World Economics "Back-to-school" for college students means big business for some retailers. While sales in some areas of the home furnishings business in America may be weak, companies that cater to back-to-school shoppers do not suffer from the effects of high energy prices or slower housing sales. Each fall, when thousands of students return to school, stores that sell items such as desk supplies, computers, and dorm-room furnishings can count on a high demand.

▼ **College student in Texas tests possible dorm chair's comfort**

Changes in Demand

Main Idea **Several different factors can cause market demand for a good or service to change.**

Economics & You Can you remember a toy that you absolutely had to have when you were younger? Read to find out how a product's popularity affects demand.

The demand for any product or service is not the same over time. Sometimes people are willing to buy higher quantities of a good or a service at a particular price. At other times they are less willing to do so. As a result, demand can increase or decrease.

Why Does Demand Change?

Several factors cause market demand to change. Market demand can change when more consumers enter the market. Market demand can also change when the incomes, tastes, and expectations of the consumers in the market change. Finally, changes in the prices of related goods affect demand.

Demand and Choice The huge variety of magazines produced is made possible by consumer tastes. ***Predicting*** **What would happen to demand if there were only one magazine about a particular topic?**

These changes can all be graphed using a market demand curve. When demand goes down, people are willing to buy fewer items at all possible prices (see the graph showing a decrease in demand on page 575). In this case, the demand curve shifts to the left. When demand goes up, people are willing to buy more of the same item at any given price. This pushes the entire demand curve to the right. Look at the graph on page 575 that shows an increase in demand.

What Determines Demand?

Demand curves do not shift to the right or left without cause. They shift because of changes in income, preferences, price of related goods, and changes in population. You as a consumer need to be aware of these factors.

Changes in Population Demand for a good in a particular market area is related to the number of consumers in the area. More people means the higher the demand; the smaller the population, the lower the demand.

For example, suppose a company puts up a new apartment building and the building is soon filled with families. These new residents begin to buy products and services from area businesses. As a result, demand for gasoline, food, and video rentals in this area will go up. In this case, the demand curve will shift to the right.

The same factor can cause a change in the opposite direction. When many people move out of an area, demand in that area for goods and services goes down. Here the demand curve shifts to the left.

Why Population Changes The number of consumers in a particular market area may change for a number of reasons. A higher birthrate or increased **immigration**—the arrival of people from another region—increases the number of consumers. Factors such as a higher death rate or the migration of people out of a region can also cause the number of consumers to fall.

Changes in Income Demand also changes when consumers' incomes change. When the economy is healthy, people receive raises or move to better-paying jobs. With more money to spend, they are willing to buy more of a product at any particular price.

The opposite can happen, too. In hard times, people lose their jobs. They have less money to spend, so demand goes down.

Changes in Tastes Changing tastes and fading popularity of a product can affect demand as well. When a product becomes popular, the demand curve shifts to the right. More people are willing to buy the product at a particular price. We often see this during the holiday shopping season when a new product becomes the "must-buy" of the year.

Many products, though, fade in popularity over time. When that happens, fewer are sold at a particular price, and the demand curve shifts to the left.

Changes in Expectations Expectations refer to the way people think about the future. For example, suppose that a leading maker of audio products announces a technological breakthrough that would allow more music to be recorded on a smaller disk at a lower cost than before. Even if the new product might not be available for another year, some consumers might decide to buy fewer music CDs today because they want to wait for the new product.

Expectations can also affect demand in another way. In late 2001, following the September 11 terrorist attacks, people were worried about the economy. As a result, they were less willing to spend money on holiday gifts. The demand for goods was reduced.

Expectations can also force demand higher. If people expect a shortage of a good, such as gasoline, they tend to stock up and demand increases. This shifts the demand curve to the right.

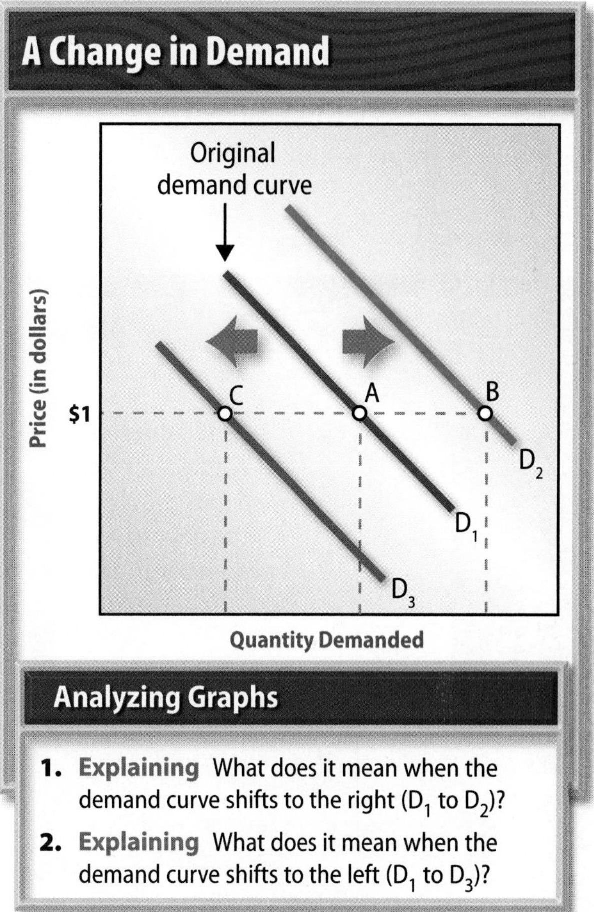

Analyzing Graphs

1. **Explaining** What does it mean when the demand curve shifts to the right (D_1 to D_2)?
2. **Explaining** What does it mean when the demand curve shifts to the left (D_1 to D_3)?

Product-Related Changes

You have learned that demand curves do not shift to the right or left without cause. Factors that also affect demand are related to the products themselves.

Demand can be influenced by changes in the price or quality of related products. The demand for older computers falls when new models with faster processors come out. The demand for a certain brand of tire may increase when another tire has safety problems.

Price of Related Goods

The demand for a good is affected by the prices of related goods. There are two types of related goods; substitutes and complements. Competing products are called **substitutes** because consumers can use one in place of the other.

Change in Demand for Substitutes

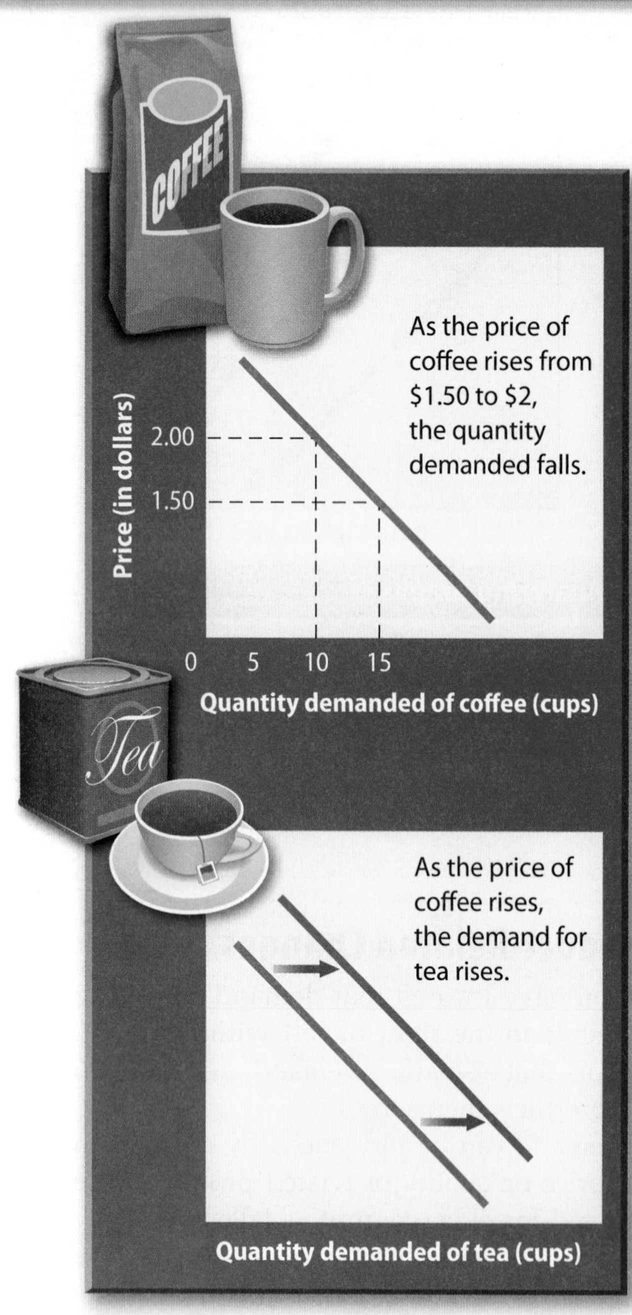

COFFEE

As the price of coffee rises from $1.50 to $2, the quantity demanded falls.

Price (in dollars)

2.00
1.50

0 5 10 15

Quantity demanded of coffee (cups)

Tea

As the price of coffee rises, the demand for tea rises.

Quantity demanded of tea (cups)

Analyzing Graphs

1. **Explaining** What happens to the demand for coffee if the price of coffee increases?
2. **Analyzing** How would an increase in the price of coffee affect demand for tea?

Changes in Substitutes When two goods are substitutes, a change in the price of one good causes the demand for the other good to move in the *same* direction. For example, for many people, butter is a substitute for margarine. If the price of margarine increases, the demand for butter also increases (shifts to the right).

Changes in Complements Some products are **complements**—they are used together. For example, computers and software are complements. With complementary goods, the demand for one moves in the opposite direction as the price of the other. So if computer prices rise, fewer computers will be demanded, and the demand for computer software will go down.

You can also see the same effect when the price goes down instead of up. When the price of DVD players goes down, more DVD players are demanded, which also results in an increase in the demand for DVDs. Other examples of complements (or complementary goods) include cars and gasoline, and lightbulbs and lamps.

A Change in Quantity Demanded

You learned that a change in demand refers to a shift in the *entire* demand curve. You learned that factors that can shift the demand curve include the number of buyers, income, taste, preferences, and price of related goods.

A change in quantity demanded refers to a movement from one point to another along a given demand curve. The only factor that can directly cause a change in the quantity of a good is a change in the price—its own price. For example, as shown here, the price of coffee increased from $1.50 to $2 per cup. The change in the price of coffee brings about a change in the quantity demanded.

Reading Check **Comparing** Are butter and margarine substitute goods? Why or why not?

Demand Elasticity Auto sales can be affected by changes in price. ***Explaining*** **If these young men purchase a car at a recently reduced price, how does the purchase illustrate the elasticity of demand?**

Elasticity of Demand

Main Idea **Demand elasticity is the extent to which a change in price causes a change in the quantity demanded.**

Economics & You Does your family always have turkey at Thanksgiving? Read to find out what might happen if stores raised the price of turkey at Thanksgiving.

The law of demand states that price and quantity demanded move in opposite directions. If price goes up, quantity demanded goes down; and if price goes down, quantity demanded goes up.

Now suppose price goes up from $1 to $1.25, a 25 percent increase. We know that quantity demanded will go down, but we do not know by how much. Quantity demanded could go down by 25 percent, by less than 25 percent, or by more than 25 percent.

All products and services are not affected by these factors in the same way. Economists call this **phenomenon,** or rare occurrence, **demand elasticity.** Demand elasticity is the extent to which a change in price causes a change in the quantity demanded.

Elastic Demand

For some goods and services, demand is elastic. This means that each change in price causes a relatively larger percentage of change in quantity demanded. For example, when automakers reduce car prices modestly, the quantity sold goes up greatly. When they raise the price of their cars, the quantity sold goes down a great deal.

When there are attractive substitutes for a good or service, demand tends to be elastic. That is because consumers can choose to buy the substitute. Expensive items generally have elastic demand. That is because consumers are less willing to pay even more for goods that are expensive in the first place.

Finally, demand is usually elastic when a purchase can be postponed until later. In this case, consumers delay buying the good or service in the hopes that the price will go down. Again, this usually happens when consumers are dealing with higher priced items.

Inelastic Demand

You know that demand for a good or service is elastic if it is very responsive to a change in price. For other goods and services, demand is inelastic. This means that price changes have little effect on the quantity demanded. For example, the demand for turkey at Thanksgiving tends to be inelastic. Many people make turkey a central part of their Thanksgiving meal. If supermarkets slightly raise the price of turkey, they would probably not lose many customers. At another time of year, higher turkey prices might cause consumers to purchase other meat products instead.

The demand for goods with very few or no substitutes, such as pepper, electricity, and some medicines, is likely to be inelastic. Heart medicine, for example, has relatively few substitutes; many people must have it to stay well. Even if the price of heart medicine doubled, quantity demanded probably would not fall by much.

Necessities and Luxuries Demand for heart medicine and food is inelastic because these are necessities. Necessities are goods that people need in order to survive. If the price of a necessity increases, people cannot cut back very much on the quantity demanded. However, demand for luxuries is likely to be elastic. If the price of a luxury good increases, buyers are more able to cut back on the quantity demanded.

Reading Check **Inferring** Why is the demand for insulin, a medicine for people with diabetes, inelastic?

Vocabulary

1. **Write** a paragraph in which you use each of these terms correctly: *substitute, complement, demand elasticity.*

Main Ideas

2. **Explaining** If income and population increase, what tends to happen to demand?
3. **Comparing** What is the distinction between elastic and inelastic demand?

Critical Thinking

4. **Concluding** Will products that are very important to us and that have no close substitutes have elastic or inelastic demand? Why? What is an example of such a product?
5. **BIG Ideas** Re-create the diagram below. Use arrows to indicate the direction of movement on the demand curve for tennis balls if the price of tennis rackets increases.

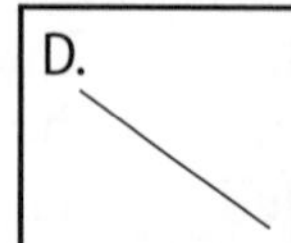

CITIZENSHIP Activity

6. **Research** Find an example of the law of demand or elasticity of demand in a newspaper or magazine article or advertisement. Share your findings with the class.
7. **Creative Writing** Working with a partner, write a dialogue between a store owner and a customer about some aspect of demand, as discussed in this section. Perform your dialogue with a partner for the class.

Study Central™ To review this section, go to glencoe.com.

Writing a Résumé: Dos and Don'ts

A résumé is a brief summary of your abilities, education, experience, and skills. To get an employer's attention, prepare a one- to two-page résumé that highlights your talents and skills. Prevent it from landing in the recycle bin by keeping these ideas in mind.

Résumé Dos

- Include your contact information.
- Make the layout easy to read.
- Highlight your special skills.
- Print your résumé on high-quality paper.
- Review your résumé for any grammar errors or other mistakes.
- Use action words to describe your experience and accomplishments.
- Always include a cover letter with your résumé. Get right to the point in your letter. State your employment goal and highlight reasons that you are qualified for the job.

Résumé Don'ts

- Do not include any personal information such as your race, religion, family, or marital status.
- Do not use inaccurate dates or pad your résumé with things you have not actually done.
- Do not write long paragraphs; use bulleted lists instead.

Your Résumé

Ima Ginary
800 Fernhill Way
Middletown, KS 12347
(555) 555-5610
fake@randomemailserver.com

Contact Information

Objective

OBJECTIVE:
Seeking a summer internship at Middletown Bank

EDUCATION:
West Prairie Land High School, Middletown, KS
Diploma expected June 2008
GPA: 3.7/4.0

Education

EXPERIENCE:
Jerry's Pizza Shop, Middletown, KS
Crew Leader (March 2005–present)
- Managed employees and time sheets

Experience

COMMUNITY SERVICE:
Riverside General Hospital, Middletown, KS (Summer 2007)
- Contributed 8 hours per week in pediatrics

HONORS:
National Honor Society, member, 2007–present
- Honor Society Treasurer (2008)

Honors & Activities

Analyzing Economics

Writing a résumé Be sure to include these parts: name and contact information, objective statement (your career goals), education, professional experience, and skills.

Section Audio

Spotlight Video

Supply and the Supply Curve

Guide to Reading

Big Idea

Supply and demand in a market interact to determine price and the quantities bought and sold.

Content Vocabulary

- supply *(p. 581)*
- law of supply *(p. 581)*
- supply schedule *(p. 581)*
- supply curve *(p. 583)*
- profit *(p. 583)*
- market supply *(p. 584)*
- productivity *(p. 585)*
- technology *(p. 585)*
- subsidy *(p. 585)*
- supply elasticity *(p. 586)*

Academic Vocabulary

- motive *(p. 583)*
- restrict *(p. 585)*

Reading Strategy

Organizing As you read the section, complete a diagram like the one below to identify the factors that affect supply.

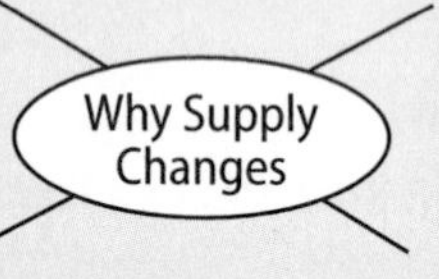

Real World Economics Organic farming is changing the face of American agriculture. Why? Because of the growing demand for its products from customers. In addition to concerns about pesticides that nonorganic growers use, consumers now want to "buy local" to avoid using extra fuel to transport food from thousands of miles away. Organic farmers Dennis and Sandy Dierks find customers are willing to pay extra for their organic produce. So organic farmers are reporting rising profits, which help recoup their increased production costs.

▼ **Dennis and Sandy Dierks harvest vegetables on their organic farm**

Supply and Choice Consumers must choose from a huge number of snack foods, each with a different price and nutritional value. ***Comparing*** **What do you think affects the supply of snack foods the most—the price or ingredients? Why?**

An Introduction to Supply

Main Idea **Supply is the quantities of a good or service that producers are willing to sell at all possible market prices.**

Economics & You If you were paid overtime, would you want to work extra hours? Read to find out what economic theory is at work.

What is supply? **Supply** refers to the various quantities of a good or service that producers are willing to sell at all possible market prices. Supply normally refers to the output of a single business or producer. However, it is also possible to add together the supply of all producers to get the supply for the entire market.

Supply is the opposite of demand. Buyers demand different quantities of a good depending on the price sellers ask. Suppliers offer different quantities of a product depending on the price buyers are willing to pay.

The Law of Supply

Remember that as the price rises for a good, the quantity demanded goes down. As the price of a good goes down, the quantity demanded rises. The quantity supplied also varies according to price—but in the opposite direction. As the price rises for a good, the quantity supplied rises. As the price falls, the quantity supplied also falls. This is the **law of supply,** the principle that suppliers will normally offer more for sale at higher prices and less at lower prices. The higher the price of a good, the greater the incentive is for a producer to produce more.

We can represent the law of supply with numbers, just as we did with the law of demand. The table at the top left of page 582 shows this. As the price goes up from $5 to $10 to $20 and to $50, the quantity supplied goes up from 1 to 10 to 30 and to 100. Producers create more items in the hopes of selling more at the higher price. A numerical chart that illustrates the law of supply is called a **supply schedule.**

Reading Check **Explaining** What does a supply schedule show?

The Law of Supply

Supply Schedule	
Price per video game	Quantity
$50	100
$40	90
$30	70
$20	30
$10	10
$5	1

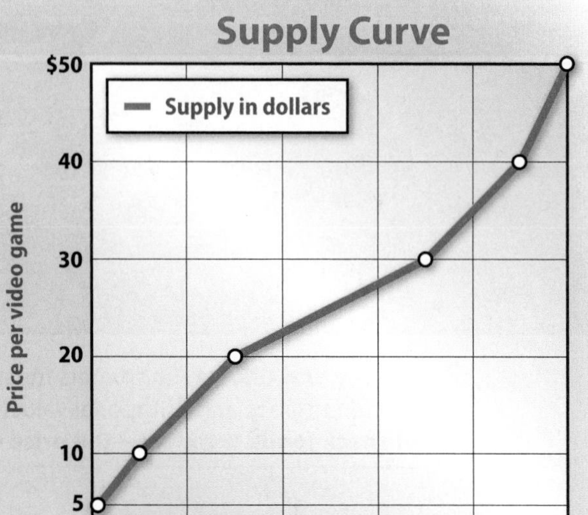

Market Supply Schedule	
Price per video game	Total Quantity Supplied
$50	275
$40	225
$30	180
$20	105
$10	55
$5	30

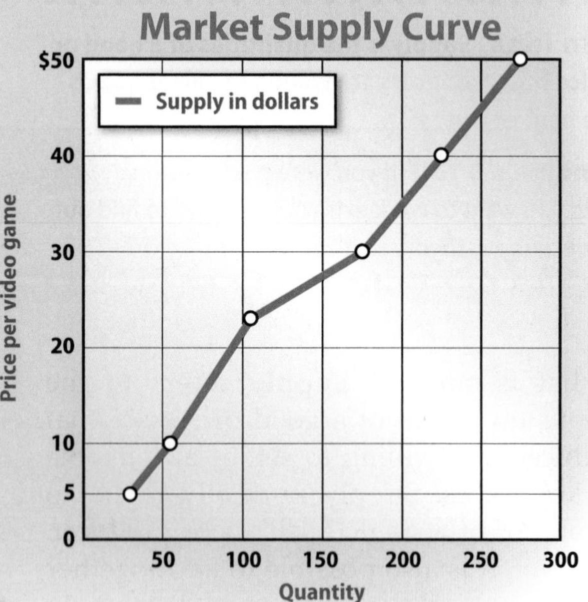

Analyzing Charts and Graphs

1. **Describing** What is the relationship between the price of a good and the quantity supplied?
2. **Explaining** The supply curve is the graphic representation of the law of supply. Why does the supply curve slope upward?

Graphing the Supply Curve

Main Idea **As with the law of demand, special tables and graphs can show the law of supply.**

Economics & You Suppose you own a company that sells television sets and the price of a set falls from $500 to $400. Would you want to supply more or fewer TV sets? Read on to find how the law of supply operates.

You have learned that we can represent the law of supply in a numerical chart called a supply schedule. We can also illustrate the law of supply with a graph.

The Individual Supply Curve

A **supply curve** is a graph that shows the amount of a product that would be supplied at all possible prices in the market. Like the demand curve, the supply curve graph is drawn with prices on the vertical axis and quantities on the horizontal axis. In the supply curve on the previous page, the quantities are the amounts of the good or service that the business will supply. Unlike the demand curve, the supply curve slopes upward. This reflects the fact that suppliers are generally willing to offer more goods and services at a higher price and fewer at a lower price.

The Profit Motive

Businesses invest time, money, and other capital resources to make money. Businesses try to set prices at a level that allows them to cover their costs. If they do not, they will lose money.

In our economy, businesses provide goods and services, hoping to make a **profit.** Profit is the money a business receives for its products or services *over and above* its costs. It is a primary **motive,** or purpose, in business.

Changes in Supply When a leak was discovered in this oil pipeline in Prudhoe Bay, Alaska, the BP company shut it down. ***Describing*** **How could this shutdown affect the price and supply of oil?**

If it costs Software House $40 to make a video game and it sells the game for $40, the company gains nothing from the sale. Making money on the sale requires selling the game for more than $40. The additional money is the owner's profit.

Producers can choose to use their profits in many different ways. They can increase wages, invest the money in the business, acquire more space, buy new equipment, or hire new workers. They can also keep the money for themselves.

Market Supply

The total of all consumers' demand is called the market demand. If you combine the supply schedules of all the businesses that provide the same good or service, the total is called the **market supply.**

An Upward Slope The figure on page 582 shows the market supply for video games in one community. Notice that the market supply for all producers is larger than the supply for the Software House alone. (Compare the graphs on page 582.) Still, the market supply curve has the same shape as the individual supply curve. The upward slope shows that all of the producers in the market would prefer to sell more video games at higher prices and fewer games at lower prices.

Price and Other Factors Keep in mind that the price is the most significant influence on the quantity supplied of any product. For example, you are offering your services for sale when you look for a job. Your economic product is your labor, and you would probably be willing to supply more labor for a high wage, or price, than you would for a low one.

However, other factors affect supply. The supply curve is drawn assuming that these and other things are fixed and do not change. If any of these factors do change, a change in supply will occur.

Reading Check **Explaining** How is market supply determined?

Changes in Supply

Main Idea **Supply increases or decreases depending on many different factors.**

Economics & You Would you expect to pay a high price for a tomato if it were the only one in the whole grocery store? Read to find out why that tomato would probably be costly.

Just like demand, supply can increase or decrease, depending on many different factors.

Why Does Supply Change?

The profit incentive is a factor that motivates people in a market economy which pushes other factors. For a change in supply to take place, producers must decide to offer a different quantity of output at each possible price in the market.

Shifts in the Supply Curve

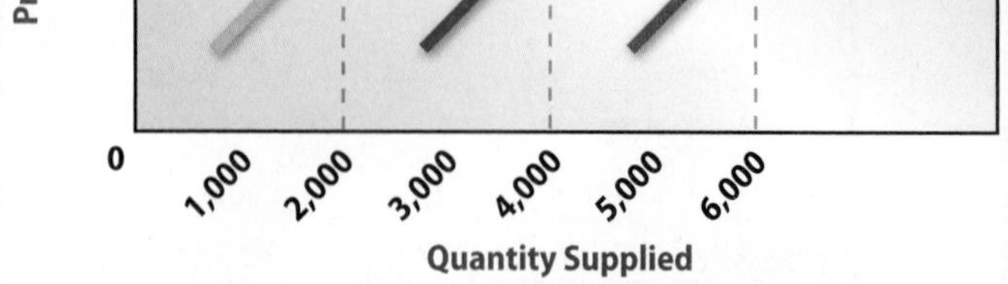

Analyzing Charts

1. **Explaining** What does it mean when the supply curve shifts to the left?
2. **Deducing** In what direction would new technology push the supply curve? Explain.

When supply goes down, the supply curve moves to the left. When supply goes up, the supply curve is pushed to the right. This means suppliers are willing to sell a larger quantity of goods and services at the original price and all other prices. You can see these changes in the figure on page 584.

Factors that can affect supply include the following:

- **The Cost of Resources** When the prices of resources used to produce goods and services fall, production costs fall. Sellers are able to produce and sell more of the good. When resource prices rise, sellers are less able to produce and sell the same quantities of the good because production costs rise.
- **Productivity** When workers are more productive, a company's costs go down. More products are produced at every price. When productivity falls, it costs more for a company to produce the same amount of goods and services.
- **Technology** **Technology** refers to the methods, or processes, used to make goods and services. New technology can speed up ways of doing things and cut a business's costs. The business is willing to supply more goods and services at the same price.
- **Government Policies** In general, increased government regulations **restrict,** or limit, supply, causing the supply curve to shift to the left. A rise in the minimum wage or new safety requirements in cars can result in higher production costs, which, in turn, lead to lower production levels.
- **Taxes** To businesses, higher taxes mean higher costs, pushing the supply curve to the left. Lower taxes—lower costs—move the supply curve to the right.
- **Subsidies** A **subsidy** is a government payment to an individual, business, or other group for certain actions. Subsidies lower the cost of production. When subsidies are repealed, costs go up, and the supply curve shifts to the left.
- **Expectations** If businesses believe that consumer demand will not be very high in the near future, they will produce less of their products. If they expect demand to go up, they will produce more at all possible prices.
- **Number of Suppliers** The larger the number of suppliers, the greater the market supply. If some suppliers leave the market, market supply decreases, shifting the curve to the left.

Reading Check **Explaining** How does productivity affect supply?

Student Web Activity Visit glencoe.com and complete the Chapter 21 Web Activity.

Quality Control An inspector at the Indian Motorcycle plant in California works at the end of the assembly line. ***Analyzing*** **What happens to company costs if workers at the plant are more productive?**

Elasticity of Supply

Main Idea **Supply elasticity measures how the quantity supplied of a good or service changes in response to changes in price.**

Economics & You What is the price of a gallon of gasoline right now? Read to find out why gasoline producers react slowly to a change in the price of gas.

Like demand, supply can be elastic or inelastic. **Supply elasticity** is a measure of how the quantity supplied of a good or service changes in response to changes in price. If the quantity changes a great deal when prices go up or down, the product is said to be supply elastic. It is elastic in the sense that like a piece of elastic it can expand out or decrease in size. If the quantity changes very little, the supply is inelastic.

Supply elasticity depends on how quickly a company can change the amount of a product it makes in response to price changes. For example, oil is supply inelastic. When oil prices go up, oil companies cannot quickly dig a new well, build a pipeline to move the oil, and build a refinery to turn it into gasoline. The same is true of other products that require producers to invest large sums of money in order to produce them.

The supply curve is likely to be elastic, however, for kites, candy, and other products that can be made quickly without huge amounts of capital and skilled labor. This is especially true of food items whose production can be quickly increased, and often is during special holiday time during the year. If consumers are willing to pay twice the price for any of these products, most producers will be able to gear up quickly to increase production.

Reading Check **Explaining** What is supply elasticity?

Vocabulary

1. **Write** sentences in which you use these key terms: *supply, law of supply, supply schedule, supply curve, profit, market supply, productivity, technology, subsidy, supply elasticity.*

Main Ideas

2. **Explain** the law of supply.
3. **Identify** four factors that can cause changes in supply.
4. **Describing** What kinds of products are considered supply elastic?

Critical Thinking

5. **Describing** What is an example of how business expectations can increase or decrease supply?
6. **BIG Ideas** Use a chart like the one below to illustrate the effect of price on supply.

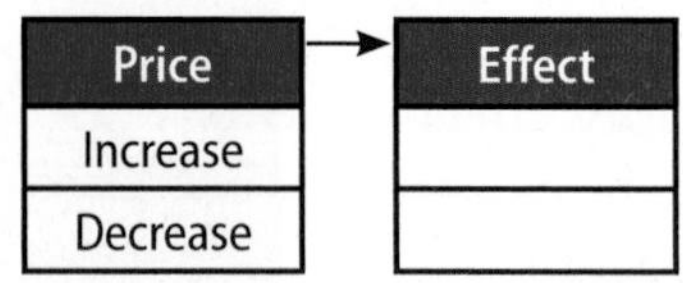

Price	→	Effect
Increase		
Decrease		

7. **Analyzing Visuals** Study the two supply schedules on page 582. How are they similar? How are they different?

CITIZENSHIP Activity

8. **Research** Make a list of products manufactured in your town, city, or community. Decide if each one is supply elastic or supply inelastic. Share your list with the class.
9. **Descriptive Writing** Write a short chalk talk for first graders in which you explain the law of supply. Be sure to include examples and graphic aids that your audience will understand.

Study Central™ To review this section, go to glencoe.com.

Spotlight Video

Demand and Supply at Work

Guide to Reading

Big Idea

Supply and demand in a market interact to determine price and the quantities bought and sold.

Content Vocabulary

- surplus *(p. 588)*
- shortage *(p. 589)*
- equilibrium price *(p. 589)*
- price ceiling *(p. 589)*
- price floor *(p. 589)*
- minimum wage *(p. 589)*

Academic Vocabulary

- mechanism *(p. 588)*
- purchase *(p. 588)*
- focus *(p. 590)*

Reading Strategy

Analyzing Cause and Effect

As you read the section, complete a diagram like the one below by describing three advantages of using prices to distribute goods and services.

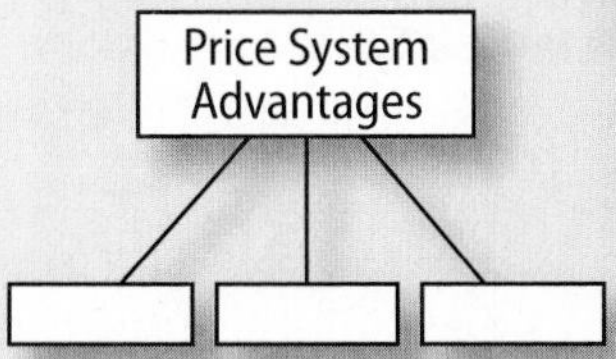

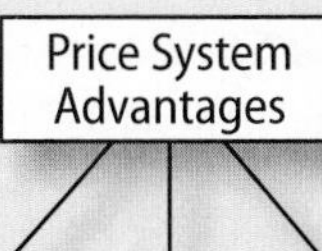

Real World Economics In 1974, U.S. gasoline customers waited in line for hours for a chance to buy fuel. At the time, several Middle Eastern nations had decided not to ship any oil to the United States. The resulting oil shortage caused the price for a gallon of gasoline to quadruple and the supply to diminish. Gas stations often could not meet the demand and refused to sell their product to anyone who brought in an empty container rather than the item itself. This forced customers to wait in line with their lawn mowers and other fuel-powered tools.

▼ **A man in San Jose, California, lines up with his lawn mower to buy gas during a fuel shortage**

Markets and Prices

Main Idea **The forces of supply and demand work together in markets to establish prices.**

Economics & You Have you ever tried to bargain for a lower price on something you bought? Read to find out how economists view the process of setting prices.

As you learned earlier, a market is any **mechanism,** or place, where buyers and sellers of a good or service get together to exchange that good or service. For example, to buy corn, people might go to a farmers market or a supermarket. Someone who wants to buy stock might use a computer to **purchase,** or buy, it from a stock market. In each case, markets bring buyers and sellers together.

The forces of supply and demand work together in markets to establish prices. In our economy, prices form the basis for economic decisions.

The Price Adjustment Process

A market consists of all buyers and sellers of a product. To see how supply and demand work together, we need to combine the supply and demand curves. Look at the graph on page 589. It shows the market demand curve for video games (the line marked "D" on the graph) and the market supply curve (marked "S") for those games.

Surplus Suppose we start by watching how buyers and sellers react to a price of $40 in this market for video games. The graph shows that sellers will supply 225 video games to the market at this price. Buyers, however, are willing to buy only 150 games at $40 each. This leaves a surplus of 75 video games.

A **surplus** is the amount by which the quantity supplied is higher than the quantity demanded. The surplus also appears as the horizontal distance between the supply and demand curves at any point above where the demand and supply curves intersect.

TIME™

Political Cartoons

Sidney Harris/ScienceCartoonsPlus.com

Every year, more than half of all Americans do volunteer work ... role in it. One of the responsibilities of citizens is to help make their ... of volunteer grou... small. Perha... dad who ...

In this cartoon, Sidney Harris is making a comment on supply and demand.

1. **Why is the store shown in the cartoon holding a sale?**
2. **What are some options that businesses have when supply exceeds demand?**
3. **Is this situation economically healthy for businesses? For consumers?**

A surplus signals that the price is too high. In that case, consumers are unwilling to pay the price in large enough numbers to satisfy producers. If the market is competitive, this surplus will not exist for long. Sellers will have to lower their prices if they want to sell their goods.

Shortage What if the price had been $20? Look at the graph again. At this price, suppliers offer only 105 video games for sale. Consumers, though, are willing to buy 230 games. This difference is a shortage. A **shortage** is the amount by which the quantity demanded is higher than the quantity supplied. The shortage is shown as the horizontal distance between the two curves at any price below the point where demand and supply cross.

A shortage signals that the price is too low. In this situation, suppliers are unwilling to sell their goods or services in large enough numbers to meet all the demand. If the market is competitive, the shortage will not last. The price will have to rise.

The Price Adjustment Process

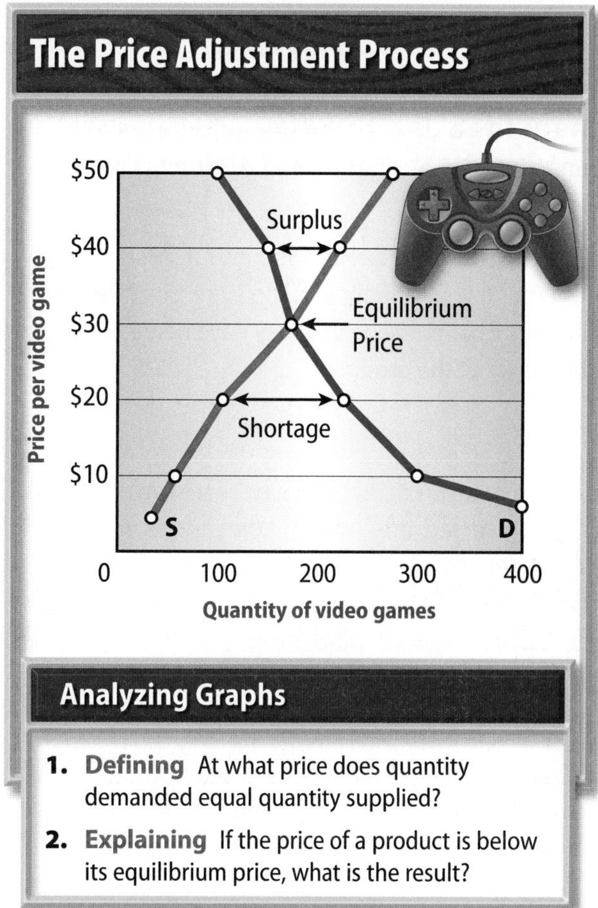

Analyzing Graphs

1. **Defining** At what price does quantity demanded equal quantity supplied?
2. **Explaining** If the price of a product is below its equilibrium price, what is the result?

Market Forces

One of the benefits of the market economy is that it eliminates shortages and surpluses when it operates without restriction. Over time, a surplus forces the price down and a shortage forces the price up. This process goes on until supply and demand are balanced. The point where they achieve balance is the **equilibrium price.** At this price, there is neither a surplus nor a shortage. In the figure on this page, the equilibrium price for video games is $30.

Once the market price reaches equilibrium, it will tend to stay there until either supply or demand changes. Once that happens, the market will have a temporary surplus or shortage. If there is a surplus, the price will be driven down. If there is a temporary shortage, the price will be driven up. The price will move in this way until the market establishes a new equilibrium price.

Price Controls

Occasionally the government sets the price of a product because it believes that the forces of supply and demand are unfair. When this happens, the new price may favor either consumers or producers.

A **price ceiling** is a maximum price set by the government that can be charged for goods and services. For example, city officials might set a price ceiling on what landlords may charge for rent. A **price floor** is a government minimum price that can be charged for goods and services. Price floors—more common than price ceilings—prevent prices from dropping too low. The **minimum wage,** the lowest legal wage that can be paid to most workers, is a price floor.

Reading Check **Explaining** If the price of a product is above its equilibrium price, what is the result?

Prices as Signals

Main Idea **In our economy, prices are signals that help businesses and consumers make decisions.**

Economics & You Have you ever refused to buy something you thought was too expensive? Read to find out what message you may have been sending to the maker of the product.

The different parts of the economy need a system of signals so they can work smoothly together. In our economy, prices are signals. They help businesses and consumers make decisions. Prices also help answer the basic economic questions—*what* to produce, *how* to produce, and *for whom* to produce.

What Do Prices Tell Us?

For example, consumers' purchases help producers decide *what* to produce. They **focus,** or center, on providing the goods and services that consumers are willing to buy at prices that allow the suppliers to earn profits. A company will make video games as long as consumers are willing to buy them at a price that generates profits. If consumers are not willing to pay that price, the company will not be willing to make video games.

Prices also help businesses and consumers decide the question of *how* to produce. Suppose it costs a hair salon $20 in labor and supplies to provide a haircut. Consumers, though, are willing to pay only $15 for the haircut. To stay in business, the salon needs to find less costly ways of providing that haircut.

Housing Market Even when the sale of houses slows down, price reductions eventually balance supply and demand. ***Identifying*** **What is the term for a price showing there is no surplus or shortage?**

American Biography

Dick Burke (1935 – 2008)

Like most entrepreneurs, **Dick Burke** started out thinking small. He never dreamed of leading a huge corporation. In fact, his first job at a large equipment manufacturer convinced him otherwise. "I entered a training program in Caterpillar's finance department," he explained. "After 18 months I knew that large corporations were not for me and I was not for them. Just before they fired me, I quit."

In the mid-1970s, Burke was working in Milwaukee, Wisconsin, when two things happened: Gas prices shot up, and Americans began to become more interested in physical fitness. Burke put the two together and started a small business in a red barn in the town of Waterloo, Wisconsin.

What was the product that addressed both issues? Dick Burke began making bicycle frames. He called the company Trek.

Today the company is world famous, thanks to providing the bicycles Lance Armstrong used to win seven Tour de France titles. Today, Trek has about 1,700 employees and annual revenues around $600 million.

Although the company has grown tremendously, some things have not changed. It is still located near that red barn in Waterloo. And the firm's original goals—quality products for our customers at competitive value and deliver them on time—have not changed either.

Making a Difference CITIZENSHIP

Analyzing What qualities do you think have helped make Trek a success?

Prices also help businesses and consumers decide the question of *for whom* to produce. Some businesses aim their goods or services at those consumers who are willing to pay higher prices. Other businesses aim their goods or services at the larger number of people who want to spend less.

Advantages of Prices

You know that consumers look for the best values for what they spend, while producers seek the best price and profit for what they have to sell. The information that prices provide allows people to work together to get more of the things that people want. Without prices, the economy would not run as smoothly, and decisions about allocating goods and services would have to be made some other way.

Prices Are Neutral First, prices in a competitive market economy are neutral because they favor neither the producer nor the consumer. Prices are the result of competition between buyers and sellers. In this way, prices represent compromises with which both sides can live. The more competitive the market is, the more efficient the price adjustment process.

Prices Are Flexible Second, prices in a market economy are flexible. Unforeseen events such as war and natural disasters affect the supply and demand for items. Buyers and sellers react to the new level of prices and adjust their consumption and production accordingly. Before long, the system functions as smoothly as it had before. The ability of the price system to absorb unexpected "shocks" is one of its strengths.

Prices and Freedom of Choice Third, the price system provides for freedom of choice. Because a market economy typically provides a variety of products at a wide range of prices, consumers have many choices. If the price is too high, a lower-priced product can usually be found. Even if a suitable alternative cannot be found, no one forces the consumer to pay a certain price for a product in a competitive market economy.

Competitive markets tend to find their own prices without outside help or interference. No bureaucrats need to be hired, no committees formed, no laws passed, or other decisions made. Even when prices adjust from one level to another, the change is usually so gradual that people hardly notice.

In command economies, such as those found in Cuba and North Korea, consumers face limited choices. Government planners determine the total quantity of goods produced—the number of radios, cars, toasters, and so on. The government then limits the product's variety to keep production costs down. Items such as food, transportation, and housing are offered to citizens at artificially low prices, but seldom are enough produced to satisfy everyone. Many people go without.

Prices Are Familiar Finally, prices are something that we have known about all our lives—from the time we were old enough to ask our parents to buy us something to the age where we were old enough to buy it ourselves. As a result, prices are familiar and easily understood. There is no doubt about a price—if something costs $4.99, then we know exactly what we have to pay for it. This allows people to make decisions quickly and efficiently.

Reading Check **Explaining** What signal does a high price send to buyers and sellers?

Section 4 Review

Vocabulary

1. **Write** a paragraph in which you use these key terms: *surplus, shortage, equilibrium price, price ceiling, price floor, minimum wage.*

Main Ideas

2. **Identifying** What is the point called at which the quantity demanded of a product and the quantity supplied meet?
3. **Explaining** What causes prices to rise—a shortage or a surplus of a good or service? Explain why.

Critical Thinking

4. **Demonstrating** If a firm charges a price below the equilibrium price, what will be the result? Explain.
5. **BIG Ideas** Create a diagram like the one below to show how shortages and surpluses affect prices of goods and services.

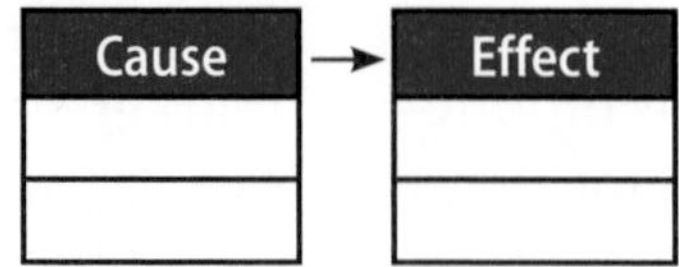

Cause	→	Effect

6. **Analyzing Visuals** Study the graph of the price adjustment process on page 589. Does a price of $40 result in a surplus or a shortage? What is the equilibrium price?

CITIZENSHIP Activity

7. **Research** Compare the prices of the same product at three different stores. What conclusion can you draw about the equilibrium price for the product from the individual prices?
8. **Persuasive Writing** Do you think the government should ever set price ceilings or price floors? Write a letter to the editor of your local newspaper stating and supporting your view.

Study Central™ To review this section, go to glencoe.com.

Chapter 21

Visual Summary

Demand and Supply

Demand is the desire, willingness, and ability to buy a good or service.

Market demand is the total demand of all consumers for a product or service.

Several different factors can cause market demand for a product or service to change.

Demand elasticity is the extent to which a change in price causes a change in the quantity demanded.

Supply is the quantity of a good or service that producers are willing to sell at all possible market prices.

Farmers market in California

Supply increases or decreases depending on many different factors.

Supply elasticity measures how the quantity supplied of a good or service changes in response to changes in price.

The forces of supply and demand work together in markets to establish prices. In our economy, prices are signals that help businesses and consumers make decisions.

Supply of soccer balls for sale

Shoppers at bulk store

Study anywhere, anytime! Download quizzes and flash cards to your PDA from glencoe.com.

Chapter

21 Assessment

Standardized Test Practice

TEST-TAKING TIP

When working numerical problems out on scrap paper, make sure you copy numbers correctly, not transposing or dropping any figures.

Reviewing Vocabulary

Directions: Choose the word(s) that best completes the sentence.

1. A ______ is a graph that shows the amount of a product that would be bought at all prices in the market.

A supply curve
B law of demand
C demand curve
D market demand

2. Some products, such as DVD players and DVDs, are called ______ because demand for one moves in the opposite direction as the price of the other.

A substitutes
B surplus
C elastic
D complements

3. The methods or services used to make goods and services are called ______.

A factors
B technology
C resources
D production

4. At the ______ price there is neither a surplus nor a shortage.

A profitable
B ceiling
C exchange
D equilibrium

Reviewing Main Ideas

Directions: Choose the best answer for each question.

Section 1 *(pp. 568–572)*

5. According to the law of demand, quantity demanded and price ______.

A move in the same direction
B depend on marginal utility
C move in opposite directions
D are not related

6. Diminishing marginal utility is the explanation for the consumer's decision to ______.

A spend less money for sale items
B buy only one dessert with a meal
C purchase more CDs of a favorite singer
D buy expensive gifts for close friends

Section 2 *(pp. 573–578)*

7. Total demand may change if more consumers enter the market, consumer tastes change, or ______.

A consumer expectations change
B substitutes become popular
C demand is inelastic
D supply remains the same

Section 3 *(pp. 580–586)*

8. Businesses invest time, money, and other capital resources for the primary motive of ______.

A paying good wages
B supplying better products
C making a profit
D satisfying customers' needs

Section 4 *(pp. 587–592)*

9. One of the strengths of a market economy is that ______.

A prices absorb some of the shocks or unexpected changes in the economy
B most consumers can afford plenty of the goods and services they want
C producers almost always make a profit
D demand is never greater than supply

GO ON

Critical Thinking

Directions: Base your answers to questions 10 and 11 on the graph below and your knowledge of Chapter 21.

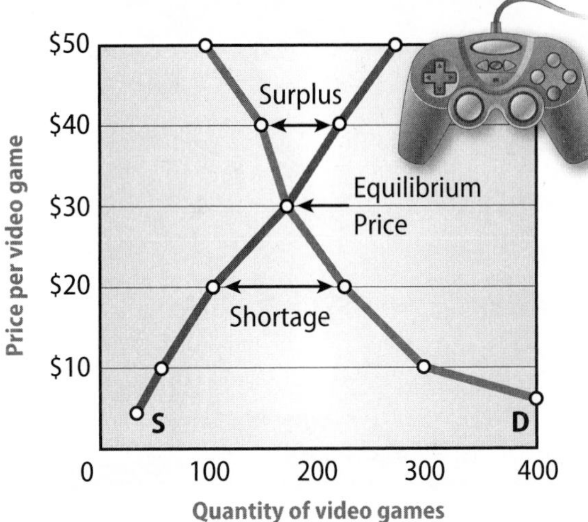

10. The price adjustment graph shows that at a price of more than $30 ______.

A consumer demand would increase

B the cost of production would have to be more than $40

C supply would increase and cause a surplus

D supply would decrease, causing a shortage

11. The graph illustrates that at the equilibrium price of video games ______.

A producers will supply nearly 200 units

B consumers will demand more than 200 units

C demand will fall

D there may be a shortage of games

Document-Based Questions

Directions: Analyze the following document and answer the short-answer questions that follow.

A price ceiling is a government-set maximum price that can be charged for goods and services. Below, a city sets such a maximum price for rent in the Washington, D.C., area.

> *No landlord shall charge a monthly rent for any controlled rental unit in an amount more than the fair market rent level established annually by the Department of Housing and Urban Development for the Washington Metropolitan Statistical Area for a four-bedroom unit or 1% of the property's assessed value for property taxes in a given year, whichever is greater. . . . Beginning in January 2007 and every three years thereafter, the City Council may reconsider the criteria for the establishment of rent ceilings based, among other factors, on the triennial reassessments of properties in the City.*
>
> —City of College Park (Md.)

12. For what period of time will each rent ceiling be set by the city government? Why will the council review the rent ceiling periodically?

13. Does a ceiling benefit renters or landlords? If the price of a product is set below its equilibrium price, what is the likely result?

Extended-Response Question

14. Do you think that the rent ceiling will provide more low cost housing in the area in the long term? Write a paragraph describing the possible results of rent ceilings that are set below the equilibrium price.

STOP

For additional test practice, use Self-Check Quizzes—Chapter 21 on glencoe.com.

Need Extra Help?

If you missed question...	1	2	3	4	5	6	7	8	9	10	11	12	13	14
Go to page...	569	576	585	589	569	572	574	583	589	589	589	584	584	584

TIME REPORTS

Oil and Gas Consumption in the U.S.

America's addiction to oil is getting ever more costly for car-loving consumers and energy-dependent industries

1 The U.S. is the world's biggest oil consumer—and importer

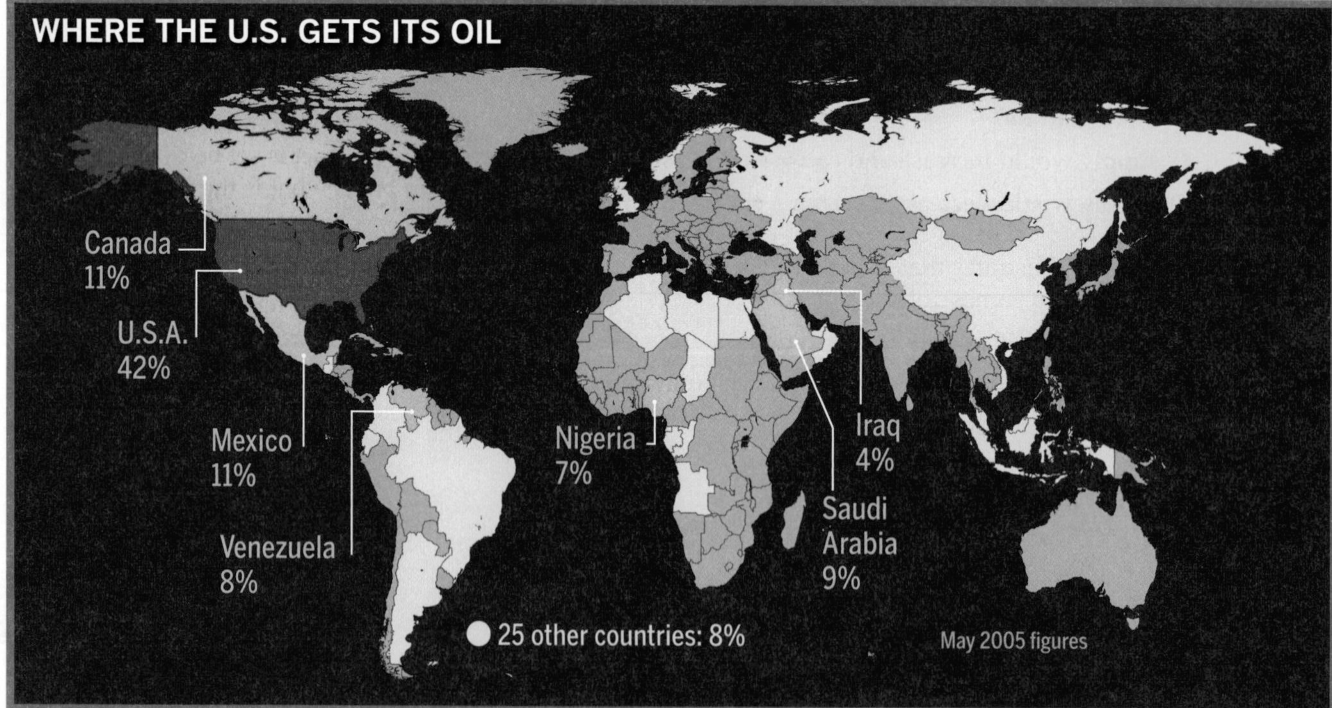

- Americans account for **4.5%** of the world's population but guzzle **25%** of the planet's petroleum output. On a typical day, the U.S. consumes **21 million barrels** of oil—more than any other country.

- About **58%** of America's oil is imported from other countries. As the map above shows, most of America's oil imports come from **outside the Middle East**. Canada and Mexico are major suppliers of U.S. oil.

- The U.S. holds **700 million barrels** of oil in the **Strategic Petroleum Reserve**. That's equivalent to about 70 days' worth of imports. This emergency oil supply is stored at four sites on the Gulf of Mexico.

2 Demand for oil is soaring

The U.S. has long been the dominant customer for the world's oil, buying more than China, Japan, and Germany combined in 2005. By 2025, U.S. oil consumption is projected to increase 32%. At current rates of consumption, the known oil supply will be exhausted by the middle of the 21st century.

3 As oil prices rise, the effects ripple through the economy

Higher oil prices mean higher gasoline prices, since gasoline is produced by refining crude oil. The U.S. consumes nearly 400 million gallons of gasoline every day, most of it going into cars and trucks. The impact of rocketing gas prices stretches well beyond the pump:

- **Airlines** are among the hardest hit, with each penny increase in the per-gallon price of jet fuel costing the industry $180 million annually. For the first time in decades, major carriers are spending more for fuel than they are for labor. That means higher fares for passengers.
- **Delivery companies** like FedEx and U.P.S. also suffer; many have added surcharges to help cover rising costs.
- **Farmers** from coast to coast are affected as the cost of operating machinery and irrigation systems rises.
- And **retailers** suffer because it costs more for goods—and for customers—to reach stores.

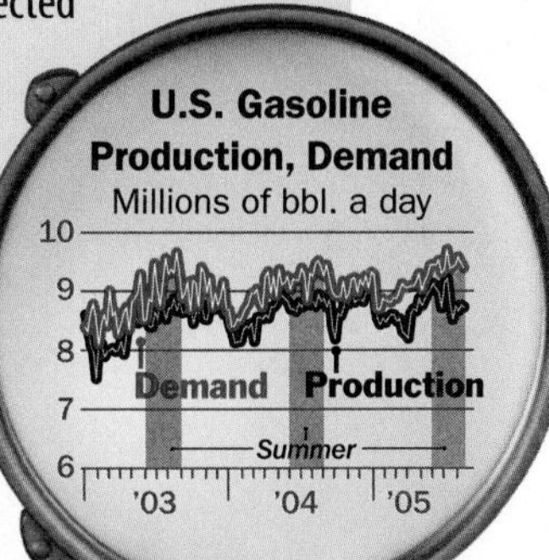

Sources: Energy Information Administration; Bureau of Labor Statistics; TIME Graphic by Lon Tweeten, Jackson Dykman, Kristina Dell and Jeremy Caplan.

FEELING THE IMPACT Every dollar jump in the price of oil costs the major U.S. airlines $365 million more in fuel per year.

Chapter 22

Business and Labor

Why It Matters

Businesses and labor organizations play a major role in our nation and communities. They work separately, as well as together, to make people's lives better by keeping the economy as healthy as possible.

Civics ONLINE
Visit glencoe.com and enter QuickPass™ code CIV3093c22 for Chapter 22 resources.

Chapter Audio

BIG Ideas

Section 1: Types of Businesses

Market economies rest upon the fundamental principle of individual freedom for consumers, producers, and workers. The three basic types of business organizations in the United States are sole proprietorship, partnership, and corporation.

Section 2: The American Labor Force

Market economies rest upon the fundamental principle of individual freedom for consumers, producers, and workers. Labor unions represent about 14 percent of U.S. workers and play an important role in the nation's economy and political life. They negotiate wages and workplace agreements with management.

Section 3: Businesses in Our Economy

Market economies rest upon the fundamental principle of individual freedom for consumers, producers, and workers. Businesses play many different roles in our economy, including that of consumer, employer, and producer. Businesses also have responsibilities to their consumers, owners, employees, and communities.

◀ Technician works on jet engine compressor

FOLDABLES™ Study Organizer

Comparing Information Study Foldable Make the following Foldable to help you compare the differences and similarities between business and labor practices.

Step 1 Fold a two inch tab along the long edge of a sheet of paper.

Step 2 Fold the paper in half so the tab is on the inside.

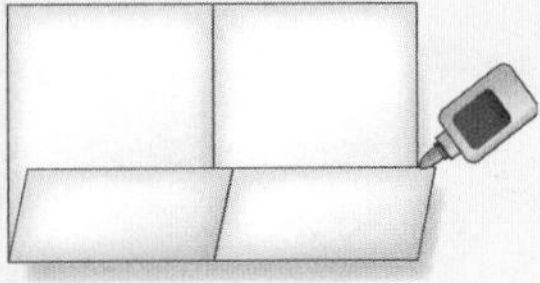

Step 3 Open the paper pocket Foldable and glue or staple the edges together. Store note cards in the pockets.

Reading and Writing
As you read the chapter, collect information about business and labor practices. Write a summary paragraph about each using your note cards.

Section 1

Types of Businesses

Guide to Reading

Big Idea
Market economies rest upon the fundamental principle of individual freedom for consumers, producers, and workers.

Content Vocabulary
- sole proprietorship *(p. 601)*
- financial capital *(p. 601)*
- partnership *(p. 602)*
- articles of partnership *(p. 602)*
- corporation *(p. 603)*
- charter *(p. 604)*
- stock *(p. 604)*
- stockholder *(p. 604)*
- board of directors *(p. 604)*
- cooperative *(p. 606)*

Academic Vocabulary
- sole *(p. 601)*
- consult *(p. 601)*
- clarify *(p. 602)*

Reading Strategy
Organizing Create a diagram like the one below, then analyze the similarities and differences between partnerships and sole proprietorships. Where the ovals overlap, write the characteristics that both share.

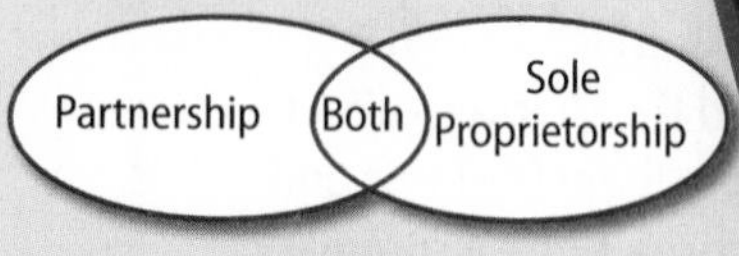

Partnership | Both | Sole Proprietorship

Real World Economics Small businesses are very important to the American economy and employ thousands of young people. Many teens, such as this girl who works in a small market, put in hours on the job after school and on weekends. Without these workers, small businesses could not survive. Support also comes from the U.S. Small Business Administration (SBA). It has been guaranteeing loans to businesses that are high-risk, not traditional, or are competing with much larger competitors.

▼ **New York teen works after school in neighborhood market**

Proprietorships

Main Idea **The most common, and simplest, form of business organization in the United States is the sole proprietorship.**

Economics & You What kind of business could you start right now? Read to find out how you would organize that business.

There are three main kinds of business organizations in the economy today—the sole proprietorship, the partnership, and the corporation. Each offers its owners important advantages and disadvantages.

The most common form of business organization in the United States is the **sole proprietorship,** or simply, proprietorship—a business owned and operated by a **sole,** or single person. You have seen such businesses in your neighborhood—beauty salons, cleaners, and pizza restaurants.

Have you ever earned money mowing lawns or babysitting? If so, you were a sole proprietor. Important advantages of sole proprietorships are that the proprietor has full pride in owning the business and receives all the profits. The proprietor can make decisions quickly, without having to **consult,** or check with, a co-owner or boss.

The biggest disadvantage is that the proprietor has unlimited liability, or complete legal responsibility for all debts and damages arising from doing business. If the business has debts, the owner's personal assets, such as houses, cars, and jewelry, may be seized to pay the debts.

Sole proprietors also find it difficult to raise **financial capital**—the money needed to run a business or enable it to grow larger. Another disadvantage is the difficulty of attracting qualified employees. Many high school and college graduates are more likely to be attracted to positions with larger firms that can offer better benefits—paid vacations, sick leave, and health and medical insurance.

Reading Check **Identifying** Who makes the decisions in a sole proprietorship?

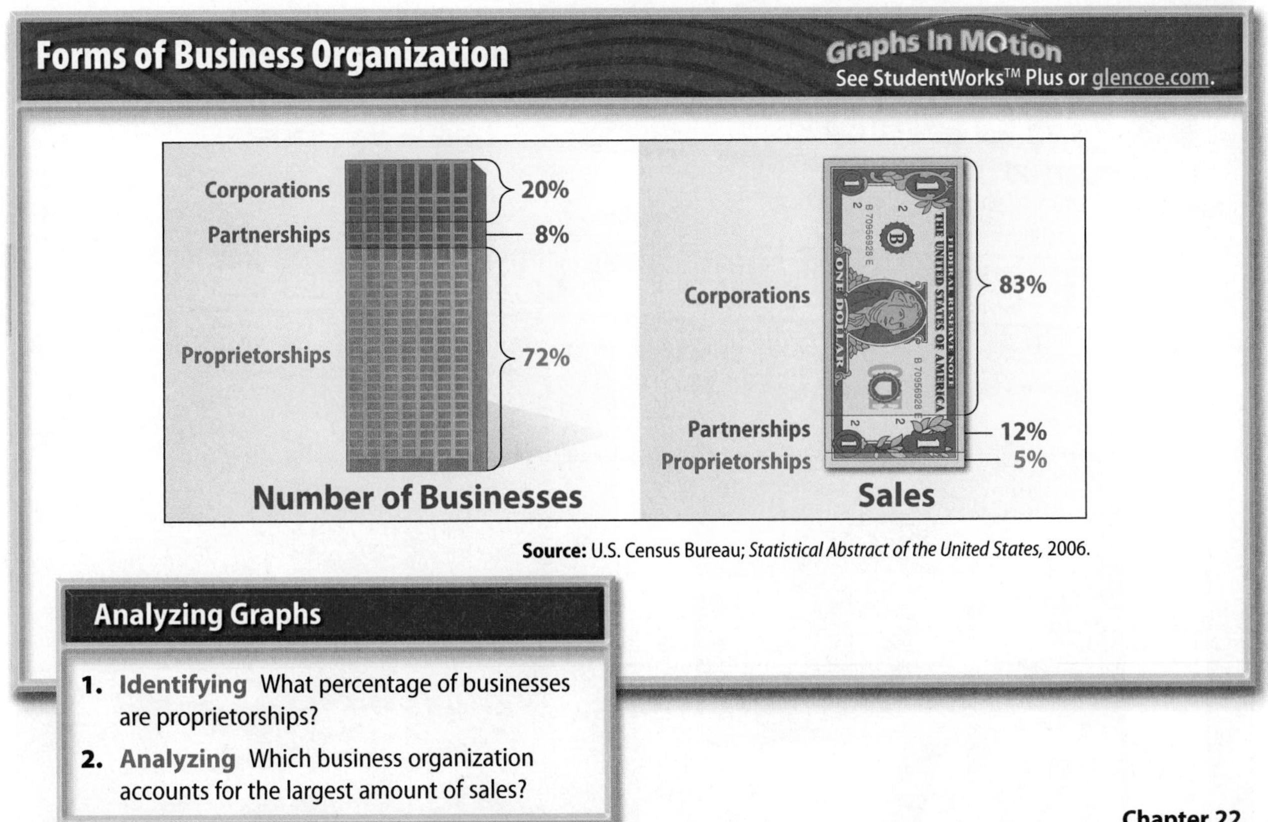

Source: U.S. Census Bureau; *Statistical Abstract of the United States,* 2006.

Analyzing Graphs

1. **Identifying** What percentage of businesses are proprietorships?
2. **Analyzing** Which business organization accounts for the largest amount of sales?

Partnerships

Main Idea **A partnership is a business owned by two or more people.**

Economics & You Can you think of someone with whom you would be willing to go into business? Read to find out more about this type of organization.

Suppose you are a proprietor, and your workload increases so much that you have little time to do anything else. You could expand your business by hiring an employee. However, you also need money to buy new equipment, and you would rather not take out a loan. You decide to take on a partner.

The best solution is to look for someone who can keep books, order supplies, handle customers, and invest in the business. You offer to form a **partnership,** a business that two or more people own and operate.

Structure

When you start the business, you and your partner draw up a legal agreement called **articles of partnership.** This document identifies how much money each of you will contribute and what role each partner will play in the business. It **clarifies,** or spells out, how you will share profits or losses. Finally, the document describes how to add or remove partners, or even how to break up the business if you want to close it down.

Kinds of Partnerships There are two kinds of partnerships. The most common form of partnership is a *general* partnership, one in which all partners are responsible for the management and financial obligations of the business. In a *limited* partnership, at least one partner is not active in the daily running of the business, although he or she may have contributed funds to finance the operation.

Partnerships Many small businesses like this New York City bodega are owned by more than one person. ***Analyzing*** **Why would a business owner want to share ownership?**

Advantages Much like sole proprietorships, an advantage of partnerships is the pride of sharing ownership in a business. Partnerships also overcome some disadvantages of a proprietorship. Because there are multiple owners, partnerships can usually raise more money. If money cannot be borrowed, the partners can always take in new partners to provide funds. Like sole proprietors, partners pay no corporate income tax.

Another advantage of partnerships is that each owner often brings special talent to the business. If, for example, one partner in an advertising agency is better at public relations and another is better at artwork, each can work at the tasks for which he or she is most capable. The ad agency then has a better chance of succeeding than if only one person ran it.

Another advantage of a partnership is the slightly larger size, which often makes for more efficient operations. In some areas, such as medicine and law, a relatively small firm with three or four partners may be just the right size for the market. Other partnerships, such as accounting firms, may have hundreds of partners offering services throughout the United States.

Disadvantages One disadvantage of the partnership is that the legal structure is complex. When a partner is added or removed, a new agreement has to be made.

The main disadvantage is that the owners have unlimited liability. This means that each owner is fully responsible for all the debts of the partnership. Suppose that you and four others form an equal partnership. The articles of partnership state that you own one-fifth of the business and have the right to one-fifth of its profits. Suppose, though, that someone was injured by the company and sued for damages. If the other owners cannot pay, you could be required to pay 100 percent of the damages.

Reading Check **Describing** What is the main disadvantage of a partnership?

Corporations

Main Idea **The corporation is a business recognized by law and is the most complicated of the three main types of business.**

Economics & You Think of a big company whose name you see everywhere. Chances are, it is organized in the manner you are going to read about.

The **corporation** is an organized business recognized by law that has many of the rights and responsibilities of an individual.

Successful Corporation Yahoo!'s corporate headquarters in California often holds meetings with the board of directors of this fast-growing Web provider. ***Explaining*** **What is the role of a board of directors?**

Corporate Chain of Command

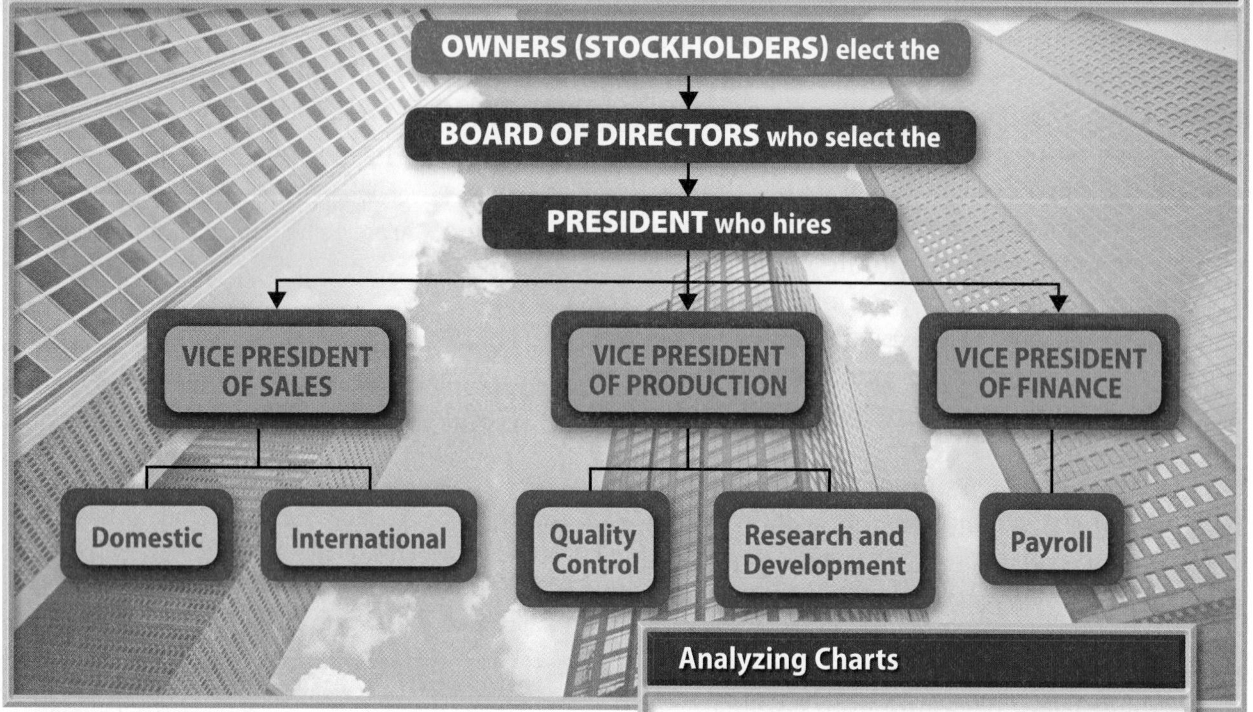

OWNERS (STOCKHOLDERS) elect the

↓

BOARD OF DIRECTORS who select the

↓

PRESIDENT who hires

- VICE PRESIDENT OF SALES
  - Domestic
  - International
- VICE PRESIDENT OF PRODUCTION
  - Quality Control
  - Research and Development
- VICE PRESIDENT OF FINANCE
  - Payroll

Analyzing Charts

1. **Identifying** To whom does the Director of Quality Control report?
2. **Analyzing** If the board of directors needed to raise capital, to whom would it appeal?

In fact, a corporation can do anything a person can do—own property, pay taxes, sue or be sued—except vote. One-fifth of all businesses are corporations.

Structure

Someone who wants to start a corporation must get a **charter**—a government document granting permission to organize. The charter includes the name, purpose, address, and other features of the business. The charter also specifies the amount of **stock,** or ownership shares of the corporation, that will be issued. The people who buy this stock—the **stockholders**—become part owners of the corporation. The corporation uses the money received from selling the stock to set up and run the business.

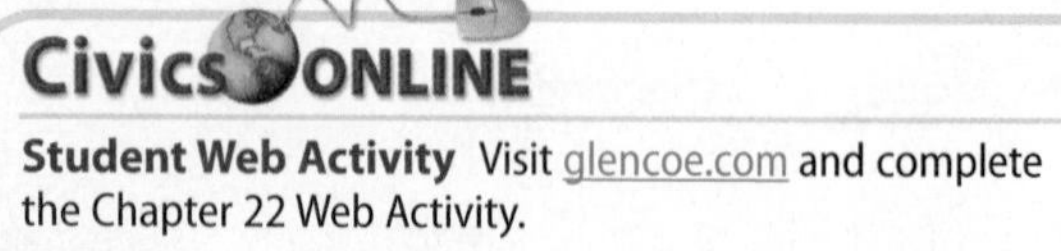

Civics ONLINE

Student Web Activity Visit glencoe.com and complete the Chapter 22 Web Activity.

The stockholders elect a **board of directors** to act on their behalf. The board hires managers to run the corporation on a daily basis. The chart above shows the relationship of these groups. As you can see, the business owners and the managers of a corporation are different groups of people.

Advantages The first advantage of the corporation is the ease of raising financial capital. If it needs additional money to expand, for example, the corporation can sell new shares of stock. Corporations also find it easier than the other types of businesses to borrow large sums of money.

The second advantage results from the ease of raising capital. This allows corporations to grow to be huge. Today's large corporations employ thousands of workers and carry out business around the world.

The Largest Corporations A recent study found that some corporations are bigger than the economies of many countries. Of the world's largest 150 economic entities, 95 are corporations, according to data released in 2005 by *Fortune* magazine and the World Bank. The ranking is based on corporations by revenue and countries by GDP. Wal-Mart is the world's largest corporation and ranks number 22. Other high ranking corporations are BP at 23, Exxon Mobil at 24, and General Motors at 33. Each of these corporations was larger than the domestic economies of Finland (34th), Ireland (35th), and Argentina (48th).

A third advantage of corporations is that the board of directors can hire professional managers to run the business. Many corporations hire professional managers. If those managers do not succeed, the board can replace them.

A fourth advantage is that ownership of the corporation can be easily transferred. If you own shares in one corporation and would rather have shares in another, you simply sell the first stock and buy the second.

A final advantage of the corporation is limited liability. Only the corporation, not its owners, is responsible for the debts of the corporation. For instance, if you paid $1,000 for stock in a corporation that later went bankrupt, you would lose your $1,000 investment—but no more than that. Unlike the proprietorship or the partnership, you would not be liable for the company's debts.

Disadvantages Corporations have their disadvantages as well. First, they often are expensive and complex to set up. In addition, the business owners have very little say in the management of the business. Millions of people own the shares of major corporations, but it is difficult for them to unite to force the managers to act in a particular way.

Third, corporations are subject to more regulation by government than the other forms of business. They must release certain reports on a regular basis. These reports give detailed financial information about the company. The reports are designed to keep potential and current shareholders informed about the state of the business.

Profit Sharing This assembly worker at Ford Motor Company may also be a stockholder in the corporation. ***Explaining*** **How are the funds raised by stock used?**

Finally, stockholders are subject to double taxation, or paying taxes twice on corporate profits. First, the corporation pays a tax on its profits. Then, when the profits are distributed to the stockholders, the stockholders have to pay tax on those earnings. Because of double taxation, corporations are required to keep detailed records of sales and expenses so that it can compute and pay taxes on its profits. Sole proprietors and partners also must pay taxes on the profits they earn. However, proprietorships and partnerships do not pay a separate profit tax.

Other Business Organizations

Profit-seeking proprietorships, partnerships, and corporations are not the only types of business organizations. Other organizations operate on a "not-for-profit" basis. Examples of nonprofit institutions include churches, hospitals, and social service agencies.

What Are Cooperatives? Another example of a nonprofit organization is the **cooperative,** a voluntary association of people formed to carry on an economic activity that benefits its members. Consumer cooperatives buy bulk amounts of goods on behalf of their members. Members usually help keep the cost of the operation down by devoting several hours a week or month to the operation. Service cooperatives provide services, such as insurance and credit, rather than goods to their members.

Producers can also have cooperatives. A producer cooperative helps members promote or sell their products. For example, farmers cooperatives help members sell their crops directly to central markets or to companies that use the products.

Reading Check **Describing** Why is double taxation a disadvantage for corporations?

Review

Vocabulary

1. **Define** these terms from the section and make a set of flash cards to help you learn them: *sole proprietorship, financial capital, partnership, articles of partnership, corporation, charter, stock, stockholder, board of directors, cooperative.*

Main Ideas

2. **Explaining** Why is a proprietorship the easiest form of business to set up? What is the most complex form?
3. **Comparing** What are the advantages and disadvantages of forming a partnership?

Critical Thinking

4. **Evaluating** If you were planning to open your own business, which form of business organization would you prefer—sole proprietorship, partnership, or corporation? Justify your answer.
5. **BIG Ideas** On a chart similar to the one below, identify the advantages of the corporation.

Corporation Advantages

6. **Analyzing Visuals** Study the graphs on page 601. What can you conclude about the form of business having the largest number of organizations and sales generated by that form of business?

CITIZENSHIP Activity

7. **Persuasive Writing** Write a paragraph either supporting or disagreeing with this statement: The sole proprietorship is the basis of U.S. business. Give reasons for your opinion.

Study Central™ To review this section, go to glencoe.com.

Financial Literacy

The Job Interview: First Impressions Count

If your résumé is what opens the door to job opportunity, keep the door open by making a good first impression. Do your homework by researching information about the company before you arrive. Have specific job goals in mind. Then practice interviewing with a friend or relative.

On the day of the interview, plan to arrive early. Dress to impress—nothing flashy, just well-groomed clothes suitable to the job.

When you meet the interviewer, shake hands firmly. Address the person as Mr., Mrs., or Ms. unless told otherwise. Relax promptly and use good manners. Maintain eye contact throughout the interview, be enthusiastic, and answer questions clearly and honestly. Focus on the training or experience you can bring to the job. Ask questions about the organization and the position. Thank the interviewer when you leave, and as a follow-up, send a thank-you note.

The company offered me the job. Now what?

- Take time to make your decision.
- Consider the salary and benefits of the job. If you have not already done so, research the job turnover of the company. High turnover might reveal employee dissatisfaction or a lack of job stability.
- Confirm the opportunities open to you, such as chances for advancement or additional training.
- Create a balance sheet weighing the pros and cons of the job. If the pros outweigh the cons, take a deep breath and jump into the job market. You are on the way to building your career!

Analyzing Economics

1. **Summarizing** What can you do to prepare for a job interview?
2. **Hypothesizing** What should you do if an employer asks you a question you cannot answer? Explain.

The American Labor Force

Guide to Reading

Big Idea

Market economies rest upon the fundamental principle of individual freedom for consumers, producers, and workers.

Content Vocabulary

- labor union *(p. 609)*
- right-to-work law *(p. 610)*
- collective bargaining *(p. 611)*
- mediation *(p. 611)*
- arbitration *(p. 611)*
- strike *(p. 612)*
- boycott *(p. 612)*

Academic Vocabulary

- comprise *(p. 609)*
- technique *(p. 611)*
- option *(p. 611)*

Reading Strategy

Organizing As you read the section, complete a diagram like the one below that shows the goals of collective bargaining.

Bargaining Goals

Real World Economics Since the first immigrants came to America and formed a huge labor force, unions have played a part in American industry. These AFL-CIO members are raising their voices in Pittsburgh to draw attention to national union issues. Unions represent more than 15 million workers in the United States and offer a powerful voice for workers to negotiate for better wages and working conditions. Some economists believe that unions are good for the economy, as they produce members who are better trained and stay on the job longer than employees who are not union members.

▼ **Union members showing support at a labor rally**

Political Cartoons

Michael Ramirez/Copley News Service

Every year, more than half of all Americans do volunteer work | role in it. One of the responsibilities of citizens is to help make their | of volunteer grou small. Perha

This cartoon, by Michael Ramirez, makes a statement about unions in the United States.

1. **What animals does Ramirez use to represent unions?**
2. **Why do you think he selected these symbols?**
3. **Do you think Ramirez believes the SEIU and Teamsters' decision to break away from the AFL-CIO will be effective? Explain.**

Organized Labor

Main Idea Labor unions play an important role in the nation's economy and political life.

Economics & You Do you think people working together have a greater chance of success than individuals? Read to find out how American workers put this idea into action.

The population of the United States by October 2006 was approximately 300 million people. Slightly more than half, or about 151 million, belonged to the civilian labor force—men and women 16 years old and over who are either working or actively looking for a job.

Some workers choose to organize. They form **labor unions,** groups of workers who band together to have a better chance to obtain higher pay and better working conditions. Only about 14 percent of American workers belong to unions. The percentage of U.S. workers who are union members has fallen since the 1980s. One of the major reasons for the decrease is the shift from a manufacturing to a service economy. Still, unions play an important role in the nation's economy and political life.

Types of Unions

There are two types of unions. Workers who perform the same skills join together in a craft or trade union, such as a printers' union. Industrial unions bring together different types of workers from the same industry. An example is the United Auto Workers. In the past, unions were formed mainly by workers in industry. Today, though, people in jobs as different as airline workers, teachers, and professional athletes join unions.

Local Unions A local union is **comprised** of, or includes, the members of a union in a factory, company, or geographic area. Unions that also have members in Canada or Mexico are often called international unions.

Right-to-Work States

Maps In MOtion
See StudentWorks™ Plus or glencoe.com.

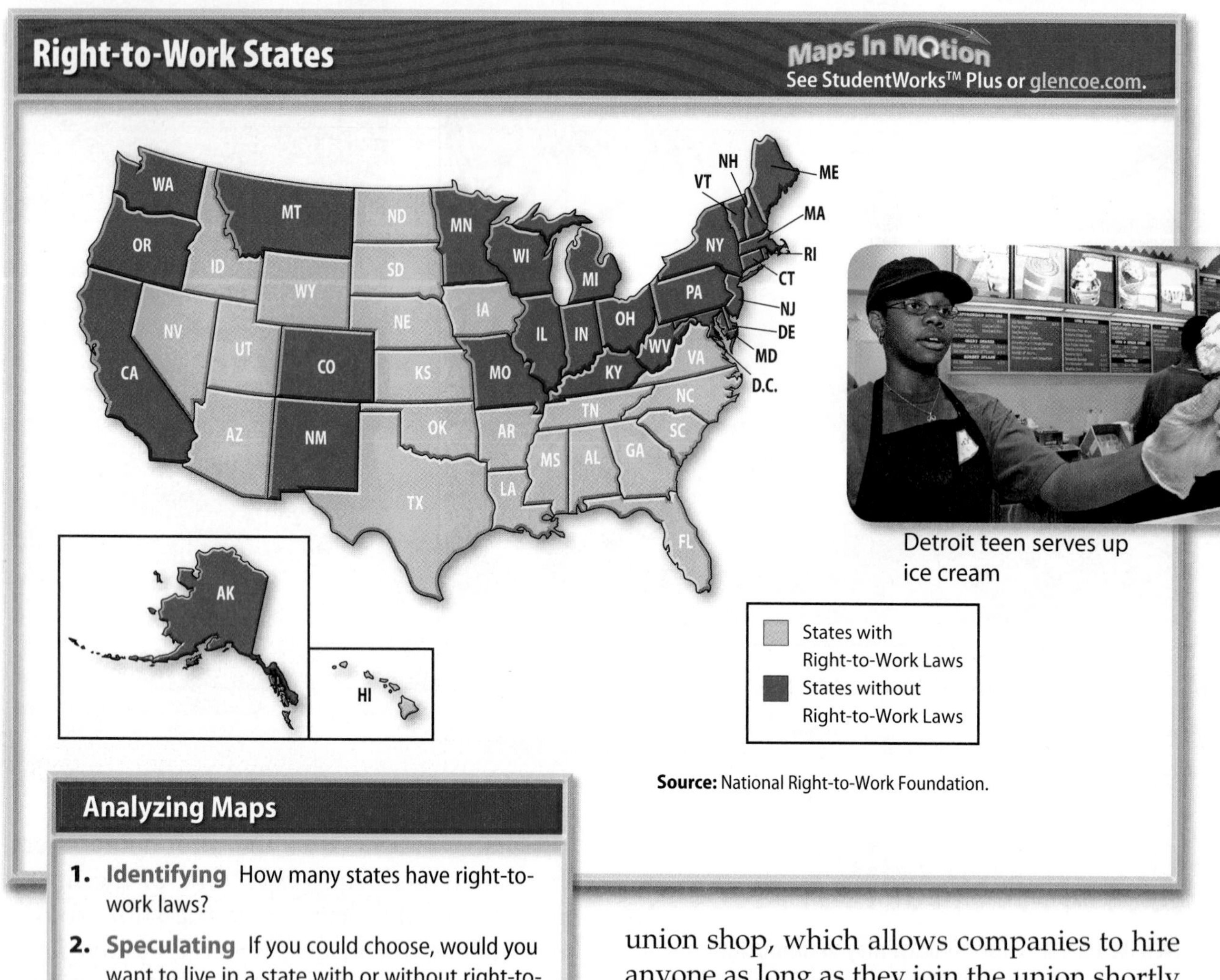

Detroit teen serves up ice cream

Source: National Right-to-Work Foundation.

Analyzing Maps

1. **Identifying** How many states have right-to-work laws?
2. **Speculating** If you could choose, would you want to live in a state with or without right-to-work laws? Why?

National Unions Above the locals are the national unions. These organizations are the individual craft or industrial unions that represent locals on a nationwide level. The American Federation of Labor-Congress of Industrial Organizations, or AFL-CIO, is a national union. The federation represents more than 13 million working men and women nationwide.

Union Arrangements

Before they were declared illegal in 1947, closed shops were one kind of union arrangement. In closed shops, a worker had to first join a union in order to be hired by a company. A common arrangement today is the union shop, which allows companies to hire anyone as long as they join the union shortly after they begin working.

However, 22 states have passed **right-to-work laws,** which prevent mandatory union membership required by the union shop. This led to the modified union shop, which does not require a worker to join a union to be hired or keep the job. Workers must, however, remain in the union if they decide to join. Finally, the agency shop requires workers to pay a fee to the union for representing them even if they do not join the union.

A union cannot be brought into a workplace unless a majority of the workers votes in favor of it. A federal government agency, the National Labor Relations Board (NLRB), makes sure that these union elections are carried out fairly and honestly.

Reading Check **Summarizing** Is the union shop illegal in right-to-work states? Explain.

Negotiations

Main Idea **Labor and management negotiate workplace agreements.**

Economics & You Have you ever had a third person help you and a friend reach a compromise? Read to find out how labor and management use this method.

Once workers choose to be represented by a union, the union carries out **collective bargaining** for them. Officials from the union and the company meet to discuss the workers' new contract. The negotiations focus on wages and benefits, including health care, holidays, working conditions, and procedures for changing rules.

Getting Outside Help

If the parties cannot agree on the terms for the new contract, they have different **options,** or choices. They might try **mediation,** in which they bring in a third party who tries to help them reach a compromise agreement. In some cases, the two sides choose **arbitration:** A third party listens to both sides, then decides how to settle the disagreement. Both parties agree in advance to accept the arbitrator's decision.

Labor-Management Conflict

Most contracts are settled at the bargaining table. Sometimes, however, negotiations break down. Unions and management use different **techniques,** or methods to pressure the other side to accept their positions.

American Biography

César Estrada Chávez (1927–1993)

César Chávez knew the suffering of farmworkers. He had labored in the fields since age 10, when his family lost their Arizona farm during the Great Depression. Like thousands of other farmers, the Chávez family became migrant workers, constantly moving to be near work. Chávez attended some 65 schools before dropping out at the end of eighth grade.

After serving in World War II, Chávez took a paid job with a Latino civil rights group to win greater rights for Mexican Americans. However, he could not forget the migrant workers. In 1962, with the support of his wife, Helen Fabela Chávez, he returned to the fields and his dream of organizing farmworkers into a union.

In 1965, Chávez launched La Huelga—"the strike"—in which he battled the power of grape growers in the San Joaquin Valley. Chávez, who lived on a salary of $5 a week, asked Americans to boycott grapes until growers signed union contracts. Some 17 million Americans stopped buying grapes, and industry profits tumbled. "For the first time," Chávez said, "the farmworker got some power." The power came in the form of the United Farm Workers, the first successful farmworkers union in the nation's history.

Making a Difference CITIZENSHIP

Explaining Chávez spent much of his life trying to help farmworkers. How did Chávez force grape growers to sign union contracts with farmworkers?

Labor Tools Workers can call a **strike,** in which all workers in the union refuse to go to work. The workers hope that the business will have to shut down without any employees, forcing the company to accept the union's contract terms. Strikers usually walk up and down in front of their workplace carrying picket signs that state their disagreement with the company. Picketing is meant to discourage workers from crossing the picket line to work for the employer. It is also aimed at embarrassing the company and building public support for the strike. Unions can also encourage members and the public to **boycott,** or refuse to buy, the business's products.

Strikes can drag on for months and even years. After a long period of time, strikers sometimes become discouraged. Some may decide to go back to work without gaining what they wanted. In most cases, however, strikes are settled as management and labor return to the negotiating table and work out an agreement.

Management Tools When faced with a strike by its workers, management has methods of its own to use against strikers. Its strongest tool is the lockout. In a lockout, the company prevents workers from entering its buildings until they accept its contract terms. The business hopes that the loss of income will convince workers to accept the company's position.

Injunctions Management sometimes requests a court injunction to limit picketing or to prevent a strike from continuing or even occurring. An injunction is a legal order of a court preventing some activity.

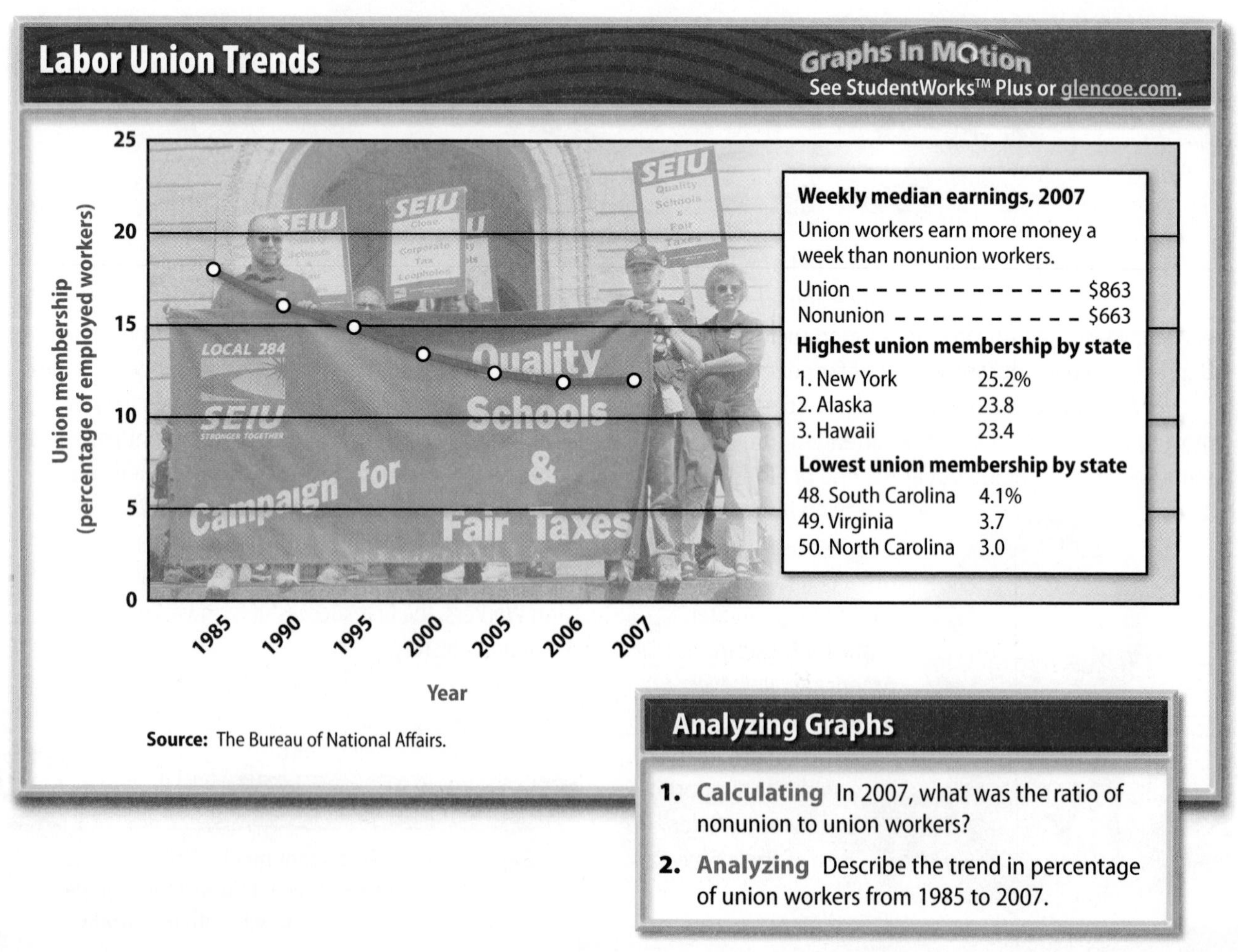

Analyzing Graphs

1. **Calculating** In 2007, what was the ratio of nonunion to union workers?
2. **Analyzing** Describe the trend in percentage of union workers from 1985 to 2007.

In the early days of the labor union movement, the courts had treated unions as illegal conspiracies. Union leaders were regularly prosecuted and sued for damages. Even up to the early 1900s, injunctions were used against labor unions to prevent strikes and some other activities. Because of the use of injunctions by employers during this period, labor unions found it very difficult to strike.

Both companies and unions may ask for an injunction. If issued against a union, the injunction may direct the union not to strike. If issued against a company, it may direct the company not to lock out its workers. In 1995, after professional baseball players ended their strike and went back to work, the owners promptly called a lockout. The players then went to court and got an injunction against the owners, and the 1995 baseball season began—without a labor agreement between the two sides.

Seizure Under extreme circumstances, the government may resort to seizure—a temporary takeover of operations—to allow the government to negotiate with the union. This occurred in 1946, when the government seized the bituminous coal industry. The government felt the welfare of the entire country was at stake because of its need for coal. While operating the mines, government officials worked out a settlement with the miners' union.

Public Employee Unions

An important development in the labor movement in the 1960s and 1970s was the growth in public employee union membership. A public employee union is a union whose members work for the local, state, or federal government. The American Federation of Government Employees (AFGE) is the largest federal employee union representing 600,000 workers.

Reading Check **Contrasting** What is the difference between a strike and a lockout?

Section 2 Review

Vocabulary

1. **Write** a true statement *and* a false statement for each of the following terms: *labor union, right-to-work law, collective bargaining, mediation, arbitration, strike, boycott.* Indicate which statements are true and which are false. Below each false statement explain why it is false.

Main Ideas

2. **Comparing** What is the difference between a union closed shop and a union shop?
3. **Explaining** When is mediation used with labor unions? What are its goals?

Critical Thinking

4. **Summarizing** How does a right-to-work law protect independent workers?
5. **BIG Ideas** Assume that you have been given the job of mediating a strike between the workers in a print shop and its management. On a diagram like the one below, identify three things you would want to know before you suggested a solution.

What I need to know		

Citizenship Activity

6. **Persuasive Writing** Write a newspaper editorial supporting or opposing one of the following practices: closed shop, right-to-work laws, boycott, or lockout. Give reasons, and if possible, cite examples to support your position.

Study Central™ To review this section, go to glencoe.com.

Issues to Debate

Should Congress raise the minimum wage?

Minimum wage is a term that identifies the hourly income that employers must pay their workers. Congress established a minimum wage of 25 cents per hour in 1938. It applied only to those employees engaged in interstate commerce. Congress revised the law in 1961 and 1968, extending coverage to most workers. Every few years thereafter, Congress raised the rate. For many years, the minimum wage of $5.15 remained unchanged. Some states passed higher minimum wage rates than the federal government. When a minimum wage issue appears on a state ballot, voters often approve it. Should Congress respond to the people's desire for a higher minimum wage?

Minimum wage jobs include retail and service jobs, such as poultry processing, fruit and vegetable picking, and restaurant service.

YES

One reason that the minimum wage should be raised every few years is because inflation gradually erodes the wages of everyone. If the purpose of the minimum wage is to lift the earnings of low-wage workers, the delay in raising it defeats the original intent of the law. The AFL-CIO, a major labor union, reported, "If the minimum wage had just kept pace with inflation since 1968 when it was a $1.60 an hour, minimum wage would have been $8.88 (an hour) in 2005." Supporters believe that raising the minimum wage would help women and children, and also have a ripple effect throughout the whole economy, improving the purchasing power of consumers.

—AFL-CIO, 2006

NO

The main argument against minimum wage laws is that raising minimum wages forces employers to dismiss low-productivity workers. This policy negatively affects those with the least education, job experience, and maturity. Teenagers are likely to face unemployment when the minimum wage is increased. According to Tim Kane of the Heritage Foundation, most economists believe a minimum wage does not work in free markets. Kane says, "Although the minimum wage will not work according to economic theory—and it has not worked in reality—what makes it especially tragic is that it hits poor Americans hardest. . . . Average pay in America has been increasing steadily in recent years, despite the fact that the minimum wage has not changed since 1997. Real wages rise when productivity rises."

—Tim Kane, PhD, March 4, 2005

Debating the Issue

1. **Describing** What is the purpose of a minimum wage law?
2. **Recalling** When did Congress begin passing minimum wage laws?
3. **Explaining** What workers are most likely to be affected by an increase in the minimum wage?
4. **Concluding** Why do you think Congress refused to increase the minimum wage for several years?

Section 3

Businesses in Our Economy

Guide to Reading

Big Idea

Market economies rest upon the fundamental principle of individual freedom for consumers, producers, and workers.

Content Vocabulary

- transparency *(p. 617)*
- discrimination *(p. 618)*
- social responsibility *(p. 618)*

Academic Vocabulary

- foundation *(p. 616)*
- crucial *(p. 617)*
- reveal *(p. 617)*

Reading Strategy

Organizing As you read the section, complete a diagram like the one below by identifying at least one responsibility of business in each category.

Responsibility of Business	
To consumers	To employees

Real World Economics Have you ever thought about starting your own business? These plumbers are fulfilling that dream as they service homes in the Miami, Florida, area. They promote their own business and welfare by running an honest company while at the same time being part of America's construction industry—a booming industry that fuels America's economy. Businesses like theirs have a responsibility to provide quality service to consumers. They also have a responsibility when hiring others, to pay a fair wage.

▼ **Adjusting the plumbing on a Florida condominium**

Roles of Business

Main Idea **Businesses play many different roles in our economy. Businesses also have many responsibilities.**

Economics & You Have you ever played in a park that was paid for by a local business? Read to find out other ways businesses assist our economies.

You may have eaten a square, onion-smothered White Castle hamburger. But did you know that the Ingram family, founders of that fast-food chain, have given $11 million to support education through its family **foundation** (an institution created to promote the public good)?

Businesspeople such as the Ingrams can be very generous. This generosity comes not only from major corporate givers like the Ingrams. Many local businesses, also, make similar efforts. They donate money or supplies to school fund-raisers. They give money to support children's athletic teams. This community involvement is just one way that business plays a role in society.

Businesses play many different roles in our economy. Sometimes businesses act as consumers—they buy goods and services from other businesses. Manufacturers buy energy and raw materials, while insurance companies buy office furniture and supplies. Stores purchase computers and software to track sales. Businesses are also employers. They provide jobs to millions of workers.

Of course, businesses are also producers. Businesses large and small produce the food, clothing, and shelter that meet people's basic needs, as well as the cars, movies, and appliances that make life more enjoyable and comfortable.

✓ Reading Check **Explaining** Businesses are producers. In what way are businesses also consumers?

Generosity Many businesspeople, such as James H. Quigley, the CEO of the North Carolina-based Deloitte & Touche USA, participate in community service. ***Describing*** **How else can businesses help a community in addition to donating employees' time?**

Responsibilities

Main Idea **Businesses have responsibilities to their consumers, owners, employees, and communities.**

Economics & You Can you think of anything in your school that was donated by a local company? Read to find out why more and more businesses feel a responsibility to their communities.

As they carry out their roles, businesses have different responsibilities. Sometimes laws spell out those responsibilities. Business managers may suffer serious consequences if they do not act responsibly.

Responsibilities to Consumers

Businesses have the responsibility of selling products that are safe. Products and services should also work as promised. A new video game should run without flaws. An auto mechanic should change a car's oil correctly. Businesses also have the responsibility of being truthful in their advertising. Finally, businesses should treat all customers fairly.

Responsibilities to Owners

Another responsibility is to the owners of the business. This is especially **crucial,** or key, in corporations, in which the managers and owners are different groups of people. To protect stockholders, corporations are required to release important financial information regularly.

Revealing, or making public, this information is called **transparency.** The purpose of publishing this information is to provide investors with full disclosure before they choose to invest, or continue to invest, in the company.

Sometimes the managers of a corporation are not completely honest in what they say about the business. When that happens, the government can prosecute them for breaking the law.

TIME™ Teens in *Action*

Brittany Clifford

Brittany Clifford, 16, of Scottsdale, Arizona, does not have cold feet when it comes to soliciting businesses for donations. A few companies foot the bill for Fuzzy Feet, Clifford's foundation that provides children with slippers to warm their feet during hospital stays.

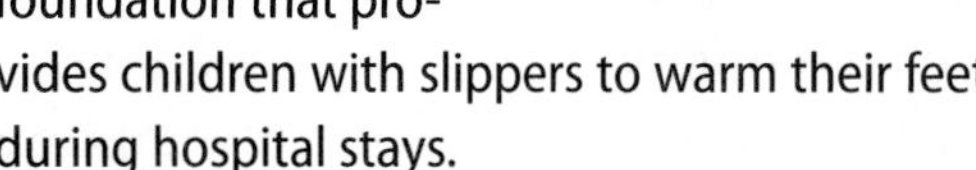

QUESTION: Why did you start Fuzzy Feet?

ANSWER: My friend Michael had heart surgery. In the hospital, he always seemed to be cold. I found out that most of the children in the hospital wore only socks, and many had bare feet. I had an idea to establish a program that would donate slippers to sick children to ease their hospital stay.

Q: How many kids have you reached?

A: Through the generosity of businesses that donate slippers, Fuzzy Feet brings comfort and smiles to hospitalized children across the United States. We delivered our first slippers on Valentine's Day, 2002. Since then, Fuzzy Feet has given away more than 8,000 slippers to sick children in Phoenix, Los Angeles, and New York City.

Q: What kind of reaction do you get when you give kids the slippers?

A: Tons of smiles and lots of laughter. Some people have even cried.

Q: What about the future?

A: My goal is to have different chapters all around the U.S. and maybe in other countries. I want to go to Kenya, Africa, and give out slippers to the kids there. I want to go everywhere to give slippers to everyone!

ACTION FACT: Clifford loves to dance and cheerlead. She has a terrier named Tinker Bell.

Making a Difference — CITIZENSHIP

Describing How did Brittany get the idea for Fuzzy Feet?

The scandal involving bankrupt energy company Enron showed the damage that can be done to investors when critical financial information is not reported by auditors.

Responsibilities to Employees

Businesses also have responsibilities to their employees. Businesses are required to give their workers a safe workplace and to treat all workers fairly and without **discrimination.** This means that they cannot treat employees differently on the basis of race, religion, color, gender, age, or disability.

Some companies are recognized for working hard to meet the needs of their employees. Johnson & Johnson, which makes baby and health care products, takes an active role in fulfilling its responsibilities to its employees. *Latina* and *Working Mother* magazines cited Johnson & Johnson as one of the best U.S. companies in this area.

Responsibilities to the Community

More and more businesses are emphasizing their **social responsibility**—the obligation to pursue goals that benefit society as well as themselves. Gifts to charities are one example of how businesses meet this social responsibility. Many businesses take an active role in meeting the needs of their communities. The retail store Target, for example, promotes programs of community and national volunteering.

American Express has a tradition of responding to emergencies and providing assistance to disaster victims through grants to relief agencies. Another company program promotes historical and environmental preservation.

Reading Check **Defining** What is social responsibility?

Review

Vocabulary

1. **Write** a paragraph describing the social responsibility of businesses using the following terms: *transparency, discrimination.*

Main Ideas

2. **Describing** How do businesses act as producers?
3. **Explaining** Why is it important for corporations to publish their financial information regularly?

Critical Thinking

4. **Evaluating** Which of the business responsibilities described in this section do you feel makes the biggest impact on your community? Why?

5. **BIG Ideas** On a diagram like the one below, identify as many of the responsibilities of businesses to consumers as you can.

CITIZENSHIP Activity

6. **Analyzing** Contact a local business and ask how the business contributes to the community. Describe the actions of the business and what you think the effects are. Share your findings with the class.

Writing

7. **Descriptive Writing** Research on the Internet and describe the corporate responsibility program of a large, well-known U.S. company. Share your findings with the class.

Study Central™ To review this section, go to glencoe.com.

Chapter 22

Visual Summary

Mine workers support those pursuing safety laws

Business

- Sole proprietorships are small, easy-to-manage enterprises owned by one person.
- Proprietorships are relatively numerous and profitable.
- Disadvantages include raising financial capital and attracting qualified employees.
- Partnerships are owned by two or more persons.
- Corporations are owned by shareholders.
- One of the major advantages of a corporation is limited liability.
- A major disadvantage of corporations is that they are taxed more heavily than other forms of business organizations.

Independent beekeeper in North Carolina

Responsibilities

- Businesses have a responsibility to provide safe, working products to their customers.
- Businesses have an obligation to pursue goals that benefit society as a whole as well as themselves.

Labor

- For much of its history, organized labor in the United States has been split into two groups: craft unions and industrial unions
- Organized labor operates at three levels:
  - local union
  - national union
  - federation
- The closed shop (now illegal) required that employers hire only union members.

Small businesses employ local workers

Collective Bargaining

- Collective bargaining is the process by which unions and employers negotiate the conditions of employment.
- When collective bargaining fails, several other methods are available to settle labor disputes.

STUDY TO GO

Study anywhere, anytime! Download quizzes and flash cards to your PDA from glencoe.com.

Chapter 22 Assessment

TEST-TAKING TIP

Question 8 asks you about mediation. Reading all the answer choices may help you remember information about this topic.

Reviewing Vocabulary

Directions: Choose the word(s) that best completes the sentence.

1. Among the advantages of corporations are the ease of raising financial capital, professional management, and ______.

A rapid promotions **C** limited liability
B lower taxes **D** specialization

2. The stockholders of a corporation elect a ______ to act on their behalf.

A board of directors **C** manager
B vice president **D** proprietor

3. Union and management discussion about wages and working conditions is an example of ______.

A arbitration **C** conflict
B collective bargaining **D** open shop

4. The purpose of ______ is to provide investors with full disclosure before they choose to invest.

A insurance **C** arbitration
B insight **D** transparency

Reviewing Main Ideas

Directions: Choose the best answer for each question.

Section 1 *(pp. 600–606)*

5. The most common form of business organization in the United States is the ______.

A sole proprietorship
B limited partnership
C department store
D corporation

6. At least one partner is not active in the daily running of the business in a ______.

A proprietorship
B limited partnership
C general partnership
D corporation

Section 2 *(pp. 608–613)*

7. In a union shop, workers are required to join a union ______.

A before they begin working
B after their first paycheck
C after they begin working
D before arbitration

8. Mediation is used in negotiations over wages and benefits when ______.

A a strike is about to occur
B the parties cannot agree
C the government orders it
D everything else has failed

Section 3 *(pp. 615–618)*

9. Businesses have the obligation to pursue goals that benefit society as well as themselves. This is called ______.

A transparency
B full disclosure
C social responsibility
D unlimited liability

10. Corporations are required to release important financial information regularly to ______.

A citizens
B employees
C competitors
D stockholders

GO ON

Critical Thinking

Directions: Base your answers to questions 11 and 12 on the map below and your knowledge of Chaper 22.

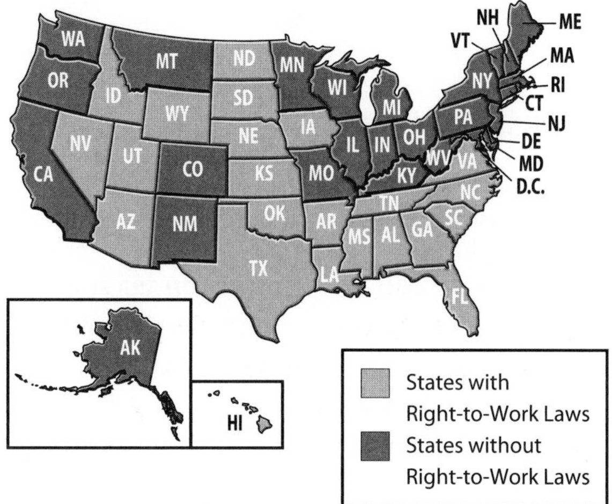

Source: National Right to Work Foundation.

11. What statement best explains the map's division of states in the eastern half of the United States?

A The northern states have more people than the southern states.

B Right-to-work laws are popular in vacation areas.

C Union influence is stronger in the industrial Northeast.

D The closed shop is more popular in the South.

12. Which of the following states does not permit union shops?

A Idaho

B Ohio

C California

D Missouri

Document-Based Questions

Directions: Analyze the following document and answer the short-answer questions that follow.

The Securities and Exchange Commission is the federal government's agency that regulates the sale of securities, such as stocks and bonds. Recently its chairman, William H. Donaldson, talked about business ethics to the Caux Roundtable in Minnesota.

> *As we all know, much of American business is defined by its dynamism and frequent change—new products, new systems, and vigorous competition. In this climate, business practices will frequently outpace any government regulator's ability to develop specific rules governing these practices. . . .*
>
> *This is where having a culture of doing what is right—in the absence of specific rules and even in the face of your competitors' choosing a different path—is vital. This is where the courage and commitment of the firm's leaders is needed to question whether a particular firm practice—no matter what the lawyers say—is truly ethical or is truly in the best interests of client and customers. . . . What I'm talking about is creating a renewed culture of compliance in American business.*

13. According to William H. Donaldson, why is it difficult for regulators to govern everyday business practices in America?

14. What is a "culture of compliance," and why is it needed?

Extended-Response Question

15. The free market has its own way of weeding out bad businesses. Should government also have a role in that process? Explain your answer.

For additional test practice, use Self-Check Quizzes—Chapter 22 on glencoe.com.

Need Extra Help?

If you missed question. . .	1	2	3	4	5	6	7	8	9	10	11	12	13	14	15
Go to page. . .	605	604	611	617	601	602	610	611	618	617	610	610	617	617	617

Analyzing Primary Sources

Economic Concepts

Reading Focus

Capitalism is a system in which government plays a limited role in the nation's economic activity. Demand and supply have an important effect on production and pricing.

Read to Discover

As you read, think about the following:

- How do freedom of enterprise and freedom of choice apply to the American economy?
- How can prices serve as signals to both producers and consumers?

Reader's Dictionary

endeavours: makes an effort
effectually: fully adequately
monopolist: one who has exclusive control or ownership
affluence: wealth, abundance
brevity: shortness

The Invisible Hand

The central principles of capitalism are found in the words of Scottish economist Adam Smith.

[E]very individual, therefore, **endeavours** as much as he can [to direct his resources toward his own business so] that its produce may be of the greatest value; every individual ... neither intends to promote the public interest, nor knows how much he is promoting it ... he intends only his own gain, and he is in this, as in many other cases, led by an invisible hand to promote an end which was no part of his intention. ... By pursuing his own interest he frequently promotes that of the society more **effectually** than when he really intends to promote it.

—from *The Wealth of Nations* by Adam Smith

The Free Market

Economists and political philosophers Friedrich Hayek and Henry Hazlitt were strong defenders of free market capitalism.

Our freedom of choice in a competitive society rests on the fact that, if one person refuses to satisfy our wishes, we can turn to another. But if we face a **monopolist** we are at his mercy. And an authority directing the whole economic system would be the most powerful monopolist imaginable.

—from *Road to Serfdom* by Friedrich A. Hayek

Benefits of Capitalism

Capitalism, the system of private property and free markets, is not only a system of freedom and of natural justice—which tends in spite of exceptions to distribute rewards in accordance with production—but it is a great co-operative and creative system that has produced for our generation an **affluence** that our ancestors did not dare dream of.

—from *Man vs. the Welfare State* by Henry Hazlitt

Supply and Demand and Prices

British economist Alfred Marshall popularized the idea that prices are determined by *both* supply and demand.

The remainder of the present volume will be chiefly occupied with interpreting and limiting this doctrine that the value of a thing tends in the long run to correspond to its cost of production. In particular … [we will consider] the controversy whether "cost of production" [supply] or "utility" [demand] governs value.

We might as reasonably dispute whether it is the upper or the under blade of a pair of scissors that cuts a piece of paper, as whether value is governed by utility or cost of production. It is true that when one blade is held still, and the cutting is effected by moving the other, we may say with careless **brevity** that the cutting is done by the second; but the statement is not strictly accurate, and is to be excused only so long as it claims to be merely a popular and not a strictly scientific account of what happens.

In the same way, when a thing already made has to be sold, the price which people will be willing to pay for it will be governed by their desire to have it, together with the amount they can afford to spend on it. Their desire to have it depends partly on the chance that, if they do not buy it, they will be able to get another thing like it at as low a price: this depends on the causes that govern the supply of it, and this again upon cost of production. …

—from *Principles of Economics* by Alfred Marshall

Photographs as Primary Sources What do you know for sure by looking at the photograph? What can you infer by looking at the photograph? Write a caption explaining how this photograph can be used to illustrate the effect that supply and demand have on price.

DBQ Document-Based Questions

1. **Analyzing** Would Adam Smith agree that the benefits of free enterprise are a consequence of people's desire to make life better for others? Explain.
2. **Explaining** What does Hayek say is an important benefit of a free market economy? What benefit does Hazlitt stress?
3. **Connecting** What example does Marshall use to depict the workings of supply and demand on price? Do you think this is a good example? Explain.
4. **Categorizing** Some prices in our economy very seldom change, whereas others change all the time, even daily. Make a list of products whose prices change slowly, if at all. Make another list of products whose prices you think change quickly. Write a paragraph explaining in your own words why the price of some items is unchanging while the price of others changes often.

UNIT 7

The Free Enterprise System

Encounter Restaurant suspended above Los Angeles International Airport

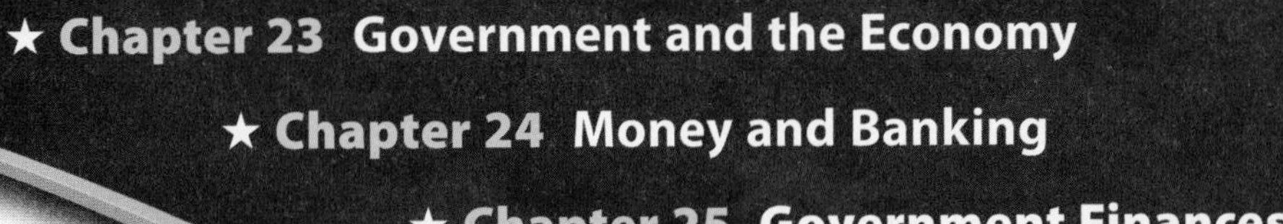

★ **Chapter 23** Government and the Economy

★ **Chapter 24** Money and Banking

★ **Chapter 25** Government Finances

Be An Active Citizen

CITIZENSHIP The free enterprise system takes a look at the economy as a whole. Talk to two or three business owners in your community. Ask about the general state of their businesses, how they feel about governmental economic policies, and their outlook. Write a summary of your findings.

Reading Social Studies

Making Inferences

1 Learn It!

Writers do not always state directly what they want to say. Often, they expect readers to make inferences or draw conclusions. Making an inference is "reading between the lines" by using clues and details the author provides to gain additional meaning from the text.

- Read the paragraph below.
- Pay attention to the facts provided by the writer.
- Read the inference that was drawn by the reader.

A chart like the one below can help you identify information you can use to make inferences.

> Suppose that an ice-cream cone that costs you a dollar doubles in price. This price increase causes the purchasing power of your dollar to fall because you have to use twice as many dollars to buy the same item. This is why inflation is particularly hard on people who have fixed incomes. . . . Inflation also reduces the value of money in a savings account because it will buy less after inflation than before.
>
> *—from page 642*

Information from Text

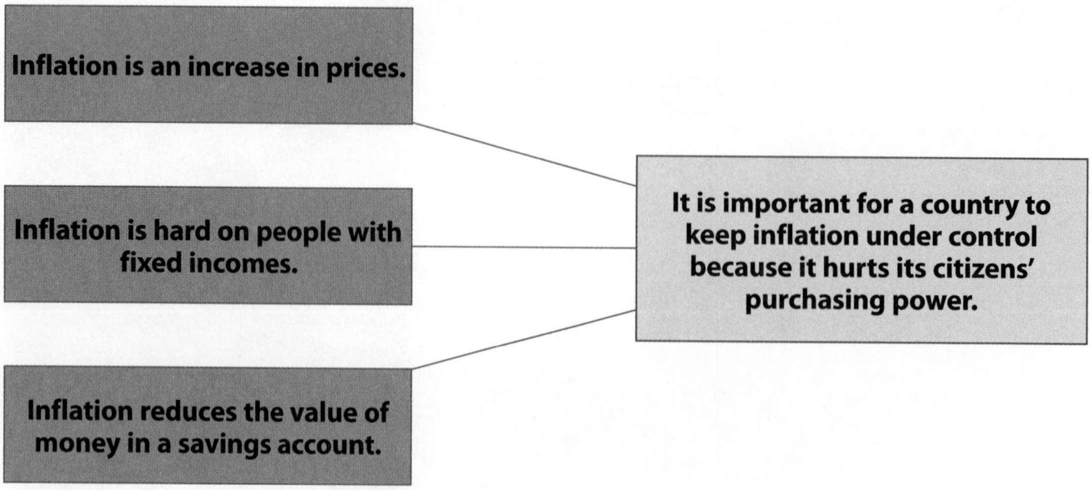

Inflation is an increase in prices.

Inflation is hard on people with fixed incomes.

Inflation reduces the value of money in a savings account.

It is important for a country to keep inflation under control because it hurts its citizens' purchasing power.

2 Practice It!

Read the following paragraph from this unit.

- Draw a chart like the one shown below.
- Write three important facts from the paragraph in the boxes on the left-hand side.
- Make an inference about the sensitivity of the stock market based upon the information from the text and write it in the box on the right.

> The price of a company's stock, like most other things, is determined by supply and demand. Factors such as changes in sales or profits, rumors of a possible takeover, or news of a technological breakthrough can change the demand for a company's stock and, therefore, its price.
>
> —*from page 643*

Read to Write Activity

Read the section titled *Safeguarding Our Financial System* in Chapter 24. Jot down any relevant facts. Then, write a statement in which you make an inference about how safe you feel using the banking system.

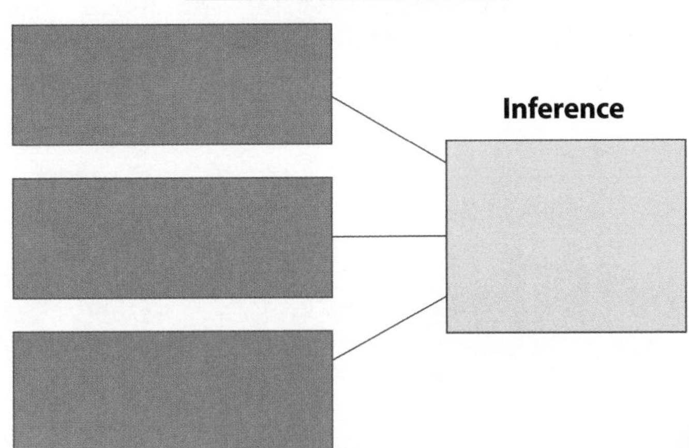

3 Apply It!

Choose one section from each chapter in this unit and create a chart like the one above. Read your facts to a partner and ask if your partner made a similar inference based on the facts you provided.

Chapter 23

Government and the Economy

Why It Matters

Promoting a stable, growing economy is a major goal of the federal government. The decisions that government makes affect our economic lives every day. As you read the chapter, list the specific ways in which the government affects you economically.

Civics ONLINE
Visit glencoe.com and enter QuickPass™ code CIV3093c23 for Chapter 23 resources.

Chapter Audio

BIG Ideas

Section 1: The Role of Government

Free enterprise is the freedom of individuals and businesses to operate and compete with a minimum of government interference or regulation. In order to encourage competition and prevent monopolies, governments take steps to regulate economies.

Section 2: Measuring the Economy

An economic system is the way a society organizes the production and consumption of goods and services. Our government plays a limited, but important, role in measuring and trying to balance the alternating periods of growth and decline called the business cycle.

Section 3: Government, the Economy, and You

People form governments to establish order, provide security, and accomplish common goals. A major focus of government programs is to help people in poverty.

Suspension bridge construction across the Houston, Texas, ship channel

FOLDABLES™ Study Organizer

Summarizing Information Study Foldable Make the following Foldable to help you summarize what you read about the role of government, how it measures the economy, and how you are involved.

Step 1 Mark the midpoint of the side edge of a sheet of paper.

Step 2 Fold the outside edges in to touch at the midpoint.

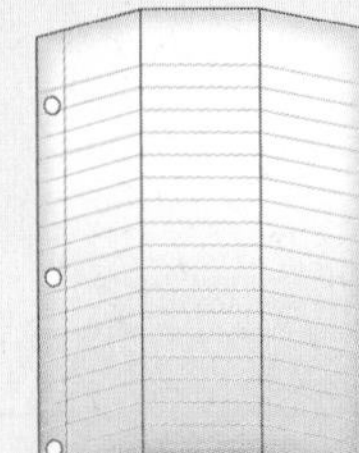

Step 3 Unfold the paper and label the three columns as shown.

Reading and Writing
As you read the chapter, note information about the three economics topics in each of the columns. Then write a summary of each topic using the information you noted.

Section Audio Spotlight Video

The Role of Government

Guide to Reading

Big Idea

Free enterprise is the freedom of individuals and businesses to operate and compete with a minimum of government interference or regulation.

Content Vocabulary

- private good *(p. 631)*
- public good *(p. 631)*
- externality *(p. 631)*
- monopoly *(p. 633)*
- antitrust law *(p. 633)*
- merger *(p. 633)*
- natural monopoly *(p. 634)*
- recall *(p. 635)*

Academic Vocabulary

- exclude *(p. 631)*
- achieve *(p. 632)*
- minimize *(p. 634)*

Reading Strategy

Analyzing Cause and Effect As you read, record the results of the government passing antitrust laws on a graphic organizer like the one below.

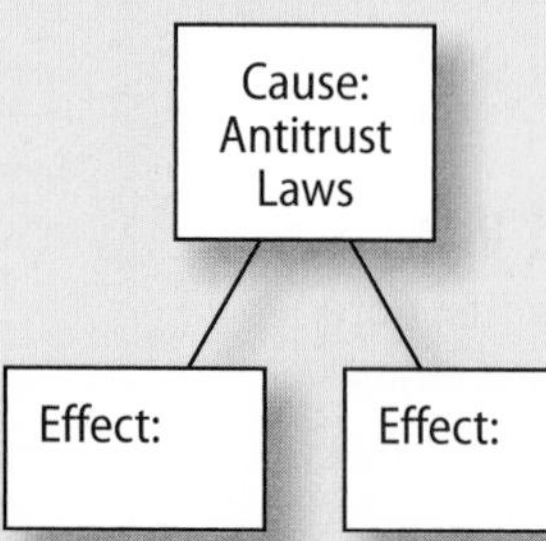

Real World Economics Fuels of the future are brought to life at a government-sponsored design exposition in Washington, DC. Scientists, businesspeople, and students are brought together to compete against each other with new ideas about technology and design. This student from Appalachian State University won an award for building a production facility that makes biodiesel fuel from used cooking oil and then recycles the oil's waste to make soap.

▼ **Award-winning student with biodiesel fuel**

Providing Public Goods

Main Idea **Governments usually provide public goods, while businesses usually provide private goods.**

Economics & You Would you like to live near an airport? Read to find out what economic idea might influence your decision.

Government plays several important roles in the economy. One role is providing goods and services—such as national defense—that private businesses do not provide.

What Are Private Goods? Most goods and services that businesses produce are **private goods,** or goods that, when consumed by one individual, cannot be consumed by another. Consumption of private goods and services is subject to the exclusion principle. This means that a person is **excluded,** or prevented, from using that good or service unless he or she pays for it. Private goods are the items we buy and replace, for example, clothes and food. Private services include such things as insurance, haircuts, medical services, auto care, and telephone services.

What Are Public Goods? This is in contrast to **public goods,** or goods that can be consumed by one person without preventing the consumption of the good by another. Consumption of public goods is subject to the nonexclusion principle. This means that no one is excluded from consuming the benefits of a public good whether or not he or she pays. Examples of public goods include public parks, public libraries, museums, highways, and street lighting.

Because of the difficulty of charging for public goods, the government usually provides them. If government did not provide these public goods and services, then the private sector would not provide them in adequate amounts because it is so difficult to get people to pay for them.

Public Goods Public goods include the highway system, national defense, and space exploration. ***Analyzing*** **Would the private sector provide these goods and services if the government did not?**

As a result, the production of public goods is one of the responsibilities of government. The government still has to pay for them, but it raises the money through taxes and then provides the products to everyone.

Dealing with Externalities

The government also plays a role in handling externalities. An **externality** is the unintended side effect of an action that affects someone not involved in the action. Suppose a company pays end-of-year bonuses to its workers. Restaurants and stores in the area will probably see their sales go up because the workers have more money to spend. These businesses experience externalities. They were not involved in the paying of bonuses, but they were affected by it.

Federal Regulatory Agencies

Federal Agency	Responsibility
Environmental Protection Agency (EPA)	Prevents air and water pollution
Centers for Disease Control and Prevention (CDC)	Considers all factors that affect the health of the nation
Occupational Safety and Health Administration (OSHA)	Makes sure that workplaces are safe and healthful
National Institutes of Health (NIH)	Serves as the nation's medical research agency
Food and Drug Administration (FDA)	Makes sure that food, drugs, and cosmetics are pure, effective, and truthfully labeled

Analyzing Charts

1. **Identifying** Which agency would regulate a kind of filtering system on a factory smokestack?
2. **Analyzing** Why do you think the National Institutes of Health is a national agency rather than a state-run agency?

Positive Externalities One reason that governments provide public goods is that these goods produce positive externalities. Everyone—not just drivers—benefits from good roads. Good roads make it cheaper to transport goods. As a result, those transported goods can sell for lower prices, which benefits everybody.

Governments can also take actions that indirectly lead to positive externalities. In the 1960s, the government wanted to put a man on the moon. The space program needed someone to develop smaller computers to **achieve,** or reach, this goal. The government provided money to researchers who developed tiny computer chips. Today, those chips are found in calculators, cars, household appliances, and cell phones, benefiting many people. Many government activities encourage positive externalities.

Negative Externalities Some externalities can be negative. That happens when an action harms an uninvolved third party. Suppose a chemical company tried to cut costs by dumping poisonous waste into a river. People who relied on the river water would suffer a negative externality from this pollution. One of the roles of government is to prevent these and other kinds of negative externalities.

Student Web Activity Visit glencoe.com and complete the Chapter 23 Web Activity.

Reading Check **Describing** How does a government usually pay for public goods and services?

Maintaining Competition

Main Idea **One government role is to ensure competition in the economy.**

Economics & You Have you ever played the game Monopoly? Read to find out for which economic idea this game is named.

Markets work best when there are large numbers of buyers and sellers. Sometimes, however, a market becomes controlled by a **monopoly,** a sole provider of a good or service. With no competition, a monopoly can charge any price it wants, and consumers may suffer.

Antitrust Laws

Historically, one of the goals of government in the United States has been to encourage competition in the economy. The government tries to meet this objective through its **antitrust laws,** or laws to control monopoly power and to preserve and promote competition.

Sherman Antitrust Act In 1890, the federal government passed the Sherman Antitrust Act. This law banned monopolies and other forms of business that prevented competition. In 1911, the government used it to break up the Standard Oil Company, which had a monopoly on oil. More than 70 years later, the government used the act again to regulate American Telephone and Telegraph (AT&T). This action created more competition in telephone service.

Clayton Act In 1914 Congress passed the Clayton Act to clarify the Sherman Act. The Clayton Act prohibited or limited a number of business practices that lessened competition; for example, charging high prices in an area where little competition existed. Another part of the Clayton Act restricted the use of the injunction against labor unions. It also gave legal support to peaceful strikes and boycotts.

Mergers

Whenever a **merger,** a combination of two or more companies to form a single business, threatens competition, government may step in to prevent it. For example, when the two leading office-supply stores, Staples and OfficeMax, wanted to merge, the federal government prevented it, arguing that a merger of these two giant firms would result in less competition and higher prices for consumers. On the other hand, the government did not prevent the 2001 merger of Hewlett-Packard and Compaq Computer, two leading personal-computer makers.

Oil Trust John D. Rockefeller took almost total control of the oil industry in the late 1800s until the government broke up his Standard Oil empire. ***Explaining*** **Why did the government want the Standard Oil Company broken up?**

American Biography

Elaine L. Chao (1953 –)

Elaine Chao is the first Asian American to hold the position of Secretary of Labor. She was named to the position in 2001 by President George W. Bush.

Chao's father came to the United States in 1958 as an employee of a Chinese shipping company and later opened his own shipping business. He brought his family to America three years later. Elaine graduated from Syosset High School in Westchester County, New York, and earned her bachelor's degree in economics from Mount Holyoke College. She was awarded an MBA from Harvard Business School and also studied at Columbia University, MIT, and Dartmouth College.

Before entering government service, Chao worked for Gulf Oil Corporation and as a loan specialist in the ship financing department of Citicorp. She was accepted as a White House Fellow in 1983 as a special assistant in the Office of Policy Development in the Ronald Reagan administration. Chao's other government positions include Deputy Secretary at the U.S. Department of Transportation, Chairman of the Federal Maritime Commission, and Deputy Maritime Administrator in the U.S. Department of Transportation. President George H. W. Bush nominated her to head the Peace Corps in 1991.

Chao, the mother of three daughters, is married to the former Assistant Majority Leader of the United States Senate, Senator Mitch McConnell of Kentucky.

Making a Difference CITIZENSHIP

Describing In what departments of government has Chao worked?

Regulating Market Activities

Recall that governments want to reduce negative externalities. To carry out this work, they regulate some activities by businesses. That is, government agencies make sure that businesses act fairly and follow the laws. Some of the federal agencies that regulate businesses are shown on the chart on page 632. Government regulation is needed in three important areas.

Natural Monopolies Sometimes it makes sense to have a single firm produce all of a particular good or service for a market. For example, it would not make sense to have three or four telephone companies compete in a local community if each company had to put up its own set of telephone poles.

This often leads to a **natural monopoly,** a market situation in which the costs of production are **minimized,** or lessened, by having a single firm produce the product. In exchange for having the market all to itself, the firm agrees to government regulation. This is why many public services such as natural gas and water are delivered by a single firm.

In the past, the telecommunications industry was usually considered a natural monopoly. Like water companies and railway companies, the existence of several telecommunications companies serving the same area would result in inefficiency.

The large size, or scale, of most natural monopolies seemed to give them economies of scale—by which they could produce the largest amount for the lowest cost. However, advances in technology are making these industries more competitive.The government is making moves to deregulate and open natural monopolies up for competition.

Advertising and Product Labels Government is also involved when it comes to truth in advertising and product labeling information. For example, some sellers may be tempted to give misleading information about a product in order to sell it. Even the content of food labels is important because some people are allergic to certain products such as eggs, milk, and peanuts.

The Food and Drug Administration (FDA) is the agency that deals with the purity, effectiveness, and labeling of food, drugs, and cosmetics. The Federal Trade Commission (FTC) deals with problems of false advertising and product claims. The FTC also administers antitrust laws forbidding unfair competition and price fixing.

The FTC has the power to review the advertising claims made about all products sold in interstate commerce. It may determine whether an advertisement for a product is false or unfair. If it is, the FTC can order the company to change the ad to comply with FTC standards. As a result of one ruling, cigarette manufacturers must place a health warning on cigarette packages.

Product Safety Product safety is another important area of regulation. From time to time, the Consumer Product Safety Commission recalls products that pose a safety hazard. In a **recall,** a company pulls a product off the market or agrees to change it to make it safe. In September 2006 producers needed to recall fresh spinach because of suspected E-coli contamination. That same month, 7 million Sony laptop batteries were recalled.

Reading Check **Explaining** What is a recall? Why are some products recalled?

Vocabulary

1. **Write** a paragraph related to government's role in the economy using the following terms: *private good, public good, externality, monopoly, antitrust law, merger, natural monopoly, recall.*

Main Ideas

2. **Explaining** What is a positive externality?
3. **Describing** How can a monopoly control the price of a product?

Critical Thinking

4. **Concluding** Think about something that your local government provides for citizens. Could this good or service be supplied by a private business? Why or why not?
5. **BIG Ideas** On a diagram like the one below, give an example of a negative externality and a positive externality of having an airport built near your home.

Airport	
Negative Externality	Positive Externality

CITIZENSHIP Activity

6. **Research** Interview a local business owner. Find out what he or she feels about government regulations that affect his or her business. Ask how the business owner would change government policies and programs.
7. **Persuasive Writing** Write a paragraph either supporting or disagreeing with this statement: Private businesses can do a better job than government of supplying water, sewer, and electricity to our community. Give reasons for your opinion.

Study Central™ To review this section, go to glencoe.com.

Issues to Debate

Does outsourcing jobs to other countries hurt America?

How would you feel if you had a good job for several years, then your company closed its American office and opened a new branch in another country? National news media often report the number of "jobs lost" in the United States from this outsourcing of jobs. Outsourcing is a controversial issue because it causes plant closings and unemployment in the United States. The number of jobs being outsourced has been growing. Who supports outsourcing? Not only do businesses like the idea, but some economists support it because it helps American business to be competitive in world markets. Outsourcing also helps consumers by lowering prices. So, does outsourcing hurt the American economy?

The Vietnamese workers at a Nike plant help the company export about 22 million pairs of shoes each year.

YES

Kathleen Madigan, a Business Outlook editor for *BusinessWeek,* warns that outsourcing is not only growing, but it is now hitting skilled and service jobs. Former jobs such as writing computer code are no longer complex enough to be secure, and American technology companies are moving them to other continents. What can be done? Madigan says, "The only way the U.S. will keep one rung ahead of the rest of the world is to ensure that we have a broadly educated workforce that keeps learning. At the corporate level, training programs would help current employees move up to better positions. And the government should overhaul jobless benefits to allow displaced workers the time and money to enter new careers."

—Kathleen Madigan, August 25, 2003

NO

Michael J. Mandel, *BusinessWeek* chief economist, believes that the United States should not fear outsourcing as long as we continue to be the most innovative economy. Our new technologies are providing more jobs than we are losing. "Despite anecdotes of well-paying jobs being sucked overseas, there's little evidence that educated workers, overall, are worse off than they were after the last recession." Mandel believes the key is staying at the top of the innovation ladder. "The biggest danger to U.S. workers isn't overseas competition. It's that we worry too much about other countries climbing up the ladder and not enough about finding the next higher rung for ourselves."

—Michael J. Mandel, August 25, 2003

Debating the Issue

1. **Defining** What is outsourcing?
2. **Identifying** What kind of jobs used to be secure from outsourcing?
3. **Comparing** What do the authors quoted above suggest the United States should do about outsourcing?
4. **Analyzing** Why might a stockholder or owner of an American company disagree with a worker in that company about outsourcing?

Section Audio   Spotlight Video

Section 2

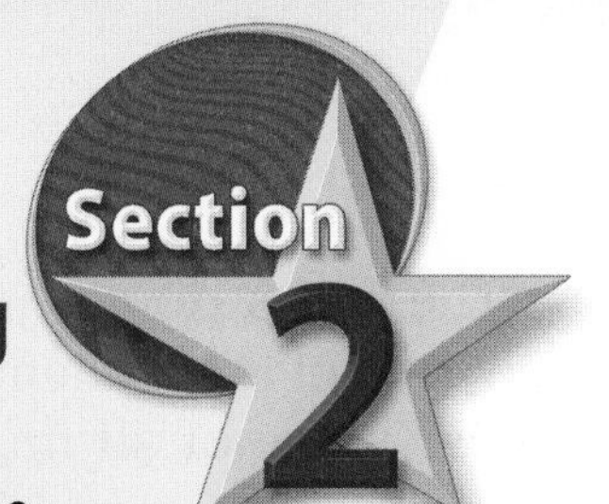

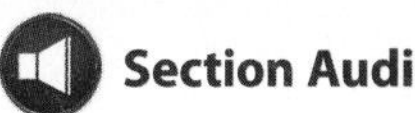

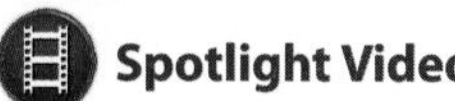

Measuring the Economy

Guide to Reading

Big Idea

An economic system is the way a society organizes the production and consumption of goods and services.

Content Vocabulary

- real GDP *(p. 638)*
- business cycle *(p. 638)*
- civilian labor force *(p. 640)*
- unemployment rate *(p. 640)*
- fiscal policy *(p. 641)*
- inflation *(p. 641)*
- consumer price index (CPI) *(p. 642)*

Academic Vocabulary

- period *(p. 638)*
- implement *(p. 641)*

Reading Strategy

Organizing Information

Create a graphic organizer like the one below to describe the expansion and recession that can take place in an economy.

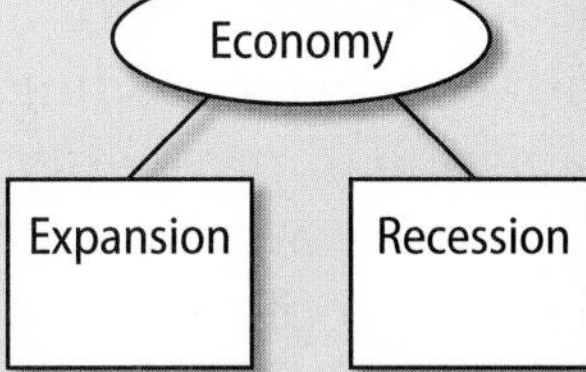

Real World Economics Traders at the Chicago Stock Exchange cheer after receiving encouraging news from the Federal Reserve. Organized in 1848, the Chicago Board of Trade was the first grain futures exchange in the United States. In its early history, the CBOT monitored only the business of agriculture. Today, cotton, grain, soy, and silver are just some of the items bought and sold in the electronic hubbub of the Chicago Board of Trade.

▼ **Traders in the Dow Pit of The Chicago Board of Trade**

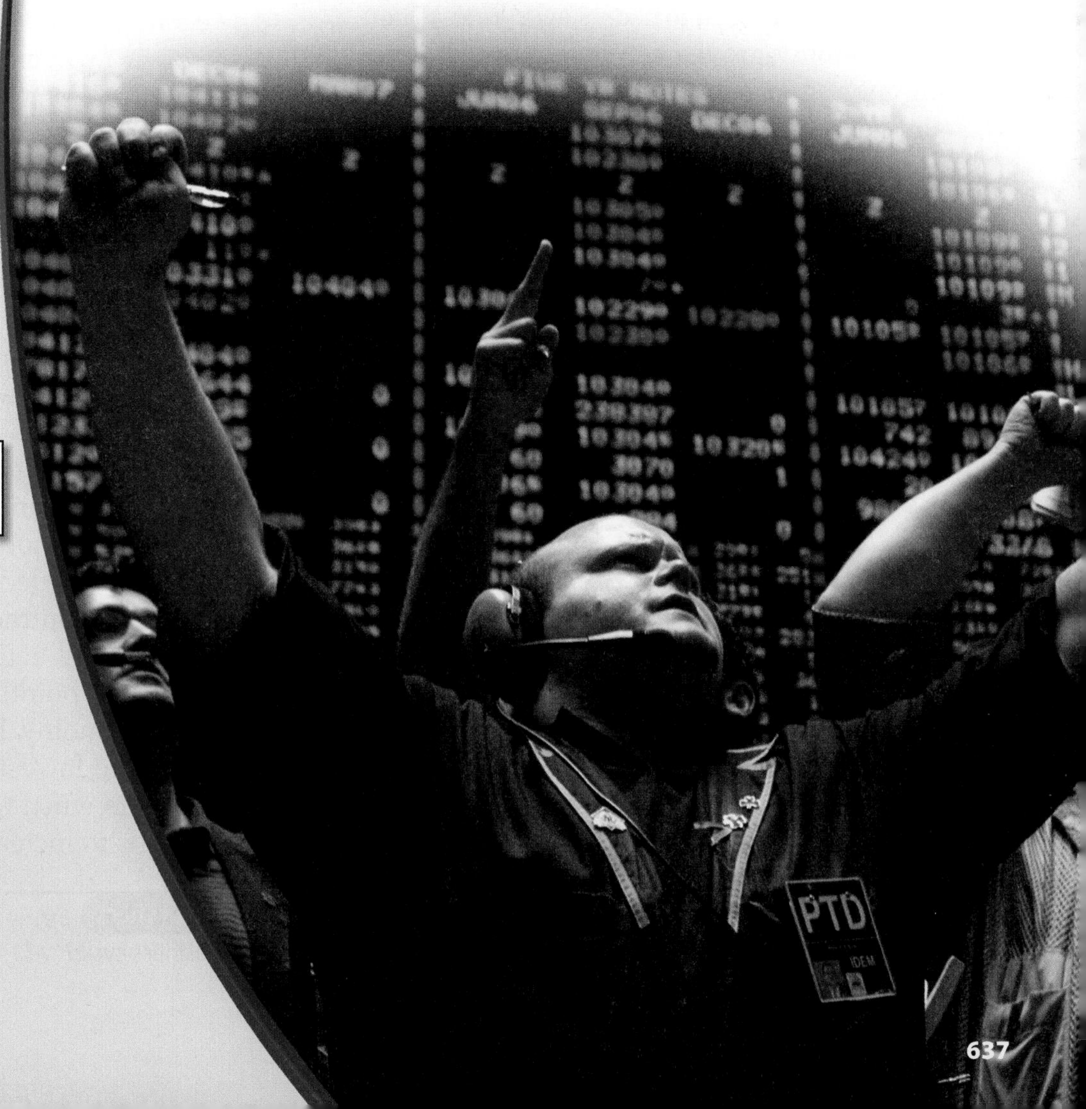

Measuring Growth

Main Idea **The real gross domestic product is the most accurate measure of an economy's performance.**

Economics & You Have you ever found that an item you wanted to buy had gone up in price? Read to find out how we have to adjust for this phenomenon when we measure economic growth.

Sometimes the economy grows, but sometimes it falters. How do economists decide which **period,** or phase, the economy is in? How do government leaders decide what to do about these changes in economic performance? You will learn the answers to these questions.

One measure of an economy's performance is whether or not it is growing. Economic growth is beneficial to nearly everyone. When the economy grows, businesses are producing more goods and services, and they usually have to hire more workers. People then have more money and buy more.

Model of the Business Cycle

Analyzing Graphs

1. **Identifying** What is the lowest point of the cycle called?
2. **Explaining** At what point in the cycle is the economy the strongest? What leads up to this point?

The gross domestic product (GDP) is a measure of the economy's output. GDP is the dollar value of all final goods and services produced in a country in a year.

Real GDP

Even if the country produces the same amount of goods and services from one year to the next, the gross domestic product could go up simply because prices increase. That would make it *seem* that the economy was growing even though it really was not. To avoid being misled in this way, another measure, **real GDP,** is used. Real GDP shows an economy's production after the distortions of price increases have been removed. This eliminates the false impression that output has gone up when prices go up.

The Business Cycle

The economy tends to grow over time, but it does not grow at a constant rate. Instead it goes through alternating intervals of growth and decline that we call the **business cycle.** The graph on this page shows an idealized business cycle. The line on the graph tracks real GDP. When the line moves upward, real GDP is growing. A downward slope shows a decline in real GDP.

According to this model, the phases of a business cycle begin with expansion leading to an economic peak—a period of prosperity. New businesses open, factories are producing at full capacity, and most people can find work. Eventually, however, real GDP levels off and begins to decline. During this part of the cycle, a contraction of the economy occurs. Business activity begins to slow down. At some point, the downward direction of the economy levels off in a trough. A trough is the lowest point in the business cycle. It occurs when real GDP levels off and slowly begins to increase.

Reading Check **Explaining** What are the phases of a business cycle?

Political Cartoons

Gary Markstein/Copley News Service

Every year, more than half of all Americans do volunteer work

role in it. One of the responsibilities of citizens is to help make their

Wages for American workers are the topic of this cartoon by Gary Markstein.

1. **What railroad symbolism do you see in this image?**
2. **How does Markstein use these symbols to comment on wages and on the economy?**
3. **Do you think Markstein is optimistic or pessimistic about higher wages for American workers? Explain.**

Business Fluctuations

Main Idea The economy goes through alternating periods of growth and decline.

Economics & You What did you do the last time you were a little short of cash? Read to find out one way our country copes with economic ups and downs.

In the real world, the business cycles are not as regular as the model shows. An entire business cycle is measured from peak to peak.

Expansions

An economic expansion takes place when real GDP goes up. It does not matter whether the economy is growing by a little or by a lot. As long as the real GDP is higher from one period to the next, the economy is expanding. At some point, real GDP reaches its highest point in an expansion. Then it starts to decline.

Expansions are normally longer than recessions. The longest peacetime expansion in U.S. history lasted from March of 1991 until March of 2001, exactly 10 years.

Recession

A recession takes place when real GDP goes down for six straight months, although most last longer than that. On the business cycle graph, the recessions are shown by a colored background. Fortunately, recessions tend to be shorter than expansions, with the average recession lasting about one year. Even so, recessions are painful times. When the economy declines, many people lose their jobs.

If a recession becomes severe, it may turn into a depression—a state of the economy with large numbers of people out of work, acute shortages, and excess capacity in manufacturing plants.

Unemployment

Another way of measuring the economy is to look at employment. Economists start by identifying the civilian labor force, which includes all civilians 16 years old or older who are either working or are looking for work. In the United States, about half of all people belong to the **civilian labor force.**

The **unemployment rate** is the percentage of people in the civilian labor force who are not working but are looking for jobs. As the graph on page 642 shows, the unemployment rate tends to rise sharply during recessions and then comes down slowly afterward.

Changes in the unemployment rate are important in terms of the economy as a whole. A 1 percent drop in the unemployment rate results in a 2 percent rise in total income in the economy. In 2006, total income in the American economy was about $13.3 trillion. As a result, a 1 percent drop in unemployment would increase total income by about $266 *billion.*

Of course, the personal impact of unemployment and lost income can be tremendous. Some people cut back on luxuries, while others must cut back on basic needs such as health care. Some families go deeper into debt by buying more goods on credit.

Times of high unemployment create stress for many people. High unemployment becomes a problem that requires some government action.

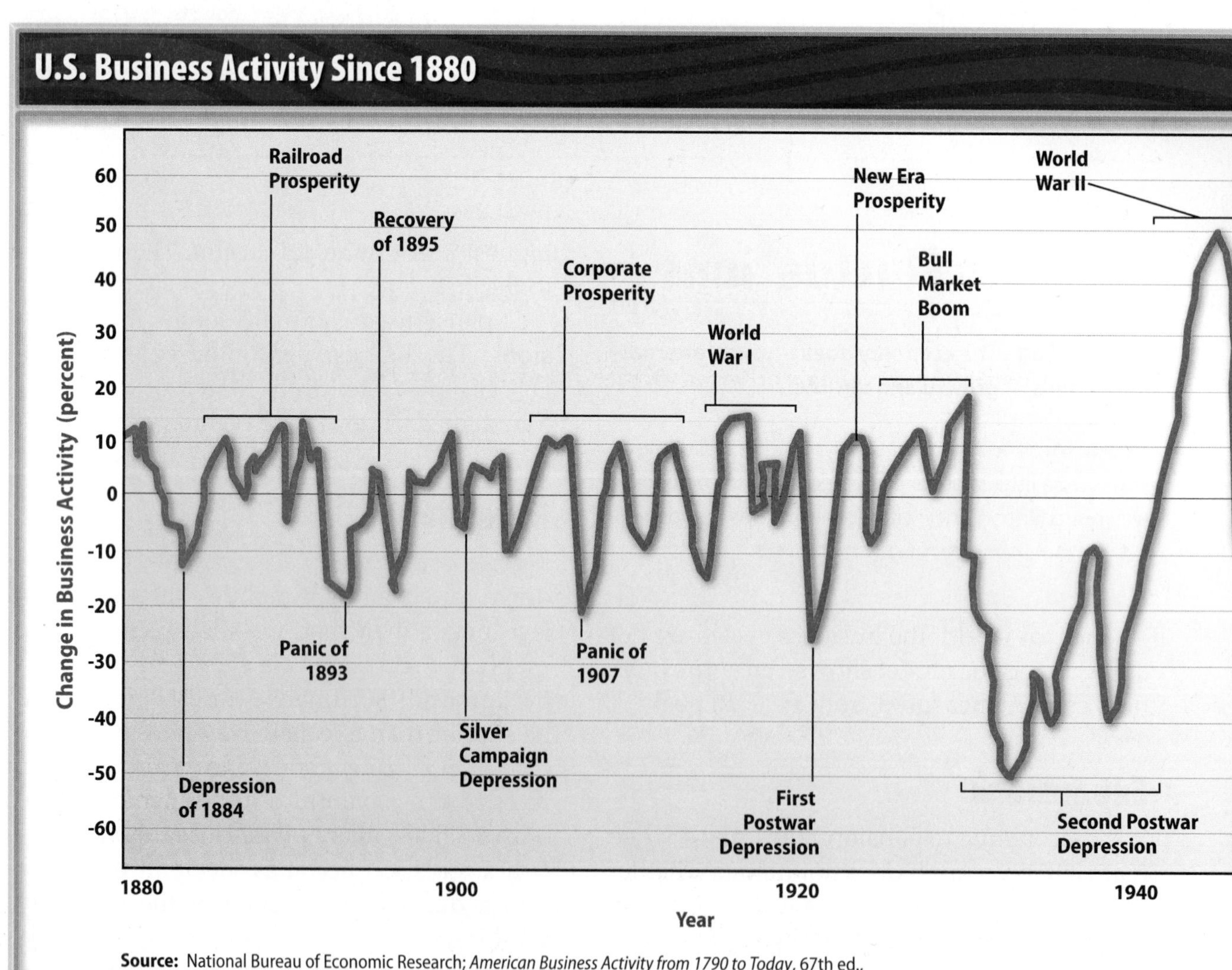

Source: National Bureau of Economic Research; *American Business Activity from 1790 to Today*, 67th ed., Ameritrust Co., January 1996, plus author's projections.

Fiscal Policy

When the government does step in, it uses **fiscal policy,** or changes in government spending or taxation. The government might cut taxes, expecting people to spend more and businesses to hire more workers. Sometimes, it increases spending to spur businesses to hire workers and boost production. Fiscal policy is a key tool because it can affect the total amount of output—gross domestic product.

Unfortunately, political differences often prevent the best use of fiscal policy. Effective fiscal policies are difficult to **implement,** or carry out, when politicians differ about whether to cut taxes or to increase spending.

When crises are especially severe, the government may take drastic action. In 2008, turmoil hit financial markets. Investment banks collapsed or faced bankruptcy due to bad loans and a housing slump. With the economic crisis spreading globally, Congress passed a gigantic rescue plan that called for pumping 700 billion dollars into the shattered U.S. financial system.

Price Stability

Another important indicator of an economy's performance is **inflation.** This is a sustained increase in the general level of prices. Inflation hurts the economy because it reduces the purchasing power of money and may alter the decisions people make.

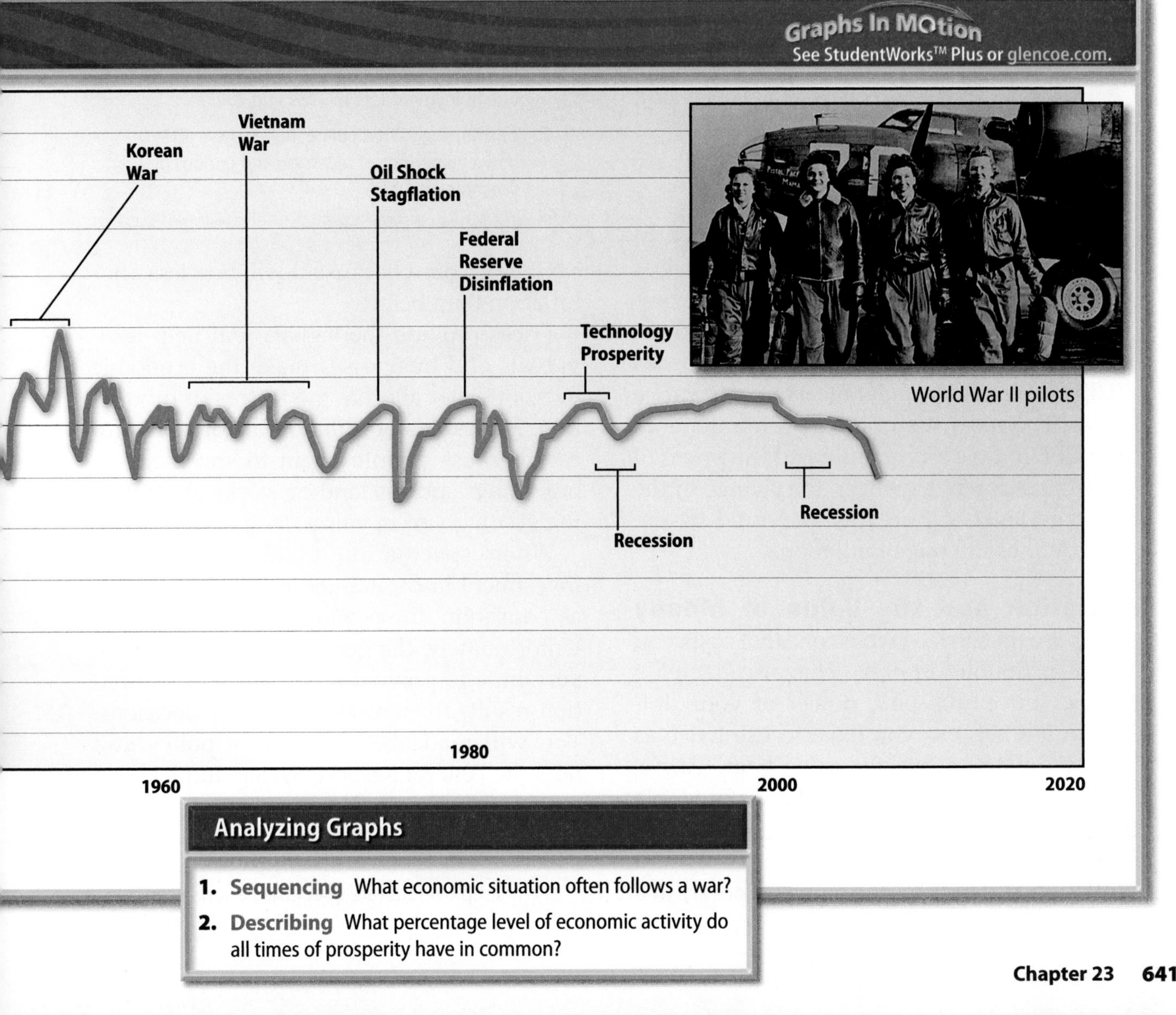

World War II pilots

Analyzing Graphs

1. **Sequencing** What economic situation often follows a war?
2. **Describing** What percentage level of economic activity do all times of prosperity have in common?

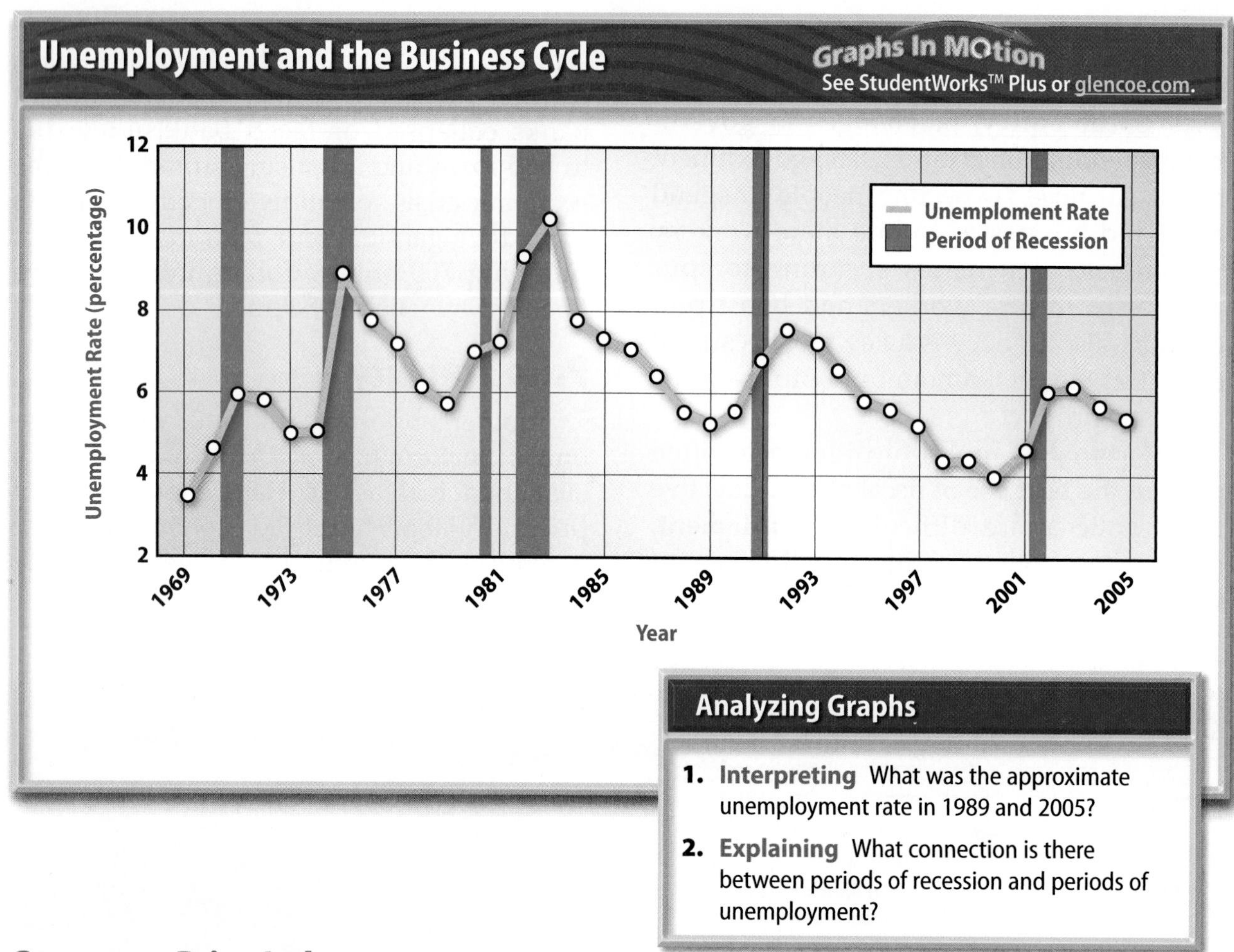

Analyzing Graphs

1. **Interpreting** What was the approximate unemployment rate in 1989 and 2005?
2. **Explaining** What connection is there between periods of recession and periods of unemployment?

Consumer Price Index To keep track of inflation, the government samples prices every month for about 400 products commonly used by consumers. The prices of these 400 items make up the **consumer price index (CPI),** which is a popular measure of the price level. Typically, the prices of some items in the CPI go up every month, and the prices of others go down. However, the change in the average level of prices as measured by the CPI defines the rate of inflation.

Inflation and the Value of Money

Suppose that an ice-cream cone that costs you a dollar doubles in price. This price increase causes the purchasing power of your dollar to fall because you have to use twice as many dollars to buy the same item. This is why inflation is particularly hard on people who have fixed incomes—people who get a pension or other fixed amount of money. Inflation also reduces the value of money in a savings account because it will buy less after inflation than before.

Prices provide the signals that help individuals and businesses make the economic decisions that allocate the factors of production. High rates of inflation distort this process because people begin to speculate, or buy things such as land or works of art they think will go up in value.

When speculation takes the place of investment in capital goods or services such as education, the economy begins to suffer. Unfortunately, the government itself can do very little to prevent inflation because inflation results from monetary policy decisions. You will read about monetary policy and how the Federal Reserve System implements monetary policy in the next chapter.

Reading Check **Describing** How does a drop in the unemployment rate affect the nation's economy?

Stocks and Stock Markets

Main Idea **Stock markets are usually good indicators of the health of the economy.**

Economics & You You have probably heard a statement like this on the news: "The Dow Jones Industrial Average rose 2 percent today." Read to find out what statements like these tell us about the economy.

Investors normally want to buy stock if they think they will make money on it. Profits from stock come in two ways—from dividends or from capital gains. Dividends are a share of the corporation's profits that are distributed to shareholders. A capital gain occurs when stock can be sold for more than it originally cost to buy. Suppose a person buys stock at $20 a share and sells it for $30. The person has had an increase in his or her capital, or wealth, of $10 a share. Of course, the value of stock may also fall. If a person decides to sell stock at a lower price than he or she paid for it, that person suffers a capital loss. Money may be made or lost on government bonds in much the same way.

Why Stock Prices Change

The price of a company's stock, like most other things, is determined by supply and demand. Factors such as changes in sales or profits, rumors of a possible takeover, or news of a technological breakthrough can change the demand for a company's stock and, therefore, its price.

The NYSE To be listed on the New York Stock Exchange, a corporation must prove to the exchange that it is in good financial condition. ***Analyzing*** **How does inflation affect the value of stocks sold on the NYSE?**

Stock Market Indexes Because most investors are concerned about the performance of their stocks, they often consult stock indexes. These are statistical measures that track stock prices over time and give us an idea of the well-being of the stock market as a whole. The Dow-Jones Industrial Average (DJIA) and Standard and Poor's (S&P) are the two most popular indexes. The DJIA tracks prices of 30 representative stocks. The S&P 500 index tracks the prices of 500 large stocks.

Stock Exchanges Stocks in publicly traded companies are bought and sold in a stock market, or a stock exchange, a specific location where shares of stock are bought and sold. The exchange makes buying and selling easy, but you do not have to actually travel to a stock exchange in order to buy or sell stock. Instead, you can call a stockbroker, who can buy or sell your stocks.

Most stocks in the United States are traded on the New York Stock Exchange (NYSE), the American Stock Exchange, or an electronic stock market like the NASDAQ. Computer technology and electronic trading allow investors to trade major stocks around the clock, anywhere in the world.

The Stock Market and the Economy

Indexes like the DJIA and the S&P 500 do more than tell us about the level of stock prices—they reveal investors' expectations about the future. If investors expect economic growth to be rapid, profits high, and unemployment low, then stock prices tend to rise in what is referred to as a "bull market." If investors are pessimistic, stock prices could fall in what is called a "bear market."

Reading Check **Explaining** What are two ways investors make money on stocks?

Vocabulary

1. **Write** complete sentences using each of the following terms that will help explain its meaning: *real GDP, business cycle, civilian labor force, unemployment rate, fiscal policy, inflation, consumer price index (CPI).*

Main Ideas

2. **Comparing** How do GDP and real GDP differ?
3. **Describing** How is the unemployment rate computed?
4. **Explaining** How does supply and demand affect a stock's price?

Critical Thinking

5. **Evaluating** Do you think it is the government's responsibility to try to balance the ups and downs of the business cycle? Justify your answer.
6. **BIG Ideas** On a chart like the one below, evaluate how a sharp increase in inflation might affect people.

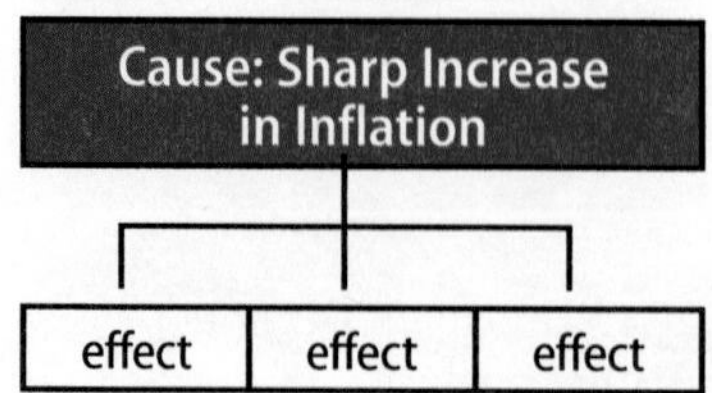

7. **Analyzing Visuals** Study the graph showing the phases of the business cycle on page 638. How are the recessionary periods in this graph illustrated?

CITIZENSHIP Activity

8. **Creative Writing** Write a play, short story, poem, or song about a family coping with a down period in the business cycle or a time of high inflation. Share your creative work with the class.

Study Central™ To review this section, go to glencoe.com.

Financial Literacy

How Much Does It Cost?

If something cost $64 in 1965, what would be the equivalent price in 2008 dollars? Using the Consumer Price Index (CPI) provides an answer. The CPI is a measure of the average change in prices over time for a specific collection of goods and services.

Average Gas Prices, 1950-2008

Year	Price Per Gallon	Price Per Gallon (adjusted for inflation)
1950	$0.23	$2.06
1955	$0.24	$1.85
1960	$0.26	$1.89
1965	$0.26	$1.78
1970	$0.30	$1.67
1975	$0.48	$1.92
1980	$1.05	$2.75
1985	$1.01	$2.02
1990	$0.97	$1.60
1995	$0.96	$1.36
2001	$1.45	$1.77
2002	$1.31	$1.60
2003	$1.38	$1.62
2004	$1.67	$1.92
2005	$2.20	$2.43
2006	$3.03	$3.24
2007	$3.26	$3.39
2008*	$3.94	$3.94

Source: U.S. Department of Energy.

*May 2008

Measuring Price Changes

The CPI can be used to compare the price level in one year with price levels in earlier or later periods.

Use this formula to calculate:

2008 Price = 1965 Price x (2008 CPI/1965 CPI)

Here's the calculation:

2008 Price = $64 x (216.5/31.5)

2008 Price = $64 x 6.87

2008 Price = $439.68

If something cost $64 in 2008, what would be the equivalent price in 1965? To calculate, use this formula:

1965 price = 2008 price x (1965 CPI/2008 CPI)

Here's the calculation:

1965 Price = $64 x (31.5/216.5)

1965 Price = $64 x .145

1965 Price = $9.28

Analyzing Economics

1. **Analyzing** What, if anything, surprises you about the average price of gasoline over time?
2. **Calculating** From one year to the next, which year shows the biggest increase in the actual price?
3. **Calculating** From one year to the next, which year shows the biggest increase in price adjusted for inflation?

Section 3

Government, the Economy, and You

Guide to Reading

Big Idea
People form governments to establish order, provide security, and accomplish common goals.

Content Vocabulary
- food stamps *(p. 648)*
- Women, Infants, and Children (WIC) *(p. 648)*
- workfare *(p. 649)*
- progressive income tax *(p. 649)*
- Earned Income Tax Credit (EITC) *(p. 649)*

Academic Vocabulary
- survive *(p. 648)*
- supplement *(p. 649)*

Reading Strategy
Comparing Information On a diagram like the one below, identify four major government programs or policies that are meant to ease the problem of poverty.

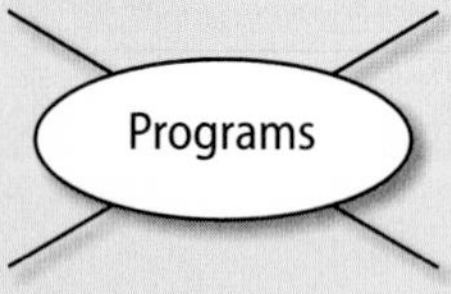

Programs

Real World Economics "Give me a head start!" exclaims this student enrolled in the federally funded preschool program Head Start. For over 40 years, the Head Start program has been a vital educational resource for lower-income families and their preschoolers. It provides educational support to improve children's readiness level for public school. Additional programs are offered in the areas of health, nutrition, and family support. Today, Head Start supporters are urging Congress to increase funding.

Louisiana 5-year-old successfully finishes lesson with Head Start teacher

Income Inequality

Main Idea **Education, family wealth, and discrimination are reasons for income differences.**

Economics & You Think of a wealthy family in your community. How did they earn their wealth? Read to find out three key factors that can influence a person's income.

Though the United States is a wealthy country, not all Americans are personally wealthy. Income levels vary for many reasons. Some people—such as Tiger Woods, Beyoncé, and Stephen King—have special talents that enable them to earn huge amounts of money.

Education Opportunities Students from Columbia University in New York City celebrate graduation. ***Explaining*** **What other factors besides education determine a person's future income?**

Three Influences on Income

Incomes differ for several reasons. Education, family wealth, and discrimination are common reasons for income differences.

Education Level of education has a major impact on a person's income. The average income of a college graduate—someone with a bachelor's degree—is nearly twice the average income of a high school graduate. More advanced degrees increase income even more. Education puts people in a better position to get the higher-paying jobs that require a higher level of skills.

Because education contributes so much to income, the federal government tries to encourage people to improve their education. This is why there are many programs that encourage education, from free or subsidized lunches to college grants and low-interest loans.

Family Wealth Some people are born into wealth. Having wealthy parents often gives people access to excellent colleges. In addition, wealthy parents can set up their children in a business or pass on their own business.

Discrimination Discrimination is one of the reasons some people do not receive higher incomes. Women and members of minority groups may not be hired into jobs that pay well, or they may not receive promotions for which they are eligible. In addition, salaries for men are normally higher than those for women. This difference is partly a result of discrimination against women.

The government has passed several laws to reduce discrimination. The Equal Pay Act of 1963 requires equal pay for jobs that require equivalent skills and responsibilities. The Civil Rights Act of 1964 bans discrimination on the basis of gender, race, color, religion, and national origin. The Equal Employment Opportunity Act of 1972 strengthened earlier laws. The Americans with Disabilities Act of 1990 extended this protection to people with physical and mental disabilities. People who suffer discrimination can use the courts to enforce these laws.

Reading Check **Explaining** How does the government encourage people to obtain an education?

Poverty

Main Idea **Poverty is a major problem in America.**

Economics & You Do you know a person with a disability who receives money from the government? Read to find out why government helps support people with disabilities.

People living in poverty or those who are at the bottom of the income scale receive special attention from the government. The most effective government programs are those that have incentives that encourage people to go back to work.

Poverty Guidelines and Programs

The government uses poverty guidelines to determine whether someone is eligible for certain programs. These guidelines are revised annually and are based on conservative estimates of how much it costs to buy enough food, clothing, and shelter to **survive,** or exist.

People in Poverty In 2006, a single person was considered to be in poverty if his or her annual income was $9,800, or about $27 a day. Today, there are almost 37 million people who fall *below* this income guideline.

Welfare Programs Most welfare programs are federal programs. The federal **food stamp** program serves millions of Americans. The goal of the food stamp program is to alleviate hunger and malnutrition by allowing low-income households to obtain a more healthful diet.Some states use electronic debit systems in place of coupons. The program gives low-income families the opportunity to buy food with Electronic Benefits Transfer (EBT) cards.

Another federal welfare program is the **Women, Infants, and Children (WIC)** program. It provides help with nutrition and health care to low-income women, infants, and children up to age 5.

TIME™ Teens in *Action*

Erika Herman

Erika Herman, 18, of Bethesda, Maryland, sees potential in people—that is why she started Project Hidden GEMS (Giving, Educating, Making Solutions).

QUESTION: Why did you create Hidden GEMS?

ANSWER: The idea clicked in 2004 at a conference about poverty that I attended in Washington, D.C. I met a homeless man who said poetry was his passion but that no one was ever willing to publish his work. I talked to my friend Emily Grunewald about creating a magazine [Hidden GEMS] for people like him. Our goals are to provide an outlet for expression for homeless and inner-city writers; to break down stereotypes and promote awareness among diverse groups of people; and to raise money for individuals and organizations in need.

Q: Have you seen changes in people that work on the magazine?

A: It gives hope to many homeless individuals whose talents would otherwise be ignored. In one case, a homeless man gained enough self-confidence from seeing that people cared about his writing that he worked hard to get a job. Now he's supporting himself in his own apartment.

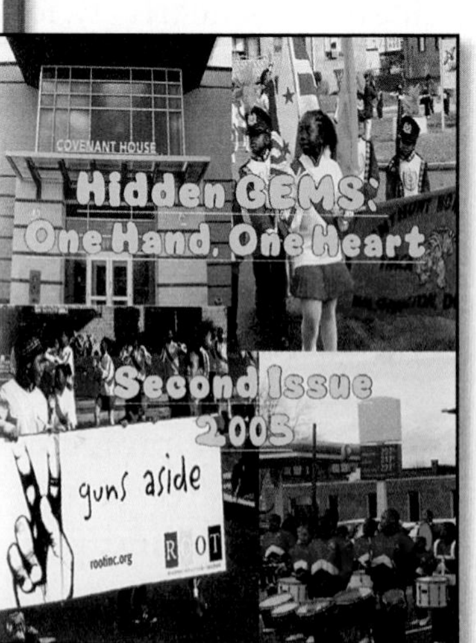

Making a Difference — CITIZENSHIP

Explaining What does Erika mean by breaking down stereotypes?

Income Assistance Other programs pay cash to certain people. Additional, or **Supplemental** Security Income (SSI), for instance, gives payments to blind or disabled people and to persons age 65 and older. Temporary Assistance to Needy Families (TANF) is another direct cash program. TANF makes payments to families who need help because a parent is dead, disabled, or absent. The number of months that a recipient can receive benefits is limited. The intent of this limit is to make sure that people do not rely on the program but look for paying work.

Workfare **Workfare** is a term used to describe programs that require welfare recipients to exchange some of their labor in exchange for benefits. Most of the programs are run at the state level, and most are designed to teach people the skills they need to succeed in a job. Many states also require some form of workfare if families want to receive TANF benefits. People who are part of workfare often assist law enforcement officials, sanitation and highway crews, or perform other community service work.

Tax Policies Another way the government helps poor people is with a **progressive income tax.** That means that the tax rate is lower at lower incomes and higher for higher incomes. This helps lower-income people by taking a smaller proportion of their income in taxes. The federal government provides additional help for low-income families and individuals. Many workers use the federal **Earned Income Tax Credit (EITC),** which gives tax credits and even cash payments to qualified workers. This program benefits about 20 million working families every year.

Reading Check **Summarizing** How does the government use poverty guidelines?

Vocabulary

1. **Define** these terms from the section and make a set of flash cards to help you learn them: *food stamps; Women, Infants, and Children (WIC); workfare; progressive income tax; Earned Income Tax Credit (EITC).*

Main Ideas

2. **Describing** What does the Americans with Disabilities Act provide?
3. **Describing** What does Supplemental Security Income provide?

Critical Thinking

4. **BIG Ideas** Which of the antipoverty programs do you think is the most effective? Explain your answer.
5. **Identifying** On a graphic organizer like the one below, identify the groups of people who are helped by government income assistance programs.

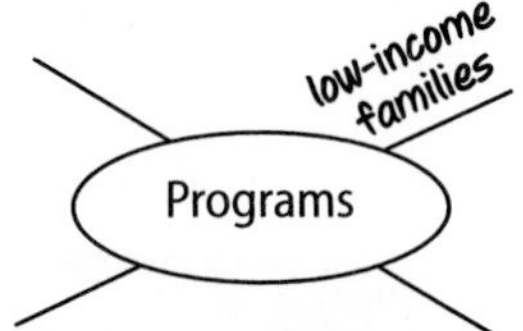

CITIZENSHIP Activity

6. **Summarizing** Scan a local newspaper for a short editorial or article about income. Take notes by writing down the main idea and supporting facts. Summarize the article using only your notes.
7. **Persuasive Writing** Write a paragraph either supporting or disagreeing with this statement: Welfare programs have a negative effect on poor people and should be eliminated. Give reasons for your opinion.

Study Central™ To review this section, go to glencoe.com.

Landmark Supreme Court Case Studies

McCulloch v. Maryland

How did the national government expand its financial powers to meet the needs of a growing nation?

Background of the Case

Alexander Hamilton, the nation's first secretary of the Treasury, urged Congress to pass a law establishing a national bank. With the backing of President George Washington, Congress did so in 1791. The bank's funds were used to build roads, canals, and other projects that would help the nation grow. The first bank lasted until 1811; a second bank was chartered in 1816.

Many citizens withdrew deposits from state banks and reinvested them in the new national bank. Angry over the competition from the national bank, states worked to weaken it. Some states, including Maryland, taxed national bank branches operating inside their boundaries. James McCulloch of the Baltimore branch bank refused to pay the state's $15,000 tax. Maryland sued him and won in a state court. McCulloch appealed to the Supreme Court.

The Decision

The Court had to decide if the national bank was constitutional, even though not mentioned in the Constitution. Chief Justice John Marshall wrote the unanimous decision on March 6, 1819:

> ***"[T]here is no phrase . . . [that] excludes incidental or implied powers; and which requires that everything granted shall be expressly and minutely described. . . . [T]he states have no power, by taxation or otherwise . . . to impede the . . . operations of the constitutional laws enacted by Congress."***
>
> —Justice John Marshall

Federal Reserve Bank, Washington, D.C.

Marshall based the ruling on Article I, Section 8, which gives Congress powers to "make all laws . . . necessary and proper" for carrying out its duties.

Why It Matters

The Court's unpopular decision upheld the national bank and denied states the power to tax it. The modern Federal Reserve System eventually grew out of the national bank concept.

The case established the implied powers doctrine, which meant Congress had, under the "necessary and proper" clause, a wide range of powers to carry out the powers that the Constitution *expressly* gave it. *McCulloch v. Maryland* also established the principle of national supremacy, which forbids the states from intruding into the constitutional operations of the national government.

Analyzing the Court Decision

1. **Describing** How did Marshall justify the *McCulloch* decision?
2. **Analyzing** Do you think the decision affected the ways Americans viewed our federal system?

Chapter 23

Visual Summary

Government and the Economy

Government's Role

- Government provides public goods.
- Government regulates the economy to ensure competition.

Measuring the Economy

- Real GDP is GDP that has been adjusted for inflation.
- The real gross domestic product is the most accurate measure of an economy's performance.

Workers with more education earn more money

The health of the Stock Exchange is important to the economy

- Government must deal with unemployment, inflation, and periods of growth and decline called the business cycle.
- Stock markets are usually good indicators of the health of the economy.

The Problem of Poverty

- Education, family wealth, and discrimination are reasons for income differences.
- Government uses several different programs and policies to combat poverty.

Laborers benefit from working for government-funded programs

STUDY TO GO Study anywhere, anytime! Download quizzes and flash cards to your PDA from glencoe.com.

Chapter

23 ASSESSMENT

TEST-TAKING TIP

Stay focused on your own test. Do not be distracted if others are finishing early.

Reviewing Vocabulary

Directions: Choose the word(s) that best completes the sentence.

1. Whenever two or more companies try to form a(n) _______ that threatens competition, the government may take action to stop it.

A antitrust
B monopoly
C merger
D externality

2. What is the term for a nation's economic production that has been adjusted for price changes?

A TANF
B real GDP
C business cycle
D inflation

3. Changes in the _______ determine inflation.

A fiscal policy
B consumer price index
C stock market
D unemployment rate

4. What is the term for an income tax whose rate increases as income level rises?

A public good
B progressive tax
C regressive tax
D real GDP

Reviewing Main Ideas

Directions: Choose the best answer for each question.

Section 1 *(pp. 630–635)*

5. A(n) _______ is a good in which one person's consumption takes away from another person's consumption.

A public good
B private good
C monopoly
D externality

6. One of the roles of the Federal Trade Commission is to _______.

A produce public goods
B reduce negative externalities
C supervise corporate mergers
D deal with the problems of false advertising

Section 2 *(pp. 637–644)*

7. A period of business recovery when economic activity increases is called _______.

A a recession
B real GDP
C the business cycle
D an expansion

8. Which explanation best explains the effects of inflation?

A Consumers have more products to choose from.
B Inflation erodes the purchasing power of the dollar.
C Inflation results in lower prices.
D Demand increases because prices are higher.

Section 3 *(pp. 646–649)*

9. What law provides protection for people with physical and mental disabilities?

A Clayton Act
B Sherman Antitrust Act
C Americans with Disabilities Act
D Supplemental Security Income

10. What program provides help for nutrition and health care to low-income families?

A Clayton Act
B Federal Trade Commission
C Americans with Disabilities Act
D Women, Infants, and Children (WIC) program

GO ON

Critical Thinking

Directions: Choose the best answer for each question.

2006 Poverty Guidelines

Size of Family Unit	Poverty Guidelines
1	$ 9,800
2	$13,200
3	$16,600
4	$20,000
5	$23,400
6	$26,800
7	$30,200
8	$33,600

Source: Department of Health and Human Services.

Poverty guidelines help the government determine financial eligibility for certain federal programs.

11. What was the measure of poverty in 2006 for a family of four?

A $13,200

B $16,600

C $20,000

D $41,000

12. For family units with more than eight members, how much must be added for each additional member to meet the poverty guidelines?

A $1,000

B $2,200

C $3,400

D $9,800

Document-Based Questions

Directions: Analyze the following document and answer the short-answer questions that follow.

In speaking before Congress, former U.S. Treasury secretary John W. Snow discusses inflation.

> ***Government and Inflation***
>
> *But clearly an economy that's growing and expanding like this one—and it certainly is doing that with a high GDP output, employment numbers strong, capacity utilization strong—that's an environment in which the Fed needs to continually be alert to early signs of inflation.*
>
> —John W. Snow, Secretary of the Treasury

13. What things about the economy does Snow recognize are strong?

14. Evaluate how a sharp increase in inflation might affect the following people:

- a person who has just withdrawn a considerable amount from a savings account
- a doctor on staff at a large hospital
- a retired autoworker on a fixed pension

Extended-Response Question

15. If we were to enter a period of recession, what would likely happen to demand? What would likely happen to the unemployment rate? The poverty rate? Write an essay in which you answer these questions and provide the reasons for your answers.

STOP

For additional test practice, use Self-Check Quizzes—Chapter 23 on glencoe.com.

Need Extra Help?

If you missed question...	1	2	3	4	5	6	7	8	9	10	11	12	13	14	15
Go to page...	633	638	642	649	631	635	639	641	647	648	648	648	642	642	639

Chapter 24

Money and Banking

Why It Matters

Our market economy is based on the idea of voluntary exchange—we exchange money for the goods and services we need. You live in a world where this exchange usually involves money. It is the primary medium of exchange for goods and services.

Civics ONLINE
Visit glencoe.com and enter QuickPass™ code CIV3093c24 for Chapter 24 resources.

Chapter Audio

BIG Ideas

Section 1: What Is Money?

The basis of the market economy is voluntary exchange. In the American economy, the exchange usually involves money in return for a good or service. People are willing to accept money in exchange for goods, and financial institutions give people a safe place to deposit their money or take out loans.

Section 2: The Federal Reserve System

Political and economic institutions evolve to help individuals and groups accomplish their goals. The central bank of the United States is the Federal Reserve System. It controls the money supply, serves as the government's bank, and watches over the banking industry.

Section 3: How Banks Operate

Political and economic institutions evolve to help individuals and groups accomplish their goals. Banks offer important financial services to millions of people.

Sorting $100 bills at the U.S. Department of the Treasury

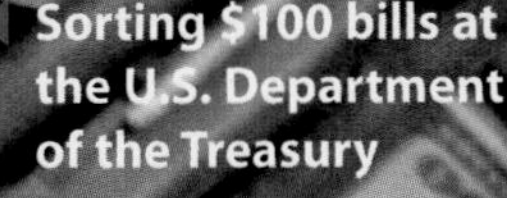

FOLDABLES™ Study Organizer

Evaluating Information Study Foldable Make the following Foldable to help you evaluate the workings of the Federal Reserve.

Step 1 Mark the midpoint of the side edge of a sheet of paper. Then fold in the outside edges to meet at the midpoint.

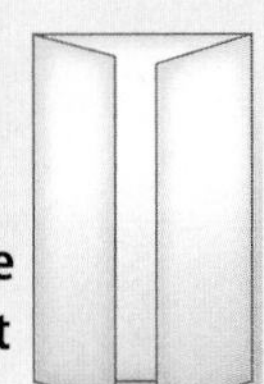

Step 2 Fold in half from side to side.

Step 3 Open and cut the inside fold lines to form four tabs. Label the tabs *what, when, where* and *why.*

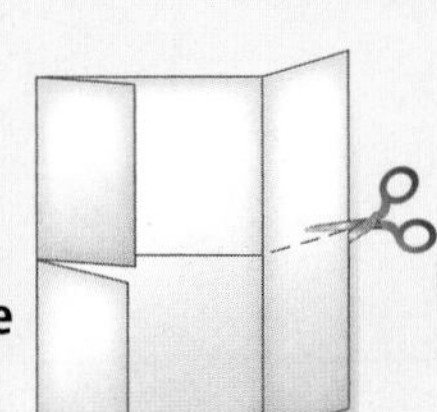

Reading and Writing
As you read the chapter, note information about the Federal Reserve under the appropriate tab.

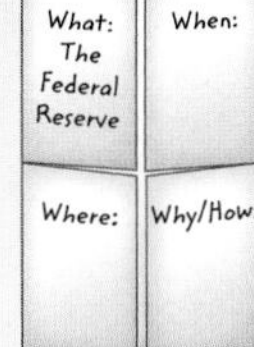

Section Audio

Spotlight Video

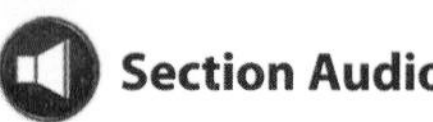

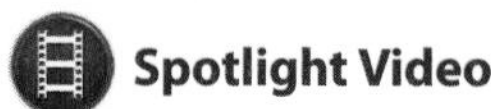

Section 1

What Is Money?

Guide to Reading

Big Idea

The basis of the market economy is voluntary exchange. In the American economy, the exchange usually involves money in return for a good or service.

Content Vocabulary

- coin *(p. 657)*
- currency *(p. 657)*
- commercial bank *(p. 658)*
- savings and loan association (S&L) *(p. 658)*
- credit union *(p. 658)*

Academic Vocabulary

- obvious *(p. 657)*
- medium *(p. 657)*

Reading Strategy

Describing As you read the section, complete a graphic organizer like the one below that illustrates three functions of money.

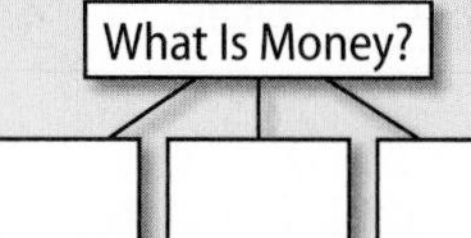

Real World Economics No flaws allowed here. This Treasury Department expert examines new sheets of $100 bills as they shoot off the presses. The money is actually made at the Bureau of Engraving and Printing. The first $100 bills, issued in 1862, were called "legal tenders." Benjamin Franklin became the face on the $100 bill in 1914. Today this bill, which may stay in circulation for up to five years, is the largest denomination in use.

▼ **U.S. Treasury worker inspects newly printed $100 bills**

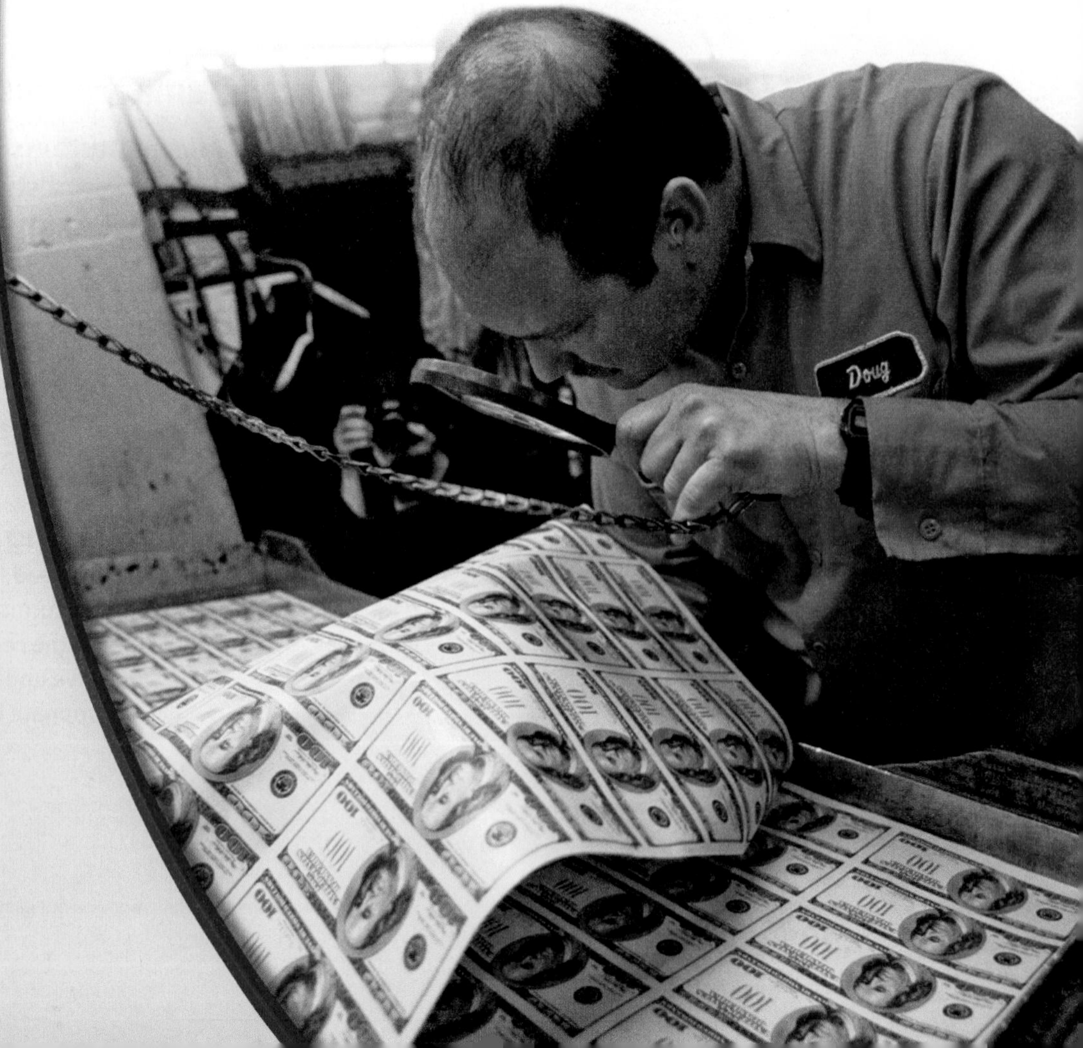

Money

Main Idea **People are willing to accept money in exchange for goods.**

Economics & You How much money do you have in your pocket or purse? Read to find out why this money has value to you and everyone else.

Money is more interesting than you might think. It serves different functions, comes in several different forms, and has value for reasons that are not immediately **obvious,** or clear.

Functions and Types of Money

Money has three functions. First, it serves as a **medium,** or form, of exchange—we can trade money for goods and services. Without money, people would have to barter—exchange goods and services for other goods and services. Second, money serves as a store of value. We can hold our wealth in the form of money until we are ready to use it. Third, money serves as a measure of value. Money is like a measuring stick that can be used to assign value to a good or service. When somebody says that something costs $10, we know exactly what that means.

Types of Money How would you define money? According to economists, money is anything that people are willing to accept in exchange for goods. At various times in history, salt, animal hides, gems, and tobacco have been used as mediums of exchange.

The most familiar types of money today are coins and currency. **Coins** are metallic forms of money such as pennies and nickels. **Currency** includes both coins and paper money. There are other forms of money as well.

Civics ONLINE

Student Web Activity Visit glencoe.com and complete the Chapter 24 Web Activity.

What Gives Money Value?

Why do we value and accept money? The simple reason is that we are absolutely sure that someone else will accept its value as well. Without this confidence in money, we would not accept it from someone else for payment in the first place.

Money by itself generally has no other value. A $10 bill costs only a few cents to make and has no alternative use. Coins contain only small amounts of precious metal. The same is true of checking and savings accounts—they have value only because we accept that they have value.

Reading Check **Explaining** Why does money have value?

Bartering People have used different goods for buying or trading. Kyle MacDonald from Montreal, Quebec, spent a year trading items on the Internet through Craigslist. He started trading with a red paper clip and ended up trading for a home. ***Identifying*** **What two types of money are most commonly used today?**

The Financial System

Main Idea **Financial institutions give people a safe place to deposit their money or take out loans.**

Economics & You Do you have a savings account? Read to find out what happens to your money when you make a deposit.

Do you know what happens when people and businesses with money to save take it to financial institutions? These institutions do not simply put the money in a safe and leave it there. Instead, they put the money to work by lending it to other people or businesses that need funds. They use the money to make more money. The financial institution covers its costs—and makes a profit—from the interest, or fees, it charges for those loans.

Financial Institutions

Commercial banks are financial institutions that offer full banking services to individuals and businesses. They are probably the most important part of our financial system because of their large areas of influence. Most people have their checking and savings accounts in commercial banks.

Savings and loan associations (S&L) are financial institutions that traditionally loaned money to people buying homes. They also take deposits and issue savings accounts in return. Today, S&Ls perform many of the activities that commercial banks do.

Credit unions work on a not-for-profit basis. They are open only to members of the group that sponsors them, usually businesses, labor unions, and government institutions. Generally, credit unions offer better rates on savings and loans than do other financial institutions.

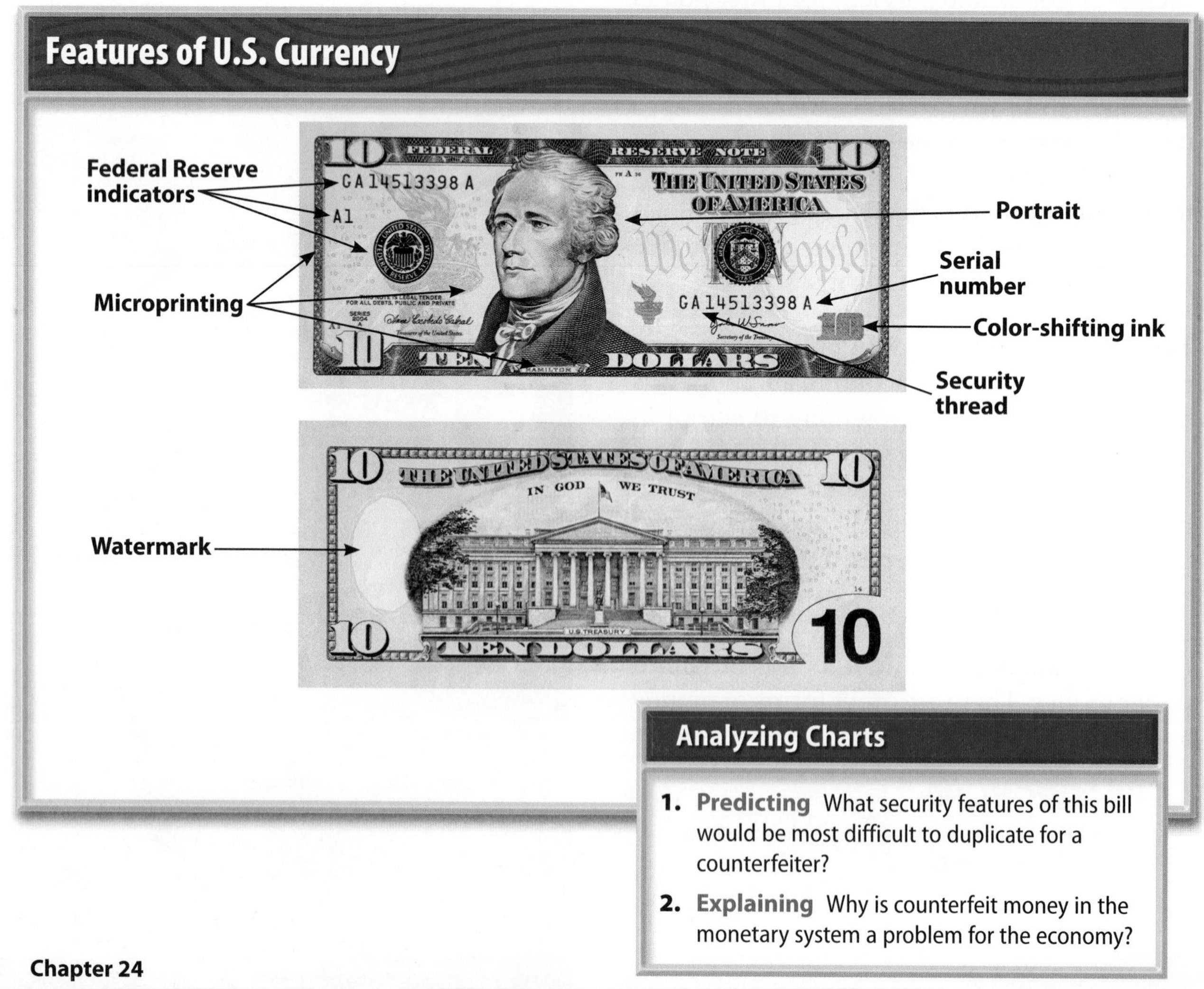

Analyzing Charts

1. **Predicting** What security features of this bill would be most difficult to duplicate for a counterfeiter?
2. **Explaining** Why is counterfeit money in the monetary system a problem for the economy?

Each of these types of banking institutions performs a similar function. They all act to bring together savers and borrowers. They give people a safe place to deposit their money when they want to save it and a source for borrowing when they need a loan. You will learn more about this system in Section 3.

Safeguarding Our Financial System

The financial system of the United States is one of the safest in the world. This safety results from two factors—regulation and insurance.

Banking is one of the most regulated industries in the country primarily because of the banking disaster of the 1920s. Most financial institutions have to report to one or more regulatory agencies. They are required to follow rules and accounting practices that minimize unnecessary risk.

The FDIC When financial institutions fail, federal deposit insurance protects consumers' deposits. The most important insurance agency is the Federal Deposit Insurance Corporation (FDIC), a national corporation that insures individual accounts in financial institutions for up to $100,000. The collapse of the banking system during the Great Depression of the 1930s wiped out people's entire savings. Now if a bank fails, depositors do not lose their savings.

Consumer Confidence Because accounts in financial institutions have some type of government insurance, consumers feel safer wherever they deposit their money. As a result, they continue to make deposits—and those deposits give financial institutions the funds they need to make loans that help fuel economic growth.

Reading Check **Explaining** How do financial institutions make a profit?

Vocabulary

1. **Write** a paragraph about the U.S. financial system that uses each of these terms: *coin, currency, commercial bank, savings and loan association (S&L), credit union.*

Main Ideas

2. **Name** two forms of money in addition to currency and coin.
3. **Describing** What is the purpose of the FDIC?

Critical Thinking

4. **Explaining** What advantage do credit unions offer their customers? Why?
5. **BIG Ideas** In a graphic organizer like the one below, describe the types of institutions in the American financial system.

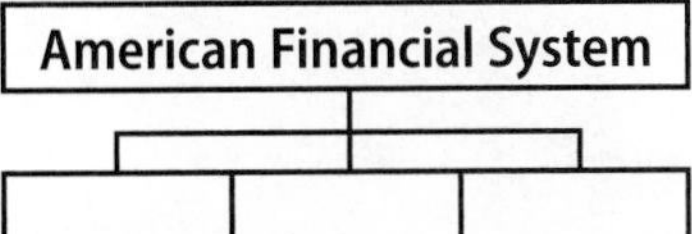

CITIZENSHIP Activity

6. **Comparing** Obtain brochures from several banks, credit unions, and savings and loans. Compare their services and fees. If you had $1,000 to deposit, which institution would you choose? Explain your choice.
7. **Descriptive Writing** Write a paragraph describing which financial institution services you expect to use over the next five years.

Study Central™ To review this section, go to glencoe.com.

Section Audio · Spotlight Video

The Federal Reserve System

Guide to Reading

Big Idea
Political and economic institutions evolve to help individuals and groups accomplish their goals.

Content Vocabulary
- central bank *(p. 661)*
- Federal Open Market Committee (FOMC) *(p. 661)*
- monetary policy *(p. 664)*
- discount rate *(p. 664)*
- reserve *(p. 665)*
- open market operations *(p. 665)*

Academic Vocabulary
- manipulate *(p. 661)*
- contract *(p. 664)*

Reading Strategy
Classifying As you read this section, complete a graphic organizer like the one below by listing the components that make up the Federal Reserve System.

Real World Economics The Federal Reserve System, usually known as the Fed, is the United States bank from which all other banks borrow. Chairperson Ben Bernanke is shown here with the president of the European Central Bank at an international monetary conference. Previously a professor and economic analyst, Bernanke replaced Alan Greenspan, longtime chairperson of the Fed. The Fed enters your life every day as the agency that controls interest rates on loans and controls the money supply, affecting inflation in America.

▼ **Ben Bernanke, right, became the Fed chairperson in February 2006**

Structure and Organization

Main Idea **The central bank of the United States is the Federal Reserve System.**

Economics & You Do you remember hearing about "the Fed" raising interest rates? Read to find out what this important body does.

The **central bank** of the United States is the Federal Reserve System, known as the Fed. When people or corporations need money, they borrow from banks. When banks need money, they borrow from the Fed. The Federal Reserve System is a banker's bank.

The United States is divided into 12 Federal Reserve districts. Each district has one main Federal Reserve Bank, along with branch banks. Thousands of banks in the United States are members of the Federal Reserve System. Member banks are owners of the Fed because they buy stock in the Fed and earn dividends from it.

Board of Governors

The Fed was established in 1913. At that time the largest banks were required to buy stock in the Fed. To prevent these banks from having too great an influence over the Fed, the law also required that the president appoint and the Senate ratify the seven members who make up the Board of Governors. The president selects one of the board members to chair the Board of Governors for a four-year term.

The Board of Governors controls and coordinates the Fed's activities. It sets general policies for the Federal Reserve and its member banks to follow. Board members and the chairperson are independent of both the president and the Congress. This allows the Board of Governors to make economic decisions independent of political pressure.

The Fed The headquarters of the Federal Reserve System is in Washington, D.C. The Board of Governors sets the Fed's policies. ***Explaining*** **Why is it important that the Board remain independent of the legislative and executive branches?**

Advisory Councils

The Fed has several advisory councils. One council reports on the general condition of the economy in each district. Another reports on financial institutions. A third reports on issues related to consumer loans. Officials of the district banks serve on these councils.

The FOMC A major policy-making group within the Fed is the **Federal Open Market Committee (FOMC).** The FOMC makes the decisions that affect the economy as a whole by **manipulating,** or controlling, the money supply. The FOMC has 12 members.

Reading Check **Explaining** How is the Fed's Board of Governors chosen?

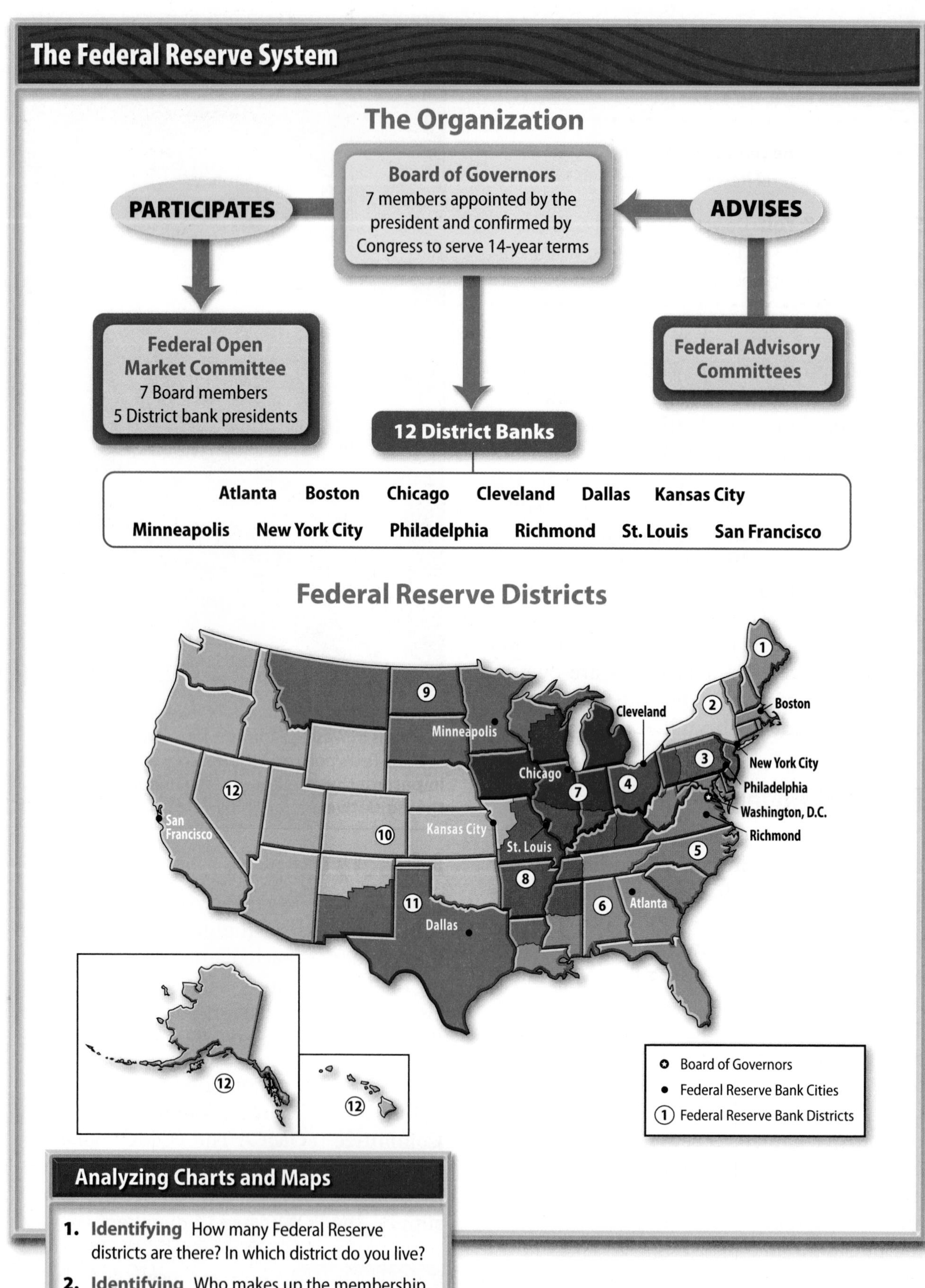

Analyzing Charts and Maps

1. **Identifying** How many Federal Reserve districts are there? In which district do you live?
2. **Identifying** Who makes up the membership of the FOMC?

TIME™

Political Cartoons

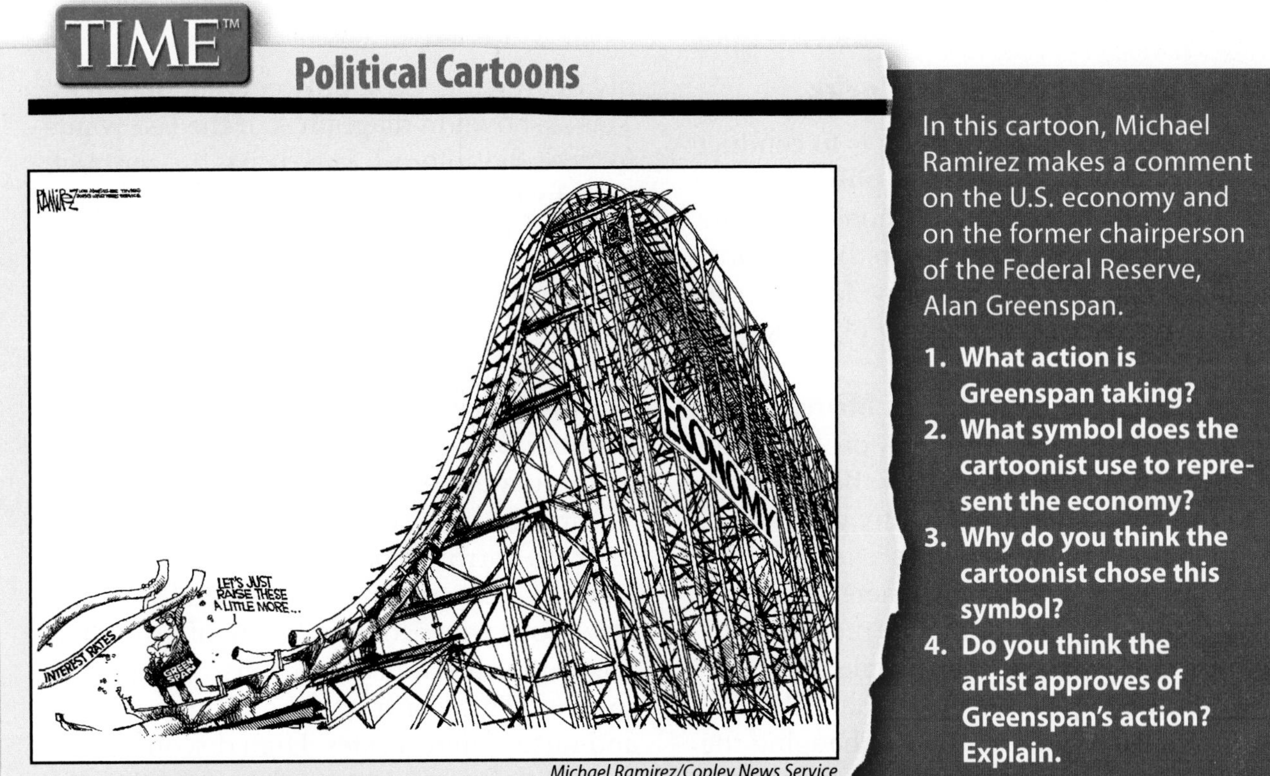

Michael Ramirez/Copley News Service

In this cartoon, Michael Ramirez makes a comment on the U.S. economy and on the former chairperson of the Federal Reserve, Alan Greenspan.

1. **What action is Greenspan taking?**
2. **What symbol does the cartoonist use to represent the economy?**
3. **Why do you think the cartoonist chose this symbol?**
4. **Do you think the artist approves of Greenspan's action? Explain.**

Functions of the Fed

Main Idea **The Fed controls the money supply, serves as the government's bank, and watches over the banking industry.**

Economics & You Can money ever be "cheap" or "expensive"? Read to find out how the Fed can raise or lower the "price" of money.

The Fed has two main regulatory functions: it deals with banking regulation and consumer credit.

The Fed as Regulator

The Fed oversees and regulates large commercial banks. If two national banks wish to merge, the Fed will decide whether the action will lessen competition. If so, the Fed could block the merger. It also regulates connections between American and foreign banking and oversees the international business of banks that operate in this country.

The Fed also enforces many laws that deal with consumer borrowing. For example, lenders must spell out the details of a loan before a consumer borrows money. The Fed specifies what information lenders must provide.

Acting as the Government's Bank

The Fed also acts as the government's bank. First, it holds the government's money. Government revenues are deposited in the Fed. When the government buys goods, it draws on these accounts. Second, the Fed sells U.S. government bonds and Treasury bills, which the government utilizes to borrow money. Third, the Fed manages the nation's currency, including paper money and coins. This money is produced by government agencies, but the Fed controls its circulation. When coins and currency become damaged, banks send them to the Fed for replacement.

How Monetary Policy Works

One of the Fed's major tasks is to conduct monetary policy. **Monetary policy** is the controlling of the supply of money and the cost of borrowing money—credit—according to the needs of the economy. The Fed can increase or decrease the supply of money.

Changing the Supply of Money The supply and demand diagrams on this page help explain monetary policy. Because the amount of money is fixed at any given time, the money supply is shown as a vertical line. In the diagrams, the point where supply of money and demand for money meet sets the interest rate—the rate that people and businesses must pay to borrow money. The Fed can change the interest rate by changing the money supply. So, if the Fed wants a *lower* interest rate, it must expand the money supply by moving the supply curve to the right. This is shown in diagram A. If the Fed wants to *raise* the interest rate, it has to **contract,** or reduce, the money supply by shifting the supply curve to the left (see diagram B).

Monetary Policy Tools Several tools help the Fed manipulate the money supply. First, the Fed can raise or lower the **discount rate.** The discount rate is the rate the Fed charges member banks for loans. If the Fed wants to stimulate the economy, it lowers the discount rate. Low discount rates encourage banks to borrow money from the Fed to make loans to their customers. If the Fed wants to slow down the economy's rate of growth, it raises the discount rate to discourage borrowing. This contracts the money supply and raises interest rates. High discount rates mean banks will borrow less money from the Fed.

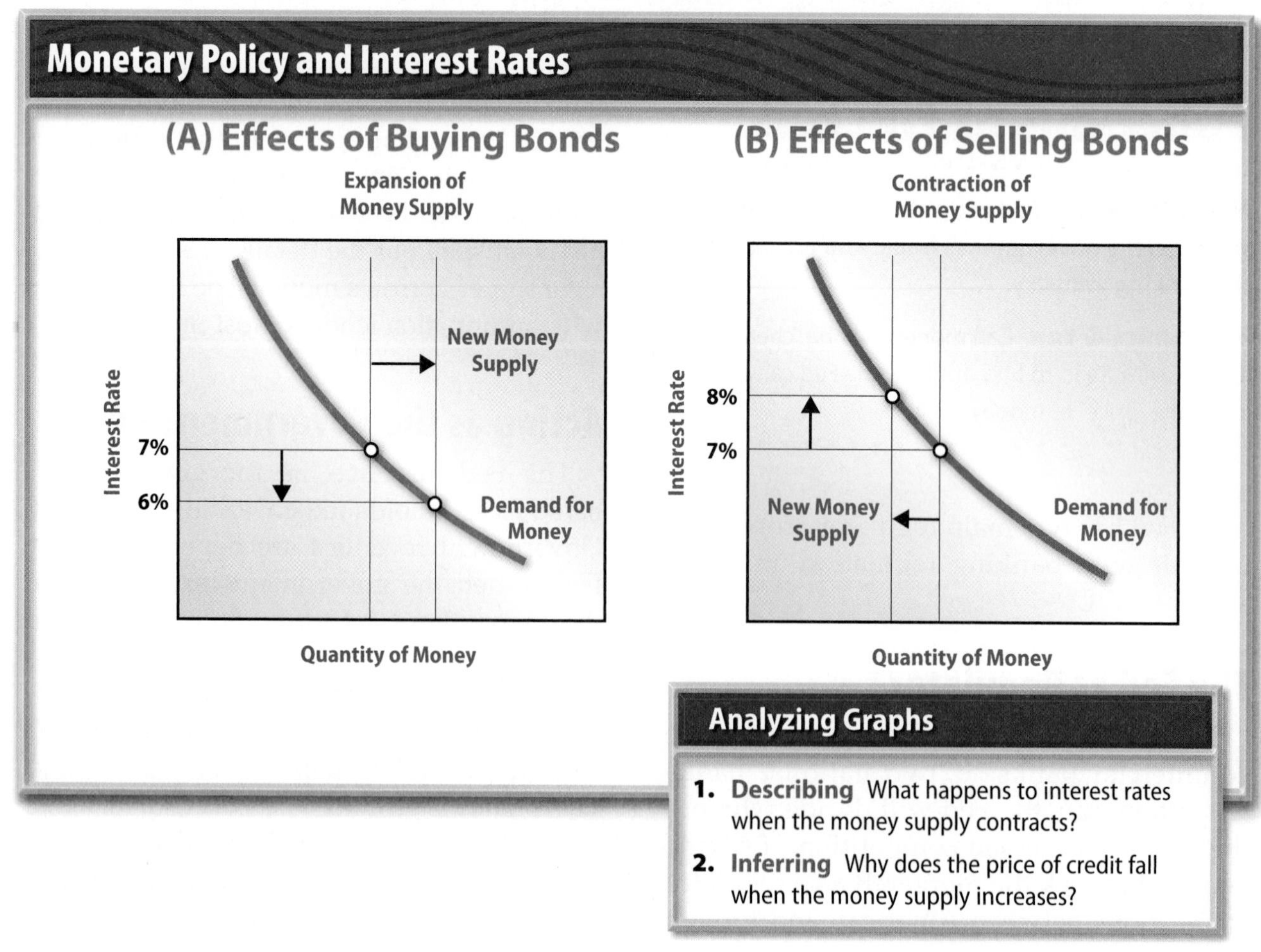

Analyzing Graphs

1. **Describing** What happens to interest rates when the money supply contracts?
2. **Inferring** Why does the price of credit fall when the money supply increases?

Second, the Fed may raise or lower the **reserve** requirement for member banks. Member banks must keep a certain percentage of their money in Federal Reserve Banks as a reserve against their deposits. This money is called the reserve. If the Fed raises the reserve requirement, banks must leave more money with the Fed, and they have less money to lend. When the Fed lowers the reserve requirement, member banks have more money to lend.

Finally, the Fed can change the money supply through **open market operations.** These are the purchase or sale of U.S. government bonds and Treasury bills. Buying bonds from investors puts more cash in investors' hands, increasing the money supply. This shifts the supply curve of money to the right, which lowers interest rates. Consumers and businesses then borrow more money, which increases consumer demand and business production. As a result, the economy grows. If the Fed decides that interest rates are too low, the Fed can sell bonds. When people buy those bonds, money comes out of the economy. This shifts the supply curve to the left, and raises interest rates.

Why Is Monetary Policy Effective?

Monetary policy can be implemented quickly and Fed officials can also easily fine-tune its policy. They can watch the results of selling bonds or raising the discount rate. If the desired result has not occurred, they can act again, selling more or fewer bonds or raising or lowering the discount rate.

Interest Rates and Business Interest rates influence business investment and consumer spending. The Fed can affect these activities by manipulating interest rates. For example, if the Fed wants to encourage business investment, it can lower interest rates. Raising rates will have the opposite effect.

Reading Check **Describing** How does the Fed protect consumer borrowers?

Vocabulary

1. **Create** a fill-in-the-blank quiz for a partner using these words: *central bank, Federal Open Market Committee (FOMC), monetary policy, discount rate, reserve, open market operations.*

Main Ideas

2. **Describing** In what way are member banks the owners of the Fed?

3. **Explaining** In what ways does the Fed act as the government's bank?

Critical Thinking

4. **Concluding** What would Fed officials likely do if prices rise too quickly?

5. **BIG Ideas** On a diagram like the one below, list five of the functions of the Federal Reserve System.

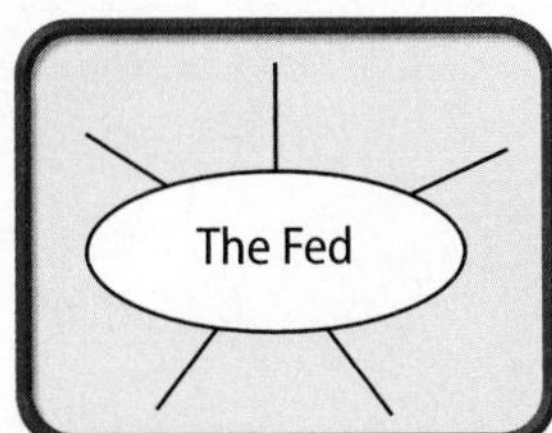

CITIZENSHIP Activity

6. **Comparing** Contact three banks in your community. Find out what interest rate they are charging on loans for a three-year loan on a new car. Compare this to the current Fed discount rate. Which is higher or lower?

7. **Expository Writing** Write a short newspaper article that explains how the Fed can use its powers to encourage or discourage business activity.

Study Central™ To review this section, go to glencoe.com.

Section Audio

Spotlight Video

How Banks Operate

Guide to Reading

Big Idea

Political and economic institutions evolve to help individuals and groups accomplish their goals.

Content Vocabulary

- checking account *(p. 667)*
- savings account *(p. 667)*
- certificate of deposit (CD) *(p. 667)*

Academic Vocabulary

- initial *(p. 667)*
- principal *(p. 667)*
- behalf *(p. 668)*

Reading Strategy

Classifying On a graphic organizer like the one below, identify three types of bank deposits.

Real World Economics Imagine what might happen if all your money were held in a bank that went bankrupt. This is what happened during the Great Depression in 1929. When the stock market crashed, stock prices fell nearly 25 percent in two days. As banks tried to collect the money investors had borrowed and invested in the stock market, many people lost everything that they owned. Banks went bankrupt, too.

▼ **Wall Street speculator tries to sell his car to make up for losses**

Banking Services

Main Idea **Banks offer important financial services to millions of people.**

Economics & You Do you know the difference between a savings and a checking account? Read to find out how these accounts differ.

Banks are started by investors. They pool financial investments, money, property, and other funds to provide banking services to people in their communities. If 10 investors each put up $10,000, the new bank would have $100,000 in funds.

A bank that relied on only the funds raised by its **initial,** or first, investors would not grow. It would have a limited amount of money available for loans. Banks need to attract depositors to survive.

Banking Transactions A New York City bank in the early 1930s handles the day-to-day transactions of its customers. ***Explaining*** **What are the advantages of a checking account?**

What Banks Do

To earn money, banks accept deposits to create different types of accounts and then use these deposited funds to make loans.

Accepting Deposits Banks hope to attract customers who make deposits. They offer **checking accounts,** which allow customers to write checks or to use check or debit cards. Checks can be used to pay bills or to transfer money from one person to another. These accounts, however, usually pay no or only a low rate of interest. People do not keep money in checking accounts for very long. They deposit the money and then use the funds to meet their regular expenses.

Sometimes people have some money that they can leave untouched for longer periods of time. With **savings accounts,** banks pay interest to customers based on how much money they have deposited. Because the bank pays interest, the money grows larger the longer it is left in a savings account.

Banks also offer **certificates of deposit (CDs)** to customers. CDs require a saver to deposit his or her funds for a certain period of time. CDs offer higher interest rates than checking accounts or savings accounts. The longer the maturity—the period of time—the higher the interest rate that the bank pays. Depositors cannot withdraw their money any sooner unless they pay a substantial penalty. Thus they lose control of their money for some time.

Making Loans One of the **principal,** or main, activities of banks is to lend money to businesses and consumers. Loans can actually increase the supply of money.

Suppose that Maria deposits $1,000 in the bank. The bank can use some of that money to make loans to other customers. Those people then deposit the money they have borrowed, and that money, too, can be loaned to new customers. In that way, the amount of money in circulation continues to accumulate.

Reading Check **Explaining** Where do banks get the money they loan to customers?

TIME™ Teens in *Action*

Andres Mendoza

Andres Mendoza, 16, of George, in the state of Washington, is all business when it comes to . . . well, business. So he signed up for a weeklong camp called Washington Business Week (WBW), which was hosted by Gonzaga University in Spokane.

QUESTION: You're originally from Oaxaca, Mexico?

ANSWER: My family moved to the United States four years ago. We didn't speak English, but luckily we learn really fast; it wasn't as difficult as it seemed.

Q: What's up with WBW?

A: WBW shows what's involved in working for a business—or running your own.

Q: What did you do there?

A: We formed mock companies. I was named Chief Executive Officer—or CEO—of my company. Everyone had to develop ideas for new products—ours was a microwave that not only warmed but also *froze* the food.

Before going to WBW, I really had no idea what went into running a business. I thought everything was about making money. But at WBW, you learn there's so much more to it—like behaving ethically.

For more info on Washington Business Week go to www.wbw.org.

Making a Difference — CITIZENSHIP

Analyzing Do you think there is a market for Mendoza's product? Explain.

Changes in Banking

Main Idea **Throughout American history, banking has become safer and more efficient.**

Economics & You Look closely at a dollar bill. Who issued it? Read to find out why this was not always the case in the United States.

The banking system of the United States has changed through the years. Often, crises led to key developments that helped strengthen American banks and safeguard the rights of citizens.

Early Banking

In the early days of our nation, leaders found that the country needed a central bank to bring order to the nation's finances. The Bank of the United States, chartered in 1791, collected fees and made payments on **behalf** of, or on the part of, the federal government. In 1816, the Second Bank of the United States was chartered for 20 years. The Bank, however, aroused much opposition, and when its charter lapsed, it was allowed to go out of business.

After that, the only banks in the nation were those chartered by the states. Because the federal government did not print paper currency until the Civil War, most of the money supply was paper currency that privately owned, state-chartered banks issued.

The end of the Bank of the United States removed a vital check on the activities of state-chartered banks. Freed from the Bank's regulations, private banks expanded the volume of bank notes, leading to an increased money supply and inflation.

The National Banking Act In 1863, Congress passed the National Banking Act. Federally chartered private banks issued national banknotes, or national currency, which were uniform in appearance and backed by U.S. government bonds.

The Federal Reserve The National Banking Act corrected some of the weaknesses of the pre-Civil War banking system. Bank crises, however, did not disappear. The Panic of 1907 resulted in the passage of the Federal Reserve Act of 1913, which you read about earlier in this chapter.

The Great Depression The Great Depression of the 1930s dealt a severe blow to the banking industry. When Franklin D. Roosevelt became president, he closed all banks. Each bank was allowed to reopen only after it proved it was financially sound. Congress established the Federal Deposit Insurance Corporation (FDIC), which insured funds of individual depositors.

Recent Developments

Several more recent developments have also changed the face of American banking. Among these were the savings and loan crisis and congressional legislation.

The Savings and Loan Crisis In the late 1970s Congress began to ease regulation of banking activities. Savings and Loans (S&Ls) were allowed to make higher-risk loans and investments. When these investments went bad, hundreds of S&Ls failed in the late 1980s and early 1990s. Because the federal government insured the savings of most depositors, the cost of bailing out these institutions cost taxpayers an estimated $200 billion. As a result, the FDIC intervened and took over regulation of the S&L industry.

The Gramm-Leach-Bliley Act The Gramm-Leach-Bliley Act, passed in 1999, permits bank holding companies greater freedom to engage in a full range of financial services, including banking, insurance, and securities. The act also requires all financial institutions to establish safeguards to protect their customers' personal financial information.

Reading Check **Identifying** Which banks issued paper currency before the Civil War?

Vocabulary

1. **Write** a paragraph about the activities of a bank using each of these terms: *checking account, savings account, certificate of deposit (CD).*

Main Ideas

2. **Describing** How do bank loans increase the supply of money?
3. **Explaining** What effect did the National Banking Act of 1863 have on banking in the United States?

Critical Thinking

4. **Predicting** What do you think would happen if everyone who had money deposited at a bank wanted to withdraw it at the same time?
5. **BIG Ideas** Using a diagram like the one below for certificates of deposit, compare the advantages and disadvantages of putting money into CDs.

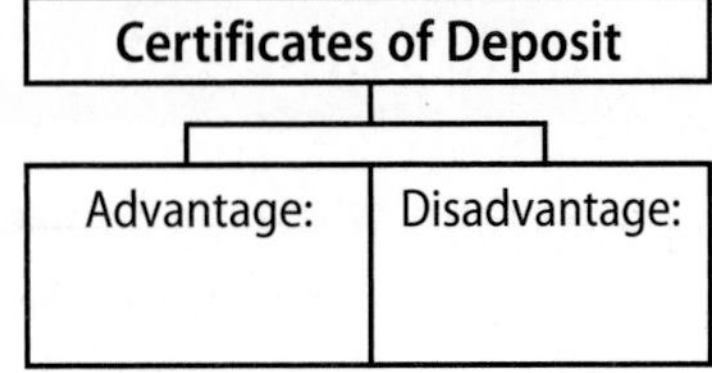

CITIZENSHIP Activity

6. **Comparing** Obtain brochures from at least three banks that explain the banks' services to customers. How are the services alike? How are they different?
7. **Creative Writing** Use what you learned in this section to write a TV or radio commercial for a bank, stressing its services.

Study Central™ To review this section, go to glencoe.com.

Life of a Check

A check is a written order directing your bank to transfer money from your account to the account of whomever receives your check. Millions of checks are moved around the country, sorted, tabulated, and credited or debited to the accounts of financial institutions. This is known as check clearing.

1. Jennifer has a checking account with Home Bank of Detroit, Michigan. She buys a CD player for $150 from Online Electronics.

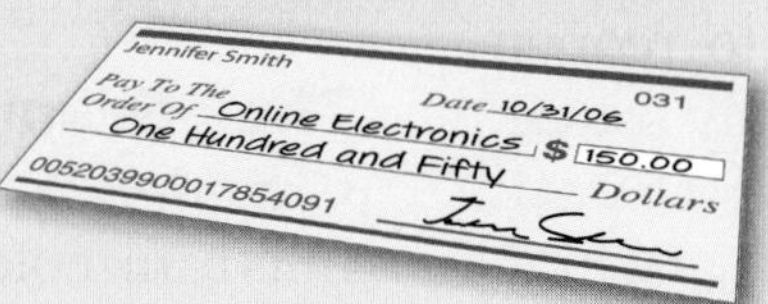

2. Online Electronics deposits the check in its account with City Bank of Toledo. City Bank credits Online Electronics' account + $150.

3. City Bank of Toledo sends the check electronically to the Federal Reserve Bank of Chicago to be cleared.

4. FRB of Chicago credits City Bank of Toledo (Online Electronics' financial institution) + $150.

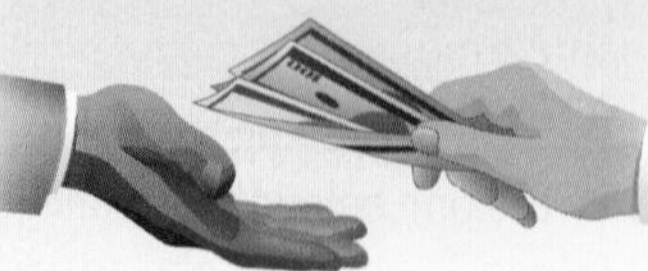

5. After processing, FRB of Chicago sends the check to Home Bank (Jennifer's financial institution).

6. Home Bank then pays FRB of Chicago $150 and it reduces (debits) Jennifer's account by $150. She receives a summary statement.

The circular flow chart illustrates the steps a check takes as it goes from a purchase through the Federal Reserve System, and back to your bank.

Analyzing Economics

1. **Explaining** What does the statement "my check cleared" mean?
2. **Explaining** You receive $50 and deposit it into your bank. What is one way to make sure this transaction was completed?

Chapter 24

Visual Summary

What is money?

- anything that people are willing to accept in exchange for goods
- a measure of value
- part of the broad financial system
- a medium of exchange
- a store of value

U.S. Treasury worker

What is the Federal Reserve?

The Federal Reserve

- serves as the nation's central bank
- wields a great deal of power in our economy
- controls monetary policy
- regulates commercial banks
- affects business through its decisions

What do banks do?

A bank ATM customer

- provide services to consumers, such as savings and checking accounts and CDs
- make a profit by lending deposited money to consumers

Study anywhere, anytime! Download quizzes and flash cards to your PDA from glencoe.com.

Standardized Test Practice

Chapter 24 ASSESSMENT

TEST-TAKING TIP

Try not to go back and change your answers unless you are very sure they are wrong. Usually your first thought is your best thought.

Reviewing Vocabulary

Directions: Choose the word(s) that best completes the sentence.

1. _______ includes both coins and paper money.

A Bank notes
B Currency
C Checking accounts
D Federal Reserve notes

2. An institution owned and operated by its members that provides low-interest loans to its members is called a _______.

A credit union
B commercial bank
C state bank
D board of governors

3. The interest rate that the Federal Reserve charges on loans to its member banks is the _______.

A dividend
B money supply
C discount rate
D medium of exchange

4. An account in which deposited money can be withdrawn at any time by writing an order is called a _______.

A savings account
B checking account
C discount rate
D certificate of deposit

Reviewing Main Ideas

Directions: Choose the best answer for each question.

Section 1 *(pp. 656–659)*

5. How do banks and other financial institutions that lend money make a profit?

A by charging interest
B by borrowing money
C by printing currency
D through promissory notes

6. What is the main purpose of the Federal Deposit Insurance Corporation?

A buy and sell for investors
B approve changes in the interest rate
C insure checking and savings deposits
D make decisions that affect the economy as a whole

Section 2 *(pp. 660–665)*

7. The central bank of the United States is the ___.

A Board of Governors
B Federal Reserve System
C Federal Open Market Committee
D Federal Deposit Insurance Corporation

8. The Fed requires banks to keep a ___, or a percentage of their money.

A reserve
B discount rate
C interest rate
D growth rate

Section 3 *(pp. 666–669)*

9. In what kind of account do savers have the most control over their money?

A savings accounts
B certificates of deposit
C open market operation
D legal tender

GO ON

10. A deposit account that requires savers to deposit their money for a certain period of time is a ______.

A savings account

B certificate of deposit

C open market operation

D legal tender

Critical Thinking

Directions: Base your answers to questions 11 and 12 on the chart below and your knowledge of Chapter 24.

Functions of Money
Medium of exchange
Store of value
Measure of value

11. If you read in the newspaper that the Federal Reserve had just lowered the discount rate, what might you conclude about the economy?

A The nation is in a financial crisis.

B The economy is operating at full capacity.

C The Fed wants to discourage bank loans.

D The economy is sluggish and needs to be stimulated.

12. Money serves as a measure of value. What does this mean?

A Your money is safe in a savings account.

B Money is a value medium everyone understands.

C Money owed must be paid.

D CDs are a good investment.

13. To say that money is a medium of exchange means that ______.

A money is durable

B an item for sale is marked with a price

C money can be deposited in a bank

D a seller will accept it in exchange for a good or service

Document-Based Questions

Directions: Analyze the document and answer the short-answer questions that follow.

Ben S. Bernanke was sworn in on February 1, 2006, as chairman of the Board of Governors of the Federal Reserve System. This passage is from a speech given by Bernanke in November 2006.

> *Inflation, which picked up earlier this year, has been somewhat better behaved of late. Overall inflation was pushed up this spring by a surge in energy prices, but the recent declines in energy prices have largely reversed those effects. Price inflation for consumer goods and services excluding energy and food, the so-called core inflation rate, has also moderated a bit in the past few months. But the level of the core inflation rate remains uncomfortably high.*
>
> —Ben S. Bernanke

14. How does Bernanke characterize the rate of inflation—in positive terms, negative terms, or both? Explain.

15. Is Bernanke calling for any specific action or policy to combat inflation? Based on your reading, what could cause the Fed to take action?

Extended-Response Question

16. When the Federal Reserve was started, it was to serve the function of a "lender of last resorts." Do you think banks need the Federal Reserve to act as a lender of last resorts more often during good economic times or bad economic times? Explain.

STOP

For additional test practice, use Self-Check Quizzes—Chapter 24 on glencoe.com.

Need Extra Help?

If you missed question...	1	2	3	4	5	6	7	8	9	10	11	12	13	14	15	16
Go to page...	657	658	664	667	658	659	661	665	667	667	664	657	657	660	660	660

Chapter 25

Government Finances

Why It Matters

As taxpayers, American citizens share most of the burden of financing local, state, and federal governments. In return, we receive a host of services that makes our lives better and more secure. These services range from education, entitlement programs, and police and fire protection to national defense and highway construction.

Civics ONLINE
Visit glencoe.com and enter QuickPass™ code CIV3093c25 for Chapter 25 resources.

BIG Ideas

Section 1: The Federal Government

Under our federal system, the executive, legislative, and judicial branches share the responsibility of governing the nation. The president and Congress work together to create the budget—a blueprint for raising and spending the nation's money.

Section 2: State and Local Governments

Political and economic institutions evolve to help individuals and groups accomplish their goals. State and local governments have their own revenue sources and decide how to spend the money they take in.

Section 3: Managing the Economy

Political and economic institutions evolve to help individuals and groups accomplish their goals. Governments use various tools to manage the economy.

Coast Guard helicopter on patrol with Guard cutter

FOLDABLES™ Study Organizer

Comparing Information Foldable Make the following Foldable to help you compare the revenues and expenditures of the different levels of government.

Step 1 Fold a sheet of paper into thirds from top to bottom.

Step 2 Open the paper and refold it into thirds from side to side.

Step 3 Unfold the paper and draw lines along the folds.

Government Finances	Federal Government	State and Local Government
Revenues		
Expenditures		

Reading and Writing
As you read the chapter, use your Foldable chart to compare how money is administered among the federal, state, and local governments.

Section Audio · Spotlight Video

The Federal Government

Guide to Reading

Big Idea

Under our federal system, the executive, legislative, and judicial branches share the responsibility of governing the nation.

Content Vocabulary

- budget *(p. 677)*
- mandatory spending *(p. 677)*
- discretionary spending *(p. 677)*
- appropriations bill *(p. 677)*
- Social Security *(p. 678)*
- Medicare *(p. 678)*

Academic Vocabulary

- enormous *(p. 677)*

Reading Strategy

Representing Create a diagram like the one below to identify the three largest federal expenditures and the three largest sources of federal revenue.

Expenditures	Revenues
1. Social Security	1.
2.	2.
3.	3.

Real World Economics Will the money be there when you retire? Social Security, the federal program designed to provide economic security for people once they retire, is often the subject of protest. Today, many younger generations of Americans are afraid they will pay into the system but never reap the benefits. That is because the Social Security system's long-term financial stability is in question, although economists have offered possible solutions.

▼ **Protesters rally against changing Social Security**

Preparing the Budget

Main Idea **The federal budget, created by the president and Congress, is the government's blueprint for raising and spending money.**

Economics & You Does your family spend money on things it must have then spend what is left over on things it wants but does not really need? Read to find out how your family is like the government.

Did you know that total federal government spending accounts for more than 20 percent of our gross domestic product (GDP)? This is an **enormous,** or very large, amount of money. Each year, the president and Congress work together to create a **budget.** This budget is a blueprint of how the government will raise and spend money.

The government's budget year differs from a calendar year. The government uses a fiscal year (FY), a 12-month period that may or may not match the calendar year. The federal government's budget year begins October 1 and ends on September 30 of the following year and must be renewed at that time.

The Budget Process

By the first Monday in February, the president proposes a budget to Congress outlining how the government should spend its money. The president then formally sends the proposed budget to Congress along with an annual budget message.

Congress then passes a budget resolution. This document totals revenues and spending for the year and sets targets for how much will be spent in various categories. Spending is divided into two types: mandatory and discretionary.

Spending that does not need annual approval is called **mandatory spending.** Examples are Social Security benefit checks and interest payments on the government debt, which must be paid every year. **Discretionary spending** is government expenditures that must be approved each year. These include things such as money for the Coast Guard, highway construction, and defense. Discretionary spending makes up only about one-third of the federal budget.

Appropriations Bills Another step remains before the government can actually spend any money: Congress must pass **appropriations bills.** These are laws that approve spending for a particular activity. Appropriations bills always begin in the House of Representatives. The Senate then works with the House to pass all appropriations bills by October 1, the beginning of the fiscal year. Appropriations bills must be approved by both houses and either signed into law or vetoed by the president.

Reading Check **Explaining** How does a fiscal year differ from a calendar year?

Budget of the U.S. Government The federal government publishes a collection of documents that contains the president's budget message and other budget-related publications. ***Identifying*** **What is the first step in the federal budget process?**

Revenues and Expenditures

Main Idea **The federal budget has two main parts—revenues and expenditures.**

Economics & You Do you sometimes have trouble matching what you earn to what you spend? Read to find out why the government faces the same challenge.

The federal budget contains two main parts—revenues and expenditures. The main sources of federal revenues are shown in the graph on page 679.

Revenues

Nearly half of the federal government's revenue comes from the income tax paid by individual Americans. Each year, every worker files a tax return, or a report that calculates the tax a worker must pay on his or her income. Corporations also pay income tax on profits they earn.

The second-largest source of federal income is payroll taxes, which are deducted from a worker's paycheck to fund **Social Security** and **Medicare.** Social Security provides money to people who are retired or disabled. Medicare pays some health care costs of elderly people.

Other taxes are also sources of revenue. Consumers pay an excise tax when they purchase goods such as gasoline, tobacco, and telephone services. When wealthy people die, the federal government collects estate taxes on the wealth passed on to their heirs. The government charges a tax on certain gifts. Miscellaneous sources such as entry fees to national parks also add to federal revenues.

Forms of Taxation

Taxes can be classified according to the effect they have on those who are taxed. In the United States today, these classifications include progressive, regressive, and proportional taxes.

Taxation Whenever we buy gasoline, we not only must pay for the gasoline, but also federal and state taxes on the gasoline. ***Identifying*** **What form of taxation is the tax on gasoline?**

Progressive Tax With a *progressive* tax, like our federal income tax, the tax rate (the proportion of earnings taken in taxes) increases as income increases. Therefore, the higher the income, the larger the percentage of income is paid as taxes.

Regressive Tax The opposite of a progressive tax is a *regressive* tax: the percentage you pay goes down as you make more money. One example of regressive taxes is the gasoline tax. Poorer families spend a larger proportion of their income on gasoline. Therefore, the sales tax they pay on gasoline takes up a larger proportion of their total income than a wealthier family pays.

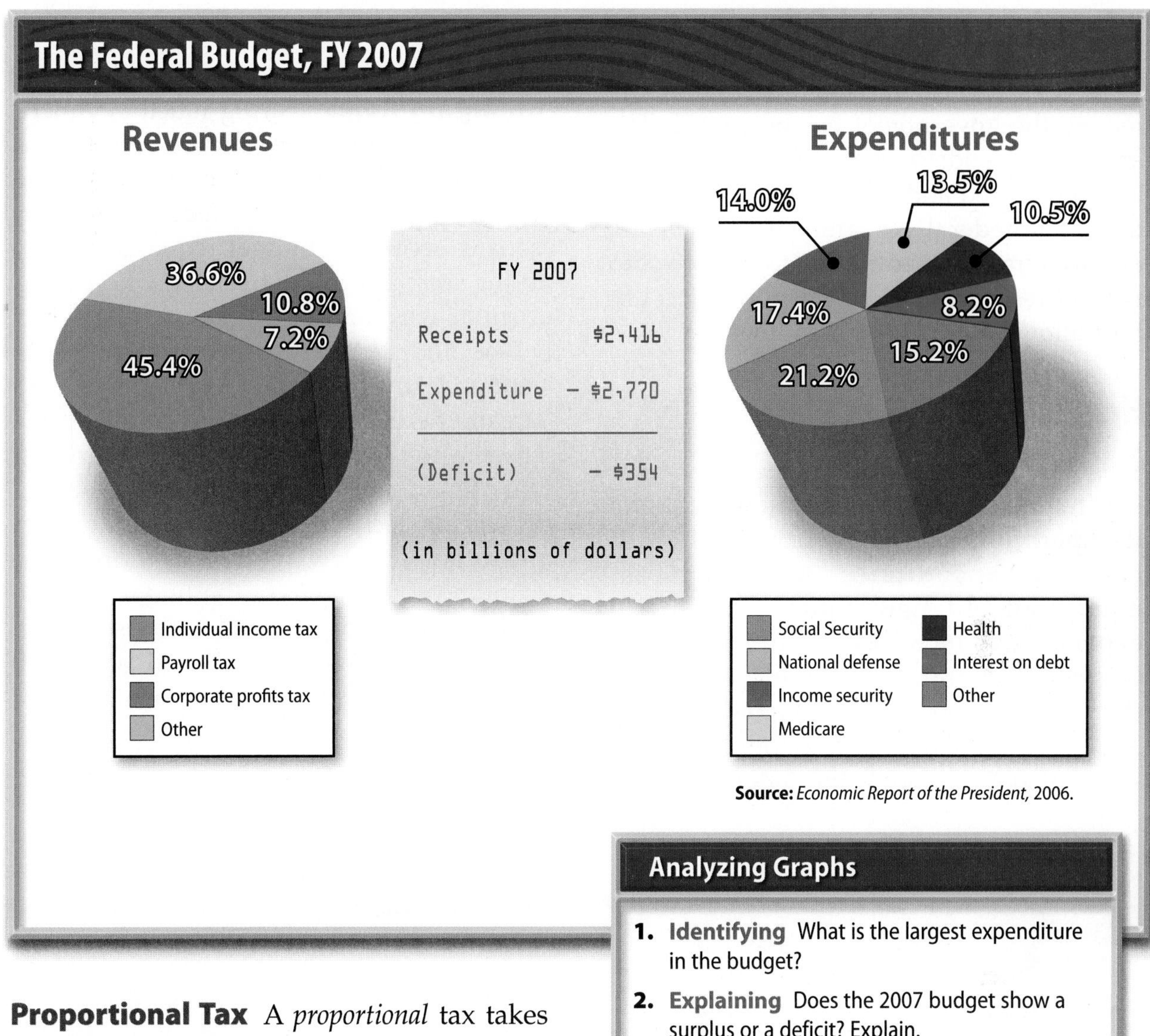

Source: *Economic Report of the President,* 2006.

Analyzing Graphs

1. **Identifying** What is the largest expenditure in the budget?
2. **Explaining** Does the 2007 budget show a surplus or a deficit? Explain.

Proportional Tax A *proportional* tax takes the same percentage of income from everyone, regardless of how much he or she earns. If there is a tax of 10 percent on all income and you earn $1,000, you pay $100 in taxes; if you earn $10,000, you pay $1,000 in taxes, and so on.

Federal Expenditures The graphs above show where the federal government planned to spend its money in 2007. Social Security was the largest single spending category. Because the number of older people in the population is growing, this expense is expected to grow in the future.

Medicare costs are also likely to rise as the population continues to age. Income security includes retirement benefits for some government workers and others, along with payments to poorer Americans for housing and child nutrition. Health costs include payments for medical research and Medicaid, which pays for health care for people with low incomes.

Defense National defense is the second-largest category of federal expenditures. The original FY 2007 budget set defense spending at more than 17 cents of every federal dollar spent. During times of conflict or war, spending for national defense is increased. Because of the war on terrorism, the 17 percent represents an increase over the percentage of defense spending before September 11, 2001.

Interest on Debt and Other Expenditures A portion of the federal budget each year goes toward paying interest on the money the government has borrowed. The amount depends on how much money has been borrowed and the interest rates of that debt. The federal government also spends on programs from education to highways to natural resources. These categories account for billions of dollars of spending.

How the Budget Process Has Changed

When the federal government began its operation under the Constitution, it had few expenditures. As the government took on new functions, federal expenditures increased greatly. President George Washington was able to put all the figures for the national government's expenditures for one year on one large sheet of paper. Today the federal budget consists of more than 1,000 pages of small type.

Changing Roles During much of American history, presidents traditionally played a limited role in researching and drawing up the budget. Various federal agencies usually sent their budget requests directly to the secretary of the treasury, who passed them on to Congress.

The Budget and Accounting Act of 1921 changed this procedure in an effort to streamline the process. As a result of this law, the president is responsible for directing the preparation of the budget and making the major decisions about national budget priorities. The law requires the president to propose to Congress the budget for the entire federal government, each fiscal year. This budget must be delivered within 15 days after Congress convenes each January.

Reading Check **Explaining** Why are Medicare and Social Security costs expected to rise?

Vocabulary

1. **Define** the following terms and use them in sentences related to federal budgeting: *budget, mandatory spending, discretionary spending, appropriations bill, Social Security, Medicare.*

Main Ideas

2. **Identifying** What is an example of mandatory government spending?
3. **Contrasting** How does a progressive tax differ from a proportional tax?
4. **Evaluating** If the government needed to increase government revenue, which kind of tax do you think it should increase? Why?

Critical Thinking

5. **BIG Ideas** In a graphic organizer like the one below, show how the president and Congress cooperate to create the federal budget.

1	President sends budget to Congress
2	
3	
4	

6. **Analyzing Visuals** Study the 2007 federal budget on page 679. What two major categories are represented? What percentage of expenditures was budgeted for health?

CITIZENSHIP Activity

7. **Persuasive Writing** Write a newspaper editorial supporting a position for or against this statement: The federal government should be required to balance its budget each year.

Study Central™ To review this section, go to glencoe.com.

State and Local Governments

Guide to Reading

Big Idea

Political and economic institutions evolve to help individuals and groups accomplish their goals.

Content Vocabulary

- intergovernmental revenue *(p. 682)*
- sales tax *(p. 682)*
- property tax *(p. 682)*
- entitlement program *(p. 684)*
- subsidize *(p. 684)*

Academic Vocabulary

- revenue *(p. 682)*
- utilize *(p. 684)*
- resource *(p. 684)*

Reading Strategy

Categorizing As you read, complete a graphic organizer like the one below to show the four major expenditures of local government.

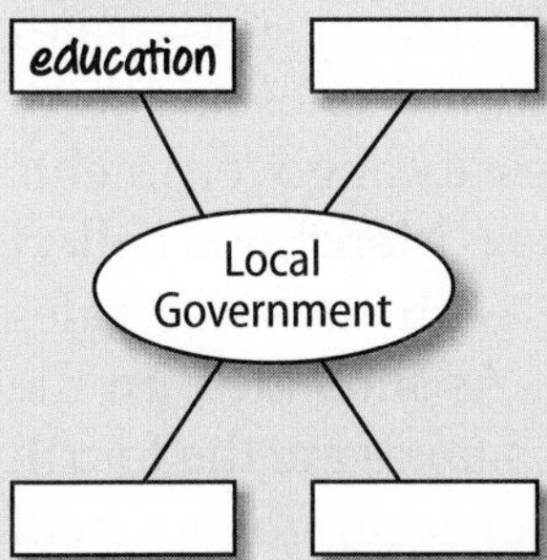

Real World Economics Have you shopped on a "sales tax holiday"? It has been initiated in many states as a day when consumers do not have to pay any sales tax to the state. The sales tax holiday allows shoppers to save as much as 10 percent by eliminating the sales tax on certain products—school supplies, clothing, computers, and other items—for as many as 10 days at a time. In New York City, where the events of September 11th, 2001, caused economic devastation, store owners have looked to the sales tax holiday to help them rebound from difficult times.

▼ **Store manager arranges stock for Alabama's sales tax holiday**

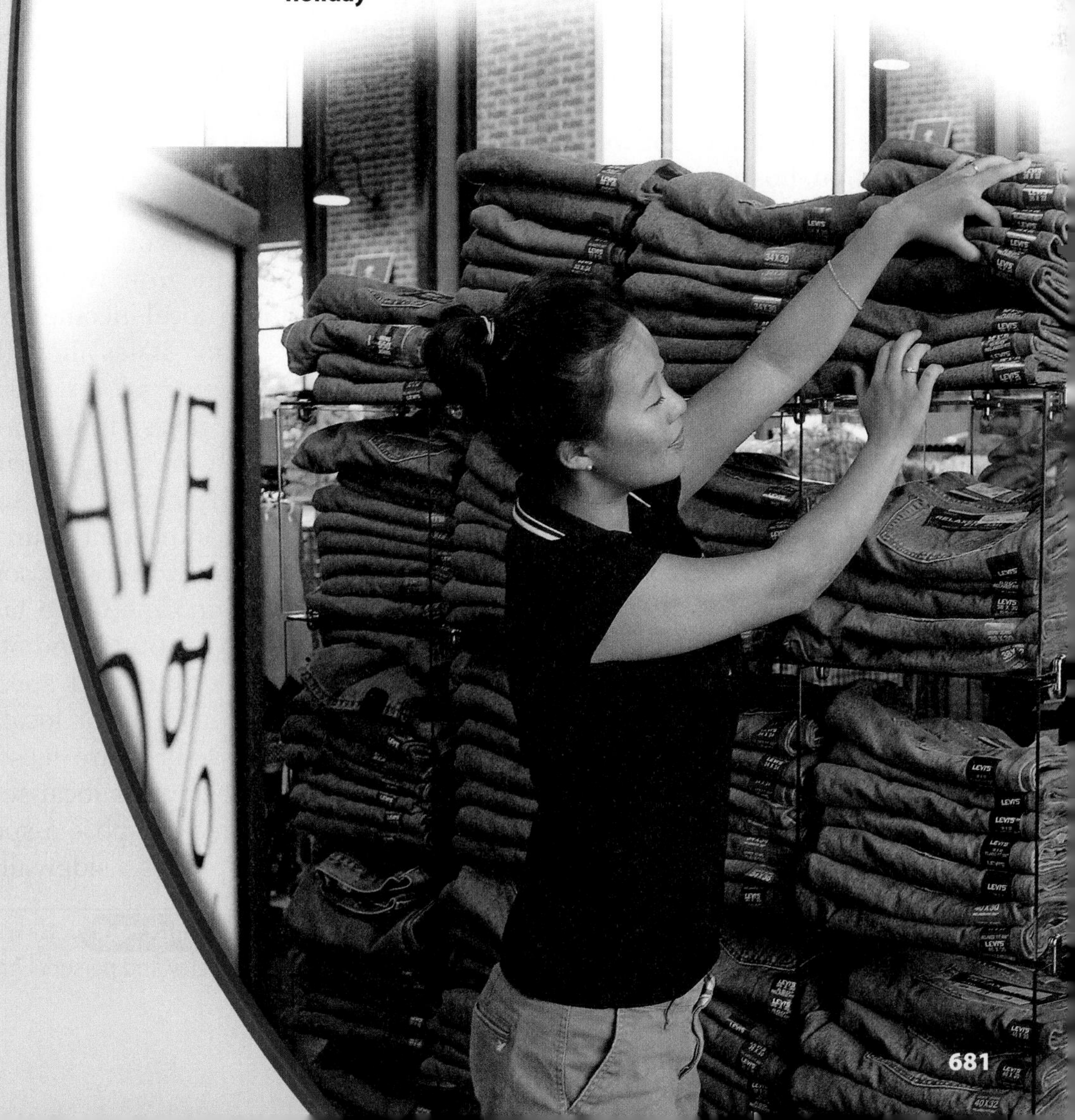

Revenues

Main Idea **State and local governments have their own revenue sources.**

Economics & You Sales taxes raise the price of things you buy. Read to find out why this source of revenue is important to cities and states.

State and local governments have their own budget approval processes, **revenues,** and expenditures. The major sources of revenue for each are described below.

State Governments

The most important sources of state government revenues, shown in the graph on page 683, are **intergovernmental revenues.** This revenue is money that one level of government receives from another level. For states, most of this revenue comes from the federal government. The federal government gives states money for welfare, highway construction, hospitals, and other needs.

Sales Tax Next in importance is the state **sales tax.** A sales tax is a general tax levied on consumer purchases of nearly all products. The tax is a percentage of the purchase price, which is added to the final price the consumer pays. The merchant regularly turns over the taxes to the proper state government agency. Five states do not have sales taxes. Rates in the other states range from 2.9 percent to 7.25 percent.

Contributions A third source of state revenue is the contributions that states and state government workers make to their retirement plans. This money is invested until it is needed to pay retirement benefits.

Student Web Activity Visit glencoe.com and complete the Chapter 25 Web Activity.

Income Tax The last major category of revenue is state income taxes. As with sales tax rates, state income tax rates vary a great deal. Some states tax a percentage of the federal income tax. A few states charge a single rate to all taxpayers. In the other states, the rate goes up as income goes up. Seven states have no state income tax.

Local Governments

Intergovernmental revenues are even more important for many local governments than they are for states. The states provide most of this money.

Property Tax The second-largest source of local revenue is local **property taxes.** These are taxes that people pay on the land and houses they own. Property taxes are collected on real property and personal property. Real property includes lands and buildings. Personal property consists of portable objects—things that can be moved—such as stocks and bonds, jewelry, and furniture. Most local governments now tax only real property.

Other Sources Local governments have other revenue sources as well. These include revenue from water and utility systems, sales taxes, local income taxes, and fines and fees.

Many states allow their local governments to impose a local sales tax. Merchants collect these taxes right along with the state sales tax, at the point of sale. As indicated on the graphs on page 683, sales taxes are the fourth most important source of local government revenues. Another source of revenue is the local income tax, a tax on personal income. Fines for traffic and other violations and fees for permits and special services also provide income for local governments. Special assessments are fees that property owners must pay for local services. For example, a city may impose a special assessment when it improves a sidewalk.

Reading Check **Contrasting** How do real property and personal property taxes differ?

State and Local Governments

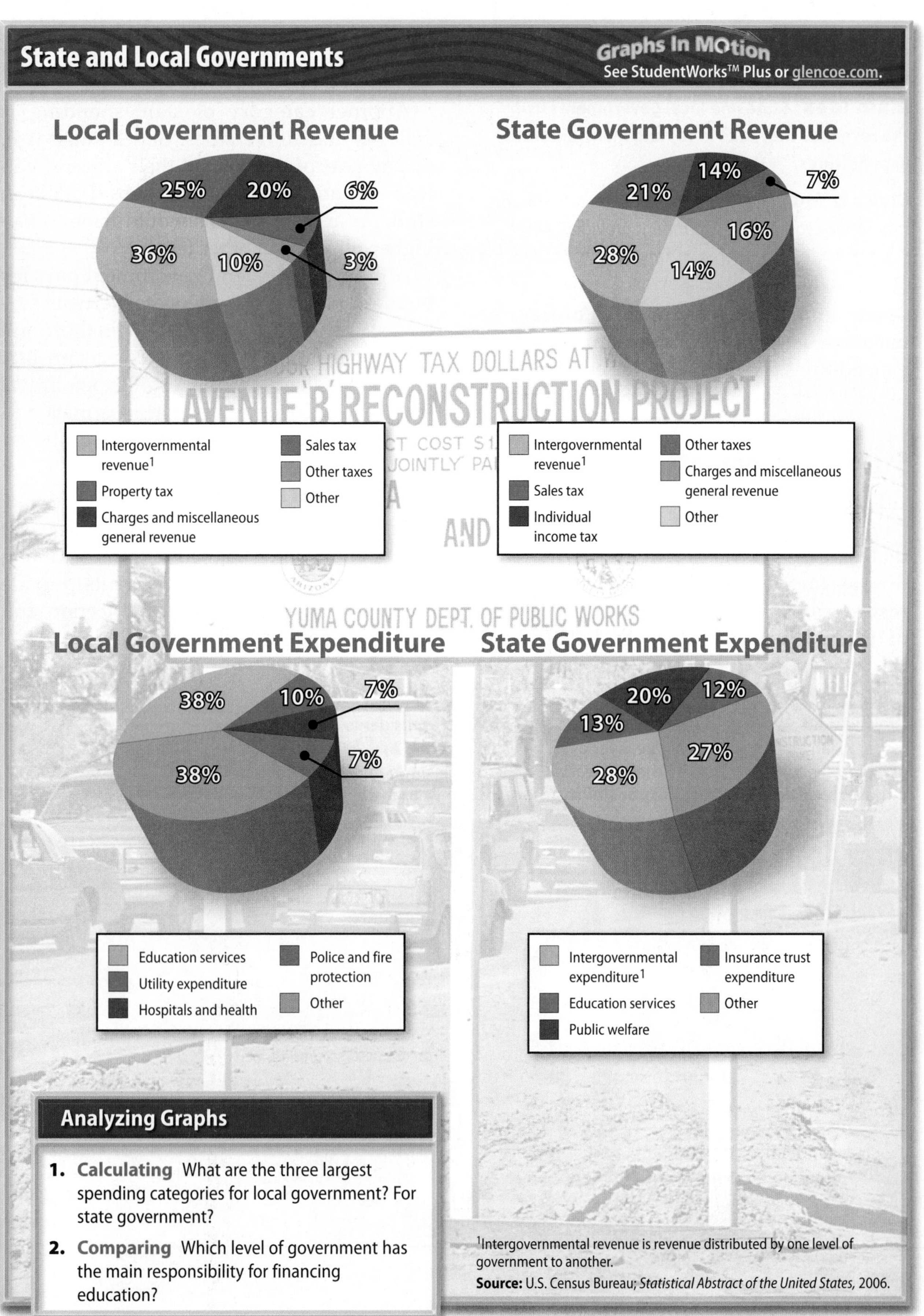

Analyzing Graphs

1. **Calculating** What are the three largest spending categories for local government? For state government?
2. **Comparing** Which level of government has the main responsibility for financing education?

[1]Intergovernmental revenue is revenue distributed by one level of government to another.

Source: U.S. Census Bureau; *Statistical Abstract of the United States*, 2006.

Expenditures

Main Idea **State and local governments use the revenues they take in to fund many different expenditures.**

Civics & You What do you think is the most important service your local government provides? Why?

State and local governments **utilize,** or make use of, their revenues to fund various expenditures. These expenditures are shown in the lower graph on page 683.

State Governments

Public welfare, or human services, is the name we give to government expenditures that maintain basic health and living conditions for people who have insufficient **resources,** or money, of their own. Most of these expenditures cover **entitlement programs,** such as health, nutritional, or income payments to people who meet established eligibility requirements.

Another category of state spending is colleges and universities. States **subsidize,** or pay part of the cost of, their citizens' college education. Without this subsidy, college students at state schools would have to pay higher tuition and other fees.

Although the federal government pays for building much of the interstate highway system, states are required to maintain those and additional highways. Other categories that take up smaller percentages of expenditures include employee retirement, hospitals and health facilities, and corrections institutions.

Local Governments

Local governments also provide services that they pay for with their revenues. Among the services that local governments provide are education, police and fire protection, and water, sewage, and sanitation services.

Government Services A street sweeper cleans the streets as residents of Trenton, New Jersey, clean up after the Delaware River overflowed its banks in July 2006. Different levels of government must work together to deal with emergencies. ***Identifying*** **Which branch of government has primary responsibility for maintaining highways?**

Education A large share of local tax revenues in many states goes to pay for public schools. Some states pay a large percentage of local public school costs, but local school districts generally provide a large share of the money and make the key decisions regarding operation of the public schools.

Police and Fire Protection Police and fire protection also make up a large part of local budgets. Fire protection is a local function that varies with the size of the community. In small towns, volunteers usually staff the fire department. In large cities, professional, full-time fire departments provide fire protection.

Water Supply Local governments make the vital decisions regarding water service. Smaller communities may contract with privately-owned companies to supply water. The threat of pollution has prompted some local governments to create special water districts. In case of a water shortage, such districts or local governments may try to limit the amount of water used.

Sewage and Sanitation Local governments are responsible for sewage disposal. Proper sewage treatment is vital to the conservation of useful water supplies. Many local governments maintain sewage treatment plants.

In the past, most trash and garbage was buried. Because of environmental concerns, these landfills are no longer the simple solution to sanitation. Some local governments use garbage-processing plants to dispose of a community's solid wastes.

Reading Check **Identifying** What level of government makes most of the key decisions regarding operation of the public schools?

Section 2 Review

Vocabulary

1. **Write** sentences related to state and local governments using the following terms: *intergovernmental revenue, sales tax, property tax, entitlement program, subsidize.*

Main Ideas

2. **Identifying** What are the largest sources of revenue for state and local governments?
3. **Describing** What is the effect of state subsidies on the cost of public colleges and universities?

Critical Thinking

4. **Evaluating** If you needed to raise local government revenues, which source of revenue would you target for an increase? Explain.
5. **BIG Ideas** In a graphic organizer like the one below, explain how a state government gets its revenue.

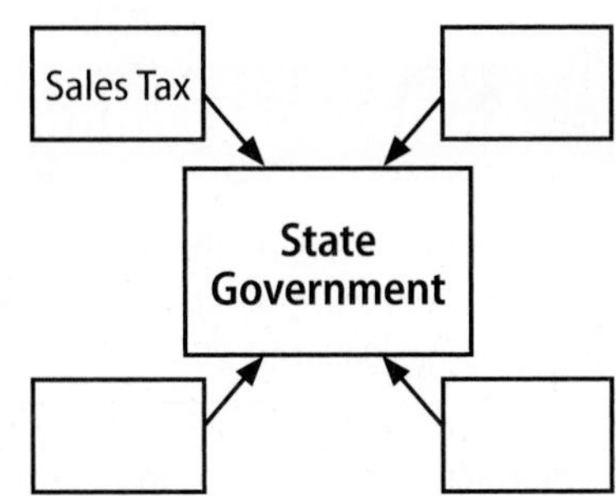

6. **Analyzing Visuals** Study the two graphs that appear on page 683. Are police and fire protection the responsibility of state or local government?

CITIZENSHIP Activity

7. **Expository Writing** Write a newspaper article that includes your own experiences with local government. Focus on one of these issues: police or fire protection, sewer or water services, trash disposal, or education.

Study Central™ To review this section, go to glencoe.com.

Financial Literacy

How Do You Calculate Unit Prices?

Trying to compare the prices of different amounts of a product—one pound of Product A versus one-half pound of Product B—can be confusing. To get the most for your money, it is important to compare the price, amount, and quality of similar products. Unit pricing can help. The unit price tells you the costs per "unit" (such as per ounce, per pound, per sheet) to buy the product.

Your supermarket offers three sizes of the same cereal.

Cereal	Cereal	Cereal
32 oz.	20 oz.	14 oz.
$5.76	**$3.40**	**$2.52**

To compute the unit price—the price per ounce, in this case—you need to divide the price of each item by its weight. Here is the formula:

$$\text{Unit price} = \frac{\text{Price}}{\text{Weight}}$$

Which one is the best buy?

$5.76 divided by 32 ounces = 18¢
$3.40 divided by 20 ounces = 17¢
$2.52 divided by 14 ounces = 18¢

In this case, the 20-ounce box offers the best price at 17 cents per ounce.

Analyzing Economics

1. **Calculating** Figure the unit price and compare accuracy to the unit price sticker. For example, which is the better buy: a 16-oz. loaf of bread at $.96 or a 25-oz. loaf at $1.20?
2. **Explaining** Can you think of a situation in which you would *not* buy a product at the most economical price? Explain your reasons.

Section Audio

Spotlight Video

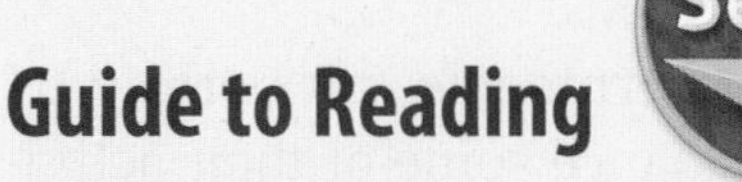

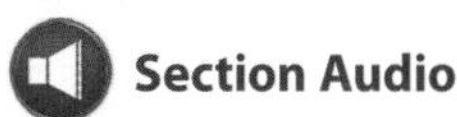

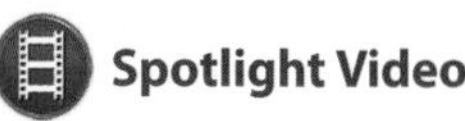

Section 3

Managing the Economy

Guide to Reading

Big Idea

Political and economic institutions evolve to help individuals and groups accomplish their goals.

Content Vocabulary

- surplus *(p. 688)*
- deficit *(p. 688)*
- bond *(p. 688)*
- debt *(p. 688)*
- balanced budget *(p. 688)*
- automatic stabilizer *(p. 692)*

Academic Vocabulary

- precise *(p. 688)*
- ideological *(p. 691)*

Reading Strategy

Explaining As you read, complete a graphic organizer like the one below to explain the differences between a federal deficit and the federal debt.

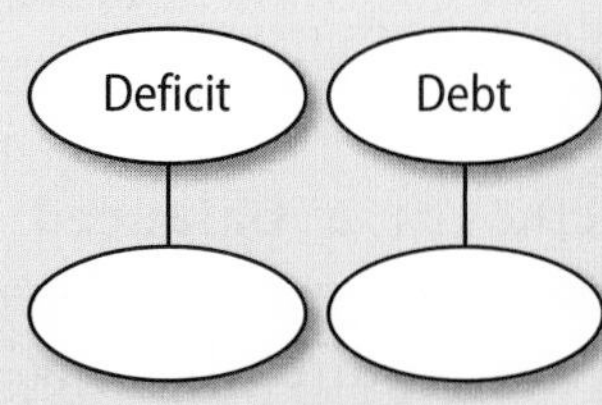

Real World Economics This clock is the same in all time zones. The National Debt Clock, created by New York City historian Seymour Durst, acts as a wake-up call to citizens in the United States, making them aware of how much the nation has economically overextended itself—how much money it owes. Today, the national debt is approaching the $10 trillion mark, an amount so enormous most people cannot understand it. The clock spells it out.

▼ **National Debt Clock in midtown Manhattan, New York City**

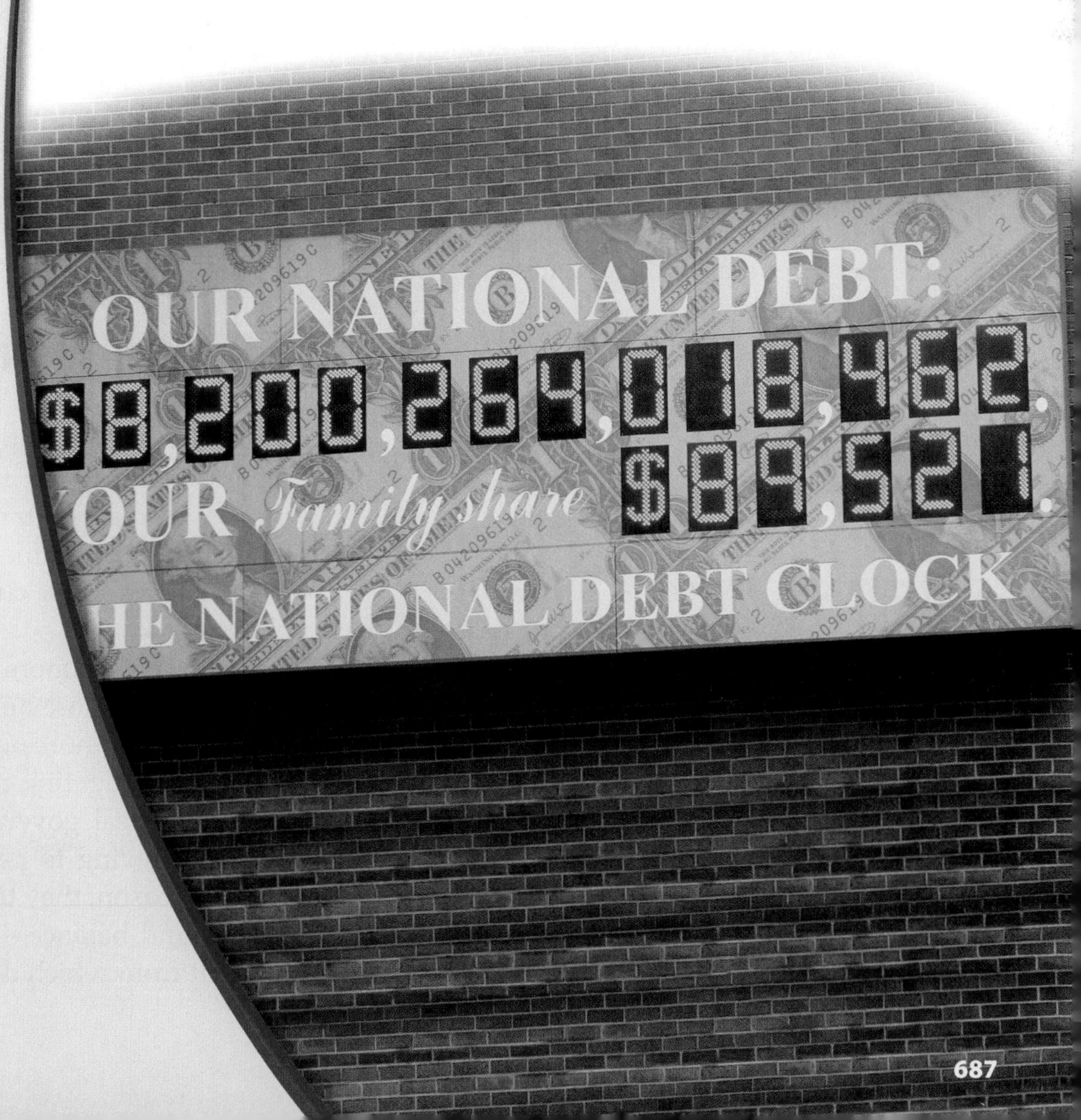

Surpluses and Deficits

Main Idea **Governmental budgeting can result in either a surplus, a deficit, or a balanced budget.**

Economics & You Do you find it easy to estimate how much money you will need over a week or a month? Read to find out why estimating is a challenge for most governments.

Governmental budgeting can be difficult. A budget, after all, is built on forecasts, which are not always **precise,** or exact. If tax revenues are lower than expected, the budget is in trouble. The same is true if expenses are higher than anticipated because of some emergency. In this section, you will learn what happens when the government spends more—or collects more—than it planned. You will also see what steps governments can take to try to influence the economy in certain ways.

When a government spends less than it collects in revenues, it enjoys a **surplus.** A government runs a **deficit** when it spends more than it collects in revenues. Review the proposed federal budget from Section 1 on page 679. As you can see, the federal government planned to end the fiscal year with a deficit of $354 billion. Look at graph A on page 690. You will see that the federal government had deficits for almost all the years shown on the graph.

From the Deficit to the Debt

When the federal government runs a deficit, it must borrow money so it can pay its bills. This borrowing is similar to an individual overspending his or her income and using credit. The government borrows money by selling **bonds.** A bond is a contract to repay the borrowed money with interest at a specific time in the future. When you buy United States savings bonds, you are also lending funds to the federal government. State and local governments can borrow by selling bonds to finance some of their activities. All the money that has been borrowed over the years and has not yet been paid back is the government's **debt,** also known as the national debt.

When a government runs deficits, its total debt goes up. On the other hand, surpluses can be used to cut the debt. Suppose, for example, that the U.S. government had a deficit of $100 billion in one year, followed by a deficit of $75 billion the next. If the country had no earlier debt, it would have a total debt of $175 billion after two years. Suppose it then had a surplus of $50 billion in the third year. That money could be used to reduce the debt to $125 billion.

How Big Is the Debt? The national debt has grown almost continuously since 1900, when the debt was $1.3 billion. By 1940 it was $50.7 billion. Huge budget deficits in the early 1990s and early 2000s have pushed the national debt held by the public to approximately $4.9 trillion by October 2006. This equals about $16,365 for every man, woman, and child in America.

A Balanced Budget

The government achieves a **balanced budget** when spending equals revenues. The federal government is not required by law to have a balanced budget, but 48 states and many local governments are. In these cases, governments must cut spending when revenues go down.

During bad economic times, revenues often go down. Yet those are the times when states need to spend more on entitlements. This can make the budgeting process difficult. Many state and local governments are prohibited from borrowing to pay operating expenses. For that reason, they try to maintain an emergency fund balance—a government savings account from which deficits can be paid.

Political Cartoons

Michael Ramirez/Copley News Service

America's major entitlement programs are the subject of this cartoon by Michael Ramirez.

1. **How are Social Security and Medicare represented?**
2. **What does the wave stand for?**
3. **What do you think the cartoonist's outlook is for the future of Social Security and Medicare?**

Impact of the National Debt

When the government spends more than it collects in tax revenues, it has to borrow the difference. You have learned that deficits lead to debt. But what does debt lead to?

Even though we owe most of the national debt to ourselves—through the purchase of bonds—the debt can affect the economy in several ways.

Paying Interest The national debt's most direct impact on the federal budget is the amount of tax money needed each year to finance past borrowing. Every year the interest on the national debt must be paid. U.S. taxpayers shoulder the responsibility of paying the interest. In fiscal year 2006, interest on the publicly held debt amounted to $218 billion. This total is roughly equal to one-quarter of all personal income tax revenue collected for 2006, and is a larger amount than the federal share of the payments for Medicaid.

The larger the national debt, the larger the interest payments, and, therefore, the more taxes needed to pay them. When people pay more taxes to the government, they have less money to spend on their own needs.

Interest Rate Additionally, when the federal government borrows money, it leaves less for citizens and private business to borrow. According to the law of supply and demand, an increase in the government's demand for credit will push up the price of credit—the interest rate. A Federal Reserve study in 2003 concluded that for every percentage point increase in the deficit as a share of GDP, long-term interest rates will rise by one-quarter percent. For example, you purchase an automobile for $20,000. Based on a four-year loan at 8 percent interest, your cumulative payments total $23,436.48, of which $3,436.48 is interest. If the interest rate is 9 percent, you pay an additional $453.21 in interest over the life of the loan.

Reading Check **Explaining** How does the federal government get money when it runs a budget deficit?

Graphs In MOtion
See StudentWorks™ Plus or glencoe.com.

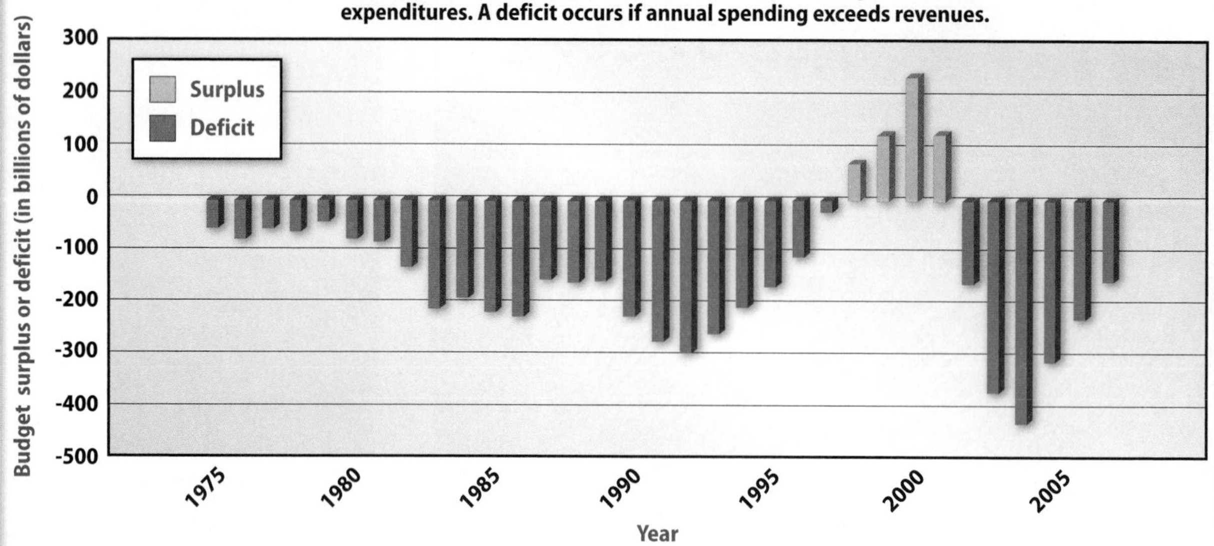

Source: U.S. Office of Management and Budget; U.S. Treasury Department.

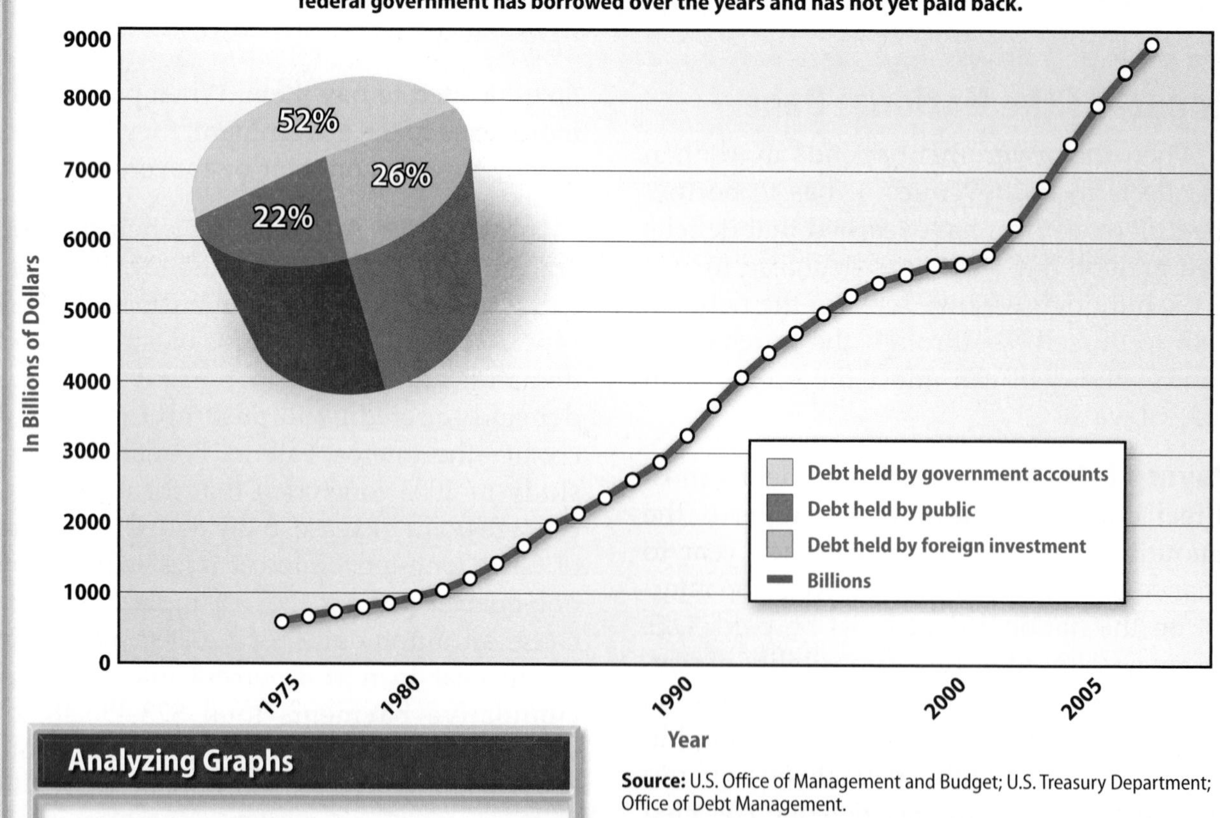

Source: U.S. Office of Management and Budget; U.S. Treasury Department; Office of Debt Management.

Analyzing Graphs

1. **Analyzing** During what years did the federal budget show a surplus?
2. **Summarizing** Describe the changes in the national debt during each of the decades shown on the graph.

Fiscal Policy

Main Idea **The tool of fiscal policy can help governments control the economy.**

Economics & You Do you need to talk your friends into doing something they already want to do? Of course not! Read how this idea applies to fiscal policy.

The role of government in the nation's economy extends beyond its activities as a regulator of specific industries. The government also manages the pace of economic activity. As you learned in Chapter 23, the federal government can try to use taxes and spending to help the economy grow. This practice is known as fiscal policy.

In theory, the government can stimulate the economy during a recession by increasing spending and cutting taxes. When the economy begins to grow again, less stimulus is needed. In those times, the government can reduce spending and increase taxes.

Fiscal Policy in Practice

Nonetheless, these decisions are difficult to make. Many people want lower taxes regardless of the state of the economy. Many people also want government services, so the federal government has a difficult time cutting spending even when the economy is strong.

Does Fiscal Policy Work? Some lawmakers oppose increased spending or tax cuts on **ideological** grounds, or sets of beliefs they hold. Even when leaders agree that a stimulus is needed, they often argue over where and how to spend the money.

Moreover, government action does not always have the desired effect. Sometimes it takes a long time for political leaders to agree on a plan to stimulate the economy. By then, many months may have passed, and the economic situation may have changed.

TIME™ Teens in Action

Katie Anderton

The homeless shelter Bethesda House in Schenectady, New York, has found the perfect volunteer in Katie Anderton. This 16-year-old from the same city says, "A lot of people my age are afraid of anyone different from them, but I don't see differences—I see people."

QUESTION: What is Bethesda House?

ANSWER: It's the lead agency serving the homeless in Schenectady. They're trying to end homelessness and make our community a welcoming place for everyone to live.

Q: What does it do to help?

A: Everything! Bethesda House has things like hot meals, showers, and a laundry. There's a medical clinic for people with no health insurance and case managers to assist people to find affordable housing. The agency also helps to educate the community about homelessness, to advocate for fairness in jobs, salaries, and health insurance.

Q: Wow! How many people does it assist?

A: Almost 8,000 different people come to Bethesda House each year. More than 60,000 meals are served. Over 500 homeless people are placed in emergency shelters and 85 percent of them are helped to move into permanent housing.

Making a Difference — **CITIZENSHIP**

Explaining What is the purpose of Bethesda House?

Automatic Stabilizers

It is difficult for the federal government to use fiscal policy to effectively stabilize the economy. However, the economy has a number of **automatic stabilizers.** These are programs that begin working to stimulate the economy as soon as they are needed. The main advantage of these programs is that they are already in place and do not need further government action to begin.

Unemployment Benefits Unemployment insurance programs are one example of automatic stabilizers. When people lose their jobs—as may happen in a recession—they collect unemployment payments. These payments are not very large. Still, they do give people some help until they can find a new job—or until the economy improves and they are hired back by their former employers.

Income Tax The fact that the federal income tax is progressive is another stabilizer. Remember that a progressive tax is based on a taxpayer's ability to pay. The higher a person's taxable income, the higher the tax rate. Progressive tax rates are lower at lower income levels. When people lose their jobs, their income goes down, pushing them into a lower tax bracket. The lower bracket helps ease the impact of the cut in income.

When the economy recovers, the opposite happens. People make more money and, therefore, need and receive less help from entitlements. Generally, automatic stabilizers go into effect much more rapidly than discretionary fiscal policies—policies that governments *choose* to implement.

Reading Check **Explaining** Why is fiscal policy difficult to implement?

Vocabulary

1. **Define** the following terms and use them in sentences related to governmental management of the economy: *surplus, deficit, bond, debt, balanced budget, automatic stabilizer.*

Main Ideas

2. **Explaining** What two situations can cause a budget deficit?
3. **Describing** What is the main advantage of an automatic stabilizer?

Critical Thinking

4. **Concluding** Do you think the federal government should be required, like most state governments, to balance the budget every year? Explain.
5. **BIG Ideas** In a graphic organizer like the one below, explain the effect of a government budget deficit.

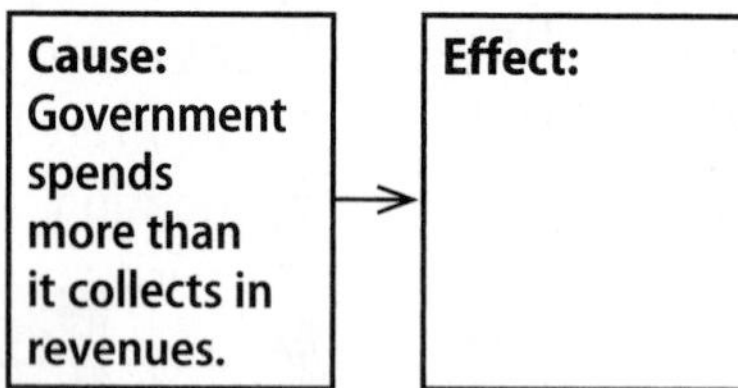

6. **Analyzing Visuals** Look at the graphs on page 690 that show the deficit and the debt. Describe the deficit in the 1970s compared to that of the 1990s.

CITIZENSHIP Activity

7. **Persuasive Writing** Write a paragraph that supports a position on the following statement: In a free-market system like ours, it should never be the government's job to stimulate the economy.

Study Central™ To review this section, go to glencoe.com.

Chapter 25 Visual Summary

American taxpayers finance most local, state, and federal governments.

↓

In return, they receive services such as education, entitlement programs, police and fire protection, national defense, and highway construction.

↓

The federal budget is the government's blueprint for raising revenues and spending money—its expenditures.

↓

Governmental budgeting can result in either a surplus, a deficit, or a balanced budget.

↓

State and local governments also have revenues and expenditures.

↓

Fiscal policy is a tool that can help governments control the economy.

Government prints money

The published U.S. budget

The price of gasoline includes an excise tax

Taxes pay for city services

Study anywhere, anytime! Download quizzes and flash cards to your PDA from glencoe.com.

Chapter

25 ASSESSMENT

Standardized Test Practice

TEST-TAKING TIP

When reading a question, note words that tell you that your answer is to be in the negative, such as *Which of these is NOT. . . or All of these EXCEPT. . . .*

Reviewing Vocabulary

Directions: Choose the word(s) that best completes the sentence.

1. Each year the president and Congress have to agree on a plan for spending called a ______.

A revenue **C** budget
B progressive tax **D** regressive tax

2. ______ provides government money to people who are retired or disabled.

A Social Security **C** Appropriations bill
B Medicare **D** Proportional tax

3. A(n) ______ is usually levied on consumer purchases of almost all products.

A property tax **C** education tax
B entitlement **D** sales tax

4. The government borrows money by selling ______.

A deficits **C** entitlement programs
B bonds **D** appropriations

Reviewing Main Ideas

Directions: Choose the best answer for each question.

Section 1 *(pp. 676–680)*

5. The federal income tax is a progressive tax, which means the ______.

A tax rate increases as income increases
B tax rate decreases as income increases
C tax rate decreases as income decreases
D tax rate and income are not related

6. A portion of the federal budget each year pays for the interest on ______.

A money lent to Great Britain
B money collected in taxes
C money spent on scientific research
D money borrowed by the government

Section 2 *(pp. 681–685)*

7. The largest source of revenues for local governments is ______.

A property taxes
B intergovernmental revenues
C local income taxes
D fines and fees

8. Which of the following is funding that state governments are NOT responsible for?

A welfare and health programs
B universities and colleges
C interstate highway maintenance
D water supplies and sewers

Section 3 *(pp. 687–692)*

9. Managing the nation's fiscal policy ______.

A requires the president and Congress to work together
B is left entirely to Congress
C is voted on by the people of Washington, D.C.
D must be approved by the Supreme Court

10. The best financial situation for the United States is to have ______.

A deficits exceed surpluses
B surpluses exceed deficits
C deficits exceed revenues
D deficits and surpluses to be equal

GO ON

Critical Thinking

Directions: Choose the best answer for each question.

11. What trend can be seen when looking at the size of the national debt over decades?

A It gets smaller every year and could be paid off in ten years.

B It is a very small part of the federal budget.

C It grows larger every year and will be difficult to pay off.

D It developed because the government had a revenue surplus every year.

12. What trend is expected with Medicare costs in the future?

A The costs will go up steadily.

B The costs will go down dramatically.

C The costs will remain stable with little change.

D The government will do away with the Medicare program.

Base your answer to question 13 on the diagram below and your knowledge of Chapter 25.

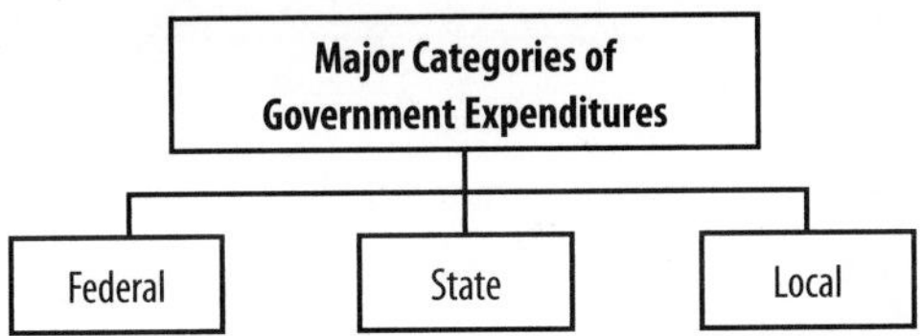

13. Expenditures for Social Security and national defense best fit under which level of government?

A Federal

B State

C Local

D Federal and State

Document-Based Questions

Merton Miller was a well-respected American economist and teacher who lived from 1923–2000.

> *. . . if you take money out of your left pocket and put it in your right pocket, you're no richer.*
>
> —Merton Miller

14. How do you think Miller feels about the government investing its money to make it grow?

A He would disagree with investing.

B He thinks saving is the best way to manage funds.

C He would be in favor of investing funds.

D He doesn't believe in income taxes for investing.

15. What do you think Miller believed the government's role in managing its money should be?

A The government should stay out of money management.

B The government is doing a good job of balancing the budget.

C The government has to make its funds increase for the country to prosper.

D The government should ask individual citizens to manage its money.

Extended-Response Question

16. Some people believe more power over spending money should be given to the states rather than the federal government controlling it. What do you think? Write a Pro/Con list for giving the states more power over spending. Conclude with a paragraph about what your list shows.

STOP

For additional test practice, use Self-Check Quizzes—Chapter 25 on glencoe.com.

Need Extra Help?

If you missed question...	1	2	3	4	5	6	7	8	9	10	11	12	13	14	15	16
Go to page...	677	678	682	688	678	680	682	684	691	688	690	680	680	678	678	684

TIME REPORTS

The Federal Deficit

As government spending grows and tax revenues shrink, the United States racks up record-breaking debt

AFP/Getty Images

ADDING IT UP This electronic clock, located in New York City, shows the total U.S. government debt as of August 2006 (top) and the estimated share for each American family (bottom). The *national debt* is the total amount of money that the government owes; the *deficit* is the yearly amount by which spending exceeds revenue. The clock does not have enough digits to show the debt when it reaches the $10 trillion mark, which is expected to occur by 2008.

Back in 2000, when Bill Clinton was completing his second term as President, the United States had a budget surplus of $236 billion—meaning that the federal government took in 236 billion more dollars than it spent that year. Under President George W. Bush, the surplus has become an annual deficit of $400 billion. About a quarter of what the government has spent since Bush entered the White House has been borrowed.

In Bush's defense, Josh Bolten—who served as Director of the Office of Management and Budget before becoming White House Chief of Staff—points to the economy the President inherited. "We had this burst bubble. Revenues just disappeared, and this was all before the President's tax cuts." But when Bush came into office, the nonpartisan Congressional Budget Office (CBO) was projecting surpluses for years to come, until Bush's tax cuts went into effect. CBO estimates show that if Bush's tax cuts are made permanent—as he is advocating—deficits will persist for at least 10 years.

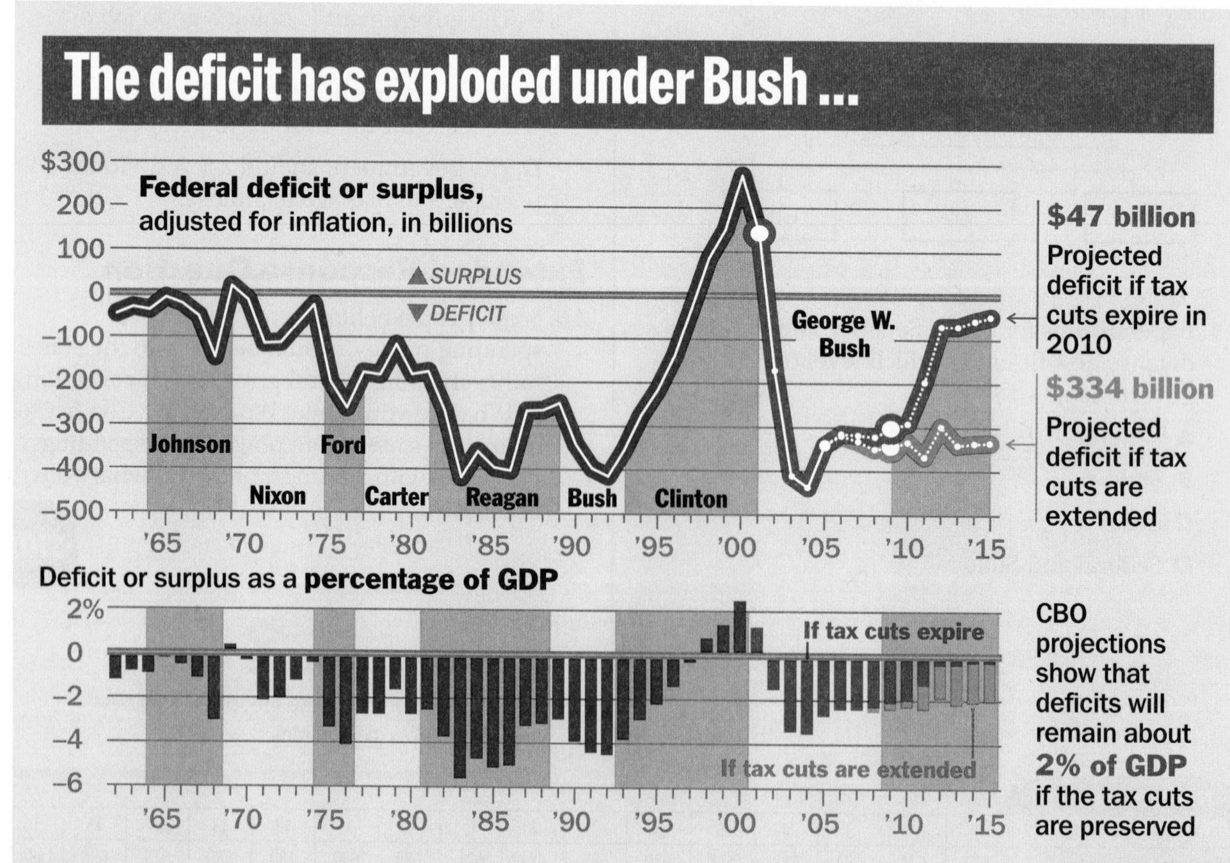

... and spending has increased rapidly ...

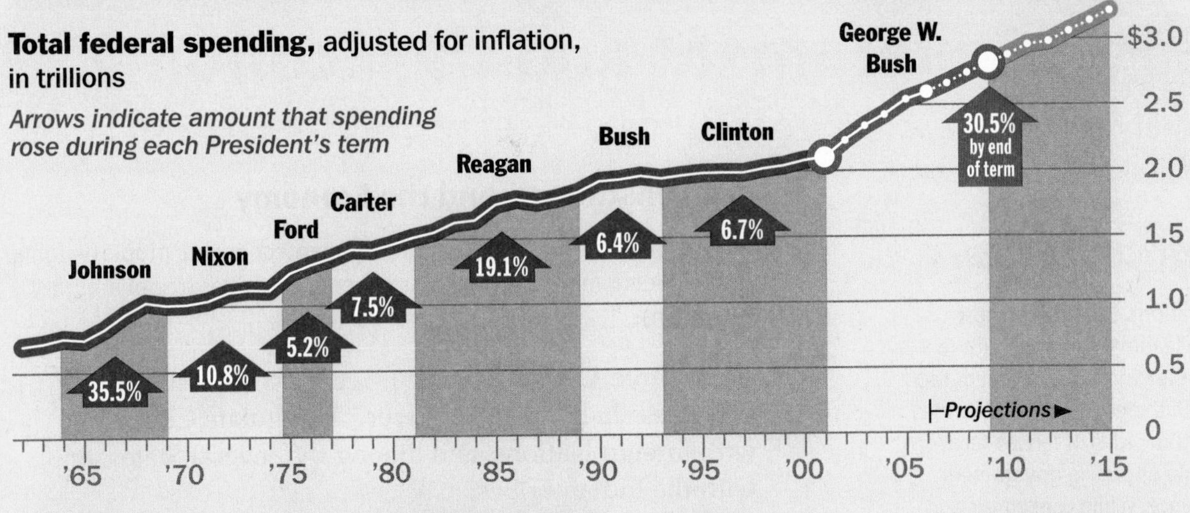

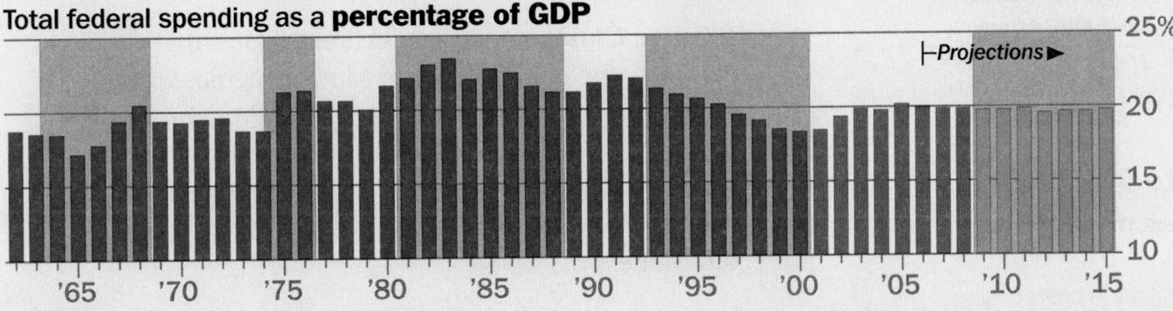

... across the entire government

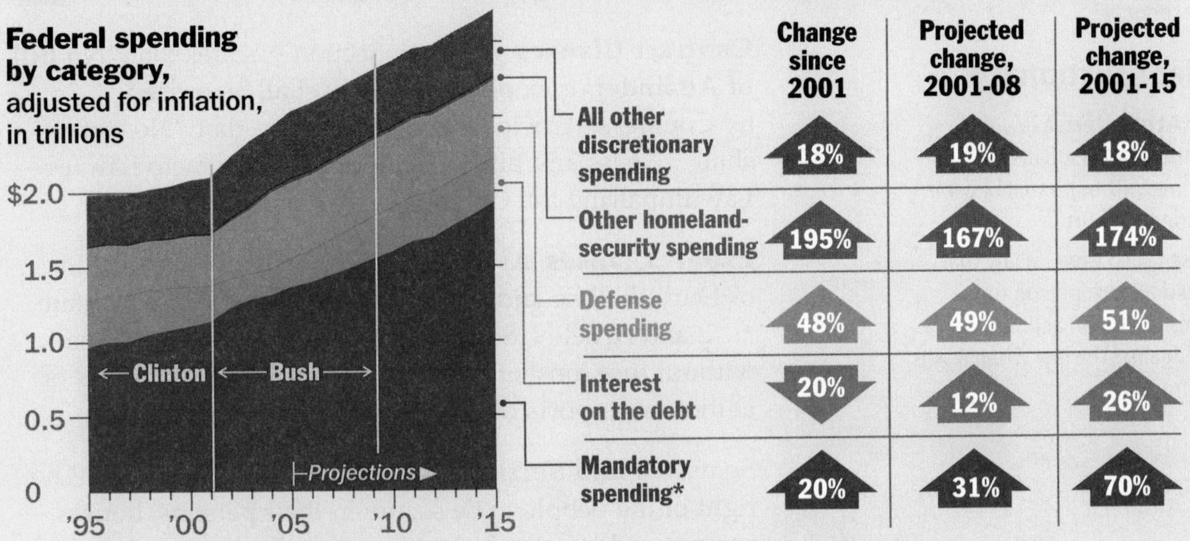

	Change since 2001	Projected change, 2001-08	Projected change, 2001-15
All other discretionary spending	18%	19%	18%
Other homeland-security spending	195%	167%	174%
Defense spending	48%	49%	51%
Interest on the debt	20%	12%	26%
Mandatory spending*	20%	31%	70%

*Programs such as Social Security, Medicare, Medicaid, veterans' benefits, unemployment, food stamps

Sources: Congressional Budget Office, Bureau of Labor Statistics, Center on Budget and Policy Priorities. All inflation-adjusted figures are 2006 dollars

Analyzing Primary Sources

Government and the Economy

Reading Focus

In the nation's early years, most political leaders were reluctant to involve the federal government too heavily in the economic sector. They accepted the idea of laissez-faire, a doctrine opposing government interference. While consumers and producers make most economic decisions, government activities have a powerful effect on the U.S. economy.

Read to Discover

As you read, think about the following:

- Why did the Framers believe it was necessary that the Constitution include the commerce clause?
- How much influence should the government have over the economy?

Reader's Dictionary

Bill of Attainder: a law that punishes a person accused of a crime without a trial or a fair hearing in court

ex post facto law: a law that would allow a person to be punished for an action that was not against the law when it was committed

The Constitution and the Economy

Some provisions in the U.S. Constitution protect private property rights and the freedom to take part in commercial activities free of arbitrary restrictions.

Commerce Clause Article I, Section 8, states that Congress shall have the power "To regulate Commerce with foreign Nations, and among the several States, and with the Indian Tribes; . . ."

Coinage Clause Article I, Section 8, states that Congress shall have the power "To coin Money, regulate the value thereof, . . ." and "To provide for the Punishment of counterfeiting the Securities and current Coin of the United States; . . ." Article I, Section 10, gives Congress this power exclusively by stating that "No State shall . . . coin Money; . . ."

Copyright Clause Article I, Section 8, states that Congress shall have the power "To promote the Progress of Science and useful Arts, by securing for limited Times to Authors and Inventors the exclusive Right to their respective Writing and Discoveries; . . ."

Contract Clauses Article I, Section 9, states that "**No Bill of Attainder** or **ex post facto Law** shall be passed . . ." by Congress. Article I, Section 10, states that "No state shall . . . pass any Bill of Attainder, ex post facto Law, or Law impairing the Obligations of Contracts, . . ."

Export Clauses Article I, Section 9, states that "No Tax or Duty shall be laid on Articles exported from any State . . .", and Article I, Section 10, states that "No State shall, without the Consent of the Congress, lay any Imposts or Duties on Imports or Exports, . . ."

Searches and Seizures Amendment IV states that "The right of the people to be secure in their persons, houses, papers, and effects, against unreasonable searches and seizures, shall not be violated, . . ."

Due Process Amendment V states that "No person shall . . . be deprived of life, liberty, or property, without due process of the law; . . ." and Amendment XIV, Section 1, states, "nor shall any State deprive any person of life, liberty, or property, without due process of law; . . ."

Reserved Rights and Powers Amendment IX states that "The enumeration in the Constitution, of certain rights, shall not be construed to deny or disparage others retained by the people." And Amendment X states, "The powers not delegated to the United States by the Constitution, nor prohibited by it to the States, are reserved to the States respectively, or to the people."

Photographs as Primary Sources A new $1 coin was introduced in 2007. The United States Mint will mint and issue four presidential $1 coins per year. Why do you think the coin features the presidents?

Role of Government

Two presidents provide their views on the role of government in the economy.

> [A] wise and frugal government, which shall restrain men from injuring one another, which shall leave them otherwise free to regulate their own pursuits of industry and improvement, and shall not take from the mouth of labor the bread it has earned. This is the sum of good government.
>
> —Thomas Jefferson, First Inaugural Address, March 4, 1801

> Government ought to have the right and will have the right, after surveying and planning for an industry to prevent, with the assistance of the overwhelming majority of that industry, unfair practice and to enforce this agreement by the authority of government. The so-called anti-trust laws were intended to prevent the creation of monopolies and to forbid unreasonable profits to those monopolies. That purpose of the anti-trust laws must be continued, but these laws were never intended to encourage the kind of unfair competition that results in long hours, starvation wages and overproduction.
>
> —President Franklin D. Roosevelt, Fireside chat, Sunday, May 7, 1933

DBQ Document-Based Questions

1. **Explaining** What restrictions does the U.S. Constitution place on state and local taxing powers?
2. **Describing** Which excerpt supports a laissez-faire position regarding government and the economy? Explain.
3. **Evaluating and Connecting** Originally the Framers of the Constitution wanted to ensure that Congress could not involve itself in the states' internal affairs. Yet, the necessary and proper clause has been expanded so that Congress now has some control over virtually all economic activities, even within each state's borders. Do you think this is a fair exercise of congressional power? Give reasons for your answer.

UNIT 8

The United States and the World

Panamanian ship *United Caroline* guided through the port of Los Angeles

★ Chapter 26 Comparing Economic Systems

★ Chapter 27 An Interdependent World

Be an Active Citizen

CITIZENSHIP The world seems smaller than it did only 50 years ago. Modern transportation and communication have brought people around the globe closer together. As citizens of the United States and members of the global community, we have a responsibility to stay informed about developments in other nations and the world.

UNIT 8

Reading Social Studies

Monitoring and Clarifying

1 Learn It!

When you read something that is difficult, monitor your comprehension to determine when your understanding breaks down. Clarify, or clear up, confusing parts by rereading, defining unfamiliar words, and asking questions.

- Read the following paragraph and look at the chart below. Write what you understand from the text in the column labeled √.
- Write what is confusing in the column labeled **?**.

> The German thinker and writer Karl Marx was a socialist who predicted violent revolution. Marx believed that the population in industrialized nations is divided into capitalists, or bourgeoisie, who own the means of production and workers, or proletariat, who work to produce the goods. Marx interpreted human history as a class struggle between the workers and the capitalists. Eventually, he thought the workers would revolt and overthrow the capitalists.
>
> —*from page 717*

Clarifying Text

√	?
Karl Marx was a socialist who predicted violent revolution.	What is a socialist?
Workers, or the proletariat, work to produce goods.	*Capitalists, or bourgeoisie, own the means of production.* What does it mean to "own the means of production"?
Eventually, the workers would revolt and overthrow the capitalists.	*Marx interpreted human history as a class struggle between the workers and the capitalists.* Does that mean that he thinks every civilization will have a class struggle?

Reading Tip

If you read something confusing, slow down and think about the text. Look at pictures, words in bold, and other hints to figure out the meaning.

② Practice It!

- Read the following paragraph. Draw a chart like the one below.
- Write what you understand from the text in the column labeled √.
- Write what is confusing in the column labeled **?**.

Read to Write Activity

Read "Issues to Debate" on page 714, titled "Should the United States Open ANWR for Oil Drilling?" Write at least two questions about the selection to help clarify your thoughts. Write the answers.

> Nevertheless, the United Nations has helped bring about peace in some areas and helped those who live in war-torn countries. In nations such as El Salvador, Cambodia, and Haiti, UN peacekeeping operations have helped sustain cease-fires, conduct free elections, monitor troop withdrawals, and prevent violence.
>
> —*from page 741*

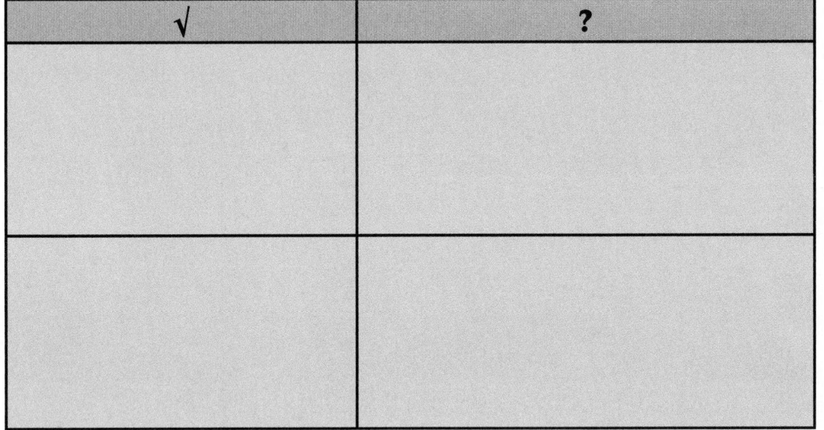

√	?

③ Apply It!

In a paragraph, identify two things you understand and two things that are confusing for:

- **Chapter 27, Section 2**

Chapter 26

Comparing Economic Systems

Why It Matters

The world is becoming more interconnected every day. One aspect of growing globalization is the vast number of foreign-made products you can buy. These products are in your stores because of international trade. Most of our trading partners are either developed or developing market economies.

Civics ONLINE
Visit glencoe.com and enter QuickPass™ code CIV3093c26 for Chapter 26 resources.

Chapter Audio

BIG Ideas

Section 1: International Trade

The exchange of goods and services helps create economic interdependence among peoples in different places and different countries. Nations trade with one another to obtain goods and services they themselves cannot produce efficiently.

Section 2: Economic Systems

An economic system is the way a society organizes the production and consumption of goods and services. Market and command economies approach economic decision making in very different ways.

Section 3: Economies in Transition

An economic system is the way a society organizes the production and consumption of goods and services. Both former command economies and developing nations face severe challenges in creating market economies.

◀ Workers at a plant that is part of Steel Authority of India Limited (SAIL), the leading steelmaking company in India

FOLDABLES™ Study Organizer

Analyzing Information Study Foldable Make the following Foldable to help you analyze the purposes and powers of world regional economic trade agreements.

Step 1 Fold a sheet of paper in half from side to side, leaving a two-inch tab at the bottom. Turn the paper and fold it into thirds.

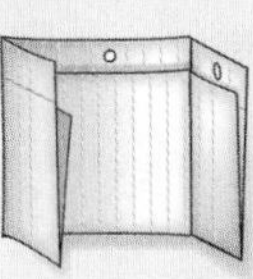

Step 2 Unfold and cut along the top fold lines to create three tabs.

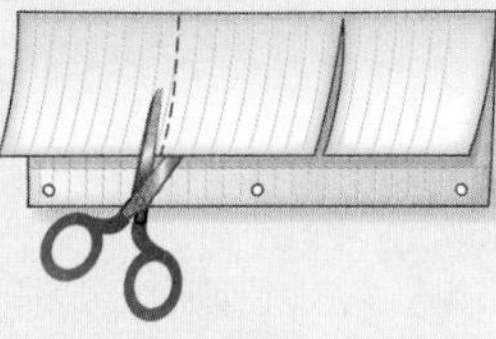

Step 3 Label the three tabs as shown.

Reading and Writing
As you read the chapter, note information about the three trade agreements. Then write a paragraph describing the agreement that you think is strongest and explain why.

Spotlight Video

International Trade

Guide to Reading

Big Idea

The exchange of goods and services helps create economic interdependence among peoples in different places and different countries.

Content Vocabulary

- export *(p. 707)*
- import *(p. 707)*
- comparative advantage *(p. 708)*
- tariff *(p. 708)*
- quota *(p. 708)*
- free trade *(p. 710)*
- exchange rate *(p. 712)*
- balance of trade *(p. 712)*
- trade surplus *(p. 712)*
- trade deficit *(p. 713)*

Academic Vocabulary

- consequently *(p. 708)*
- eventually *(p. 710)*
- flexible *(p. 712)*

Reading Strategy

Classifying On a graphic organizer like the one below, identify three reasons that nations trade.

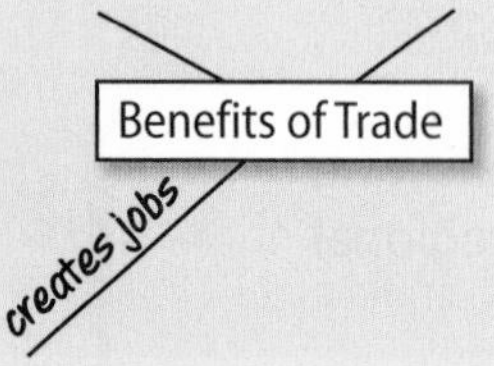

Benefits of Trade

creates jobs

Real World Economics Opening celebrations at the Hong Kong Stock Exchange include the giving of "Lai See," or red packets of lucky money, to the crowd. International trade—which is transacted in this stock exchange—is important to the U.S. economy. China is the second-largest exporter of goods to the United States. It is also the fastest growing market for U.S. goods. U.S. exports to China have grown over 300 percent since China joined the World Trade Organization in 2001.

▼ **Traders at Hong Kong Stock Exchange wave traditional lucky money**

Industry Workers craft athletic shoes at a factory in South Korea. The nation's major exports include motor vehicles and petrochemicals as well as footwear. ***Explaining*** **Why do nations trade?**

Why Nations Trade

Main Idea **Nations trade with one another to obtain goods and services they themselves cannot produce efficiently.**

Economics & You What do you think would happen if the United States could no longer sell goods to other countries or buy goods in return? Read to find out how this situation might affect our standard of living.

No country produces everything it needs to survive. Every country depends on other countries. Because of international trade, Americans can eat fruit during the winter grown in Central America. Through international trade, American computers are sold in Africa and Asia. More than 12 percent of all the goods produced in the United States are **exported,** or sold to other countries. A larger amount of goods are **imported,** or purchased from abroad. These purchases give Americans products they might not otherwise be able to enjoy.

Obtaining Scarce Goods

Trade is one way that nations solve the problem of scarcity. Nations trade for some goods and services because they could not otherwise have them or have them as cheaply. The United States buys industrial diamonds from other countries because it has almost no deposits of this mineral. Other nations trade for goods they cannot produce but that the United States can produce. Commercial aircraft built in California are sold to other countries that do not have the necessary factories or the skilled workers.

Comparative Advantage

The main reason countries trade with one another is **comparative advantage.** This is the ability of a country to produce a good at a relatively lower cost than another country can. The United States could make color televisions. Other countries, however, can make them at a lower cost. **Consequently,** the United States now buys color televisions that are made abroad.

Specialization Because of comparative advantage, nations can specialize. They use their scarce resources to produce those things that they produce better than other countries. Specialization can lead to overproduction—when a country produces more of a good than all the people in the country could consume. The answer to this problem is to sell the extra amount that is produced to other countries.

Factors of Production Comparative advantage can be based on natural resources. Saudi Arabia's comparative advantage, its huge deposits of oil, allows it to export oil. Sometimes comparative advantage is based on labor and capital. The United States has large supplies of wealth, many highly skilled workers, and advanced technology. As a result, it has a comparative advantage in making expensive products such as airplanes and weapons.

Creating Jobs

Finally, international trade creates jobs. Suppose, for example, that American airplane makers built planes for only American airline companies. If so, they would have a limited market, because each airline needs only so many new planes each year. By exporting the planes, the companies have a chance to win more orders, which leads to the hiring of more workers.

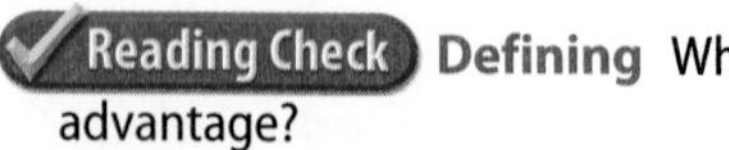

Defining What is comparative advantage?

Restrictions and Integration

Main Idea **Countries sometimes try to protect their economies by setting up trade barriers.**

Economics & You How important is price to you when you are shopping? If you are like most people, it is pretty important. In this section, you will learn how government actions can raise the price of imported goods.

Many consumers like to buy foreign-produced goods because they are cheaper. When they do so, companies in the consumers' own country lose sales. The companies are then likely to lower production and to lay off workers. When this happens, the affected workers and industries often demand that the government step in on their behalf to remedy the situation. The two most common kinds of barriers to trade that governments can apply are tariffs and quotas.

A tax on imported goods is called a **tariff,** or customs duty. If the United States wants to protect American steel producers, it can put a 20 percent tariff on all imported steel, thus adding 20 percent to its price. The goal of most tariffs is to make the price of imported goods higher than the price of the same goods produced domestically.

Sometimes people want a product so badly that higher prices have little effect—they will purchase it anyway. In this case, countries can block trade by using **quotas,** or limits on the amount of foreign goods imported. For example, during most of the 1970s, Japanese-made automobiles were so popular in the United States that the jobs of American autoworkers were threatened. As a result, President Ronald Reagan placed quotas on Japanese-made automobiles.

Student Web Activity Visit glencoe.com and complete the Chapter 26 Web Activity.

Imports and Exports, Selected Nations

Maps In MOtion
See StudentWorks™ Plus or glencoe.com.

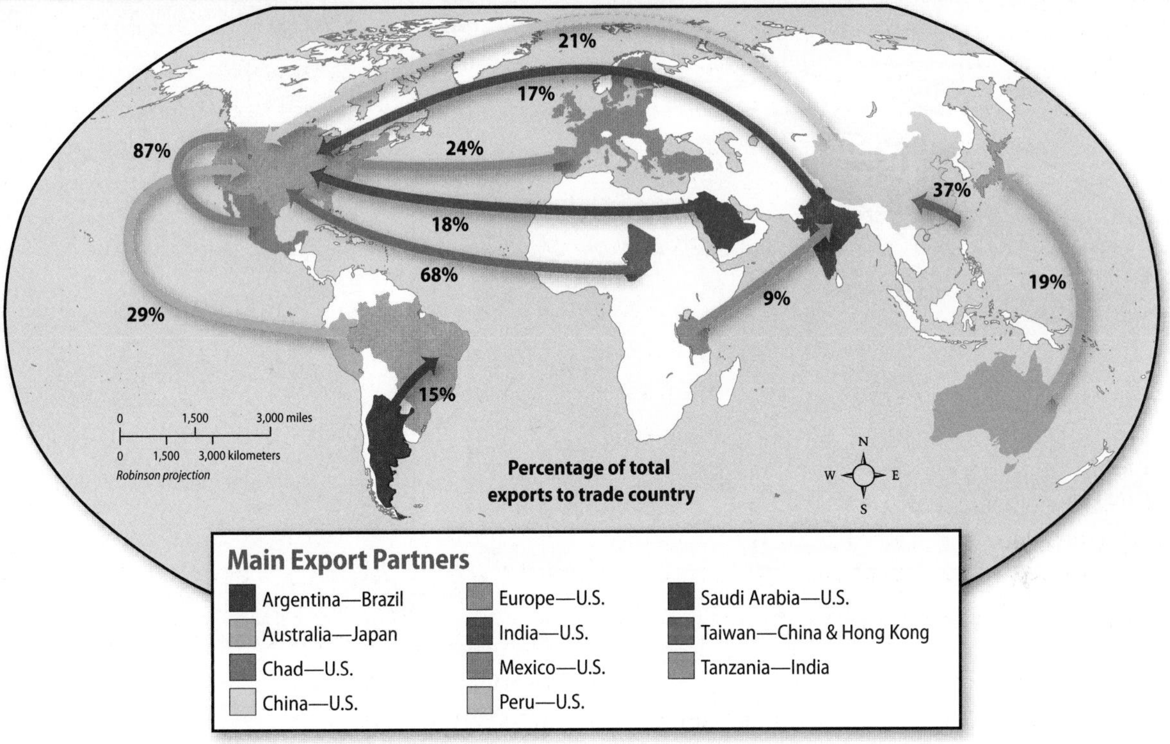

21%
17%
24%
87%
18%
37%
68%
19%
9%
29%
15%

0 1,500 3,000 miles
0 1,500 3,000 kilometers
Robinson projection

Percentage of total exports to trade country

N W E S

Main Export Partners

Argentina—Brazil	Europe—U.S.	Saudi Arabia—U.S.
Australia—Japan	India—U.S.	Taiwan—China & Hong Kong
Chad—U.S.	Mexico—U.S.	Tanzania—India
China—U.S.	Peru—U.S.	

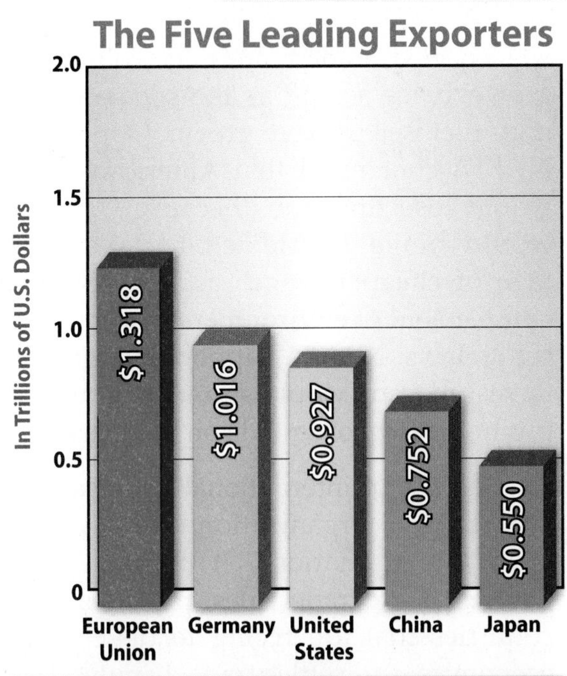

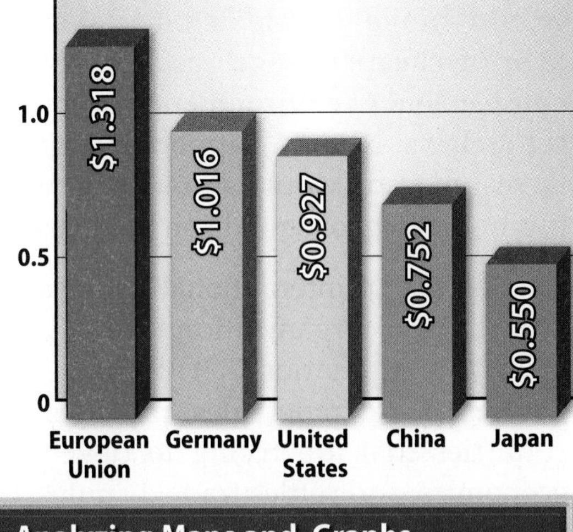

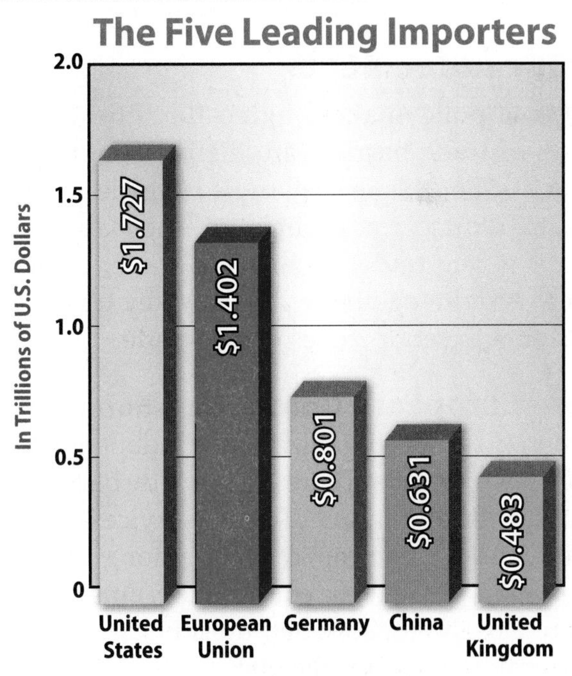

Source: *CIA The World Factbook*, 2006.

Analyzing Maps and Graphs

1. **Identifying** What nation is Brazil's chief import partner?
2. **Describing** Identify Mexico's chief export partner. What percentage of Mexico's exports go to that nation?

TIME Political Cartoons

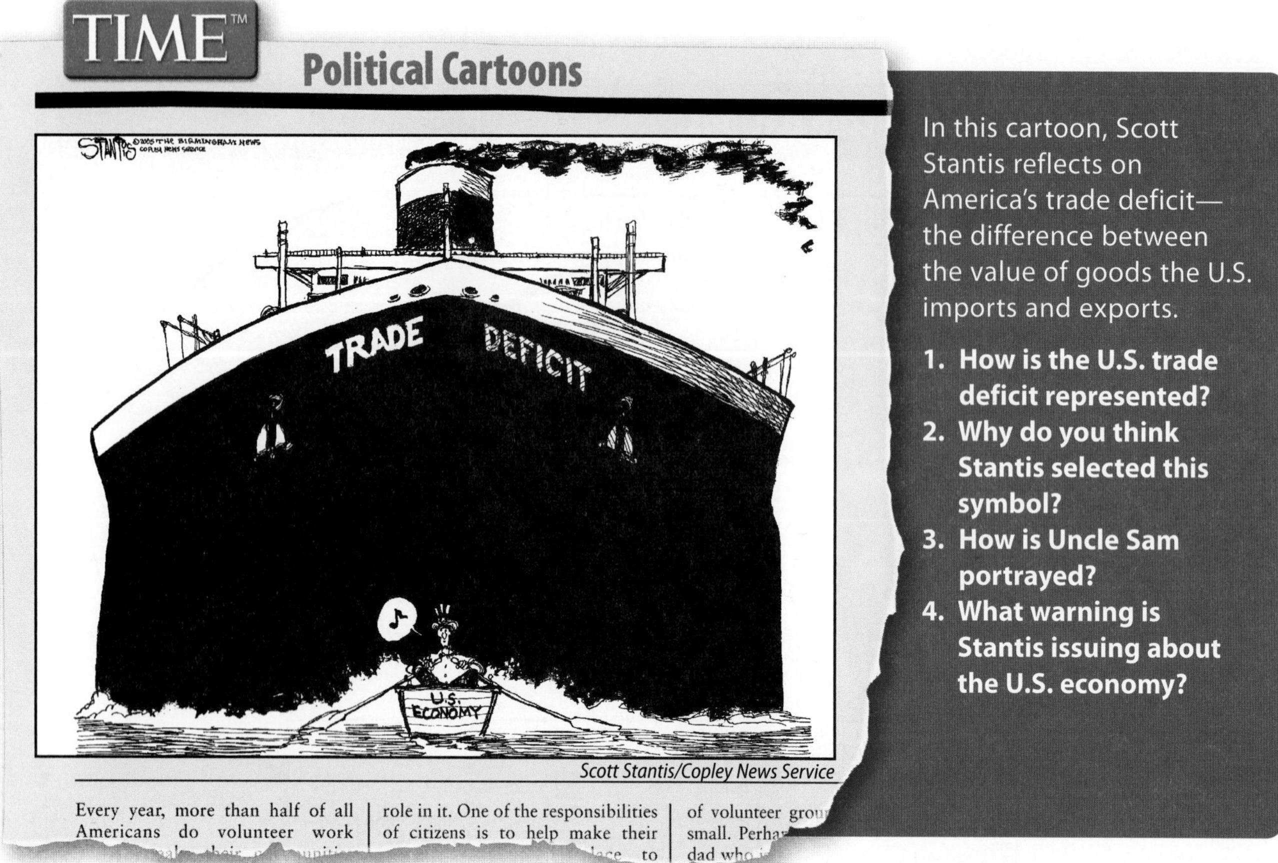

Scott Stantis/Copley News Service

In this cartoon, Scott Stantis reflects on America's trade deficit—the difference between the value of goods the U.S. imports and exports.

1. **How is the U.S. trade deficit represented?**
2. **Why do you think Stantis selected this symbol?**
3. **How is Uncle Sam portrayed?**
4. **What warning is Stantis issuing about the U.S. economy?**

Trade Agreements

Most policymakers agree that the total costs of trade barriers are higher than their benefits. For this reason, most countries now try to reduce trade barriers. They aim to achieve **free trade.** To increase trade, countries can join together with a few key trading partners to set up zones of free trade.

The European Union The European Union (EU) is an organization of independent European nations. There are no trade barriers among these nations. Goods, services, and even workers can move freely among them. In January 2002, these countries became even more closely linked when most began using a common currency, the euro.

NAFTA In the 1990s, the United States, Canada, and Mexico signed the North American Free Trade Agreement (NAFTA). This pact will **eventually** eliminate all barriers to trade among the three countries. Since NAFTA was enacted, trade among the countries has grown twice as fast as the separate economies themselves have grown. Opponents of NAFTA contended that American workers would lose their jobs because U.S. plants would move to Mexico to take advantage of cheaper wages and less stringent enforcement of environmental and workers' rights laws. NAFTA supporters argued that increased trade would stimulate growth and put more low-cost goods on the market.

The WTO An international body called the World Trade Organization (WTO) oversees trade among nations. It organizes negotiations about trade rules, provides help to countries that are trying to develop their economies, and settles trade disputes. Critics say that WTO policies favor major corporations at the expense of workers, the environment, and poor countries.

Reading Check **Explaining** Why do nations sometimes place quotas on an imported good?

The North American Free Trade Agreement (NAFTA)

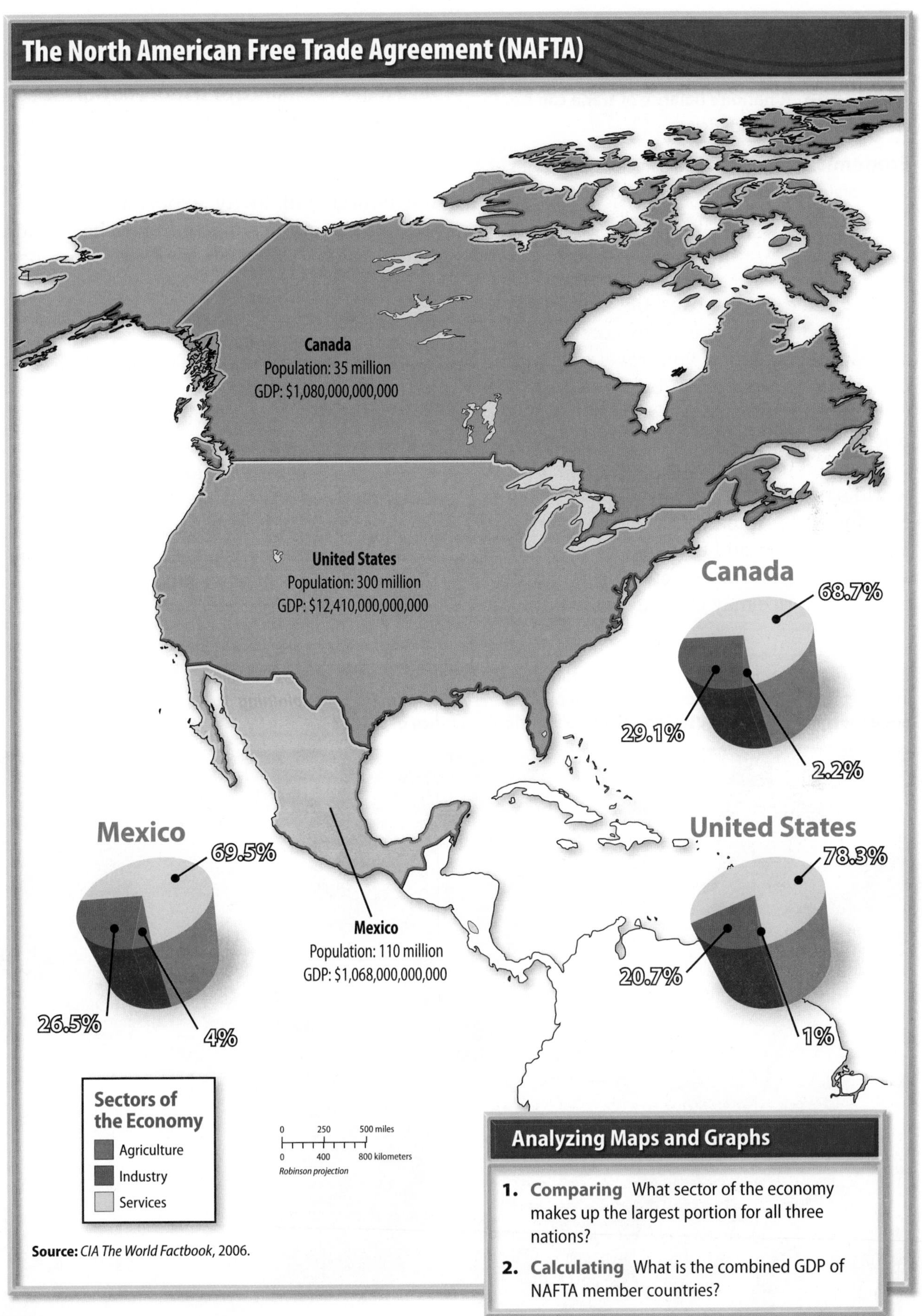

Source: *CIA The World Factbook*, 2006.

Analyzing Maps and Graphs

1. **Comparing** What sector of the economy makes up the largest portion for all three nations?
2. **Calculating** What is the combined GDP of NAFTA member countries?

Financing Trade

Main Idea **A nation's balance of trade can be either a surplus or a deficit.**

Economics & You Can you name the currencies of some foreign countries? Read to find out how these currencies are valued against our dollar.

The United States uses the dollar as its medium of exchange; Mexico, the peso; and Japan, the yen. If you travel outside the U.S. or invest in foreign business, you will want to know the **exchange rate**—what the price of your nation's currency is in terms of another nation's currency. Most of the world's nations use a **flexible,** or adjustable, exchange rate system. Under this system, the forces of supply and demand are allowed to set the price of various currencies. Thus, a currency's price may change each day.

The Balance of Trade

Exchange rates have an important effect on a nation's balance of trade. The **balance of trade** is the difference between the value of a nation's exports and its imports. If a nation's currency depreciates, or becomes "weak," the nation will likely export more goods because its products will become cheaper for other nations to buy. If a nation's currency appreciates in value, or becomes "strong," the amount of its exports will decline.

Positive Balance of Trade When the value of a nation's exports exceeds the value of its imports, a positive balance of trade exists. For example, if the value of a country's exports is $100 billion and the value of its imports is $50 billion, then the country has a positive balance of trade ($50 billion). In this case, the nation is bringing in more money than it is paying out. A positive balance of trade is known as a **trade surplus.**

Balance of Trade Bananas are the most profitable export fruit in the world. Most bananas imported to the United States are grown on plantations in Latin America. ***Explaining*** **How are exports and imports used to calculate a nation's balance of trade?**

Negative Balance of Trade A negative balance of trade exists when the value of goods coming into a country is greater than the value of those going out. For example, if the value of a country's exports is $70 billion and the value of its imports is $120 billion, then the country has a negative balance of trade (–$50 billion). A negative balance of trade is known as a **trade deficit.** A trade deficit can affect other factors in a country's economy.

Effects of a Trade Deficit

What are the effects of a trade deficit? A trade imbalance tends to erode the value of a country's currency on foreign exchange markets. The devalued currency then causes a chain reaction that affects income and employment in that country's industries. For example, the large deficit in the United States's balance of payments in late 2006 flooded the foreign exchange markets with dollars. As economists predicted, the rise in the supply of dollars caused the dollar to lose some of its value. The weaker dollar caused unemployment in import industries as imports became more expensive. However, this had an opposite effect in the area of exports. It caused employment to rise in export industries as the prices of these goods became more competitive.

Under flexible exchange rates, trade deficits will correct themselves through the price system. Historically this has been the case with regards to the American economy. A strong currency generally leads to a deficit in the balance of payment and a subsequent decline in the value of the currency. A weak currency tends to cause trade surpluses, which eventually pull up the value of the currency.

Reading Check **Describing** What is a trade deficit?

Section 1 Review

Vocabulary

1. **Create** a set of flash cards to use when you review the section; write the definitions on the backs of the cards for these terms: *export, import, comparative advantage, tariff, quota, free trade, exchange rate, balance of trade, trade surplus, trade deficit.*

Main Ideas

2. **Identifying** What are three reasons that nations trade among themselves?
3. **Explaining** How can trade barriers raise prices?
4. **Identifying** What is the name for the condition that exists when the value of a nation's exports exceeds the value of its imports?

Critical Thinking

5. **BIG Ideas** In a graphic organizer like the one below, explain the likely effects of weak and strong currencies on a nation's exports.

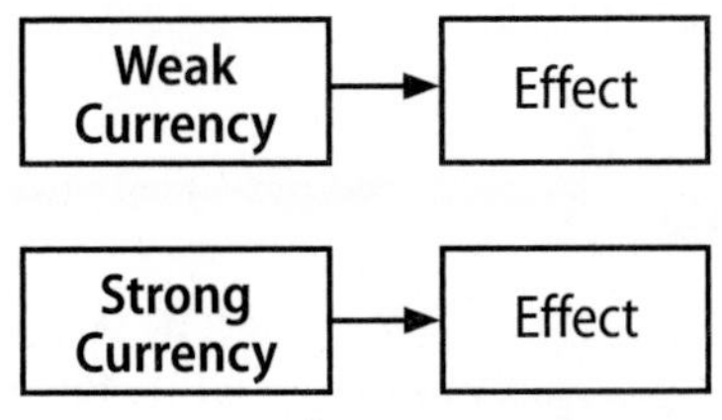

6. **Evaluating** Is a trade deficit a bad situation for a country? Explain your answer.

CITIZENSHIP Activity

7. **Creative Writing** Write a song, poem, short story, or dialogue about an effect of international trade, such as the demand for cheaper goods or the loss of jobs, on individuals in a community like yours. Share your work with the class.

Study Central™ To review this section, go to glencoe.com.

Issues to Debate

Should the United States Open ANWR for Oil Drilling?

More than 40 years ago, the United States government set aside lands in northeast Alaska to protect its wildlife, wilderness, and recreation values. The 1980 Alaska National Interest Lands Conservation Act doubled the size of the Arctic Range to 19 million acres and renamed it the Arctic National Wildlife Refuge (ANWR). About 100 miles west of ANWR is Prudhoe Bay, North America's largest oil field. Americans' increasing dependence on foreign oil and the rising price of gasoline has raised the issue of whether the federal government should allow oil companies to drill in ANWR. The issue has sparked heated debate in Congress and among interest groups.

Discovered in 1968, the oil fields at Prudhoe Bay in northern Alaska are the largest in North America.

YES

Supporters of drilling in ANWR claim that only a small area of the wildlife refuge would be affected. New drilling technology would protect the environment, while a major oil discovery would reduce the nation's dependence on foreign oil. Representative Don Young of Alaska, in an open letter to Congress, said, "According to the U.S. Energy Administration, the mean estimate of technically recoverable oil in ANWR is 10.4 billion barrels. That is almost half of the total U.S. proven reserve of 21 billion barrels. So in basic economic terms, if we open up ANWR, we would be increasing our supply, which in turn would lower prices. . . . Getting ANWR passed would provide Congress a tangible answer for its constituents when they want to know what we are doing about the high energy costs. ANWR is American oil. ANWR is 30 years worth of Saudi Arabian imports."

—Representative Don Young, May 24, 2006

NO

Defenders of Wildlife is one of the many environmental interest groups that opposes drilling in ANWR. These groups believe that oil development in the region would require a large web of industrial companies, hundreds of miles of roads and pipelines, refineries, and power plants that would change the environment. The grizzly bears, wolves, caribou, whales, and other species would be at risk. Defenders of Wildlife reports, "At the Prudhoe Bay oil field just west of the Arctic Refuge, spills of oil products and hazardous substances happen *every single day,* and noise and air pollution are rampant. According to Alaska's Department of Environmental Conservation, there are 55 contaminated waste sites already associated with this development." And they add, "Drilling for oil in the Arctic National Wildlife Refuge will not end America's dependence on Persian Gulf or other oil imports."

—Defenders of Wildlife, 2006

Debating the Issue

1. **Identifying** What is ANWR?
2. **Describing** What is the location and size of ANWR?
3. **Explaining** Why has Congress considered drilling for oil in this area?
4. **Concluding** Do the benefits outweigh the risks of drilling for oil in ANWR? Explain.

Section Audio Spotlight Video

Section 2

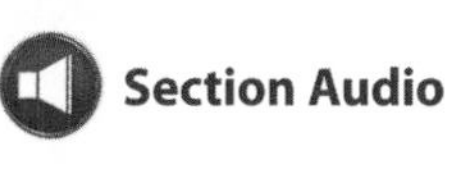

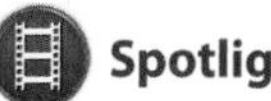

Economic Systems

Guide to Reading

Big Idea

An economic system is the way a society organizes the production and consumption of goods and services.

Content Vocabulary

- market economy *(p. 716)*
- per capita GDP *(p. 716)*
- command economy *(p. 717)*
- socialism *(p. 717)*
- communism *(p. 718)*
- mixed economy *(p. 719)*

Academic Vocabulary

- intervene *(p. 716)*
- exploit *(p. 717)*

Reading Strategy

Describing As you read, complete a diagram like the one below by describing characteristics of a market economy.

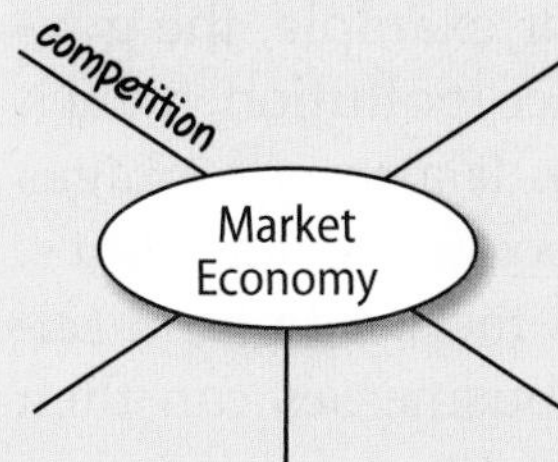

Real World Economics Suppose the government told you that you could not operate your own business. That is exactly what happened to this Cuban woman in 2005. The Cuban government—one of the best-known examples of a command economy—told her that she could no longer sell flowers to make extra money. In Cuba, the government makes all the economic decisions. Many Americans hope that Cuba moves toward a freer market economy.

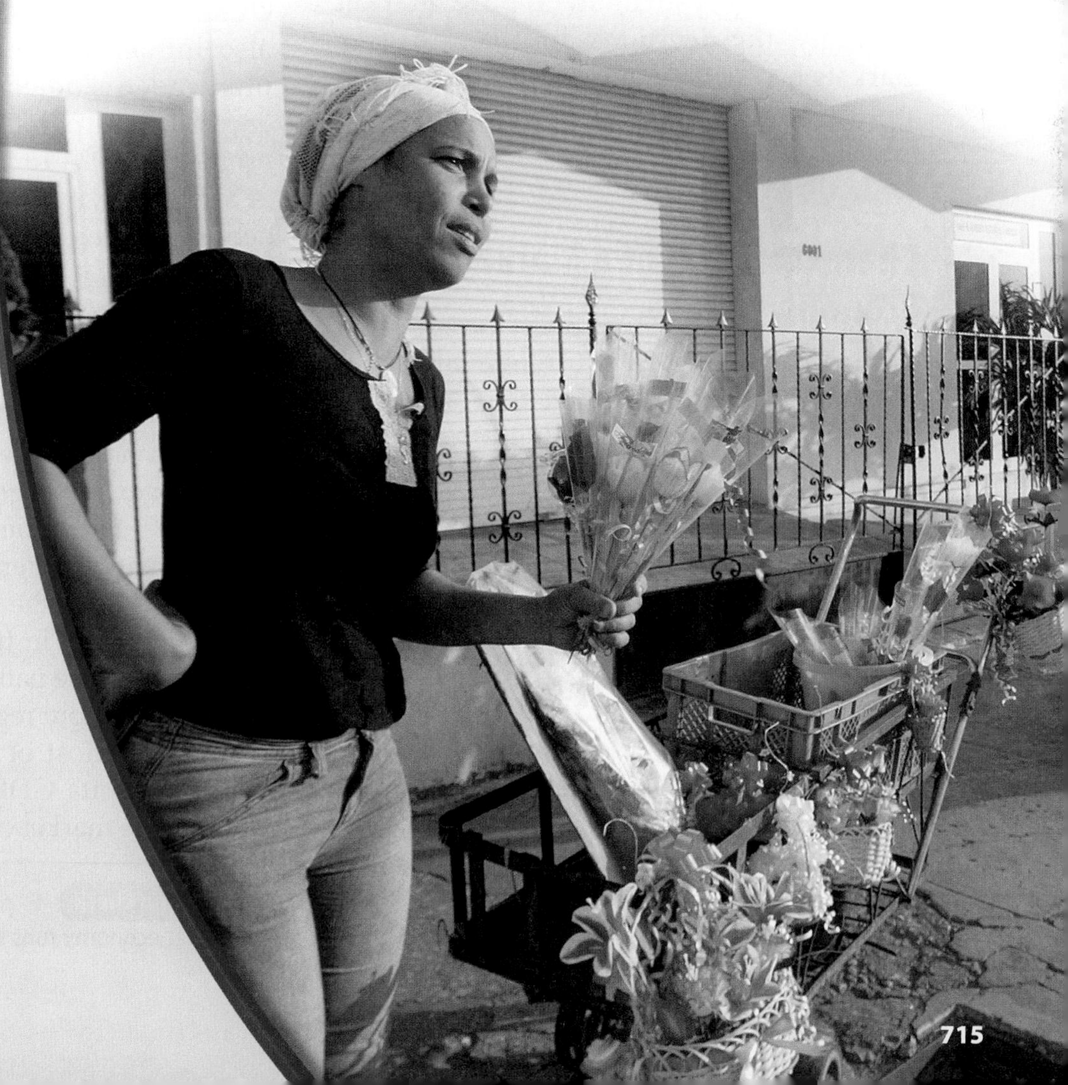

▼ **Havana native Laura Sanchez had her license to sell flowers revoked**

Market Economies

Main Idea **Market economies are characterized by individual freedom, competition, and less government control.**

Economics & You Would having more pizza parlors in your town lower pizza prices or improve pizza quality? Read to find out why governments work to ensure competition.

Economic systems around the world vary. Some, like the one in the United States, are based on markets. Others, like China's, feature far greater government control. These different economies deal with scarcity in different ways. All societies face the basic questions of *what* to produce, *how* to produce, and *for whom* to produce. How society answers these questions determines its economic system. In a pure **market economy,** the decisions are made in free markets based on the interaction of supply and demand. Capitalism is another name for this system.

Characteristics of a Market Economy

In a market economy, private citizens—not the government—own the factors of production. As you recall, those factors are natural resources, capital, labor, and entrepreneurship.

Individual Freedom A market economy offers a high degree of individual freedom. Businesses decide *what* to produce, *how* to produce, and *for whom* to produce. Driving those decisions is the business owner's desire to earn a profit. At the same time, consumers decide what to buy. In a market economy, supply and demand interact to set prices, and producers and consumers make their own decisions.

Decisions in a market economy are made by all the people in the economy, not by just a few. Therefore, we say a market economy is decentralized. The economy seems to run by itself because no one coordinates the decisions.

Pure market economies seldom exist. Even in the United States, for example, the government provides public goods such as national defense and a system of justice.

Competition Governments play another role in an economy: they make sure markets stay competitive. As a consumer in a market economy, you are likely to benefit from competition between sellers. Effective competition requires a large number of sellers. The U.S. government can ensure this by regulating businesses. It also **intervenes,** or interferes, to punish businesses that break laws meant to ensure competition.

Dealing with Externalities Governments also influence externalities. These are the unintended side effects that have an influence on third parties. For example, the government works to reduce pollution, which is a negative externality. It also encourages activities that generate positive externalities. For instance, it provides money to fund scientific research, which businesses can then use to develop new products.

Higher Per Capita GDPs Most of the largest economies are market economies. Look at the map on page 718, which shows the per capita gross domestic product (GDP) for selected nations. **Per capita GDP** is the total GDP divided by the country's population. By expressing GDP in terms of each person, we can compare one nation's economic success to another's without regard to the size of the two economies. Most of the countries that have high per capita GDPs, including the United States, have market economies.

Reading Check **Explaining** Why do we say a market economy runs itself?

Command Economy North Korean leader Kim Jong Il (far right) inspects a new food processing plant operated by the Korea People's Army (KPA) Unit 543. A factor contributing to the nation's poor economic performance is that North Korea focuses on producing weapons and not consumer goods. ***Identifying*** **Who owns most of North Korea's productive resources?**

Command Economies

Main Idea **In command economies, the government tells producers what to do.**

Economics & You Would you like the government to choose your job for you? In some economies, governments exert vast control over individuals.

Characteristics of a Command Economy

The opposite of a market economy is called a **command economy.** In a pure command economic system, the individual has little, if any, influence over how the basic economy functions. Major economic decisions are made by the central government. The government tells producers what to do—it *commands* what actions they should take. This economic system is also called a controlled economy.

Socialism Starting in the early 1800s, some people came to believe that aiding **exploited,** or oppressed, workers required eliminating capitalism completely. They advocated **socialism,** the belief that the means of production should be owned and controlled by society, either directly or through the government. Socialists felt that this system would distribute wealth more equally among all citizens.

Communism The German thinker and writer Karl Marx was a socialist who predicted violent revolution. Marx believed that the population in industrialized nations is divided into capitalists, or bourgeoisie, who own the means of production and workers, or proletariat, who work to produce the goods. Marx interpreted human history as a class struggle between the workers and the capitalists. Eventually, he thought the workers would revolt and overthrow the capitalists.

Per Capita GDP, Selected Nations

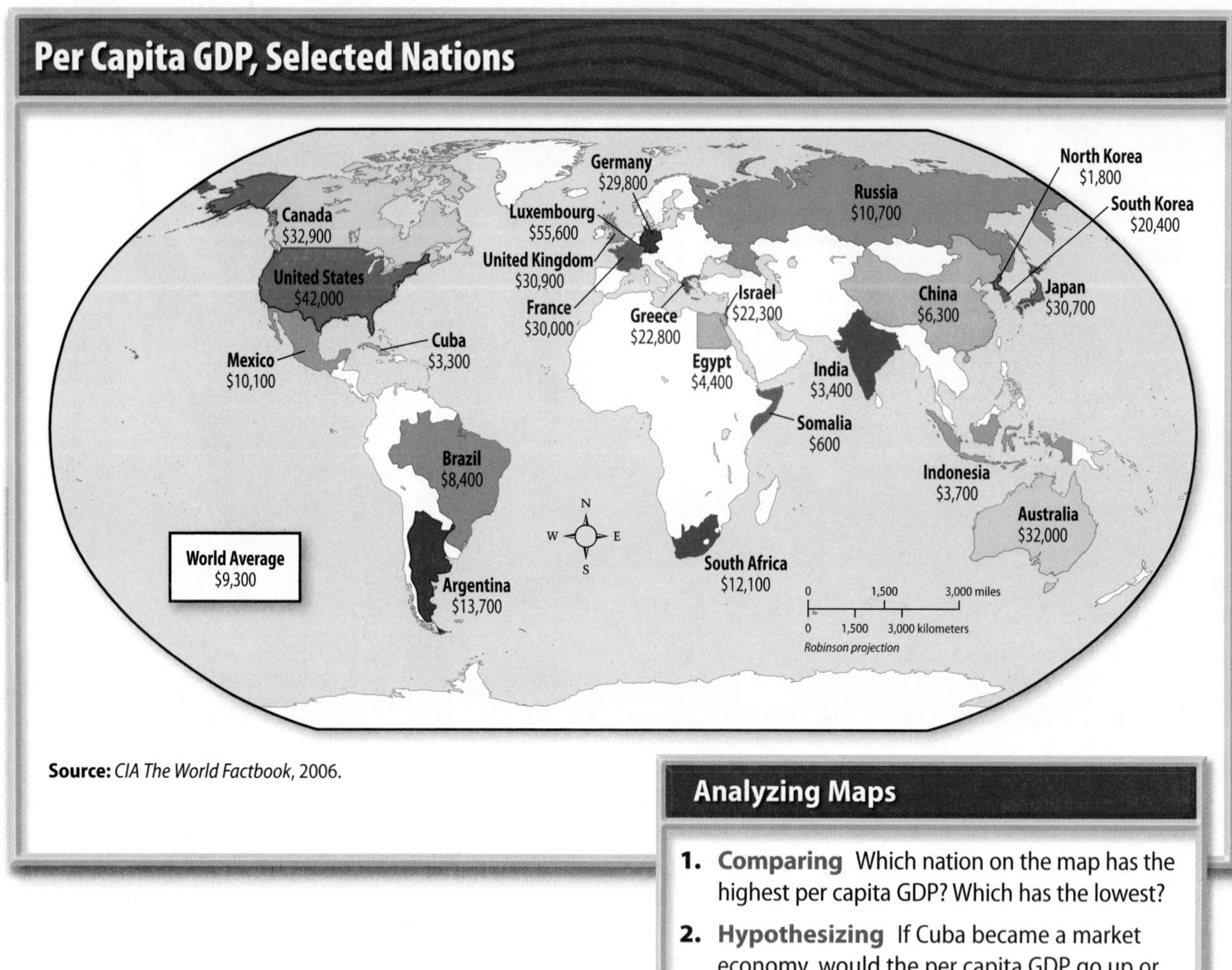

Source: *CIA The World Factbook*, 2006.

Analyzing Maps

1. **Comparing** Which nation on the map has the highest per capita GDP? Which has the lowest?
2. **Hypothesizing** If Cuba became a market economy, would the per capita GDP go up or down? Why?

Marx believed socialism would develop into **communism.** Under communism, one class would evolve, all property would be held in common, and there would be no need for government.

Government Control In a command economy, most productive resources—especially land and capital—are owned by government, not by private individuals. The government makes the three basic allocation decisions. It decides *what* to produce; it tells factory managers whether to make cars, buses, or military vehicles. The government also regulates *how* goods will be produced. It tells managers where to buy their raw materials, for example. Finally, the government decides for *whom* to produce. It fixes the wages of all workers and sets prices as well.

Unsurprisingly, governments in command economies have planning agencies with a great deal of power. These organizations make the important decisions for different parts of the economy, such as agriculture, steel production, and consumer products manufacturing.

Slow Growth Because of their inefficiency, command economies tend to grow more slowly and attain a lower per capita GDP than do market economies. Cuba and North Korea are perhaps the two best current examples of command economies. Look at the map on this page to see how low their per capita GDPs are.

Reading Check **Contrasting** What is the difference between a pure market economy and a pure command economy?

Mixed Economies

Main Idea **Today the American economy and others like it are described as mixed economies.**

Economics & You Do you think it is possible for a nation to have a pure market economy? Read to find out about how some nations combine elements of different economic systems.

Pure forms of command or market economies are rare. In most cases, a country's economic system combines these principles in what is known as a mixed economy. In a **mixed economy,** individuals carry on their economic affairs freely, but are subject to some government intervention. Many countries of the world have a mixed economy.

In the United States, free enterprise is combined with and supported by government decisions in the marketplace. The government keeps competition free and fair and protects the public interest.

The United States also promotes the economy by providing services to businesses and consumers. For example, the federal and state governments have built extensive highway systems that have helped promote travel and the transportation of goods.

Many government agencies produce and distribute goods and services to consumers, giving government a direct role in the economy. The role is "direct" because the government supplies a good or service that competes with private businesses. Perhaps the best known is the U.S. Postal Service.

The government plays an indirect role when it acts as an umpire to make sure the economy operates smoothly and efficiently. One such case is the regulation of public utilities, investor- or municipal-owned companies that offer important products to the public, such as water or electric service.

Reading Check **Explaining** In what ways can mixed economies be considered a combination of other economic systems?

Review

Vocabulary

1. **Write** complete sentences about the world economic system using each of the following terms: *market economy, per capita GDP, command economy, socialism, communism, mixed economy.*

Main Ideas

2. **Describing** Why is per capita GDP a good way to compare the economic success of different countries?
3. **Explaining** What did advocates of socialism hope to achieve?

Critical Thinking

4. **Assessing** Why do you think most of the world's most successful economies are market economies? Explain your answer.
5. **BIG Ideas** In a graphic organizer like the one below, compare and contrast market and command economies.

Market Economy	Command Economy

6. **Analyze Visuals** Examine the map on page 718. What five countries had the highest per capita GDPs?

CITIZENSHIP Activity

7. **Persuasive Writing** Write an editorial that supports a position on the following statement: *Any government intervention in the U.S. economy is harmful.* Use your editorial to debate the idea with classmates.

Study Central™ To review this section, go to glencoe.com.

Financial Literacy

Help Wanted: Tomorrow's Job Market

The Bureau of Labor Statistics (BLS) predicts that more than 18.9 million new jobs will be added between 2004 and 2014, increasing the workforce from 147.4 million to more than 162 million. Young people ages 16–24 are projected to fill more than 22 million jobs.

- Employment growth will be concentrated in the service industries.
- Five of the 10 occupations adding the most jobs are service occupations.
- An associate or bachelor's degree is the major source of postsecondary education or training for 6 of the 10 fastest-growing occupations.

Fastest-Growing Occupations, 2004–2014

Percentage Growth

Occupation	Total employment 2014 (in thousands)	Percentage growth 2004–2014	Most significant source of postsecondary education or training
Home health aides	974	56	On-the-job training
Network systems and data communications analysts	357	55	Bachelor's degree
Medical assistants	589	52	On-the-job training
Physician assistants	93	50	Bachelor's degree
Computer software engineers	682	48	Bachelor's degree

Jobs Gaining the Most Workers

Occupation	Total employment 2014 (in thousands)	Employment growth 2004–2014 (in thousands)	Most significant source of postsecondary education or training
Retail salespersons	4,992	736	On-the-job training
Registered nurses	3,096	703	Associate degree
Postsecondary teachers	2,153	524	Doctoral degree
Customer service representatives	2,534	471	On-the-job training
Janitors and cleaners	2,813	440	On-the-job training

Source: Bureau of Labor Statistics.

Analyzing Economics

1. **Classifying** Is most of the growth concentrated in the service or the manufacturing sector? Explain.
2. **Describing** What are three factors that will change the job market?

Section Audio
Spotlight Video

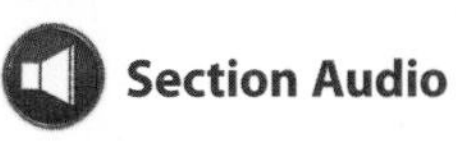

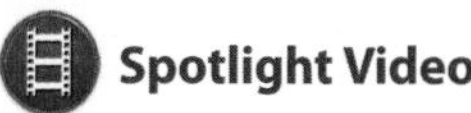

Section 3

Economies in Transition

Guide to Reading

Big Idea
An economic system is the way a society organizes the production and consumption of goods and services.

Content Vocabulary
- developing country *(p. 724)*
- traditional economy *(p. 724)*

Academic Vocabulary
- collapse *(p. 722)*
- nevertheless *(p. 723)*

Reading Strategy
Identifying As you read, note the ways developing countries can overcome some of their obstacles.

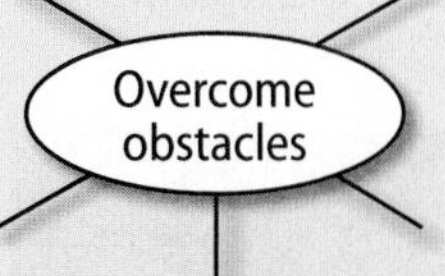

Real World Economics The economy of Vietnam is in a state of transition. This woman sells appliances in an electronics shop in Hanoi that may soon feature products from Japan, China, and the United States. Vietnam, once a fiercely communist country, has been moving toward a market economy, which replaced its earlier command economy. Now, slightly more than 35 years after the Vietnam War ended, Vietnam is a member of the World Trade Organization (WTO).

▼ **Customer and salesperson at a Hanoi electronics store**

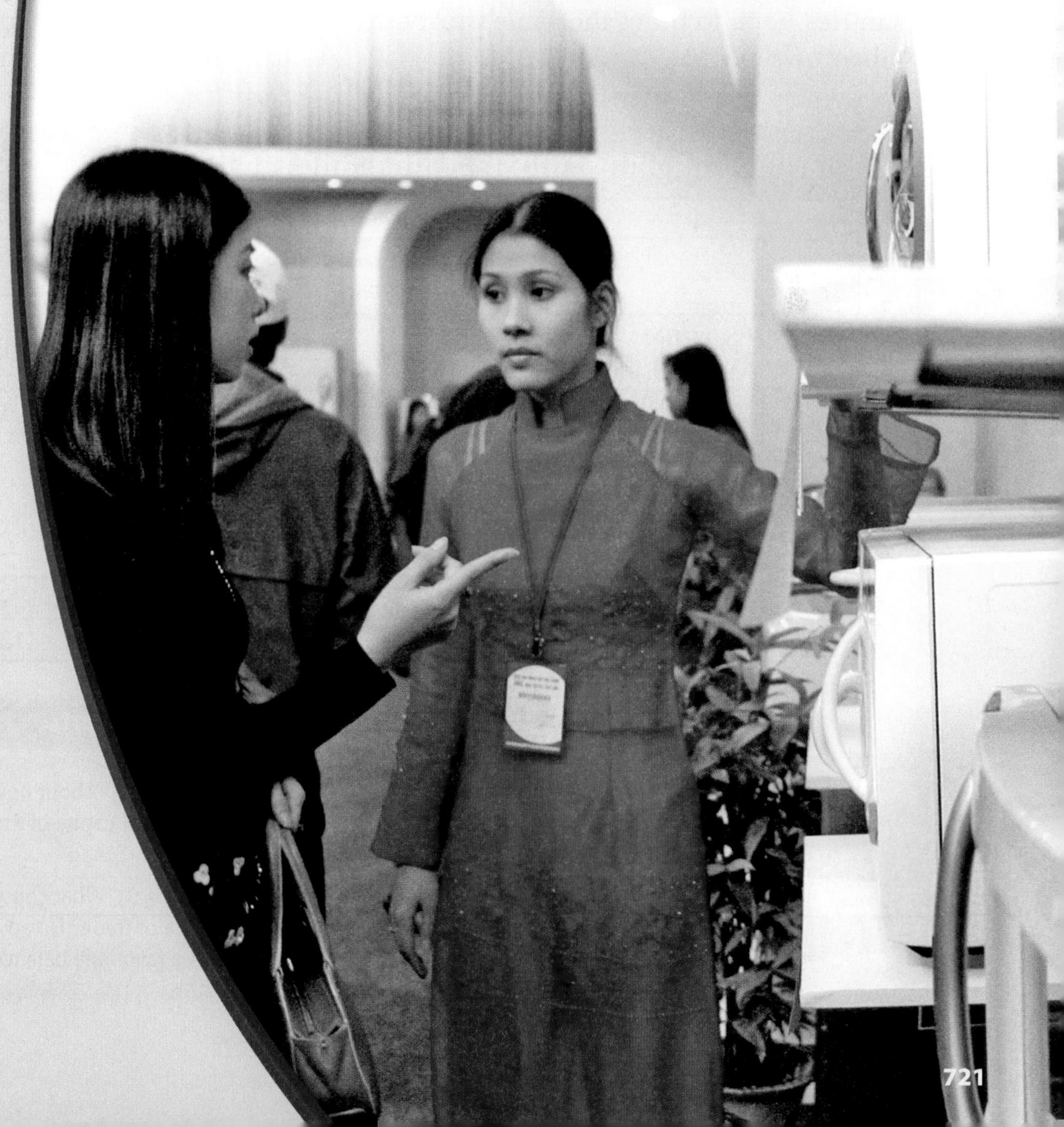

Changing Economies

Main Idea **Russia and China are making the difficult transition from command to market economies.**

Civics & You Have you ever decided to make a big change in your life? Major changes are difficult for countries, too.

Many nations in the world are making the transition from one type of economy to another. Some are moving from a traditional economy to a more developed system. Others are shifting from a command economy to a market system. The main reason for the transition is the remarkable success of the major market economies in the world. Many countries hope to bring the same prosperity to their own people.

Failure of Command Economies

In the 1980s, command economies began to seem increasingly unattractive. They were unable to achieve the economic growth that market economies could. The Soviet Union, China, and the countries of Eastern Europe had command economies. By 1991, however, they were all in the process of changing. In Eastern Europe, this economic change was accompanied by political changes. The countries moved toward greater democracy in addition to market economies.

Russia

The same transition took place in the Soviet Union, where change came with the actual breakup of the country. In 1991, the Soviet Union **collapsed,** or fell apart. Communist leaders could no longer keep the economy going. Russia emerged as the largest country to come out of the former Soviet Union.

Comparing Economies: Russia, China, and the U.S.

	Russia	China	United States
Population (July 2006 est.)	142,894,000	1,313,974,000	300,000,000
GDP per capita	$11,000	$6,800	$41,600
Labor Force -Agriculture -Industry -Services	 5.4% 21.4% 57.5%	 12.5% 47.3% 40.3%	 1% 20.4% 78.7%
Exports	$245 billion	$752.2 billion	$927.5 billion
Imports	$125 billion	$631.8 billion	$1.727 trillion

Source: *CIA The World Factbook,* 2006; Statistics based on 2005, 2006 estimates.

Analyzing Charts

1. **Calculating** About how many times larger is the GDP per capita of the United States than of China?
2. **Explaining** What constitutes a favorable balance of trade? Do any of the nations listed show a favorable balance of trade?

Economic Change in China A worker at a construction site in Yantai, China still uses hand tools. In the background, several cranes are operating. ***Describing*** **What economic problems is China facing?**

Economic Change Most economic decisions during Soviet times were made by a central planning body. Soviet production was inefficient. Supplies did not arrive on time, too much or too little of a good was produced, and goods were not always delivered to the places that needed them most. The process became too complicated to work effectively.

Following the breakup of the Soviet Union, Russia's leaders wanted to use some elements of a market-based economy. State-owned factories had to be put in the hands of private ownership. Stock markets had to be created so that people could own the factories. People had to learn to make decisions based on supply and demand and market prices. This ongoing transition has been difficult, and the process will probably continue for many more years.

China

Like Russia, China is trying to incorporate certain elements of a market economy. The Chinese economy had been modeled on the Soviet system of central planning. By the 1980s, China was falling far behind the market-based economies of its neighbors Taiwan, South Korea, Hong Kong, and Singapore. China began introducing market reforms to catch up. For example, it converted many state-owned factories to privately owned factories. The reunification of Hong Kong with China in 1997 gave China further motivation to change. Chinese leaders hoped to learn more about markets from Hong Kong.

China's economy has averaged 10 percent annual, or yearly, growth over the past 20 years—a high level of growth. Many workers in China's cities can now buy goods they were never able to have in the old economy. **Nevertheless,** along with these successes, there are some serious problems. Farmers find it hard to compete with cheaper foreign food. About 160 million Chinese are unemployed. China's leaders must find solutions to these problems.

Reading Check **Explaining** Why did China introduce market reforms?

Developing Countries

Main Idea **Developing countries face many problems as they try to create market economies.**

Civics & You How do you feel when you owe a friend money? Does your debt nag at you until you pay it back? A similar problem affects developing countries around the world.

Economic Characteristics

Of the nearly 200 countries in the world, only about 35 are considered developed nations. These nations include the United States, Japan, Australia, the Republic of China, and Spain. Dozens of other countries are trying to make the transition to a market-based economy. Most of the countries are **developing countries,** or countries whose average per capita income is only a fraction of that in more industrialized countries.

Many of the countries trying to make this transition have **traditional economies.** Economic decisions are based on custom or habit. For example, if your grandparents and parents fished for a living, you also will fish for a living. Traditional methods and materials are used to make items in this economy.

Problems Developing Countries Face

Developing countries face numerous obstacles that make economic growth difficult. A major obstacle to economic growth is a high rate of population growth. When population grows faster than GDP, per capita GDP declines—each person has a smaller share of what the economy produces. Countries with higher rates of population growth tend to have lower per capita GDPs (see the map on page 718). Countries with high per capita GDPs, on the other hand, have low rates of population growth. Rapid population growth is often the source of many other problems, such as lack of food and housing.

TIME™ Teens in *Action*

Jacorey Patterson

Jacorey Patterson, 17, goes to a local school in his hometown of Brooklyn, New York. But with the help of Global Kids, Inc., Jacorey thinks worldwide.

QUESTION: What is Global Kids?

ANSWER: An educational organization that provides school-based and after-school programs to build young people's understanding of complex global issues.

Q: Like what?

A: Diversity and discrimination, human rights, education, the environment, immigration—and many other issues!

Q: What kinds of kids are involved?

A: They are racially, ethnically, and socioeconomically diverse. The majority identify themselves as African American, Latino, South Asian, Middle Eastern, East Asian, or Caribbean.

Q: How does the organization affect the community?

A: In many ways; for example, following September 11, Global Kids youth conducted training for peers on Muslim stereotypes and facilitated an online dialogue for youth to share their fears and concerns about the attacks.

For more information about Global Kids, please visit www.globalkids.org.

Making a Difference CITIZENSHIP

Describing Write a paragraph describing how you could adapt Jacorey's Global Kids plan to your school.

Social Statistics Comparison, Selected Regions

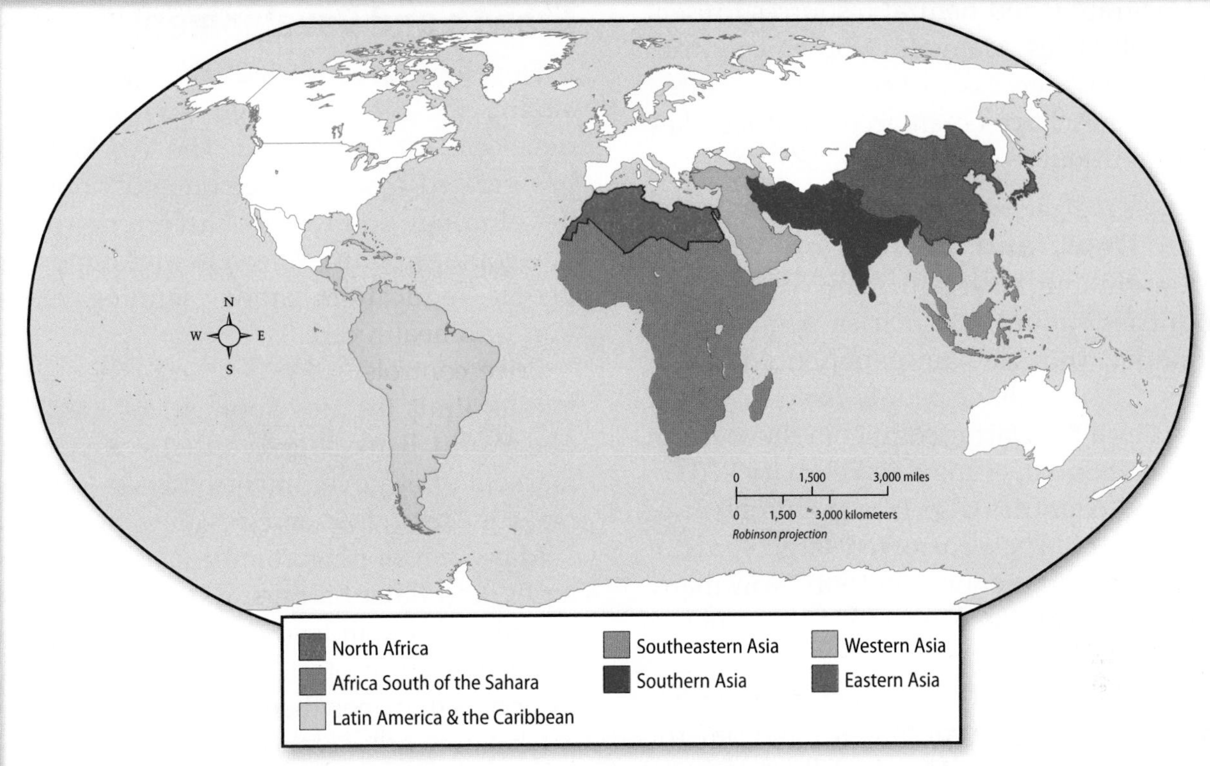

	Africa		Asia				Latin America & Caribbean	World
	Northern	South of Sahara	Eastern	Southeastern	Southern	Western		
Mortality Rate								
Deaths per 1,000 live births	33	102	30	35	65	48	27	55
Under 5 years of age mortality rate, per 1,000	38	172	37	46	90	60	32	80
Unemployment rate of young people								
Percentage of females aged 15–24 unemployed	14.2	39.1	5.8	17.7	17.1	22.5	20.8	14.2
Percentage of males aged 15–24 unemployed	14.5	25.5	8.1	15.6	13.5	20.1	14.0	14.5
Literacy								
Literacy rate of 15–24-year-old females	72.5	69.3	98.6	95.1	62.8	80.3	95.9	83.8
Literacy rate of 15–24-year-old males	84.1	79.0	99.2	96.4	81.6	90.7	95.2	90.7

Source: United Nations, 2005.

Analyzing Maps and Charts

1. **Comparing** What region has the lowest percentage of young people employed?
2. **Comparing** How does the literacy rate in Latin America and the Caribbean compare with the world literacy rate?

Geography and natural resources present other obstacles. Many developing countries do not have access to ocean trade routes. Others may have ocean access but lack key natural resources.

War, Debt, and Corruption War has left a chilling legacy in many developing countries. Countries such as Afghanistan, Ethiopia, and Vietnam experienced recent wars. Thousands of people have lost their lives since the Darfur conflict in the western region of Sudan erupted in February 2003.

Many countries also face the problem of severe debt. They borrowed large sums of money to spur economic growth. Now many cannot pay off the loans or even the interest on their debt.

Finally, corruption delays the development of some economies. Nigeria, for example, is rich in oil but is still a relatively poor nation because of the alleged corruption of its government officials.

Growth and Development

Developing countries face the responsibility for directing their own economic development and future. The World Bank has created a set of recommendations for developing countries. Governments in developing countries need to invest more in people—education, family planning, nutrition, and health care.

Price controls, subsidies, and other regulations limit the development of markets. The World Bank suggests that competitive markets—not government officials—should make the *what, how,* and for *whom* decisions.

Many developing countries have quotas, tariffs, and other barriers to protect domestic jobs and young industries. At the same time, trade barriers protect inefficient industries. Countries that open their markets to the world can begin to grow economically.

Reading Check **Describing** What economic challenges do developing nations face?

Vocabulary

1. **Write** complete sentences about two nations of the world using each of the following terms: *developing country, traditional economy.*

Main Ideas

2. **Explaining** Why did the former Soviet Union economy collapse?
3. **Identifying** What problems do developing nations face?

Critical Thinking

4. **Evaluating** Which of the problems that face developing countries do you think is the most challenging? Why?
5. **BIG Ideas** In a graphic organizer like the one below, list some of Russia's and China's achievements in their efforts to change economically.

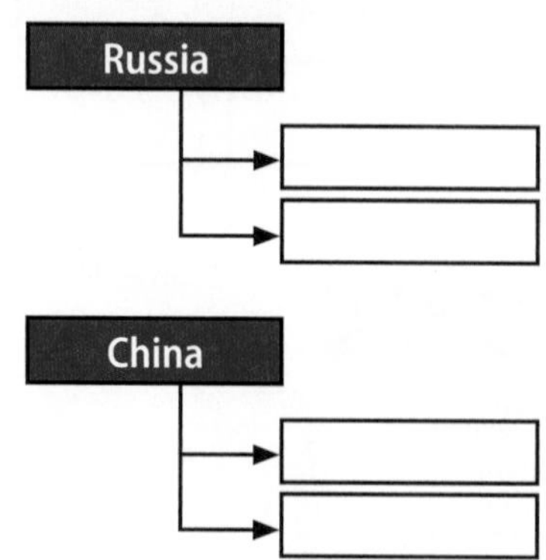

6. **Analyzing Visuals** Examine the map and chart on page 725. In what region is female literacy the lowest? In what region is the mortality rate the highest?

CITIZENSHIP Activity

7. **Expository Writing** Write a paragraph explaining how large amounts of debt can hamper development in developing nations and what has been proposed to address the problem.

Study Central™ To review this section, go to glencoe.com.

Chapter 26

Visual Summary

International Trade

- Nations trade with one another to obtain goods and services that they themselves cannot produce efficiently.
- Comparative advantage is the ability of a country to produce a good at a relatively lower cost than another country can.
- Countries sometimes try to protect their economies by setting up trade barriers, such as tariffs and quotas.
- A nation's balance of trade can be either a surplus or a deficit.
- A nation's currency can be strong or weak.

Flower seller, Havana, Cuba

Economic Systems

South Korean athletic shoe factory

- Market economies, or capitalist systems, are characterized by individual freedom, competition, and less government control.
- In command economies, the government tells producers what to do, resulting in inefficiency and slow economic growth.

Economies in Transition

- Russia and China, two former command economies, with the nations of Eastern Europe, are making the difficult transition from command to market economies.

North Korean leaders inspect newly built food processing plant

- Developing nations are nations with little industrial development and low standards of living.
- Developing countries with traditional economies, many in Africa and Asia, also face problems as they try to create market economies.

STUDY TO GO

Study anywhere, anytime! Download quizzes and flash cards to your PDA from glencoe.com.

ASSESSMENT

TEST-TAKING TIP

When learning about international topics it helps to look at a world map or globe to see where major countries are located.

Reviewing Vocabulary

Directions: Choose the word(s) that best completes the sentence.

1. A nation may put a limit on the amount of foreign goods imported by placing a(n) _______ on these goods.

A export
B quota
C deficit
D trade surplus

2. In a pure _______, economic decisions are made based on the interaction of supply and demand.

A mixed economy
B socialism
C communism
D market economy

3. The belief that society should own and control the means of production is part of the philosophy of _______.

A a traditional economy
B a mixed economy
C socialism
D free enterprise

4. In a _______ the per capita GDP is very low.

A developed country
B traditional economy
C developing country
D all of the above

Reviewing Main Ideas

Directions: Choose the best answers for each question.

Section 1 *(pp. 706–713)*

5. The ability of a country to produce a product at a lower cost than another country is called _______.

A free trade
B comparative advantage
C balance of trade
D import quota

6. The NAFTA trade agreement was made among _______.

A United States, Canada, and Mexico
B European countries
C developing countries
D United States, Russia, and China

Section 2 *(pp. 715–719)*

7. The way a society organizes the production and consumption of goods and services is its _______.

A trade economy
B economic system
C communism
D socialism

8. In a command economy, trade decisions are made by _______.

A the individuals in the society
B factory owners
C one class of people
D the government

Section 3 *(pp. 721–726)*

9. Many command economies have failed because of _______.

A the greater success of market economies
B the greater success of socialism
C the greater success of the Soviet Union's economy
D the greater success of China's economy

10. A major challenge facing developing countries is _______.

A below average temperatures
B huge population growth
C lack of roadways
D lack of organized religion

GO ON

Critical Thinking

Directions: Choose the best answer for each question.

11. Why do some countries have trade barriers?

A to encourage trade

B to do away with quotas

C to become communist

D to protect their economies

Base your answers to questions 12 and 13 on the graph below and your knowledge of Chapter 26.

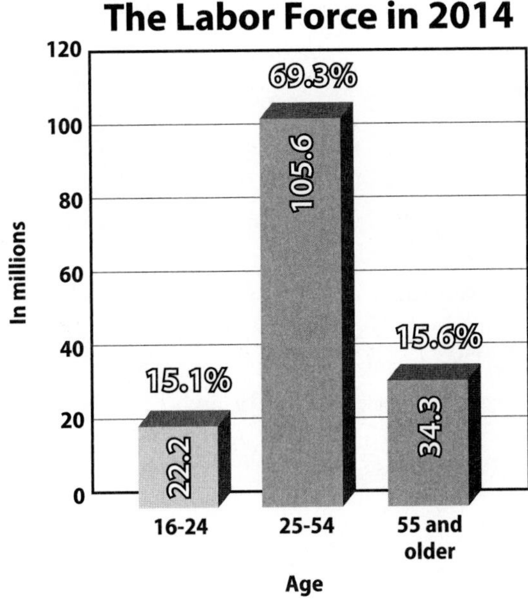

Source: Monthly Labor Review estimate.

12. What is the projected size of the total U.S. labor force in 2014?

A 105.6 million

B 34.3 million

C 162.1 million

D 120 million

13. According to the estimates, for every 100 workers in 2014, how many will be between the ages of 16 and 24?

A 5

B about 15

C about 25

D 22.2

Document-Based Questions

Directions: Analyze the following document and answer the short-answer questions that follow.

Milton Friedman, who died in 2006, was considered one of the greatest economists of the twentieth century. Here he comments on society and economics.

> Freedom requires individuals to be free to use their own resources in their own way, and modern society requires cooperation among a large number of people...The only way that has ever been discovered to have a lot of people cooperate together voluntarily is through the free market.
>
> —Milton Friedman, Nobel Prize-winning economist

14. From this quotation, would you say Friedman is a supporter of capitalism or a non-supporter? Explain.

15. Why do you think Friedman sees a connection between society—people—and economics?

Extended-Response Question

16. Developing countries have several challenges they face in improving their economies. What one thing do you think is the most challenging and what suggestion could you make to help that challenge?

STOP

For additional test practice, use Self-Check Quizzes—Chapter 26 on glencoe.com.

Need Extra Help?

If you missed question...	1	2	3	4	5	6	7	8	9	10	11	12	13	14	15	16
Go to page...	708	716	717	724	708	710	716	717	722	724	708	720	720	716	716	724

New Technology for the Developing World

From pedal-powered laptops to wireless Internet, high-tech tools are reaching those who need them most

fuse-project

The $100 Laptop

When Nicholas Negroponte took a year off from his job as a professor at the Massachusetts Institute of Technology, he launched an ambitious project: to build a laptop so cheap that developing countries could buy them by the millions to help their kids leapfrog into the 21st century.

With the support of the United Nations, the "$100 laptop" quickly found backing from a wide range of corporations. On the latest prototype, a new foot pedal supplies power in areas lacking electricity.

Negroponte hopes to start in seven countries—Nigeria, India, China, Thailand, Brazil, Argentina, and Egypt—with a combined total of at least 5 million orders. "If this makes the industry address low-power, low-cost laptops that can be used in very remote places, that's perfect," he says.

The New Electric Lamp

Artificial lighting may not seem a necessity like food or shelter, but 1.6 billion people around the globe lack access to electricity and the on-off switches we take for granted. Inspired by the Light Up the World Foundation, which promotes the use of energy-efficient light-emitting diodes (LEDs), Matt Scott and Amit Chugh teamed up to devise a replacement for the kerosene lamp.

Courtesy of Cosmos Ignite Innovations

NEW POWER Mightylight is replacing kerosene lamps in India.

The result is the Mightylight, a water-proof, shockproof, LED lamp that can be used as a flashlight, reading lamp, or ceiling fixture. Solar-powered, capable of holding an eight-hour charge, and designed to last 100,000 hours, the Mightylight is safer and more cost effective than kerosene lamps. Not only do kerosene lamps start a lot of fires, but they are also a primary source of indoor air pollution, a major killer in developing countries.

More than 4,000 Mightylights have been distributed for earthquake relief in Pakistan and to the poor in Afghanistan, Guatemala, and Kashmir. In India, weavers and fishermen are using the lights to extend their work hours. Says Scott: "The exciting thing—more than just the light itself—is the model of using a sustainable approach to effect social change."

Villagewide Wi-Fi

To reach the village of Nyarukamba in western Uganda, visitors have to climb up a thin, almost vertical dirt track. It's not the kind of place you would expect to find farmers surfing the Web with wi-fi computers or making VOIP (voice over Internet protocol) phone calls. But that's exactly what the village's 800 or so inhabitants have been doing—thanks to a wireless, solar-powered communications system installed in the Ruwenzori mountains by Inveneo, a San Francisco nonprofit group.

Inveneo's founders had done enough volunteer work overseas to see how wireless communications could improve and save lives—through phone calls to health clinics, fast reporting of natural disasters, support for trading co-ops, and better educational opportunities. So they designed a solar-powered Internet network that is easy to install, inexpensive, and nearly maintenance-free. At its heart is a regional hub from which wireless relay stations—some bolted to trees—fan out for up to four miles and connect a network of PCs. The total cost, including solar panels, was just $1,995.

Nyarukamba is already reaping the benefits. Village income is rising, buying power has increased, and more people are learning to read. And in case the sun doesn't shine, the system can be powered up with a retrofitted bicycle.

IT TAKES A VILLAGE Local residents carried equipment to Nyarukamba in the foothills of Uganda's Rwenzori mountains (top) and helped set up the solar panel that powers the village's wireless Internet system (right). An old tree trunk is being used as a mounting pole for the network's antenna (above).

Chapter 27 An Interdependent World

Why It Matters

As global economic interdependence grows, the different parts of the world are growing closer together. What happens in other countries affects the United States in many ways, while what Americans believe and do has a greater impact around the world than ever before.

Civics ONLINE
Visit glencoe.com and enter QuickPass™ code CIV3093c27 for Chapter 27 resources.

Chapter Audio

BIG Ideas

Section 1: Global Developments

The exchange of goods and services helps create economic interdependence among people in different places and different countries. We live today in an era of a global economy, in which countries depend on one another for goods, services, and natural resources.

Section 2: The United Nations

Political and economic institutions evolve to help individuals and groups accomplish their goals. The United Nations was formed to promote common aims of the world's countries and has won some successes, but has suffered some failures as well.

Section 3: Human Rights

Economic, social, and political changes create new traditions, values, and beliefs. In spite of important advances around the world for human rights and democracy, many people still do not live in freedom.

◀ **Young refugees return to their homes in Kabul, Afghanistan, after Taliban leaders are overthrown**

FOLDABLES™ Study Organizer

Defining Study Foldable Make the following Foldable to help you define the content vocabulary that you will encounter in this chapter.

Step 1 Stack four sheets of paper, one on top of the other. On the top sheet of paper, trace a large circle.

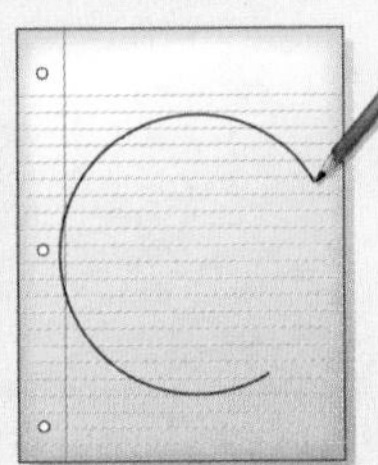

Step 2 With the papers still stacked, cut along the circle line you traced.

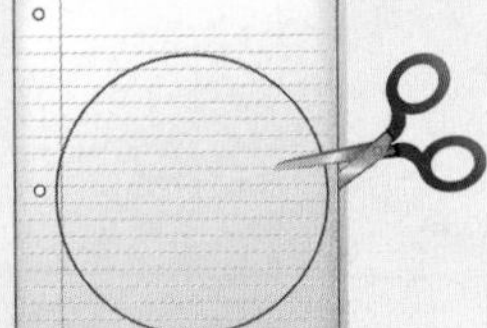

Step 3 Staple the paper circles together at one point around the edge.

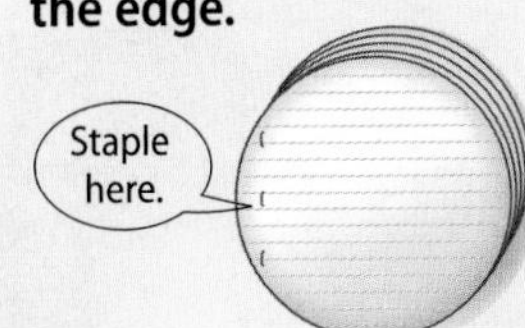

Step 4 Label the front circle Content Vocabulary.

Reading and Writing

As you read the chapter, record the content vocabulary terms with definitions for each section of Chapter 27 on the front and back of the sheets of your booklet for easy reference.

Section Audio Spotlight Video

Global Developments

Guide to Reading

Big Idea

The exchange of goods and services helps create economic interdependence among people in different places and different countries.

Content Vocabulary

- protectionism *(p. 735)*
- acid rain *(p. 737)*
- conservation *(p. 737)*
- refugee *(p. 738)*

Academic Vocabulary

- cooperate *(p. 735)*
- access *(p. 736)*

Reading Strategy

Explaining As you read, complete a graphic organizer like the one below by identifying three global challenges. Then explain why each of these is a problem.

Real World Civics Independent workers, such as this tailor surrounded by mounds of fabric in Beijing, China, are part of the American economy. The United States more than doubled its imports of clothing from China and other Asian nations in a five-year period beginning in 1998—and imports continue to grow. International trade, quotas, and imports and exports are powerful tools in the area of American foreign relations.

▼ **Tailor at outdoor market in Beijing**

Global Interdependence

Main Idea **We live today in an era of global economic interdependence, in which countries depend on one another for goods, services, and natural resources.**

Economics & You Think of five products you use every day. Do you know many of these items were made in a foreign country? Read more to find out how global trade has created an interdependent world.

Global interdependence means that people and nations all over the world now depend on one another for many goods and services. An important part of global interdependence is trade. As you learned in Chapter 26, trade includes both competition and **cooperation,** or assistance. Nations compete to sell their products. They also cooperate to make trade beneficial for everyone.

Global trade has many advantages. Businesses can make more profit. Greater competition may result in lower prices and a wider choice of products. However, global trade can also lead to problems worldwide. Competition may force weak companies out of business, hurting some national economies and costing workers their jobs. Nations sometimes try to protect their industries from foreign competition by placing tariffs on imports. This forces the price of foreign goods up and makes local prices more competitive. This policy, called **protectionism,** can cause harm as well as good. Price increases can lead to trade wars, in which nations set up even greater trade barriers.

The European Union (EU)—an organization that continues to grow—has eliminated most trade and many other barriers in Europe. The North American Free Trade Agreement (NAFTA) will gradually abolish all trade barriers among the United States, Mexico, and Canada.

Interdependence Hyundai autos are loaded for export at the port city of Ulsan. Hyundai, South Korea's largest carmaker, depends on the U.S. market, which accounts for about one-third of Korean vehicle exports. ***Explaining*** **What is global interdependence?**

The U.S. and Trade

The fuel to power our cars, planes, trains, trucks, and buses; to heat and light our homes; and to run our factories is an important example of growing interdependence. The United States must import more than two-thirds of the oil it uses, and the percentage is expected to keep rising.

In addition, the United States imports many of the minerals its industries need to keep working. For instance, 98 percent of the manganese, 93 percent of the bauxite, 81 percent of the tin, and 62 percent of the mercury used in American industries comes from other countries.

Global interdependence also means that other countries depend on us. The United States sells wheat, computers, telecommunications equipment, aircraft, medical equipment, machinery, and other high-technology products around the world. American services and entertainment products are also in demand. In addition, many poorer countries look to the United States for food, medicine, and defense weaponry.

✓ Reading Check **Explaining** Why does the United States trade with other countries?

Global Issues

Main Idea **The world community faces many serious global problems.**

Economics & You What do you think makes a family rich or poor? Read to find out how countries can also be rich or poor and what factors make them so.

One of the biggest global problems is the growing economic inequality among nations. There is a growing divide between the rich and poor nations of the world. As this gap grows, conflicts flare, and the United States faces difficult decisions. On one side of the divide are about 35 rich, industrialized countries, including the United States, Japan, Germany, Canada, Great Britain, and France.

These developed countries have natural resources such as coal and iron, or they have easy **access,** or connection, to such resources. They have many large industries, such as steel, electronics, and carmaking. These countries produce many of the manufactured goods sold around the world. They also consume much of the world's natural resources, enjoying a high standard of living. On the other side of the divide are about 165 poorer and less developed nations. Because most of the poor countries are trying to develop industrial economies, they are called developing countries.

Comparing Developing Nations

Some developing countries, such as Chad, Albania, and Paraguay, are very poor. They have few natural resources and cannot

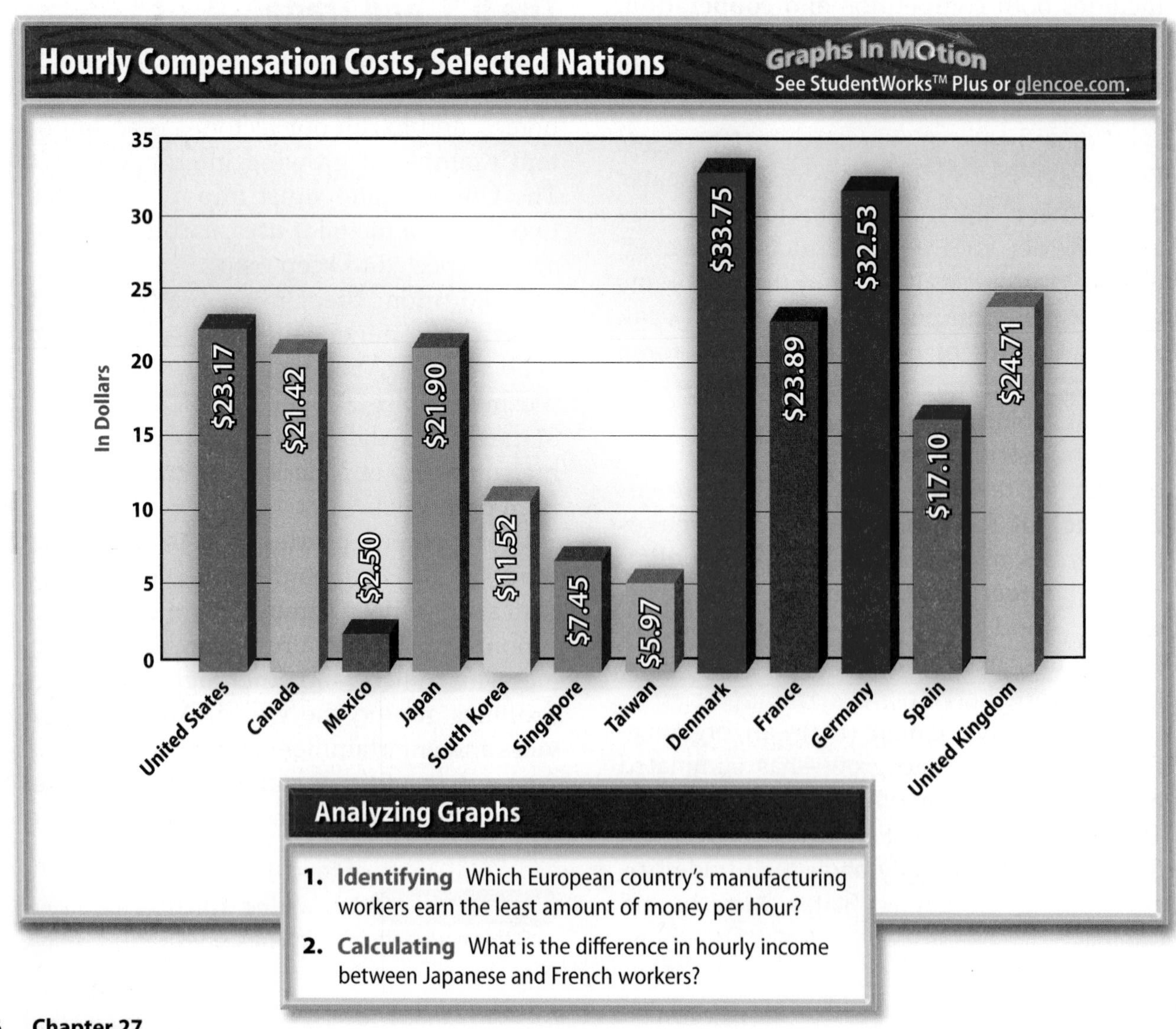

Analyzing Graphs

1. **Identifying** Which European country's manufacturing workers earn the least amount of money per hour?
2. **Calculating** What is the difference in hourly income between Japanese and French workers?

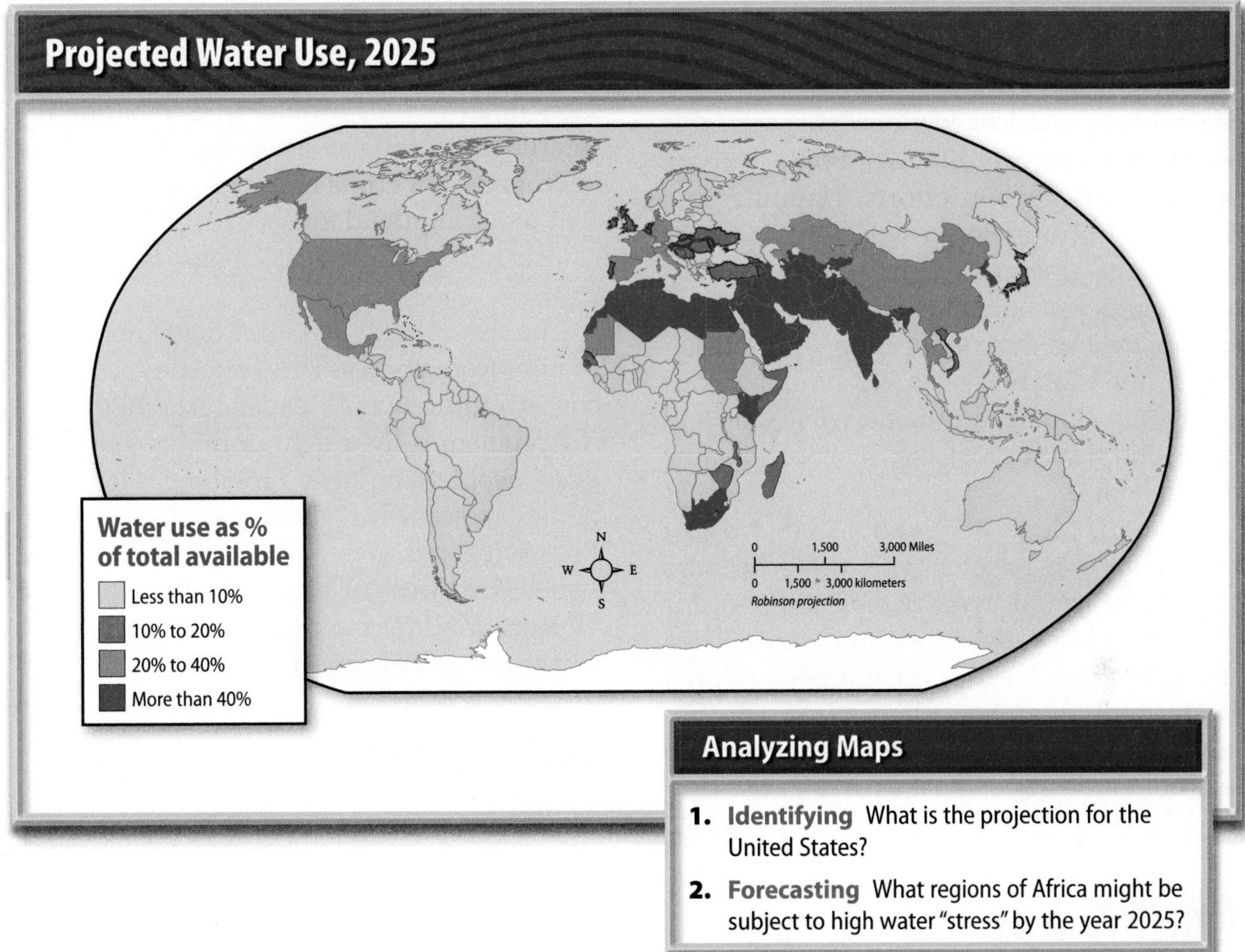

Analyzing Maps

1. **Identifying** What is the projection for the United States?
2. **Forecasting** What regions of Africa might be subject to high water "stress" by the year 2025?

produce enough food to feed their populations. They manufacture few products for export. They have high levels of unemployment, disease, and poverty. The average life expectancy in these countries is under 40 years.

Other developing countries have valuable natural resources. Countries such as Saudi Arabia and Venezuela have oil. Colombia grows coffee. The Democratic Republic of the Congo has copper. Some of these countries have little industry, though. Some do not have the governmental, health, and educational facilities to develop their human resources. It generally takes able leaders, scientists, engineers, bankers, and businesspeople to develop industry.

Cooperation Developed and developing nations need each other. Rich nations sell their products to the poorer nations. Developed nations also get raw materials from developing countries. For their part, the developing nations badly need the food, technology, and money that developed nations can supply.

Environmental Destruction

Another global problem is the destruction of the natural environment. Industries and motor vehicles have pumped poisonous metals, such as mercury and lead, into the air and water. Coal-burning factories release sulfur dioxide gas into the air. Sulfur dioxide mixes with water vapor and later falls to the earth as **acid rain,** damaging forests and lakes. To save the environment, countries must work to end pollution both within their borders and internationally. An important way to reduce pollution is through **conservation**—limiting the use of polluting substances.

Conserving gasoline, for example, cuts the amount of gases that pollute the atmosphere. Conserving wood protects forests and wildlife habitats and leaves more trees available to absorb carbon dioxide. Some people oppose conservation efforts, claiming that they slow economic growth. Others argue that lack of conservation may produce short-term gains but long-term problems. Many experts believe that not dealing with air pollution, for example, may lead to dangerous changes in climate, destruction of forests and lakes, and health problems as people breathe polluted air.

Many people in poor nations believe that antipollution regulations are unfair because such rules would make it more difficult for them to develop their own industries. They argue that the developed countries polluted freely while they were becoming rich, but now the developed countries do not want to let poor countries do the same.

Other Global Challenges

An interdependent world community also faces other serious problems. Combating the international traffic in drugs and the influence of cross-border crime requires cooperation, as will repairing the damage caused by natural catastrophes such as the Asian tsunami of 2004.

Coping with the pressures of greater immigration from poor to rich countries is sure to concern future world leaders. Another growing problem is the plight of millions of **refugees,** people who have unwillingly left their homes to escape war, famine, or other disaster. Preserving peace remains a pressing global issue. The threat of war and other forms of violence continues to grow. Terrorism persists as a major global concern.

Describing What are the effects of acid rain?

Vocabulary

1. **Define** the following terms and use them in sentences related to economic and environmental issues: *protectionism, acid rain, conservation, refugee.*

Reviewing Main Ideas

2. **Explaining** What do industrialized nations have in common?
3. **Comparing** How do developing countries differ from developed countries?

Critical Thinking

4. **Evaluating** What is the most serious problem the world community faces? Why?
5. **BIG Ideas** Create a diagram like the one below to explain four characteristics of developing nations.

6. **Analyzing Visuals** Study the graph on page 736. In what country are production workers' costs between $10 and $15 per hour?

CITIZENSHIP Activity

7. **Expository Writing** Select a developing nation and write a research report about its economic and social conditions. Consider including information in your report about the nation's housing, food production, and medical care.

Study Central™ To review this section, go to glencoe.com.

Section 2

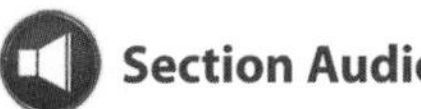

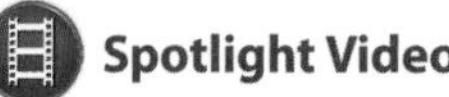

The United Nations

Section Audio | Spotlight Video

Guide to Reading

Big Idea
Political and economic institutions evolve to help individuals and groups accomplish their goals.

Content Vocabulary
- internationalism *(p. 740)*
- charter *(p. 740)*
- globalization *(p. 742)*
- multinational *(p. 742)*

Academic Vocabulary
- maintain *(p. 740)*
- promote *(p. 740)*
- mutual *(p. 741)*

Reading Strategy
Describing As you read, complete a graphic organizer like the one below by describing how the UN has responded to these global issues.

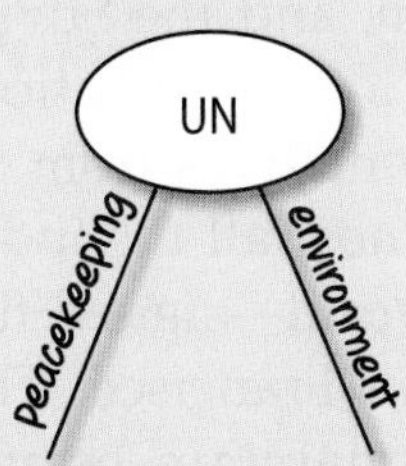

Real World Civics These Afghan girls are learning to play guitar today in a country—Afghanistan—that until recently banned all music. How is this possible? The United Nations has funded an educational program, which will soon be self-supporting, to provide them with lessons. The girls are now also allowed to attend school under the protection of the United Nations.

▼ **Women of the northern Afghan city of Mazār-e Sharīf playing guitars**

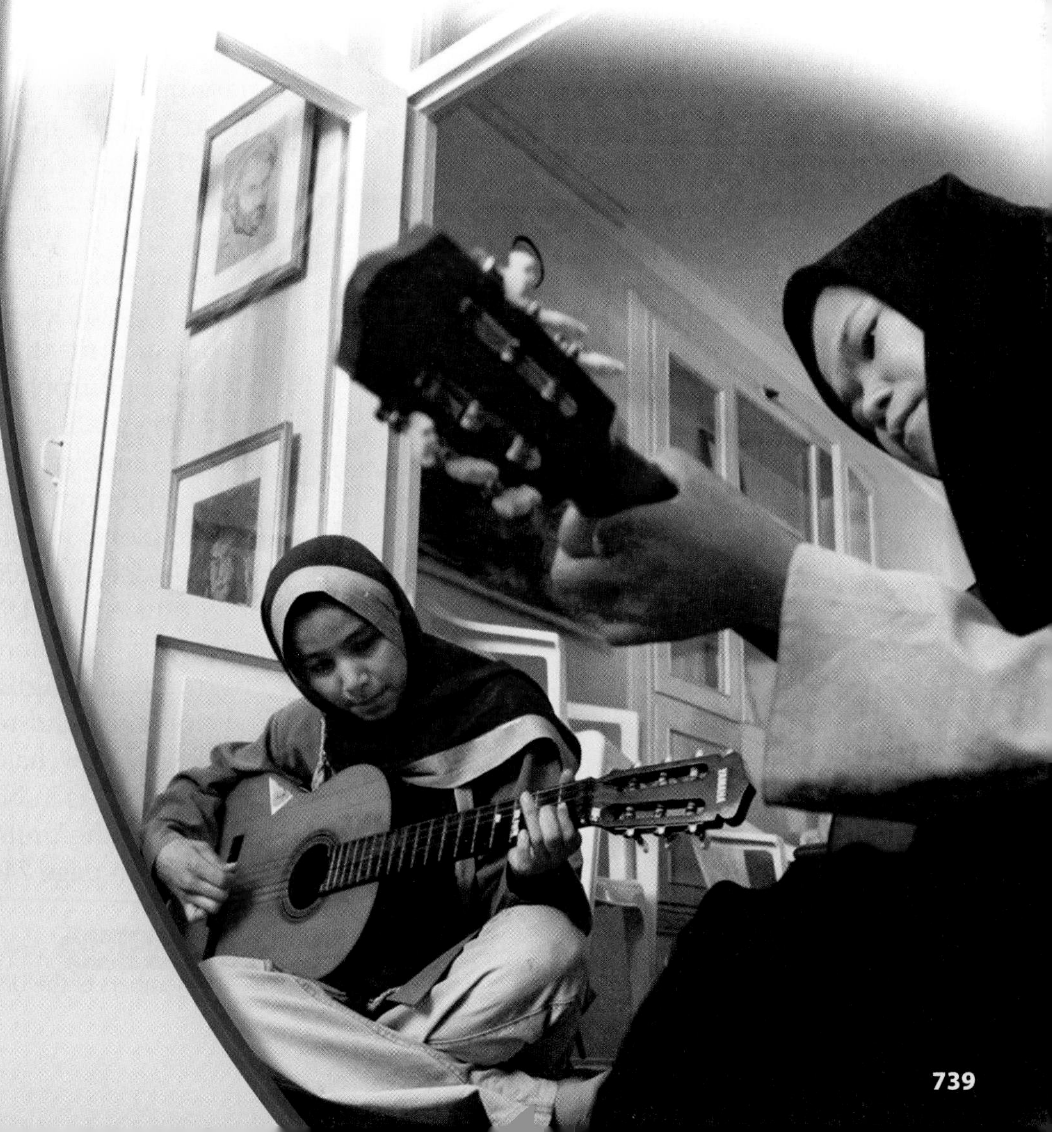

TIME™ Teens in *Action*

Kevin McGregor

What would it be like to represent the United States at the United Nations? How about China? Or maybe Burkina-Faso? Students like Kevin McGregor, 17, of Russellville, Arkansas, who take part in Model United Nations (MUN), have a pretty good idea. When these American teens get together at MUN conferences, they act as if they are delegates from different countries.

QUESTION: Where can people find MUN?

ANSWER: All over the United States and the globe. The conferences provide an awesome chance to learn about diplomacy and the intricacies of international relations—while developing public speaking and research skills.

Q: How has MUN changed you?

A: I think it's made me a more responsible world citizen. I took up biking to school because I felt it was a more efficient use of resources. It makes you think more about what is going on in the world. You start to see people that look different from you are fellow world citizens.

Q: How will MUN help your future?

A: Students that participate in Model UN are more aware of global issues and adopt more analytical ways of looking at problems. Those same students become voters and leaders in their community, maybe even politicians.

ACTION FACT: Kevin loves to be outside doing things like backpacking and mountain biking.

Making a Difference — CITIZENSHIP

Explaining In what way has Kevin changed because of his participation in the program?

Purpose of the UN

Main Idea **The United Nations was formed to promote the common aims of the world's countries.**

Civics & You Think about a time you tried to get a group of your friends to agree on a movie or activity. What did you do? Read to find out how the nations of the world succeeded when they decided to form an international organization.

Internationalism is the idea that nations should cooperate to promote common aims, such as supporting economic development and fighting terrorism. They do this through membership in an organization, the United Nations, which is made up of many nations.

UN Goals

The United States and its allies started planning for the United Nations during World War II. In 1944 delegates from the United States, Great Britain, and the Soviet Union drafted a **charter,** or constitution, for the UN. In 1945 representatives from 50 countries—at that time, almost all the independent countries in the world—signed the charter at a meeting in San Francisco. The UN's main purposes are to **maintain**, or preserve, international peace; develop friendly relations among nations; **promote,** or encourage, justice and cooperation; and seek solutions to global problems. On United Nations Day, October 24, 2001, President George W. Bush praised the UN for its commitment to "promoting human rights, protecting the environment, fighting disease, fostering development, and reducing poverty."

The UN now has 192 members. Its main headquarters is in New York City. The different parts of the United Nations are shown on the chart on page 741.

Reading Check **Describing** How many nations are members of the UN?

UN Activities

Main Idea **The United Nations had some success in solving world problems, but lack of cooperation has hampered its efforts.**

Civics & You Do you think it is difficult to get all your friends to agree on something? Read more to find out how the United Nations has struggled with the same problem.

The UN has been successful in several ways. It has served as a meeting place where representatives from many nations can discuss **mutual,** or common, problems. Special agencies of the UN have done a great deal to fight sickness, poverty, and ignorance. However, a lack of cooperation among the Security Council's permanent members has made the UN less effective in settling disputes and preventing conflict.

Efforts to Promote Peace

Nevertheless, the United Nations has helped bring about peace in some areas and helped those who live in war-torn countries. In nations, such as El Salvador, Cambodia, and Haiti, UN peacekeeping operations have helped sustain ceasefires, conduct free elections, monitor troop withdrawals, and prevent violence. The UN has also provided aid for more than 30 million refugees.

Organization of the United Nations

Principal Units	
International Court of Justice	Also known as the World Court, this is the main judicial agency of the UN. Consisting of 15 judges selected by the General Assembly and the Security Council, the court decides disputes between countries.
Security Council	The Security Council is the UN's principal agency for maintaining international peace and security. Of the 15 Council members, 5 members—China, France, Russian Federation, the United Kingdom, and the United States—are permanent members. The other 10 are elected by the General Assembly for two-year terms. Decisions of the Council require nine yes votes.
General Assembly	All UN member states are represented in the General Assembly. It meets to consider important matters such as international peace and security, the UN budget, and admission of new members. Each member state has one vote.
Secretariat	The Secretariat carries out the administration work of the United Nations as directed by the General Assembly, the Security Council, and the other agencies. Its head is the secretary-general.
Economic and Social Council	The Economic and Social Council recommends economic and social policies.
Trusteeship Council	The Trusteeship Council was established to ensure the rights of territories as they took the steps toward self-government or independence.

Analyzing Charts

1. **Describing** What are the six main units of the UN?
2. **Explaining** What nations make up the General Assembly?

Responses to Global Problems

The United Nations was created in the early twentieth century to respond to global problems. Countries around the world have established progressively closer contacts over time, but recently the pace has increased significantly. This interdependence and interaction among individuals and nations working across barriers of distance, culture, and technology is called **globalization.** Former Secretary-General Kofi A. Annan of Ghana wrote, "Globalization is transforming the world. . . . Our challenge today is to make globalization an engine that lifts people out of hardship and misery, not a force that holds them down."

The Environment In 1992 a major conference on the environment was held in Rio de Janeiro, Brazil. This Earth Summit brought together representatives from 178 nations who discussed ways of protecting the environment. Leaders signed treaties pledging to safeguard animal and plant life and limit the pollution that causes global warming. In 1997 world leaders gathered at the United Nations for Earth Summit II. They agreed that, while some progress had been made, much remained to be done.

Economic Inequality In 2006 the United Nations addressed the problem of growing economic inequality that divides the world into rich and poor nations. The UN found that countries with weak economic structures (laws, institutions, and markets), and low infrastructure (roads, transportation, and water access) gain less from global markets. Globalization has been led by **multinationals,** large firms that do business or have offices in many countries. The UN has called on leaders of private enterprise to play a stronger role in integrating economic, social, and environmental development in the countries in which they operate.

Reading Check **Identifying** What factor makes the UN less effective in settling disputes than many had hoped?

Vocabulary

1. **Write** a short paragraph in which you use the following key terms: *internationalism, charter, globalization, multinational.*

Main Ideas

2. **Explaining** What is the purpose of the UN?
3. **Identifying** To which UN body do all member nations belong?

Critical Thinking

4. **Analyzing** What do you think is the most important role of the UN in the world today? Explain.
5. **BIG Ideas** On a diagram like the one below, describe how the General Assembly operates.

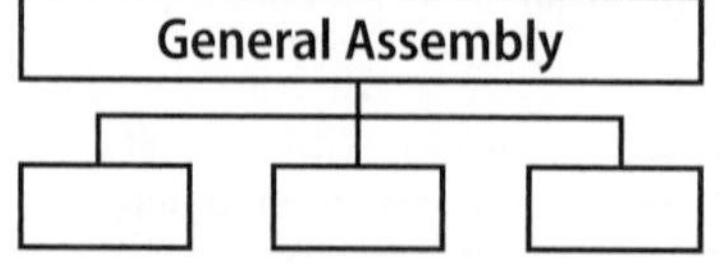

6. **Analyzing Visuals** Study the chart on page 741. How many judges sit on the World Court? How are the judges of the World Court selected?

CITIZENSHIP Activity

7. **Research** Take a poll of several adults in your community. Find out their opinions about the work of the United Nations and about U.S. involvement in that organization.
8. **Persuasive Writing** Every member nation has an equal vote in the UN General Assembly. Do you think this one-nation, one-vote system is fair? Explain in a one-page paper.

Study Central™ To review this section, go to glencoe.com.

Section 3

Human Rights

Guide to Reading

Big Idea
Economic, social, and political changes create new traditions, values, and beliefs.

Content Vocabulary
- human rights *(p. 744)*
- tribunal *(p. 745)*
- genocide *(p. 745)*
- apartheid *(p. 746)*
- sanction *(p. 746)*
- satellite *(p. 747)*
- Cold War *(p. 748)*

Academic Vocabulary
- commission *(p. 744)*
- adequate *(p. 744)*
- policy *(p. 745)*

Reading Strategy
Describing As you read, complete a graphic organizer like the one below by describing how the UN has responded to these global issues.

Real World Civics Human rights issues for migrant workers are huge questions in the Dominican Republic and elsewhere in the world. These Haitian children's parents are migrant workers who cut cane in the sugar fields and work in the processing plants in the Dominican Republic. They are allowed to go to school only because a nongovernmental organization associated with the United Nations has intervened and set up the school.

▼ **Young Haitian girls attend school on the grounds of a sugar plantation**

Standards for Human Rights

Main Idea **Although basic human rights have spread to more countries, they are still not respected in many parts of the world.**

Civics & You What basic rights do you think all people should have? Read to find out about the spread of basic human rights around the world.

Human rights are the basic freedoms that all people should enjoy. Human rights include the right to safety, to food, and to shelter, among other things. In democracies like the United States, citizens and noncitizens can worship as they please, and speak, read, and write freely. In recent decades, the issue of human rights has captured world attention.

A Mixed Picture

Despite democratic advances, however, many governments still imprison and abuse people for speaking their minds. Among the countries accused of human rights violations are China, Indonesia, Myanmar (Burma), Iran, Cuba, and Sudan. The good news is that human rights abuses are more carefully monitored than in the past. In South Africa, Haiti, and El Salvador, for example, national **commissions,** or committees, have investigated abuses of past governments. International groups have also called on individuals to account for their war crimes.

Right to Safety A returning refugee surveys the damage in her family's apartment due to fighting in southern Lebanon. The right to safety is one of the basic freedoms for all people. ***Explaining*** **What are other human rights?**

The Universal Declaration of Human Rights

In 1948 the United Nations adopted what has become the most important human rights document of the post-World War II years—the Universal Declaration of Human Rights. Addressing social and economic freedoms as well as political rights worldwide, the articles of the Declaration form a statement not of the way things are but of the way they should be with a unified effort.

Protection of Rights Articles 1 and 2 proclaim that "all human beings are born equal in dignity and rights." Articles 3–21 state the civil and political rights of all human beings, including many of the same liberties and protections of the U.S. Constitution. They also include other rights, such as freedom of movement, the right to seek asylum, the right to a nationality, the right to marry and found a family, and the right to own property.

Raising Standards of Living Articles 22 to 27 spell out the economic, social, and cultural rights of all people. These include the right to security, the right to work, the right to receive equal pay for equal work, and the right to form and join trade unions. The Declaration also lists the right to enjoy rest and leisure, the right to have a standard of living **adequate,** or acceptable, for health and well being, the right to education, and the right to participate in the cultural life of the community.

Protecting Human Rights

The UN High Commissioner for Human Rights directs programs that promote and protect human rights. For example, the UN Commission on Human Rights monitors and reports rights violations in all parts of the world. By drawing attention to these abuses, the UN hopes to bring pressure to halt them.

International Tribunals The Security Council has acted to punish human rights violators by establishing international **tribunals.** These courts have authority from the UN to hear cases and make judgments about violations of international human rights law.

Genocide During the 1990s, ethnic tensions in the East African nations of Rwanda and Burundi led to violent conflict. In a **genocide,** or the deliberate killing of members of a racial or cultural group, Hutu forces killed more than 500,000 people, mostly Tutsis. The International Criminal Tribunal Court for Rwanda began bringing to justice people accused of participating in the genocide.

Working for Human Rights The efforts of individuals make a difference in fighting for human rights. Salih Mahmoud Osman is an attorney from the Darfur region of Sudan. For 20 years, Osman has given free legal aid to people who have been taken into custody unfairly and tortured by the Sudanese government. Now a member of Sudan's parliament, Osman has led investigations of ethnic cleansing and other crimes against the people of Darfur.

Omid Memarian, an Iranian journalist and blogger, was arrested and tortured for his defense of human rights. He was released from prison after the international community campaigned for his freedom. He continues to expose arbitrary imprisonment, torture, and mistreatment of prisoners in Iran.

Reading Check **Describing** What is genocide? How might an international tribunal deal with a case of genocide?

Spread of Democracy and Liberty

Main Idea **Democracy has spread to more countries over the last 50 years, aided by support from democratic nations and the collapse of the Soviet Union.**

Civics & You How do you define *freedom?* Read more to find out how freedom is described and encouraged around the world.

The United Nations has encouraged the spread of democracy and human rights throughout the world. So has the United States, which has made these causes an important part of its foreign **policy,** or guidelines.

Growth of Democracy

At the beginning of the twentieth century, only about 12 percent of the world's people lived in a democracy. By 1950 there were 22 democratic nations, with 31 percent of the world's population. Over the next 50 years, democracy grew rapidly, especially after 1980. Today nearly 64 percent of the world's population in 150 countries live under politically democratic conditions. This has all taken place during the time the UN has been established.

A publication called *Freedom in the World* provides an annual evaluation of political rights and civil liberties for more than 190 countries. At a minimum, "a democracy is a political system in which the people choose their authoritative leaders freely in public elections from among competing groups and individuals who were not chosen by the government." Countries that go beyond this standard for democracy offer the broadest range of human rights. These countries are "fully free" democracies. In 2007, there were 90 countries with free and democratic governments.

There were 58 "partly free" countries; none of these countries guaranteed a broad range of individual liberties beyond holding free and fair elections, however. In 2006 about 37 percent of the world's population lived in 49 countries that were not free. These nondemocracies often practiced or permitted terrible violations of human rights.

Fight for Rights in South Africa

A success story of the late twentieth century is South Africa. White leaders of South Africa enforced a policy of racial separation between blacks and whites called **apartheid.** Apartheid laws dictated where blacks could travel, eat, and go to school. Black people could not vote or own property, and they could be jailed indefinitely without cause. For more than 40 years, people inside and outside South Africa protested against apartheid. Both the United States and the European Economic Community (now known as the European Union) ordered economic **sanctions,** or coercive measures, against South Africa. Mounting pressure brought a gradual end to apartheid. In April 1994, South Africa held its first election open to all races. Voters elected antiapartheid leader Nelson Mandela as the first black president.

Population Living Under Various Types of Government

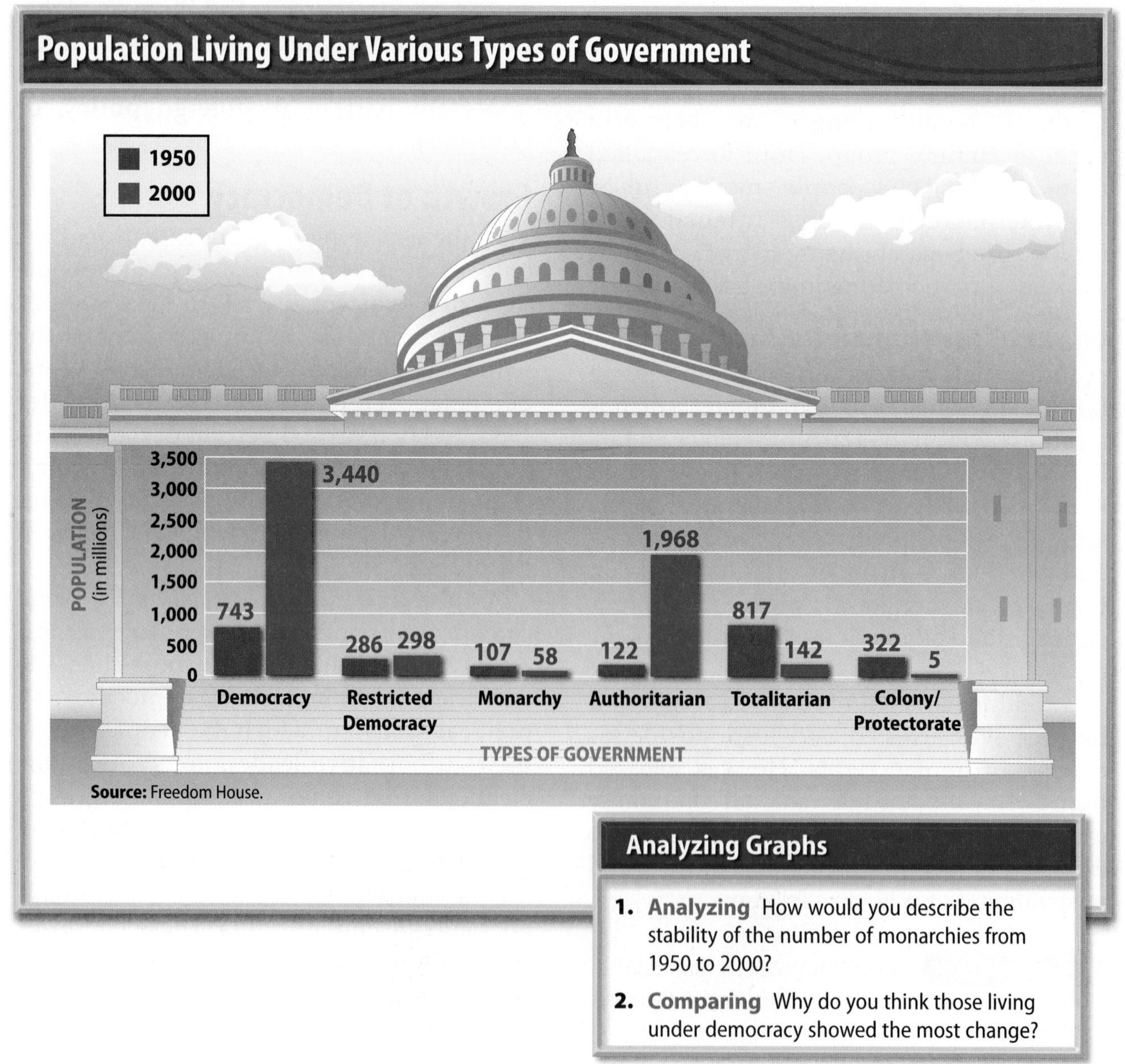

Source: Freedom House.

Analyzing Graphs

1. **Analyzing** How would you describe the stability of the number of monarchies from 1950 to 2000?
2. **Comparing** Why do you think those living under democracy showed the most change?

TIME™ **Political Cartoons**

Michael Ramirez/Copley News Service

Every year, more than half of all Americans do volunteer work | role in it. One of the responsibilities of citizens is to help make their | of volunteer grou small. Perha

This cartoon, drawn by Michael Ramirez, focuses on laws regarding Internet use.

1. **What is the setting for this image?**
2. **In the cartoon, where does the Information Superhighway lead?**
3. **What does the "great wall" symbolize?**
4. **What do you think Ramirez's intention was in creating this cartoon?**

Fight for Rights in Afghanistan

After Afghanistan collapsed into civil war in the 1990s, many people turned to the Taliban for leadership. By 1996 the Taliban had taken control of about 80 percent of the country. They put in place harsh policies based on a strict interpretation of Islam. Basic freedoms were severely restricted, especially for women. In late 2001 the United States accused the Taliban of supporting terrorists. The U.S. and a coalition of European forces have been waging war on the Taliban ever since. The United Nations began working with the nation's leaders to create a climate that protected human rights.

Safeguarding Democracy

During most of the twentieth century, the global advancement of democracy and liberty was a main objective of the U.S. government. President Woodrow Wilson declared during and after World War I that the United States and its allies should "make the world safe for democracy." During World War II, President Franklin D. Roosevelt said that the United States and its allies were fighting for democracy and freedom in the world. Roosevelt said,

> *"Freedom means the supremacy of human rights everywhere. Our support goes to those who struggle to gain those rights or to keep them."*
>
> —Franklin D. Roosevelt

The Cold War After World War II, the Soviet Union dominated Eastern Europe. It forced countries there to become **satellites**—countries politically and economically dominated or controlled by another more powerful country. Soviet actions during these years convinced the United States and its allies that the Soviet goal was to expand its power and influence.

Most of the world soon divided into two hostile camps—the democratic nations and the Communist nations. This bitter struggle between the two sides was known as the **Cold War** because it more often involved a clash of ideas than a clash of arms. The struggle was between the American ideas of democracy and freedom and the Soviets' communism and totalitarianism.

Soviet Domination Ends From 1945 until the fall of the Soviet Union in 1991, American presidents declared their commitment to the spread of democracy and liberty. After the collapse of Soviet totalitarianism, American presidents promoted the advance of democracy in the former Soviet Union and in other countries in central and eastern Europe that had suffered under Soviet domination. The spread of democracy elsewhere in the world continued to be a goal of U.S. foreign policy.

War Against Terror In response to the September 11, 2001, terrorist attacks on the United States, President George W. Bush repeated America's commitment to democracy and liberty around the world. He said in a speech to Congress,

> *"The advance of human freedom—the great achievement of our time, and the hope of every time—now depends on us."*
>
> —President George W. Bush

A world that is increasingly democratic and free means that the United States and other nations will have an easier time maintaining peace, prosperity, and national security. Thus, it is in the national interest of the United States to promote the global advancement of democracy and liberty.

Reading Check **Identifying** What was the Cold War?

Vocabulary

1. **Write** a paragraph that summarizes key points of this section. Use all of the following terms: *human rights, tribunal, genocide, apartheid, sanction, satellite, Cold War.*

Main Ideas

2. **Explaining** What are human rights? List two important political rights.
3. **Explaining** What actions are being taken to safeguard human rights?

Critical Thinking

4. **BIG Ideas** Why are many nations turning to a more democratic form of government?
5. **Classifying** In a diagram like the one below, describe the characteristics of these types of government.

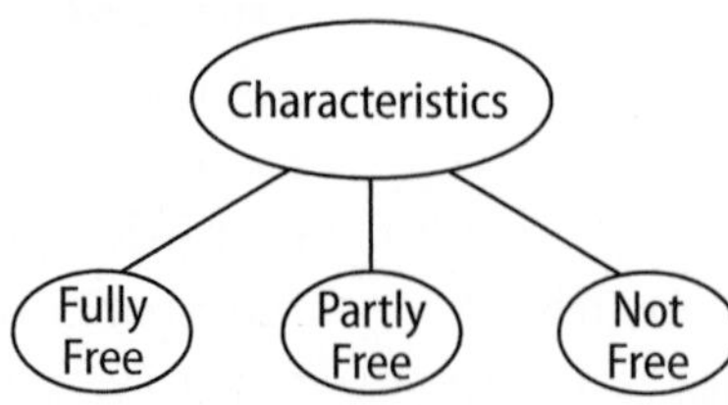

CITIZENSHIP Activity

6. **Expository Writing** Choose a country discussed in this section. Research the country. Imagine that you are traveling to the country. Write a letter to a friend describing the country and the extent to which the government affects people's everyday lives.

Study Central™ To review this section, go to glencoe.com.

Chapter 27 Visual Summary

Main Idea	Supporting Details
We live in an era of global economic interdependence, in which countries depend on one another for goods, services, and natural resources.	Trade among nations is a major part of global interdependence.
The world faces many serious global challenges.	Challenges include the growing split between developed and developing nations, destruction of the natural environment, international traffic in drugs and other crime, damage caused by natural catastrophes, greater immigration from poor to rich countries, and the plight of millions of refugees.
The United Nations was established to provide a forum for nations to settle their disputes by peaceful means.	The UN's main purposes are to maintain international peace, develop friendly relations among nations, promote justice and cooperation, and seek solutions to global problems.
The UN has had some success in solving world difficulties, but a lack of cooperation has hampered its efforts.	The UN has battled sickness, poverty, and ignorance around the world, but has had less success in narrowing the gap between rich and poor and in protecting the environment.
Although acknowledgment of basic human rights has spread to more countries, rights are still not respected in many parts of the world.	The Universal Declaration of Human Rights lists basic human rights of all people, but these rights have been limited in places like Rwanda, the former Yugoslavia, China, Indonesia, Myanmar, Iran, Cuba, and Sudan.
Democracy has spread to more countries over the last 50 years, aided by support from democratic nations and the collapse of the Soviet Union.	A growing number of countries have instituted democratic reforms.

STUDY TO GO

Study anywhere, anytime! Download quizzes and flash cards to your PDA from glencoe.com.

Chapter

27 ASSESSMENT

Standardized Test Practice

TEST-TAKING TIP

Read through all of the answer choices before choosing the one that provides a general restatement of the information.

Reviewing Vocabulary

Directions: Choose the word(s) that best completes the sentence.

1. The policy of _______ involves a nation guarding its own industries against outside competition.

A internationalism **C** globalization
B protectionism **D** sanctions

2. _______ are courts with UN authority to hear cases involving international human rights violations.

A Tribunals **C** Satellites
B Sanctions **D** Charters

3. During the Cold War, many nations became _______ of the Soviet Union.

A satellites **C** sanctions
B charters **D** multinationals

4. Basic freedoms that should be available to all people are called _________.

A charters **C** human rights
B multinationals **D** sanctions

Reviewing Main Ideas

Directions: Choose the best answers for each question.

Section 1 *(pp. 734–738)*

5. Which of the following is NOT a way in which developed and developing nations help one other?

A Developed nations get raw materials from developing nations.
B Developed nations sell products to developing nations.
C Developed nations are less strict with antipollution regulations for developing nations.
D Developed nations send aid to developing nations.

6. Many developing nations have _________.

A abundant natural resources
B low unemployment
C high levels of poverty
D many industries

Section 2 *(pp. 739–742)*

7. The principal agency of the United Nations for maintaining peace and security is the _________.

A Secretariat
B Security Council
C General Assembly
D Earth Summit

8. An important force that is driving globalization are multinationals, which are _________.

A UN peacekeeping forces
B large firms that do business in many countries
C organizations that promote conservation
D made up of business leaders from developing countries

Section 3 *(pp. 743–748)*

9. The deliberate killing of members of a racial or cultural group is called _________.

A genocide
B apartheid
C domestic terror
D totalitarianism

10. Apartheid laws dictated where blacks could travel, eat, and go to school in _________.

A Sudan
B China
C Myanmar
D South Africa

GO ON

Critical Thinking

Directions: Base your answers to questions 11–13 on the chart and your knowledge of Chapter 27.

U.S. International Trade, 2000 and 2005 (in millions of dollars)		
Exports:	2000	2005
Goods	$771,994	$894,631
Services	$298,603	$380,614
Imports:	2000	2005
Goods	$1,224,408	$1,677,371
Services	$223,748	$314,604

Source: U.S. Census Bureau, *U.S. International Trade in Goods and Services*

11. This comparison of U.S. trade statistics shows that ________.

A trade decreased between 2000 and 2005

B the United States imported more goods than it exported

C the United States exported more goods than it imported

D services made up a larger share of U.S. trade than did goods

12. In both 2000 and 2005, the United States imported more goods and services than it exported, which means that the nation had ________.

A a positive balance of trade

B a negative balance of trade

C a system of tariffs in place

D instituted protectionist policies

13. In 2005 the United States exported about ______ times as many goods as it did services.

A two

B five

C ten

D fifteen

Document-Based Questions

Directions: Analyze the document and answer the short-answer questions that follow.

In December 2006, Ban Ki-moon of the Republic of Korea was sworn in as the eighth secretary-general of the United Nations. The excerpt is from a news story.

> *[I will do] everything in my power to ensure that our United Nations can live up to its name, and be truly united, so that we can live up to the hopes that so many people around the world place in this institution, which is unique in the annals of human history. . . .*
>
> *You could say that I am a man on a mission. And my mission could be dubbed 'Operation Restore Trust': trust in the Organization, and trust between Member States and the Secretariat.*
>
> *I hope this mission is not 'Mission Impossible, ...'*
>
> *Member States need a dynamic and courageous Secretariat, not one that is passive and risk-averse. The time has come for a new day in relations between the Secretariat and Member States. The dark night of distrust and disrespect has lasted far too long.*
>
> —UN News Service

14. What does Ban Ki-moon convey as one of the problems facing the UN? Why do you think he considers this a problem?

15. What is the Secretariat? Do you think Ban is criticizing it? Explain.

Extended Response

16. Why might industrialized nations such as the United States exercise influence on developing nations to develop free market economies and democracy? Express your answer in a one-page essay.

STOP

For additional test practice, use Self-Check Quizzes—Chapter 27 on glencoe.com.

Need Extra Help?

If you missed question...	1	2	3	4	5	6	7	8	9	10	11	12	13	14	15	16
Go to page...	735	745	747	744	736	736	741	742	745	746	735	735	735	741	741	745

Analyzing Primary Sources

Comparing Constitutions

Reading Focus

The Preamble to the U.S. Constitution sets forth the general purposes for which our government was established. The Preamble also declares that the power of government comes from the people. Have you ever wondered how the Preamble to our Constitution compares to the preambles of other nations' constitutions?

Read to Discover

Each nation has its own unique culture and history. As you read, think about these points:

- How do the words in each preamble relate to the shared experiences of the people who live in that country?
- What values and beliefs expressed in each preamble are similar to the expressions in the other preambles?

Reader's Dictionary

multinational: originating from several countries

immutable: never changing

Constitution of the Russian Federation

The Constitution of the Russian Federation was ratified December 12, 1993.

We, the **multinational** people of the Russian Federation, united by a common destiny on our land, asserting human rights and liberties, civil peace and accord, preserving the historic unity of the state, proceeding from the commonly recognized principles of equality and self-determination of the peoples honoring the memory of our ancestors, who have passed on to us love of and respect for our homeland and faith in good and justice, reviving the sovereign statehood of Russia and asserting its **immutable** democratic foundations, striving to secure the well-being and prosperity of Russia and proceeding from a sense of responsibility for our homeland before the present and future generations, and being aware of ourselves as part of the world community, hereby approve the Constitution of the Russian Federation.

Constitution of the Argentine Nation

This constitution was adopted by the people of Argentina in 1853 and, like the United States Constitution, has had a number of amendments added to it since its adoption.

We, the representatives of the people of the Argentine Nation, gathered in General Constituent Assembly by the will and election of the Provinces which compose it, in fulfillment of pre-existing pacts, in order to form a national union, guarantee justice, secure domestic peace, provide for the common defense, promote the general welfare and secure the blessings of liberty to ourselves, to our posterity, and to all men of the world who wish to dwell on Argentine soil: invoking the protection of God, source of all reason and justice: do ordain, decree, and establish this Constitution for the Argentine Nation.

Constitution of India

India is the world's largest democracy. This constitution became the law of the land on November 26, 1949, shortly after India received its independence from Great Britain.

WE, THE PEOPLE OF INDIA, having solemnly resolved to constitute India into a SOVEREIGN SOCIALIST SECULAR DEMOCRATIC REPUBLIC and to secure to all its citizens:
JUSTICE, social, economic and political
LIBERTY of thought, expression, belief, faith and worship
EQUALITY of status and of opportunity
FRATERNITY, assuring the dignity of the individual and the unity and integrity of the Nation.
IN OUR CONSTITUENT ASSEMBLY this twenty-sixth day of November, 1949, do HEREBY ADOPT, ENACT AND GIVE TO OURSELVES THIS CONSTITUTION.

Photographs as Primary Sources An Iraqi woman displays her ink-stained finger after voting. Why do you think voters' fingers were marked with ink? Some Iraqis call it the "ink of freedom." What does that phrase tell you about what voting means to them?

Constitution of Iraq

In October 2005, more than 63 percent of eligible Iraqi voters went to the polls to decide whether to accept or reject the nation's new constitution. The constitution was overwhelmingly ratified.

We the people of Iraq, newly arisen from our disasters and looking with confidence to the future through a democratic, federal, republican system, are determined—men and women, old and young—to respect the rule of law, reject the policy of aggression, pay attention to women and their rights, the elderly and their cares, the children and their affairs, spread the culture of diversity and defuse terrorism.

[We accept this constitution] which shall preserve for Iraq its free union of people, land and sovereignty.

DBQ Document-Based Questions

1. **Analyzing** What does this statement from the Russian constitution "multinational people . . . united by a common destiny" mean?
2. **Responding** What do you think it means to "promote the general welfare and secure the blessing of liberty"?
3. **Predicting** In what ways do racist and extreme policies affect countries and bring harm to the people?
4. **Connecting** Compare the preambles that are presented in this activity. Describe how they are similar and how they are different. Explain what you believe is the purpose of a preamble to a constitution. Then identify which preamble best expresses that purpose.

Appendix

Contents

What Is an Appendix and How Do I Use One?

An appendix is the additional material you often find at the end of books. The following information will help you learn how to use the appendix in Civics Today: Citizenship, Economics, & You.

Skills Handbook

The Skills Handbook offers you information and practice using critical thinking and social study skills. Mastering these skills will help you in all your courses.

Historical Documents

This is a collection of some of the most important writings in American history. Each document begins with an introduction describing the author and placing the selection within its historical context.

Data Bank

A data bank is a collection of data organized for rapid search and retrieval. This data bank supplies information about the government and economy of the United States. It also includes information about state governments and economies.

Supreme Court Case Summaries

Supreme Court case summaries provide readable discussions of important Supreme Court cases. The summaries are listed in alphabetical order and include a summary of the facts of each case and its impact.

United States Facts

This quick resource lists all the states and territories of the Union along with the year each was admitted and its population, land area, and number of representatives in Congress.

United States Presidents

The presidents have served as our nation's leaders. In this resource you will find information of interest on the nation's presidents, including their terms in office, political affiliations, and occupations before they became president.

National Geographic Reference Atlas

Helpful maps of the United States and world are available for your easy reference.

Glossary/Glosario

A glossary is a list of important or difficult terms found in a textbook. The glossary gives a definition of each term as it is used in the book. The glossary also includes page numbers telling you where in the textbook each term is used. This glossary combines the English term with the Spanish translation and definition to aid Spanish-speaking students.

Index

An index is an alphabetical listing that includes the subjects of the book and the page numbers where those subjects can be found. The index in this book also lets you know that certain pages contain maps, graphs, or photos about the subjects.

Acknowledgments

This section lists photo credits and/or literary credits for the book. You can look at this section to find out where the publisher obtained the permission to use a photograph or to use excerpts from other books.

Test Yourself

Find the answers to these questions by using the Appendix on the following pages.

1. What are "intergovernmental revenues"?
2. Who was the sixth president of the United States and what term did he serve?
3. On what page can I find out about John Peter Zenger?
4. What year was Michigan admitted to the Union?
5. What was the Supreme Court's decision in *Marbury* v. *Madison*?

Skills Handbook

Contents

Interpreting Political Cartoons

Why Learn This Skill?

Political cartoons express the cartoonist's opinions through art. The cartoons appear in newspapers, magazines and books, and on the Internet. Political cartoons usually focus on public figures, political events, or economic or social conditions. This type of art can give you a summary of an event or circumstance, along with the artist's opinion, sometimes with exaggeration.

1 Learn It!

Follow these steps to interpret political cartoons:

- Read the title, caption, or conversation balloons. They help you identify the subject of the cartoon.
- Identify the characters or people in the cartoon. They may be caricatures, or unrealistic drawings that exaggerate the characters' physical features.
- Identify any symbols. Symbols are objects that stand for other things. An example is the American flag, which is a symbol of our country. Commonly recognized symbols may not be labeled. Unusual symbols might be labeled.
- Examine the actions in the cartoon—what is happening and why?
- Identify the cartoonist's purpose. What statement or idea is he or she trying to express? Decide if the cartoonist wants to persuade, criticize, or just make people think.

2 Practice It!

On a separate piece of paper, answer these questions about the political cartoon below.

1. What is the subject of the cartoon?
2. What words give clues to the meaning of the cartoon?
3. Why is the picture on a milk carton?
4. What message do you think the cartoonist is trying to send?

3 Apply It!

Bring a newsmagazine to class. With a partner, analyze the message in each political cartoon you find in the magazine.

TIME™

Political Cartoons

Gary Markstein/Copley News Service

Every year, more than half of all Americans do volunteer work ... role in it. One of the responsibilities of citizens is to help make their ... of volunteer grou... small. Perha... dad who...

Predicting

Why Learn This Skill?

You have probably read about people making difficult decisions based on something they think *might* happen. You will have a better understanding of why people make certain choices when you consider the factors that influenced their decisions, or predictions.

1 Learn It!

As you read a paragraph or section in your book, think about what might happen next. What you think will happen is your *prediction.* A prediction does not have a correct or incorrect answer. A prediction is an educated guess of what might happen next based on facts.

To make a prediction, ask yourself:

- What happened in this paragraph or section that I just read?
- What prior knowledge do I have about the information in the text?
- What similar circumstances do I know of?
- What do I think might happen next?
- Test your prediction: read further to see if you were correct.

2 Practice It!

To practice the skill, read the following paragraph about a possible case of discrimination. Then answer the questions.

A high school student who uses a wheelchair needs a ramp installed to reach the stage during a graduation ceremony held at an auditorium. The principal says no, the diploma can be awarded down in front of the stage.

1. What action do you predict the student will take? Why?
2. What action do you think the principal will take as a result of your predicted student action?
3. If you were the principal in this situation, what do you predict you would do?

3 Apply It!

Watch a television show or a movie. Halfway through the show, write down your prediction of how it will end. At the end of the show, check your prediction. Were you correct? What clues did you use to make your prediction? What clues did you miss?

Analyzing Library and Research Resources

Why Learn This Skill?

Imagine that your teacher has sent you to the library or to the Internet to research and to write a report about the current makeup of the United States Congress. Knowing how to choose sources that contain accurate and current information will help you save time in the library or on the Internet. You will also be able to write a better and more accurate report.

1 Learn It!

Not all sources will be useful for your report on the members of the Senate and House of Representatives. Even some sources that involve topics about government will not always provide the information you want. In analyzing sources for your research project, choose items that are nonfiction and that contain the most information about your topic. Also choose sources based on their depth and how timely they are.

When choosing research resources, ask these questions:

- Is the information up-to-date?
- Does a book's or journal's index have several page references listed for the topic?
- Is the research written in a way that is easy to understand?
- Are there helpful statistical graphs, charts, and photos?

2 Practice It!

Look at the following list of sources. Which would be most helpful in writing a report on the United States Congress? Explain your choices.

(1) The Declaration of Independence
(2) The current *Information Please* Almanac
(3) A children's storybook about the U.S. Congress
(4) A student's notes on the Internet about a family trip to Washington, D.C.
(5) A book about U.S. history
(6) A Web site, www.thomas.loc.gov
(7) A journal article written by the current president of the United States
(8) a biographical dictionary

3 Apply It!

Go to your local library or use the Internet to create a bibliography of sources you might use to write a report on the current membership of the U.S. Congress. Explain why you would choose each source. Make sure you include information about both the House of Representatives and the Senate, including a breakdown of the membership of each.

Interpreting a Chart

Why Learn This Skill?

To make learning easier, you can organize information into groups of related facts and ideas. One way to organize information is with a chart. A chart presents written or numerical information in lists, columns, and rows. It helps you remember and compare information more easily. Cross-referencing data is an important comparison that can be made on a chart.

1 Learn It!

To organize information in a chart, follow these steps:

- Decide what information you must organize.
- Identify several major categories of ideas or facts about the topic, and use these categories as column headings.
- Find information that fits into each category, and write those facts or ideas under the appropriate column heading.

2 Practice It!

On a separate sheet of paper, answer the following questions using the chart on this page.

Time Management Tips for High School Students
1. Make a "To Do" list every day. 2. Use spare minutes wisely. 3. It's okay to say "No!" when keeping your study priorities in mind. 4. Find the right time of the day to work. 5. Review your notes every day. 6. Get a good night's sleep. 7. Communicate your schedule to others so they do not interrupt your study time. 8. Become a taskmaster and budget your time. 9. Don't waste time agonizing over setbacks or procrastinating. 10. Keep things in perspective by setting realistic goals.
Source: collegeboard.com.

1. What type of information does the chart contain?
2. Whom would this chart help?
3. What features of the chart help you read ideas easily?

3 Apply It!

Create a chart to track your school assignments. Work with five areas of information: Subject, Assignment, Description, Due Date, and Completed Assignments. Be sure to keep your chart up-to-date.

Making Comparisons

Why Learn This Skill?

Suppose you want to buy a portable CD player, and you must choose among three models. To make this decision, you would probably compare various features of the three models, such as price, sound quality, size, and so on. After you compare the models, you will choose the one that is best for you.

In your studies of civics and economics, you must often compare forms of government and different economic plans, identify patterns, make predictions, and make generalizations about them.

 Learn It!

When making comparisons, you identify and examine two or more places and their economies, or their forms of government. Then you identify any similarities between two types, or ways the two types are alike. Finally, you also note their differences—the things about them that are not alike.

When making comparisons, apply the following steps:

- Decide what types of government or economies to compare. Clue words such as *also, as well as, like, same as,* and *similar to* can help you identify when topics are being compared.
- Read the information about each type carefully.
- Identify what information is similar for both topics.
- Make note of aspects of both that are different or dissimilar.

2 Practice It!

To practice the skill, analyze the information in the chart at the bottom of this page. Then answer these questions:

1. What types of government are being compared?
2. What categories for each government are being compared?
3. In what ways, if any, are the United States and Cuba similar?
4. Suppose you wanted to compare the two governments in more detail. What other categories might you use?

Democratic vs. Totalitarian		
	Democratic	**Totalitarian**
Country	United States	Cuba
Control of Economy	Individual Development	Government
Control of Laws	Citizens Vote, Government Enforces	Government Dictates
Choice of Leaders	Citizens Vote	Government Selects or Appoints

3 Apply It!

Think about two sports that are played at your school. Make a chart comparing categories such as where the games are played, who plays them, what equipment is used, and so on.

Analyzing Primary Sources

Why Learn This Skill?

People who study civics and government examine pieces of evidence to understand their government, laws, and economy. These types of evidence—both written and illustrated—are called *primary sources.* Examining primary sources can help you understand your government. They are called primary sources because a specific source or origin of the information can be identified.

1 Learn It!

Primary sources of civics are firsthand accounts that describe an event, law, or constitutional development. They can include letters, diaries, photographs, pictures, news articles, legal documents, stories, literature, and artwork.

Ask yourself the following questions when analyzing primary sources:

- What is the primary source?
- Who created it?
- What is its original format or source?
- When was it created?
- What does it reveal about the topic I am studying?
- Why was it created and for what audience?

2 Practice It!

The following primary source is the first verse of the song "The Star-Spangled Banner" written by Francis Scott Key during the War of 1812. Read the verse, and then answer the questions that follow.

> *Oh, say, can you see, by the dawn's early light*
> *What so proudly we hailed at the twilight's last gleaming,*
> *Whose broad stripes and bright stars through the perilous fight,*
> *O'er the ramparts we watched were so gallantly streaming?*
> *And the rocket's red glare, the bombs bursting in air,*
> *Gave proof through the night that our flag was still there.*
> *Oh, say, does that star-spangled banner yet wave*
> *O'er the land of the free, and the home of the brave?*
>
> —Excerpt from "The Star-Spangled Banner" by Francis Scott Key, 1812

1. What is the main topic?
2. What details let you know he is talking about the American flag?
3. How do we know there is a war going on?
4. What emotion is the songwriter trying to convey?

3 Apply It!

Find a primary source from your past, such as a photo, newspaper clipping, or diary entry. Explain to the class what it shows about that time in your life.

Recognizing Bias

Why Learn This Skill?

If you say, "Summer is a prettier season of the year than winter," you are stating a bias. A *bias* is an attitude that favors one way of thinking over another. A bias can also be thought of as a form of an opinion. That is someone's personal attitude, but not necessarily a true fact. It can prevent you from looking at a situation in a reasonable or truthful way.

Learn It!

Most people have feelings and ideas that affect their points of view. Their viewpoints, or *biases*, influence the way they interpret events. For this reason, an idea that is stated as a fact may really be only an opinion. Recognizing bias will help you judge the accuracy of what you read and sort opinions from true facts.

To recognize bias, follow these steps:

- Identify the speaker or writer and examine the views presented. Why did the person speak or write about a particular issue?
- Look for language that shows emotion or opinion. Look for words such as *all, never, best, worst, might,* or *should.*
- Examine the information for imbalances. Is it written from one point of view? Does it take into consideration other points of view?
- Identify statements of fact. Factual statements usually answer the *who, what, where,* and *when* questions.
- Does the writer use facts to support his or her point of view? Statements such as *I think,* or *I believe* often indicate a point of view—not a fact.

2 Practice It!

Read the following statement by an author who writes about what goes on in American politics and government.

> *Misusing words is, in politics, an art form. The politician who uses plain English is not likely to be a politician for long. Often it is better to be obscure.*

1. What problem is the speaker addressing?
2. What reason does the speaker give for the problem?
3. What is the speaker's point of view, or bias?
4. What words give clues as to the speaker's bias?

3 Apply It!

Choose a "Letter to the Editor" from a newspaper. Summarize the issue being discussed and the writer's bias about the issue. Describe a possible opposing opinion and who might have that opinion and why.

Interpreting a Circle Graph

Why Learn This Skill?

Have you ever watched someone serve pieces of pie? When the pie is cut evenly, everyone's slice is the same size. If one slice is cut a little larger, however, someone else gets a smaller piece.

A *circle graph* is like a sliced pie. It is often called a pie chart. In a circle graph, the complete circle represents a whole group—or 100 percent. The circle is divided into "slices," or wedge-shaped sections representing parts of the whole.

1 Learn It!

To read a circle graph, follow these steps:

- Read the title of the circle graph to find the subject.
- Study the labels or the key to see what each "slice" represents.
- Compare the sizes of the circle slices.
- Draw conclusions from your comparison.

2 Practice It!

The circle graph below represents that same information shown on this chart, but in a different format. Study the circle graph, and answer the following questions.

1. What is the subject of the circle graph?
2. Which region of the U.S. has produced the most presidents?
3. Which states on the graph produced the fewest presidents?
4. What conclusion could you draw from this circle graph?

3 Apply It!

Quiz some friends about the first names of 10 presidents of which you supply them the last names. Create a circle graph showing percentages of correct and noncorrect results of those who answered your questions.

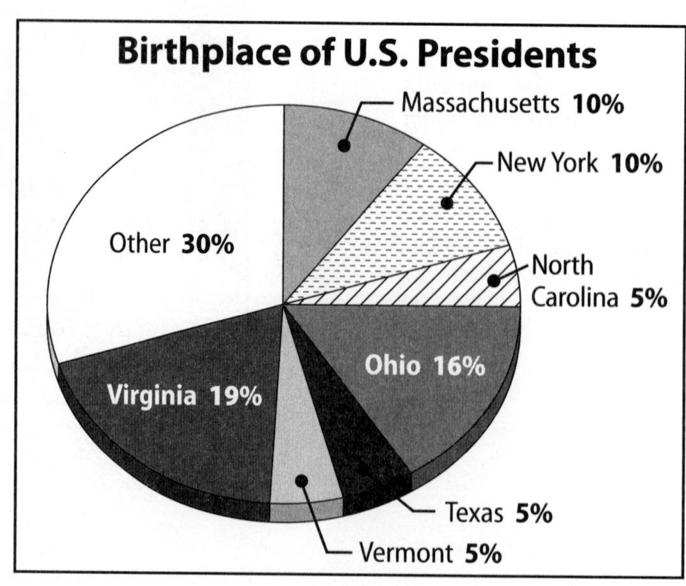

Sequencing Events

Why Learn This Skill?

Have you ever had to remember events and their dates in the order in which they happened? *Sequencing* means listing facts in the correct order that they occurred. A time line helps you do this. A time line is a diagram that shows how dates and events relate to one another. The years are evenly spaced on most time lines. Time lines may be horizontal or vertical. Events on time lines are described beside the date on which they occurred.

1 Learn It!

To understand how to sequence events, follow these steps:

- As you read, look for dates or clue words that hint at chronological order, such as *in 2006, the late 1900s, first, then, finally,* and *after.*
- To read a time line, find the dates on the opposite ends of the time line. These dates show the range of time that is covered.
- Note the equal spacing between dates on the time line. These are the time intervals.
- Study the order of events.
- Look to see how the events relate to one another.

2 Practice It!

Examine the time line below and answer the questions.

1. When does the time line begin? When does it end?
2. What major event for a UN agency happened in 1965?
3. In what country did the UN monitor a cease-fire in 1991?
4. During what decade did South Africa hold its first free elections?

3 Apply It!

List key events from one of the chapters in Unit 1 of your textbook that covers the history of the United States. Decide what time period to cover and what time intervals you will put on your time line. Create a time line that lists these events in the order they occurred.

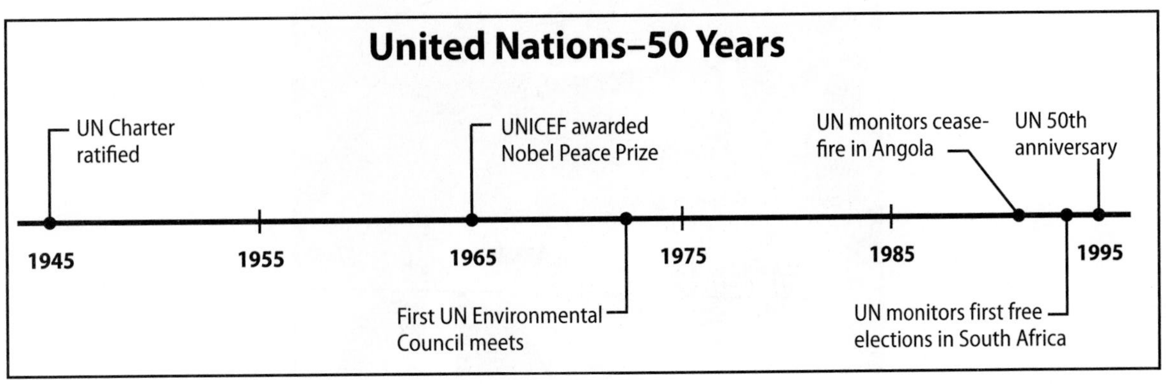

Categorizing and Analyzing Information

Why Learn This Skill?

If you looked at the season statistics for your favorite football game to decide if they have a chance at the championship, you would be categorizing and analyzing information about the team.

Categorizing information means you sort information into related groups or topics. Then in analyzing that information, you determine its accuracy and reliability. In the case of football statistics, this process would involve looking at scores, player injuries, yards gained rushing, and other data from the past season.

1 Learn It!

To learn to categorize and analyze information, follow these steps:

- As you read, sort information into categories or groups according to related topics.
- Choose headings for your categories to help you identify relationships.
- Look at the source of information to determine its accuracy. Is it a primary or secondary source?
- Compare the same information from different sources to check reliability and look for contradictions.

2 Practice It!

Read the following excerpt describing laws in the United States, and then answer the questions.

Laws fall into two major groups: criminal and civil. Criminal laws regulate public conduct and set duties owed to society. Criminal laws have penalties and offenders can be imprisoned, fined, or punished in some other way. Civil laws regulate relations between individuals or groups of individuals. A civil action is a lawsuit. As a result, the courts may award the injured person money for his or her loss or require the offender to make amends in some other way.

1. What major categories are discussed in the paragraph?
2. Under what subtopics would you list information in each category?
3. Which would be the more reliable source for this information—a textbook or the newspaper? Why?

3 Apply It!

Choose an article from your newspaper describing the details of a crime. Categorize and analyze to explain it to a classmate. Does the information seem complete and accurate? What is the source? Share your findings.

Flag Etiquette

For Americans, the flag has always had a special meaning. It is a symbol of our nation's freedom and democracy. Over the years, Americans have developed rules and customs concerning the use and display of the flag. One of the most important things every American should remember is to treat the flag with respect.

- ★ **The flag should be raised and lowered by hand and displayed only from sunrise to sunset. On special occasions, the flag may be displayed at night, but it should be illuminated.**
- ★ **The flag may be displayed on all days, weather permitting, particularly on national and state holidays and on historic and special occasions.**
- ★ **No flag may be flown above the American flag or to the right of it at the same height.**
- ★ **The flag should never touch the ground or floor beneath it.**
- ★ **The flag may be flown at half-staff by order of the president, usually to mourn the death of a public official.**
- ★ **The flag may be flown upside down only to signal distress.**
- ★ **The flag should never be carried flat or horizontally, but always carried aloft and free.**
- ★ **When the flag becomes old and tattered, it should be destroyed by burning. According to an approved custom, the Union (stars on blue field) is first cut from the flag; then the two pieces, which no longer form a flag, are burned.**

Historical Documents

The Magna Carta

The Magna Carta, signed by King John in 1215, marked a decisive step forward in the development of constitutional government in England. Later, it became a model for colonists who carried the Magna Carta's guarantees of legal and political rights to America.

1. . . . [T]hat the English Church shall be free, and shall have its rights entire, and its liberties unimpaired. . . . we have also granted for us and our heirs forever, all the liberties written out below, to have and to keep for them and their heirs, of us and our heirs:

39. No free man shall be seized or imprisoned, or stripped of his rights or possessions, or outlawed or exiled, or deprived of his standing in any other way, nor will we proceed with force against him, or send others to do so, except by the lawful judgment of his equals, or by the law of the land.

40. To no one will we sell, to no one deny or delay right or justice.

41. All merchants may enter or leave England unharmed and without fear, and may stay or travel within it, by land or water, for purposes of trade, free from all illegal exactions, in accordance with ancient and lawful customs. This, however, does not apply in time of war to merchants from a country that is at war with us. . . .

42. In future it shall be lawful for any man to leave and return to our kingdom unharmed and without fear, by land or water, preserving his allegiance to us, except in time of war, for some short period, for the common benefit of the realm. . . .

60. All these customs and liberties that we have granted shall be observed in our kingdom in so far as concerns our own relations with our subjects. Let all men of our kingdom, whether clergy or laymen, observe them similarly in their relations with their own men. . . .

63. . . . Both we and the barons have sworn that all this shall be observed in good faith and without deceit. Witness the abovementioned people and many others. Given by our hand in the meadow that is called Runnymede, between Windsor and Staines, on the fifteenth day of June in the seventeenth year of our reign.

Illuminated manuscript, Middle Ages

The Mayflower Compact

On November 21, 1620, 41 colonists aboard the Mayflower drafted this agreement. The Mayflower Compact was the first plan of self-government ever put in force in the English colonies.

In the Name of God, Amen. We, whose names are underwritten, the Loyal Subjects of our dread Sovereign Lord King James, by the Grace of God, of Great Britain, France, and Ireland, King, Defender of the Faith, etc. Having undertaken for the Glory of God, and Advancement of the Christian Faith, and the Honour of our King and Country, a Voyage to plant the first Colony in the northern Parts of Virginia; Do by these Presents, solemnly and mutually, in the Presence of God and one another, covenant and combine ourselves together into a civil Body Politick, for our better Ordering and Preservation, and Furtherance of the Ends aforesaid: And by Virtue hereof do enact, constitute, and frame, such just and equal Laws, Ordinances, Acts, Constitutions, and Officers, from time to time, as shall be thought most meet and convenient for the general Good of the Colony; unto which we promise all due Submission and Obedience. In Witness whereof we have hereunto subscribed our names at Cape-Cod the eleventh of November, in the Reign of our Sovereign Lord King James, of England, France, and Ireland, the eighteenth, and of Scotland, the fifty-fourth, Anno Domini, 1620.

The Federalist, No. 10

James Madison wrote several articles supporting ratification of the Constitution for a New York newspaper. In the excerpt below, Madison argues for the idea of a federal republic.

By a faction, I understand a number of citizens . . . who are united and actuated by some common impulse . . . adverse to the rights of other citizens. . . .

The inference to which we are brought is that the causes of faction cannot be removed and that relief is only to be sought in the means of controlling its effects. . . .

A republic, by which I mean a government in which the scheme of representation takes place . . . promises the cure for which we are seeking. . . .

The two great points of difference between a democracy and a republic are: first, the delegation of the government, in the latter, to a small number of citizens elected by the rest; secondly, the greater number of citizens, and greater sphere of country, over which the latter may be extended.

James Madison

The effect of the first difference is . . . to refine and enlarge the public views, by passing them through the medium of a chosen body of citizens, whose wisdom may best discern the true interest of their country, and whose patriotism and love of justice will be least likely to sacrifice it to temporary or partial considerations. . . .

Washington's Farewell Address

At the end of his second term as president, George Washington spoke of the dangers facing the young nation. He warned against the dangers of political parties and sectionalism, and he advised the nation against permanent alliances with other nations.

. . . Citizens by birth or choice of a common country, that country has a right to concentrate your affections. The name of American, which belongs to you in your national capacity, must always exalt the just pride of patriotism more than any appellation derived from local discriminations. With slight shades of difference, you have the same religion, manners, habits, and political principles. You have in a common cause fought and triumphed together. . . .

In contemplating the causes which may disturb our union it occurs as matter of serious concern that any ground should have been furnished for characterizing parties by geographical discriminations. . . .

George Washington

No alliances, however strict, between the parts can be an adequate substitute. They must inevitably experience the infractions and interruptions which all alliances in all times have experienced. . . .

The great rule of conduct for us in regard to foreign nations is, in extending our commercial relations to have with them as little political connection as possible. . . .

. . . I anticipate with pleasing expectation that retreat in which I promise myself to realize . . . the sweet enjoyment of partaking in the midst of my fellow citizens the benign influence of good laws under a free government—the ever-favorite object of my heart, and the happy reward, as I trust, of our mutual cares, labors, and dangers.

The Star-Spangled Banner

During the British bombardment of Fort McHenry during the War of 1812, a young Baltimore lawyer named Francis Scott Key was inspired to write the words to "The Star-Spangled Banner." Although it became popular immediately, it was not until 1931 that Congress officially declared "The Star-Spangled Banner" as our national anthem.

O! say can you see by the dawn's early light,
What so proudly we hailed at the twilight's last gleaming,
Whose broad stripes and bright stars through the perilous fight,
O'er the ramparts we watch'd, were so gallantly streaming?
And the Rockets' red glare, the Bombs bursting in air,
Gave proof through the night that our Flag was still there;
O! say does that star-spangled Banner yet wave,
O'er the Land of the free, and the home of the brave!

The Monroe Doctrine

In 1823 President James Monroe proclaimed the Monroe Doctrine. Designed to end European influence in the Western Hemisphere, it became a cornerstone of United States foreign policy.

. . . With the existing colonies or dependencies of any European power we have not interfered and shall not interfere. But with the Governments who have declared their independence and maintained it, and whose independence we have, on great consideration and on just principles, acknowledged, we could not view any interposition for the purpose of oppressing them, or controlling in any other manner their destiny, by any European power in any other light than as the manifestation of any unfriendly disposition toward the United States. . . .

James Monroe

Our policy in regard to Europe, which was adopted at an early stage of the wars which have so long agitated that quarter of the globe, nevertheless remains the same, which is, not to interfere in the internal concerns of any of its powers; to consider the government de facto as the legitimate government for us; to cultivate friendly relations with it, and to preserve those relations by a frank, firm, and manly policy, meeting in all instances the just claims of every power, submitting to injuries from none. . . .

Memorial of the Cherokee Nation

The Indian Removal Act of 1830 called for the relocation of Native Americans to territory west of the Mississippi River. Cherokee leaders protested the policy.

We are aware that some persons suppose it will be for our advantage to remove beyond the Mississippi. We think otherwise. Our people universally think otherwise. . . .

We wish to remain on the land of our fathers. We have a perfect and original right to remain without interruption or molestation. The treaties with us, and laws of the United States made in pursuance of treaties, guaranty our residence and our privileges, and secure us against intruders. Our only request is, that these treaties may be fulfilled, and these laws executed. . . .

. . . We have been called a poor, ignorant, and degraded people. We certainly are not rich; nor have we ever boasted of our knowledge, or our moral or intellectual elevation. But there is not a man within our limits so ignorant as not to know that he has a right to live on the land of his fathers, in the possession of his immemorial privileges, and that this right has been acknowledged by the United States; nor is there a man so degraded as not to feel a keen sense of injury, on being deprived of his right and driven into exile. . . .

The Seneca Falls Declaration

One of the first documents to express the desire for equal rights for women is the Declaration of Sentiments and Resolutions, issued in 1848 at the Seneca Falls Convention in Seneca Falls, New York. Led by Lucretia Mott and Elizabeth Cady Stanton, the delegates adopted a set of resolutions that called for woman suffrage and opportunities for women in employment and education. Excerpts from the Declaration follow.

When, in the course of human events, it becomes necessary for one portion of the family of man to assume among the people of the earth a position different from that which they have hitherto occupied, but one to which the laws of nature and of nature's God entitle them, a decent respect to the opinions of mankind requires that they should declare the causes that impel them to such a course.

We hold these truths to be self-evident: that all men and women are created equal; that they are endowed by their Creator with certain inalienable rights; that among these are life, liberty, and the pursuit of happiness; that to secure these rights governments are instituted, deriving their just powers from the consent of the governed. Whenever any form of government becomes destructive of these ends, it is the right of those who suffer from it to refuse allegiance to it, and to insist upon the institution of a new government, laying its foundation on such principles, and organizing its powers in such form as to them shall seem most likely to effect their safety and happiness. Prudence, indeed, will dictate that governments long established should not be changed for light and transient causes; . . . But when a long train of abuses and usurpations, pursuing invariably the same object, evinces a design to reduce them under absolute despotism, it is their duty to throw off such government, and to provide new guards for their future security. . . .

The history of mankind is a history of repeated injuries and usurpations on the part of man toward woman, having in direct object the establishment of an absolute tyranny over her. To prove this, let facts be submitted to a candid world. . . .

Now, in view of the entire disfranchisement of one-half the people of this country, their social and religious degradation—in view of the unjust laws above mentioned, and because women do feel themselves aggrieved, oppressed, and fraudulently deprived of their most sacred rights, we insist that they have immediate admission to all the rights and privileges which belong to them as citizens of these United States. . . .

Elizabeth Cady Stanton

The Emancipation Proclamation

On January 1, 1863, President Abraham Lincoln issued the Emancipation Proclamation, which freed all enslaved people in states under Confederate control. The Proclamation was a step toward the Thirteenth Amendment (1865), which ended slavery in all of the United States.

. . . That on the 1st day of January, in the year of our Lord 1863, all persons held as slaves within any state or designated part of a state, the people whereof shall then be in rebellion against the United States, shall be then, thenceforward, and forever free; and the Executive Government of the United States, including the military and naval authority thereof, will recognize and maintain the freedom of such persons, and will do no act or acts to repress such persons, or any of them, in any efforts they may make for their actual freedom.

That the Executive will, on the 1st day of January aforesaid, by proclamation, designate the states and parts of states, if any, in which the people thereof, respectively, shall then be in rebellion against the United States; and the fact that any state, or the people thereof, shall on that day be in good faith represented in the Congress of the United States, by members chosen thereto at elections wherein a majority of the qualified voters of such states shall have participated, shall, in the absence of strong countervailing testimony, be deemed conclusive evidence that such state, and the people thereof, are not then in rebellion against the United States. . . .

And, by virtue of the power and for the purpose aforesaid, I do order and declare that all persons held as slaves within said designated states and parts of states are, and henceforward shall be, free; and that the Executive Government of the United States, including the military and naval authorities thereof, will recognize and maintain the freedom of said persons.

And I hereby enjoin upon the people so declared to be free to abstain from all violence, unless in necessary self-defense; and I recommend to them that, all cases when allowed, they labor faithfully for reasonable wages.

And I further declare and make known that such persons, of suitable condition, will be received into the armed service of the United States. . . .

And upon this act, sincerely believed to be an act of justice, warranted by the Constitution upon military necessity, I invoke the considerate judgement of mankind and the gracious favor of Almighty God. . . .

Abraham Lincoln

The Gettysburg Address

On November 19, 1863, President Abraham Lincoln gave a short speech at the dedication of a national cemetery on the battlefield of Gettysburg. His simple yet eloquent words expressed his hopes for a nation divided by civil war.

Four score and seven years ago our fathers brought forth on this continent a new nation, conceived in liberty, and dedicated to the proposition that all men are created equal.

Now we are engaged in a great civil war, testing whether that nation, or any nation so conceived and so dedicated, can long endure. We are met on a great battlefield of that war. We have come to dedicate a portion of that field as a final resting place for those who here gave their lives that that nation might live. It is altogether fitting and proper that we should do this.

But, in a larger sense, we can not dedicate—we can not consecrate—we can not hallow—this ground. The brave men, living and dead, who struggled here, have consecrated it far above our poor power to add or detract. The world will little note nor long remember what we say here, but it can never forget what they did here. It is for us, the living, rather, to be dedicated here to the unfinished work which they who fought here have thus far so nobly advanced. It is rather for us to be here dedicated to the great task remaining before us—that from these honored dead we take increased devotion to that cause for which they gave the last full measure of devotion; that we here highly resolve that these dead shall not have died in vain; that this nation, under God, shall have a new birth of freedom; and that government of the people, by the people, for the people, shall not perish from the earth.

Current day photo of Gettysburg battlefield

I Will Fight No More

In 1877 the Nez Perce fought the government's attempt to move them to a smaller reservation. After a remarkable attempt to escape to Canada, Chief Joseph realized that resistance was hopeless and advised his people to surrender.

Tell General Howard I know his heart. What he told me before I have in my heart.

I am tired of fighting. . . . The old men are all dead. It is the young men who say yes or no. He who led the young men is dead. It is cold and we have no blankets. The little children are freezing to death. My people, some of them have run away to the hills, and have no blankets, no food; no one knows where they are—perhaps freezing to death. I want to have time to look for my children and see how many of them I can find. Maybe I shall find them among the dead. Hear me, my chiefs.

I am tired; my heart is sick and sad. From where the sun now stands I will fight no more forever.

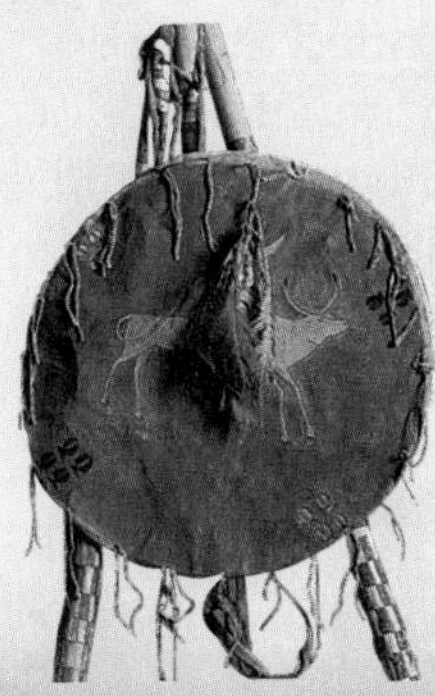

Cheyenne shield

The Pledge of Allegiance

In 1892 the nation celebrated the 400th anniversary of Columbus's landing in America. In connection with this celebration, Francis Bellamy, a magazine editor, wrote and published the Pledge of Allegiance. The words "under God" were added by Congress in 1954 at the urging of President Dwight D. Eisenhower.

I pledge allegiance to the Flag of the United States of America and to the Republic for which it stands, one Nation under God, indivisible, with liberty and justice for all.

Students in a New York City school recite the Pledge of Allegiance

The American's Creed

William Tyler Page of Friendship Heights, Maryland, wrote The American's Creed. This statement of political faith summarizes the true meaning of freedom available to all Americans. The U.S. House of Representatives adopted the creed on behalf of the American people on April 3, 1918.

I believe in the United States of America as a Government of the people, by the people, for the people; whose just powers are derived from the consent of the governed; a democracy in a republic; a sovereign Nation of many sovereign States; a perfect union, one and inseparable; established upon those principles of freedom, equality, justice, and humanity for which American patriots sacrificed their lives and fortunes.

I therefore believe it is my duty to my Country to love it, to support its Constitution, to obey its laws, to respect its flag, and to defend it against all enemies.

The Fourteen Points

On January 8, 1918, President Woodrow Wilson went before Congress to offer a statement of aims called the Fourteen Points. Wilson's plan called for freedom of the seas in peace and war, an end to secret alliances, and equal trading rights for all countries. The excerpt that follows is taken from the president's message.

. . . We entered this war because violations of right had occurred which touched us to the quick and made the life of our own people impossible unless they were corrected and the world secured once for all against their recurrence. What we demand in this war, therefore, is nothing peculiar to ourselves. It is that the world be made fit and safe to live in; and particularly that it be made safe for every peace-loving nation which, like our own, wishes to live its own life, determine its own institutions, be assured of justice and fair dealing by the other peoples of the world as against force and selfish aggression. All the peoples of the world are in effect partners in this interest, and for our own part we see very clearly that unless justice be done to others it will not be done to us. The program of the world's peace, therefore, is our program; and that program, the only possible program, as we see it, is this:

I. Open covenants of peace, openly arrived at, after which there shall be no private international understandings of any kind but diplomacy shall proceed always frankly and in the public view.

II. Absolute freedom of navigation upon the seas, outside territorial waters, alike in peace and in war, except as the seas may be closed in whole or in part by international action for the enforcement of international covenants.

XIV. A general association of nations must be formed under specific covenants for the purpose of affording mutual guarantees of political independence and territorial integrity to great and small states alike. . . .

Brown v. Board of Education

On May 17, 1954, the Supreme Court ruled in Brown v. Board of Education of Topeka, Kansas, that racial segregation in public schools was unconstitutional. This decision provided the legal basis for court challenges to segregation in every aspect of American life.

. . . The plaintiffs contend that segregated public schools are not "equal" and cannot be made "equal" and that hence they are deprived of the equal protection of the laws. Because of the obvious importance of the question presented, the Court took jurisdiction. . . .

Our decision, therefore, cannot turn on merely a comparison of these tangible factors in the Negro and white schools involved in each of the cases. We must look instead to the effect of segregation itself on public education.

In approaching this problem, we cannot turn the clock back to 1868 when the Amendment was adopted, or even to 1896 when Plessy v. Ferguson was written. We must consider public education in the light of its full development and its present place in American life throughout the Nation. Only in this way can it be determined if segregation in public schools deprives these plaintiffs of the equal protection of the laws.

Today, education is perhaps the most important function of state and local governments. Compulsory school attendance laws and the great expenditures for education both demonstrate our recognition of the importance of education to our democratic society. . . . In these days, it is doubtful that any child may reasonably be expected to succeed in life if he is denied the opportunity of an education. Such an opportunity, where the state has undertaken to provide it, is a right which must be made available to all on equal terms.

We come then to the question presented: Does segregation of children in public schools solely on the basis of race, even though the physical facilities and other "tangible" factors may be equal, deprive the children of the minority group of equal educational opportunities? We believe that it does.

. . . We conclude that in the field of public education the doctrine of "separate but equal" has no place. Separate educational facilities are inherently unequal. Therefore, we hold that the plaintiffs and others similarly situated for whom the actions have been brought are, by reason of the segregation complained of, deprived of the equal protection of the laws guaranteed by the Fourteenth Amendment. . . .

Armed guards escort African American students

John F. Kennedy's Inaugural Address

President Kennedy's Inaugural Address on January 20, 1961, set the tone for his administration. In his address Kennedy stirred the nation by calling for "a grand and global alliance" to fight tyranny, poverty, disease, and war.

We observe today not a victory of party but a celebration of freedom—symbolizing an end as well as a beginning—signifying renewal as well as change. For I have sworn before you and Almighty God the same solemn oath our forebears prescribed nearly a century and three-quarters ago.

The world is very different now. For man holds in his mortal hands the power to abolish all forms of human poverty and all forms of human life. And yet the same revolutionary beliefs for which our forebears fought are still at issue around the globe—the belief that the rights of man come not from the generosity of the state but from the hand of God.

We dare not forget today that we are the heirs of that first revolution. Let the word go forth from this time and place, to friend and foe alike, that the torch has been passed to a new generation of Americans—born in this century, tempered by war, disciplined by a hard and bitter peace, proud of our ancient heritage—and unwilling to witness or permit the slow undoing of those human rights to which this nation has always been committed, and to which we are committed today at home and around the world.

Let every nation know, whether it wishes us well or ill, that we shall pay any price, bear any burden, meet any hardship, support any friend, oppose any foe to assure the survival and the success of liberty.

This much we pledge—and more.

To those old allies whose cultural and spiritual origins we share, we pledge the loyalty of faithful friends. United, there is little we cannot do in a host of cooperative ventures. Divided, there is little we can do. . . .

Let us never negotiate out of fear. But let us never fear to negotiate.

Let both sides explore what problems unite us instead of belaboring those problems which divide us. . . .

Let both sides seek to invoke the wonders of science instead of its terrors. Together let us explore the stars, conquer the deserts, eradicate disease, tap the ocean depths, and encourage the arts and commerce. . . .

And so, my fellow Americans: ask not what your country can do for you—ask what you can do for your country.

My fellow citizens of the world: ask not what America will do for you, but what together we can do for the freedom of man. . . .

President Kennedy speaking

I Have a Dream

On August 28, 1963, while Congress debated wide-ranging civil rights legislation, Dr. Martin Luther King, Jr., led more than 200,000 people in a march on Washington, D.C. On the steps of the Lincoln Memorial he gave a stirring speech in which he eloquently spoke of his dreams for African Americans and for the United States. Excerpts of the speech follow.

. . . There are those who are asking the devotees of civil rights, "When will you be satisfied?"

We can never be satisfied as long as the Negro is the victim of the unspeakable horrors of police brutality. . . .

We cannot be satisfied as long as the Negro's basic mobility is from a smaller ghetto to a larger one.

We can never be satisfied as long as a Negro in Mississippi cannot vote and a Negro in New York believes he has nothing for which to vote. . . .

I say to you today, my friends, that in spite of the difficulties and frustrations of the moment I still have a dream. It is a dream deeply rooted in the American dream. I have a dream that one day this nation will rise up and live out the true meaning of its creed: "We hold these truths to be self-evident, that all men are created equal."

I have a dream that one day on the red hills of Georgia the sons of former slaves and the sons of former slaveowners will be able to sit down together at the table of brotherhood.

I have a dream that one day even the state of Mississippi, a desert state sweltering with the heat of injustice and oppression, will be transformed into an oasis of freedom and justice.

I have a dream that my four little children will one day live in a nation where they will not be judged by the color of their skin but by the content of their character. . . .

. . . When we let freedom ring, when we let it ring from every village and every hamlet, from every state and every city, we will be able to speed up that day when all of God's children, black men and white men, Jews and Gentiles, Protestants and Catholics, will be able to join hands and sing in the words of the old Negro spiritual: "Free at last! Free at last! Thank God Almighty, we are free at last!"

Dr. Martin Luther King, Jr.

Data Bank

Contents

United States Population Growth, 1980–2006

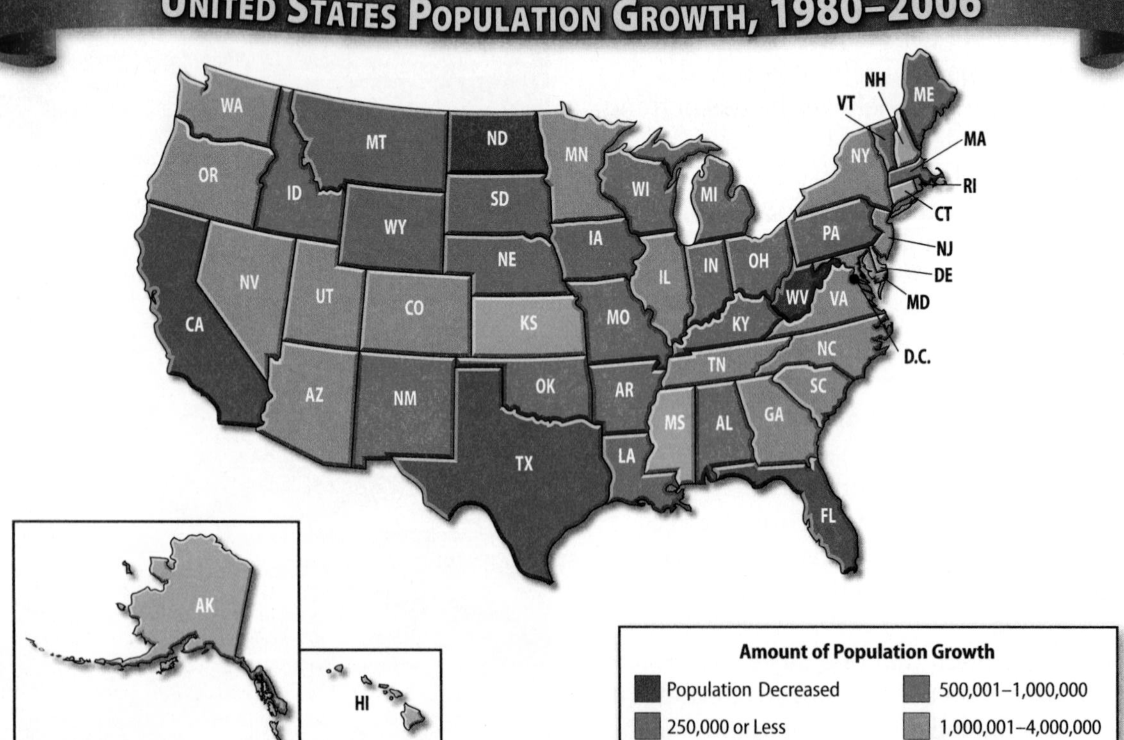

Source: U.S. Bureau of the Census, *Statistical Abstract of the United States*, 2006.

CRIME AND THE JUSTICE SYSTEM

Supreme Court Cases

10,000
9,000
8,000
7,000
6,000
5,000
4,000
Number of Pending Cases
1970
1980
1990
2000
2006
Year

Supreme Court Decisions

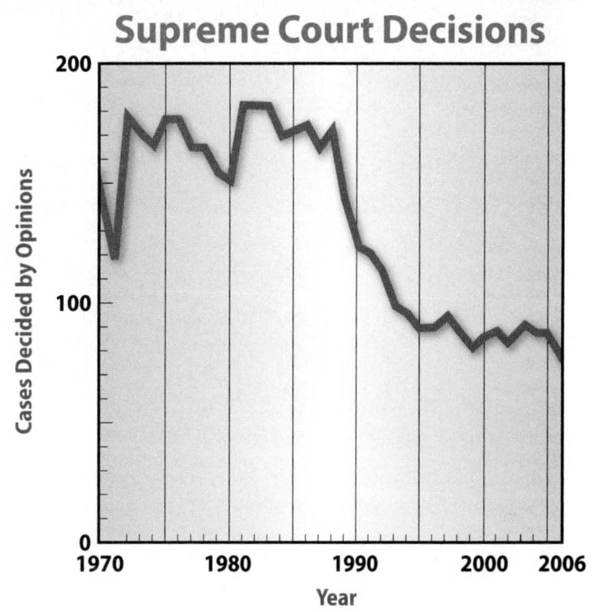

Types of Cases in Federal District Courts, 2007

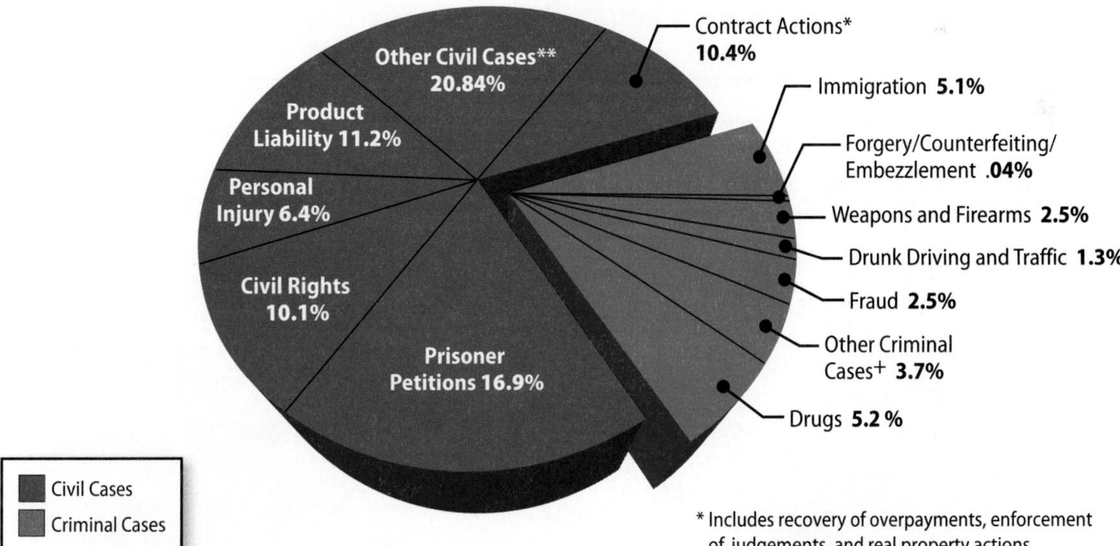

* Includes recovery of overpayments, enforcement of judgements, and real property actions

** Includes bankruptcy, tax suits, labor laws, social security issues, protected property rights, RICO, other statutory actions, and forfeiture and penalty

+ Includes federal statute violations, sex offenses, larceny/theft, homicide, robbery, assault, and burglary

Sources: U.S. Bureau of the Census, *Statistical Abstract of the United States,* 2008 (Washington, D.C.: 2008); Administrative Office of the U.S. Courts, *Statistical Tables for the Federal Judiciary,* 2007.

Bills Introduced, Passed, and Enacted by Congress, 1961–2006

CONGRESS (Years)	BILLS INTRODUCED* House	BILLS INTRODUCED* Senate	BILLS PASSED* House	BILLS PASSED* Senate	BILLS ENACTED
87th (1961–62)	15,751	4,565	2,424	2,345	1,569
88th (1963–64)	15,299	3,937	1,734	1,691	1,026
89th (1965–66)	21,999	4,567	2,148	1,968	1,283
90th (1967–68)	24,227	4,906	1,659	1,731	1,002
91st (1969–70)	23,575	5,466	1,712	1,676	941
92nd (1971–72)	20,458	4,896	1,469	1,371	768
93rd (1973–74)	21,095	5,127	1,524	1,564	774
94th (1975–76)	19,371	4,913	1,624	1,552	729
95th (1977–78)	17,800	4,513	1,615	1,596	803
96th (1979–80)	10,400	4,194	1,478	1,482	736
97th (1981–82)	9,175	3,172	1,058	1,209	528
98th (1983–84)	8,104	4,097	1,348	1,322	677
99th (1985–86)	7,522	4,080	1,368	1,330	690
100th (1987–88)	7,269	4,013	1,502	1,430	758
101st (1989–90)	7,611	4,184	1,370	1,321	666
102nd (1991–92)	7,771	4,245	1,338	1,277	609
103rd (1993–94)	6,647	3,177	1,126	938	473
104th (1995–96)	5,329	2,661	1,012	822	337
105th (1997–98)	5,982	3,161	1,186	891	404
106th (1999–2000)	6,942	3,898	1,534	1,245	604
107th (2001–2002)	7,029	3,770	1,215	948	383
108th (2003–2004)	6,954	3,716	1,421	1,253	281
109th (2005–2006)	7,568	4,543	1,113	972	281

Source: thomas.loc.gov
*Includes House and Senate resolutions, joint resolutions, and concurrent resolutions.

Federal Revenue by Source, 2007

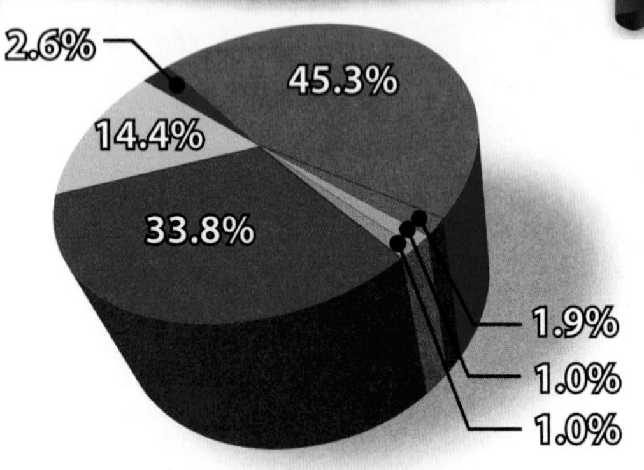

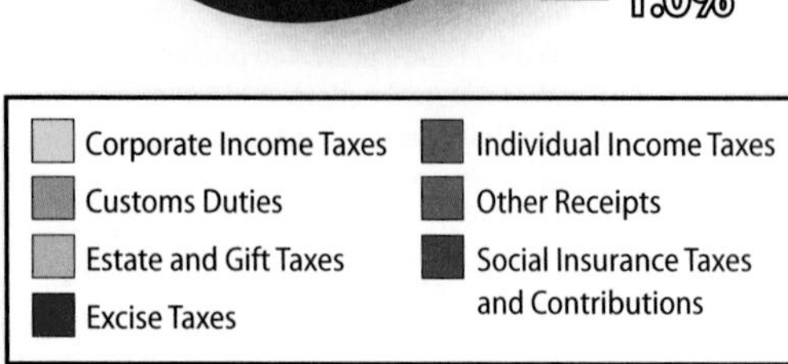

Expenditures by Type, 2007

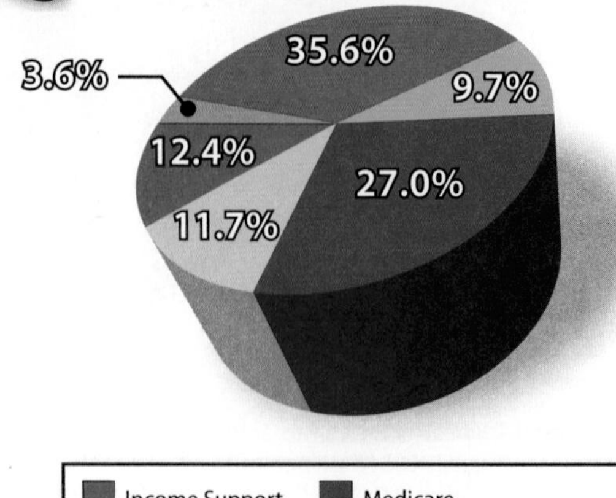

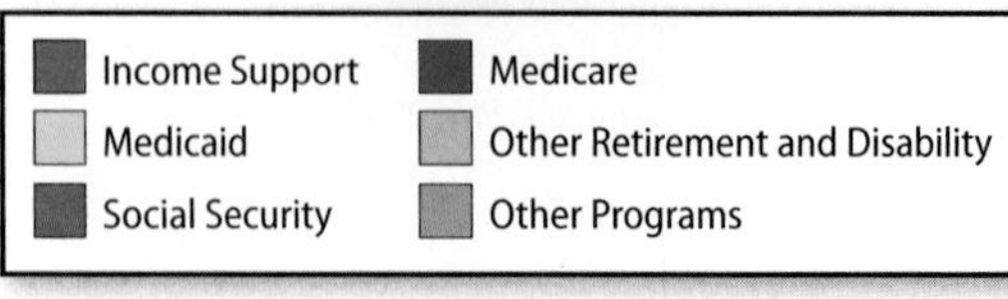

* Percentages may not total 100% due to rounding.

Source: U.S. Congressional Budget Office, U.S. Congress, www.cbo.gov

FEDERAL REVENUES, EXPENDITURES, AND DEBTS, 1960–2006

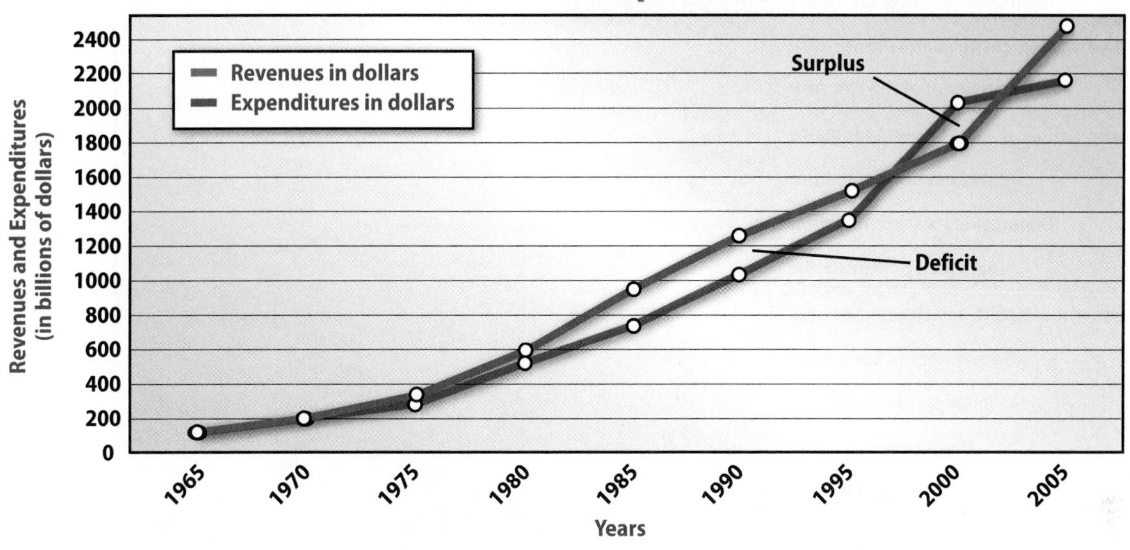

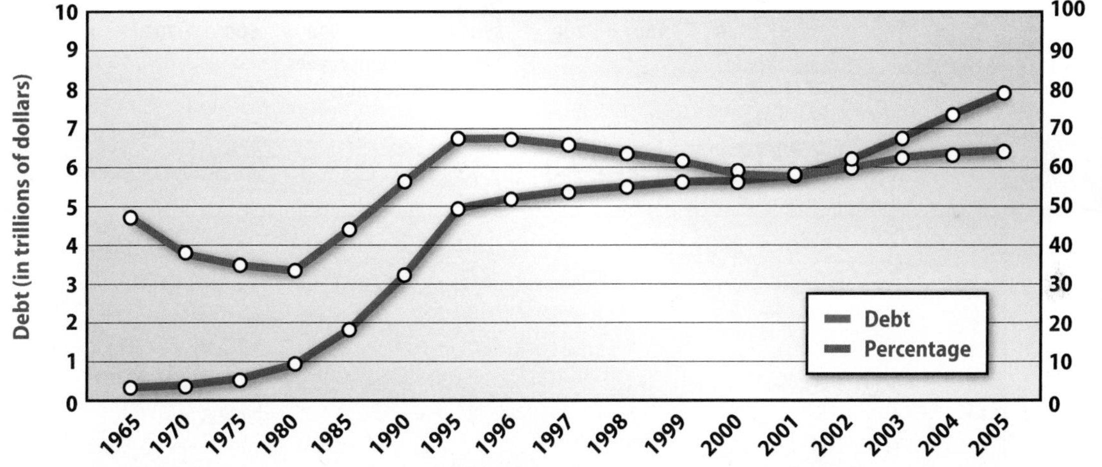

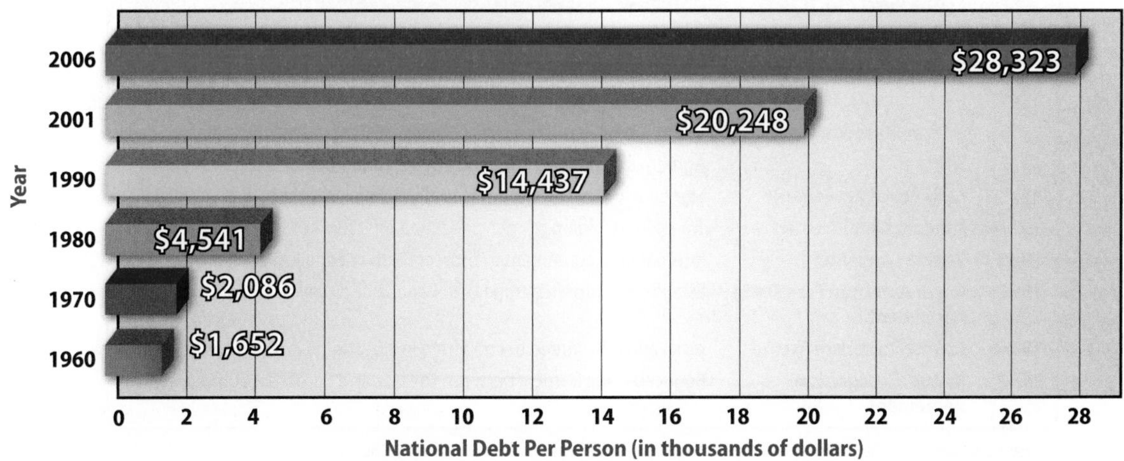

* Includes federal debt held by public and by the federal government.

Source: U.S. Bureau of the Census; U.S. Bureau of Public Debt; *Statistical Abstract of the United States*, 2006.

Executive Department Civilian Employees*

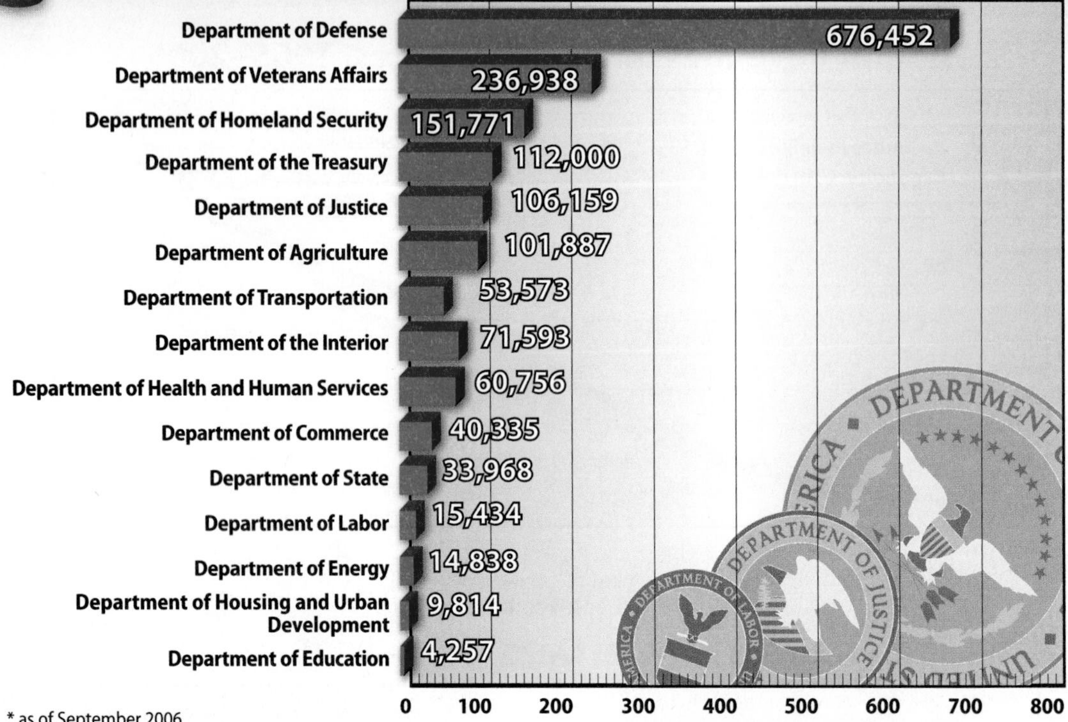

* as of September 2006

Source: U.S. Bureau of the Census, *Statistical Abstract of the United States*, 2008 (Washington, D.C.: 2008).

Major United States Treaties

Year	Treaty	Major Provisions
1783	**Treaty of Paris**	Great Britain recognized U.S. independence
1795	**Pinckney's Treaty**	Spain granted U.S. navigation rights on Mississippi River
1803	**Louisiana Purchase**	U.S. gained Louisiana Territory from France
1818	**Convention of 1818**	Set border with Canada west from Great Lakes as the 49th parallel
1819	**Adams-Onís Treaty**	Spain ceded Florida; U.S. border set with Spanish territory in West
1846	**Oregon Treaty**	Signed with Great Britain to settle claims to Oregon Country
1848	**Treaty of Guadalupe Hidalgo**	Ended Mexican War; U.S. gained Southwest and California
1867	**Alaska Purchase**	U.S. gained Alaska from Russia
1898	**Treaty of Paris**	Ended Spanish-American War; U.S. gained Puerto Rico and Philippines
1903	**Hay-Buneau-Varilla Treaty**	Signed with Panama to give U.S. right to build Panama Canal
1949	**North Atlantic Treaty**	Multinational agreement for defense of Western Europe; created NATO
1968	**Nonproliferation Treaty**	International agreement to prevent spread of nuclear weapons
1972	**SALT I**	Agreements between U.S. and Soviet Union to limit nuclear weapons
1973	**Paris Peace Agreement**	Signed with North Vietnam to end U.S. involvement in Vietnam War
1977	**Panama Canal Treaties**	Transferred Panama Canal to Panama effective in 1999
1985	**Vienna Convention**	International agreement to protect Earth's ozone layer
1993	**North American Free Trade Agreement**	Established duty-free trade with Canada and Mexico
1996	**Counterterrorism Accord**	Israel and U.S. agreed to cooperate in investigation of terrorist acts
1997	**Mutual Recognition Agreement**	Reduced trade barriers between the U.S. and European Community

Sources: U.S. State Department, *Treaties in Force;* Findling, *Dictionary of American Diplomatic History,* 2nd ed. (New York: Greenwood Press, 1989).

THE WHITE HOUSE . . .
The President's Home

White House Statistics

3 Elevators
5 Major Floors with:
2 Basements
7 Staircases
12 Chimneys
32 Bathrooms
132 Rooms
160 Windows
412 Doors

White House Technology Firsts

1834 Indoor Plumbing
1845 Central Heating
1848 Gas Lighting
1866 Telegraph
1877 Telephone
1891 Electricity
1921 Radio
1926 Electric Refrigerator
1933 Air Conditioning
1942 Bomb Shelter
1947 Television
1979 Computer

Did You Know?

- ***The first baby born in the White House*** was Thomas Jefferson's grandson in 1806.
- ***The first White House wedding held*** was for Dolley Madison's sister in 1812.
- ***General Lafayette visited the White House in 1825*** with his pet alligator, which he kept in the East Room.
- ***Cows grazed on the front lawn of the White House*** up until 1913.
- ***The only president married in the White House*** was Grover Cleveland, in 1886.

State Revenues and Expenditures, 2004

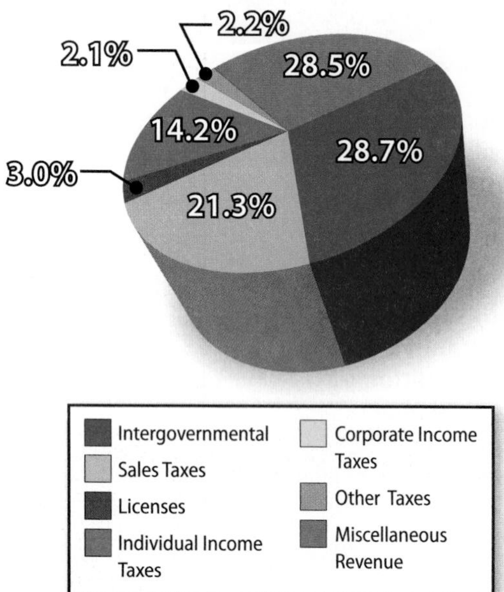

Intergovernmental
Sales Taxes
Licenses
Individual Income Taxes
Corporate Income Taxes
Other Taxes
Miscellaneous Revenue

* Percentages may not total 100% due to rounding.

Expenditures by Category

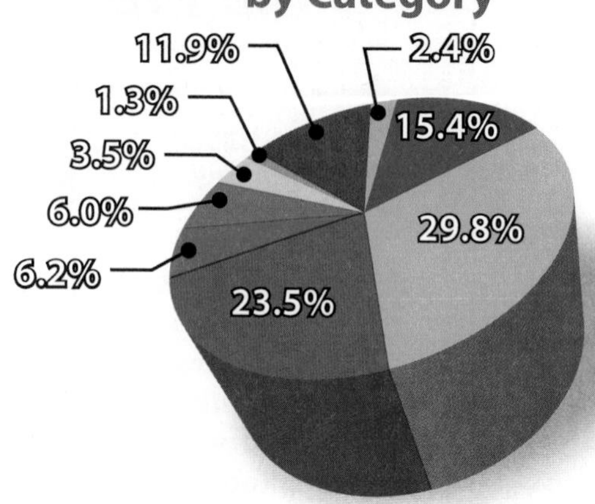

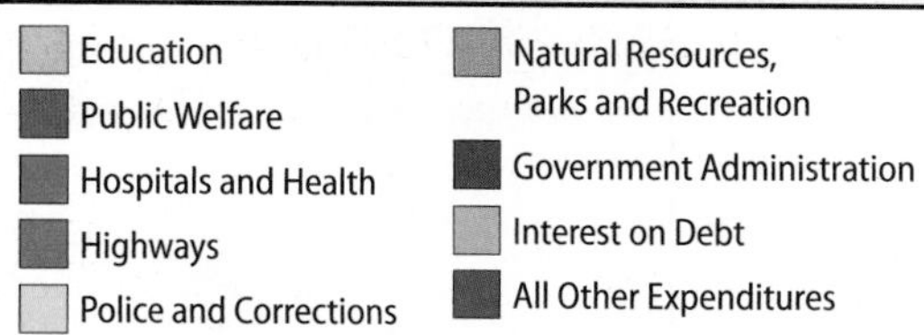

Source: U.S. Bureau of the Census.

State Expenditures for Public Education

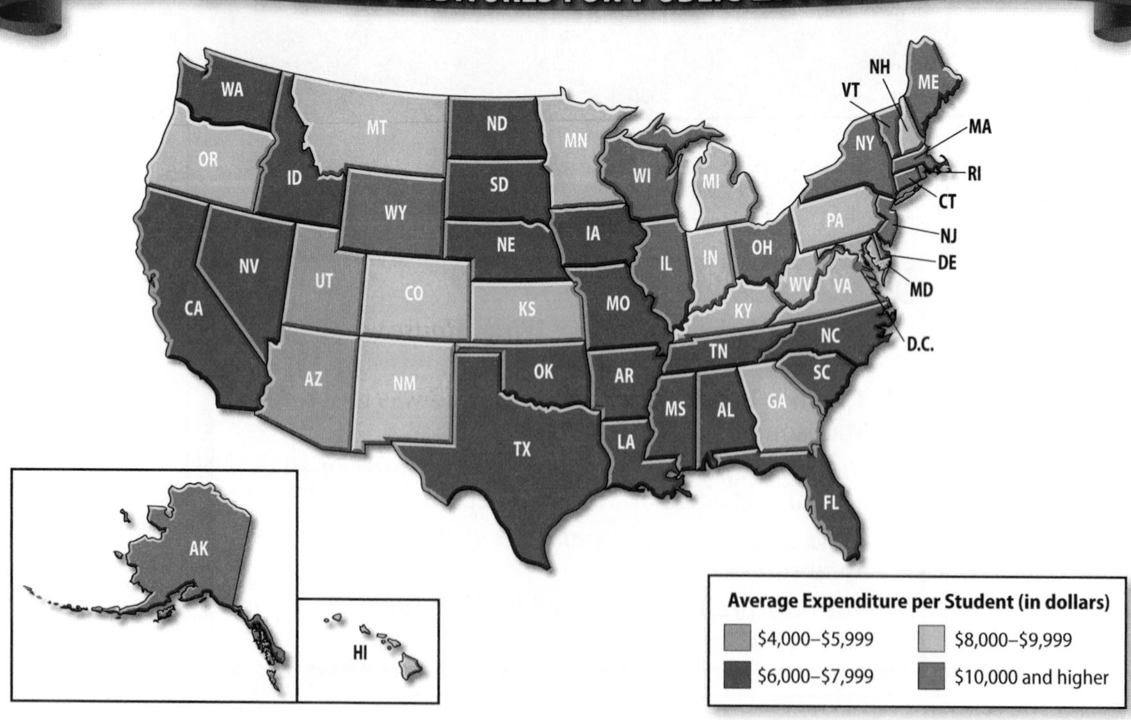

Source: U.S Bureau of the Census.

SIZE OF STATE LEGISLATURES

State	House Members	Senate Members
Alabama	105	35
Alaska	40	20
Arizona	60	30
Arkansas	100	35
California	80	40
Colorado	65	35
Connecticut	151	36
Delaware	41	21
Florida	120	40
Georgia	180	56
Hawaii	51	25
Idaho	70	35
Illinois	118	59
Indiana	100	50
Iowa	100	50
Kansas	125	40
Kentucky	100	38
Louisiana	105	39
Maine	151	35
Maryland	141	47
Massachusetts	160	40
Michigan	110	38
Minnesota	134	67
Mississippi	122	52
Missouri	163	34
Montana	100	50
Nebraska	N/A	49
Nevada	42	21
New Hampshire	400	24
New Jersey	80	40
New Mexico	70	42
New York	150	62
North Carolina	120	50
North Dakota	94	47
Ohio	99	33
Oklahoma	101	48
Oregon	60	30
Pennsylvania	203	50
Rhode Island	75	38
South Carolina	124	46
South Dakota	70	35
Tennessee	99	33
Texas	150	31
Utah	75	29
Vermont	150	30
Virginia	100	40
Washington	98	49
West Virginia	100	34
Wisconsin	99	33
Wyoming	60	30

Source: *The World Almanac and Book of Facts*, 2005.

STATE LEGISLATORS' COMPENSATION

State	Salary	Expense allowance during session
Alabama	$10/day*	$2,280/month
Alaska	$24,012	$163–218/day
Arizona	$24,000	$35–60/day
Arkansas	$14,765	$130/day
California	$113,098	$162/day
Colorado	$30,000	$45–99/day
Connecticut	$28,000	$0
Delaware	$42,000	$0
Florida	$30,996	$126/day
Georgia	$17,342	$173/day
Hawaii	$35,900	$10–120/day
Idaho	$16,116	$49–122/day
Illinois	$57,619	$125/day
Indiana	$11,600	$137/day
Iowa	$25,000	$88–118/day
Kansas	$84.80/day*	$99/day
Kentucky	$180.54/day*	$108.90/day
Louisiana	$16,800	$138/day
Maine	$12,713	$70/day
Maryland	$43,500	$157/day
Massachusetts	$58,237.15	$10–100/day
Michigan	$79,650	$12,000/year
Minnesota	$31,140.90	$77–96/day
Mississippi	$10,000	$91/day
Missouri	$31,351	$79.20/day
Montana	$82.67/day+	$98.75/day
Nebraska	$12,000	$39–99/day
Nevada	$137.90/day*	federal rate
New Hampshire	$200	$0
New Jersey	$49,000	$0
New Mexico	$0	$142/day
New York	$79,500	varies
North Carolina	$13,951	$104/day
North Dakota	$125/day*	up to $900/month
Ohio	$58,933.56	$0
Oklahoma	$38,400	$122/day
Oregon	$18,408	$99/day
Pennsylvania	$73,613	$129/day
Rhode Island	$13,089.44	$0
South Carolina	$10,400	$119/day
South Dakota	$6,000	$110/day
Tennessee	$18,123	$153/day
Texas	$7,200	$139/day
Utah	$130/day*	$144/day
Vermont	$600.78/week+	$51–139/day
Virginia	$18,000	$135–140/day
Washington	$36,311	$90/day
West Virginia	$15,000	$115/day
Wisconsin	$47,413	$88/day
Wyoming	$150/day+	$85/day

* calendar day
+ legislative day
Source: National Conference of State Legislatures, www.ncsl.org ,2007

DATA BANK

Supreme Court Case Summaries

CONTENTS

Brown v. *Board of Education*

1954

In *Brown* v. *Board of Education of Topeka, Kansas,* the Supreme Court overruled *Plessy* v. *Ferguson* (1896) [see p. 259] making the separate-but-equal doctrine in public schools unconstitutional. The Supreme Court rejected the idea that truly equal but separate schools for African American and white students would be constitutional. The Court explained that the Fourteenth Amendment's requirement that all persons be guaranteed equal protection of the law is not met simply by ensuring that African American and white schools "have been equalized . . . with respect to buildings, curricula, qualifications and salaries, and other tangible factors."

The Court then ruled that racial segregation in public schools violates the Equal Protection Clause of the Constitution because it is inherently unequal. In other words, nothing can make racially segregated public schools equal under the Constitution because the very fact of separation marks the separated race as inferior. In practical terms, the Court's decision in this case has been extended beyond public education to virtually all public accommodations and activities.

George E.C. Hayes, Thurgood Marshall, and James Nabrit, Jr., were attorneys who argued the case against segregation in *Brown* v. *Board of Education.*

Bush v. *Gore*

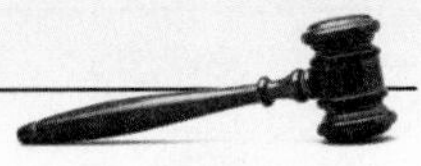

2000

The 2000 presidential election was hanging in the balance as the state of Florida recounted its disputed ballots. Candidates George W. Bush, Republican, and Al Gore, Democrat, were so close in the polls that there was a manual recount of the votes.

Bush went to the Court to stop the recount, stating that it violated the Fourteenth Amendment. The Court ruled that since the manual recount had no uniform way to judge each disputed vote equally, it did violate the Constitution and had to be stopped. As a result, Bush won Florida's electoral votes and became President.

District of Columbia v. *Heller*

2008

In *District of Columbia* v. *Heller* the Supreme Court for the first time ruled that the Constitution protects an individual's right to have a gun. In a landmark decision, the justices stated that the Second Amendment guaranteed a citizen the right to possess a gun "for traditionally lawful purposes, such as self-defense within the home," in addition to the right of governments to form militias. The case stemmed from protests that the Washington, D.C., strict gun law made it nearly impossible to legally possess a gun within the District of Columbia.

Dred Scott v. *Sandford*

1857

Dred Scott was taken by slaveholder John Sanford to the free state of Illinois and to the Wisconsin Territory, which had also banned slavery. Later they returned to Missouri, a slave state. Several years later, Scott sued for his freedom under the Missouri legal principle of "once free, always free." In other words, under Missouri law, enslaved people were entitled to freedom if they had lived in a free state at any time. Missouri courts ruled against Scott, but he appealed the case all the way to the United States Supreme Court.

Dred Scott

The Supreme Court decided this case before the Fourteenth Amendment was added to the Constitution. (The Fourteenth Amendment provides that anyone born or naturalized in the United States is a citizen of the nation and of his or her state of residence.) The Court held that enslaved African Americans were property, not citizens, and thus had no rights under the Constitution.

Furman v. *Georgia*

1972

This decision put a halt to the application of the death penalty under state laws then in effect. For the first time, the Supreme Court ruled that the death penalty amounted to cruel and unusual punishment, which is outlawed in the Constitution. The Court explained that existing death penalty laws did not give juries enough guidance in deciding whether or not to impose the death penalty. As a result, the death penalty in many cases was imposed arbitrarily, that is, without a reasonable basis in the facts and circumstances of the offender or the crime.

The *Furman* decision halted all executions in the 39 states that had death penalty laws at that time. Since the decision, 38 states have rewritten death penalty laws to meet the requirements established in the *Furman* case.

Gibbons v. *Ogden*

1824

Thomas Gibbons had a federal license to operate a steamboat along the coast, but he did not have a license from the state of New York to travel on New York waters. He wanted to run a steamboat line between Manhattan and New Jersey that would compete with Aaron Ogden's company. Ogden had a New York license. Gibbons sued for the freedom to use his federal license to compete against Ogden on New York waters.

Gibbons won the case. The Supreme Court made it clear that the authority of Congress to regulate interstate commerce (among states) includes the authority to regulate intrastate commerce (within a single state) that bears on, or relates to, interstate commerce.

Gideon v. *Wainwright*

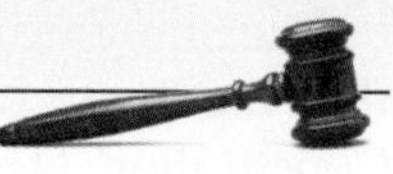

1963

After being accused of robbery, Clarence Gideon defended himself in a Florida court because the judge in the case refused to appoint a free lawyer. The jury found Gideon guilty. Eventually, Gideon appealed his conviction to the United States Supreme Court, claiming that by failing to appoint a lawyer, the lower court had violated his rights under the Sixth and Fourteenth Amendments.

The Supreme Court agreed with Gideon. In *Gideon* v. *Wainwright* the Supreme Court held for the first time that poor defendants in criminal cases have the right to a state-paid attorney under the Sixth Amendment. The rule announced in this case has been refined to apply whenever the defendant, if convicted, can be sentenced to more than six months in jail or prison.

In 1983 Fred Korematsu (center) won a reversal of his conviction.

Korematsu v. *United States*

1944

After the Japanese bombing of Pearl Harbor in 1941, thousands of Japanese Americans on the West Coast were forced to abandon their homes and businesses, and they were moved to internment camps in California, Idaho, Utah, Arizona, Wyoming, Colorado, and Arkansas. The prison-like camps offered poor food and cramped quarters.

The Supreme Court's decision in *Korematsu* v. *United States* upheld the authority of the federal government to move Japanese Americans, many of whom were citizens, from designated military areas that included almost the entire West Coast. The government defended the so-called exclusion orders as a necessary response to Japan's attack on Pearl Harbor. Only after his reelection in 1944 did President Franklin Roosevelt rescind the evacuation orders, and by the end of 1945 the camps were closed.

Marbury v. *Madison*

1803

During his last days in office, President John Adams commissioned William Marbury and several other men as judges. This action by Federalist president Adams angered the incoming Democratic-Republican president Thomas Jefferson. Jefferson then ordered James Madison, his secretary of state, not to deliver the commissions, thus blocking the appointments. William Marbury sued, asking the Supreme Court to order Madison to deliver the commission that would make him a judge.

The Court ruled against Marbury, but more importantly, the decision in this case established one of the most significant principles of American constitutional law. The Supreme Court held that it is the Court itself that has the final say on what the Constitution means. This is known as judicial review. It is also the Supreme Court that has the final say in whether or not an act of government—legislative or executive at the federal, state, or local level—violates the Constitution.

McCulloch v. Maryland

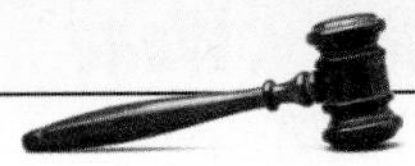

1819

Following the War of 1812, the United States experienced years of high inflation and general economic turmoil. In an attempt to stabilize the economy, the United States Congress chartered a Second Bank of the United States in 1816. Maryland and several other states, however, opposed the competition that the new national bank created and passed laws taxing its branches. In 1818, James McCulloch, head of the Baltimore branch of the Second Bank of the United States, refused to pay the tax to the state of Maryland. The case worked its way through the Maryland state courts all the way to the United States Supreme Court.

The Supreme Court declared the Maryland tax unconstitutional and void. More importantly, the decision established the foundation for expanded congressional authority. The Court held that the necessary and proper clause of the Constitution allows Congress to do more than the Constitution expressly authorizes it to do. The decision allows Congress to enact nearly any law that will help it achieve any of its duties as set forth in the Constitution. For example, Congress has the express authority to regulate interstate commerce. The necessary and proper clause permits Congress to do so in ways not actually specified in the Constitution.

Minnesota v. Mille Lacs Band of Chippewa Indians

1999

An 1855 treaty with the United States set aside lands in present-day Minnesota and Wisconsin to several Chippewa bands as reservations at Mille Lacs, but made no mention of, among other things, whether it abolished rights guaranteed by previous treaties. Minnesota was admitted to the Union in 1858. In 1990, the Mille Lacs Band and several members sued Minnesota, its Department of Natural Resources, and state officials (collectively State), seeking, among other things, a declaratory judgment that they retained their ownership rights to the land without state interference. The District Court ultimately concluded that the Chippewa retained their claim under the 1837 treaty and resolved several resource allocation and regulation issues. The State's argument under the "equal footing doctrine," that Minnesota's entrance into the Union in 1855 extinguished any Indian treaty rights, was considered void. The Supreme Court ruled in favor of the Chippewa and the existing 1837 treaty.

Miranda v. Arizona

1966

In 1963, police in Arizona arrested Ernesto Miranda for kidnapping. The court found Miranda guilty on the basis of a signed confession. The police admitted that neither before nor during the questioning had Miranda been advised of his right to consult with an attorney before answering any questions or of his right to have an attorney present during the interrogation. Miranda appealed his conviction, claiming that police had violated his right against self-incrimination under the Fifth Amendment by not informing him of his legal rights during questioning.

Miranda won the case. The Supreme Court held that a person in police custody cannot be questioned unless told that: 1) he or she has the right to remain silent, 2) he or she has the right to an attorney (at government expense if the accused is unable to pay), and 3) anything the person says after stating that he or she understands these rights can be used as evidence of guilt at trial. These rights have come to be called the Miranda warning. They are intended to ensure that an accused person in custody will not unknowingly give up the Fifth Amendment's protection against self-incrimination.

In 1963, the arrest of Ernesto Miranda (left) led to a landmark decision.

SUPREME COURT CASES

New York Times Company v. *United States*
1971

In June 1971, the *New York Times* published the "Pentagon Papers," a classified document about government actions in the Vietnam War era. The secret document had been leaked to the *Times* by antiwar activist Daniel Ellsberg. President Richard Nixon went to court to block further publication of the Pentagon Papers. The *New York Times* appealed to the Supreme Court to allow it to continue publishing without government interference.

The Supreme Court's ruling in this case upheld earlier decisions establishing the doctrine of prior restraint. This doctrine protects the press (broadly defined to include newspapers, television and radio, filmmakers and distributors, etc.) from government attempts to block publication. Except in extraordinary circumstances, the press must be allowed to publish.

Plessy v. *Ferguson*
1896

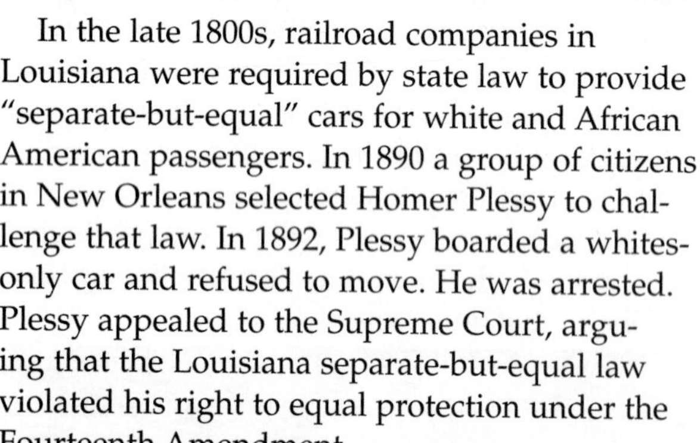

In the late 1800s, railroad companies in Louisiana were required by state law to provide "separate-but-equal" cars for white and African American passengers. In 1890 a group of citizens in New Orleans selected Homer Plessy to challenge that law. In 1892, Plessy boarded a whites-only car and refused to move. He was arrested. Plessy appealed to the Supreme Court, arguing that the Louisiana separate-but-equal law violated his right to equal protection under the Fourteenth Amendment.

Homer Plessy lost the case. The *Plessy* decision upheld the separate-but-equal doctrine used by Southern states to perpetuate segregation following the Civil War. The court ruled that the Fourteenth Amendment's clause required only equal public facilities for the two races, not equal access to the same facilities. This decision was overruled in 1954 by *Brown* v. *Board of Education of Topeka, Kansas.*

Roe v. *Wade*
1973

Roe v. *Wade* challenged restrictive abortion laws in both Texas and Georgia. The suit was brought in the name of Jane Roe, an alias.

In this decision, the Supreme Court ruled that females have a constitutional right under various provisions of the Constitution—most notably, the due process clause—to decide whether or not to terminate a pregnancy. The Court's decision was the most significant in decisions over a period of 50 years that recognized a constitutional right of privacy, even though the word *privacy* is not found in the Constitution.

Tinker v. *Des Moines School District*
1969

During the Vietnam War, some students in Des Moines, Iowa, wore black armbands to school to protest American involvement in the conflict and were suspended. Two days earlier, school officials had adopted a policy banning the wearing of armbands. The students argued that school officials violated their First Amendment right to free speech.

The Supreme Court sided with the students. The Court said that "it can hardly be argued that either students or teachers shed their constitutional rights of freedom of speech or expression at the schoolhouse gate." It ruled that a public school could not suspend students who wore black armbands to school to symbolize their opposition to the Vietnam War. In so holding, the Court likened the students' conduct to pure speech.

United States v. *Nixon*
1974

In the early 1970s, President Nixon was named an unindicted co-conspirator in the criminal investigation that arose in the aftermath of a break-in at the offices of the Democratic Party in Washington, D.C. A federal judge had ordered President Nixon to turn over tapes of conversations he had with

President Nixon encounters angry protesters in 1974 during the Watergate scandal.

his advisers about the break-in. Nixon resisted the order, claiming that the conversations were entitled to absolute confidentiality by Article II of the Constitution.

The decision in this case made it clear that the president is not above the law. The Supreme Court held that only those presidential conversations and communications that relate to performing the duties of the office of president are confidential and protected from a judicial order of disclosure. The Court ordered Nixon to give up the tapes, which revealed evidence linking the president to the conspiracy to obstruct justice. He resigned from office shortly thereafter.

Worcester v. Georgia

1832

State officials in Georgia wanted to remove the Cherokees from land that had been guaranteed to them in earlier treaties. Samuel Worcester was a congregational missionary who worked with the Cherokee people. He was arrested for failure to have a license that the state required to live in Cherokee country and for refusing to obey an order from the Georgia militia to leave Cherokee lands. Worcester then sued the state of Georgia. He claimed that Georgia had no legal authority on Cherokee land because the United States government recognized the Cherokee in Georgia as a separate nation.

The Supreme Court agreed with Worcester by a vote of 5 to 1. Chief Justice John Marshall wrote the majority opinion, which said that Native American nations were a distinct people with the right to have independent political communities and that only the federal government had authority over matters that involved the Cherokee.

President Andrew Jackson supported Georgia's efforts to remove the Cherokee to Indian Territory and refused to enforce the Court's ruling. After the ruling Jackson remarked, "John Marshall has made his decision. Now let him enforce it." As a result of Jackson's refusal to enforce the Court's order, thousands of Cherokees died on the long, forced trek to Indian Territory, known as the "Trail of Tears."

United States Facts

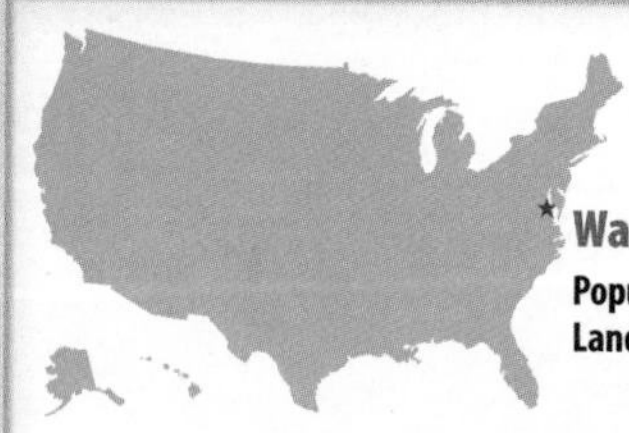

Washington, D.C.
Population: 551,136
Land area: 61 sq. mi.

U.S. Territories

Puerto Rico
Population: 3,912,000
Land area: 3,425 sq. mi.

Guam
Population: 168,564 (est.)
Land area: 209 sq. mi.

U.S. Virgin Islands
Population: 108,708 (est.)
Land area: 134 sq. mi.

American Samoa
Population: 57,881 (est.)
Land area: 77 sq. mi.

The states are listed in the order they were admitted to the Union.

Population figures are based on the U.S. Bureau of the Census projection for July 2005. House of Representatives figures from the 2000 census are from the Clerk of the House of Representatives. States are not drawn to scale.

1 Delaware
Year Admitted: 1787
Population: 836,687
Land area: 1,955 sq. mi.
Representatives: 1
Dover

2 Pennsylvania
Year Admitted: 1787
Population: 12,426,603
Land area: 44,820 sq. mi.
Representatives: 19
Harrisburg

3 New Jersey
Year Admitted: 1787
Population: 8,745,279
Land area: 7,419 sq. mi.
Representatives: 13
Trenton

9 New Hampshire
Year Admitted: 1788
Population: 1,314,821
Land area: 8,969 sq. mi.
Representatives: 2
Concord

10 Virginia
Year Admitted: 1788
Population: 7,552,581
Land area: 39,598 sq. mi.
Representatives: 11
Richmond

11 New York
Year Admitted: 1788
Population: 19,258,082
Land area: 47,224 sq. mi.
Representatives: 29
Albany

17 Ohio
Year Admitted: 1803
Population: 11,477,557
Land area: 40,953 sq. mi.
Representatives: 18
Columbus

18 Louisiana
Year Admitted: 1812
Population: 4,534,310
Land area: 43,566 sq. mi.
Representatives: 7
Baton Rouge

19 Indiana
Year Admitted: 1816
Population: 6,249,617
Land area: 35,870 sq. mi.
Representatives: 9
Indianapolis

24 Missouri
Year Admitted: 1821
Population: 5,765,166
Land area: 68,898 sq. mi.
Representatives: 9
Jefferson City

25 Arkansas
Year Admitted: 1836
Population: 2,777,007
Land area: 52,075 sq. mi.
Representatives: 4
Little Rock

26 Michigan
Year Admitted: 1837
Population: 10,207,421
Land area: 56,809 sq. mi.
Representatives: 15
Lansing

27 Florida
Year Admitted: 1845
Population: 17,509,827
Land area: 53,997 sq. mi.
Representatives: 25
Tallahassee

28 Texas
Year Admitted: 1845
Population: 22,775,004
Land area: 261,914 sq. mi.
Representatives: 32
Austin

33 Oregon
Year Admitted: 1859
Population: 3,596,083
Land area: 96,003 sq. mi.
Representatives: 5
Salem

34 Kansas
Year Admitted: 1861
Population: 2,751,509
Land area: 81,823 sq. mi.
Representatives: 4
Topeka

35 West Virginia
Year Admitted: 1863
Population: 1,818,887
Land area: 24,087 sq. mi.
Representatives: 3
Charleston

36 Nevada
Year Admitted: 1864
Population: 2,352,086
Land area: 109,806 sq. mi.
Representatives: 3
Carson City

37 Nebraska
Year Admitted: 1867
Population: 1,744,370
Land area: 76,878 sq. mi.
Representatives: 3
Lincoln

42 Washington
Year Admitted: 1889
Population: 6,204,632
Land area: 66,582 sq. mi.
Representatives: 9
Olympia

43 Idaho
Year Admitted: 1890
Population: 1,407,060
Land area: 82,751 sq. mi.
Representatives: 2
Boise

44 Wyoming
Year Admitted: 1890
Population: 507,268
Land area: 97,105 sq. mi.
Representatives: 1
Cheyenne

45 Utah
Year Admitted: 1896
Population: 2,417,998
Land area: 82,168 sq. mi.
Representatives: 3
Salt Lake City

46 Oklahoma
Year Admitted: 1907
Population: 3,521,379
Land area: 68,679 sq. mi.
Representatives: 5
Oklahoma City

4 Georgia
Year Admitted: 1788
Population: 8,925,796
Land area: 57,919 sq. mi.
Representatives: 13

5 Connecticut
Year Admitted: 1788
Population: 3,503,185
Land area: 4,845 sq. mi.
Representatives: 5

Hartford

6 Massachusetts
Year Admitted: 1788
Population: 6,518,868
Land area: 7,838 sq. mi.
Representatives: 10

Boston

7 Maryland
Year Admitted: 1788
Population: 5,600,563
Land area: 9,775 sq. mi.
Representatives: 8

Annapolis

8 South Carolina
Year Admitted: 1788
Population: 4,239,310
Land area: 30,111 sq. mi.
Representatives: 6

Columbia

12 North Carolina
Year Admitted: 1789
Population: 8,702,410
Land area: 48,718 sq. mi.
Representatives: 13-

13 Rhode Island
Year Admitted: 1790
Population: 1,086,575
Land area: 1,045 sq. mi.
Representatives: 2

14 Vermont
Year Admitted: 1791
Population: 630,979
Land area: 9,249 sq. mi.
Representatives: 1

15 Kentucky
Year Admitted: 1792
Population: 4,163,360
Land area: 39,732 sq. mi.
Representatives: 6

16 Tennessee
Year Admitted: 1796
Population: 5,965,317
Land area: 41,220 sq. mi.
Representatives: 9

Nashville

20 Mississippi
Year Admitted: 1817
Population: 2,915,696
Land area: 46,914 sq. mi.
Representatives: 4

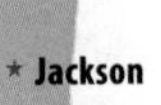

21 Illinois
Year Admitted: 1818
Population: 12,699,336
Land area: 55,593 sq. mi.
Representatives: 19

22 Alabama
Year Admitted: 1819
Population: 4,527,1660
Land area: 50,750 sq. mi.
Representatives: 7

Montgomery

23 Maine
Year Admitted: 1820
Population: 1,318,557
Land area: 30,865 sq. mi.
Representatives: 2

29 Iowa
Year Admitted: 1846
Population: 2,973,700
Land area: 55,875 sq. mi.
Representatives: 5

Des Moines

30 Wisconsin
Year Admitted: 1848
Population: 5,554,343
Land area: 54,314 sq. mi.
Representatives: 8

31 California
Year Admitted: 1850
Population: 36,038,859
Land area: 155,973 sq. mi.
Representatives: 53

32 Minnesota
Year Admitted: 1858
Population: 5,174,743
Land area: 79,617 sq. mi.
Representatives: 8

Saint Paul

38 Colorado
Year Admitted: 1876
Population: 4,617,962
Land area: 103,730 sq. mi.
Representatives: 7

Denver

39 North Dakota
Year Admitted: 1889
Population: 635,468
Land area: 68,994 sq. mi.
Representatives: 1

Bismarck

40 South Dakota
Year Admitted: 1889
Population: 771,803
Land area: 75,898 sq. mi.
Representatives: 1

Pierre

41 Montana
Year Admitted: 1889
Population: 933,005
Land area: 145,556 sq. mi.
Representatives: 1

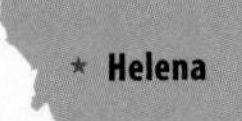

47 New Mexico
Year Admitted: 1912
Population: 1,902,057
Land area: 121,365 sq. mi.
Representatives: 3

Santa Fe

48 Arizona
Year Admitted: 1912
Population: 5,868,004
Land area: 113,642 sq. mi.
Representatives: 8

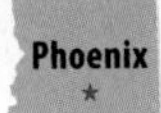

49 Alaska
Year Admitted: 1959
Population: 661,110
Land area: 570,374 sq. mi.
Representatives: 1

50 Hawaii
Year Admitted: 1959
Population: 1,276,552
Land area: 6,432 sq. mi.
Representatives: 2

Honolulu

United States Presidents

In this resource you will find portraits of the individuals who served as presidents of the United States, along with their occupations, political party affiliations, and other interesting facts.

George Washington 1

Presidential term: 1789–1797
Lived: 1732–1799
Born in: Virginia
Elected from: Virginia
Occupations: Soldier, Planter
Party: None
Vice President: John Adams

John Adams 2

Presidential term: 1797–1801
Lived: 1735–1826
Born in: Massachusetts
Elected from: Massachusetts
Occupations: Teacher, Lawyer
Party: Federalist
Vice President: Thomas Jefferson

Thomas Jefferson 3

Presidential term: 1801–1809
Lived: 1743–1826
Born in: Virginia
Elected from: Virginia
Occupations: Planter, Lawyer
Party: Republican**
Vice Presidents: Aaron Burr, George Clinton

James Madison 4

Presidential term: 1809–1817
Lived: 1751–1836
Born in: Virginia
Elected from: Virginia
Occupation: Planter
Party: Republican**
Vice Presidents: George Clinton, Elbridge Gerry

James Monroe 5

Presidential term: 1817–1825
Lived: 1758–1831
Born in: Virginia
Elected from: Virginia
Occupation: Lawyer
Party: Republican**
Vice President: Daniel D. Tompkins

John Quincy Adams 6

Presidential term: 1825–1829
Lived: 1767–1848
Born in: Massachusetts
Elected from: Massachusetts
Occupation: Lawyer
Party: Republican**
Vice President: John C. Calhoun

Andrew Jackson 7

Presidential term: 1829–1837
Lived: 1767–1845
Born in: South Carolina
Elected from: Tennessee
Occupations: Lawyer, Soldier
Party: Democratic
Vice Presidents: John C. Calhoun, Martin Van Buren

Martin Van Buren 8

Presidential term: 1837–1841
Lived: 1782–1862
Born in: New York
Elected from: New York
Occupation: Lawyer
Party: Democratic
Vice President: Richard M. Johnson

William H. Harrison 9

Presidential term: 1841
Lived: 1773–1841
Born in: Virginia
Elected from: Ohio
Occupations: Soldier, Planter
Party: Whig
Vice President: John Tyler

** *The Republican Party during this period developed into today's Democratic Party. Today's Republican Party originated in 1854.*

John Tyler 10

Presidential term: 1841–1845
Lived: 1790–1862
Born in: Virginia
Elected as V.P. from: Virginia
Succeeded Harrison
Occupation: Lawyer
Party: Whig
Vice President: None

James K. Polk 11

Presidential term: 1845–1849
Lived: 1795–1849
Born in: North Carolina
Elected from: Tennessee
Occupation: Lawyer
Party: Democratic
Vice President: George M. Dallas

Zachary Taylor 12

Presidential term: 1849–1850
Lived: 1784–1850
Born in: Virginia
Elected from: Louisiana
Occupation: Soldier
Party: Whig
Vice President: Millard Fillmore

Millard Fillmore 13

Presidential term: 1850–1853
Lived: 1800–1874
Born in: New York
Elected as V.P. from: New York
Succeeded Taylor
Occupation: Lawyer
Party: Whig
Vice President: None

Franklin Pierce 14

Presidential term: 1853–1857
Lived: 1804–1869
Born in: New Hampshire
Elected from: New Hampshire
Occupation: Lawyer
Party: Democratic
Vice President: William R. King

James Buchanan 15

Presidential term: 1857–1861
Lived: 1791–1868
Born in: Pennsylvania
Elected from: Pennsylvania
Occupation: Lawyer
Party: Democratic
Vice President: John C. Breckinridge

Abraham Lincoln 16

Presidential term: 1861–1865
Lived: 1809–1865
Born in: Kentucky
Elected from: Illinois
Occupation: Lawyer
Party: Republican
Vice Presidents: Hannibal Hamlin, Andrew Johnson

Andrew Johnson 17

Presidential term: 1865–1869
Lived: 1808–1875
Born in: North Carolina
Elected as V.P. from: Tennessee
Succeeded Lincoln
Occupation: Tailor
Party: Republican
Vice President: None

Ulysses S. Grant 18

Presidential term: 1869–1877
Lived: 1822–1885
Born in: Ohio
Elected from: Illinois
Occupations: Farmer, Soldier
Party: Republican
Vice Presidents: Schuyler Colfax, Henry Wilson

Rutherford B. Hayes 19

Presidential term: 1877–1881
Lived: 1822–1893
Born in: Ohio
Elected from: Ohio
Occupation: Lawyer
Party: Republican
Vice President: William A. Wheeler

James A. Garfield 20

Presidential term: 1881
Lived: 1831–1881
Born in: Ohio
Elected from: Ohio
Occupations: Laborer, Professor
Party: Republican
Vice President: Chester A. Arthur

Chester A. Arthur 21

Presidential term: 1881–1885
Lived: 1830–1886
Born in: Vermont
Elected as V.P. from: New York
Succeeded Garfield
Occupations: Teacher, Lawyer
Party: Republican
Vice President: None

Grover Cleveland 22

Presidential term: 1885–1889
Lived: 1837–1908
Born in: New Jersey
Elected from: New York
Occupation: Lawyer
Party: Democratic
Vice President: Thomas A. Hendricks

Benjamin Harrison 23

Presidential term: 1889–1893
Lived: 1833–1901
Born in: Ohio
Elected from: Indiana
Occupation: Lawyer
Party: Republican
Vice President: Levi P. Morton

Grover Cleveland 24

Presidential term: 1893–1897
Lived: 1837–1908
Born in: New Jersey
Elected from: New York
Occupation: Lawyer
Party: Democratic
Vice President: Adlai E. Stevenson

William McKinley 25

Presidential term: 1897–1901
Lived: 1843–1901
Born in: Ohio
Elected from: Ohio
Occupations: Teacher, Lawyer
Party: Republican
Vice Presidents: Garret Hobart, Theodore Roosevelt

Theodore Roosevelt 26

Presidential term: 1901–1909
Lived: 1858–1919
Born in: New York
Elected as V.P. from: New York
Succeeded McKinley
Occupations: Historian, Rancher
Party: Republican
Vice President: Charles W. Fairbanks

William H. Taft 27

Presidential term: 1909–1913
Lived: 1857–1930
Born in: Ohio
Elected from: Ohio
Occupation: Lawyer
Party: Republican
Vice President: James S. Sherman

Woodrow Wilson 28

Presidential term: 1913–1921
Lived: 1856–1924
Born in: Virginia
Elected from: New Jersey
Occupation: College Professor
Party: Democratic
Vice President: Thomas R. Marshall

Warren G. Harding 29

Presidential term: 1921–1923
Lived: 1865–1923
Born in: Ohio
Elected from: Ohio
Occupations: Newspaper Editor, Publisher
Party: Republican
Vice President: Calvin Coolidge

Calvin Coolidge 30

Presidential term: 1923–1929
Lived: 1872–1933
Born in: Vermont
Elected as V.P. from: Massachusetts–Succeeded Harding
Occupation: Lawyer
Party: Republican
Vice President: Charles G. Dawes

Herbert C. Hoover 31

Presidential term: 1929–1933
Lived: 1874–1964
Born in: Iowa
Elected from: California
Occupation: Engineer
Party: Republican
Vice President: Charles Curtis

Franklin D. Roosevelt 32

Presidential term: 1933–1945
Lived: 1882–1945
Born in: New York
Elected from: New York
Occupation: Lawyer
Party: Democratic
Vice Presidents: John N. Garner, Henry A. Wallace, Harry S. Truman

Harry S. Truman 33

Presidential term: 1945–1953
Lived: 1884–1972
Born in: Missouri
Elected as V.P. from: Missouri Succeeded Roosevelt
Occupations: Clerk, Farmer
Party: Democratic
Vice President: Alben W. Barkley

Dwight D. Eisenhower 34

Presidential term: 1953–1961
Lived: 1890–1969
Born in: Texas
Elected from: New York
Occupation: Soldier
Party: Republican
Vice President: Richard M. Nixon

John F. Kennedy 35

Presidential term: 1961–1963
Lived: 1917–1963
Born in: Massachusetts
Elected from: Massachusetts
Occupations: Author, Reporter
Party: Democratic
Vice President: Lyndon B. Johnson

Lyndon B. Johnson 36

Presidential term: 1963–1969
Lived: 1908–1973
Born in: Texas
Elected as V.P. from: Texas Succeeded Kennedy
Occupation: Teacher
Party: Democratic
Vice President: Hubert H. Humphrey

Richard M. Nixon 37

Presidential term: 1969–1974
Lived: 1913–1994
Born in: California
Elected from: New York
Occupation: Lawyer
Party: Republican
Vice Presidents: Spiro T. Agnew, Gerald R. Ford

Gerald R. Ford 38

Presidential term: 1974–1977
Lived: 1913–2006
Born in: Nebraska
Appointed as V.P. upon Agnew's resignation; succeeded Nixon
Occupation: Lawyer
Party: Republican
Vice President: Nelson A. Rockefeller

James E. Carter, Jr. 39

Presidential term: 1977–1981
Lived: 1924–
Born in: Georgia
Elected from: Georgia
Occupations: Business, Farmer
Party: Democratic
Vice President: Walter F. Mondale

Ronald W. Reagan 40

Presidential term: 1981–1989
Lived: 1911–2004
Born in: Illinois
Elected from: California
Occupations: Actor, Lecturer
Party: Republican
Vice President: George H.W. Bush

George H. W. Bush 41

Presidential term: 1989–1993
Lived: 1924–
Born in: Massachusetts
Elected from: Texas
Occupation: Business
Party: Republican
Vice President: J. Danforth Quayle

William J. Clinton 42

Presidential term: 1993–2001
Lived: 1946–
Born in: Arkansas
Elected from: Arkansas
Occupation: Lawyer
Party: Democratic
Vice President: Albert Gore, Jr.

George W. Bush 43

Presidential term: 2001–2008
Lived: 1946–
Born in: Connecticut
Elected from: Texas
Occupation: Business
Party: Republican
Vice President: Richard B. Cheney

Barack H. Obama 44

Presidential term: 2009–
Lived: 1961–
Born in: Hawaii
Elected from: Illinois
Occupation: Attorney
Party: Democratic
Vice President: Joseph Biden

Reference Atlas

NATIONAL GEOGRAPHIC

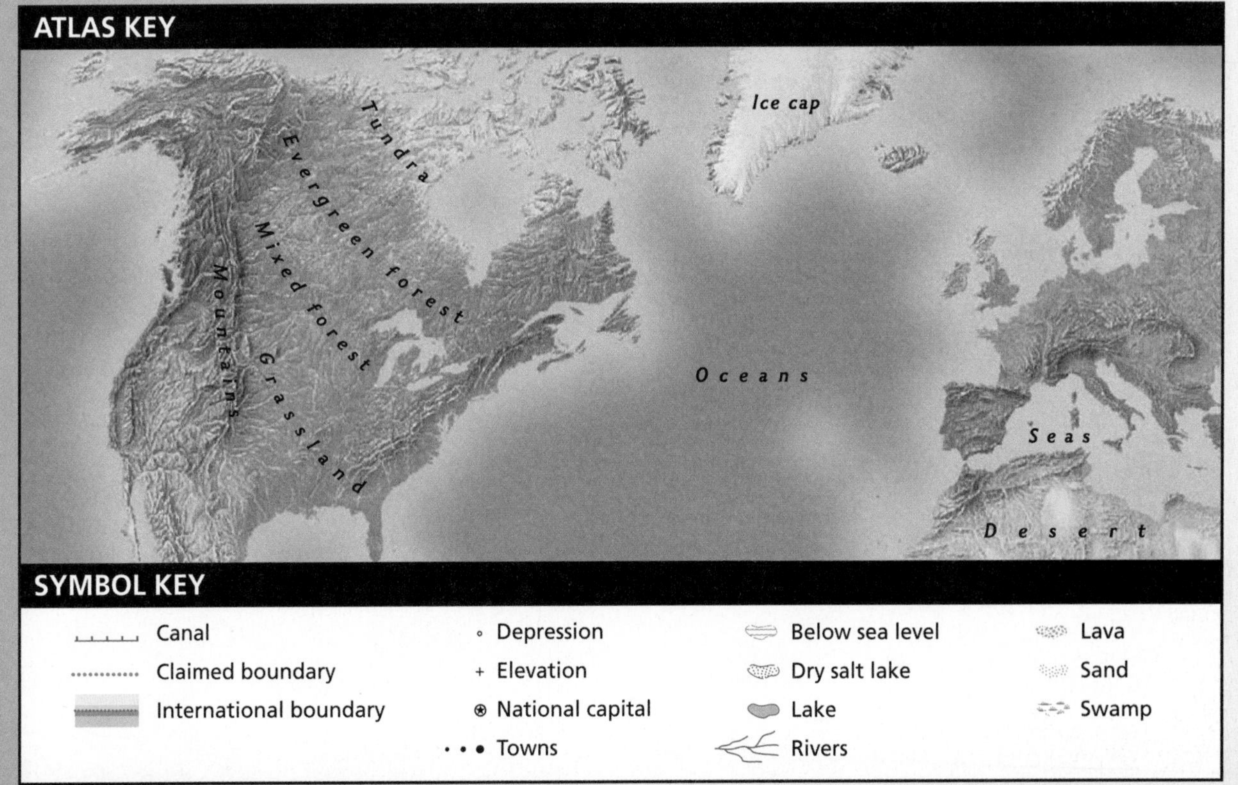

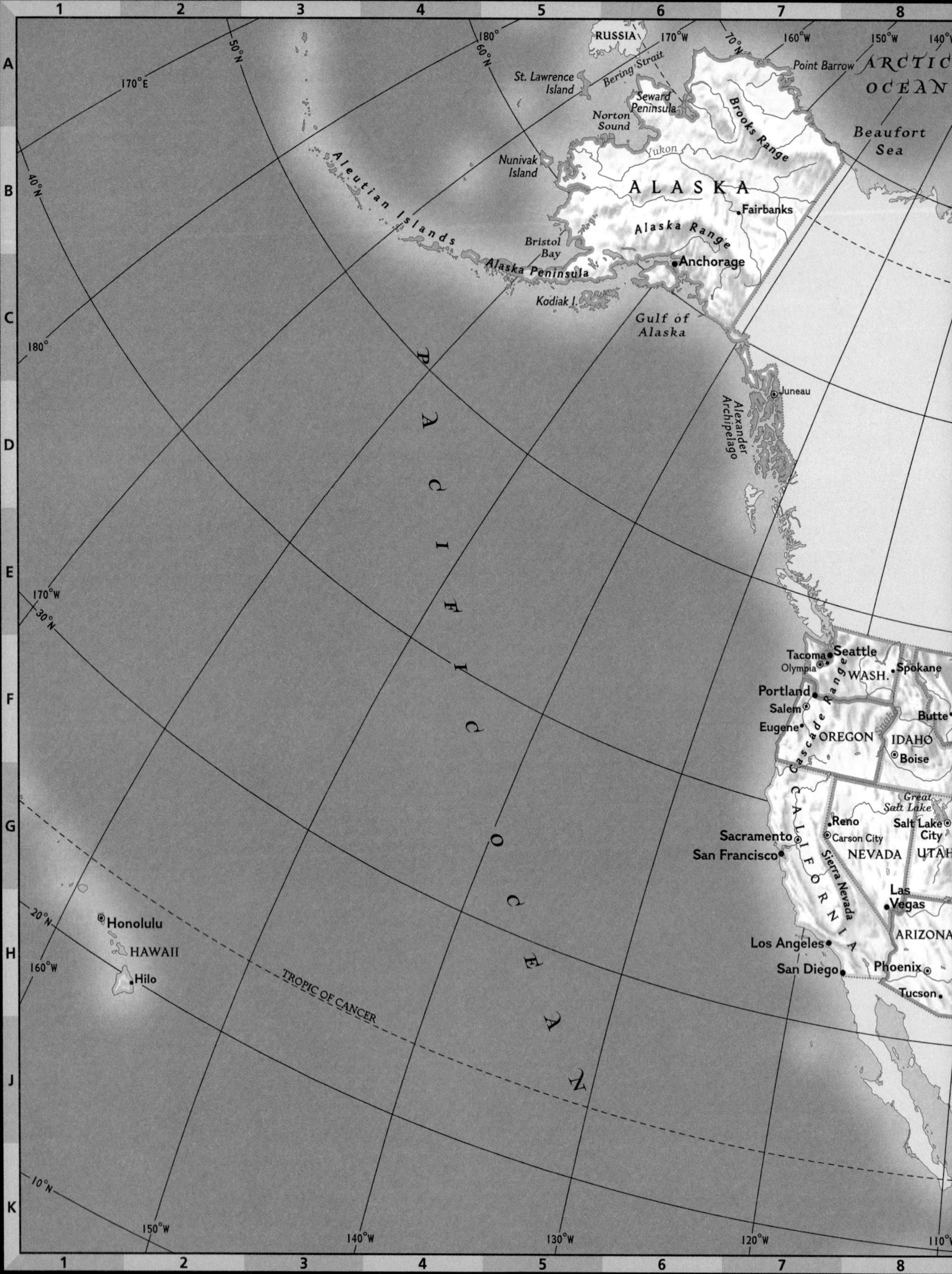

1 2 3 4 5 6 7 8

A B C D E F G H J K

RUSSIA
St. Lawrence Island
Bering Strait
Seward Peninsula
Norton Sound
Point Barrow
ARCTIC OCEAN
Brooks Range
Beaufort Sea
Yukon
Nunivak Island
ALASKA
Fairbanks
Aleutian Islands
Alaska Range
Bristol Bay
Anchorage
Alaska Peninsula
Kodiak I.
Gulf of Alaska
Juneau
Alexander Archipelago
PACIFIC OCEAN
Tacoma
Seattle
Olympia
WASH.
Spokane
Portland
Salem
Cascade Range
Eugene
OREGON
Snake
IDAHO
Boise
Butte
Great Salt Lake
Salt Lake City
Reno
Carson City
Sacramento
San Francisco
NEVADA
UTAH
CALIFORNIA
Sierra Nevada
Las Vegas
ARIZONA
Los Angeles
San Diego
Phoenix
Tucson
Honolulu
HAWAII
Hilo
TROPIC OF CANCER

180° 170°W 70°N 160°W 150°W 140°W
170°E 50°N 60°N
40°N 180° 170°W 30°N 20°N 160°W 10°N
150°W 140°W 130°W 120°W 110°W

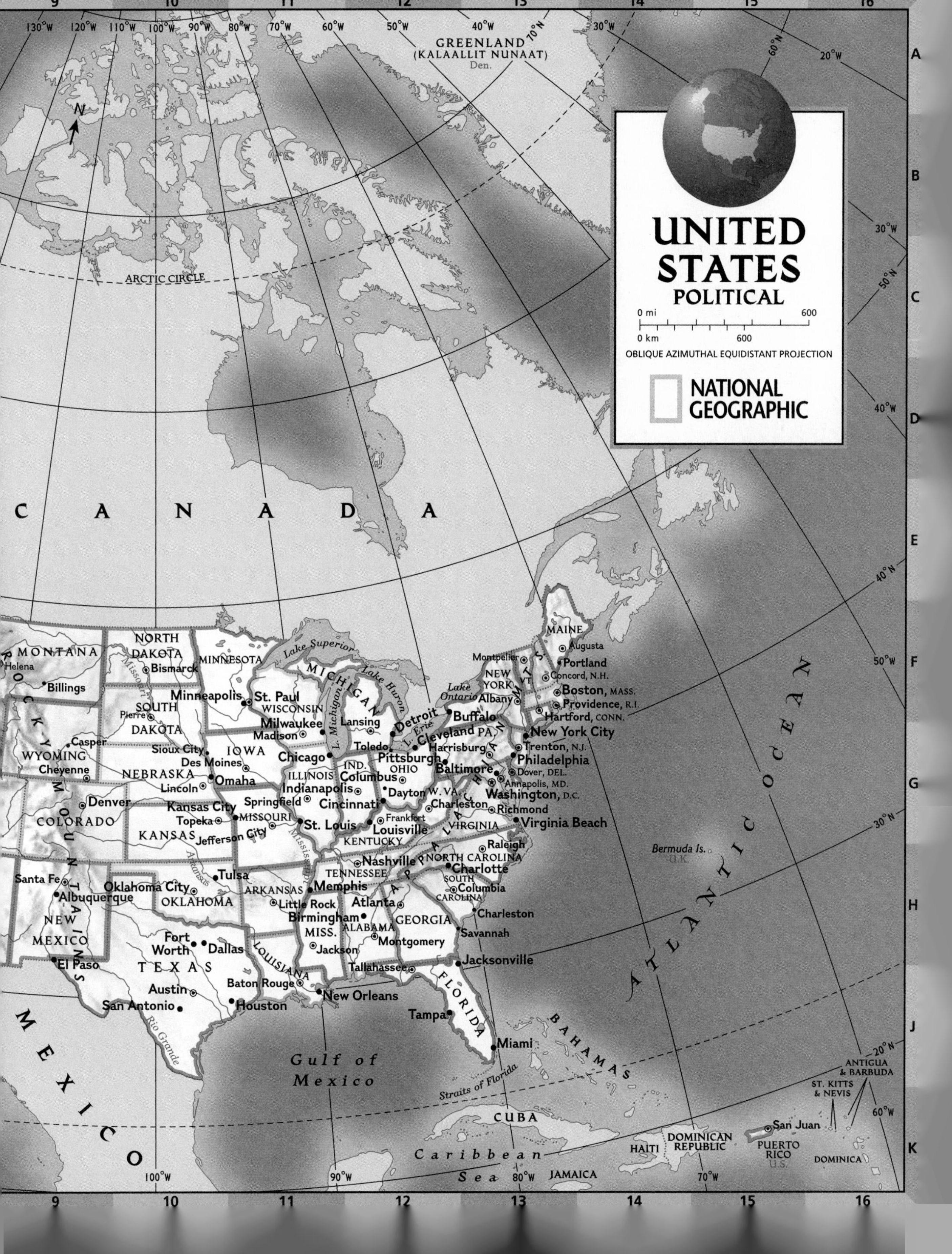
UNITED STATES
POLITICAL
0 mi 600
0 km 600
OBLIQUE AZIMUTHAL EQUIDISTANT PROJECTION
NATIONAL GEOGRAPHIC
GREENLAND
(KALAALLIT NUNAAT)
Den.
ARCTIC CIRCLE
C A N A D A
MONTANA
Helena
Billings
NORTH DAKOTA
Bismarck
MINNESOTA
Minneapolis
St. Paul
SOUTH DAKOTA
Pierre
WISCONSIN
Milwaukee
Madison
MICHIGAN
Lansing
Detroit
Lake Superior
Lake Huron
L. Michigan
L. Erie
Lake Ontario
WYOMING
Casper
Cheyenne
IOWA
Sioux City
Des Moines
NEBRASKA
Omaha
Lincoln
Chicago
ILLINOIS
IND.
Indianapolis
Springfield
OHIO
Toledo
Cleveland
Columbus
Dayton
Cincinnati
Pittsburgh
PA
Harrisburg
Buffalo
NEW YORK
Albany
Montpelier
VT
N.H.
Concord, N.H.
MAINE
Augusta
Portland
Boston, MASS.
Providence, R.I.
Hartford, CONN.
New York City
Trenton, N.J.
Philadelphia
Baltimore
Dover, DEL.
Annapolis, MD.
Washington, D.C.
Richmond
Virginia Beach
VIRGINIA
W. VA.
Charleston
COLORADO
Denver
KANSAS
Kansas City
Topeka
MISSOURI
Jefferson City
St. Louis
Louisville
Frankfort
KENTUCKY
Nashville
TENNESSEE
NORTH CAROLINA
Raleigh
Charlotte
SOUTH CAROLINA
Columbia
Charleston
NEW MEXICO
Santa Fe
Albuquerque
Oklahoma City
OKLAHOMA
Tulsa
ARKANSAS
Little Rock
Memphis
MISS.
Jackson
ALABAMA
Birmingham
Montgomery
GEORGIA
Atlanta
Savannah
Jacksonville
Tallahassee
FLORIDA
Tampa
Miami
TEXAS
El Paso
Fort Worth
Dallas
Austin
San Antonio
Houston
LOUISIANA
Baton Rouge
New Orleans
ROCKY MOUNTAINS
APPALACHIAN MTS.
Missouri
Mississippi
Arkansas
Rio Grande
MEXICO
Gulf of Mexico
Straits of Florida
BAHAMAS
CUBA
Caribbean Sea
JAMAICA
HAITI
DOMINICAN REPUBLIC
PUERTO RICO
U.S.
San Juan
ST. KITTS & NEVIS
ANTIGUA & BARBUDA
DOMINICA
Bermuda Is.
U.K.
ATLANTIC OCEAN
ARCTIC CIRCLE
130°W 120°W 110°W 100°W 90°W 80°W 70°W 60°W 50°W 40°W 30°W 20°W
70°N 60°N 50°N 40°N 30°N 20°N
9 10 11 12 13 14 15 16
A B C D E F G H J K

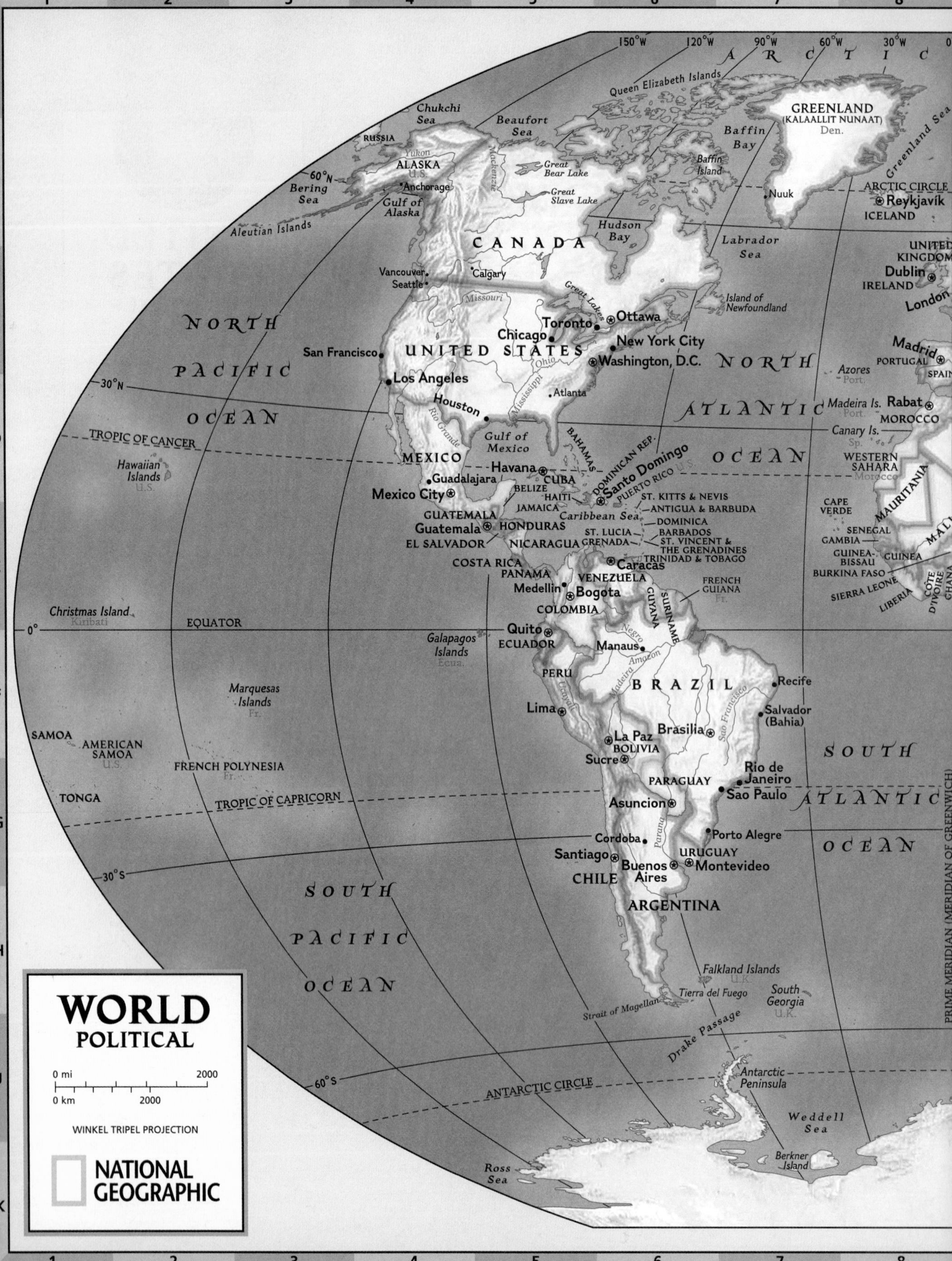
WORLD
POLITICAL
0 mi 2000
0 km 2000
WINKEL TRIPEL PROJECTION
NATIONAL GEOGRAPHIC
ARCTIC
Queen Elizabeth Islands
GREENLAND (KALAALLIT NUNAAT) Den.
Greenland Sea
Baffin Bay
Baffin Island
Nuuk
ARCTIC CIRCLE
Reykjavík
ICELAND
Chukchi Sea
Beaufort Sea
RUSSIA
Yukon
ALASKA U.S.
Mackenzie
Great Bear Lake
Great Slave Lake
Bering Sea
Anchorage
Gulf of Alaska
Aleutian Islands
Hudson Bay
Labrador Sea
CANADA
UNITED KINGDOM
Dublin
IRELAND
London
Vancouver
Calgary
Seattle
Missouri
Great Lakes
Island of Newfoundland
Toronto
Ottawa
Chicago
New York City
San Francisco
UNITED STATES
Ohio
Washington, D.C.
Madrid
PORTUGAL
SPAIN
Azores Port.
NORTH PACIFIC OCEAN
NORTH ATLANTIC OCEAN
Los Angeles
Mississippi
Atlanta
Houston
Rio Grande
Madeira Is. Port.
Rabat
MOROCCO
Canary Is. Sp.
Gulf of Mexico
BAHAMAS
DOMINICAN REP.
Santo Domingo
PUERTO RICO U.S.
TROPIC OF CANCER
Hawaiian Islands U.S.
MEXICO
Havana
CUBA
Guadalajara
Mexico City
BELIZE
HAITI
JAMAICA
Caribbean Sea
WESTERN SAHARA Morocco
MAURITANIA
CAPE VERDE
ST. KITTS & NEVIS
ANTIGUA & BARBUDA
DOMINICA
BARBADOS
ST. VINCENT & THE GRENADINES
TRINIDAD & TOBAGO
ST. LUCIA
GRENADA
GUATEMALA
Guatemala
HONDURAS
EL SALVADOR
NICARAGUA
COSTA RICA
PANAMA
Caracas
VENEZUELA
SENEGAL
GAMBIA
GUINEA-BISSAU
GUINEA
BURKINA FASO
SIERRA LEONE
LIBERIA
CÔTE D'IVOIRE
GHANA
MALI
Medellín
Bogota
COLOMBIA
GUYANA
SURINAME
FRENCH GUIANA Fr.
Christmas Island Kiribati
EQUATOR
0°
Quito
ECUADOR
Galapagos Islands Ecua.
Negro
Manaus
Amazon
PERU
Ucayali
Madeira
BRAZIL
São Francisco
Recife
Salvador (Bahia)
Marquesas Islands Fr.
Lima
Brasília
La Paz
BOLIVIA
Sucre
SAMOA
AMERICAN SAMOA U.S.
FRENCH POLYNESIA Fr.
TONGA
SOUTH ATLANTIC OCEAN
Rio de Janeiro
PARAGUAY
Sao Paulo
TROPIC OF CAPRICORN
Asuncion
Parana
Cordoba
Porto Alegre
URUGUAY
Santiago
Buenos Aires
Montevideo
CHILE
ARGENTINA
SOUTH PACIFIC OCEAN
PRIME MERIDIAN (MERIDIAN OF GREENWICH)
Falkland Islands U.K.
Tierra del Fuego
South Georgia U.K.
Strait of Magellan
Drake Passage
ANTARCTIC CIRCLE
Antarctic Peninsula
Weddell Sea
Berkner Island
Ross Sea
150°W
120°W
90°W
60°W
30°W
60°N
30°N
30°S
60°S

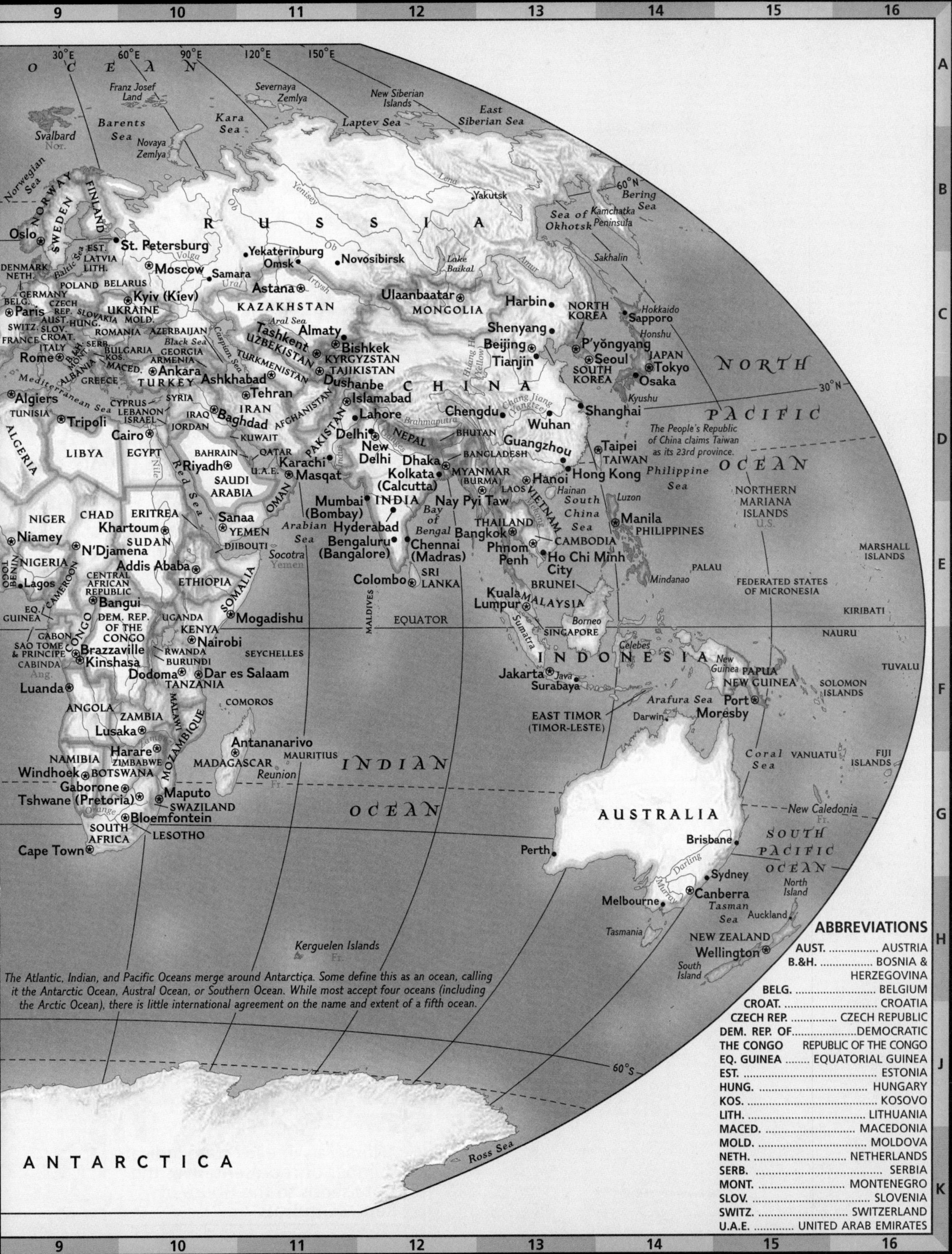

The People's Republic of China claims Taiwan as its 23rd province.

The Atlantic, Indian, and Pacific Oceans merge around Antarctica. Some define this as an ocean, calling it the Antarctic Ocean, Austral Ocean, or Southern Ocean. While most accept four oceans (including the Arctic Ocean), there is little international agreement on the name and extent of a fifth ocean.

ABBREVIATIONS

AUST.	AUSTRIA
B.&H.	BOSNIA & HERZEGOVINA
BELG.	BELGIUM
CROAT.	CROATIA
CZECH REP.	CZECH REPUBLIC
DEM. REP. OF THE CONGO	DEMOCRATIC REPUBLIC OF THE CONGO
EQ. GUINEA	EQUATORIAL GUINEA
EST.	ESTONIA
HUNG.	HUNGARY
KOS.	KOSOVO
LITH.	LITHUANIA
MACED.	MACEDONIA
MOLD.	MOLDOVA
NETH.	NETHERLANDS
SERB.	SERBIA
MONT.	MONTENEGRO
SLOV.	SLOVENIA
SWITZ.	SWITZERLAND
U.A.E.	UNITED ARAB EMIRATES

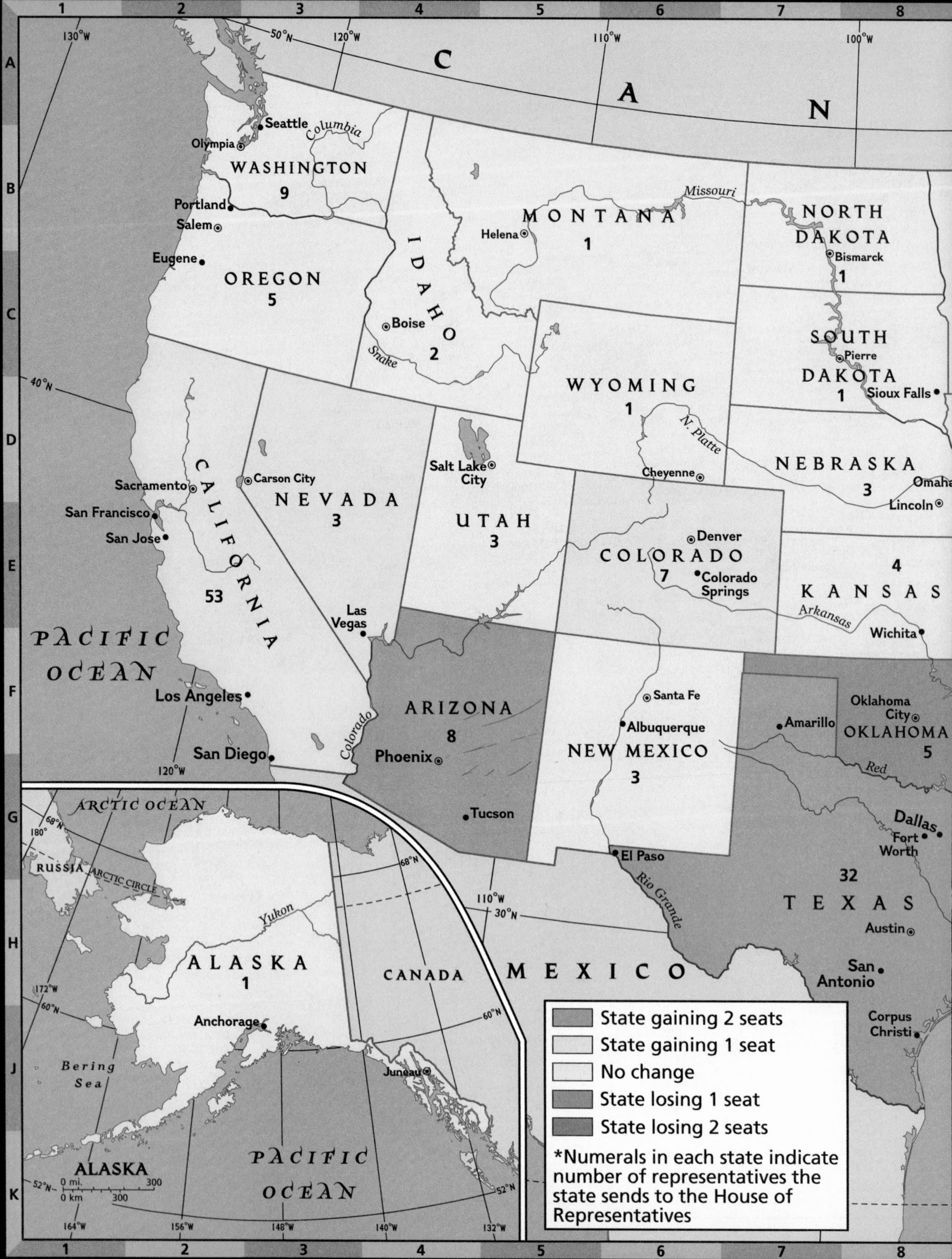

NGS REFERENCE ATLAS

CANADA

PACIFIC OCEAN

WASHINGTON 9
Seattle
Olympia
Columbia
Portland

OREGON 5
Salem
Eugene

IDAHO 2
Boise
Snake

MONTANA 1
Helena
Missouri

NORTH DAKOTA 1
Bismarck

SOUTH DAKOTA 1
Pierre
Sioux Falls

WYOMING 1
Cheyenne
N. Platte

NEBRASKA 3
Omaha
Lincoln

CALIFORNIA 53
Sacramento
San Francisco
San Jose
Los Angeles
San Diego

NEVADA 3
Carson City
Las Vegas

UTAH 3
Salt Lake City

COLORADO 7
Denver
Colorado Springs

KANSAS 4
Arkansas
Wichita

ARIZONA 8
Colorado
Phoenix
Tucson

NEW MEXICO 3
Santa Fe
Albuquerque

OKLAHOMA 5
Oklahoma City
Amarillo
Red

TEXAS 32
Dallas
Fort Worth
El Paso
Rio Grande
Austin
San Antonio
Corpus Christi

MEXICO

ARCTIC OCEAN
RUSSIA
ARCTIC CIRCLE
Yukon

ALASKA 1
Anchorage
Juneau
CANADA
Bering Sea
PACIFIC OCEAN
ALASKA
0 mi. 300
0 km 300

130°W 120°W 110°W 100°W 50°N 40°N 30°N 180° 172°W 164°W 156°W 148°W 140°W 132°W 68°N 60°N 52°N

State gaining 2 seats
State gaining 1 seat
No change
State losing 1 seat
State losing 2 seats

*Numerals in each state indicate number of representatives the state sends to the House of Representatives

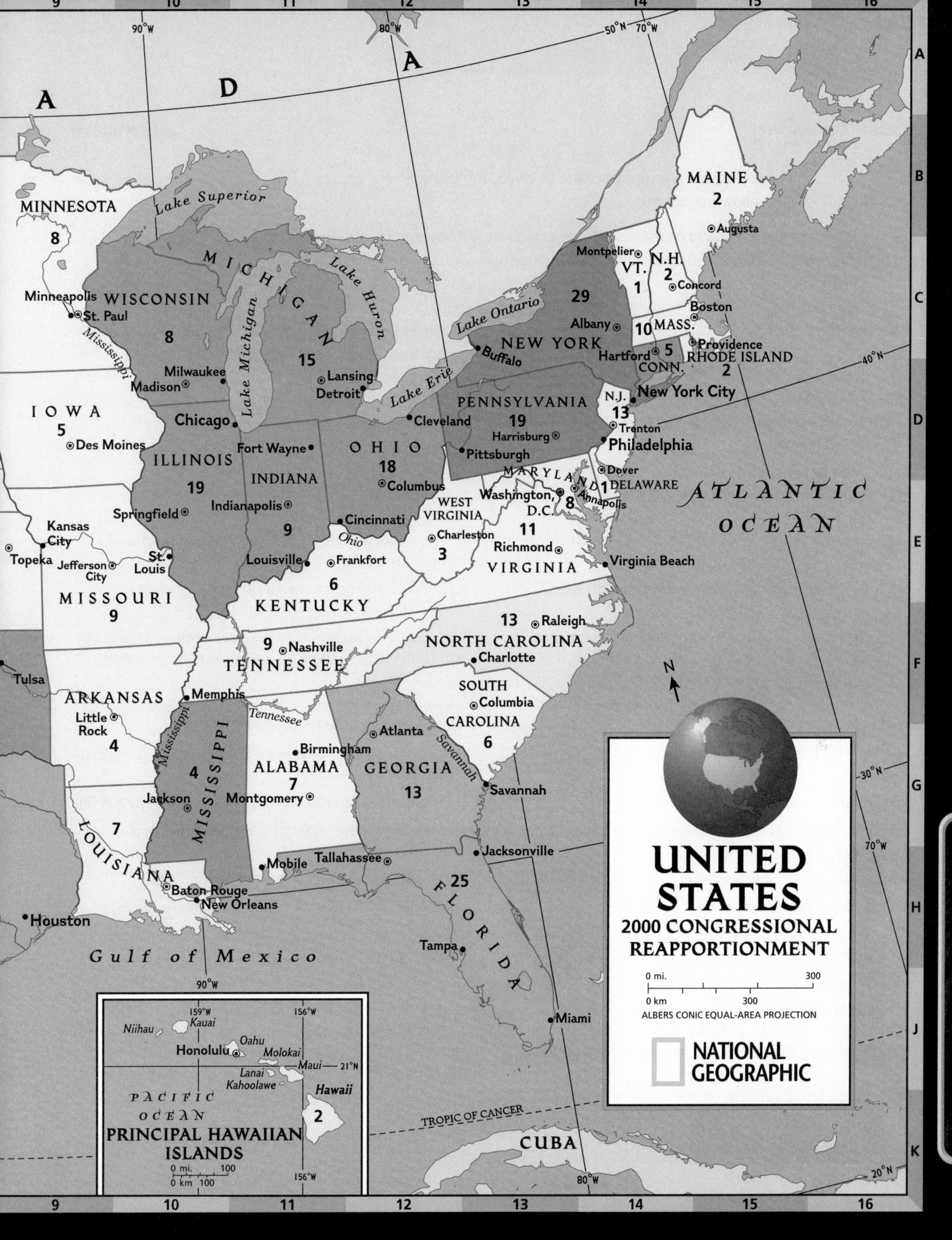
UNITED STATES
2000 CONGRESSIONAL REAPPORTIONMENT
0 mi. 300
0 km 300
ALBERS CONIC EQUAL-AREA PROJECTION
NATIONAL GEOGRAPHIC
ATLANTIC OCEAN
Gulf of Mexico
MINNESOTA 8
WISCONSIN 8
MICHIGAN 15
IOWA 5
ILLINOIS 19
INDIANA 9
OHIO 18
MISSOURI 9
KENTUCKY 6
TENNESSEE 9
ARKANSAS 4
MISSISSIPPI 4
ALABAMA 7
GEORGIA 13
LOUISIANA 7
FLORIDA 25
SOUTH CAROLINA 6
NORTH CAROLINA 13
VIRGINIA 11
WEST VIRGINIA 3
MARYLAND 8
DELAWARE 1
PENNSYLVANIA 19
N.J. 13
NEW YORK 29
CONN. 5
RHODE ISLAND 2
MASS. 10
VT. 1
N.H. 2
MAINE 2
PRINCIPAL HAWAIIAN ISLANDS
PACIFIC OCEAN
Hawaii 2
Niihau
Kauai
Oahu
Honolulu
Molokai
Maui
Lanai
Kahoolawe
CUBA
TROPIC OF CANCER
Lake Superior
Lake Michigan
Lake Huron
Lake Erie
Lake Ontario
NGS REFERENCE ATLAS

Glossary/Glosario

- Content vocabulary are words that relate to civics and government content. They are highlighted yellow in your text.
- Words below that have an asterisk (*) are academic vocabulary. They help you understand your school subjects and are **boldfaced** in your text.

ENGLISH

absentee ballot one that allows a person to vote without going to the polls on Election Day (p. 297)

access* as a way or means of approach (p. 736)

accumulate* to increase in quantity or size (p. 528)

achieve* to accomplish or successfully gain (p. 632)

acid rain rain containing high amounts of chemical pollutants (p. 737)

acknowledge* to recognize the existence of or to make something known (pp. 239, 328)

acquire* to gain or get possession of (p. 39)

acquittal a vote of not guilty (p. 458)

adapt* to adjust or become adjusted to a situation or condition (p. 45)

adequate* acceptable (p. 744)

adjacent* neighboring or near (p. 281)

adjust* to change or alter in order to fit or conform (p. 179)

affect* to produce an effect on (p. 244)

affirmative action programs intended to make up for past discrimination by helping minority groups and women gain access to jobs and opportunities (p. 143)

alien a noncitizen (p. 16)

alternative* a choice or possibility (p. 541)

ESPAÑOL

absentee ballot/boleta electoral por correspondencia aquélla que permite que una persona vote sin ir al lugar de votación el día de la elección (pág. 297)

access/acceso* una forma o medio de acercamiento (pág. 736)

accumulate/acumular* aumentar en cantidad o tamaño (pág. 528)

achieve/lograr* alcanzar u obtener algo con éxito (pág. 632)

acid rain/lluvia ácida lluvia que contiene grandes cantidades de sustancias químicas contaminantes (pág. 737)

acknowledge/reconocer* aceptar la existencia de o dar a conocer algo (págs. 239, 328)

acquire/adquirir* obtener o conseguir la posesión de (pág. 39)

acquittal/absolución un voto de inocente (pág. 458)

adapt/adaptarse* ajustarse a una situación o condición (pág. 45)

adequate/adecuado* aceptable (pág. 744)

adjacent/adyacente* vecino o cercano (pág. 281)

adjust/ajustar* cambiar o alterar a fin de corresponder o cumplir con algo (pág. 179)

affect/afectar* producir un efecto en (pág. 244)

affirmative action/acción afirmativa programas con el fin de compensar la discriminación pasada al ayudar a los grupos minoritarios y las mujeres a obtener acceso a empleos y oportunidades (pág. 143)

alien/extranjero una persona que no es ciudadana (pág. 16)

alternative/alternativa* una opción o posibilidad (pág. 541)

ambassador an official representative of a country's government (p. 222)

amendment any change in the Constitution (p. 82)

amnesty a pardon to a group of people (p. 217)

annual* covering the period of a year or occurring once a year (p. 162)

annual percentage rate (APR) annual cost of credit expressed as a percentage of the amount borrowed (p. 547)

Anti-Federalists those who opposed ratification of the Constitution (p. 78)

antitrust law legislation to prevent new monopolies from forming and police those that already exist (p. 633)

apartheid system of laws that separated racial and ethnic groups and limited the rights of blacks in South Africa (p. 746)

apathy a lack of interest (p. 299)

appeals court a court that reviews decisions made in lower district courts (p. 244)

appellate jurisdiction the authority of a court to hear a case appealed from a lower court (p. 244)

apportion divide among districts (p. 359)

appropriations bill legislation earmarking funds for certain purposes (p. 677)

arbitration situation in which union and company officials submit the issues they cannot agree on to a third party for a final decision (p. 611)

archives files of older stories (p. 471)

area* a region or section (p. 69)

arraignment a hearing in which a suspect is charged and pleads guilty or not guilty (p. 456)

articles of partnership formal legal papers specifying the arrangement between partners (p. 602)

assign* to dole out or give as a task (p. 88)

assist* to help or aid (p. 48)

assume* to take over a job or responsibility (p. 84)

ambassador/embajador un representante oficial del gobierno de un país (pág. 222)

amendment/enmienda cualquier cambio en la Constitución (pág. 82)

amnesty/amnistía un perdón a un grupo de personas (pág. 217)

annual/anual* que cubre el período de un año u ocurre una vez por año (pág. 162)

annual percentage rate (APR)/tasa de interés anual (TPA) costo de crédito anual expresado como un porcentaje de la cantidad tomada en préstamo (pág. 547)

Anti-Federalists/antifederalistas aquéllos que se oponían a la ratificación de la Constitución (pág. 78)

antitrust law/ley antimonopolista ley para evitar la formación de nuevos monopolios y supervisar a aquéllos que ya existen (pág. 633)

apartheid/*apartheid* sistema de leyes que separaba a los grupos raciales y étnicos y limitaba los derechos de los negros en Sudáfrica (pág. 746)

apathy/apatía falta de interés (pág. 299)

appeals court/tribunal de apelación un tribunal que revisa las decisiones tomadas en tribunales de distrito inferiores (pág. 244)

appellate jurisdiction/jurisdicción de apelación la autoridad de un tribunal de ver un caso apelado de un tribunal inferior (pág. 244)

apportion/asignar dividir entre distritos (pág. 359)

appropriations bill/proyecto de ley de apropiación presupuestaria ley que destina fondos para ciertos propósitos (pág. 677)

arbitration/arbitraje situación en la que jefes de sindicatos y compañías presentan las cuestiones sobre las que no pueden llegar a un acuerdo a un tercero para que tome una decisión final (pág. 611)

archives/archivos registros de historias antiguas (pág. 471)

area/área* una región o sección (pág. 69)

arraignment/comparecencia una audiencia en la que un sospechoso es acusado y se declara culpable o inocente (pág. 456)

articles of partnership/artículos de asociación documentos legales formales que especifican el acuerdo entre socios (pág. 602)

assign/asignar* repartir o dar como una tarea (pág. 88)

assist/ayudar* brindar ayuda o asistencia (pág. 48)

assume/asumir* hacerse cargo de un empleo o una responsabilidad (pág. 84)

at-large election an election for an area as a whole; for example, statewide (p. 380)

at-large election/elección general una elección para un área en general; por ejemplo, en todo el estado (pág. 380)

attitude* a feeling or way of thinking (p. 409)

attitude/actitud* una forma de pensar o sentir (pág. 409)

authoritarian a government in which one leader or group of people holds absolute power (p. 475)

authoritarian/autoritario un gobierno en el que un líder o grupo de personas tiene poder absoluto (pág. 475)

authority* power or influence over other people or groups; person or persons having the power of government (pp. 33, 409)

authority/autoridad* poder o influencia sobre otras personas o grupos; persona o personas que tienen el poder del gobierno (págs. 33, 409)

automatic stabilizer program that when needed provides benefits to offset a change in people's incomes (p. 692)

automatic stabilizer/estabilizador automático programa que brinda beneficios automáticamente para compensar un cambio en los ingresos de la gente (pág. 692)

B

bail a sum of money used as a security deposit to ensure that an accused person returns for his or her trial (p. 440)

bail/fianza una suma de dinero usada como depósito de garantía para asegurar que una persona acusada regrese para su juicio (pág. 440)

balance of trade the difference between the value of a nation's exports and its imports (p. 712)

balance of trade/balanza comercial la diferencia entre el valor de las exportaciones y las importaciones de una nación (pág. 712)

balanced budget annual budget in which expenditures equal revenues (p. 688)

balanced budget/presupuesto equilibrado presupuesto anual en el que los gastos equivalen a los ingresos (pág. 688)

ballot the list of candidates on which you cast your vote (p. 296)

ballot/boleta electoral la lista de candidatos sobre la que emites tu voto (pág. 296)

bankruptcy inability to pay debts (p. 549)

bankruptcy/quiebra bancarrota imposibilidad para pagar las deudas (pág. 549)

behalf* in the interest of (p. 668)

behalf/defensa, favor* en beneficio de (pág. 668)

benefit* to be useful or profitable to (p. 328)

benefit/beneficio* ser útil o rentable para (pág. 328)

bicameral a legislature consisting of two parts, or houses (pp. 67, 177, 358)

bicameral/bicameral un cuerpo legislativo que consiste en dos partes o cámaras (págs. 67, 177, 358)

bill of attainder a law that punishes a person accused of a crime without a trial or a fair hearing in court (p. 436)

bill of attainder/ley de proscripción un ley que castiga a una persona acusada de un delito sin un juicio o una audiencia justa en un tribunal (pág. 436)

board of directors people elected by the shareholders of a corporation to act on their behalf (p. 604)

board of directors/junta directiva personas elegidas por los accionistas de una corporación para que actúen en su nombre (pág. 604)

bond contract to repay borrowed money with interest at a specific time in the future (pp. 557, 688)

bond/bono contrato para devolver el dinero tomado en préstamo con interés en un tiempo específico en el futuro (págs. 557, 688)

boycott the refusal to purchase certain goods (p. 612)

boycott/boicot la negativa de comprar ciertos bienes (pág. 612)

brief a written document explaining the position of one side or the other in a case (p. 256)

budget a plan for making and spending money (pp. 22, 545, 677)

bureaucracy complex systems with many departments, many rules, and many people in the chain of command (p. 157)

burglary unlawful entry into any dwelling or structure (p. 432)

business cycle alternating periods of growth and decline that the economy goes through (p. 638)

brief/expediente un documento escrito que explica la posición de una parte o la otra en un caso (pág. 256)

budget/presupuesto un plan para generar y gastar dinero (págs. 22, 545, 677)

bureaucracy/burocracia sistemas complejos con muchos departamentos, muchas reglas y muchas personas en la cadena de mando (pág. 157)

burglary/robo ingreso ilegal a una vivienda o estructura (pág. 432)

business cycle/ciclo de negocios períodos alternos de crecimiento y descenso por los que pasa la economía (pág. 638)

cabinet a group of advisers to the president that includes the heads of 15 top-level executive departments (p. 226)

capable* having ability or competence (p. 501)

capital previously manufactured goods used to make other goods and services (p. 517)

capitalism a system in which private citizens own most, if not all, of the means of production and decide how to use them within legislated limits (pp. 500, 528)

casework the work that a lawmaker does to help constituents with a problem (p. 195)

category* a division or grouping used to classify something (p. 198)

caucus a meeting of political party members to conduct party business (p. 279)

censorship the banning of printed materials or films due to alarming or offensive ideas (p. 122)

census a population count taken by the Census Bureau (pp. 179, 359)

central bank an institution that lends money to other banks; also, the place where the government does its banking business (p. 661)

certificate of deposit timed deposit that states the amount of the deposit, maturity, and rate of interest being paid (p. 667)

cabinet/gabinete un grupo de asesores del presidente que incluye a los jefes de 15 departamentos ejecutivos de alto nivel (pág. 226)

capable/capaz* que posee habilidad o competencia (pág. 501)

capital/capital bienes previamente fabricados que se utilizan para hacer otros bienes y servicios (pág. 517)

capitalism/capitalismo un sistema en el que los ciudadanos privados son propietarios de la mayoría de, si no todos, los medios de producción y deciden cómo usarlos dentro de límites legales (págs. 500, 528)

casework/proyecto particular el trabajo que realiza un legislador para ayudar a los electores con un problema (pág. 195)

category/categoría* una división o agrupación usada para clasificar algo (pág. 198)

caucus/*caucus* una reunión de miembros de un partido político para tratar los asuntos del partido (pág. 279)

censorship/censura la prohibición de materiales impresos o películas debido a ideas ofensivas o inquietantes (pág. 122)

census/censo un recuento de la población que realiza la Oficina de Censos (págs. 179, 359)

central bank/banco central una institución que presta dinero a otros bancos; también, el lugar donde el gobierno realiza sus operaciones bancarias (pág. 661)

certificate of deposit/certificado de depósito depósito a plazo que especifica la cantidad del depósito, el vencimiento y la tasa de interés que debe pagarse (pág. 667)

challenge* a demand for justification or a dispute (p. 54)

charter a written document granting land and the authority to set up colonial governments (p. 36); or a government document granting permission to organize a corporation (pp. 604, 740)

charter schools schools that receive state funding, but are excused from meeting many public school regulations (p. 402)

checking account an account in which deposited money can be withdrawn at any time by writing a check (p. 667)

checks and balances a system in which each branch of government is able to check, or restrain, the power of the others (p. 88)

circuit the area of jurisdiction of a federal court of appeals (p. 240)

circumstance* an incident or occurrence (p. 242)

citizen community member who owes loyalty to the government and is entitled to protection from it (p. 7)

citizenship rights and duties of members of a state (p. 7)

city charter a document granting power to a local government (p. 377)

civics the study of the rights and duties of citizens (p. 7)

civil case person or group taking legal action against another person or group (p. 367)

civil liberties freedoms to think and act without government interference or fear of unfair legal treatment (p. 121)

civil rights the rights of full citizenship and equality under the law (p. 140)

civil service system the practice of hiring government workers on the basis of open, competitive examinations and merit (p. 229)

civil service worker person hired into a government position (p. 229)

civilian labor force all civilians 16 years old or older who are either working or are looking for work (p. 640)

challenge/desafío* demanda de justificación o un conflicto (pág. 54)

charter/carta de privilegio un documento escrito que otorga territorio y la autoridad de establecer gobiernos coloniales; o un documento gubernamental que otorga permiso para organizar una corporación (págs. 604, 740)

charter schools/escuelas con carta de privilegio escuelas que reciben financiación del estado, pero se las libera de la obligación de cumplir muchas reglamentaciones de las escuelas públicas (pág. 402)

checking account/cuenta de cheques una cuenta en la que el dinero depositado puede retirarse en cualquier momento al emitir un cheque (pág. 667)

checks and balances/controles y balances un sistema en el que cada poder del gobierno puede controlar, o limitar, el poder de los demás (pág. 88)

circuit/circuito el área de jurisdicción de un tribunal federal de apelación (pág. 240)

circumstance/circunstancia* un incidente o acontecimiento; una condición que acompaña o determina un hecho o evento (pág. 242)

citizen/ciudadano miembro de una comunidad que le deben lealtad al gobierno y tienen derecho a recibir protección de éste (pág. 7)

citizenship/ciudadanía derechos y deberes de los miembros de un estado (pág. 7)

city charter/carta municipal un documento que otorga poder a un gobierno local (pág. 377)

civics/civismo o cívica el estudio de los derechos y las obligaciones de los ciudadanos (pág. 7)

civil case/caso civil persona o grupo que realiza acciones legales contra otra persona o grupo (pág. 367)

civil liberties/libertades civiles libertades para pensar y actuar sin la interferencia del gobierno o miedo a un trato legal injusto (pág. 121)

civil rights/derechos civiles los derechos de ciudadanía e igualdad total según la ley (pág. 140)

civil service system/sistema de servicio civil la práctica de contratar empleados gubernamentales basándose en su mérito y en exámenes abiertos y competitivos (pág. 229)

civil service worker/trabajador de servicio civil persona contratada para un puesto federal (pág. 229)

civilian labor force/fuerza laboral civil todos los civiles mayores de 16 años que están trabajando o buscando un empleo (pág. 640)

clarify* to make something more understandable (p. 602)

closed primary an election in which only the declared members of a party are allowed to vote for that party's nominees (p. 283)

cloture a procedure used in the Senate to limit debate on a bill (p. 200)

coin metallic form of money such as pennies, nickels, and dimes (p. 657)

Cold War conflict between the United States and the Soviet Union dating from the later 1940s to the late 1980s, when the two countries competed for world influence without declared military action (p. 748)

collapse* to fall apart (p. 722)

collateral property or valuable item serving as security for a loan (p. 547)

collective bargaining process by which unions and employers negotiate the conditions of employment (p. 611)

colony a group of people in one place who are ruled by a parent country elsewhere (p. 36)

command economy an economic system in which the major economic decisions are made by the central government (p. 717)

commercial bank a financial institution that offers full banking services to individuals and businesses (p. 658)

commission* a special committee (p. 744)

commit* to pledge or assign oneself to a particular action (p. 562)

common law a system of law based on precedent and customs (p. 429)

communicate* to exchange information, thoughts, or feelings (p. 256)

communism economic system in which the central government directs all major economic decisions (p. 718)

community a group of people who share the same interests and concerns (p. 21)

community policing local police force visibly keeping the peace and patrolling neighborhoods (p. 405)

clarify/aclarar* hacer que algo sea más comprensible (pág. 602)

closed primary/elección primaria cerrada una elección en la que sólo los miembros declarados de un partido pueden votar por los candidatos de ese partido (pág. 283)

cloture/clausura un procedimiento usado en el Senado para limitar el debate sobre un proyecto de ley (pág. 200)

coin/moneda forma metálica de dinero como "pennies" (monedas de un centavo), "nickels" (monedas de cinco centavos) y "dimes" (monedas de diez centavos) (pág. 657)

Cold War/Guerra Fría conflicto entre los Estados Unidos y la Unión Soviética desde fines de los años 40 hasta fines de los años 80, cuando los dos países compitieron por la influencia mundial sin acción militar declarada (pág. 748)

collapse/colapsar* desploarse (pág. 722)

collateral/garantía aval propiedad u objeto de valor que sirve como caución para un préstamo (pág. 547)

collective bargaining/negociación colectiva proceso mediante el cual sindicatos y empleadores negocian las condiciones de empleo (pág. 611)

colony/colonia un grupo de personas en un lugar que están gobernados por un país matriz en otro lugar (pág. 36)

command economy/economía de mando un sistema económico en el que las principales decisiones económicas las toma el gobierno central (pág. 717)

commercial bank/banco comercial una institución financiera que ofrece servicios bancarios completos a personas y empresas (pág. 658)

commission/ comisón* comité especial (pág. 744)

commit/comprometer commit/cometer* prometer o hacerse cargo de una acción particular (pág. 562)

common law/derecho consuetudinario un sistema legal basado en precedentes y costumbres (pág. 429)

communicate/comunicar* intercambiar información, pensamientos o sentimientos (pág. 256)

communism/comunismo sistema económico en el cual el gobierno central toma todas las decisiones económicas principales (pág. 718)

community/comunidad un grupo de personas que comparten los mismos intereses e inquietudes (pág. 21)

community policing/control de la comunidad fuerza policial local que visiblemente mantiene la paz y patrulla los vecindarios (pág. 405)

commute to reduce a criminal's sentence (p. 364)

compact an agreement, or contract, among a group of people (p. 36)

comparative advantage the ability of a country to produce a good at a lower opportunity cost (p. 708)

comparison shopping buying strategy to get best buy for the money (p. 541)

competition the struggle that goes on between buyers and sellers to get the best products at the lowest prices (p. 530)

complaint a formal notice that a lawsuit is being brought (p. 450)

complement product often used with another product (p. 576)

complex* complicated or intricate (pp. 193, 389)

comprise* to consist or be made up of (p. 609)

compute* to determine or calculate (p. 506)

concurrent jurisdiction authority for both state and federal courts to hear and decide cases (p. 242)

concurrent powers powers shared by the state and federal governments (pp. 89, 353)

concurring opinion a statement written by a justice who votes with the majority, but for different reasons (p. 256)

confederation a group of individuals or state governments (p. 68)

confine* to restrict or imprison (p. 453)

confirm* to approve (p. 369)

conflict* a struggle or disagreement (p. 252)

consent* to express willingness or to agree (p. 351)

consequently* as a result (p. 708)

conservation the careful preservation and protection of natural resources (pp. 410, 737)

consist* to be made up of (p. 80)

constituent a person from a legislator's district (p. 179)

constitution a detailed, written plan for government (p. 67)

commute/conmutar reducir la sentencia de un delincuente (pág. 364)

compact/convenio un acuerdo, o contrato, entre un grupo de personas (pág. 36)

comparative advantage/ventaja comparativa la habilidad de un país de producir un bien a un costo de oportunidad menor (pág. 708)

comparison shopping/comparar antes de comprar estrategia de compras para obtener la mejor compra por el dinero empleado (pág. 541)

competition/competencia la lucha que tiene lugar entre compradores y vendedores para obtener los mejores productos a los precios más bajos (pág. 530)

complaint/queja un aviso formal de que se entabló. Una demanda (pág. 450)

complement/complemento producto a menudo usado con otro producto (pág. 576)

complex/complejo* complicado o intrincado (págs. 193, 389)

comprise/constar* estar compuesto o conformado por (pág. 609)

compute/computar* determinar o calcular (pág. 506)

concurrent jurisdiction/jurisdicción concurrente autoridad de tribunales estatales y federales para ver y decidir casos (pág. 242)

concurrent powers/poderes concurrentes poderes compartidos por los gobiernos estatales y federales (págs. 89, 353)

concurring opinion/opinión concurrente una declaración escrita por un juez que vota con la mayoría, pero por diferentes razones (pág. 256)

confederation/confederación un grupo de personas o gobiernos estatales (pág. 68)

confine/confinar* restringir o encerrar (pág. 453)

confirm/confirmar* aprobar (pág. 369)

conflict/conflicto* una lucha o un desacuerdo (pág. 252)

consent/consentir estar dispuesto o aceptar (pág. 351)

consequently/consiguientemente* como resultado (pág. 708)

conservation/conservación la cuidadosa preservación y protección de los recursos naturales (págs. 410, 737)

consist/consistir* estar compuesto por (pág. 80)

constituent/elector una persona del distrito de un legislador (pág. 179)

constitution/constitución un plan de gobierno escrito y detallado (pág. 67)

constitutional in accordance with the Constitution (p. 252)

Constitutional Convention meeting of state delegates in 1787 leading to adoption of new Constitution (p. 73)

constitutional law branch of law dealing with formation, construction, and interpretation of constitutions (p. 434)

constrain* to force, limit, or hold back (p. 25)

consult* to seek information or advice from a person or resource (p. 601)

consume* to use up (p. 522)

consumer someone who buys a good or service (p. 539)

consumer price index measure of change in price over time of specific group of goods and services (p. 642)

consumer sovereignty the role of consumer as the ruler of the market, determining what products will be produced (p. 529)

consumerism a movement to educate buyers about the purchases they make and to demand better and safer products from manufacturers (p. 540)

contract* to become smaller (p. 664)

contrary* opposite or different (p. 476)

convert* to change from one belief, form, or use to another (p. 67)

convince* to persuade through argument or evidence (p. 397)

cooperative a voluntary association of people formed to carry on some kind of economic activity that will benefit its members (p. 606)

copyright the owner's exclusive right to control, publish, and sell an original work (p. 483)

corporation type of business organization owned by many people but treated by law as though it were a person (p. 603)

cost-benefit analysis economic model that compares the marginal costs and marginal benefits of a decision (p. 508)

constitutional/constitucional de acuerdo con la Constitución (pág. 252)

Constitutional Convention/Convención Constitucional reunión de delegados estatales en 1787 que llevó a la adopción de una nueva Constitución (pág. 73)

constitutional law/ley constitucional rama del derecho que trata de la información, construcción e interpretación de las constituciones. (pág. 434)

constrain/constreñir* forzar, limitar o retener (pág. 25)

consult/consultar* buscar información o consejos de una persona o un recurso (pág. 601)

consume/consumir* agotar (pág. 522)

consumer/consumidor alguien que compra un bien o un servicio (pág. 539)

consumer price index/índice de precios de consumo medida del cambio en el precio con el paso del tiempo de un grupo específico de bienes y servicios (pág. 642)

consumer sovereignty/soberanía del consumidor la función del consumidor como el gobernante del mercado, donde determina qué productos se producirán (pág. 529)

consumerism/protección al consumidor un movimiento para educar a los compradores sobre las compras que hacen y para demandar productos mejores y más seguros a los fabricantes (pág. 540)

contract/contraer* reducir a menor tamaño (pág. 664)

contrary/contrario* opuesto o diferente (pág. 476)

convert/convertir* cambiar de una creencia, forma o uso a otra (pág. 67)

convince/convencer* persuadir mediante argumentos o evidencia (pág. 397)

cooperative/cooperativa una asociación voluntaria de personas formada para realizar algún tipo de actividad económica que beneficie a sus miembros (pág. 606)

copyright/derecho de autor el derecho exclusivo del propietario de controlar, publicar y vender una obra original (pág. 483)

corporation/sociedad anónima tipo de organización comercial propiedad de varias personas pero tratada por la ley como si fuera una persona (pág. 603)

cost-benefit analysis/análisis costo-beneficio modelo económico que compara los costos marginales y los beneficios marginales de una decisión (pág. 508)

county normally the largest territorial and political subdivision of a state (p. 384)

county seat a town where the county courthouse is located (p. 384)

credit money borrowed to pay for a good or service p. 547

credit union nonprofit service cooperative that accepts deposits, makes loans, and provides other financial services (p. 658)

crime an act that breaks a law and causes harm to people or society in general (p. 453)

cross-examine to question a witness at a trial or a hearing to check or discredit the testimony (p. 457)

crucial* of vital importance (p. 617)

currency both coins and paper money (p. 657)

county/condado normalmente, la subdivisión territorial y política más grande de un estado (pág. 384)

county seat/capital del condado una ciudad en la que está ubicado el palacio de justicia del condado (pág. 384)

credit/crédito dinero tomado en préstamo para pagar un bien o un servicio (pág. 547)

credit union/asociación de crédito cooperativa de servicio sin fines de lucro que acepta depósitos, otorga préstamos y presta otros servicios financieros (pág. 658)

crime/delito un acto que viola una ley y provoca un daño la gente o a la sociedad en general (pág. 453)

cross-examine/interrogar hacer preguntas a un testigo en un juicio o una audiencia para confirmar o desacreditar el testimonio (pág. 457)

crucial/crucial* de importancia vital (pág. 617)

currency/moneda dinero en monedas y en papel (pág. 657)

D

debt money borrowed and not yet paid back (p. 688)

decade* a period of 10 years (p. 39)

decline* to lessen or diminish (p. 390)

defendant an individual or group being sued or charged with a crime (pp. 368, 431)

deficit situation in which government spends more than it collects in revenues (p. 688)

delegate a representative to a meeting (p. 54)

demand the desire, willingness, and ability to buy a good or service (p. 569)

demand curve downward-sloping line that graphically shows the quantities demanded at each possible price (p. 569)

demand elasticity measure of responsiveness relating change in quantity demanded to a change in price (p. 577)

demand schedule table showing quantities demanded at different possible prices (p. 569)

democracy a government in which citizens hold the power to rule (p. 23)

deny* refusal to grant, agree, or believe (p. 17)

deport to send an alien or immigrant back to his or her own country (p. 19)

debt/deuda dinero prestado y aún no pagado (pág. 688)

decade/década* un período de 10 años (pág. 39)

decline/declinar* reducir o disminuir (pág. 390)

defendant/acusado una persona o un grupo demandado o acusado de un delito (págs. 368, 431)

deficit/déficit situación en la que el gobierno gasta más de lo que recauda en ingresos (pág. 688)

delegate/delegado un representante en una reunión (pág. 54)

demand/demanda el deseo, la disposición y la habilidad de comprar un bien o servicio (pág. 569)

demand curve/curva de demanda línea en declive que muestra gráficamente las cantidades demandadas a cada precio posible (pág. 569)

demand elasticity/elasticidad de demanda medida de respuesta que relaciona un cambio en la cantidad demandada con un cambio en el precio (pág. 577)

demand schedule/tabla de demanda tabla que muestra las cantidades demandadas a los diferentes precios posibles (pág. 569)

democracy/democracia un gobierno en el que los ciudadanos tienen el poder para gobernar (pág. 23)

deny/negar* negativa de otorgar, aceptar o creer (pág. 17)

deport/deportar enviar a un extranjero o inmigrante a su propio país (pág. 19)

despite* in spite of (p. 73)

developing country a country whose average per capita income is only a fraction of that in more industrialized countries (p. 724)

devote* to dedicate oneself to (p. 297)

diminish* to lessen or reduce (p. 509)

direct democracy a form of democracy in which the people vote firsthand (p. 23)

direct primary an election in which voters choose candidates to represent each party in a general election (p. 283)

discount rate the interest rate the Fed charges on its loans (p. 664)

discovery process by which attorneys have opportunity to check facts and gather evidence (p. 450)

discretionary income money income left after necessities have been bought and paid for (p. 539)

discretionary spending spending for federal programs that must receive annual approval (p. 677)

discrimination unfair treatment based on prejudice against a certain group (pp. 140, 618)

display* to put in plain view (p. 210)

disposable income money income left after all taxes on it have been paid (p. 539)

dispose* to throw away or discard (p. 529)

dissenting opinion a statement written by a justice who disagrees with the majority opinion, presenting his or her opinion (p. 256)

dissident person or group that disagrees with established systems (p. 475)

district court federal court where trials are held and lawsuits are begun (p. 244)

diverse* differing from one another (p. 8)

dividend payment of a portion of a company's earnings (p. 557)

division of labor the breaking down of a job into separate, smaller tasks to be performed individually (p. 524)

docket a court's calendar, showing the schedule of cases it is to hear (p. 255)

despite/a pesar* en contra de (pág. 73)

developing country/país en desarrollo un país cuyo ingreso per cápita promedio es sólo una fracción del valor en países más industrializados (pág. 724)

devote/dedicarse* destinar la atención de uno a (pág. 297)

diminish/disminuir* reducir (pág. 509)

direct democracy/democracia directa una forma de democracia en la que el pueblo vota directamente (pág. 23)

direct primary/elección primaria directa una elección en la que los votantes eligen a los candidatos para representar a cada partido en una elección general (pág. 283)

discount rate/tipo reducido la tasa de interés que el Fed cobra en sus préstamos (pág. 664)

discovery/descubrimiento proceso mediante el que los abogados pueden verificar los hechos y obtener evidencia (pág. 450)

discretionary income/ingresos discrecionales ingreso de dinero restante luego de haber comprado y pagado las necesidades básicas (pág. 539)

discretionary spending/gasto discrecional gastos para programas federales que deben recibir aprobación anual (pág. 677)

discrimination/discriminación trato injusto basado en el prejuicio contra cierto grupo (págs. 140, 618)

display/exhibir* colocar a la vista de todos (pág. 210)

disposable income/ingreso disponible ingreso de dinero restante luego de haber pagado todos los impuestos sobre éste (pág. 539)

dispose/desechar* tirar o descartar (pág. 529)

dissenting opinion/opinión disidente declaración escrita que presenta la opinión de un juez que está en desacuerdo con la opinión mayoritaria (pág. 256)

dissident/disidente persona o grupo que está en desacuerdo con los sistemas establecidos (pág. 475)

district courts/tribunales distrito tribunales federales en los que se llevan a cabo juicios y se inician demandas (pág. 244)

diverse/diverso* que difieren entre sí (pág. 8)

dividend/dividendo pago de una parte de las ganancias de una empresa (pág. 557)

division of labor/división de trabajo la separación de un trabajo en tareas separadas y más pequeñas que deben realizarse de manera individual (pág. 524)

docket/registro el calendario de un tribunal, que detalla el programa de casos que debe ver (pág. 255)

document* a written paper that provides information or proof of something (p. 33)

domestic* relating to or occurring in one's own country (p. 160)

dominate* to have command or control over (p. 379)

double jeopardy putting someone on trial for a crime of which he or she was previously acquitted (p. 128)

draft* to call up (p. 152)

due process following established legal procedures (p. 128)

due process of law procedures established by law and guaranteed by the Constitution (p. 437)

duty a thing we are required to do (p. 151)

document/documento* un documento escrito que brinda información o prueba de algo (pág. 33)

domestic/doméstico* que se relaciona con u ocurre en el país de uno (pág. 160)

dominate/dominar* dirigir o tener el control sobre (pág. 379)

double jeopardy/riesgo doble llevar a una persona a juicio por un delito por el que había sido absuelta anteriormente (pág. 128)

draft/llamamiento* a filas reclutar (pág. 152)

due process/proceso correspondiente seguir los procedimientos legales establecidos (pág. 128)

due process of law/proceso legal correspondiente procedimientos establecidos por la ley y garantizados por la Constitución (pág. 437)

duty/deber una cosa que debemos hacer (pág. 151)

E

Earned Income Tax Credit (EITC) a program that gives tax credits and even cash payments to qualified workers (p. 649)

economic interdependence a reliance on others, as they rely on you, to provide goods and services to be consumed (p. 525)

economic model simplified representation of the real world that economists develop to describe how the economy behaves and is expected to perform in the future (p. 500)

economics the study of how individuals and nations make choices about ways to use scarce resources to fulfill their needs and wants (p. 499)

economic system nation's way of producing things its people want and need (p. 500)

egalitarianism the philosophy or spirit of equality (p. 48)

elastic clause clause in Article I, Section 8 of the Constitution that gives Congress the right to make all laws "necessary and proper" to carry out its expressed powers (p. 185)

elector person appointed to vote in presidential elections for the major candidates (p. 210)

Earned Income Tax Credit (EITC)/crédito fiscal sobre ingresos un programa que otorga créditos fiscales e incluso pagos en efectivo a trabajadores calificados (pág. 649)

economic interdependence/interdependencia económica dependencia en otros, mientras que ellos dependen de ti, a fin de suministrar bienes y servicios para el consumo (pág. 525)

economic model/modelo económico representación simplificada del mundo real que los economistas crean para describir la forma en que la economía se comporta y se espera que actúe en el futuro (pág. 500)

economics/economía el estudio de la forma en que personas y naciones toman decisiones sobre las maneras de usar los recursos escasos, para satisfacer sus necesidades y deseos (pág. 499)

economic system/sistema económico manera de una nación de producir cosas que su población necesita y desea (pág. 500)

egalitarianism/igualitarismo la filosofía o el espíritu de igualdad (pág. 48)

elastic clause/cláusula elástica cláusula en el artículo I, sección 8 de la Constitución que otorga al Congreso el derecho de crear todas las leyes "necesarias y adecuadas" para ejercer sus poderes explícitos (pág. 185)

elector/elector persona designada para votar en elecciones presidenciales por los principales candidatos (pág. 210)

Electoral College a group of people named by each state legislature to select the president and vice president (pp. 76, 210, 301)

electorate all the people who are eligible to vote (p. 299)

electronic media radio, television, and the Internet (p. 327)

element* a component of a whole (p. 198)

eliminate* to get rid of (p. 562)

embargo an agreement among a group of nations that prohibits them all from trading with a target nation (p. 223)

eminent domain the right of government to take private property for public use (p. 128)

emphasis* placing stress or special importance on something (p. 463)

enable* to make able or possible (p. 476)

enforce* to carry out by force or ensure compliance (p. 21)

Enlightenment movement that spread the idea that reason and science could improve society (p. 33)

enormous* very large (p. 677)

ensure* to secure or make sure (p. 87)

entitlement program a program using eligibility requirements to provide health, nutritional, or income supplements to individuals (p. 684)

entrepreneur individual who starts a new business, introduces a new product, and improves a management technique (p. 517)

environmentalism movement concerned with protecting environment (p. 409)

equilibrium price the price at which the amount producers are willing to supply is equal to the amount consumers are willing to buy (p. 589)

equivalent* alike or equal to in number or meaning (p. 463)

erode* to wear away or destroy gradually (p. 483)

establish* to bring into existence or create (p. 553)

estimate* to judge the approximate nature, value, quality, or amount of a thing (pp. 193, 386)

Electoral College/Colegio Electoral un grupo de personas designadas por cada cuerpo legislativo estatal para elegir al presidente y al vicepresidente (págs. 76, 210, 301)

electorate/electorado todas las personas que tienen derecho a votar (pág. 299)

electronic media/medios electrónicos de comunicación radio, televisión e Internet (pág. 327)

element/elemento* un componente de un todo (pág. 198)

eliminate/eliminar* deshacerse de (pág. 562)

embargo/embargo un acuerdo entre un grupo de naciones que les prohíbe a todas comerciar con una nación en particular (pág. 223)

eminent domain/dominio eminente el derecho del gobierno de tomar propiedad privada para uso público (pág. 128)

emphasis/énfasis* hacer hincapié o dar especial importancia a algo (pág. 463)

enable/permitir* hacer posible (pág. 476)

enforce/hacer cumplir* llevar a cabo por fuerza o asegurar la conformidad (pág. 21)

Enlightenment/Iluminismo movimiento que sostenía la idea de que la razón y la ciencia podían mejorar a la sociedad (pág. 33)

enormous/enorme* muy grande (pág. 677)

ensure/asegurar* garantizar (pág. 87)

entitlement program/programa de derechos un programa que utiliza requisitos de elegibilidad para dar suplementos de ingresos, salud o nutricionales a personas (pág. 684)

entrepreneur/empresario persona que inician nuevos negocios, presentan nuevos productos y mejoran las técnicas de administración (pág. 517)

environmentalism/ecología movimiento dedicado a la protección del medio ambiente (pág. 409)

equilibrium price/precio de equilibrio el precio al que los productores están dispuestos a ofertar es igual al monto que los consumidores están dispuestos a comprar (pág. 589)

equivalent/equivalente* similar o igual en número o significado (pág. 463)

erode/desgastar* gastar o destruir gradualmente (pág. 483)

establish/establecer* dar vida o crear (pág. 553)

estimate/estimar* juzgar la naturaleza, el valor, la calidad o la cantidad aproximada de algo (págs. 193, 386)

ethnic* relating to races or groups of people who share common traits and customs (p. 9)

evaluate* to assess or find the value of (p. 560)

eventually* in the end (p. 710)

exceed* to be or go beyond a limit (p. 545)

exchange rate the price of one nation's currency in terms of another nation's currency (p. 712)

exclude* to shut out (p. 631)

exclusive jurisdiction authority of only federal courts to hear and decide cases (p. 242)

executive agreement an agreement between the president and the leader of another country (p. 222)

executive branch the branch of government that carries out laws (p. 80)

executive order a rule or command that has the force of law (p. 216)

exit poll a survey taken at polling places of how people voted (p. 297)

expand* to increase in size or amount (p. 353)

expense money spent on goods and services (p. 546)

exploit* to take advantage of (p. 717)

export to sell goods to other countries; a good produced in one country, then sold to another (p. 707)

ex post facto law a law that would allow a person to be punished for an action that was not against the law when it was committed (p. 188)

expressed powers powers that Congress has that are specifically listed in the Constitution (pp. 89, 185)

externality the unintended side effect of an action that affects someone not involved in the action (p. 631)

extremist group organization that promotes ideas that are farthest from the political center (p. 476)

ethnic/étnico* relativo a razas o grupos de personas que comparten los mismos rasgos y costumbres (pág. 9)

evaluate/evaluar* encontrar el valor de (pág. 560)

eventually/finalmente* por ultimo (pág. 710)

exceed/exceder* estar o ir más allá de un límite (pág. 545)

exchange rate/tipo de cambio el precio de la moneda de una nación en términos de la moneda de otra nación (pág. 712)

exclude/excluir* dejar afuera (pág. 631)

exclusive jurisdiction/jurisdicción exclusiva autoridad de los tribunales federales únicamente de ver y decidir casos (pág. 242)

executive agreement/acuerdo ejecutivo un acuerdo entre el presidente y el líder de otro país (pág. 222)

executive branch/poder ejecutivo el poder del gobierno que crea las leyes (pág. 80)

executive order/orden ejecutiva una regla que tiene la fuerza de una ley (pág. 216)

exit poll/encuesta de votación una encuesta que se realiza en los lugares de votación sobre cómo votó la gente (pág. 297)

expand/expandir* incrementar en tamaño o cantidad (pág. 353)

expense/gasto dinero gastado en bienes y servicios (pág. 546)

exploit/explotar* aprovecharse de (pág. 717)

export/exportar, exportación vender bienes a otros países; un bien producido en un país y luego vendido a otro (pág. 707)

ex post facto law/ley con efecto retroactivo una ley que permitiría que una persona sea castigada por una acción que no era contra la ley cuando la realizó (pág. 188)

expressed powers/poderes explícitos poderes que tiene el Congreso y que están detallados específicamente en la Constitución (págs. 89, 185)

externality/exterioridad el efecto secundario no planificado de una acción que afecta a alguien que no forma parte en la acción (pág. 631)

extremist group/grupo extremista organización que promueve ideas totalmente alejadas del centro político (pág. 476)

F

factor* an element contributing to a result (p. 437)

factor market a market where productive resources are bought and sold (p. 521)

factors of production resources necessary to produce goods and services (p. 517)

federal* of or involving the federal government (p. 411)

federal bureaucracy agencies and the employees of the executive branch of government (p. 228)

federalism a form of government in which power is divided between the federal, or national, government and the states (p. 77)

Federalists supporters of the Constitution (p. 77)

Federal Open Market Committee (FOMC) the most powerful committee of the Fed, because it makes the decisions that affect the economy as a whole by manipulating the money supply (p. 661)

federal system the sharing of power between the central and state governments (p. 351)

fee* a charge (p. 307)

felony a serious crime such as murder, rape, kidnapping, or robbery (pp. 368, 432)

file* to submit or register (p. 449)

filibuster a tactic for defeating a bill in the Senate by talking until the bill's sponsor withdraws it (p. 200)

financial capital money used to buy the tools and equipment used in production (p. 601)

fiscal policy the federal government's use of spending and taxation policies to affect overall business activity (p. 641)

flexible* able to adapt easily (p. 712)

factor/factor* un elemento que contribuye a un resultado (pág. 437)

factor market/mercado de factores un mercado en el que se compran y venden recursos productivos (pág. 521)

factors of production/factores de producción recursos necesarios para producir bienes y servicios (pág. 517)

federal/federal* perteneciente o relacionado con el gobierno federal (pág. 411)

federal bureaucracy/burocracia federal las agencias colectivas y los empleados del poder ejecutivo (pág. 228)

federalism/federalismo una forma de gobierno en la que el poder está dividido entre el gobierno federal, o nacional, y los estados (pág. 77)

Federalists/federalistas defensores de la Constitución (pág. 77)

Federal Open Market Committee (FOMC)/ Comité Federal del Mercado Abierto el comité más poderoso del Fed, ya que toma las decisiones que afectan la economía en general al manipular la oferta monetaria (pág. 661)

federal system/sistema federal la posesión conjunta del poder entre los gobiernos centrales y estatales (pág. 351)

fee/costo* un cargo (pág. 307)

felony/felonía un delito grave como asesinato, violación, secuestro o robo (págs. 368, 432)

file/presentar* enviar o registrar (pág. 449)

filibuster/maniobra obstruccionista una táctica para rechazar un proyecto de ley en el Senado al hablar hasta que el patrocinador del proyecto de ley la retire (pág. 200)

financial capital/capital financiero dinero usado para comprar las herramientas y los equipos usados en la producción (pág. 601)

fiscal policy/política fiscal el uso de políticas sobre gastos e impuestos por parte del gobierno federal para afectar la actividad comercial en general (pág. 641)

flexible/flexible* que se adapta con facilidad (pág. 712)

focus* a central point of attention or activity (p. 590)

food stamps government coupons that can be used to purchase food (p. 648)

foreign policy a nation's overall plan for dealing with other nations (p. 220)

foundation* an organization (p. 616)

franking privilege the right of senators and representatives to send job-related mail without paying postage (p. 192)

free enterprise economic system in which individuals and businesses are allowed to compete for profit with a minimum of government interference (p. 528)

function* to serve a purpose (p. 453)

fund* a sum of money (p. 553)

furthermore* in addition, moreover (p. 379)

focus/centro* un punto central de atención o actividad (pág. 590)

food stamps/estampillas para alimentos cupones del gobierno que pueden usarse para comprar alimentos (pág. 648)

foreign policy/política extranjera el plan global de una nación para el trato con otras naciones (pág. 220)

foundation/fundación* una organización (pág. 616)

franking privilege/privilegio de franqueo el derecho de los senadores y representantes de enviar correo relacionado con el trabajo sin pagar franqueo (pág. 192)

free enterprise/empresa libre sistema económico en el que personas y negocios pueden competir por las ganancias con mínima interferencia del gobierno (pág. 528)

function/función* servir para un propósito (pág. 453)

fund/fondo* una suma de dinero (pág. 553)

furthermore/además* lo que es más, por otra parte (pág. 379)

G

gender* a notation of the sex of a person (pp. 141, 319)

generate* to bring into existence (p. 502)

genocide mass murder of a people because of their race, religion, ethnicity, politics, or culture (p. 745)

gerrymander an oddly-shaped election district designed to increase the voting strength of a particular group (p. 179)

global* relating to the entire world (p. 151)

globalization individuals and nations working across barriers of distance, culture, and technology (p. 742)

good tangible product that we use to satisfy our wants and needs (p. 517)

government the ruling authority for a community (p. 21)

government corporation a business owned and operated by the federal government (p. 229)

grand jury a group of citizens that decides whether there is sufficient evidence to accuse someone of a crime (pp. 128, 439)

gender/género* una notación del sexo de una persona (págs. 141, 319)

generate/generar* dar vida (pág. 502)

genocide/genocidio asesinato en masa de un pueblo debido a su raza, religión, origen étnico, política o cultura (pág. 745)

gerrymander/*gerrymander* un distrito formado de manera extraña para incrementar la fuerza de votación de un grupo particular (pág. 179)

global/global* relativo a todo el mundo (pág. 151)

globalization/globalización personas y naciones que trabajan a través de las barreras de distancia, cultura y tecnología (pág. 742)

good/biene producto tangible que usamos para satisfacer nuestros deseos y necesidades (pág. 517)

government/gobierno la autoridad que gobierna a una comunidad (pág. 21)

government corporation/corporación gubernamental una empresa que es propiedad del gobierno federal y es operada por éste (pág. 229)

grand jury/jurado un grupo de ciudadanos que decide si hay suficiente evidencia para acusar a una persona de un delito (págs. 128, 439)

grant to allow or permit (p. 33)

grants-in-aid money awarded to the states by the federal government (p. 353)

Great Compromise agreement providing a dual system of congressional representation (p. 75)

Gross Domestic Product (GDP) total dollar value of all final goods and services produced in a country during a single year (p. 518)

guarantee* to promise or give security (p. 337)

guideline* an outline or guide for a future course of action (p. 364)

grant/otorgar permitir (pág. 33)

grants-in-aid/subsidios dinero otorgado a los estados por parte del gobierno federal (pág. 353)

Great Compromise/Gran Compromiso acuerdo que estipula un sistema dual de representación del Congreso (pág. 75)

Gross Domestic Product (GDP)/Producto Interno Bruto (PIB) valor total en dólares de todos los bienes y servicios finales producidos en un país durante un único año (pág. 518)

guarantee/garantizar* prometer o dar seguridad (pág. 337)

guideline/directriz* un esquema o una guía para un curso de acción futuro (pág. 364)

home rule allows cities to write their own charters, choose their own type of government, and manage their own affairs (p. 377)

human rights fundamental freedoms of individuals (p. 744)

hung jury a jury that cannot agree on a verdict (p. 458)

home rule/autonomía política permite que las ciudades redacten sus propias cartas, elijan a su propio tipo de gobierno y administren sus propios asuntos (pág. 377)

human rights/derechos humanos libertades fundamentales de las personas (pág. 744)

hung jury/jurado en desacuerdo un jurado que no puede llegar a un veredicto (pág. 458)

identify* to find or show the identity of (p. 570)

ideological* relating to a body of opinions (p. 691)

illustrate* to show or make clear by example (p. 572)

image* a representation or public perception (p. 307)

immigrant a person who moves permanently to a new country (p. 16)

impact* to influence or affect (pp. 69, 216)

impeach to accuse government officials of misconduct in office (p. 187)

implement* to put into practice (p. 641)

implied powers powers that Congress has that are not stated explicitly in the Constitution (p. 185)

identify/identificar* encontrar o mostrar la identidad de (pág. 570)

ideological/ideólogical* relativo un conjunto de ideas u opiniones (pág. 691)

illustrate/ilustrar* mostrar o aclarar mediante un ejemplo (pág. 572)

image/imagen* una representación o percepción pública (pág. 307)

immigrant/inmigrante una persona que se muda de manera permanente a un nuevo país (pág. 16)

impact/impactar* influir o afectar (págs. 69, 216)

impeach/impugnar acusar a funcionarios del gobierno de mala conducta en el desempeño de su cargo (pág. 187)

implement/implementar* poner en práctica (pág. 641)

implied powers/poderes implícitos poderes que tiene el Congreso y que no están detallados explícitamente en la Constitución (pág. 185)

imply* to suggest something rather than directly state it (p. 123)

import a good purchased from one country by another (p. 707)

impose* to establish as a charge or penalty (p. 401)

impulse buying purchasing an item on the spot because of an emotional rather than planned decision (p. 561)

incentive* reward offered to try to persuade people to take certain economic actions (p. 529)

income* money received from labor, business, or property (pp. 152, 545)

incorporate to receive a state charter, officially recognizing the government of a locality (p. 377)

incumbent a politician who has already been elected to office (p. 309)

indentured servant workers who contracted with American colonists for food and shelter in return for their labor (p. 42)

independence self-reliance and freedom from outside control (p. 54)

independent agency federal board or commission that is not part of any cabinet department (p. 229)

indictment a formal charge by a grand jury (p. 128)

inflation sustained increase in the general level of prices (p. 641)

infrastructure a community's system of roads, bridges, water, and sewers (p. 399)

initial* the very first (p. 667)

initiative a procedure by which citizens can propose new laws or state constitutional amendments (p. 301)

innovate* to introduce or create something new (p. 517)

input* resources factored into the economy (p. 523)

institution sets of ideas that people have about relationships, obligations, roles, and functions of society (p. 13)

intellectual property things that people create, such as songs, movies, books, poetry, art, and software (p. 482)

imply/insinuar* algo sugerido en vez de dicho directamente (pág. 123)

import/importación un bien que compra un país a otro (pág. 707)

impose/imponer* establecer como un cargo o una pena (pág. 401)

impulse buying/comprar por impulso comprar un artículo en el momento debido a una decisión emocional en lugar de una planificada (pág. 561)

incentive/incentivo* recompensa ofrecida para tratar de persuadir a que la gente tome ciertas decisiones económicas (pág. 529)

income/ingresos* dinero recibido del trabajo, negocio o propiedad (págs. 152, 545)

incorporate/incorporar recibir una carta del estado, mediante la que se reconoce oficialmente el gobierno de una localidad (pág. 377)

incumbent/titular un político que ya ha sido elegido para un cargo (pág. 309)

indentured servant/sirvientes por contrato trabajadores que se empleaban con los colonos estadounidenses por alimento y casa a cambio de su trabajo (pág. 42)

independence/independencia dependencia en sí mismo y libertad del control externo (pág. 54)

independent agency/agencia independiente comisión o junta federal que no forma parte de ningún departamento del gabinete (pág. 229)

indictment/acusación un cargo formal de un jurado (pág. 128)

inflation/inflación incremento sostenido en el nivel general de los precios (pág. 641)

infrastructure/infraestructura el sistema de calles, puentes, agua y desagües de una comunidad (pág. 399)

initial/inicial* el primero de todos (pág. 667)

initiative/iniciativa un procedimiento mediante el que los ciudadanos pueden proponer nuevas leyes o exponer enmiendas constitucionales (pág. 301)

innovate/innovar* introducir o crear algo nuevo (pág. 517)

input/insumos* recursos ingresados a la economía (pág. 523)

institution/institución conjuntos de ideas que las personas tienen sobre las relaciones, las obligaciones, los papeles y las funciones de la sociedad (pág. 13)

intellectual property/propiedad intelectual cosas que la gente crea, como canciones, películas, libros, poesía, arte y software (pág. 482)

interact* to act upon one another (p. 471)

interest the payment people receive when they lend money or allow someone else to use their money (p. 554)

interest group a group of people who share a point of view about an issue and unite to promote their beliefs (p. 321)

intergovernmental revenues funds one level of government receives from another level of government (p. 682)

intermediate* being or occurring in the middle or between two points (p. 368)

internationalism involvement in world affairs (p. 740)

Internet a mass communication system of millions of networked computers and databases all over the world (p. 471)

interpret* to explain or translate (p. 436)

interval* a break or period of time between two events (p. 557)

intervene* to come between (p. 716)

involve* to take part in or include as a necessary component (p. 131)

isolate* to separate or keep apart (p. 476)

issue* a matter of debate or dispute (p. 301); to distribute or send out (p. 363)

J

joint resolution a resolution that is passed by both houses of Congress (p. 198)

joint-stock company investors provide partial ownership in a company organized for profit (p. 36)

judicial branch the branch of government that interprets laws (p. 81)

judicial review the power of the Supreme Court to say whether any federal, state, or local law or government action goes against the Constitution (p. 252)

jurisdiction a court's authority to hear and decide cases (p. 240)

justice of the peace the judge of a small, local court (p. 367)

interact/interactuar* actuar recíprocamente (pág. 471)

interest/interés el pago que recibe la gente cuando presta dinero o permite que otra persona use su dinero (pág. 554)

interest group/grupo de interés un grupo de personas que comparten un punto de vista sobre una cuestión y se unen para promover sus creencias (pág. 321)

intergovernmental revenues/ingresos intergubernamentales fondos que recibe un nivel del gobierno de otro nivel del gobierno (pág. 682)

intermediate/intermedio* que está u ocurre en el medio o entre dos puntos (pág. 368)

internationalism/internacionalismo participación en los asuntos mundiales (pág. 740)

Internet/Internet un sistema de comunicación masiva de millones de computadoras y bases de datos conectados en red en todo el mundo (pág. 471)

interpret/interpretar* explicar o traducir (pág. 436)

interval/intervalo* un descanso o período de tiempo entre dos eventos (pág. 557)

intervene/intervener* interponerse entre (pág. 716)

involve/involucrar* formar parte de o incluir como un componente necesario (pág. 131)

isolate/aislar* separar o mantener alejado (pág. 476)

issue/cuestión* un asunto de debate o conflicto (pág. 301) **issue/expedir*** distribuir o enviar (pág. 363)

joint resolution/resolución colectiva una resolución que es aprobada por ambas cámaras del Congreso (pág. 198)

joint-stock company/sociedad anónima inversores con propiedad parcial de una empresa organizada para obtener ganancias (pág. 36)

judicial branch/poder judicial el poder del gobierno que interpreta las leyes (pág. 81)

judicial review/revisión judicial el poder de la Suprema Corte de decir si alguna acción gubernamental o ley federal, estatal o local va en contra de la Constitución (pág. 252)

jurisdiction/jurisdicción la autoridad de un tribunal de ver y decidir casos (pág. 240)

justice of the peace/juez de paz el juez de un tribunal local pequeño (pág. 367)

juvenile a person not yet legally an adult (p. 461)

juvenile delinquent a child or teenager who commits a serious crime or repeatedly breaks the law (p. 461)

juvenile/menor una persona que aún no es legalmente un adulto (pág. 461)

juvenile delinquent/delincuente juvenil un niño o adolescente que comete un delito grave o viola la ley repetidamente (pág. 461)

L

labor human effort directed toward producing goods and services (p. 517)

labor union association of workers organized to improve wages and working conditions (p. 609)

laissez-faire economics economic system where government should not interfere in the marketplace (p. 531)

landfill place where garbage is dumped (p. 409)

larceny the unlawful taking away of another person's property with the intent never to return it (p. 432)

law of demand the concept that people are normally willing to buy less of a product if the price is high and more of it if the price is low (p. 569)

law of supply suppliers will normally offer more for sale at higher prices and less at lower prices (p. 581)

lawsuit a legal action in which a person or group sues to collect damages for some harm that is done (p. 432)

leak the release of secret government information by anonymous government officials to the media (p. 328)

legislative branch the lawmaking branch of government (p. 80)

legislature a group of people that makes laws (p. 33)

levy* to require taxes to be paid (p. 385)

libel written untruths that are harmful to someone's reputation (pp. 124, 330, 433)

likewise* similarly or in addition (p. 572)

line-item veto to veto only a specific part of a bill (p. 364)

labor/trabajo esfuerzo humano con el objetivo de producir bienes y servicios (pág. 517)

labor union/sindicato asociación de trabajadores organizada para mejorar los salarios y las condiciones de trabajo (pág. 609)

laissez-faire economics/economía laissez-faire sistema económico en el que el gobierno no intervendría en el mercado (pág. 531)

landfill/vertedero lugar donde se vierte la basura (pág. 409)

larceny/robo tomar ilegalmente la propiedad de otra persona sin intención alguna de devolverla (pág. 432)

law of demand/ley de demanda el concepto de que la gente normalmente está dispuesta a comprar menos de un producto si el precio es alto y más si el precio es bajo (pág. 569)

law of supply/ley de oferta los proveedores normalmente ofrecen más para la venta a precios más altos y menos a precios más bajos (pág. 581)

lawsuit/pleito una acción legal en la que una persona o un grupo realiza una demanda para cobrar una compensación por algún daño que se le ha hecho (pág. 432)

leak/filtración de información la revelación de información gubernamental confidencial por parte de funcionarios gubernamentales anónimos a los medios de comunicación (pág. 328)

legislative branch/poder legislativo el poder del gobierno que crea las leyes (pág. 80)

legislature/asamblea legislativa un grupo de personas que crea leyes (pág. 33)

levy/recaudar* exigir que se paguen los impuestos (pág. 385)

libel/difamación falsedades escritas que son perjudiciales para la reputación de alguien (págs. 124, 330, 433)

likewise/igualmente* asimismo o también (pág. 572)

line-item veto/veto parcial vetar sólo una parte específica de un proyecto de ley (pág. 364)

lobbyist representative of an interest group who contacts lawmakers or other government officials directly to influence their policy making (pp. 192, 335)

long-term plan a government plan for policy that can span 10 to 50 years (p. 398)

lobbyist/lobista representante de un grupo de interés que contacta a legisladores u otros funcionarios gubernamentales directamente para influir en su creación de políticas (págs. 192, 335)

long-term plan/plan a largo plazo plan del gobierno por política que se puede extender de 10 a 50 años (pág. 398)

M

macroeconomics economic behavior and decision-making by government or whole industries or societies (p. 500)

macroeconomics/macroeconomía conducta económica y toma de decisiones por parte de un gobierno, las industrias en conjunto o las sociedades (pág. 500)

magistrate courts police courts generally located in larger towns, may handle traffic violations, civil cases involving small amounts of money, etc. (p. 367)

magistrate courts/cortes de magistrados juzgados de guardia generalmente ubicados en pueblos más grandes; pueden encargarse de las violaciones de tránsito, casos civiles relacionados con pequeñas cantidades de dinero, etc. (pág. 367)

maintain* to keep up (p. 740)

maintain/mantener* continuar con (pág. 740)

majority a number that is more than 50 percent of the total (p. 284)

majority/mayoría cantidad que es más del 50 por ciento del total (pág. 284)

majority opinion a statement that presents the views of the majority of Supreme Court justices regarding a case (p. 256)

majority opinion/opinión mayoritaria declaración que presenta la opinión de la mayoría de los jueces de la Suprema Corte sobre un caso (pág. 256)

majority party in both the House of Representatives and the Senate, the political party to which more than half the members belong (p. 180)

majority party/partido mayoritario tanto en la Cámara de Representantes como en el Senado, el partido político al que pertenece más de la mitad de los miembros (pág. 180)

majority rule political principle providing that a majority of the members of a community has the power to make laws binding upon all the people (p. 25)

majority rule/principio mayoritario principio político que estipula que una mayoría de los miembros de una comunidad tiene el poder de crear leyes vinculantes para toda la gente (pág. 25)

malapportionment unequal representation in state legislatures (p. 359)

malapportionment/mala asignación representación desigual en las legislaturas estatales (pág. 359)

malice evil intent (p. 330)

malice/malicia propósito maligno (pág. 330)

mandatory sentencing punishment that judges must impose according to what the law directs (p. 454)

mandatory sentencing/sentencias obligatorias castigos que los jueces deben imponer de acuerdo a lo que dicta la ley (pág. 454)

mandatory spending federal spending required by law that continues without the need for annual approvals by Congress (p. 677)

mandatory spending/gastos obligatorios gastos federales requeridos por ley que tienen lugar sin la necesidad de aprobaciones anuales del Congreso (pág. 677)

manipulate* to handle with skill (p. 661)

manipulate/manipular* manejar hábilmente (pág. 661)

marginal benefit the additional or extra benefit associated with an action (p. 508)

marginal benefit/beneficio marginal el beneficio extra o adicional asociado con una acción (pág. 508)

marginal cost the additional or extra opportunity cost associated with an action (p. 507)

marginal cost/costo marginal el costo de oportunidad extra o adicional asociado con una acción (pág. 507)

marginal utility additional use that is derived from each unit acquired (p. 572)

market free and willing exchange of goods and services between buyers and sellers (p. 521)

market demand the total demand of all consumers for a product or service (p. 570)

market economy system in which individuals own the factors of production and make economic decisions through free interaction (p. 716)

market supply the total of the supply schedules of businesses that provide the same good or service (p. 584)

mass media a mechanism of mass communication, including television, radio, newspapers, magazines, recordings, movies, the Internet, and books (p. 320)

master plan a plan that states a set of goals and explains how the government will carry them out to meet changing needs over time (p. 399)

mechanism* the steps that compose a process or activity (p. 588)

media* a means of communication with large influence (p. 122)

mediation situation in which union and company officials bring in a third party to try to help them reach an agreement (p. 611)

Medicare government program that provides health care for the aged (p. 678)

medium* a means of doing (p. 657)

mercantilism the theory that a country should sell more goods to other countries than it buys (p. 51)

merger a combination of two or more companies to form a single business (p. 633)

merit system hiring people into government jobs on the basis of their qualifications (p. 230)

method* a procedure or process of doing something (p. 222)

metropolitan area a large city and its suburbs (p. 382)

marginal utility/utilidad marginal uso adicional que se obtiene de cada unidad adquirida (pág. 572)

market/mercado intercambio de bienes y servicios libre y voluntario entre compradores y vendedores (pág. 521)

market demand/demanda de mercado la demanda total de todos los consumidores para un producto o servicio (pág. 570)

market economy/economía de mercado sistema en el que las personas son propietarias de los factores de producción y toman decisiones económicas a través de una interacción libre (pág. 716)

market supply/oferta de mercado el total de los programas de oferta de los negocios que proporcionan el mismo bien o servicio (pág. 584)

mass media/medios masivos de información un mecanismo de comunicación masiva, que incluye televisión, radio, periódicos, revistas, grabaciones, películas, Internet y libros (pág. 320)

master plan/plan maestro un plan que especifica un conjunto de objetivos y explica la forma en que el gobierno los llevará a cabo para satisfacer las necesidades cambiantes con el tiempo (pág. 399)

mechanism/mecanismo* los pasos que componen un proceso o una actividad (pág. 588)

media/medios de comunicación* un medio de comunicación con gran influencia (pág. 122)

mediation/mediación situación en la que los jefes de compañías y sindicatos requieren a un tercero para que los ayude a llegar a un acuerdo (pág. 611)

Medicare/Medicare programa gubernamental que brinda atención médica a las personas mayores (pág. 678)

medium/medio* cosa que puede servir para un determinado fin (pág. 657)

mercantilism/mercantilismo la teoría de que un país debería vender más bienes a otros países de los que compra (pág. 51)

merger/fusión empresarial una combinación de dos o más compañías para formar un único negocio (pág. 633)

merit system/sistema de méritos la contratación de personas en empleos gubernamentales sobre la base de sus calificaciones (pág. 230)

method/método* un procedimiento o proceso para hacer algo (pág. 222)

metropolitan area/área metropolitana una gran ciudad y sus suburbios (pág. 382)

microeconomics the economic behavior and decision-making by individuals and small businesses (p. 500)

minimize* to make as small as possible (p. 634)

minimum wage lowest legal wage that can be paid to most U.S. workers (p. 589)

minority party in both the House of Representatives and the Senate, the political party to which fewer than half the members belong (p. 180)

misdemeanor a relatively minor offense such as vandalism or stealing inexpensive items (pp. 367, 432)

mixed economy system combining characteristics of more than one type of economy (p. 719)

monarch king or queen (p. 33)

monarchy a government with a hereditary, single leader (p. 24)

monetary policy policy that involves changing the rate of growth of the money supply in circulation in order to affect the cost and availability of credit (p. 664)

monitor* to watch or observe (p. 225)

monopoly when the market creates a sole provider for a good or service (p. 633)

motive* something that causes a person to act (p. 583)

multinational firm that does business or has offices in many countries (p. 742)

mutual* shared feelings (p. 741)

mutual funds pools of money from many people who are invested in a selection of individual stocks and bonds chosen by financial experts (p. 558)

microeconomics/microeconomía conducta económica y toma de decisiones realizada por individuos y pequeñas empresas (pág. 500)

minimize/minimizar* hacer lo más pequeño posible (pág. 634)

minimum wage/salario mínimo el más bajo sueldo legal que se le puede pagar a la mayoría de trabajadores en Estados Unidos (pág. 589)

minority party/partido minoritario tanto en la Cámara de Representantes como en el Senado, el partido político al que pertenece menos de la mitad de los miembros (pág. 180)

misdemeanor/delito menor una falta relativamente menor como vandalismo o el robo de artículos sin valor (págs. 367, 432)

mixed economy/economía mixta sistema que combina características de más de un tipo de economía (pág. 719)

monarch/monarca rey o reina (pág. 33)

monarchy/monarquía gobierno con un único líder hereditario (pág. 24)

monetary policy/política monetaria política que implica el cambio de la tasa de crecimiento de la oferta monetaria en circulación a fin de afectar el costo y la disponibilidad del crédito (pág. 664)

monitor/monitorear* mirar u observar (pág. 225)

monopoly/monopolio situación en la que el mercado crea un solo proveedor para un bien o servicio (pág. 633)

motive/motivo* algo que hace que una persona actúe (pág. 583)

multinational/multinacional empresa que hace negocios o posee oficinas en varios países (pág. 742)

mutual/mutuo* sentimientos compartidos (pág. 741)

mutual funds/fondos mutuos montos de dinero proveniente de muchos individuos que se invierten en una variedad de acciones y bonos individuales seleccionados por expertos financieros. (pág. 558)

N

national committee representatives from the 50 state party organizations who run a political party (p. 279)

national security the ability to keep the country safe from attack or harm (p. 220)

natural monopoly a market situation in which the costs of production are minimized by having a single firm produce the product (p. 634)

national committee/comité nacional representantes de las organizaciones de partidos de los 50 estados que dirigen un partido político (pág. 279)

national security/seguridad nacional la habilidad de mantener al país seguro frente a ataques o daños (pág. 220)

natural monopoly/monopolio natural una situación de mercado en la que los costos de producción se ven minimizados al haber una única empresa que produce el bien (pág. 634)

natural resources gifts of nature that make production possible (p. 517)

natural resources/recursos naturales regalos de la naturaleza que posibilitan la producción (pág. 517)

natural rights freedoms people possess relating to life, liberty, and property (p. 34)

natural rights/derechos naturales libertades que las personas poseen relativas a la vida, a la libertad y a la propiedad (pág. 34)

naturalization a legal process to obtain citizenship (p. 15)

naturalization/naturalización proceso legal para obtener la ciudadanía (pág. 15)

need requirement for survival, such as food, clothing, and shelter (p. 499)

need/necesidad requisito para la supervivencia, como alimentos, vestimenta y alojamiento (pág. 499)

network* a group of broadcasting stations; a system of connected or related parts (p. 471)

network/red* un grupo de estaciones de radiodifusión; un sistema de partes conectadas o relacionadas (pág. 471)

nevertheless* even so (p. 723)

nevertheless/sin embargo* no obstante, a pesar de ello (pág. 723)

newsgroup Internet discussion forum (p. 472)

newsgroup/grupo de noticias foro de conversación en Internet (pág. 472)

nonetheless* nevertheless, however (p. 482)

nonetheless/sin embargo* no obstante, a pesar de ello (pág. 482)

nonpartisan free from party ties or bias (p. 471)

nonpartisan/no partidario libre de vínculos partidarios o parcialidad (pág. 471)

O

obtain* to gain or acquire (p. 17)

obtain/obtener* ganar o adquirir (pág. 17)

obvious* easily found, seen, or understood (p. 657)

obvious/obvio* fácil de encontrar, ver o entender (pág. 657)

occur* to happen or take place (p. 178)

occur/ocurrir* suceder o tener lugar (pág. 178)

odd* additional to what is usual (p. 301)

odd/impar* adicional a lo que es usual (pág. 301)

open market operations purchase or sale of U.S. government bonds and Treasury bills (p. 665)

open market operations/operaciones de mercado libre compra o venta de letras del Tesoro y bonos del gobierno de los EE. UU. (pág. 665)

open primary an election in which voters need not declare their party preference (p. 283)

open primary/elección primaria abierta una elección en la que los votantes no deben declarar su partido de preferencia (pág. 283)

opinion a detailed explanation of the legal thinking behind a court's decision in a case (p. 245)

opinion/opinión una explicación detallada del pensamiento legal detrás de la decisión de un tribunal en un caso (pág. 245)

opportunity cost the cost of the next best use of time and money when choosing to do one thing or another (p. 505)

opportunity cost/costo de oportunidad el costo del próximo mejor uso de tiempo y dinero cuando se elige hacer una cosa u otra (pág. 505)

option* an alternative or choice (p. 611)

option/opción* una alternativa (pág. 611)

ordinance a law, usually of a city or county (p. 378)

ordinance/ordenanza una ley, normalmente de una ciudad o un condado (pág. 378)

original jurisdiction the authority to hear cases for the first time (p. 244)

original jurisdiction/jurisdicción original la autoridad para ver casos por primera vez (pág. 244)

outcome* the result of an action or event (p. 210)

outcome/resultado* las consecuencias de una acción o un evento (pág. 210)

output* something produced (p. 517)

output/producto* algo producido (pág. 517)

P

pardon a declaration of forgiveness and freedom from punishment (p. 217)

parole to grant a prisoner an early release from prison, with certain restrictions (p. 454)

partnership a business owned by two or more people (p. 602)

penal code a state's written criminal laws (p. 453)

per capita GDP Gross Domestic Product per person (p. 716)

percent* a portion of 100 (p. 158)

period* a length of time (p. 638)

petition a formal request for government action (p. 123); or, a process by which candidates who are not affiliated with one of the two major parties can get on the ballot for the general election in most states (p. 284)

phenomenon* a rare or important fact or event (p. 577)

philosophy* a system of beliefs or principles about practical affairs (p. 250)

Pilgrim colonial Puritans who considered themselves people on a religious journey (p. 41)

plaintiff a person or party filing a lawsuit (pp. 368, 431)

plank each individual part of a political party's platform (p. 277)

planning commission an advisory group to a community (p. 398)

plantation a large estate (p. 43)

platform a series of statements expressing the party's principles, beliefs, and positions on election issues (p. 277)

plea bargain negotiation between the defense attorney and the prosecutor (p. 440)

plurality the most votes among all those running for a political office (p. 284)

pocket veto president's power to kill a bill, if Congress is not in session, by not signing it for 10 days (p. 202)

pardon/indulto una declaración de perdón y liberación de una pena (pág. 217)

parole/libertad condicional otorgar a un prisionero una liberación anticipada de la prisión, con ciertas restricciones (pág. 454)

partnership/asociación un negocio que es propiedad de una o más personas (pág. 602)

penal code/código penal leyes penales escritas de un estado (pág. 453)

per capita GDP/PIB per cápita producto interno bruto por persona (pág. 716)

percent/porcentaje* una porción de 100 (pág. 158)

period/período* un tiempo determinado (pág. 638)

petition/petición una solicitud formal de acción gubernamental (pág. 123); o, un proceso mediante el cual candidatos no que están afiliados a uno de los dos partidos principales pueden ingresar a la boleta electoral para la elección general en la mayoría de los estados (pág. 284)

phenomenon/fenómeno* un hecho o evento raro o importante (pág. 577)

philosophy/filosofía* un sistema de creencias o principios sobre cuestiones prácticas (pág. 250)

Pilgrim/Peregrino puritanos coloniales que se consideraban individuos en un viaje religioso (pág. 41)

plaintiff/demandante una persona o un partido que presenta una demanda (págs. 368, 431)

plank/punto cada parte individual de la plataforma de un partido político (pág. 277)

planning commission/comisión de planificación grupo asesor de una comunidad (pág. 398)

plantation/plantación propiedad extensa (pág. 43)

platform/plataforma una serie de declaraciones que expresan los principios, las creencias y las posiciones del partido político sobre los temas de la elección (pág. 277)

plea bargain/acuerdo de reducción de sentencia negociación entre el abogado defensor y el fiscal (pág. 440)

plurality/pluralidad la mayor cantidad de votos entre aquellas personas que se postulan a un cargo político (pág. 284)

pocket veto/veto indirecto el poder del presidente de acabar con un proyecto de ley, si el Congreso no está en sesión, al no firmarlo durante 10 días (pág. 202)

policy* a guiding course of action (pp. 217, 397, 745)

political action committee (PAC) political organization established by a corporation, labor union, or other special-interest group designed to support candidates by contributing money (pp. 308, 334)

political appointee a person appointed to a federal position by the president (p. 229)

political machine a strong party organization that can control political appointments and deliver votes (p. 282)

political party an association of voters with broad common interests who want to influence or control decision making in government by electing the party's candidates to public office (p. 273)

poll tax a sum of money required of voters before they are permitted to cast a ballot (p. 137)

polling place the location where voting is carried out (p. 295)

pollster a specialist whose job is to conduct polls regularly (p. 323)

popular sovereignty the notion that power lies with the people (pp. 12, 86)

pork-barrel project government project grant that primarily benefits the home district or state (p. 196)

portion* a share or part of a whole (p. 367)

potential* capable of being or becoming (p. 427)

Preamble the opening section of the Constitution (p. 80)

precedent a ruling that is used as the basis for a judicial decision in a later, similar case (pp. 34, 245, 429)

precinct a geographic area that contains a specific number of voters (pp. 281, 295)

precise* to be exact (p. 688)

preliminary* coming before the main part or item (p. 463)

presume* to assume or suppose to be true (p. 438)

previous* coming before or prior (p. 504)

price ceiling maximum price that can be charged for goods and services, set by the government (p. 589)

policy/política* un curso de acción guía (págs. 217, 397, 745)

political action committee (PAC)/comité de acción política organización política establecida por una corporación, un sindicato u otro grupo de interés especial diseñada para apoyar a los candidatos al contribuir con dinero (págs. 308, 334)

political appointee/político asignado una persona asignada a un cargo federal por parte del presidente (pág. 229)

political machine/maquinaria política una fuerte organización partidaria que puede controlar los nombramientos políticos y dar votos (pág. 282)

political party/partido político una asociación de votantes con numerosos intereses comunes que desean influir en o controlar la toma de decisiones en el gobierno al elegir a los candidatos del partido para un cargo público (pág. 273)

poll tax/impuesto de contribución una suma de dinero que deben pagar los votantes antes de que se les permita emitir un voto (pág. 137)

polling place/lugar de votación la ubicación en la que se lleva a cabo la votación (pág. 295)

pollster/encuestador un especialista cuyo trabajo es realizar encuestas con regularidad (pág. 323)

popular sovereignty/soberanía popular la noción de que el poder lo tiene el pueblo (págs. 12, 86)

pork-barrel projects/*proyectos pork-barrel* proyectos y subsidios del gobierno que benefician principalmente al estado o distrito local (pág. 196)

portion/porción* una parte de un todo (pág. 367)

potential/potencial* capaz de ser o convertirse en (pág. 427)

Preamble/Preámbulo la sección de apertura de la Constitución (pág. 80)

precedent/precedente un fallo que se utiliza como base para una decisión judicial de un caso similar posterior (págs. 34, 245, 429)

precinct/precinto un área geográfica que contiene un número específico de votantes (págs. 281, 295)

precise* que es exacto (pág. 688)

preliminary/preliminar* que viene antes de la parte o el artículo principal (pág. 463)

presume/presumir* asumir o suponer que es verdadero (pág. 438)

previous/previo* que viene antes (pág. 504)

price ceiling/precio máximo precio máximo que se puede cobrar por bienes y servicios, establecido por el gobierno (pág. 589)

price floor minimum price that can be charged for goods and services, set by the government (p. 589)

primary* first in time or importance (p. 334)

principal* the most important (p. 667)

principle* a rule of conduct or belief (p. 11)

print media newspapers, magazines, newsletters, and books (p. 327)

prior restraint government censorship of material before it is published (p. 329)

priority* the goals a community considers most important or most urgent (pp. 18, 399)

private good good that, when consumed by one individual, cannot be consumed by another (p. 631)

private property rights the freedom to own and use our own property as we choose as long as we do not interfere with the rights of others (p. 529)

process* an action or a series of actions directed toward a result (p. 72)

product market a market where producers offer goods and services for sale (p. 522)

productivity the degree to which resources are being used efficiently to produce goods and services (pp. 524, 585)

professional* engaging or working in a profession (p. 398)

profit the money a business receives for its products or services over and above its costs (pp. 530, 583)

profit motive the driving force that encourages individuals and organizations to improve their material well-being (p. 530)

progressive income tax a tax that takes a larger percentage of higher incomes than lower incomes (p. 649)

prohibition* an order forbidding something (p. 431)

promote* to encourage the acceptance or recognition of (pp. 274, 740)

price floor/precio mínimo precio mínimo que se puede cobrar por bienes y servicios, establecido por el gobierno (pág. 589)

primary/primario, primero* primero en tiempo o en importancia (pág. 334)

principal/principal* el más importante (pág. 667)

principle/principio* una regla de conducta o creencia (pág. 11)

print media/medios de comunicación impresos periódicos, revistas, boletines informativos y libros (pág. 327)

prior restraint/restricción anterior censura gubernamental de material antes de que se publique (pág. 329)

priority/prioridad* algo a lo que se le da más atención o importancia (págs. 18, 399)

private goods/bienes privados bienes que, cuando los consume una persona, no pueden ser consumidos por otra (pág. 631)

private property rights/derechos de propiedad privada la libertad de ser propietario y usar nuestra propiedad como queramos siempre que no interfiramos con los derechos de otros (pág. 529)

process/proceso* una acción o una serie de acciones con el fin de obtener un resultado (pág. 72)

product market/mercado de productos un mercado en el que los productores ofrecen bienes y servicios para la venta (pág. 522)

productivity/productividad el grado al que se utilizan los recursos de manera eficaz para producir bienes y servicios (págs. 524, 585)

professional/profesional* que participa o trabaja en una profesión (pág. 398)

profit/ganancia el dinero que recibe un negocio por sus productos o servicios y que supera sus costos (págs. 530, 583)

profit motive/motivo lucrativo el impulso que incentiva a las personas y las organizaciones a mejorar su bienestar material (pág. 530)

progressive income tax/impuesto progresivo sobre la renta un impuesto que toma un porcentaje mayor de ingresos superiores que de ingresos inferiores (pág. 649)

prohibition/prohibición* una orden que no permite algo (pág. 431)

promote/promover* incentivar la aceptación o el reconocimiento de (págs. 274, 740)

propaganda certain ideas that may involve misleading messages designed to manipulate people (pp. 307, 476)

property tax tax on land and property (p. 682)

proportion* the size or amount of something in relation to something else or to a whole (p. 129)

proposition a petition asking for a new law (p. 301)

proprietary colony area with owner-controlled land and government (p. 39)

prosecution party who starts the legal proceedings against another party for a violation of the law (p. 453)

protectionism policy of trade restrictions to protect domestic industries (p. 735)

public agenda issues considered most significant by government officials (p. 327)

public goods economic goods that are consumed collectively, such as highways and national defense (p. 631)

public interest group an organization that supports causes that affect the lives of Americans in general (p. 334)

public opinion the ideas and attitudes that most people hold about elected officials, candidates, government, and political issues (p. 319)

public opinion poll a survey in which individuals are asked to answer questions about a particular issue or person (p. 323)

public policy the course of action the government takes in response to an issue or problem (pp. 22, 397)

purchase* to buy or pay for (p. 588)

Puritan religious dissenter who came to the colonies to purify, or reform, the Anglican Church (p. 41)

propaganda/propaganda ciertas ideas que pueden incluir mensajes falsos o erróneos diseñados para manipular a la gente (págs. 307, 476)

property tax/impuesto a la propiedad impuesto sobre la tierra y la propiedad (pág. 682)

proportion/proporción* el tamaño o la cantidad de algo en relación con otra cosa o con un todo (pág. 129)

proposition/proposición una petición que solicita una nueva ley (pág. 301)

proprietary colony/colonia propietaria zona con la tierra y el gobierno controlados por un propietario (pág. 39)

prosecution/fiscalía parte que inicia los procedimientos legales contra otra parte por una violación a las leyes (pág. 453)

protectionism/proteccionismo política de restricciones comerciales para proteger a las industrias nacionales (pág. 735)

public agenda/agenda pública cuestiones consideradas más importantes por los funcionarios de gobierno (pág. 327)

public goods/bienes públicos bienes económicos que se consumen colectivamente, como las carreteras y la defensa nacional (pág. 631)

public interest group/grupo de interés público una organización que apoya causas que afectan las vidas de los estadounidenses en general (pág. 334)

public opinion/opinión pública las ideas y actitudes que tiene la mayoría de la gente sobre los funcionarios electos, los candidatos, el gobierno y los asuntos políticos (pág. 319)

public opinion poll/encuesta de opinión pública una encuesta en la que se pide a las personas que respondan preguntas sobre un asunto o una persona en particular (pág. 323)

public policy/política pública el curso de acción que toma el gobierno en respuesta a un asunto o problema (págs. 22, 397)

purchase/comprar* adquirir o pagar por (pág. 588)

Puritan/puritano disidente religioso que llegó hasta las colonias para purificar, o reformar, la Iglesia Anglicana (pág. 41)

Q

quota a limit on the amount of foreign goods imported into a country (p. 708)

quota/cupo un límite en la cantidad de bienes extranjeros importados a un país (pág. 708)

R

racial profiling singling out an individual as a suspect due to appearance of ethnicity (p. 143)

range* a variation between limits (p. 279)

ratify to vote approval of (p. 68)

ratio* the relationship between two or more things (p. 404)

rational* showing reason (p. 499)

real GDP GDP after adjustments for inflation (p. 638)

recall a special election in which citizens can vote to remove a public official from office (p. 301); situation in which a company pulls a product off the market or agrees to change it to make it safe (p. 635)

recover* to regain or reclaim (p. 433)

recycle reusing old materials to make new ones (p. 410)

referendum a way for citizens to vote on state or local laws (p. 301)

refugee a person who has unwillingly left his or her home to escape war, famine, or other disaster (p. 738)

register* to record or enroll (p. 160)

regulate* to control or govern (p. 185)

regulatory* used to describe an agency or body whose function is to control or govern (p. 330)

rehabilitate to correct a person's behavior (p. 462)

reject* to refuse or throw away (p. 539)

religious dissenter those who followed a religious faith other than the official religion of England (p. 41)

reluctant* having doubt or unwillingness (p. 379)

remand to send a case back to a lower court to be tried again (p. 245)

repeal to cancel a law (p. 52)

representative democracy a government in which citizens choose a smaller group to govern on their behalf (p. 24)

racial profiling/prácticas discriminatorias raciales señalar a una persona como sospechosa debido al origen étnico (pág. 143)

range/rango* una variación entre límites (pág. 279)

ratify/ratificar votar la aprobación de algo (pág. 68)

ratio/relación* el vínculo entre dos o más cosas (pág. 404)

rational/racional* que muestra razón (pág. 499)

real GDP/PIB real PIB luego de ajustes por inflación (pág. 638)

recall/revocación una elección especial en la que los ciudadanos pueden votar para quitar a un funcionario público de un cargo (pág. 301); **recall/retirada** situación en la que una compañía retira un producto del mercado o acepta cambiarlo para hacerlo seguro (pág. 635)

recover/recuperar* volver a obtener (pág. 433)

recycle/reciclar volver a usar de materiales viejos para hacer nuevos (pág. 410)

referendum/referéndum una forma en que los ciudadanos pueden votar sobre las leyes estatales o locales (pág. 301)

refugee/refugiando persona que ha dejado su hogar de buena voluntad para escaparse de la guerra , la hambre, o de otra desasrte (pág. 738)

register/registrar* anotar o inscribir (pág. 160)

regulate/regular* controlar o determinar (pág. 185)

regulatory/regulatorio* se usa para describir a una agencia o un organismo cuya función es controlar o determinar (pág. 330)

rehabilitate/rehabilitar corregir el comportamiento de una persona (pág. 462)

reject/rechazar* no aceptar o desechar (pág. 539)

religious dissenter/disidente religioso persona que seguía una fe religiosa distinta a la religión oficial de Inglaterra (pág. 41)

reluctant/reacio* que tiene duda o no está dispuesto (pág. 379)

remand/remitir enviar un caso a un tribunal inferior para ser juzgado nuevamente (pág. 245)

repeal/revocar cancelar una ley (pág. 52)

representative democracy/democracia representativa un gobierno en que los ciudadanos escogen un grupo pequeño para gobernar en su representación (pág. 24)

reprieve an order to delay a person's punishment until a higher court can hear the case (p. 217)

reprieve/aplazamiento una orden para retrasar la pena de una persona hasta que un tribunal superior pueda ver el caso (pág. 217)

republic a representative democracy where citizens choose their lawmakers (p. 24)

republic/república democracia representativa en la que los ciudadanos eligen a sus legisladores (pág. 24)

require* to have a need for or to order (p. 215)

require/requerir* tener una necesidad u ordenar (pág. 215)

reserve a certain percentage of deposits that banks have to set aside as cash in their own vaults or as deposits in their Federal Reserve district bank (p. 665)

reserve/reserva cierto porcentaje de los depósitos que los bancos deben separar como dinero en efectivo en sus propias bóvedas o como depósitos en su banco de distrito de la Reserva Federal (pág. 665)

reserved powers powers that the Constitution does not give to the national government that are kept by the states (pp. 89, 352)

reserved powers/poderes reservados poderes que la Constitución no otorga al gobierno nacional y que mantienen los estados (págs. 89, 352)

resolve* to find a solution or reach a decision (p. 427)

resolve/resolver* encontrar una solución o llegar a una decisión (pág. 427)

resource* the money, people, and materials available to accomplish a community's goals (pp. 399, 501, 684)

resource/recurso* el dinero, las personas y los materiales disponibles para alcanzar las metas de una comunidad (págs. 399, 501, 684)

respond* to answer or react (p. 450)

respond/responder* contestar o reaccionar (pág. 450)

responsibility an obligation that we fulfill voluntarily (p. 151)

responsibility/responsabilidad una obligación que cumplimos voluntariamente (pág. 151)

restore* to bring back into existence or put back in an original condition (p. 54)

restore/restaurar* volver a dar vida o colocar en una condición original (pág. 54)

restrict* to place limits on or keep within bounds (p. 585)

restrict/restringir* colocar límites en o mantener entre límites (pág. 585)

retain* to keep or to hold secure (p. 450)

retain/retener* conservar o mantener seguro (pág. 450)

return profit earned through investing (p. 557)

return/rendimiento ganancia que se obtiene mediante la inversión (pág. 557)

returns ballots and results of an election (p. 297)

returns/resultados boletas electorales y consecuencias de una elección (pág. 297)

reveal* to make known or show plainly (p. 617)

reveal/revelar* dar a conocer o mostrar directamente (pág. 617)

revenue* the income that a government collects for public use (pp. 485, 682)

revenue/ingreso* la renta que un gobierno recauda para uso público (págs. 485, 682)

revise* to correct or improve (p. 359)

revise/revisar* corregir o mejorar (pág. 359)

right-to-work laws state laws forbidding unions from forcing workers to join (p. 610)

right-to-work laws/leyes de derecho a trabajar leyes estatales que prohíben a los sindicatos obligar a los trabajadores a unirse (pág. 610)

robbery the taking of property from a person's possession by using force or threats (p. 432)

robbery/robo toma de una propiedad de las posesiones de una persona mediante el uso de fuerza o amenazas (pág. 432)

role* the function of a person or thing (pp. 225, 401)

role/papel* la función de una persona o cosa (págs. 225, 401)

roll-call vote a voting method in the Senate in which members voice their votes in turn (p. 202)

roll-call vote/votación por nómina un método de votación en el Senado en el que cada uno de los miembros expresa su voto (pág. 202)

royal colony a colonial area of land controlled directly by a king or other monarch (p. 39)

rule of law principle that the law applies to everyone, even those who govern (p. 87)

royal colony/colonia real zona de tierra colonial controlada directamente por un rey u otro monarca (pág. 39)

rule of law/reglamento de ley principio de que la ley se aplica a todos, incluso a aquéllos que gobiernan (pág. 87)

S

sales tax tax levied on a product at the time of sale (p. 682)

sanction measure such as withholding economic aid used to influence a foreign government's actions (p. 746)

satellite nation politically and economically dominated or controlled by another, more powerful country (p. 747)

save to set aside income for a period of time so that it can be used later (p. 553)

savings account an account in which customers receive interest based on how much money they have deposited (p. 667)

savings and loan association (S&L) financial institutions that traditionally loaned money to people buying homes (p. 658)

scarcity not having enough resources to produce all of the things we would like to have (p. 501)

search warrant a court order allowing law enforcement officers to search a suspect's home or business and take specific items as evidence (pp. 127, 438)

section* an area or division (p. 140)

sector* a segment or distinct part (p. 521)

segregation the social separation of the races (p. 140)

seniority years of service, which is used as a consideration for assigning committee members (p. 182)

separation of powers the split of authority among the legislative, executive, and judicial branches (p. 88)

service work performed by a person for someone else (p. 517)

service economy where the majority of people earn their living by providing a service rather than manufacturing a product (p. 10)

sales tax/impuesto a las ventas impuesto aplicado a un producto en el momento de la venta (pág. 682)

sanction/sanción medida como la negación de ayuda económica para influir en las acciones de un gobierno extranjero (pág. 746)

satellite/satélite nación dominada o controlada política y económicamente por otro país más poderoso (pág. 747)

save/ahorro separar y acumular ingresos durante un tiempo para poder usarlos luego (pág. 553)

savings account/cuenta de ahorros una cuenta en la que los clientes reciben intereses según la cantidad de dinero que tienen depositado (pág. 667)

savings and loan association (S&L)/asociación de ahorros y préstamos instituciones financieras que tradicionalmente prestaban dinero a personas que compraban viviendas (pág. 658)

scarcity/escasez no tener suficientes recursos para producir todo lo que quisiéramos tener (pág. 501)

search warrant/orden de allanamiento una orden judicial que permite a los agentes de policía revisar la vivienda o el negocio de un sospechoso y tomar ciertos artículos como evidencia (págs. 127, 438)

section/sección* un área o una división (pág. 140)

sector/sector* un segmento o parte diferenciada (pág. 521)

segregation/segregación la separación social de las razas (pág. 140)

seniority/antigüedad años de servicio, que se utilizan como consideración para la designación de miembros del comité (pág. 182)

separation of powers/separación de poderes la división de la autoridad entre los poderes, legislativo, ejecutivo y judicial (pág. 88)

service/servicio trabajo realizado por una persona para otra (pág. 517)

service economy/economía de servicio en la que la mayoría de las personas se ganan la vida al proporcionar un servicio en lugar de fabricar un producto (pág. 10)

settlement in a legal case, the amount of money the defendant agrees to pay the plaintiff (p. 450)

settlement/acuerdo en un caso legal, monto de dinero que el acusado acuerda pagar al demandante (pág. 450)

shortage situation in which quantity demanded is greater than quantity supplied (p. 589)

shortage/déficit situación en la que la cantidad demandada es mayor que la cantidad ofertada (pág. 589)

short-term plan a government policy being carried out over the next few years (p. 398)

short-term plan/plan a corto plazo política del gobierno que se lleva a cabo durante los próximos siguientes años (pág. 398)

similar* having qualities in common or resembling (p. 389)

similar/similar* que tienen cualidades en común o se parecen (pág. 389)

slander spoken untruths that are harmful to someone's reputation (p. 124)

slander/calumnia falsedades escritas que son perjudiciales para la reputación de alguien (pág. 124)

social contract an agreement among people in a society with a government (p. 35)

social contract/contrato social acuerdo entre las personas en una sociedad con el gobierno (pág. 35)

social responsibility the obligation a business has to pursue goals that benefit society as well as themselves (p. 618)

social responsibility/responsabilidad social la obligación que tiene un negocio de buscar metas que beneficien a la sociedad así como a él mismo (pág. 618)

Social Security federal program that provides monthly payments to people who are retired or unable to work (p. 678)

Social Security/Seguro Social programa federal que proporciona pagos mensuales a la gente jubilada o que no puede trabajar (pág. 678)

socialism economic system in which government owns some factors of production and distributes the products and wages (p. 717)

socialism/socialismo sistema económico en el que el gobierno es propietario de algunos factores de producción y distribuye los productos y los salarios (pág. 717)

soft money donations given to political parties and not designated for a particular candidate's election campaign (p. 308)

soft money/*soft money* donaciones otorgadas a los partidos políticos y no designadas para la campaña electoral de un candidato particular (pág. 308)

sole* being the only one (p. 601)

sole/único* ser exclusivo (pág. 601)

sole proprietorship a business owned and operated by a single person (p. 601)

sole proprietorship/propietario único un negocio que es propiedad de una sola persona y es manejado por ésta (pág. 601)

solid waste the technical name for garbage (p. 409)

solid waste/desecho sólido el nombre técnico para basura (pág. 409)

special district a unit of government that deals with a specific function, such as education, water supply, or transportation (p. 382)

special district/distrito especial una unidad de gobierno que trata con una función específica, como educación, suministro de agua o transporte (pág. 382)

special-interest group an organization of people with some common interest who try to influence government decisions (p. 199)

special-interest group/grupo de interés especial una organización de personas con algún interés común que intentan influir en las decisiones del gobierno (pág. 199)

specialization when people, businesses, regions, and/or nations concentrate on goods and services that they can produce better than anyone else (p. 524)

specialization/especialización cuando las personas, los negocios, las regiones o las naciones se concentran en los bienes y servicios que pueden producir mejor que cualquier otro (pág. 524)

specific* clearly specified, precise, or explicit (p. 399)

specific/específico* especificado claramente, preciso o explícito (pág. 399)

specify* to mention exactly or clearly (p. 137)

specify/especificar* mencionar con exactitud o claridad (pág. 137)

spoils system rewarding people with government jobs on the basis of their political support (p. 230)

spoils system/sistema de despojo recompensar a la gente con empleos gubernamentales sobre la base de su apoyo político (pág. 230)

standard of living the material well-being of an individual, group, or nation measured by how well their necessities and luxuries are satisfied (p. 518)

standard of living/estándar de vida el bienestar material de una persona, un grupo o una nación medido según la eficacia con la que satisfacen sus necesidades y lujos (pág. 518)

standing committee permanent committee that continues its work from session to session in Congress (p. 181)

standing committee/comité permanente aquéllos que continúan su trabajo de sesión en sesión en el Congreso (pág. 181)

standing vote in Congress, when members stand to be counted for a vote on a bill (p. 202)

standing vote/voto de pie en el Congreso, cuando los miembros se paran y se los cuenta para votar por una ley (pág. 202)

stare decisis the practice of using earlier judicial rulings as a basis for deciding cases (pp. 257, 436)

stare decisis/*stare decisis* la práctica de usar fallos judiciales anteriores como base para decidir casos (págs. 257, 436)

status* a position or rank (p. 547)

status/estatus* una posición o un rango (pág. 547)

statute a law written by a legislative branch (p. 429)

statute/estatuto una ley escrita por un poder legislativo (pág. 429)

stock ownership share of a corporation (pp. 557, 604)

stock/acciones participación en la propiedad de una corporación (págs. 557, 604)

stockholder an individual who has invested in a corporation and owns some of its stock (p. 604)

stockholder/accionista una persona que ha invertido en una corporación y es propietaria de parte de sus acciones (pág. 604)

stress* to place special importance or emphasis on something (p. 273)

stress/hincapié* dar especial importancia o poner énfasis en algo (pág. 273)

strike when workers deliberately stop working in order to force an employer to give in to their demands (p. 612)

strike/huelga cuando los trabajadores dejan de trabajar deliberadamente para obligar a su empleador a satisfacer sus demandas (pág. 612)

strong-mayor system a type of government, usually in large cities, under which the mayor has strong executive powers (p. 379)

strong-mayor system/sistema de alcalde fuerte un tipo de gobierno, normalmente en grandes ciudades, en el que el acalde posee poderes ejecutivos contundentes (pág. 379)

submit* to present for review or decision (p. 246)

submit/presentar* enviar para revisión o decisión (pág. 246)

subsidize to aid or promote with money (p. 684)

subsidize/subvencionar ayudar o promover con dinero (pág. 684)

subsidy a government payment to an individual, business, or group in exchange for certain actions (p. 585)

subsidy/subvención un pago del gobierno a una persona, un negocio o un grupo a cambio de ciertas acciones (pág. 585)

substitute a competing product that consumers can use in place of another (p. 575)

substitute/sustituto un producto de la competencia que los consumidores pueden usar en lugar de otro (pág. 575)

suburb community that is near or surrounds a larger city (p. 382)

suburb/suburbio comunidad que se encuentra cerca de una ciudad más grande o la rodea (pág. 382)

sufficient* to be adequate for a purpose (p. 456)

sufficient/suficiente* ser adecuado para un propósito (pág. 456)

suffrage the right to vote (p. 135)

suffrage/sufragio el derecho al voto (pág. 135)

summons a notice directing someone to appear in court to answer a complaint or a charge (p. 450)

summons/requerimiento judicial un aviso que indica a una persona que debe comparecer ante un tribunal para dar respuesta a una queja o a un cargo (pág. 450)

supplement* something that supplies what is needed or makes an addition (p. 649)

supplement/suplemento* algo que suministra lo que se necesita o que se añade a otra cosa (pág. 649)

supply the amount of goods and services that producers are able and willing to sell at various prices during a specified time period (p. 581)

supply/oferta la cantidad de bienes y servicios que los productores son capaces y están dispuestos a vender a diferentes precios durante un tiempo específico (pág. 581)

supply curve upward-sloping line that graphically shows the quantities supplied at each possible price (p. 583)

supply curve/curva de oferta línea en aumento que muestra gráficamente las cantidades ofertadas a cada precio posible (pág. 583)

supply elasticity responsiveness of quantity supplied to a change in price (p. 586)

supply elasticity/elasticidad de oferta respuesta de la cantidad ofertada a un cambio en el precio (pág. 586)

supply schedule table showing quantities supplied at different possible prices (p. 581)

supply schedule/tabla de oferta tabla que muestra las cantidades ofertadas a los diferentes precios posibles (pág. 581)

surplus situation in which quantity supplied is greater than quantity demanded; situation in which government spends less than it collects in revenues (pp. 588, 688)

surplus/excedente situación en la que la cantidad ofertada es mayor que la cantidad demandada; situación en la que el gobierno gasta menos de lo que recauda en ingresos (págs. 588, 688)

survey* to gather information about, as in a poll (p. 323)

survey/sondear* reunir información sobre, como en una encuesta (pág. 323)

survive* to continue to exist (p. 648)

survive/sobrevivir* continuar existiendo (pág. 648)

T

target* a goal or aim (p. 223)

target/objetivo* una meta o un propósito (pág. 223)

tariff a customs duty; a tax on an imported good (p. 708)

tariff/tarifa un derecho aduanero; un impuesto sobre un producto importado (pág. 708)

technique* procedure or method by which something is done (p. 611)

technique/técnica* procedimiento o método mediante lo que se hace algo (pág. 611)

technology the methods or processes used to make goods and services (p. 585)

technology/tecnología los métodos o procesos usados para producir bienes y servicios (pág. 585)

testimony the statement a witness makes under oath (p. 457)

testimony/testimonio la declaración que hace un testigo bajo juramento (pág. 457)

third party a party that challenges the two major parties (p. 274)

third party/tercer partido un partido que desafía a los dos partidos principales (pág. 274)

Three-fifths Compromise agreement providing that enslaved persons would count as three-fifths of other persons in determining representation in Congress (p. 75)

Three-fifths Compromise/Compromiso de Tres Quintos acuerdo que estipulaba que los esclavos se contarían como tres quintos de otras personas para determinar la representación en el Congreso (pág. 75)

Tidewater areas of low, flat plains near the seacoast of Virginia and North Carolina (p. 46)

Tidewater/región de aguas de marea zonas de planicies llanas y bajas cerca de la costa marina de Virginia y Carolina del Norte (pág. 46)

tolerance respecting and accepting others, regardless of their beliefs, practices, or differences (p. 154)

toleration acceptance of other groups, such as religious groups (p. 41)

torts wrongful acts for which an injured party has the right to sue (p. 433)

totalitarian a system in which government control extends to almost all aspects of people's lives (p. 26)

town political unit that is larger than a village and smaller than a city (p. 388)

town meeting a gathering of local citizens to discuss and vote on important issues (p. 388)

township a subdivision of a county that has its own government (p. 389)

toxic poisonous or deadly (p. 409)

trade deficit situation in which the value of the products imported by a country exceeds the value of its exports (p. 713)

trade sanction an effort to punish another nation by imposing trade barriers (p. 223)

trade surplus situation in which the value of the products exported by a country exceeds the value of its imports (p. 712)

trade-off the alternative you face if you decide to do one thing rather than another (p. 504)

tradition* a way of thinking or acting that is long established (p. 427)

traditional economy an economic system in which the decisions of what, how, and for whom to produce are based on custom or habit (p. 724)

transparency process of making business deals more visible to everyone (p. 617)

treaty a formal agreement between the governments of two or more countries (p. 222)

triangular trade pattern of trade that developed in colonial times among the Americas, Africa, and Europe (p. 43)

tribunal courts established by the UN to hear cases of violations of international human rights laws (p. 745)

tolerance/tolerancia el respeto y la aceptación de los demás, independientemente de sus creencias, prácticas o diferencias (pág. 154)

toleration/tolerancia aceptación de otros grupos, como los grupos religiosos (pág. 41)

torts/agravios actos ilegales por los que la parte perjudicada tiene derecho a demandar (pág. 433)

totalitarian/totalitario un sistema en el que el control del gobierno se extiende a casi todos los aspectos de las vidas de la gente (pág. 26)

town/pueblo unidad política que es más grande que una aldea y más pequeña que una ciudad (pág. 388)

town meeting/reunión municipal asamblea de ciudadanos locales para debatir y votar sobre cuestiones importantes (pág. 388)

township/municipio una subdivisión de un condado que tiene su propio gobierno (pág. 389)

toxic/tóxico pernicioso o mortal (pág. 409)

trade deficit/déficit comercial situación en la que el valor de los productos importados por un país supera el valor de sus exportaciones (pág. 713)

trade sanction/sanción comercial una acción para castigar a otra nación al imponer barreras comerciales (pág. 223)

trade surplus/excedente comercial situación en la que el valor de los productos exportados por un país supera el valor de sus importaciones (pág. 712)

trade-off/*trade-off* la alternativa que uno enfrenta si decide hacer una cosa en vez de otra (pág. 504)

tradition/tradición* una forma de pensar o actuar que está muy arraigada (pág. 427)

traditional economy/economía tradicional un sistema económico en el que las decisiones sobre qué, cómo y para quién producir se basan en costumbres o hábitos (pág. 724)

transparency/transparencia proceso mediante el que los negocios se hacen más visibles para todos (pág. 617)

treaty/tratado un acuerdo formal entre los gobiernos de dos o más países (pág. 222)

triangular trade/comercio triangular patrón de comercio que se desarrolló en la época colonial entre las Américas, África y Europa (pág. 43)

tribunal/tribunal corte establecida por las Naciones Unidas para atender casos internacionales de violaciones a las leyes de derechos humanos (pág. 745)

tuition voucher program providing subsidies for education payments, allowing families the option of sending students to private schools (p. 403)

two-party system a system of government in which two parties compete for power (p. 273)

tuition vouchers/vale educativo programa que otorga subvenciones para pagos educativos, con lo que se las familias pueden enviar a los estudiantes a escuelas privadas (pág. 403)

two-party system/sistema bipartita un sistema de gobierno en el que dos partidos compiten por el poder (pág. 273)

U

ultimate* the most basic or final (p. 293)

unanimous opinion the Supreme Court rules on a case in which all justices agree on the ruling (p. 256)

unemployment rate the percentage of people in the civilian labor force who are not working but are looking for jobs (p. 640)

unicameral one-house legislature (p. 358)

uniform* consistent or unvarying (p. 319)

utility the amount of satisfaction one gets from a good or service (p. 570)

utilize* to make use of (p. 684)

ultimate/primordial, final* el más básico o en el último lugar (pág. 293)

unanimous opinion/opinión unánime la Suprema Corte dictamina en un caso en el que todos los jueces acuerdan en el fallo (pág. 256)

unemployment rate/tasa de desempleo el porcentaje de personas en la fuerza laboral civil que no trabajan pero que buscan un empleo (pág. 640)

unicameral/unicameral cuerpo legislativo de una cámara (pág. 358)

uniform/uniforme* consistente o sin variación (pág. 319)

utility/utilidad la cantidad de satisfacción que se obtiene de un bien o servicio (pág. 570)

utilize/utilizar* hacer uso de (pág. 684)

value the general principles or beliefs people use to make judgments and decisions (p. 11)

version* a particular form or type (p. 473)

veto refusal to sign a bill or resolution (p. 202)

village smallest unit of local government (p. 390)

violate* to fail to keep or to break, as in a law (p. 134)

voice vote a voting method in which those in favor say "Yea" and those against say "No" (p. 202)

voluntary exchange the act of buyers and sellers freely and willingly engaging in market transactions (p. 530)

volunteerism the practice of offering your time and services to others without payment (p. 158)

value/valor principio o creencia general que las personas utilizan para emitir juicios y tomar decisiones (pág. 11)

version/versión* una forma o un tipo particular de otra ya existente (pág. 473)

veto/veto negativa de firmar un proyecto de ley o una resolución (pág. 202)

village/aldea la unidad más pequeña de gobierno local (pág. 390)

violate/violar* no cumplir o romper, como una ley (pág. 134)

voice vote/voto en voz alta un método de votación en el que aquéllos a favor dicen "Sí" y aquéllos en contra dicen "No" (pág. 202)

voluntary exchange/intercambio voluntario el acto de compradores y vendedores que realizan transacciones de mercado de manera libre y voluntaria (pág. 530)

volunteerism/voluntarismo la práctica de ofrecer tu tiempo y servicios a otros sin pago (pág. 158)

want a thing we would like to have, such as entertainment, vacation, or an item, that makes life comfortable and enjoyable (p. 499)

ward several adjoining precincts making up a larger election unit (p. 281)

warranty the promise made by a manufacturer or a seller to repair or replace a product within a certain time period if it is faulty (p. 542)

weak-mayor system a type of government under which the mayor has limited executive powers (p. 379)

Web site a "page" on the World Wide Web that may contain text, images, audio, and video (p. 471)

welfare the health, prosperity, and happiness of the members of a community (pp. 158, 406)

whereas* while; on the contrary (p. 360)

winner-take-all system a system in which the candidate who wins the popular vote in a state usually receives all of the state's electoral votes (p. 303)

Women, Infants, and Children (WIC) program a program that provides help for nutrition and health care to low-income women, infants, and children up to age 5 (p. 648)

workfare programs that require welfare recipients to exchange some of their labor in return for benefits (p. 649)

World Wide Web operating within the Internet, it allows users to interact with the billions of documents stored on computers across the Net (p. 471)

writ of habeas corpus a court order that requires police to bring a prisoner to court to explain why they are holding the person (pp. 188, 436)

want/deseo cosas que te gustaría tener, como entretenimiento, vacaciones y artículos que hacen que la vida sea cómoda y agradable (pág. 499)

ward/distrito varios precintos contiguos que conforman una unidad electoral más grande (pág. 281)

warranty/garantía la promesa que hace un fabricante o vendedor de reparar o cambiar un producto dentro de un período determinado si éste tiene una falla (pág. 542)

weak-mayor system/sistema de alcalde débil un tipo de gobierno en el que el alcalde tiene poderes ejecutivos limitados (pág. 379)

Web site/página web un sitio en la World Wide Web que puede contener texto, imágenes, audio y vídeo (pág. 471)

welfare/bienestar la salud, prosperidad y felicidad de los miembros de una comunidad (págs. 158, 406)

whereas/mientras que* en tanto que por otro lado (pág. 360)

winner-take-all system/sistema de ganador toma todo un sistema en el cual el candidato que gana el voto popular en un estado normalmente recibe todos los votos electorales del estado (pág. 303)

Women, Infants, and Children (WIC) program/programa para Mujeres, Bebés y Niños un programa que brinda ayuda para la nutrición y asistencia médica a mujeres de bajos ingresos, bebés y niños de hasta 5 años (pág. 648)

workfare/trabajo requerido programas que requieren que beneficiarios del bienestar social cambien parte de su trabajo por beneficios (pág. 649)

World Wide Web funciona dentro de Internet y permite que los usuarios interactúen con los miles de millones de documentos guardados en las computadoras por la red (pág. 471)

writ of habeas corpus/escrito de hábeas corpus una orden judicial que requiere que la policía lleve a un prisionero a un tribunal para explicar por qué retienen a la persona (págs. 188, 436)

Index

*The following abbreviations are used in the index: *c* = chart, *crt* = cartoon, *d* = diagrams, *g* = graph, *m* = map, *p* = photograph or picture; and *q* = quotes.

INDEX

Acknowledgments

Text and Art Credits

361 From "Let's List the Lottery Losers" by Andy Rooney. CBS News, August 6, 2006. Reprinted by permission of Andy Rooney.

Glencoe would like to acknowledge the artists and agencies who participated in illustrating this program: Anthology Inc.; Kenneth Batelman; Bill Dickson, represented by Contact Jupiter.

Photo Credits

Cover (t)CORBIS, (b)Miles Ertman/Masterfile; **iv** (bl)Crittenden Studio/Jupiter Images; (br)Getty Images; **v** Bettmann/CORBIS; **vi** Marleen Cate/Jupiter Images; **vii** Dennis Halliman/Jupiter Images; **viii** Jupiter Images; **xx** BananaStock/PunchStock; **xxi** (l)Don Farrall/Getty Images; (c)The McGraw-Hill Companies Inc./Ken Cavanagh Photographer; (r)Don Farrall/Photodisc/Getty Images; **2** Justin Lane/epa/CORBIS; **4** Carlos Barria/Reuters/CORBIS; **5** Mark Gibson/Index Stock Imagery; **6** Joe Raedle/Getty Images; **7** Panoramic Images; **9** Catherine Karnow/CORBIS; **10** (t)Freeman Patterson/Masterfile, (c)Robert Fried/Alamy, (r)CORBIS, (b)blickwinkel/Alamy; **11** Panoramic Images/Getty Images; **12** Steve Breen/Copley News Service; **14** Denis Poroy/AP Images; **15** John Moore/AP Images; **16** Reuters/CORBIS; **17** (t)Rob O'Neal, (b)WWF/South Florida Program; **18** Jim Sugar/CORBIS; **20** Judy Fahys/AP Images; **21** David Butow/CORBIS SABA; **23** Getty Images; **27** (t)CORBIS, (bl)Marianna Day Massey/ZUMA/CORBIS, (br)Spencer Grant/PhotoEdit; **30** Panoramic Images/Getty Images; **32** Alden Pellett/AP Images; **33** The Granger Collection, New York; **35** Bettmann/CORBIS; **36** Gibson Stock Photography; **38** Chuck Liddy/AP Images; **39** North Wind/North Wind Picture Archives; **40** (t)Ingram Publishing/Alamy, (b)Comstock/SuperStock; **41** The Art Archive/Culver Pictures; **44** AP Images; **46** North Wind/North Wind Picture Archives; **47** Yale University Art Gallery, Bequest of Eugene Phelps Edwards; **48** Bita Emrani; **50** Comstock/Imagestate; **51** The Art Archive/Musèe des Arts Africains et Ocèaniens/Dagli Orti; **52** Library of Congress; **53** Bettmann/CORBIS; **55** Kean Collection/Getty Images; **57** (tcl)The Granger Collection, New York, (tcr)The Colonial Williamsburg Foundation, (tr)File Photo, (cl)The Colonial Williamsburg Foundation, (bc)Military & Historical Image Bank, (c)The Colonial Williamsburg Foundation, (cr)Military & Historical Image Bank, (bl)Lee Snider/Photo Images/CORBIS; **59** Mike Peters, reprinted by permission of UFS, Inc.; **61** CORBIS; **63** (t)CORBIS, (b)Bettmann/CORBIS; **64** Scott Frances/Esto; **66** Leif Skoogfors/CORBIS; **67** James Lemass/Index Stock; **68** CORBIS; **71** Diana Walker/Time Life Pictures/Getty Images; **72** George Widman/AP Images; **73** (t)Bettmann/CORBIS, (c)CORBIS; **74** Dennis Degnan/CORBIS; **75** file photo; **76** Bettman/CORBIS; **77** National Archives; **79** Rick Bowmer/AP Images; **81** CORBIS; **82** (t)Russ Curtis, (b)Russ Curtis; **85** Gerald Herbert/AP Images; **86** Scott Stantis/Copley News Service; **87** Getty Images; **91** (tl)Art Resource, NY, (tr)Dave Bartruff/CORBIS, (bl)Dennis Degnan/CORBIS, (br)Bettmann/CORBIS; **94** Steve Allen/Brand X Pictures/Jupiter Images; **96** White House Historical Association; **102** Greg Gibson/AP Images; **106** George Widman/AP Images; **112** General Photographic Agency/Getty Images; **116** Bettmann/CORBIS; **117** Sandy Schaeffer/TimePix; **118** Justin Sullivan/Getty Images; **120** Evan Vucci/AP Images; **122** (bl)David Paul Morris/Getty Images, (br)Peter Hvizdak/The Image Works; **123** ANA/The Image Works; **125** BananaStock/PunchStock; **126** David Duprey/AP Images; **127** Teri L. Gilman; **128** Mikael Karlsson/Alamy; **129** Porter Gifford/Liaison Agency/Getty Images; **130** Ann Purcell; **132** Bettmann/CORBIS; **133** AP Images; **134** North Wind/North Wind Picture Archives; **136** Bettmann/CORBIS; **139** Danny Johnston/AP Photo; **140** Mike Thompson/Copley News Service; **141** MPI/Getty Images; **142** David J. & Janice L. Frent Collection/CORBIS; **144** Bettmann/CORBIS; **145** (t)Robert A. Reeder/Pool/Reuters/CORBIS, (c)Bruce Roberts/Photo Researchers, (b)MPI/Getty Images; **148** Dima Gavrysh/AP Images; **150** John Sandy Santucci/AP Images; **151** Bod Daemmrich/PhotoEdit; **152** (t)Nicole Robinson,(b)Ben Baker; **153** (t)Brand X Pictures/PunchStock, (c)Bob Daemmrich; **155** (t)The McGraw-Hill Companies, Inc./Emily and David Tietz, (b)StudiOhio; **156** Marc Lester/AP Images; **157** Ben Sklar/AP Images; **158** Marshall Ramsey/Copley News Service; **159** Getty Images; **160** James L. Amos/CORBIS; **163** (t)Las Cruces Sun-News, Norm Dettlaff/AP Images, (bl)Joe Rowley/AP Images, (br)Peter Turnley/CORBIS; **166 167** Bettmann/CORBIS; **168** (t)Comstock, Culver Pictures, (br)Time Life Pictures/Getty Images; **169** (t)Brooks Kraft/CORBIS, (c)Ethan Miller/Getty Images, (bl)Time Life Pictures/Getty Images, (br)Bettmann/CORBIS; **170** Matthew Borkoski/Index Stock; **174** Lester Lefkowitz/Getty Images; **176** Steve Warmowski/Jacksonville Journal-Courier/The Image Works; **177** Roberto Schmidt/AFP/Getty Images; **180** Mark Wilson/Getty Images; **184** David McNew/Getty Images; **185** U.S. Navy photo; **186** (t)Department of the Army, (b)Department of the Navy; **187** Jason Reed/Reuters/CORBIS; **189** Bob Daemmrich/PhotoEdit; **190** Chip Somodevilla/Getty Images; **191** Mark Humphrey/AP Images; **192** Mike Theiler/Getty Images; **193** (t)Sarah Seufer, (b)Chuck Kennedy/KRT/Newscom; **194** Courtesy Ileana Ros-Lehtinen; **195** Michael Ramirez/Copley News Service; **197** William Lovelace/Express/Getty Images; **198** Richard Broadwell/Alamy; **199** Bettmann/CORBIS; **203** (t)PCL/Alamy, (c)Jurgen Vogt/Getty Images; **205** Mark Cullum; **206** Stan Honda/AFP/Getty Images; **208** Paul J. Richards/AFP/Getty Images; **209** Susan Walsh/AP Images; **211** (inset) Hulton Archive, (others) White House Historical Association; **212** Alex Wong/Getty Images; **214** Susan Walsh/AP Images; **216** Courtesy AMillionThanks.org; **217** Mandel Ngan/AFP/Getty Images; **219** Tim Graham Picture Library/AP Images; **220** Marshall Ramsey/Copley News Service; **221** Brooks Kraft/CORBIS; **222** Evan F. Sisley-Pool/Getty Images; **224** Jean Louis Atlan/CORBIS; **226** AP Images; **227** Martin H. Simon/CORBIS; **228** Jim Watson AFP/Getty Images; **231** (t)Alex Wong/Getty Images, (cl)John F. Kennedy Presidential Library and Museum, Boston, (c)Bettmann/CORBIS, (b)Terry Ashe/Time Life Pictures/Getty Images; **235** Steven P. Widoff for TIME; **236** Olivier Doubiery/Abaca/Time; **238** National Park Service/AP Images; **239** ART LIEN/AFP/Getty Images; **241** Gary Sargent; **243** Pablo Martinez/CORBIS; **244** Jennifer Altman/Bloomberg News /Landov; **245** Richard Cummins/Lonely Planet Images; **246** NILS JUUL-HANSEN; **248** Mike Theiler/Getty Images; **249** Matthew Cavanaugh/epa/CORBIS; **250** Mark Wilson/Getty Images; **251** Pablo Martinez Monsivais/AP Images; **252** Joseph Mirachi/The Cartoon Bank; **254** Staff/AP Images; **257** Jim Rassol/CORBIS SYGMA; **260** Liza Biganzoli, National Geographic Society Image Collection; **261** (t)Getty Images, (bl)MIKE THEILER/AFP/Getty Images, (br)Richard A. Bloom/CORBIS; **265** Public Domain; **266** Bob Daemmrich/The Image Works; **270** Mark Wilson/Getty Images; **272** Staff/AP Images; **273** Ramin Talaie/CORBIS; **274** (t)National Museum of American History, Smithsonian Institution, Smithsonian Institution, Behring Center, (b)Collection of David J. & Janice L. Frent; **275** Jim Mone/AP Images; **276** David J. & Janice L. Frent Collection/CORBIS; **278** Peter Thompson/Getty Images; **279** George Skadding/Time Life Pictures/Getty Images; **280** (t)Democratic National Committee. All rights reserved, (b)Republican National Committee. All rights reserved; **281** (t)Susan Liebold, **282** Michael Ramirez/Copley News Service; **283** Jim Cole/AP Images; **285** David McNew/Getty Images; **287** (tl)Jim Cole/AP Images, (tr)David Bacon/The Image Works, (b)AP Images; **290** Orjan F. Ellingvag/CORBIS; **292** Kathy Willens/AP Images; **293** Spencer Platt/Getty Images; **294** Jack Star/PhotoLink/Getty Images; **295** CORBIS; **296** William Lovelace/Express/Getty Images; **298** Mike Thompson/Copley News Service; **300** Jon Readle/Getty Images; **302** (b)Nancy Pierce; **305** Kenneth Lambert/AP Images; **306** Herald-Mail, Kevin G. Gilbert/AP Images; **307** Michael Newman/PhotoEdit; **311** (t)B. Ray/Cedar Rapids Gazette/ZUMA/CORBIS, (bl)Bettmann/CORBIS, (br)Marianne Todd/Getty Images; **314** (c)Courtesy TIME, (b)Tim Boyles/Stringer/Getty Images; **315** (t)Charles Bennett/AP Images, (c)Stuart Ramson, (bl)Vincent Lerz/AP Images, (br)Comstock; **316** JIM BOURG/Reuters/Landov; **318** Daniel Shanken/AP Images; **319** Tim Boyle/Getty Images; **320** White House Historical Association; **321** (t)David Joel, (b)David Joel; **322** Bettmann/CORBIS; **323** (inset)AP Images, Larry Downing/Reuters/Landov; **325** Kayte M. Deioma/PhotoEdit; **326** Jim Bourg/Reuters; **327** Alex Brandon/AP Images; **328** Bettmann/CORBIS; **329** Federal Communications Commission; **331** Harley Schwadron/CartoonStock; **332** Brian Kersey/AP Images; **333** Alex Wong/Getty Images; **334** William Thomas Cain/Getty Images; **335** Steve Breen/Copley News Service; **339** (tl)Radhika Chalasani/Getty Images, (tr)David Young-Wolff/PhotoEdit, (b)William Thomas Cain/Getty Images; **342 343** Flip Schulke/CORBIS; **344** Karen Kasmauski/CORBIS; **346** A. Ramey/Stock Boston; **348** Bob Daemmrich/CORBIS; **350** Reuters; **351** George Steinmetz/CORBIS; **353** James W. Porter/CORBIS; **354** (t)Courtesy of Prateek Pere-da-Silva, (b)Gerry Broome/AP Images; **357** Allen Fredrickson/Reuters; **358** Tony Kurdzuk/Star Ledger/CORBIS; **359** Chris Britt/Copley News Service; **361** Scott Olson/Getty Images; **362** Koji Sasahara/AP Images; **363** Mark Kegans/Getty Images; **366** Scott Sharpe/AP Images; **367** Michael Kelley/Getty Images; **370** AP Images; **371** (l)Joseph Sohm, ChromoSohm/CORBIS, (c)Florida Department of State; (r)Reuters/CORBIS; **373** Steve Greenberg courtesy Seattle Post-Intelligencer; **374** Dave L. Ryan/Index Stock; **376** Library of Congress; **377** Charles Shoffner/Index Stock; **379** (t)Christian Science Monitor/Getty Images, (b)Rebecca Cook/Reuters; **380** Courtesy John Liu; **383** David McNew/Getty Images; **384** Robin Nelson/PhotoEdit; **387** Toby Talbot/AP Images; **388** Lee Marriner/AP Images; **389** Jeff Parker, Florida Today; **391** (t)Thinkstock/Jupiter Images, (bl)Scenics of America/PhotoLink/Getty Images, (br)Pete Fisher/911 Pictures; **393** By permission of Steve Breen and Creators Syndicate, Inc.; **394** Ethel Wolvovitz/The Image Works; **396** Bill Haber/AP Images; **397** Jeff Greenberg/The Image Works; **398** Russ Curtis; **400** Ben Chrisman/AP Images; **401** Marshall Ramsey/Copley News Service; **403** Courtesy Charlotte Hawkins Brown Museum at Historic Palmer Memorial Institute; **404** Peter Hvizdak/The Image Works;

405 Design Pics Inc./Alamy; **408** Sylvain Grandadam/Getty Images; **409** Paul Sancya/AP Images; **410** Jim West/The Image Works; **411** CORBIS; **413** (t)Jeff Greenberg/The Image Works, (bl)Gerry Broome/AP Images, (br)Steve Cole/Getty Images; **417** (t)Bettmann/CORBIS, (c)Alfred Eisenstaedt/Time Life Pictures/Getty Images; **419** Lon Tweeten; **420** Bob Daemmrich/PhotoEdit; **424** Nancy Richmond/The Image Works; **426** Kat Wade/San Francisco Chronicle/CORBIS; **427** Gibson Stock Photography; **430** LOU KRASKY/AP Images; **431** Cumberland Times-News, Steve Bittner/AP Images; **432** (t)Lee Anderlite/Stage 3 Productions, (b)Grantpix/Index Stock; **433** Dennis MacDonald/PhotoEdit; **435** Bettmann/CORBIS; **437** Steve Breen/Copley News Service; **438** Fat Chance Productions/CORBIS, (inset)Comstock Images/Alamy; **441** (t)Robertstock, (b)Las Cruces Sun-News, Norm Dettlaff/AP Images; **446** Andre Jenny/Alamy; **448** Michael Newman/PhotoEdit; **449** Chris Britt/Copley News Service; **452** Danny Johnston/AP Images; **453** Bob Daemmrich/The Image Works; **455** Ramin Talaie/CORBIS; **456** Mikael Karlsson/Arresting Images; **459** AP Images; **460** A. Ramey/PhotoEdit; **461** Larry Kolvoord/The Image Works; **462** Katja Heinemann/Aurora Photos; **464** SARGENT ©2005 Austin American-Statesman; **465** (t)Richard Lord/PhotoEdit, (c b)Bob Daemmrich; **468** Peter Hvizdak/The Image Works; **470** Mario Tama/Getty Images; **471** China Photos/Getty Images; **472** The Plain Dealer, Marvin Fong/AP Images; **474** Paul Sakuma/AP Images; **475** Ken James/CORBIS; **476** Reuters/CORBIS; **480** Mannie Garcia/Reuters/CORBIS; **481** Gary Markstein/Copley News Service; **482** Tom Sobolik; **483** Everett Kennedy Brown/epa/CORBIS; **485** Ed Kashi/CORBIS; **487** (t)Mel Evans/AP Images, (c)Ken James/CORBIS, (b)Reuters/CORBIS; **489** Tribune Media Services, Inc.; **491** Photri; **492** Spencer Grant/PhotoEdit; **495** Frank Siteman/PhotoEdit; **496** Wendell Metzen/Index Stock; **498** Paul Sancya/AP Images; **499** Rick Bowmer/AP Images; **500** Cynthia Johnson/Time Life Pictures/Getty Images; **503** Dan Reiland/AP Images; **504** David Young-Wolff/PhotoEdit; **505** Steve Breen/Copley News Service; **506** Author's Image - Celestial Panoramas Ltd/Alamy; **507** (b)Courtesy Jessica Painter; **508** Robert Glusic/Getty Images; **511** (tl)David Frazier/PhotoEdit, (tr)Don Ryan/AP Images, (b)Wally Santana/AP Images; **514** Andy Sacks/Getty Images; **516** Mike Cardew/Akron Beacon Journal/AP Images; **517** Jeff Greenberg/The Image Works; **520** Elliott Minor/AP Images; **521** Justin Sullivan/Getty Images; **523** (t)Anthony Gray, (b)Courtesy Ohio Fair Schools Campaign; **524** Brownie Harris/CORBIS; **527** Catherine Karnow/CORBIS; **528** Gary Markstein/Copley News Service; **529** Courtesy Liberty Power; **530** The Granger Collection, New York; **532** The Art Archive/Museum of the City of New York; **533** (t)Myrleen Ferguson Cate/PhotoEdit, (bl)Spencer Grant/Stock Boston, (br)AP Images; **536** Rob Gage; **538** David Young-Wolff/Photo Edit; **539** Michael Newman/PhotoEdit; **540** Scott Olson/Getty Images; **541** Rich Pedroncelli/AP Images; **542** Mango Productions/CORBIS; **544** Ken Ruinard/AP Images; **545** Bill Aron/PhotoEdit; **546** Chris Britt/Copley News Service; **547** Jerry Arcieri/CORBIS; **550 551** C Squared Studios; **552** David Duprey/AP Images; **553** Creatas/SuperStock, (inset)Thomas Northcut/Getty Images; **554** Rohanna Mertens for ACCION International; **557** Daniel Acker/Bloomberg News/Landov; **559** Robert Jordan/AP Images; **561** (t)Tim Byrne; **563** (t)Barry Austin Photography/Getty Images, (bl)Directphoto.org/Alamy, (br)Spencer Grant/PhotoEdit; **566** Denis Poroy/AP Images; **568** Pat Wellenbach/AP Images; **569** Paul Sakuma/AP Images; **570** Gary Heatherly; **573** Ron Heflin/AP Images; **574** Tom Carter/PhotoEdit; **577** Spencer Grant/PhotoEdit; **580** George Nikitin/AP Images; **581** Spencer Platt/Getty Images; **583** Al Grillo/AP Images; **585** Mike Fiala/AP Images; **587** AP Images; **588** Sidney Harris/ScienceCartoonsPlus.com; **590** David Zalubowski/AP Images, (inset)Don Ryan/AP Images; **591** Trek Bikes; **593** (t)Phil Klein/CORBIS, (bl)Mark Richards/PhotoEdit, (br)CORBIS; **597** George Hall/CORBIS; **598** Jeff Greenberg/Index Stock; **600** Dick Blume/The Image Works; **602** Jeremy Horner/CORBIS; **603** Justin Sullivan/Getty Images; **604** Skip Nall/Getty Images; **605** Carlos Osorio/AP Images; **608** Keith Srakocic/AP Images; **609** Michael Ramirez/Copley News Service; **610** Paul Sancya/AP Images; **611** Arthur Schatz/Time Life Pictures/Getty Images; **612** Michael Siluk/The Image Works; **614** Mike Stewart/Time Life Pictures/Getty Images; **615** Jeff Greenberg/PhotoEdit; **616** Business Wire/Getty Images; **617** Courtesy Fuzzy Feet Foundation; **619** (t)Seth Perlman/AP Images, (c)M. Spencer Green/AP Images, (b)Gerry Broome/AP Images; **622** The Granger Collection, New York; **623** David Duprey/AP Images; **624** Chris Daniels/CORBIS; **627** Sam C. Pierson, Jr./Photo Researchers; **628** Bill Pogue/Getty Images; **630** Chip Somodevilla/Getty Images; **631** NASA; **633** Bettmann/CORBIS; **634** Shawn Thew/epa/CORBIS; **636** Steve Raymer/CORBIS; **637** Joe Tabacca/Bloomberg News/Landov; **639** Gary Markstein/Copley News Service; **641** US Air Force Museum; **643** AP Images; **646** Mario Villafuerte/Getty Images; **647** Spencer Platt/Getty Images; **648** Courtesy Erika Herman; **650** Mark Burnett/Stock Boston; **651** (t)William Manning/CORBIS, (bl)Gary Conner/PhotoEdit, (br)Warren Morgan/CORBIS; **654 656** James Leynse/CORBIS; **657** Canadian Press, David Boily/AP Images; **658** (t)Michael Houghton, StudiOhio; **660** PAUL J. RICHARDS/AFP/Getty Images; **661** Hisham Ibrahim/Getty Images; **663** Michael Ramirez/Copley News Service; **666 667** Bettmann/CORBIS; **668** (t)©Gavin Seim Photography, (b)Courtesy Washington Business Week; **671** (t)Rob Crandall/Stock Boston, (c)Mark Burnett/Stock Boston, (b)AP Images; **674** Michael Newman/PhotoEdit; **676** Manuel Balce Ceneta/AP Images; **677** Kevin Lamarque/Reuters; **678** Spencer Grant/PhotoEdit; **681** Jamie Martin/AP Images; **683** Tony Freeman/PhotoEdit; **684** William Thomas Cain/Getty Images; **687** Stan Honda/AFP/Getty Images; **689** Michael Ramirez/Copley News Service; **691** Fred Ricard; **693** (t)Digital Vision, (cl)JupiterImages/ComStock, (cr)Kevin Lamarque/Reuters, (bl)Spencer Grant/PhotoEdit, (br)William Thomas Cain/Getty Images; **696** AFP/Getty Images; **699** (t)Kevin Wolf/United States Mint/AP Images (c b)Bettmann/CORBIS; **700** Richard Cummins/CORBIS; **703** IT Stock Free/JupiterImages; **704** Indiapicture/Alamy; **706** Mike Clarke/AFP/Getty Images; **707** Ahn Youngjoon/AP Images; **710** Scott Stantis/Copley News Service; **712** Elmer Martinez/AFP/Getty Images; **714** British Petrolium Handout/epa/CORBIS; **715** Jorge Rey/AP Images; **717** KCNA/epa/CORBIS; **721** Kham Kham/CN/Reuters; **723** Reuters/CORBIS; **724** (t)Courtesy Global Kids, (b)Joe Robinson; **727** (t)Ahn Youngjoon/AP Images, (c)KCNA/epa/CORBIS, (b)Jorge Rey/AP Images; **732** Silvia Izquierdo/AP Images; **734** Guang Niu/Reuters/CORBIS; **735** KIM JAE-HWAN/AFP/Getty Images; **736** (t)fuse-project, (b)Courtesy of Cosmos Ignite Innovations; **737** Courtesy Inveneo, **739** Ahmad Masood/REUTERS/Landov; **740** (t)Susan Liebold, (b)Jonathan Nourok/PhotoEdit; **743** Gideon Mendel/CORBIS; **744** Marco Di Lauro/Getty Images; **747** Michael Ramirez/Copley News Service; **749** (t) KIM JAE-HWAN/AFP/Getty Images, (c)IT Stock Free/JupiterImages, (b)Marco Di Lauro/Getty Images; **753** Thaier Al-Sudani/Reuters/CORBIS; **757** By permission of Gary Markstein and Creators Syndicate, Inc.; **758** Dennis MacDonald/PhotoEdit; **760** Michael Newman/PhotoEdit; **763** Koji Sasahara/AP Images; **772** National Portrait Gallery/Smithsonian Institution, Art Resource; **773** Smithsonian Institution; **774** Mark Burnett; **775** (t)Denver Art Museum (b) CORBIS; **777** CORBIS; **778** CORBIS; **779** Flip Schulke/CORBIS; **790** CORBIS; **791** Bettmann/CORBIS; **797 798 799 800** White House Historical Association; **801** White House Historical Association, (bl)Bush 2000 Campaign, (br)Brooks Kraft/CORBIS.